Legislation and
the Regulatory State

Legislation and the Regulatory State

SECOND EDITION

Samuel Estreicher

Dwight D. Opperman Professor of Law
Director, Center for Labor and Employment Law
Co-Director, Institute of Judicial Administration
New York University School of Law

David L. Noll

Associate Professor of Law
Rutgers Law School

Carolina Academic Press

Durham, North Carolina

Print ISBN: 978-1-5310-0558-0
E-ISBN: 978-1-5310-0559-7
LCCN: 2017939784

Carolina Academic Press, LLC
700 Kent Street
Durham, North Carolina 27701
Telephone (919) 489-7486
Fax (919) 493-5668
www.cap-press.com

Printed in the United States of America

Contents

Table of Cases

Foreword

This book addresses two subjects critically important to the practice of law in the twenty-first century: legislation and the regulatory or administrative state. Most students are familiar with the idea of legislation. Each year, Congress and state legislatures enact tens or sometimes hundreds of statutes, which are the major form of positive law in the United States. Approaches to interpreting statutes, and the policy and regulatory choices underlying them, may be less familiar. By the regulatory state, we mean the vast apparatus of governmental bodies, agencies, and institutions charged with implementing and enforcing statutes and executive orders.

Legislation and regulation are central to many aspects of what lawyers do. Among other practice areas, compliance, corporate governance, health care law, securities regulation, consumer law, and criminal practice all require attorneys to understand how legislation is enacted and why, and the relationship between the legislature, administrative agencies, regulated parties, and reviewing courts. Because of its importance to legal practice, many law schools have recently added "LegReg" courses to their curriculum, often as a required course in the 1L year. As this volume went to press, Harvard, NYU, Michigan, Vanderbilt, Wake Forest, Brigham Young, Fordham, Colorado (Boulder), Richmond, Houston, Case Western, Pittsburgh and West Virginia all required LegReg in the first three semesters of law school. Other law schools offer students the option of taking LegReg in the 1L year, offer it as part of specialized degree programs, and integrate elements of LegReg into courses in Administrative Law and Legislation.

Under the principle of dual sovereignty recognized by the Constitution, the federal government and the states share authority to regulate many areas of social life. Legislation and regulation can accordingly be found at the federal, state, and local levels—and for the ordinary American, state and local law is more important than anything the federal government does. When buying a house, starting a business, or seeking permission to drive a car, state legislation supplies the governing law. The individual's primary contact with government will be with a state agency.

Our focus in this volume is on *federal* legislation and regulation. This is principally because state laws vary. We also believe that an understanding of federal law enables students better to deal with state and local laws, because the principles shaping federal administrative law and statutory interpretation influence the resolution of similar issues under state and local government law.

There are now several casebooks on legislation and regulation and related subjects. Three features distinguish this book. First, a central goal is to help students develop fluency with the *concepts* and *vocabulary* that are necessary to the practice of law in the modern regulatory state. We have sought to follow Judge Posner's suggestion that a text on legislation and regulation should introduce the legislative process, the real-world factors that influence the design and content of legislation, techniques for judicial interpretation of statutes, and the process of researching legislative history.[1] The chapters on administrative agencies and judicial review similarly emphasize the building blocks of administrative law and court oversight of the regulatory state.

Second, we emphasize the creative, pragmatic aspects of lawyering. Legal theory is important but subordinate to the actual considerations lawyers will present and judges will be influenced by. There is no single universally accepted theory of statutory interpretation; we are all promiscuous users of diverse authorities and forms of argument. The notes and questions therefore encourage students to develop the ability to switch back and forth among different perspectives and modes of argument and to make use of different authorities when explaining the meaning of a statute, regulation, agency order, or court decision. This should not be a course in catechism. What courts say is never as important as what they in fact do in the case and holdings can never be assessed without considering to what extent the verbal formulations are necessary to the result. The interpretation of statutes and regulation is "a multifarious enterprise."[2]

Finally, while including a healthy dose of statutory interpretation and administrative law classics, the text features a substantial number of recently decided cases. Our sense is that these more recent cases lend the text an immediacy that will resonate with many readers, and help students develop fluency with the forms of analysis and argumentative moves they will encounter the minute they enter practice.

In preparing the volume, we have sought to preserve as much texture of the original sources as possible. To help students understand the mechanics of the legislative process, the documentary appendix contains excerpted legislative histories of two statutes that are the subject of several cases in the main text, the Civil Rights Attorney's Fees Awards Act of 1976, Pub. L. No. 94-559, 90 Stat. 2641, and the Driver's Privacy Protection Act of 1994, Pub. L. No. 103-322, 108 Stat. 2099. In editing cases, we have preserved many citations and procedural details to give a full picture of the context in which a case was decided.

The principal readings have been closely edited. We omit courts' analysis of issues and other details not pertinent to the subject at hand, including footnotes rehashing the debates between judges. Where a substantial amount of text has been omitted, the omission is noted with asterisks or a summary of the omitted material. The text does not indicate where citations and footnotes have been omitted, but footnotes retain their original numbering. Footnotes that we have added are indicated by an asterisk or dagger.

---

1. *See* Richard A. Posner, *Statutory Interpretation-in the Classroom and in the Courtroom*, 50 U. Chi. L. Rev. 800, 804 (1983).

2. Todd D. Rakoff, *Statutory Interpretation as a Multifarious Enterprise*, 104 Nw. U. L. Rev. 1559 (2010).

A course on legislation and the regulatory state is an amalgam of traditional law school courses on legislation and the legislative process, statutory interpretation, administrative law, regulation, and economic analysis of law. We are indebted to the many scholars working in these fields whose work the volume builds upon, and to Rachel Barkow, Rick Hills, Jonathan Nash, Bethany Davis Noll, Bobby Papazian, Ricky Revesz, Dick Stewart, Peter Strauss, and students in courses at NYU and Rutgers for invaluable feedback. Larry Gold deserves special thanks for reading multiple drafts of the manuscript and making countless contributions to the book.

S.E. & D.N.
New York
April 2017

Legislation and
the Regulatory State

Chapter 1

Why Regulate—And How?

This volume focuses on federal as opposed to state legislation and regulation. It must be borne in mind, however, that most areas of social life are governed by state court decisions (often termed "common law") and state legislation. Federal law, if any, builds on the baseline of state law. We begin in Section A with a historical overview of federal regulation. Subsequent sections consider the justifications for legislative changes to the common law, the justifications for regulating at the federal level (Section B), and the modes of regulation Congress considers (Section C).

A. Historical Background for Federal Regulation

Federal agencies first came into being as executive departments of the Federal Government, personified in the "Secretaries" who led them. Soon after the ratification of the Constitution, Congress in 1789 created the Departments of State (then denominated the Department of Foreign Affairs), Defense (called the Department of War until 1947), and the Treasury.[1] The secretaries of these departments were all members of the President's "cabinet," an unofficial term that refers to the most senior appointed officers of the executive branch.

Though these departments today employ millions of individuals, their scope in the early decades of the republic was more modest. Indeed, some of the highest-ranking officers of government were not even full-time employees. In 1790, Edmund Randolph, the first Attorney General, complained to a friend that his $1,500 per year retainer was not enough to cover his financial needs. Randolph "was expected to support himself by an independent law practice, and thus seemed halfway between an officer of the United States and a mere hired attorney or contractor."[2]

In the first half of the nineteenth century, the largest federal bureaucracy was the Post Office. "In 1831, the postal system, with more than 8,800 postmasters, employed

---

1. An Act for Establishing an Executive Department, to be Denominated the Department of Foreign Affairs, 1 Stat. 28 (July 27, 1789); An Act to Establish an Executive Department, to be Denominated the Department of War, 1 Stat. 49 (Aug. 7, 1789); An Act to Establish the Treasury Department, 1 Stat. 65 (Sept. 2, 1789).

2. Jerry L. Mashaw, *Recovering American Administrative Law: Federalist Foundations, 1787–1801,* 115 YALE L.J. 1256, 1289 (2006).

History of agencies

3

just over three-quarters of the *entire* federal civil work force, mostly as part-time post-masters in villages and towns scattered throughout the countryside." In contrast, the federal army "consisted of 3,332 men, most of whom were located at isolated army posts in the transappalachian West."[3] Other early agencies often were housed in the same physical building as the Post Office. They included the courts, the offices of the United States Attorneys, the Patent Office, and the Land Office.

The relatively small 18th and 19th century federal government reflects the understanding that states would be the principal governmental force dealing with the lives and affairs of their citizens and residents. Although Congress was given enumerated powers in Article I, Section 8 of the Constitution, including power to declare war and regulate interstate commerce, "the most fundamental social choices—from the organization of capitalism to the regulation of family life—[were] firmly lodged in state legal codes."[4] Early federal bureaucracies generated most of the revenue needed to operate the national government. Handling mail, collecting patent fees, adjudicating cases, and collecting customs and tariffs all generated revenue that the federal government needed to fund its operations.

These two features combined in a model of the federal government as a self-supporting, interstitial regulator. What federal law there was afforded the states ample authority to regulate social and economic conditions within their borders, but always subject to competition from other states. The federal government's operations were limited to discrete areas of national concern, and paid for themselves.

Westward expansion, the displacement of Native American populations it entailed, and the Civil War all challenged this model of the federal government's role. Throughout the nineteenth century, the Land Office administered the western holdings of the United States—a function that required it to survey federal holdings, conduct land sales, manage land grants to veterans who had been promised land in exchange for military service, and monitor compliance with the terms of grants to settlers. "Settlement on lands in which Indian claims had not been extinguished by treaty or purchase created constant conflict."[5]

The Civil War led to a significant expansion of the War Department, which oversaw the two million soldiers of the Union army. At the war's end in 1865, the federal government confronted thousands of claims by veterans and their dependents seeking pensions for wartime service. "Between 1874 and 1878, the Pension Office [the unit of the executive responsible for paying pensions to Civil War soldiers and their families] adjudicated between 30,000 and 45,000 claims a year, and provided benefits to about 230,000 persons at an expenditure of roughly thirty million dollars. In 1880, the office adjudicated 50,000 new claims, and by 1883 the number exceeded

---

3. RICHARD R. JOHN, SPREADING THE NEWS: THE AMERICAN POSTAL SYSTEM FROM FRANKLIN TO MORSE 3 (1995).

4. STEPHEN SKOWRONEK, THE EXPANSION OF NATIONAL ADMINISTRATIVE CAPACITIES, 1877–1920, at 23 (1982).

5. Jerry L. Mashaw, *Reluctant Nationalists: Federal Administration and Administrative Law in the Republican Era,* 1801–1829, 116 YALE L.J. 1636, 1700 (2007).

100,000."[6] The reintegration of the South gave rise to administrative challenges that were no less daunting. During Reconstruction, the federal army maintained a large presence in southern states, which required an administrative infrastructure to support it. Section 3 of the Fourteenth Amendment barred thousands of Southerners who supported the Confederacy from holding "any office, civil or military, under the United States, or under any state" without Congress's permission. Many petitioned Congress to remove this disability, necessitating the creation of a special claims-processing apparatus within Congress.

By the 1880s, the growth of a national market required a larger federal role in the economy. The railroads were a major impetus. Particularly in the West, small businesses complained that national railroads were abusing their economic power by charging discriminatory rates and engaging in other unfair practices. In the Interstate Commerce Act of 1887,[7] Congress created the Interstate Commerce Commission (ICC) to regulate the rates and business practices of railroads (and eventually, other forms of interstate commerce).

It is often said that the ICC was the first true federal administrative agency. To be sure, executive departments exercised some characteristics of administrative agencies from the beginning of the republic. However, the ICC was the first federal entity that had a largely regulatory mission and possessed all of the features now considered hallmarks of an administrative agency: independent legal status, a mandate to oversee a particular area of the economy, authority to elaborate legal requirements and investigate violations of the law within the area of the agency's delegated authority, and structural mechanisms designed to ensure that the agency did not overstep the limits of its authority and operated free of improper influence.[8]

As specified in the 1887 Act, the ICC consisted of five "commissioners" who would be appointed by the President with the advice and consent of the Senate. Commissioners could be removed from office only "for inefficiency, neglect of duty, or malfeasance in office." They would serve staggered terms, limiting the President's ability to influence the Commission's political and ideological makeup.

Since the creation of the ICC, the federal regulatory state has grown exponentially. As of November 2013, the *U.S. Government Manual* lists some 400 federal agencies. Some, such as the Environmental Protection Agency, have significant budgets and make decisions that affect the day-to-day business of many individuals and corporations. Others, such as the United States Botanic Garden, are concerned primarily with the management of federal property.

Growth of the federal government has been concentrated in three time periods. During the "progressive era" that lasted from roughly the 1890s to the outbreak of

---

6. Jerry L. Mashaw, *Federal Administration and Administrative Law in the Gilded Age*, 119 Yale L.J. 1362, 1419 (2010).

7. 24 Stat. 379.

8. Jerry L. Mashaw, *Foreword: The American Model of Federal Administrative Law: Remembering the First One Hundred Years*, 78 Geo. Wash. L. Rev. 975, 977–81 (2010).

World War I, national political leaders focused on the threat to the economy presented by large corporations and trusts such as the railroads, U.S. Steel, and Standard Oil. During the administration of Theodore Roosevelt, Congress created the Department of Commerce and Labor and charged it with promoting foreign and domestic commerce and the labor interests of the United States.[9] On March 4, 1913, President Taft signed legislation that separated the Departments of Labor and Commerce and established both as cabinet departments.[10] The next year, President Wilson signed the Federal Trade Commission Act,[11] which created the Federal Trade Commission (FTC), an independent agency that regulates anticompetitive, deceptive, and unfair business practices. The progressive era also saw the enactment of legislation regulating the working conditions of railroad employees. The 1898 Erdman Act barred railroads from restricting employees from unionizing and provided for arbitration of labor-management disputes.[12] The Federal Employers Liability Act, enacted in 1908, made railroads liable for death or injury resulting from a railroad's negligence, and provided that an employee's contributory negligence would merely diminish recovery, not bar it entirely as many courts held.[13]

As is familiar, the Great Depression beginning in 1929, the 1932 election of Franklin D. Roosevelt, and Roosevelt's "New Deal" led to another significant expansion of the federal regulatory state. In the decade between 1930 and 1940, Congress created seventeen new federal regulatory agencies. The New Deal agencies included the Commodity Exchange Commission, the Federal Deposit Insurance Corporation, the Federal Home Loan Bank Board, the National Labor Relations Board, the Railroad Retirement Board, the Securities and Exchange Commission, the Selective Service Administration, and the Social Security Board.[14]

Third, during the 1960s and 1970s, Congress enacted major regulatory statutes in the areas of civil rights, social insurance, and the environment. Each of these statutes was implemented in part by a federal administrative agency. However, the style of governance favored by Congress had evolved. Whereas New Deal era statutes relied heavily on administrative enforcement, the later statutes tended to use a mix of agency enforcement, external checks on agencies, private enforcement, and informal proceedings to accomplish Congress's objectives. For example, the major federal employment discrimination statute, Title VII of the Civil Rights Acts of 1964,[15] divides enforcement authority between the federal Equal Employment Opportunity Commission and private, civil litigation.

An important factor in the growth of the federal government was the passage of the Sixteenth Amendment in 1913. As previously noted, the federal government in the

---

9. Act of Feb. 14, 1903 § 3, 32 Stat. 825.

10. Act of March 14, 1913 § 1, Pub. L. No. 62-426, 37 Stat. 736.

11. Pub. L. No. 63-203, 38 Stat. 717 (Sept. 26, 1914).

12. Erdman Act of 1898, 30 Stat. 424 (June 1, 1898).

13. Pub. L. No. 60-106, 35 Stat. 65 (Apr. 22, 1908).

14. *See* Cass R. Sunstein, *Constitutionalism After the New Deal*, 101 Harv. L. Rev. 421, 424 n.9 (1987).

15. 42 U.S.C. § 2000e *et seq.*

nineteenth century relied heavily on fees and customs to finance its operations. This funding mechanism, however, proved inadequate as the end of the nineteenth century approached.

In 1894, Congress passed a uniform federal income tax of 2% on income over $4,000. The Supreme Court ruled that the income tax was a "direct" tax that, under Article I, Section 2 of the Constitution, had to be "apportioned" among the states of the Union "according to their respective numbers."[16] Liberalizing the federal government's power to tax, the Sixteenth Amendment provided Congress with "power to lay and collect taxes on incomes, from whatever source derived, without apportionment among the several States, and without regard to any census or enumeration." (Many state governments have similar powers under state constitutions but until recently were less likely to tax the income of their citizens because of competition from other states without such taxes. Compared to the federal government, state governments rely extensively on real estate taxes, user fees, and sales taxes.)

Freed of the apportionment requirement and called upon to perform a growing number of functions, the federal government increased expenditures substantially over the twentieth century. Figure 1, below, shows per capita growth in federal expenditures from 1792 to 2004 on an inflation-adjusted basis. As the figure shows, per capita federal spending increased about seven-fold over the twentieth century, with spikes during the Civil War and two World Wars.

Figure 1[17]

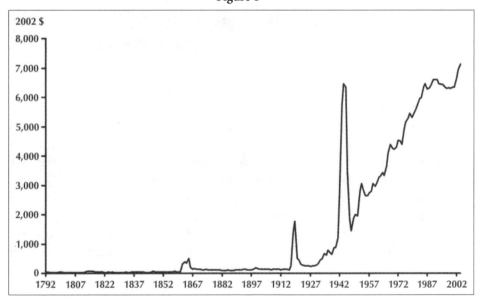

16. Pollock v. Farmers' Loan & Trust Co., 158 U.S. 601, 637 (1895).

17. Source: Thomas A. Garrett & Russell M. Rhine, *On the Size and Growth of Government*, FED. RESERVE BANK OF ST. LOUIS REV., Jan./Feb. 2006, at 15 fig. 1.

Today, most federal revenue comes from two kinds of individual taxes: the income tax, and payroll taxes that fund Social Security, Medicare, and Medicaid programs. In contrast to the situation that prevailed in the nineteenth century, the amount of federal revenue currently derived from excise taxes is relatively small. Figure 2, below, shows the percentage of federal revenue derived from the four largest sources of federal revenue between 1934 and 2013.

Figure 2[18]

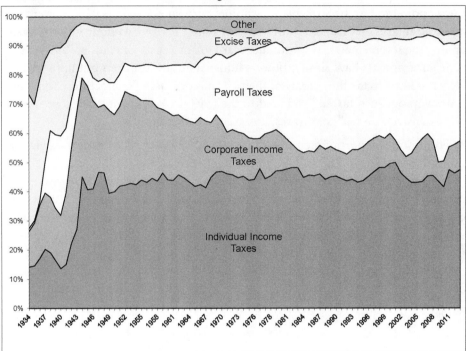

The growth of federal spending parallels an increase in the size of the federal workforce. Figure 3, below, shows the number of executive branch employees (excluding legislative and judicial branch employees) between 1816 and 2012, in ten-year increments. In 2012, the executive branch employed about 2.1 million individuals. As the chart shows, executive-branch employment increased approximately seven-fold over the twentieth century. Even so, the size of the federal government is somewhat smaller on a per capita basis than the governments of other advanced democracies. A 1999 survey found that while the "central" governments of members of the Organization for Economic Cooperation and Development (OECD) employ, on average, 1.8% of the workforce, the federal government employed 1.2% of the U.S. workforce. (State governments, however, employed more civilian employees, per capita, than the "non central governments" of OECD members.)[19]

---

18. Source: Office of Management & Budget, Budget of the U.S. Government, historical tbl. 2.1 (2016).

19. Salvatore Schiavo-Campo et. al, An International Statistical Survey of Government Employment and Wages at 39, tbl. A-2 (1999).

Figure 3[20]

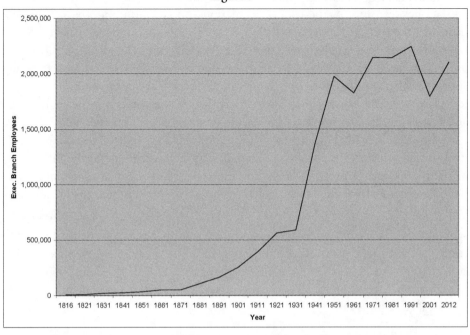

The "rise and rise of the administrative state"[21] reflects a judgment on the part of federal lawmakers that many social problems warrant federal legislation and the creation of a federal regulatory apparatus. Nevertheless, American government generally operates on the premise that markets operating under common law rules are an effective way to produce, distribute, and allocate resources; for example, New Yorkers consume thousands of lattes each day without the benefit of a Central Coffee Administrator. Moreover, some observers share the sense of the framing generation that when governmental intervention in addition to common law rules is needed, states rather than the federal government should take the lead. What, then, are the precise justifications for regulation and, if regulation is required, regulating at the federal level?

B. Justifications for Regulation

To paraphrase Justice Harlan's famous definition of "substantive" law, regulation can be understood as any legal directive designed to affect "primary decisions respecting

---

20. Prior to 1942, data on federal government employment were collected by the Bureau of the Census. Historical data from 1942 on is maintained by the Office of Personnel Management, an agency that functions as the government's employment bureau. 5 U.S.C. § 1101. Data for years prior to 1942 are from Bureau of the Census, Historical Statistics of the United States, 1794–1945, at 294 (1949). Data for years after 1942 are from Office of Personnel Management, Historical Federal Workforce Tables: Executive Branch Civilian Employment Since 1940, http://goo.gl/sbESIj.

21. Gary Lawson, *The Rise and Rise of the Administrative State*, 107 Harv. L. Rev. 1231 (1994).

human conduct."[22] This understanding is a modern one. Writers traditionally distinguished between the "public law" of legislation and constitutional law, on the one hand, and the "private" law of property, torts, and contract, on the other. But increasingly informed observers have questioned the viability of a clean distinction between public law and private law, and public rights and private ones. Even quintessentially "private" rights such as the right to be free of tortious behavior by others or the right to enforce a private contract can affect the real-world decisions of other individuals and firms and certainly implicate the system of rights, responsibilities, and remedies. Even though it is created by judicial decisions and kept in place by a respect for precedent (the doctrine of "stare decisis," or "standing by that which is decided") rather than by statute and agency regulations, the common law is just as much a form of regulation as regulatory programs that are defined by statute and enforced by an administrative agency.

Regulation is accordingly a broad subject. Given that this volume is specifically concerned with federal legislation and regulation, our focus here is narrower. We consider two questions. First, when is it appropriate to alter the common law rule by legislation? Second, should the new rule be set by the federal government or by state and local governments?

1. Reasons for Changes in Common Law Arrangements

We begin with a hypothetical made famous by the late University of Chicago Nobel laureate Ronald H. Coase.[23] Suppose that a farmer and a rancher operate a farm and a ranch on neighboring properties, and that there is no fence separating the properties. In the absence of a fence, the rancher's cattle sometimes wander into the farmer's fields and damage the farmer's crops. Suppose furthermore that an increase in the size of the rancher's herd will cause an increase in damage to the farmer's crop; that the annual cost of installing and maintaining a fence is $9; that the annual profit from a single cow is $3; and that the farmer's crops sell for $1 per ton. Finally, assume that the relationship between the number of cattle in the rancher's herd and the farmer's annual crop loss is, as follows:

Number in Herd (Cows)	Annual Crop Loss (Tons)	Crop Loss per Additional Cow (Tons)
1	1	1
2	3	2
3	6	3
4	10	4

At common law, the owner of real property had a near-absolute right to exclude others from the owner's property. Recognized exceptions to an owner's right to exclude,

---

22. Hanna v. Plumer, 380 U.S. 460, 475 (1965) (Harlan, J., concurring).
23. R.H. Coase, *The Problem of Social Cost*, 3 J. L. & ECON. 1. 2–3 (1960).

such as for necessity and custom, were narrow.[24] A property owner could recover damages from a trespasser even if the trespass did not physically damage the owner's property.[25] Where a trespasser caused damage to an owner's land, the trespasser was responsible for the damages caused by the trespass. In most jurisdictions, this rule applied to "trespassing animals" that were permitted by their owner to wander onto adjacent land.[26]

How would this system of rules influence the rancher's decision whether to add more cattle to the rancher's herd? Suppose for example that the rancher had one cow and was considering adding one more cow to the herd. Under what circumstances, if any, would the rancher decide *not* to add additional cattle to her herd? Under what circumstances would the rancher decide to build a fence to keep her cows within the ranch? What should the law do in this case?

a. Government Provision of Public Goods

In the above example, there does not appear to be a compelling need for a legislature to intervene in the common law and establish special standards for the regulation of farms and ranches. Under common law liability rules, the rancher must pay for the damage that the rancher's cattle cause to the farmer's crops. Because the rancher captures both the gains and bears the costs of the rancher's actions, the rancher will add cows until the rancher's damages liability to the farmer exceeds the value the rancher obtains from the additional cows. For example, if the rancher has four cattle that produce income of $12, the rancher will install a fence ($9) and thus avoid having to pay $10 for damaged crops. The decision to install a fence saves the rancher $1 on net.

This conclusion depends on a number of assumptions that may not be true in the real world. For example, we have assumed that it costs nothing for the farmer to enforce the farmer's rights when in reality, courts impose filing fees and almost all lawyers charge for their services. We have also assumed that the rancher can accurately predict the amount of damage the rancher's cattle will cause, and that the rancher will rationally weigh the costs and benefits of the rancher's actions. Nonetheless, the common law seems to produce a sensible outcome, at least when the parties are reasonably certain of what the law requires and can costlessly enforce those rules or reach agreements to alter the impact of legal rules. (In such circumstances, "transaction costs" are low.)

At the same time, mutually beneficial transactions between the parties do not always produce results that are desirable from a societal perspective. One classic justification for government intervention is the underproduction of "public goods" in a purely market-based society. To function effectively, a modern state must provide certain forms of infrastructure: e.g., police to ensure public safety; a military to provide national defense; and highways to carry goods among producers and consumers. For

---

24. *See* Ploof v. Putnam, 71 A. 188 (Vt. 1908).
25. *See* Jacque v. Steenberg Homes, Inc., 563 N.W.2d 154 (Wis. 1997).
26. *See* Restatement Third, Torts: Liability for Physical and Emotional Harm § 21 (2009).

self-interested reasons, it is unlikely that individuals acting on their own will produce these goods at a socially optimal level.

Goods or services such as police protection and national defense are "non-excludable"; access to the benefits of the good cannot be easily limited once the good is provided to some. Consider public provision of police protection. We can have private guards patrol private gated residences against crime, but criminal actors will then victimize other communities. A general climate of lawlessness outside the gated communities would likely increases risk to residents even of those communities. Any system of law and courts to try perpetrators of crime in gated communities could not long be limited to crimes in those communities.

"Public goods" are also "non-rivalrous"; the incremental cost of providing the good to another person is zero once the good is provided to some individuals. These goods or services entail a "free rider" effect allowing individuals or entities to benefit from their provision without contributing a proportionate share of the costs of their provision. Without state compulsion, such goods or services tend to be underproduced (below the socially optimal level) because investors cannot recoup the same level of profits as they would from investment in private goods or services.

If a society is small enough that its citizens or residents can apply social pressure to ensure that responsibility is relatively equally shared, the free-rider effect can be mitigated. Thus, for example, a small town can maintain a volunteer fire department. As the town gets bigger and its population becomes more heterogeneous, social sanctions lose their force, and the town must consider establishing a professional fire department maintained by tax revenues.[27]

For another example, Alexander Hamilton argued in the Federalist Papers that "[t]he militia in times of profound peace would not long, if at all, submit to be dragged from their occupations and families to performe [sic] that most disagreeable duty" of defending the Western frontier. "And if they could be prevailed upon or compelled to do it, the increased expense of a frequent rotation of service, and the loss of labor and disconcertion of the industrious pursuits of individuals, would form conclusive objections to the scheme." The solution, Hamilton argued, was a "permanent corps in the pay of the [federal] government."[28]

b. Externalities

The need to provide public goods is related to another standard justification for government intervention—the need to control externalities. Classical economic theory assumes that the costs and benefits of a transaction are borne entirely by the parties to the transaction. For example, the farmer and the rancher might decide to build a fence between their properties and split the costs, because doing so allows them to increase the amount of crops and cattle they respectively produce. This kind of private

---

27. *See generally* Robert C. Ellickson, Order Without Law: How Neighbors Settle Disputes (1991).

28. The Federalist No. 24, at 150 (Hamilton) (Robert Scigliano ed., 2000).

transaction improves social welfare because the farmer and the rancher will agree to the transaction only if it improves their respective positions in the absence of such a fence.

But the agreement between the farmer and the rancher may affect other people, in ways that are both beneficial and harmful. Suppose that, in addition to keeping the rancher's cattle off the farmer's field, the fence protected neighborhood children who, in the absence of a fence, would wander onto parts of the farm that were dangerous for children. Or, suppose that a mail carrier crossed back and forth across the farm and ranch when delivering the mail, and that construction of the fence required a different, more time-consuming route resulting in late mail delivery. (Assume that the farmer and rancher have no objection to the mail carrier using this route, or that mail carriers have been using the route since time immemorial.)

In the first scenario, the farmer-rancher agreement creates a "positive" externality. Society is better off because the farmer and rancher agree to build a fence, and fewer children will be injured after entering the farm. In the second scenario, the agreement creates a "negative" externality. Society is worse off because of the agreement if the fence disrupts timely delivery of the mail. Moreover, the costs of that disruption may be greater than the benefits that the farmer and rancher capture from erecting the fence. If the fence causes a delay in the delivery of extremely time-sensitive documents that recipients depend on for their livelihood, the overall social cost of the project may be negative.

The classic regulatory response to externalities, first put forward by the English economist Arthur C. Pigou, is to attempt to equalize an activity's private and social costs through taxation or subsidy. To increase the amount of an activity that produces a positive externality, the government subsidizes the activity, reducing its private cost. When an activity harms third parties, the government increases the private cost of the activity through a penalty or tax.

By reallocating the costs of an externality-generating activity, regulation attempts to change the calculus of individuals who are contemplating engaging in the activity. Ideally, individuals in the post-regulation world will undertake the activity only if its net *social* benefits outweigh its net *social* costs. This reasoning underlies the imposition of "sin taxes" on goods such as alcohol, cigarettes, and, more recently, sugary drinks. As Pigou observed, nearly all countries tax alcohol because of its costs "in disablement, inefficiency, illness, and crime, with all their depressing effects on industrial productivity, and with the direct costs in doctors, policemen, prisons, etc. etc. etc."[29]

Recognition that private transactions generate external costs or benefits that can be influenced by regulation raises the possibility that *all* externalities should be taxed or subsidized, to ensure that individuals are taking into account the social costs and benefits of their actions. But is government intervention really warranted every time an activity generates externalities? In 1960, Ronald Coase challenged that idea in the

---

29. A.C. Pigou, Welfare and Welfare 163–64 (1912) (quoting Bernard Shaw, The Common Sense of Municipal Trading 19–20 (1908)).

paper which introduced the hypothetical at the beginning of this section, *The Problem of Social Cost*.

Coase's paper focuses on how liability rules affect the rancher's decision to add cattle to the rancher's herd. Coase first considers what will happen if the rancher is liable to the farmer for the cost of the damaged crops. He predicts that the rancher will add cows so long as the rancher's gain from doing so outweighs the costs of damaged crops or the costs of building a fence. When the gains from an additional cow outweigh the costs, the rancher will compensate the farmer for the farmer's damages or pay for a fence.

Coase then considers what would happen *without* a rule that assigns liability for losses to the rancher. He concludes that the absence of such a liability rule will not affect the bottom-line decisions that the rancher and farmer arrive at about the appropriate level of cattle and whether to build a fence. Compared to a world with a liability rule, the only thing different about a world without one is that the farmer will internalize the cost of harms to the farmer's crops and pay the rancher not to add more cattle or build a fence when the damage caused by the new cattle exceeds the cost of a fence. If one party has potential gains that exceed the other's losses, that party can induce the other to act by compensating the other for his or her losses.

Coase concludes that *in a world of no transaction costs where the parties can bargain costlessly*, the initial allocation of entitlements and existence of a liability rule have no effect on parties' ability to produce resources efficiently. A baseline rule is needed: "It is necessary to know whether the damaging business is liable or not for damage caused since without the establishment of this initial delimitation of rights there can be no market transactions to transfer and recombine them. But the ultimate result (which maximizes the value of production) is independent of the legal position if the pricing system is assumed to work without cost."[30]

Transaction costs, however, are pervasive. Large numbers of parties, the cost of communication, differential access to information, contractual complexity, the costs of hiring a lawyer and invoking the court system, and myriad other factors keep parties from bargaining to reach an efficient allocation of resources. Moreover, parties sometimes *create* transaction costs in the hopes of securing a larger share of a smaller pie.[31] How should legal policymakers approach externalities given this reality?

Coase contends that in the real world of transaction costs, policymakers should consider two questions. First, are transaction costs sufficiently high to justify regulation? Second, if transaction costs are high enough to warrant regulation, what form of regulation best approximates the outcome that parties would reach in a world without transaction costs?

The first question reflects the fact that regulation, like bargaining, is not costless. Legal rules can be over- and under-inclusive, and often are enacted on the basis of

---

30. R.H. Coase, *The Problem of Social Cost*, 3 J.L. & Econ. 1, 8 (1960).

31. *See generally* Jordan M. Barry, John William Hatfield & Scott Duke Kominers, *Coasean Keep-Away: Voluntary Transaction Costs* (San Diego Legal Studies Paper No. 14–149, 2014), http://ssrn.com/abstract=2403839.

imperfect information. Thus, the choice between private ordering and regulation involves a comparative assessment. Both private ordering and regulation entail costs. Regulation is warranted only if it will do a better job than private ordering at allocating resources.

The second question assumes that regulation is warranted, and asks how regulation should be designed. For Coase, regulation seeks to approximate the outcomes that would obtain in a world of costless bargaining. If ranchers and their neighbors would erect fences for ranches with more than one cow and transaction costs keep them from reaching an agreement to do so, the law should impose that result.

Importantly, it does *not* follow that any externality-generating activity should be taxed or subsidized. According to Coase, policymakers undertaking to regulate an area should focus on whether regulation improves on the status quo, not whether an activity, taken in isolation, generates externalities.

c. Moral Hazard

Externalities are only one of many ways in which individuals' real-world behavior departs from the simplified ideal posited by classical economic theory. Another problem involves an individual's failure to internalize the costs of that person's actions, or "moral hazard."

Classical economic theory assumes that individuals will take actions that are in their self-interest because they will bear the costs of those actions. For example, drivers will drive carefully to avoid the costs of hospitalization, time off from work, and vehicle damage caused by accidents. When the costs of an actor's actions are paid by someone else, the actor may engage in riskier behavior than the actor would if the actor internalized all the costs and benefits of her actions. The driver of a fully-insured Volvo may drive less carefully than he would if he had to face unlimited personal liability. On the other hand, unlimited personal liability as a routine prospect might discourage useful social activity requiring the use of an automobile.

The standard policy response to moral hazard is to require the risk-taking actor to bear some of the costs of his actions. Thus, most insurance policies have a deductible that must be paid by the policyholder before insurance proceeds become available to pay losses. Alternatively, the law may prohibit shifting losses to another party. Many states prohibit insurance policies from covering criminal fines. Underlying the prohibition are concerns about moral hazard. Fines are intended to deter criminal behavior, and would fail to have this deterrent effect if they were paid by a third-party.

d. Flawed Decisionmaking

In the past decade, considerable attention has been devoted to another way in which individuals' behavior diverges from the ideal posited by classical economic theory. Even when individuals bear the costs of their own actions, they frequently make decisions that are irrational or fail to advance their self-interest. In a famous study, employees at a large firm gave up thousands of dollars in employer contributions by failing to participate in their firm's retirement plan, even though it was possible to participate in the plan at little cost and the process of enrolling took only a few minutes.[32]

i. *Information Failure or Asymmetry*

One obvious reason for bad decisions is that people lack information needed to make good ones. Consumers may not appreciate that products such as air fresheners, dishwasher detergent, and non-stick cookware contain dangerous chemicals. Few people are capable of evaluating whether a new pharmaceutical is safe and effective.

Policymakers often address this kind of "information failure" or "information asymmetry" (one party to the transaction knows more about the costs and benefits of a product or service than the other) by mandating disclosure of more information. For example, rules promulgated under the Occupational Safety and Health Act of 1970[33] require manufacturers of chemical products to describe the hazards of the chemicals they produce, and to prepare labels and safety data sheets to convey information about hazards to customers.[34] Likewise, Food and Drug Administration (FDA) regulations promulgated under the federal Food, Drug, and Cosmetic Act require manufacturers to include information on a pharmaceutical's safety, effectiveness, and intended use on the pharmaceutical's packaging.[35]

Mandatory disclosure will not always eliminate or even significantly mitigate flawed decisionmaking. Disclosure can cause "information overload"—too much information can be counterproductive when not readily assimilated by the intended audience. In addition, if a significant amount of time and effort is necessary for people to read and interpret information, individuals may ignore the information. Individuals are "boundedly rational" when presented with information; that is, they digest information only if the expected benefits outweigh the time and effort necessary to do so.[36]

ii. *Paternalism and "Choice Architecture"*

Inability or unwillingness to process large amounts of information is only one reason people may fail to make decisions that would advance their long-term interests. Recent research in behavioral science has identified numerous cognitive biases that negatively affect individuals' ability to make good decisions.[37] Some examples include:

---

32. Brigitte C. Madrian & Dennis F. Shea, *The Power of Suggestion: Inertia in 401(k) Participation and Savings Behavior*, 116 Q.J. Econ. 1149 (2001). *See also* James J. Choi et al., *Defined Contribution Pensions: Plan Rules, Participant Choices, and the Path of Least Resistance*, in 16 Tax Policy and the Economy 67 (James M. Poterba ed. 2002).

33. Pub. L. No. 91-596, 84 Stat. 1590, 29 U.S.C. § 651 et seq.

34. *See* 29 C.F.R. pt. 1900.

35. *See* 21 C.F.R. pt. 201.

36. *See generally* Howard Latin, *Good Warnings, Bad Products, and Cognitive Limitations*, 41 U.C.L.A. L. Rev. 1193, 1211–12 (1994).

37. *See* Richard H. Thaler & Cass R. Sunstein, Nudge: Improving Decisions about Health, Wealth, and Happiness 22–39 (2009).

- *Anchoring and adjustment.* When individuals estimate the value of an unknown variable (e.g., the population of Milwaukee), they begin with an "anchor" value they know (e.g., the population of Chicago) and make a ballpark adjustment (e.g., Milwaukee is a third the size of Chicago). However, the adjustment is often too low (or high).

- *Availability bias.* Individuals assess the likelihood of a risk based on the availability of high-salience examples. Thus, a familiar risk like the risk of terrorism following the September 11, 2001, attacks will be given more weight than a less familiar risk, such as the risk of global warming.

- *Representativeness bias.* When asked to assess whether something belongs in a particular category, people respond based on the average characteristics of members of that category. For example, students are more likely to believe that a balding, middle-aged man is a law professor than a young, athletic woman.

- *Optimism and overconfidence.* Individuals are claimed to systematically overestimate their own abilities and the likelihood that they will succeed.

- *Loss aversion.* Individuals are willing to pay more to prevent giving up something that they possess than to purchase the same thing, even though the same thing is at stake in both scenarios.

- *Status quo bias.* People generally tend to stick with their current situation, rather than make welfare-improving changes.

- *Framing.* People make different choices based on the way in which information is presented. For example, a liquor store will sell more bottles of 18-year-old whiskey if they are placed on a shelf between 10-year-old and 25-year-old bottles, compared to being placed next to 10-year-old bottles alone.

With respect to all of these biases, it is not always clear how potent they are in particular circumstances and to what extent information or experience can diminish their potency.

Cognitive biases present difficult problems for regulatory policies that rely on individuals acting in their own self-interest. One well-known problem is the "divided self." Individuals may acknowledge that activities such as saving for retirement are in their long-term self-interest, but fail to do so because self-control is difficult. Faced with a choice between saving for retirement and taking a nice vacation, many people choose the vacation, even if saving would make them better off in the long run. Addiction to harmful drugs may be another example.

The simplest regulatory response is to mandate the "correct" choice by law—or at least the choice that is correct for most individuals. For example, the Social Security Act requires that individuals set aside a portion of their wages via a payroll tax to pay for old-age, survivors, and disability insurance.[38] Money deducted from wages is used

---

38. *See* 26 U.S.C. § 3101.

to pay current Social Security benefits. When a worker retires, she receives benefits keyed to her former income.

Critics of regulatory programs that mandate particular choices or take choices off the table charge that they are an unattractive form of "paternalism." As a philosophical matter, critics maintain that *any* denial of individuals' decisionmaking authority is inappropriate. On economic grounds, critics charge that the decisions made by the government are often worse than those that individuals would make on their own.

Responding to these critiques, some regulatory programs have attempted to guide or "nudge" individuals toward good decisions rather than overriding individual choice. For example, the 2006 Pension Protection Act[39] encourages employers to establish voluntary retirement-savings programs that automatically enroll participants, and gradually increase employees' retirement contributions over time. Employees remain free to opt out of the savings programs and save nothing, however.

The Act's automatic enrollment feature is an example of a "default rule." Enrollment will occur unless the individuals makes an affirmative decision to opt out of the program. The program thus takes advantage of the status quo and loss aversion tendencies of individuals in order to promote pension-plan participation. The Act's provision for greater contributions over time is an example of a "commitment device." When individuals display preferences that are "dynamically inconsistent"—preferring A to B at time 1, but B to A at time 2—a commitment device ensures that the earlier decision, presumably made after deliberation and not in the heat of passion, sticks.

Whether such programs succeed in practice is contested, however. A recent article suggests that automatic enrollment may reduce the retirement savings rates of many employees, despite increased initial participation rates. Paradoxically, the explanation for this anomaly involves inertia and status quo bias: workers join opt-out savings plans at higher rates than traditional plans but, having done so, are less likely to change contribution rates than they are in traditional opt-in plans, and thus end up saving less.[40] The authors of this article conclude that in a situation where inertial forces are strong, the task of designing a default rule is not fundamentally different than designing a hard mandate.

Default rules and commitment devices are two examples of the broader project of "choice architecture." Rather than overriding individual decisionmaking, regulatory programs allow individual choice while encouraging individuals to make good decisions by exploiting the cognitive biases that lead to bad decisions in the first instance. Choice architecture thus seeks to provide the benefits of governmental intervention

---

39. Pub. L. 109-280, 120 Stat. 780.
40. Ryan Bubb & Richard H. Pildes, *How Behavioral Economics Trims Its Sails and Why*, 127 Harv. L. Rev. 1593, 1618 (2014). For a counterpoint, see Cass R. Sunstein, Why Nudge?: The Politics of Libertarian Paternalism (2014).

while permitting individuals to avoid the government's suggested solution if it is not right for their situation.

e. Inequality/Limited Bargaining Power

The discussion thus far has focused on ways the law might help individuals and entities to allocate resources to their most valued use (what economists call "efficiency" or "efficient resource allocation"), including ways certain "market failures" might be addressed. Regulation might also be premised on the advancement of nonmarket values, such as reducing social inequity and distributing income and benefits to less-well-off individuals and families.

The Civil Rights Act of 1964,[41] for example, prohibits discrimination in public accommodations, governmental facilities, education, and employment. In doing so, this measure sought to redress "the deprivation of personal dignity that surely accompanies denials of equal access to public establishments."[42]

Legislation may seek to redress inequality through the provision of "social insurance." Most prominently, the Social Security system seeks to protect individuals against poverty caused by old age or disability through the Social Security Old-Age and Disability Insurance Programs. These programs are premised on the same insight as private insurance programs: that by pooling resources, a group of individuals can mitigate the effects of risks that cannot be predicted with certainty. They differ from private insurance programs in that members of the insurance pool are required, by law, to participate in the scheme. In the case of Social Security, retirement benefits begin to accrue when an individual has paid payroll taxes for the equivalent of ten working years.[43]

Lastly, legislation may seek to redress inequality by overcoming collective action problems or transferring resources to particular groups. Laws protecting collective bargaining, for example, are thought "to remedy the individual worker's inequality of bargaining power by 'protecting the exercise . . . of full freedom of association, self-organization, and designation of representatives of [workers'] own choosing.'"[44] A similar rationale motivates laws that encourage credit unions and agricultural marketing cooperatives. In permitting individuals and companies who are less well-off to pool their resources, these laws seek to improve the welfare of a favored group by giving them greater bargaining power in the marketplace.[45]

---

41. Pub. L. No. 88-352, 78 Stat. 241 (1964).

42. Report of the Senate Judiciary Committee to Accompany S. 1732, S. Rep. No. 88-872 (2d Sess. 1964), available at 1964 U.S.C.C.A.N. 2355, 2370.

43. *See* 42 U.S.C. §414.

44. NLRB v. Hearst Publ'ns, 322 U.S. 111, 126 (1944).

45. *See, e.g.,* Amendments to Federal Credit Union Act §2, Pub. L. 105-219, §112 Stat. 913 (Aug. 7, 1998) (affording legal recognition to credit unions as "member-owned, democratically operated, not-for-profit organizations [with] the specified mission of meeting the credit and savings needs of consumers, especially persons of modest means"); Capper-Volstead Act of 1922 §1, Pub. L. No. 67-146,

Is the use of regulation to deal with problems of inequality less effective than the use of taxing-and-spending measures to redistribute resources directly to the benefited group? If Congress wants to raise the living standards of the working poor, is it better to raise minimum wages for all who work or to supplement directly the income of poor workers through tax credits or cash subsidies? A minimum wage hike raises wages for all minimum-wage workers, some of whom may be middle-class college students engaged in part-time work. Some employers may respond to such a hike by introducing labor-saving technology, lowering work hours, or hiring only higher-quality workers—moves that may hurt some in the purportedly benefited class. On the other hand, tax credits or cash subsidies may have the effect of subsiding the low-wage employer who reduces or does not increase wages in the knowledge that the public benefit will kick in. It also may be easier for politicians to enact across-the-board mandates rather than targeted benefits for politically weak groups.[46]

Redistributive regulation also affects the supply of goods. Suppose, for example, that because of a legislated minimum price floor, the retail price of apples increases above the price most consumers are willing to pay. The imposition of a price floor will reduce the production and consumption of apples compared to the level that prevails in an unregulated market.[47]

Another non-market value that regulation might seek to promote is political participation For example, the National Voter Registration Act of 1993 mandates that states give citizens opportunities to register to vote at government motor vehicle agencies. Through this mandate, the Act sought to "increase the number of eligible citizens who register to vote in elections for Federal office."[48]

2. Why Federal Rather than State Regulation?

The prior section highlights some of the most common reasons why the government might decide to enact legislation that alters the common law rule. In the United States, there is the further question: whether Congress or state and local governments should make that decision.

---

42 Stat. 388 (codified at 7 U.S.C. § 291) (exempting agricultural marketing cooperatives from anti-trust regulation in order to improve the market power of farmer-members).

46. *See generally* Louis Kaplow & Steven Shavell, *Why the Legal System Is Less Efficient Than the Income Tax in Redistributing Income*, 23 J. Legal Stud. 667 (1994). *See also* Zachary D. Liscow, Note, *Reducing Inequality on the Cheap: When Legal Rule Design Should Incorporate Equity as Well as Efficiency*, 123 Yale L.J. 2478 (2014).

47. *See* Alan Schwartz & Robert E. Scott, *Contract Theory and the Limits of Contract Law*, 113 Yale L.J. 541 (2003).

48. 42 U.S.C. § 1973gg(b)(1).

United States v. Sullivan

332 U.S. 689 (1948)

MR. JUSTICE BLACK delivered the opinion of the Court.

Respondent, a retail druggist in Columbus, Georgia, was charged in two counts of an information with a violation of § 301(k) of the Federal Food, Drug, and Cosmetic Act of 1938. [52 Stat. ch. 675, 21 U.S.C. § 331(k).] That section prohibits "the doing of any . . . act with respect to, a . . . drug . . . if such act is done while such article is held for sale after shipment in interstate commerce and results in such article being misbranded."[1] Section 502(f) of the Act declares a drug "to be misbranded . . . unless its labeling bears (1) adequate directions for use; and (2) such adequate warnings against use . . . dangerous to health, or against unsafe dosage . . . as are necessary for the protection of users." [21 U.S.C. § 352(f)] The information charged specifically that the respondent had performed certain acts which resulted in sulfathiazole being "misbranded" while "held for sale after shipment in interstate commerce."

The facts alleged were these: A laboratory had shipped in interstate commerce from Chicago, Illinois, to a consignee at Atlanta, Georgia, a number of bottles, each containing 1,000 sulfathiazole tablets. These bottles had labels affixed to them, which, as required by § 502(f)(1) and (2) of the Act, set out adequate directions for the use of the tablets and adequate warnings to protect ultimate consumers from dangers incident to this use.[2] Respondent bought one of these properly labeled bottles of sulfathiazole tablets from the Atlanta consignee, transferred it to his Columbus, Georgia, drugstore, and there held the tablets for resale. On two separate occasions twelve tablets were removed from the properly labeled and branded bottle, placed in pill boxes, and sold to customers. These boxes were labeled "sulfathiazole." They did not contain the statutorily required adequate directions for use or warnings of danger.

Respondent's motion to dismiss the information was overruled, a jury was waived, evidence was heard, and respondent was convicted under both counts.

---

1. "Sec. 301. The following acts and the causing thereof are hereby prohibited:

. . . . .

"(k) The alteration, mutilation, destruction, obliteration, or removal of the whole or any part of the labeling of, or the doing of any other act with respect to, a food, drug, device, or cosmetic, if such act is done while such article is held for sale after shipment in interstate commerce and results in such article being misbranded." 52 Stat. 1042, 21 U.S.C. § 331(k).

2. The following inscription appeared on the bottle labels as a compliance with § 502 (f) (1) which requires directions as to use: "Caution.—To be used only by or on the prescription of a physician." This would appear to constitute adequate directions since it is required by regulation issued by the Administrator pursuant to authority of the Act. 21 C.F.R. Cum. Supp. § 2.106(b)(3). The following appeared on the label of the bottles as a compliance with § 502(f)(2) which requires warnings of danger: "Warning.—In some individuals Sulfathiazole may cause severe toxic reactions. Daily blood counts for evidence of anemia or leukopenia and urine examinations for hematuria are recommended.

"Physicians should familiarize themselves with the use of this product before it is administered. A circular giving full directions and contraindications will be furnished upon request."

The Circuit Court of Appeals reversed. The court thought that as a result of respondent's action the sulfathiazole became "misbranded" within the meaning of the Federal Act, and that in its "broadest possible sense" the Act's language "may include what happened." However, it was also of the opinion that the Act ought not to be taken so broadly "but held to apply only to the holding for the first sale by the importer after interstate shipment." Thus the Circuit Court of Appeals interpreted the statutory language of § 301(k) "while such article is held for sale after shipment in interstate commerce" as though Congress had said "while such article is held for sale by a person who had himself received it by way of a shipment in interstate commerce." We granted certiorari to review this important question concerning the Act's coverage.

First. The narrow construction given § 301(k) rested not so much upon its language as upon the Circuit Court's view of the consequences that might result from the broader interpretation urged by the Government. The court pointed out that the retail sales here involved were made in Columbus nine months after this sulfathiazole had been shipped from Chicago to Atlanta. It was impressed by the fact that, if the statutory language "while such article is held for sale after shipment in interstate commerce" should be given its literal meaning, the criminal provisions relied on would "apply to all intrastate sales of imported drugs after any number of intermediate sales within the State and after any lapse of time; and not only to such sales of drugs, but also to similar retail sales of foods, devices and cosmetics, for all these are equally covered by these provisions of the Act." The court emphasized that such consequences would result in far-reaching inroads upon customary control by local authorities of traditionally local activities, and that a purpose to afford local retail purchasers federal protection from harmful foods, drugs and cosmetics should not be ascribed to Congress in the absence of an exceptionally clear mandate***. Another reason of the court for refraining from construing the Act as applicable to articles misbranded while held for retail sale even though the articles had previously been shipped in interstate commerce, was its opinion that such a construction would raise grave doubts as to the Act's constitutionality. In support of this position the court cited *Labor Board v. Jones & Laughlin Steel Corp.*, 301 U.S. 1, 30, and *Schechter Poultry Corp. v. United States*, 295 U.S. 495 [*infra* Chapter 3[B][1][a]].

A restrictive interpretation should not be given a statute merely because Congress has chosen to depart from custom or because giving effect to the express language employed by Congress might require a court to face a constitutional question. And none of the foregoing cases, nor any other on which they relied, authorizes a court in interpreting a statute to depart from its clear meaning.*** Although criminal statutes must be so precise and unambiguous that the ordinary person can know how to avoid unlawful conduct, even in determining whether such statutes meet that test, they should be given their fair meaning in accord with the evident intent of Congress.

Second. Another consideration that moved the Circuit Court of Appeals to give the statute a narrow construction was its belief that the holding in this case with reference to misbranding of drugs by a retail druggist would necessarily apply also to "similar retail sales of foods, devices and cosmetics, for all of these," the court said, "are equally covered by the same provisions of the Act." And in this Court the effect of such a possible coverage of the Act is graphically magnified. We are told that its application to these local sales of sulfathiazole would logically require all retail grocers and beauty parlor operators to reproduce the bulk container labels on each individual item when it is taken from the container to sell to a purchaser. It is even prophesied that, if § 301(k) is given the interpretation urged by the Government, it will later be applied so as to require retail merchants to label sticks of candy and sardines when removed from their containers for sale.

The scope of the offense which Congress defined is not to be judicially narrowed as applied to drugs by envisioning extreme possible applications of its different misbranding provisions which relate to food, cosmetics, and the like. There will be opportunity enough to consider such contingencies should they ever arise. It may now be noted, however, that the Administrator of the Act is given rather broad discretion—broad enough undoubtedly to enable him to perform his duties fairly without wasting his efforts on what may be no more than technical infractions of law.*** The provisions of § 405 with regard to food apparently are broad enough to permit the relaxation of some of the labeling requirements which might otherwise impose a burden on retailers out of proportion to their value to the consumer.*

Third. When we seek the meaning of § 301(k) from its language we find that the offense it creates and which is here charged requires the doing of some act with respect to a drug (1) which results in its being misbranded, (2) while the article is held for sale "after shipment in interstate commerce." Respondent has not seriously contended that the "misbranded" portion of § 301(k) is ambiguous. Section 502(f), as has been seen, provides that a drug is misbranded unless the labeling contains adequate directions and adequate warnings. The labeling here did not contain the information which § 502(f) requires. There is a suggestion here that, although alteration, mutilation, destruction, or obliteration of the bottle label would have been a "misbranding," transferring the pills to non-branded boxes would not have been, so long as the labeling on the empty bottle was not disturbed. Such an argument cannot be sustained. For the chief purpose of forbidding the destruction of the label is to keep it intact for the information and protection of the consumer. That purpose would be frustrated when the pills the consumer buys are not labeled as required, whether the label has been torn from the original container or the pills have been transferred from it to a non-labeled one. We find no ambiguity in the misbranding language of the Act.

---

* Section 405 provided:

The Secretary shall promulgate regulations exempting from any labeling requirements of this Act (1) small open containers of fresh fruits and vegetables and (2) food which is, in accordance with the practice of the trade, to be processed, labeled, or repacked in substantial quantities at establishments other than those where originally processed or packed, on condition that such food is not adulterated or misbranded under the provisions of this Act upon removal from such processing, labeling, or repacking establishment.

Pub. L. No. 75-717 § 405, 52 Stat. ch. 675, at 1059 (1938).—*Eds.*

Furthermore, it would require great ingenuity to discover ambiguity in the additional requirement of § 301(k) that the misbranding occur "while such article is held for sale after shipment in interstate commerce." The words accurately describe respondent's conduct here. He held the drugs for sale after they had been shipped in interstate commerce from Chicago to Atlanta. It is true that respondent bought them over six months after the interstate shipment had been completed by their delivery to another consignee. But the language used by Congress broadly and unqualifiedly prohibits misbranding articles held for sale after shipment in interstate commerce, without regard to how long after the shipment the misbranding occurred, how many intrastate sales had intervened, or who had received the articles at the end of the interstate shipment. Accordingly we find that the conduct of the respondent falls within the literal language of § 301(k).

Fourth. Given the meaning that we have found the literal language of § 301(k) to have, it is thoroughly consistent with the general aims and purposes of the Act. For the Act as a whole was designed primarily to protect consumers from dangerous products.*** Its purpose was to safeguard the consumer by applying the Act to articles from the moment of their introduction into interstate commerce all the way to the moment of their delivery to the ultimate consumer. Section 301(a) forbids the "introduction or delivery for introduction into interstate commerce" of misbranded or adulterated drugs; § 301(b) forbids the misbranding or adulteration of drugs while "in interstate commerce"; and § 301(c) prohibits the "receipt in interstate commerce" of any misbranded or adulterated drug, and "the delivery or proffered delivery thereof for pay or otherwise." But these three paragraphs alone would not supply protection all the way to the consumer. The words of paragraph (k) "while such article is held for sale after shipment in interstate commerce" apparently were designed to fill this gap and to extend the Act's coverage to every article that had gone through interstate commerce until it finally reached the ultimate consumer. Doubtless it was this purpose to insure federal protection until the very moment the articles passed into the hands of the consumer by way of an intrastate transaction that moved the House Committee on Interstate and Foreign Commerce to report on this section of the Act as follows: "In order to extend the protection of consumers contemplated by the law to the full extent constitutionally possible, paragraph (k) has been inserted prohibiting the changing of labels so as to misbrand articles held for sale after interstate shipment."[3] We hold that § 301(k) prohibits the misbranding charged in the information.***

Mr. Justice Frankfurter, dissenting.

* * * [I]t cannot be that a transfer from a jar, the bulk container, to a small paper bag, without transferring the label of the jar to the paper bag, is "any other act" when applied to a drug, but not "any other act" when applied to candies or cosmetics.*** Therefore, it cannot be put off to some other day to determine whether "any other act" in § 301(k) applies to the ordinary retail sale of candies or cosmetics in every drug store or grocery throughout the land, and so places every corner grocery and drug store under the

---

3. H.R. Rep. 2139, 75th Cong., 3d Sess., 3.

hazard that the Administrator may report such conduct for prosecution. That question is now here. It is part of this very case, for the simple reason that the prohibited conduct of §301(k) applies with equal force, through the same phrase, to food, drugs and cosmetics insofar as they are required to be labeled. See §403, 502, and 602 of the Act.

It is this inescapable conjunction of food, drugs and cosmetics in the prohibition of §301(k) that calls for a consideration of the phrase "or the doing of any other act," in the context of the rest of the sentence and with due regard for the important fact that the States are also deeply concerned with the protection of the health and welfare of their citizens on transactions peculiarly within local enforcing powers. So considered, "the doing of any other act" should be read with the meaning which radiates to that loose phrase from the particularities that precede it, namely "alteration, mutilation, destruction, obliteration, or removal" of any part of the label.*** I would affirm the judgment below.

MR. JUSTICE REED and MR. JUSTICE JACKSON join in this dissent.

[Opinion of JUSTICE RUTLEDGE, concurring, omitted.]

Notes and Questions

1. **The Need to Regulate?** The common law tort of fraud allows a party to recover damages caused by false statements about a product's composition or quality. To recover, a plaintiff must prove that (1) the defendant made a "misrepresentation of fact, opinion, intention or law," (2) "for the purpose of inducing another to act or to refrain from action in reliance upon it," (3) the plaintiff justifiably relied upon the defendant's misrepresentation, and (4) thereby suffered a "pecuniary loss." Restatement Second of Torts §525 (1977). A party is liable for failing to disclose a fact "if, but only if, he is under a duty to the other to exercise reasonable care to disclose the matter in question." §551(1).

Why might a legislature conclude that these common law protections are inadequate to protect consumers against the dangers posed by misbranded pharmaceuticals? Prior to the enactment of food and drug legislation, assuming competent counsel could be obtained, what hurdles would a plaintiff face attempting to establish that a manufacturer intended to induce buyers to act in reliance on a misstatement? That the buyer's reliance was reasonable?

Even if the common law tort system did not provide a remedy for all instances of misbranding, don't firms face strong market incentives to label their goods accurately? A consumer who purchases a misbranded drug will presumably complain to others, causing demand for the mislabeled drug to drop. This, in turn, creates an incentive for firms to label drugs accurately. When are consumers likely to learn of such mislabeling? What will they need to do to communicate their complaint to the mislabeling firm? Even if a complaint is lodged, how will this information be incorporated into prices and market demand for the mislabeled product?

2. The Need for *Federal* Regulation? Shortly after the release of Upton Sinclair's *The Jungle*, which detailed horrific conditions in Chicago's meatpacking plants, Congress passed and President Theodore Roosevelt signed the Pure Food and Drugs Act, Pub. L. No, 59-384, 34 Stat. 768 (June 30, 1906) (Wiley Act). The 1906 Act prohibited "misbranding" and "adulteration" of food and drugs moving in interstate commerce and required manufacturers to disclose the presence of ten "dangerous" chemicals in products, including cannabis, cocaine, and opium. Violations of the Act were misdemeanors. In addition to bringing criminal prosecutions, the Wiley Act authorized U.S. attorneys to seize shipments of food and drugs that violated the act's standards through an action for libel, a form of action inherited from admiralty.

The modern era of food and drug regulation began in 1938, when Congress overhauled the Wiley Act in the Food, Drug, and Cosmetic Act (FDCA), Pub. L. No. 75-717, 52 Stat. 1040 (June 25, 1938). The Report of the House Committee on Interstate and Foreign Commerce on the 1938 Act explained that "[w]hile the old law has been of incalculable benefit to American consumers, it contains serious loopholes and is not sufficiently broad in its scope to meet the requirements of consumer protection under modern conditions." H.R. Rep. No 75-2139, at 1 (3d Sess., 1938). Among other changes, the 1938 Act prohibited the adulteration and misbranding of cosmetics, required that new drugs be tested for safety before they were placed on the market, and required that food sold in interstate commerce bear labeling identifying its quality and composition.

The 1938 Act created the Food and Drug Administration (FDA), an executive branch agency that is part of the Department of Health and Human Services (previously, the Department of Health, Education, and Welfare). The FDA states that it is "responsible for protecting the public health by ensuring the safety, efficacy, and security of human and veterinary drugs, biological products, and medical devices; and by ensuring the safety of our nation's food supply, cosmetics, and products that emit radiation."[1] It is authorized to seize food, drugs, and cosmetics that do not comply with standards established by law and regulation, *see, e.g.,* 21 U.S.C. §334, and regulates the entry of new pharmaceuticals and medical devices onto the market through an extensive pre-market review process. *See Riegel v. Medtronic, Inc.,* 552 U.S. 312 (2008), *infra* Chapter 1[C][4]. The agency regulates the sale of prescription drugs and adjudicates requests to make prescription drugs available over-the-counter. *See Tummino v. Torti,* 603 F. Supp. 2d 519 (E.D.N.Y. 2009). Since 2009, the FDA has regulated the manufacturing, marketing, and distribution of tobacco products under the Family Smoking Prevention and Tobacco Control Act, Pub. L. No. 111-31, 123 Stat. 1776. The FDA historically has enjoyed a substantial degree of independence from political interference and has cultivated a reputation for independent, science-based policymaking. Its budget for fiscal year 2015 was $4.74 billion.

The Court in *Sullivan* writes that the 1938 FDCA amendments sought "to safeguard the consumer by applying the [1906 Wiley] Act to articles from the moment of their

---

1. U.S. Food and Drug Administration, What We Do, http://www.fda.gov/AboutFDA/WhatWeDo/.

introduction into interstate commerce all the way to the moment of their delivery to the ultimate consumer." Why do you suppose Congress concluded that *federal* legislation was necessary to protect consumers from adulterated and misbranded food, drugs, and cosmetics as opposed to regulation at the state or local level? Consider the following possible rationales:

a. **"Race to the Bottom"?** To begin, might competition among the states have resulted in a "race to the bottom," in which no state was able to regulate at the level it judged optimal because of competition from other states? In the period prior to the Wiley Act, "[r]egulatory law on food, beverages, and drugs was piecemeal. Early laws regulating drugs and other medicinal products included . . . a state law that the New York College of Pharmacy used in 1831 to regulate or supervise the importation of drugs from other countries [and a] 1848 federal law provided for the examination of drugs, medicines, and other medicinal preparations." Ilyse D. Barkan, *Industry Invites Regulation: The Passage of the Pure Food and Drug Act of 1906*, 75 Am. J. Pub. Health 18 (1985). Will competition among jurisdictions necessarily *reduce* the level of regulation? Barkan notes that at the end of the nineteenth century, English and German legislation required "food and beverage exports to meet standards of product quality and inspection," and that foreign manufacturers touted their products' compliance with these standards to appeal to American consumers suspicious of unregulated American goods.

b. **Special federal expertise?** Might the federal government have special expertise to determine how food, drugs, and cosmetics should be labeled? Does it have access to information or expertise that is unavailable to or could not be shared among state and local governments?

c. **Coordinating market activity?** Might federal regulation be desirable on the ground that it helps to coordinate regulatory activity and thus reduces the cost of doing business in the national market? "As early as the 1880s, most domestic food, beverage, and drug industries had recognized the need for product certification to increase the competitiveness of their products" vis-à-vis foreign goods. Barkan, *supra*, at 23. When early efforts at standardization failed, industries in the 1890s began to express the need for federal legislation that would regulate and certify product quality.

Does a federal law establishing a uniform floor of regulatory standards necessarily ensure the *consumer* interest in safety is safeguarded? Will federal regulation lead in some cases to over-regulation, disserving consumer interests in lower prices for the goods they purchase? Is it possible that federal legislation might *benefit* manufacturers of food, drug, and cosmetics as opposed to imposing an unwanted regulatory burden on them?

d. **The extent of state authority.** Recall that, at the time of the 1938 FDCA amendments, a state's authority to regulate out-of-state defendants based on activities directed at the state's market was uncertain. It was not until 1945 that the Supreme Court expressly recognized that a state could regulate an out-of-state defendant to the extent that the defendant, through its agents, was "present" in the state, and that an out-of-state defendant could be compelled to defend itself in the state's courts where it had "minimum contacts" with the state and the exercise of judicial jurisdiction was consistent with "traditional notions of fair play and substantial justice." *International Shoe Co. v. Washington*, 326 U.S. 310, 316 (1945).

3. **The Government's Theory of the Case?** What was the government's theory for how Sullivan violated the FDCA? Which provision of the statute did the government claim that Sullivan violated? (*See* note 1, *supra*.) When in the government's view did this violation occur? What was the procedural posture of the dispute when it reached the Supreme Court?

4. **The Interpretive Dispute.** Sullivan argued—and the court of appeals agreed—that the sulfathiazole tablets he sold were not "held for sale after shipment in interstate commerce" because the tablets had passed through an Atlanta intermediary before Sullivan acquired them. In arguing that the pills lacked the requisite connection to interstate commerce, Sullivan invoked three canons of statutory interpretation, interpretive rules of thumb that courts use to determine the meaning of indeterminate statutory language. *See infra* Chapter 2[B][1][a].

First, Sullivan invoked the principle that "an exceptionally clear mandate" is necessary if Congress wishes to make "far-reaching inroads upon customary control by local authorities of traditionally local activities." This principle, sometimes termed the "federalism" canon, is based on the assumption that Congress is aware of, and intends to respect, states' authority over essentially local matters. *See Gregory v. Ashcroft*, 501 U.S. 452 (1991), *infra* Chapter 2[B][2][f]. Second, Sullivan invoked the principle that "criminal statutes must be so precise and unambiguous that the ordinary person can know how to avoid unlawful conduct." This canon, often called the doctrine of lenity, is based in part on the due process consideration that the government give notice of actions that it intends to punish. *See FCC v. Fox Television Stations, Inc.*, 132 S. Ct. 2307, 2317 (2012). Finally, Sullivan argued that Congress could not have intended § 301(k) to apply drugs that passed through an intermediary before they were sold, because the section also applied to food products which are often resold and broken into smaller units before it is sold to consumers. Congress could not have intended to criminalize this common practice, Sullivan argued. This is an example of the "absurdity" canon: "If a literal construction of the words of a statute be absurd, the act must be so construed as to avoid the absurdity." *Holy Trinity Church v. United States*, 143 U.S. 457, 460 (1892), *infra* Chapter 2[B][1][b].

How did the Court respond to Sullivan's invocation of the federalism canon? In *NLRB v. Catholic Bishop of Chicago*, 440 U.S. 490 (1979), *infra* Chapter 2[B][2][f], the Supreme Court observed that "an Act of Congress ought not be construed to violate the Constitution if any other possible construction remains available." To the *Catholic Bishop* Court, it followed that an interpretation which "presents a significant risk" of a constitutional violation (there, a violation of the First Amendment's Establishment and Free Exercise Clauses) was to be avoided. Does the risk of constitutional invalidity play the same role in the Court's decision in *Sullivan*?

How does the Court respond to Sullivan's claim that § 301(k) did not provide sufficiently clear notice of the conduct that it prohibited? The argument that Congress could not have intended § 301(k) to apply to all downstream sales?

In dissent, Justice Frankfurter advances a different argument. He contends that Sullivan's act of removing sulfathiazole pills from a properly labeled bottle was too remote from the pills' movement in interstate commerce to fall within § 301(k). Why was the majority not persuaded? Are we?

Note on Justifications for *Federal* Regulation

Nearly every significant proposal for a new federal law encounters two objections. The first, which we term the "assumption of private ordering," is the idea that private parties are generally competent to order their affairs in the manner they think best, without governmental interference.

The private ordering premise posits that voluntary transactions among self-interested parties have the long-term effect of allocating goods and services to the persons and organizations that value them most highly. Individuals' pursuit of their self-interest therefore produces a socially optimal—sometimes called "efficient"—allocation of resources, meaning that resources are assigned to the actors who value them the most and will put them to the most valuable use. An efficient allocation of resources, in turn, is thought to improve the overall welfare of society. On this view, a new federal law is undesirable because it interferes with the ability of private parties to arrange their own affairs. (This objection is also invoked against significant new state and local laws.)

The second objection to a new federal law is "the presumption in favor of state regulation." According to this view, state governments are better at regulating social problems than the federal government, because they have more information about problems that require regulation, and experience the costs and benefits of regulation more directly than the geographically distant federal government.

This view has deep roots in U.S. political thought. James Madison wrote in the Federalist Papers:

> Many considerations . . . seem to place it beyond doubt that the first and most natural attachment of the people will be to the governments of their respective States. Into the administration of these a greater number of individuals will expect to rise. From the gift of these a greater number of offices and emoluments will flow. By the superintending care of these, all the more domestic and personal interests of the people will be regulated and provided for. With the affairs of these, the people will be more familiarly and minutely conversant. And with the members of these, will a greater proportion of the people have the ties of personal acquaintance and friendship, and of family and party attachments; on the side of these, therefore, the popular bias may well be expected most strongly to incline.[49]

---

49. THE FEDERALIST No. 46, at 302 (Madison) (Robert Scigliano ed., 2000).

Given the private ordering and state regulation objections, when is federal regulation appropriate? The four rationales for federal action that are most frequently invoked are the following.

First, federal regulation might be warranted because the federal government is better situated to deal with the problem than state and local governments. In a national economy, states and municipalities will not always experience all of the costs and benefits of a given activity or its possible regulatory mitigation. Coal-producing states, for example, are likely to feel differently about air quality standards than, say, the coastal states and yet the environmental impact of coal production will not be confined to the producing states. The federal government is more likely to reflect the interests of all affected states.[50]

Second, federal legislation can overcome collective action problems that prevent state and local governments from regulating a problem effectively on their own. States may desire to regulate a problem but be unable to do so because of the possibility that other states will capture business or residents by offering havens from regulation. In its most famous form, this argument posits a "race to the bottom" in which states, unable to resist pressure from regulated industries for less stringent regulation, adopt suboptimal regulatory standards. The solution, some claim, is to enact federal regulatory standards from which the states cannot compete away to the lowest common denominator.[51]

Third, federal legislation may be needed to correct failures of the political process at the state level. Prior to the passage of the Voting Rights Act of 1965,[52] for example, racial minorities were systematically excluded from voting in states of the former confederacy and some northern jurisdictions. Under these circumstances, Congress was the only forum in which proponents of civil rights legislation could hope to succeed. Similarly, the federal government may use its superior taxing base to subsidize improvements in public education that local governments cannot afford.

Fourth, federal regulation might be thought desirable even for regulated entities because compliance costs are likely to be lower with respect to a uniform federal rule than with having to navigate 50 or more different rules and regulatory processes. Thus, for example, federal regulation of employee pension and welfare plans under the Employee Retirement Income Security Act (ERISA) is broadly preemptive of state and local laws "relating to" such plans in order to preserve the benefits of uniformity.[53]

---

50. *See generally* Bruce Ackerman & William T. Hassler, Clean Coal/Dirty Air: Or How the Clean Air Act Became a Multibillion-Dollar Bail-Out for High-Sulfur Coal Producers (1981).

51. *See generally* Richard B. Stewart, *Pyramids of Sacrifice? Problems of Federalism in Mandating State Implementation of National Environmental Policy*, 86 Yale L.J. 1196 (1977); Richard L. Revesz, *Rehabilitating Interstate Competition: Rethinking the "Race to the Bottom" Rationale for Federal Environmental Regulation*, 67 N.Y.U. L. Rev. 1210 (1992); Robert D. Cooter & Neil S. Siegel, *Collective Action Federalism: A General Theory of Article I, Section 8*, 63 Stan. L. Rev. 115 (2010).

52. Pub. L. No. 89-110, 79 Stat. 437, codified as amended at 52 U.S.C. § 10101 et seq.

53. *See* 29 U.S.C. § 1144(a).

We will return to the justifications for federal regulation throughout this volume. Now, we turn to the choices that policymakers confront when designing a federal legislative and regulatory program.

C. How to Regulate?

The goal in making public policy is not only to identify *the problem* that regulation will address but also to determine *how best to address the problem*. Indeed, how to regulate may be more important than identifying problems for regulation. Few would dispute that, all other things being equal, it is beneficial for society to produce more wealth, reduce inequality, or encourage political participation. The difficult question is how to accomplish those goals.

1. Regulation vs. Common Law

An initial question for policymakers is whether particular choices should be controlled through governmental regulation or left to market dynamics within a common law system that generally protects private property and freedom of contract. Consider the following case involving the Fair Labor Standards Act of 1938, a statute that restricts market arrangements over the wages paid to employees.

Brooklyn Savings Bank v. O'Neil

324 U.S. 697 (1945)

Mr. Justice Reed delivered the opinion of the Court.

The petitioner, Brooklyn Savings Bank, owned and operated an eleven-story office building in which the respondent was employed as a night watchman during a two-year period from November 5, 1938, to August 30, 1940. Since a substantial portion of that building was devoted to the production of goods for commerce, the respondent was entitled to overtime compensation under the provisions of §7 of the Fair Labor Standards Act.[3] No such compensation was paid at that time. However, in November, 1942, over two years after the respondent had left petitioner's service, the petitioner computed the statutory overtime compensation due the respondent and offered him a check for $423.16 in return for a release of all of his rights under the Act. The respondent signed the release and took the check. Since this sum did not include any payment

---

3. Section 7(a) provides:

"No employer shall, except as otherwise provided in this section, employ any of his employees who is engaged in commerce or in the production of goods for commerce*** for a workweek longer than forty hours*** unless such employee receives compensation for his employment in excess of the hours above specified at a rate not less than one and one-half times the regular rate at which he is employed."

for liquidated damages provided for in § 16(b) of the Act,* the respondent subsequently instituted the present proceeding in a New York City Municipal Court to recover liquidated damages due him under § 16(b). The complaint was dismissed on the grounds that respondent failed to prove a cause of action and also that the respondent "released any claim for liquidated damages or counsel fees." The Appellate Term reversed, per curiam, holding that respondent was employed in the production of goods for commerce within the meaning of the Fair Labor Standards Act and was entitled therefore to recover liquidated damages by reason of petitioner's default in making overtime payments as required by § 7 of the Act. This decision was affirmed by the New York Appellate Division, and by the New York Court of Appeals.***

It has been held in this and other courts that a statutory right conferred on a private party, but affecting the public interest, may not be waived or released if such waiver or release contravenes the statutory policy. Where a private right is granted in the public interest to effectuate a legislative policy, waiver of a right so charged or colored with the public interest will not be allowed where it would thwart the legislative policy which it was designed to effectuate. With respect to private rights created by a federal statute, such as § 16(b), the question of whether the statutory right may be waived depends upon the intention of Congress as manifested in the particular statute.***

Neither the statutory language, the legislative reports nor the debates indicates that the question at issue was specifically considered and resolved by Congress. In the absence of evidence of specific Congressional intent, it becomes necessary to resort to a broader consideration of the legislative policy behind this provision as evidenced by its legislative history and the provisions in and structure of the Act. Such consideration clearly shows that Congress did not intend that an employee should be allowed to waive his right to liquidated damages.

The legislative history of the Fair Labor Standards Act shows an intent on the part of Congress to protect certain groups of the population from sub-standard wages and excessive hours which endangered the national health and well-being and the free flow of goods in interstate commerce. The statute was a recognition of the fact that due to the unequal bargaining power as between employer and employee, certain segments of the population required federal compulsory legislation to prevent private contracts on their part which endangered national health and efficiency and as a result the free movement of goods in interstate commerce. To accomplish this purpose

---

* Section 16 (b) provides:

"Any employer who violates the provisions of section 6 or section 7 of this Act shall be liable to the employee or employees affected in the amount of their unpaid minimum wages, or their unpaid overtime compensation, as the case may be, and in an additional equal amount as liquidated damages. Action to recover such liability may be maintained in any court of competent jurisdiction by any one or more employees for and in behalf of himself or themselves and other employees similarly situated, or such employee or employees may designate an agent or representative to maintain such action for and in behalf of all employees similarly situated. The court in such action shall, in addition to any judgment awarded to the plaintiff or plaintiffs, allow a reasonable attorney's fee to be paid by the defendant, and costs of the action."

—*Eds.*

standards of minimum wages and maximum hours were provided. Neither petitioner nor respondent suggests that the right to the basic statutory minimum wage could be waived by any employee subject to the Act. No one can doubt but that to allow waiver of statutory wages by agreement would nullify the purposes of the Act. We are of the opinion that the same policy considerations which forbid waiver of basic minimum and overtime wages under the Act also prohibit waiver of the employee's right to liquidated damages.

The same policy which forbids waiver of the statutory minimum as necessary to the free flow of commerce requires that reparations to restore damage done by such failure to pay on time must be made to accomplish Congressional purposes. Moreover, the same policy which forbids employee waiver of the minimum statutory rate because of inequality of bargaining power, prohibits these same employees from bargaining with their employer in determining whether so little damage was suffered that waiver of liquidated damage is called for.

Notes and Questions

1. **The Procedural Posture?** In *Brooklyn Savings Bank*, an employee entitled to statutory overtime pay accepted a settlement payment from his employer before bringing suit. How, then, did the case end up in court? In the Supreme Court?

A major issue for any regulatory scheme that relies on private suits is access to legal assistance. Most beneficiaries of statutes like the FLSA do not earn enough income nor will their claims be large enough to attract competent lawyers. Under the "American rule" concerning attorney's fees, litigants are generally responsible for their own litigation costs, including attorney's fees. *See Alyeska Pipeline v. Wilderness Society*, 421 U.S. 240, 247 (1975). Congress in § 16(b) of FLSA specified that "[t]he court in such actions shall, in addition to any judgment award to the plaintiff or plaintiffs, allow a reasonable attorney's fee to be paid by the defendant and the costs of the action." Does this provision have any bearing on how the case ended up in court?

Note that the *Brooklyn Bank* lawsuit was brought in New York state court. What is the purpose of concurrent jurisdiction in a case where the defendant can remove to federal court? Why do you think this case was not removed to federal court?

2. **The Justification for Minimum Labor Standards?** The FLSA operates within a legal and social context in which privately-negotiated or employer-imposed labor contracts are the norm. At common law, parties were free to negotiate terms of employment, including hours of work and employee compensation. The common law implied various duties in employment contracts governing matters such as the employee's duty to serve in good faith and termination of the employment relationship. *See* Restatement of Employment Law, chs. 2–3 & 8 (2015). However, the common law did not establish a floor for compensation.

According to a standard theory in labor economics, freedom of contract in the labor area permits the employer to pay the minimum compensation necessary to attract and retain employees needed to carry out its business objectives. This lowers the employer's cost of producing goods and services, which in turn leads to lower consumer prices. *See generally* Samuel Estreicher & Gillian Lester, Employment Law 2–5 (2008).

Within this context, the FLSA imposes a federal minimum wage and requires time-and-a-half pay for work beyond a forty-hour workweek. What problems with the common law's treatment of the employment relationship motivated Congress to intervene in this manner? Are employees who work more than forty hours a week incapable of negotiating increased compensation for higher working hours? Without statutory labor standards, will there be a "race to the bottom" among workers? Does the FLSA improve the bargaining leverage of workers by placing a value on their leisure that employers, wanting more hours from their workforce, must pay more for? *See generally* John T. Addison & Barry T. Hirsch, *The Economic Effects of Employment Regulation: What Are the Limits?*, *in* Government Regulation of the Employment Relationship 141–42 (Bruce Kaufman ed., 1997); Todd D. Rakoff, A Time for Every Purpose: Law and the Balance of Life 65–66 (2002).

The time-and-a-half requirement has the indirect effect of spreading work among potential workers. Because of the FLSA and similar state laws, all other things being equal, it costs more for an employer to have an existing employee work more than forty hours per week than to hire a new employee. Thus, for self-interested reasons, employers are encouraged to bring on new employees rather than asking existing employees to work more. Work-spreading might not occur, however, if benefit and training costs for new workers are greater than the overtime premium.

Is this job-spreading effect something that could be accomplished through negotiation of individual employment agreements under common law contract rules? Is it a kind of public good, like interstate highways or national defense, that government generally has a duty to provide?

What is the net effect of the FLSA on job creation? Insofar as the Act sets minimum wages for new employees, does it discourage employment by raising the cost of hiring and retaining workers? (The extent of any job-displacement effect would depend on how easily employers could replace labor with machines or raise consumer prices.) Or does it lead to the creation of more work by attaching a penalty to having employees work more than 40 hours in a work week?

In June 2014, the City of Council of Seattle, Washington voted to raise Seattle's minimum wage to $15 per hour through a series of increases that take effect between 2015 and 2021. The Seattle vote was the first major success for a national movement that seeks a higher minimum wage for workers in low-wage industries. (The FLSA does not preempt state laws imposing higher minimum wages.) Which is more desirable social policy: requiring that employers pay a particular amount, or increasing work opportunities by leaving the labor market lightly regulated? One argument advanced by supporters of the $15/hour minimum wage suggests that private wage-setting imposes externalities: if workers are not paid enough to cover their basic needs, the state will end up paying for those needs through other, more costly mechanisms. The business community typically counters that higher minimum wages will negatively affect unemployment rates; if a firm's labor budget is fixed, the only way to satisfy a minimum-wage law is to raise prices or reduce the overall number of employees. A famous study of fast food workers conducted after New Jersey raised its minimum wage found no evidence that this actually occurred, raising the possibility that employers can meet at least modest increases in the minimum wage through means other than reducing the size of the workforce. *See* David Card & Alan B. Krueger, *Minimum Wages and Employment: A Case Study of the Fast-Food Industry in New Jersey and Pennsylvania*, 84 Am. Econ. Rev. 772 (1994); David Card & Alan B. Krueger, Myth and Measurement: The New Economics of the Minimum Wage (1997). *But see* Daniel Shaviro, *The Minimum Wage, the Earned Income Tax Credit, and Optimal Subsidy Policy*, 64 U. Chi. L. Rev. 405 (1997). Does the policy response to low wages depend on whether a minimum wage in fact increases unemployment? Is the debate over facts, or deeper social norms?

3. **The Justification for *Federal* Minimum Labor Standards?** If one accepts that wages should be regulated by law rather than established by the market, what is the argument for *federal* minimum wage laws? Given variations in the cost of living, are minimum wages better set at the state or local level? Without a national wage floor, is there a risk that a state will be able to export suboptimal wage standards to other states? How might this occur? *Cf. United States v. Darby*, 312 U.S. 100, 109–10 (1941) (suggesting that the FLSA sought to prevent the "spreading and perpetuating [of] substandard labor conditions among the workers of the several states").

4. **Role of the Statutory Text?** Which statutory provisions are pertinent to the Court's conclusion that an employee may not waive liquidated damages due under the FLSA? Does the Court offer an argument based on statutory text for why damages may not be waived? What is the strongest textual argument that can be made in support of the Court's conclusion? What is the strongest textual argument *against* the Court's conclusion?

Should the case come out differently if the question is not whether the minimum wage was paid for hours that were concededly worked but, rather, a dispute over whether the worker *in fact* worked the number of hours claimed? Say the employee claims 50 hours of unpaid work but the employer's records show that unpaid hours are less than 25. Should a private agreement between the employer and the worker compromising their differences to provide for payment of the 25 hours of conceded work and 12 hours of disputed work be enforceable? Is it relevant that the Department of Labor, which enforces the Act, does not have adequate resources to bring suit in every claim of unpaid work under the Act? *See Schulte, Inc. v. Gangi*, 328 U.S. 108 (1946). On the private settlement of claims under the Age Discrimination in Employment Act (ADEA), also enforced by the same mixture of private action and litigation by the Department of Labor, see 29 U.S.C. §626(f); *Runyan v. National Cash Register Corp.*, 787 F.2d 1039 (6th Cir. 1986) (comparing average ADEA and FLSA claimants).

5. **Role of Legislative History?** In concluding that the Act impliedly precludes waivers of liquidated damages, the Court relies on the legislative history of the FLSA. How is this understanding of the statute's history pertinent to the question before the Court? What specifically does the Court glean from the FLSA's legislative history?

6. **Public and Private Enforcement.** The version of the FLSA in effect at the time of the decision in *Brooklyn Savings Bank* contained overlapping public and private enforcement mechanisms. The Department of Labor (DOL) was authorized to bring criminal actions for willful violations of the statute's minimum wage and overtime standards and to sue to recover unpaid compensation owed under the law. Congress in §16(b) authorized suits by employees acting either individually or on behalf of themselves and others "similarly situated." The right to bring a private suit terminates upon the filing of a DOL court action. What might be the reasons for this division of enforcement authority?

Note that the DOL was not given the authority to adjudicate violations using its administrative processes. The agency was charged with investigating conditions in industries regulated by the Act and promulgating guidance for the benefit of regulated firms. The effect of such administrative guidance on judicial interpretation of the FLSA is discussed in *Skidmore v. Swift & Co.*, in Section [C][3], below.

2. Rules vs. Standards

Beyond deciding *whether* to regulate through legislation, Congress must decide *how precise* its regulatory directives should be. Legislation can be written at various levels of generality, ranging from a general directive ("Act reasonably") to an extremely specific command ("No deduction shall be allowed for any expense incurred between June 1, 2014, and June 10, 2014, in New York, New York."). Consider the prohibition of "unfair" trade practices in the Federal Trade Commission Act.

FTC v. R.F. Keppel & Bro.

291 U.S. 304 (1934)

Mr. Justice Stone delivered the opinion of the Court.

This case comes here on certiorari to review a decree of the Court of Appeals for the Third Circuit, which set aside an order of the Federal Trade Commission forbidding certain trade practices of respondent as an unfair method of competition. 63 F.(2d) 81; section 5, Federal Trade Commission Act, 38 Stat. 717, 719 (15 U.S.C. §45).

The Commission found that respondent, one of numerous candy manufacturers similarly engaged, manufactures, sells, and distributes, in interstate commerce, package assortments of candies known to the trade as 'break and take' packages, in competition with manufacturers of assortments known as 'straight goods' packages. Both types are assortments of candies in packages in convenient arrangement for sale by the piece at a small price in retail stores in what is known as the penny candy trade. The break and take assortments are so arranged and offered for sale to consumers as to avail of the element of chance as an inducement to the retail purchasers. One assortment, consisting of 120 pieces retailing at 1 cent each, includes four pieces, each having concealed within its wrapper a single cent, so that the purchasers of those particular pieces of candy receive back the amount of the purchase price and thus obtain the candy without cost.***

The Commission found that the use of the break and take package in the retail trade involves the sale or distribution of the candy by lot or chance; that it is a lottery or gambling device which encourages gambling among children; that children, enticed by the element of chance, purchase candy so sold in preference to straight goods candy; and that the competition between the two types of package results in a substantial diversion of trade from the manufacturers of the straight goods package to those distributing the break and take type.***

Although the method of competition adopted by respondent induces children, too young to be capable of exercising an intelligent judgment of the transaction, to purchase an article less desirable in point of quality or quantity than that offered at a comparable price in the straight goods package, we may take it that it does not involve any fraud or deception. It would seem also that competing manufacturers can adopt the break and take device at any time and thus maintain their competitive position.***

[However, neither] the language nor the history of the act suggests that Congress intended to confine the forbidden methods to fixed and unyielding categories. The common law afforded a definition of unfair competition and, before the enactment of the Federal Trade Commission Act, the Sherman Anti-Trust Act (15 U.S.C. §§ 1–7, 15 note) had laid its inhibition upon combinations to restrain or monopolize interstate commerce which the courts had construed to include restraints upon competition in interstate commerce. It would not have been a difficult feat of draftsmanship to have restricted the operation of the Trade Commission Act to those methods of competition in interstate commerce which are forbidden at common law or which are likely to grow into violations of the Sherman Act, if that had been the purpose of the legislation.

The act undoubtedly was aimed at all the familiar methods of law violation which prosecutions under the Sherman Act had disclosed. But as this Court has pointed out it also had a broader purpose. As proposed by the Senate Committee on Interstate Commerce and as introduced in the Senate, the bill which ultimately became the Federal Trade Commission Act declared 'unfair competition' to be unlawful.

[I]t was because the meaning which the common law had given to those words was deemed too narrow that the broader and more flexible phrase 'unfair methods of competition' was substituted.[2] Congress, in defining the powers of the Commission, thus

---

2. The phrase 'unfair methods of competition' was substituted for 'unfair competition' in the Conference Committee. This change seems first to have been suggested by Senator Hollis in debate on the floor of the Senate in response to the suggestion that the words 'unfair competition' might be construed as restricted to those forms of unfair competition condemned by the common law. 51 Cong. Record 12145. The House Managers of the conference committee, in reporting this change said, House Report No. 1142, 63d Congress, 2d Sess., September 4, 1914, at page 19:

advisedly adopted a phrase which, as this Court has said, does not "admit of precise definition, but the meaning and application of which must be arrived at by what this Court elsewhere has called 'the gradual process of judicial inclusion and exclusion.'"

The argument that a method used by one competitor is not unfair if others may adopt it without any restriction of competition between them was rejected by this Court in *Federal Trade Commission v. Winsted Hosiery Co.,* [258 U.S. 483 (1922)]; compare *Federal Trade Commission v. Algoma Lumber Co.,* 291 U.S. 67. There it was specifically held that a trader may not, by pursuing a dishonest practice, force his competitors to choose between its adoption or the loss of their trade. A method of competition which casts upon one's competitors the burden of the loss of business unless they will descend to a practice which they are under a powerful moral compulsion not to adopt, even though it is not criminal, was thought to involve the kind of unfairness at which the statute was aimed.***

While this Court has declared that it is for the courts to determine what practices or methods of competition are to be deemed unfair, in passing on that question the determination of the Commission is of weight. It was created with the avowed purpose of lodging the administrative functions committed to it in 'a body specially competent to deal with them by reason of information, experience and careful study of the business and economic conditions of the industry affected,' and it was organized in such a manner, with respect to the length and expiration of the terms of office of its members, as would 'give to them an opportunity to acquire the expertness in dealing with these special questions concerning industry that comes from experience.' Report of Senate Committee on Interstate Commerce, No. 597, June 13, 1914, 63d Cong., 2d Sess., pp. 9, 11. If the point were more doubtful than we think it, we should hesitate to reject the conclusion of the Commission, based as it is upon clear, specific and comprehensive findings supported by evidence.***

Notes and Questions

1. **The Justification for Regulation?** In a leading English decision, the Queen's Bench Division of the High Court of Justice concluded: "No man [can] justify damaging another in his commercial business by fraud or misrepresentation. Intimidation, obstruction, and molestation are forbidden; so is the intentional procurement of a violation of individual rights, contractual or other, assuming always that there is no just cause for it." However, a person's "pursu[it] to the bitter end a war of

---

[continuation of footnote 2]

'It is impossible to frame definitions which embrace all unfair practices. There is no limit to human inventiveness in this field. Even if all known unfair practices were specifically defined and prohibited, it would be at once necessary to begin over again. If Congress were to adopt the method of definition, it would undertake an endless task. It is also practically impossible to define unfair practices so that the definition will fit business of every sort in every part of this country. Whether competition is unfair or not generally depends upon the surrounding circumstances of the particular case. What is harmful under certain circumstances may be beneficial under different circumstances.'

competition waged in the interest of their own trade," is lawful. *Mogul Steamship Co. v. McGregor, Gow, & Co.*, 23 Q.B.D. 598 (1889). Under these standards, would the use of break-and-take candy packaging be considered lawful?

Section 5(a)(1) of the Federal Trade Commission Act (FTC Act) provides: "Unfair methods of competition in or affecting commerce, and unfair or deceptive acts or practices in or affecting commerce, are hereby declared unlawful." 15 U.S.C. § 45 (a)(1). According to the FTC, the use of break-and-take candy packaging presented at least four problems that warranted a regulatory response. That practice: (1) "encourage[d] gambling among children"; (2) induced children to buy inferior candy; (3) diverted business "from the manufacturers of the straight goods package to those distributing the break and take type"; and (4) disadvantaged retailers who regarded break-and-take packaging as "a reprehensible encouragement of gambling among children" and therefore refused to make use of it. To what extent would common law prohibitions on unfair competition address these problems?

2. **The Justification for Federal Regulation?** To the extent that break-and-take candy packaging presents problems that are not adequately addressed by the common law, what is the justification for regulating those problems through federal rather than state law? Is there a need for national uniformity in the way that candy is marketed? Are states likely to engage in a "race to the bottom" in the absence of a uniform federal standard? Does the federal government have access to information or expertise that is unavailable to state and local governments?

3. **The FTC Act's Mode of Regulation?** The FTC Act gives the FTC substantial authority to determine what methods of competition are lawful. Rather than Congress determining whether a particular business practice is lawful, the FTC does so, through a combination of rulemaking, agency adjudication (as in the principal reading but unlike the DOL in FLSA cases), and statements of policy. What are the advantages of this structure from the perspective of Congress? Why might Congress be reluctant to identify specific practices that it believes to be unfair?

Congress's failure to specify the conduct believed to be unlawful may have negative consequences for businesses' ability to plan their affairs. Suppose that you represent a company that makes breakfast cereal, which is thinking of introducing a new kind of children's cereal called "Tasty Os." Scientists working in the firm's research and development department report that when miniscule amounts of monosodium glutamate (MSG) are added to Tasty Os, children become enthralled with the cereal and, if left unattended, consume large amounts of it. The CEO of the cereal maker would very much like to release a version of Tasty Os that contains MSG. Based on *R.F. Keppel*, would you advise her that doing so is an unfair method of competition? Could you predict with confidence that the FTC would or would not deem the use of MSG an unfair trade practice? Would an agency practice of providing advisory opinions mitigate the regulatory uncertainty? From the standpoint of agency regulatory objectives, are there any costs to providing such guidance to regulated industries?

4. **The Procedural Posture?** Who initiated the dispute between the FTC and R.F. Keppel & Brother? What was the nature of the administrative action under review by the Supreme Court?

5. **"Unfair" Methods of Competition?** Just what is "unfair" about the use of break-and-take candy packages? Is there any indication in the legislative history cited by the Court that Congress was concerned with the problem of break-and-take packaging? Is there any indication that Congress was even concerned with the general kind of problem exemplified by break-and-take packaging? Thinking back to the prior section, what policy justification could be offered in support of a prohibition of break-and-take packaging?

6. **The Federal Trade Commission.** Congress established the Federal Trade Commission (FTC) in 1914 for the twofold purpose of improving administration of the antitrust laws and regulating anticompetitive conduct that did not fall within the scope of the Sherman Antitrust Act of 1890. *See* Report of the Senate Committee on Interstate Commerce, S. Rep. No. 63-597, at 10 (June 13, 1914). The FTC was modeled on the Interstate Commerce Commission, and contains five members who serve staggered terms and enjoy "for cause" removal protection.

At its creation, Congress contemplated that the FTC would work primarily through case-by-case agency adjudication. The 1914 FTC Act provided that "Whenever the commission shall have reason to believe that any . . . person, partnership, or corporation has been or is using any unfair method of competition in commerce, . . . it shall issue and serve upon such person, partnership, or corporation a complaint stating its charges in that respect, and containing a notice of a hearing . . . ." Pub. L. No. 63-203 § 5, 37 Stat. 717, 719 (1914). Hearings were to be conducted on the record. If the Commission concluded that the respondent had engaged in an unfair method of competition, it was to "make a report in writing in which it shall state its findings as to the facts, and shall issue and cause to be served on [the respondent] requiring [it] to cease and desist from using such method of competition." *Id.*, 37 Stat. at 720. The respondent could seek judicial review in a court of appeals, and the Commission could petition for enforcement of its order in the same courts if the respondent failed to comply with a cease-and-desist order.

The FTC Act also gave the FTC authority to investigate the activities "of any corporation engaged in commerce, excepting banks and common carriers." *Id.* § 6, 37 Stat. at 721. The Commission was authorized to require reports from corporations, publish information it deemed to be in the public interest, and make annual reports to Congress. Although the FTC held informal "conferences" to clarify standards governing particular areas of the economy, it did not promulgate any significant legislative rules until 1964, when it issued a controversial rule governing cigarette labelling. The Commission obtained express authority to promulgate substantive rules in the 1975 Federal Trade Improvements Act, Pub. L. No. 93-637, 88 Stat. 2183, codified at 15 U.S.C. § 57a. *See* Thomas W. Merrill & Kathryn Tongue Watts, *Agency Rules with the Force of Law: The Original Convention*, 116 HARV. L. REV. 467, 549–557 (2002).

7. **Judicial Deference to the FTC?** The Court in *R.F. Keppel* maintains that the judicial branch has ultimate authority "to determine what practices or methods of competition are to be deemed unfair," but says that "in passing on that question the determination of the Commission is of weight." Later, writing about the unfairness of break-off candy packages, the Court says, "we should hesitate to reject the conclusion of the Commission, based as it is upon clear, specific and comprehensive findings supported by evidence." The Court further clarified the relationship between judicial and agency interpretation of the FTC Act in *Skidmore v. Swift & Co.*, below.

3. Agency vs. Court

Still another decision Congress must make when undertaking to regulate an area involves which institution should be responsible for first-order implementation of the statute. Typically, the choice for Congress is between an agency, on the one hand (whether pre-existing or newly created), and a court on the other. The following cases illustrate two prototypical justifications for assigning responsibilities to an agency rather than a court: (1) the need for an expert body to elaborate a statute's meaning in diverse factual circumstances, and (2) the need to adjudicate a large number of cases.

Skidmore v. Swift & Co.

323 U.S. 134 (1944)

Mr. Justice Jackson delivered the opinion of the Court.

Seven employees of the Swift and Company packing plant at Fort Worth, Texas, brought an action under the Fair Labor Standards Act to recover overtime, liquidated damages, and attorneys' fees, totaling approximately $77,000. The District Court rendered judgment denying this claim wholly, and the Circuit Court of Appeals for the Fifth Circuit affirmed.

It is not denied that the daytime employment of these persons was working time within the Act. Two were engaged in general fire-hall duties and maintenance of fire-fighting equipment of the Swift plant. The others operated elevators or acted as relief men in fire duties. They worked from 7:00 a.m. to 3:30 p.m., with a half-hour lunch period, five days a week. They were paid weekly salaries.

Under their oral agreement of employment, however, petitioners undertook to stay in the fire hall on the Company premises, or within hailing distance, three and a half to four nights a week. This involved no task except to answer alarms, either because of fire or because the sprinkler was set off for some other reason. No fires occurred during the period in issue, the alarms were rare, and the time required for their answer rarely exceeded an hour. For each alarm answered the employees were paid in addition to their fixed compensation an agreed amount, fifty cents at first, and later sixty-four cents. The Company provided a brick fire hall equipped with steam heat and air-conditioned rooms. It provided sleeping quarters, a pool table, a domino table, and a radio. The men used their time in sleep or amusement as they saw fit, except that they were required to stay in or close by the fire hall and be ready to respond to alarms. It is stipulated that "they agreed to remain in the fire hall and stay in it or within hailing distance, subject to call, in event of fire or other casualty, but were not required to perform any specific tasks during these periods of time, except in answering alarms." The trial court [found] as a "conclusion of law" that "the time plaintiffs spent in the fire hall subject to call to answer fire alarms does not constitute hours worked, for which overtime compensation is due them under the Fair Labor Standards Act, as interpreted by the Administrator and the Courts," and in its opinion observed, "of course we know pursuing such pleasurable occupations or performing such personal chores, does not constitute work." The Circuit Court of Appeals affirmed.

[N]o principle of law found either in the statute or in Court decisions precludes waiting time from also being working time. We have not attempted to, and we cannot, lay down a legal formula to resolve cases so varied in their facts as are the many situations in which employment involves waiting time. Whether in a concrete case such time falls within or without the Act is a question of fact to be resolved by appropriate findings of the trial court. This involves scrutiny and construction of the agreements between the particular parties, appraisal of their practical construction of the working agreement by conduct, consideration of the nature of the service, and its relation to the waiting time, and all of the surrounding circumstances. Facts may show that the employee was engaged to wait, or they may show that he waited to be engaged. His compensation may cover both waiting and task, or only performance of the task itself. Living quarters may in some situations be furnished as a facility of the task and in another as a part of its compensation. The law does not impose an arrangement upon the parties. It imposes upon the courts the task of finding what the arrangement was.***

Congress [in the FLSA] did not utilize the services of an administrative agency to find facts and to determine in the first instance whether particular cases fall within or without the Act. Instead, it put this responsibility on the courts. But it did create the office of Administrator [of the Department of Labor's Wage and Hour Division], impose upon him a variety of duties, endow him with powers to inform himself of conditions in industries and employments subject to the Act, and put on him the duties of bringing injunction actions to restrain violations. Pursuit of his duties has accumulated a considerable experience in the problems of ascertaining working time in employments involving periods of inactivity and a knowledge of the customs prevailing in reference to their solution. From these he is obliged to reach conclusions as to conduct without the law, so that he should seek injunctions to stop it, and that within the law, so that he has no call to interfere. He has set forth his views of the application of the Act under different circumstances in an interpretative bulletin and in informal rulings. They provide a practical guide to employers and employees as to how the office representing the public interest in its enforcement will seek to apply it. Wage and Hour Division, Interpretative Bulletin No. 13.

The Administrator thinks the problems presented by inactive duty require a flexible solution, rather than the all-in or all-out rules respectively urged by the parties in this case, and his Bulletin endeavors to suggest standards and examples to guide in particular situations. In some occupations, it says, periods of inactivity are not properly counted as working time even though the employee is subject to call. Examples are an operator of a small telephone exchange where the switchboard is in her home and she ordinarily gets several hours of uninterrupted sleep each night; or a pumper of a stripper well or watchman of a lumber camp during the off season, who may be on duty twenty-four hours a day but ordinarily "has a normal night's sleep, has ample time in which to eat his meals, and has a certain amount of time for relaxation and entirely private pursuits." Exclusion of all such hours the Administrator thinks may be justified. In general, the answer depends "upon the degree to which the employee is free to engage in personal activities during periods of idleness when he is subject to call and the number of consecutive hours that the employee is subject to call without being required to perform active work." "Hours worked are not limited to the time spent in active labor but include time given by the employee to the employer. . . ."

The facts of this case do not fall within any of the specific examples given, but the conclusion of the Administrator, as expressed in the brief amicus curiae, is that the general tests which he has suggested point to the exclusion of sleeping and eating time of these employees from the workweek and the inclusion of all other on-call time: although the employees were required to remain on the premises during the entire time, the evidence shows that they were very rarely interrupted in their normal sleeping and eating time, and these are pursuits of a purely private nature which would presumably occupy the employees' time whether they were on duty or not and which apparently could be pursued adequately and comfortably in the required circumstances; the rest of the time is different because there is nothing in the record to suggest that, even though pleasurably spent, it was spent in the ways the men would have chosen had they been free to do so.

There is no statutory provision as to what, if any, deference courts should pay to the Administrator's conclusions. And, while we have given them notice, we have had no occasion to try to prescribe their influence. The rulings of this Administrator are not reached as a result of hearing adversary proceedings in which he finds facts from evidence and reaches conclusions of law from findings of fact. They are not, of course, conclusive, even in the cases with which they directly deal, much less in those to which they apply only by analogy. They do not constitute an interpretation of the Act or a standard for judging factual situations which binds a district court's processes, as an authoritative pronouncement of a higher court might do. But the Administrator's policies are made in pursuance of official duty, based upon more specialized experience and broader investigations and information than is likely to come to a judge in a particular case. They do determine the policy which will guide applications for enforcement by injunction on behalf of the Government. Good administration of the Act and good judicial administration alike require that the standards of public enforcement and those for determining private rights shall be at variance only where justified by very good reasons. The fact that the Administrator's policies and standards are not reached by trial in adversary form does not mean that they are not entitled to respect. This Court has long given considerable and in some cases decisive weight to Treasury Decisions and to interpretative regulations of the Treasury and of other bodies that were not of adversary origin.

We consider that the rulings, interpretations and opinions of the Administrator under this Act, while not controlling upon the courts by reason of their authority, do constitute a body of experience and informed judgment to which courts and litigants may properly resort for guidance. The weight of such a judgment in a particular case will depend upon the thoroughness evident in its consideration, the validity of its reasoning, its consistency with earlier and later pronouncements, and all those factors which give it power to persuade, if lacking power to control.

[I]n this case, although the District Court referred to the Administrator's Bulletin, its evaluation and inquiry were apparently restricted by its notion that waiting time may not be work, an understanding of the law which we hold to be erroneous. Accordingly, the judgment is reversed and the cause remanded for further proceedings consistent herewith.

Notes and Questions

1. **The Procedural Posture?** *Skidmore v. Swift* is the second decision we have seen under the Fair Labor Standards Act (FLSA), 29 U.S.C. § 201 et seq. How was this lawsuit commenced? How did this dispute make its way to the Supreme Court? How do you suppose that the plaintiffs in *Skidmore* realized they potentially had a claim against Swift under the FLSA?

2. **The Statutory Issue?** As described in *Brooklyn Savings Bank*, § 7(a) of the FLSA requires time-and-a-half compensation for "a workweek longer than forty hours." The question in *Skidmore* and its companion case, *Armour & Co. v. Wantock*, 323 U.S. 126 (1944), was whether "on call" or waiting time counted toward the forty-hour threshold for overtime purposes. Refer to the text of the FLSA quoted in the first footnote to *Brooklyn Savings Bank*. What is the strongest textual argument for counting waiting time toward the 40-hour threshold? What is the strongest textual argument *against* doing so?

3. **The Agency's Role in Statutory Interpretation?** Generally, courts decide issues of statutory interpretation. According to the *Skidmore* decision, what role does the DOL's Wage and Hour Administrator play in elaborating the meaning of the FLSA? How much independent interpretation is the Court performing compared to relying on the agency's view? What benefit is there to having multiple institutions—the courts and the agency—decide what constitutes working time and how to handle "on

call" arrangements? What sources of information did the Wage-Hour Division have available to it that the courts do not?

Would the interpretative function have been better performed if the Administrator had the authority to bring complaints against the employer in an internal administrative proceeding? If the Administrator had the authority to issue binding rules, after notice to the affected public and opportunity to comment?

4. **Agencies as "Expert" Decisionmakers?** Do agencies have greater expertise in a regulated area than either Congress or the courts? Consider the view of a New Deal theorist and one-time Harvard Law Dean: "the art of regulating an industry requires knowledge of the details of its operation, ability to shift requirements as the condition of the industry may dictate, the pursuit of energetic measures upon the appearance of an emergency, and the power through enforcement to realize conclusions as to policy." JAMES LANDIS, THE ADMINISTRATIVE PROCESS 23–24 (1938).

How do agencies develop expertise? Is it relevant that agency members sit only for limited terms, and are usually drawn from the ranks of lawyers and lobbyists without any technical background in the field? Is the expertise rather, drawn, from the staff of the agency who tend to remain there for their careers? How is this expertise imparted to the agency decisionmakers?

5. **Agencies as "Independent" or Politically Insulated Decisionmakers?** Another frequently cited reason for deferring to agency views is that it is desirable (and Congress presumably desires) that policy decisions be made by an institution that operates free of improper interest-group or political influence. Recall the Federal Trade Commission, discussed in *R.F. Keppel*, in Section [C][2], above. The FTC is composed of five commissioners, no more than three of whom can be members of the same political party. Commissioners may be dismissed only "for cause"; the President may not fire a Commissioner because the Commissioner disagrees with the administration's general approach to competition policy or regulation. Commissioners, furthermore, are prohibited from "engag[ing] in any other business, vocation, or employment." 15 U.S.C. § 41. Together, these provisions are intended to make the FTC "a body of experts who shall gain experience by length of service," which is "free to exercise its judgment without the leave or hindrance of any other official or any department of the government." *Humphrey's Executor v. United States*, 295 U.S. 602, 625–26 (1935), *infra* Chapter 3[B][1][d].

The concept of a government agency that operates independently of the three branches of government established by the Constitution is, at a glance, in tension with separation-of-powers principles. In many ways, however, "independent" agencies like the FTC are subject to considerable legislative and executive controls. Chapter 3 considers the constitutionality of this institutional structure and the limits on Congress's ability to delegate legislative, executive, and judicial authority to "independent" agencies.

6. **Agency Decisionmaking and Stare Decisis.** Agencies traditionally have not been thought to be strictly bound by the doctrine of *stare decisis* ("stand by that which is decided"), which forms the basis for the system of judicial precedent. This is because "[a]djudicated cases may and do*** serve as vehicles for the formulation of agency

policies, which are applied and announced therein," and that "policies announced in [agency] adjudication are [not] 'rules' in the sense that they must, without more, be obeyed by the affected public." *NLRB v. Wyman-Gordon Co.*, 394 U.S. 759, 765–66 (1969) (plurality op.), *infra* Chapter 4[D]. Nonetheless, an agency decision may be set aside if it is "arbitrary, capricious, an abuse of discretion, or otherwise not in accordance with law," 5 U.S.C. §706(2)(a), a principle that constrains the agency's decision to depart from a previous agency order or rule. *See Motor Vehicle Mfgr's Ass'n v. State Farm Mut. Automobile Ins. Co.*, 463 U.S. 29 (1983), *infra* Chapter 5[D]; *FCC v. Fox*, 129 S. Ct. 1800 (2009), *infra* Chapter 5[D].

———

In addition to elaborating a statute's meaning, agencies can address large numbers of disputes that would overwhelm the courts if they were litigated as traditional cases or controversies. The decision below explores this function.

Heckler v. Campbell

461 U.S. 458 (1983)

Justice Powell delivered the opinion of the Court.

The issue is whether the Secretary of Health and Human Services may rely on published medical-vocational guidelines to determine a claimant's right to Social Security disability benefits.

I

The Social Security Act defines "disability" in terms of the effect a physical or mental impairment has on a person's ability to function in the work place. It provides disability benefits only to persons who are unable "to engage in any substantial gainful activity by reason of any medically determinable physical or mental impairment." 42 U.S.C. §423(d)(1)(A). And it specifies that a person must "not only [be] unable to do his previous work but [must be unable], considering his age, education, and work experience, [to] engage in any other kind of substantial gainful work which exists in the national economy, regardless of whether such work exists in the immediate area in which he lives, or whether a specific job vacancy exists for him, or whether he would be hired if he applied for work." 42 U.S.C. §423(d)(2)(A).

In 1978, the Secretary of Health and Human Services promulgated regulations implementing this definition. See 43 Fed.Reg. 55349 (1978) (codified as amended at 20 CFR pt. 404, subpt. P (1982)). The regulations recognize that certain impairments are so severe that they prevent a person from pursuing any gainful work. See 20 CFR §404.1520(d) (1982) (referring to impairments listed at 20 CFR pt. 404, subpt. P, app. 1). A claimant who establishes that he suffers from one of these impairments will be considered disabled without further inquiry. If a claimant suffers from a less severe impairment, the Secretary must determine whether the claimant retains the ability to perform either his former work or some less demanding employment. If a claimant can pursue his former occupation, he is not entitled to disability benefits. See

§ 404.1520(e). If he cannot, the Secretary must determine whether the claimant retains the capacity to pursue less demanding work. See § 404.1520(f)(1).

The regulations divide this last inquiry into two stages. First, the Secretary must assess each claimant's present job qualifications. The regulations direct the Secretary to consider the factors Congress has identified as relevant: physical ability, age, education and work experience.[1] See 42 U.S.C. § 423(d)(2)(A); 20 CFR § 404.1520(f). Second, she must consider whether jobs exist in the national economy that a person having the claimant's qualifications could perform. 20 CFR § 404.1520(f); §§ 404.1566–404.1569.

Prior to 1978, the Secretary relied on vocational experts to establish the existence of suitable jobs in the national economy. After a claimant's limitations and abilities had been determined at a hearing, a vocational expert ordinarily would testify whether work existed that the claimant could perform. Although this testimony often was based on standardized guides, see 43 Fed.Reg. 9286 (1978), vocational experts frequently were criticized for their inconsistent treatment of similarly situated claimants.*** To improve both the uniformity and efficiency[2] of this determination, the Secretary promulgated medical-vocational guidelines as part of the 1978 regulations. See 20 CFR pt. 404, subpt. P, app. 2 (1982).

These guidelines relieve the Secretary of the need to rely on vocational experts by establishing through rulemaking the types and numbers of jobs that exist in the national economy. They consist of a matrix of the four factors identified by Congress— physical ability, age, education, and work experience—and set forth rules that identify whether jobs requiring specific combinations of these factors exist in significant numbers in the national economy. Where a claimant's qualifications correspond to the job requirements identified by a rule,[5] the guidelines direct a conclusion as to whether work exists that the claimant could perform. If such work exists, the claimant is not considered disabled.

---

1. The regulations state that the Secretary will inquire into each of these factors and make an individual assessment of each claimant's abilities and limitations. See 20 CFR §§ 404.1545–404.1565 (1982); cf. 20 CFR § 404.944. In determining a person's physical ability, she will consider, for example, the extent to which his capacity for performing tasks such as lifting objects or his ability to stand for long periods of time has been impaired. See § 404.1545.

2. ***Approximately 2.3 million claims for disability benefits were filed in fiscal year 1981. Department of Health and Human Services, Social Security Annual Report to the Congress for Fiscal Year 1981, pp. 32, 35 (1982). More than a quarter of a million of these claims require a hearing before an Administrative Law Judge. *Id.*, at 38. The need for efficiency is self-evident.

5. The regulations recognize that the rules only describe "major functional and vocational patterns." 20 CFR pt. 404, subpt. P, app. 2, § 200.00(a). If an individual's capabilities are not described accurately by a rule, the regulations make clear that the individual's particular limitations must be considered. See app. 2, §§ 200.00(a), (d). Additionally, the regulations declare that the Administrative Law Judge will not apply the age categories "mechanically in a borderline situation," 20 CFR § 404.1563(a), and recognize that some claimants may possess limitations that are not factored into the guidelines, see app. 2, § 200.00(e). Thus, the regulations provide that the rules will be applied only when they describe a claimant's abilities and limitations accurately.

II

In 1979, Carmen Campbell applied for disability benefits because a back condition and hypertension prevented her from continuing her work as a hotel maid. After her application was denied, she requested a hearing *de novo* before an Administrative Law Judge.*** Relying on the medical-vocational guidelines, the Administrative Law Judge found that a significant number of jobs existed that a person of Campbell's qualifications could perform. Accordingly, he concluded that she was not disabled.

This determination was upheld by both the Social Security Appeals Council and the District Court for the Eastern District of New York. The Court of Appeals for the Second Circuit reversed.***

III***

The Court of Appeals held that "[i]n failing to show suitable available alternative jobs for Ms. Campbell, the Secretary's finding of 'not disabled' is not supported by substantial evidence."*** Accordingly, we think the decision below requires us to consider whether the Secretary may rely on medical-vocational guidelines in appropriate cases.

The Social Security Act directs the Secretary to "adopt reasonable and proper rules and regulations to regulate and provide for the nature and extent of the proofs and evidence and the method of taking and furnishing the same" in disability cases. 42 U.S.C. § 405(a). As we previously have recognized, Congress has "conferred on the Secretary exceptionally broad authority to prescribe standards for applying certain sections of the [Social Security] Act." *Schweiker v. Gray Panthers*, 453 U.S. 34, 43 (1981); see *Batterton v. Francis*, 432 U.S. 416, 425 (1977). Where, as here, the statute expressly entrusts the Secretary with the responsibility for implementing a provision by regulation, our review is limited to determining whether the regulations promulgated exceeded the Secretary's statutory authority and whether they are arbitrary and capricious.

We do not think that the Secretary's reliance on medical-vocational guidelines is inconsistent with the Social Security Act. It is true that the statutory scheme contemplates that disability hearings will be individualized determinations based on evidence adduced at a hearing. See 42 U.S.C. § 423(d)(2)(A) (specifying consideration of each individual's condition); 42 U.S.C. § 405(b) (1976 ed., Supp. V) (disability determination to be based on evidence adduced at hearing). But this does not bar the Secretary from relying on rulemaking to resolve certain classes of issues. The Court has recognized that even where an agency's enabling statute expressly requires it to hold a hearing, the agency may rely on its rulemaking authority to determine issues that do not require case-by-case consideration. A contrary holding would require the agency continually to relitigate issues that may be established fairly and efficiently in a single rulemaking proceeding.

The Secretary's decision to rely on medical-vocational guidelines is consistent with [*FPC v. Texaco*, 377 U.S. 33 (1964)] and [*United States v. Storer Broadcasting*, 351 U.S. 192 (1956)]. As noted above, in determining whether a claimant can perform less strenuous work, the Secretary must make two determinations. She must assess each claimant's individual abilities and then determine whether jobs exist that a person having the claimant's qualifications could perform. The first inquiry involves a determination of historic facts, and the regulations properly require the Secretary to make these findings on the basis of evidence adduced at a hearing. We note that the regulations afford claimants ample opportunity both to present evidence relating to their own abilities and to offer evidence that the guidelines do not apply to them.[11] The second inquiry requires the Secretary to determine an issue that is not unique to each claimant—the types and numbers of jobs that exist in the national economy. This type of general factual issue may be resolved as fairly through rulemaking as by introducing the testimony of vocational experts at each disability hearing. See *American Airlines, Inc. v. CAB*, 359 F.2d 624, 633 (1966) (en banc).

As the Secretary has argued, the use of published guidelines brings with it a uniformity that previously had been perceived as lacking. To require the Secretary to relitigate the existence of jobs in the national economy at each hearing would hinder needlessly an already overburdened agency. We conclude that the Secretary's use of medical-vocational guidelines does not conflict with the statute, nor can we say on the record before us that they are arbitrary and capricious.***

IV

The Court of Appeals' decision would require the Secretary to introduce evidence of specific available jobs that respondent could perform. It would limit severely her ability to rely on the medical-vocational guidelines. We think the Secretary reasonably could choose to rely on these guidelines in appropriate cases rather than on the testimony of a vocational expert in each case.***

Notes and Questions

1. **The Statutory Issue?** *Heckler* addresses whether the Social Security Administration (SSA), previously a unit of the Department of Health and Human Services and an independent agency since 1995, *see* Pub. L. No. 103-296, 108 Stat. 1464, can rely on medical-vocational guidelines colloquially known as "grids" to process claims for Social Security benefits. What is the nature of the agency action under review in the Supreme Court? How did this dispute reach the Court? What is the textual basis for the Court's conclusion that the agency's reliance on the grids is lawful? What is the strongest textual argument against the Court's conclusion?

2. **The Need for Federal Disability Insurance?** The Social Security Act establishes a scheme of disability insurance that applies to most workers in the United States.

---

11. Both *FPC v. Texaco, Inc.*, 377 U.S. 33, 40 (1964), and *United States v. Storer Broadcasting Co.*, 351 U.S. 192, 205 (1956), were careful to note that the statutory scheme at issue allowed an individual applicant to show that the rule promulgated should not be applied to him. The regulations here provide a claimant with equal or greater protection since they state that an Administrative Law Judge will not apply the rules contained in the guidelines when they fail to describe a claimant's particular limitations. See n. 5, *supra*.

Covered workers are required to contribute a portion of their payroll earnings to a trust fund, *see* 26 U.S.C. § 3101, which is used to pay benefits to workers who become disabled. Disability insurance is also available in the private market, and private insurance permits individuals to customize the level of insurance to their individual circumstances. The CEO of a Fortune 500 company can purchase a "gold plated" policy; a young person who is physically fit and has no dependents can purchase a cheaper one.

Given the availability of private disability insurance, why did Congress in the SSA undertake to establish a public social insurance program for disabled workers? Why did Congress require employees to participate in that program as opposed to making participation voluntary or "nudging" employees to participate with financial incentives? What is the justification for establishing a *federal* disability insurance program?

MICHAEL J. GRAETZ & JERRY L. MASHAW, TRUE SECURITY: RETHINKING AMERICAN SOCIAL INSURANCE (1999), note a number of factors that may limit the private market's ability to provide reliable and efficient insurance. First, the likelihood of a disabling occurrence may be so difficult to predict that actuaries cannot make reliable estimates about exposure, even over large groups. Second, risks may "covary": rather than policyholders experiencing losses over time, all policymakers may experience a loss simultaneously, depleting the insurance pool. Third, if participants in the insurance pool have better information about risk than insurance companies, the market will be characterized by "adverse selection": individuals will purchase insurance only when they are at high risk, or have already suffered an injury. Finally, an insurance market may be characterized by moral hazard if participants in the pool change their behavior because they know they are insured. Uncertainty, covariance, adverse selection, and moral hazard can lead private insurance markets to fail.

Graetz and Mashaw suggest that social insurance—which they define as a government-sponsored insurance program involving mandatory participation, a national risk pool and financing, and "an intergenerational social contract"—is warranted when market failure in the private insurance market prevents a major life risk from being insurable. They also observe that social insurance may be justified by other traditional justifications for regulation, such as citizens' moral obligations to one another, maximizing social welfare, and paternalism. Which of these justifications is at work in the federal disability insurance program?

3. **Agency as Claims Processor?** In fiscal year 2012, the SSA's Office of Disability Adjudication and Review adjudicated 820,484 claims for disability benefits.[54] By contrast, federal district courts nationwide disposed of 288,330 cases.[55] Does the volume of claiming explain why Congress chose to have the SSA resolve disability claims in the first instance?

---

54. *See* Social Security Administration, Hearing Office Workload Data, FY 2012, http://www.socialsecurity.gov/policy/docs/statcomps/supplement/2013/2f8-2f11.html.

55. Administrative Office of the United States Courts, Federal Judicial Caseload Statistics, March 31, 2012, tbl. C.

The various Social Security insurance programs account for approximately $800 billion in federal spending per year, or about 7% of the United States' Gross Domestic Product. Spending on benefits payments required by the Social Security Act is considered "mandatory" spending, and does not need to be appropriated by Congress on a yearly basis. However, the administrative costs of operating the Social Security system—currently about $12 billion per year—are considered discretionary spending, which must be appropriated by Congress each year.

4. **Internal Agency Process and Judicial Review.** A recent report of the Administrative Conference of the United States, an independent federal agency dedicated to the study and reform of the administrative process, describes the early stages of the disability claims process, as follows:

> The quest for disability benefits begins with an application filed in one of SSA's 1,300 field offices, or online or by telephone. A "claims representative," the first SSA employee the applicant encounters, assembles some of the information necessary to determine whether a claimant is entitled to benefits. The claims representative prepares a "disability report," which includes information on the claimant's work history, the alleged disability onset date, and the claimant's medical providers. The claims representative also creates a "certified electronic folder," or a digital receptacle into which the claims representative, the claimant, her representative, and other personnel throughout the adjudication process deposit medical records and other claim-related information.
>
> The claims representative verifies non-medical aspects of the claim. She then forwards the claim to a "Disability Determination Service" ("DDS"), a state-run agency that operates under the SSA's guidance and pursuant to federal law. A "disability examiner" gathers as many of the claimant's medical records as possible and then determines whether the claimant is disabled. In the majority of DDS offices, a medical or psychological consultant who works for the state agency may assist the disability examiner with this determination. Some DDS offices have followed a "single decision maker" model that allows the disability examiner to decide some claims without a medical consultant's signature. In most states, the claimant can ask for reconsideration if the DDS office denies the claim. A different pair of examiners and consultants decides these requests.

JONAH GELBACH & DAVID MARCUS, A STUDY OF SOCIAL SECURITY LITIGATION IN THE FEDERAL COURTS 17–18 (July 2016).

The SSA is authorized under 42 U.S.C. §§ 421 and 1352 to approve state plans for the administration of disability insurance benefits. Pursuant to such plans, Administrative Law Judges ("ALJs") are employed by state departments of social services rather than the SSA. This structure is an example of a "cooperative federalism" program that is administered by both the state and federal governments. *See* Note 6 to *Riegel v. Mectronic, Inc., infra* p. 68.

If the disability examiner denies a claim, claimant has sixty days to request a hearing before an ALJ. After the ALJ makes a decision on a disability claim, the decision is subject to review by the Social Security Appeals Council, an administrative body that is currently made up of approximately 68 Administrative Appeals Judges, 42 Appeals Officers, and several hundred support personnel.[56] The Appeals Council can affirm, reverse, or modify the ALJ's benefits determination, or remand for further proceedings. 20 C.F.R. § 404.979.

After the SSA issues its final decision, the claimant "may obtain a review of such decision by a civil action" filed in district court. The government may not appeal an award of benefits. (Can you see why?) 42 U.S.C. § 405(g) directs the Commissioner of Social Security, the SSA agency head, when answering such a civil action to file "a certified copy of the transcript of the record including the evidence upon which the findings and decision complained of are based." *Id.* The district court "shall have power to enter, upon the pleadings and transcript of the record, a judgment affirming, modifying, or reversing the decision of the Commissioner of Social Security, with or without remanding the cause for a rehearing." The SSA's findings of fact are conclusive if supported by "substantial evidence," a standard we discuss in Chapter 4[B]. However, the district court "may at any time order additional evidence to be taken before the Commissioner of Social Security . . . upon a showing that there is new evidence which is material and that there is good cause for the failure to incorporate such evidence into the record in a prior proceeding." § 405(g). The district court's decision is subject to review by the court of appeals and Supreme Court.

In all, disability determinations are potentially subject to four levels of appellate review. What explains the decision to provide for review of disability determinations in a district court, court of appeals, and the Supreme Court? In many other statutory schemes, if the agency issues an order through an internal adjudication, the order is reviewable in the court of appeals on the basis of the record before the agency. In the social security context, we have an agency adjudication, district court review where the case can be remanded for expansion of the record, and appellate review. *See generally* Henry J. Friendly, Federal Jurisdiction: A General View 34–35 & n.108 (1973) (discussing multi-tier review of SSA determinations).

5. **The Role of Administrative Law Judge in SSA Disability Proceedings?** The Administrative Law Judge (ALJ) in disability proceedings functions less like U.S. trial court judge than a French *juge d'instruction*. Rather than acting as an impartial referee who rules after hearing competing presentations put on by the parties, the ALJ judge actively investigates the claim and is expected to develop a complete record upon which the claim is resolved.

The ALJ's duties in this respect derive from statutory and regulatory provisions that assume many claimants will not be represented by counsel. Section 405 of the Social Security Act provides the SSA with authority, "on the Commissioner's own

---

56. Social Security Administration, Brief History and Current Information about the Appeals Council, http://www.ssa.gov/appeals/about_ac.html.

motion, to hold such hearings and to conduct such investigations and other proceedings as the Commissioner may deem necessary or proper for the administration of this subchapter." SSA regulations provide that before making a disability determination, the agency will make "every reasonable effort" to obtain relevant medical records, 20 C.F.R. § 404.1512, and that "the administrative law judge [will] look[] fully into the issues," 20 C.F.R. § 404.944. Decisional law holds "there is a 'basic obligation' on the ALJ in these nonadversarial proceedings to develop a full and fair record, which obligation rises to a 'special duty*** to scrupulously and conscientiously explore for all relevant facts' where an unrepresented claimant has not waived counsel." *Broz v. Schweiker*, 677 F.2d 1351, 1364 (11th Cir. 1982).

What explains the Social Security Act's departure from the traditional adversarial model of legal proceedings followed by U.S. courts? Wouldn't benefits determinations be more reliable if claimants were appointed counsel and a claimant and the government put on competing evidentiary presentations? Dean Landis contended that the adversarial model's reliance on private litigants to develop facts and legal arguments failed to ensure that the overall system would further the public interest. *See* JAMES M. LANDIS, THE ADMINISTRATIVE PROCESS 38–39 (1938) ("[T]he common law system left too much in the way of the enforcement of claims and interests to private initiative.... For [administrative] process to be successful in a particular field, it is imperative that controversies be decided as 'rightly' as possible."). Are these contentions persuasive? Are there specific types of disputes where it is more appropriate for an administrative judge to assume an inquisitorial role? How should the costs of additional safeguards be factored in?

6. **"Legislative" vs. "Adjudicative Facts."** Note the *kind* of "fact" that is established by the SSA grids. As the Court points out, ALJs consult the grids to determine "whether jobs requiring specific combinations of [physical ability, age, education, and work experience] exist in significant numbers in the national economy." This kind of a fact—which is relatively stable over time, and should not normally vary from one adjudication to the next—is often referred to as a "legislative" fact. KENNETH CULP DAVIS, 3 ADMINISTRATIVE LAW TREATISE § 15.10, at 178 (2d ed. 1980). *See also* LOUIS L. JAFFE, JUDICIAL CONTROL OF ADMINISTRATIVE ACTION 636 (1965). By contrast, an "adjudicative" fact is one having to do with the specific facts concerning the claimant in the SSA proceeding. Legislative facts are often the assumptions or premises underlying legislative or regulatory actions; they are accepted as a matter of judicial or administrative notice without hearing or argument. Adjudicative facts, by contrast, are the subject of adversarial proceedings.

7. **"Bail Out"/Variance Mechanisms.** Note, further, that the Social Security grids contain a "bail out" mechanism for cases in which the grids do not supply a reliable answer to whether the benefits applicant could find suitable work. The grids do not apply to individuals whose capabilities are not described accurately by them, and the regulations "recognize that some claimants may possess limitations that are not factored into the guidelines." *Heckler, supra* at n.5, n.11. How important are these mechanisms to the Court's conclusion that the Social Security Administration's reliance on the grids

was lawful? Would the Court have reached the same decision if the grids were applied mechanically in all cases?

8. **Further Reading.** There is an extensive literature on agencies as providers of mass retail justice. *See, e.g.,* Jerry L. Mashaw, Bureaucratic Justice: Managing Social Security Disability Claims (1995); Lawrence M. Friedman, Total Justice (1985); Jaya Ramji-Nogales, Andrew I. Schoenholtz & Philip G. Schrag, Refugee Roulette: Disparities in Asylum Adjudication and Proposals for Reform (2011); Jonah B. Gelbach & David Marcus, A Study of Social Security Disability Litigation in the Federal Courts: Final Report to the Administrative Conference of the United States (July 28, 2016); Adam S. Zimmerman, *Distributing Justice*, 86 N.Y.U. L. Rev. 500 (2012).

———

As the cases involving the Fair Labor Standards Act illustrate, Congress often seeks to combine agency enforcement with private enforcement. Reliance on private enforcers, however, creates its own problems. To succeed in having private litigation supplement or even replace an administrative agency as the primary mechanism for enforcing a regulatory regime, the legislature must create sufficient incentives to encourage persons harmed by violations of the law to sue, and for attorneys to represent them.

Christiansburg Garment Co. v. EEOC
434 U.S. 412 (1978)

Mr. Justice Stewart delivered the opinion of the Court.

Section 706(k) of Title VII of the Civil Rights Act of 1964 provides:

> "In any action or proceeding under this title the court, in its discretion, may allow the prevailing party ... a reasonable attorney's fee ...."

The question in this case is under what circumstances an attorney's fee should be allowed when the defendant is the prevailing party in a Title VII action—a question about which the federal courts have expressed divergent views.

I

Two years after Rosa Helm had filed a Title VII charge of racial discrimination against the petitioner Christiansburg Garment Co. (company), the Equal Employment Opportunity Commission notified her that its conciliation efforts had failed and that she had the right to sue the company in federal court. She did not do so. Almost two years later, in 1972, Congress enacted amendments to Title VII. Section 14 of these amendments authorized the Commission to sue in its own name to prosecute "charges pending with the Commission" on the effective date of the amendments. Proceeding under this section, the Commission sued the company, alleging that it had engaged in unlawful employment practices in violation of the amended Act. The company moved for summary judgment on the ground, *inter alia*, that the Rosa Helm charge had not been "pending" before the Commission when the 1972 amendments took effect. The District Court agreed and granted summary judgment in favor of the company.

The company then petitioned for the allowance of attorney's fees against the Commission pursuant to § 706(k) of Title VII. Finding that "the Commission's action in bringing the suit cannot be characterized as unreasonable or meritless," the District Court concluded that "an award of attorney's fees to petitioner is not justified in this case." A divided Court of Appeals affirmed, and we granted certiorari to consider an important question of federal law.

II

It is the general rule in the United States that in the absence of legislation providing otherwise, litigants must pay their own attorney's fees. *Alyeska Pipeline Co. v. Wilderness Society*, 421 U.S. 240. Congress has provided only limited exceptions to this rule "under selected statutes granting or protecting various federal rights." Some of these statutes make fee awards mandatory for prevailing plaintiffs; others make awards permissive but limit them to certain parties, usually prevailing plaintiffs. But many of the statutes are more flexible, authorizing the award of attorney's fees to either plaintiffs or defendants, and entrusting the effectuation of the statutory policy to the discretion of the district courts. Section 706(k) of Title VII of the Civil Rights Act of 1964 falls into this last category, providing as it does that a district court may in its discretion allow an attorney's fee to the prevailing party.

In *Newman v. Piggie Park Enterprises*, 390 U.S. 400, the Court considered a substantially identical statute authorizing the award of attorney's fees under Title II of the Civil Rights Act of 1964. In that case the plaintiffs had prevailed, and the Court of Appeals had held that they should be awarded their attorney's fees "only to the extent that the respondents' defenses had been advanced 'for purposes of delay and not in good faith.'" We ruled that this "subjective standard" did not properly effectuate the purposes of the counsel-fee provision of Title II. Relying primarily on the intent of Congress to cast a Title II plaintiff in the role of "a 'private attorney general,' vindicating a policy that Congress considered of the highest priority," we held that a prevailing plaintiff under Title II "should ordinarily recover an attorney's fee unless special circumstances would render such an award unjust."***

In *Albemarle Paper Co. v. Moody*, 422 U.S. 405, the Court made clear that the *Piggie Park* standard of awarding attorney's fees to a successful plaintiff is equally applicable in an action under Title VII of the Civil Rights Act. It can thus be taken as established, as the parties in this case both acknowledge, that under § 706(k) of Title VII a prevailing *plaintiff* ordinarily is to be awarded attorney's fees in all but special circumstances.

III

The question in the case before us is what standard should inform a district court's discretion in deciding whether to award attorney's fees to a successful *defendant* in a Title VII action. Not surprisingly, the parties in addressing the question in their briefs and oral arguments have taken almost diametrically opposite positions.

The company contends that the *Piggie Park* criterion for a successful plaintiff should apply equally as a guide to the award of attorney's fees to a successful defendant. Its submission, in short, is that every prevailing defendant in a Title VII action should receive an allowance of attorney's fees "unless special circumstances would render such an award unjust." The respondent Commission, by contrast, argues that the prevailing defendant should receive an award of attorney's fees only when it is found that the plaintiff's action was brought in bad faith. We have concluded that neither of these positions is correct.

A

Relying on what it terms "the plain meaning of the statute," the company argues that the language of §706(k) admits of only one interpretation: "A prevailing defendant is entitled to an award of attorney's fees on the same basis as a prevailing plaintiff." But the permissive and discretionary language of the statute does not even invite, let alone require, such a mechanical construction. The terms of §706(k) provide no indication whatever of the circumstances under which either a plaintiff *or* a defendant should be entitled to attorney's fees. And a moment's reflection reveals that there are at least two strong equitable considerations counseling an attorney's fee award to a prevailing Title VII plaintiff that are wholly absent in the case of a prevailing Title VII defendant.

First, as emphasized so forcefully in *Piggie Park*, the plaintiff is the chosen instrument of Congress to vindicate "a policy that Congress considered of the highest priority." Second, when a district court awards counsel fees to a prevailing plaintiff, it is awarding them against a violator of federal law. As the Court of Appeals clearly perceived, "these policy considerations which support the award of fees to a prevailing plaintiff are not present in the case of a prevailing defendant." A successful defendant seeking counsel fees under §706(k) must rely on quite different equitable considerations.

But if the company's position is untenable, the Commission's argument also misses the mark. It seems clear, in short, that in enacting §706(k) Congress did not intend to permit the award of attorney's fees to a prevailing defendant only in a situation where the plaintiff was motivated by bad faith in bringing the action. As pointed out in *Piggie Park*, if that had been the intent of Congress, no statutory provision would have been necessary, for it has long been established that even under the American common-law rule attorney's fees may be awarded against a party who has proceeded in bad faith.

Furthermore, while it was certainly the policy of Congress that Title VII plaintiffs should vindicate "a policy that Congress considered of the highest priority," it is equally certain that Congress entrusted the ultimate effectuation of that policy to the adversary judicial process. A fair adversary process presupposes both a vigorous prosecution and a vigorous defense. It cannot be lightly assumed that in enacting §706(k), Congress intended to distort that process by giving the private plaintiff substantial incentives to sue, while foreclosing to the defendant the possibility of recovering his expenses in resisting even a groundless action unless he can show that it was brought in bad faith.

B

The sparse legislative history of § 706(k) reveals little more than the barest outlines of a proper accommodation of the competing considerations we have discussed. The only specific reference to § 706(k) in the legislative debates indicates that the fee provision was included to "make it easier for a plaintiff of limited means to bring a meritorious suit."[14]***

[The Court discusses court of appeals decisions holding that attorneys' fee awards to defendants should be permitted "not routinely, not simply because he succeeds, but only where the action brought is found to be unreasonable, frivolous, meritless or vexatious."]

To the extent that abstract words can deal with concrete cases, we think that the concept embodied in the language adopted by these two Courts of Appeals is correct. We would qualify their words only by pointing out that the term "meritless" is to be understood as meaning groundless or without foundation, rather than simply that the plaintiff has ultimately lost his case, and that the term "vexatious" in no way implies that the plaintiff's subjective bad faith is a necessary prerequisite to a fee award against him. In sum, a district court may in its discretion award attorney's fees to a prevailing defendant in a Title VII case upon a finding that the plaintiff's action was frivolous, unreasonable, or without foundation, even though not brought in subjective bad faith.***

That § 706(k) allows fee awards only to *prevailing* private plaintiffs should assure that this statutory provision will not in itself operate as an incentive to the bringing of claims that have little chance of success. To take the further step of assessing attorney's fees against plaintiffs simply because they do not finally prevail would substantially add to the risks inhering in most litigation and would undercut the efforts of Congress to promote the vigorous enforcement of the provisions of Title VII. Hence, a plaintiff should not be assessed his opponent's attorney's fees unless a court finds that his claim was frivolous, unreasonable, or groundless, or that the plaintiff continued to litigate after it clearly became so. And, needless to say, if a plaintiff is found to have brought or continued such a claim in *bad faith*, there will be an even stronger basis for charging him with the attorney's fees incurred by the defense.

IV

In denying attorney's fees to the company in this case, the District Court focused on the standards we have discussed. The court found that "the Commission's action in bringing the suit could not be characterized as unreasonable or meritless" because "the basis upon which petitioner prevailed was an issue of first impression requiring judicial resolution" and because the "Commission's statutory interpretation of § 14

---

14. Remarks of Senator Humphrey, 110 Cong.Rec. 12724 (1964).

of the 1972 amendments was not frivolous." The court thus exercised its discretion squarely within the permissible bounds of § 706(k).

Notes and Questions

1. **Justification for Federal Regulation?** Title VII of the Civil Rights Act of 1964, 42 U.S.C. § 2000e et seq., prohibits discrimination against an employee on the basis of her race, color, religion, sex, or national origin. Today, prohibitions on discrimination are commonplace. Nevertheless, it is useful to consider what would have motivated Congress to enact such prohibitions in the first instance. What was Congress's interest in outlawing employment discrimination? Is discrimination a simple question of fairness, or does it also reflect a kind of market failure or collective action problem? Consider the effect of excluding a large proportion of the working-age population from the workforce (or most desirable positions in the workforce) and the consequences for the economy. Why was *federal* legislation needed to address discrimination in employment?

2. **The Procedural Posture?** How was Rosa Helm's claim against Christiansburg Garment resolved? How was the issue of Christiansburg Garment's entitlement to attorneys' fees raised? How did the issue reach the Supreme Court?

3. **The Statutory Issue?** The question in *Christianburg Garment* was: when may a defendant who has prevailed in a Title VII action recover its attorneys' fees from the plaintiff? The language of § 706(k) seems to be clear: "the court, in its discretion, may allow the prevailing party . . . a reasonable attorney's fee . . . ." Section 706(k) does not refer to the prevailing plaintiff or prevailing defendant, but rather to the prevailing "party," a term that is ordinarily used to refer to anyone bound by a judgment. *Cf.* Fed. R. Civ. P. 17. Nevertheless, the Court rejects this reading. What is the textual basis for the Court's interpretation? Is the Court's position consistent with the text of § 706(k)? If not, what are the grounds for the Court's decision? What role does prior precedent from the Court or the lower courts play? What role does Title VII's legislative history play? What role do judicial policy judgments play?

4. **The Decline of the Agency Enforcement Model and the Rise of the Private Enforcement Model.** Prior to the enactment of the Civil Rights of 1964, almost all employment discrimination legislation vested enforcement authority in an administrative agency. "The centerpiece of this approach was a fair employment practices commission, or FEPC, with the authority to mediate disputes and, where necessary, order that a defendant cease and desist from discriminatory practices. Every major state that enacted a fair employment law in the immediate postwar period adopted the FEPC approach." David Freeman Engstrom, *The Lost Origins of American Fair Employment Law: Regulatory Choice and the Making of Modern Civil Rights,* 1943–1972, 63 Stan. L. Rev. 1071, 1073–74 (2011).

The inclusion of a private right of action with statutory fee-shifting in the Civil Rights Act of 1964 transformed this enforcement model. Today, private civil lawsuits are the dominant means of enforcing Title VII and other civil rights laws. The decision that Title VII should be enforced primarily through private civil litigation originally reflected a compromise between conservative Republican supporters of the Civil Rights Act who feared creating a new federal bureaucracy and liberal democrats who favored enforcement by a powerful administrative agency modelled on the National Labor Relations Board, which has exclusive enforcement authority under its organic statute. *See* Sean Farhang, *The Political Development of Job Discrimination Litigation, 1963–1976,* 23 Stud. Am. Pol. Devel. 23, 27 (2009); Daniel B. Rodriguez & Barry R. Weingast, *The Positive Political Theory of Legislative History: New Perspectives on the 1964 Civil Rights Act and Its Interpretation,* 151 U. Pa. L. Rev. 1417, 1491 (2003).

As a general matter, what are the advantages of enforcement through private, civil litigation compared to administrative enforcement? Consider in this respect the resources available for enforcement of the statute; the information available to actors considering whether to file charges and then to bring suit; the motivations of such actors; and the risk of "capture" by factions that have interests other than carrying out the policy embodied in legislation; and the likely role of the courts. Is private enforcement superior to public enforcement on all of these dimensions? On which, if any?

For discussion of the comparative costs and benefits of public and private enforcement, see, e.g., Sean Farhang, Litigation State: Public Regulation and Private Lawsuits in the United States (2010); David Freeman Engstrom, *Agencies as Litigation Gatekeepers,* 123 Yale L.J. 616 (2013); Matthew C. Stephenson, *Public Regulation of Private Enforcement: The Case for Expanding the Role of Administrative Agencies,* 91 Va. L. Rev. 93 (2005); John C. Coffee, Jr., *Understanding the Plaintiff's Attorney: The Implications of Economic Theory for Private Enforcement of Law Through Class and Derivative Actions,* 86 Colum. L. Rev. 669 (1986).

5. **The Relationship Between Agency Adjudication and Private Enforcement.** The Civil Rights Act makes use of a hybrid public/private structure to address claims of discrimination brought by private parties. A person complaining of discrimination must first file a charge with the Equal Employment Opportunity Commission (EEOC), as well as a state civil rights agency, if any. The EEOC serves notice of the charge on the respondent and, according to the statute, will conduct an investigation and determine if there is "reasonable cause" to believe the charge is true. If reasonable cause is lacking, the EEOC dismisses the case and the charging party may file an action in federal district court. If reasonable cause is found, EEOC attempts to conciliate the dispute. If conciliation fails, either EEOC or the charging party may bring an action in federal district court. *See* 42 U.S.C. § 2000e-5.

One consequence of the charge-filing process is that EEOC is given early notice of claims and may step into the shoes of a private charging party and effectively take control of a lawsuit. Why might EEOC do so? To begin with, the charging party may lack counsel. Moreover, the EEOC as a public agency is able to take advantage of more liberal court procedures than private litigants. EEOC may bring an action to enjoin a "pattern or practice" of employment discrimination without having to satisfy the requirements of Fed. R. Civ. P. 23. 42 U.S.C. § 2000e-6(a); *see General Tel. Co. of the Northwest, Inc. v. EEOC,* 446 U.S. 318 (1980). Furthermore, while an individual employee may agree to submit employment discrimination claims to binding arbitration, *see Gilmer v. Interstate/Johnson Lane Corp.*, 500 U.S. 20 (1991), such agreements are not binding on the EEOC. *See EEOC v. Waffle House, Inc.*, 534 U.S. 279 (2002). Litigation by the EEOC is therefore a way of securing court review of claims that otherwise would be subject to mandatory arbitration.

For many plaintiffs, however, presentation of a charge to the EEOC is merely a procedural formality. Due to large backlogs and chronic underfunding, the EEOC cannot investigate or conciliate many employment discrimination claims. Statistics maintained by the agency show that in fiscal year 2012, it received 99,412 charges under Title VII and other civil rights statutes. 8.6% of the charges resulted in settlements. 4.9% of the charges were withdrawn "with benefits"—the claimant withdrew the charge upon receiving the results she desired. 14.8% were administratively closed—for example, for failure to prosecute; 67.9% resulted in a finding by the EEOC that there was no reasonable cause to believe discrimination had occurred; and 3.8% resulted in a reasonable cause finding. All told, 17.2% of charges were resolved on the merits, and claimants received total compensation of $365.4 million, for a mean payment of $22,074.54 per successful claimant. During the same fiscal year, the EEOC initiated only 155 lawsuits. *See generally* Laura Beth Nielson & Robert L. Nelson, *Rights Realized? An Empirical Analysis of Employment Discrimination Litigation as a Claiming System*, 2005 Wis. L. Rev. 663.

6. **The Costs of Private Enforcement.** Private enforcement "gives the United States the most politically and socially responsive court system in the world." Robert A. Kagan, Adversarial Legalism: The American Way of Law 16 (2001). But it is not without costs. Among other things, critics contend that privatizing enforcement of the law leads to inefficient levels of law-enforcement, eliminates prosecutorial discretion, interferes with public officials' ability to coordinate enforcement, empowers unaccountable parties to enforce the law, results in windfalls to those parties, and generates work for the courts. *See, e.g.*, Samuel Estreicher & Zev Eigen, *The Forum for Adjudication of Employment Disputes*, in Research Handbook on the Economics of Labor and Employment Law (Michael L. Wachter & Cynthia L. Estlund, eds. 2012).

Are these symptoms necessary features of a private enforcement regime? What steps could Congress could take when drafting a statute to minimize the negative consequences of private enforcement? Is "optimal" enforcement of the law through private enforcement—i.e., enforcement directed at the most serious violations, to the extent necessary to secure compliance in the real world—a realistic goal?

4. Federal vs. State Regulation

As noted in the preceding section, there is a deep-seated presumption in favor of state and local regulation. On this view, if a problem requires governmental regulation, a state or local government should be the default body that is responsible for regulating. The potential overlap of state and federal regulation raises questions of coordination and preemption.

In recent decades, debate has focused on the question of when federal regulation "preempts" or precludes the operation of state regulation. The problem is particularly acute when federal and state law follow different strategies for regulating the same harm—for example, when federal law operates through ex ante controls on market entry, and state law operates by imposing ex post liability for unreasonably dangerous conduct. The following decision presents a concrete example of this problem, as well as the general legal framework the Supreme Court uses for determining if federal law preempts state regulation.

Riegel v. Medtronic, Inc.

552 U.S. 312 (2008)

JUSTICE SCALIA delivered the opinion of the Court.

We consider whether the pre-emption clause enacted in the Medical Device Amendments of 1976, 21 U.S.C. § 360k, bars common-law claims challenging the safety and effectiveness of a medical device given premarket approval by the Food and Drug Administration (FDA).

I

A

The Federal Food, Drug, and Cosmetic Act (FDCA), 52 Stat. 1040, as amended, 21 U.S.C. § 301 *et seq.*, has long required FDA approval for the introduction of new drugs into the market. Until the statutory enactment at issue here, however, the introduction of new medical devices was left largely for the States to supervise as they saw fit. See *Medtronic, Inc. v. Lohr*, 518 U.S. 470, 475–476 (1996).

The regulatory landscape changed in the 1960's and 1970's, as complex devices proliferated and some failed. Most notably, the Dalkon Shield intrauterine device, introduced in 1970, was linked to serious infections and several deaths, not to mention a large number of pregnancies. Thousands of tort claims followed.*** Several states adopted regulatory measures, including California, which in 1970 enacted a law requiring premarket approval of medical devices.***

Congress stepped in with passage of the Medical Device Amendments of 1976 (MDA), 21 U.S.C. § 360c *et seq.*, which swept back some state [law] obligations and imposed a regime of detailed federal oversight. The MDA includes an express pre-emption provision that states:

"Except as provided in subsection (b) of this section, no State or political subdivision of a State may establish or continue in effect with respect to a device intended for human use any requirement—

"(1) which is different from, or in addition to, any requirement applicable under this chapter to the device, and

"(2) which relates to the safety or effectiveness of the device or to any other matter included in a requirement applicable to the device under this chapter." § 360k(a).

The exception contained in subsection (b) permits the FDA to exempt some state and local requirements from pre-emption.

The new regulatory regime established various levels of oversight for medical devices, depending on the risks they present. Class I, which includes such devices as elastic bandages and examination gloves, is subject to the lowest level of oversight: "general controls," such as labeling requirements. § 360c(a)(1)(A). Class II, which includes such devices as powered wheelchairs and surgical drapes, *ibid.*, is subject in addition to "special controls" such as performance standards and postmarket surveillance measures, § 360c(a)(1)(B).

The devices receiving the most federal oversight are those in Class III, which include replacement heart valves, implanted cerebella stimulators, and pacemaker pulse generators. In general, a device is assigned to Class III if it cannot be established that a less stringent classification would provide reasonable assurance of safety and effectiveness, and the device is "purported or represented to be for a use in supporting or sustaining human life or for a use which is of substantial importance in preventing impairment of human health," or "presents a potential unreasonable risk of illness or injury." § 360c(a)(1)(C)(ii).

Although the MDA established a rigorous regime of premarket approval for new Class III devices, it grandfathered many that were already on the market. Devices sold before the MDA's effective date may remain on the market until the FDA promulgates, after notice and comment, a regulation requiring premarket approval. §§ 360c(f)(1), 360e(b)(1). A related provision seeks to limit the competitive advantage grandfathered devices receive. A new device need not undergo premarket approval if the FDA finds it is "substantially equivalent" to another device exempt from premarket approval. § 360c(f)(1)(A). The agency's review of devices for substantial equivalence is known as the § 510(k) process, named after the statutory provision describing the review. Most new Class III devices enter the market through § 510(k). In 2005, for example, the FDA authorized the marketing of 3,148 devices under § 510(k) and granted premarket approval to just 32 devices. P. Hutt, R. Merrill, & L. Grossman, Food and Drug Law 992 (3d ed.2007).

Premarket approval is a "rigorous" process. *Lohr*, 518 U.S., at 477. A manufacturer must submit what is typically a multivolume application. FDA, Device Advice— Premarket Approval (PMA) 18. It includes, among other things, full reports of all studies and investigations of the device's safety and effectiveness that have been published or should reasonably be known to the applicant; a "full statement" of the device's "components, ingredients, and properties and of the principle or principles of operation"; "a full description of the methods used in, and the facilities and controls used for, the manufacture, processing, and, when relevant, packing and installation of, such device"; samples or device components required by the FDA; and a specimen of the proposed labeling. § 360e(c)(1). Before deciding whether to approve the application, the agency may refer it to a panel of outside experts, 21 CFR § 814.44(a) (2007), and may request additional data from the manufacturer, § 360e(c)(1)(G).

The FDA spends an average of 1,200 hours reviewing each application, and grants premarket approval only if it finds there is a "reasonable assurance" of the device's "safety and effectiveness," § 360e(d). The agency must "weig[h] any probable benefit to health from the use of the device against any probable risk of injury or illness from such use." § 360c(a)(2)(C).***

The premarket approval process includes review of the device's proposed labeling. The FDA evaluates safety and effectiveness under the conditions of use set forth on the label, § 360c(a)(2)(B), and must determine that the proposed labeling is neither false nor misleading, § 360e(d)(1)(A).

After completing its review, the FDA may grant or deny premarket approval. § 360e(d). It may also condition approval on adherence to performance standards, 21 CFR § 861.1(b)(3), restrictions upon sale or distribution, or compliance with other requirements, § 814.82. The agency is also free to impose device-specific restrictions by regulation. § 360j(e)(1).***

Once a device has received premarket approval, the MDA forbids the manufacturer to make, without FDA permission, changes in design specifications, manufacturing processes, labeling, or any other attribute, that would affect safety or effectiveness. § 360e(d)(6)(A)(i). If the applicant wishes to make such a change, it must submit, and the FDA must approve, an application for supplemental premarket approval, to be evaluated under largely the same criteria as an initial application. § 360e(d)(6); 21 CFR § 814.39(c).

After premarket approval, the devices are subject to reporting requirements. § 360i.*** The FDA has the power to withdraw premarket approval based on newly reported data or existing information and must withdraw approval if it determines that a device is unsafe or ineffective under the conditions in its labeling. § 360e(e)(1); see also § 360h(e) (recall authority).

B

***The device at issue is an Evergreen Balloon Catheter marketed by defendant-respondent Medtronic, Inc. It is a Class III device that received premarket approval from the FDA in 1994; changes to its label received supplemental approvals in 1995 and 1996.

Charles Riegel underwent coronary angioplasty in 1996, shortly after suffering a myocardial infarction. His right coronary artery was diffusely diseased and heavily calcified. Riegel's doctor inserted the Evergreen Balloon Catheter into his patient's coronary artery in an attempt to dilate the artery, although the device's labeling stated that use was contraindicated for patients with diffuse or calcified stenoses. The label also warned that the catheter should not be inflated beyond its rated burst pressure of eight atmospheres. Riegel's doctor inflated the catheter five times, to a pressure of 10 atmospheres; on its fifth inflation, the catheter ruptured. Riegel developed a heart block, was placed on life support, and underwent emergency coronary bypass surgery.

Riegel and his wife Donna brought this lawsuit in April 1999, in the United States District Court for the Northern District of New York. Their complaint alleged that Medtronic's catheter was designed, labeled, and manufactured in a manner that violated New York common law, and that these defects caused Riegel to suffer severe and permanent injuries. The complaint raised a number of common-law claims. The District Court held that the MDA pre-empted Riegel's claims of strict liability; breach of implied warranty; and negligence in the design, testing, inspection, distribution, labeling, marketing, and sale of the catheter. It also held that the MDA pre-empted a negligent manufacturing claim insofar as it was not premised on the theory that Medtronic violated federal law. Finally, the court concluded that the MDA pre-empted Donna Riegel's claim for loss of consortium to the extent it was derivative of the pre-empted claims.

The United States Court of Appeals for the Second Circuit affirmed these dismissals.***

II

Since the MDA expressly pre-empts only state requirements "different from, or in addition to, any requirement applicable . . . to the device" under federal law, § 360k (a)(1), we must determine whether the Federal Government has established requirements applicable to Medtronic's catheter. If so, we must then determine whether the Riegels' common-law claims are based upon New York requirements with respect to the device that are "different from, or in addition to" the federal ones, and that relate to safety and effectiveness. § 360k(a).

We turn to the first question. In *Lohr*, a majority of this Court interpreted the MDA's pre-emption provision in a manner "substantially informed" by the FDA regulation set forth at 21 CFR § 808.1(d). 518 U.S., at 495; see also *id.*, at 500–501. That regulation says that state requirements are pre-empted "only when the Food and Drug Administration has established specific counterpart regulations or there are other specific requirements applicable to a particular device . . . ." 21 CFR § 808.1(d). Informed by the regulation, we concluded that federal manufacturing and labeling requirements applicable across the board to almost all medical devices did not pre-empt the common-law claims of negligence and strict liability at issue in *Lohr*.***

Even though substantial-equivalence review under § 510(k) is device specific, *Lohr* also rejected the manufacturer's contention that § 510(k) approval imposed device-specific "requirements." We regarded the fact that products entering the market through § 510(k) may be marketed only so long as they remain substantial equivalents of the relevant pre-1976 devices as a qualification for an exemption rather than a requirement. *Id.*, at 493–494; see also *id.*, at 513 (O'Connor, J., concurring in part and dissenting in part).

Premarket approval, in contrast, imposes "requirements" under the MDA as we interpreted it in *Lohr*. Unlike general labeling duties, premarket approval is specific to individual devices. And it is in no sense an exemption from federal safety review—it *is* federal safety review. Thus, the attributes that *Lohr* found lacking in § 510(k) review are present here.***

III

We turn, then, to the second question: whether the Riegels' common-law claims rely upon "any requirement" of New York law applicable to the catheter that is "different from, or in addition to" federal requirements and that "relates to the safety or effectiveness of the device or to any other matter included in a requirement applicable to the device." § 360k(a). Safety and effectiveness are the very subjects of the Riegels' common-law claims, so the critical issue is whether New York's tort duties constitute "requirements" under the MDA.

A

***Congress is entitled to know what meaning this Court will assign to terms regularly used in its enactments. Absent other indication, reference to a State's "requirements" includes its common-law duties. As the plurality opinion said in *Cipollone* [*v. Liggett Group, Inc.*, 505 U.S. 504], common-law liability is "premised on the existence of a legal duty," and a tort judgment therefore establishes that the defendant has violated a state-law obligation. And while the common-law remedy is limited to damages, a liability award "'can be, indeed is designed to be, a potent method of governing conduct and controlling policy.'"

In the present case, there is nothing to contradict this normal meaning. To the contrary, in the context of this legislation excluding common-law duties from the scope of pre-emption would make little sense. State tort law that requires a manufacturer's catheters to be safer, but hence less effective, than the model the FDA has approved disrupts the federal scheme no less than state regulatory law to the same effect. Indeed, one would think that tort law, applied by juries under a negligence or strict-liability standard, is less deserving of preservation. A state statute, or a regulation adopted by a state agency, could at least be expected to apply cost-benefit analysis similar to that applied by the experts at the FDA: How many more lives will be saved by a device which, along with its greater effectiveness, brings a greater risk of harm? A jury, on the other hand, sees only the cost of a more dangerous design, and is not concerned with its benefits; the patients who reaped those benefits are not represented in court.***[4]

B

The dissent would narrow the pre-emptive scope of the term "requirement" on the grounds that it is "difficult to believe that Congress would, without comment, remove

---

4. The Riegels point to § 360k(b), which authorizes the FDA to exempt state "requirements" from pre-emption under circumstances that would rarely be met for common-law duties. But a law that permits an agency to exempt certain "requirements" from pre-emption does not suggest that no other "requirements" exist. The Riegels also invoke § 360h(d), which provides that compliance with certain FDA orders "shall not relieve any person from liability under Federal or State law." This indicates that some state-law claims are not pre-empted, as we held in *Lohr*. But it could not possibly mean that *all* state-law claims are not pre-empted, since that would deprive the MDA pre-emption clause of all content. And it provides no guidance as to which state-law claims are pre-empted and which are not.

all means of judicial recourse" for consumers injured by FDA-approved devices. But, as we have explained, this is exactly what a pre-emption clause for medical devices does by its terms. The operation of a law enacted by Congress need not be seconded by a committee report on pain of judicial nullification.***

[Opinions of JUSTICE STEVENS, concurring in part and concurring in the judgment, and JUSTICE GINSBURG, dissenting, omitted.]

Notes and Questions

1. **The Regulatory Context?** *Riegel v. Medtronic* concerns the preemptive effect of the 1976 Medical Device Amendments to the Federal Food, Drug, and Cosmetic Act on common law product liability and negligence claims under New York law. In contrast to cases we have seen thus far, the Riegels invoked common law liability standards rather than asserting rights under a statutory or administrative scheme. What causes of action did they invoke? What judgment(s) were they seeking from the courts?

What might motivate a legislature to supplement or supplant common law standards governing the safety of medical devices? What are the advantages of establishing safety standards through tort litigation? Does such litigation provide a decentralized, cost-efficient means of establishing device standards, in which enforcers have strong incentives to ensure the safety of devices? On the other hand, what is the case for uniform national standards for device safety?

2. **The Statutory Issue?** What is the textual basis for the Court's conclusion that Riegels' claims are preempted? How much work does the statutory text do in support of the Court's conclusion?

3. **The Multiple Layers of Regulation in a Federal System.** *Riegel* illustrates the complexity of regulating in a system of government that divides regulatory authority among multiple governments who in turn variously make use of legislation, administrative law, and the common law to accomplish their regulatory objectives. A number of questions to be addressed: (a) Who *promulgates* legal norms—Congress, state legislatures, federal agencies, state agencies, or some combination of the above? (b) Who *enforces* those norms—federal agencies, state agencies, private parties? (c) Which *forum* will adjudicate contested violations of legal norms—federal courts, state courts, federal agencies, state agencies? (d) Does federal law *preempt* state law or do federal and state law operate in tandem—the question in *Riegel*.

How would you rate Congress's performance in drafting the preemption provision of the Medical Device Act? Did Congress fail to address a question of significant economic and social importance? Could Congress have foreseen that question when it enacted the MDA?

4. **Why Did Congress Require Pre-Market Clearance by the FDA?** The Medical Device Amendments to the FDCA are unusual in requiring that medical devices be approved by the FDA before they may enter the market. This is often called "pre-market review." This process is a powerful way of preventing harm but may also delay the introduction of new products. In the United States, the safety and effectiveness of

products is more typically controlled through the imposition of ex post liability or sanctions. If a product injures a consumer, the consumer can seek compensation through a tort suit. If the injury is serious enough or endangers the public, the manufacturer may be subject to criminal penalties.

Ex post forms of liability, such as damages awards, fines, and criminal penalties, are premised on the assumption that manufacturers will adjust their behavior to avoid future liability. Ideally, manufacturers will internalize the costs of harms that their products lead to, and invest in safety so long as those investments are less expensive than the costs that unsafe products generate, taking into account regulatory sanctions and reputational harm. *See generally* Samuel Issacharoff, *Regulating After the Fact*, 56 DePaul L. Rev. 375.

Why did Congress depart from ex post regulation when it enacted the Medical Device Amendments? Do medical devices involve risks that cannot be managed adequately through the imposition of liability ex post? What are the costs of requiring government preclearance of new medical devices? Note that restrictions on market entry and the imposition of ex post liability are not necessarily exclusive of one another. *See generally* Charles D. Kolstad, Thomas S. Ulen & Gary V. Johnson, Ex Post *Liability for Harm vs.* Ex Ante *Safety Regulation: Substitutes or Complements?*, 80 Am. Econ. Rev. 888 (1990).

5. **Tort Duties as Preempted State-Law "Requirements" and Interpretive Canons.** A central point in the Court's analysis is the conclusion that duties imposed through tort law—such as a jury's determination that a product is unreasonably dangerous—are "requirements" as that the term is used in the MDA's preemption provision. That conclusion is not inevitable. The term "requirement" could also be read to apply to directives that are expressly intended to change the device's design. Under this view, the fact that tort liability is imposed ex post and as a means of compensating for harm would prevent it from being an MDA "requirement." Alternatively, the term "requirement" might apply only to statutes and regulations promulgated by legislatures and administrative agencies, not to decisions in individual lawsuits, which vary from case to case. *See* Catherine M. Sharkey, *Products Liability Preemption: An Institutional Approach*, 76 Geo. Wash. L. Rev. 449, 459 (2008) (observing that "[t]o our modern sensibilities, tort law wears (at least) two hats: victim-specific compensation and regulatory deterrence").

The Court's holding that "common-law causes of action for negligence and strict liability do impose 'requirement[s]' for federal preemption purposes" can be viewed as a canon of interpretation. The Court admittedly attempts to justify that holding based on the text, history, and objectives of the MDA. But the holding is also a generalization about the meaning of a term, "requirement," that appears frequently in federal legislation. "Congress," the Court says, "is entitled to know what meaning this Court will assign to terms regularly used in its enactments."

This type of a canon—a rule of thumb about the meaning of a particular term of art—is known as a "grammatical" canon. Interestingly, in *Riegel*, there is also another canon at work: the "presumption against preemption." This canon, which might be termed a "substantive" canon, teaches that when analyzing the preemptive effect of a federal law, a court "start[s] with the assumption that the historic police powers of the

States [are] not to be superseded by . . . Federal Act unless that [is] the clear and manifest purpose of Congress." *Cipollone v. Liggett Group, Inc.*, 505 U.S. 504, 516 (1992) (quoting *Rice v. Santa Fe Elevator Corp.*, 331 U.S. 218, 230 (1947)). The justification for this canon is not that Congress generally uses words in a way that leaves state law undisturbed; as a descriptive matter, there are too many federal statutes that preempt state law for this to be so. Instead, the presumption against preemption reflects a particular *substantive* view of the proper relationship among federal governments and the states: that "national and state authority is largely concurrent, not limited by exclusive subject-matter spheres." Ernest A. Young, *"The Ordinary Diet of The Law": The Presumption Against Preemption in the Roberts Court*, 2011 Sup. Ct. Rev. 253, 256. This substantive canon would apply in the absence of clear statutory text to the contrary; it acts as a "thumb on the scale" in favor of concurrent federal-state regulation.

How does the Court conceive of the relationship between these two canons? Does it offer persuasive reasons for why the newly recognized grammatical canon should trump the substantive, federalism-protecting canon?

6. **Models of the Federal-State Relationship.** Historically, most federal and state regulation operated concurrently. This overlapping federal and state regulation provides the foundation for the Court's view that Congress must clearly intend to displace the historic police powers exercised by states before a federal statute is given preemptive effect. *See Cipollone*, 505 U.S. at 516.

Perhaps the most important departure from the historical model is so-called "command and control" regulation by a federal agency. Legislation from the New Deal era typically established federal regulatory standards and a federal administrative apparatus to implement and enforce those standards. The presence of this top-down administrative apparatus often indicated Congress's intent to preempt concurrent regulation by states and local governments. For example, the Securities Act of 1933, 15 U.S.C. § 77a et seq., and Securities Exchange Act of 1934, 15 U.S.C. § 78a et seq., are enforced by the Securities Exchange Commission and Department of Justice. Cases under these statutes are adjudicated largely in federal court. As amended over the years, the Acts prohibit states from regulating many matters within their coverage. *See, e.g.*, 15 U.S.C. § 78bb(f)(1) (barring certain actions for securities fraud that are "based upon the statutory or common law of any State or subdivision thereof").

Federal statutes also have sought to enlist state actors in the implementation of federal policy. For example, the Medicare and Medicaid programs establish baseline federal criteria for benefits eligibility while giving states substantial discretion over who gets benefits and how benefits are distributed. This model of the federal-state relationship, known as "cooperative federalism," attempts to leverage states' pre-existing governmental institutions in the implementation of federal policy, generally in exchange for federal funding related to the specified program.

As a general matter, such conditional grants involve a two-step process. The first step concerns the original design of the grant: Congress enacts legislation defining the purposes of the grant, establishing the criteria for getting the money, any matching requirements, and so on.*** Congress may impose various substantive conditions on both the federal grant money and preexisting state funds to ensure the federal grant is spent for specified classes of beneficiaries or specified federal purposes. Congress may also demand that state agencies responsible for spending the federal revenue comply with various structural or procedural requirements.*** In the second stage, individual states decide whether to accept the conditions and apply for the funds.

Roderick M. Hills, Jr., *The Political Economy of Cooperative Federalism: Why State Autonomy Makes Sense and "Dual Sovereignty" Doesn't*, 96 Mich. L. Rev. 813, 859–60 (1998). *See also* Eloise Pasachoff, *Agency Enforcement of Spending Clause Statutes: A Defense of the Funding Cut-Off*, 124 Yale L.J. 248 (2014).

More recent statutes such as the No Child Left Behind Act, Pub. L. No. 107-110, 115 Stat. 1425 (2002), present a variation on the cooperative federalist structure. As enacted, No Child Left Behind imposed stringent requirements and performance standards that states must follow on pain of losing federal education funding. However, the statute also permitted the U.S. Department of Education to waive many of these requirements if they proved impractical for states to satisfy. The Obama administration made aggressive use of this authority to encourage states to develop innovative education programs that advance No Child Left Behind's underlying purposes while departing from the formal requirements of the statute. In effect, requirements established by federal legislation become a "penalty default"—a costly form of regulation that states are subjected to only if they do not undertake reasonable efforts to implement federal policy. *See* David J. Barron & Todd D. Rakoff, *In Defense of Big Waiver*, 113 Colum. L. Rev. 265 (2013); Martin A. Kurzweil, *Disciplined Devolution and the New Education Federalism*, 103 Cal. L. Rev. 565 (2015).

Which of the above models of the federal/state relationship, if any, does the Medical Device Act, at issue in *Riegel*, appear to follow? Can you identify some of the general costs and benefits of these models?

7. **Tests for Determining Whether Federal Law Preempts State Law.** Under the Supremacy Clause of Article VI of the Constitution, in any conflict between federal and state laws, the federal law is supreme. This provision accords Congress broad power to displace state law, but Congress frequently fails to address the subject of preemption or does so in ways that are difficult to make sense of. For example, it is common for federal legislation to contain a preemption clause stating that inconsistent "standards" or "requirements" are preempted as well as a "savings" clause disclaiming any intention to displace common law duties. *See* Catherine M. Sharkey, *Products Liability Preemption: An Institutional Approach*, 76 Geo. Wash. L. Rev. 449, 450–51 (2008); Roderick M. Hills, Jr., *Against Preemption: How Federalism Can Improve the National Legislative Process*, 82 N.Y.U. L. Rev. 1, 16 (2007).

As stated in *English v. General Electric Co.*, 496 U.S. 72 (1990), there are generally three circumstances in which federal law is deemed to displace state law:

First, Congress can define explicitly the extent to which its enactments preempt state law. Preemption fundamentally is a question of congressional intent, and when Congress has made its intent known through explicit statutory language, the courts' task is an easy one.

Second, in the absence of explicit statutory language, state law is preempted where it regulates conduct in a field that Congress intended the Federal Government to occupy exclusively. Such an intent may be inferred from a "scheme of federal regulation . . . so pervasive as to make reasonable the inference that Congress left no room for the States to supplement it," or where an Act of Congress "touch[es] a field in which the federal interest is so dominant that the federal system will be assumed to preclude enforcement of state laws on the same subject." Although this Court has not hesitated to draw an inference of field pre-emption where it is supported by the federal statutory and regulatory schemes, it has emphasized: "Where . . . the field which Congress is said to have pre-empted" includes areas that have "been traditionally occupied by the States," congressional intent to supersede state laws must be "'clear and manifest.'"

Finally, state law is pre-empted to the extent that it actually conflicts with federal law. Thus, the Court has found pre-emption where it is impossible for a private party to comply with both state and federal requirements, or where state law "stands as an obstacle to the accomplishment and execution of the full purposes and objectives of Congress."

Id. at 78–79 (citations omitted).

Note that the different types of preemption are premised on different theories of *how* federal law preempts state law. Express and field preemption are based on the premise that Congress exercised its power under Articles I and VI to displace state law. Here, federal law preempts state law because Congress said so, or because the statute regulates a problem so comprehensively that it supports an inference that Congress intended no other form of regulation to be available. Implied preemption (the Court's final category) functions more like a conflict-of-law rule. When both state and federal law govern the same conduct, implied-preemption doctrine identifies some circumstances where federal law displaces state law because the two are incompatible, or because the operation of state law is inconsistent with the way in which federal law is intended to work. Which form of preemption is at work in *Riegel?*

8. **Preemption and "Regulatory Competition."** Justice Brandeis famously argued, "It is one of the happy incidents of the federal system that a single courageous State may, if its citizens choose, serve as a laboratory; and try novel social and economic experiments without risk to the rest of the country." *New State Ice Co. v. Liebmann,* 285 U.S. 262, 311 (1932) (Brandeis, J., dissenting). Should the preemptive effect of federal law vary depending on whether a field would benefit from such experimentation and competition among multiple regulators?

For example, should the presumption in favor of preemption be considered most powerful in fields where inter-state externalities create a need for national regulation? Should the presumption be weakest where multiple, competing regulators coordinate their activities, or regulatory competition can be expected to lead to innovation? *See* Erin O'Hara O'Connor & Larry E. Ribstein, *Preemption and Choice-of-Law Coordination*, 111 MICH. L. REV. 647, 680 (2013). Is Congress able and likely to make these kinds of judgments? Would this kind of "regulatory competition" among states trying to achieve the most effective and efficient regulations work in the field of medical devices? What would be the real-world consequences if medical devices were subject to regulation by fifty state governments as well as the federal government? Would such a regulatory environment lead to better and safer medical devices, or stifle innovation by subjecting manufacturers to a crazy quilt of regulation? In any event, is the regulatory-competition theory attractive as a policy matter? Does it have any foundation in the Constitution?

9. **Pharmaceutical Preemption.** In a dissent not reproduced here, Justice Ginsburg maintained that decades of drug regulation indicate "Congress did not regard FDA regulation and state tort claims as mutually exclusive." Subsequent decisions partially vindicated this view. In *Wyeth v. Levine*, 555 U.S. 555 (2009), the Court concluded that FDA pre-market approval of new pharmaceuticals did not preempt state tort suits seeking damages for the manufacturer's failure to provide adequate warning of the drug's risks. Two years later, however, in *PLIVA, Inc. v. Mensing*, 131 S. Ct. 2567 (2011), the Court ruled that federal law preempted identical suits against manufacturers of generic pharmaceuticals, because generic manufacturers could not easily change a drug's labeling in response to newly-discovered risks.

The different outcomes were required, in the *PLIVA* Court's view, by the fact that name-brand and generic pharmaceuticals are governed by different statutory provisions—for name-brand pharmaceuticals, the 1962 Drug Amendments to the Federal Food, Drug, and Cosmetic Act, 76 Stat. 780, 21 U.S.C. § 301 *et seq*, and for generics, the Drug Price Competition and Patent Term Restoration Act, 98 Stat. 1585 (1984), or Hatch-Waxman Amendments. Under the 1962 Drug Amendments, "[a] brand-name manufacturer seeking new drug approval is responsible for the accuracy and adequacy of its label," whereas "[a] manufacturer seeking generic drug approval . . . is responsible for ensuring that its warning label is *the same* as the brand name's." *PLIVA*, 131 S. Ct. at 2574 (emphasis added). Because it is impossible for a generic manufacturer to update its warning label in response to new information, the Court thought, tort liability based on failure to update warnings was preempted.

Does the varying treatment of brand-name and generic pharmaceuticals affect the outcome in *Riegel*? As a policy matter, is there any reason why pharmaceuticals and medical devices, whether brand-name or generic, should be subject to different preemption rules?

10. **Further Reading.** In recent years, preemption in general and the preemptive effects of agency regulation in particular have been the subjects of much scholarship. For varying perspectives, see, e.g., Jessica Bulman-Pozen & Heather K. Gerken, *Uncooperative Federalism*, 118 YALE L.J. 1256 (2009); Mary J. Davis, *Unmasking the Presumption in Favor of Preemption*, 53 S.C. L. REV. 963 (2002); Roderick M. Hills, Jr.,

Against Preemption: How Federalism Can Improve the National Legislative Process, 82 N.Y.U. L. Rev. 1 (2007); Samuel Issacharoff & Catherine Sharkey, *Backdoor Federalization*, 53 UCLA L. Rev. 1353 (2006); Nina A. Mendelson, Chevron *and Preemption*, 102 Mich. L. Rev. 737 (2004); Thomas W. Merrill, *Preemption and Institutional Choice*, 102 Nw. U. L. Rev. 727 (2008); Caleb Nelson, *Preemption*, 86 Va. L. Rev. 225 (2000); Ernest A. Young, *The Rehnquist Court's Two Federalisms*, 83 Tex. L. Rev. 1 (2004).

5. Criminal vs. Civil Liability

Church of the Holy Trinity v. United States

143 U.S. 457 (1892)

Mr. Justice Brewer delivered the opinion of the court.

Plaintiff in error is a corporation, duly organized and incorporated as a religious society under the laws of the State of New York. E. Walpole Warren was, prior to September, 1887, an alien residing in England. In that month the plaintiff in error made a contract with him, by which he was to remove to the city of New York and enter into its service as rector and pastor; and in pursuance of such contract, Warren did so remove and enter upon such service. It is claimed by the United States that this contract on the part of the plaintiff in error was forbidden by the act of February 26, 1885, 23 Stat. 332, c. 164, and an action was commenced to recover the penalty prescribed by that act.[*] The Circuit Court held that the contract was within the prohibition of the statute, and rendered judgment accordingly, and the single question presented for our determination is whether it erred in that conclusion.

The first section describes the act forbidden, and is in these words:

> "Be it enacted by the Senate and House of Representatives of the United States of America in Congress assembled, That from and after the passage of this act it shall be unlawful for any person, company, partnership, or corporation, in any manner whatsoever, to prepay the transportation, or in any way assist

---

[*]　Section 3 of the Act provided:

[F]or every violation of any of the provisions of section one of this act the person, partnership, company, or corporation violating the same, by knowingly assisting, encouraging, or soliciting the migration or importation of any alien or aliens, foreigner or foreigners, into the United States, its Territories, or the District of Columbia, to perform labor or service of any kind under contract or agreement, express or implied, parol or special, with such alien or aliens, foreigner or foreigners, previous to becoming residents or citizens of the United States, shall forfeit and pay for every such offence the sum of one thousand dollars, which may be sued for and recovered by the United States or by any person who shall first bring his action therefor including any such alien or foreigner who may be a party to any such contract or agreement, as debts of like amount are now recovered in the circuit courts of the United States; the proceeds to be paid into the Treasury of the United States; and separate suits may be brought for each alien or foreigner being a party to such contract or agreement aforesaid. And it shall be the duty of the district attorney of the proper district to prosecute every such suit at the expense of the United States.

23 Stat. 332, 333.—Eds.

or encourage the importation or migration of any alien or aliens, any foreigner or foreigners, into the United States, its Territories, or the District of Columbia, under contract or agreement, parol or special, express or implied, made previous to the importation or migration of such alien or aliens, foreigner or foreigners, to perform labor or service of any kind in the United States, its Territories, or the District of Columbia."

It must be conceded that the act of the corporation is within the letter of this section, for the relation of rector to his church is one of service, and implies labor on the one side with compensation on the other. Not only are the general words labor and service both used, but also, as it were to guard against any narrow interpretation and emphasize a breadth of meaning, to them is added "of any kind;" and, further, as noticed by the Circuit Judge in his opinion, the fifth section, which makes specific exceptions, among them professional actors, artists, lecturers, singers and domestic servants, strengthens the idea that every other kind of labor and service was intended to be reached by the first section. While there is great force to this reasoning, we cannot think Congress intended to denounce with penalties a transaction like that in the present case. It is a familiar rule, that a thing may be within the letter of the statute and yet not within the statute, because not within its spirit, nor within the intention of its makers. This has been often asserted, and the reports are full of cases illustrating its application. This is not the substitution of the will of the judge for that of the legislator, for frequently words of general meaning are used in a statute, words broad enough to include an act in question, and yet a consideration of the whole legislation, or of the circumstances surrounding its enactment, or of the absurd results which follow from giving such broad meaning to the words, makes it unreasonable to believe that the legislator intended to include the particular act.***

Notes and Questions

1. **Historical Context.** Historically, control over immigration was thought to be a national legislative and executive prerogative as opposed to a matter regulated by state common law. The Supreme Court has long maintained "[t]he power to exclude or to expel aliens, being a power affecting international relations, is vested in the political departments of the government, and is to be regulated by treaty or by act of congress, and to be executed by the executive authority according to the regulations so established . . . ." *Fong Yue Ting v. United States*, 149 U.S. 698, 713 (1893). *But see* Gerald L. Neuman, *The Lost Century of American Immigration (1776–1875)*, 93 COLUM. L. REV. 1833 (1993).

Despite federal supremacy over immigration, state common law was not completely displaced. In 1821, the Indiana Supreme Court considered a petition for habeas corpus filed by Mary Clark, in which Clark asked to be discharged from an indenture by which she "voluntarily bound herself to serve him as an indented servant and house maid for 20 years." *In re Clark*, 1 Blackf. 122, 122 (In. 1821). Disregarding "all distinctions that might be drawn from the color of the [petitioner]," who was African American, the court concluded as a matter of general equitable principles that Clark could not be compelled to perform the indenture. "It may be laid down as a general rule," the court wrote, "that neither the common law nor the statutes in force in this State recognize the coercion of a specific performance of contracts."

2. **Was Federal Regulation Warranted?** Why did Congress conclude it was necessary to enact legislation regulating contracts for alien labor? The enactment of the Alien Contract Labor Act was driven in large measure by advocacy of U.S. labor unions, which sought to protect negotiated labor standards from competition by foreign workers. *See* WILLIAM E. FORBATH, LAW AND THE SHAPING OF THE AMERICAN LABOR MOVEMENT 12–17 (1991); CHARLOTTE ERICKSON, AMERICAN INDUSTRY AND THE EUROPEAN IMMIGRANT, 1860–1885, at 155 (1957).

In late 1883, the Knights of Labor, perhaps the most important labor organization of the 1880s, began to organize meetings and petition drives against contract labor. In hearings before the Senate Committee on Education and Labor, a representative of the Federation of Organized Trades and Labor Unions testified that "[they] hoped to prevent employers from importing strikebreakers or workers to lower the standards [of employment]." 1 SAMUEL GOMPERS, SEVENTY YEARS OF LIFE AND LABOR 154 (1925).

In January 1884, Representative Martin Foran (D-OH), a former president of the Coopers International Union, first introduced a bill restricting alien contract labor, H.R. 2550, in the House. Foran's bill was referred to the House Committee on Labor, which he chaired, and hearings were held at which representatives of the Knights of Labor testified in favor of the bill. *See* ERICKSON, *supra*, at 156.

Foran's bill passed the House during the first session of the 48th Congress. Despite being reported without amendment by the Senate Committee of Labor and Education, the Senate did not vote on the bill before the conclusion of the first session on July 7, 1884. When the second session began, the Senate took up the House bill and passed it, with substantive amendments, on February 18, 1885. 16 Cong. Rec. 1839–40. The amended bill returned to the House, which agreed to the Senate's amendments on February 23, 1885. 16 Cong. Rec. 2032.

3. **The Procedural Posture?** When *Church of the Holy Trinity* reached the U.S. Supreme Court, the Church of the Holy Trinity was the "plaintiff in error." Who was the church's adversary? What remedy had that party originally sought? What was the status of the dispute when it reached the Supreme Court?

A March 1, 1892, article in the *New York Daily Tribune* contains the following description of the origins of the suit by Reverend Warren:

> I had been here only a short time when I was told that John S. Kennedy, a Presbyterian gentleman connected with the Rev. Dr. John Hall's church, had begun suit against the vestry of the Church of the Holy Trinity, to test the application of the Contract Labor Law. The suit was an entirely friendly one, and Mr. Kennedy's object was to make odious the attempt to apply the law to clergymen and other men of the same class. He said that if he won the case he would pay the fine of $1,000 imposed. I think that he paid all the expenses

of the defence, but I am not sure. . . . Mr. Kennedy begged us to try the case squarely on the merits to the end, and not try to have it dismissed on any side issue, as might have been done. On several grounds we might have had the case dismissed, but instead we defended it simply on the ground that the Contract Labor Law did not apply to clergymen.

The Right to Import Rectors, N.Y. Daily Trib., Mar. 1, 1892 at 2, *quoted in* Adrian Vermeule, *Legislative History and the Limits of Judicial Competence: The Untold Story of Holy Trinity Church*, 50 Stan. L. Rev. 1833, 1840 (1998). *See also Importing a Rector*, N.Y. Times, Sept. 25, 1887, at 2 (letter from Kennedy suggesting that he initiated the suit because of displeasure with discriminatory enforcement against Scots).

Section 3 of the Alien Contract Labor Act authorized suits by "the United States or by any person who shall first bring his action therefor including any such alien or foreigner who may be a party to any such contract or agreement." 23 Stat. 332, 333. The "proceeds" of such actions were "to be paid into the Treasury of the United States; and separate suits may be brought for each alien or foreigner being a party to such contract or agreement aforesaid." *Id.* Section 3 further provided that "it shall be the duty of the district attorney of the proper district to prosecute every such suit at the expense of the United States." *Id.* Professor Vermeule reads these provisions to mean "that a private party could, on proper complaint, initiate a suit that district attorneys would then be obliged to prosecute." 50 Stan. L. Rev. at 1839–40.

4. **Congress's Choice of Remedy: Enforcement by Criminal Proceedings.** In general, Congress can choose to provide criminal, civil, or administrative remedies for violations of a regulatory statute. The principal criminal penalties are death, imprisonment, and fines. Civil remedies consist primarily of damages, injunctions, and declaratory judgments. Administrative remedies such as cease-and-desist orders are defined by the prosecuting agency's organic statute. Regulatory statutes often authorize multiple kinds of remedies. *See, e.g.*, Clean Air Act, 42 U.S.C. §7413 (providing for criminal, civil, and administrative enforcement).

The Court in *Holy Trinity* describes importation of alien labor as a misdemeanor. What might have motivated Congress to make violations of the act a crime? Section 3, quoted in the footnote above, imposed a $1,000 penalty for violations of §1. Why did Congress impose a $1,000 criminal fine instead of providing a private, civil action with statutory damages of $1,000?

First, consider how the decision to make violations of the statute a crime would have affected the makeup of litigated cases. As noted in the discussion of *Christiansburg Garment Co. v. EEOC*, in Section [C][3], above, a private litigant's willingness to assert a claim depends primarily on the costs and potential payoff of doing so. A private plaintiff (more precisely, a private plaintiff's attorney) who is acting in her economic self-interest will only initiate suit if the anticipated recovery, discounted by the probability of success, exceeds the costs of advancing a claim.

The "costs" of claiming include not only filing fees and the value of the attorneys' time, but social consequences for the plaintiff. A party who asserts a claim may be subject to retaliation, or people may be less willing to do business with her because of her reputation for being "litigious."

The calculus that informs a public prosecutor's decision to bring suit is different. While grand juries have some formal control over the decision to prosecute, conventional wisdom holds that the grand jury "is not a meaningful check" on the decision to prosecute or not. *See* Wayne R. LaFave et al., 4 Criminal Procedure § 13.3(d) (3d ed. 2013). Prosecutors, moreover, are rarely interested in whether prosecuting an action is cost justified in the narrow sense relevant to private, civil litigation. Administrative agencies face a different calculus:

> [A]n agency decision [to prosecute a violation of the law] often involves a complicated balancing of a number of factors which are peculiarly within its expertise. Thus, the agency must not only assess whether a violation has occurred, but whether agency resources are best spent on this violation or another, whether the agency is likely to succeed if it acts, whether the particular enforcement action requested best fits the agency's overall policies, and, indeed, whether the agency has enough resources to undertake the action at all. An agency generally cannot act against each technical violation of the statute it is charged with enforcing.

Heckler v. Chaney, 470 U.S. 821, 831 (1985).

As discussed in Chapter 5, *infra*, the decision to prosecute or not is largely immune from review by courts. Moreover, prosecutors are comparatively unlikely to be subject to retaliation for the decision to initiate suit. Most prosecutors are either elected or appointed by an elected official. On the standard account, elections are the primary mechanism through which prosecutors are held accountable for their charging decisions.

Next, consider how the decision to make violations of the Alien Contract Labor Act criminal would have affected the public's perception of the contracts that § 1 prohibited. What difference does it make that § 1 declared contracts for the importation of alien employees "unlawful" rather than simply specifying that any person who imported a foreign employee would be liable for a judgment of $1,000? From a reputational standpoint, which is worse: having to pay a $1,000 civil judgment, or being found guilty of a misdemeanor and having to pay a $1,000 fine?

5. **Congress's Choice of Frontline Enforcer.** The remedies available under a regulatory statute affect the actor or actors responsible for frontline enforcement. Again, Congress has three basic options available. Enforcement of a statute can be entrusted to (1) prosecutors (e.g., the United States Attorneys' Offices); (2) private individuals and entities; or (3) administrative agencies.

Many European nations have procedures through which a private party may initiate a criminal action. In Spain, for example, a private party may request that the prosecutor and investigating judge initiate charges or an investigation. After the investigative judge conducts a preliminary investigation, the national prosecution office decides whether to prosecute on the basis of the evidence collected. *See* Constitución Española [Spanish Constitution of 1978] § 124.

Such provisions are extremely rare in U.S. law, however. As a rule, the decision to initiate criminal proceedings is made by a prosecutor or administrative agency, not the victim of the alleged wrongdoing. The standard explanation stresses the President's responsibility under Article I § 8 to "take care that the laws be faithfully executed" and the importance of prosecutorial discretion. *See Bordenkircher v. Hayes*, 434 U.S. 357, 364 (1978) ("In our system, so long as the prosecutor has probable cause to believe that the accused committed an offense defined by statute, the decision whether or not to prosecute, and what charge to file or bring before a grand jury, generally rests entirely in his discretion.").

6. **Cease-and-Desist Orders.** Many statutes authorize an administrative agency to issue cease-and-desist orders to prevent or remedy violations of a statute the agency administers. For example, § 21C(a) of the Securities Exchange Act authorizes the Securities Exchange Commission to enter a cease-and-desist order upon a finding "that any person is violating, has violated, or is about to violate any provision of this chapter, or any rule or regulation thereunder." 15 U.S.C. § 78u-3(a). An order may direct a person to comply with the Act "upon such terms and conditions and within such time as the Commission may specify in such order" and may "require future compliance or steps to effect future compliance, either permanently or for such period of time as the Commission may specify." *Id.* An order can also require disgorgement of profits from violating the Act. § 78u-3(e). Whether a cease-and-desist order has the force of law depends on the particular statute authorizing the agency action. *Compare, e.g.*, 15 U.S.C. § 45 (specifying that orders of the Federal Trade Commission lack the force of law until enforced in court), *with* 15 U.S.C. § 78u-3 (providing that certain orders of Security Exchange Commission shall take effect immediately, notwithstanding the availability of judicial review). Historically, most agency cease-and-desist orders were not enforceable absent a court order.

Whether or not an order is immediately enforceable, contempt can result in large penalties. In *Horne v. Department of Agriculture*, 133 S. Ct. 2053 (2013), the petitioners refused to comply with an order promulgated by the Secretary of Agriculture, which required a percentage of the yearly California raisin crop to be set aside as a means of stabilizing raisin prices. An administrative law judge in the Department of Agriculture imposed more than $690,000 in civil penalties, representing assessments due to the Department, fines, and "the value of the California raisins that petitioners failed to hold in reserve" for two crop years. *Id.* at 2059. (The Supreme Court ultimately ruled that the penalties were a Fifth Amendment taking, *Horne v. Dep't of Agric.*, 135 S. Ct. 2419 (2015), but this conclusion depended on the particular regulatory scheme in *Horne*, which required physical sequestration of growers' raisins.)

Again depending on the agency's organic statute, contempt proceedings may be initiated by a private party, the administrative agency, or both. For example, the National Labor Relations Board has exclusive authority to initiate contempt proceedings for violation of a Board order. *Amalgamated Utility Workers (C.I.O.) v. Consolidated Edison Co.*, 309 U.S. 261 (1940). If a private party believes the subject of an order is in contempt, it must petition the Board to initiate contempt proceedings. Because Board orders are made enforceable by an order of a Court of Appeals, the Board must in turn petition the appeals court to find the subject of the order in contempt. *See, e.g., NLRB v. Remington Rand*, 130 F.2d 919, 924 (2d Cir. 1942). Would cease-and-desist orders have been an attractive means of enforcing the Alien Contract Labor Act? If not, why?

7. **The Statutory Issue?** In addition to illustrating the distinctions among criminal, civil, and administrative enforcement, *Church of the Holy Trinity* is one of the most famous (or infamous) statutory interpretation cases ever decided by the Supreme Court. The section of the Court's opinion interpreting the Alien Contract Labor Act and the questions raised by that interpretation are presented *infra*, in Chapter 2[B][1][b].

Chapter 2

The Legislative Process and Statutory Interpretation

The prior chapter introduced some of the leading justifications for federal regulation, and some of the choices lawmakers must take into account in determining whether to regulate in a particular area and how to do so. In this chapter, we focus on legislation. Section A introduces the process by which a legislative proposal becomes law (or more frequently, fails to do so). Section B addresses the subject of statutory interpretation — the process of determining what a statute means, how it interacts with other provisions of law, and whether and how the statute applies in particular factual circumstances.

A. The Legislative Process

1. An Overview of the Legislative Process

As we will see, the process through which a statute is enacted often informs the way in which courts, administrative agencies, and Executive branch officials interpret it. We therefore begin with a short overview of how a bill becomes law, adapted from a guide prepared by the Parliamentarian of the House of Representatives.[1]

a. Origination

Proposed legislation generally may originate in either the House of Representatives or the Senate. However, Article 1, section 7 of the Constitution specifies that revenue-raising bills are required to originate in the House. For purposes of this overview, we assume that a bill originates in the House. When a bill originates in the Senate, the steps below are more-or-less reversed.

b. The Rules of the Legislative Process

Article I, Section 1 provides that "[a]ll legislative powers herein granted shall be vested in a Congress of the United States, which shall consist of a Senate and House of Representatives." The Constitution, however, specifies only the most basic aspects of the legislative process. They include the following:

- The House and the Senate are authorized to establish "rules of [their] proceedings." Art. 1 § 5.

---

1. John V. Sullivan, How Our Laws Are Made, H.R. Doc. No. 110-49 (2007).

- The House and Senate must keep a "journal" of their proceedings. *Id.*
- A fifth of the members of either the House or Senate may demand that votes on a proposed bill be recorded. *Id.*
- Bills that have been passed by the House and Senate must be "presented" to the President before they become law. Art. 1 § 7.
- The President may veto proposed legislation by "return[ing] it, with his objections to that House in which it shall have originated." *Id.*
- If the President does not return the bill after 10 days from presentment, it becomes law, unless Congress by adjourning during the 10-day period prevents its return (in which case it is not law). *Id.* (This is sometimes referred to as the "pocket veto.")
- Congress may override a presidential veto through a two-thirds supermajority vote in both the House and Senate. *Id.*

As a practical matter, the process through which a bill becomes a law is defined largely by the rules of the House and Senate and the informal customs of both bodies. At the beginning of each Congress, the House adopts rules as one of its first orders of business. Because the Senate has a staggered membership — new members arrive every two years, while incumbent Senators continue their six-year terms — it "considers itself a continuing body."[2] Accordingly, the Senate operates under "standing" rules that it amends from time to time. Procedural questions that are not addressed in the rules may be governed by precedents—rulings by the Parliamentarian or entire Senate that are treated as binding until they are revised by rule or future precedents.

c. Preliminary Steps

The first step in the legislative process is the introduction of a proposal in one of four forms: a bill, joint resolution, concurrent resolution, or simple resolution. The most common kind of proposal used in both the House and the Senate is a bill.

Any member of the House may introduce a bill. The bill is assigned a number that it retains throughout the legislative process. For example, the bill that would later become the Alien Contract Labor Act originated as H.R. 2550. Bills introduced in the House have the prefix "H.R.," and bills introduced in the Senate have the prefix "S." Bill numbers are not necessarily unique. Because of the large number of bills that are introduced, there are for example multiple bills numbered H.R. 2550, which were introduced in different congresses. When a bill is introduced, its title is entered in the House's Journal and printed in the Congressional Record, the official record of proceedings and debates of Congress.

---

2. Sulivan, *supra* note 1, at 3.

d. Committee Consideration

The most important phase in the legislative process is action by congressional committees and subcommittees. Because it would be impractical for the House or Senate as a whole to consider every bill that is introduced, both bodies delegate initial responsibility for consideration of a bill to a committee (or committees) with jurisdiction over a particular subject matter. As of January 2014, there were twenty-five standing (permanent) committees in the House and twenty standing committees in the Senate.[3] From time to time, the House and Senate create "select" or ad hoc committees and task forces to study and report on specific issues. Each committee has a professional staff that assists the committee with its responsibilities.

Bills are referred to committees according to their subject matter. For example, the House Committee on the Judiciary has jurisdiction over measures relating to judicial proceedings and eighteen other subjects, "including constitutional amendments, immigration policy, bankruptcy, patents, copyrights, and trademarks."[4] In some cases, bills that involve several distinct subject matter areas may be referred to multiple committees.

Consideration of a bill in committee is a multi-step process. Many committees operate under rules that require bills to be referred to an appropriate subcommittee unless the full committee votes to retain jurisdiction. The subcommittee (or committee, as the case may be) may seek input from relevant departments of government and agencies. It may also submit the bill to the Government Accountability Office, the investigative office of Congress, for an official report on the necessity and desirability of the legislation. If a bill is sufficiently important, the subcommittee will hold public hearings on it. Committees often publish hearings.[5]

Following hearings, if any, the subcommittee considers the bill in one or more "markup" sessions. Reports from subcommittees are received at meetings of the full committee. Perhaps the most frequent action is for the committee to table a bill and thereby prevent the bill from being reported to the House. If the committee proceeds on the bill, it is read section by section and committee members may offer amendments.

If the committee votes to report the bill to the House, the committee's staff writes a report describing the purpose of the bill and the reasons the committee recommends its approval. A report may include supplemental, minority, or additional views that do not represent the views of the entire committee. The report is assigned a report number when it is filed, and sent to the Government Printing Office for printing.

---

3. U.S. House of Representatives, Committees, http://www.house.gov/committees/ (last accessed May 19, 2015); U.S. Senate, Committees, http://www.senate.gov/pagelayout/committees/d_three _sections_with_teasers/committees_home.htm (last accessed May 19, 2015).

4. Sullivan, *supra* note 1, at 9. *See also* House Rule X (setting out jurisdiction of House standing committees); Senate Rule XXV (same, Senate standing committees).

5. The Government Printing Office's official archive of legislative hearings is the Federal Digital System, http://www.fdsys.gov. Hearings are available on Lexis in the "LEGIS" series of databases. On Westlaw, hearings are available in the "USTESTIMONY" database.

Before a bill is reported from a House or Senate committee, the Congressional Budget Office (CBO) is required to prepare an estimate of the bill's anticipated effects on federal outlays and revenues pursuant to § 402 of the Congressional Budget Act of 1974, Pub. L. No. 93-344, 88 Stat. 297 (codified at 2 U.S.C. § 653). CBO is a nonpartisan agency within the legislative branch. It is headed by a Director who is appointed for a four-year term and selected by the Speaker of the House of Representatives and the President Pro Tempore of the Senate.

CBO's work is generally well-regarded by both political parties. Its budget estimates have played a central role in congressional budget negotiations, such as the summer 2011 debates over the extension of the federal debt ceiling, and ongoing debates about the cost of the Patient Protection and Affordable Care Act, Pub. L. No. 111-148, 124 Stat. 119 (2012). In addition to estimating the effects of a bill on the federal budget, CBO is required under the Unfunded Mandates Reform Act of 1995, Pub. L. No. 104-4, 109 Stat. 47, to prepare "a qualitative, and if practicable, a quantitative assessment of costs and benefits" anticipated from bills that impose a mandate on state, local, and tribal governments, and that are not funded by a federal appropriation. *See* 2 U.S.C. § 658b.

Reports of House and Senate committees are the most important form of legislative history relied on by courts and administrative agencies, and often provide a readable introduction to statutes which are useful to attorneys beginning research in an area.[6]

e. Consideration by the Full House

The House maintains four calendars for different types of legislation. When a bill is reported out of committee, it is placed on a calendar for consideration by the full House. Occasionally, the House allows consideration of a bill by the unanimous consent of its members. In a typical case, however, supporters of the bill obtain a special resolution or "rule" expediting consideration of the bill from the Committee on Rules, a committee with jurisdiction over the conduct of business in the House that is controlled by the Speaker of the House.[7] Such a rule permits the bill to be considered out of its usual calendar order and specifies the format that debate on the bill will take.

Debate typically occurs via the "Committee of the Whole on the State of the Nation," a parliamentary device that permits the House to operate as if it were a single large committee. When debate closes, the bill proceeds to a "second reading"—a section-by-section reading in which amendments may be offered as the bill is read. At the conclusion of the second reading, the Committee of the Whole "rises" and the bill is

---

6. Committee reports are given a prefix indicating the Congress during which the report was issued and a serial number indicating the sequential order of the report. For example, the first House report filed during the 110th Congress is numbered H.R. Rep. 110-1. Reports of Senate committees follow the same convention, and are prefixed with "S. Rep." House and Senate reports are printed in United States Code Congressional and Administrative News or "U.S.C.C.A.N.," a commercial publication available on all major commercial database services.

7. See House of Representatives Rule X(o) (vesting the Committee on Rules with jurisdiction over "the order of business of the House" and "[r]ecesses and final adjournments of Congress"); Douglas Dion & John Huber, *Procedural Choice and the House Committee on Rules*, 58 J. POLITICS 25, 26 (1996).

reported to the House with any amendments that have been adopted during consideration by the Committee of the Whole.[8]

The bill is then debated in the full House. Debate ends when the Speaker "orders the previous question," a procedure that requires a majority vote or a provision waiving the requirement for such a vote in the special rule authorizing consideration of the bill. Any amendments not voted on in the Committee of the Whole are immediately voted upon by the entire House. After voting on amendments finishes, the House votes on the bill with the amendments that have been adopted. Since the mid-1990s, the Speaker of the House (the highest-ranking member of the majority party) has followed an informal practice known as the "Hastert Rule," which prohibits a bill from being voted on by the full House unless it is supported by a majority of the majority party. Under the rules of the House, a three-fifths majority is needed to consider, pass, or agree to any bill "carrying a Federal income tax rate increase."[9] Otherwise, a simple majority suffices for the bill to pass.

When a bill is passed by the House, the Enrolling Clerk prepares an "engrossed" copy of the bill in the form in which it was passed. At this point, the bill formally becomes an "act," signifying that it is the act of one house of Congress. The bill is printed and copies are made available to Congress and the public. This printing is known as the "Act print" or the "Senate referred print."[10]

f. Senate Consideration

As already noted, the Senate also maintains standing and select committees with jurisdiction over specified subject areas. When the Senate receives a bill that has been passed by the House, the Senate Parliamentarian, an official advisor on matters of parliamentary procedure, refers the bill to the appropriate standing committee for consideration.

In the appropriate Senate committee, the bill receives the same kind of attention it received in the respective House committee. Ordinarily, a committee will refer legislation to a subcommittee before acting on it.

Once a bill is reported out of committee, the practices of the Senate differ significantly from those of the House. In the House, the Speaker and Rules Committee largely control which matters will be debated and voted upon. In contrast, the Senate relies heavily on the practice of obtaining unanimous consent to set its agenda. Thus, at the time that a bill is reported out of committee, the Majority Leader may ask unanimous consent for the immediate consideration of the bill. If the bill is uncontroversial and there is no objection, the Senate may pass the bill with little or no debate and with only a brief explanation of its purpose and effect. In the ordinary course, debate is required.

---

8. Sullivan, *supra* note 1, at 28–29.

9. House Rule XXI(5)(b).

10. Act prints can be obtained from the Library of Congress's Thomas system, http://thomas.loc .gov, the Government Printing Office Federal Digital System, http://www.fdsys.gov, and compiled legislative histories.

Debate in the Senate is less structured than debate in the House. When a Senator is recognized by the Presiding Officer, the Senator may speak for as long as she wishes and loses the floor only when she yields or takes a parliamentary action that forfeits her right to the floor.[11] Thus, Senators opposed to a measure may extend debate by making lengthy speeches or a series of speeches, a tactic known as "filibustering."[12] To end debate and cut off a filibuster, sixteen Senators must sign a motion to that effect, and the motion must be approved by three-fifths of the Senate, or sixty Senators. This procedure is known as "invoking cloture."

While a measure is being considered, any Senator may propose amendments, each of which is considered separately. After the Senate votes on amendments, the bill is ready for "final engrossment." The Presiding Officer calls for a vote on whether the bill should be passed. A simple majority is needed for passage.

The original engrossed House bill, together with the engrossed Senate amendments, if any, or the original Senate bill, as the case may be, is then returned to the House with a message indicating the action the Senate has taken. A bill that has passed the Senate is known as an engrossed bill or act.[13]

g. Reconciliation of Conflicting Bills — Conference

The Senate may pass a bill that originated in the House without making any changes to it, and the House, likewise, may pass a bill that originated in the Senate without modifications. Far more frequently, the House and Senate pass versions of legislation that differ in ways major or minor. Under article I section 7 of the Constitution, a bill may become law only if it "shall have passed the House of Representatives and the Senate"—a requirement known as "bicameral approval" or simply "bicameralism." Thus, when the House and Senate pass conflicting versions of a bill, the bills must be reconciled and the reconciled bill passed by both chambers.

The task of reconciling different versions of a bill that has passed the House and Senate is traditionally performed by a "Conference" comprised of two committees, one from each of the House and Senate. To initiate the conference process, one house amends and passes the bill of the other and requests the other house's attendance at a conference. Each house appoints "managers," known as conferees, and gives them instructions about how to reconcile the bills.

When a majority of each of the conference committees agrees on how the bills should be reconciled, they submit a "conference report" containing the agreed-upon

---

11. Sullivan, *supra* note 1, at 39–40.

12. Until November 2013, Senators also had the power to prevent a vote on Executive branch and lower-court nominees through filibuster. That month, the Senate established a precedent in a tactic colloquially known as the "nuclear option" that ended the minority party's ability to filibuster such nominees. In April 2017, the Senate extended the nuclear option to the vote on Judge Neil Gorsuch's appointment to the U.S. Supreme Court. See Note 8 following *Edmond v. United States* in Chapter 3[B][1][c].

13. *See supra* note 10 for information on locating engrossed bills.

bill to the House and Senate. The conference committee may issue a separate report that explains the conference committee's actions. This is sometimes referred to as the "conference committee report" or, confusingly, the "conference report."[14] Under House and Senate Rules, such a "conference report" is entitled to expedited consideration. A conference report is not subject to amendment in either the House or the Senate and must be accepted or rejected in its entirety pursuant to a majority vote. By custom, the house of Congress that agreed to the other's request for a conference acts first on the conference report. It can accept the report, reject the report, or recommit it to the conference committee for further consideration. Once the first house acts, the conference committee dissolves and the other house is limited to approving or disapproving the conference report. Conference reports are rarely rejected. When a report is rejected, a bill may be sent back to the committees of both houses that initially reported the bill for reconsideration, or a house may request a new conference. Conference reports are printed in the same manner as House Reports, and are also printed in the Congressional Record for the day on which the report is issued.

When a bill has been approved by both houses, a final "enrolled" copy is prepared. The enrolled bill is transmitted to the President pursuant to Article I, Section 5 of the Constitution for signature or veto.

h. Publication

When the President approves a bill or Congress overrides a presidential veto, the enrolled bill is sent from the White House to the Archivist of the United States to be published. The bill is assigned a "Public Law" number and paginated for the volume of *Statutes of Large* covering the current session of Congress.[15]

Eventually, most laws are codified in the United States Code, a subject matter codification of the public laws of the United States. The Code is prepared by the Law Revision Counsel of the House of Representatives, a nonpartisan body whose members are selected by the Speaker of the House.[16] By law, the Counsel must generate a codification that "conforms to the understood policy, intent, and purpose of the Congress in the original enactments, with such amendments and corrections as will remove ambiguities, contradictions, and other imperfections both of substance and of form . . . ."[17]

---

14. House and Senate Rules require conferences to issue explanatory reports on certain matters, *e.g.*, House Rule XXI(a), Senate Rule XXVIII(6), but are not always followed.

15. Public law numbers consist of the number of the enacting Congress and a serial number indicating when the law was passed. For example, the first public law of the 110th Congress is designated Public Law 110-1. Public laws are available from the Library of Congress's Thomas system, http://thomas.loc.gov, the Government Printing Office Federal Digital System, http://www.fdsys.gov, and commercial databases. Public laws are cited in the form "Pub. L. No. ___." The *United States Statutes at Large*, abbreviated "Stat.," is a chronological arrangement of the laws exactly as they have been enacted. A legislative history and notes on the statute appear following each law.

16. 2 U.S.C. § 285c.

17. *Id.*

Occasionally, the text of an enacted law conflicts with the text of the Code. Because the Code is not generally subject to the requirements of bicameralism and present-ment to the President, the enacted law controls in cases of conflict.[18] To eliminate such inconsistencies, Congress has begun to enact certain titles of the Code directly into positive law. As of 2013, twenty-nine of the fifty-four titles of the U.S. Code have been enacted directly into law. When Congress enacts a title of the U.S. Code into law, "the Code title itself is deemed to constitute conclusive evidence of the law; recourse to other sources is unnecessary and precluded."[19] New editions of the U.S. Code are published every six years and cumulative supplements are published after the con-clusion of each regular session of the Congress.

Figure 1, below, presents a schematic overview of the legislative process. For more detailed accounts of Congress's internal procedures, *see, e.g.,* CQ Press, Guide to Congress (7th ed. 2012); Robert A. Katzmann, Judging Statutes (2014); Abner J. Mikva & Eric Lane, Legislative Process (3d ed. 2009); Peter L. Strauss, Legislation: Understanding and Using Statutes (2006).

---

18. U.S. Nat'l Bank of Ore. v. Independent Ins. Agents of America, Inc., 508 U.S. 439, 448 (1993) ("Though the appearance of a provision in the current edition of the United States Code is 'prima facie' evidence that the provision has the force of law, it is the Statutes at Large that provides 'legal evidence of laws' . . . ." (citations omitted)).

19. United States v. Zuger, 602 F. Supp. 889, 891 (D. Conn. 1984).

Figure 1: Overview of the Legislative Process

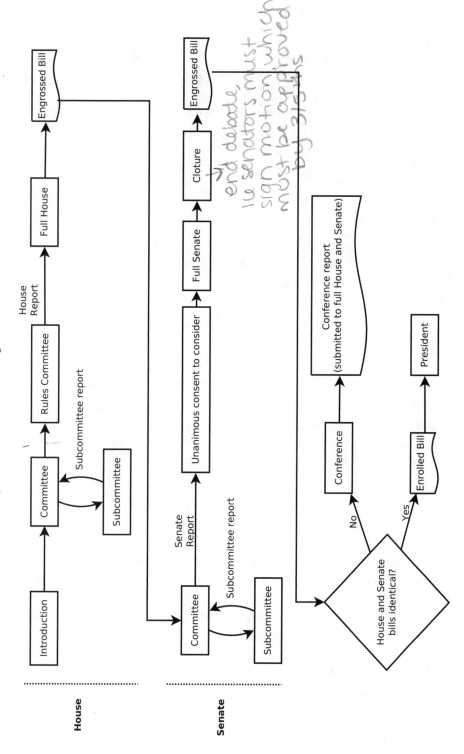

2. The Dynamics of Legislation

The formal legislative process is crucial to understanding legislation but it is far from the entire story. A bill becomes law only if it is approved in identical form by a majority of the House and the Senate and signed by the President or approved by a super-majority of the House and Senate following a presidential veto. Moreover, the internal structure of the House and Senate establish numerous points at which one or more members of Congress have the power to halt progress on a bill. Given the resulting difficulty of enacting legislation, it is important to consider the broader forces that affect which legislative proposals become law. This section introduces some of those forces.

a. The Madisonian Vision

The classic account of the American legislative process was delivered by James Madison in *Federalist No. 10* Urging voters of New York to approve the 1787 Constitution, Madison argued that a central goal of any Constitution is to limit the influence of "faction" on the exercise of governmental power in general, and the legislature in particular. The Constitution's design for the House and Senate, Madison maintained, did just that.

FEDERALIST NO. 10
James Madison

To the People of the State of New York:*** By a faction, I understand a number of citizens, whether amounting to a majority or a minority of the whole, who are united and actuated by some common impulse of passion, or of interest, [adverse] to the rights of other citizens, or to the permanent and aggregate interests of the community.***

The latent causes of faction are*** sown in the nature of man; and we see them everywhere brought into different degrees of activity, according to the different circumstances of civil society. A zeal for different opinions concerning religion, concerning government, and many other points, as well of speculation as of practice; an attachment to different leaders ambitiously contending for pre-eminence and power; or to persons of other descriptions whose fortunes have been interesting to the human passions, have, in turn, divided mankind into parties, inflamed them with mutual animosity, and rendered them much more disposed to vex and oppress each other than to co-operate for their common good.*** [T]he most common and durable source of factions has been the various and unequal distribution of property. Those who hold and those who are without property have ever formed distinct interests in society. Those who are creditors, and those who are debtors, fall under a like discrimination. A landed interest, a manufacturing interest, a mercantile interest, a moneyed interest, with many lesser interests, grow up of necessity in civilized nations, and divide them into different classes, actuated by different sentiments and views. The regulation of these various and interfering interests forms the principal task of modern legislation, and involves the spirit of party and faction in the necessary and ordinary operations of the government.

No man is allowed to be a judge in his own cause, because his interest would certainly bias his judgment, and, not improbably, corrupt his integrity. With equal, nay with greater reason, a body of men are unfit to be both judges and parties at the same time; yet what are many of the most important acts of legislation, but so many judicial determinations, not indeed concerning the rights of single persons, but concerning the rights of large bodies of citizens? And what are the different classes of legislators but advocates and parties to the causes which they determine? Is a law proposed concerning private debts? It is a question to which the creditors are parties on one side and the debtors on the other. Justice ought to hold the balance between them. Yet the parties are, and must be, themselves the judges; and the most numerous party, or, in other words, the most powerful faction must be expected to prevail. Shall domestic manufactures be encouraged, and in what degree, by restrictions on foreign manufactures? are questions which would be differently decided by the landed and the manufacturing classes, and probably by neither with a sole regard to justice and the public good. The apportionment of taxes on the various descriptions of property is an act which seems to require the most exact impartiality; yet there is, perhaps, no legislative act in which greater opportunity and temptation are given to a predominant party to trample on the rules of justice. Every shilling with which they overburden the inferior number, is a shilling saved to their own pockets.

It is in vain to say that enlightened statesmen will be able to adjust these clashing interests, and render them all subservient to the public good. Enlightened statesmen will not always be at the helm. Nor, in many cases, can such an adjustment be made at all without taking into view indirect and remote considerations, which will rarely prevail over the immediate interest which one party may find in disregarding the rights of another or the good of the whole.

The inference to which we are brought is, that the CAUSES of faction cannot be removed, and that relief is only to be sought in the means of controlling its EFFECTS.

If a faction consists of less than a majority, relief is supplied by the republican principle, which enables the majority to defeat its sinister views by regular vote. It may clog the administration, it may convulse the society; but it will be unable to execute and mask its violence under the forms of the Constitution. When a majority is included in a faction, the form of popular government, on the other hand, enables it to sacrifice to its ruling passion or interest both the public good and the rights of other citizens.***

The two great points of difference between a democracy and a republic are: first, the delegation of the government, in the latter, to a small number of citizens elected by the rest; secondly, the greater number of citizens, and greater sphere of country, over which the latter may be extended.

The effect of the first difference is, on the one hand, to refine and enlarge the public views, by passing them through the medium of a chosen body of citizens, whose wisdom may best discern the true interest of their country, and whose patriotism and love of justice will be least likely to sacrifice it to temporary or partial considerations.***

The other point of difference is, the greater number of citizens and extent of territory which may be brought within the compass of republican than of democratic government; and it is this circumstance principally which renders factious combinations less to be dreaded in the former than in the latter. The smaller the society, the fewer probably will be the distinct parties and interests composing it; the fewer the distinct parties and interests, the more frequently will a majority be found of the same party; and the smaller the number of individuals composing a majority, and the smaller the compass within which they are placed, the more easily will they concert and execute their plans of oppression. Extend the sphere, and you take in a greater variety of parties and interests; you make it less probable that a majority of the whole will have a common motive to invade the rights of other citizens; or if such a common motive exists, it will be more difficult for all who feel it to discover their own strength, and to act in unison with each other. Besides other impediments, it may be remarked that, where there is a consciousness of unjust or dishonorable purposes, communication is always checked by distrust in proportion to the number whose concurrence is necessary.

Hence, it clearly appears, that the same advantage which a republic has over a democracy, in controlling the effects of faction, is enjoyed by a large over a small republic, — is enjoyed by the Union over the States composing it. Does the advantage consist in the substitution of representatives whose enlightened views and virtuous sentiments render them superior to local prejudices and schemes of injustice? It will not be denied that the representation of the Union will be most likely to possess these requisite endowments. Does it consist in the greater security afforded by a greater variety of parties, against the event of any one party being able to outnumber and oppress the rest? In an equal degree does the increased variety of parties comprised within the Union, increase this security. Does it, in fine, consist in the greater obstacles opposed to the concert and accomplishment of the secret wishes of an unjust and interested majority? Here, again, the extent of the Union gives it the most palpable advantage.

The influence of factious leaders may kindle a flame within their particular States, but will be unable to spread a general conflagration through the other States. A religious sect may degenerate into a political faction in a part of the Confederacy; but the variety of sects dispersed over the entire face of it must secure the national councils against any danger from that source. A rage for paper money, for an abolition of debts, for an equal division of property, or for any other improper or wicked project, will be less apt to pervade the whole body of the Union than a particular member of it; in the same proportion as such a malady is more likely to taint a particular county or district, than an entire State.

Notes and Questions

1. **The Federalist Papers.** The *Federalist Papers* are a series of newspaper pieces—op-eds, essentially—printed in three New York newspapers beginning in October 1787 during state debates on the ratification of the Constitution. The articles were written by James Madison, Alexander Hamilton, and John Jay, and usually printed under the pseudonym "Publius." (Because they were printed under a pseudonym, authorship of some *Federalist Papers* is uncertain.) Many of the *Federalist Papers* respond to arguments against the proposed Constitution raised by "anti-federalists," among them William Penn, Patrick Henry, and the pseudonymous "Federal Farmer" (either Melancton Smith, Richard Henry Lee, or Mercy Otis Warren). *See generally* GORDON S. WOOD, THE CREATION OF THE AMERICAN REPUBLIC, 1776–1787 (1998); GARRY WILLS, EXPLAINING AMERICA: THE FEDERALIST (2001); CHARLES R. KESLER, SAVING THE REVOLUTION: THE FEDERALIST PAPERS AND THE AMERICAN FOUNDING (1987).

Because the *Federalist Papers* were authored by three of the Constitution's framers and read by some of those who voted to ratify the Constitution, they are considered important evidence of how the Constitution originally was understood. Argument from *The Federalist Papers* is a staple of constitutional litigation, and virtually every modern Justice has cited to the *Papers* in published opinions.

2. **Madison's Representatives.** What according to *Federalist No. 10* is the primary force that drives the enactment of legislation? When a member of Congress introduces legislation or works for passage of bill, what is her likely motivation? When a bill is passed by the House or Senate, what is the most likely reason?

According to one widely-held view, members of Congress act as *trustees* for citizens whom they represent and are expected to exercise independent judgment once in office. On this view, "(1) national legislation ought to *aim* at the national good; (2) the representative, in deliberation with other legislators, should be the ultimate *judge* of what constitutes that national good; and (3) the representative should be less responsive to electoral sanctions, motivated instead by some form of civic virtue." Andrew Rehfeld, *Representation Rethought: On Trustees, Delegates, and Gyroscopes in the Study of Political Representation and Democracy*, 103 AM. POL. SCI. REV. 214, 218 (2009). Another contrasting view holds that representatives are essentially *agents* of the citizens who elected them. On this view, the duty of a representative is to advocate for the aggregated preferences of the voters she represents, not to exercise the independent judgment of a statesman.

Is the image of representatives in *Federalist No. 10* closer to one of these views? Which of the specific assumptions noted in connection with the trustee model (if any) would Madison agree with?

3. **"Faction" and the Legislative Process.** Recall some of the defining features of the federal legislative process: (1) bicameralism (the requirement that a bill pass both Houses of Congress in identical form); (2) presentment (the requirement that a bill passed by both Houses of Congress be approved by the President, or that a presidential veto be overcome by a supermajority vote); (3) the House and Senate's authority

to determine rules of their proceedings; (4) delegation of responsibility to committees and subcommittees pursuant to that authority; (5) the requirement of public debate; and (6) the requirement of public votes upon demand.

How, if at all, do these structural features work to prevent or mitigate the risks of "faction" with which *Federalist No. 10* was concerned? Do these features also make it difficult to pass laws even if desired by a majority of the people? Is that a necessary price? Are there risks other than those identified in *Federalist No. 10* that the legislative structure envisioned by Article I *fails* to address?

Note on the Dynamics of Legislation

For Madison, a key function of the Constitution and particularly Article I was to limit the negative influence of interest groups. Madison termed interest groups "factions"—a term that encompasses modern special-interest groups such as the American Association of Retired Persons, social classes, political parties, and more local interests such as southern farmers or midwestern power plant operators. According to Madison, the legislative process created by Article I would prevent any given faction from exercising undue influence on the content of legislation.

Three structural features of Article I would help accomplish this objective. First, elections for national office would produce "representatives whose enlightened views and virtuous sentiments render them superior to local prejudices." Second, the size of the union would ensure election of representatives that served "a great[] variety of parties," preventing "any one party [from] being able to outnumber and oppress the rest." Lastly, bicameralism, presentment, and other checkpoints in the legislative process would prevent "accomplishment of the secret wishes of an unjust and interested majority."

The geographical size of the union was particularly important to Madison's account. Prior to the ratification of the Constitution, no nation as large as the United States had attempted to govern itself using a republican form of government. The federal government under the Articles of Confederation was beset by well-known problems. *See Federalist No. 15* (Hamilton) (noting that the Confederation could not honor commitments to other nations, pay debts, exercise authority over territories, make effective use of credit, or conduct foreign relations due to "the imbecility of our government"). While the framers attempted to overcome the problems of the Articles of Confederation, they also attempted to leverage the nation's size to manage the influence of faction.

At the national level, Madison anticipated that the size of the nation and resulting diversity in Congress's membership would act as a brake on legislation. Because the House and Senate are made up of representatives from different geographical areas, a faction representing local interests could not push through legislation that advanced only those interests, but would need to win over legislators from other areas of the country to enact legislation. In Madison's view, the size of the legislative districts also ensured the public-spiritedness of members of Congress. "[P]opular election of the House would vindicate popular sovereignty, but the provision for large districts would ensure that only gentlemen with established reputations for public service would be elected. Senators would remain few in number, chosen by the state legislatures and given long terms to insulate them from popular pressures and encourage collegial deliberation in the public interest."[20] At the same time, the fact that local factions could not prevail at the *national* level tended to give such factions greater influence at the local level. Here, in Madison's terms, there would be "fewer ... distinct parties and interests," and it would be easier for them to "concert and execute their plans of oppression."

b. Extending Interest Group Theory

Federalist No. 10 has exercised a profound influence on American political thought. Viewed in light of contemporary political theory, however, there are several notable omissions in Madison's account.

One has to do with the *origin* of factions. Madison seems to assume that an interest group will form around any issue that citizens feel strongly about: "A zeal for different opinions concerning religion, concerning government, and many other points, as well of speculation as of practice; an attachment to different leaders ambitiously contending for pre-eminence and power; or to persons of other descriptions whose fortunes have been interesting to the human passions, have, in turn, divided mankind into parties ...." Yet Madison did not account for so-called "collective action" problems that often prevent people from banding together and seeking to change public policy.

Suppose that a majority of the citizens in a state wishes to prohibit private ownership of fireworks. The majority believes that fireworks present serious safety risks, and that efforts to restrict fireworks to persons who can use them responsibly presents an impossible administrative challenge. Assuming there are no constitutional obstacles, we might expect to see citizens form an interest group to put pressure on elected officials to regulate fireworks, or elect officials who pledge to do so. In fact, the costs of organizing and seeking legislation are likely to prevent such a group from forming or being able to effect the desired legislative change.

To continue the example, suppose that a person injured by fireworks is likely to incur costs of $1 million, and that the likelihood of a citizen being involved in a fireworks accident in a given year is 1 in 10,000. For an individual citizen, the expected cost of maintaining the status quo for one more year is therefore $100 ($1 million × .0001). Successfully lobbying for the enactment of legislation is likely to cost far more than $100, however. In theory, a fireworks ban would be enacted if it was supported by a majority of voters. But because enactment of the ban would confer a collective benefit on all citizens supporting it, no one citizen has adequate incentives to undertake the costs of seeking the ban's enactment. Those costs include organizing voters, drafting legislation, and pressuring legislators to vote in favor of it. In modern society, these functions require technology, advertising, and skilled managers.

---

20. Gerald Leonard, *Party As a "Political Safeguard of Federalism": Martin Van Buren and the Constitutional Theory of Party Politics*, 54 Rutgers L. Rev. 221, 232–33 (2001).

Accordingly, individuals will rationally choose *not* to "invest" in the enactment of fireworks legislation—even though, by hypothesis, that legislation is favored by a majority of the state's citizens.

Political theorists have been aware of these collective-action problems since before the founding, but they were first explored in a systematic way by the economist Mancur Olson in a 1965 monograph entitled *The Logic of Collective Action*. After explaining some causes of collective action problems, Olson turned to the question of why some groups are able to overcome them. While collective action problems prevent many groups of citizens from securing legislation, other groups are able to overcome them and obtain legislation that advances the group's interests. Why?

Olson's first insight was that it is easier for a group to overcome collective action problems if it serves multiple purposes. Suppose that citizens opposed to fireworks did not simply seek legislation prohibiting fireworks ownership, but also published a popular magazine devoted to parenting. If the group's publishing activities generated sufficient revenue, some of that revenue could be directed toward seeking legislation that advanced the group's legislative interests, thereby overcoming group members' rational unwillingness to invest in securing legislation directly. Olson predicted that the interest groups that were most successful in Congress would be those that provided other services to members. That prediction turns out to be supported by considerable evidence. For example, the American Association of Retired Persons (AARP) provides members with discounts on a variety of products and organizes activities such as cruises and educational seminars in addition to lobbying for legislation. The American Medical Association (AMA) supervises professional standards, publishes academic journals and provides continuing professional education to doctors. The National Rifle Association (NRA) organizes outdoor shows, hunting trips, and safety shows, in addition to opposing any form of firearms regulation.

A second mechanism for overcoming collective-action problems is "political entrepreneurship." A person or organization may take responsibility for advocating legislation favored by a majority in the expectation of being rewarded later. Policy entrepreneurs have included members of Congress, individuals running for elected office, non-governmental organizations, and even profit-seeking businesses. In each case, the entrepreneur hopes to secure some private benefit—election to office, prestige, profits—by helping to secure the enactment of a policy that is favored by a larger group.[21]

c. Political Parties

Another notable omission from Madison's account of the legislative process is political parties. Madison's omission of parties in his description of the legislative process was intentional. The framers equated parties with factions and famously sought

---

21. *See generally* John W. Kingdon, Agendas, Alternatives, and Public Policies (1984).

to create a "Constitution Against Parties."[22] But "[b]y the 1796 elections, Federalists and Republicans had coalesced into competing groupings, with party leaders controlling nominations and, at least in some states, rudimentary party machinery organizing campaigns focused more on issues and platforms than on the local stature of the candidates. When Congress convened in 1797, its members were clearly identified as Federalist or Republican and regularly voted along those lines."[23]

What explains the rise of political parties even under a Constitution designed to exclude them? To begin with, there is an urgent need to coordinate the actions of the various actors involved in a legislative process where a bill must overcome many obstacles to become law. Political parties provide such a coordinating mechanism. In exchange for support from the party, legislators commit to supporting legislation the party backs.

Another factor that contributes to the rise of political parties is the complexity of public policy and the difficulty of formulating coherent positions on all of the proposals that come before Congress. In any year, Congress might consider the budget for the federal government and its agencies; the appointment of judges, administrators, and executive branch officials; the enactment of major social legislation; revisions to the federal criminal laws; national defense policy; and countless other issues. Given limits on humans' ability to process information, it would be difficult for a voter to form sound views on each of these issues. So too for a member of Congress; even the most diligent lawmaker could not perform in-depth research on every issue that comes before her. Parties provide a crucial function in helping translate general preferences — such as a preference for limited government, or a government that seeks to reduce inequality — into positions on specific issues. For individual members of Congress, a bill's party support serves as shorthand for whether to support the bill. Parties also provide an important signaling device for voters who generally, and rationally, do not invest the time or effort to understand complex legislative issues and political dynamics. Instead, voters will look to the general policy agenda of a political party as a guide to voting.

For these reasons, political scientists have argued that the rise of political parties was inevitable and perhaps desirable in a representative democracy.[24] But why has politics in the United States been dominated by *two* political parties — the Democratic and Republican parties, currently — while other advanced democracies see three parties, four parties, or more? The answer is thought to lie in the representation structures and voting rules the United States uses in elections for federal office.

In elections for the President and Senators, states vote as a bloc. A single candidate is elected to the Senate or receives the state's presidential votes in the electoral college.

---

22. Richard Hofstadter, The Idea of a Party System: The Rise of Legitimate Opposition in the United States, 1780–1840, at 40 (1969).

23. Daryl J. Levinson & Richard H. Pildes, *Separation of Parties, Not Powers*, 119 Harv. L. Rev. 2311, 2320 (2006).

24. For a survey of the scholarly literature, see Leon D. Epstein, Political Parties in the American Mold ch. 2 (1986).

States of course elect multiple representatives to the House, but each representative is elected from a single-member district that covers a portion of the state's territory. As a matter of custom, House, Senate, and Presidential elections are decided using the "first-past-the-post rule": the candidate who receives the most votes is elected to office, even if she does not receive 50% of the vote. Some state office elections are run on a different basis, requiring a run-off if no candidate receives a majority of votes, or providing for some form of "proportional representation" (PR).

Within the context of single-member districts using first-past-the-post voting, the emergence of a new third party is thought to favor the party *ideologically opposed* to it.[25] For example, if there are two "conservative" parties and a single "liberal" party, and voters are evenly distributed along a spectrum of conservative to liberal beliefs, the conservative parties will split the conservative vote leaving the liberal party with the most votes. (According to popular wisdom, this dynamic contributed to President Bill Clinton's victory in the 1992 presidential election, in which Clinton defeated George H.W. Bush and Ross Perot with 43% of the national popular vote.) Confronted with the risk of splitting the vote, politicians who establish a new party will come under intense pressure to bring their party "into the fold" and thereby avoid splitting the vote in a way that benefits the ideological opposition. Similarly, voters will be reluctant to vote for the third party, for they will fear that, unless the party receives a third of the vote and the remaining vote is evenly split, their vote will be "wasted."[26]

Other representation structures do not share the same tendency to produce two major political parties. For example, the PR system assigns representatives based on the share of the total vote that a political party receives. If a party receives 25% of the popular vote, it is assigned approximately 25% of the representatives in the legislature. Nations that use PR typically have a large number of political parties. As of 2014, fifteen parties were represented in Spain's legislature, for example, and fourteen were represented in Israel's. Because legislatures include more parties, it can be more difficult for stable majorities to form in countries that use PR.

d. Parties and Interest Groups

How closely do parties align with interest groups in their policy preferences? Do interest groups such as big business, environmentalists, or civil rights activists consistently favor one party over the other?

One way of approaching the question is to examine which political parties and candidates individuals and political action committees (PACs) associated with interest groups contribute money to. (A PAC is a type of organization recognized by the Internal Revenue Code that pools donations from individual contributors in support of a

---

25. *See* Maurice Duverger, Political Parties: Their Organization and Activity in the Modern State (1954).

26. For further discussion, see James L. Sundquist, Dynamics of the Party System (1983); Anthony Downs, An Economic Theory of Democracy (1957).

candidate, ballot initiative, or legislative proposal.) Such analysis can reveal surprising patterns. "A few sectors—energy and natural resources for Republicans and labor for Democrats—are strongly committed to one party or another . . . . But most of the economic sectors do not put all of their eggs in one partisan basket. They give to both parties; or, more specifically they give to incumbents, which means that they give to both parties."[27] Thus, during the 2012 presidential election, employees of Goldman Sachs, a major investment bank, contributed $135,343 to the campaign of Barack Obama and $564,904 to the campaign of Mitt Romney. Employees of Whole Foods Markets—which one might expect to be more liberal—contributed $17,025 to the Obama campaign and $10,750 to the Romney campaign.[28]

Why do interest groups spread donations among the parties? One theory holds that donors fundamentally are interested in *access* to elected officials.[29] Interest groups contribute to both parties because they believe that doing so will increase their access to policymakers, regardless of the party or candidate that is currently in power. Alternatively, it is suggested that interest groups give to candidates for a mix of "strategic" and "sincere" reasons. PACs give money to both Democrats and Republicans in order to ensure a baseline level of access to whichever politicians are elected. But when they give money to a legislator who does not share their ideological preferences, they do so in a way that is unlikely to affect the overall partisan makeup of Congress by giving to incumbents who do not face a serious challenge.[30]

e. Legislative Process

Still another factor that helps explain the output of the legislative process is the internal structure of the House and Senate. As the above overview suggests, there are many points in the legislative process where a person or group of person that makes up less than the majority of a house can thwart the progress of proposed legislation.

Understanding legislators who are able to take advantage of points in the process where legislation can be halted can help explain the form that legislation ultimately takes. A classic example involves the Civil Rights Act of 1964. The Act prohibits discrimination on the basis of a protected characteristics in housing, employment, and government-subsidized programs, but as originally introduced did not prohibit discrimination on the basis of sex. During House debate, an opponent of the Civil Rights Act, former Judge Howard Smith (D-VA), proposed to add "sex" to the list of protected characteristics. Smith was the chair of the House Rules Committee, and had previously attempted to kill the bill that would become the Civil Rights Act by

---

27. David Lowrey & Holly Brasher, Organized Interests and American Government 138 (2004).

28. Data from Center for Responsive Politics, Presidential Donor Lookup, http://www.opensecrets.org/pres12/search_donor.php (last accessed Jan. 31, 2015).

29. *See* Keith T. Poole & Thomas Romer, *Patterns of Political Action Committee Contributions to the1980 Campaigns for the United States House of Representatives*, 47 Public Choice 63 (1985).

30. Thomas L. Brunell, *The Relationship Between Political Parties and Interest Groups: Explaining Patterns of PAC Contributions to Candidates for Congress*, 58 Pol. Research Q. 681 (2005).

preventing the Rules Committee from issuing a resolution that would permit debate on it. (Recall that in the House, the Rules Committee and the Speaker generally set terms for debate on a bill.)

Smith's attempt to kill the bill at the Rules Committee stage was unsuccessful. In his amendment, he hoped that by prohibiting discrimination against women, the bill would become so controversial that it would fail in the House or the Senate. Smith had the support of southern Democrats opposed to civil rights and a handful of northern Republicans who could not see a principled reason for distinguishing between discrimination on the basis of race and discrimination on the basis of sex. Backed by a coalition of Southerners opposed to any form of civil rights legislation and women who favored outlawing discrimination on the basis of sex, the Smith amendment passed.[31] The Smith stratagem resulted in Title VII covering sex discrimination but did not block enactment of the Civil Rights Act.

———————

Interest groups, parties, and legislative procedures provide three lenses through which to view the legislative process and the legislation that emerges from it. But as explanations for which bills become law, they are not necessarily exclusive. As we have seen, there is a complicated relationship between interest groups and political parties, and the involvement of interest groups and parties affects the individuals and groups that exercise control over vetogates and the behavior of those individuals. Furthermore, there clearly are factors beyond interest groups, parties, and the legislative process that influence the output of the legislative process. As just one example, we have not considered the kind of legislative quid pro quos that are deplored by critics of budget "earmarks" ("support funding for a highway in my district and I'll support construction of a school in yours").

Despite the limitations of this brief account, interest groups, parties, and legislative process provide valuable insight in understanding why legislation is enacted and why it takes the form it takes. As we continue to consider Congress's statutory output, ask: Which interest group or groups worked for the enactment of this legislation? Is the statute aligned with the policy objectives of the Democratic or Republican Party? Is it "bipartisan"? How, if at all, did key members of Congress affect the shape the legislation ultimately took?

———————

31. For a valuable account of the legislative history of the Civil Rights Act, see Daniel B. Rodriguez & Barry R. Weingast, *The Positive Political Theory of Legislative History: New Perspectives on the 1964 Civil Rights Act and Its Interpretation*, 151 U. Pa. L. Rev. 1417 (2003). On the Smith amendment, see Carl M. Brauer, *Women, Activists, Southern Conservatives, and the Prohibition of Sex Discrimination in Title VII of the 1964 Civil Rights Act*, 49 J.S. Hist. 37 (1983). *See also* Cary C. Franklin, *Inventing the "Traditional Concept" of Sex Discrimination*, 125 Harv. L. Rev. 1307 (2012).

B. Statutory Interpretation

Once a bill is enacted and becomes law, the focus shifts to understanding its meaning—the task of "statutory interpretation." Section 1 below introduces the three most important tools of statutory interpretation: text, purpose, and history. Section 2 surveys some recurring problems of statutory interpretation, and the way that courts have responded to them.

1. Tools of Statutory Interpretation

In large measure, the debate over statutory interpretation concerns the *tools* courts and other interpreters use to determine statutory meaning: When the meaning of a statute is unclear, what kind of materials can be consulted as evidence of the statute's meaning, and what inferences can properly be drawn from those materials? Debate over the tools of statutory interpretation is linked to debate over the proper role of the various branches of government. When an appointed Article III judge interprets an exacted statute, what are the limits of the judge's authority?

This section introduces the three most important tools federal courts use to interpret statutes: text, purpose, and legislative history. As you read the materials, consider not only the advantages and disadvantages of each tool of statutory interpretation but also the wisdom of relying exclusively on a *single* tool to interpret legislation. Should reliance on text preclude reliance on a statute's purpose and history, for example, or can those tools be used together to determine statutory meaning?

a. Text

The text of the statute is, and always has been, central to the task of statutory interpretation. At times, the Supreme Court has been more willing to consider aids to interpretation, such as the statute's legislative history—committee reports, debates and legislator statements—than at other times. In some decisions during New Deal period through the late 1970s, there is force to the quip that in interpreting statutes, the Supreme Court would begin with legislative history and only afterwards turn to the text. *See Citizens to Preserve Overton Park v. Volpe*, 401 U.S. 402, 412 n.29 (1971).

As *Maracich v. Spears* illustrates, the Court's attitude toward statutory text has changed dramatically since then. Before reading *Maracich*, review the statute at issue in that case, the Driver's Privacy Protection Act of 1994, reproduced in the statutory supplement.

Maracich v. Spears

133 S. Ct. 2191 (2013)

JUSTICE KENNEDY delivered the opinion of the Court.***

I

A

The State of South Carolina, to protect purchasers of motor vehicles, enacted the South Carolina Regulation of Manufacturers, Distributors, and Dealers Act (MDDA). In June 2006, respondent attorneys were approached by car purchasers who complained about administrative fees charged by car dealerships in certain South Carolina counties, allegedly in violation of the MDDA. The state statute prohibits motor vehicle dealers from engaging in "any action which is arbitrary, in bad faith, or unconscionable and which causes damage to any of the parties or to the public." S.C.Code Ann. § 56-15-40(1) (2006). The MDDA provides that "one or more may sue for the benefit of the whole" where an action is "one of common or general interest to many persons or when the parties are numerous and it is impracticable to bring them all before the court." § 56-15-110(2).

On June 23, 2006, one of the respondent attorneys submitted a state Freedom of Information Act (FOIA) request to the South Carolina DMV to determine if charging illegal administrative fees was a common practice so that a lawsuit could be brought as a representative action under the MDDA. The attorney's letter to the DMV requested information regarding "[p]rivate purchases of new or used automobiles in Spartanburg County during the week of May 1–7, 2006, including the name, address, and telephone number of the buyer, dealership where purchased, type of vehicle purchased, and date of purchase." The letter explained that the request was made "in anticipation of litigation . . . pursuant to the exception in 18 U.S.C. § 2721(b)(4) of the Driver's Privacy Protection Act [(DPPA)]." The South Carolina DMV provided the requested information. On August 24, 2006, respondents submitted a second FOIA request to the DMV, also asserting that it was made "in anticipation of litigation . . . pursuant to the exception in 18 U.S.C. § 2721(b)(4)," for car purchasers in five additional counties during the same week.

On August 29, 2006, respondents filed suit in South Carolina state court on behalf of four of the consumers who originally contacted them. The case is referred to here, and by the parties, as the *Herron* suit. The complaint in the *Herron* suit named 51 dealers as defendants and invoked the MDDA's "group action" provision to assert claims "for the benefit of all South Carolina car buyers wh[o] paid administrative fees," to those dealers during the same time period.

Some of the dealer defendants in the *Herron* suit filed motions to dismiss for lack of standing because none of the named plaintiffs purchased cars from them. On October 26, 2006, while the motions to dismiss were pending, respondents submitted a new FOIA request to the South Carolina DMV. That request, again citing subsection (b)(4) of the DPPA, sought to locate additional car buyers who could serve as plaintiffs against the dealers who had moved to dismiss. On October 31, 2006, respondents filed an amended complaint, which added four named plaintiffs and increased the number of defendant dealers from 51 to 324. As before, defendant dealerships that had not engaged in transactions with any of the now eight named plaintiffs filed motions to dismiss for lack of standing.

[Following additional FOIA requests, respondent attorneys mailed letters to potential clients.] In total, respondents used the information obtained through their FOIA requests to send letters to over 34,000 car purchasers in South Carolina.***

The letters, all essentially the same, had the heading "ADVERTISING MATERIAL." The letters explained the lawsuit against the South Carolina dealers and asked recipients to contact the respondent-lawyers if interested in participating in the case. Attached to the letter was a reply card that asked a few questions about the recipient's contact information and car purchase and ended with the sentence "I am interested in participating" followed by a signature line.***

In June 2007, respondents sought to amend their complaint to add 247 plaintiffs. The court denied leave to amend and held the named plaintiffs had standing to sue only those dealerships from which they had purchased automobiles and any alleged co-conspirators. In September 2007, respondents filed two new lawsuits on behalf of the additional car buyers. Those subsequent cases were consolidated with the *Herron* suit. All claims against dealerships without a corresponding plaintiff-purchaser were dropped.

B

In the case now before the Court, petitioners are South Carolina residents whose personal information was obtained by respondents from the South Carolina DMV and used without their consent to send solicitation letters asking them to join the lawsuits against the car dealerships.***

In 2009, petitioners filed the instant putative class-action lawsuit in the United States District Court for the District of South Carolina. The complaint alleged that respondents had violated the [DPPA, 18 U.S.C. §§ 2721–2725] by obtaining, disclosing, and using personal information from motor vehicle records for bulk solicitation without the express consent of petitioners and the other class members.

[The district court dismissed the action, finding that respondent attorneys' use of driver information was covered by 18 U.S.C. §§ 2721(b)(1) and (b)(4). The Court of Appeals affirmed, relying exclusively on § 2721(b)(4).]

II

To obtain a driver's license or register a vehicle, state DMVs, as a general rule, require an individual to disclose detailed personal information, including name, home address, telephone number, Social Security number, and medical information. The enactment of the DPPA responded to at least two concerns over the personal information contained in state motor vehicle records. The first was a growing threat from stalkers and criminals who could acquire personal information from state DMVs. The second concern related to the States' common practice of selling personal information to businesses engaged in direct marketing and solicitation. To address these concerns, the DPPA establishes a regulatory scheme that restricts the States' ability to disclose a driver's personal information without the driver's consent.***

The DPPA's disclosure ban is subject to 14 exceptions set forth in §2721(b), for which personal information "may be disclosed." The two exceptions most relevant for the purpose of this case are the litigation exception in subsection (b)(4) and the solicitation exception in (b)(12).***

The solicitation exception was originally enacted as an opt-out provision, allowing state DMVs to disclose personal information for purposes of solicitation only if the DMV gave individuals an opportunity to prohibit such disclosures. §2721(b)(12) (1994 ed.). In 1999, Congress changed to an opt-in regime, requiring a driver's affirmative consent before solicitations could be sent.

III

Respondents' liability depends on whether their use of personal information acquired from the South Carolina DMV to solicit clients constitutes a permissible purpose under the DPPA.***

A

Respondents claim they were entitled to obtain and use petitioners' personal information based on two of the phrases in (b)(4). First, disclosure of personal information is permitted for use "in connection with any civil, criminal, administrative, or arbitral proceeding." §2721(b)(4). Second, a use in connection with litigation includes "investigation in anticipation of litigation." *Ibid.* Respondents contend that the solicitation of prospective clients, especially in the circumstances of this case, is both a use "in connection with" litigation and "investigation in anticipation of litigation."

1

If considered in isolation, and without reference to the structure and purpose of the DPPA, (b)(4)'s exception allowing disclosure of personal information "for use in connection with any civil, criminal, administrative, or arbitral proceeding," and for "investigation in anticipation of litigation," is susceptible to a broad interpretation. That language, in literal terms, could be interpreted to its broadest reach to include the personal information that respondents obtained here.*** So the phrase "in connection with" provides little guidance without a limiting principle consistent with the structure of the statute and its other provisions.***

An interpretation of (b)(4) that is consistent with the statutory framework and design is also required because (b)(4) is an exception to both the DPPA's general prohibition against disclosure of "personal information" and its ban on release of "highly restricted personal information." §§2721(a)(1)–(2). An exception to a "general statement of policy" is "usually read ... narrowly in order to preserve the primary operation of the provision." *Commissioner v. Clark*, 489 U.S. 726, 739 (1989). It is true that the DPPA's 14 exceptions permit disclosure of personal information in a range of circumstances. Unless commanded by the text, however, these exceptions ought not operate to the farthest reach of their linguistic possibilities if that result would contravene the statutory design.***

If (b)(4) were read to permit disclosure of personal information whenever any connection between the protected information and a potential legal dispute could be shown, it would undermine in a substantial way the DPPA's purpose of protecting an individual's right to privacy in his or her motor vehicle records. The "in connection with" language in (b)(4) must have a limit. A logical and necessary conclusion is that an attorney's solicitation of prospective clients falls outside of that limit.***

2

An attorney's solicitation of new clients is distinct from other aspects of the legal profession. [This distinction is] recognized and regulated by state bars or their governing bodies, which treat solicitation as discrete professional conduct. See, e.g., Cal. Rule Prof. Conduct 1-400 (2013); N.Y. Rule Prof. Conduct 7.3 (2012–2013); Tex. Disciplinary Rules Prof. Conduct 7.02–7.03 (2013); Va. Rule Prof. Conduct 7.3 (Supp. 2012). That, indeed, was true here. Respondents were required by the South Carolina rules of ethics to include certain language in their solicitation letters and to file copies with the South Carolina Office of Disciplinary Counsel. See S.C. Rule Prof. Conduct 7.3.

The exclusion of solicitation from the meaning of "in connection with" litigation draws further support from the examples of permissible litigation uses in (b)(4). The familiar canon of *noscitur a sociis*, the interpretive rule that "words and people are known by their companions," provides instruction in this respect. Under this rule, the phrases "in connection with" and "investigation in anticipation of litigation," which are "capable of many meanings," can be construed in light of their accompanying words in order to avoid giving the statutory exception "unintended breadth."

The examples of uses "in connection with" litigation that Congress provided in (b)(4) include "the service of process, investigation in anticipation of litigation, and the execution or enforcement of judgments and orders, or pursuant to an order of a Federal, State, or local court." § 2721(b)(4). These uses involve an attorney's conduct when acting in the capacity as an officer of the court, not as a commercial actor. The listed examples are steps that ensure the integrity and efficiency of an existing or imminent legal proceeding.***

Similarly, "investigation in anticipation of litigation" is best understood to allow background research to determine whether there is a supportable theory for a complaint, a theory sufficient to avoid sanctions for filing a frivolous lawsuit, or to locate witnesses for deposition or trial testimony. An interpretation of "investigation" to include commercial solicitation of new clients would expand the language in a way inconsistent with the limited uses given as examples in the statutory text.***

3

An additional reason to hold that (b)(4) does not permit solicitation of clients is because the exception allows use of the most sensitive kind of information, including medical and disability history and Social Security numbers. To permit this highly personal information to be used in solicitation is so substantial an intrusion on privacy it must not be assumed, without language more clear and explicit, that Congress intended to exempt attorneys from DPPA liability in this regard.

Subsection (b)(4) is one of only four exceptions in the statute that permit disclosure of "highly restricted personal information," including a person's image, Social Security number, and medical and disability information. See § 2721(a)(2); § 2725(4). The other three exceptions that permit access to highly restricted personal information include: use by the government, including law enforcement, see § 2721 (b)(1); use by an insurer in claim investigation and antifraud activities, see § 2721(b)(6); and use by an employer to obtain or verify information as required by law, see § 2721 (b)(9). None of these exceptions are written to authorize private individuals to acquire the most restricted personal information in bulk merely to propose a commercial transaction for their own financial benefit.***

B

Limiting the reach of (b)(4) to foreclose solicitation of clients also respects the statutory design of the DPPA. The use of protected personal information for the purpose of bulk solicitation is addressed explicitly by the text of (b)(12). Congress was aware that personal information from motor vehicle records could be used for solicitation, and it permitted it in circumstances that it defined, with the specific safeguard of consent by the person contacted. So the absence of the term "solicitation" in (b)(4) is telling. Subsection (b)(12) allows solicitation only of those persons who have given express consent to have their names and addresses disclosed for this purpose. If (b)(4) were to be interpreted to allow solicitation without consent, then the structure of the Act, and the purpose of (b)(12), would be compromised to a serious degree.***

This is not to say, as petitioners contend, that this is a straightforward application of the specific (qualified solicitation permission in (b)(12)) controlling the general (the undefined reach of "in connection with" and "investigation in anticipation of litigation" in (b)(4)). As between the two exceptions at issue here, it is not clear that one is always more specific than the other. For while (b)(12) is more specific with respect to solicitation, (b)(4) is more specific with respect to litigation. The DPPA's 14 permissible use exceptions, moreover, are not in all contexts mutually exclusive. The better reading is that each exception addresses different conduct which may, on occasion, overlap.***

If the "in connection with" language of (b)(4) were read broadly to include solicitation, an attorney could acquire personal information from the state DMV to send bulk solicitations to prospective clients without their express consent. This would create significant tension in the DPPA between the litigation and solicitation exceptions. That inconsistency and the concomitant undermining of the statutory design are avoided by interpreting (b)(4) so it does not authorize the use of personal information for the purpose of soliciting clients.***

C

If the phrase "in connection with" in (b)(4) included solicitation by lawyers, then a similar reach for that phrase could apply to other exceptions, resulting in further frustration of the Act's design. Subsection (b)(6) allows an insurer and certain other parties to obtain DMV information for use "in connection with . . . underwriting." § 2721(b)(6). If that phrase extended to solicitation, then personal information protected by the DPPA could be used to solicit new customers for underwriting without their consent. It is most doubtful that Congress intended to exempt insurers from the consent requirement for bulk solicitations.***

JUSTICE GINSBURG, with whom JUSTICE SCALIA, JUSTICE SOTOMAYOR, and JUSTICE KAGAN join, dissenting.

Congress used expansive language in framing the § 2721(b)(4) exception, starting with the words "in connection with" and thrice repeating the word "any." Notably, the Court acknowledges that (b)(4) is "susceptible to a broad interpretation," and, "in literal terms," could be read "to include the personal information that [respondent-lawyers] obtained here."

This case should therefore be easy. One need not strain to see the connection between the respondent-lawyers' conduct and a specific civil proceeding. No attenuated chain of connection need be established. All the uses of DMV information at issue took place when a concrete civil action between identified parties was either imminent or pending. Thus, the uses were indisputably "in connection with" a civil proceeding.

[B]ecause the suit qualified under state law as a representative action, respondent-lawyers represented and were obligated to serve the interests of all car purchasers affected by the charged illegal conduct. Respondent lawyers' uses of DMV information in aid of the *Herron* litigation facilitated the discharge of their professional obligations to the court, their individual clients, and the "whole" group of named and unnamed purchasers that state law required the lawyers to serve. S.C.Code Ann. § 56-15-110(2).

It would be extraordinary for Congress to pass a law disturbing the processes of a state court in such a case.*** We have taken special care to emphasize "the State's strong interest in regulating members of the Bar," and have cautioned against undue "Federal interference with a State's traditional regulation of [the legal] profession." One would therefore expect Congress to speak clearly if it intended to trench on state control in this domain.***

I agree with the Court that the words "in connection with" must be contained within reasonable bounds. But the Court immediately jumps from this premise to the conclusion that "an attorney's solicitation of prospective clients falls outside of [any reasonable] limit."*** The majority's sojourn away from § 2721(b)(4)'s text in search of a limiting principle is unwarranted. A limit to the scope of (b)(4) can be readily identified by attending to the phrasing of the provision and its focus on a "proceeding." Congress used similar language in the obstruction of justice statute, which criminalizes various attempts to interfere with a "proceeding." 18 U.S.C. § 1512. The Court had no difficulty identifying a limiting principle in this term; it held that the statute applies only to persons who "have in contemplation any particular official proceeding." *Arthur Andersen LLP v. United States*, 544 U.S. 696, 708 (2005). By the same token, (b)(4) is best interpreted to permit only uses tied to a concrete, particular proceeding.

Congress' use of the phrase "in anticipation of litigation" provides further support for this interpretation. The phrase is hardly unique to (b)(4); it is commonly used to refer to the time at which the work-product privilege attaches to an attorney's work for a client and the time at which a party has a duty to preserve material evidence. *See, e.g.*, Fed. Rule Civ. Proc. 26(b)(3).*** Both now and when the DPPA was enacted, courts have understood this phrase to require a concrete dispute between parties, and to exclude the abstract possibility of a hypothetical lawsuit. *See, e.g.*, *National Union Fire Ins. Co. v. Murray Sheet Metal Co.*, 967 F.2d 980, 984 (C.A.4 1992) (the "general possibility of litigation" is not enough; a document is prepared in anticipation of litigation when there is "an actual claim or a potential claim following an actual event or series of events that reasonably could result in litigation")***.

Usage of the same words in other prescriptions indicates that (b)(4) is indeed limited by its text. A hypothetical case without identified adverse parties is not encompassed by (b)(4). To anticipate a particular civil proceeding, a lawyer must have a client whose claim presents a genuine controversy. Trolling for prospective clients with no actual or imminent proceeding, involving already identified adverse parties, in sight — apparently, the Court's primary concern — would not be a permissible use.***

The Court's second argument is no more convincing. A severe limit must be read into (b)(4), the Court urges, to respect the structure of the statute. [However, Congress sought] to provide a set of separate exceptions, any one of which makes permissible the uses therein. Consider a consulting company hired by a State to conduct research into motor vehicle safety. Depending on the particulars of the research project, the company might seek to obtain DMV information under the uses listed in (b)(1), (2), (5), (12), or (14). These exceptions entail different requirements, so the project might well fit within one or two of them but not the others. It would be ludicrous to treat the fact that the project did not fit within one exception as establishing that the project should not be allowed under any other exception. Construing the DPPA in that manner would render the statute totally unworkable.*** [W]ithout any congressional instruction to do so, the Court reads (b)(12) — the 12th on a list of 14 permissible uses — as so central a part of the DPPA that it alone narrows the scope of other exceptions.***

Notes and Questions

1. **The Enactment of the Driver's Privacy Protection Act.** The interplay of federal and state law in *Maracich* is characteristic of modern federal regulation. Respondent attorneys obtained drivers' personal information from the South Carolina DMV using that state's Freedom of Information Act, which was loosely modeled on the landmark federal Freedom of Information Act of 1966, 5 U.S.C. § 552 *et seq.* The attorneys hoped to sue under a state statute, the Regulation of Manufacturers, Distributors, and Dealers Act, that in sweeping general terms prohibits unfair trade practices by car dealers. The tables were then turned on the attorneys, who were sued under a federal statute, the Driver's Privacy Protection Act of 1994 (DPPA), 18 U.S.C. §§ 2721–2725, by the drivers whose personal information they obtained. Notably, the fact that a state DMV provided the information to the attorneys was *not* a defense to a violation of the federal DPPA.

The bill that would become the DPPA was simultaneously introduced on October 23, 1993, as H.R. 3365 by Rep. James P. Moran (D-VA) and as S. 1589 by Senator Barbara Boxer (D-CA). Upon its introduction, H.R. 3365 was referred to the House Judiciary Committee. S. 1589 was referred to the Senate Governmental Affairs Committee.

In its original form, H.R. 3365 generally prohibited the use of personal information obtained from state DMVs. The bill contained nine exceptions for the use of personal information: use by state and federal courts; use by state and federal agencies; use "in connection with matters of automobile and driver safety"; "use in the normal course of business by a legitimate business"; "use in any civil or criminal proceeding"; research activities; marketing activities; the compilation of information for marketing purposes; and insurance claims investigations. S. 1589 omitted the exception covering the compilation of information for marketing purposes and included an additional exception for uses to which drivers specifically consented.

When he introduced the legislation, Representative Moran cited the case of television actress Rebecca Schaeffer, who had been murdered by a stalker who obtained her address from the California DMV. He observed that the bill,

> acknowledges that there are many businesses that depend on access to motor vehicle records to serve their customers, including insurance companies, financial institutions, vehicle dealers, and others. By focusing this legislation on the personal information contained within a driver file, this bill does not limit those legitimate organizations in using the information. It does, however, restrict access to all those without a legitimate purpose.

139 Cong. Rec. 27,328.

No action was taken on H.R. 3365 or S. 1589. However, the bill reappeared as Title XXX of H.R. 3355, an omnibus bill that the 103rd Congress enacted as the Violent Crime Control and Law Enforcement Act of 1994, Pub. L. No. 103-322, 108 Stat. 2099 (Sept. 13 1994).

Representative Jack Bascom Brooks (D-TX) introduced H.R. 3355 on October 26, 1993, and the bill passed the House without a driver's privacy provision on November 3, 1993. 139 Cong. Rec. 8,723. Senator Barbara Boxer (D-CA) introduced Title XXX as an amendment to H.R. 3355 on the Senate floor on November 16, 1993. As introduced by Senator Boxer, Title XXX contained ten amendments, including an exception for use of personal information "in any civil criminal [sic] proceeding . . . if the case involves a motor vehicle, or if the request is pursuant to an order of a court of competent jurisdiction." 139 Cong. Rec. 29,466. Senator Oren Hatch (R-UT) was the floor manager for the omnibus bill. While acknowledging the need for legislation to protect the privacy of driver information, he expressed concern that the Senate had not had an adequate opportunity to consider Senator Boxer's amendment. Nonetheless, Hatch allowed the amendment to be included in the omnibus bill because it had bipartisan support. *See id.* at 29,467. He stated: "We are prepared to take the amendment on both sides but I have had a number of people very, very concerned about it. I would like to take it under the condition that we work on it together and see if we can perfect it somewhat between now and conference." *Id.* at 29,467.

On November 19, 1993, the Senate passed H.R. 3355 without changing Title XXX as introduced by Senator Boxer. *See id.* at 17,095. The bill then returned to the House. On February 4, 1994, the House Subcommittee on Civil and Constitutional Rights held hearings on the subject of driver privacy. See 140 Cong Rec Daily Ed. 78. No transcript of the hearing was printed. The version of Title XXX that ultimately would be enacted into law was introduced as a floor amendment by Representative Moran on April 20, 1994, during debate on the amended H.R. 3355 in the Committee on the Whole. 140 Cong. Rec. 7,922. (Recall the Committee of the Whole is a parliamentary device that permits the House to function as if it were a single, large committee.)

Representative Moran explained that his version of Title XXX,

> reflects many comments and suggestions received during hearings held by the Subcommittee on Civil and Constitutional Rights. Changes were made to the Driver's Privacy Protection Act as a result of those hearings that make this amendment very different than the amendment that was offered to the crime bill by Senator Boxer. Unlike the Boxer amendment, my amendment allows greater access for private detectives and the press and more flexibility to the States in allowing additional uses of personal information.

Id.

On April 21, 1994, the House passed H.R. 3355 — including Moran's version of Title XXX — and requested a conference. The conference committee made numerous changes to H.R. 3355 but did not change Title XXX from the version introduced by Senator Moran on April 20. On August 21, 1994, the conference committee issued its final report and the bill passed the House and Senate. President Clinton signed the enrolled bill on September 13, 1994.

The DPPA is codified in Title 18 of the U.S. Code, the federal criminal code. Section 2723(a) provides that "[a] person who knowingly violates this chapter shall be fined." "Any State department of motor vehicles that has a policy or practice of substantial noncompliance with this chapter shall be subject to a civil penalty imposed by the Attorney General of not more than $5,000 a day for each day of substantial noncompliance."

Section 2724 creates a private cause of action: "[a] person who knowingly obtains, discloses or uses personal information, from a motor vehicle record, for a purpose not permitted under this chapter shall be liable to the individual to whom the information pertains, who may bring a civil action in a United States district court." Remedies include "actual damages, but not less than liquidated damages in the amount of $2,500"; "punitive damages upon proof of willful or reckless disregard of the law"; and "reasonable attorneys' fees and other litigation costs reasonably incurred."

2. **The Justification for Regulation?** The information at issue in *Maracich* was supplied to the South Carolina DMV by individuals applying for driver's licenses. The amount of protection provided for such information by the common law is modest. Prior to the publication of Louis Brandeis and Samuel Warren's 1890 article *The Right of Privacy*, 4 HARV. L. REV. 193, no state recognized a general right of privacy. Eventually, either by judicial decision or legislation, most states recognized a limited right of privacy. As summarized by the Restatement Second of Torts § 652A (1977), that right is invaded by: (a) "unreasonable intrusion upon the seclusion of another"; (b) "appropriation of the other's name or likeness"; (c) "unreasonable publicity given to the other's private life"; or (d) "publicity that unreasonably places the other in a false light before the public." Are any of these aspects of the right to privacy implicated by the use of information at issue in *Maracich*? Are any implicated by the sort of stalking activity that motivated Representative Moran to introduce H.R. 3365?

Is there a case for regulation given the limits of privacy protection in tort and the prospect that individuals or entities having no prior relationship with drivers could obtain the DMV information? Is there reason to believe that the state DMV officers would routinely release this information? Consider the rise of "right to know" statutes and freedom of information acts, and the corresponding expansion of commercial data brokers that specialize in aggregating personal information in a form that is useful to marketers and other users. *See generally* Margaret B. Kwoka, *FOIA, Inc.*, 65 DUKE L.J. 1361 (2016).

3. **The Need for *Federal* Regulation?** Assuming that drivers' personal information needed protection through legislation, what is the justification for providing such protection at the federal as opposed to the state level? During Senate debate on DPPA, Senator John Warner (R-VA) asked Senator Chuck Robb (D-VA), a supporter of the bill and former governor of Virginia, why "this was a situation that apparently was not recognized by the Governors as being so compelling as it is today during the period [1982–1986] when he was Governor." Senator Robb responded:

In recent years, it has become increasingly evident that this information was accessible and it was being used for purposes that were certainly not intended by the framers of the [state] legislation that permitted its release.

This legislation is simply designed to close an important loophole that at this point restricts [sic] the privacy that I think most of our citizens believe they have but in some cases subjects them to stalking, abuse or other improper utilization of information which simply should not be in their hands.

Senator Warner responded: "I think this is a very important part of the legislative history that we are making tonight. It has been a relatively short period of time that the urgency for such legislation as this [to] be adopted by the Congress." 140 Cong. Rec. 29,469.

Does the Warner-Robb colloquy set out a convincing justification for federal intervention? Might states' failure to regulate the use of drivers' personal information have a financial explanation if states charged data brokers for access to their DMV records?

4. **The Procedural Posture?** By the time this case came before the Supreme Court, the parties and their attorneys were involved in multiple lawsuits. What was the status of the litigation in South Carolina state court (referred to in *Maracich* as the *Herron* litigation)? What was the status of the federal litigation alleging violations of the DPPA? Which lower-court decision was being reviewed by the Supreme Court and what did that court decide? Where does the dispute go after the Supreme Court decision? What are the issues, if any, left for litigation in the courts below?

5. **The Textual Issue: The "Litigation Exception."** The key textual question in *Maracich* is how to interpret the clause excluding "use in connection with any civil . . . proceeding." 18 U.S.C. § 2721(b)(4). According to the majority, an attorney's solicitation of a client categorically falls outside the exception because solicitation of a client precedes the filing of a lawsuit. According to the dissent, a use "in connection with . . . a civil proceeding" is one that is "tied to a concrete, particular proceeding."

In other cases, the Court had applied far broader interpretations of the phrase "in connection with." *See, e.g., United States v. O'Hagan*, 521 U.S. 642, 656 (1997) (misappropriation of confidential information from one's employer is fraud "in connection with" purchase or sale of securities, under § 10(b) of the Securities Exchange Act, 15 U.S.C. § 78j, and Rule 10(b)(5) thereunder, 17 C.F.R. § 240.10b-5, where misappropriated information provides rationale for securities transaction). As between the majority and the dissent, which interpretation is more consistent with the text of § 2721(b)(4)?

6. **The Textual Issue: The Relationship Among the DPPA Exceptions.** Both the Court and the dissent agree that the exceptions to the DPPA are *not* mutually exclusive of one another; "each exception addresses different conduct which may, on occasion, overlap." The majority reasons that "[i]f (b)(4) were to be interpreted to allow solicitation without consent, then the structure of the Act, and the purpose of (b)(12), would be compromised to a serious degree." What does the Court mean by this? Do the exceptions suggest some overall conception of the allowable uses of motor vehicle information?

7. **"Dueling Canons."** The majority says that the uses listed in § 2721(b)(4) — "service of process," "investigation in anticipation of litigation," "execution or enforcement of judgments and orders," and uses "pursuant to an order of a Federal, State, or local court"— support its conclusion that solicitation of clients is not a permitted use under this exception. The majority invokes the *noscitur a sociis* canon ("know a word by its friends") which holds that the meaning of an unclear term is informed by the words immediately surrounding it.

Is the majority's interpretation the most natural way of reading § 2721(b)(4)? Is the "including" phrase, which lists service of process, investigation, and the like, more naturally read to show the *breadth* of the phrase "use in connection with any civil . . . proceeding"? Without the "including" phrase, would "in connection with any civil . . . proceeding" include activities like pre-suit investigation and enforcement of judgments?

The majority also invokes the *in pari materia* canon when arguing that a broad interpretation of the litigation exception would unduly broaden the insurance underwriting exception. This canon holds that when statutory provisions use the same language, they should be interpreted in the same way unless context indicates otherwise. Is the majority correct in saying that a ruling which applied the litigation exception to the respondent attorneys would also allow *insurers* to obtain DMV information to solicit new clients without their consent?

The dissent responds to the majority's invocation of canons of construction with a canon of its own. "Federal interference with a State's traditional regulation of [the legal] profession" requires a clear statement, given the states' 'strong interest in regulating members of the Bar.'" As the DPPA lacks any such statement, are respondent attorneys' presumptively within § 2721(b)(4)? Is this argument any more convincing than the majority's reliance on *noscitur a sociis*? Are the canons doing real work in the Court's resolution of the interpretive question? How does the majority know that the case calls for use of *noscitur* and *in pari materia*? Do you think the Justices relied on the canons when deciding how to vote, or were the canons brought out when Justice Kennedy and his clerks turned to drafting the opinion for the Court? We return to the canons in the following case.

8. **"Statutory Design"?** The majority contends that an interpretation of § 2721(b)(4) that extends to an attorney's solicitation of clients conflicts with "the statutory design of the DPPA." It advances a patch-work of arguments to this effect.

a. The majority posits that the bulk usage of DMV information for solicitation purposes is addressed by § 2721(b)(12), the "solicitation" exception. That exception permits solicitation only if a driver has consented to the use of her personal information. For the Court, allowing solicitation under the litigation exception would be inconsistent with the consent requirement of (b)(12).

The dissent responds that the exceptions are independent of one another. A use of personal information might be covered by two, three, or more exceptions. As such, the solicitation exception is not a reliable guide to the meaning of the litigation exception.

Note that both the majority and the dissent disclaim reliance on the maxim that specific statutory language takes precedence over general language. *See Edmond v. United States*, 520 U.S. 651, 657 (1997) ("Ordinarily, where a specific provision conflicts with a general one, the specific governs.").

Who has the better of this debate?

b. The majority says that its interpretation is supported by the fact that exceptions in §§ 2721(b)(1) through (b)(4) apply to "highly personal information" such as Social Security numbers, whereas the remaining exceptions apply to all "personal information." Is this persuasive?

c. The majority further argues that its interpretation is necessary to give effect to the general purposes of the DPPA. Citing the principle that "[a]n exception to a 'general statement of policy' is 'usually read . . . narrowly in order to preserve the primary operation of the provision,'" the majority reasons that the DPPA's exceptions "ought not operate to the farthest reach of their linguistic possibilities if that result would contravene the statutory design."

Is this analysis consistent with the DPPA's enumeration of fourteen separate exceptions that permit the use of personal information obtained from the DMV? Does the limitation proposed by the dissent "operate to the farthest reach" of the litigation exception, such that "the statutory design" is "contravene[d]"?

9. **Arguments from Other Areas of Law.** Both the majority and the dissent rely on other provisions of law to support their interpretation of the litigation exception. To support the proposition that an attorney's solicitation of clients is different from her other professional duties, the majority cites state professional responsibility codes. To support its interpretation of "investigation in anticipation of litigation," the dissent cites the Federal Rules of Civil Procedure and decisions that address when a potential litigant has a duty to preserve discoverable information. Do you suppose that the members of Congress who voted on the DPPA were aware of these materials? Are persons who are regulated by the DPPA aware of them? Does usage in other areas of the law nonetheless provide a sensible clue to the meaning of the statutory phrase?

10. **Postscript.** After the Supreme Court issued its decision, *Maracich* was remanded to the District Court for the District of South Carolina. After further pre-trial proceedings, the parties agreed to a settlement. Under the settlement, the respondent attorneys agreed to an injunction that prohibited them from further violating the DPPA, and to publish an advertisement in the *South Carolina Lawyer* advising the legal community that obtaining DMV information for the purpose of soliciting legal clients is not a use "in connection with litigation" under the DPPA. The respondent attorneys also agreed to pay up to $2.6 million of the other side's attorneys' fees and costs. Settlement Agreement, *Maracich v. Spears*, No. 7:09-cv-01651 (D.S.C. July 8, 2015).

The respondent attorneys in *Maracich* are not the only parties to be caught in DPPA's crosshairs. In *Pichler v. UNITE*, 542 F.3d 380, 383 (3d Cir. 2008), union organizers recorded the license plate numbers of employees of Cintas, a laundry service company, and used the license plate numbers to locate employees' home addresses using information from the Pennsylvania DMV. The organizers then visited the employees at home, where they could discuss forming a union without Cintas managers observing them. The union organizers maintained that they were seeking not merely to organize Cintas employees, but also to organize litigation against the company for violations of a variety of federal laws.

The organizers were found to have violated the DPPA, notwithstanding their claimed desire to initiate litigation. Before the district court ruled on damages, the parties agreed to a settlement that provided $2,500 to each of 1,209 members of the plaintiffs' class, and awarded plaintiffs' counsel $1 million. *Pichler v. UNITE*, 775 F. Supp. 2d 754, 758 (E.D. Pa. 2011).

––––––––

One difficulty with relying exclusively on text and statutory structure to answer questions of statutory interpretation is that the answer does not always clearly emerge from such textual material. Even if an interpreter carefully studies a statute's text and structure, the meaning of a provision or the way in which it applies to a particular set of facts may be unclear. We might say that the statute is "ambiguous" on the point in question.

A traditional response to this problem involves use of "canons" or "maxims" of interpretation. Such canons or maxims are "rules of thumb," ways to approach the text begin to provide the beginnings of an answer without necessarily being conclusive of the inquiry. Consider the role that canons play in the case that follows.

Yates v. United States

135 S. Ct. 1074 (2015)

Justice Ginsburg, announced the judgment of the Court and delivered an opinion, in which The Chief Justice, Justice Breyer, and Justice Sotomayor join.

John Yates, a commercial fisherman, caught undersized red grouper in federal waters in the Gulf of Mexico. To prevent federal authorities from confirming that he had harvested undersized fish, Yates ordered a crew member to toss the suspect catch into the sea. For this offense, he was charged with, and convicted of, violating 18 U.S.C. § 1519, which provides:

> "Whoever knowingly alters, destroys, mutilates, conceals, covers up, falsifies, or makes a false entry in any record, document, or tangible object with the intent to impede, obstruct, or influence the investigation or proper administration of any matter within the jurisdiction of any department or agency of the United States or any case filed under title 11, or in relation to or contemplation of any such matter or case, shall be fined under this title, imprisoned not more than 20 years, or both."

Yates was also indicted and convicted under § 2232(a), which provides:

"DESTRUCTION OR REMOVAL OF PROPERTY TO PREVENT SEIZURE. —Whoever, before, during, or after any search for or seizure of property by any person authorized to make such search or seizure, knowingly destroys, damages, wastes, disposes of, transfers, or otherwise takes any action, or knowingly attempts to destroy, damage, waste, dispose of, transfer, or otherwise take any action, for the purpose of preventing or impairing the Government's lawful authority to take such property into its custody or control or to continue holding such property under its lawful custody and control, shall be fined under this title or imprisoned not more than 5 years, or both."

Yates does not contest his conviction for violating § 2232(a), but he maintains that fish are not trapped within the term "tangible object," as that term is used in §1519.

Section 1519 was enacted as part of the Sarbanes-Oxley Act of 2002, 116 Stat. 745, legislation designed to protect investors and restore trust in financial markets following the collapse of Enron Corporation. A fish is no doubt an object that is tangible; fish can be seen, caught, and handled, and a catch, as this case illustrates, is vulnerable to destruction. But it would cut § 1519 loose from its financial-fraud mooring to hold that it encompasses any and all objects, whatever their size or significance, destroyed with obstructive intent. Mindful that in Sarbanes-Oxley, Congress trained its attention on corporate and accounting deception and cover-ups, we conclude that a matching construction of § 1519 is in order: A tangible object captured by § 1519, we hold, must be one used to record or preserve information.

I

On August 23, 2007, the *Miss Katie*, a commercial fishing boat, was six days into an expedition in the Gulf of Mexico. Her crew numbered three, including Yates, the captain. Engaged in a routine offshore patrol to inspect both recreational and commercial vessels, Officer John Jones of the Florida Fish and Wildlife Conservation Commission decided to board the *Miss Katie* to check on the vessel's compliance with fishing rules. Although the *Miss Katie* was far enough from the Florida coast to be in exclusively federal waters, she was nevertheless within Officer Jones's jurisdiction. Because he had been deputized as a federal agent by the National Marine Fisheries Service, Officer Jones had authority to enforce federal, as well as state, fishing laws.

Upon boarding the *Miss Katie*, Officer Jones noticed three red grouper that appeared to be undersized hanging from a hook on the deck. At the time, federal conservation regulations required immediate release of red grouper less than 20 inches long. 50 CFR § 622.37(d)(2)(ii) (effective April 2, 2007). Violation of those regulations is a civil offense punishable by a fine or fishing license suspension. See 16 U.S.C. §§ 1857(1)(A), (G), 1858(a), (g).

Suspecting that other undersized fish might be on board, Officer Jones proceeded to inspect the ship's catch, setting aside and measuring only fish that appeared to him to be shorter than 20 inches. Officer Jones ultimately determined that 72 fish fell short of the 20-inch mark. A fellow officer recorded the length of each of the undersized fish on a catch measurement verification form. With few exceptions, the measured fish were between 19 and 20 inches; three were less than 19 inches; none were less than 18.75 inches. After separating the fish measuring below 20 inches from the rest of the catch by placing them in wooden crates, Officer Jones directed Yates to leave the fish, thus segregated, in the crates until the *Miss Katie* returned to port. Before departing, Officer Jones issued Yates a citation for possession of undersized fish.

Four days later, after the *Miss Katie* had docked in Cortez, Florida, Officer Jones measured the fish contained in the wooden crates. This time, however, the measured fish, although still less than 20 inches, slightly exceeded the lengths recorded on board. Jones surmised that the fish brought to port were not the same as those he had detected during his initial inspection. Under questioning, one of the crew members admitted that, at Yates's direction, he had thrown overboard the fish Officer Jones had measured at sea, and that he and Yates had replaced the tossed grouper with fish from the rest of the catch.

Yates was tried on the criminal charges in August 2011. At the end of the Government's case in chief, he moved for a judgment of acquittal on the § 1519 charge. [The district court denied the motion; its decision was affirmed by the Eleventh Circuit on appeal.]

For violating § 1519 and § 2232(a), the [district] court sentenced Yates to imprisonment for 30 days, followed by supervised release for three years. For life, he will bear the stigma of having a federal felony conviction.

II

The Sarbanes-Oxley Act, all agree, was prompted by the exposure of Enron's massive accounting fraud and revelations that the company's outside auditor, Arthur Andersen LLP, had systematically destroyed potentially incriminating documents. The Government acknowledges that § 1519 was intended to prohibit, in particular, corporate document-shredding to hide evidence of financial wrongdoing. Prior law made it an offense to "intimidat[e], threate[n], or corruptly persuad[e] *another* person" to shred documents. § 1512(b) (emphasis added). Section 1519 cured a conspicuous omission by imposing liability on a person who destroys records himself. See S. Rep. No. 107-146, p. 14 (2002) (describing § 1519 as "a new general anti shredding provision" and explaining that "certain current provisions make it a crime to persuade another person to destroy documents, but not a crime to actually destroy the same documents yourself"). The new section also expanded prior law by including within the provision's reach "any matter within the jurisdiction of any department or agency of the United States. "

In the Government's view, § 1519 extends beyond the principal evil motivating its passage. The words of § 1519, the Government argues, support reading the provision as a general ban on the spoliation of evidence, covering all physical items that might be relevant to any matter under federal investigation.

Yates urges a contextual reading of § 1519, tying "tangible object" to the surrounding words, the placement of the provision within the Sarbanes-Oxley Act, and related provisions enacted at the same time, in particular § 1520 and § 1512(c)(1). Section 1519, he maintains, targets not all manner of evidence, but records, documents, and tangible objects used to preserve them, e.g., computers, servers, and other media on which information is stored.***

A

The ordinary meaning of an "object" that is "tangible," as stated in dictionary definitions, is "a discrete . . . thing," Webster's Third New International Dictionary 1555 (2002), that "possess[es] physical form," Black's Law Dictionary 1683 (10th ed. 2014). From this premise, the Government concludes that "tangible object," as that term appears in § 1519, covers the waterfront, including fish from the sea.

Whether a statutory term is unambiguous, however, does not turn solely on dictionary definitions of its component words. Rather, "[t]he plainness or ambiguity of statutory language is determined [not only] by reference to the language itself, [but as well by] the specific context in which that language is used, and the broader context of the statute as a whole." *Robinson v. Shell Oil Co.*, 519 U.S. 337, 341 (1997). Ordinarily, a word's usage accords with its dictionary definition. In law as in life, however, the same words, placed in different contexts, sometimes mean different things.*** In short, although dictionary definitions of the words "tangible" and "object" bear consideration, they are not dispositive of the meaning of "tangible object" in § 1519.***

B

Familiar interpretive guides aid our construction of the words "tangible object" as they appear in § 1519.

We note first § 1519's caption: "Destruction, alteration, or falsification of records in Federal investigations and bankruptcy." That heading conveys no suggestion that the section prohibits spoliation of any and all physical evidence, however remote from records. Neither does the title of the section of the Sarbanes-Oxley Act in which § 1519 was placed, § 802: "Criminal penalties for altering documents." 116 Stat. 800. Furthermore, § 1520, the only other provision passed as part of § 802, is titled "Destruction of corporate audit records" and addresses only that specific subset of records and documents. While these headings are not commanding, they supply cues that Congress did not intend "tangible object" in § 1519 to sweep within its reach physical objects of every kind, including things no one would describe as records, documents, or devices closely associated with them. If Congress indeed meant to make § 1519 an all-encompassing ban on the spoliation of evidence, as the dissent believes Congress did, one would have expected a clearer indication of that intent.

Section 1519's position within Chapter 73 of Title 18 further signals that § 1519 was not intended to serve as a cross-the-board ban on the destruction of physical evidence of every kind. Congress placed § 1519 (and its companion provision § 1520) at the end of the chapter, following immediately after the pre-existing § 1516, § 1517, and § 1518, each of them prohibiting obstructive acts in specific contexts. *See* § 1516 (audits of recipients of federal funds); § 1517 (federal examinations of financial institutions); § 1518 (criminal investigations of federal health care offenses). *See also*

S. Rep. No. 107-146, at 7 (observing that § 1517 and § 1518 "apply to obstruction in certain limited types of cases, such as bankruptcy fraud, examinations of financial institutions, and health care fraud").***

The contemporaneous passage of § 1512(c)(1), which was contained in a section of the Sarbanes-Oxley Act discrete from the section embracing § 1519 and § 1520, is also instructive. Section 1512(c)(1) provides:

> "c) Whoever corruptly—(1) alters, destroys, mutilates, or conceals a record, document, or other object, or attempts to do so, with the intent to impair the object's integrity or availability for use in an official proceeding
>
> . . . .
>
> "shall be fined under this title or imprisoned not more than 20 years, or both."

The legislative history reveals that § 1512(c)(1) was drafted and proposed after § 1519. *See* 148 Cong. Rec. 12518, 13088–13089 (2002). The Government argues, and Yates does not dispute, that § 1512(c)(1)'s reference to "other object" includes any and every physical object. But if § 1519's reference to "tangible object" already included all physical objects, as the Government and the dissent contend, then Congress had no reason to enact § 1512(c)(1): Virtually any act that would violate § 1512(c)(1) no doubt would violate § 1519 as well, for § 1519 applies to "the investigation or proper administration of any matter within the jurisdiction of any department or agency of the United States . . . or in relation to or contemplation of any such matter," not just to "an official proceeding."

The Government acknowledges that, under its reading, § 1519 and § 1512(c)(1) "significantly overlap." Nowhere does the Government explain what independent function § 1512(c)(1) would serve if the Government is right about the sweeping scope of § 1519. We resist a reading of § 1519 that would render superfluous an entire provision passed in proximity as part of the same Act.[6] *See Marx v. General Revenue Corp.,* 568 U.S. ___, ___ (2013) (slip op., at 14) ("[T]he canon against surplusage is strongest when an interpretation would render superfluous another part of the same statutory scheme.").

The words immediately surrounding "tangible object" in § 1519—"falsifies, or makes a false entry in any record [or] document"—also cabin the contextual meaning of that term. As explained in *Gustafson v. Alloyd Co.,* 513 U.S. 561, 575 (1995), we rely on the principle of *noscitur a sociis*—a word is known by the company it keeps—to "avoid ascribing to one word a meaning so broad that it is inconsistent with its accompanying words, thus giving unintended breadth to the Acts of Congress." (internal quotation marks omitted). In *Gustafson,* we interpreted the word "communication" in § 2(10) of the Securities Act of 1933 to refer to a public communication, rather than any communication, because the word appeared in a list with other words, notably "notice, circular,

---

6. Furthermore, if "tangible object" in § 1519 is read to include any physical object, § 1519 would prohibit all of the conduct proscribed by § 2232(a), which imposes a maximum penalty of five years in prison for destroying or removing "property" to prevent its seizure by the Government.

[and] advertisement," making it "apparent that the list refer[red] to documents of wide dissemination." And we did so even though the list began with the word "any."

The *noscitur a sociis* canon operates in a similar manner here. "Tangible object" is the last in a list of terms that begins "any record [or] document." The term is therefore appropriately read to refer, not to any tangible object, but specifically to the subset of tangible objects involving records and documents, *i.e.*, objects used to record or preserve information.

This moderate interpretation of "tangible object" accords with the list of actions § 1519 proscribes. The section applies to anyone who "alters, destroys, mutilates, conceals, covers up, *falsifies*, or *makes a false entry in* any record, document, or tangible object" with the requisite obstructive intent. (Emphasis added.) The last two verbs, "falsif[y]" and "mak[e] a false entry in," typically take as grammatical objects records, documents, or things used to record or preserve information, such as logbooks or hard drives. It would be unnatural, for example, to describe a killer's act of wiping his fingerprints from a gun as "falsifying" the murder weapon. But it would not be strange to refer to "falsifying" data stored on a hard drive as simply "falsifying" a hard drive. Furthermore, Congress did not include on § 1512(c)(1)'s list of prohibited actions "falsifies" or "makes a false entry in." *See* § 1512(c)(1) (making it unlawful to "alte[r], destro[y], mutilat[e], or concea[l] a record, document, or other object" with the requisite obstructive intent). That contemporaneous omission also suggests that Congress intended "tangible object" in § 1519 to have a narrower scope than "other object" in § 1512(c)(1).

A canon related to *noscitur a sociis*, *ejusdem generis*, counsels: "Where general words follow specific words in a statutory enumeration, the general words are [usually] construed to embrace only objects similar in nature to those objects enumerated by the preceding specific words." In *Begay v. United States*, 553 U.S. 137, 142–143 (2008), for example, we relied on this principle to determine what crimes were covered by the statutory phrase "any crime . . . that . . . is burglary, arson, or extortion, involves use of explosives, or otherwise involves conduct that presents a serious potential risk of physical injury to another," 18 U.S.C. § 924(e)(2)(B)(ii). The enumeration of specific crimes, we explained, indicates that the "otherwise involves" provision covers "only similar crimes, rather than every crime that 'presents a serious potential risk of physical injury to another.'" Had Congress intended the latter "all encompassing" meaning, we observed, "it is hard to see why it would have needed to include the examples at all." Just so here. Had Congress intended "tangible object" in § 1519 to be interpreted so generically as to capture physical objects as dissimilar as documents and fish, Congress would have had no reason to refer specifically to "record" or "document." The Government's unbounded reading of "tangible object" would render those words misleading surplusage.

Having used traditional tools of statutory interpretation to examine markers of congressional intent within the Sarbanes-Oxley Act and § 1519 itself, we are persuaded that an aggressive interpretation of "tangible object" must be rejected. It is highly improbable that Congress would have buried a general spoliation statute covering objects of any and every kind in a provision targeting fraud in financial record-keeping.***

C

Finally, if our recourse to traditional tools of statutory construction leaves any doubt about the meaning of "tangible object," as that term is used in § 1519, we would invoke the rule that "ambiguity concerning the ambit of criminal statutes should be resolved in favor of lenity." *Cleveland v. United States*, 531 U.S. 12, 25 (2000). That interpretative principle is relevant here, where the Government urges a reading of § 1519 that exposes individuals to 20-year prison sentences for tampering with *any* physical object that *might* have evidentiary value in *any* federal investigation into *any* offense, no matter whether the investigation is pending or merely contemplated, or whether the offense subject to investigation is criminal or civil. In determining the meaning of "tangible object" in § 1519, "it is appropriate, before we choose the harsher alternative, to require that Congress should have spoken in language that is clear and definite."***

JUSTICE ALITO, concurring in the judgment.

This case can and should be resolved on narrow grounds. And though the question is close, traditional tools of statutory construction confirm that John Yates has the better of the argument. Three features of 18 U.S.C. § 1519 stand out to me: the statute's list of nouns, its list of verbs, and its title. Although perhaps none of these features by itself would tip the case in favor of Yates, the three combined do so.

Start with the nouns. Section 1519 refers to "any record, document, or tangible object." The *noscitur a sociis* canon instructs that when a statute contains a list, each word in that list presumptively has a "similar" meaning. A related canon, *ejusdem generis*, teaches that general words following a list of specific words should usually be read in light of those specific words to mean something "similar." Applying these canons to § 1519's list of nouns, the term "tangible object" should refer to something similar to records or documents. A fish does not spring to mind—nor does an antelope, a colonial farmhouse, a hydrofoil, or an oil derrick. All are "objects" that are "tangible." But who wouldn't raise an eyebrow if a neighbor, when asked to identify something similar to a "record" or "document," said "crocodile"?***

Next, consider § 1519's list of verbs: "alters, destroys, mutilates, conceals, covers up, falsifies, or makes a false entry in." Although many of those verbs could apply to nouns as far-flung as salamanders, satellites, or sand dunes, the last phrase in the list—"makes a false entry in"—makes no sense outside of filekeeping. How does one make a false entry in a fish? "Alters" and especially "falsifies" are also closely associated with filekeeping. Not one of the verbs, moreover, cannot be applied to filekeeping—certainly not in the way that "makes a false entry in" is always inconsistent with the aquatic.***

Finally, my analysis is influenced by § 1519's title: "Destruction, alteration, or falsification of *records* in Federal investigations and bankruptcy." (Emphasis added.) This too points toward filekeeping, not fish. Titles can be useful devices to resolve "doubt about the meaning of a statute." *Porter v. Nussle*, 534 U.S. 516, 527–528 (2002). The title is especially valuable here because it reinforces what the text's nouns and verbs independently suggest—that no matter how other statutes might be read, this particular one does not cover every noun in the universe with tangible form.***

JUSTICE KAGAN, with whom JUSTICE SCALIA, JUSTICE KENNEDY, and JUSTICE THOMAS join, dissenting.

I

While the plurality starts its analysis with § 1519's heading, I would begin with § 1519's text. When Congress has not supplied a definition, we generally give a statutory term its ordinary meaning. As the plurality must acknowledge, the ordinary meaning of "tangible object" is "a discrete thing that possesses physical form." A fish is, of course, a discrete thing that possesses physical form. *See generally* Dr. Seuss, One Fish Two Fish Red Fish Blue Fish (1960). So the ordinary meaning of the term "tangible object" in § 1519, as no one here disputes, covers fish (including too-small red grouper).

That interpretation accords with endless uses of the term in statute and rule books as construed by courts. Dozens of federal laws and rules of procedure (and hundreds of state enactments) include the term "tangible object" or its first cousin "tangible thing"—some in association with documents, others not.***

Begin with the way the surrounding words in § 1519 reinforce the breadth of the term at issue. Section 1519 refers to "any" tangible object, thus indicating (in line with that word's plain meaning) a tangible object "of whatever kind." Webster's Third New International Dictionary 97 (2002). This Court has time and again recognized that "any" has "an expansive meaning," bringing within a statute's reach *all* types of the item (here, "tangible object") to which the law refers. And the adjacent laundry list of verbs in § 1519 ("alters, destroys, mutilates, conceals, covers up, falsifies, or makes a false entry") further shows that Congress wrote a statute with a wide scope. Those words are supposed to ensure—just as "tangible object" is meant to—that § 1519 covers the whole world of evidence-tampering, in all its prodigious variety.***

The words "record, document, or tangible object" in § 1519 also track language in 18 U.S.C. § 1512, the federal witness-tampering law covering (as even the plurality accepts) physical evidence in all its forms. Section 1512, both in its original version (preceding § 1519) and today, repeatedly uses the phrase "record, document, or other object"—most notably, in a provision prohibiting the use of force or threat to induce another person to withhold any of those materials from an official proceeding. § 4(a) of the Victim and Witness Protection Act of 1982, 96 Stat. 1249, as amended, 18 U.S.C. § 1512(b)(2). That language, which itself likely derived from the Model Penal Code, encompasses no less the bloody knife than the incriminating letter, as all courts have for decades agreed. And typically "only the most compelling evidence" will persuade this Court that Congress intended "nearly identical language" in provisions dealing with related subjects to bear different meanings. Context thus again confirms what text indicates.

And legislative history, for those who care about it, puts extra icing on a cake already frosted. Section 1519, as the plurality notes, was enacted after the Enron Corporation's collapse, as part of the Sarbanes-Oxley Act of 2002, 116 Stat. 745. But the provision began its life in a separate bill, and the drafters emphasized that Enron was "only a case study exposing the shortcomings in our current laws" relating to both "corporate and criminal" fraud. S. Rep. No. 107-146, pp. 2, 11 (2002). The primary "loophole[]" Congress identified, arose from limits in the part of § 1512 just described: That provision, as uniformly construed, prohibited a person from inducing another to destroy "record[s], document[s], or other object[s]"—of every type—but not from doing so himself. § 1512(b)(2). Congress (as even the plurality agrees) enacted § 1519 to close that yawning gap. But § 1519 could fully achieve that goal only if it covered all the records, documents, and objects § 1512 did, as well as all the means of tampering with them. And so § 1519 was written to do exactly that—"to apply broadly to any acts to destroy or fabricate physical evidence," as long as performed with the requisite intent. S. Rep. No. 107-146, at 14. "When a person destroys evidence," the drafters explained, "overly technical legal distinctions should neither hinder nor prevent prosecution."***

As Congress recognized in using a broad term, giving immunity to those who destroy non-documentary evidence has no sensible basis in penal policy. A person who hides a murder victim's body is no less culpable than one who burns the victim's diary. A fisherman, like John Yates, who dumps undersized fish to avoid a fine is no less blameworthy than one who shreds his vessel's catch log for the same reason. Congress thus treated both offenders in the same way. It understood, in enacting § 1519, that destroying evidence is destroying evidence, whether or not that evidence takes documentary form.

II

A

The plurality's analysis starts with § 1519's title: "Destruction, alteration, or falsification of records in Federal investigations and bankruptcy." That's already a sign something is amiss. I know of no other case in which we have begun our interpretation of a statute with the title, or relied on a title to override the law's clear terms. Instead, we have followed "the wise rule that the title of a statute and the heading of a section cannot limit the plain meaning of the text." *Trainmen v. Baltimore & Ohio R. Co.*, 331 U.S. 519, 528–529 (1947).

The reason for that "wise rule" is easy to see: A title is, almost necessarily, an abridgment. Attempting to mention every term in a statute "would often be ungainly as well as useless"; accordingly, "matters in the text . . . are frequently unreflected in the headings."***

The plurality next tries to divine meaning from § 1519's "position within Chapter 73 of Title 18."*** The plurality claims that if § 1519 applied to objects generally,

Congress would not have placed it "after the pre-existing § 1516, § 1517, and § 1518" because those are "specialized provisions." But search me if I can find a better place for a broad ban on evidence-tampering. The plurality seems to agree that the law properly goes in Chapter 73 — the criminal code's chapter on "obstruction of justice." But the provision does not logically fit into any of that chapter's pre-existing sections. And with the first 18 numbers of the chapter already taken (starting with § 1501 and continuing through § 1518), the law naturally took the 19th place.***

The plurality's third argument, relying on the surplusage canon, at least invokes a known tool of statutory construction — but it too comes to nothing. Says the plurality: If read naturally, § 1519 "would render superfluous" § 1512(c)(1), which Congress passed "as part of the same act." But that is not so: Although the two provisions significantly overlap, each applies to conduct the other does not. The key difference between the two is that § 1519 protects the integrity of "matter[s] within the jurisdiction of any [federal] department or agency" whereas § 1512(c)(1) safeguards "official proceeding[s]" as defined in § 1515(a)(1)(A). Section 1519's language often applies more broadly than § 1512(c)(1)'s, as the plurality notes. For example, an FBI investigation counts as a matter within a federal department's jurisdiction, but falls outside the statutory definition of "official proceeding" as construed by courts. But conversely, § 1512(c)(1) sometimes reaches more widely than § 1519. For example, because an "official proceeding" includes any "proceeding before a judge or court of the United States," § 1512(c)(1) prohibits tampering with evidence in federal litigation between private parties. By contrast, § 1519 wouldn't ordinarily operate in that context because a federal court isn't a "department or agency." So the surplusage canon doesn't come into play. Overlap — even significant overlap — abounds in the criminal law. This Court has never thought that of such ordinary stuff surplusage is made.

And the legislative history to which the plurality appeals*** only cuts against it because those materials show that lawmakers knew that § 1519 and § 1512(c)(1) share much common ground. Minority Leader Lott introduced the amendment that included § 1512(c)(1) (along with other criminal and corporate fraud provisions) late in the legislative process, explaining that he did so at the specific request of the President. See 148 Cong. Rec. 12509, 12512 (2002) (remarks of Sen. Lott). Not only Lott but several other Senators noted the overlap between the President's package and provisions already in the bill, most notably § 1519. *See id.*, at 12512 (remarks of Sen. Lott); *id.*, at 12513 (remarks of Sen. Biden); *id.*, at 12517 (remarks of Sens. Hatch and Gramm). The presence of both § 1519 and § 1512(c)(1) in the final Act may have reflected belt-and-suspenders caution: If § 1519 contained some flaw, § 1512(c)(1) would serve as a backstop. Or the addition of § 1512(c)(1) may have derived solely from legislators' wish "to satisfy audiences other than courts" — that is, the President and his Justice Department. Gluck & Bressman, *Statutory Interpretation from the Inside*, 65 Stan. L. Rev. 901, 935 (2013) (emphasis deleted). Whichever the case, Congress's consciousness of overlap between the two provisions removes any conceivable reason to cast aside § 1519's ordinary meaning in service of preventing some statutory repetition.

Indeed, the inclusion of § 1512(c)(1) in Sarbanes-Oxley creates a far worse problem for the plurality's construction of § 1519 than for mine. Section 1512(c)(1) criminalizes the destruction of any "record, document, or other object"; § 1519 of any "record, document, or tangible object." On the plurality's view, one "object" is really an object, whereas the other is only an object that preserves or stores information.*** The plurality doesn't — really, can't — explain why it instead interprets the same words used in two provisions of the same Act addressing the same basic problem to mean fundamentally different things.

Getting nowhere with surplusage, the plurality switches canons, hoping that *noscitur a sociis* and *ejusdem generis* will save it.*** [A]ssigning "tangible object" its ordinary meaning comports with *noscitur a sociis* and *ejusdem generis* when applied, as they should be, with attention to § 1519's subject and purpose. Those canons require identifying a common trait that links all the words in a statutory phrase. In responding to that demand, the plurality characterizes records and documents as things that preserve information — and so they are. But just as much, they are things that provide information, and thus potentially serve as evidence relevant to matters under review. And in a statute pertaining to obstruction of federal investigations, that evidentiary function comes to the fore. The destruction of records and documents prevents law enforcement agents from gathering facts relevant to official inquiries. And so too does the destruction of tangible objects — of whatever kind. Whether the item is a fisherman's ledger or an undersized fish, throwing it overboard has the identical effect on the administration of justice. For purposes of § 1519, records, documents, and (all) tangible objects are therefore alike.***

Finally, when all else fails, the plurality invokes the rule of lenity. But even in its most robust form, that rule only kicks in when, "after all legitimate tools of interpretation have been exhausted, 'a reasonable doubt persists' regarding whether Congress has made the defendant's conduct a federal crime." *Abramski v. United States*, 573 U.S. ___, ___ (2014) (Scalia, J., dissenting) (slip op., at 12) (quoting *Moskal v. United States*, 498 U.S. 103, 108 (1990)). No such doubt lingers here. The plurality points to the breadth of § 1519, as though breadth were equivalent to ambiguity. It is not. Section 1519 *is* very broad. It is also very clear. Every traditional tool of statutory interpretation points in the same direction, toward "object" meaning object. Lenity offers no proper refuge from that straightforward (even though capacious) construction.***

III

If none of the traditional tools of statutory interpretation can produce today's result, then what accounts for it? The plurality offers a clue when it emphasizes the disproportionate penalties § 1519 imposes if the law is read broadly. Section 1519, the plurality objects, would then "expose[] individuals to 20-year prison sentences for tampering with *any* physical object that *might* have evidentiary value in any federal investigation into *any* offense." That brings to the surface the real issue: overcriminalization and excessive punishment in the U.S. Code.

[W]hatever the wisdom or folly of § 1519, this Court does not get to rewrite the law. "Resolution of the pros and cons of whether a statute should sweep broadly or narrowly is for Congress." *Rodgers*, 466 U.S., at 484. If judges disagree with Congress's choice, we are perfectly entitled to say so — in lectures, in law review articles, and even in dicta. But we are not entitled to replace the statute Congress enacted with an alternative of our own design.

Notes and Questions

1. **The Procedural Posture?** How did the case come to the Supreme Court? What happened in the courts below? What sanctions did the lower courts impose on Yates? Will the Supreme Court's resolution of the case have any practical effect on Yates, or is the Court's resolution of the case an academic exercise?

2. **The Justification for Regulation?** Why, according to the plurality, was it necessary to add § 1519 to the federal criminal code? Does the dissent disagree? Why was it necessary to create a *federal* crime to address the conduct covered by § 1519, given that all states prohibit the destruction of criminal evidence?

3. **The Interpretative Issue?** The question the Supreme Court addresses in *Yates* is deceptively simple: Does 18 U.S.C. § 1519 apply to fish? The full text of § 1519 appears at the beginning of Justice Ginsburg's plurality opinion; pertinent sections of Chapter 73 of Title 18, in which § 1519 appears, are reproduced in the documentary supplement. Note in particular § 1512(c), a separate provision that appears in a section entitled "Tampering with a witness, victim, or an informant."

As explained above in Section [A][1][h], Congress has enacted certain titles of the U.S. Code as positive law. When Congress enacts a title of the U.S. Code into law, it specifies that the U.S. Code, as opposed to enacted bills reproduced in Statutes at Large, is the authoritative written source of federal law. When Congress wishes to amend a law that appears in an enacted version of the U.S. Code, it passes a bill specifying amendments to a specific section of the Code. *See, e.g.*, 116 Stat. 768 ("Section 10A of the Securities Exchange Act of 1934 (15 U.S.C. § 78j-1) is amended by adding at the end the following . . . .").

Title 18, which contains the federal criminal code, is one of the titles enacted into positive law. Read the provisions of Chapter 73 reproduced in the documentary supplement. Based on this statutory text, does § 1519 appear to apply to fish?

4. **Dictionary Definitions of "Tangible Object"?** Is the plurality right that dictionary definitions of "tangible object" are inadequate to resolve the case, because the term is ambiguous? The plurality reasons that a term's ambiguity depends not only on the term itself, but also the context in which it is used, and that in the context of § 1519, "tangible object" is indeed ambiguous. Does the dissent disagree with the plurality on this point?

What role should dictionaries play in statutory interpretation? In an interesting article, Justice Scalia and Professor Garner argue that not all dictionaries are created equal. In their view, interpreters should be sensitive to differences in the quality and coverage of dictionaries and use dictionaries that are appropriate to the interpretative task at hand. Antonin Scalia & Bryan A. Garner, *A Note on the Use of Dictionaries*, 16 GREEN BAG 2D 419 (2013). They note, for example, that "[d]ictionaries tend to lag behind linguistic realities — so a term now known to have first occurred in print in 1900 might not have made its way into a dictionary until 1950 or even 2000. If you are seeking to ascertain the meaning of a term in an 1819 statute, it is generally quite permissible to consult an 1828 dictionary." They also warn that WEBSTER'S THIRD, NEW INTERNATIONAL DICTIONARY (1961) is "to be used cautiously because of its frequent inclusion of doubtful, slipshod meanings without adequate usage notes." *Id.* at 427 & n.21 (citing DICTIONARIES AND THAT DICTIONARY (James Sledd & Wilma R. Ebbitt, eds. 1962)).

Is this dictionary-ology pertinent in *Yates*? Are the definitions of "tangible" and "object" likely to shift depending on the dictionary the interpreter uses? Where do the Justices look for guidance about the "ordinary" meaning of those terms?

5. **Section 1519's Caption?** Having concluded that it is appropriate to look beyond dictionary definitions of "tangible" and "object," the plurality next considers § 1519's title: "Destruction, alteration, or falsification of records in Federal investigations and bankruptcy." What does the plurality take from the section's title? A statute's title may be part of the session law enacted by Congress (and reprinted in the Statutes at Large), or added by the Office of the Law Revision Counsel in the course of preparing the U.S. Code, the codification of federal statutory law. *See* Tobias A. Dorsey, *Some Reflections on Not Reading the Statutes*, 10 GREEN BAG 2D 283, 284–85 (2007) (describing example in which the Office of the Law Revision Counsel threw out the enacted title of an amendatory law and replaced it with a title that it drafted).

In *Lawson v. FMR LLC*, 134 S. Ct. 1158 (2014), the Court considered the probative worth of titles in Section 806 of the Sarbanes-Oxley Act of 2002, 116 Stat. 745, 18 U.S. § 1514A, which prohibits a publicly traded company "or any officer, employee, contractor, subcontractor, or agent of such company" from retaliating against "an employee" for reporting certain violations of the federal securities laws. As enacted by Congress, Section 806 was entitled "Protection for Employees of *Publicly Traded* Companies Who Provide Evidence of Fraud." 116 Stat. 802 (emphasis added). In the U.S. Code, this provision appears in a section titled "Civil action to protect against retaliation in fraud cases." 18 U.S.C. § 1514A (2006). The pertinent subsection is captioned "Protection for Employees of *Publicly Traded* Companies Who Provide Evidence of Fraud." § 1514A(a) (emphasis added).

In *Lawson*, former employees of privately held financial advisory companies brought suit against their former employers under § 806, alleging that they had been fired for blowing the whistle on fraud at Fidelity mutual funds, which are publicly traded. The Fidelity funds themselves have no employees, and contract with investment advisers to handle their day-to-day operations. At issue was whether privately-held advisors are subject to § 806.

The Court answered in the affirmative, notwithstanding the reference to "publicly traded" companies in § 806's title. The Court reasoned that "where, as here, the statutory text is complicated and prolific, headings and titles can do no more than indicate the provisions in a most general manner." *Id.* at 1169. Given "numerous indicators that the statute's prohibitions govern the relationship between a contractor and its own employees"—including its text, the fact that Sarbanes-Oxley was enacted in response to Arthur Anderson's failure to blow the whistle on fraud at Enron, and the structure of the statute—the Court did not "read the headings to 'undo' or 'limit' those signals." *Id.*

6. **Section 1519's Placement in Chapter 73 of Title 18?** The plurality next reasons that § 1519's placement in chapter 73 supports interpreting it not to apply to all tangible objects. In the plurality's view, the chapter begins with broad evidence-tampering offenses and concludes with narrower, more specific offenses. If one looks at the titles of the offenses included in chapter 73, is the plurality's point correct? Justice Kagan writes she does not understand how the placement of § 1519 in chapter 73 could be relevant to its meaning. Is this position consistent with the Court's analysis of statutory structure in *Maracich v. Spears*? (Note that Justice Kagan joined Justice Ginsburg's dissent in *Maracich*, which maintained that the litigation exception and bulk solicitation exception to the Driver's Privacy Protection Act "simply cover different subjects.")

The Sarbanes-Oxley Act directly amended Title 18 of the U.S. Code. *See* Pub. L. No. 107-204, title VIII, § 802(a), 116 Stat. 745, 800 ("Chapter 73 of title 18, United States Code, is amended by adding at the end the following . . . ."). Does this fact support the plurality's position? The dissent's?

7. *Noscitur a Sociis?* Both the plurality and the dissent invoke the grammatical canon *noscitur a socii*—literally "it is known by its associates." The canon recognizes that the meaning of words such as "any," "whatsoever," or "otherwise" is affected by other words with which they are associated, particularly when those words appear at the end of a list. *See* RUPERT CROSS, STATUTORY INTERPRETATION 118 (1976). For example, imagine that a statute prohibited "vehicles including cars, trucks, motorcycles, mopeds, and tractors" from entering a public park. Although airplanes fit the literal definition of a "vehicle," *noscitur a socii* suggests that they are not encompassed by the statute.

Does the canon support the plurality's interpretation of § 1519 or the dissent's? Justice Ginsburg reasons, "'Tangible object' is the last in a list of terms that begins 'any record [or] document.' The term is therefore appropriately read to refer, not to any tangible object, but specifically to the subset of tangible objects involving records and documents, *i.e.*, objects used to record or preserve information." Justice Kagan responds that the thing which unites "record[s]," "document[s]," and "tangible object[s]" is the fact that they have value as evidence. Who has the better of this debate? Note that, under the modern law of evidence, "evidence" is anything that tends to prove or disprove a fact that is material to the determination of an action. *See* Fed. R. Ev. 404.

8. *Ejusdem Generis?* Both the plurality and dissent also invoke the *ejusdem generis* canon, also known in common law jurisdictions as Lord Tenterden's rule. *Ejusdem generis* translates literally to "of the same kind or class." It holds that "when a general word or phrase follows a list of specifics, the general word or phrase will be interpreted to include only items of the same class as those listed. For example, in the phrase *horses, cattle, sheep, pigs, goats,* or *any other farm animals,* the general language *or any other farm animals*—despite its seeming breadth—would probably be held to include only four-legged, hoofed mammals typically found on farms, and thus would exclude chickens." BLACK'S LAW DICTIONARY (10th ed. 2014).

Doesn't this grammatical canon clearly cut in favor of the plurality's interpretation? During argument on Yates' motion to dismiss the § 1519 charge, the district judge asked without prompting: "Isn't there a Latin phrase [about] construction of a statute . . . . The gist of it is . . . you take a look at [a] line of words, and you interpret the words consistently. So if you're talking about documents, and records, tangible objects are tangible objects in the nature of a document or a record, as opposed to a fish." Does Justice Kagan offer a compelling response to the plurality's reliance on the canon?

9. **"Objects" and "Tangible Objects."** Justice Kagan contends that § 1519 borrows the phrase "tangible object" from § 1512(b)(2)(B), which makes it unlawful to induce another person to "alter, destroy, mutilate, or conceal *an object* with intent to impair the object's integrity or availability for use in an official proceeding." Justice Kagan contends that § 1519 was intended to expand § 1512's coverage, so that it would be unlawful both to induce another person to destroy evidence *and* to destroy evidence oneself. Congress's use of "nearly identical" language in §§ 1512 and 1519 shows that "object" and "tangible object" were intended to have the same coverage. The majority's interpretation creates a loophole in federal criminal law, Justice Kagan says, because it makes it lawful to destroy evidence that is not used to store information. Does the majority offer a convincing response to Justice Kagan's argument? For a case in which an evidence-tampering prosecution was threatened by *Yates'* narrow interpretation of § 1519, see *United States v. Tazhayakov,* No. 13-10238-DPW (D. Mass. 2015) (involving destruction of backpack used by Boston marathon bomber Dzhokhar Tsarnaev).

10. **The Rule of Lenity?** The plurality finally reasons that if there were any doubt about § 1519's applicability to fish, it would be resolved by the rule that "ambiguity concerning the ambit of criminal statutes should be resolved in favor of lenity." Several justifications have been offered in support of this "rule of lenity." Where conduct is *malum prohibitum* rather than *malum in se*—i.e., where the conduct is wrongful only because it has been proscribed by law and not because of its intrinsic wrongfulness— the rule of lenity guards against unintended expansion of criminal liability. The rule serves a notice function, ensuring that regulated parties receive advance warning of conduct that is illegal. Within the United States' federalist system, the rule acts as a weak check against the expansion of federal criminal liability and the corresponding contraction of states' regulatory authority. And finally, the rule serves separation-of-powers objectives, ensuring that crimes are defined by Congress rather than the courts. *See* WAYNE R. LaFAVE, SUBSTANTIVE CRIMINAL LAW § 2.2(d) (2d ed. 2014). In recent

decades, the Supreme Court has emphasized that the rule of lenity "is reserved for cases where, '[a]fter seiz[ing] every thing from which aid can be derived, the Court is left with an ambiguous statute.'" *Staples v. United States*, 511 U.S. 600, 619 (1994) (internal punctuation omitted). Is § 1519 ambiguous in this sense? Don't *noscitur* and *ejusdem* offer a means of resolving the case without the need to resort to the rule of lenity?

In contrast to *noscitur* and *ejusdem*, the rule of lenity is a "substantive" canon. It seeks not to capture the way that words are used within a particular interpretative community, but to give effect to deeply held constitutional or normative commitments. We consider the circumstances in which courts recognize such canons and their legitimacy in § [B][2], below.

11. **The Operative Holding.** Having concluded that § 1519 does not apply to everything that can literally be described as a "tangible object," the majority closes by holding that "a 'tangible object' within § 1519's compass is one used to record or preserve information." This gloss on § 1519 was suggested by Yates' brief. Does the plurality give an adequate justification for adopting it? Was it necessary to put a gloss on § 1519 to resolve the case? Compare Justice Alito's approach. As between the plurality and Justice Alito, who provides more guidance to prosecutors, defense counsel, and trial judges? Does the plurality's interpretation allow prosecutions for destroying "tangible object[s]" that are less intuitively worrisome than the undersized fish at issue in *Yates*? Consider the examples cited by Justice Kagan.

12. **What Work Do Grammatical Canons Perform?** In a famous law review article, Professor Karl Llewellyn, a leading figure in the legal realist movement, contended that hard interpretative questions were never truly resolved by applying canons of construction. In difficult cases, judges instead relied on "[t]he good sense of the situation and a *simple* construction of the available language," to determine statutory meaning. Karl N. Llewellyn, *Remarks on the Theory of Appellate Decision and the Rules or Canons About How Statutes Are To Be Construed*, 3 VAND. L. REV. 395 (1949).

To support his point, Llewellyn offered a table of "thrusts" and "parries" that in his view demonstrated that any argument that invoked a canon could be rebutted by another canon. That table is excerpted below.

Figure 2: Canons and Counter-Canons

THRUST	BUT	PARRY
1. A statute cannot go beyond its text.		1. To effect its purpose a statute may be implemented beyond its text.***
3. Statutes are to be read in the light of the common law and a statute affirming a common law rule is to be construed in accordance with the common law.		3. The common law gives way to a statute which is [inconsistent] with it and when a statute is designed as a revision of a whole body of law applicable to a given subject it supersedes the common law.***

6. Statutes *in pari materia* must be construed together.	6. A statute is not *in pari materia* if its scope and aim are distinct or where a legislative design to depart from the general purpose or policy of previous enactments may be apparent.***
12. If language is plain and unambiguous it must be given effect.	12. Not when literal interpretation would lead to absurd or mischievous consequences or thwart manifest purpose.***
15. Words are to be taken in their ordinary meaning unless they are technical terms or words of art.	15. Popular words may bear a technical meaning and technical words may have a popular signification and they should be so construed as to agree with evident intention or to make the statute operative.
16. Every word and clause must be given effect.	16. If inadvertently inserted or if repugnant to the rest of the statute, they may be rejected as surplusage.
17. The same language used repeatedly in the same connection is presumed to bear the same meaning through the statute.	17. This presumption will be disregarded where it is necessary to assign different meanings to make the statute consistent.***
20. Expression of one thing excludes another.	20. The language may fairly comprehend many different cases where some only are expressed by way of example.***
22. It is a general rule of construction that where general words follow an enumeration they are to be held as applying only to persons and things of the same general kind or class specifically mentioned (*ejusdem generis*).	22. General words must operate on something. Further, *ejusdem generis* is only an aid in getting the meaning and does not warrant confining the operations of a statute within narrower limits than were intended.
23. Qualifying or limiting words or clauses are to be referred to the next preceding antecedent.	23. Not when evident sense and meaning require a different construction.***

Is Llewellyn's basic point borne out by the debate in *Yates*? Would the plurality have reached the same conclusion regarding the scope of § 1519 if it had not relied on *ejusdem generis*, *noscitur a sociis*, and the rule of lenity? The dissent?

b. Purpose

Few dispute that, all other things being equal, a statute should be interpreted in a manner that is consistent with its purposes. But reliance on statutory purpose as a guide to the statute's meaning can raise difficult questions. Is there always a purpose that is pertinent to problems of statutory interpretation? How should a statute's purpose be identified? What evidence can legitimately be consulted to identify statutory purpose? When a statute's purpose is in tension with the ordinary meaning of its text, what takes precedence—the purpose or the text? Can there be multiple purposes for a provision that are in tension with one another? The following decisions illustrate two approaches, one historical and one modern, to interpreting a statute in accordance with its purpose.

Church of the Holy Trinity v. United States

143 U.S. 457 (1892)

MR. JUSTICE BREWER delivered the opinion of the court.

[Recall that under § 1 of the Alien Contract Labor Act of 1885, 23 Stat. 332, c. 164, it was unlawful "to prepay the transportation . . . of any alien or aliens, any foreigner or foreigners, into the United States, its Territories, or the District of Columbia, under contract or agreement, ... to perform labor or service of any kind in the United States, its Territories, or the District of Columbia." The Church of the Holy Trinity prepaid E. Walpole Warren's passage from England to the United States, so that Warren could serve as the church's rector and pastor. The Court wrote, "It must be conceded that the act of the corporation is within the letter of this section." Nonetheless, the Court concluded that Congress did not "intend[] to denounce with penalties a transaction like that in the present case."]

Among other things which may be considered in determining the intent of the legislature is the title of the act. We do not mean that it may be used to add to or take from the body of the statute, *Hadden v. The Collector*, 5 Wall. 107, but it may help to interpret its meaning.*** Now, the title of this act is, "An act to prohibit the importation and migration of foreigners and aliens under contract or agreement to perform labor in the United States, its Territories and the District of Columbia." Obviously the thought expressed in this reaches only to the work of the manual laborer, as distinguished from that of the professional man. No one reading such a title would suppose that Congress had in its mind any purpose of staying the coming into this country of ministers of the gospel, or, indeed, of any class whose toil is that of the brain. The common understanding of the terms labor and laborers does not include preaching and preachers; and it is to be assumed that words and phrases are used in their ordinary meaning. So whatever of light is thrown upon the statute by the language of the title indicates an exclusion from its penal provisions of all contracts for the employment of ministers, rectors and pastors.

Again, another guide to the meaning of a statute is found in the evil which it is designed to remedy; and for this the court properly looks at contemporaneous events, the situation as it existed, and as it was pressed upon the attention of the legislative body. *United States v. Union Pacific Railroad*, 91 U.S. 72, 79. The situation which called for this statute was briefly but fully stated by Mr. Justice Brown when, as District Judge, he decided the case of *United States v. Craig*, 28 Fed. Rep. 795, 798: "The motives and history of the act are matters of common knowledge. It had become the practice for large capitalists in this country to contract with their agents abroad for the shipment of great numbers of an ignorant and servile class of foreign laborers, under contracts, by which the employer agreed, upon the one hand, to prepay their passage, while, upon the other hand, the laborers agreed to work after their arrival for a certain time at a low rate of wages. The effect of this was to break down the labor market, and to reduce other laborers engaged in like occupations to the level of the assisted immigrant. The evil finally became so flagrant that an appeal was made to Congress for relief by the passage of the act in question, the design of which was to raise the standard of foreign immigrants, and to discountenance the migration of those who had not sufficient means in their own hands, or those of their friends, to pay their passage."

It appears, also, from the petitions, and in the testimony presented before the committees of Congress, that it was this cheap unskilled labor which was making the trouble, and the influx of which Congress sought to prevent. It was never suggested that we had in this country a surplus of brain toilers, and, least of all, that the market for the services of Christian ministers was depressed by foreign competition. Those were matters to which the attention of Congress, or of the people, was not directed. So far, then, as the evil which was sought to be remedied interprets the statute, it also guides to an exclusion of this contract from the penalties of the act.

A singular circumstance, throwing light upon the intent of Congress, is found in this extract from the report of the Senate Committee on Education and Labor, recommending the passage of the bill: "The general facts and considerations which induce the committee to recommend the passage of this bill are set forth in the Report of the Committee of the House. The committee report the bill back without amendment, although there are certain features thereof which might well be changed or modified, in the hope that the bill may not fail of passage during the present session. Especially would the committee have otherwise recommended amendments, substituting for the expression 'labor and service,' whenever it occurs in the body of the bill, the words 'manual labor' or 'manual service,' as sufficiently broad to accomplish the purposes of the bill, and that such amendments would remove objections which a sharp and perhaps unfriendly criticism may urge to the proposed legislation. The committee, however, believing that the bill in its present form will be construed as including only those whose labor or service is manual in character, and being very desirous that the bill become a law before the adjournment, have reported the bill without change." [Page] 6059, Congressional Record, 48th Congress. And, referring back to the report of the Committee of the House, there appears this language: "It seeks to restrain and prohibit the immigration or importation of laborers who would have never seen our shores but for the inducements and allurements of men whose only object is to obtain labor at the lowest possible rate, regardless of the social and material well-being of our own citizens and regardless of the evil consequences which result to American laborers from such immigration. This class of immigrants care nothing about our institutions, and in many instances never even heard of them; they are men whose passage is paid by the importers; they come here under contract to labor for a certain number of years; they are ignorant of our social condition, and that they may remain so they are isolated and prevented from coming into contact with Americans. They are generally from the lowest social stratum, and live upon the coarsest food and in hovels of a character before unknown to American workmen. They, as a rule, do not become citizens, and are certainly not a desirable acquisition to the body politic. The inevitable tendency of their presence among us is to degrade American labor, and to reduce it to the level of the imported pauper labor." Page 5359, Congressional Record, 48th Congress.

We find, therefore, that the title of the act, the evil which was intended to be remedied, the circumstances surrounding the appeal to Congress, the reports of the committee of each house, all concur in affirming that the intent of Congress was simply to stay the influx of this cheap unskilled labor.

But beyond all these matters no purpose of action against religion can be imputed to any legislation, state or national, because this is a religious people. [The Court here recited a litany of evidence that ostensibly demonstrated the affection of the American people for religious values, including the religion clauses of the first amendment, the appeal to the Almighty at the opening of most legislative sessions, and government offices' observance of the Christian Sabbath.] These, and many other matters which might be noticed, add a volume of unofficial declarations to the mass of organic utterances that this is a Christian nation. In the face of all these, shall it be believed that a Congress of the United States intended to make it a misdemeanor for a church of this country to contract for the services of a Christian minister residing in another nation?

Suppose in the Congress that passed this act some member had offered a bill which in terms declared that, if any Roman Catholic church in this country should contract with Cardinal Manning to come to this country and enter into its service as pastor and priest; or any Episcopal church should enter into a like contract with Canon Farrar; or any Baptist church should make similar arrangements with Rev. Mr. Spurgeon; or any Jewish synagogue with some eminent Rabbi, such contract should be adjudged unlawful and void, and the church making it be subject to prosecution and punishment, can it be believed that it would have received a minute of approving thought or a single vote? Yet it is contended that such was in effect the meaning of this statute. The construction invoked cannot be accepted as correct. It is a case where there was presented a definite evil, in view of which the legislature used general terms with the purpose of reaching all phases of that evil, and thereafter, unexpectedly, it is developed that the general language thus employed is broad enough to reach cases and acts which the whole history and life of the country affirm could not have been intentionally legislated against. It is the duty of the courts, under those circumstances, to say that, however broad the language of the statute may be, the act, although within the letter, is not within the intention of the legislature, and therefore cannot be within the statute.

Notes and Questions

1. **The Procedural Posture?** As noted above, the *Holy Trinity* case was originally filed in the Circuit Court for the Southern District of New York by John S. Kennedy, "a Presbyterian gentleman," as a test case. Pursuant to § 3 of the statute, the United States Attorney's Office for the Southern District of New York took over prosecution of the action. When the case reached the Supreme Court, the church had been found liable for a criminal penalty of $1,000 (about $25,500 in inflation-adjusted dollars). *See United States v. Church of the Holy Trinity*, 36 F. 303 (Cir. Ct. S.D.N.Y. 1888).

But for the Alien Contract Labor Act, is there any reason why paying for an Episcopal minister's passage to the United States would violate the law? As noted above, see

Note 10 following *Yates v. United States, supra* Section [B][1][a], p. 127, criminal jurisprudence traditionally has recognized a distinction between activities that are *malum in se*, or inherently evil, and those that are *malum probitum*, or illegal only by reason of a regulatory statute. Was Holy Trinity Church's payment of Reverend Walpole's passage *malum in se* or *malum probitum*?

2. **Justification for Regulation.** Recall from Chapter 1 that common law regulation of immigration, and particularly contracts for alien labor, was de minimis. See Note 2 following *Church of the Holy Trinity v. United States, supra* in Chapter 1[C][5], p. 133. Recall also that the Alien Contract Labor Act was enacted in response to a perceived influx of foreign labor that threatened American labor unions' influence by undermining their ability to call strikes and engage in other forms of collective action. What was the rationale for addressing that problem through federal legislation rather than through state contract law? Would supporters of the Alien Contract Labor Act have been content with state legislation providing that alien labor contracts could not be enforced? Would such a provision have been adequate to deal with the perceived evil?

Violations of the Act were a misdemeanor, enforcement actions could be initiated by private individuals, and the Act further declared contracts such as Reverend Walpole's void. How did these remedies help to accomplish the Act's objectives?

3. **The Statutory Issue: Text.** What were the strongest textual arguments available to the Holy Trinity Church to support the conclusion that Reverend Warren fell outside the scope of § 1? The Court reasoned that § 1's reference to "labor or service of any kind" was intended to "guard against any narrow interpretation" and "emphasize a breadth of meaning." Is this the only way to read "labor or service of any kind"? Could "labor" and "service" be read to refer to "manual labor"?

Recall the *noscitur a sociis* canon ("know a word by its neighbors"), which teaches that the meaning of a term is informed by the terms surrounding it. What argument based on *noscitur* could the church make regarding the coverage of § 1? If the church emphasized § 1's reference to "labor," how would the government likely respond? In ordinary usage, does a minister perform "labor"? "Service"? Keep in mind that churches are exempt from much legislation governing employment matters, because of the perception that a congregation's choice of minister is intertwined with questions of faith. See Note 4.

What is the relevance of the fact that a violation of § 1 was a misdemeanor, punishable by a $1,000 fine? Recall the rule of lenity from *Yates v. United States*. Is § 1 ambiguous in the way contemplated by the rule? Does the rule of lenity apply with special force in this case because the statute is a *malum prohibitum* measure?

Section 5 of the Alien Contract Labor Act provided that "the provisions of this act [shall not] apply to professional actors, artists, lecturers, or singers, nor to persons employed strictly as personal or domestic servants." The Court reasoned, quoting the circuit judge, that § 5 "strengthens the idea that every other kind of labor and service was intended to be reached by the first section." Is that correct? What arguments were available to the church under this section? How would the government respond?

The canon *expressio unius est exclusio alterius* ("the expression of one is the exclusion of others") teaches that the expression of one thing in a legal text reflects the drafter's intention to exclude things that are not mentioned. As applied to § 5, does *expressio unius* work in favor of the government's position or the church's?

4. **The Statutory Issue: Purpose.** The Court reasons that "a thing may be within the letter of the statute and yet not within the statute, because not within its spirit, nor within the intention of its makers." Following this mode of analysis, the Court concludes that while ministers, rectors and pastors fall within the literal language of § 1, they are impliedly excluded from the Act's coverage.

How does the Court know that applying the Alien Contract Labor Act to ministers, rectors and pastors would be inconsistent with the statute's purpose? The Court cites a variety of evidence:

a. **Title.** The Court first turns to the title of the statute. As it appeared in the *Statutes at Large*, the Alien Contract Labor Act was entitled "An act to prohibit the importation and migration of foreigners and aliens under contract or agreement to perform labor in the United States, its Territories and the District of Columbia." 23 Stat. 332. The Court reasons that "No one reading such a title would suppose that Congress had in mind any purpose of staying the coming into this country of ministers of the gospel, or, indeed, of any class whose toil is that of the brain." Given the similarities between the title of the Act and § 1, how can the Court reach this conclusion? How would the government have interpreted the title of the statute?

Since *Church of the Holy Trinity* was decided, the Supreme Court's attitude toward titles has shifted. Whereas *Church of the Holy Trinity* reasoned that a title might reflect Congress's intention that a statute did not apply to the full extent of its literal language, the prevailing view is that "[t]he title of a statute . . . cannot limit the plain meaning of the text. For interpretive purposes, [it is] of use only when [it] shed[s] light on some ambiguous word or phrase." *Pennsylvania Dep't of Corr. v. Yeskey*, 524 U.S. 206, 212 (1998) (quoting *Trainmen v. Baltimore & Ohio R. Co.*, 331 U.S. 519, 528–529 (1947)). *See also Lawson v. FMR LLC*, 134 S. Ct. 1158 (2014), discussed p. 125, *supra*.

b. **The "evil" to be remedied.** The *Holy Trinity* Court states that "another guide to the meaning of a statute is found in the evil which it is designed to remedy." The Court's reliance on the evil to be remedied invokes an approach to statutory interpretation that understands the enactment of legislation—similar to the decision of a case or controversy—as an official act done in response to circumstances before the legislature. To understand the meaning of legislation, the interpreter must understand the legislature's reasons for acting and what the legislature intended to accomplish in passing the statute that was enacted.

The *locus classicus* for this approach to statutory interpretation is *Heydon's Case* (1584) 76 Eng. Rep. 637 (Exchequer). In 1531, Henry VIII declared himself Supreme Head of the Church of England after Rome refused to nullify his marriage to

Catherine of Aragon. Following the split with Rome, the English government undertook to disband the many Catholic monasteries, priories, convents, and friaries that were located throughout England, Wales, and Ireland in a process known as the Dissolution of Monasteries. As part of the dissolution, Parliament passed the Suppression Act of 1539, 31 Hen. VII, c. 13, which dissolved 552 monasteries and religious houses that had survived prior dissolution acts. A provision of the statute provided that "if any abbot, etc., or other religious and ecclesiastical house or place ... make any lease or grant for life, or for term of years, of any manors, messuages, lands, etc., and in the which any estate or interest for life, year or years ... then had his being or continuance ... every such lease shall be utterly void." The purpose of this provision—"known to all, even to the common lawyers"—was to prevent monasteries from transferring their property to friendly buyers, thereby preventing the land from being acquired by the Crown. *See* S.E. Thorne, *The Equity of a Statute and* Heydon's Case, 31 U. Ill. L. Rev. 202, 216 (1936).

The prior of Bodwin Priory leased a manor called Rialton to his brother for ninety-nine years through a "copyhold," an ancient device that permits a tenant to use a manor's land in exchange for providing services established by custom. The brother in turn leased the land to Heydon, who was charged with intruding on the lands in the Court of Exchequer. The case against Heydon raised the question "whether a copyhold estate ... at the will of the lord, according to the custom of the said manor, should in judgment of law be called an estate and interest for lives, within the said general words and meaning of the said act." Although the legal debates are not recorded, they are thought to have revolved around two subsidiary questions: (1) whether the 1539 Suppression Act should be strictly construed because it was in derogation of the common law (at common law, priories were free to lease land as they saw fit), and (2) whether a copyhold fell within the statute's reference to a "lease or grant for life." Thorne, *supra*, at 216.

The barons of the Court of Exchequer "resolved ... that for the sure and true interpretation of all statutes in general (be they penal or beneficial, restrictive or enlarging of the common law,) four things are to be discerned and considered." These were:

> 1st. What was the common law before the making of the Act.
>
> 2nd. What was the mischief and defect for which the common law did not provide.
>
> 3rd. What remedy the Parliament hath resolved and appointed to cure the disease of the commonwealth.
>
> And, 4th. The true reason of the remedy; and then the office of all the Judges is always to make such construction as shall suppress the mischief, and advance the remedy, and to suppress subtle inventions and evasions for continuance of the mischief, and *pro private commodo*, and to add force and life to the cure and remedy, according to the true intent of the makers of the Act, *pro bono publico*.

Focusing on the third factor, the barons in *Heydon's Case* concluded that "copyhold and customary estates are within the general purview" of the 1539 act, because they implicated the mischief that parliament sought to remedy there. As such, the lease to the prior's brother was void, and Heydon had no claim to the land.

What is the "evil" that the Alien Contract Labor Act sought to remedy? What evidence does the Court rely on to ascertain that evil? Did the Court properly weigh evidence of a somewhat broader purpose?

Relying on a lower court opinion by Justice Brown sitting as circuit court judge, the *Holy Trinity* Court says it was "common knowledge" that the Act was intended to halt "the practice [of] large capitalists in this country to contract with their agents abroad for the shipment of great numbers of an ignorant and servile class of foreign laborers." Is applying the statute to ministers, pastors, and rectors inconsistent with Congress's judgment that *this* practice should be ended? Can this reading of the legislative purpose be reconciled with the exceptions Congress provided in Section 5 of the Act?

Recall from Chapter 1 that an inevitable characteristic of precise statutory provisions ("rules," in colloquial terms) is that they will be too broad or too narrow when judged by reference to Congress's underlying objectives. Rules sacrifice precision to reduce enforcement costs, concentrate policymaking in the lawmaking body that promulgates them, and prevent discriminatory enforcement, among other benefits. Even if Congress's primary concern was the problems associated with the importation of *manual* labor, isn't a broader prohibition of *all* pay-for-labor agreements a rational legislative response—for example, because it eliminates the appearance of class bias and simplifies enforcement?

c. **Legislative history.** The Court also invokes the history of the evolution of the Alien Contract Labor Act in Congress. It relies on two items: a report from the Senate Committee on Education and Labor, which asserted that § 1's prohibition of labor or service "of any kind" applied only to manual labor, and a report from the House Committee on Education and Labor, which first reported the bill. The House report disparaged the undesirable "class of immigrants" who "care nothing about our institutions, and in many instances never even heard of them." In contrast to Episcopal ministers, these immigrants "are generally from the lowest social stratum, and live upon the coarsest food and in the hovels of a character before unknown to American workmen." Why does the Court believe these reports are pertinent to the meaning of § 1?

Both of the reports were read by the clerk of the House and Senate when they were presented. *See* 15 Cong. Rec. 5358–59 (June 19, 1884) (House report); *id.* at 6059 (July 5, 1885) (Senate report). Does it follow that Congress as a whole was aware of the reports' contents and agreed with their understanding of the proposed legislation? Compared to the statute's text, its title, and "common knowledge" of the evil that the Act sought to remedy, how persuasive are the reports as evidence of the statute's purpose and legal effect? What arguments would you make to discount the probative value of the legislative history cited by the Court?

During Senate floor debate on the bill that became the Alien Contract Labor Act, several Senators noted its apparent overbreadth as a means of regulating manual labor. The bill was introduced for debate on July 15, 1884, by Senator Henry W. Blair (R-NH), the chair of the Committee on Education and Labor. Blair noted that he intended to propose an amendment "so that the provision of the bill would then be restricted to the evil that exists . . . . It would apply only to those engaged in manual labor or service." *See* 15 Cong. Rec. 6059 (July 5, 1884). (The amendment was never introduced.) Debate resumed on February 13, 1885. Senator John Tyler Morgan (D-NH) noted that if an immigrant "happens to be a lawyer, an artist, a painter, an engraver, a sculptor, a great author, or what not, and he comes under employment to write for a newspaper, or to write books, or to paint pictures, as we are informed that a recent Secretary of State sent abroad for an artist to paint his picture, he comes under the general provisions of the bill." 16 Cong. Rec. 1632–33 (Feb. 13, 1885). Senator McPherson explained that he "deplore[d] . . . the organizations that are gotten up for the purpose of depriving American labor of employment; but I want to do it by some measure of legislation that will be just and fair and proper, that will reach exactly that class of cases, and at the same time will not be so sweeping in its provisions as to deter honest and proper laborers from coming to this country seeking to better their condition." *Id.* at 1635–56 (Feb. 13, 1885). (He did not propose an amendment to this effect.)

Are statements to the effect that § 1's language was overbroad evidence that the Supreme Court interpreted § 1 correctly? Or do they show, rather, that members of Congress understood the statute to sweep more broadly than necessary to accomplish its objectives, and that Congress failed to correct the problem? Scholarly opinion is divided over the intended reach of the Act. *Compare* Adrian Vermeule, *Legislative History and the Limits of Judicial Competence: The Untold Story of* Holy Trinity Church, 50 Stan. L. Rev. 1833, 1844–45 (1998), *with* Carol Chomsky, *Unlocking the Mysteries of* Holy Trinity: *Spirit, Letter, and History in Statutory Interpretation*, 100 Colum. L. Rev. 901, 940 (2000).

d. **Presumption against interference with church autonomy.** The Court's final argument is that Congress could not have intended to prohibit the importation of ministers, rectors, and pastors, because "this is a Christian nation," and it would be unthinkable for "a Congress of the United States . . . to make it a misdemeanor for a church of this country to contract for the services of a Christian minister residing in another nation."

Assuming that it was accurate to characterize the United States as a "Christian nation" in 1892, is application of the Act to a Christian minister really absurd? The Court seems to assume that Congress could not conceivably enact a law that was overbroad relative to its purposes. But isn't it equally possible that Congress did so to simplify enforcement and prevent evasion of its commands?

Although the Court's proclamation that "this is a Christian nation" may sound odd to modern ears, other doctrines of statutory interpretation similarly privilege the role of religion in American public life. *NLRB v. Catholic Bishop of Chicago*, 440 U.S. 490 (1979), in Section [B][2][f], below, construed the National Labor Relations Act, 29

U.S.C. §§ 151 *et seq.*, not to extend to lay teachers of parochial schools, based on concerns that government regulation of catholic schools' personnel decisions would violate the Establishment Clause.

In *Hosanna-Tabor Evangelical Lutheran Church and School v. EEOC*, 132 S. Ct. 694 (2012), the Supreme Court unanimously ruled that the First Amendment's Religion Clauses required an implied "ministerial exception" that precluded application of the Americans with Disabilities Act, 42 U.S.C. § 12101 *et seq.* (ADA), to a "called" teacher (as opposed to a lay teacher) at a small Lutheran school, who taught a religion class, led students in prayer and devotional exercises, and attended a weekly school-wide chapel service, in addition to teaching secular subjects. This implied exception ensures the "freedom of a religious organization to select its ministers."

The Court was clear that were it not for this exception, application of anti-discrimination laws to religious organizations would violate the Constitution. Yet, it did not "adopt a rigid formula for deciding when an employee qualifies as a minister," ruling instead that the exception covered the *Hosanna-Tabor* plaintiff, "given all the circumstances of her employment."

5. **"Absurdity" and Prosecutorial Discretion.** The Court declares that applying the Alien Contract Labor Act to a Christian minister would be unthinkable. If the application of the Alien Contract Labor Act to a Christian minister was really absurd, could it still be the basis for a criminal conviction? Why was it the responsibility of the Court, as opposed to another institution, to remedy the absurdity? The U.S. Attorney's Office for the Southern District of New York was responsible for the prosecution of the Church of the Holy Trinity. Although a private individual initiated the prosecution, the U.S. Attorney's Office could have dropped the prosecution at any time.

Congress, too, was capable of addressing the problem created by the Act's overbreadth, and in fact did so in 1891. Section 5 of the Act of Mar. 3, 1891, 26 Stat. 1084, 1085, amended § 5 of the Alien Contract Labor Act to exempt "ministers of any religious denomination," "persons belonging to any recognized profession," and "professors for colleges and seminaries." The bill specified that it did not apply to "any prosecution or other proceeding, criminal or civil, begun under any existing act or any acts hereby amended, but such prosecution or other proceedings, criminal or civil, shall proceed as if this act had not been passed." *Id.* § 12.

6. **Further Reading.** For more on *Holy Trinity*, see, e.g., Antonin Scalia, *Common Law Courts in a Civil-Law System, The Role of the United States Federal Courts in Interpreting the Constitution and Laws, in* A MATTER OF INTERPRETATION: FEDERAL COURTS AND THE LAW (Amy Guttman, ed. 1998); Steven K. Green, *Justice David Josiah Brewer and the "Christian Nation" Maxim*, 63 ALB. L. REV. 427, 430 (1999); Anita S. Krishnakumar, *The Hidden Legacy of* Holy Trinity Church: *The Unique National Institution Canon*, 51 WM. & MARY L. REV. 1053 (2009); John F. Manning, *The Absurdity Doctrine*, 116 HARV. L. REV. 2387 (2003).

Church of the Holy Trinity is notable because considerations of statutory purpose trumped what the Court perceived to be the plain meaning of the Alien Contract Labor Act, and the Court acknowledged it was elevating purpose over text. But the tension between a statute's purpose and plain meaning is not always as stark.

General Dynamics Land Systems, Inc. v. Cline

540 U.S. 581 (2004)

JUSTICE SOUTER delivered the opinion of the Court.***

I

In 1997, a collective-bargaining agreement between petitioner General Dynamics and the United Auto Workers eliminated the company's obligation to provide health benefits to subsequently retired employees, except as to then-current workers at least 50 years old. Respondents (collectively, Cline) were then at least 40 and thus protected by the Act, see 29 U.S.C. § 631(a), but under 50 and so without promise of the benefits. All of them objected to the new terms, although some had retired before the change in order to get the prior advantage, some retired afterwards with no benefit, and some worked on, knowing the new contract would give them no health coverage when they were through.

Before the Equal Employment Opportunity Commission (EEOC or Commission) they claimed that the agreement violated the [Age Discrimination in Employment Act of 1967 (ADEA or Act), 81 Stat. 602, 29 U.S.C. § 621 et seq.], because it "discriminate[d against them] . . . with respect to . . . compensation, terms, conditions, or privileges of employment, because of [their] age," § 623(a)(1). The EEOC agreed, and invited General Dynamics and the union to settle informally with Cline.

When they failed, Cline brought this action against General Dynamics, combining claims under the ADEA and state law. The District Court called the federal claim one of "reverse age discrimination," upon which, it observed, no court had ever granted relief under the ADEA. It dismissed in reliance on the Seventh Circuit's opinion in *Hamilton v. Caterpillar Inc.*, 966 F.2d 1226 (1992), that "the ADEA 'does not protect . . . the younger against the older.'"

A divided panel of the Sixth Circuit reversed, with the majority reasoning that the prohibition of § 623(a)(1), covering discrimination against "any individual . . . because of such individual's age," is so clear on its face that if Congress had meant to limit its coverage to protect only the older worker against the younger, it would have said so.*** The Sixth Circuit drew support for its view from the position taken by the EEOC in an interpretive regulation.[1]

---

1. 29 CFR § 1625.2(a) (2003) ("[I]f two people apply for the same position, and one is 42 and the other 52, the employer may not lawfully turn down either one on the basis of age, but must make such decision on the basis of some other factor").***

II

The common ground in this case is the generalization that the ADEA's prohibition covers "discriminat[ion] . . . because of [an] individual's age," 29 U.S.C. § 623(a)(1), that helps the younger by hurting the older. In the abstract, the phrase is open to an argument for a broader construction, since reference to "age" carries no express modifier and the word could be read to look two ways. This more expansive possible understanding does not, however, square with the natural reading of the whole provision prohibiting discrimination, and in fact Congress's interpretive clues speak almost unanimously to an understanding of discrimination as directed against workers who are older than the ones getting treated better.

Congress chose not to include age within discrimination forbidden by Title VII of the Civil Rights Act of 1964, § 715, 78 Stat. 265, being aware that there were legitimate reasons as well as invidious ones for making employment decisions on age. Instead it called for a study of the issue by the Secretary of Labor who concluded that age discrimination was a serious problem, but one different in kind from discrimination on account of race.[2] The Secretary spoke of disadvantage to older individuals from arbitrary and stereotypical employment distinctions (including then-common policies of age ceilings on hiring), but he examined the problem in light of rational considerations of increased pension cost and, in some cases, legitimate concerns about an older person's ability to do the job. When the Secretary ultimately took the position that arbitrary discrimination against older workers was widespread and persistent enough to call for a federal legislative remedy, he placed his recommendation against the background of common experience that the potential cost of employing someone rises with age, so that the older an employee is, the greater the inducement to prefer a younger substitute. The report contains no suggestion that reactions to age level off at some point, and it was devoid of any indication that the Secretary had noticed unfair advantages accruing to older employees at the expense of their juniors.

Congress then asked for a specific proposal, Fair Labor Standards Amendments of 1966, § 606, 80 Stat. 845, which the Secretary provided in January 1967. 113 Cong. Rec. 1377 (1967); see also Public Papers of the Presidents, Lyndon B. Johnson, Vol. 1, Jan. 23, 1967, p. 37 (1968) (message to Congress urging that "[o]pportunity . . . be opened to the many Americans over 45 who are qualified and willing to work"). Extensive House and Senate hearings ensued. See Age Discrimination in Employment: Hearings on H. R. 3651 et al. before the General Subcommittee on Labor of the House Committee on Education and Labor, 90th Cong., 1st Sess. (1967) (hereinafter House Hearings); Age

---

2. That report found that "[e]mployment discrimination because of race is identified . . . with . . . feelings about people entirely unrelated to their ability to do the job. There is no significant discrimination of this kind so far as older workers are concerned. The most closely related kind of discrimination in the non-employment of older workers involves their rejection because of assumptions about the effect of age on their ability to do a job *when there is in fact no basis for these assumptions*." Report of the Secretary of Labor, The Older American Worker: Age Discrimination in Employment 2 (June 1965) (hereinafter Wirtz Report) (emphasis in original).

Discrimination in Employment: Hearings on S. 830 and S. 788 before the Subcommittee on Labor of the Senate Committee on Labor and Public Welfare, 90th Cong., 1st Sess. (1967) (hereinafter Senate Hearings).

The testimony at both hearings dwelled on unjustified assumptions about the effect of age on ability to work. See, e. g., House Hearings 151 (statement of Rep. Joshua Eilberg) ("At age 40, a worker may find that age restrictions become common . . . . By age 45, his employment opportunities are likely to contract sharply; they shrink more severely at age 55 and virtually vanish by age 65"); *id.*, at 422 (statement of Rep. Claude Pepper) ("We must provide meaningful opportunities for employment to the thousands of workers 45 and over who are well qualified but nevertheless denied jobs which they may desperately need because someone has arbitrarily decided that they are too old"); Senate Hearings 34 (statement of Sen. George Murphy) ("[A]n older worker often faces an attitude on the part of some employers that prevents him from receiving serious consideration or even an interview in his search for employment"). The hearings specifically addressed higher pension and benefit costs as heavier drags on hiring workers the older they got. See, e.g., House Hearings 45 (statement of Norman Sprague) (Apart from stereotypes, "labor market conditions, seniority and promotion-from-within policies, job training costs, pension and insurance costs, and mandatory retirement policies often make employers reluctant to hire older workers"). The record thus reflects the common facts that an individual's chances to find and keep a job get worse over time; as between any two people, the younger is in the stronger position, the older more apt to be tagged with demeaning stereotype. Not surprisingly, from the voluminous records of the hearings, we have found (and Cline has cited) nothing suggesting that any workers were registering complaints about discrimination in favor of their seniors.

Nor is there any such suggestion in the introductory provisions of the ADEA, 81 Stat. 602, which begins with statements of purpose and findings that mirror the Wirtz Report and the committee transcripts. *Id.*, § 2. The findings stress the impediments suffered by "older workers . . . in their efforts to retain . . . and especially to regain employment," *id.*, § 2(a)(1); "the [burdens] of arbitrary age limits regardless of potential for job performance," *id.*, § 2(a)(2); the costs of "otherwise desirable practices [that] may work to the disadvantage of older persons," *ibid.*; and "the incidence of unemployment, especially long-term unemployment[, which] is, relative to the younger ages, high among older workers," *id.*, § 2(a)(3). The statutory objects were "to promote employment of older persons based on their ability rather than age; to prohibit arbitrary age discrimination in employment; [and] to help employers and workers find ways of meeting problems arising from the impact of age on employment." *Id.*, § 2(b).***

Such is the setting of the ADEA's core substantive provision, § 4 (as amended, 29 U.S.C. § 623), prohibiting employers and certain others from "discriminat[ion] . . . because of [an] individual's age," whenever (as originally enacted) the individual is "at least forty years of age but less than sixty-five years of age," § 12, 81 Stat. 607. The prefatory provisions and their legislative history make a case that we think is beyond reasonable doubt, that the ADEA was concerned to protect a relatively old worker from discrimination that works to the advantage of the relatively young.

Nor is it remarkable that the record is devoid of any evidence that younger workers were suffering at the expense of their elders, let alone that a social problem required a federal statute to place a younger worker in parity with an older one. Common experience is to the contrary, and the testimony, reports, and congressional findings simply confirm that Congress used the phrase "discriminat[ion] . . . because of [an] individual's age" the same way that ordinary people in common usage might speak of age discrimination any day of the week. One commonplace conception of American society in recent decades is its character as a "youth culture," and in a world where younger is better, talk about discrimination because of age is naturally understood to refer to discrimination against the older.

This same, idiomatic sense of the statutory phrase is confirmed by the statute's restriction of the protected class to those 40 and above. If Congress had been worrying about protecting the younger against the older, it would not likely have ignored everyone under 40. The youthful deficiencies of inexperience and unsteadiness invite stereotypical and discriminatory thinking about those a lot younger than 40, and prejudice suffered by a 40-year-old is not typically owing to youth, as 40-year-olds sadly tend to find out. The enemy of 40 is 30, not 50.***

The federal reports are as replete with cases taking this position as they are nearly devoid of decisions like the one reviewed here.***

III

Cline and *amicus* EEOC proffer three rejoinders in favor of their competing view that the prohibition works both ways.***

A

The first response to our reading is the dictionary argument that "age" means the length of a person's life, with the phrase "because of such individual's age" stating a simple test of causation: "discriminat[ion] . . . because of [an] individual's age" is treatment that would not have occurred if the individual's span of years had been longer or shorter. The case for this reading calls attention to the other instances of "age" in the ADEA that are not limited to old age, such as 29 U.S.C. § 623(f), which gives an employer a defense to charges of age discrimination when "age is a bona fide occupational qualification." Cline and the EEOC argue that if "age" meant old age, § 623(f) would then provide a defense (old age is a bona fide qualification) only for an employer's action that on our reading would never clash with the statute (because preferring the older is not forbidden).

The argument rests on two mistakes. First, it assumes that the word "age" has the same meaning wherever the ADEA uses it. But this is not so, and Cline simply misemploys the "presumption that identical words used in different parts of the same act are intended to have the same meaning." *Atlantic Cleaners & Dyers, Inc. v. United States*, 286 U.S. 427, 433 (1932). Cline forgets that "the presumption is not rigid and readily yields whenever there is such variation in the connection in which the words are used as reasonably to warrant the conclusion that they were employed in different parts of the act with different intent."***

"Age" is that kind of word.*** [T]he word "age" standing alone can be readily understood either as pointing to any number of years lived, or as common shorthand for the longer span and concurrent aches that make youth look good. Which alternative was probably intended is a matter of context; we understand the different choices of meaning that lie behind a sentence like "Age can be shown by a driver's license," and the statement, "Age has left him a shut-in." So it is easy to understand that Congress chose different meanings at different places in the ADEA, as the different settings readily show. Hence the second flaw in Cline's argument for uniform usage: it ignores the cardinal rule that "[s]tatutory language must be read in context [since] a phrase 'gathers meaning from the words around it.'" *Jones v. United States*, 527 U.S. 373, 389 (1999). The point here is that we are not asking an abstract question about the meaning of "age"; we are seeking the meaning of the whole phrase "discriminate . . . because of such individual's age," where it occurs in the ADEA, 29 U.S.C. § 623(a)(1).***

B

The second objection has more substance than the first, but still not enough. The record of congressional action reports a colloquy on the Senate floor between two of the legislators most active in pushing for the ADEA, Senators [Jacob] Javits [(D-NY)] and [Ralph] Yarborough [(D-TX)]. Senator Javits began the exchange by raising a concern mentioned by Senator Dominick, that "the bill might not forbid discrimination between two persons each of whom would be between the ages of 40 and 65." 113 Cong. Rec. 31255 (1967). Senator Javits then gave his own view that, "if two individuals ages 52 and 42 apply for the same job, and the employer selected the man aged 42 solely . . . because he is younger than the man 52, then he will have violated the act," and asked Senator Yarborough for his opinion. Senator Yarborough answered that "[t]he law prohibits age being a factor in the decision to hire, as to one age over the other, whichever way [the] decision went."

Although in the past we have given weight to Senator Yarborough's views on the construction of the ADEA because he was a sponsor, his side of this exchange is not enough to unsettle our reading of the statute.*** [T]he Senator's remark, "whichever way [the] decision went," is the only item in all the 1967 hearings, reports, and debates going against the grain of the common understanding of age discrimination. Even from a sponsor, a single outlying statement cannot stand against a tide of context and history, not to mention 30 years of judicial interpretation producing no apparent legislative qualms. See *Consumer Product Safety Comm'n v. GTE Sylvania, Inc.*, 447 U.S. 102, 118 (1980) ("[O]rdinarily even the contemporaneous remarks of a single legislator who sponsors a bill are not controlling in analyzing legislative history").

C

The third objection relies on a reading consistent with the Yarborough comment, adopted by the agency now charged with enforcing the statute, as set out at 29 CFR § 1625.2(a) (2003), and quoted in full, n. 1, *supra*. When the EEOC adopted § 1625.2(a) in 1981, shortly after assuming administrative responsibility for the ADEA, it gave no reasons for the view expressed, beyond noting that the provision was carried forward from an earlier Department of Labor regulation, see 44 Fed. Reg. 68858 (1979); 46 Fed. Reg. 47724 (1981); that earlier regulation itself gave no reasons, see 33 Fed. Reg. 9172 (1968) (reprinting 29 CFR § 860.91, rescinded by 46 Fed. Reg. 47724 (1981)).

The parties contest the degree of weight owed to the EEOC's reading, with General Dynamics urging us that *Skidmore v. Swift & Co.*, 323 U.S. 134 (1944), sets the limit, while Cline and the EEOC say that § 1625.2(a) deserves greater deference under *Chevron U.S.A. Inc. v. Natural Resources Defense Council, Inc.*, 467 U.S. 837 (1984).*** In *Edelman v. Lynchburg College*, 535 U.S. 106, 114 (2002), we found no need to choose between *Skidmore* and *Chevron*, or even to defer, because the EEOC was clearly right; today, we neither defer nor settle on any degree of deference because the Commission is clearly wrong.

Even for an agency able to claim all the authority possible under *Chevron*, deference to its statutory interpretation is called for only when the devices of judicial construction have been tried and found to yield no clear sense of congressional intent. Here, regular interpretive method leaves no serious question, not even about purely textual ambiguity in the ADEA. The word "age" takes on a definite meaning from being in the phrase "discriminat[ion] ... because of such individual's age," occurring as that phrase does in a statute structured and manifestly intended to protect the older from arbitrary favor for the younger.

IV

We see the text, structure, purpose, and history of the ADEA, along with its relationship to other federal statutes, as showing that the statute does not mean to stop an employer from favoring an older employee over a younger one.***

[Justice Thomas, joined by Justice Kennedy, dissented on the ground that the ADEA's plain language extended to discrimination against the young in favor of the old. Justice Scalia dissented separately, arguing that 29 C.F.R. § 1625.2(a) reasonably interpreted an ambiguous statutory term and was entitled to deference.]

Notes and Questions

1. **The Procedural Posture?** What was the interpretative issue that the Court addressed in *Cline*? What was the case's procedural posture when it arrived at the Supreme Court? Where did the plaintiffs initially turn to advance their claim that they had been discriminated against in violation of the ADEA?

2. **Justification for Regulation.** At common law, the employment relationship was considered to be terminable "at will." An employer could hire or refuse to hire a potential employee for any reason or no reason at all. Both the employer and the employee were free to terminate the relationship without notice or cause. *See generally* Restatement of Employment Law ch. 2 (2015). The common law provided no protection against discrimination on the basis of race, sex, disability, or other characteristics. Indeed, a standard formulation held that an employer could hire or discharge an

employee "for cause morally wrong, without thereby being guilty of a legal wrong." *Payne v. W. & Atl. R. Co.*, 81 Tenn. 507, 519–20 (1884), *overruled on other grounds*, *Hutton v. Watters*, 179 S.W. 134 (Tenn. 1915).

In the aftermath of World War II, northern states began to regulate employment discrimination through legislation modeled on New Deal administrative statutes. As noted above in connection with *Christiansburg Garment Co. v. EEOC*, the centerpiece of the states' post-war response to employment discrimination was a "Fair Employment Practices Commission," or FEPC, that had the authority to mediate disputes and order employers to cease and desist from engaging in employment discrimination. See Chapter 1[C][3], above. Eliminating employment discrimination at least in theory gave employers a competitive advantage over those that continued to discriminate, because non-discriminating employers had access to a larger base of potential employees. However, market dynamics were inadequate to end racial discrimination, particularly in the deep South, where it was kept in place by violence and social ostracism. The persistence of discriminatory employment practices in the South—combined with televised violence against civil rights demonstrators in cities such as Birmingham, Alabama and the advocacy of civil rights leaders including Martin Luther King, Jr.—created critical momentum for the enactment of civil rights legislation by 1963. Following President John F. Kennedy's assassination in December 1963, President Lyndon B. Johnson announced that the enactment of civil rights legislation would be a central part of Kennedy's legacy.

When Congress enacted the Civil Rights Act of 1964, it prohibited discrimination on the basis of race, color, religion, sex, or national origin. At the same time, it authorized a study of whether similar federal legislation was needed to deal with age discrimination in employment. A year later, Secretary of Labor W. Willard Wirtz issued a report to Congress that was central to the ADEA's enactment. *See* REPORT OF THE SECRETARY OF LABOR, THE OLDER AMERICAN WORKER: AGE DISCRIMINATION IN EMPLOYMENT (June 1965).

The Wirtz Report found "there is persistent and widespread use of age limits in hiring that in a great many cases can be attributed only to arbitrary discrimination against older workers on the basis of age and regardless of ability." More specifically, the report found that employers required employees to retire when they reached a predetermined age regardless of whether they were still able to perform their duties, and that employers used age cutoffs when advertising positions (e.g., "persons over 50 need not apply").

As the Court observes, Congress did not vote on the Wirtz Report. Rather, in the Fair Labor Standards Amendments of 1966, § 606, 80 Stat. 845, Congress directed the Secretary of Labor to propose specific legislation to remedy the problem the Wirtz Report describes. The draft bill submitted in response was modeled on the 1964 Civil Rights Act. Its operative provision defined various forms of age discrimination as an unlawful employment practice. Enforcement authority was divided between the Department of Labor and private lawsuits. *See* 113 Cong. Rec. 1377 (Jan. 24, 1967).

3. **The Statutory Issue: Discrimination "Because of Age."** The ADEA's principal operative provision, 29 U.S.C. § 623(a)(1), provides: "It shall be unlawful for an employer . . . to fail or refuse to hire or to discharge any individual or otherwise discriminate against any individual with respect to his compensation, terms, conditions, or privileges of employment, because of such individual's age . . . ."

The Court had construed nearly identical language in Title VII of the Civil Rights Act of 1964 to prohibit race-based discrimination not only against blacks but also against whites. *See McDonald v. Santa Fe Transportation Co.*, 427 U.S. 273 (1976) (interpreting 42 U.S.C. § 2000e-2's prohibition on discrimination because of "such individual's race"). While acknowledging that the 1964 Civil Rights Act was enacted in response to discrimination against African Americans, the *Cline* Court reasoned that Title VII's "terms are not limited to discrimination against members of any particular race." If the ADEA was read *in pari materia* with Title VII, its prohibition of discrimination "because of age" would have applied to individuals of all ages who complained that they were discriminated against because they were older or younger than the decisionmaker would have preferred.

4. **ADEA's Statement of Findings and Purpose.** The Court relies on a variety of evidence in determining that the ADEA has the limited purpose of prohibiting discrimination against workers because of relative elderliness, rather than seeking to prohibit any consideration of age.

The Act sets out four findings, drawn from the Wirtz Report and committee hearings on the ADEA:

> (1) in the face of rising productivity and affluence, older workers find themselves disadvantaged in their efforts to retain employment, and especially to regain employment when displaced from jobs;

> (2) the setting of arbitrary age limits regardless of potential for job performance has become a common practice, and certain otherwise desirable practices may work to the disadvantage of older persons;

> (3) the incidence of unemployment, especially long-term unemployment with resultant deterioration of skill, morale, and employer acceptability is, relative to the younger ages, high among older workers; their numbers are great and growing; and their employment problems grave;

> (4) the existence in industries affecting commerce, of arbitrary discrimination in employment because of age, burdens commerce and the free flow of goods in commerce.

29 U.S.C. § 621(a).

How much weight should be given to these findings? They are part of the enacted law but they are not operational provisions. Finding (4) speaks of "arbitrary discrimination in employment because of age" which, standing alone, might support a reading of ADEA that protected younger workers (over the age of 40) from preferential treatment of older workers. Is such a reading foreclosed by the references to "older workers" and "older persons" in Findings 1–3 and in the Act's statement of purpose: "the purpose of this chapter is to promote employment of older persons based on their ability rather than age; to prohibit arbitrary age discrimination in employment; to help employers and workers find ways of meeting problems arising from the impact of age on employment," *id.* § 621(b)?

5. **Explaining the Age Cut-Off.** The Court in *Cline* drew affirmative support from the ADEA provision, 29 U.S.C. § 631(a), limiting the protection against age discrimination to those who are at least 40 years old: "The youthful deficiencies of inexperience and unsteadiness invite stereotypical and discriminatory thinking about those a lot younger than 40, and prejudice suffered by a 40-year-old is not typically owing to youth, as 40-year-olds sadly tend to find out." If Congress had been worried about discrimination against the young, the Court reasoned, it would have defined the ADEA's protected class more broadly, to also include persons younger than 40 years old.

Dissenting, Justice Thomas countered that there was a "perfectly rational explanation" for the 40-year-old cutoff, which did not create a conflict with 29 U.S.C. § 623(a)(1)'s plain meaning. "Congress could [have] easily conclude[d] that age discrimination directed against those under 40 is not as damaging, since a young worker unjustly fired is likely to find a new job or otherwise recover from the discrimination." 540 U.S. at 605. As support for this argument Justice Thomas cited the Secretary Wirtz's report and the findings set out in 29 U.S.C. §§ 621(a)(1) and (3). Who has the better of this debate?

6. **Comparing *Cline* and *Holy Trinity*.** The *Cline* Court in footnote 5 (not included above) denies that it is narrowing the scope of a general statutory mandate to cover only the specific problem that motivated Congress to enact legislation. Instead, the Court states that "Congress expressed a prohibition by using a term in a commonly understood, narrow sense ('age' as 'relatively old age')." Is this an accurate description of the ADEA? Is there a "narrow sense" of "labor or service of any kind" that the *Holy Trinity* Court could have invoked?

How does the *Cline* Court's analysis of the ADEA differ from the *Holy Trinity* Court's analysis of the Alien Contract Labor Act? Does *Cline* have a stronger or weaker foundation in statutory text than *Church of the Holy Trinity*?

How does the *Cline* Court's reliance on statutory purpose differ from *Holy Trinity*? Recall that in *Church of the Holy Trinity*, the Court relied on two House and Senate committee reports and a lower court opinion which posited it was "common knowledge" that the Alien Contract Labor Act addressed the "the practice [of] large capitalists in this country to contract with their agents abroad for the shipment of great numbers of an ignorant and servile class of foreign laborers." Is the evidence of statutory purpose cited in *Cline* more reliable than the evidence *Church of the Holy Trinity* relied on? More persuasive?

7. **The Relevance of Title VII Precedents.** The Supreme Court had previously recognized that because "the ADEA and Title VII share a common purpose, the

elimination of discrimination in the workplace," and that in many places the language of the ADEA is "almost *in haec verba*" with Title VII (because the ADEA was modeled after Title VII), there is often good reason to interpret the measures in like fashion. *See Oscar Mayer & Co. v. Evans*, 441 U.S. 750 (1979). If so, perhaps the strongest argument against the Court's interpretation is that Title VII had been interpreted to prohibit all discrimination on the basis of race and sex, not just discrimination against the group that was historically discriminated against. As noted above, *McDonald v. Santa Fe Transportation Co.*, 427 U.S. 273 (1976), held that a white plaintiff could bring a claim for discrimination because of race under Title VII. Title VII precedents antedating *Cline, see, e.g., Oncale v. Sundowner Offshore Services, Inc.*, 523 U.S. 75 (1998); *Wilson v. Southwest Airlines*, 517 F. Supp. 292 (N.D. Tex. 1981), similarly held that Title VII's prohibition of discrimination because of sex protects men as well as women. Moreover, the *in pari materia* canon teaches that because Title VII and the ADEA share the same structure and prohibit discrimination "because of" a protected characteristic, they should be interpreted consistently. *See Northcross v. Bd. of Ed. of Memphis City Sch.*, 412 U.S. 427, 428 (1973) (statutes containing similar language and sharing common raison d'etre should be interpreted consistently).

On the other hand, can this reading be reconciled with the emphasis on protecting "older workers" in Findings (1) and (3), and the Wirtz Report's focus on the "arbitrary" use of age classifications to disadvantage older workers in hiring and mandatory retirement programs? *See also* Older Workers Benefit Protection Act of 1990, Pub. L. No. 101-433, 104 Stat. 978 (amending ADEA "to prohibit discrimination against older workers in all employee benefits except when age-based reductions in employee benefit plans are justified by significant cost considerations").

8. **Why No Deference to the EEOC?** The Court concludes that "regular interpretive method leaves no serious question" that the ADEA does not prohibit discrimination against the young. Accordingly, the Court gives no deference to the EEOC's contrary position, set out in a codified interpretation, that "if two people apply for the same position, and one is 42 and the other 52, the employer may not lawfully turn down either one on the basis of age, but must make such decision on the basis of some other factor." 29 C.F.R. § 1625.2(a) (2003). Chapter 5, below, considers the forms of deference courts extend to agency statutory interpretations, and the EEOC's track record in interpreting civil rights laws.

c. Legislative History

As *Holy Trinity* and *Cline* illustrate, U.S. courts often look to "legislative history" as an aid to understanding the circumstances that prompted the enactment of legislation, the intent of lawmakers, and the meaning of statutory language. Legislative history in this sense is another tool of statutory interpretation — one that is particularly important for interpretation that relies upon statutory purpose or the intent of the enacting legislature.

The term "legislative history" is often used to include *both* (i) materials such as the text of bills and conference reports that have been voted upon by either chamber and thus track the evolution of a statute as it is understood by members of the House and Senate, and (ii) other materials such as committees reports and colloquy on proposed amendments that were not voted on by either chamber. The former we would suggest is the "enactment history" of a statute and should not be lumped together with category (ii) materials. *See also* Note on "Hierarchy" of Legislative History, Note 5 following *Hanrahan v. Hampton*, p. 152, *infra*. Whatever the nomenclature, courts must determine whether legislative history is actually probative of statutory meaning, what kinds of legislative materials to look at, and the weight to give to those materials. More fundamentally, courts must decide whether there are circumstances where the use of legislative history as a guide to the meaning of enacted statutory language is consistent with the judicial role.

Hanrahan v. Hampton

446 U.S. 754 (1980)

PER CURIAM.

In the Civil Rights Attorney's Fees Awards Act of 1976, Congress amended 42 U.S.C. § 1988 to permit the award of a reasonable attorney's fee to the "prevailing party" as part of the taxable costs in a suit brought under any of several specified civil rights statutes. The respondents brought suit under three of those statutes in the United States District Court for the Northern District of Illinois, alleging that their constitutional rights had been violated by the petitioners, and seeking money damages from them.[1] The District Court directed verdicts for the petitioners, but the Court of Appeals reversed and remanded the case to the District Court for a new trial. The Court of Appeals also awarded to the respondents their costs on appeal, including attorney's fees which it believed to be authorized by § 1988.

The final sentence of § 1988, as amended, provides as follows:

> "In any action or proceeding to enforce a provision of sections 1981, 1982, 1983, 1985, and 1986 of this title, . . . the court, in its discretion, may allow the prevailing party, other than the United States, a reasonable attorney's fee as part of the costs." 42 U.S.C. § 1988.

---

1. The controversy arose from the execution in 1969 of a judicial warrant to search for and seize illegal weapons within an apartment in Chicago occupied by nine members of the Black Panther Party. In the course of the search two of the apartment's occupants were killed by gunfire, and four others were wounded. The police seized various weapons and arrested the seven surviving occupants of the apartment. The survivors were indicted by a state grand jury on charges of attempted murder and aggravated battery, but the indictments ultimately were dismissed. Those seven persons and the legal representatives of the two persons killed are the respondents in these cases. Named as defendants in the respondents' suits were Cook Country, the City of Chicago, and various state and local officials allegedly involved in the search or its aftermath. Those officials are the petitioners in No. 79-912. After proceedings in the District Court and the Court of Appeals resulted in the dismissal of the complaint against the city and the county, the respondents filed an amended complaint naming as additional defendants the three Federal Bureau of Investigation agents and an informant who are the petitioners in No. 79-914. The respondents based their claims on 42 U.S.C. §§ 1983, 1985(3) (1976 ed., Supp. II), and 1986, and on provisions of the Constitution. They also alleged various causes of action under state law.

The statute by its terms thus permits the award of attorney's fees only to a "prevailing party." Accordingly, in the present cases, the Court of Appeals was authorized to award to the respondents the attorney's fees attributable to their appeal only if, by reason of obtaining a partial reversal of the trial court's judgment, they "prevailed" within the meaning of § 1988. The Court of Appeals believed that they had prevailed with respect to the appeal in this case, resting its conclusion upon the following appellate rulings favorable to the respondents: (1) the reversal of the District Court's judgment directing verdicts against them, save with respect to certain of the defendants; (2) the reversal of the District Court's denial of their motion to discover the identity of an informant; and (3) the direction to the District Court on remand to consider allowing further discovery, and to conduct a hearing on the respondents' contention that the conduct of some of the petitioners in response to the trial court's discovery orders warranted the imposition of sanctions under Federal Rule of Civil Procedure 37(b)(2). While the respondents did prevail on these matters in the sense that the Court of Appeals overturned several rulings against them by the District Court, they were not, we have concluded, "prevailing" parties in the sense intended by 42 U.S.C. § 1988, as amended.

The legislative history of the Civil Rights Attorney's Fees Awards Act of 1976 indicates that a person may in some circumstances be a "prevailing party" without having obtained a favorable "final judgment following a full trial on the merits," H. R. Rep. No. 94-1558, p. 7 (1976). See also S. Rep. No. 94-1011, p. 5 (1976). Thus for example, "parties may be considered to have prevailed when they vindicate rights through a consent judgment or without formally obtaining relief," *ibid. See also* H. R. Rep. No. 94-1558, *supra*, at 7, and cases cited.

It is evident also that Congress contemplated the award of fees *pendente lite* in some cases. S. Rep. No. 94-1011, *supra*, at 5; H. R. Rep. No. 94-1558, *supra*, at 7–8. But it seems clearly to have been the intent of Congress to permit such an interlocutory award only to a party who has established his entitlement to some relief on the merits of his claims, either in the trial court or on appeal. The congressional Committee Reports described what were considered to be appropriate circumstances for such an award by reference to two cases — *Bradley v. Richmond School Board*, 416 U.S. 696 (1974), and *Mills v. Electric Auto-Lite Co.*, 396 U.S. 375 (1970). S. Rep. No. 94-1011, *supra*, at 5; H.R. Rep. No. 94-1558, *supra*, at 8. In each of those cases the party to whom fees were awarded had established the liability of the opposing party, although final remedial orders had not been entered. The House Committee Report, moreover, approved the standard suggested by this Court in *Bradley*, that "'the entry of any order that determines substantial rights of the parties may be an appropriate occasion upon which to consider the propriety of an award of counsel fees ... ,'" H.R. Rep. No. 94-1558, *supra*, at 8, quoting *Bradley v. Richmond School Board, supra*, at 723, n. 28. Similarly, the Senate Committee Report explained that the award of counsel fees *pendente lite* would be "especially appropriate where a party has prevailed on an important matter in the course of litigation, even when he ultimately does not prevail on *all* issues." S. Rep. No. 94-1011, *supra*, at 5 (emphasis added). It seems apparent from these passages that Congress intended to permit the interim award of counsel fees only when a party has prevailed on the merits of at least some of his claims. For only in that event has there been a determination of the "substantial rights of the parties," which Congress determined was a necessary foundation for departing from the usual rule in this country that each party is to bear the expense of his own attorney.[4]

The respondents have of course not prevailed on the merits of any of their claims. The Court of Appeals held only that the respondents were entitled to a trial of their cause. As a practical matter they are in a position no different from that they would have occupied if they had simply defeated the defendants' motion for a directed verdict in the trial court. The jury may or may not decide some or all of the issues in favor of the respondents. If the jury should not do so on remand in these cases, it could not seriously be contended that the respondents had prevailed. Nor may they fairly be said to have "prevailed" by reason of the Court of Appeals' other interlocutory dispositions, which affected only the extent of discovery. As is true of other procedural or evidentiary rulings, these determinations may affect the disposition on the merits, but were themselves not matters on which a party could "prevail" for purposes of shifting his counsel fees to the opposing party under § 1988.

[Justice Powell, joined by Chief Justice Burger and Justice Rehnquist, concurred in part and dissented in part. He expressed concern that the litigation imposed too great a burden on the federal defendants who had been added after the dismissal of claims against Chicago and Cook County. Justice Marshall dissented and would have set the case for argument rather than disposing of it summarily. He also argued: "Obtaining an appellate order requiring that a new trial be held after an action to enforce civil rights has been prematurely terminated similarly is an achievement reflecting on the merits of the case. The decision of the Court of Appeals, establishing that respondents produced sufficient evidence to warrant sending their case to the jury, breathes new life into an otherwise dead lawsuit."]

Notes and Questions

1. **The Procedural Posture?** What was the procedural posture in which *Hanrahan* was heard by the Supreme Court? When the Supreme Court issued this decision? What had happened in the lower courts? What was still to come?

2. **The Statutory Issue?** 42 U.S.C. § 1988 encourages private, civil enforcement of the civil rights laws by modifying the ordinary "American rule" that each side pay its own attorney's fees, win or lose. The Supreme Court has said that the plaintiff in an action to enforce the civil rights laws is "a 'private attorney general,' vindicating a

---

4. The provision for counsel fees in § 1988 was patterned upon the attorney's fees provisions contained in Titles II and VII of the Civil Rights Act of 1964, 42 U.S.C. §§ 2000a-3(b) and 2000e-5(k), and § 402 of the Voting Rights Act Amendments of 1975, 42 U.S.C. § 1973l(e). S. Rep. No. 94-1011, p. 2 (1976); H.R. Rep. No. 94-1558, p. 5 (1976). Those provisions have been construed by the Courts of Appeals to permit the award of counsel fees only to a party who has prevailed on the merits of a claim.***

policy that Congress considered of the highest priority." *Christiansburg Garment Co. v. EEOC*, 434 US 412, 416 (1978), in Chapter 1[C][3], above.

At issue in *Hanrahan* is whether "by reason of obtaining a partial reversal of the trial court's judgment" on appeal, a party has "prevailed" within the meaning of § 1988. What is the pertinent statutory text? Does the statutory text answer the question the Court must decide? Are any of the canons of interpretation helpful in answering the interpretive question?

What are the strongest textual arguments for the conclusion the Court reaches — that such a party is not a "prevailing party" under § 1988? In ordinary usage, is such an appeal an "action or *proceeding* to *enforce* a provision of [the civil rights laws]" (emphasis added)? Do at least partially successful appeals help "enforce" substantive laws? What are the strongest textual arguments for the conclusion reached by the court of appeals below — that a party who prevails on an interlocutory appeal is a prevailing party under § 1988? Note that costs are typically awarded at the conclusion of a case in the district court, and that the party who wins an appeal is usually entitled to recover costs such as filing and duplication fees as a matter of course. *See* Fed. R. Civ. P. 54(d)(1); Fed. R. App. P. 39(a). Attorney's fees, however, are not as a general matter included in "costs" unless otherwise provided by law. *See Marek v. Chesney*, 473 U.S. 1 (1985).

What are the strongest arguments based on the purpose of § 1988 (as gleaned from this case and *Christiansburg Garment*, which interpreted the fee-shifting provision in Title VII of the Civil Rights Act of 1962, 42 U.S.C. § 2000e-5(g)(2)(B)) for the conclusion the Court reached? Is limiting awards of attorney's fees to litigants who have established the defendant's liability on the merits consistent with Congress's policy of encouraging private, civil enforcement of the civil rights laws discussed in *Christiansburg Garment*? Are there not many situations where private enforcement will advance the purposes of the civil rights laws without resulting in a judgment against the defendant?

3. **The Court's Reliance on Legislative History.** Rather than relying primarily on § 1988's text or purpose to answer the question presented, the Court turns to the statute's legislative history. The Court relies on two congressional reports, which are included in the documentary supplement to this volume: a report of the Senate Committee on the Judiciary on the Civil Rights Attorney's Fees Act of 1976, S. Rep. No. 94-1011 (June 29, 1976), and a report of the House Committee on the Judiciary on the same act, H.R. Rep. No. 94-1558 (Sept. 15, 1976). Recalling the discussion of the legislative process above, what role would these reports have played in the enactment of the Civil Rights Attorneys' Fees Act? Are they materials that a typical member of the House or Senate would have relied upon in deciding how to vote on the bill? Chief Judge Katzmann's recent monograph notes it is "commonplace for committee reports accompanying proposed legislation to be disseminated to the full chamber so that members [will] have a fuller appreciation of the bills on which they were called to vote. Committee reports are generally circulated at least two days before legislation is considered on the floor." ROBERT A. KATZMANN, JUDGING STATUTES 20 (2014).

Based on its review of House and Senate Judiciary Committee reports, the Court acknowledges that fees may be awarded under § 1988 before the entry of final judgment or *pendente lite*. The Court's rejection of the fee award in *Hanrahan* turns on the fact that, in the Court's judgment, the plaintiff's successful interlocutory appeal did not affect the "substantial rights of the parties."

This standard appeared in the House Judiciary Committee Report, which quoted a footnote from *Bradley v. Richmond School Board*, 416 U.S. 696 (1974). In relevant part, the *Bradley* footnote read: "Without wishing affirmatively to construe the statute in detail in the absence of consideration of the issue by the lower courts, we venture to say only that the entry of any order that determines substantial rights of the parties may be an appropriate occasion upon which to consider the propriety of an award of counsel fees in school desegregation cases." *Id.* at 723 n.28.

Do the materials quoted by the Court show that a majority of Congress in fact intended "to permit such an interlocutory award *only* to a party who has established his entitlement to some relief on the merits of his claims, either in the trial court or on appeal?" (emphasis added). More to the point, do those materials show that the Committee members or Congress as a whole had *any* intention with respect to interlocutory matters where the plaintiff prevailed but had yet to establish the defendant's liability on the merits?

Is the Court correct that the successful prosecution of an interlocutory appeal that, in Justice Marshall's phrase, "breathes new life into an otherwise dead lawsuit" does not affect the "substantial rights" of the parties? The Court maintains that "[a]s a practical matter [the plaintiffs] are in a position no different from that they would have occupied if they had simply defeated the defendants' motion for a directed verdict in the trial court." Is this assertion correct? If you were representing the plaintiffs and negotiating a settlement, would you rather be in the position of having (a) just defeated a motion for a directed verdict, or (b) having just won an interlocutory appeal that revived a dead lawsuit?

4. **Uses of Legislative History.** Why does the Court believe that the House and Senate Judiciary Committee reports are probative of § 1988's meaning? Consider several possibilities:

First, some jurists and commentators believe that in interpreting a statute, a court ideally acts as an *agent* of the legislature. The court must faithfully carry out Congress' commands, such as a subordinate employee carries out the commands of her supervisor. "[T]he function of the courts" on this account "is to construe the language so as to give effect to the intent of Congress." *United States v. American Trucking Ass'n*, 310 U.S. 534, 542 (1940). "[O]nce the legislature has formulated public policy," the courts "must carry out the defined policy and disregard their own determination of what the public good demands." *United States v. Atlantic Mut. Ins. Co.*, 343 U.S. 236, 245 (1952). Because legislative history provides evidence of what Congress intended to accomplish in enacting a statute, it is the best evidence of Congress' wishes, and thus should be consulted to ensure that the agent (court) performs its duties faithfully.

Second, legislative history can supply information about the context in which a statute was adopted. In doing so, it can help courts understand "specialized meanings of terms or phrases in a statute which were previously understood by the community of specialists (or others) particularly interested in the statute's enactment." Stephen Breyer, *On the Uses of Legislative History in Interpreting Statutes*, 65 S. Cal. L. Rev. 845, 853 (1992).

Third, legislative history may be used to help understand the purpose of a statute. Then-Judge Breyer noted:

> Sometimes [a court] can simply look to the surrounding language in the statute or to the entire statutory scheme and ask, "Given this statutory background, what would a reasonable human being intend this specific language to accomplish?" Often this question has only one good answer, but sometimes the surrounding statutory language and the "reasonable human purpose" test cannot answer the question. In such situations, legislative history may provide a clear and helpful resolution.

Id. at 853–54.

Fourth, legislative history can be used to guide the choice among interpretations of a politically controversial statute. Where a statute is susceptible to multiple interpretations that are equally compatible with its text and purpose, and equally supported by canons of interpretation, legislative history can be used as a tie-breaker to resolve the interpretative question. Use of legislative history in this way has the arguable advantage of allowing courts to avoid the appearance of partisanship, and to resolve the interpretive question in the manner that appears most consistent with the will of democratically legitimate representatives of the people. *See id.* at 858–60.

Which of these theories is at work in *Hanrahan*?

5. **The "Hierarchy" of Legislative History.** As the discussion of the legislative process above describes, a large amount of material may be generated during the process that leads to a bill's ultimate enactment as a law. Congress as a whole does not consider all of this material, nor does each and every piece of internal legislative history necessarily reflect the reasons that the statute was enacted in a particular form or the intentions of the majority of the House or Senate voting for a bill. Rather, some materials, such as conference committee reports, are predictably considered by a large number of congresspersons, while others, such as statements made to an empty chamber in the middle of the night, or inserted without publicity into the Congressional Record, are considered by none. *See* Abner J. Mikva, *Reading and Writing Statutes*, 28 S. Tex. L. Rev. 185 (1986) (describing speech made by then-representative Mikva to a mostly empty House that was subsequently cited as evidence of the Racketeer Influence and Corrupt Organization Act's breadth).

Courts and commentators who look to legislative history as evidence of Congress's intent have suggested there exists an implied hierarchy of legislative history. This hierarchy captures the likelihood that a given item of legislative history reflects

Congress's intent (or more precisely, the intent of those members necessary for the bill's passage). The standard account organizes legislative history as follows:

- The most reliable evidence of congressional intent is the text of a bill emerging from the conference committee and the statements of the managers accompanying the bill (collectively, the "conference report").

- The next most reliable evidence of congressional intent is the text of the bill reported out by the House and Senate Committees with primary jurisdiction over a bill and accompanying report of the relevant committee, with particular focus on the bill that becomes law.

- The next most reliable evidence of congressional intent is statements by members of Congress who were sponsors and managers during floor debates or committee hearings, especially statements offered to explain their position on proposed amendments to the bill.

- "Statements by Members not associated with sponsorship or committee consideration of a bill are accorded little weight and statements by bill opponents generally are discounted or considered unreliable."[32]

- Finally, post-enactment statements are generally given littleweight. See Note 10 following *TVA v. Hill*, in Section [B][1][a], below.

Where in this hierarchy do the legislative materials relied on in *Hanrahan* fall? Those relied on in *Cline* fall? *Holy Trinity*? Considering all three cases, does the hierarchy of legislative history identify materials that accurately reflect congressional intent?

Is legislative history relevant only because it reveals Congress's intentions? Or does it also inform interpretation by shedding light on the reasons a statute was enacted in a particular form? If the objective is to understand how a statute would be understood as an act of communication, what types of evidence should interpreters consult? *See generally* Ryan Doerfler, *Who Cares How Congress Really Works?*, 66 DUKE L.J. 979 (2017).

Note on the Textualist Critique of Legislative History

Beginning with *Holy Trinity* and accelerating in the 1930s foreword, courts and lawyers began to place increasing reliance on legislative history when resolving questions of statutory interpretation. Particularly in briefs filed by the federal government, arguments about the meaning of a statute often set forth a lengthy history of the statute's evolution in Congress, including its progress through the House and Senate, the views of committees that worked on it, and the views of individual Senators and Representatives as expressed in floor debates and other proceedings. The fact that a committee, senator, or representative supported a litigant's interpretation of a statute was considered to be a powerful argument in favor of the litigant's interpretation. *See generally*

---

32. George A. Costello, *Average Voting Members and Other "Benign Fictions": The Relative Reliability of Committee Reports, Floor Debates, and Other Sources of Legislative History*, 1990 DUKE L.J. 39, 41–42.

Nicholas R. Parrillo, *Leviathan and Interpretive Revolution: The Administrative State, the Judiciary, and the Rise of Legislative History, 1890–1950*, 123 Yale L.J. 266, 287–300 (2013).

Beginning in the 1980s, a group of judges and scholars led by Justice Scalia began to advance a broad-ranging attack on the use of legislative history to interpret statutes. This "textualist" critique involves four central claims.

1. *Legislative history is not law.* Textualists charge that use of legislative history to determine statutory meaning is *illegitimate*, because committee reports, floor debates, and other materials produced by Congress before a law is enacted are not law under the Constitution. Unlike duly enacted laws, legislative materials are not passed in identical form by the House and Senate and presented to the President for signature or veto. According to textualists, these materials are not law under the Article I, Section 7 process and their use to ascertain a statute's meaning enables members of Congress to circumvent the Constitution's process for making law.

Defenders of legislative history respond that they do not give legislative materials the force of law, but merely consult it as evidence of what a statute means. Communications from committee chairs, floor managers, and party leaders "can provide reliable signals to the whole chamber" regarding the meaning of legislation. Moreover, "members and their staffs, who well understand that maintaining credibility with colleagues is essential to effective legislating, have every incentive to represent accurately the meaning of proposed statutes to colleagues, as written and discussed in legislative history." Robert A Katzmann, Judging Statutes 49 (2014).

2. *Legislative history reflects the views of fewer than all or even a majority of legislators.* Textualists further charge that, even if the use of legislative history is legitimate, it rarely captures the intentions of Congress as a whole. Congress consists of 100 Senators and 435 Representatives, and there is no guaranty that a given committee report or floor statement captures the way that Congress *as a whole* understands a bill. As expressed by Kenneth Shepsle, "Congress is a 'They,' not an 'It.'" *See generally* Kenneth A. Shepsle, *Congress is a "They," Not an "It":Legislative Intent as Oxymoron*, 12 Int'l Rev. L. & Econ. 239, 239 (1992).

Furthermore, as courts place greater reliance on legislative history, members of Congress and lobbyists aligned with them realize they can shape judicial interpretations of statutes by strategically inserting material into the legislative record that did not reflect Congress's intentions. Senator John Danforth famously stated: "It is very common for members of the Senate to try to affect the way in which a court will interpret a statute by putting things into the Congressional Record . . . . I remember one night literally following one of my colleagues around the floor of the Senate for fear that he would slip something into the Congressional Record, and I would have to slip [in] something else." Joan Biscupic, *Skirmish over Spin*, Cong. Q., Nov. 2, 1991, at 3204, 3204.

While acknowledging that some statements made prior to the enactment of a statement are not probative of Congress's general intentions, defenders of legislative history stress that certain communications are good evidence of what Congress intended to accomplish in enacting a law. Under the House and Senate's practices, conference reports, committee reports, and statements by floor managers are considered to be authoritative statements of a statute's objectives and legal effect. *See* KATZMANN, JUDGING STATUTES, *supra*, at 26–27. Thus, a court sensitive to the pathways of Congress can separate true legislative history from that inserted to bias later interpretations.

3. *Legislative history promotes sloppy drafting.* If courts turn to legislative history to resolve interpretative questions, the argument goes, there is no reason for members of Congress to take care in drafting statutory language, or specify the details of how a statute will operate. Congress can instead enact poorly drafted statutes and rely on courts to figure out what it "intended" to accomplish, perhaps by relying on a committee report that was never reviewed by a majority of Congress.

Defenders of legislative history again concede that there is some truth to the textualist critique. But they note that statutes will always contain ambiguities and blind spots, no matter how diligent Congress is when drafting them. Moreover, some ambiguity is beneficial insofar as it helps difficult legislation obtain passage. *See* KATZMANN, *supra*, at 47 ("[I]t may be that the sponsors were unable or deliberately chose not to craft legislation that was both precise and enactable. The language may be imprecise to facilitate the bill's passage, such that even competing interests can find language in the bill that supports their positions.").

4. *Legislative history is a waste of resources.* Finally, textualists charge that use of legislative history is a waste of resources. Reconstructing how a statute came to be written a particular way is a time-consuming endeavor, one that privileges the government and litigants who are able to employ attorneys that work as lobbyists, and one that many judges and lawyers, who are unfamiliar with the details of how Congress functions, cannot reliably perform.

To what extent does the decision in *Hanrahan* exemplify the problems with judicial reliance on legislative history highlighted by textualists? Does the Court treat the reports of the House and Senate Judiciary Committees as law? Are those reports good evidence of what Congress as a whole intended to accomplish in the Civil Rights Attorneys Fees Act of 1976? Did the Court's reliance on those reports encourage sloppy drafting? Did it require the Court to undertake a herculean research effort? As between the critics of legislative history and its defenders, who is more persuasive as a general matter?

2. Recurring Problems of Statutory Interpretation

The cases in the preceding section all involve the interpretation and application of unclear or ambiguous statutory terms: "in connection with litigation," "labor or service," "discrimination because of an individual's age," etc. But while courts and other statutory interpreters are often called upon to explain the meaning of unclear and ambiguous terms, Congress's use of such terms is only one of many reasons why the meaning of a statute may be uncertain. The cases below present six common scenarios that represent recurring problems of statutory interpretation.

a. Government-Wide Statutes

Consistent with the model of the federal government as an interstitial regulator, much federal legislation works in a discrete subject area and affects the work of a small number of administrative agencies. Other statutes, such as the National Environmental Policy Act, Pub. L. No. 91-190, 83 Stat. 852 (1969), and Religious Freedom Restoration Act of 1993, Pub. L. No. 103-141, 107 Stat. 1488, establish standards for the entire federal government. When Congress enacts such a "government-wide" statute, determining how the statute applies to the diverse activities of hundreds of federal agencies can be challenging.

Tennessee Valley Authority v. Hill
437 U.S. 153 (1978)

Mr. Chief Justice Burger delivered the opinion of the Court.

The questions presented in this case are (a) whether the Endangered Species Act of 1973 requires a court to enjoin the operation of a virtually completed federal dam — which had been authorized prior to 1973 — when, pursuant to authority vested in him by Congress, the Secretary of the Interior has determined that operation of the dam would eradicate an endangered species; and (b) whether continued congressional appropriations for the dam after 1973 constituted an implied repeal of the Endangered Species Act, at least as to the particular dam.

I

The Tellico Dam has never opened despite the fact that construction has been virtually completed and the dam is essentially ready for operation. Although Congress has appropriated monies for Tellico every year since 1967, progress was delayed, and ultimately stopped, by a tangle of lawsuits and administrative proceedings. After unsuccessfully urging [the Tennessee Valley Authority (TVA)] to consider alternatives to damming the Little Tennessee [River], local citizens and national conservation groups brought suit in the District Court, claiming that the project did not conform to the requirements of the National Environmental Policy Act of 1969 (NEPA), 83 Stat. 852, 42 U.S.C. § 4321 et seq. After finding TVA to be in violation of NEPA, the District Court enjoined the dam's completion pending the filing of an appropriate environmental impact statement. The injunction remained in effect until late 1973, when the District Court concluded that TVA's final environmental impact statement for Tellico was in compliance with the law.[5]

A few months prior to the District Court's decision dissolving the NEPA injunction, a discovery was made in the waters of the Little Tennessee which would profoundly affect the Tellico Project. Exploring the area around Coytee Springs, which is

---

5. The NEPA injunction was in effect some 21 months; when it was entered TVA had spent some $29 million on the project. Most of these funds have gone to purchase land, construct the concrete portions of the dam, and build a four-lane steel-span bridge to carry a state highway over the proposed reservoir.

about seven miles from the mouth of the river, a University of Tennessee ichthyologist, Dr. David A. Etnier, found a previously unknown species of perch, the snail darter, or *Percina (Imostoma) tanasi*. This three-inch, tannish-colored fish, whose numbers are estimated to be in the range of 10,000 to 15,000, would soon engage the attention of environmentalists, the TVA, the Department of the Interior, the Congress of the United States, and ultimately the federal courts, as a new and additional basis to halt construction of the dam.

Until recently the finding of a new species of animal life would hardly generate a cause celebre. This is particularly so in the case of darters, of which there are approximately 130 known species, 8 to 10 of these having been identified only in the last five years.[7] The moving force behind the snail darter's sudden fame came some four months after its discovery, when the Congress passed the Endangered Species Act of 1973 (Act), 87 Stat. 884, 16 U.S.C. § 1531 et seq. (1976 ed.). This legislation, among other things, authorizes the Secretary of the Interior to declare species of animal life "endangered"[8] and to identify the "critical habitat"[9] of these creatures. When a species or its habitat is so listed, the following portion of the Act—relevant here—becomes effective:

> "The Secretary [of the Interior] shall review other programs administered by him and utilize such programs in furtherance of the purposes of this chapter. All other Federal departments and agencies shall, in consultation with and with the assistance of the Secretary, utilize their authorities in furtherance of the purposes of this chapter by carrying out programs for the conservation of endangered species and threatened species listed pursuant to section 1533 of this title and *by taking such action necessary to insure that actions authorized, funded, or carried out by them do not jeopardize the continued existence of such endangered species and threatened species or result in the destruction or modification of habitat of such species* which is determined

---

7. In Tennessee alone there are 85 to 90 species of darters, of which upward to 45 live in the Tennessee River system. New species of darters are being constantly discovered and classified—at the rate of about one per year. This is a difficult task for even trained ichthyologists since species of darters are often hard to differentiate from one another.

8. An "endangered species" is defined by the Act to mean "any species which is in danger of extinction throughout all or a significant portion of its range other than a species of the Class Insecta determined by the Secretary to constitute a pest whose protection under the provisions of this chapter would present an overwhelming and overriding risk to man." 16 U.S.C. § 1532(4) (1976 ed.) . . . .

9. The Act does not define "critical habitat," but the Secretary of the Interior has administratively construed the term:

> "'Critical habitat' means any air, land, or water area (exclusive of those existing man-made structures or settlements which are not necessary to the survival and recovery of a listed species) and constituent elements thereof, the loss of which would appreciably decrease the likelihood of the survival and recovery of a listed species or a distinct segment of its population. The constituent elements of critical habitat include, but are not limited to: physical structures and topography, biota, climate, human activity, and the quality and chemical content of land, water, and air. Critical habitat may represent any portion of the present habitat of a listed species and may include additional areas for reasonable population expansion." 43 Fed. Reg. 874 (1978) (to be codified as 50 CFR § 402.02).

by the Secretary, after consultation as appropriate with the affected States, to be critical." 16 U.S.C. § 1536 (1976 ed.) (emphasis added).

In January 1975, the respondents in this case[10] and others petitioned the Secretary of the Interior[11] to list the snail darter as an endangered species. After receiving comments from various interested parties, including TVA and the State of Tennessee, the Secretary formally listed the snail darter as an endangered species on October 8, 1975. 40 Fed. Reg. 47505–47506; see 50 CFR § 17.11(i) (1976). In so acting, it was noted that "the snail darter is a living entity which is genetically distinct and reproductively isolated from other fishes." 40 Fed. Reg. 47505. More important for the purposes of this case, the Secretary determined that the snail darter apparently lives only in that portion of the Little Tennessee River which would be completely inundated by the reservoir created as a consequence of the Tellico Dam's completion.***

Subsequent to this determination, the Secretary declared the area of the Little Tennessee which would be affected by the Tellico Dam to be the "critical habitat" of the snail darter. 41 Fed. Reg. 13926–13928 (1976) (to be codified as 50 CFR § 17.81). Using these determinations as a predicate, and notwithstanding the near completion of the dam, the Secretary declared that pursuant to § 7 of the Act, "all Federal agencies must take such action as is necessary to insure that actions authorized, funded, or carried out by them do not result in the destruction or modification of this critical habitat area." 41 Fed. Reg. 13928 (1976) (to be codified as 50 CFR § 17.81(b)). This notice, of course, was pointedly directed at TVA and clearly aimed at halting completion or operation of the dam.***

Meanwhile, Congress had also become involved in the fate of the snail darter. Appearing before a Subcommittee of the House Committee on Appropriations in April 1975 — some seven months before the snail darter was listed as endangered — TVA representatives described the discovery of the fish and the relevance of the Endangered Species Act to the Tellico Project. Hearings on Public Works for Water and Power Development and Energy Research Appropriation Bill, 1976, before a Subcommittee of the House Committee on Appropriations, 94th Cong., 1st Sess., pt. 7, pp. 466–467 (1975); Hearings on H. R. 8122, Public Works for Water and Power Development and Energy Research Appropriations for Fiscal Year 1976, before a Subcommittee of the Senate Committee on Appropriations, 94th Cong., 1st Sess., pt. 4, pp. 3775–3777 (1975). At that time TVA presented a position which it would advance in successive forums thereafter, namely, that the Act did not prohibit the completion of a project authorized, funded, and substantially constructed before the Act was passed. TVA also described its efforts to transplant the snail darter, but contended that the dam should be finished regardless of the experiment's success. Thereafter, the House Committee

10. Respondents are a regional association of biological scientists, a Tennessee conservation group, and individuals who are citizens or users of the Little Tennessee Valley area which would be affected by the Tellico Project.

11. The Act authorizes "interested [persons]" to petition the Secretary of the Interior to list a species as endangered. 16 U.S.C. § 1533(c)(2) (1976 ed.); see 5 U.S.C. § 553(e) (1976 ed.).

on Appropriations, in its June 20, 1975, Report, stated the following in the course of recommending that an additional $29 million be appropriated for Tellico:

> "The *Committee* directs that the project, for which an environmental impact statement has been completed and provided the Committee, should be completed as promptly as possible . . . ." H.R. Rep. No. 94-319, p. 76 (1975). (Emphasis added.)

Congress then approved the TVA general budget, which contained funds for continued construction of The Tellico Project.[14] In December 1975, one month after the snail darter was declared an endangered species, the President signed the bill into law. Public Works for Water and Power Development and Energy Research Appropriation Act, 1976, 89 Stat. 1035, 1047.

In February 1976, pursuant to § 11(g) of the Endangered Species Act, 87 Stat. 900, 16 U.S.C. § 1540(g) (1976 ed.), respondents filed the case now under review, seeking to enjoin completion of the dam and impoundment of the reservoir on the ground that those actions would violate the Act by directly causing the extinction of the species *Percina (Imostoma) tanasi.* The District Court denied respondents' request for a preliminary injunction and set the matter for trial. Shortly thereafter the House and Senate held appropriations hearings which would include discussions of the Tellico budget.

At these hearings, TVA Chairman Wagner reiterated the agency's position that the Act did not apply to a project which was over 50% finished by the time the Act became effective and some 70% to 80% complete when the snail darter was officially listed as endangered. It also notified the Committees of the recently filed lawsuit's status and reported that TVA's efforts to transplant the snail darter had "been very encouraging." Hearings on Public Works for Water and Power Development and Energy Research Appropriation Bill, 1977, before a Subcommittee of the House Committee on Appropriations, 94th Cong., 2d Sess., pt. 5, pp. 261–262 (1976); Hearings on Public Works for Water and Power Development and Energy Research Appropriations for Fiscal Year 1977, before a Subcommittee of the Senate Committee on Appropriations, 94th Cong., 2d Sess., pt. 4, pp. 3096–3099 (1976).

Trial was held in the District Court on April 29 and 30, 1976, and on May 25, 1976, the court entered its memorandum opinion and order denying respondents their requested relief and dismissing the complaint. The District Court found that closure of the dam and the consequent impoundment of the reservoir would "result in the adverse modification, if not complete destruction, of the snail darter's critical habitat," making it "highly probable" that "the continued existence of the snail darter" would be "[jeopardized]." Despite these findings, the District Court declined to embrace the plaintiffs' position on the merits: that once a federal project was shown

---

14. TVA projects generally are authorized by the Authority itself and are funded—without the need for specific congressional authorization—from lump-sum appropriations provided in yearly budget grants. See 16 U.S.C. §§ 831c(j) and 831z (1976 ed.).

to jeopardize an endangered species, a court of equity is compelled to issue an injunction restraining violation of the Endangered Species Act.

In reaching this result, the District Court stressed that the entire project was then about 80% complete and, based on available evidence, "there [were] no alternatives to impoundment of the reservoir, short of scrapping the entire project." The District Court also found that if the Tellico Project was permanently enjoined, "some $53 million would be lost in nonrecoverable obligations," meaning that a large portion of the $78 million already expended would be wasted. The court also noted that the Endangered Species Act of 1973 was passed some seven years after construction on the dam commenced and that Congress had continued appropriations for Tellico, with full awareness of the snail darter problem. Assessing these various factors, the District Court concluded:

> "At some point in time a federal project becomes so near completion and so incapable of modification that a court of equity should not apply a statute enacted long after inception of the project to produce an unreasonable result . . . . Where there has been an irreversible and irretrievable commitment of resources by Congress to a project over a span of almost a decade, the Court should proceed with a great deal of circumspection."

To accept the plaintiffs' position, the District Court argued, would inexorably lead to what it characterized as the absurd result of requiring "a court to halt impoundment of water behind a fully completed dam if an endangered species were discovered in the river on the day before such impoundment was scheduled to take place. We cannot conceive that Congress intended such a result."

Less than a month after the District Court decision, the Senate and House Appropriations Committees recommended the full budget request of $9 million for continued work on Tellico. See S. Rep. No. 94-960, p. 96 (1976); H.R. Rep. No. 94-1223, p. 83 (1976). In its Report accompanying the appropriations bill, the Senate Committee stated:

> "During subcommittee hearings, TVA was questioned about the relationship between the Tellico project's completion and the November 1975 listing of the snail darter (a small 3-inch fish which was discovered in 1973) as an endangered species under the Endangered Species Act. TVA informed the Committee that it was continuing its efforts to preserve the darter, while working towards the scheduled 1977 completion date. TVA repeated its view that the Endangered Species Act did not prevent the completion of the Tellico project, which has been under construction for nearly a decade. The subcommittee brought this matter, as well as the recent U.S. District Court's decision upholding TVA's decision to complete the project, to the attention of the full Committee. *The Committee does not view* the Endangered Species Act as prohibiting the completion of the Tellico project at its advanced stage and directs that this project be completed as promptly as possible in the public interest." S. Rep. No. 94-960, *supra*, at 96. (Emphasis added.)

On June 29, 1976, both Houses of Congress passed TVA's general budget, which included funds for Tellico; the President signed the bill on July 12, 1976. Public Works for Water and Power Development and Energy Research Appropriation Act, 1977, 90 Stat. 889, 899.

Thereafter, in the Court of Appeals, respondents argued that the District Court had abused its discretion by not issuing an injunction in the face of "a blatant statutory violation." The Court of Appeals agreed, and on January 31, 1977, it reversed, remanding "with instructions that a permanent injunction issue halting all activities incident to the Tellico Project which may destroy or modify the critical habitat of the snail darter." The Court of Appeals directed that the injunction "remain in effect until Congress, by appropriate legislation, exempts Tellico from compliance with the Act or the snail darter has been deleted from the list of endangered species or its critical habitat materially redefined."***

Following the issuance of the permanent injunction, members of TVA's Board of Directors appeared before Subcommittees of the House and Senate Appropriations Committees to testify in support of continued appropriations for Tellico. The Subcommittees were apprised of all aspects of Tellico's status, including the Court of Appeals' decision. TVA reported that the dam stood "ready for the gates to be closed and the reservoir filled," Hearings on Public Works for Water and Power Development and Energy Research Appropriation Bill, 1978, before a Subcommittee of the House Committee on Appropriations, 95th Cong., 1st Sess., pt. 4, p. 234 (1977), and requested funds for completion of certain ancillary parts of the project, such as public use areas, roads, and bridges. As to the snail darter itself, TVA commented optimistically on its transplantation efforts, expressing the opinion that the relocated fish were "doing well and [had] reproduced."

Both Appropriations Committees subsequently recommended the full amount requested for completion of the Tellico Project. In its June 2, 1977, Report, the House Appropriations Committee stated:

> "It is *the Committee's view* that the Endangered Species Act was not intended to halt projects such as these in their advanced stage of completion, and [the Committee] strongly recommends that these projects not be stopped because of misuse of the Act." H.R. Rep. No. 95-379, p. 104. (Emphasis added.).

As a solution to the problem, the House Committee advised that TVA should cooperate with the Department of the Interior "to relocate the endangered species to another suitable habitat so as to permit the project to proceed as rapidly as possible." Toward this end, the Committee recommended a special appropriation of $2 million to facilitate relocation of the snail darter and other endangered species which threatened to delay or stop TVA projects. Much the same occurred on the Senate side[.]*** TVA's budget, including funds for completion of Tellico and relocation of the snail darter, passed both Houses of Congress and was signed into law on August 7, 1977. Public Works for Water and Power Development and Energy Research Appropriation Act, 1978, 91 Stat. 797.***

II

We begin with the premise that operation of the Tellico Dam will either eradicate the known population of snail darters or destroy their critical habitat. Petitioner does not now seriously dispute this fact. In any event, under § 4(a)(1) of the Act, 87 Stat. 886, 16 U.S.C. § 1533(a)(1) (1976 ed.), the Secretary of the Interior is vested with exclusive authority to determine whether a species such as the snail darter is "endangered" or "threatened" and to ascertain the factors which have led to such a precarious existence. By § 4(d) Congress has authorized—indeed commanded—the Secretary to "issue such regulations as he deems necessary and advisable to provide for the conservation of such species." 16 U.S.C. § 1533(d) (1976 ed.). As we have seen, the Secretary promulgated regulations which declared the snail darter an endangered species whose critical habitat would be destroyed by creation of the Tellico Reservoir. Doubtless petitioner would prefer not to have these regulations on the books, but there is no suggestion that the Secretary exceeded his authority or abused his discretion in issuing the regulations. Indeed, no judicial review of the Secretary's determinations has ever been sought and hence the validity of his actions are not open to review in this Court.***

One would be hard pressed to find a statutory provision whose terms were any plainer than those in § 7 of the Endangered Species Act. Its very words affirmatively command all federal agencies "to *insure* that actions *authorized, funded, or carried out* by them do not *jeopardize* the continued existence" of an endangered species or "*result in the destruction or modification of habitat of such species . . . .*" 16 U.S.C. § 1536 (1976 ed.). (Emphasis added.) This language admits of no exception. Nonetheless, petitioner urges, as do the dissenters, that the Act cannot reasonably be interpreted as applying to a federal project which was well under way when Congress passed the Endangered Species Act of 1973. To sustain that position, however, we would be forced to ignore the ordinary meaning of plain language. It has not been shown, for example, how TVA can close the gates of the Tellico Dam without "carrying out" an action that has been "authorized" and "funded" by a federal agency. Nor can we understand how such action will "insure" that the snail darter's habitat is not disrupted.[18] Accepting the Secretary's determinations, as we must, it is clear that TVA's proposed operation of the dam will have precisely the opposite effect, namely the eradication of an endangered species.

---

18. In dissent, Mr. Justice Powell argues that the meaning of "actions" in § 7 is "far from 'plain,'" and that "it seems evident that the 'actions' referred to are not all actions that an agency can ever take, but rather actions that the agency is deciding whether to authorize, to fund, or to carry out."*** Aside from being unexplicated, the dissent's reading of § 7 is flawed on several counts. First, under its view, the words "or carry out" in § 7 would be superfluous since all prospective actions of an agency remain to be "authorized" or "funded." Second, the dissent's position logically means that an agency would be obligated to comply with § 7 only when a project is in the planning stage. But if Congress had meant to so limit the Act, it surely would have used words to that effect, as it did in the National Environmental Policy Act, 42 U.S.C. §§ 4332(2)(A), (C).

Concededly, this view of the Act will produce results requiring the sacrifice of the anticipated benefits of the project and of many millions of dollars in public funds.[19] But examination of the language, history, and structure of the legislation under review here indicates beyond doubt that Congress intended endangered species to be afforded the highest of priorities.

When Congress passed the Act in 1973, it was not legislating on a clean slate. The first major congressional concern for the preservation of the endangered species had come with passage of the Endangered Species Act of 1966, 80 Stat. 926, repealed, 87 Stat. 903. In that legislation Congress gave the Secretary power to identify "the names of the species of native fish and wildlife found to be threatened with extinction," § 1(c), 80 Stat. 926, as well as authorization to purchase land for the conservation, protection, restoration, and propagation of "selected species" of "native fish and wildlife" threatened with extinction. §§ 2(a)–(c), 80 Stat. 926–927. Declaring the preservation of endangered species a national policy, the 1966 Act directed all federal agencies both to protect these species and "insofar as is practicable and consistent with [their] primary purposes," § 1(b), 80 Stat. 926, "preserve the habitats of such threatened species on lands under their jurisdiction."*** The 1966 statute was not a sweeping prohibition on the taking of endangered species, however, except on federal lands, § 4(c), 80 Stat. 928, and even in those federal areas the Secretary was authorized to allow the hunting and fishing of endangered species. § 4(d)(1), 80 Stat. 928.

In 1969 Congress enacted the Endangered Species Conservation Act, 83 Stat. 275, repealed, 87 Stat. 903, which continued the provisions of the 1966 Act while at the same time broadening federal involvement in the preservation of endangered species. Under the 1969 legislation, the Secretary was empowered to list species "threatened with worldwide extinction," § 3(a), 83 Stat. 275; in addition, the importation of any species so recognized into the United States was prohibited. § 2, 83 Stat. 275. An indirect approach to the taking of endangered species was also adopted in the Conservation Act by way of a ban on the transportation and sale of wildlife taken in violation of any federal, state, or foreign law. §§ 7(a)–(b), 83 Stat. 279.

Despite the fact that the 1966 and 1969 legislation represented "the most comprehensive of its type to be enacted by any nation" up to that time, Congress was soon persuaded that a more expansive approach was needed if the newly declared national policy of preserving endangered species was to be realized. By 1973, when Congress held hearings on what would later become the Endangered Species Act of 1973, it was informed that species were still being lost at the rate of about one per year, 1973 House Hearings 306 (statement of Stephen R. Seater, for Defenders of Wildlife), and "the pace of disappearance of species" appeared to be "accelerating." H.R. Rep. No. 93-412, p. 4 (1973). Moreover, Congress was also told that the primary cause of this trend was something other than the normal process of natural selection:

---

19. The District Court determined that failure to complete the Tellico Dam would result in the loss of some $53 million in nonrecoverable obligations . . . . Respondents dispute this figure, and point to a recent study by the General Accounting Office, which suggests that the figure could be considerably less. . . .

"[Man] and his technology has [sic] continued at an ever-increasing rate to disrupt the natural ecosystem. This has resulted in a dramatic rise in the number and severity of the threats faced by the world's wildlife. The truth in this is apparent when one realizes that half of the recorded extinctions of mammals over the past 2,000 years have occurred in the most recent 50-year period." 1973 House Hearings 202 (statement of Assistant Secretary of the Interior).***

The legislative proceedings in 1973 are, in fact, replete with expressions of concern over the risk that might lie in the loss of any endangered species.***

In shaping legislation to deal with the problem thus presented, Congress started from the finding that "[the] two major causes of extinction are hunting and destruction of natural habitat." S. Rep. No. 93-307, p. 2 (1973).***

As it was finally passed, the Endangered Species Act of 1973 represented the most comprehensive legislation for the preservation of endangered species ever enacted by any nation. Its stated purposes were "to provide a means whereby the ecosystems upon which endangered species and threatened species depend may be conserved," and "to provide a program for the conservation of such . . . species . . . ." 16 U.S.C. § 1531(b) (1976 ed.). In furtherance of these goals, Congress expressly stated in § 2(c) that "all Federal departments and agencies shall seek to conserve endangered species and threatened species . . . ." 16 U.S.C. § 1531(c) (1976 ed.).*** Lest there be any ambiguity as to the meaning of this statutory directive, the Act specifically defined "conserve" as meaning "to use and the use of *all methods and procedures which are necessary* to bring *any endangered species* or threatened species to the point at which the measures provided pursuant to this chapter are no longer necessary." § 1532(2). (Emphasis added.) Aside from § 7, other provisions indicated the seriousness with which Congress viewed this issue: Virtually all dealings with endangered species, including taking, possession, transportation, and sale, were prohibited, 16 U.S.C. § 1538 (1976 ed.), except in extremely narrow circumstances, see § 1539(b). The Secretary was also given extensive power to develop regulations and programs for the preservation of endangered and threatened species. § 1533(d).***

Section 7 of the Act, which of course is relied upon by respondents in this case, provides a particularly good gauge of congressional intent. As we have seen, this provision had its genesis in the Endangered Species Act of 1966, but that legislation qualified the obligation of federal agencies by stating that they should seek to preserve endangered species only "insofar as is practicable and consistent with [their] primary purposes . . . ." Likewise, every bill introduced in 1973 contained a qualification similar to that found in the earlier statutes.***

What is very significant*** is that the final version of the 1973 Act carefully omitted . . . the reservation[] described above. In the bill which the Senate initially approved (S. 1983), however, the version of the current § 7 merely required federal agencies to "carry out such programs *as are practicable* for the protection of species listed . . . ." 27 S. 1983, § 7(a). (Emphasis added.) By way of contrast, the bill that originally passed the House, H.R. 37, contained a provision which was essentially a mirror image of the subsequently passed § 7—indeed all phrases which might have qualified an agency's responsibilities had been omitted from the bill. In explaining the expected impact of this provision in H.R. 37 on federal agencies, the House Committee's Report states:

> "This subsection *requires* the Secretary and the heads of all other Federal departments and agencies to use their authorities in order to carry out programs for the protection of endangered species, and it further requires that those agencies take *the necessary action* that will *not jeopardize* the continuing existence of endangered species or result in the destruction of critical habitat of those species." H.R. Rep. No. 93-412, p. 14 (1973). (Emphasis added.)

Resolution of this difference in statutory language, as well as other variations between the House and Senate bills, was the task of a Conference Committee. See 119 Cong. Rec. 30174–30175, 31183 (1973). The Conference Report, H.R. Conf. Rep. No. 93-740 (1973), basically adopted the Senate bill, S. 1983; but the conferees rejected the Senate version of § 7 and adopted the stringent, mandatory language in H.R. 37. While the Conference Report made no specific reference to this choice of provisions, the House manager of the bill, Representative Dingell, provided an interpretation of what the Conference bill would require, making it clear that the mandatory provisions of § 7 were not casually or inadvertently included:

> "[Section 7] substantially [amplifies] the obligation of [federal agencies] to take steps within their power to carry out the purposes of this act. A recent article ... illustrates the problem which might occur absent this new language in the bill. It appears that the whooping cranes of this country, perhaps the best known of our endangered species, are being threatened by Air Force bombing activities along the gulf coast of Texas. Under existing law, the Secretary of Defense has some discretion as to whether or not he will take the necessary action to see that this threat disappears .... [Once] the bill is enacted, [the Secretary of Defense] would be required to take the proper steps.*** The purposes of the bill included the conservation of the species and of the ecosystems upon which they depend, and every agency of government is committed to see that those purposes are carried out .... [The] agencies of Government can no longer plead that they can do nothing about it. They can, and they must. The law is clear." 119 Cong. Rec. 42913 (1973) ....

It is against this legislative background[29] that we must measure TVA's claim that the Act was not intended to stop operation of a project which, like Tellico Dam, was near completion when an endangered species was discovered in its path. While there is no discussion in the legislative history of precisely this problem, the totality of congressional action makes it abundantly clear that the result we reach today is wholly in accord with both the words of the statute and the intent of Congress. The plain intent

---

29. ***Here it is not necessary to look beyond the words of the statute. We have undertaken such an analysis only to meet MR. JUSTICE POWELL's suggestion that the "absurd" result reached in this case ... is not in accord with congressional intent.

of Congress in enacting this statute was to halt and reverse the trend toward species extinction, whatever the cost. This is reflected not only in the stated policies of the Act, but in literally every section of the statute. All persons, including federal agencies, are specifically instructed not to "take" endangered species, meaning that no one is "to harass, harm, pursue, hunt, shoot, wound, kill, trap, capture, or collect" such life forms. 16 U.S.C. §§ 1532(14), 1538(a)(1)(B) (1976 ed.). Agencies in particular are directed by §§ 2(c) and 3(2) of the Act to "use . . . *all methods* and procedures which are necessary" to preserve endangered species. 16 U.S.C. §§ 1531(c), 1532(2) (1976 ed.) (emphasis added). In addition, the legislative history undergirding § 7 reveals an explicit congressional decision to require agencies to afford first priority to the declared national policy of saving endangered species. The pointed omission of the type of qualifying language previously included in endangered species legislation reveals a conscious decision by Congress to give endangered species priority over the "primary missions" of federal agencies.

Furthermore, it is clear Congress foresaw that § 7 would, on occasion, require agencies to alter ongoing projects in order to fulfill the goals of the Act.*** [An] example is provided by the House Committee Report:

> "Under the authority of [§ 7], the Director of the Park Service would be required *to conform the practices of his agency* to the need for protecting the rapidly dwindling stock of grizzly bears within Yellowstone Park. These bears, which may be endangered, and are undeniably threatened, should at least be protected by supplying them with carcasses from excess elk within the park, *by curtailing the destruction of habitat by clear cutting National Forests surrounding the Park*, and by preventing hunting until their numbers have recovered sufficiently to withstand these pressures." H.R. Rep. No. 93-412, p. 14 (1973). (Emphasis added.)

One might dispute the applicability of th[is] example[] to the Tellico Dam by saying that in this case the burden on the public through the loss of millions of unrecoverable dollars would greatly outweigh the loss of the snail darter.[33] But neither the Endangered Species Act nor Art. III of the Constitution provides federal courts with authority to make such fine utilitarian calculations. On the contrary, the plain language of the Act, buttressed by its legislative history, shows clearly that Congress viewed the value of endangered species as "incalculable." Quite obviously, it would be difficult for a court to balance the loss of a sum certain — even $100 million — against a congressionally declared "incalculable" value, even assuming we had the power to engage in such a weighing process, which we emphatically do not.

---

33. MR. JUSTICE POWELL's dissent places great reliance on *Church of the Holy Trinity v. United States*, 143 U.S. 457, 459 (1892), . . . to support his view of the 1973 Act's legislative history. This Court, however, later explained *Holy Trinity* as applying only in "rare and exceptional circumstances . . . . And there must be something to make plain the intent of Congress that the letter of the statute is not to prevail." *Crooks v. Harrelson*, 282 U.S. 55, 60 (1930). As we have seen from our explication of the structure and history of the 1973 Act, there is nothing to support the assertion that the literal meaning of § 7 should not apply in this case.

In passing the Endangered Species Act of 1973, Congress was also aware of certain instances in which exceptions to the statute's broad sweep would be necessary. Thus, § 10, 16 U.S.C. § 1539 (1976 ed.), creates a number of limited "hardship exemptions," none of which would even remotely apply to the Tellico Project. In fact, there are no exemptions in the Endangered Species Act for federal agencies, meaning that under the maxim *expressio unius est exclusio alterius*, we must presume that these were the only "hardship cases" Congress intended to exempt.

Notwithstanding Congress' expression of intent in 1973, we are urged to find that the continuing appropriations for Tellico Dam constitute an implied repeal of the 1973 Act, at least insofar as it applies to the Tellico Project.*** There is nothing in the appropriations measures, as passed, which states that the Tellico Project was to be completed irrespective of the requirements of the Endangered Species Act. These appropriations, in fact, represented relatively minor components of the lump-sum amounts for the entire TVA budget.[35] To find a repeal of the Endangered Species Act under these circumstances would surely do violence to the "'cardinal rule . . . that repeals by implication are not favored.'"***

The doctrine disfavoring repeals by implication "applies with full vigor when . . . the subsequent legislation is an appropriations measure." This is perhaps an understatement since it would be more accurate to say that the policy applies with even greater force when the claimed repeal rests solely on an Appropriations Act. We recognize that both substantive enactments and appropriations measures are "Acts of Congress," but the latter have the limited and specific purpose of providing funds for authorized programs. When voting on appropriations measures, legislators are entitled to operate under the assumption that the funds will be devoted to purposes which are lawful and not for any purpose forbidden. Without such an assurance, every appropriations measure would be pregnant with prospects of altering substantive legislation, repealing by implication any prior statute which might prohibit the expenditure. Not only would this lead to the absurd result of requiring Members to review exhaustively the background of every authorization before voting on an appropriation, but it would flout the very rules the Congress carefully adopted to avoid this need. House Rule XXI(2), for instance, specifically provides:

> "No appropriation shall be reported in any general appropriation bill, or be in order as an amendment thereto, for any expenditure not previously authorized by law, unless in continuation of appropriations for such public works as are already in progress. *Nor shall any provision in any such bill or amendment thereto changing existing law be in order.*" (Emphasis added.)

---

35. The Appropriations Acts did not themselves identify the projects for which the sums had been appropriated; identification of these projects requires reference to the legislative history.*** Thus, unless a Member scrutinized in detail the Committee proceedings concerning the appropriations, he would have no knowledge of the possible conflict between the continued funding and the Endangered Species Act.

See also Standing Rules of the Senate, Rule 16.4. Thus, to sustain petitioner's position, we would be obliged to assume that Congress meant to repeal pro tanto §7 of the Act by means of a procedure expressly prohibited under the rules of Congress.

Perhaps mindful of the fact that it is "swimming upstream" against a strong current of well-established precedent, TVA argues for an exception to the rule against implied repealers in a circumstance where, as here, Appropriations Committees have expressly stated their "understanding" that the earlier legislation would not prohibit the proposed expenditure. We cannot accept such a proposition. Expressions of committees dealing with requests for appropriations cannot be equated with statutes enacted by Congress, particularly not in the circumstances presented by this case. First, the Appropriations Committees had no jurisdiction over the subject of endangered species, much less did they conduct the type of extensive hearings which preceded passage of the earlier Endangered Species Acts, especially the 1973 Act. We venture to suggest that the House Committee on Merchant Marine and Fisheries and the Senate Committee on Commerce would be somewhat surprised to learn that their careful work on the substantive legislation had been undone by the simple — and brief — insertion of some inconsistent language in Appropriations Committees' Reports.

Second, there is no indication that Congress as a whole was aware of TVA's position, although the Appropriations Committees apparently agreed with petitioner's views. Only recently, in *SEC v. Sloan*, 436 U.S. 103 (1978), we declined to presume general congressional acquiescence in a 34-year-old practice of the Securities and Exchange Commission, despite the fact that the Senate Committee having jurisdiction over the Commission's activities had long expressed approval of the practice.*** A fortiori, we should not assume that petitioner's views — and the Appropriations Committees' acceptance of them — were any better known, especially when the TVA is not the agency with primary responsibility for administering the Endangered Species Act.***

Having determined that there is an irreconcilable conflict between operation of the Tellico Dam and the explicit provisions of §7 of the Endangered Species Act, we must now consider what remedy, if any, is appropriate. It is correct, of course, that a federal judge sitting as a chancellor is not mechanically obligated to grant an injunction for every violation of law. This Court made plain in *Hecht Co. v. Bowles*, 321 U.S. 321, 329 (1944), that "[a] grant of jurisdiction to issue compliance orders hardly suggests an absolute duty to do so under any and all circumstances." As a general matter it may be said that "[since] all or almost all equitable remedies are discretionary, the balancing of equities and hardships is appropriate in almost any case as a guide to the chancellor's discretion." D. Dobbs, Remedies 52 (1973).***

But these principles take a court only so far.*** Once Congress, exercising its delegated powers, has decided the order of priorities in a given area, it is for the Executive to administer the laws and for the courts to enforce them when enforcement is sought. *** Congress has spoken in the plainest of words, making it abundantly clear that the balance has been struck in favor of affording endangered species the highest of priorities, thereby adopting a policy which it described as "institutionalized caution."*** We agree with the Court of Appeals that [a permanent injunction enjoining the completion of the dam should be entered].

MR. JUSTICE POWELL, with whom MR. JUSTICE BLACKMUN joins, dissenting.

The Court today holds that § 7 of the Endangered Species Act requires a federal court, for the purpose of protecting an endangered species or its habitat, to enjoin permanently the operation of any federal project, whether completed or substantially completed. This decision casts a long shadow over the operation of even the most important projects, serving vital needs of society and national defense, whenever it is determined that continued operation would threaten extinction of an endangered species or its habitat.***

***Today the Court, like the Court of Appeals below, adopts a reading of § 7 of the Act that gives it a retroactive effect and disregards 12 years of consistently expressed congressional intent to complete the Tellico Project. With all due respect, I view this result as an extreme example of a literalist construction, not required by the language of the Act and adopted without regard to its manifest purpose. Moreover, it ignores established canons of statutory construction.

A

The starting point in statutory construction is, of course, the language of § 7 itself. I agree that it can be viewed as a textbook example of fuzzy language, which can be read according to the "eye of the beholder." The critical words direct all federal agencies to take "such action [as may be] necessary to insure that actions authorized, funded, or carried out by them do not jeopardize the continued existence of . . . endangered species . . . or result in the destruction or modification of [a critical] habitat of such species . . . ." Respondents—as did the Sixth Circuit—read these words as sweepingly as possible to include all "actions" that any federal agency ever may take with respect to any federal project, whether completed or not.

The Court today embraces this sweeping construction. Under the Court's reasoning, the Act covers every existing federal installation, including great hydroelectric projects and reservoirs, every river and harbor project, and every national defense installation—however essential to the Nation's economic health and safety. The "actions" that an agency would be prohibited from "carrying out" would include the continued operation of such projects or any change necessary to preserve their continued usefulness. The only precondition, according to respondents, to thus destroying the usefulness of even the most important federal project in our country would be a finding by the Secretary of the Interior that a continuation of the project would threaten the survival or critical habitat of a newly discovered species of water spider or amoeba.***

The critical word in § 7 is "actions" and its meaning is far from "plain." It is part of the phrase: "actions authorized, funded or carried out." In terms of planning and executing various activities, it seems evident that the "actions" referred to are not all actions that an agency can ever take, but rather actions that the agency is deciding whether to authorize, to fund, or to carry out. In short, these words reasonably may be read as applying only to *prospective actions, i.e.,* actions with respect to which the agency has reasonable decision-making alternatives still available, actions not yet carried out. At the time respondents brought this lawsuit, the Tellico Project was 80% complete at a cost of more than $78 million. The Court concedes that as of this time and for the purpose of deciding this case, the Tellico Dam Project is "completed" or "virtually completed and the dam is essentially ready for operation." Thus, under a prospective reading of § 7, the action already had been "carried out" in terms of any remaining reasonable decision-making power.

This is a reasonable construction of the language and also is supported by the presumption against construing statutes to give them a retroactive effect. As this Court stated in *United States Fidelity & Guaranty Co. v. United States ex rel. Struthers Wells Co.*, 209 U.S. 306, 314 (1908), the "presumption is very strong that a statute was not meant to act retrospectively, and it ought never to receive such a construction if it is susceptible of any other." This is particularly true where a statute enacts a new regime of regulation. For example, the presumption has been recognized in cases under the National Environmental Policy Act, 42 U.S.C. § 4321 et seq., holding that the requirement of filing an environmental impact statement cannot reasonably be applied to projects substantially completed.*** Similarly under § 7 of the Endangered Species Act, at some stage of a federal project, and certainly where a project has been completed, the agency no longer has a reasonable choice simply to abandon it. When that point is reached, as it was in this case, the presumption against retrospective interpretation is at its strongest. The Court today gives no weight to that presumption.

B

***While the Court's review of the legislative history establishes that Congress intended to require governmental agencies to take endangered species into account in the planning and execution of their programs, there is not even a hint in the legislative history that Congress intended to compel the undoing or abandonment of any project or program later found to threaten a newly discovered species.[17]

If the relevant Committees that considered the Act, and the Members of Congress who voted on it, had been aware that the Act could be used to terminate major federal projects authorized years earlier and nearly completed, or to require the abandonment of essential and long-completed federal installations and edifices, we can be certain

---

17. The Senate sponsor of the bill [that became the ESA] Senator [John V.] Tunney [(D-NY)], apparently thought that the Act was merely precatory and would not withdraw from the agency the final decision on completion of the project:

"[A]s I understand it, after the consultation process took place, the Bureau of Public Roads, or the Corps of Engineers, would not be prohibited from building a road if they deemed it necessary to do so.

"[A]s I read the language, there has to be consultation. However, the Bureau of Public Roads or any other agency would have the final decision as to whether such a road should be built. That is my interpretation of the legislation at any rate." 119 Cong. Rec. 25689–25690 (1973).

that there would have been hearings, testimony, and debate concerning consequences so wasteful, so inimical to purposes previously deemed important, and so likely to arouse public outrage. The absence of any such consideration by the Committees or in the floor debates indicates quite clearly that no one participating in the legislative process considered these consequences as within the intendment of the Act.***

[Justice Rehnquist dissented separately. He argued that in light of the uncertainty over how § 7 applied to the Tellico Dam project, the district court was within its discretion in refusing to enjoin completion of the dam even if the project was covered by § 7.]

Notes and Questions

1. **The Challenge of Government-Wide Legislation.** When Congress, as in the Endangered Species Act, enacts a statute that applies to the entire federal government, it cannot readily address all the programs the statute will affect. As *TVA* illustrates, application of a government-wide statute to a program the statute does not explicitly address can produce results that are surprising—and arguably unintended. A court in this scenario has at least four interpretative options open to it. It can: (a) apply the statute according to its literal terms; (b) consider what Congress intended with respect to the case or kind of case in question; (c) consider what Congress *would have* intended had it explicitly considered the question (so-called "imaginative reconstruction"); or (d) apply other sources of law—statutes, common law, canons of construction, etc.— to explain the application of the government-wide statute.

Which strategy (or strategies) does the Court in *TVA* follow? Which strategy (or strategies) does Justice Powell follow in dissent? What do those choices reflect about the Court's and the dissent's understanding of the judicial role? Under the Court's approach, is a court permitted to use common sense when determining the effect of government-wide legislation? Under the dissent's approach?

2. **The Enactment of the ESA.** The Court's opinion gives a glimpse of the history of and justifications for the modern Endangered Species Act (ESA), which was enacted in 1973. The ESA originated with a 1966 act "for the conservation, protection, and propagation of native species of fish and wildlife," Pub. L. No., 89-669, 80 Stat. 926. The 1966 act authorized the Secretary of the Interior to identify fish and wildlife that were threatened with extinction and to purchase land to conserve threatened species. The act further directed federal agencies "insofar as is practicable and consistent with [their] primary purposes" to "preserve the habitats of such threatened species on lands under their jurisdiction." *Id.* § 1(b), 80 Stat. 926. A 1969 act expanded the geographical coverage of the 1966 act to any species threatened with extinction worldwide, and prohibited the importation of endangered species into the territorial United States. Pub. L. No. 91-135, 83 Stat. 275.

These statutes, however, were perceived by critics to be inadequate to the preservation of endangered species—an objective defended on economic, moral, and aesthetic grounds. A 1969 article describing protests against the fur trade noted that environmental and conservation groups "all agreed that if animals are wantonly destroyed, the ecological balance of the earth will be upset and society will suffer for the lack of even such unendearing creatures as alligators." Angela Taylor, *Fur Coats: Facing Extinction at Conservationists' Hand?*, N.Y. TIMES, Dec. 30, 1969, at 28. The Washington Post editorial board was harsher in its assessment of technology's impact on the environment:

> Our land, air, water and food are so poisoned that no longer is progress our most important product, no longer is better living to be found through chemistry, no longer are the skies friendly, no longer are lead fuel cars the mark of excellence . . . . The deep horror concerning the environment is not that we have ravaged and poisoned our section of the planet—but that we live with the horror so calmly.*** Today America is under siege from its own waste, blind technology and arrogant abuse of Nature; instead of resisting these horrors, we have adjusted—like mule-beasts with a heavier and heavier load.

The Environment: Clean Up or Patch Up?, WASH. POST, Feb. 11, 1970, at A20.

In a February 8, 1972, message to Congress, President Nixon stated he would propose "legislation to provide for early identification and protection of endangered species. My new proposal would make the taking of endangered species a Federal offense for the first time, and would permit protective measures to be undertaken before a species is so depleted that regeneration is difficult or impossible." Richard M. Nixon, Public Papers of the Presidents of the United States, 1972, at 183 (1974). That same day, Representative John Dingell (D-MI) introduced the Nixon administration's proposed bill as H.R. 13081 (92d Cong.). Ten days later, Mark Hatfield (R-OR) introduced an identical bill in the Senate, S. 3199. On December 28, 1973, Congress passed the Endangered Species Act of 1973, Pub. L. No. 93-205, 87 Stat. 884, the statute at issue in *TVA*. Since the ESA's enactment, it has been amended in 1976, 1977, 1978, 1979, 1980, 1982, 1988, and 2003. M. Lynne Corn, Kristina Alexander & Eugene H. Buck, The Endangered Species Act: A Primer 1 (Cong. Research Serv. 2012).

3. **The Justification for Regulation?** What, according to the Court, were Congress's reasons for wishing to protect endangered species? Insofar as the ESA categorically prohibits actions that threaten endangered species, why did Congress undertake to protect endangered species at all costs, rather than when practical, or not inconsistent with other national needs? Would the Secretary of Defense be justified destroying the habitat of an endangered species if doing so helped accomplish a crucial national defense objective—for example, building a facility that provided reliable early warnings of biological and chemical attacks?

4. **The Mode of Regulation?** The ESA incorporates two important judgments about how endangered species should be managed. First, the enactment of federal legislation reflects Congress's judgment that management of endangered species should be performed largely at the federal rather than state level. What is the reason for this decision? In particular, why would state regulation of the trade in endangered species be perceived to be inadequate?

An article published in 1970 argued that "[w]ithout the protection of an interstate commerce law, an animal such as the alligator could be poached in its home territory and then transported to a hide market in New York . . . . The soft belly skin of the reptiles (the only part that poachers use) sells for as much as $10 a linear foot, and reptile poaching is reportedly a $1 million industry in southern Florida alone." Mark Oberle, *Endangered Species: Congress Curbs International Trade in Rare Animals*, 167 Science 152 (Jan. 9, 1970).

Does the problem of trade in alligator hides necessarily require regulation through federal legislation? Consider the possibility that a *consumer*-oriented state could regulate trade in endangered species by enacting laws that restrict the use, sale, or possession of endangered species. *See* N.Y. Code § 11-0536 (restricting sales of leopard, snow leopard, clouded leopard (neofelis nebulosa), tiger, asiatic lion, cheetah, alligators, and caiman or crocodile of the order crocodylia, among other species). Does the problem necessarily call for regulation through a federal *mandate* as opposed to, say, federal funding conditioned on the enactment of state regulation restricting the trade in endangered species? What are the advantages of a federal mandate? What are the costs?

Second, the ESA centralizes the first task related to the management of endangered species—the listing of "endangered" or "threatened" species—in the Department of Interior. The ESA provides that "[t]he Secretary shall by regulation . . . determine whether any species is an endangered species or a threatened species because of" specified factors. 16 U.S.C. § 1533(a). The listing determination is to be made following the Administrative Procedure Act's notice-and-comment procedures, *see infra* Chapter 4, "solely on the basis of the best scientific and commercial data available to him after conducting a review of the status of the species and after taking into account those efforts, if any, being made by any State or foreign nation, or any political subdivision of a State or foreign nation, to protect such species." § 1533(b). When a species is "listed," the Secretary is required to identify its "critical habitat," defined as areas where the species is found or where features essential to its conservation are present, even if the species is not physically located there. *Id.* § 1533(b)(2); § 1532(5). Once a species is listed and its critical habitat defined, it becomes unlawful to take and, in some circumstances, possess the species. *Id.* § 1538. The Act further provides: "Each Federal agency shall, in consultation with and with the assistance of the Secretary, insure that any action authorized, funded, or carried out by such agency . . . is not likely to jeopardize the continued existence of any endangered species or threatened species or result in the destruction or adverse modification of habitat of such species which is determined by the Secretary . . . to be critical . . . ." § 1536(a)(2).

Why would Congress have centralized listing decisions in the Department of Interior? Consider not only the Department's technical and scientific expertise, but also the way in which the Department's institutional priorities might affect listing decisions.

Section 1533(a) provides that the Secretary "shall" determine whether "any" species is endangered or threatened, but does not describe how the Secretary will learn about such species. That question is addressed in part by subsection (b)(3)(a), which requires the Secretary to accept petitions to list new species. That subsection further provides that "[t]o the maximum extent practicable, within 90 days after receiving the petition of an interested person . . . the Secretary shall make a finding as to whether the petition presents substantial scientific or commercial information indicating that the petitioned action may be warranted. If such a petition is found to present such information, the Secretary shall promptly commence a review of the status of the species concerned."

At each of the steps in the listing process, a private litigant acting under the ESA's "citizen suit" provision can file suit to force agency action. *See id.* § 1540(g). "A failure to list species, or delays in listing decisions, are a significant source of lawsuits . . . ." Corn et al., *supra*, at 15. What explains Congress's decision to make the Secretary and her delegates accountable to the public in this way? What effect does the availability of a private right of action have on enforcement of the ESA? Keeping in mind that litigation against the government can be costly and time-consuming, what kind of parties are likely to file suit for failure to list a threatened species? How would enforcement of the Act differ if authority to force agency action was vested in a politically sensitive agency, such as the Department of Justice?

5. **The Tennessee Valley Authority.** Congress created the Tennessee Valley Authority (TVA) in May 1933 to stimulate economic development in the Tennessee Valley, a region of the country that was severely affected by the Depression. President Roosevelt envisioned the TVA as "a corporation clothed with the power of Government but possessed of the flexibility and initiative of a private enterprise." He suggested that TVA "be charged with the broadest duty of planning for the proper use, conservation and development of the natural resources of the Tennessee River drainage basin and its adjoining territory for the general social and economic welfare of the Nation." Franklin D. Roosevelt, Message to Congress Suggesting the Tennessee Valley Authority (Apr. 10, 1933).

Following Roosevelt's suggestion, Congress established the TVA as "a body corporate" with the powers of a private corporation as well as the right to dispose of federal government property and acquire property through eminent domain. *See* Tennessee Valley Act, 48 Stat. 58, ch. 32 (May 18, 1933), codified at 16 U.S.C. § 831 et seq. TVA is managed by a board of directors whose nine members are appointed by the President with advice and consent of the Senate and a Chief Executive Officer appointed by the Board. *See* 16 U.S.C. § 831a.

During its heyday in the 1930s, the TVA was headed by prominent New Deal lawyer David E. Lilienthal, a mentee of Harvard law professor and Supreme Court Justice Felix Frankfurter. The authority sought to raise the standard of living in the Tennessee Valley through a range of projects. It provided navigation and flood control services; generated electricity and installed electric infrastructure throughout the Tennessee Valley; manufactured fertilizer and advised farmers on how to increase output; and engaged in other activities intended to spur economic development. During this time, TVA was also a major employer in the Tennessee Valley region, hiring a large number of unemployed workers. *See generally* BRUCE J. SCHULMAN, FROM COTTON BELT TO SUNBELT: FEDERAL POLICY, ECONOMIC DEVELOPMENT, AND THE TRANSFORMATION OF THE SOUTH 1938–1980 (1994).

Today, TVA is engaged primarily in generating electric power. The Authority operates eleven fossil-fuel power plants, three nuclear plants, and twenty-nine hydro-electric plants, which supply electricity to 9 million people in seven southeastern states. TVA stopped receiving federal appropriations for electricity generation in 1959, and now operates as a self-financing non-profit, that is funded by fees from selling power.

6. The Snail Darter's Listing as an Endangered Species. As the Court's opinion notes, the Snail Darter was listed as a result of a citizen petition filed by the respondents in *TVA v. Hill*, among them a group of biologists and citizens opposed to the construction of the Tellico Dam. When the Interior Department received the petition, it elicited comments from TVA as well as the Governor of Tennessee.

The TVA opposed the listing of the darter. It advanced four arguments: (1) "[l]isting of the fish would have no valid basis since the taxonomic status of the fish has not been determined, there is no known publication of its description, and it has never been classified as a new and distinct species"; (2) there was "scientific opinion that the fish undoubtedly exists elsewhere in the Tennessee River system, unaffected by the Tellico project" (a contention that turned out to be true); (3) "[l]isting the snail darter would not enhance the likelihood that this fish would survive," because "TVA and others already are undertaking a scientifically recognized program to conserve the snail darter"; and (4) "Tellico is a lawfully authorized federal project which . . . has been repeatedly funded by Congress, over objections of opponents . . . ." Amendment Listing the Snail Darter as an Endangered Species, 40 Fed. Reg. 47,505 (Oct 6, 1975) (reprinting TVA's comments to the Department of the Interior).

The Department of Interior's Fish and Wildlife Service rejected all of TVA's arguments. With respect to the lawfulness of the Tellico project, the Service noted that while it was "aware of the Congressional authorization of the Tellico project," it had "no evidence to indicate that the Tennessee Valley Authority ha[d] given adequate consideration to the snail darter" subsequent to the enactment of the Endangered Species Act. *Id.* at 47,506.

Thus, TVA and the Department of Interior did not *coordinate* the performance of their respective statutory duties in connection with the Tellico project, but instead took opposite positions as to the desirability and lawfulness of completing the project. The conflict between TVA and Interior persisted as *TVA v. Hill* was litigated. In the Supreme Court, TVA was represented by the U.S. Solicitor General's office, which is responsible for representing the interests of the United States before the Court. The Solicitor General's brief argued that the ESA's prohibition of actions that "jeopardize the continued existence of such endangered species . . . or result in the destruction or modification of [a critical] habitat of such species" should not be read to apply to projects that are substantially complete. Instead, the Solicitor General argued, the prohibition applies "to those points in the decision-making process when an agency is deciding whether an action should be 'authorized, funded, or carried out'—when it has before it reasonable alternatives, choices that are consistent with commitments already made and that do not exact substantial waste of unrecoverable resources." Brief for Petitioner at 20, *TVA v. Hill*, 437 U.S. 153 (1978).

The Solicitor General's brief did not comment on the Department of Interior's listing of the Snail Darter or the propriety of an injunction in the event that the Court concluded completion of the Tellico Dam would violate the ESA. Nor did it mention any efforts by the Nixon or Ford administrations to encourage TVA and Interior to resolve their differences informally. The Solicitor General's brief included an appendix setting out the "Views of the Secretary of Interior." There, the Secretary of Interior advanced the arguments the Court eventually adopted and contended that if the Court were to adopt TVA's position, it would undermine recently promulgated Interior regulations that "expressly apply [the ESA] to previously initiated projects where Federal involvement or control remains."

We return to the problem of coordinating agency action below, in the materials on the Office of Management and Budget and its Office of Information and Regulatory Affairs. *See* Chapter 3[D][1].

7. **The Statutory Dispute.** The overarching issue in *TVA* was whether the enactment of the ESA prohibited the completion of the Tellico Dam project. In the majority's view, the precise issue was whether §7 of the Act, 16 U.S.C. §1536, directing federal agencies "to *insure* that actions *authorized, funded,* or *carried out* by them do not *jeopardize* the continued existence" of an endangered species or "*result* in the destruction or modification of habitat of such species," prohibited completion of the dam. In Justice Powell's view, the question was whether §7 "requires a federal court, for the purpose of protecting an endangered species or its habitat, to enjoin permanently the operation of any federal project, whether completed or substantially completed."

Both sides accepted that at the time of the Supreme Court's decision, the project was "virtually complete and ready for the closing of the gates to impound the reservoir." The only work that remained was the "completion of roads and bridges" and involved "minor expenditures" relative to the cost of the entire project. Brief of the United States at 4 & n.2, *TVA v. Hill*, 437 U.S. 153 (1978).

As between the majority and the dissent, which framing of the statutory issue is more compelling? Is the Court correct that §7's reference to actions "authorized, funded, or carried out" addresses the temporal scope of the ESA? Wouldn't Congress have used more explicit language if it had intended to prohibit agencies from continuing to fund or maintain long-completed facilities ("actions . . . carried out" by the agency) that would threaten the habitat of a newly-listed endangered species? *See* Brief of the United States, *supra*, at 19.

8. **Probative Worth of Floor Statements by Sponsors of the Legislation?** In note 17 of his dissent, Justice Powell invokes a statement made during debate on the ESA by Senator John V. Tunney (D-CA), the bill's sponsor, to the effect that an agency such as TVA would have final authority to determine whether to go through with a project

that threatened the habitat of an endangered species. Recall from the notes on *Hanra-han* that sponsor statements are considered to be particularly reliable evidence of congressional intent. The rationale is that Congress as a practical matter must rely on representations of sponsors because of the volume and complexity of legislation it enacts, and because there are long-term reputational consequences if a sponsor misrepresents a bill's content. In this case, however, how much weight can be given to Senator Tunney's statement? Was his assurance that the TVA would complete its dam based on any language in the ESA?

9. **The "Dog that Didn't Bark"?** Is Justice Powell correct to think that members of Congress necessarily would have commented on the Tellico project if they intended the ESA to prevent its completion? Powell's argument rests on the assumptions that (a) if something of consequence is happening, members of Congress will comment on it and (b) those comments will be captured in the legislative record. In the years since *TVA v. Hill*, the Court has occasionally endorsed similar arguments. *E.g., Koons Buick Pontiac GMC, Inc. v. Nigh*, 543 U.S. 50, 73 (2004); *Chisom v. Roemer*, 501 U.S. 380, 396 (1991). In a reference to the Sherlock Holmes story *Silver Blaze*, these are known as "the dog that didn't bark" arguments. Justice Scalia uses a similar turn of phrase when he suggests that Congress does not usually hide "elephants in a molehill." *See, e.g., Gonzales v. Oregon*, 546 U.S. 243, 267 (2006) (Scalia, J., dissenting).

10. **Post-Enactment Evidence of Legislative Intent?** The *TVA v. Hill* Court gives no weight to statements contained in a report of the House Appropriations Committee, issued after the court of appeals enjoined completion of the Tellico Dam, to the effect that the ESA did not prohibit the dam's completion. H.R. Rep. No. 95-379, at 104 (1st Sess. 1977). One possible reason, discussed in the note that follows, is that the statements of the Appropriations Committee do not represent the views of the House as a whole. Another reason is that the statements were issued *after* the ESA's enactment and thus could not inform the understanding of Representatives who voted on it.

Are post-enactment materials ever reliable evidence of a statute's meaning? If someone wrote a letter three weeks ago whose meaning was unclear, wouldn't it be perfectly valid to ask her what she intended to express? Indeed, wouldn't testimony of the letter writer ordinarily be powerful evidence of the letter's original meaning? What distinguishes this situation from the use of post-enactment legislative history?

In *Jones v. United States*, 526 U.S. 227 (1999), the Court considered whether serious bodily injury was an element of the offense created by the federal carjacking statute, 18 U.S.C. § 2119, or simply a factor that the trial judge could consider when imposing sentence. To support its argument that bodily injury was a sentencing factor, the government relied on the Carjacking Correction Act of 1996, 110 Stat. 3020, and several statements in the act's legislative history that referred to bodily injury as a "penalty enhancement." The Supreme Court gave no weight to these materials, reasoning that "subsequent legislative history is a 'hazardous basis for inferring the intent of an earlier' Congress." *Id.* at 236 (quoting *Pension Benefit Guaranty Corporation v. LTV Corp.*, 496 U.S. 633, 650 (1990)). Is the problem with post-enactment legislative history that it is not created by the same Congress that enacted the statute under consideration? Or does post-enactment legislative history present an especially acute version of the risks highlighted in the broader textualist critique of legislative history?

11. **Impact of Appropriations Legislation and Committee Reports.** Article I, § 9 of the Constitution provides, "No money shall be drawn from the treasury, but in consequence of appropriations made by law." Congress appropriates money for agencies in two ways: through provisions in agencies' organic statutes ("direct" or "mandatory" appropriations) and through yearly appropriations measures. Today, direct funding accounts for approximately 55% of federal spending. Yearly appropriations account for the rest. *See* Bill Heniff Jr., Congressional Research Service, Overview of the Authorization-Appropriations Process, at 1 (Nov. 26, 2012).

Appropriations acts generally provide budget authority for the fiscal year beginning October 1. Subcommittees of the House and Senate Appropriations Committees are responsible for promulgating yearly appropriations bills. The Rules of the House and Senate attempt to limit the content of appropriations bills.

First, the House and Senate rules restrict appropriations for programs not authorized by law. *See* House Rule XXI, clause 2; Senate Rule XVI. Second, House Rule XXI and Senate Rule XVI prohibit substantive legislative language in appropriations measures. Third, the House in Rule XXI prohibits appropriations language in legislation that authorizes new government agencies and programs. *See generally* Heniff, *supra*, at 2. These protections, however, are not foolproof. A point of order (i.e., procedural objection) must be raised to enforce the rules, and the rules may be waived. In addition, the Senate "may allow legislative language in an appropriations act if it determines, by an affirmative vote, that such language is germane to legislative language already in the act as passed by the House." *Id.*

In *TVA v. Hill*, the government argued that the appropriation of money for the Tellico Dam after the passage of the ESA demonstrated Congress did not understand the ESA to prohibit completion of the dam. The Court rejected the argument on two grounds. First, the Court explained that the appropriations bills Congress passed did not appropriate money specifically for the Dam as opposed to the TVA's general operations. Second, the Court reasoned, the rule against implied repeals—which holds that later legislation is presumed not to affect earlier legislation absent express language showing an intent to repeal or modify the earlier enactment—applies with special force to appropriations measures, because they are not supposed to affect the content of substantive legislation under House and Senate rules. Justice Powell, by contrast, read the history of appropriations measures to confirm the lawfulness of the Tellico project.

Is there something odd about the Court enforcing the House and Senate's internal *procedural* rules in the context of interpreting *enacted* law? Considering that the House and Senate rules governing the content of appropriations measures can be waived, are they a reliable guide to statutory meaning? Two years after *TVA*, the Court held that "when Congress desires to suspend or repeal a statute in force, [t]here can be no doubt that . . . it could accomplish its purpose by an amendment to an appropriation bill, or otherwise. The whole question depends on the intention of Congress as expressed in the statutes." *United States v. Will*, 449 U.S. 200, 222 (1980) (internal punctuation omitted). Is this view consistent with *TVA v. Hill*'s contention that appropriations bills "have the limited and specific purpose of providing funds for authorized programs"?

12. **Was ESA Being Applied Retroactively to Bar Completion of the Tellico Dam?** To support his reading of the ESA, Justice Powell invokes the canon against retroactivity. A standard statement of that canon provides:

> If there is no congressional directive on the temporal reach of a statute, we determine whether the application of the statute to the conduct at issue would result in a retroactive effect. If so, then in keeping with our "traditional presumption" against retroactivity, we presume that the statute does not apply to that conduct.

Martin v. Hadix, 527 U.S. 343, 352 (1999) (quoting *Landgraf v. USI Film Products*, 511 U.S. 244, 280 (1994)).

As noted above, the Tellico project was basically complete at the time of the Court's decision in *TVA v. Hill*. All that remained to be done was for ancillary roads and bridges to be constructed and the floodgates to be closed. What is the conduct that in the Court's view would "jeopardize the continued existence of [an] endangered species . . . or result in the destruction or modification of habitat of such species"? The Court denies that its interpretation of the ESA gives the statute retroactive effect and posits that § 7 applies only to activities "which *remain* to be authorized, funded, or carried out." What is the basis for this understanding of the ESA? Does it render the presumption against retroactivity toothless, as Justice Powell contends?

13. **The Question of Remedy.** The Court in *TVA v. Hill* assumes that if a violation of ESA § 7 is established, a court must issue an injunction prohibiting completion of the violating project. In *Hecht Co. v. Bowles*, 321 U.S. 321 (1944), the Court considered whether a district court was required to issue an injunction prohibiting violations of the Emergency Price Control Act of 1942, Pub. L. No. 77-729, 56 Stat. 23, once it determined that a firm had violated the act's maximum price and recordkeeping provisions. The pertinent section of the act provided:

> Whenever in the judgment of the [Price] Administrator any person has engaged . . . in any acts or practices which constitute . . . a violation of any provision of section 4 of this Act, he may make application to the appropriate court for an order enjoining such acts or practices . . . . and upon a showing by the Administrator that such person has engaged . . . in any such acts or practices a permanent or temporary injunction, restraining order, or other order shall be granted without bond.

Despite seemingly mandatory language in the statute that upon proof of a violation, an order "shall be granted without bond," the Court ruled that the district court retained discretion to deny an injunction if, for example, a business was attempting in good faith to comply with the law. The Court reasoned that "[a] grant of *jurisdiction* to issue compliance orders hardly suggests an absolute duty to do so under any and all circumstances . . . . [I]f Congress had intended to make such a drastic departure from the traditions of equity practice, an unequivocal statement of its purpose would have been made." 321 U.S. at 329.

Does the ESA contain an "unequivocal statement" of congressional purpose that all violations of the Act be enjoined? What would the respondents in *TVA v. Hill* have argued? In a dissent not reproduced above, Justice Rehnquist observed: "the District Court recognized that Congress, when it enacted the Endangered Species Act, made the preservation of the habitat of the snail darter an important public concern. But it concluded that this interest on one side of the balance was more than outweighed by other equally significant factors." 437 U.S. at 213. Justice Rehnquist thus concluded that even if completion of the Tellico Dam technically violated the ESA, the district court was within its discretion to deny an injunction. Is this reasoning persuasive?

In *Winter v. Natural Resources Defense Council*, 555 U.S. 7 (2008), an environmental group and filmmaker brought suit against the Navy under the National Environmental Policy Act (NEPA), Pub. L. No. 91-190, 83 Stat. 852 (1969), to enjoin active "MFA" sonar training exercises conducted off the coast of southern California. According to plaintiffs, the Navy's sonar exercises harmed marine animals by inhibiting their ability to navigate under water and led to several "mass strandings" of marine animals. Because the Navy had not addressed the strandings in an environmental impact statement, plaintiffs contended that the sonar exercises violated NEPA. The district court entered a preliminary injunction that established restrictive conditions for the exercises, and the court of appeals affirmed.

The Supreme Court vacated the injunction. After noting some uncertainty over the risk of irreparable harm the plaintiffs were required to establish, the Court concluded that a preliminary injunction was inappropriate because any injury to the plaintiffs was "outweighed by the public interest and the Navy's interest in effective, realistic training of its sailors." 555 U.S. at 23. The Court explained:

> While we do not question the seriousness of [the plaintiffs'] interests, we conclude that the balance of equities and consideration of the overall public interest in this case tip strongly in favor of the Navy. For the plaintiffs, the most serious possible injury would be harm to an unknown number of the marine mammals that they study and observe. In contrast, forcing the Navy to deploy an inadequately trained antisubmarine force jeopardizes the safety of the fleet. Active sonar is the only reliable technology for detecting and tracking enemy diesel-electric submarines, and the President—the Commander in Chief—has determined that training with active sonar is "essential to national security."

Id. at 26.

Permanent injunctions are governed by a slightly different standard than preliminary injunctions. *See eBay Inc. v. MercExchange, L.L.C.*, 547 U.S. 388, 391 (2006). Nevertheless, the Court in *Winter* stated that "what we have said makes clear that it would be an abuse of discretion to enter a permanent injunction, after final decision on the merits, along the same lines as the preliminary injunction. An injunction is a matter of equitable discretion; it does not follow from success on the merits as a matter of course." 129 S. Ct. at 381. The Court's opinion did not cite *TVA v. Hill*.

Could the *TVA* plaintiffs have obtained an injunction under the *Winter* standard? In particular, did the "public interest" weigh in favor of or against completion of the Tellico Dam? What would the plaintiffs argue? How would the government respond?

14. **Postscript.** The Endangered Species Amendments Act of 1978, Pub. L. No. 95-632, 92 Stat. 3751 (1978), created a scheme for exempting projects from the requirements of ESA § 7. The process begins when an agency petitions the Secretary of the Interior for an exemption. The petition is reviewed by an Endangered Species Committee (colloquially known as the "God Squad") comprised of the Secretary of Agriculture, the Secretary of the Army, the Chairman of the Council of Economic Advisors, the Administrator of the Environmental Protection Agency, the Secretary of the Interior, the Administrator of the National Oceanic and Atmospheric Administration, and representatives of states the project affects.

After collecting evidence and soliciting public comment, the Endangered Species Committee votes on whether to grant an exemption. Granting an exemption requires a super-majority vote of five members. The Committee is charged to grant an exemption only if:

(A) it determines on the record . . . that—

(i) there are no reasonable and prudent alternatives to the agency action;

(ii) the benefits of such action clearly outweigh the benefits of alternative courses of action consistent with conserving the species or its critical habitat, and such action is in the public interest;

(iii) the action is of regional or national significance; and

(iv) neither the Federal agency concerned nor the exemption applicant made any irreversible or irretrievable commitment of resources prohibited by subsection (d) of this section [prohibiting resource commitments that foreclose alternative measures for complying with the ESA]; and

(B) it establishes such reasonable mitigation and enhancement measures, including, but not limited to, live propagation, transplantation, and habitat acquisition and improvement, as are necessary and appropriate to minimize the adverse effects of the agency action upon the endangered species, threatened species, or critical habitat concerned.

16 U.S.C. § 1536(h)(1).

TVA petitioned for an exemption for the Tellico Dam under the exemption process. On January 23, 1979, the Endangered Species Committee rejected the petition in a unanimous vote. In a press account, Charles Schultze, Chair of the Council of Economic Advisers, explained: "The costs [of the dam] clearly outweigh the benefits. It would have cost $35 million to complete it and we would be inundating $40 million worth of land. You would lose important Indian archelogical [sic] sites, scenic values and the river in its natural state." Margot Hornblower, *Panel Junks TVA Dam; Cites Cost, Not Snail Darter*, WASH. POST, Jan. 24, 1979, at A12. Interior Secretary Cecil D. Andrus commented, "I hate to see the snail darter get the credit for stopping a project that was ill-conceived and uneconomic in the first place." *Id.*

In 1979, Congress passed an appropriations rider that specifically exempted the Tellico Dam project from the ESA. Title IV of Pub. L. No. 96-69, 93 Stat. 437 (Sept. 25, 1979), provided: "[N]otwithstanding the provisions of 16 U.S.C., chapter 35 or any other law, the [TVA] is authorized and directed to complete construction, operate and maintain the Tellico Dam and Reservoir project for navigation, flood control, electric power generation and other purposes, including the maintenance of a normal summer reservoir pool of 813 feet above sea level." Despite a veto threat, President Carter eventually signed the bill. He wrote in a signing statement that he was "convinced that this resolution of the Tellico matter will help assure the passage of the Endangered Species Act reauthorization without weakening amendments or further exemptions." Statement on Signing H.R. 4388 into Law, in Jimmy Carter, Public Papers of the Presidents of the United States, 1979, at 1760 (1980). *See generally* Zygmunt J.B. Plater, *In the Wake of the Snail Darter: An Environmental Law Paradigm and its Consequences*, 19 U. MICH. J.L. REFORM 805, 813 n.32 (1986).

What is the significance of this legislation for the debate between the Court and Justice Powell in *TVA v. Hill*? Does it show that Justice Powell's understanding of Congress's intent was correct? Does it prove that the Court has no business correcting "errors" that can be corrected through the legislative process? Are later developments irrelevant to the correctness of the Court's 1978 decision?

Construction of the dam was completed in 1979 and the downriver snail darter population was destroyed. Several small populations were later found upstream in the Tennessee River and its tributaries. Today, the species is listed as "threatened" rather than "endangered."

b. Shared Regulatory Space

Another recurring problem of statutory interpretation involves conflicting regulatory regimes. A case may implicate two or more statutory schemes that seemingly command contradictory or incompatible results. The task of a court in this circumstance is less to divine the meaning of the language Congress used than to make sense of Congress's enactments. Does the court try to reconcile the regulatory requirements or does it adhere to the maxim that statutes are presumed not to impliedly repeal one another?

POM Wonderful LLC v. Coca-Cola Co. *Skip for 1/28*

134 S. Ct. 2228 (2014)

JUSTICE KENNEDY delivered the opinion of the Court.

POM Wonderful LLC makes and sells pomegranate juice products, including a pomegranate-blueberry juice blend. One of POM's competitors is the Coca-Cola Company. Coca-Cola's Minute Maid Division makes a juice blend sold with a label that, in describing the contents, displays the words "pomegranate blueberry" with far more prominence than other words on the label that show the juice to be a blend of five juices. In truth, the Coca-Cola product contains but 0.3% pomegranate juice and 0.2% blueberry juice.

Alleging that the use of that label is deceptive and misleading, POM sued Coca-Cola under § 43 of the Lanham Act. 60 Stat. 441, as amended, 15 U.S.C. § 1125. That provision allows one competitor to sue another if it alleges unfair competition arising from false or misleading product descriptions. The Court of Appeals for the Ninth Circuit held that, in the realm of labeling for food and beverages, a Lanham Act claim like POM's is precluded by a second federal statute. The second statute is the Federal Food, Drug, and Cosmetic Act (FDCA), which forbids the misbranding of food, including by means of false or misleading labeling. §§ 301, 403, 52 Stat. 1042, 1047, as amended, 21 U.S.C. §§ 331, 343.

I***

POM Wonderful LLC is a grower of pomegranates and a distributor of pomegranate juices. Through its POM Wonderful brand, POM produces, markets, and sells a variety of pomegranate products, including a pomegranate/blueberry juice blend.

POM competes in the pomegranate-blueberry juice market with the Coca-Cola Company. Coca-Cola, under its Minute Maid brand, created a juice blend containing 99.4% apple and grape juices, 0.3% pomegranate juice, 0.2% blueberry juice, and 0.1% raspberry juice. Despite the minuscule amount of pomegranate and blueberry juices in the blend, the front label of the Coca-Cola product displays the words "pomegranate blueberry" in all capital letters, on two separate lines. Below those words, Coca-Cola placed the phrase "flavored blend of 5 juices" in much smaller type.***

Claiming that Coca-Cola's label tricks and deceives consumers, all to POM's injury as a competitor, POM brought suit under the Lanham Act. POM alleged that the name, label, marketing, and advertising of Coca-Cola's juice blend mislead consumers into believing the product consists predominantly of pomegranate and blueberry juice when it in fact consists predominantly of less expensive apple and grape juices. That confusion, POM complained, causes it to lose sales. POM sought damages and injunctive relief.

The District Court granted partial summary judgment to Coca-Cola on POM's Lanham Act claim, ruling that the FDCA and regulations [governing the labelling of blended juices] preclude challenges [under the Lanham Act] to the name and label of Coca-Cola's juice blend. The District Court reasoned that in the juice blend regulations the "FDA has directly spoken [to] the issues that form the basis of Pom's Lanham Act claim against the naming and labeling of" Coca-Cola's product, but has not prohibited any, and indeed expressly has permitted some, aspects of Coca-Cola's label.*** The Court of Appeals for the Ninth Circuit affirmed in relevant part.***

Congress enacted the Lanham Act nearly seven decades ago. *See* 60 Stat. 427 (1946).*** Section 45 of the Lanham Act provides:

> "The intent of this chapter is to regulate commerce within the control of Congress by making actionable the deceptive and misleading use of marks in such commerce; to protect registered marks used in such commerce from interference by State, or territorial legislation; to protect persons engaged in such commerce against unfair competition; to prevent fraud and deception in such commerce by the use of reproductions, copies, counterfeits, or colorable imitations of registered marks; and to provide rights and remedies stipulated by treaties and conventions respecting trademarks, trade names, and unfair competition entered into between the United States and foreign nations." 15 U.S.C. § 1127.***

The Lanham Act creates a cause of action for unfair competition through misleading advertising or labeling[, 15 U.S.C. § 1125(a).]*** The cause of action*** imposes civil liability on any person who "uses in commerce any word, term, name, symbol, or device, or any combination thereof, or any false designation of origin, false or misleading description of fact, or false or misleading representation of fact, which . . . misrepresents the nature, characteristics, qualities, or geographic origin of his or her or another person's goods, services, or commercial activities." 15 U.S.C. § 1125(a)(1).*** POM's cause of action would be straightforward enough but for Coca-Cola's contention that a separate federal statutory regime, the [Federal Food, Drug, and Cosmetic Act (FDCA), 52 Stat. 1042, 21 U.S.C. § 331], allows it to use the label in question and in fact precludes the Lanham Act claim.

***The FDCA statutory regime is designed primarily to protect the health and safety of the public at large. *See 62 Cases of Jam v. United States*, 340 U.S. 593, 596 (1951); FDCA, § 401, 52 Stat. 1046, 21 U.S.C. § 341 (agency may issue certain regulations to "promote honesty and fair dealing in the interest of consumers"). The FDCA prohibits the misbranding of food and drink. 21 U.S.C. §§ 321(f), 331. A food or drink is deemed misbranded if, inter alia, "its labeling is false or misleading," § 343(a), information required to appear on its label "is not prominently placed thereon," § 343(f), or a label does not bear "the common or usual name of the food, if any there be," § 343(i). To implement these provisions, the Food and Drug Administration (FDA) promulgated regulations regarding food and beverage labeling, including the labeling of mixes of different types of juice into one juice blend. *See* 21 CFR § 102.33 (2013). One provision of those regulations is particularly relevant to this case: If a juice blend does not name all the juices it contains and mentions only juices that are not predominant in the blend, then it must either declare the percentage content of the named juice or "[i]ndicate that the named juice is present as a flavor or flavoring," e.g., "raspberry and cranberry flavored juice drink." § 102.33(d). The Government represents that the FDA does not preapprove juice labels under these regulations. That contrasts with the FDA's regulation of other types of labels, such as drug labels, see 21 U.S.C. § 355(d), and is consistent with the less extensive role the FDA plays in the regulation of food than in the regulation of drugs.

Unlike the Lanham Act, which relies in substantial part for its enforcement on private suits brought by injured competitors, the FDCA and its regulations provide the United States with nearly exclusive enforcement authority, including the authority to seek criminal sanctions in some circumstances. 21 U.S.C. §§ 333(a), 337. Private parties may not bring enforcement suits. § 337. Also unlike the Lanham Act, the FDCA contains a provision pre-empting certain state laws on misbranding. That provision, which Congress added to the FDCA in the Nutrition Labeling and Education Act of 1990, § 6, 104 Stat. 2362-2364, forecloses a "State or political subdivision of a State" from establishing requirements that are of the type but "not identical to" the requirements in some of the misbranding provisions of the FDCA. 21 U.S.C. § 343-1(a). It does not address, or refer to, other federal statutes or the preclusion thereof.

II

A

[T]his is not a pre-emption case. In pre-emption cases, the question is whether state law is pre-empted by a federal statute, or in some instances, a federal agency action. See *Wyeth v. Levine*, 555 U.S. 555, 563 (2009). This case, however, concerns the alleged preclusion of a cause of action under one federal statute by the provisions of another federal statute. So the state-federal balance does not frame the inquiry. Because this is a preclusion case, any "presumption against pre-emption" has no force. In addition, the preclusion analysis is not governed by the Court's complex categorization of the types of pre-emption. See *Crosby v. National Foreign Trade Council*, 530 U.S. 363, 372–373 (2000).***

[T]his is a statutory interpretation case and the Court relies on traditional rules of statutory interpretation.*** A principle of interpretation is "often countered, of course, by some maxim pointing in a different direction." *Circuit City Stores, Inc. v. Adams*, 532 U.S. 105, 115 (2001). It is thus unsurprising that in this case a threshold dispute has arisen as to which of two competing maxims establishes the proper framework for decision. POM argues that this case concerns whether one statute, the FDCA as amended, is an "implied repeal" in part of another statute, i.e., the Lanham Act. See, *e.g.*, *Carcieri v. Salazar*, 555 U.S. 379, 395 (2009). POM contends that in such cases courts must give full effect to both statutes unless they are in "irreconcilable conflict," and that this high standard is not satisfied here. Coca-Cola resists this canon and its high standard. Coca-Cola argues that the case concerns whether a more specific law, the FDCA, clarifies or narrows the scope of a more general law, the Lanham

Act. See, *e.g.*, *United States v. Fausto*, 484 U.S. 439, 453 (1988). The Court's task, it claims, is to "reconcil[e]" the laws, and it says the best reconciliation is that the more specific provisions of the FDCA bar certain causes of action authorized in a general manner by the Lanham Act.

The Court does not need to resolve this dispute. Even assuming that Coca-Cola is correct that the Court's task is to reconcile or harmonize the statutes and not, as POM urges, to enforce both statutes in full unless there is a genuinely irreconcilable conflict, Coca-Cola is incorrect that the best way to harmonize the statutes is to bar POM's Lanham Act claim.

B

Beginning with the text of the two statutes, it must be observed that neither the Lanham Act nor the FDCA, in express terms, forbids or limits Lanham Act claims challenging labels that are regulated by the FDCA. By its terms, the Lanham Act subjects to suit any person who "misrepresents the nature, characteristics, qualities, or geographic origin" of goods or services. 15 U.S.C. § 1125(a). This comprehensive imposition of liability extends, by its own terms, to misrepresentations on labels, including food and beverage labels. No other provision in the Lanham Act limits that understanding or purports to govern the relevant interaction between the Lanham Act and the FDCA. And the FDCA, by its terms, does not preclude Lanham Act suits. In consequence, food and beverage labels regulated by the FDCA are not, under the terms of either statute, off limits to Lanham Act claims. No textual provision in either statute discloses a purpose to bar unfair competition claims like POM's.

This absence is of special significance because the Lanham Act and the FDCA have coexisted since the passage of the Lanham Act in 1946. 60 Stat. 427 (1946); ch. 675, 52 Stat. 1040 (1938). If Congress had concluded, in light of experience, that Lanham Act suits could interfere with the FDCA, it might well have enacted a provision addressing the issue during these 70 years. Congress enacted amendments to the FDCA and the Lanham Act, *see, e.g.*, Nutrition Labeling and Education Act of 1990, 104 Stat. 2353; Trademark Law Revision Act of 1988, § 132, 102 Stat. 3946, including an amendment that added to the FDCA an express pre-emption provision with respect to state laws addressing food and beverage misbranding, § 6, 104 Stat. 2362. Yet Congress did not enact a provision addressing the preclusion of other federal laws that might bear on food and beverage labeling. This is powerful evidence that Congress did not intend FDA oversight to be the exclusive means of ensuring proper food and beverage labeling.

Perhaps the closest the statutes come to addressing the preclusion of the Lanham Act claim at issue here is the pre-emption provision added to the FDCA in 1990 as part of the Nutrition Labeling and Education Act. *See* 21 U.S.C. § 343-1. But, far from expressly precluding suits arising under other federal laws, the provision if anything suggests that Lanham Act suits are not precluded.

This pre-emption provision forbids a "State or political subdivision of a State" from imposing requirements that are of the type but "not identical to" corresponding FDCA requirements for food and beverage labeling.*** [T]he provision does not refer to requirements imposed by other sources of law, such as federal statutes. For purposes of deciding whether the FDCA displaces a regulatory or liability scheme in another statute, it makes a substantial difference whether that other statute is state or federal. By taking care to mandate express pre-emption of some state laws, Congress if anything indicated it did not intend the FDCA to preclude requirements arising from other sources.***

The Lanham Act and the FDCA complement each other in major respects, for each has its own scope and purpose. Although both statutes touch on food and beverage labeling, the Lanham Act protects commercial interests against unfair competition, while the FDCA protects public health and safety. The two statutes impose "different requirements and protections."

The two statutes complement each other with respect to remedies in a more fundamental respect. Enforcement of the FDCA and the detailed prescriptions of its implementing regulations is largely committed to the FDA. The FDA, however, does not have the same perspective or expertise in assessing market dynamics that day-to-day competitors possess. Competitors who manufacture or distribute products have detailed knowledge regarding how consumers rely upon certain sales and marketing strategies. Their awareness of unfair competition practices may be far more immediate and accurate than that of agency rulemakers and regulators. Lanham Act suits draw upon this market expertise by empowering private parties to sue competitors to protect their interests on a case-by-case basis.***

Unlike other types of labels regulated by the FDA, such as drug labels, *see* 21 U.S.C. § 355(d), it would appear the FDA does not preapprove food and beverage labels under its regulations and instead relies on enforcement actions, warning letters, and other measures. Because the FDA acknowledges that it does not necessarily pursue enforcement measures regarding all objectionable labels, if Lanham Act claims were to be precluded then commercial interests—and indirectly the public at large—could be left with less effective protection in the food and beverage labeling realm than in many other, less regulated industries. It is unlikely that Congress intended the FDCA's protection of health and safety to result in less policing of misleading food and beverage labels than in competitive markets for other products.

Notes and Questions

1. **Justification for and Mode of Regulation.** How would POM Wonderful and Coca-Cola's dispute over Coca-Cola's misleading pomegranate juice label have been handled at common law? Recall from the notes to *FTC v. R.F. Keppel & Brother*, in Chapter 1[C][2], *supra*, that the common law prohibition of unfair competition extended only to "fraud," "misrepresentation," "[i]ntimidation," "obstruction," "molestation," and "the intentional procurement of a violation of individual rights, contractual or other."

Mogul Steamship Co. v. McGregor, Gow, & Co., 23 Q.B.D. 598 (1889). Insofar as the Minute Maid pomegranate juice label was fraudulent, would POM Wonderful have been able to recover damages for the business it lost? Why was legislation thought necessary in the case of the Lanham Act? The Food, Drug and Cosmetic Act (FDCA)?

Recall from the notes to *United States v. Sullivan* in Chapter 1 that Congress enacted the FDCA in 1938 to prohibit the movement of "adulterated" and "misbranded" food, drugs, devices, and cosmetics in interstate commerce. Pub. L. No. 75-717, 52 Stat. 1040. What choices did Congress make regarding the way in which food safety would be regulated under the FDCA? Is safety ensured through ex ante controls on market entry, the imposition of ex post liability, or a combination of the two? Is enforcement primarily the responsibility of an agency, or entrusted to individuals who are empowered to bring private, civil actions? What kind of penalties is a manufacturer subject to if it distributes misbranded beverages?

What choices regarding the means of regulation did Congress make in the Lanham Act? Are deceptive and misleading statements regulated through ex ante controls on market entry or ex post liability? Does an administrative agency oversee implementation and enforcement of the Act? Who is the primary frontline enforcer?

2. **Posture of the Dispute.** Before POM Wonderful filed this lawsuit, had the federal government taken any actions with respect to the labeling of Minute Maid pomegranate/blueberry juice? If Minute Maid's juice label did not comply with the FDA's regulations, how would the issue have been raised before an administrative agency or court? How did POM's lawsuit against Coca-Cola end up in the Supreme Court? What happened in the courts below? What was POM's theory of the case? What sort of proceedings do you expect after the Supreme Court's decision?

3. **The Statutory Dispute: Conflict Between Dual Federal Schemes.** At issue in *POM Wonderful* is whether the FDA's promulgation of standards for blended juice labels under the FDCA precluded POM from bringing a private, civil damages action alleging that the label was misleading under the Lanham Act. Note that the terminology used to describe this question differs slightly from the terminology used when considering whether a federal statute displaces state regulation and tort law. In the federal vs. state context, the federal statute is said to *preempt* state regulation. When a federal statute displaces a cause of action created by another federal statute, the federal statute is said to *preclude* the federal cause of action.

In the decision below, the Ninth Circuit reasoned that requiring Coca-Cola to change the design of its label might require it to do something more than the FDA's regulations required. The court wrote:

> [A]s best we can tell, FDA regulations authorize the name Coca-Cola has chosen. The FDA has concluded that a manufacturer may name a beverage using the name of a flavoring juice that is not predominant by volume. See 21 C.F.R. § 102.33(c), (d). Section 102.33(c) recognizes, for example, that a blend of juices can represent a juice in its name or label even if the blend "also

contains a juice other than the . . . juice" named or represented on the label. And the FDA has explained, by way of example, that a three-juice blend where apple is the juice identified on the label can be named "Apple blend; apple juice in a blend of two other fruit juices." *Id.* § 102.33(c) (internal quotation marks omitted). The FDA has also said that a "named" juice need "not [be] the predominant juice" by volume. *Id.* § 102.33(d).*** Taken together, these provisions reflect that: (1) Coca-Cola may give its product a name that refers to juices that provide the characterizing flavor, and (2) those juices need not be predominant by volume if Coca-Cola states that those juices are not predominant. Thus, Pom's challenge to the name "Pomegranate Blueberry Flavored Blend of 5 Juices" would create a conflict with FDA regulations and would require us to undermine the FDA's apparent determination that so naming the product is not misleading.

679 F.3d 1170, 1177 (2012).

What did the Supreme Court say with respect to this precise point? Is the Ninth Circuit correct that permitting POM to sue for false advertising under the Lanham Act could create a regime in which a label that does not conflict with FDA regulations is still actionable under a different federal law? The Supreme Court observes that the FDCA and Lanham Act "complement each other." Would this still be the case if a label that was unquestionably lawful under the FDA's regulations was found to violate the Lanham Act?

The FDCA and the Lanham Act were enacted eight years apart, in 1938 and 1946 respectively. Why did Congress fail to address the relationship between FDA approval of a label and the availability of a private, damages cause of action under the Lanham Act when it enacted the Lanham Act in 1946? Note that the FDCA regulated beverage labels from the start. *See* Pub. L. No. 75-717 § 301(b), 52 Stat. 1042 (1938) (prohibiting "[t]he adulteration or misbranding of any food . . . in interstate commerce); *id.* § 201(f), 52 Stat. 1050 (defining "food" as "articles used for food or drink for man or other animals"). Could Congress have foreseen all the forms of regulatory activity that were potentially inconsistent with the outcome of a private suit under the Lanham Act?

4. **Reconciling the FDCA and the Lanham Act—Canons.** The relationship between FDA regulation of juice labels and the Lanham Act's cause of action is an example of a problem that constantly occurs in the interpretation and application of federal statutes. Because of the volume and complexity of federal legislation, courts and other statutory interpreters are often called upon to determine how one statute affects another. As Coca-Cola argued here, Statute *A* may preclude or displace application of Statute *B*. Statute *A* might inform the way in which Statute *B* is interpreted. Or *A* and *B* might be interpreted as establishing independent legal regimes, which have no effect upon one another.

Several canons of construction are potentially relevant to that problem, two of which are noted in the Court's opinion:

- The "canon against implied repeals" teaches that "repeals by implication are not favored and will not be presumed unless the intention of the legislature to repeal is clear and manifest." *Hui v. Castaneda*, 559 U.S. 799, 810 (2010). "[A]n implied repeal will only be found where provisions in two statutes are in 'irreconcilable conflict,' or where the latter Act covers the whole subject of the earlier one and 'is clearly intended as a substitute.'" *Carcieri v. Salazar*, 555 U.S. 379, 395 (2009).

- The "specific over general" canon teaches that specific statutory language takes precedence over more general language. *See, e.g., Busic v. United States*, 446 U.S. 398, 406 (1980).

- The "last in time" rule teaches that "the more recent of two irreconcilably conflicting statutes governs." *Watt v. Alaska*, 451 U.S. 259, 266 (1981).

- The "rule against surplusage" or "rule against superfluities" teaches that statutes should be read so that each provision and term carries a distinct meaning. *See, e.g., Mackey v. Lanier Collection Agency & Service, Inc.*, 486 U.S. 825, 837 (1988).

- The "sense and purpose" rule teaches that "[a court] must read [conflicting] statutes to give effect to each if [it] can do so while preserving their sense and purpose." *Watt*, 451 U.S. at 267.

The Court maintains that none of these canons is relevant to the interpretative question in *POM Wonderful*. Do you see any reliance on these canons in the Court's decision? *See generally* Carlos González, *Trumps, Inversions, Balancing, Presumptions, Institution Prompting and Interpretive Canons: New Ways for Adjudicating Conflicts between Legal Norms*, 45 Santa Clara L. Rev. 233 (2005).

5. **Reconciling the FDCA and the Lanham Act — Text.** The Court's analysis of the relationship between the FDCA and the Lanham Act proceeds in two steps, which focus on the statutes' text and structure. The Court begins by noting that the Lanham Act generally prohibits misleading descriptions of a product's nature or characteristics. Neither the Lanham Act nor the FDCA describe how the statutes interact. From this, the Court concludes that a claim asserting that a label violates the Lanham Act may be asserted even when the label that is the subject of the Lanham Act claim complies with regulations promulgated under the FDCA.

Is the statutes' silence with respect to the relationship between them as probative as the Court maintains? Suppose that (counter-factually) FDA regulations provided a juice label could not be used until it was pre-approved by the agency, and that a label, once approved by the agency, could not be changed without the FDA's permission. Would the statutes' silence with respect to their effect on one another lead to the same conclusion in this scenario?

Following *expressio unius*, the Court next reasons that the Nutrition Labeling and Education Act's preemption of certain *state* law claims reflects Congress's judgment that claims under *federal* laws such as the Lanham Act are *not* precluded by the FDCA. According to the Court, the preemption of state law claims only is "'powerful evidence that Congress did not intend FDA oversight to be the exclusive means' of ensuring proper food and beverage labeling."

Is the Court's analysis persuasive? Recall from *Riegel v. Medtronic*, in Chapter 1[C][5], that federal law is presumed not to preempt state law, at least in certain traditional areas of state concern. No such presumption against preemption applies to federal law; Congress is free to revise prior legislation subject only to constitutional requirements. Isn't the need to overcome the presumption against preemption an equally plausible reason for Congress to have spoken to preemption of state claims in the Nutrition Labeling and Education Act?

6. Reconciling the FDCA and the Lanham Act — Structure. Turning from text to structure, the Court observes that although both the FDCA and the Lanham Act "touch on" beverage labelling, "the Lanham Act protects commercial interests against unfair competition, while the FDCA protects public health and safety." It follows that "[t]he Lanham Act and the FDCA complement each other in major respects, for each has its own scope and purpose."

The Court's conclusion that the FDCA and the Lanham Act "complement each other" is based in part on the observation that the FDA and private litigants have different competencies. What function, according to the Court, does the FDA excel at? What function are private litigants better able to perform? Why are private litigants better able to perform this function than a regulatory agency staffed with scientific and technical experts?

The Court also observes that "the FDA does not preapprove food and beverage labels under its regulations and instead relies on enforcement actions, warning letters, and other measures." What is the significance of the fact that the FDA does not pre-approve labels? What would be the result if a private litigant were allowed to challenge a label that had been pre-approved by the FDA in a Lanham Act action, and the defendant could not make further changes to the label without the FDA's permission? Would the Ninth Circuit's conclusion be on firmer ground in this scenario?

7. Intra-Statute Conflicts. At times, conflicts between statutory provisions occur at a finer-grained level than in *POM Wonderful*. Consider a current controversy involving §111(d) of the Clean Air Act (CAA). Section 111(d) is one of three programs in the Clean Air Act that regulate air pollution from stationary sources such as power plants. Under the National Ambient Air Quality Standards (NAAQS) program, established in §§108 and 110 of the Act, 42 U.S.C. §§7408 and 7410, the Environmental Protection Agency (EPA) is required to promulgate and states are required to implement emissions standards for six pollutants that are harmful to public health and the environment. The Hazardous Air Pollutants program, established in §112, 42 U.S.C. §7412, similarly requires EPA to promulgate and states to implement standards for emissions of certain toxic chemicals. Section 111(d), added to the Act by the Clean Air Amendments Act of 1990, Pub. L. No. 101-549, 104 Stat. 2399, broadly authorizes EPA to establish standards for emissions from existing stationary sources that endanger public health or welfare that are not regulated under the other two programs.

When Congress enacted current § 111(d), it attempted to update a cross-reference to § 112 in the prior version of § 111. However, the House and Senate passed conflicting conforming amendments, *both* of which were signed into law by the President and appear in the Statutes at Large. The Senate bill replaced the former cross-reference to § 112(b)(1)(A), which was eliminated in the 1990 amendments, with a new cross-reference to that section's replacement, § 112(b). It directed EPA to promulgate standards for "any air pollutant (i) for which air quality criteria have not been issued or which is not included on a list published under section 108(a) or *section 112(b)*." Pub. L. No. 101-549, § 302(a), 104 Stat. 2399, 2574 (1990) (amendment emphasized). The House bill, by contrast, replaced the pre-existing cross-reference to § 112 with entirely new language. It required EPA to promulgate standards for "any air pollutant (i) for which air quality criteria have not been issued or which is not included on a list published under section 108(a) *or emitted from a source category which is regulated under section 112 of this title*." Pub. L. No. 101-549, § 108(g), 104 Stat. 2399, 2467 (1990) (amendment emphasized).

On August 3, 2015, EPA issued the Clean Power Plan Final Rule. *Carbon Pollution Emission Guidelines for Existing Stationary Sources: Electric Utility Generating Units; Final Rule*, 80 Fed. Reg. 64,662 (October 23, 2015). Relying on section 111(d), the Clean Power Plan sets carbon dioxide (CO_2) emissions performance rates for power plants that reflect the "best system of emission reduction." States are required to develop and implement plans that comply with the EPA-established rates. If a state fails to do so, a federal plan regulates emissions within the state.

Immediately after the rule was promulgated, power plants and states represented by Republican attorneys general filed petitions for review in the U.S. Court of Appeals for the D.C. Circuit and moved for an order staying implementation of the Rule pending judicial review. With respect to EPA's statutory authority, the power plants argued that because they were subject to regulation under the NAAQS and Hazardous Air Pollutants program, their emissions could not also be regulated under § 111(d). The House amendment to § 111(d) controlled, the power plants claimed, because it was a "substantive" amendment as that term is used in drafting manuals of the House and Senate Offices of Legislative Counsel, and therefore took priority over the "conforming" amendment the Senate passed. Once the House amendment was executed by amending the U.S. Code, there was nothing left for the Senate's amendment to § 111(d) to amend: "Having already executed the Substantive Amendment, the [House] Law Revision Counsel [which compiles the U.S. Code] properly found the Conforming Amendment to be extraneous." Opening Brief of Petitioners on Core Legal Issues at 72, *West Virginia v. EPA*, No. 15-1363 (D.C. Cir. 2016). EPA responded that both the House and the Senate amendments were validly promulgated law. It maintained the agency had authority to regulate the release of CO_2 under either amendment, and that its interpretation of the Clean Air Act was entitled to deference under *Chevron U.S.A. Inc. v. Natural Resources Defense Council, Inc.*, 467 U.S. 837 (1984), *infra* Chapter 5[C][3].

On January 21, 2016, a panel of the D.C. Circuit unanimously denied petitioners' application for a stay and established an expedited briefing schedule for the challenge to the Clean Power Plan. On February 9, 2016, the Supreme Court stayed implementation of the Rule by a 5-4 vote in an unexplained order. Four days after the Supreme Court's order issued, Justice Scalia passed away. The D.C. Circuit announced that it would hear the petitions for review *en banc*, and heard argument on September 27, 2016. On April 28, 2017, the court announced that it would hold the petitions for review in abeyance while the EPA, now led by Administrator Scott Pruitt, reconsidered the Clean Power Plan.

c. Technical vs. Lay Meaning

Another recurring problem of statutory interpretation involves terms that carry different meanings for different audiences. Think for example of how you understood "negligence" or "intent" before enrolling in law school, and how you understand those terms now. When a statute uses a term that carries different meanings for different people, which of the meanings controls? The following two cases explore this problem.

Nix v. Hedden

149 U.S. 304 (1893)

MR. JUSTICE GRAY, after stating the case, delivered the opinion of the court.

The single question in this case is whether tomatoes, considered as provisions, are to be classed as "vegetables" or as "fruit," within the meaning of the Tariff Act of 1883.

The only witnesses called at the trial testified that neither "vegetables" nor "fruit" had any special meaning in trade or commerce, different from that given in the dictionaries; and that they had the same meaning in trade to-day that they had in March, 1883.

The passages cited from the dictionaries define the word "fruit" as the seed of plants, or that part of plants which contains the seed, and especially the juicy, pulpy products of certain plants, covering and containing the seed. These definitions have no tendency to show that tomatoes are "fruit," as distinguished from "vegetables," in common speech, or within the meaning of the Tariff Act.

There being no evidence that the words "fruit" and "vegetables" have acquired any special meaning in trade or commerce, they must receive their ordinary meaning. Of that meaning the court is bound to take judicial notice, as it does in regard to all words in our own tongue; and upon such a question dictionaries are admitted, not as evidence, but only as aids to the memory and understanding of the court. *Brown v. Piper*, 91 U.S. 37, 42; *Jones v. United States*, 137 U.S. 202, 216; *Nelson v. Cushing*, 2 Cush. 519, 532, 533; *Page v. Fawcet*, 1 Leon. 242; Taylor on Evidence, (8th ed.) §§ 16, 21.

Botanically speaking, tomatoes are the fruit of a vine, just as are cucumbers, squashes, beans and peas. But in the common language of the people, whether sellers or consumers of provisions, all these are vegetables, which are grown in kitchen gardens, and which, whether eaten cooked or raw, are, like potatoes, carrots, parsnips, turnips, beets, cauliflower, cabbage, celery and lettuce, usually served at dinner in, with or after the soup, fish or meats which constitute the principal part of the repast, and not, like fruits generally, as dessert.

The attempt to class tomatoes with fruit is not unlike a recent attempt to class beans as seeds, of which Mr. Justice Bradley, speaking for this court, said: "We do not see why they should be classified as seeds, any more than walnuts should be so classified. Both are seeds in the language of botany or natural history, but not in commerce nor in common parlance. On the other hand, in speaking generally of provisions, beans may well be included under the term 'vegetables.' As an article of food on our tables, whether baked or boiled, or forming the basis of soup, they are used as a vegetable, as well when ripe as when green. This is the principal use to which they are put. Beyond the common knowledge which we have on this subject, very little evidence is necessary, or can be produced." *Robertson v. Salomon*, 130 U.S. 412, 414.

Notes and Questions

1. **The Justification for Regulation.** *Nix v. Hedden* involved the Tariff Act of 1883, ch. 121, 22 Stat. 488, which imposed fairly significant duties on the importation of foreign goods. Under the Act, "vegetables" were subject to a 10% duty. "[F]ruits, green, ripe, or dried" were exempt. *Id.* at 519.

Recall from the introduction to Chapter 1 that prior to the enactment of the Sixteenth Amendment in 1913, tariffs were a major source of revenue for the federal government. The 1883 Act arguably represents the high-point of this financing model, and reflected a desire not only to generate revenue but also to protect domestic industry from increasing foreign competition and trade. Before the 1883 Act was enacted, "[o]rganizations such as the American Iron and Steel Association, the Boston Home Market Club, and the American Protective Tariff League disseminated pro-tariff pamphlets, raised campaign funds, and lobbied lawmakers on behalf of protectionism." Ajay K. Mehrotra, *Envisioning the Modern American Fiscal State: Progressive-Era Economists and the Intellectual Foundations of the U.S. Income Tax*, 52 UCLA L. Rev. 1793, 1806 (2005).

2. **The Procedural Posture.** In *Nix v. Hedden*, the collector of the port of New York demanded that Nix pay duties after classifying tomatoes that Nix imported from Bermuda as "vegetables." Nix maintained that tomatoes were covered by the Tariff Act's exemption for "fruits, green, ripe, or dried" and paid the duties under protest. Nix brought suit to recover the duties he had paid. After hearing from two witnesses and counsel who cited Webster's Dictionary, Worcester's Dictionary, and the Imperial Dictionary, the trial court directed a verdict for defendant. The case was appealed directly to the Supreme Court via a writ of error.

3. **The Statutory Issue.** The interpretive question is whether the 1883 Tariff Act used the term "vegetable" in its lay or technical meaning. What, according to the Court, is the ordinary or lay meaning of a "vegetable"? What is the technical or specialized meaning of that term? Why does the Court conclude that the Tariff Act used vegetable in its lay as opposed to its technical sense?

Corning Glass Works v. Brennan

417 U.S. 188 (1974)

MR. JUSTICE MARSHALL delivered the opinion of the Court.

These cases arise under the Equal Pay Act of 1963, 77 Stat. 56, § 3, 29 U.S.C. § 206(d)(1), which added to § 6 of the Fair Labor Standards Act of 1938 the principle of equal pay for equal work regardless of sex.[*] The principal question posed is whether Corning Glass Works violated the Act by paying a higher base wage to male night shift inspectors than it paid to female inspectors performing the same tasks on the day shift, where the higher wage was paid in addition to a separate night shift differential paid to all employees for night work.[***]

I

Prior to 1925, Corning operated its plants in Wellsboro and Corning only during the day, and all inspection work was performed by women. Between 1925 and 1930, the company began to introduce automatic production equipment which made it desirable to institute a night shift. During this period, however, both New York and Pennsylvania law prohibited women from working at night.[2] As a result, in order to fill inspector positions on the new night shift, the company had to recruit male employees from among its male day workers. The male employees so transferred demanded and received wages substantially higher than those paid to women inspectors engaged on the two day shifts.[3] During this same period, however, no plant-wide shift

---

[*] The version of the Equal Pay Act in effect at the time of the Court's decision provided as follows: No employer having employees subject to any provisions of this section shall discriminate, within any establishment in which such employees are employed, between employees on the basis of sex by paying wages to employees in such establishment at a rate less than the rate at which he pays wages to employees of the opposite sex in such establishment for equal work on jobs the performance of which requires equal skill, effort, and responsibility, and which are performed under similar working conditions, except where such payment is made pursuant to (i) a seniority system; (ii) a merit system; (iii) a system which measures earnings by quantity or quality of production; or (iv) a differential based on any other factor other than sex: Provided, That an employer who is paying a wage rate differential in violation of this subsection shall not, in order to comply with the provisions of this subsection, reduce the wage rate of any employee.
29 U.S.C. § 206(d)(1) (1973), quoted in *Hodgson v. Corning Glass Works*, 474 F.2d 226, 228 (2d Cir. 1973). — Eds.

2. New York prohibited the employment of women between 10 p.m. and 6 a.m. See 1927 N.Y. Laws, c. 453; 1930 N.Y. Laws, c. 868. Pennsylvania also prohibited them from working between 10 p.m. and 6 a.m. See Act of July 25, 1913, Act No. 466, Pa. Laws 1913.

3. Higher wages were demanded in part because the men had been earning more money on their day shift jobs than women were paid for inspection work. Thus, at the time of the creation of the new night shift, female day shift inspectors received wages ranging from 20 to 30 cents per hour. Most of the men designated to fill the newly created night shift positions had been working in the blowing room where the lowest wage rate was 48 cents per hour and where additional incentive pay could be earned. As night shift inspectors these men received 53 cents per hour. There is also some evidence in the record that additional compensation was necessary because the men viewed inspection jobs as "demeaning" and as "women's work."

differential existed and male employees working at night, other than inspectors, received the same wages as their day shift counterparts. Thus a situation developed where the night inspectors were all male, the day inspectors all female, and the male inspectors received significantly higher wages.

In 1944, Corning plants at both locations were organized by a labor union and a collective-bargaining agreement was negotiated for all production and maintenance employees. This agreement for the first time established a plant-wide shift differential, but this change did not eliminate the higher base wage paid to male night inspectors. Rather, the shift differential was superimposed on the existing difference in base wages between male night inspectors and female day inspectors.

Prior to June 11, 1964, the effective date of the Equal Pay Act, the law in both Pennsylvania and New York was amended to permit women to work at night. It was not until some time after the effective date of the Act, however, that Corning initiated efforts to eliminate the differential rates for male and female inspectors. Beginning in June 1966, Corning started to open up jobs on the night shift to women. Previously separate male and female seniority lists were consolidated and women became eligible to exercise their seniority, on the same basis as men, to bid for the higher paid night inspection jobs as vacancies occurred.

On January 20, 1969, a new collective-bargaining agreement went into effect, establishing a new "job evaluation" system for setting wage rates. The new agreement abolished for the future the separate base wages for day and night shift inspectors and imposed a uniform base wage for inspectors exceeding the wage rate for the night shift previously in effect. All inspectors hired after January 20, 1969, were to receive the same base wage, whatever their sex or shift. The collective-bargaining agreement further provided, however, for a higher "red circle" rate for employees hired prior to January 20, 1969, when working as inspectors on the night shift. This "red circle" rate served essentially to perpetuate the differential in base wages between day and night inspectors.

The Secretary of Labor brought these cases to enjoin Corning from violating the Equal Pay Act and to collect back wages allegedly due female employees because of past violations.***

II

Congress' purpose in enacting the Equal Pay Act was to remedy what was perceived to be a serious and endemic problem of employment discrimination in private industry—the fact that the wage structure of "many segments of American industry has been based on an ancient but outmoded belief that a man, because of his role in society, should be paid more than a woman even though his duties are the same." S. Rep. No. 176, 88th Cong., 1st Sess., 1 (1963). The solution adopted was quite simple in principle: to require that "equal work will be rewarded by equal wages."

The Act's basic structure and operation are similarly straightforward. In order to make out a case under the Act, the Secretary must show that an employer pays different wages to employees of opposite sexes "for equal work on jobs the performance of which requires equal skill, effort, and responsibility, and which are performed under similar working conditions." Although the Act is silent on this point, its legislative history makes plain that the Secretary has the burden of proof on this issue,[9] as both of the courts below recognized.

The Act also establishes four exceptions — three specific and one a general catchall provision — where different payment to employees of opposite sexes "is made pursuant to (i) a seniority system; (ii) a merit system; (iii) a system which measures earnings by quantity or quality of production; or (iv) a differential based on any other factor other than sex." Again, while the Act is silent on this question, its structure and history also suggest that once the Secretary has carried his burden of showing that the employer pays workers of one sex more than workers of the opposite sex for equal work, the burden shifts to the employer to show that the differential is justified under one of the Act's four exceptions.***

Corning argues that the Secretary has failed to prove that Corning ever violated the Act because day shift work is not "performed under similar working conditions" as night shift work. The Secretary maintains that day shift and night shift work are performed under "similar working conditions" within the meaning of the Act.[13] Although the Secretary recognizes that higher wages may be paid for night shift work, the Secretary contends that such a shift differential would be based upon a "factor other than sex" within the catchall exception to the Act and that Corning has failed to carry its burden of proof that its higher base wage for male night inspectors was in fact based on any factor other than sex.

The courts below relied in part on conflicting statements in the legislative history having some bearing on this question of statutory construction. The Third Circuit found particularly significant a statement of Congressman Goodell, a sponsor of the Equal Pay bill, who, in the course of explaining the bill on the floor of the House, commented that "standing as opposed to sitting, pleasantness or unpleasantness of surroundings, periodic rest periods, hours of work, *difference in shift*, all would logically fall within the working condition factor." 109 Cong. Rec. 9209 (1963) (emphasis added). The Second Circuit, in contrast, relied on a statement from the House Committee Report which, in describing the broad general exception for differentials "based on any other factor other than sex," stated: "Thus, among other things, shift differentials ... would also be excluded ...." H.R. Rep. No. 309, 88th Cong., 1st Sess., 3 (1963).

We agree with Judge Friendly['s opinion for the Second Circuit], however, that in this case a better understanding of the phrase "performed under similar working conditions" can be obtained from a consideration of the way in which Congress arrived

---

9. See 109 Cong. Rec. 9196 (1963) (Rep. Frelinghuysen); 109 Cong. Rec. 9208 (Rep. Goodell).

13. The Secretary also advances an argument that even if night and day inspection work is assumed not to be performed under similar working conditions, the differential in base wages is nevertheless unlawful under the Act. The additional burden of working at night, the argument goes, was already fully reflected in the plant-wide shift differential, and the shifts were made "similar" by payment of the shift differential.***

at the statutory language than from trying to reconcile or establish preferences between the conflicting interpretations of the Act by individual legislators or the committee reports.***

As originally introduced, the Equal Pay bill required equal pay for "equal work on jobs the performance of which requires equal skills." There were only two exceptions— for differentials "made pursuant to a seniority or merit increase system which does not discriminate on the basis of sex . . . ."[14]

In both the House and Senate committee hearings, witnesses were highly critical of the Act's definition of equal work and of its exemptions. Many noted that most of American industry used formal, systematic job evaluation plans to establish equitable wage structures in their plants.[15] Such systems, as explained coincidentally by a representative of Corning Glass Works who testified at both hearings, took into consideration four separate factors in determining job value—skill, effort, responsibility and working conditions—and each of these four components was further systematically divided into various subcomponents.[16] Under a job evaluation plan, point values are assigned to each of the subcomponents of a given job, resulting in a total point figure representing a relatively objective measure of the job's value.

In comparison to the rather complex job evaluation plans used by industry, the definition of equal work used in the first drafts of the Equal Pay bill was criticized as unduly vague and incomplete. Industry representatives feared that as a result of the bill's definition of equal work, the Secretary of Labor would be cast in the position of second-guessing the validity of a company's job evaluation system. They repeatedly urged that the bill be amended to include an exception for job classification systems, or otherwise to incorporate the language of job evaluation into the bill.[17] Thus Corning's own representative testified:

> "Job evaluation is an accepted and tested method of attaining equity in wage relationship.

> "A great part of industry is committed to job evaluation by past practice and by contractual agreement as the basis for wage administration.

> "'Skill' alone, as a criterion, fails to recognize other aspects of the job situation that affect job worth.

---

14. See S. 882, 88th Cong., 1st Sess., § 4 (1963); cf. S. 910, 88th Cong., 1st Sess., § 4(a) (1963).

15. *See, e.g.,* Hearings On Equal Pay Act of 1963 before the Subcommittee on Labor of the Senate Committee on Labor and Public Welfare, 88th Cong., 1st Sess., 26, 73, 79, 124, 140, 178 (1963) (hereinafter Senate Hearings); Hearings on Equal Pay Act before the Special Subcommittee on Labor of the House Committee on Education and Labor, 88th Cong., 1st Sess., 145–146 (1963) (hereinafter House Hearings).

16. *See* Senate Hearings 96-104; House Hearings 232–240. *See also* House Hearings 304–305, 307–308.

17. *See, e.g.,* Senate Hearings 73, 74, 79, 124, 130, 138, 140, 178; House Hearings 145, 146, 159, 199–200.

"We sincerely hope that this committee in passing legislation to eliminate wage differences based on sex alone, will recognize in its language the general role of job evaluation in establishing equitable rate relationship."[18]

We think it plain that in amending the bill's definition of equal work to its present form, the Congress acted in direct response to these pleas. Spokesmen for the amended bill stated, for example, during the House debates:

"The concept of equal pay for jobs demanding equal skill has been expanded to require also equal effort, responsibility, and similar working conditions. These factors are the core of all job classification systems. They form a legitimate basis for differentials in pay."[19]

Indeed, the most telling evidence of congressional intent is the fact that the Act's amended definition of equal work incorporated the specific language of the job evaluation plan described at the hearings by Corning's own representative—that is, the concepts of "skill," "effort," "responsibility," and "working conditions."

Congress' intent, as manifested in this history, was to use these terms to incorporate into the new federal Act the well-defined and well-accepted principles of job evaluation so as to ensure that wage differentials based upon bona fide job evaluation plans would be outside the purview of the Act. The House Report emphasized:

"This language recognizes that there are many factors which may be used to measure the relationships between jobs and which establish a valid basis for a difference in pay. These factors will be found in a majority of the job classification systems. Thus, it is anticipated that a bona fide job classification program that does not discriminate on the basis of sex will serve as a valid defense to a charge of discrimination." H.R. Rep. No. 309, *supra*, at 3.

It is in this light that the phrase "working conditions" must be understood, for where Congress has used technical words or terms of art, "it [is] proper to explain them by reference to the art or science to which they [are] appropriate." *Greenleaf v. Goodrich*, 101 U.S. 278, 284 (1880). See also *NLRB v. Highland Park Mfg. Co.*, 341 U.S. 322, 326 (1951) (Frankfurter, J., dissenting). This principle is particularly salutary where, as here, the legislative history reveals that Congress incorporated words having a special meaning within the field regulated by the statute so as to overcome objections by industry representatives that statutory definitions were vague and incomplete.

While a layman might well assume that time of day worked reflects one aspect of a job's "working conditions," the term has a different and much more specific meaning in the language of industrial relations. As Corning's own representative testified at the hearings, the element of working conditions encompasses two subfactors: "surroundings" and "hazards."[20] "Surroundings" measures the elements, such as toxic

---

18. Senate Hearings 98; House Hearings 234.

19. 109 Cong. Rec. 9195 (1963) (Rep. Frelinghuysen). *See also* H.R. Rep. No. 309, 88th Cong., 1st Sess., 8 (1963).

20. Senate Hearings 98–99; House Hearings 234–236.

chemicals or fumes, regularly encountered by a worker, their intensity, and their frequency. "Hazards" takes into account the physical hazards regularly encountered, their frequency, and the severity of injury they can cause. This definition of "working conditions" is not only manifested in Corning's own job evaluation plans but is also well accepted across a wide range of American industry.

Nowhere in any of these definitions is time of day worked mentioned as a relevant criterion. The fact of the matter is that the concept of "working conditions," as used in the specialized language of job evaluation systems, simply does not encompass shift differentials. Indeed, while Corning now argues that night inspection work is not equal to day inspection work, all of its own job evaluation plans, including the one now in effect, have consistently treated them as equal in all respects, including working conditions.

And Corning's Manager of Job Evaluation testified*** that time of day worked was not considered to be a "working condition." Significantly, it is not the Secretary in this case who is trying to look behind Corning's bona fide job evaluation system to require equal pay for jobs which Corning has historically viewed as unequal work. Rather, it is Corning which asks us to differentiate between jobs which the company itself has always equated. We agree with the Second Circuit that the inspection work at issue in this case, whether performed during the day or night, is "equal work" as that term is defined in the Act.***

The question remains, however, whether Corning carried its burden of proving that the higher rate paid for night inspection work, until 1966 performed solely by men, was in fact intended to serve as compensation for night work, or rather constituted an added payment based upon sex.*** The differential in base wages originated at a time when no other night employees received higher pay than corresponding day workers, and it was maintained long after the company instituted a separate plant-wide shift differential which was thought to compensate adequately for the additional burdens of night work. The differential arose simply because men would not work at the low rates paid women inspectors, and it reflected a job market in which Corning could pay women less than men for the same work. That the company took advantage of such a situation may be understandable as a matter of economics, but its differential nevertheless became illegal once Congress enacted into law the principle of equal pay for equal work.

III

We now must consider whether Corning continued to remain in violation of the Act after 1966 when, without changing the base wage rates for day and night inspectors, it began to permit women to bid for jobs on the night shift as vacancies occurred. It is evident that this was more than a token gesture to end discrimination, as turnover in the night shift inspection jobs was rapid.***

But the issue before us is not whether the company, in some abstract sense, can be said to have treated men the same as women after 1966. Rather, the question is whether the company remedied the specific violation of the Act which the Secretary proved. We agree with the Second Circuit, as well as with all other circuits that have had occasion to consider this issue, that the company could not cure its violation except by equalizing the base wages of female day inspectors with the higher rates paid the night inspectors.***

Notes and Questions

1. **Justification for Regulation?** The statute at issue in *Corning* is the Equal Pay Act, Pub. L. No. 88-38, 77 Stat. 56, an amendment to the Fair Labor Standards Act (FLSA), Pub. L. No. 75-718, 52 Stat. 1060, codified as amended at 29 U.S.C. § 201 et seq. Like the FLSA, Title VII of the Civil Rights Act of 1964, 42 U.S.C. § 2000e et seq., and the Americans with Disabilities Act (ADA), 42 U.S.C. § 12101 et seq., the Equal Pay Act is part of the federal statutory framework governing the employment process and employer-employee relationship.

Recall from above that the FLSA was enacted in part to overcome a collective action problem faced by employees who demanded minimum wages and compensation for working more than 40 hours per week. In the absence of legislation, employers could respond to an individual employee's demand for improved wages by hiring an employee who accepted less than a sustenance wage or did not demand compensation for overtime. *See Brooklyn Savings Bank v. O'Neil*, and the notes following, in Chapter 1[C][1]. Title VII and the ADA, while advancing important dignity and moral goals, also responded to a form of market failure by mandating the inclusion of racial minorities and disabled individuals in the workforce—a move that improved society's overall welfare that would not necessarily have occurred under ordinary market dynamics.

Which of these policy rationales are applicable to the Equal Pay Act? Is the requirement of equal pay for equal work a simple matter of fairness? Does it overcome a form of market failure, similar to the dynamics that led to the enactment of the FLSA, Title VII, and the ADA? In the absence of protective laws like the Equal Pay Act, why would women stay in a job where they are paid less for the same work than men?

Notice Congress's reliance on job evaluation systems of private industry. Is such reliance consistent with Congress's basic objective of equalizing pay? Is Congress simply rationalizing systems that had kept in place gender-based stereotypes from a time women were excluded from the workforce? Notice also that the Equal Pay Act is administered by the Department of Labor as opposed to the Equal Employment Opportunity Commission (EEOC), which administers Title VII and the ADA. The most obvious explanation for this choice is that, at the time of the Equal Pay Act's enactment in 1963, the EEOC did not yet exist.

2. **Posture of the Dispute.** Before the Supreme Court heard *Corning Glass Works*, the Second and Third Circuits had issued conflicting rulings on whether Corning's pay scheme violated the Equal Pay Act. In both cases, the Secretary of Labor brought

an action to enjoin Corning from violating the Act. Actions were brought in both New York and Pennsylvania because Corning operated plants in both locations. The Second Circuit ruled in favor of the Secretary; the Third Circuit ruled against him.

3. **The Statutory Dispute: Text and Context.** The Equal Pay Act applied to all employers covered by the FLSA. The Act mandated equal pay for jobs "performed under similar working conditions." What, according to the Court, is the ordinary meaning of "working conditions"? What is the technical or specialized meaning of that term?

4. **The Interpretive Audience for the Statute?** As both *Nix* and *Corning* illustrate, terms used in a statute often have different meanings, depending on whether they are read in their technical or lay sense. Why does the Court in *Corning* conclude that, "[w]hile a layman might well assume that time of day worked reflects one aspect of a job's 'working conditions,' the term has a different and much more specific meaning" as used in the Equal Pay Act? How did the statute at issue in each case indicate whether a lay or technical meaning was intended?

Is *Corning* consistent with *Nix*? How can the Court in *Corning* apply a specialized understanding of "working conditions" without even alluding to *Nix*'s conclusion that the ordinary and not the technical meaning of "vegetable" controlled in that case? Do either *Nix* or *Corning* establish a "rule" for determining whether a statute uses a term in the lay sense or the technical sense — or are they examples of judicial intuition based in the statutory context?

A well-known approach to the lay-versus-technical-meaning problem is to choose based on the *audience* the statute speaks to. As expressed by Justice Frankfurter: "If a statute is written for ordinary folk, it would be arbitrary not to assume that Congress intended its words to be read with the minds of ordinary men. If they are addressed to specialists, they must be read by judges with the minds of specialists." Felix Frankfurter, *Some Reflections on the Reading of Statutes*, 47 COLUM. L. REV. 527, 536 (1947). *See also* Frank Easterbrook, *Statutes' Domains*, 50 U. CHI. L. REV. 533, 536 (1983).

What audience does the tariff statute in *Nix* speak to? Customs officials? Persons and business who import "fruit" and "vegetables"? What audience does the Equal Pay Act address? Employees? Employers? Note that the Act applies, among others, to "[e]very employer . . . who in any workweek is engaged in commerce or in the production of goods for commerce, or is employed in an enterprise engaged in commerce or in the production of goods for commerce." 29 U.S.C. § 206(a). Does it make sense to apply to this entire category of employers an understanding of "working conditions" that does not reflect ordinary usage but was advocated by a few large manufacturers in a congressional hearing? What evidence does the Court marshal to suggest that Congress was embracing this technical meaning in the Equal Pay Act?

5. An Alternative Path? Footnote 13 of the Court's opinion flags an alternative argument the Secretary of Labor advanced for why Corning's pay system violated the Equal Pay Act, which did not depend on the conclusion that day and night work are performed under similar "working conditions." Even if night and day inspection work were performed under dissimilar working conditions, the difference in working conditions "was already fully reflected in the plant-wide *shift* differential, and the shifts were made 'similar' by payment of the shift differential." As such, the fact that night inspection workers were paid above that differential could only reflect compensation for their being male.

If the Supreme Court adopted this argument, what would have been the effect on litigation of Equal Pay Act claims? Who would have the burden of proving that differences in pay for day and night work were reflected in the plant-wide shift differential? Would that issue be simple to resolve? All things considered, is the Secretary's alternative argument a better way of interpreting the Act?

d. Unanticipated Changes in Regulated Activity

Experience with a statute can reveal problems that the statute does not address, or that the statute addresses imperfectly. When this occurs, how should courts and other interpreters respond?

Board of Governors of the Federal Reserve System v. Dimension Financial Corp.

474 U.S. 361 (1986)

CHIEF JUSTICE BURGER delivered the opinion of the Court.***

I

A

Section 2(c) of the Bank Holding Company Act defines "bank" as any institution "which (1) accepts deposits that the depositor has a legal right to withdraw on demand, and (2) engages in the business of making commercial loans." 70 Stat. 133, as amended, 12 U.S.C. § 1841(c).

This case is about so-called "nonbank banks"—institutions that offer services similar to those of banks but which until recently were not under [Federal Reserve] Board regulation because they conducted their business so as to place themselves arguably outside the narrow definition of "bank" found in § 2(c) of the Act. Many nonbank banks, for example, offer customers NOW (negotiable order of withdrawal) accounts which function like conventional checking accounts but because of prior notice provisions do not technically give the depositor a "legal right to withdraw on demand." 12 U.S.C. § 1841(c)(1). Others offer conventional checking accounts, but avoid classification as "banks" by limiting their extension of commercial credit to the purchase of money market instruments such as certificates of deposit and commercial paper.

In 1984, the Board promulgated rules providing that nonbank banks offering the functional equivalent of traditional banking services would thereafter be regulated as banks. 49 Fed. Reg. 794. The Board accomplished this by amending its definition of a bank, found in "Regulation Y," in two significant respects. First, the Board defined "demand deposit" to include deposits, like NOW accounts, which are "as a matter of practice" payable on demand. 12 CFR § 225.2 (a)(1)(A) (1985). Second, the Board defined the "making of a commercial loan" as "any loan other than a loan to an individual for personal, family, household, or charitable purposes," including "the purchase of retail installment loans or commercial paper, certificates of deposit, bankers' acceptances, and similar money market instruments." 12 CFR § 225.2(a)(1)(B) (1985).

B

Cases challenging the amended Regulation Y were commenced in three Circuits and were consolidated in the United States Court of Appeals for the Tenth Circuit. The Court of Appeals set aside both the demand deposit and commercial loan aspects of the Board's regulation.*** Accordingly, the Court of Appeals invalidated the amended regulations.***

II

The Bank Holding Company Act of 1956, 12 U.S.C. § 1841 *et seq.*, vests broad regulatory authority in the Board over bank holding companies* "to restrain the undue concentration of commercial banking resources and to prevent possible abuses related to the control of commercial credit." S. Rep. No. 91-1084, p. 24 (1970). The Act authorizes the Board to regulate "any company which has control over any bank." 12 U.S.C. § 1841(a)(1).

The breadth of that regulatory power rests on the Act's definition of the word "bank." The 1956 Act gave a simple and broad definition of bank: "any national banking association or any State bank, savings bank, or trust company." 12 U.S.C. § 1841(c) (1964 ed.). Experience soon proved that literal application of the statute had the unintended consequence of including within regulation industrial banks offering limited checking account services to their customers. These institutions accepted "'funds from the public that are, in actual practice, repaid on demand.'"*** Congress*** amended the statutory definition of a bank in 1966 [to include only] institutions that accept "deposits that the depositor has a legal right to withdraw on demand."

The 1966 definition proved unsatisfactory because it too included within the definition of "bank" institutions that did not pose significant dangers to the banking system. Because one of the primary purposes of the Act was to "restrain undue concentration of . . . commercial credit," it made little sense to regulate institutions that

---

* As relevant here, the Act defines a "bank holding company" as "any company which has control over any bank or over any company that is or becomes a bank holding company." 12 U.S.C. § 1841(a)(1).—Eds.

did not, in fact, engage in the business of making commercial loans. S. Rep. No. 91-1084, p. 24 (1970). Congress accordingly amended the definition, excluding all institutions that did not "engag[e] in the business of making commercial loans." Since 1970 the statute has provided that a bank is any institution that

> "(1) accepts deposits that the depositor has a legal right to withdraw on demand, and (2) engages in the business of making commercial loans." 12 U.S.C. § 1841(c).

III

In 1984, the Board initiated rulemaking to respond to the increase in the number of nonbank banks. After hearing views of interested parties, the Board found that nonbank banks pose three dangers to the national banking system. *First*, by remaining outside the reach of banking regulations, nonbank banks have a significant competitive advantage over regulated banks despite the functional equivalence of the services offered. *Second*, the proliferation of nonbank banks threatens the structure established by Congress for limiting the association of banking and commercial enterprises. *See* 12 U.S.C. § 1843(c)(8) (bank holding company can purchase nonbanking affiliate only if entity "closely related to banking"). *Third*, the interstate acquisition of nonbank banks undermines the statutory proscription on interstate banking without prior state approval. [See 12 U.S.C. § 1842(d) (1970) (to acquire bank located in another state, bank holding company must generally secure approval from acquiree's state).] Since the narrowed statutory definition required that both the demand deposit and the commercial loan elements be present to constitute the institution as a bank, the Board proceeded to amend Regulation Y redefining both elements of the test. We turn now to the two elements of this definition.

A

The Board amended its definition of "demand deposit" primarily to include within its regulatory authority institutions offering NOW accounts. A NOW account functions like a traditional checking account—the depositor can write checks that are payable on demand at the depository institution. The depository institution, however, retains a seldom exercised but nevertheless absolute right to require prior notice of withdrawal. Under a literal reading of the statute, the institution—even if it engages in full-scale commercial lending—is not a "bank" for the purposes of the Holding Company Act because the prior notice provision withholds from the depositor any "legal right" to withdraw on demand. The Board in its amended definition closes this loophole by defining demand deposits as a deposit, not that the depositor has a "legal right to withdraw on demand," but a deposit that "as a matter of practice is payable on demand."***

By the 1966 amendments to § 2(c), Congress expressly limited the Act to regulation of institutions that accept deposits that "the depositor has a legal right to withdraw on demand." 12 U.S.C. § 1841(c). The Board would now define "legal right" as meaning the same as "a matter of practice." But no amount of agency expertise—however sound may be the result—can make the words "legal right" mean a right to do something "as a matter of practice." A legal right to withdraw on demand means just that: a right to withdraw deposits without prior notice or limitation. Institutions offering NOW accounts do not give the depositor a legal right to withdraw on demand; rather, the institution itself retains the ultimate legal right to require advance notice of withdrawal. The Board's definition of "demand deposit," therefore, is not an accurate or reasonable interpretation of §2(c).

B

Section 2(c) of the Act provides that, even if an institution accepts deposits that the depositor has a legal right to withdraw on demand, the institution is not a bank unless it "engages in the business of making commercial loans." Under Regulation Y, "commercial loan" means "any loan other than a loan to an individual for personal, family, household, or charitable purposes," including "the purchase of retail installment loans or commercial paper, certificates of deposit, bankers' acceptances, and similar money market instruments."

The purpose of the amended regulation is to regulate as banks institutions offering "commercial loan substitutes," that is, extensions of credit to commercial enterprises through transactions other than the conventional commercial loan. In its implementing order, the Board explained that "it is proper to include these instruments within the scope of the term commercial loan as used in the Act in order to carry out the Act's basic purposes: to maintain the impartiality of banks in providing credit to business, to prevent conflicts of interest, and to avoid concentration of control of credit." 49 Fed. Reg., at 841.

As the Board's characterization of these transactions as "commercial loan substitutes" suggests, however, money market transactions do not fall within the commonly accepted definition of "commercial loans." The term "commercial loan" is used in the financial community to describe the direct loan from a bank to a business customer for the purpose of providing funds needed by the customer in its business. The term does not apply to, indeed is used to distinguish, extensions of credit in the open market that do not involve close borrower-lender relationships. Cf. G. Munn & F. Garcia, Encyclopedia of Banking and Finance 607 (1983). These latter money market transactions undoubtedly involve the indirect extension of credit to commercial entities but, because they do not entail the face-to-face negotiation of credit between borrower and lender, are not "commercial loans."

This common understanding of the term "commercial loan" is reflected in the Board's own decisions. Throughout the 1970's the Board applied the term "commercial loan" to exclude from regulation institutions engaging in money market transactions. [The Court discussed *D.H. Baldwin Co.*, 63 Fed. Res. Bull. 280 (1977), and *American Fletcher Corp.*, 60 Fed. Res. Bull. 868 (1974).] A 1981 internal memorandum summarized the Board's longstanding interpretation of the commercial loan definition:

> "The Board also has concluded that, although commercial in nature, the purchase of federal funds, money market instruments (certificates of deposit,

commercial paper, and bankers acceptances) are not considered commercial loans *for the purposes of section 2(c) of the Act*, despite the fact that for other statutory and regulatory purposes these instruments may be considered commercial loans." Federal Reserve System, Office Correspondence (Feb. 10, 1981) (App. 97A) (emphasis in original).[5]

The Board now contends that the new definition conforms with the original intent of Congress in enacting the "commercial loan" provision. The provision, the Board argues, was a "technical amendment to the Act designed to create a narrowly circumscribed exclusion from the Act's coverage." The Board supports this revisionist view of the purpose of the "commercial loan" provision by citing a comment in the "legislative history" indicating that at the time the provision was enacted, it operated to exclude only one institution, the Boston Safe Deposit & Trust Co. The Board does not go so far as to claim that the commercial loan amendment was a private bill, designed only to exempt Boston Safe. It suggests, however, that because the amendment was prompted by the circumstances of one particular institution, the language "commercial loan" should be given something other than its commonly accepted meaning.

The statute by its terms, however, exempts from regulation *all* institutions that do not engage in the business of making commercial loans. The choice of this general language demonstrates that, although the legislation may have been prompted by the needs of one institution, Congress intended to exempt the class of institutions not making commercial loans. Furthermore, the legislative history supports this plain reading of the statute. The Senate Report explained:

> "The definition of 'bank' adopted by Congress in 1966 was designed to include commercial banks and exclude those institutions not engaged in commercial banking, since the purpose of the act was to restrain undue concentration of commercial banking resources and to prevent possible abuses related to the control of commercial credit. However, the Federal Reserve Board has noted that this definition may be too broad and may include institutions which are not in fact engaged in the business of commercial banking in that they do not make commercial loans. The committee, accordingly, adopted a provision which would exclude institutions that are not engaged in the business of making commercial loans from the definition of 'bank.'" S. Rep. No. 91-1084, p. 24 (1970).

The only reference to Boston Safe is in a lengthy banking journal article that Representative Gonzalez entered into the Congressional Record. See 116 Cong. Rec. 25846, 25848 (1970) (indicating that Boston Safe was "[v]irtually the only bank that does no commercial lending"). Such a passage is not "legislative history" in any meaningful

---

5. The Board contends that these decisions "represented a willingness by the Board to refrain from applying the full scope of the Act in conditions that did not appear to generate the potential for its evasion." 49 Fed. Reg., at 842. But the decisions themselves make no mention of such self-imposed restraint. Rather, the decisions represented the Board's interpretation of the meaning of the statute based on the language of the Act and the legislative history of its passage.

sense of the term and cannot defeat the plain application of the words actually chosen by Congress to effectuate its will.***

C

Unable to support its new definitions on the plain language of § 2(c), the Board contends that its new definitions fall within the "plain purpose" of the Bank Holding Company Act. Nonbank banks must be subject to regulation, the Board insists, because "a statute must be read with a view to the 'policy of the legislation as a whole' and cannot be read to negate the plain purpose of the legislation." The plain purpose of the legislation, the Board contends, is to regulate institutions "functionally equivalent" to banks. Since NOW accounts are the functional equivalent of a deposit in which the depositor has a legal right to withdraw on demand and money market transactions involve the extension of credit to commercial entities, institutions offering such services should be regulated as banks.[6]

The "plain purpose" of legislation, however, is determined in the first instance with reference to the plain language of the statute itself. Application of "broad purposes" of legislation at the expense of specific provisions ignores the complexity of the problems Congress is called upon to address and the dynamics of legislative action. Congress may be unanimous in its intent to stamp out some vague social or economic evil; however, because its Members may differ sharply on the means for effectuating that intent, the final language of the legislation may reflect hard-fought compromises. Invocation of the "plain purpose" of legislation at the expense of the terms of the statute itself takes no account of the processes of compromise and, in the end, prevents the effectuation of congressional intent.

Without doubt there is much to be said for regulating financial institutions that are the functional equivalent of banks. NOW accounts have much in common with traditional payment-on-demand checking accounts; indeed we recognize that they generally serve the same purpose. Rather than defining "bank" as an institution that offers the functional equivalent of banking services, however, Congress defined with specificity certain transactions that constitute banking subject to regulation. The statute may be imperfect, but the Board has no power to correct flaws that it perceives in the statute it is empowered to administer. Its rulemaking power is limited to adopting regulations to carry into effect the will of Congress as expressed in the statute.***

Notes and Questions

1. **The Procedural Posture.** After the Federal Reserve Board promulgated Regulation Y, the newly regulated non-bank banks sought judicial review under 12 U.S.C. § 1848. That section provides that "[a]ny party aggrieved by an order of the Board

---

6. In a related argument, the Board contends that it has the power to regulate these institutions under § 5(b), which provides that the Board may issue regulations "necessary to enable it to administer and carry out the purposes of this chapter and prevent evasions thereof." 12 U.S.C. § 1844(b). But § 5 only permits the Board to police within the boundaries of the Act; it does not permit the Board to expand its jurisdiction beyond the boundaries established by Congress in § 2(c).

under this chapter may obtain a review of such order in the United States Court of Appeals within any circuit wherein such party has its principal place of business or in the Court of Appeals in the District of Columbia, by filing in the court, within thirty days after the entry of the Board's order, a petition praying that the order of the Board be set aside." What was the status of Regulation Y when the Supreme Court decided *Dimension Financial*? Had any non-bank bank been subject to regulation or any sanctions by the Federal Reserve Board?

2. **The Federal Reserve System.** The Federal Reserve System or "Fed" is the central bank of the United States. Congress created the Federal Reserve as an independent government agency in the Federal Reserve Act of 1913, ch. 6, 38 Stat. 25. The Fed is responsible for conducting the nation's monetary policy, supervising and regulating banks and other major financial institutions, ensuring the stability of the financial system, and providing financial services to the U.S. government.

3. **The Regulatory Problem.** What is the regulatory problem that led the Fed to issue Regulation Y? Why did the Fed believe that non-bank banks should be subject to regulation under the Bank Holding Company Act? Why do you suppose that the Fed promulgated a regulation advancing a new interpretation of § 2(c) of the Bank Holding Company Act rather than asking Congress to amend the Act to cover non-bank banks? Could Congress have anticipated the problem that led the Fed to promulgate Regulation Y? Did Congress provide any mechanism for reinterpreting or adjusting the Act in response to unanticipated changes in regulated parties' activities?

4. **The Statutory Issue.** Under the Bank Holding Company Act, as amended in 1966, the Fed was authorized to regulate any company organized as a bank, defined as an institution which "accepts deposits that the depositor has a legal right to withdraw on demand," and "engages in the business of making commercial loans." In an effort to avoid regulation as banks, the "non-bank banks" made a technical change to their customer agreements so that deposits were not technically payable on demand. Nevertheless, they continued to make payments on demand as a practical matter. The non-bank banks additionally stopped extending commercial loans to business with which they had a personal relationship, and instead made short term investments in the money market (i.e., the market for short-term loans among banks).

Regulation Y responded to the non-bank banks' efforts to avoid regulation by expanding the activities that subjected an entity to regulation by the Fed. To do so, Regulation Y reinterpreted the Bank Holding Company Act's definition of a bank, to include institutions which accepted deposits that "as a matter of practice [are] payable on demand" and made "any loan[s] other than a loan to an individual for personal, family, household, or charitable purposes." The question for the Court was whether Regulation Y was a permissible interpretation of the Bank Holding Company Act's definition of "bank." That is, is a "bank" that accepts deposits which are payable on demand as a matter of practice but not contract, and which makes loans to parties other than to individuals, a "bank" within the meaning of the Bank Holding Company Act?

5. **Unanticipated Changes in Regulated Activity.** Efforts by regulated parties to avoid regulation are pervasive, and are only one of many reasons why a statute might be thought to require updating. Technological and social change may lead to new kinds of activities not contemplated by the statute's drafters, or make the statute's coverage over- or under-inclusive. The statute may have been drafted based on factual assumptions that turn out to have been incorrect or outdated. Application of the statute may reveal problems that the drafter could not have contemplated. Under what circumstances do changes in regulated activity justify interpreting a statute in a manner that departs from a prior interpretation? Does it matter whether the institution that decides to reopen the question is an agency to which Congress has expressly delegated interpretive authority? Recall that the need for regulatory flexibility is a standard justification for charging an agency with implementation of a statute.

6. **"Dynamic" Statutory Interpretation.** Is it ever permissible for an agency or a court to "update" a statute? William N. Eskridge, Jr., *Dynamic Statutory Interpretation*, 135 U. Pa. L. Rev. 1479 (1987), contends that just as courts "typically consider not only the constitutional text and its historical background, but also its subsequent interpretational history, related constitutional developments, and current societal facts," courts should also interpret — and reinterpret — statutes "in light of their present societal, political, and legal context." In Professor Eskridge's view, such "lawmaking from statutes" contributes to a society "that is deliberative and promotes the common good . . . especially in light of the tendency of the legislature to produce too little up-to-date public-seeking policy and not to produce well-integrated policies." *See also Hively vs. Ivy Tech. Comm. College*, 853 F.3d 339, 352 (7th Cir. 2017) (Posner, J., concurring) ("[I]nterpretation can mean giving a fresh meaning to a statement. . . that infuses the statement with vitality and significance today.").

Is the proposed judicial updating function consistent with the understanding of the judicial role that underlies *TVA v. Hill*? *POM Wonderful v. Coca-Cola*? *Corning*? Is such judicial renovation of statutes sufficiently attentive to the rule-of-law concern that parties have reasonably clear notice of how the law will apply to their actions?

Does the legitimacy of judicial updating depend on the specificity of the text that Congress enacts? Consider §1 of the Sherman Antitrust Act, 15 U.S.C. §1: "Every contract, combination in the form of trust or otherwise, or conspiracy, in restraint of trade or commerce among the several States, or with foreign nations, is declared to be illegal." The Supreme Court has reasoned that "[t]he general presumption that legislative changes should be left to Congress has less force with respect to the Sherman Act," because "[f]rom the beginning [the Court] has treated the Sherman Act as a common-law statute. Just as the common law adapts to modern understanding and greater experience, so too does the Sherman Act's prohibition on 'restraint[s] of trade' evolve to meet the dynamics of present economic conditions." *Leegin Creative Leather Products, Inc. v. PSKS, Inc.*, 551 U.S. 877, 899 (2007). Other arguably "common law" statutes include 42 U.S.C. §1983 (creating a cause of action that runs against "[e]very person who, under color of [law], subjects, or causes to be subjected, any citizen of the United States or other person within the jurisdiction thereof to the deprivation of any rights, privileges, or immunities secured by the Constitution and laws"); the Lanham Act, 15 U.S.C. § 1051 et seq. (providing for recognition and enforcement of trade and servicemarks); and § 301 of the Taft-Hartley Act of 1947, 29 U.S.C. § 185 (providing for the enforcement of collective bargaining agreements).

What explains the Court's willingness to treat the Sherman Act as a common law statute? Does the text of § 1 reflect Congress's intention to delegate broad interpretative authority to the courts? If so, how? In *Textile Workers v. Lincoln Mills*, 353 U.S. 448 (1957), the Court considered § 301(a) of the Taft-Hartley Act, 29 U.S.C. § 185(a). Section 301(a) provides that "[s]uits for violation of contracts between an employer and a labor organization representing employees . . . may be brought in any district court of the United States having jurisdiction of the parties, without respect to the amount in controversy or without regard to the citizenship of the parties." The Court reasoned that the section's history and the structure of the Taft-Hartley Act indicated that Congress intended courts to elaborate federal rules of decision in disputes over collective bargaining agreements:

> The . . . Act expressly furnishes some substantive law. It points out what the parties may or may not do in certain situations. Other problems will lie in the penumbra of express statutory mandates. Some will lack express statutory sanction but will be solved by looking at the policy of the legislation and fashioning a remedy that will effectuate that policy. The range of judicial inventiveness will be determined by the nature of the problem.

353 U.S. at 457.

Why does the Court believe the common law approach is *not* warranted when it comes to the Bank Holding Company Act? Does the text, purpose, or history of the Bank Holding Company Act reflect an intention that the Federal Reserve Board *not* interpret the statute in a common law fashion? Note that the precise issue in *Dimension Financial* is not whether courts have authority to update the Bank Holding Company Act in common law fashion, but whether the Board can update the statute through a regulation that alters the definition of "bank." *See generally* Margaret H. Lemos, *The Other Delegate: Judicially Administered Statutes and the Nondelegation Doctrine*, 81 S. Cal. L. Rev. 406 (2008).

7. **Regulation of Non-Bank Banks — Text, History, and Purpose.** The Supreme Court's analysis of whether Regulation Y was a permissible interpretation of the Bank Holding Company Act focused on the Act's text, history, and purpose.

With respect to the first prong of the bank definition — the legal right to withdraw on demand — the Fed maintained in Regulation Y that the term,

> cannot be interpreted to turn on the technicality of whether the account is subject to a notice of withdrawal requirement that in practice is never imposed. Such an interpretation would permit the fundamental purposes of the Act to be circumvented or rendered meaningless simply through the offering of checking accounts that perform the same function as demand deposits, that are advertised as checking accounts, and that for all intents and

purposes are the equivalent of a conventional demand checking deposit, but that are not treated as demand checking deposits only because they are subject to a never exercised right of the depository institution to require prior notice of withdrawals.

Board of Governors of the Federal Reserve System, Final Rule: Bank Holding Companies and Change in Bank Control; Revision of Regulation Y, 49 Fed. Reg. 794, 836 (Jan. 5, 1984).

The Supreme Court responded that "[a] legal right to withdraw on demand means just that: a right to withdraw deposits without prior notice or limitation." Is the Court correct that the literal language of § 2(c) forecloses the Fed's definition? Perhaps sensing that its definition was in tension with the statutory text, the Fed noted in Regulation Y: "It is a fundamental principle of statutory construction that a statute must be interpreted to give effect to its purposes and to avoid an absurd or unreasonable result." 49 Fed. Reg. at 836. Is permitting non-bank banks to evade Fed regulation in fact absurd? From what perspective?

With respect to the second, "commercial loan" prong of the bank definition, the Fed reasoned: "these instruments as a matter of law establish a debtor-creditor relationship and constitute an extension of credit or loan. Since these loans result in the provision of funds to commercial enterprises, including banks, which are also commercial enterprises, and since they are not made for personal, family, household or charitable purposes, these loans are commercial loans for purposes of the bank definition in the Act." 48 Fed. Reg. at 839. The Fed observed that a definition which excluded loans in the money market "would deny to the Board any authority to prevent evasion of the Act by covering instruments that are in fact loans to commercial enterprises but take non-traditional forms. This approach would permit banks to structure their lending transactions to avoid the coverage of the Act and to circumvent its purposes." *Id.*

The Court concludes, however, that a "commercial loan" describes only "the direct loan from a bank to a business customer for the purpose of providing funds needed by the customer in its business." Key to the Court's interpretation is the evolution of the Bank Holding Company Act. The Act initially defined a "bank" as "any national banking association or any State bank, savings bank, or trust company." In response to the Act's perceived overbreadth, Congress in 1966 added the requirement that the bank accept "deposits that the depositor has a legal right to withdraw on demand." In 1970, Congress added a requirement that a bank "engage[] in the business of making commercial loans." In the financial community and Board decisions from the 1970s, "commercial loan" was used "to describe the direct loan from a bank to a business customer for the purpose of providing funds needed by the customer in its business," and not transactions in the money market. In the Court's view, this history reflected Congress's judgment that the initial definition of a bank was too broad, and that the range of regulated institutions should be narrowed.

Does the Court give sufficient attention to the problem of regulatory evasion that motivated the Fed to expand the bank definition? Did anything in the legislative history cited by the Court address the specific problem that prompted Regulation Y—banks' efforts to avoid regulation by making technical changes to the way in which they did business that had no real-world effect? In other words, had Congress spoken to whether the Fed could adjust its interpretation of "bank" in response to activities designed to evade regulation? Who has the better of the debate with respect to the first prong of the bank definition? The second prong?

8. **The "Public Choice" Approach to Statutory Interpretation.** The Court's treatment of the Fed's arguments about the purpose of the Bank Holding Company Act reflects the influence of the public choice approach to statutory interpretation. The approach stresses that passing legislation usually requires members of Congress to make many compromises about the coverage and operation of a bill. The reasons for those compromises are not always apparent from a reading of the statutory text, enactment history, and legislative history. In order to "respect the compromises" that Congress has made, the statute is applied according to its literal text; its scope is not expanded or contracted based on the interpreter's view of what Congress thought the legislation sought to accomplish. *See generally* Frank H. Easterbrook, *Text, History, and Structure in Statutory Interpretation*, 17 Harv. J. L. & Pub. Pol'y 61 (1994); Philip P. Frickey & Daniel A. Farber, Law and Public Choice: A Critical Introduction (1991).

Does the Bank Holding Company Act reflect compromises that are not evident in the statutory text, enactment history, or reliable sources of legislative history? What does the Court mean when it says, "Invocation of the 'plain purpose' of legislation at the expense of the terms of the statute itself takes no account of the processes of compromise and, in the end, prevents the effectuation of congressional intent"? Is there any "compromise" relevant to the regulation of non-bank banks in the history of the Bank Holding Company Act or is the loophole the non-bank banks exploited an artifact of the language used by congressional drafters? Can one tell based upon the materials cited by the Court?

9. **Non-Deference to the Fed.** Regulation Y is an example of an agency statutory interpretation that affects the agency's regulatory jurisdiction. The Court did not consider whether the Fed's interpretation was entitled to judicial deference, because it concluded that interpretation was inconsistent with congressional intent reflected in the Bank Holding Company Act.

10. **Postscript.** The Competitive Equality Banking Act of 1987, Pub. L. No. 100-86, § 101(a)(1), amended the Bank Holding Company's definition of "bank" by replacing the requirement that a bank "accept[] deposits that the depositor has a legal right to withdraw on demand" with a requirement that the bank "accept[] demand deposits or deposits that the depositor may withdraw by check or similar means for payment to third parties or others." Reports of the Senate Banking, Housing, and Urban Affairs

Committee and House/Senate Conference explained that the amendment was needed to close the "the nonbank bank loophole," and noted that "lawyers looking for a way around the Bank Holding Company Act [had] advised their clients that the Act could be circumvented if the bank gave up either its demand deposits or commercial lending." S. Rep. No. 100-19, at 5–6 (1987). *See also* H.R. Conf. Rep. 100-261, at 119–20 (1987). Does the enactment of this legislation say anything about the correctness of the Court's decision in *Dimension Financial*?

11. **Further reading.** For more on the problem of unanticipated changes in regulated activity, see, e.g., EINER ELHAUGE, STATUTORY DEFAULT RULES: HOW TO INTERPRET UNCLEAR LEGISLATION (2009); WILLIAM N. ESKRIDGE, JR., DYNAMIC STATUTORY INTERPRETATION (1994); Martin H. Redish & Theodore T. Chung, *Democratic Theory and the Legislative Process: Mourning the Death of Originalism in Statutory Interpretation*, 68 TUL. L. REV. 803 (1994); Lawrence C. Marshall, *"Let Congress Do It:" The Case for an Absolute Rule of Statutory Stare Decisis*, 88 MICH. L. REV. 177 (1989); T. Alexander Aleinikoff, *Updating Statutory Interpretation*, 87 MICH. L. REV. 22 (1988).

e. Statutory "Blindspots"

The preceding sections deal with situations in which Congress expresses itself imperfectly, whether by choosing language that fails to capture its intentions, enacting statutes that arguably conflict, using terms that have both technical and lay meanings, or using language that imperfectly addresses activity that occurs after a statutory enactment. Another interpretative problem is more basic. Congress can simply fail to address questions that arise in the implementation of a statute, in which case interpreters must determine how to resolve the question using the materials the statute does provide. The following case grapples with a question Congress often leaves unanswered—a statute's geographic reach.

Morrison v. National Australia Bank Ltd.
130 S. Ct. 2869 (2010)

JUSTICE SCALIA delivered the opinion of the Court.

We decide whether § 10(b) of the Securities Exchange Act of 1934 provides a cause of action to foreign plaintiffs suing foreign and American defendants for misconduct in connection with securities traded on foreign exchanges.

I

Respondent National Australia Bank Limited (National) was, during the relevant time, the largest bank in Australia. Its Ordinary Shares—what in America would be called "common stock"—are traded on the Australian Stock Exchange Limited and on other foreign securities exchanges, but not on any exchange in the United States. There are listed on the New York Stock Exchange, however, National's American Depositary Receipts (ADRs), which represent the right to receive a specified number of National's Ordinary Shares. 547 F.3d 167, 168, and n. 1 (C.A.2 2008).

The complaint alleges the following facts, which we accept as true. In February 1998, National bought respondent HomeSide Lending, Inc., a mortgage servicing company headquartered in Florida. HomeSide's business was to receive fees for servicing mortgages (essentially the administrative tasks associated with collecting mortgage payments, see J. Rosenberg, Dictionary of Banking and Financial Services 600 (2d ed. 1985)). The rights to receive those fees, so-called mortgage-servicing rights, can provide a valuable income stream.*** How valuable each of the rights is depends, in part, on the likelihood that the mortgage to which it applies will be fully repaid before it is due, terminating the need for servicing. HomeSide calculated the present value of its mortgage-servicing rights by using valuation models designed to take this likelihood into account. It recorded the value of its assets, and the numbers appeared in National's financial statements.

From 1998 until 2001, National's annual reports and other public documents touted the success of HomeSide's business, and respondents Frank Cicutto (National's managing director and chief executive officer), Kevin Race (HomeSide's chief operating officer), and Hugh Harris (HomeSide's chief executive officer) did the same in public statements. But on July 5, 2001, National announced that it was writing down the value of HomeSide's assets by $450 million; and then again on September 3, by another $1.75 billion. The prices of both Ordinary Shares and ADRs slumped. After downplaying the July write-down, National explained the September write-down as the result of a failure to anticipate the lowering of prevailing interest rates (lower interest rates lead to more refinancings, i.e., more early repayments of mortgages), other mistaken assumptions in the financial models, and the loss of goodwill. According to the complaint, however, HomeSide, Race, Harris, and another HomeSide senior executive who is also a respondent here had manipulated HomeSide's financial models to make the rates of early repayment unrealistically low in order to cause the mortgage-servicing rights to appear more valuable than they really were. The complaint also alleges that National and Cicutto were aware of this deception by July 2000, but did nothing about it.

As relevant here, petitioners Russell Leslie Owen and Brian and Geraldine Silverlock, all Australians, purchased National's Ordinary Shares in 2000 and 2001, before the write-downs.[1] They sued National, HomeSide, Cicutto, and the three HomeSide executives in the United States District Court for the Southern District of New York for alleged violations of §§ 10(b) and 20(a) of the Securities and Exchange Act of 1934, 48 Stat. 891, 15 U.S.C. §§ 78j(b) and 78t(a), and SEC Rule 10b-5, 17 CFR § 240.10b-5 (2009), promulgated pursuant to § 10(b). They sought to represent a class of foreign purchasers of National's Ordinary Shares during a specified period up to the September write-down.

Respondents moved to dismiss for lack of subject-matter jurisdiction under Federal Rule of Civil Procedure 12(b)(1) and for failure to state a claim under Rule 12(b)(6).

---

1. Robert Morrison, an American investor in National's ADRs, also brought suit, but his claims were dismissed by the District Court because he failed to allege damages.***

The District Court granted the motion on the former ground, finding no jurisdiction because the acts in this country were, "at most, a link in the chain of an alleged overall securities fraud scheme that culminated abroad." The Court of Appeals for the Second Circuit affirmed on similar grounds.***

III

A

It is a "longstanding principle of American law 'that legislation of Congress, unless a contrary intent appears, is meant to apply only within the territorial jurisdiction of the United States.'" *EEOC v. Arabian American Oil Co.*, 499 U.S. 244, 248 (1991) (*Aramco*) (quoting *Foley Bros., Inc. v. Filardo*, 336 U.S. 281, 285 (1949)). This principle represents a canon of construction, or a presumption about a statute's meaning, rather than a limit upon Congress's power to legislate, see *Blackmer v. United States*, 284 U.S. 421, 437 (1932). It rests on the perception that Congress ordinarily legislates with respect to domestic, not foreign matters. *Smith v. United States*, 507 U.S. 197, 204, n. 5 (1993).*** When a statute gives no clear indication of an extraterritorial application, it has none.

Despite this principle of interpretation, long and often recited in our opinions, the Second Circuit believed that, because the Exchange Act is silent as to the extraterritorial application of § 10(b), it was left to the court to "discern" whether Congress would have wanted the statute to apply. This disregard of the presumption against extraterritoriality did not originate with the Court of Appeals panel in this case. It has been repeated over many decades by various courts of appeals in determining the application of the Exchange Act, and § 10(b) in particular, to fraudulent schemes that involve conduct and effects abroad. That has produced a collection of tests for divining what Congress would have wanted, complex in formulation and unpredictable in application.***

The Second Circuit [held] that application of § 10(b) could be premised upon either some effect on American securities markets or investors*** or significant conduct in the United States***. It later formalized these two applications into (1) an "effects test," "whether the wrongful conduct had a substantial effect in the United States or upon United States citizens," and (2) a "conduct test," "whether the wrongful conduct occurred in the United States." These became the north star of the Second Circuit's § 10(b) jurisprudence, pointing the way to what Congress would have wished.*** The Second Circuit never put forward a textual or even extratextual basis for these tests.***

As they developed, these tests were not easy to administer. The conduct test was held to apply differently depending on whether the harmed investors were Americans or foreigners: When the alleged damages consisted of losses to American investors abroad, it was enough that acts "of material importance" performed in the United States "significantly contributed" to that result; whereas those acts must have "directly caused" the result when losses to foreigners abroad were at issue. And "merely preparatory activities in the United States" did not suffice "to trigger application of the securities laws for injury to foreigners located abroad." This required the court to distinguish between mere preparation and using the United States as a "base" for fraudulent activities in other countries. But merely satisfying the conduct test was sometimes insufficient without "'some additional factor tipping the scales'" in favor of the application of American law. District courts have noted the difficulty of applying such vague formulations. There is no more damning indictment of the "conduct" and "effects" tests than the Second Circuit's own declaration that "the presence or absence of any single factor which was considered significant in other cases . . . is not necessarily dispositive in future cases."***

Commentators have criticized the unpredictable and inconsistent application of § 10(b) to transnational cases. Some have challenged the premise underlying the Courts of Appeals' approach, namely that Congress did not consider the extraterritorial application of § 10(b) (thereby leaving it open to the courts, supposedly, to determine what Congress would have wanted). Others, more fundamentally, have noted that using congressional silence as a justification for judge-made rules violates the traditional principle that silence means no extraterritorial application.***

The criticisms seem to us justified. The results of judicial-speculation-made-law— divining what Congress would have wanted if it had thought of the situation before the court—demonstrate the wisdom of the presumption against extraterritoriality. Rather than guess anew in each case, we apply the presumption in all cases, preserving a stable background against which Congress can legislate with predictable effects.

B

Rule 10b-5, the regulation under which petitioners have brought suit,[6] was promulgated under § 10(b), and "does not extend beyond conduct encompassed by § 10(b)'s prohibition." Therefore, if § 10(b) is not extraterritorial, neither is Rule 10b-5.

On its face, § 10(b) contains nothing to suggest it applies abroad:

> "It shall be unlawful for any person, directly or indirectly, by the use of any means or instrumentality of interstate commerce or of the mails, or of any facility of any national securities exchange . . . [t]o use or employ, in connection with the purchase or sale of any security registered on a national securities exchange or any security not so registered, . . . any manipulative or

---

6. Rule 10b-5 makes it unlawful:

"for any person, directly or indirectly, by the use of any means or instrumentality of interstate commerce, or of the mails or of any facility of any national securities exchange,

"(a) To employ any device, scheme, or artifice to defraud,

"(b) To make any untrue statement of a material fact or to omit to state a material fact necessary in order to make the statements made, in the light of the circumstances under which they were made, not misleading, or

"(c) To engage in any act, practice, or course of business which operates or would operate as a fraud or deceit upon any person, in connection with the purchase or sale of any security." 17 CFR § 240.10b-5 (2009).

The Second Circuit considered petitioners' appeal to raise only a claim under Rule 10b-5(b), since it found their claims under subsections (a) and (c) to be forfeited. We do likewise.

deceptive device or contrivance in contravention of such rules and regulations as the [Securities and Exchange] Commission may prescribe . . . ." 15 U.S.C. § 78j(b).

Petitioners and the Solicitor General contend, however, that three things indicate that § 10(b) or the Exchange Act in general has at least some extraterritorial application.

First, they point to the definition of "interstate commerce," a term used in § 10(b), which includes "trade, commerce, transportation, or communication . . . between any foreign country and any State." 15 U.S.C. § 78c(a)(17). But "we have repeatedly held that even statutes that contain broad language in their definitions of 'commerce' that expressly refer to 'foreign commerce' do not apply abroad." The general reference to foreign commerce in the definition of "interstate commerce" does not defeat the presumption against extraterritoriality.

Petitioners and the Solicitor General next point out that Congress, in describing the purposes of the Exchange Act, observed that the "prices established and offered in such transactions are generally disseminated and quoted throughout the United States and foreign countries." 15 U.S.C. § 78b(2). The antecedent of "such transactions," however, is found in the first sentence of the section, which declares that "transactions in securities as commonly conducted upon securities exchanges and over-the-counter markets are affected with a national public interest." § 78b. Nothing suggests that this national public interest pertains to transactions conducted upon foreign exchanges and markets. The fleeting reference to the dissemination and quotation abroad of the prices of securities traded in domestic exchanges and markets cannot overcome the presumption against extraterritoriality.

Finally, there is § 30(b) of the Exchange Act, 15 U.S.C. § 78dd(b), which does mention the Act's extraterritorial application: "The provisions of [the Exchange Act] or of any rule or regulation thereunder shall not apply to any person insofar as he transacts a business in securities without the jurisdiction of the United States," unless he does so in violation of regulations promulgated by the Securities and Exchange Commission "to prevent . . . evasion of [the Act]." (The parties have pointed us to no regulation promulgated pursuant to § 30(b).) The Solicitor General argues that "[this] exemption would have no function if the Act did not apply in the first instance to securities transactions that occur abroad."

We are not convinced. In the first place, it would be odd for Congress to indicate the extraterritorial application of the whole Exchange Act by means of a provision imposing a condition precedent to its application abroad. And if the whole Act applied abroad, why would the Commission's enabling regulations be limited to those preventing "evasion" of the Act, rather than all those preventing "violation"? The provision seems to us directed at actions abroad that might conceal a domestic violation, or might cause what would otherwise be a domestic violation to escape on a technicality. At most, the Solicitor General's proposed inference is possible; but possible interpretations of statutory language do not override the presumption against extraterritoriality.

The Solicitor General also fails to account for § 30(a), which reads in relevant part as follows:

> "It shall be unlawful for any broker or dealer . . . to make use of the mails or of any means or instrumentality of interstate commerce for the purpose of effecting on an exchange not within or subject to the jurisdiction of the United States, any transaction in any security the issuer of which is a resident of, or is organized under the laws of, or has its principal place of business in, a place within or subject to the jurisdiction of the United States, in contravention of such rules and regulations as the Commission may prescribe . . . ." 15 U.S.C. § 78dd(a).

Subsection 30(a) contains what § 10(b) lacks: a clear statement of extraterritorial effect. Its explicit provision for a specific extraterritorial application would be quite superfluous if the rest of the Exchange Act already applied to transactions on foreign exchanges — and its limitation of that application to securities of domestic issuers would be inoperative. Even if that were not true, when a statute provides for some extraterritorial application, the presumption against extraterritoriality operates to limit that provision to its terms. No one claims that § 30(a) applies here.

The concurrence claims we have impermissibly narrowed the inquiry in evaluating whether a statute applies abroad, citing for that point the dissent in *Aramco*. But we do not say, as the concurrence seems to think, that the presumption against extraterritoriality is a "clear statement rule," if by that is meant a requirement that a statute say "this law applies abroad." Assuredly context can be consulted as well. But whatever sources of statutory meaning one consults to give "the most faithful reading" of the text, there is no clear indication of extraterritoriality here. The concurrence does not even try to refute that conclusion, but merely puts forward the same (at best) uncertain indications relied upon by petitioners and the Solicitor General. As the opinion for the Court in *Aramco* (which we prefer to the dissent) shows, those uncertain indications do not suffice.

In short, there is no affirmative indication in the Exchange Act that § 10(b) applies extraterritorially, and we therefore conclude that it does not.

IV

A

Petitioners argue that the conclusion that § 10(b) does not apply extraterritorially does not resolve this case. They contend that they seek no more than domestic application anyway, since Florida is where HomeSide and its senior executives engaged in the deceptive conduct of manipulating HomeSide's financial models; their complaint also alleged that Race and Hughes made misleading public statements there. This is less an answer to the presumption against extraterritorial application than it is an assertion — a quite valid assertion — that that presumption here (as often) is not self-evidently dispositive, but its application requires further analysis. For it is a rare case of prohibited extraterritorial application that lacks all contact with the territory of the United States. But the presumption against extraterritorial application would be a craven watchdog indeed if it retreated to its kennel whenever some domestic activity is involved in the case.***

[W]e think that the focus of the Exchange Act is not upon the place where the deception originated, but upon purchases and sales of securities in the United States. Section 10(b) does not punish deceptive conduct, but only deceptive conduct "in connection with the purchase or sale of any security registered on a national securities exchange or any security not so registered." 15 U.S.C. § 78j(b). Those purchase-and-sale transactions are the objects of the statute's solicitude. It is those transactions that the statute seeks to "regulate"; it is parties or prospective parties to those transactions that the statute seeks to "protec[t]." And it is in our view only transactions in securities listed on domestic exchanges, and domestic transactions in other securities, to which § 10(b) applies.

The primacy of the domestic exchange is suggested by the very prologue of the Exchange Act, which sets forth as its object "[t]o provide for the regulation of securities exchanges ... operating in interstate and foreign commerce and through the mails, to prevent inequitable and unfair practices on such exchanges ...." 48 Stat. 881. We know of no one who thought that the Act was intended to "regulat[e]" foreign securities exchanges — or indeed who even believed that under established principles of international law Congress had the power to do so. The Act's registration requirements apply only to securities listed on national securities exchanges. 15 U.S.C. § 78l(a).

With regard to securities not registered on domestic exchanges, the exclusive focus on domestic purchases and sales is strongly confirmed by § 30(a) and (b), discussed earlier. The former extends the normal scope of the Exchange Act's prohibitions to acts effecting, in violation of rules prescribed by the Commission, a "transaction" in a United States security "on an exchange not within or subject to the jurisdiction of the United States." § 78dd(a). And the latter specifies that the Act does not apply to "any person insofar as he transacts a business in securities without the jurisdiction of the United States," unless he does so in violation of regulations promulgated by the Commission "to prevent evasion [of the Act]." § 78dd(b). Under both provisions it is the foreign location of the transaction that establishes (or reflects the presumption of) the Act's inapplicability, absent regulations by the Commission.

The same focus on domestic transactions is evident in the Securities Act of 1933, 48 Stat. 74, enacted by the same Congress as the Exchange Act, and forming part of the same comprehensive regulation of securities trading. That legislation makes it unlawful to sell a security, through a prospectus or otherwise, making use of "any means or instruments of transportation or communication in interstate commerce or of the mails," unless a registration statement is in effect. 15 U.S.C. § 77e(a)(1). The Commission has interpreted that requirement "not to include ... sales that occur outside the United States." 17 CFR § 230.901 (2009).

Finally, we reject the notion that the Exchange Act reaches conduct in this country affecting exchanges or transactions abroad for the same reason that *Aramco* rejected overseas application of Title VII to all domestically concluded employment contracts or all employment contracts with American employers: The probability of incompatibility with the applicable laws of other countries is so obvious that if Congress intended such foreign application "it would have addressed the subject of conflicts with foreign laws and procedures." 499 U.S., at 256. Like the United States, foreign countries regulate their domestic securities exchanges and securities transactions occurring within their territorial jurisdiction. And the regulation of other countries often differs from ours as to what constitutes fraud, what disclosures must be made, what damages are recoverable, what discovery is available in litigation, what individual actions may be joined in a single suit, what attorney's fees are recoverable, and many other matters. *See, e.g.,* Brief for United Kingdom of Great Britain and Northern Ireland as Amicus Curiae 16–21. The Commonwealth of Australia, the United Kingdom of Great Britain and Northern Ireland, and the Republic of France have filed amicus briefs in this case. So have (separately or jointly) such international and foreign organizations as the International Chamber of Commerce, the Swiss Bankers Association, the Federation of German Industries, the French Business Confederation, the Institute of International Bankers, the European Banking Federation, the Australian Bankers' Association, and the Association Francaise des Entreprises Privées. They all complain of the interference with foreign securities regulation that application of § 10(b) abroad would produce, and urge the adoption of a clear test that will avoid that consequence. The transactional test we have adopted—whether the purchase or sale is made in the United States, or involves a security listed on a domestic exchange— meets that requirement.

B

The Solicitor General suggests a different test, which petitioners also endorse: "[A] transnational securities fraud violates [§] 10(b) when the fraud involves significant conduct in the United States that is material to the fraud's success." Neither the Solicitor General nor petitioners provide any textual support for this test.***

[T]he Solicitor General argues that the Commission has adopted an interpretation similar to the "significant and material conduct" test, and that we should defer to that. In the two adjudications the Solicitor General cites, however, the Commission did not purport to be providing its own interpretation of the statute, but relied on decisions of federal courts—mainly Court of Appeals decisions that in turn relied on the*** decisions of the Second Circuit that we discussed earlier.*** We need "accept only those agency interpretations that are reasonable in light of the principles of construction courts normally employ." *Aramco,* 499 U.S., at 260 (Scalia, J., concurring in part and concurring in judgment). Since the Commission's interpretations relied on cases we disapprove, which ignored or discarded the presumption against extraterritoriality, we owe them no deference.

Section 10(b) reaches the use of a manipulative or deceptive device or contrivance only in connection with the purchase or sale of a security listed on an American stock exchange, and the purchase or sale of any other security in the United States. This case involves no securities listed on a domestic exchange, and all aspects of the purchases complained of by those petitioners who still have live claims occurred outside the United States. Petitioners have therefore failed to state a claim on which relief can be granted. We affirm the dismissal of petitioners' complaint on this ground.

[Justice Stevens, joined by Justice Ginsburg, concurred in the judgment but dissented from the Court's repudiation of the Second Circuit's conduct-and-effects test.]

Notes and Questions

1. **The Procedural Posture.** At issue in *Morrison* is whether § 10(b) of the Securities Exchange Act of 1934, 15 U.S.C. § 78j(b), applies to the securities transactions at issue in the plaintiffs' suit, and, more generally, how to determine whether a securities transaction that involves some domestic elements and some foreign elements is regulated by § 10(b). What did the courts below decide with respect to those questions? How did the case get to the Supreme Court? Would additional fact-finding have shed any light on the questions the Supreme Court addressed? What do you recommend the petitioners do after the Supreme Court's decision?

2. **Justification for Regulation and Mode of Regulation.** The Securities Exchange Act of 1934 (Exchange Act), Pub. L. No. 730-291, 48 Stat. 881, codified as amended at 15 U.S.C. § 78a et seq., was enacted at the height of the Depression and governs the secondary securities market in the United States — i.e., the market for securities sold by persons other than the security's issuer. Congress recognized that the public had lost confidence in public securities markets and the national securities exchanges because "prices of securities on such exchanges and markets are susceptible to manipulation and control, and the dissemination of such prices gives rise to excessive speculation, resulting in sudden and unreasonable fluctuations in the prices of securities which . . . cause alternately unreasonable expansion and unreasonable contraction of the volume of credit available for trade, transportation, and industry in interstate commerce." 15 U.S.C. § 78b(3). The Act justified federal legislation on the ground that it was necessary for "reasonably complete and effective" regulation of the securities markets, and to prevent "[n]ational emergencies, which produce widespread unemployment and the dislocation of trade, transportation, and industry, and which burden interstate commerce." § 78b(4). The Act created the Securities Exchange Commission (SEC), a five-member body that is designed to operate relatively free of political interference, and establishes a regulatory structure for national exchanges such as the New York Stock Exchange.

Section 10(b) prohibits parties to securities transactions from making fraudulent statements in connection with those transactions "in contravention of such rules and regulations as the Commission." SEC Rule 10b-5, 17 C.F.R. § 240.10b-5, implements § 10(b) and makes it unlawful for participants in securities transactions "[t]o engage in any act, practice, or course of business which operates or would operate as a fraud or deceit upon any person," among other things. Rule 10b-5 was promulgated with little discussion in 1942 when SEC lawyers learned that the president of a company was buying up its stock while making false statements about the company's financial performance that drove down the stock price. *See Blue Chip Stamps v. Manor Drug Stores*, 421 U.S. 723, 767 (1975). Four years after Rule 10b-5 was promulgated, a court first recognized a private right of action for persons who lost money because of fraud prohibited by Rule 10b-5. *Kardon v. Natl. Gypsum Co.*, 69 F. Supp. 512, 513 (E.D. Pa. 1946). In a case involving the SEC proxy solicitation rules pursuant to § 14(a) of the Exchange Act, 15 U.S.C. § 78n, the Supreme Court recognized an implied private right of action for violations of the proxy rules. *See J.I. Case Co. v. Borak*, 377 U.S. 426 (1964). Since then, the Supreme Court has reviewed a number of cases involving private suits under Rule 10b-5.

In recent decades, private enforcement of Rule 10b-5 has grown into a major area of litigation. In a much-litigated theory, the so-called "fraud on the market" action, a class of plaintiffs alleges that it purchased securities in reliance on the integrity of a security's market price, and that that price was distorted by false statements made by executives of the security's issuer. Such suits typically seek to recover damages plaintiffs suffered by reason of the artificially inflated stock price. *See, e.g., Halliburton v. Erica P. John Fund, Inc.*, 134 S. Ct. 2398 (2014).

Between 1996 and 2013, 1,049 cases were settled in which the plaintiff's only claim was for a violation of Rule 10b-5. The median settlement was $6.8 million. The largest recorded settlement in a Rule 10b-5 action, which alleged other statutory violations and arose out of the failure of Enron Corp., had a value of approximately $7.2 billion. Cornerstone Research, Securities Class Action Settlements, 2013 Review and Analysis, at 12. SEC enforcement of Rule 10b-5 is an order of magnitude less prominent than private enforcement. The SEC often describes private enforcement "a 'necessary supplement' to the Commission's own enforcement proceedings," Brief for the SEC at 1, *Transamerica Mortgage Advisers, Inc. v. Lewis*, 444 U.S. 11 (1979), a formulation that has been adopted by the Supreme Court.

Congress's decision to regulate securities fraud via a federal statute is often attributed to the difficulty of proving fraud at common law. In an impersonal market where counter-parties do not conduct business face-to-face, it may be difficult for a plaintiff to show that she relied on the seller's statements, or that the seller intended the buyer to rely on her statements — both elements of a claim for common law fraud. What might explain the decision of Congress, the courts, and the SEC to leave enforcement of Rule 10b-5 primarily to private parties? What advantages do private litigants have vis-à-vis the Commission in prosecuting violations of Rule 10b-5? What costs does reliance on private litigants impose compared to enforcement by the SEC?

3. **The Problem of Extraterritoriality.** The only part of § 10(b) that speaks to its territorial scope is its reference to "interstate commerce." That reference, however, is simply a jurisdictional hook, which ensures the statute applies only to activity Congress may regulate under Article I, § 8 of the Constitution.

Section 10(b)'s silence with respect to its territorial reach is a common blindspot in statutory drafting. Congress occasionally specifies the territorial reach of statutes it enacts, *see, e.g.*, Foreign Trade Antitrust Improvements Act, Pub. L. 97-290, 96 Stat. 1246 (1982), but more frequently says nothing on the subject. This failure creates predictable interpretative problems. In an interconnected global economy, activities that are subject to regulation often take place in more than one nation. When this happens, courts and agencies must sort out whether the activity that took place in the United States, or the effects on U.S. markets, trigger the application of U.S. law. *See generally* David L. Noll, *The New Conflicts Law*, 2 STAN. J. COMPLEX LIT. 40 (2014).

Why do you suppose that Congress failed to specify the territorial scope of § 10(b) when it enacted the Securities Exchange Act in 1934? Did Congress have information necessary to make a judgment about the statute's territorial scope when it was enacted? Would members of Congress have even been aware of the possibility of cross-border securities transactions before the electronic communications developments of the post-World War II era?

Of course, Congress has amended the Exchange Act several times since it was first enacted. *See, e.g.*, Williams Act, Pub. L. No. 90-439, 82 Stat. 455 (1968); Sarbanes-Oxley Act of 2002, Pub. L. No. 107-204, 116 Stat. 745 (2002). Congress has also amended other statutes to deal expressly with extraterritorial application. *See, e.g.*, Civil Rights Act of 1991, Pub. L. No. 102-168, 105 Stat. 1071 (1991); Foreign Trade Antitrust Improvements Act, Pub. L. No. 97-290, 96 Stat. 1246 (1982). Why did parties subject to the string of appellate decisions *Morrison* criticized not seek an amendment clarifying § 10(b)'s application to transactions that did not take place entirely within in the United States? Would such an amendment be desirable for the plaintiffs in § 10(b) actions (or more to the point, law firms that specialize in representing them)? Would it be desirable for the SEC? Regulated issuers? As between Congress, the Supreme Court, and the SEC, who would plaintiffs want to clarify § 10(b)'s territorial scope? Issuers and other sellers of securities? Other countries with a possible regulatory interest in the transaction at issue?

4. **Section 10(b)'s Territorial Scope.** The Court's analysis of § 10(b)'s territorial scope proceeds in two steps. The Court begins from the premise that § 10(b) cannot apply to all transactions in the world. Insofar as the "presumption against extraterritoriality" captures this intuition, it is uncontroversial and even obvious. Indeed, despite *Morrison*'s criticism of the Second Circuit's "disregard" of the presumption against extraterritoriality, that court had long recognized that the Securities Exchange Act did not apply worldwide. *See, e.g., Bersch v. Drexel Firestone, Inc.*, 519 F.2d 974, 985 (2d Cir. 1975) ("When . . . a court is confronted with transactions that on any view are predominantly foreign, it must seek to determine whether Congress would have wished the precious resources of United States courts and law enforcement agencies to be devoted to them rather than leave the problem to foreign countries.").

The second, more important step in the Court's analysis involves the "trigger" for the application of § 10(b). Where a transaction involves both foreign and domestic elements, courts must identify what kinds of connections to the United States are needed for § 10(b) to apply.

Courts have historically followed two approaches when considering that kind of question. Under a "conduct" test, a statute applies when one or more of the activities that trigger liability occur within the United States. *See American Banana Co. v. United Fruit Co.*, 213 U.S. 347, 356 (1909) (Holmes, J.). Under an "effects" test, a statute applies when the regulated transaction affects an interest of the United States—prototypically by harming a U.S. citizen. *See Steele v. Bulova Watch Co.*, 344 U.S. 280, 288 (1952). *See generally* William S. Dodge, *Understanding the Presumption Against Extraterritoriality*, 16 BERKELEY J. INT'L L. 85 (1998).

By the time of *Morrison*, Second Circuit caselaw held that either U.S. conduct *or* effects on the market, or a combination of the two, supported the application of § 10(b). Overruling that precedent, *Morrison* holds that § 10(b) applies only to "transactions in securities listed on domestic exchanges, and domestic transactions in other securities." One of this volume's authors has written that this holding reflects a particular, rule-like form of the "conduct" test. Section 10(b) applies only to frauds that culminate in a *transaction* that takes place in the United States. If such a transaction exists, § 10(b) applies regardless of where other conduct related to the fraud took place and regardless of whether the fraud affected U.S. investors or interests of the United States. Absent a transaction on a U.S. exchange, § 10(b) does not apply—again, regardless of whether conduct related to the fraud took place in the United States or the fraud affected U.S. interests. Noll, *supra*, at 81.

What explains the Court's decision to link the applicability of § 10(b) to a transaction that takes place on a U.S. exchange? The Court contends that transactions on U.S. exchanges "are the objects of the statute's solicitude" and the preamble to the Securities Exchange Act reflects a concern with fraud and other misconduct on U.S. exchanges. Is this explanation convincing? Doesn't § 10(b)'s reference to fraud "*in connection with the purchase or sale of any security registered on a national securities exchange or any security not so registered*" suggest a far broader territorial scope, if anything? Why doesn't the Court interpret § 10(b) to reach frauds perpetrated in the United States that affect U.S. investors but are effected through in transactions on foreign exchanges? Does Justice Scalia explain why?

5. **Substantive Canons of Construction.** If the Court's test is not dictated by the text or purpose of the Exchange Act, what else might explain it? Note in this respect the Court's observation that foreign countries and industry groups had complained "of the interference with foreign securities regulation that application of § 10(b) abroad would produce, and urge the adoption of a clear test that will avoid that consequence." The idea that federal legislation should be construed so as to avoid conflicts with other nations' laws is an example of a "substantive canon." Such canons give effect to deeply held values that are not necessarily captured in the text, history, or structure of legislation—for example, avoiding conflicts with foreign governments, preserving the traditional functions of state government, or ensuring that Congress rather than an agency makes major policy decisions. Substantive canons are justified on the ground that if Congress sought to intrude on one of these values, it would say so clearly. We return to substantive canons in the following section.

6. **Why No Deference to the SEC?** The SEC adopted the Second Circuit's conduct-and-effects test in two administrative decisions that arose out of SEC enforcement actions, *In re United Securities Clearing Corp.*, 52 S.E.C. 92 (1994), and *In re Robert F. Lynch*, Exchange Act Release No. 11737, 8 S.E.C. Docket 75 (1975). *Morrison* declined to defer to the SEC's interpretation of the Exchange Act's territorial scope on the ground that it was not "reasonable in light of the principles of construction courts normally employ." Is the Court's explanation for why it did not defer to the SEC convincing?

7. **Statutory "Blindspots" and the "Checklist" Proposal.** The territorial scope of a statute is only one of many issues that Congress may fail to address when enacting legislation. In 1990, Chief Justice Rehnquist convened a "Federal Courts Study Committee" to study problems in the administration of the federal courts and recommend reforms. One of the committee's central recommendations was that Congress develop a "checklist" for legislative staff to use in reviewing legislation. The checklist would remind legislative staff of items that needed to be addressed in new legislation, including the statute of limitations, whether Congress intended to create a private cause of action, whether pre-emption of state law is intended, the definition of key terms, and whether the statute applied retroactively. Report of the Federal Courts Study Committee, at 91 (Apr., 1990). *See also* Robert A. Katzmann, *The Continuing Challenge, in* JUDGES AND LEGISLATORS: TOWARD INSTITUTIONAL COMITY 180, 184 (1988) (advocating similar checklist). Congress, however, has not institutionalized the use of a legislative drafting checklist.

8. **Postscript.** The Dodd-Frank Wall Street Reform and Consumer Protection Act, Pub. L. No. 111-203, 124 Stat. 1376 (2010), was signed into law soon after the Court handed down *Morrison*. Section 929P(b)(2) of Dodd Frank adds the following provision to the Securities Exchange Act of 1934:

> EXTRATERRITORIAL JURISDICTION. — The district courts of the United States and the United States courts of any Territory shall have jurisdiction of an action or proceeding brought or instituted by the Commission or the United States alleging a violation of the antifraud provisions of this title involving —
>
> (1) conduct within the United States that constitutes significant steps in furtherance of the violation, even if the securities transaction occurs outside the United States and involves only foreign investors; or
>
> (2) conduct occurring outside the United States that has a foreseeable substantial effect within the United States.

124 Stat. 1865

With respect to private actions, Dodd Frank directs the Commission to undertake a study of whether the conduct-and-effects test should be restored along similar lines. The SEC was to study:

> (1) the scope of such a private right of action, including whether it should extend to all private actors or whether it should be more limited to extend just to institutional investors or otherwise; (2) what implications such a private

right of action would have on international comity; (3) the economic costs and benefits of extending a private right of action for transnational securities frauds; and (4) whether a narrower extraterritorial standard should be adopted.

Id. at 1871.

Why would Congress make the territorial reach of a statute depend on who was enforcing it? What reasons are suggested by the study Congress directed the SEC to undertake? Does the fact that Congress responded to *Morrison* show that the presumption against extraterritoriality is working the way that the Court envisioned? How might the dynamics of the legislative process affect the "dialogue" between the Court and Congress over extraterritoriality that *Morrison* seems to envision?

The SEC released its study in April 2012. It concluded that "the conflicting evidence in the academic literature and the results of our event study on the *Morrison* decision are inconclusive as to the net benefits or costs of a cross-border extension of private rights of action." Securities & Exchange Commission, Study on the Cross-Border Scope of the Private Right of Action Under Section 10(b) of the Securities Exchange Act of 1934, at B13 (Apr. 2012), available at http://www.sec.gov/news/studies/2012/929y -study-cross-border-private-rights.pdf.

9. **Further Reading.** For more on the causes of statutory blindspots and the interpretative challenges they create, *see, e.g.*, JUDGES AND LEGISLATORS: TOWARD INSTITUTIONAL COMITY (Robert A. Katzmann, ed., 1988); Robert A. Katzmann & Russell R. Wheeler, *A Mechanism for Statutory Housekeeping: Appellate Courts Working with Congress*, 9 J. APP. PRAC. & PROCESS 131 (2007); Amanda Frost, *Certifying Questions to Congress*, 101 NW. U. L. REV. 1 (2007); Victoria F. Nourse & Jane S. Schacter, *The Politics of Legislative Drafting: A Congressional Case Study*, 77 N.Y.U. L. REV. 575 (2002); Gregory E. Maggs, *Reducing the Costs of Statutory Ambiguity: Alternative Approaches and the Federal Courts Study Committee*, 29 HARV. J. ON LEGIS. 123 (1992).

f. Application of Statute Raises Risk of Constitutional Invalidity

To this point, the cases in this section have largely concerned problems "internal" to statutes. Questions arise because Congress fails to articulate the meaning of a statutory provision or address questions that arise in the statute's implementation. Or, the way in which the statute's provisions interact with one another, or with other statutes, is unclear.

But questions of statutory interpretation also arise for reasons "external" to the statute. Most prominently, application of a statute can run up against deeply held values in the common law, Constitution, or political history of the nation, raising questions about whether Congress in fact intended to violate those values. The following cases consider this problem and the judicial doctrine that has evolved in response to it.

NLRB v. Catholic Bishop of Chicago

440 U.S. 490 (1979)

Mr. Chief Justice Burger delivered the opinion of the Court.

This case arises out of the National Labor Relations Board's exercise of jurisdiction over lay faculty members at two groups of Catholic high schools. We granted certiorari to consider two questions: (a) Whether teachers in schools operated by a church to teach both religious and secular subjects are within the jurisdiction granted by the National Labor Relations Act; and (b) if the Act authorizes such jurisdiction, does its exercise violate the guarantees of the Religion Clauses of the First Amendment?

I

One group of schools is operated by the Catholic Bishop of Chicago, a corporation sole; the other group is operated by the Diocese of Fort Wayne-South Bend, Inc. The group operated by the Catholic Bishop of Chicago consists of two schools, Quigley North and Quigley South. Those schools are termed "minor seminaries" because of their role in educating high school students who may become priests. At one time, only students who manifested a positive and confirmed desire to be priests were admitted to the Quigley schools. In 1970, the requirement was changed so that students admitted to these schools need not show a definite inclination toward the priesthood. Now the students need only be recommended by their parish priest as having a potential for the priesthood or for Christian leadership. The schools continue to provide special religious instruction not offered in other Catholic secondary schools. The Quigley schools also offer essentially the same college-preparatory curriculum as public secondary schools. Their students participate in a variety of extra-curricular activities which include secular as well as religious events. The schools are recognized by the State and accredited by a regional educational organization.

The Diocese of Fort Wayne-South Bend, Inc., has five high schools. Unlike the Quigley schools, the special recommendation of a priest is not a prerequisite for admission. Like the Quigley schools, however, these high schools seek to provide a traditional secular education but oriented to the tenets of the Roman Catholic faith; religious training is also mandatory. These schools are similarly certified by the State.

In 1974 and 1975, separate representation petitions were filed with the Board by interested union organizations for both the Quigley and the Fort Wayne-South Bend schools; representation was sought only for lay teachers. The schools challenged the assertion of jurisdiction on two grounds: (a) that they do not fall within the Board's discretionary jurisdictional criteria; and (b) that the Religion Clauses of the First Amendment preclude the Board's jurisdiction. The Board rejected the jurisdictional arguments on the basis of its decision in *Roman Catholic Archdiocese of Baltimore*, 216 N.L.R.B. 249 (1975). There the Board explained that its policy was to decline jurisdiction over religiously sponsored organizations "only when they are completely religious, not just religiously associated." Because neither group of schools was found to fall within the Board's "completely religious" category, the Board ordered elections.

In the Board-supervised election at the Quigley schools, the Quigley Education Alliance, a union affiliated with the Illinois Education Association, prevailed and was certified as the exclusive bargaining representative for 46 lay teachers. In the Diocese of Fort Wayne-South Bend, the Community Alliance for Teachers of Catholic High Schools, a similar union organization, prevailed and was certified as the representative for the approximately 180 lay teachers. Notwithstanding the Board's order, the schools declined to recognize the unions or to bargain. The unions filed unfair labor practice complaints with the Board under §§ 8(a)(1) and (5) of the National Labor Relations Act, 49 Stat. 452, as amended, 29 U.S.C. §§ 158(a)(1) and (5). The schools opposed the General Counsel's motion for summary judgment, again challenging the Board's exercise of jurisdiction over religious schools on both statutory and constitutional grounds.

The Board reviewed the record of previous proceedings and concluded that all of the arguments had been raised or could have been raised in those earlier proceedings. Since the arguments had been rejected previously, the Board granted summary judgment, holding that it had properly exercised its statutory discretion in asserting jurisdiction over these schools.[7] The Board concluded that the schools had violated the Act and ordered that they cease their unfair labor practices and that they bargain collectively with the unions.

II

The schools challenged the Board's orders in petitions to the Court of Appeals for the Seventh Circuit. That court denied enforcement of the Board's orders.***

IV

That there are constitutional limitations on the Board's actions has been repeatedly recognized by this Court even while acknowledging the broad scope of the [National Labor Relations Act's] grant of jurisdiction. The First Amendment, of course, is a limitation on the power of Congress. Thus, if we were to conclude that the Act granted the challenged jurisdiction over these teachers we would be required to decide whether that was constitutionally permissible under the Religion Clauses of the First Amendment.

Although the respondents press their claims under the Religion Clauses, the question we consider first is whether Congress intended the Board to have jurisdiction over teachers in church-operated schools. In a number of cases the Court has heeded the

---

7. The Board relied on its reasoning in *Cardinal Timothy Manning, Roman Catholic Archbishop of the Archdiocese of Los Angeles*, 223 N.L.R.B. 1218 (1976): "We also do not agree that the schools are religious institutions intimately involved with the Catholic Church. It has heretofore been the Board's policy to decline jurisdiction over institutions only when they are completely religious, not just religiously associated. The schools perform in part the secular function of educating children, and in part concern themselves with religious instruction. Therefore, we will not decline to assert jurisdiction over these schools on such a basis."

essence of Mr. Chief Justice Marshall's admonition in *Murray v. The Charming Betsy*, 2 Cranch 64, 118 (1804), by holding that an Act of Congress ought not be construed to violate the Constitution if any other possible construction remains available. Moreover, the Court has followed this policy in the interpretation of the Act now before us and related statutes.***

The values enshrined in the First Amendment plainly rank high in the scale of our national values. In keeping with the Court's prudential policy it is incumbent on us to determine whether the Board's exercise of its jurisdiction here would give rise to serious constitutional questions. If so, we must first identify "the affirmative intention of the Congress clearly expressed" before concluding that the Act grants jurisdiction.

In recent decisions involving aid to parochial schools we have recognized the critical and unique role of the teacher in fulfilling the mission of a church-operated school. What was said of the schools in *Lemon v. Kurtzman*, 403 U.S. 602, 617 (1971), is true of the schools in this case: "Religious authority necessarily pervades the school system." The key role played by teachers in such a school system has been the predicate for our conclusions that governmental aid channeled through teachers creates an impermissible risk of excessive governmental entanglement in the affairs of the church-operated schools.***

The Board argues that it can avoid excessive entanglement since it will resolve only factual issues such as whether an anti-union animus motivated an employer's action. But at this stage of our consideration we are not compelled to determine whether the entanglement is excessive as we would were we considering the constitutional issue. Rather, we make a narrow inquiry whether the exercise of the Board's jurisdiction presents a significant risk that the First Amendment will be infringed.

Moreover, it is already clear that the Board's actions will go beyond resolving factual issues. The Court of Appeals' opinion refers to charges of unfair labor practices filed against religious schools. The court observed that in those cases the schools had responded that their challenged actions were mandated by their religious creeds. The resolution of such charges by the Board, in many instances, will necessarily involve inquiry into the good faith of the position asserted by the clergy-administrators and its relationship to the school's religious mission. It is not only the conclusions that may be reached by the Board which may impinge on rights guaranteed by the Religion Clauses, but also the very process of inquiry leading to findings and conclusions.

The Board's exercise of jurisdiction will have at least one other impact on church-operated schools. The Board will be called upon to decide what are "terms and conditions of employment" and therefore mandatory subjects of bargaining. See 29 U.S.C. § 158(d). Although the Board has not interpreted that phrase as it relates to educational institutions, similar state provisions provide insight into the effect of mandatory bargaining.***

The Pennsylvania Supreme Court aptly summarized the effect of mandatory bargaining when it observed that the "introduction of a concept of mandatory collective bargaining, regardless of how narrowly the scope of negotiation is defined, necessarily represents an encroachment upon the former autonomous position of management." Inevitably the Board's inquiry will implicate sensitive issues that open the door to conflicts between clergy-administrators and the Board, or conflicts with negotiators for unions.***

The church-teacher relationship in a church-operated school differs from the employment relationship in a public or other nonreligious school. We see no escape from conflicts flowing from the Board's exercise of jurisdiction over teachers in church-operated schools and the consequent serious First Amendment questions that would follow. We therefore turn to an examination of the National Labor Relations Act to decide whether it must be read to confer jurisdiction that would in turn require a decision on the constitutional claims raised by respondents.

VI

There is no clear expression of an affirmative intention of Congress that teachers in church-operated schools should be covered by the Act. Admittedly, Congress defined the Board's jurisdiction in very broad terms; we must therefore examine the legislative history of the Act to determine whether Congress contemplated that the grant of jurisdiction would include teachers in such schools.

In enacting the National Labor Relations Act in 1935, Congress sought to protect the right of American workers to bargain collectively.*** Our examination of the statute and its legislative history indicates that Congress simply gave no consideration to church-operated schools. It is not without significance, however, that the Senate Committee on Education and Labor chose a college professor's dispute with the college as an example of employer-employee relations not covered by the Act. S. Rep. No. 573, 74th Cong., 1st Sess., 7 (1935).

Congress' next major consideration of the jurisdiction of the Board came during the passage of the Labor Management Relations Act of 1947 — the Taft-Hartley Act. In that Act Congress amended the definition of "employer" in § 2 of the original Act to exclude nonprofit hospitals.* 61 Stat. 137, 29 U.S.C. § 152(2) (1970 ed.). There was some discussion of the scope of the Board's jurisdiction but the consensus was that nonprofit institutions in general did not fall within the Board's jurisdiction because they did not affect commerce. *See* H.R. 3020, 80th Cong., 1st Sess. (1947); H.R. Rep.

---

* The amended definition of employer applied to "any person acting as an agent of an employer, directly or indirectly, but shall not include the United states or any Federal Reserve Bank, or any State or political subdivision thereof, *or any corporation or association operating a hospital, if no part of the net earnings inures to the benefits of any private shareholder or individual,* or any person subject to the Railway Labor Act, as amended from time to time, or any labor organization (other than when acting as an employer), or anyone acting in the capacity of officer or agent of such labor organization" (emphasis added). — Eds.

No. 245, 80th Cong., 1st Sess., 12 (1947); H.R. Conf. Rep. No. 510, 80th Cong., 1st Sess., 3, 32 (1947); 93 Cong. Rec. 4997 (1947) (remarks of Sens. Tydings and Taft).

The most recent significant amendment to the Act was passed in 1974, removing the exemption of nonprofit hospitals. Pub. L. 93-360, 88 Stat. 395. The Board relies upon that amendment as showing that Congress approved the Board's exercise of jurisdiction over church-operated schools. A close examination of that legislative history, however, reveals nothing to indicate an affirmative intention that such schools be within the Board's jurisdiction. Since the Board did not assert jurisdiction over teachers in a church-operated school until after the 1974 amendment, nothing in the history of the amendment can be read as reflecting Congress' tacit approval of the Board's action.

During the debate there were expressions of concern about the effect of the bill on employees of religious hospitals whose religious beliefs would not permit them to join a union. 120 Cong. Rec. 12946, 16914 (1974) (remarks of Sen. Ervin and Rep. Erlenborn). The result of those concerns was an amendment which reflects congressional sensitivity to First Amendment guarantees:

> "Any employee of a health care institution who is a member of and adheres to established and traditional tenets or teachings of a bona fide religion, body, or sect which has historically held conscientious objections to joining or financially supporting labor organizations shall not be required to join or financially support any labor organization as a condition of employment; except that such employee may be required, in lieu of periodic dues and initiation fees, to pay sums equal to such dues and initiation fees to a nonreligious charitable fund exempt from taxation under section 501(c)(3) of title 26, chosen by such employee from a list of at least three such funds, designated in a contract between such institution and a labor organization, or if the contract fails to designate such funds, then to any such fund chosen by the employee." 29 U.S.C. § 169.

The absence of an "affirmative intention of the Congress clearly expressed" fortifies our conclusion that Congress did not contemplate that the Board would require church-operated schools to grant recognition to unions as bargaining agents for their teachers.*** [I]n the absence of a clear expression of Congress' intent to bring teachers in church-operated schools within the jurisdiction of the Board, we decline to construe the Act in a manner that could in turn call upon the Court to resolve difficult and sensitive questions arising out of the guarantees of the First Amendment Religion Clauses.***

MR. JUSTICE BRENNAN, with whom MR. JUSTICE WHITE, MR. JUSTICE MARSHALL, and MR. JUSTICE BLACKMUN join, dissenting.

The general principle of construing statutes to avoid unnecessary constitutional decisions is a well-settled and salutary one. The governing canon, however, is not that expressed by the Court today. The settled canon for construing statutes wherein constitutional questions may lurk was stated in [*Machinists v. Street*, 367 U.S. 740 (1961):]

> "When the validity of an act of the Congress is drawn in question, and even if a serious doubt of constitutionality is raised, it is a cardinal principle that this Court will first ascertain whether a construction of the statute is fairly possible by which the question may be avoided."

This limitation to constructions that are "fairly possible," and "reasonable," acts as a brake against wholesale judicial dismemberment of congressional enactments. It confines the judiciary to its proper role in construing statutes, which is to interpret them so as to give effect to congressional intention. The Court's new "affirmative expression" rule releases that brake.

The interpretation of the National Labor Relations Act announced by the Court today is not "fairly possible." The Act's wording, its legislative history, and the Court's own precedents leave "the intention of the Congress . . . revealed too distinctly to permit us to ignore it because of mere misgivings as to power." Section 2(2) of the Act, 29 U.S.C. § 152(2), defines "employer" as

> ". . . any person acting as an agent of an employer, directly or indirectly, *but shall not include* the United States or any wholly owned Government corporation, or any Federal Reserve Bank, or any State or political subdivision thereof, or any person subject to the Railway Labor Act, as amended from time to time, or any labor organization (other than when acting as an employer), or anyone acting in the capacity of officer or agent of such labor organization." (Emphasis added.)

Thus, the Act covers all employers not within the eight express exceptions. The Court today substitutes amendment for construction to insert one more exception — for church-operated schools. This is a particularly transparent violation of the judicial role: The legislative history reveals that Congress itself considered and rejected a very similar amendment.

The pertinent legislative history of the NLRA begins with the Wagner Act of 1935, 49 Stat. 449. Section 2(2) of that Act, identical in all relevant respects to the current section, excluded from its coverage neither church-operated schools nor any other private nonprofit organization.[3] Accordingly, in applying that Act, the National Labor Relations Board did not recognize an exception for nonprofit employers, even when religiously associated. An argument for an implied nonprofit exemption was rejected

---

3. Section 2(2), 49 Stat. 450, stated:
"The term 'employer' includes any person acting in the interest of an employer, directly or indirectly, but shall not include the United States, or any State or political subdivision thereof, or any person subject to the Railway Labor Act, as amended from time to time, or any labor organization (other than when acting as an employer), or anyone acting in the capacity of officer or agent of such labor organization."

because the design of the Act was as clear then as it is now: "[N]either charitable institutions nor their employees are exempted from operation of the Act by its terms, although certain other employers and employees are exempted." Both the lower courts and this Court concurred in the Board's construction.

The Hartley bill, which passed the House of Representatives in 1947, would have provided the exception the Court today writes into the statute:

> "The term 'employer' . . . shall not include . . . any corporation, community chest, fund, or foundation organized and operated exclusively for *religious*, charitable, scientific, literary, or *educational* purposes, . . . no part of the net earnings of which inures to the benefit of any private shareholder or individual . . . ." (Emphasis added.) H.R. 3020, 80th Cong., 1st Sess., § 2(2) (Apr. 18, 1947).

But the proposed exception was not enacted.[5] The bill reported by the Senate Committee on Labor and Public Welfare did not contain the Hartley exception. See S. 1126, 80th Cong., 1st Sess., § 2(2) (Apr. 17, 1947). Instead, the Senate proposed an exception limited to nonprofit hospitals, and passed the bill in that form. See H.R. 3020, 80th Cong., 1st Sess., § 2(2) (Senate, May 13, 1947). The Senate version was accepted by the House in conference, thus limiting the exception for nonprofit employers to nonprofit hospitals. Ch. 120, 61 Stat. 136.

Even that limited exemption was ultimately repealed in 1974. Pub. L. 93-360, 88 Stat. 395. In doing so, Congress confirmed the view of the Act expressed here: that it was intended to cover all employers—including nonprofit employers—unless expressly excluded, and that the 1947 amendment excluded only nonprofit hospitals.[7] ***Moreover, it is significant that in considering the 1974 amendments, the Senate expressly rejected an amendment proposed by Senator Ervin that was analogous to the one the Court today creates—an amendment to exempt nonprofit hospitals operated by religious groups. 120 Cong. Rec. 12950, 12968 (1974). Senator Cranston, floor manager of the Senate Committee bill and primary opponent of the proposed religious exception, explained:

> "[S]uch an exception for religiously affiliated hospitals would seriously erode *the existing national policy which holds religiously affiliated institutions*

---

5. A number of reasons were offered for the rejection of the Hartley bill's exception. Some Congressmen strongly opposed the exception, *see* 93 Cong. Rec. 3446 (1947) (remarks of Rep. Klein); some were opposed to additional exceptions to the Board's jurisdiction, *see id.*, at 4997 (remarks of Sen. Taft); and some thought it unnecessary, *see* H.R. Conf. Rep. No. 510, 80th Cong., 1st Sess., 32 (1947). But whatever the reasons, it is clear that an amendment similar to that made by the Court today was proposed and rejected in 1947.

7. The House Report stated: "Currently, the only broad area of charitable, eleemosynary, educational institutions wherein the Board does not now exercise jurisdiction concerns the nonprofit hospitals, explicitly excluded by section 2(2) of the Act . . . . [T]he bill removes the existing Taft-Hartley exemption in section 2(2) of the Act. It restores to the employees of nonprofit hospitals the same rights and protections enjoyed by the employees of proprietary hospitals and most all other employees." H.R. Rep. No. 93-1051, p. 4 (1974).***

generally such as proprietary nursing homes, residential communities, and educational facilities to the same standards as their nonsectarian counterparts." 120 Cong. Rec. 12957 (1974) (emphasis added).

See also ibid. (Sen. Javits); 120 Cong. Rec. 12957 (1974) (Sen. Williams).[8]

In construing the Board's jurisdiction to exclude church-operated schools, therefore, the Court today is faithful to neither the statute's language nor its history.***

Thus, the available authority indicates that Congress intended to include—not exclude—lay teachers of church-operated schools. The Court does not counter this with evidence that Congress did intend an exception it never stated. Instead, despite the legislative history to the contrary, it construes the Act as excluding lay teachers only because Congress did not state explicitly that they were covered. In Mr. Justice Cardozo's words, this presses "avoidance of a difficulty . . . to the point of disingenuous evasion."

Notes and Questions

1. **Justification for Regulation and Mode of Regulation.** The National Labor Relations Act (NLRA) regulates the employer-union relationship; provides legal recognition of the bargaining authority of organizations such as unions that represent some or all of an employer's employees; and prohibits employers and unions alike from engaging in "unfair labor practices" (ULPs). The independent National Labor Relations Board (NLRB) is central to operation of the Act. Through its General Counsel's office, the Board investigates and prosecutes ULP cases. Case adjudication is performed in the first instance by Board-employed administrative law judges, whose decisions are subject to review and revision by the Board.

The justifications for this regulatory regime are twofold: (1) collective representation helps workers negotiate fairer contracts as a group than they could on their own and, in the process, boosts consumer demand for U.S. products and services (the "equality-of-bargaining-power" rationale) and (2) an administrative process for resolving labor relations disputes will reduce the incidence of industrial conflict with spillover effects on society at large (the "industrial-peace" rationale). *See* Samuel Estreicher, *"Easy In, Easy Out": A Future for U.S. Workplace Representation*, 98 Minn. L. Rev. 1615, 1617 (2014).

---

8. The Court relies upon the fact that the 1974 amendments provided that "[a]ny *employee* of a health care institution who is a member of . . . a bona fide religion . . . which has historically held conscientious objections to joining . . . labor organizations shall not be required to join . . . any labor organization as a condition of employment . . . ." 29 U.S.C. § 169 (emphasis added). This is, of course, irrelevant to the instant case, as no employee has alleged that he was required to join a union against his religious principles and not even the respondent employers contend that collective bargaining itself is contrary to their religious beliefs. Recognizing this, the Court has limited its inference from the amendment to the proposition that it reflects "congressional sensitivity to First Amendment guarantees." This is quite true, but its usefulness as support for the Court's opinion is completely negated by the rejection of the Ervin amendment, which makes clear the balance struck by Congress. While Congress agreed to exclude conscientiously objecting employees, it expressly refused to sanction an exclusion for all religiously affiliated employers.

2. **The Statutory Question.** The provisions of the NLRA most pertinent to *Catholic Bishops* are §§ 2, 8, and 10 of the Act. Section 10 provides, "The Board is empowered . . . to prevent any person from engaging in any unfair labor practice . . . affecting commerce." 29 U.S.C. § 160. Section 8 prohibits an "employer" from engaging in five unfair labor practices, among them "refus[ing] to bargain collectively with the representatives of his employees." 29 U.S.C. § 158(a)(5). Section 2 defines an "employer" as:

> any person acting as an agent of an employer, directly or indirectly, but shall not include the United States or any wholly owned Government corporation, or any Federal Reserve Bank, or any State or political subdivision thereof, or any person subject to the Railway Labor Act, as amended from time to time, or any labor organization (other than when acting as an employer), or anyone acting in the capacity of officer or agent of such labor organization.

29 U.S.C. § 152(2).

3. **Procedural and Regulatory Posture.** What was the action of the NLRB under review? Was there any evidence of the impact of the Board's assertion of jurisdiction on the operation of the religious schools? Or was the courts' analysis based on speculation?

4. **The Trigger for Constitutional Avoidance: Constitutional Violations vs. Constitutional Doubt?** The doctrine of constitutional avoidance entered our jurisprudence with Justice Brandeis's concurring opinion in *Ashwander v. TVA*, 297 U.S. 288 (1936). Protesting the Court's choice to resolve a constitutional question about the constitutionality of the Tennessee Valley Authority, Brandeis catalogued seven principles the Court had developed "for its own governance in the cases confessedly within its jurisdiction," through which the Court "has avoided passing upon a large part of all the constitutional questions pressed upon it for decision." *Id.* at 346 (Brandeis, J., concurring). The seventh of these was that "When the validity of an act of the Congress is drawn in question, and even if a serious doubt of constitutionality is raised, it is a cardinal principle that this Court will first ascertain whether a construction of the statute is fairly possible by which the question may be avoided." *Id.* at 348. A standard formulation of constitutional avoidance doctrine holds that "if an otherwise acceptable construction of a statute would raise serious constitutional problems, and where an alternative interpretation of the statute is 'fairly possible,' we are obligated to construe the statute to avoid such problems." *INS v. St. Cyr*, 533 U.S. 289, 299–300 (2001). *See generally* Samuel Estreicher, *Judicial Nullification: Guido Calabresi's Uncommon Common Law for an Age of Statutes*, 57 N.Y.U. L. Rev. 1126 (1982).

What is the specific constitutional violation the Court fears will occur if the NLRB is permitted to assert jurisdiction over the collective bargaining rights of lay teachers at Chicago and South Bend catholic schools? How likely was that violation? Is the court identifying a likely violation or a mere concern? According to the Court, how great does the risk of a constitutional violation have to be?

Recall that in *United States v. Sullivan*, 332 U.S. 689, 693 (1948), *supra* Chapter 1[B][2], the Court stated: "A restrictive interpretation should not be given a statute merely because Congress has chosen to depart from custom or because giving effect to the express language employed by Congress might require a court to face a constitutional question." By contrast, the Court in *Catholic Bishop* writes that the Board's interpretation of the NLRA should be avoided because the Board's assertion of jurisdiction creates a "significant risk" that the First Amendment will be violated. Given that the Supreme Court has the authority to determine whether the First Amendment was in fact violated, does it make sense to speak about the "risk" that a statute will be found unconstitutional? In Justice Brandeis's formulation, constitutional avoidance seems to involve adopting an alternate construction to avoid declaring a statute unconstitutional. The Court in *Catholic Bishops* follows more of a prophylactic approach, construing the statute to avoid the necessity of even considering its constitutionality, if there is a sufficiently high risk that deciding the constitutional question would result in invalidation of the statute. Is there a practical difference between these approaches? What is gained by adopting an alternate interpretation of the NLRA instead of deciding the constitutional question outright?

5. **The Requirement of a "Fairly Possible" Alternate Construction.** Justice Brennan in dissent objects that the Court's interpretation of the National Labor Relations Act, exempting religiously affiliated schools from the Act's coverage, is not "fairly possible." But for the constitutional objection, is there any way to construe the sections of the Act quoted in question 2 above to deny the Board jurisdiction over religiously affiliated schools? How might the schools invoke the Act's text and purpose to support such an interpretation?

The Court advances two main arguments for exempting religiously affiliated schools from the NLRB's jurisdiction. The Court first posits that there was a "consensus" to this effect when Congress adopted the Taft-Hartley Act in 1947, and specifically, that members of Congress did not think that non-profit hospitals were engaged in commerce under the prevailing understanding of the commerce power. Justice Brennan responds that Congress rejected an amendment that would have exempted religious employees, which would have been senseless if the act did not apply to non-profits in the first place. Who has the better of this exchange?

The Court next invokes the 1974 amendment to the NLRA that permitted certain health care workers to opt out of otherwise mandatory payment of union dues. The Court reads the amendment to reflect a general "congressional sensitivity to First Amendment guarantees." Is this argument persuasive? How should it inform a proper reading of the statutory definition of a covered "employer" or a covered "employee"?

Justice Brennan counters that the Court's interpretation conflicts with § 2's definition of an employer, and that the history of the NLRA shows that Congress intended to exert its regulatory authority to the full extent permitted by the Commerce Clause. The Court responds by invoking the dog-that-didn't-bark canon. Its review of the NLRA's legislative history did not reveal any instances in which a member of Congress *affirmatively indicated* that the NLRB had authority to regulate religiously affiliated schools.

Considering all of the materials cited by the Court, is an interpretation of the NLRA that does not apply to religious schools plausible, much less "fairly possible"? If not, why is the Court willing to engage in what effectively amounts to a judicial revision of the statute? Does it matter how difficult or simple it would be for Congress to amend the Act? Compare the Federal Reserve Board's decision in *Dimension Financial, supra* Section [B][2][d], to reinterpret the coverage of the Bank Holding Company Act rather than asking Congress to amend the Act in a way that applied to "non-bank banks." Is the Court in *Catholic Bishops* doing what it said the Federal Reserve in *Dimension Financial* could not do? Is the Court's interpretation legitimate?

Much debate has focused on how plausible an interpretation must be to satisfy the "fairly possible" standard. In *United States v. Five Gambling Devices Labeled in Part "Mills," & Bearing Serial Nos. 593-221*, 346 U.S. 441, 447 (1953), the government argued that a statute regulating gambling devices required the registration of all covered devices, regardless of whether a device was involved in interstate commerce — a litigating position that invited "a far-reaching [holding] as to the extent of congressional power." In a plurality opinion, Justice Jackson wrote:

> [T]his Court will construe a statute in a manner that requires decision of serious constitutional questions only if the statutory language leaves no reasonable alternative. This is not because we would avoid or postpone difficult decisions. The predominant consideration is that we should be sure Congress has intentionally put its power in issue by the legislation in question before we undertake a pronouncement which may have far-reaching consequences upon the powers of the Congress or the powers reserved to the several states. To withhold passing upon an issue of power until we are certain it is knowingly precipitated will do no great injury, for Congress, once we have recognized the question, can make its purpose explicit and thereby necessitate or avoid decision of the question.

Id. at 448–49.

More recent cases take a somewhat more restrictive view of courts' power to interpret statutes to avoid constitutional questions. For example, in *Almendarez-Torres v. United States*, 523 U.S. 224, 238 (1998), the Court wrote:

> The [constitutional avoidance] doctrine seeks in part to minimize disagreement between the branches by preserving congressional enactments that might otherwise founder on constitutional objections. It is not designed to aggravate that friction by creating (through the power of precedent) statutes foreign to those Congress intended, simply through fear of a constitutional difficulty that, upon analysis, will evaporate. Thus, those who invoke the doctrine must believe that the alternative is a serious likelihood that the statute will be held unconstitutional. Only then will the doctrine serve its basic

democratic function of maintaining a set of statutes that reflect, rather than distort, the policy choices that elected representatives have made. For similar reasons, the statute must be genuinely susceptible to two constructions after, and not before, its complexities are unraveled. Only then is the statutory construction that avoids the constitutional question a "fair" one.

In *Clark v. Martinez*, 543 U.S. 371 (2005), Justice Scalia purported to add a textual limitation to the doctrine. He said in an opinion for the Court: "The canon of constitutional avoidance comes into play only when, after the application of ordinary textual analysis, the statute is found to be susceptible of more than one construction; and the canon functions *as a means of choosing between them.*" *Id.* at 385.

6. **Constitutional Avoidance and the Sequencing of Constitutional Decisionmaking.** In *National Federation of Independent Businesses v. Sebelius*, 132 S. Ct. 2566 (2011), the Supreme Court considered the constitutionality of the "individual mandate" in the Patient Protection and Affordable Care Act, Pub. L. No. 111-148, 124 Stat. 119 (2012). *See* 26 U.S.C. § 5000A (Supp. IV 2010). Chief Justice Roberts argued in a section of his opinion joined by no other Justice that, because the Solicitor General principally defended the constitutionality of the mandate as an exercise of the commerce power, the Court was required to address that argument before considering whether the mandate was a permissible exercise of the taxing power:

> [T]he statute reads more naturally as a command to buy insurance than as a tax, and I would uphold it as a command if the Constitution allowed it. It is only because the Commerce Clause does not authorize such a command that it is necessary to reach the taxing power question. And it is only because we have a duty to construe a statute to save it, if fairly possible, that § 5000A can be interpreted as a tax. Without deciding the Commerce Clause question, I would find no basis to adopt such a saving construction.

Id. at 2600–01.

Concurring in the Chief Justice's ultimate conclusion that the mandate was constitutional, Justice Ginsburg objected that the Chief Justice's "Commerce Clause essay" was unnecessary. "The Chief Justice ultimately concludes . . . that interpreting the provision as a tax is a 'fairly possible' construction. That being so, I see no reason to undertake a Commerce Clause analysis that is not outcome determinative." Is the Chief Justice's use of the canon of constitutional avoidance consistent with *Ashwander* and *Catholic Bishops*? Does it matter that the Court in *Sebelius* undertook not to interpret the Affordable Care Act but to decide its constitutionality?

Note on "Substantive" Canons of Statutory Interpretation

Toward the beginning of this chapter, we introduced a number of linguistic canons that courts use to resolve recurring problems of statutory interpretation. The canons discussed there are justified on the ground that they capture the way in which Congress or the broader legal community uses particular verbal formulations. For example, the *expressio unius* canon teaches that when a statute identifies specific things that are regulated (e.g., stocks, bonds, and mutual funds), the listing of those things connotes a decision *not* to regulate other things (e.g., futures contracts). In general legal usage, the expression of one thing implies the exclusion of others.

In contrast to these grammatical or semantic canons, the canon of constitutional avoidance teaches that courts should interpret statutes in light of constitutional values—namely, minimizing the need to strike down legislation as unconstitutional and preserving comity between Congress and the courts. Other substantive canons similarly promote values extrinsic to the statute under interpretation. The justification for invoking these canons is that we should not assume Congress means to trench on these values; if Congress truly wished to intrude on the value a canon protects, it would express its intention to do so clearly. Thus, the canons impose "clear statement" rules.

Other prominent substantive canons include the following:

- The *presumption against extraterritoriality*, introduced in *Morrison*, holds that federal statutes do not apply outside the United States unless it is clear that a statute was intended to apply extraterritorially.

- The Administrative Procedure Act-based *presumption of reviewability* holds that "judicial review of a final agency action by an aggrieved person will not be cut off unless there is persuasive reason to believe that such was the purpose of Congress." *Abbott Laboratories v. Gardner*, 387 U.S. 136, 140 (1967).

- The *rule of lenity* teaches that "when choice has to be made between two readings of what conduct Congress has made a crime, it is appropriate, before we choose the harsher alternative, to require that Congress should have spoken in language that is clear and definite." *United States v. Universal C.L.T. Credit Corp.*, 344 U.S. 218, 221–22 (1952).

- The *Charming Betsy* canon teaches that "an Act of congress ought never to be construed to violate the law of nations, if any other possible construction remains." *Murray v. Schooner Charming Betsy*, 6 U.S. (2 Cranch) 64, 118 (1804).

- The Eleventh Amendment-based *presumption of state sovereign immunity* holds that "Congress may abrogate the States' constitutionally secured immunity from suit in federal court only by making its intention unmistakably clear in the language of the statute." *Atascadero State Hospital v. Scanlon*, 473 U.S. 234 (1985).

- The *Native American sovereignty canon* holds that "statutes are to be construed liberally in favor of Indians with ambiguous provisions interpreted to their benefit." *Chickasaw Nation v. United States*, 534 U.S. 84, 88 (2001).

The substantive canons' reliance on non-statutory substantive values raises questions about how courts identify the values that deserve protection via doctrines of statutory interpretation, and whether courts in this manner are developing a general federal common law that they ordinarily do not have the authority to expound. How, for example, did the Court in *Morrison* know that avoiding conflict with foreign regulatory regimes was important enough to restrict § 10(b) of the Exchange Act to frauds that culminate in a transaction in the United States? Does the Court's judgment about the desirability of avoiding regulatory conflicts originate in the Constitution? Other statutes? Common sense? These questions run throughout the following decision on the Age Discrimination in Employment Act, a statute we previously encountered in *General Dynamics Land Systems, Inc. v. Cline*, in Section [B][1][b], above.

Gregory v. Ashcroft
501 U.S. 452 (1991)

JUSTICE O'CONNOR delivered the opinion of the Court.

Article V, § 26, of the Missouri Constitution provides that "[a]ll judges other than municipal judges shall retire at the age of seventy years." We consider whether this mandatory retirement provision violates the federal Age Discrimination in Employment Act of 1967 (ADEA or Act), 81 Stat. 602, as amended, 29 U.S.C. §§ 621–634.***

I

Petitioners are Missouri state judges. Judge Ellis Gregory, Jr., is an associate circuit judge for the Twenty-first Judicial Circuit. Judge Anthony P. Nugent, Jr., is a judge of the Missouri Court of Appeals, Western District. Both are subject to the § 26 mandatory retirement provision. Petitioners were appointed to office by the Governor of Missouri, pursuant to the Missouri Non-Partisan Court Plan, Mo. Const., Art. V, §§ 25(a)-25(g). Each has, since his appointment, been retained in office by means of a retention election in which the judge ran unopposed, subject only to a "yes or no" vote. See Mo. Const., Art. V, § 25(c)(1).

Petitioners and two other state judges filed suit against John D. Ashcroft, the Governor of Missouri, in the United States District Court for the Eastern District of Missouri, challenging the validity of the mandatory retirement provision. The judges alleged that the provision violated both the ADEA and the Equal Protection Clause of the Fourteenth Amendment to the United States Constitution. The Governor filed a motion to dismiss. [The District Court granted the motion and the Court of Appeals for the Eighth Circuit affirmed.]

II

The ADEA makes it unlawful for an "employer" "to discharge any individual" who is at least 40 years old "because of such individual's age." 29 U.S.C. §§ 623(a), 631(a). The term "employer" is defined to include "a State or political subdivision of a State." § 630(b)(2). Petitioners work for the State of Missouri. They contend that the Missouri mandatory retirement requirement for judges violates the ADEA.

A

As every schoolchild learns, our Constitution establishes a system of dual sovereignty between the States and the Federal Government. This Court also has recognized this fundamental principle. In *Tafflin v. Levitt*, 493 U.S. 455, 458 (1990), "[w]e beg[a]n with the axiom that, under our federal system, the States possess sovereignty concurrent with that of the Federal Government, subject only to limitations imposed by the Supremacy Clause." Over 120 years ago, the Court described the constitutional scheme of dual sovereigns:

> "'[T]he people of each State compose a State, having its own government, and endowed with all the functions essential to separate and independent existence,'... '[W]ithout the States in union, there could be no such political body as the United States.' Not only, therefore, can there be no loss of separate and independent autonomy to the States, through their union under the Constitution, but it may be not unreasonably said that the preservation of the States, and the maintenance of their governments, are as much within the design and care of the Constitution as the preservation of the Union and the maintenance of the National government. The Constitution, in all its provisions, looks to an indestructible Union, composed of indestructible States." *Texas v. White*, 7 Wall. 700, 725 (1869), quoting *Lane County v. Oregon*, 7 Wall. 71, 76 (1869).

The Constitution created a Federal Government of limited powers. "The powers not delegated to the United States by the Constitution, nor prohibited by it to the States, are reserved to the States respectively, or to the people." U.S. Const., Amdt. 10. The States thus retain substantial sovereign authority under our constitutional system. As James Madison put it:

> "The powers delegated by the proposed Constitution to the federal government are few and defined. Those which are to remain in the State governments are numerous and indefinite.... The powers reserved to the several States will extend to all the objects which, in the ordinary course of affairs, concern the lives, liberties, and properties of the people, and the internal order, improvement, and prosperity of the State." The Federalist No. 45, pp. 292–293 (C. Rossiter ed. 1961).

This federalist structure of joint sovereigns preserves to the people numerous advantages. It assures a decentralized government that will be more sensitive to the diverse needs of a heterogenous society; it increases opportunity for citizen involvement in democratic processes; it allows for more innovation and experimentation in government; and it makes government more responsive by putting the States in competition for a mobile citizenry.

Perhaps the principal benefit of the federalist system is a check on abuses of government power. "The 'constitutionally mandated balance of power' between the States and the Federal Government was adopted by the Framers to ensure the protection of 'our fundamental liberties.'" *Atascadero State Hospital v. Scanlon*, 473 U.S. 234, 242 (1985), quoting *Garcia v. San Antonio Metropolitan Transit Authority*, 469 U.S. 528, 572 (1985) (Powell, J., dissenting). Just as the separation and independence of the coordinate branches of the Federal Government serve to prevent the accumulation of excessive power in any one branch, a healthy balance of power between the States and the Federal Government will reduce the risk of tyranny and abuse from either front. Alexander Hamilton explained to the people of New York, perhaps optimistically, that the new federalist system would suppress completely "the attempts of the government to establish a tyranny":

> "[I]n a confederacy the people, without exaggeration, may be said to be entirely the masters of their own fate. Power being almost always the rival of power, the general government will at all times stand ready to check the usurpations of the state governments, and these will have the same disposition towards the general government. The people, by throwing themselves into either scale, will infallibly make it preponderate. If their rights are invaded by either, they can make use of the other as the instrument of redress." The Federalist No. 28, pp. 180–181 (C. Rossiter ed. 1961).

James Madison made much the same point:

> "In a single republic, all the power surrendered by the people is submitted to the administration of a single government; and the usurpations are guarded against by a division of the government into distinct and separate departments. In the compound republic of America, the power surrendered by the people is first divided between two distinct governments, and then the portion allotted to each subdivided among distinct and separate departments. Hence a double security arises to the rights of the people. The different governments will control each other, at the same time that each will be controlled by itself." *Id.*, No. 51, p. 323.

One fairly can dispute whether our federalist system has been quite as successful in checking government abuse as Hamilton promised, but there is no doubt about the design. If this "double security" is to be effective, there must be a proper balance between the States and the Federal Government. These twin powers will act as mutual restraints only if both are credible. In the tension between federal and state power lies the promise of liberty.

The Federal Government holds a decided advantage in this delicate balance: the Supremacy Clause. U.S. Const., Art. VI, cl. 2. As long as it is acting within the powers granted it under the Constitution, Congress may impose its will on the States. Congress may legislate in areas traditionally regulated by the States. This is an extraordinary power in a federalist system. It is a power that we must assume Congress does not exercise lightly.

The present case concerns a state constitutional provision through which the people of Missouri establish a qualification for those who sit as their judges. This provision goes beyond an area traditionally regulated by the States; it is a decision of the most fundamental sort for a sovereign entity. Through the structure of its government, and the character of those who exercise government authority, a State defines itself as a sovereign.***

Congressional interference with this decision of the people of Missouri, defining their constitutional officers, would upset the usual constitutional balance of federal and state powers. For this reason, "it is incumbent upon the federal courts to be certain of Congress' intent before finding that federal law overrides" this balance. We explained recently:

> "[I]f Congress intends to alter the 'usual constitutional balance between the States and the Federal Government,' it must make its intention to do so 'unmistakably clear in the language of the statute.'" *Atascadero State Hospital v. Scanlon*, 473 U.S. 234, 242 (1985); see also *Pennhurst State School and Hospital v. Halderman*, 465 U.S. 89, 99 (1984).

> "*Atascadero* was an Eleventh Amendment case, but a similar approach is applied in other contexts. Congress should make its intention 'clear and manifest' if it intends to pre-empt the historic powers of the States, ... 'In traditionally sensitive areas, such as legislation affecting the federal balance, the requirement of clear statement assures that the legislature has in fact faced, and intended to bring into issue, the critical matters involved in the judicial decision.'"

This plain statement rule is nothing more than an acknowledgment that the States retain substantial sovereign powers under our constitutional scheme, powers with which Congress does not readily interfere.***

Here, we must decide what Congress did in extending the ADEA to the States, pursuant to its powers under the Commerce Clause. See *EEOC v. Wyoming*, 460 U.S. 226 (1983) (the extension of the ADEA to employment by state and local governments was a valid exercise of Congress' powers under the Commerce Clause). As against Congress' powers "[t]o regulate Commerce . . . among the several States," U.S. Const., Art. I, § 8, cl. 3, the authority of the people of the States to determine the qualifications of their government officials may be inviolate.

We are constrained in our ability to consider the limits that the state-federal balance places on Congress' powers under the Commerce Clause. *See Garcia v. San Antonio Metropolitan Transit Authority*, 469 U.S. 528 (1985) (declining to review limitations placed on Congress' Commerce Clause powers by our federal system). But there is no need to do so if we hold that the ADEA does not apply to state judges. Application of the plain statement rule thus may avoid a potential constitutional problem. Indeed, inasmuch as this Court in *Garcia* has left primarily to the political process the protection of the States against intrusive exercises of Congress' Commerce Clause powers, we must be absolutely certain that Congress intended such an exercise. "[T]o give the state-displacing weight of federal law to mere congressional ambiguity would evade the very procedure for lawmaking on which *Garcia* relied to protect states' interests." L. Tribe, American Constitutional Law § 6-25, p. 480 (2d ed. 1988).

B

In 1974, Congress extended the substantive provisions of the ADEA to include the States as employers. Pub. L. 93-259, § 28(a), 88 Stat. 74, 29 U.S.C. § 630(b)(2). At the same time, Congress amended the definition of "employee" to exclude all elected and most high-ranking government officials. Under the Act, as amended:

> "The term 'employee' means an individual employed by any employer except that the term 'employee' shall not include any person elected to public office in any State or political subdivision of any State by the qualified voters thereof, or any person chosen by such officer to be on such officer's personal staff, or an appointee on the policymaking level or an immediate adviser with respect to the exercise of the constitutional or legal powers of the office." 29 U.S.C. § 630(f).

Governor Ashcroft contends that the § 630(f) exclusion of certain public officials also excludes judges, like petitioners, who are appointed to office by the Governor and are then subject to retention election. The Governor points to two passages in § 630(f). First, he argues, these judges are selected by an elected official and, because they make policy, are "appointee[s] on the policymaking level."

Petitioners counter that judges merely resolve factual disputes and decide questions of law; they do not make policy. Moreover, petitioners point out that the policymaking-level exception is part of a trilogy, tied closely to the elected official exception. Thus, the Act excepts elected officials and: (1) "any person chosen by such officer to be on such officer's personal staff"; (2) "an appointee on the policymaking level"; and (3) "an immediate advisor with respect to the exercise of the constitutional or legal powers of the office." Applying the maxim of statutory construction *noscitur a sociis*— that a word is known by the company it keeps—petitioners argue that since (1) and (3) refer only to those in close working relationships with elected officials, so too must (2). Even if it can be said that judges may make policy, petitioners contend, they do not do so at the behest of an elected official.

Governor Ashcroft relies on the plain language of the statute: It exempts persons appointed "at the policymaking level." The Governor argues that state judges, in fashioning and applying the common law, make policy. Missouri is a common law state. See Mo. Rev. Stat. § 1.010 (1986) (adopting "[t]he common law of England" consistent with federal and state law). The common law, unlike a constitution or statute, provides no definitive text; it is to be derived from the interstices of prior opinions and a well-considered judgment of what is best for the community.***

Governor Ashcroft contends that Missouri judges make policy in other ways as well. The Missouri Supreme Court and Courts of Appeals have supervisory authority over inferior courts. Mo. Const., Art. V, § 4. The Missouri Supreme Court has the constitutional duty to establish rules of practice and procedure for the Missouri court system, and inferior courts exercise policy judgment in establishing local rules of practice. See Mo. Const., Art. V, § 5. The state courts have supervisory powers over the state bar, with the Missouri Supreme Court given the authority to develop disciplinary rules.

The Governor stresses judges' policymaking responsibilities, but it is far from plain that the statutory exception requires that judges actually make policy. The statute refers to appointees "on the policymaking level," not to appointees "who make policy."

It may be sufficient that the appointee is in a position requiring the exercise of discretion concerning issues of public importance. This certainly describes the bench, regardless of whether judges might be considered policymakers in the same sense as the executive or legislature.

Nonetheless, "appointee at the policymaking level," particularly in the context of the other exceptions that surround it, is an odd way for Congress to exclude judges; a plain statement that judges are not "employees" would seem the most efficient phrasing. But in this case we are not looking for a plain statement that judges are excluded. We will not read the ADEA to cover state judges unless Congress has made it clear that judges are included. This does not mean that the Act must mention judges explicitly, though it does not. Rather, it must be plain to anyone reading the Act that it covers judges. In the context of a statute that plainly excludes most important state public officials, "appointee on the policymaking level" is sufficiently broad that we cannot conclude that the statute plainly covers appointed state judges. Therefore, it does not.***

[Justice White, joined by Justice Stevens, concurred in the result but argued that the Court's clear statement rule conflicted with its modern Commerce Clause doctrine. Justice Blackmun, joined by Justice Marshall, dissented. In his view, the Missouri judges were covered by the ADEA.]

Notes and Questions

1. **Procedural Posture.** What was the judgment of the court below that was being reviewed in *Gregory*? From where did the Supreme Court derive the facts of the case? What if anything remains to be litigated after the Supreme Court's decision?

2. **Statutory Context.** As we have seen, the ADEA broadly prohibits age discrimination in employment (defined by *General Dynamics v. Cline*, Section [B][1][b], *supra*, to mean discrimination against individuals over 40 relative to younger workers). The provisions at issue in *Gregory* were added in 1974 and extended the ADEA to state and local governments. 29 U.S.C. §630(b)(2) defines the employers subject to the Act to include "a State or political subdivision of a State." 29 U.S.C. §630(f) excludes from the Act "any person elected to public office in any State or political subdivision of any State by the qualified voters thereof, or any person chosen by such officer to be on such officer's personal staff, or an appointee on the policymaking level or an immediate adviser with respect to the exercise of the constitutional or legal powers of the office."

3. **The Statutory Question.** At issue in *Gregory* is whether an appointed state judge who has continued in office pursuant to a vote of the electorate is covered by the ADEA. If not for the perceived intrusion on state sovereignty, would there be any question that appointed state court judges are subject to the statute? In ordinary usage, are Missouri judges reasonably described as having been "elected to public office"? Are they "appointee[s] on the policymaking level"?

Missouri argued that judges fall within this exemption because the elaboration of common law rules creates public policy, and the Missouri Supreme Court exercises policymaking functions in promulgating court rules and supervising lower courts. Channeling statements by Supreme Court Justices at Senate confirmation hearings, the Missouri judges responded that judges merely apply law to fact. Who has the better of this debate? Even if the characterization of the judicial role put forward by the judges is inaccurate, are judges naturally described as "appointee[s] on the policy-making level"? Are there other aspects of that provision that support holding it inapplicable to judges who are appointed and then subject to a retention election?

4. **The Federalism Canon.** The Court's analysis turns on the "federalism canon." Because the selection of state judges "is a decision of the most fundamental sort for a sovereign entity," the ADEA will not be read to apply to state judges absent a "plain statement" to that effect. The Court does not fully explain, however, which activities are "of the most fundamental sort for a sovereign entity." Is everything that a state does an exercise of its sovereign authority? Is there a judicially manageable standard for separating "fundamental" activities from those that are "non-fundamental," or is this a chancellor's foot type of question? What is the underlying characteristic of the "fundamental" activities of a sovereign?

The Court argues that its plain statement rule "may avoid a potential constitutional problem." What is the specific constitutional problem that the Court has in mind? Is the Court right to worry about "constitutional problem[s]" given *Garcia v. San Antonio Metropolitan Transit Authority*, 469 U.S. 528 (1985)? The Court held there "that States must find their protection from congressional regulation through the national political process, not through judicially defined spheres of unregulable state activity." *Id.* at 512. The Court rejected as "unsound in principle and unworkable in practice" limits on Congress's authority that turned on whether a state activity was "traditional," "integral" or "necessary" to state government. *Id.* at 546.

The Court justifies its clear statement rule on the ground that it ensures Congress takes federalism concerns into account when enacting legislation: "inasmuch as this Court in *Garcia* has left primarily to the political process the protection of the States against intrusive exercises of Congress' Commerce Clause powers, we must be absolutely certain that Congress intended such an exercise." Note in this respect that the 1974 amendments at issue in *Gregory* were enacted eleven years prior to *Garcia*.

5. *Gregory's* **Practical Effect.** How does the kind of plain statement rule articulated in *Gregory* differ from a ruling under the Commerce Clause that Congress may not regulate in areas of fundamental importance to state governments? Note the Court's dictum that "the authority of the people of the States to determine the qualifications of their government officials may be inviolate." Also recall Justice Jackson's admonition to the effect that the Court "should be sure Congress has intentionally put its power in issue by the legislation in question before we undertake a pronouncement which may have far-reaching consequences upon the powers of the Congress or the powers reserved to the several states." *See United States v. Five Gambling Devices Labeled in Part "Mills," & Bearing Serial Nos. 593-221*, 346 U.S. 441, 447 (1953).

Does recognizing a clear statement rule permit the Court to engage in a form sub-constitutional lawmaking without having to, as it were, pay the price of declaring legislation unconstitutional? Is such lawmaking likely to be less disciplined than more typical exercises of judicial review?

6. **Further Reading.** For further discussion of substantive canons, see, e.g., Richard L. Hasen, *The Democracy Canon*, 62 Stan. L. Rev. 69 (2009); Einer Elhauge, *Preference-Eliciting Statutory Default Rules*, 102 Colum. L. Rev. 2162 (2002); David L. Shapiro, *Continuity and Change in Statutory Interpretation*, 67 N.Y.U. L. Rev. 921, 945–46 (1992); William N. Eskridge, Jr. & Philip P. Frickey, *Quasi-Constitutional Law: Clear Statement Rules as Constitutional Lawmaking*, 45 Vand. L. Rev. 593 (1992).

Chapter 3

Administrative Agencies in the Federal System

A. Introduction

To this point, this volume has considered the issues lawmakers must resolve in deciding whether to regulate an area of society, the nature of the legislative process, and the rules, canons, and customs governing the interpretation of statutes. A century ago, a course on legislation and regulation would go no further. On the federal level, prior to the creation of the Interstate Commerce Commission in 1887, Congress typically relied on criminal enforcement and civil lawsuits to implement regulatory policy. The situation was much the same on the state and local government level.

Congress today has a more complex set of issues to address once it decides to regulate in an area. Should legislation be implemented through litigation in the courts, where Article III judges will elaborate the statute's meaning in a more-or-less (federal) common law fashion, or should Congress make use of an agency to make policy judgments within the statutory framework and enforce the statute by administrative proceedings or in the courts? For a variety of reasons—including concern over expanding the federal judiciary, judicial resistance to Congress's regulatory goals, and a desire to take advantage of a staff and administrative leadership dedicated to the statute— Congress often has opted for administrative regulation subject to judicial review.

Not surprisingly, as Congress has made greater use of agencies, the federal government has grown. In Fiscal Year 2012, the federal government employed approximately 4.3 million individuals, or about 1.7% of the nation's working age population.[1] The budget enacted by Congress anticipated revenues of $2.77 trillion, and authorized expenditures of $3.45 trillion, $518 billion allocated to the Defense Department, and $115 billion allocated separately to funding the wars in Iraq and Afghanistan.[2] By way of contrast, the Fiscal Year 2012 budget for California, the state with the largest individual budget, anticipated revenues of $95.9 billion and expenditures of $91 billion.[3] The documentary supplement contains organizational charts for the entire federal government, the Department of Justice (an executive department), and the Social

---

1. Office of Personnel Management, Historical Federal Workforce Tables, https://www.opm.gov/policydata-oversight/data-analysis-documentation/federal-employment-reports/historical-tables/totalgovernment-employment-since-1962/

2. Pub. L. No. 113-06, 127 Stat. 198 (Mar. 26, 2013).

3. Edmund G. Brown, California State Budget: 2012–13, at 12–13.

Security Administration (a freestanding agency). Note the size of the DOJ and SSA and the number of layers of bureaucracy between the agency heads and their front-line personnel.

This chapter introduces administrative agencies; their legal position within the federal government and the constitutional constraints on Congress's design of agencies; and the levers through which Congress and the President influence agency action. The legal frameworks for administrative action and judicial review are addressed in Chapters 4 and 5, below.

B. The Constitutional Position of Administrative Agencies

The Constitution says little about the structure of the federal government. Article I provides that "[a]ll legislative powers herein granted shall be vested in a Congress of the United States," and sets out a list of powers that Congress may exercise. The "executive power" is vested in the President (Art. II, § 1) who, with the Senate's advice and consent, is given the power to appoint "Officers of the United States" and to require in writing opinions from "the principal officer in each of the executive departments" on any subject relating to their duties (Art. II, § 2). ("Heads of Departments" are also referenced in the Appointments Clause, *id.*, cl. 2). Article III contemplates that the "[t]he judicial power of the United States, shall be vested in one Supreme Court, and in such inferior courts as the Congress may from time to time ordain and establish." Beyond these broad outlines, little is said about how the government is to be structured and the important questions of how the executive and judicial functions are to be performed. Rather, the federal government as we know it is largely the product of statutes passed by Congress.

As Congress responded to the growth of the national economy by expanding the number of administrative agencies and the scope of their responsibilities, the position of administrative agencies within the constitutional scheme became a source of debate. At the broadest level, debates about the constitutional position of administrative agencies have focused on two questions: how does the Constitution constrain the organizational design of administrative agencies (Section 1, below), and how does the Constitution limit congressional efforts to *influence* the actions of administrative agencies (Section 2)?

1. Limits on the Statutory Design of Administrative Agencies

a. Delegation of Legislative Functions to Agencies

The most basic question about the design of administrative agencies involves their ability to promulgate regulations having the force of law. For example, the Federal Trade Commission (FTC) in 2004 promulgated a regulation that provides as follows:

Availability of contact lens prescriptions to patients.

(a) *In general.* When a prescriber completes a contact lens fitting, the prescriber:

(1) Whether or not requested by the patient, shall provide to the patient a copy of the contact lens prescription; and

(2) Shall, as directed by any person designated to act on behalf of the patient, provide or verify the contact lens prescription by electronic or other means.***

69 Fed. Reg. 40,508 (July 2, 2004) (codified at 16 C.F.R. § 315.3.)

The FTC stated that this regulation was issued under the Fairness to Contact Lens Consumers Act, Pub. L. No. 108-164, 117 Stat. 2024 (2003). Article I, § 1 of the Constitution provides that "[a]ll legislative powers herein granted shall be vested in a Congress of the United States." If one reads Article I, § 1 as a statement about which institutions can make laws on behalf of the federal government, can Congress delegate some aspect of its legislative authority to administrative agencies like the FTC, which issue rules and regulations having the force of law?[4] Does the FTC regulation involve an exercise of lawmaking that derogates from the vested authority of Congress?

From the early years of the republic, Congress has delegated authority to other institutions of the federal government. Early statutes delegated authority to cabinet heads to regulate pensions, land grants, and the operations of the Departments of War and State, often with little direction as to how the delegated authority should be exercised.[5]

The Supreme Court's general view is that Congress does not have to spell out all the details of a regulatory scheme, and that Congress does not impermissibly delegate its legislative power if a statute contains an "intelligible principle" to guide the discretion of the agency to whom regulatory authority is delegated. This test originated in *J.W. Hampton, Jr., & Co. v. United States*, 276 U.S. 394 (1928). There, the Court rejected a non-delegation challenge to Title III § 315 of the Tariff Act of September 21, 1922, Pub. L. No. 67-318, 42 Stat. 858, 941. That provision permitted the President to adjust tariffs to equalize differences in costs of production for goods between the United States and the "principal competing country." Changes to tariffs were proposed by the United States Tariff Commission,[6] which had authority to investigate costs of

---

4. A note on terminology: the terms "rules" and "regulations" are generally used to refer to directives promulgated by agencies that establish standards of conduct and have the force of law. Such directives are called "substantive" or "legislative" rules. A regulation has the "force and effect of law," *Chrysler Corp. v. Brown*, 441 U.S. 281, 295 (1979), when a violation of the regulation constitutes a violation of law.

5. *See* Jerry L. Mashaw, *Foreword: The American Model of Federal Administrative Law: Remembering the First One Hundred Years*, 78 Geo. Wash. U. L. Rev. 975, 982 (2010).

6. The Commission was established by the 1916 Revenue Ac, ch. 463, § 700, tit. VII, 39 Stat.756, 795 (Sept. 8, 1916), as a six-member body whose members, equally divided between the two political

production in the United States and competitor nations. In adjusting tariffs, the President and the Commission were to consider differences in the conditions of production among the United States and foreign competitors, differences in wholesale prices of goods, advantages granted to a foreign producer by a foreign government, and "any other advantages or disadvantages in competition."

In an opinion by Chief Justice Taft, the Court wrote that in determining what Congress "may do in seeking assistance from another branch, the extent and character of that assistance must be fixed according to common sense and the inherent necessities of the governmental co-ordination." The delegation of authority to set tariffs involved a delegation of legislative authority only "in a sense" that was not constitutionally relevant, because legislative power "has already been exercised legislatively by the body vested with that power under the Constitution." "If," as in § 315 of the Tariff Act, "Congress shall lay down by legislative act an intelligible principle to which the person or body authorized to fix such rates is directed to conform, such legislative action is not a forbidden delegation of legislative power. If it is thought wise to vary the customs duties according to changing conditions of production at home and abroad, Congress may authorize the Chief Executive to carry out this purpose, with the advisory assistance of a Tariff Commission appointed under congressional authority."

Notwithstanding *Hampton*'s "intelligible principle" standard, the Supreme Court in the 1930s for a brief time seriously considered enforcing limits on Congress's power to delegate "quasi-legislative" authority to administrative agencies through judicial review. As you read the following decisions, try to identify the benefits and drawbacks of the approach each takes to determining whether a statute impermissibly delegates "legislative powers" to an institution other than Congress.

A.L.A. Schechter Poultry Corp. v. United States

295 U.S. 495 (1935)

Mr. Chief Justice Hughes delivered the opinion of the Court.

Petitioners*** were convicted in the District Court of the United States for the Eastern District of New York on eighteen counts of an indictment charging violations of what is known as the "Live Poultry Code," and on an additional count for conspiracy to commit such violations. By demurrer to the indictment and appropriate motions on the trial, the defendants contended . . . that the Code had been adopted pursuant to an unconstitutional delegation by Congress of legislative power.***

---

parties, were appointed by the President and confirmed by the Senate. Its function was to investigate tariff conditions and make recommendations. As one commentator noted: "For the first time in U.S. trade history, Congress established an administratively separate institution to supplement its own tariff information-gathering. Moreover, the creation of the Tariff Commission marks the beginning of ever-greater delegations of congressional trade policy authority to other political actors and institutions." Karen E. Schnietz, *The 1916 Tariff Commission: Democrats' Use of Expert Information to Constrain Republican Tariff Protection*, 23 Bus. & Econ. Hist. 176 (no. 1, fall 1994).

New York City is the largest live-poultry market in the United States. Ninety-six per cent. of the live poultry there marketed comes from other States.*** The commission men transact by far the greater part of the business on a commission basis, representing the shippers as agents, and remitting to them the proceeds of sale, less commissions, freight and handling charges. Otherwise, they buy for their own account. They sell to slaughterhouse operators who are also called market-men.

The defendants are slaughterhouse operators of the latter class.***

The "Live Poultry Code" was promulgated under § 3 of the National Industrial Recovery Act [of 1933 (NIRA), Pub. L. No. 73-67, 48 Stat. 195]. That section . . . authorizes the President to approve "codes of fair competition." Such a code may be approved for a trade or industry, upon application by one or more trade or industrial associations or groups, if the President finds (1) that such associations or groups "impose no inequitable restrictions on admission to membership therein and are truly representative," and (2) that such codes are not designed "to promote monopolies or to eliminate or oppress small enterprises and will not operate to discriminate against them, and will tend to effectuate the policy" of Title I of the Act.*** Violation of any provision of a code (so approved or prescribed) "in any transaction in or affecting interstate or foreign commerce" is made a misdemeanor punishable by a fine of not more than $500 for each offense, and each day the violation continues is to be deemed a separate offense.

The "Live Poultry Code" was approved by the President on April 13, 1934.*** The Code fixes the number of hours for work-days. It provides that no employee, with certain exceptions, shall be permitted to work in excess of forty (40) hours in any one week, and that no employee, save as stated, "shall be paid in any pay period less than at the rate of fifty (50) cents per hour." The article containing "general labor provisions" prohibits the employment of any person under sixteen years of age, and declares that employees shall have the right of "collective bargaining," and freedom of choice with respect to labor organizations, in the terms of § 7(a) of the Act.***

Of the eighteen counts of the indictment upon which the defendants were convicted, aside from the count for conspiracy, two counts charged violation of the minimum wage and maximum hour provisions of the Code, and ten counts were for violation of the requirement (found in the "trade practice provisions") of "straight killing." This requirement was really one of "straight" selling. The term "straight killing" was defined in the Code as "the practice of requiring persons purchasing poultry for resale to accept the run of any half coop, coop, or coops, as purchased by slaughterhouse operators, except for culls."***

The question of the delegation of legislative power. We recently had occasion to review the pertinent decisions and the general principles which govern the determination of this question. *Panama Refining Co. v. Ryan*, 293 U.S. 388. The Constitution provides that "All legislative powers herein granted shall be vested in a Congress of the United States, which shall consist of a Senate and House of Representatives." Art I, § 1. And the Congress is authorized "To make all laws which shall be necessary and proper for carrying into execution" its general powers. Art. I, § 8, par. 18. The

Congress is not permitted to abdicate or to transfer to others the essential legislative functions with which it is thus vested. We have repeatedly recognized the necessity of adapting legislation to complex conditions involving a host of details with which the national legislature cannot deal directly. [But] the constant recognition of the necessity and validity of such provisions, and the wide range of administrative authority which has been developed by means of them, cannot be allowed to obscure the limitations of the authority to delegate, if our constitutional system is to be maintained.

Accordingly, we look to the statute to see whether Congress has overstepped these limitations, — whether Congress in authorizing "codes of fair competition" has itself established the standards of legal obligation, thus performing its essential legislative function, or, by the failure to enact such standards, has attempted to transfer that function to others.***

For a statement of the authorized objectives and content of the "codes of fair competition" we are referred repeatedly to the "Declaration of Policy" in section one of Title I of the Recovery Act.*** It is there declared to be "the policy of Congress"—

> "to remove obstructions to the free flow of interstate and foreign commerce which tend to diminish the amount thereof; and to provide for the general welfare by promoting the organization of industry for the purpose of cooperative action among trade groups, to induce and maintain united action of labor and management under adequate governmental sanctions and supervision, to eliminate unfair competitive practices, to promote the fullest possible utilization of the present productive capacity of industries, to avoid undue restriction of production (except as may be temporarily required), to increase the consumption of industrial and agricultural products by increasing purchasing power, to reduce and relieve unemployment, to improve standards of labor, and otherwise to rehabilitate industry and to conserve natural resources."

Under § 3, whatever "may tend to effectuate" these general purposes may be included in the "codes of fair competition." We think the conclusion is inescapable that the authority sought to be conferred by § 3 was not merely to deal with "unfair competitive practices" which offend against existing law, and could be the subject of judicial condemnation without further legislation, or to create administrative machinery for the application of established principles of law to particular instances of violation. Rather, the purpose is clearly disclosed to authorize new and controlling prohibitions through codes of laws which would embrace what the formulators would propose, and what the President would approve, or prescribe, as wise and beneficient measures for the government of trades and industries in order to bring about their rehabilitation, correction and development, according to the general declaration of policy in section one. Codes of laws of this sort are styled "codes of fair competition."***

The Government urges that the codes will "consist of rules of competition deemed fair for each industry by representative members of that industry — by the persons most vitally concerned and most familiar with its problems." Instances are cited in which Congress has availed itself of such assistance; as e.g., in the exercise of its authority over the public domain, with respect to the recognition of local customs or rules of miners as to mining claims, or, in matters of a more or less technical nature, as in designating the standard height of drawbars. But would it be seriously contended that Congress could delegate its legislative authority to trade or industrial associations or groups so as to empower them to enact the laws they deem to be wise and beneficent for the rehabilitation and expansion of their trade or industries? Could trade or industrial associations or groups be constituted legislative bodies for that purpose because such associations or groups are familiar with the problems of their enterprises? And, could an effort of that sort be made valid by such a preface of generalities as to permissible aims as we find in section 1 of title I? The answer is obvious. Such a delegation of legislative power is unknown to our law and is utterly inconsistent with the constitutional prerogatives and duties of Congress.***

Accordingly we turn to the Recovery Act to ascertain what limits have been set to the exercise of the President's discretion. First, the President, as a condition of approval, is required to find that the trade or industrial associations or groups which propose a code, "impose no inequitable restrictions on admission to membership" and are "truly representative." That condition, however, relates only to the status of the initiators of the new laws and not to the permissible scope of such laws. Second, the President is required to find that the code is not "designed to promote monopolies or to eliminate or oppress small enterprises and will not operate to discriminate against them." And, to this is added a proviso that the code "shall not permit monopolies or monopolistic practices." But these restrictions leave virtually untouched the field of policy envisaged by section one, and, in that wide field of legislative possibilities, the proponents of a code, refraining from monopolistic designs, may roam at will and the President may approve or disapprove their proposals as he may see fit. That is the precise effect of the further finding that the President is to make—that the code "will tend to effectuate the policy of this title." While this is called a finding, it is really but a statement of an opinion as to the general effect upon the promotion of trade or industry of a scheme of laws. These are the only findings which Congress has made essential in order to put into operation a legislative code having the aims described in the "Declaration of Policy."

Nor is the breadth of the President's discretion left to the necessary implications of this limited requirement as to his findings. As already noted, the President in approving a code may impose his own conditions, adding to or taking from what is proposed, as "in his discretion" he thinks necessary "to effectuate the policy" declared by the Act.***

Section 3 of the Recovery Act*** supplies no standards for any trade, industry or activity. It does not undertake to prescribe rules of conduct to be applied to particular states of fact determined by appropriate administrative procedure. Instead of prescribing rules of conduct, it authorizes the making of codes to prescribe them. For that legislative undertaking, § 3 sets up no standards, aside from the statement of the general aims of rehabilitation, correction and expansion described in section one. In view of the scope of that broad declaration, and of the nature of the few restrictions that are imposed, the discretion of the President in approving or prescribing codes, and thus enacting laws for the government of trade and industry throughout the country, is virtually unfettered. We think that the code-making authority thus conferred is an unconstitutional delegation of legislative power.

Notes and Questions

1. **The Procedural Posture?** The case arose as a federal criminal prosecution in which the defendants asserted the unconstitutionality of the National Industrial Recovery Act (NIRA) as a defense. *See generally* Amity Shlaes, The Forgotten Man: A New History of the Great Depression 204, 215 (2007).

2. **Justification for Regulation?** A response to the continuing economic depression, which began with the stock market crash of 1929, NIRA sought to improve economic conditions by, inter alia, "promoting the organization of industry for the purpose of cooperative action among trade groups to induce and maintain united action of labor and management under adequate supervision," "eliminat[ing] unfair competitive practices," "increas[ing] the consumption of industrial and agricultural products by increasing purchasing power," "reduc[ing] and reliev[ing] unemployment," and "improv[ing] standards of labor." The legislation reflected a demand-side diagnosis of the depression — that what was needed was an improvement in purchasing power through a corporatist organization of the economy that would rein in some of the destructive forces of "excessive competition." NIRA § 1, 48 Stat. 195. *See generally* Alfred E. Kahn, The Economics of Regulation: Principles and Institutions ch. 5 (1998 ed.); James Q. Whitman, *Of Corporatism, Fascism and the First New Deal*, 39 Am. J. Comp. L. 747 (1991).

3. **The Constitutional Defect?** Only two statutes in the history of the republic have been invalidated by the Supreme Court on the ground that they impermissibly delegated Congress's legislative power. The first is the NIRA.

The centerpiece of NIRA, at issue in *Schechter Poultry*, was § 3. That section authorized the President to establish codes of "fair competition" — price controls, essentially — for an industry upon finding that the code of competition promoted the objectives of the statute set out in § 1. NIRA § 9(c), invalidated in *Panama Refining Co. v. Ryan*, 293 U.S. 388 (1935), authorized the President "to prohibit the transportation in interstate and foreign commerce of petroleum and the products thereof produced or withdrawn from storage in excess of the amount permitted to be produced or withdrawn from storage by any state law or valid regulation." Violations of a presidential order were punishable by fine or imprisonment.

Exactly what was constitutionally objectionable about §§ 3 and 9(c)? Consider three possibilities:

a. **Policy Indeterminacy: "Delegation Run Riot"?** *Schechter Poultry* states that because § 3 did not "establish[] the standards of legal obligation," Congress failed to "perform[] its essential legislative function." What does the Court mean by this? Doesn't § 3 obligate the President to consider a specific set of objectives when deciding whether to approve codes of fair competition? It is true that these objectives are in some tension with one another. But legal directives frequently require a decision-maker to accommodate competing goals. *Cf.* Fed. R. Civ. P. 1 (Federal Rules of Civil Procedure to be "administered to secure the just, speedy, and inexpensive determination of every action and proceeding"). Should this level of indeterminacy be a sufficient basis for the Court to strike down a statute?

As we have seen in *FTC v. R.F. Keppel & Bro.*, in Chapter 1, the Federal Trade Commission Act (FTCA) authorizes the FTC to restrain acts of "unfair competition." Does the *Schechter Poultry* Court persuasively distinguish the NIRA authorization of codes of "fair competition"?

Consider Justice Cardozo's concurrence (joined in by Justice Stone) in *Schechter Poultry* (295 U.S. at 552-53):

> But there is another conception of codes of fair competition***. By this other conception a code is not to be restricted to the elimination of business practices that would be characterized by general acceptance as oppressive or unfair. It is to include whatever ordinances may be desirable or helpful for the well-being or prosperity of the industry affected. In that view, the function of its adoption is not merely negative, but positive; the planning of improvements as well as the extirpation of abuses. What is fair, as thus conceived, is not something to be contrasted with what is unfair or fraudulent or tricky. The extension becomes as wide as the field of industrial regulation. If that conception shall prevail, anything that Congress may do within the limits of the commerce clause for the betterment of business may be done by the President upon the recommendation of a trade association by calling it a code. This is delegation running riot. No such plenitude of power is susceptible of transfer. The statute, however, aims at nothing less, as one can learn both from its terms and from the administrative practice under it. Nothing less is aimed at by the code now submitted to our scrutiny.

The provision struck down in *Panama Refining*, NIRA § 9(c), was considerably more cabined than § 3 insofar as it applied only when petroleum was produced in violation of a quota established by state law or valid regulation. The *Panama Refining* Court determined that this provision —

> leaves to the States and to their constituted authorities the determination of what production shall be permitted. It does not qualify the President's authority by reference to the basis, or extent, of the State's limitation of production. Section 9(c) does not state whether, or in what circumstances or under what conditions, the President is to prohibit the transportation of the amount of petroleum or petroleum products produced in excess of the State's permission. It establishes no criterion to govern the President's course. It does not require any finding by the President as a condition of his action. The Congress in § 9(c) thus declares no policy as to the transportation of the excess production. So far as this section is concerned, it gives to the President an

> unlimited authority to determine the policy and to lay down the prohibition, or not to lay it down, as he may see fit.

293 U.S. at 415.

b. **The Nature of the Delegatee?** Another possible defect with delegations in the NIRA involves the kind of actor or institution to which Congress delegated regulatory authority. Under § 3, the development of codes of competition was entrusted to private organizations. These organizations would draft a code of conduct in the first instance, and the code would take effect when it was approved by the President. Under § 9(c), states determined the petroleum quotas in the first instance that, at the President's option, would have the force of federal law.

In *Carter v. Carter Coal Co.*, 298 U.S. 238 (1936), the Supreme Court invalidated a provision of the Bituminous Coal Conservation Act of 1935, 49 Stat. 991, ch. 824, that gave the force of law to labor agreements "negotiated between the producers of more than two-thirds of the annual national tonnage production [of bituminous coal] for the preceding calendar year and the representatives of more than one-half of the mine workers employed." The Court reasoned that this provision gave private parties the ability to make law in a manner that was inconsistent with basic requirements of the democratic process: "The power conferred upon the majority is, in effect, the power to regulate the affairs of an unwilling minority. This is legislative delegation in its most obnoxious form; for it is not even delegation to an official or an official body, presumptively disinterested, but to private persons whose interests may be and often are adverse to the interests of others in the same business." 298 U.S. at 311. Could the same be said of §§ 3 and 9(c) of the NIRA?

c. **Inadequate Oversight of the Delegatee?** Still another possible defect with §§ 3 and 9(c) was the failure to establish appropriate *procedures* for self-regulatory organizations and states to follow when implementing legislative policy. According to one commentator, "the fact that the National Industrial Recovery Act imposed no procedural requirements on the president contributed to the Court's conclusion that the Act exceeded the bounds of permissible delegation. And since *Schechter*, the Supreme Court's tolerance of broad congressional delegations may be attributable, at least in part, to the greater procedural constraints imposed on statutory delegates." Kevin M. Stack, *The Statutory President*, 90 Iowa L. Rev. 539, 591 (2005). Why would the kind of *procedure* followed by a delegatee affect the validity of a *delegation* of regulatory authority? Professor Stack observes that "[p]rocedure provides a check on the potential abuses of statutory delegations, and its absence, particularly when the president is involved, may raise a concern about the arbitrary exercise of power." Does this have any bearing on whether Congress has impermissibly delegated legislative power?

Do any of these considerations justify the Court's decision to strike §§ 3 and 9(c)? Which of the three is the most persuasive?

4. **The Birth of the Federal Register Act.** During oral argument in *Panama Refining*, lawyers for the United States had to acknowledge that the petroleum regulation they were trying to enforce had been inadvertently revoked. On July 26, 1935, Congress enacted the Federal Register Act, Pub. L. No. 74-220, ch. 417, 49 Stat. 500 (1935),

codified as amended at 44 U.S.C. § 1501 et seq., to require that all federal regulations be published in the Federal Register.

Yakus v. United States

321 U.S. 414 (1944)

MR. CHIEF JUSTICE STONE delivered the opinion of the Court.***

Petitioners in both of these cases were tried and convicted by the District Court for Massachusetts upon several counts of indictments charging violation of §§ 4(a) and 205(b) of the Act by the willful sale of wholesale cuts of beef at prices above the maximum prices prescribed by §§ 1364.451-1364.455 of Revised Maximum Price Regulation No. 169, 7 Fed.Reg. 10381 et seq. Petitioners have not availed themselves of the procedure set up by §§ 203 and 204 by which any person subject to a maximum price regulation may test its validity by protest to and hearing before the Administrator, whose determination may be reviewed on complaint to the Emergency Court of Appeals and by this Court on certiorari, *see Lockerty v. Phillips*, 319 U.S. 182. When the indictments were found the 60 days period allowed by the statute for filing protests had expired.***

The Emergency Price Control Act [of 1942 (EPCA), Pub. L. No. 77-729, 56 Stat. 765,] provides for the establishment of the Office of Price Administration under the direction of a Price Administrator appointed by the President, and sets up a comprehensive scheme for the promulgation by the Administrator of regulations or orders fixing such maximum prices of commodities and rents as will effectuate the purposes of the Act and conform to the standards which it prescribes. The Act was adopted as a temporary wartime measure, and provides in § 1(b) for its termination on June 30, 1943, unless sooner terminated by Presidential proclamation or concurrent resolution of Congress. By the amendatory act of October 2, 1942, it was extended to June 30, 1944.

Section 1(a) declares that the Act is "in the interest of the national defense and security and necessary to the effective prosecution of the present war", and that its purposes are:

> "to stabilize prices and to prevent speculative, unwarranted, and abnormal increases in prices and rents; to eliminate and prevent profiteering, hoarding, manipulation, speculation, and other disruptive practices resulting from abnormal market conditions or scarcities caused by or contributing to the national emergency; to assure that defense appropriations are not dissipated by excessive prices; to protect persons with relatively fixed and limited incomes, consumers, wage earners, investors, and persons dependent on life insurance, annuities, and pensions, from undue impairment of their standard of living; to prevent hardships to persons engaged in business,*** and to the Federal, State, and local governments, which would result from abnormal increases in prices; to assist in securing adequate production of commodities and facilities; to prevent a post emergency collapse of values;***."

The standards which are to guide the Administrator's exercise of his authority to fix prices, so far as now relevant, are prescribed by § 2(a) and by § 1 of the amendatory Act of October 2, 1942, and Executive Order 9250, promulgated under it. 7 Fed. Reg. 7871. By § 2(a) the Administrator is authorized, after consultation with representative members of the industry so far as practicable, to promulgate regulations fixing prices of commodities which "in his judgment will be generally fair and equitable and will effectuate the purposes of this Act" when, in his judgment, their prices "have risen or threaten to rise to an extent or in a manner inconsistent with the purposes of this Act."

The section also directs that

> "So far as practicable, in establishing any maximum price, the Administrator shall ascertain and give due consideration to the prices prevailing between October 1 and October 15, 1941 (or if, in the case of any commodity, there are no prevailing prices between such dates, or the prevailing prices between such dates are not generally representative because of abnormal or seasonal market conditions or other cause, then to the prices prevailing during the nearest two-week period in which, in the judgment of the Administrator, the prices for such commodity are generally representative) ... and shall make adjustments for such relevant factors as he may determine and deem to be of general applicability, including ... Speculative fluctuations, general increases or decreases in costs of production, distribution, and transportation, and general increases or decreases in profits earned by sellers of the commodity or commodities, during and subsequent to the year ended October 1, 1941."

By the Act of October 2, 1942, the President is directed to stabilize prices, wages and salaries "so far as practicable" on the basis of the levels which existed on September 15, 1942, except as otherwise provided in the Act. By Title I, § 4 of Executive Order No. 9250, he has directed "all departments and agencies of the Government" "to stabilize the cost of living in accordance with the Act of October 2, 1942."***

That Congress has constitutional authority to prescribe commodity prices as a war emergency measure, and that the Act was adopted by Congress in the exercise of that power, are not questioned here .... Congress enacted the Emergency Price Control Act in pursuance of a defined policy and required that the prices fixed by the Administrator should further that policy and conform to standards prescribed by the Act. The boundaries of the field of the Administrator's permissible action are marked by the statute. It directs that the prices fixed shall effectuate the declared policy of the Act to stabilize commodity prices so as to prevent wartime inflation and its enumerated disruptive causes and effects. In addition the prices established must be fair and equitable, and in fixing them the Administrator is directed to give due consideration, so far as practicable, to prevailing prices during the designated base period, with prescribed administrative adjustments to compensate for enumerated disturbing factors affecting prices.***

The Act is unlike the National Industrial Recovery Act of June 16, 1933, 48 Stat. 195, considered in *Schechter Corp. v. United States*, 295 U.S. 495, which proclaimed in the broadest terms its purpose "to rehabilitate industry and to conserve natural resources." It prescribed no method of attaining that end save by the establishment of codes of fair competition, the nature of whose permissible provisions was left undefined. It provided no standards to which those codes were to conform. The function of formulating the codes was delegated, not to a public official responsible to Congress or the Executive, but to private individuals engaged in the industries to be regulated.

The Constitution as a continuously operative charter of government does not demand the impossible or the impracticable. It does not require that Congress find for itself every fact upon which it desires to base legislative action or that it make for itself detailed determinations which it has declared to be prerequisite to the application of the legislative policy to particular facts and circumstances impossible for Congress itself properly to investigate. The essentials of the legislative function are the determination of the legislative policy and its formulation and promulgation as a defined and binding rule of conduct.***

Nor does the doctrine of separation of powers deny to Congress power to direct that an administrative officer properly designated for that purpose have ample latitude within which he is to ascertain the conditions which Congress has made prerequisite to the operation of its legislative command. Acting within its constitutional power to fix prices it is for Congress to say whether the data on the basis of which prices are to be fixed are to be confined within a narrow or a broad range.***

Congress is not confined to that method of executing its policy which involves the least possible delegation of discretion to administrative officers. It is free to avoid the rigidity of such a system, which might well result in serious hardship, and to choose instead the flexibility attainable by the use of less restrictive standards. Only if we could say that there is an absence of standards for the guidance of the Administrator's action, so that it would be impossible in a proper proceeding to ascertain whether the will of Congress has been obeyed, would we be justified in overriding its choice of means for effecting its declared purpose of preventing inflation.

Notes and Questions

1. **The Procedural Posture?** This case, like *Schechter Poultry*, began as a criminal prosecution. Arguing they could challenge the validity of the maximum price regulation as a defense to the prosecution, the defendants sought to bypass a specific statutory procedure for challenging maximum price regulations under the Emergency Price Control Act. In a portion of the opinion reproduced below in Chapter 5[B], the Court held that Congress intended the statutory procedure to be exclusive and that failure to comply with the procedure could be excused only if the defendants were denied due process. (The Court held they were not.) The Court presumably could have barred the challenge solely on this ground of statutory preclusion without reaching the

merits of the challenge to the validity of the ECPA and maximum price regulations. Is it fair to preclude the ability to challenge a regulation's validity in the course of an agency enforcement action? Is there an *in terrorem* effect to the enforcement action that will unduly induce settlement and hence diminish the likelihood of a challenge altogether? On the availability of judicial review to challenge agency regulations before they have been enforced, see Chapter 5[A], *infra*.

2. **Justification for Regulation?** Wartime mobilization often requires the economy to function at full capacity, which likely induces shortages in some goods and materials. In ordinary times, the price system adjusts to such shortages by raising prices, which has the effect of reducing demand. When the economy is on a wartime footing, the government may wish to avoid the inflationary and solidarity-undermining effects of price increases and attendant demands for wage increases. This is a unique form of market failure: the market is unable to produce goods and services at prices that are necessary to national policy objectives rather than simply the maximization of profits. *See generally* Mariano-Florentino Cuéllar, *Administrative War*, 82 Geo. Wash. L. Rev. 1343 (2014).

3. **Unavoidable Delegation?** The Court rejects a rule that would require Congress to use the "least possible delegation." Such a rule would have required the Court to find that the ECPA's delegation to the Administrator was necessary and could not have been avoided by greater legislative specification.

But wasn't that in fact the case under the EPCA? Congress can specify a baseline period for evaluation of price and wage increases, but unless it wishes to invite the scarcity-inducing rigidity of ruling out all such increases, were not the factors identified in the statute the inevitable factors for evaluating permissible increases?

———

Given *Yakus'* broad endorsement of Congress's authority to delegate subsidiary questions of administrative policy, *Schechter Poultry* and *Panama Refining* mark the high points of the non-delegation doctrine. Despite academic criticism from some quarters, *see, e.g.*, David Schoenbrod, Power Without Responsibility: How Congress Abuses the People through Delegation (2005), the Court has accepted broad delegations of regulatory authority that do not approach the unbounded sweep of the NIRA. In the decision of the D.C. Circuit that is the subject of the Supreme Court decision that follows, Judge Steven Williams for the majority held that § 109(b)(1) of the Clean Air Act delegated legislative power to the Administrator in contravention of the Constitution because the *delegatee*, the Environmental Protection Agency (EPA), had interpreted the statute in a way that provided no "intelligible principle" to guide the agency's exercise of authority. *See American Trucking Assns., Inc. v. EPA*, 175 F.3d 1027, 1034 (D.C. Cir. 1999). The appeals court thought, however, that the EPA could perhaps avoid the unconstitutional delegation by adopting a narrower construction of § 109(b)(1), so instead of declaring the section unconstitutional, the court remanded the case back to the agency. *Id.* at 1038. (On this delegation point, Judge David Tatel dissented, finding the statute constitutional as written. *Id.* at 1057.)

Whitman v. American Trucking Associations, Inc.

531 U.S. 457 (2001)

JUSTICE SCALIA delivered the opinion of the Court.

These cases present the following questions: (1) Whether § 109(b)(1) of the Clean Air Act (CAA) delegates legislative power to the Administrator of the Environmental Protection Agency (EPA). (2) Whether the Administrator may consider the costs of implementation in setting national ambient air quality standards (NAAQS) under § 109(b)(1).***

I

Section 109(a) of the CAA, as added, 84 Stat. 1679, and amended, 42 U.S.C. § 7409(a), requires the Administrator of the EPA to promulgate NAAQS for each air pollutant for which "air quality criteria" have been issued under § 108, 42 U.S.C. § 7408. Once a NAAQS has been promulgated, the Administrator must review the standard (and the criteria on which it is based) "at five-year intervals" and make "such revisions . . . as may be appropriate." CAA § 109(d)(1), 42 U.S.C. § 7409(d)(1). These cases arose when, on July 18, 1997, the Administrator revised the NAAQS for particulate matter (PM) and ozone. American Trucking Associations, Inc., and its co-respondents in No. 99-1257—which include, in addition to other private companies, the States of Michigan, Ohio, and West Virginia—challenged the new standards in the Court of Appeals for the District of Columbia Circuit, pursuant to 42 U.S.C. § 7607(b)(1).***

II

In *Lead Industries Assn., Inc. v. EPA*, [647 F.1d 1130, 1148 (D.C. Cir. 1980)], the District of Columbia Circuit held that "economic considerations [may] play no part in the promulgation of ambient air quality standards under Section 109" of the CAA. In the present cases, the court adhered to that holding, as it had done on many other occasions.*** Respondents argue that these decisions are incorrect. We disagree; and since the first step in assessing whether a statute delegates legislative power is to determine what authority the statute confers, we address that issue of interpretation first and reach respondents' constitutional arguments in Part III, *infra*.

Section 109(b)(1) instructs the EPA to set primary ambient air quality standards "the attainment and maintenance of which . . . are requisite to protect the public health" with "an adequate margin of safety." 42 U.S.C. § 7409(b)(1). Were it not for the hundreds of pages of briefing respondents have submitted on the issue, one would have thought it fairly clear that this text does not permit the EPA to consider costs in setting the standards. The language, as one scholar has noted, "is absolute." D. Currie, Air Pollution: Federal Law and Analysis 4-15 (1981). The EPA, "based on" the information about health effects contained in the technical "criteria" documents compiled under § 108(a)(2), 42 U.S.C. § 7408(a)(2), is to identify the maximum airborne concentration of a pollutant that the public health can tolerate, decrease the concentration to provide an "adequate" margin of safety, and set the standard at that level. Nowhere are the costs of achieving such a standard made part of that initial calculation.***

The text of § 109(b), interpreted in its statutory and historical context and with appreciation for its importance to the CAA as a whole, unambiguously bars cost considerations from the NAAQS-setting process, and thus ends the matter for us as well as the EPA. We therefore affirm the judgment of the Court of Appeals on this point.

III

Section 109(b)(1) of the CAA instructs the EPA to set "ambient air quality standards the attainment and maintenance of which in the judgment of the Administrator, based on [the] criteria [documents of § 108] and allowing an adequate margin of safety, are requisite to protect the public health." 42 U.S.C. § 7409(b)(1). The Court of Appeals held that this section as interpreted by the Administrator did not provide an "intelligible principle" to guide the EPA's exercise of authority in setting NAAQS. "[The] EPA," it said, "lacked any determinate criteria for drawing lines. It has failed to state intelligibly how much is too much." The court hence found that the EPA's interpretation (but not the statute itself) violated the nondelegation doctrine. We disagree.

In a delegation challenge, the constitutional question is whether the statute has delegated legislative power to the agency. Article I, § 1, of the Constitution vests "all legislative Powers herein granted . . . in a Congress of the United States." This text permits no delegation of those powers, *Loving v. United States*, 517 U.S. 748, 771 (1996); *see id.* at 776-777 (Scalia, J., concurring in part and concurring in judgment), and so we repeatedly have said that when Congress confers decisionmaking authority upon agencies Congress must "lay down by legislative act an intelligible principle to which the person or body authorized to [act] is directed to conform." *J. W. Hampton, Jr., & Co. v. United States*, 276 U.S. 394, 409 (1928). We have never suggested that an agency can cure an unlawful delegation of legislative power by adopting in its discretion a limiting construction of the statute.*** The idea that an agency can cure an unconstitutionally standardless delegation of power by declining to exercise some of that power seems to us internally contradictory. The very choice of which portion of the power to exercise—that is to say, the prescription of the standard that Congress had omitted—would itself be an exercise of the forbidden legislative authority. Whether the statute delegates legislative power is a question for the courts, and an agency's voluntary self-denial has no bearing upon the answer.

We agree with the Solicitor General that the text of § 109(b)(1) of the CAA at a minimum requires that "for a discrete set of pollutants and based on published air quality criteria that reflect the latest scientific knowledge, [the] EPA must establish uniform national standards at a level that is requisite to protect public health from the adverse effects of the pollutant in the ambient air." Requisite, in turn, "means sufficient, but not more than necessary."***

The scope of discretion § 109(b)(1) allows is in fact well within the outer limits of our nondelegation precedents. In the history of the Court we have found the requisite "intelligible principle" lacking in only two statutes, one of which provided literally no guidance for the exercise of discretion, and the other of which conferred authority to regulate the entire economy on the basis of no more precise a standard than stimulating the economy by assuring "fair competition." *See Panama Refining Co. v. Ryan*, 293 U.S. 388 (1935); *A. L. A. Schechter Poultry Corp. v. United States*, 295 U.S. 495 (1935). We have, on the other hand, upheld the validity of § 11(b)(2) of the Public Utility Holding Company Act of 1935, 49 Stat. 821, which gave the Securities and Exchange Commission authority to modify the structure of holding company systems so as to ensure that they are not "unduly or unnecessarily complicated" and do not "unfairly or inequitably distribute voting power among security holders." *American Power & Light Co. v. SEC*, 329 U.S. 90, 104 (1946). We have approved the wartime conferral of agency power to fix the prices of commodities at a level that "'will be generally fair and equitable and will effectuate the [in some respects conflicting] purposes of the Act.'" *Yakus v. United States*, 321 U.S. 414, 420 (1944). And we have found an "intelligible principle" in various statutes authorizing regulation in the "public interest." *See, e.g., National Broadcasting Co. v. United States*, 319 U.S. 190, 225-226 (1943) (FCC's power to regulate airwaves); *New York Central Securities Corp. v. United States*, 287 U.S. 12, 24-25 (1932) (ICC's power to approve railroad consolidations). In short, we have "almost never felt qualified to second-guess Congress regarding the permissible degree of policy judgment that can be left to those executing or applying the law." *Mistretta v. United States*, 488 U.S. 361, 416 (1989) (Scalia, J., dissenting); *see id.* at 373 (majority opinion).***

We therefore reverse the judgment of the Court of Appeals remanding for reinterpretation that would avoid a supposed delegation of legislative power.***

Justice Stevens, with whom Justice Souter joins, concurring in part and concurring in the judgment.

***The Court has two choices. We could choose to articulate our ultimate disposition of this issue by frankly acknowledging that the power delegated to the EPA is "legislative" but nevertheless conclude that the delegation is constitutional because adequately limited by the terms of the authorizing statute. Alternatively, we could pretend, as the Court does, that the authority delegated to the EPA is somehow not "legislative power." Despite the fact that there is language in our opinions that supports the Court's articulation of our holding, I am persuaded that it would be both wiser and more faithful to what we have actually done in delegation cases to admit that agency rulemaking authority is "legislative power."

The proper characterization of governmental power should generally depend on the nature of the power, not on the identity of the person exercising it. If the NAAQS that the EPA promulgated had been prescribed by Congress, everyone would agree that those rules would be the product of an exercise of "legislative power." The same characterization is appropriate when an agency exercises rulemaking authority pursuant to a permissible delegation from Congress.

My view is not only more faithful to normal English usage, but is also fully consistent with the text of the Constitution. In Article I, the Framers vested "All legislative Powers" in the Congress, Art. I, § 1, just as in Article II they vested the "executive Power" in the President, Art. II, § 1. Those provisions do not purport to limit the authority of either recipient of power to delegate authority to others. Surely the authority granted to members of the Cabinet and federal law enforcement agents is properly characterized as "Executive" even though not exercised by the President.

It seems clear that an executive agency's exercise of rulemaking authority pursuant to a valid delegation from Congress is "legislative." As long as the delegation provides a sufficiently intelligible principle, there is nothing inherently unconstitutional about it.

Notes and Questions

1. **The Procedural Posture?** Who are the challengers of the EPA regulation? Was the challenge made as a defense to a criminal prosecution or EPA civil enforcement proceeding or, rather, as an affirmative lawsuit to restrain EPA from enforcing the regulation — what today would be termed "pre-enforcement review"? On the costs and benefits of pre-enforcement review, see *Abbott Labs. v. Gardner, infra,* Chapter 5[A][2].

2. **Justification for and Mode of Regulation?** The Clean Air Act (CAA or Act) is a classic example of regulation to deal with negative externalities: firms that emit air pollution do not bear its full costs. To address this problem, the Act imposes a system of licensing and fees on emitters. *See infra* Chapter 4[E]; Richard L. Revesz, *Rehabilitating Interstate Competition: Rethinking the "Race-to-the-Bottom" Rationale for Federal Environmental Regulation,* 67 N.Y.U. L. Rev. 1210, 1224–25 (1992) (citing provisions of the Act which are expressly directed at interstate externalities).

The EPA was established via a government reorganization plan on December 2, 1970, to implement the CAA and the National Environmental Policy Act of 1969 (NEPA), Pub. L. No. 91-190, 83 Stat. 852, codified as amended 42 U.S.C. § 4321 et seq. *See* Reorganization Plan of July 9, 1970, 5 U.S.C. app., at 202 (2006 & Supp. 2011). The Act authorizes the EPA to pass on state plans for emission controls and to set standards, such as the National Ambient Air Quality Standards, State Implementation Plans (SIPs), New Source Performance Standards (NSPS), and National Emission Standards for Hazardous Air Pollutants (NESHAPs).

3. **Costs and Air Quality Standards?** Why is the Court in *Whitman* so intent on excluding consideration of costs from the promulgation of national air quality standards? Would allowing such consideration have made it too difficult to argue that the Clean Air Act satisfied the "intelligible principle" standard for evaluating nondelegation challenges? What is the regulatory strategy behind disallowing consideration of costs when *promulgating* safety standards but requiring a comparison of attendant costs and benefits when *implementing* such regulations? For a criticism of the Court's approach, see Michael A. Livermore & Richard L. Revesz, *Rethinking Health-Based Environmental Standards,* 89 N.Y.U. L. Rev. 1184 (2014).

In *Michigan v. EPA,* 135 S. Ct. 2699 (2015), the Court (per Justice Scalia) held that cost was relevant in deciding whether regulation of power-plant emissions was "appropriate and necessary" under 42 U.S.C. § 7412(a)(1)(A) of the CAA. The Court distinguished *Whitman* (135 S. Ct. at 2709):

American Trucking ... establishes the modest principle that where the Clean Air Act expressly directs EPA to regulate on the basis of a factor that on its face does not include cost, the Act normally should not be read as implicitly allowing the Agency to consider cost anyway. That principle has no application here. "Appropriate and necessary" is a far more comprehensive criterion than "requisite to protect the public health"; read fairly and in context, ... the term plainly subsumes consideration of cost.

4. **Role of Narrowing Construction?** The *Whitman* Court concludes that an agency cannot cure an unconstitutional legislative delegation of power by adopting an interpretation of the statute which has the effect of reducing the agency's scope of discretion: "Whether the statute delegates legislative power is a question for the courts, and an agency's voluntary self-denial has no bearing upon the answer." Consider the D.C. Circuit's reasoning that was rejected by the Court:

> Where ... statutory language and an existing agency interpretation involve an unconstitutional delegation of power, but an interpretation without the constitutional weakness is or may be available, our response is not to strike down the statute but to give the agency an opportunity to extract a determinate standard on its own. Doing so serves at least two of three basic rationales for the nondelegation doctrine. If the agency develops determinate, binding standards for itself, it is less likely to exercise the delegated authority arbitrarily. And such standards enhance the likelihood that meaningful judicial review will prove feasible. A remand of this sort of course does not serve the third key function of non-delegation doctrine, to ensure[] to the extent consistent with orderly governmental administration that important choices of social policy are made by Congress [.]*** The agency will make the fundamental policy choices. But the remand does ensure that the courts not hold unconstitutional a statute that an agency, with the application of its special expertise, could salvage.

American Trucking Associations, Inc. v. EPA, 175 F.3d 1027, 1038 (D.C. Cir. 1999).

Note also that in *Yakus*, the Court gave weight to the fact that the ECPA required the Administrator to provide a "statement of considerations" informing its price regulations: "The standards prescribed by the present Act, with the aid of the 'statement of considerations' required to be made by the Administrator, are sufficiently definite and precise to enable Congress, the courts and the public to ascertain whether the Administrator, in fixing the designated prices, has conformed to those standards." 321 U.S. at 426.

5. **Delegation to Private Parties Redux.** Section 207(a) of the Passenger Rail Investment and Improvement Act of 2008, Pub. L. No. 110-432, Div. B, 122 Stat. 4916, requires the Federal Railroad Administration (FRA) and the National Railroad Passenger Corporation (better known as Amtrak) to "jointly*** develop" metrics and standards for measuring passenger trains' on-time performance. Those metrics, in turn, are used by the Surface Transportation Board in investigations of whether

freight railroads have complied with a preference for passenger rail service established by 49 U.S.C. § 24308(c) (Supp. V 2011).

If the FRA and Amtrak cannot agree on metrics for Amtrak's performance, the metrics are established through an arbitration in which the FRA and Amtrak appear as opposing parties. The D.C. Circuit concluded, in an opinion by Judge Janice Rogers Brown, that this scheme worked an unconstitutional delegation of legislative power because both Amtrak and the arbitrator who set standards in the event of an impasse were private parties for purposes of the non-delegation doctrine. In the court of appeals' view, "[e]ven an intelligible principle cannot rescue a statute empowering private parties to wield regulatory authority," and Amtrak was a private party for purposes of this rule. *Association of Am. Railroads v. Dep't of Transp.*, 721 F.3d 666, 671 (D.C. Cir. 2013).

The Supreme Court reversed on the ground that Amtrak, though nominally a private, for-profit corporation, was a government entity for purposes of the non-delegation doctrine. *Department of Transp. v. Ass'n of Am. Railroads*, 135 S. Ct. 1225 (2015). Summarizing its analysis, the Court observed that Amtrak's "priorities, operations, and decisions are extensively supervised and funded by the political branches. A majority of its Board is appointed by the President and confirmed by the Senate and is understood by the Executive to be removable by the President at will. Amtrak was created by the Government, is controlled by the Government, and operates for the Government's benefit. Thus, in its joint issuance of the metrics and standards with the FRA, Amtrak acted as a governmental entity for purposes of the Constitution's separation of powers provisions." *Id.* at 1232-33.

The Supreme Court remanded to the D.C. Circuit to address petitioners' remaining challenges to the Passenger Rail Act. The court of appeals on remand ruled that the Passenger Rail Act "violates the Fifth Amendment's Due Process Clause by authorizing an economically self-interested actor to regulate its competitors and violates the Appointments Clause [by] delegating regulatory power to an improperly appointed arbitrator." *Association of Am. Railroads v. Dep't of Transp.*, 821 F.3d 19, 23 (D.C. Cir. 2016).

What if anything is special about delegations to actors who are not officers of the federal government? Are federal officers likely to exercise discretion differently than delegates who are not employed by the federal government? Are federal employees accountable in ways that non-employees are not? For extended analyses, see Gillian Metzger, *Privatization as Delegation*, 103 Colum. L. Rev. 1367 (2003); Jody Freeman, *The Private Role in the Public Governance*, 75 N.Y.U. L. Rev. 543 (2000).

6. **Constitutional Basis for the Non-Delegation Doctrine?** Does the Court in any of the decisions discussed in this section explain the constitutional basis for the principle that legislation must contain an intelligible principle to guide the discretion of a delegatee promulgating implementing regulations? The most obvious possibility is Article I, § 1's Vesting Clause, which provides that "All legislative powers herein granted shall be vested in a Congress of the United States, which shall consist of a Senate and House of Representatives." Note that, in contrast to Article II, § 1, and Article III, § 1, the Article I vesting clause vests "*all*" legislative powers in Congress.

While textually plausible, the inference that the Vesting Clause prohibits institutions other than Congress from establishing rules of conduct pursuant to congressional authorization is difficult to reconcile with history. Consider the early administrative delegations noted by Professor Mashaw, *Foreword: The American Model of Federal Administrative Law: Remembering the First One Hundred Years*, 78 Geo. Wash. U. L. Rev. 975, 982 (2010).

Another possible textual source for the non-delegation doctrine is found in the legislative process established by Article I, § 7. Under Article I, § 7, a bill must be passed by the House and Senate in identical form and presented to the President. In contrast, a regulation promulgated by an agency, while subject to significant procedural requirements discussed below, is not subject to the requirements of bicameralism and presentment.

But if bicameralism and presentment are required anytime that the federal government establishes a generally applicable conduct regulating rule, wouldn't *all* federal law that is not defined by statute be unconstitutional? Moreover, even when Congress delegates power to promulgate rules to other institutions, the statute that effects the delegation must be passed by both the House and the Senate and presented to the President for a possible veto.

Eric A. Posner & Adrian Vermeule, *Interring the Nondelegation Doctrine*, 69 U. Chi. L. Rev. 1721 (2002), contend that the nondelegation doctrine "lacks any foundation in constitutional text and structure, in standard originalist sources, or in sound economic and political theory . . . . The Court's invocation of the rule to invalidate two statutes in 1935 was nothing more than a local aberration." Posner and Vermeule maintain that the only way that Congress can impermissibly delegate legislative power is for it "or its individual members*** to cede to anyone else the members' de jure powers as federal legislative officers, such as the power to vote on proposed statutes.*** [A] statutory grant of authority to the executive branch or other agents can *never* amount to a delegation of legislative power. A statutory grant of authority to the executive isn't a *transfer* of legislative power, but an *exercise* of legislative power." Is this analysis persuasive? Is it consistent with the Court's analysis in *Whitman Trucking*?

7. **The Issue of Administrability.** Whatever the defects of the current non-delegation doctrine, it is simple for courts to administer. Provided that a statute contains an "intelligible principle" to guide presidential or agency decisionmaking, it does not impermissibly delegate legislative authority. Would a more vigorous version of the doctrine share this feature? Can you devise a judicially administrable standard for identifying impermissible delegations of Congress's legislative powers?

8. **Non-Delegation Doctrine as a Substantive Canon?** If concerns about delegation of legislative authority do not yield a judicially administrable test for determining the constitutionality of legislation, might they nevertheless be a useful guide to interpreting statutes? On one account, non-delegation concerns influence courts to interpret statutes in a manner that forces Congress to address difficult policy questions rather than delegating authority over them to other institutions. "Rather than invalidating

federal legislation as excessively open-ended, courts hold that federal administrative agencies may not engage in certain activities unless and until Congress has expressly authorized them to do so." Cass R. Sunstein, *Nondelegation Canons*, 67 U. CHI. L. REV. 315, 316 (2000). How would this non-delegation canon apply to § 3 of the NIRA? What would be the predicate for requiring express authorization? Wasn't there express authorization in § 3? Recall the discussion of substantive canons in Chapter 2[B][2][f], and the criticism that substantive canons allow courts to engage in judicial review without paying a price for invalidating duly-enacted laws, and to negate central compromises in such legislation. Is the canon suggested by Professor Sunstein foreclosed by the Court's decision in *Whitman*?

b. Delegation of Judicial Functions to Agencies

When creating an administrative agency, Congress can delegate authority to the agency to resolve disputes as well as authority to promulgate regulations having the force of law. Indeed, as indicated in Note 3 following *Heckler v. Campbell*, Chapter 1[C][3], *supra* p. 50, administrative agencies adjudicate a far greater number of disputes, on an absolute basis, than Article III courts. Just as the delegation of rulemaking authority to an administrative agency might be thought to violate Article I, § 1's Vesting Clause, the delegation of adjudicatory authority to an administrative agency might be thought inconsistent with Article III, § 1's vesting of "[t]he judicial power of the United States" in "one Supreme Court, and in such inferior courts as the Congress may from time to time ordain and establish." The two decisions that follow introduce the framework used to analyze whether a statute that assigns adjudicative functions to a non-Article III tribunal is consistent with Article III.

Crowell v. Benson

285 U.S. 22 (1932)

MR. CHIEF JUSTICE HUGHES delivered the opinion of the Court.

[The Longshoremen's and Harbor Workers' Compensation Act (LHWA), Pub. L. No. 69-803, 44 Stat. 1424 (1927), liberalized common law tort standards for workers who died or became disabled because of "an injury occurring upon the navigable waters of the United States." Among other things, the Act provided for compensation "irrespective of fault as a cause for the injury."

The Act was administered by the U.S. Employees' Compensation Commission, a three-member, bipartisan body modeled on the Interstate Commerce Commission. The Commission determined whether claims fell within the coverage of the Act, resolved factual disputes about specific claims, and entered orders awarding compensation to injured employees. Under the Act, district courts were authorized to enter judgment on orders of the Commission that were made "in accordance with law." The Act further provided that a compensation order not made in accordance with law "'may be suspended or set aside, in whole or in part, through injunction proceedings, mandatory or otherwise, brought by any party in interest against the deputy commissioner making the order and instituted in the Federal district court for the judicial district in which the injury occurred."

Benson challenged the Act's constitutionality. He contended, among other things, that adjudication of claims by the Commission in the first instance violated Article III.—Eds.]

The contention based upon the judicial power of the United States, as extended "to all cases of admiralty and maritime jurisdiction" (Const. Art. III), presents a distinct question. In *Murray's Lessee v. Hoboken Land and Improvement Co.*, 18 How. 272, 284, this Court, speaking through Mr. Justice Curtis, said: "To avoid misconstruction upon so grave a subject, we think it proper to state that we do not consider congress can either withdraw from judicial cognizance any matter which, from its nature, is the subject of a suit at the common law, or in equity, or admiralty; nor, on the other hand, can it bring under the judicial power a matter which, from its nature, is not a subject for judicial determination."

The question in the instant case, in this aspect, can be deemed to relate only to determinations of fact.*** The Congress did not attempt to define questions of law, and the generality of the description leaves no doubt of the intention to reserve to the Federal court full authority to pass upon all matters which this Court had held to fall within that category.***

As to determinations of fact, the distinction is at once apparent between cases of private right and those which arise between the Government and persons subject to its authority in connection with the performance of the constitutional functions of the executive or legislative departments. The Court referred to this distinction in *Murray's Lessee v. Hoboken Land and Improvement Co.*, *supra*, pointing out that "there are matters, involving public rights, which may be presented in such form that the judicial power is capable of acting on them, and which are susceptible of judicial determination, but which Congress may or may not bring within the cognizance of the courts of the United States, as it may deem proper." Thus the Congress, in exercising the powers confided to it, may establish "legislative" courts (as distinguished from "constitutional courts in which the judicial power conferred by the Constitution can be deposited") which are to form part of the government of territories or of the District of Columbia, or to serve as special tribunals "to examine and determine various matters, arising between the government and others, which from their nature do not require judicial determination and yet are susceptible of it." But "the mode of determining matters of this class is completely within congressional control. Congress may reserve to itself the power to decide, may delegate that power to executive officers, or may commit it to judicial tribunals." Familiar illustrations of administrative agencies created for the determination of such matters are found in connection with the exercise of the congressional power as to interstate and foreign commerce, taxation, immigration, the public lands, public health, the facilities of the post office, pensions and payments to veterans.

The present case does not fall within the categories just described but is one of private right, that is, of the liability of one individual to another under the law as defined.

But in cases of that sort, there is no requirement that, in order to maintain the essential attributes of the judicial power, all determinations of fact in constitutional courts shall be made by judges. On the common law side of the Federal courts, the aid of juries is not only deemed appropriate but is required by the Constitution itself. In cases of equity and admiralty, it is historic practice to call to the assistance of the courts, without the consent of the parties, masters and commissioners or assessors, to pass upon certain classes of questions, as, for example, to take and state an account or to find the amount of damages.***

The statute has a limited application, being confined to the relation of master and servant, and the method of determining the questions of fact, which arise in the routine of making compensation awards to employees under the Act, is necessary to its effective enforcement. The Act itself, where it applies, establishes the measure of the employer's liability, thus leaving open for determination the questions of fact as to the circumstances, nature, extent and consequences of the injuries sustained by the employee for which compensation is to be made in accordance with the prescribed standards. Findings of fact by the deputy commissioner upon such questions are closely analogous to the findings of the amount of damages that are made, according to familiar practice, by commissioners or assessors; and the reservation of full authority to the court to deal with matters of law provides for the appropriate exercise of the judicial function in this class of cases.***

What has been said thus far relates to the determination of claims of employees within the purview of the Act. A different question is presented where the determinations of fact are fundamental or "jurisdictional" in the sense that their existence is a condition precedent to the operation of the statutory scheme. These fundamental requirements are that the injury occurs upon the navigable waters of the United States, and that the relation of master and servant exists. These conditions are indispensable to the application of the statute not only because the Congress has so provided explicitly (§3), but also because the power of the Congress to enact the legislation turns upon the existence of these conditions.***

In relation to these basic facts, the question is not the ordinary one as to the propriety of provision for administrative determinations. Nor have we simply the question of due process in relation to notice and hearing. It is, rather, a question of the appropriate maintenance of the federal judicial power in requiring the observance of constitutional restrictions. It is the question whether the Congress may substitute for constitutional courts, in which the judicial power of the United States is vested, an administrative agency—in this instance, a single deputy commissioner—for the final determination of the existence of the facts upon which the enforcement of the constitutional rights of the citizen depend.

[The Court concluded that the Act should be interpreted so as to permit trial *de novo* on the question of whether an employee fell within the Act's scope. The existence of a master-servant relationship and an injury within the navigable waters of the United States underpinned Congress's assertion of regulatory power; absent those facts, there would be no authority in article I, §8 to modify common law rules of liability. The Court wrote that in these circumstances, "the argument that the Congress has constituted the deputy commissioner a fact-finding tribunal is unavailing, as the contention makes the untenable assumption that the constitutional courts may be deprived in all cases of the determination of facts upon evidence even though a constitutional right may be involved."]

MR. JUSTICE BRANDEIS, dissenting.

***The "judicial power" of Article III of the Constitution is the power of the federal government, and not of any inferior tribunal. There is in that Article nothing which requires any controversy to be determined as of first instance in the federal district courts. The jurisdiction of those courts is subject to the control of Congress. Matters which may be placed within their jurisdiction may instead be committed to the state courts. If there be any controversy to which the judicial power extends that may not be subjected to the conclusive determination of administrative bodies or federal legislative courts, it is not because of any prohibition against the diminution of the jurisdiction of the federal district courts as such, but because, under certain circumstances, the constitutional requirement of due process is a requirement of judicial process.

Notes and Questions

1. **The Procedural Posture?** Charles Benson filed the action in *Crowell* in the U.S. District Court for the Southern District of Alabama and sought an injunction prohibiting enforcement of a compensation order issued by Letus N. Crowell, the Deputy Commissioner for the Seventh Compensation District, an employee of the U.S. Employees' Compensation Commission. The lower courts granted the injunction on the ground that J.B. Knudsen, the claimant whom Crowell ruled in favor of, was not in fact an employee of Benson, and thus fell outside the coverage of the Longshoremen's and Harbor Workers' Compensation Act (LHWCA). *Crowell v. Benson*, 45 F.2d 66, 70 (5th Cir. 1930). The issue before the Supreme Court was whether the lower courts were correct that a trial *de novo* was required on the issue of whether there was an employment relationship between Knudsen and Benson. *See generally* Mark Tushnet, *The Story of* Crowell: *Grounding the Administrative State, in* FEDERAL COURTS STORIES (Vicki C. Jackson & Judith Resnik eds., 2010).

2. **Justification for Regulation?** The LHWCA established new standards of tort liability for injuries and deaths that occurred "upon the navigable waters of the United States." Claims under the Act were heard in the first instance by a deputy commissioner of the U.S. Employees' Compensation Commission, a three-member body modeled after the Interstate Commerce Commission. District courts were authorized under §21 of the Act to review the Commission's legal conclusions *de novo*, but the standard of review for the Commission's factual findings was not specified.

Admiralty law has always been considered a province of the federal government. *See* Henry J. Friendly, *In Praise of* Erie — *And of the New Federal Common Law*, 39 N.Y.U. L. REV. 383, 404–05 (1964). The LHWCA brought to bear the no-fault principles of state workers' compensation laws to injuries occurring in the course of employment in the country's navigable waters. As was true of state workers' compensation laws, the no-fault principle sought to provide greater likelihood of compensation for employment-related injuries free of common-law defenses, such as contributory negligence, assumption of risk and the fellow-servant doctrine, that often stymied recovery. Employers, on the other hand, benefited from being freed of the uncertainty of jury awards.

Why do you think Congress channeled compensation claims to the Commission rather than the district courts in the first instance? Is this an area where adjudication by an expert adjudicator is necessary to accomplish a statute's objectives? Would the handling of LHWCA claims have caused a significant increase in the district courts' caseload, requiring additional federal judges? Is it also possible that by making the Commission the initial forum for the adjudication of LHWCA claims, Congress was seeking to make the claiming process more accessible for injured workers?

3. **"Public Rights" Doctrine.** *Crowell* teaches that Congress has wide discretion to structure dispute resolution systems for questions "which arise between the Government and persons subject to its authority in connection with the performance of the constitutional functions of the executive or legislative departments." This principle is known as the "public rights" doctrine, because the rights at issue are created by statute and involve the operation of the government. *Crowell* also teaches that Congress can give an agency jurisdiction over a category of claims and direct the agency to perform fact finding functions analogous to those performed by a master, commissioner, or assessor in an action at law or admiralty. Here, the validity of the jurisdictional grant depends on the availability of judicial review in an Article III court. As stated by *Crowell*, an Article III court must have "full authority . . . to deal with matters of law."

The Court has also offered the "public rights" doctrine as an explanation for the why the Seventh Amendment's civil jury trial guarantee does not apply in administrative proceedings. *See Atlas Roofing Co. v. Occupational Safety and Health Comm'n*, 430 U.S. 442 (1977).

4. **"Jurisdictional"/"Constitutional Facts."** *Crowell* marks an important turning point in the history of U.S. administration, because the Court broadly sustained the power of Congress to assign fact finding functions to administrative agencies. But the Court's ruling was not unqualified. As to facts upon which the jurisdiction of the agency and the constitutional authority of Congress depended — in this case, whether there was an employment relation between Knudsen and Benson and whether the injury occurred in the navigable waters of the United States — the Court held that factual determinations could be made only by an Article III court. Justice Brandeis, dissenting, maintained that the Commission's factual determination should be upheld and that trial *de novo* in an Article III court was not required: "The existence of a relation of employment is a question going to the applicability of the substantive law, not to the jurisdiction of the tribunal. Jurisdiction is the power to adjudicate between the parties concerning the subject-matter."

Justice Brandeis's view prevailed in *St. Joseph Stock Yards v. United States*, 298 U.S. 38 (1936). Although a claim that a government action deprived a regulated party of

its property without due process raised a constitutional question requiring the independent scrutiny of an Article III court, de novo review by an Article III tribunal court
was not required. Chief Justice Hughes wrote for the Court (at 53):

> But this judicial duty to exercise an independent judgment does not require
> or justify disregard of the weight which may properly attach to findings
> upon hearing and evidence. On the contrary, the judicial duty is performed
> in the light of the proceedings already had, and may be greatly facilitated by
> the assembling and analysis of the facts in the course of the legislative deter-
> mination. Judicial judgment may be nonetheless appropriately indepen-
> dent because informed and aided by the sifting procedure of an expert
> legislative agency.

Today, it is commonplace for agencies to find facts that underpin the exercise of federal authority, and such facts are not generally reviewed differently than others found
by an agency. *See generally* Henry P. Monaghan, *Constitutional Fact Review*, 85 COLUM.
L. REV. 231 (1985); John Dickinson, Crowell v. Benson: *Judicial Review of Administrative Determinations of Questions of "Constitutional Fact,"* 80 U. PENN. L. REV. 1055
(1932). The "jurisdictional fact" doctrine re-emerged for a brief period in the different context of judicial review of agency statutory interpretation in *City of Arlington v.
FCC*, 133 S. Ct. 1863 (2013), *infra* Chapter 5[C][3].

To what extent may Congress go beyond the limits suggested by *Crowell* and assign
adjudication of common law claims to an administrative agency? The Supreme Court
considered that question in a case that arose out of proceedings before the Commodities Futures Trading Commission.

Commodity Futures Trading Commission v. Schor

478 U.S. 833 (1986)

JUSTICE O'CONNOR delivered the opinion of the Court.

The question presented is whether the Commodity Exchange Act (CEA or Act), 7
U.S.C. § 1 et seq., empowers the Commodity Futures Trading Commission (CFTC or
Commission) to entertain state law counterclaims in reparation proceedings and, if
so, whether that grant of authority violates Article III of the Constitution.

I

The CEA broadly prohibits fraudulent and manipulative conduct in connection
with commodity futures transactions. In 1974, Congress "overhaul[ed]" the Act in
order to institute a more "comprehensive regulatory structure to oversee the volatile
and esoteric futures trading complex." H.R. Rep. No. 93-975, p. 1 (1974). See Pub. L.
93-463, 88 Stat. 1389. Congress also determined that the broad regulatory powers of
the CEA were most appropriately vested in an agency which would be relatively
immune from the "political winds that sweep Washington." H.R. Rep. No. 93-975, at

44, 70. It therefore created an independent agency, the CFTC, and entrusted to it sweeping authority to implement the CEA.

Among the duties assigned to the CFTC was the administration of a reparations procedure through which disgruntled customers of professional commodity brokers could seek redress for the brokers' violations of the Act or CFTC regulations. Thus, § 14 of the CEA, 7 U.S.C. § 18 (1976 ed.), provides that any person injured by such violations may apply to the Commission for an order directing the offender to pay reparations to the complainant and may enforce that order in federal district court. Congress intended this administrative procedure to be an "inexpensive and expeditious" alternative to existing fora available to aggrieved customers, namely, the courts and arbitration. S. Rep. No. 95-850, p. 11 (1978).

In conformance with the congressional goal of promoting efficient dispute resolution, the CFTC promulgated a regulation in 1976 which allows it to adjudicate counterclaims "aris[ing] out of the transaction or occurrence or series of transactions or occurrences set forth in the complaint." *Id.*, at 3995, 4002 (codified at 17 CFR § 12.23(b)(2) (1983)). This permissive counterclaim rule leaves the respondent in a reparations proceeding free to seek relief against the reparations complainant in other fora.

The instant dispute arose in February 1980, when respondents Schor and Mortgage Services of America, Inc., invoked the CFTC's reparations jurisdiction by filing complaints against petitioner ContiCommodity Services, Inc. (Conti), a commodity futures broker, and Richard L. Sandor, a Conti employee. Schor had an account with Conti which contained a debit balance because Schor's net futures trading losses and expenses, such as commissions, exceeded the funds deposited in the account. Schor alleged that this debit balance was the result of Conti's numerous violations of the CEA.

Before receiving notice that Schor had commenced the reparations proceeding, Conti had filed a diversity action in Federal District Court to recover the debit balance. Schor counterclaimed in this action, reiterating his charges that the debit balance was due to Conti's violations of the CEA.***

Although the District Court declined to stay or dismiss the suit, Conti voluntarily dismissed the federal court action and presented its debit balance claim by way of a counterclaim in the CFTC reparations proceeding. Conti denied violating the CEA and instead insisted that the debit balance resulted from Schor's trading, and was therefore a simple debt owed by Schor.

After discovery, briefing, and a hearing, the Administrative Law Judge (ALJ) in Schor's reparations proceeding ruled in Conti's favor on both Schor's claims and Conti's counterclaims. After this ruling, Schor for the first time challenged the CFTC's statutory authority to adjudicate Conti's counterclaim. The ALJ rejected Schor's challenge.*** The Commission declined to review the decision and allowed it to become final, at which point Schor filed a petition for review with the Court of Appeals for the District of Columbia Circuit.***

After briefing and argument, the Court of Appeals upheld the CFTC's decision on Schor's claim in most respects, but ordered the dismissal of Conti's counterclaims on the ground that "the CFTC lacks authority (subject matter competence) to adjudicate" common law counterclaims.***

II

[The Supreme Court rejected the argument that the CFTC lacked statutory authority to consider Schor's counterclaims.]

III

Schor claims that [Article III] prohibit[s] Congress from authorizing the initial adjudication of common law counterclaims by the CFTC, an administrative agency whose adjudicatory officers do not enjoy the tenure and salary protections embodied in [the constitutional provision].

A

Article III, § 1, serves both to protect "the role of the independent judiciary within the constitutional scheme of tripartite government," and to safeguard litigants' "right to have claims decided before judges who are free from potential domination by other branches of government." Although our cases have provided us with little occasion to discuss the nature or significance of this latter safeguard, our prior discussions of Article III, § 1's guarantee of an independent and impartial adjudication by the federal judiciary of matters within the judicial power of the United States intimated that this guarantee serves to protect primarily personal, rather than structural, interests.

Our precedents also demonstrate, however, that Article III does not confer on litigants an absolute right to the plenary consideration of every nature of claim by an Article III court. Moreover, as a personal right, Article III's guarantee of an impartial and independent federal adjudication is subject to waiver, just as are other personal constitutional rights that dictate the procedures by which civil and criminal matters must be tried.***

In the instant cases, Schor indisputably waived any right he may have possessed to the full trial of Conti's counterclaim before an Article III court. Schor expressly demanded that Conti proceed on its counterclaim in the reparations proceeding rather than before the District Court, and was content to have the entire dispute settled in the forum he had selected until the ALJ ruled against him on all counts; it was only after the ALJ rendered a decision to which he objected that Schor raised any challenge to the CFTC's consideration of Conti's counterclaim.***

B

As noted above, our precedents establish that Article III, § 1, not only preserves to litigants their interest in an impartial and independent federal adjudication of claims within the judicial power of the United States, but also serves as "an inseparable element of the constitutional system of checks and balances." Article III, § 1, safeguards the role of the Judicial Branch in our tripartite system by barring congressional attempts "to transfer jurisdiction [to non-Article III tribunals] for the purpose of emasculating" constitutional courts,*** and thereby preventing "the encroachment or aggrandizement of one branch at the expense of the other." *Buckley v. Valeo*, 424 U.S. 1, 122 (1976) (per curiam). To the extent that this structural principle is implicated in a given case, the parties cannot by consent cure the constitutional difficulty for the same reason that the parties by consent cannot confer on federal courts subject-matter jurisdiction beyond the limitations imposed by Article III, §2. When these Article III limitations are at issue, notions of consent and waiver cannot be dispositive because the limitations serve institutional interests that the parties cannot be expected to protect.***

An examination of the relative allocation of powers between the CFTC and Article III courts in light of the considerations given prominence in our precedents demonstrates that the congressional scheme does not impermissibly intrude on the province of the judiciary. The CFTC's adjudicatory powers depart from the traditional [administrative] agency model in just one respect: the CFTC's jurisdiction over common law counterclaims. While wholesale importation of concepts of pendent or ancillary jurisdiction into the agency context may create greater constitutional difficulties, we decline to endorse an absolute prohibition on such jurisdiction out of fear of where some hypothetical "slippery slope" may deposit us.***

In the instant cases, we are*** persuaded that there is little practical reason to find that this single deviation from the agency model is fatal to the congressional scheme.*** The CFTC*** deals only with a "particularized area of law,"*** CFTC orders*** are enforceable only by order of the district court. *See* 7 U.S.C. §18(f). CFTC orders are also reviewed under the*** "weight of the evidence" standard.*** The legal rulings of the CFTC*** are subject to de novo review. Finally, the CFTC *** does not exercise "all ordinary powers of district courts," and thus may not, for instance, preside over jury trials or issue writs of habeas corpus.

Of course, the nature of the claim has significance in our Article III analysis quite apart from the method prescribed for its adjudication. The counterclaim asserted in this litigation is a "private" right for which state law provides the rule of decision. It is therefore a claim of the kind assumed to be at the "core" of matters normally reserved to Article III courts.***

[T]he state law character of a claim is significant for purposes of determining the effect that an initial adjudication of those claims by a non-Article III tribunal will have on the separation of powers for the simple reason that private, common law rights were historically the types of matters subject to resolution by Article III courts. The risk that Congress may improperly have encroached on the federal judiciary is obviously magnified when Congress "withdraw[s] from judicial cognizance any matter which, from its nature, is the subject of a suit at the common law, or in equity, or admiralty" and which therefore has traditionally been tried in Article III courts, and allocates the decision of those matters to a non-Article III forum of its own creation. Accordingly, where private, common law rights are at stake, our examination of the congressional attempt to control the manner in which those rights are adjudicated has been searching. In this litigation, however, looking beyond form to the substance of what Congress has done, we are persuaded that the congressional authorization of limited CFTC jurisdiction over a narrow class of common law claims as an incident to the CFTC's primary, and unchallenged, adjudicative function does not create a substantial threat to the separation of powers.

It is clear that Congress has not attempted to "withdraw from judicial cognizance" the determination of Conti's right to the sum represented by the debit balance in Schor's account. Congress gave the CFTC the authority to adjudicate such matters, but the decision to invoke this forum is left entirely to the parties and the power of the federal judiciary to take jurisdiction of these matters is unaffected. In such circumstances, separation of powers concerns are diminished, for it seems self-evident that just as Congress may encourage parties to settle a dispute out of court or resort to arbitration without impermissible incursions on the separation of powers, Congress may make available a quasi-judicial mechanism through which willing parties may, at their option, elect to resolve their differences.***

It also bears emphasis that the CFTC's assertion of counterclaim jurisdiction is limited to that which is necessary to make the reparations procedure workable. *See* 7 U.S.C. § 12a(5). The CFTC adjudication of common law counterclaims is incidental to, and completely dependent upon, adjudication of reparations claims created by federal law, and in actual fact is limited to claims arising out of the same transaction or occurrence as the reparations claim.

In such circumstances, the magnitude of any intrusion on the Judicial Branch can only be termed de minimis. Conversely, were we to hold that the Legislative Branch may not permit such limited cognizance of common law counterclaims at the election of the parties, it is clear that we would defeat the obvious purpose of the legislation to furnish a prompt, continuous, expert and inexpensive method for dealing with a class of questions of fact which are peculiarly suited to examination and determination by an administrative agency specially assigned to that task. We do not think Article III compels this degree of prophylaxis.

[JUSTICE BRENNAN, joined by JUSTICE MARSHALL, dissented.]

Notes and Questions

1. **The Procedural Posture?** What actions had taken place before the CFTC by the time the Supreme Court issued its decision? What actions had taken place in the lower courts? What did the lower courts conclude? Why is the Commodities Futures Trading Commission a party in the Supreme Court?

2. **Justification for Regulation?** The federal government has regulated trading of options contracts for certain commodities since the Grain Futures Act of 1922, ch. 369, 42 Stat. 998. The Supreme Court sustained the Grain Futures Act as a constitutional exercise of Congress' power to regulate interstate commerce in *Board of Trade v. Olsen*, 262 U.S. 1 (1923). In 1936, Congress enacted the Commodity Exchange Act (CEA), ch. 545, 49 Stat. 1491, 7 U.S.C. § 1 et seq., which replaced the 1922 measure. The CEA provides federal regulation of all commodities and futures trading activities

and requires all futures and commodity options to be traded on organized exchanges. In 1974 amendments, Congress established the Commodities Futures Trading Commission (CFTC) to provide more comprehensive regulation of commodities futures transactions.

The CEA protects commodities market participants by broadly prohibiting commodities brokers from engaging in fraud in commodities transactions and authorizes the CFTC to resolve claims for reparation by parties who claim to have been defrauded in connection with a commodities transaction. The CFTC may resolve claims under the CEA, as well as factually related state law counterclaims by commodities brokers against parties who seek reparations from them. The CFTC's jurisdiction is concurrent with the district courts. That is, reparation claims can be filed either in district court or before the CFTC.

Why did Congress decide to give the CFTC jurisdiction to resolve claims under the CEA in the first instance? Does resolution of claims under the CEA require expertise in a specialized subject area? Could district courts efficiently handle the volume of claims that Congress anticipated under the CEA? Aside from the possible Article III issues, is there any policy reason why Congress provided concurrent jurisdiction in the CFTC and the district courts? What incentives does concurrent jurisdiction create for the CFTC? For district courts? What strategic choices does concurrent jurisdiction present for parties filing a reparations claim? Consider that, according to one press account, one ALJ at the CFTC has ruled in investors' favor only a handful of times over a decades-long career. *See* Michael Miltzik, *Strange Doings at the CFTC*, LA TIMES, Oct. 27, 2010, at B1 (quoting an attorney to the effect that "[i]t's an open secret among my brethren that if you get [this ALJ], he's not going to rule for the investor.").

3. *Schor's* **Framework for Agency Adjudication of "Private Rights" Disputes.** Insofar as the CFTC in *Schor* provided an adjudicatory forum for resolving customers' claims against commodities brokers for violating the CEA, there would seem to be no serious Article III issue under *Crowell*. The difficulty *Schor* presents was the Commission's adjudication of counterclaims based on state law that Conti, the broker, had against the customer arising out of the same trading transaction. Conti's counterclaim involved an adjudication of "private rights" under *Crowell*. Here, the Court introduces a two-part test. First, Congress may authorize an agency to adjudicate private-rights claims if the delegation of dispute-resolution authority does not compromise "the institutional integrity of the Judicial Branch." What factors govern this inquiry? How was the authority of Article III courts in any way adversely affected by allowing CFTC adjudication of factually-related state-law counterclaims?

Second, provided that the delegation of dispute-resolution authority to an agency does not compromise the Article III judiciary's institutional integrity, a litigant may waive her right to an Article III forum by taking advantage of a non-Article III forum. Presenting a claim to the agency and litigating the claim to judgment "indisputably" effects such a waiver. Should a waiver be found given the fact that Conti was a respondent in the CFTC proceeding?

Would a reading of the CEA that barred resolution of factually-related state law counterclaims have been fair to Conti? Would it have promoted efficient dispute resolution?

4. Constitutional Basis for Judicial Non-Delegation Doctrine? What is the relationship between agency adjudication and Article III, § 1's vesting of the judicial power in the Supreme Court and inferior courts established by Congress? Analogous to the legislative non-delegation doctrine, Article III, § 1 might be read to say by negative implication that no institution of federal government other than an Article III court may exercise "the judicial power of the United States." A central difficulty with this position, pointed out by Justice Brandeis in *Crowell*, is that Article III does not require the establishment of *any* federal courts aside from the Supreme Court. (The Supreme Court functions as a court of first instance only in rare circumstances.) Indeed the framers of both the Constitution and the Judiciary Act of 1789, which created lower federal courts, assumed that state courts rather than federal courts would be the central site for resolution of disputes arising under federal law. Only in 1875, *see* Act of March 3, 1875 § 1, ch. 137, 18 Stat. 470, did Congress give the lower federal courts general subject matter jurisdiction to try claims arising under federal law.

The framework *Schor* elaborates might also be understood as an effort to protect separation of powers values—and more particularly, the role of the Article III judiciary in the federal government. Adjudicating cases and controversies provides the occasion for the judiciary to say what the law is, and allocating too much dispute resolution authority to agencies might disrupt its ability to do so. But isn't such a view equally difficult to square with the premise of the founding era that state courts would be adjudicating most disputes governed by federal law? In any event, are federal courts ousted from their law-declaration role if review of questions of law remain the province of the courts (as *Crowell* plainly requires)?

Does the Article III jurisprudence have anything to do with preserving Seventh Amendment rights to a civil jury trial? *See Atlas Roofing, Inc. v. OSHA*, 430 U.S. 442 (1977) (rejecting Seventh Amendment challenge to agency adjudication in "public rights" case). Is *Schor* a "public rights" case for Seventh Amendment purposes?

5. Delegation of Legislative vs. Judicial Functions. How does the Supreme Court's approach to Congress's assignment of dispute resolution functions to agencies differ from its approach to Congress's assignment of quasi-legislative functions to agencies? As we saw, a delegation of quasi-legislative authority will be upheld if the delegation contains an "intelligible principle" to guide the discretion of the delegate exercising regulatory authority. By contrast, delegations of dispute resolution authority must respect the Article III courts' monopoly on adjudication of traditional common law claims, and cannot impermissibly infringe the "integrity of the Judicial Branch."

What might justify the comparatively greater scrutiny given to delegations of dispute-resolution authority? Do the textual bases for the legislative and judicial non-delegation doctrines suggest that delegations of quasi-legislative and quasi-judicial power should be treated differently? Are there prudential reasons why courts should be more careful about delegations of judicial authority than delegations of legislative authority? In particular, might delegations of legislative authority be self-correcting— that is, revisited by Congress—in a way that delegations of dispute-resolution authority are not?

6. **Article III and Bankruptcy Proceedings.** In *Stern v. Marshall*, 131 S. Ct. 2594 (2011), the Supreme Court seemed to take a significantly more restrictive view toward the delegation of dispute-resolution functions to non-Article III tribunals than it did in *Crowell* and *Schor*. At issue was a counterclaim for tortious interference with expectancy of inheritance that the late model Anna Nicole Smith asserted against E. Pierce Marshall in Smith's individual bankruptcy proceeding. Bankruptcy courts are Article I courts, whose judges serve for 14-year terms. The Supreme Court concluded that Article III prohibited the bankruptcy court from adjudicating Smith's counterclaim.

The Court in *Stern* acknowledged the public-rights doctrine but concluded that Smith's counterclaim fell outside of it. The counterclaim was "the stuff of the traditional actions at common law tried by the courts at Westminster in 1789," and "within the bounds of federal jurisdiction." Marshall did not consent to the bankruptcy court adjudicating his claim, so the claim had to be resolved by an Article III court.

Discussing *Schor*, the *Stern* Court stated that "the customer's reparations claim before the agency and the broker's counterclaim were competing claims to the same amount, [so] it was 'necessary' to allow the agency to exercise jurisdiction over the broker's claim, or else 'the reparations procedure would have been confounded.'" The Court emphasized that in *Schor*, "(1) the claim and the counterclaim concerned a 'single dispute'—the same account balance; (2) the CFTC's assertion of authority involved only 'a narrow class of common law claims' in a 'particularized area of law'; (3) the area of law in question was governed by 'a specific and limited federal regulatory scheme' as to which the agency had 'obvious expertise'; (4) the parties had freely elected to resolve their differences before the CFTC; and (5) CFTC orders were 'enforceable only by order of the district court.'" 131 S. Ct. at 2613. *Stern* did not apply *Schor*'s analysis for determining whether the bankruptcy courts' adjudication of counterclaims impinged the integrity of Article III courts.

In *Executive Benefits Ins. Agency v. Arkison*, 134 S. Ct. 2165 (2014), the Court considered how district courts should approach bankruptcy court judgments that finally resolved so-called "*Stern*" claims—that is, claims which *Stern* held must be resolved by an Article III court. The Supreme Court ruled that even where the bankruptcy court enters a final judgment, *de novo* review of the judgment by the district court and entry of a fresh judgment cures any violation of Article III.

c. Appointment of Administrative Officials

The preceding two sections address the *functions* performed by agencies: to what extent can agencies perform functions that resemble those performed by Congress and Article III courts consistent with the Constitution? A separate set of questions about congressional control of the structure of agencies involves their personnel, specifically, the way in which high-level agency personnel are appointed and removed. We turn initially to the Constitution's Appointments Clause. Art. II, § 2, cl. 2.*

During the colonial period, one of the colonists' perennial complaints against the Crown involved its use of biased administrators and judges. In an effort to address the problem of judicial bias, the 1701 Act of Settlement provided that English judges would serve during good behavior and could only be removed by a vote of both houses of parliament. But the Board of Trade (the committee of the Privy Council that oversaw colonial affairs) declined to follow the Settlement Act in the colonies, leaving in place an appointments system that facilitated corruption. After the American Revolution, state constitutions took a variety of approaches to the appointment of judges and other officers. In six states, the executive had virtually no role other than commissioning appointees selected by the legislature. In four states, "the governor's participation [in appointments] was directly restrained by councils composed of, or elected by, legislators." In two other states, "the governor's choices were subject to approval by councils elected by those qualified to vote." Finally, in New York, "a separate Council of Appointment was constituted in reaction to the colony's long history of appointment patronage." Theodore Y. Blumoff, *Separation of Powers and the Origins of the Appointment Clause*, 34 Syracuse L. Rev. 1037, 1055–56 (1987). Article IX of the Articles of Confederation provided: "The United States in Congress assembled shall have authority to appoint a committee, to sit in the recess of Congress, to be denominated 'A Committee of the States', and to consist of one delegate from each State; and to appoint such other committees and civil officers as may be necessary for managing the general affairs of the United States under their direction . . . ." However, the Articles did not provide for a President, executive departments or agencies, or a judiciary.

Against this backdrop, there was no clear consensus at the 1787 constitutional convention about where the appointment power should be vested in the new federal government. Debate focused on two questions: "Was the Executive or the Legislature more likely to abuse its power? And which entity, the Executive or the Legislature, was more likely to be jealous and create discord if it was not given a role in the [appointment] process?" Blumoff, *supra*, at 1066.

As it was originally drafted by the Committee on Detail, the Constitution's Appointments Clause provided that "[t]he Senate . . . shall have power to make treaties, and to appoint Ambassadors, and Judges of the Supreme Court," and gave the President power to appoint "officers in all cases not otherwise provided for by this Constitution." 2 Max Farrand, The Records of the Federal Convention of 1787, at 183, 185 (1966). On August 24, the Convention "with little discussion began to rewrite the appointment provision." On September 7, the Convention fashioned what is now the

---

* "[The President]*** shall nominate, and by and with the advice and consent of the Senate, shall appoint ambassadors, other public ministers and consuls, judges of the Supreme Court, and all other officers of the United States, whose appointments are not herein otherwise provided for, and which shall be established by law: but the Congress may by law vest the appointment of such inferior officers, as they think proper, in the President alone, in the courts of law, or in the heads of departments."

Appointments Clause. The "least discussed" provision of the Clause was the Delegation Clause under which Congress, by law, could vest the appointment of "inferior officers" in the President, the courts of law, or the heads of departments. The motion to adopt the Delegation Clause "was at first defeated by an even vote. An unidentified member, however, 'urged that it be put a second time, some such provision being too necessary, to be omitted,' and on a second vote, it was approved unanimously." Blumoff, *supra*, at 1068–69 (quoting 2 FARRAND at 627–28).

The first Supreme Court decision to deal with the Appointments Clause in any depth was *Buckley v. Valeo*, 424 U.S. 1 (1976), a challenge to the Federal Election Campaign Act (FECA) of 1971 passed in the wake of the Watergate scandal. Pub. L. No. 92-225, 86 Stat. 3. FECA established the Federal Election Commission (FEC), an independent, bipartisan agency that was charged with administering and enforcing federal campaign finance laws. The members of the FEC were appointed as follows: Two voting members were appointed by the President *pro tempore* of the Senate and two by the Speaker of the House; in each case, upon the recommendation of the majority and minority leaders in the chamber. The remaining two members were appointed by the President. Each of the six voting members had be to be confirmed by the majority of both Houses of Congress, and each of the three appointing authorities were forbidden to choose both of their appointees from the same political party.

The Supreme Court in *Buckley* ruled that the "fair import" of the Appointments Clause "is that any appointee exercising significant authority pursuant to the laws of the United States is an 'Officer of the United States.'" The FEC's members were not appointed in conformity with the Appointments Clause because, if they were principal officers of the United States, four of the members were not appointed by the President. Even if they were inferior officers, they were not appointed by the President, courts of law, or heads of departments.

In the following decisions, the Supreme Court continued to grapple with the meaning of the Appointments Clause.

Freytag v. Commissioner of Internal Revenue
501 U.S. 868 (1991)

JUSTICE BLACKMUN delivered the opinion of the Court.***

By the Tax Reform Act of 1969, §951, 83 Stat. 730, 26 U.S.C. §7441, Congress "established, under article I of the Constitution of the United States, a court of record to be known as the United States Tax Court." It also empowered the Tax Court to appoint commissioners to assist its judges. §958, 83 Stat. 734. By the Tax Reform Act of 1984, §464(a), 98 Stat. 824, the title "commissioner" was changed to "special trial judge." By §463(a) of that Act, 98 Stat. 824, and by §1556(a) of the Tax Reform Act of 1986, 100 Stat. 2754, Congress authorized the Chief Judge of the Tax Court to appoint and assign these special trial judges to hear certain specifically described proceedings and "any other proceeding which the chief judge may designate." 26 U.S.C. §§7443A(a) and (b). The Tax Court presently consists of 19 judges appointed to

15-year terms by the President, by and with the advice and consent of the Senate. §§ 7443(a), (b), and (e).***

[After Tax Court Judge Richard C. Wilbur became ill, Special Trial Judge Carleton D. Powell presided over petitioners' trial. Judge Powell prepared written findings and an opinion finding that petitioners had engaged in a $1.5 billion tax shelter and ordering them to pay back tax and penalties.] The Chief Judge adopted Judge Powell's opinion as that of the Tax Court.

[On appeal, petitioners contended that the court's opinion was invalid because Special Trial Judge Powell had not been appointed in conformity with the Appointments Clause. The Court of Appeals rejected petitioners' claim.]

Petitioners submit that [§ 7443A(b)] violates the Appointments Clause of the Constitution, Art. II, § 2, cl. 2. According to petitioners, a special trial judge is an "Office[r]" of the United States who must be appointed in compliance with the Clause.***

[T]he Constitution limits congressional discretion to vest power to appoint "inferior Officers" to three sources: "the President alone," "the Heads of Departments," and "the Courts of Law." Petitioners argue that a special trial judge is an "inferior Office[r]," and also contend that the Chief Judge of the Tax Court does not fall within any of the Constitution's three repositories of the appointment power.***

[Respondent] Commissioner reasons that special trial judges may be deemed employees in subsection (b)(4) cases because they lack authority to enter a final decision. But this argument ignores the significance of the duties and discretion that special trial judges possess. The office of special trial judge is "established by Law," Art. II, § 2, cl. 2, and the duties, salary, and means of appointment for that office are specified by statute. These characteristics distinguish special trial judges from special masters, who are hired by Article III courts on a temporary, episodic basis, whose positions are not established by law, and whose duties and functions are not delineated in a statute. Furthermore, special trial judges perform more than ministerial tasks. They take testimony, conduct trials, rule on the admissibility of evidence, and have the power to enforce compliance with discovery orders. In the course of carrying out these important functions, the special trial judges exercise significant discretion.

Even if the duties of special trial judges under subsection (b)(4) were not as significant as we and the two courts have found them to be, our conclusion would be unchanged. Under §§ 7443A(b)(1), (2), and (3), and (c), the Chief Judge may assign special trial judges to render the decisions of the Tax Court in declaratory judgment proceedings and limited-amount tax cases. The Commissioner concedes that in cases governed by subsections (b)(1), (2), and (3), special trial judges act as inferior officers who exercise independent authority.***

Special trial judges are not inferior officers for purposes of some of their duties under § 7443A, but mere employees with respect to other responsibilities. The fact that an inferior officer on occasion performs duties that may be performed by an employee not subject to the Appointments Clause does not transform his status under the Constitution. If a special trial judge is an inferior officer for purposes of subsections (b)(1), (2), and (3), he is an inferior officer within the meaning of the Appointments Clause and he must be properly appointed.***

Can the Chief Judge of the Tax Court constitutionally be vested by Congress with the power to appoint? The Appointments Clause names the possible repositories for the appointment power. It is beyond question in this litigation that Congress did not intend to grant to the President the power to appoint special trial judges. We therefore are left with three other possibilities. First, as the Commissioner urges, the Tax Court could be treated as a department with the Chief Judge as its head. Second,*** the Tax Court could be considered one of "the Courts of Law." Third,*** the Tax Court is neither a "Departmen[t]" nor a "Cour[t] of Law."

We cannot accept the Commissioner's assumption that every part of the Executive Branch is a department, the head of which is eligible to receive the appointment power.*** This Court for more than a century has held that the term "Department" refers only to a part or division of the executive government, as the Department of State, or of the Treasury, expressly created and given the name of a department by Congress.[4]***Having so concluded, we now must determine whether it is one of the "Courts of Law"[.]***

The text of the Clause does not limit the "Courts of Law" to those courts established under Article III of the Constitution. The Appointments Clause does not provide that Congress can vest appointment power only in "one supreme Court" and other courts established under Article III, or only in tribunals that exercise broad common-law jurisdiction. Petitioners argue that Article II's reference to the "Courts of Law" must be limited to Article III courts because Article III courts are the only courts mentioned in the Constitution. It of course is true that the Constitution "nowhere makes reference to 'legislative courts.'"*** Petitioners, however, underestimate the importance of this Court's time-honored reading of the Constitution as giving Congress wide discretion to assign the task of adjudication in cases arising under federal law to legislative tribunals. *See, e.g., American Insurance Co. v. Canter*, 1 Pet. 511, 546 (1828) (the judicial power of the United States is not limited to the judicial power defined under Article III and may be exercised by legislative courts); *Williams v. United States*, 289 U.S. 553, 565-567 (1933) (same). [As such, and because the Tax Court did not exercise any non-judicial functions, it was a "Court of Law" for Appointments Clause purposes.]

JUSTICE SCALIA, with whom JUSTICE O'CONNOR, JUSTICE KENNEDY, and JUSTICE SOUTER join, concurring in part and concurring in the judgment.

***I agree with the Court that a special trial judge is an "inferior Office[r]" within the meaning of this Clause, with the result that, absent Presidential appointment, he must be appointed by a court of law or the head of a department. I do not agree,

---

4. * * * We do not address here any question involving an appointment of an inferior officer by the head of one of the principal agencies, such as the Federal Trade Commission, the Securities and Exchange Commission, the Federal Energy Regulatory Commission, the Central Intelligence Agency, and the Federal Reserve Bank of St. Louis.

however, with the Court's conclusion that the Tax Court is a "Cour[t] of Law" within the meaning of this provision. I would find the appointment valid because the Tax Court is a "Departmen[t]" and the Chief Judge is its head.***

The Framers' experience with post-revolutionary self-government had taught them that combining the power to create offices with the power to appoint officers was a recipe for legislative corruption. The foremost danger was that legislators would create offices with the expectancy of occupying them themselves. This was guarded against by the Incompatibility and Ineligibility Clauses, Article I, § 6, cl. 2. But real, if less obvious, dangers remained. Even if legislators could not appoint themselves, they would be inclined to appoint their friends and supporters. This proclivity would be unchecked because of the lack of accountability in a multimember body . . . . And not only would unaccountable legislatures introduce their friends into necessary offices, they would create unnecessary offices into which to introduce their friends.***

For these good and sufficient reasons, then, the federal appointment power was removed from Congress. The Framers knew, however, that it was not enough simply to define in writing who would exercise this power or that . . . . Thus, it was not enough simply to repose the power to execute the laws (or to appoint) in the President; it was also necessary to provide him with the means to resist legislative encroachment upon that power. The means selected were various, including a separate political constituency, to which he alone was responsible, and the power to veto encroaching laws, see Art. I, § 7, or even to disregard them when they are unconstitutional. See Easterbrook, *Presidential Review*, 40 Case W. Res. L. Rev. 905, 920–924 (1990).***

A power of appointment lodged in a President surrounded by such structural fortifications could be expected to be exercised independently, and not pursuant to the manipulations of Congress. The same is true, to almost the same degree, of the appointment power lodged in the heads of departments. Like the President, these individuals possess a reputational stake in the quality of the individuals they appoint; and though they are not themselves able to resist congressional encroachment, they are directly answerable to the President, who is responsible to his constituency for their appointments and has the motive and means to assure faithful actions by his direct lieutenants.***

[T]he Tax Court, like its predecessors, exercises the executive power of the United States. This does not, of course, suffice to make it a "Departmen[t]" for purposes of the Appointments Clause. If, for instance, the Tax Court were a subdivision of the Department of the Treasury—as the Board of Tax Appeals used to be—it would not qualify. In fact, however, the Tax Court is a free-standing, self-contained entity in the Executive Branch, whose Chief Judge is removable by the President (and, save impeachment, no one else).***

I must confess that in the case of the Tax Court, as with some other independent establishments (notably, the so-called "independent regulatory agencies" such as the FCC and the Federal Trade Commission) permitting appointment of inferior officers by the agency head may not ensure the high degree of insulation from congressional control that was the purpose of the appointments scheme elaborated in the Constitution. That is a consequence of our decision in *Humphrey's Executor v. United States*, 295 U.S. 602 (1935), which approved congressional restriction upon arbitrary dismissal of the heads of such agencies by the President, a scheme avowedly designed to made such agencies less accountable to him, and hence he less responsible for them.*** [W]hatever may be the distorting effects of later innovations that this Court has approved, considering the Chief Judge of the Tax Court to be the head of a department seems to me the only reasonable construction of Article II, § 2.

Edmond v. United States

520 U.S. 651 (1997)

Justice Scalia, delivered the opinion of the Court.

We must determine in this case whether Congress has authorized the Secretary of Transportation to appoint civilian members of the Coast Guard Court of Criminal Appeals, and if so, whether this authorization is constitutional under the Appointments Clause of Article II.

I

The Coast Guard Court of Criminal Appeals (formerly known as the Coast Guard Court of Military Review) is an intermediate court within the military justice system. It is one of four military Courts of Criminal Appeals; others exist for the Army, the Air Force, and the Navy-Marine Corps. The Coast Guard Court of Criminal Appeals hears appeals from the decisions of courts-martial, and its decisions are subject to review by the United States Court of Appeals for the Armed Forces (formerly known as the United States Court of Military Appeals).

Appellate military judges who are assigned to a Court of Criminal Appeals must be members of the bar, but may be commissioned officers or civilians. Art. 66(a), Uniform Code of Military Justice (UCMJ), 10 U.S.C. § 866(a). During the times relevant to this case, the Coast Guard Court of Criminal Appeals has had two civilian members, Chief Judge Joseph H. Baum and Associate Judge Alfred F. Bridgman, Jr. These judges were originally assigned to serve on the court by the General Counsel of the Department of Transportation, who is, ex officio, the Judge Advocate General of the Coast Guard, Art. 1(1), UCMJ, 10 U.S.C. § 801(1). Subsequent events, however, called into question the validity of these assignments.

[In response to *Weiss v. United States*, 510 U.S. 163 (1994), which held that military trial and appellate judges are officers of the United States and must be appointed pursuant to the Appointments Clause, Chief Judge Baum sent a memorandum to the Chief Counsel of the Coast Guard requesting that the Secretary, in his capacity as a department head, reappoint the judges so the court would be constitutionally valid beyond any doubt.] On January 15, 1993, the Secretary of Transportation issued a memorandum "adopting" the General Counsel's assignments to the Coast Guard Court of Military Review "as judicial appointments of my own." The memorandum then listed the names of "[t]hose judges presently assigned and appointed by me," including Chief Judge Baum and Judge Bridgman.***

Each of the petitioners in the present case was convicted by court-martial. In each case the conviction and sentence were affirmed, in whole or in part, by the Coast Guard Court of Criminal Appeals (or its predecessor the Court of Military Review) after the January 15, 1993, secretarial appointments. Chief Judge Baum participated in each decision, and Judge Bridgman participated in the appeals involving two of the petitioners. The Court of Appeals for the Armed Forces affirmed the convictions.***

II

Petitioners argue that the Secretary's civilian appointments to the Coast Guard Court of Criminal Appeals are invalid for two reasons: First, the Secretary lacks authority under 49 U.S.C. § 323(a) to appoint members of the court; second, judges of military Courts of Criminal Appeals are principal, not inferior, officers within the meaning of the Appointments Clause, and must therefore be appointed by the President with the advice and consent of the Senate.

[The Supreme Court initially concluded that the Secretary had authority under § 323(a) to appoint members of the Coast Guard Court of Criminal Appeals.]

III

As we recognized in *Buckley v. Valeo*, 424 U.S. 1, 125 (1976) (per curiam), the Appointments Clause of Article II is more than a matter of "etiquette or protocol"; it is among the significant structural safeguards of the constitutional scheme. By vesting the President with the exclusive power to select the principal (noninferior) officers of the United States, the Appointments Clause prevents congressional encroachment upon the Executive and Judicial Branches. This disposition was also designed to assure a higher quality of appointments: The Framers anticipated that the President would be less vulnerable to interest-group pressure and personal favoritism than would a collective body.

The prescribed manner of appointment for principal officers is also the default manner of appointment for inferior officers. "[B]ut," the Appointments Clause continues, "the Congress may by Law vest the Appointment of such inferior Officers, as they think proper, in the President alone, in the Courts of Law, or in the Heads of Departments." This provision, sometimes referred to as the "Excepting Clause," was added to the proposed Constitution on the last day of the Grand Convention, with little discussion. [I]ts obvious purpose is administrative convenience—but that convenience was deemed to outweigh the benefits of the more cumbersome procedure only with respect to the appointment of "inferior Officers." Section 323(a), which confers appointment power upon the Secretary of Transportation, can constitutionally be applied to the appointment of Court of Criminal Appeals judges only if those judges are "inferior Officers."

Our cases have not set forth an exclusive criterion for distinguishing between principal and inferior officers for Appointments Clause purposes. Among the offices that we have found to be inferior are that of a district court clerk, *Ex parte Hennen*, 13 Pet. 225, 258 (1839), an election supervisor, *Ex parte Siebold*, 100 U.S. 371, 397-398 (1880), a vice consul charged temporarily with the duties of the consul, *United States v. Eaton*, 169 U.S. 331, 343 (1898), and a "United States commissioner" in district court proceedings, *Go-Bart Importing Co. v. United States*, 282 U.S. 344, 352-354 (1931). Most recently, in *Morrison v. Olson*, 487 U.S. 654 (1988), we held that the independent counsel created by provisions of the Ethics in Government Act of 1978, 28 U.S.C. §§ 591-599, was an inferior officer. In reaching that conclusion, we relied on several factors: that the independent counsel was subject to removal by a higher officer (the Attorney General), that she performed only limited duties, that her jurisdiction was narrow, and that her tenure was limited.

Petitioners are quite correct that the last two of these conclusions do not hold with regard to the office of military judge at issue here. It is not "limited in tenure," as that phrase was used in *Morrison* to describe "appoint[ment] essentially to accomplish a single task [at the end of which] the office is terminated." Nor are military judges "limited in jurisdiction," as used in *Morrison* to refer to the fact that an independent counsel may investigate and prosecute only those individuals, and for only those crimes, that are within the scope of jurisdiction granted by the special three-judge appointing panel. However, *Morrison* did not purport to set forth a definitive test for whether an office is "inferior" under the Appointments Clause.***

To support principal-officer status, petitioners emphasize the importance of the responsibilities that Court of Criminal Appeals judges bear. They review those court-martial proceedings that result in the most serious sentences, including those "in which the sentence, as approved, extends to death, dismissal . . . , dishonorable or bad-conduct discharge, or confinement for one year or more." Art. 66(b)(1), UCMJ, 10 U.S.C. § 866(b)(1). They must ensure that the court-martial's finding of guilt and its sentence are "correct in law and fact," which includes resolution of constitutional challenges. And finally, unlike most appellate judges, Court of Criminal Appeals judges are not required to defer to the trial court's factual findings, but may independently "weigh the evidence, judge the credibility of witnesses, and determine controverted questions of fact, recognizing that the trial court saw and heard the witnesses." We do not dispute that military appellate judges are charged with exercising significant authority on behalf of the United States. This, however, is also true of offices that we have held were "inferior" within the meaning of the Appointments Clause. *See, e.g., Freytag v. Commissioner*, 501 U.S., at 881-882 (special trial judges having "significan[t] . . . duties and discretion" are inferior officers). The exercise of "significant authority pursuant to the laws of the United States" marks, not the line between principal and inferior officer for Appointments Clause purposes, but rather, as we said in *Buckley*, the line between officer and nonofficer.

Generally speaking, the term "inferior officer" connotes a relationship with some higher ranking officer or officers below the President: Whether one is an "inferior" officer depends on whether he has a superior. It is not enough that other officers may be identified who formally maintain a higher rank, or possess responsibilities of a greater magnitude. If that were the intention, the Constitution might have used the phrase "lesser officer." Rather, in the context of a Clause designed to preserve political accountability relative to important Government assignments, we think it evident that "inferior officers" are officers whose work is directed and supervised at some level by others who were appointed by Presidential nomination with the advice and consent of the Senate.***

Supervision of the work of Court of Criminal Appeals judges is divided between the Judge Advocate General (who in the Coast Guard is subordinate to the Secretary of Transportation) and the Court of Appeals for the Armed Forces. The Judge Advocate General exercises administrative oversight over the Court of Criminal Appeals. He is charged with the responsibility to "prescribe uniform rules of procedure" for the court, and must "meet periodically [with other Judge Advocates General] to formulate policies and procedure in regard to review of court-martial cases." It is conceded by the parties that the Judge Advocate General may also remove a Court of Criminal Appeals judge from his judicial assignment without cause. The power to remove officers, we have recognized, is a powerful tool for control.

The Judge Advocate General's control over Court of Criminal Appeals judges is, to be sure, not complete. He may not attempt to influence (by threat of removal or otherwise) the outcome of individual proceedings, and has no power to reverse decisions of the court. This latter power does reside, however, in another Executive Branch entity, the Court of Appeals for the Armed Forces. [Thus,] the judges of the Court of Criminal Appeals have no power to render a final decision on behalf of the United States unless permitted to do so by other Executive officers.

Finally, petitioners argue that *Freytag v. Commissioner*, 501 U.S. 868 (1991), which held that special trial judges charged with assisting Tax Court judges were inferior officers and could be appointed by the Chief Judge of the Tax Court, suggests that Court of Criminal Appeals judges are principal officers. Petitioners contend that Court of Criminal Appeals judges more closely resemble Tax Court judges—who we implied (according to petitioners) were principal officers—than they do special trial judges. We note initially that *Freytag* does not hold that Tax Court judges are principal officers; only the appointment of special trial judges was at issue in that case. Moreover, there are two significant distinctions between Tax Court judges and Court of Criminal Appeals judges. First, there is no Executive Branch tribunal comparable to the Court of Appeals for the Armed Forces that reviews the work of the Tax Court; its decisions are appealable only to courts of the Third Branch. And second, there is no officer comparable to a Judge Advocate General who supervises the work of the Tax Court, with power to determine its procedural rules, to remove any judge without cause, and to order any decision submitted for review. *Freytag* does not control our decision here.***

We conclude that 49 U.S.C. § 323(a) authorizes the Secretary of Transportation to appoint judges of the Coast Guard Court of Criminal Appeals; and that such appointment is in conformity with the Appointments Clause of the Constitution, since those judges are "inferior Officers" within the meaning of that provision, by reason of the supervision over their work exercised by the General Counsel of the Department of Transportation in his capacity as Judge Advocate General and the Court of Appeals for the Armed Forces. The judicial appointments at issue in this case are therefore valid.***

Notes and Questions

1. **The Organizational Structure of the Tax Court and the Coast Guard Court of Criminal Appeals.** What is the basic organizational structure of the Tax Court, the court at issue in *Freytag*? Who is the top official within the Tax Court? How is he or she selected and appointed? Where do "Special Trial Judges" fall within the structure of the court? How are Special Trial Judges selected and appointed?

What is the basic organizational structure of the Coast Guard Court of Criminal Appeals, the court at issue in *Edmond*? How are judges of the court selected and appointed?

2. **The Posture of the Disputes.** The petitioners in both *Freytag* and *Edmond* contended that the judges who heard their cases had not been appointed in a manner that complied with the Appointments Clause. What, specifically, did the *Freytag* petitioners contend was wrong with the way in which Special Trial Judges Powell and Wilbur were appointed? What, according to the petitioners in *Edmond*, was the defect with the way in which judges of the Coast Guard Court of Criminal Appeals were appointed? How were these arguments raised in the courts below? What did the lower courts conclude? What is the practical significance of whether the judges were validly appointed?

3. **The Political Theory of the Appointments Clause?** According to the opinions in *Freytag* and *Edmond*, what is the Appointments Clause intended to accomplish? What are the abuses that the Clause was adopted to prevent? How do *Freytag* and *Edmond* differ on that question? How does the requirement that officers be appointed by the President with the advice and consent of the Senate prevent those risks from occurring?

4. **Who Is an "Officer" of the United States?** The Court in *Freytag* grapples with two questions. Is a Special Trial Judge of the Tax Court an "officer of the United States" who must be appointed in the manner specified by the Appointments Clause? If so, where does the Tax Court fall within the three-part appointment structure contemplated by the Appointments Clause, which gives authority to appoint inferior officers to the President, the heads of department, and courts of law?

With respect to the first question, all of the Justices agreed that a Special Trial Judge is an officer of the United States. Such an officer is someone who "exercises significant authority pursuant to the laws of the United States." What is the rationale for requiring such officials to be appointed in conformity with the Appointments Clause?

What is the "authority" that a Special Trial Judge exercises that bring her within this standard? What distinguishes a Special Trial Judge from, say, a judicial law clerk who helps the judge prepare opinions and orders, or a court security officer responsible for protecting the courthouse in which the Tax Court sits? What distinguishes a Special Trial Judge from staff counsel who help Article III judges prepare orders and opinions in non-argued cases? If Special Trial Judges were appointed on an ad hoc basis, would they be subject to the Appointments Clause? *Compare* Fed. R. Civ. P. 53(a) (providing that a special master may be appointed if appointment is warranted by "some exceptional condition" or the need to perform an accounting or resolve a difficult computation of damages).

5. **What Are "Departments" and "Courts of Law"?** The Court divides 5-4 on the second question in *Freytag*—how to classify the Tax Court for purposes of the Appointments Clause. The majority concludes that, despite the fact that the Tax Court is an Article I court, it is a "Court of Law" for purposes of the Clause. Justice Scalia concludes that the Court is a "Department," which he understands to be any "free-standing, self-contained entity in the Executive Branch" whose head is removable by the President. On Justice Scalia's view in this case, are multi-member independent regulatory agencies a "Department" for Appointments Clause purposes? Even if the President's ability to remove the members of these agencies is restricted by statute? Who is the "Head" of such a Department?

6. **Who Are "Inferior" Officers?** Under the Appointments Clause, so-called "principal" officers must be appointed by the President with the advice and consent of the Senate. In contrast, Congress "may by law vest the appointment of such inferior officers, as they think proper, in the President alone, in the courts of law, or in the heads of departments." According to the Court in *Edmond*, what distinguishes a principal officer, subject to the requirement of senatorial confirmation, from an inferior officer, who is not? Seen in terms of the political theory underlying the Appointments Clause, is this a sensible distinction? Is the Appointments Clause's treatment of inferior officers consistent with the framers' intent to maintain relatively clear lines of governmental accountability? If an inferior officer misapplies the law or carries out her duties ineptly, will citizens affected by her decisions blame the President? Congress?

7. **The *Free Enterprise Fund* Decision.** In *Free Enterprise Fund v. PCAOB*, 130 S. Ct. 3138 (2010), the Supreme Court addressed a constitutional challenge to the Public Company Accounting Oversight Board, an agency created by the Sarbanes-Oxley Act of 2002 in response to accounting scandals at Enron and WorldCom. Pub. L. No. 107-204, 116 Stat. 745 (codified in scattered sections of Titles 15, 18, 28, and 29). Pursuant to Sarbanes-Oxley, the Board extensively regulates the public accounting industry. It is authorized to issue rules and regulations, and to investigate violations of the securities laws, the Securities and Exchange Commission's rules, the Board's own rules, and professional accounting standards. Any firm that participates in auditing a company that issues securities regulated by the securities laws must register with the Board.

The Board consists of five members, who are appointed to staggered five-year terms by the Securities and Exchange Commission (SEC), a multi-member independent regulatory authority created during the New Deal administration of President Franklin D. Roosevelt. The SEC in turn exercises significant control over the Board's operations.

No rule of the Board may become public without SEC approval, 15 U.S.C. § 7217(b), and the SEC reviews sanctions imposed by the Board in the same manner that it reviews sanctions imposed by self-regulatory organizations such as the Financial Industry Regulatory Authority, § 7217(c). The SEC may remove a Board member following notice and a hearing "for good cause shown." § 7217(d)(3). To do so, the SEC is required to find that the member "willfully violated any provision of [the Sarbanes-Oxley] Act, the rules of the Board, or the securities laws," "willfully abused the authority of that member," or "without reasonable justification or excuse, ... failed to enforce compliance with any such provision or rule, or any professional standard by any registered public accounting firm or any associated person thereof." SEC Commissioners are conventionally thought to enjoy for-cause removal protection, although the Securities Exchange Act provides only that "[e]ach commissioner shall hold office for a term of five years and until his successor is appointed and has qualified." 15 U.S.C. § 78d(a). *See* Kirti Datla & Richard L. Revesz, *Deconstructing Independent Agencies (And Executive Agencies)*, 98 Cornell L. Rev. 769, 780 (2013).

In *Free Enterprise Fund*, an accounting firm that the Board investigated for improper accounting practices and an industry group that the firm belonged to sought a declaration that the Board was unconstitutional and an injunction prohibiting the Board from exercising the powers given to it in Sarbanes-Oxley. Plaintiffs argued that "(1) Board members are not 'inferior Officers' who may be appointed by 'Heads of Departments'; (2) even if they are, the [Securities Exchange] Commission is not a 'Departmen[t]'; and (3) even if it is, the several Commissioners (as opposed to the Chairman) are not its 'Hea[d].'" Petitioners also argued that Board members' "double for cause" removal protection—Board members could only be removed for cause by the SEC, whose Commissioners were in turn protected by for-cause removal protection—violated Article II.

The Supreme Court ruled that Article II prevented Congress from conferring double for-cause removal protection on agency heads and remedied the constitutional defect by striking the provision of the Sarbanes-Oxley Act that gave Board members removal protection. *See* Note 9 following *Humphrey's Executor v. United States, infra* p. 315. The Court rejected plaintiffs' Appointments Clause challenges.

The Board's members were inferior officers under *Edmond*, the Court concluded, because they could be removed at will and were subject to SEC oversight. With respect to plaintiffs' claim that the SEC could not be considered a "Department" for Appointments Clause purposes, the Court noted that in *Freytag*, it had "specifically reserved the question whether a 'principal agenc[y], such as ... the Securities and Exchange Commission' is a 'Departmen[t]' under the Appointments Clause." *See supra* p. 288 n. 4. The Court answered "yes," reasoning that this understanding of the Clause was consistent with the usage in Noah Webster's 1828 dictionary as well as with "the early practice of Congress," which treated the Postmaster General as a head of department even though the Postmaster was not part of the President's cabinet. The Court concluded: "Because the [SEC] is a freestanding component of the Executive Branch, not subordinate to or contained within any other such component, it constitutes a 'Departmen[t]' for purposes of the Appointments Clause."

With respect to plaintiffs' claim that the Commissioners of the SEC could not be considered the agency's "Head," the Court observed that the Commission's powers were generally vested in the Commissioners jointly. There was no constitutional reason why a multimember body could not be a Head of Department, because the Appointments Clause contemplates appointments by the courts and each House of Congress, both of which appoint officers collectively.

In light of these holdings, the Court concluded that the appropriate remedy was a declaration ensuring that the reporting and auditing standards the Board sought to enforce against the plaintiff accounting firm would be enforced by a constitutionally constituted agency. Plaintiffs were "not entitled to broad injunctive relief against the Board's continued operations."

8. Is the Appointments Clause a Significant Constraint on Agency Design? In light of the holdings of *Freytag*, *Edmund*, and *Free Enterprise Fund*, does the Appointments Clause significantly limit Congress's power to structure agencies? Suppose you are advising Congress on the design of a new agency to regulate U.S. companies' response to computer hacking by foreign governments. Lawmakers wish to establish the new agency as an independent regulatory authority that is headed by a five-member "Board of Cybersecurity" whose members enjoy a fixed term in office and for-cause removal protection. The Board will be authorized to promulgate rules and regulations governing computer security that are devised in the first instance by a "Technical Review Committee" consisting of full-time government employees who are selected for their expertise in cybersecurity and foreign affairs. The Technical Review Committee, in turn, is expected to devise cybersecurity standards in consultation with a board of outside advisors who are appointed from the private sector, the academy, and state governments, who also have expertise in cybersecurity and foreign affairs. Which of the proposed agency's employees must be appointed by the President and confirmed by the Senate? Which may be appointed by the Board of Cybersecurity? What would be the down-side of legislation creating a Board of Cybersecurity if members of the Board were appointed by the Secretary of Commerce, and all other positions in the agency were filled by majority vote of Board's members? Would such an arrangement violate the Appointments Clause? If so, what would be the likely remedy?

9. Non-Officer Employees. Most federal appointees are neither principal officers nor inferior officers. The Constitution does not address the manner in which such employees are selected, managed, and discharged. Congress has enacted an extensive statutory framework for these matters. *See* Note on the Federal Civil Service, following *Humphrey's Executor*, in Section [B][1][d], below.

10. The Controversy over SEC ALJs. Since the 2008 financial crisis and with enhanced authority to seek financial penalties under the Dodd-Frank Wall Street Reform and Consumer Protection Act, Pub. L. 111-203, 124 Stat. 1376 (July 21, 2010), the SEC has increased its use of internal agency proceedings where an Administrative Law Judge (ALJ) presides to adjudicate securities law violations. *See generally* Jean Eaglesham, *SEC Steers More Trials to Judges it Appoints*, WALL ST. J., Oct. 21, 2014, at A1. According to former SEC Commissioner and law professor Roberta Karmel, administrative proceedings had previously been used only against registered companies and associated persons; with Dodd-Frank, the agency assumed authority against non-registered entities. *See* Roberta S. Karmel, *Administrative Law Judges in SEC Proceedings*, N.Y.L.J., Oct. 19, 2016, at 3. Fearing bias and the loss of the civil jury trial, critics have argued that the ALJs are appointed and supervised in a manner that violates Article II. *See, e.g.*, David B. Rivkin, Jr. & Andrew M. Grossman, *When Is a Judge Not Really a Judge*, WALL St. J., Jan. 24, 2017, at A15.

Under the Securities Exchange Act, Dodd-Frank Act, and other statutes, the SEC is authorized to adjudicate alleged violations of the securities laws following the procedures set out by the Administrative Procedure Act, 5 U.S.C. §§ 556, 557. Acting pursuant to a provision of the Securities Exchange Act, 15 U.S.C. § 78d-1, the SEC has delegated authority to the Chief Administrative Law Judge (Chief ALJ) to schedule hearings and assign ALJs to cases, 17 C.F.R. § 200.30-10, and to ALJs "[t]o make an initial decision in any proceeding at which the Judge presides in which a hearing is required to be conducted in conformity with the Administrative Procedure Act," 17 C.F.R. § 200.30-9(a). An administrative prosecution typically begins with an order from the full Commission directing an ALJ to conduct a public hearing for the purpose of taking evidence. *E.g.*, Joint Appendix at 32, *Raymond J. Lucia Companies, Inc. v. SEC*, 832 F.3d 277 (D.C. Cir. 2016) *vac'd & reh'g en banc granted*, 2017 U.S. App. LEXIS 2732 (D.C. Cir. Feb. 16, 2017). When such an order issues, an ALJ selected by the Chief ALJ presides over an evidentiary hearing and issues an initial decision. Either the respondent or the SEC's Division of Enforcement may appeal an initial ALJ decision to the full Commission, which can also review an initial decision "on its own initiative." 17 C.F.R. § 201.411(c). If neither side seeks review by the full Commission and the Commission does not review the decision on its own motion, the initial decision is "deemed the action of the Commission," 15 U.S.C. § 78d-1(c).

The SEC currently employs five ALJs, one of whom is designated Chief ALJ by the Commission. Like ALJs at other agencies, the SEC's ALJs are chosen through a merit selection process that is administered by the Office of Personnel Management (OPM), the executive branch agency which oversees the civil service system. Applicants for an ALJ position take an exam that is administered by OPM, which uses the exam results to identify the top candidates. OPM then forwards the names of the top three candidates to the SEC. The Chief ALJ and an interview committee make a preliminary selection from among the candidates identified by OPM, which is "subject to final approval and processing by the Commission's Office of Human Resources." Notice of Filing at 2, *Timbervest, LLC*, File No. 3-15519, https://perma.cc/G8M2-36P3. Once appointed, an ALJ may be removed only for "good cause," which must be "established and determined" by the Merit Systems Protection Board, not the SEC. 5 U.S.C. § 7521. ALJs thus enjoy a form of "double for-cause" job protection.

An initial round of litigation focused on whether respondents in SEC enforcement proceedings could challenge the constitutionality of the SEC's internal adjudication system in an Article III court before the agency issued a final decision. *See Abbott Laboratories v. Gardner, infra* Chapter 5[A][2] (discussing ripeness limitations on review in Article III courts). These challenges largely failed, with courts holding that constitutional challenges could not be entertained until the conclusion of administrative proceedings. *See, e.g., Tilton v. SEC*, 824 F.3d 276 (2d Cir. 2016); *Jarkesy v. SEC*, 803 F.3d 9 (D.C. Cir. 2015).

When courts reached the merits on petitions for review, they divided on whether SEC ALJs were appointed in violation of the Appointments Clause. In *Raymond J. Lucia*, the D.C. Circuit concluded (in a decision that is now being review *en banc*) that SEC ALJs were employees, not officers, and therefore were not subject to the Appointments Clause. As the court of appeals read *Freytag*, "the main criteria for drawing the line between inferior officers and employees not covered by the Clause are (1) the significance of the matters resolved by the officials, (2) the discretion they exercise in reaching their decisions, and (3) the finality of those decisions." 832 F.3d at 284 (citing *Tucker v. Comm'r, Internal Revenue*, 676 F.3d 1129, 1132 (D.C. Cir. 2012), and *Landry v. FDIC*, 204 F.3d 1125 (D.C. Cir. 2000)). The third factor was dispositive for SEC ALJs. ALJs' decisions did not become final until they were affirmatively adopted by the Commission. The court reasoned: "the Commission's ALJs neither have been delegated sovereign authority to act independently of the Commission nor, by other means established by Congress, do they have the power to bind third parties, or the government itself, for the public benefit. The Commission's right of discretionary review . . . ensure[s] that the politically accountable Commissioners have determined that an ALJ's initial decision is to be the final action of the Commission." As ALJs were mere employees, there was no problem with their holding double for-cause job protection under *Free Enterprise Fund*.

In contrast, the Tenth Circuit concluded by a 2-1 vote in *Bandimere v. SEC*, 844 F.3d 1168 (10th Cir. 2016), that SEC ALJs *were* inferior officers who had to be appointed in conformity with the Appointments Clause. The court of appeals based this conclusion on ALJs' functional similarity to the Special Trial Judges in *Freytag*. Like Special Trial Judges, ALJs had authority to, for example, take testimony, rule on the admissibility of evidence, schedule proceedings, and issue initial decisions. The court thought that ALJs' authority to issue final decisions was "relevant" to whether they were constitutional officers but denied that such final decisionmaking authority was necessary to officer status. The court did not reach the question whether a validly-appointed ALJ could have double for-cause removal protection but suggested that this, too, would violate Article II.

If SEC ALJs are considered interior officers of the United States, what, if anything, would be lost by legislation authorizing their appointment by the Commission or by an external agency like OPM? For further analysis of the constitutional issues raised by the current system for appointing ALJs, see David Zaring,

Enforcement Discretion at the SEC, 94 Tex. L. Rev. 1155 (2016); Kent H. Barnett, *Resolving the ALJ Quandary*, 66 Vand. L. Rev. 797 (2013).

11. **Recess Appointments.** Under the Appointments Clause, principal and inferior officers are subject to Senate confirmation by default. However, the "Recess Appointments Clause" provides that "[t]he President shall have power to fill up all vacancies that may happen *during the recess of the Senate*, by granting commissions which shall expire at the end of their next session." U.S. Const., Art. II, § 2, cl. 3 (emphasis added).

In *NLRB v. Noel Canning*, 134 S. Ct. 2550 (2014), the Supreme Court considered whether three members of the National Labor Relations Board (Board or NLRB) had been validly appointed pursuant to the Clause. The Board members had been appointed on Jan. 4, 2012. At that time, the Board was operating without a quorum, but Senate Republicans, invoking the Senate filibuster rule, refused to allow votes on President Obama's nominees to the Board. The Senate had adjourned "*sine die*" (i.e., without specifying the day on which it would return) for the winter 2012 holiday. At the insistence of House Republicans, however, it held pro forma sessions every Tuesday and Friday, at which no business was conducted and no members were present except the President Pro Tempore or his delegate. *See* U.S. Const., Art I, § 5 ("Neither House, during the session of Congress, shall, without the consent of the other, adjourn for more than three days."). The purpose of these sessions was to prevent President Obama from making recess appointments.

Relying heavily on historical practice from the eighteenth and early nineteenth centuries, the Court (per Justice Breyer) resolved four questions about the Recess Appointments Clause. First, the Court concluded the Clause applies both to inter-session and intra-session recesses; that is, to recesses that occur *within* a session of Congress and those that occur *between* sessions of Congress. Next, the Court stated that the Clause applies to all vacancies that are open during a recess, regardless of when the vacancy first happens. Third, while declining to decide precisely how long a recess must be to trigger the President's recess appointment power, the Court agreed with the Solicitor General that a three to ten day recess was "too short." This limit originated from the Adjournments Clause, Art. 1, § 5, cl. 4, which provides: "Neither House, during the session of Congress, shall, without the consent of the other, adjourn for more than three days . . . ." The Clause's reference to three-day adjournments "reflect[ed] the fact that a 3-day break is not a significant interruption of legislative business" that would justify use of the recess appointment power.

Having reached these conclusions, the Court found that President Obama's nominees to the NLRB had not been appointed validly. Although the Senate would have been in recess but for the pro forma sessions, it retained the formal power to conduct business at those sessions, which prevented the occurrence of a genuine "recess." In the absence of such a recess, President Obama could make appointments to the Board only with the advice and consent of the Senate.

Justice Scalia concurred in the judgment but took a very different view of the Recess Appointments Clause. Writing for himself, the Chief Justice, and Justices Thomas and Alito, Scalia opined that the recess appointment power "may be exercised only in . . . the intermission between two formal legislative sessions." Moreover, the power "may be used to fill only those vacancies . . . that become vacant during that intermission." Justice Scalia objected to the majority's reliance on "late-arising historical practices" to resolve ambiguities about the Recess Appointments Clause's meaning. On the general role of historical practice in separation-of-powers analysis, see, e.g., Curtis A. Bradley & Trevor W. Morrison, *Historical Gloss and the Separation of Powers*, 126 HARV. L. REV. 411 (2012); Shalev Roisman, *Constitutional Acquiescence*, 86 GEO. WASH. L. REV. 668 (2016).

While Noel Canning was being briefed, the Obama administration in July 2013 reached an agreement with Senate Republicans to fill the vacant seats on the Board. President Obama withdrew the pending nominations of two recess appointees and nominated two other nominees in their place. Under the agreement, Republicans also agreed not to oppose another nominee to be nominated in 2014. *See* Jonathan Weisman & Jennifer Steinhauer, *Senate Strikes Filibuster Deal, Ending Logjam on Nominees*, N.Y. TIMES, July 17, 2013, at A1.

In November 2013, a simple majority of Democratic senators voted to change the Senate's rules to permit votes on Executive branch and lower court nominees to proceed without the approval of a super-majority of 60 Senators agreeing to cloture. Jeremy W. Peters, *In Landmark Vote, Senate Limits Use of the Filibuster*, N.Y. TIMES, Nov. 21, 2013, at A1. In public statements, Senate majority leader Harry Reid explained that the move was made necessary by Republican Senators' unwillingness to consider any democratic nominees for the U.S. Court of Appeals for the D.C. Circuit. In April 2017, because of a threatened filibuster by Senate Democrats, the Senate Republican majority extended the nuclear option to the vote on Judge Neil Gorsuch's appointment to the U.S. Supreme Court. As of this writing, the super-majority requirement to cut off debate remains applicable to legislation.

d. Removal of Agency Officials

As we have seen, Congress expressly deals with appointment of some executive officials. It may also enact laws limiting the circumstances in which an official may be removed.

For example, § 1 of the 1867 Tenure of Office Act provided: "every person holding any civil office to which he has been appointed by and with the advice and consent of the Senate . . . shall be entitled to hold such office until a successor shall have been in like manner appointed and duly qualified." 14 Stat. 430, ch. 154,

Such provisions raise a separate set of constitutional questions. Does the fact that the President must obtain advice and consent of the Senate to *appoint* an agency head mean that the Senate must be consulted before the President *removes* an agency head? Given the President's Article II, § 3 duty "to take care that the laws be faithfully executed," may Congress insulate agency heads from Presidential oversight by, for example, limiting the reasons for which they may be removed? Are "independent" agencies consistent with the structure of separated powers the Constitution creates? The starting point for debate on these questions is the Supreme Court's decision in *Humphrey's Executor*, which considers the legal status of the Federal Trade Commission's commissioners.

Humphrey's Executor v. United States
295 U.S. 602 (1935)

Mr. Justice Sutherland delivered the opinion of the Court.

Plaintiff brought suit in the Court of Claims against the United States to recover a sum of money alleged to be due the deceased for salary as a Federal Trade Commissioner from October 8, 1933, when the President undertook to remove him from office, to the time of his death on February 14, 1934. The court below has certified to this court two questions, in respect of the power of the President to make the removal. The material facts which give rise to the questions are as follows:

William E. Humphrey, the decedent, on December 10, 1931, was nominated by President Hoover to succeed himself as a member of the Federal Trade Commission, and was confirmed by the United States Senate. He was duly commissioned for a term of seven years expiring September 25, 1938; and, after taking the required oath of office, entered upon his duties. On July 25, 1933, President Roosevelt addressed a letter to the commissioner asking for his resignation, on the ground "that the aims and purposes of the Administration with respect to the work of the Commission can be carried out most effectively with personnel of my own selection," but disclaiming any reflection upon the commissioner personally or upon his services. The commissioner replied, asking time to consult his friends. After some further correspondence upon the subject, the President on August 31, 1933, wrote the commissioner expressing the hope that the resignation would be forthcoming and saying:

> "You will, I know, realize that I do not feel that your mind and my mind go along together on either the policies or the administering of the Federal Trade Commission, and, frankly, I think it is best for the people of this country that I should have a full confidence."

The commissioner declined to resign; and on October 7, 1933, the President wrote him:

> "Effective as of this date you are hereby removed from the office of Commissioner of the Federal Trade Commission."

Humphrey never acquiesced in this action, but continued thereafter to insist that he was still a member of the commission, entitled to perform its duties and receive the compensation provided by law at the rate of $10,000 per annum.***

The Federal Trade Commission Act, c. 311, 38 Stat. 717; 15 U.S.C. §§ 41, 42, creates a commission of five members to be appointed by the President by and with the advice and consent of the Senate, and § 1 provides:

"Not more than three of the commissioners shall be members of the same political party. The first commissioners appointed shall continue in office for terms of three, four, five, six, and seven years, respectively, from the date of the taking effect of this Act, the term of each to be designated by the President, but their successors shall be appointed for terms of seven years, except that any person chosen to fill a vacancy shall be appointed only for the unexpired term of the commissioner whom he shall succeed. The commission shall choose a chairman from its own membership. No commissioner shall engage in any other business, vocation, or employment. Any commissioner may be removed by the President for inefficiency, neglect of duty, or malfeasance in office . . . ."***

First. The question first to be considered is whether, by the provisions of § 1 of the Federal Trade Commission Act already quoted, the President's power is limited to removal for the specific causes enumerated therein.

[The Court concluded that "the language of the act, the legislative reports, and the general purposes of the legislation as reflected by the debates, all combine to demonstrate the Congressional intent to create a body of experts who shall gain experience by length of service—a body which shall be independent of executive authority, except in its selection, and free to exercise its judgment without the leave or hindrance of any other official or any department of the government."]

Second. To support its contention that the removal provision of § 1, as we have just construed it, is an unconstitutional interference with the executive power of the President, the government's chief reliance is *Myers v. United States*, 272 U.S. 52.*** [T]he narrow point actually decided was only that the President had power to remove a postmaster of the first class, without the advice and consent of the Senate as required by act of Congress. In the course of the opinion of the court, expressions occur which tend to sustain the government's contention, but these are beyond the point involved and, therefore, do not come within the rule of stare decisis. In so far as they are out of harmony with the views here set forth, these expressions are disapproved.***

The office of a postmaster is so essentially unlike the office now involved that the decision in the *Myers* case cannot be accepted as controlling our decision here. A postmaster is an executive officer restricted to the performance of executive functions. He is charged with no duty at all related to either the legislative or judicial power. The actual decision in the *Myers* case finds support in the theory that such an officer is merely one of the units in the executive department and, hence, inherently subject to the exclusive and illimitable power of removal by the Chief Executive, whose subordinate and aid he is. Putting aside dicta, which may be followed if sufficiently persuasive but which are not controlling, the necessary reach of the decision goes far enough to include all purely executive officers. It goes no farther;—much less does it include an officer who occupies no place in the executive department and who exercises no part of the executive power vested by the Constitution in the President.

The Federal Trade Commission is an administrative body created by Congress to carry into effect legislative policies embodied in the statute in accordance with the legislative standard therein prescribed, and to perform other specified duties as a legislative or as a judicial aid. Such a body cannot in any proper sense be characterized as an arm or an eye of the executive. Its duties are performed without executive leave and, in the contemplation of the statute, must be free from executive control. In administering the provisions of the statute in respect of "unfair methods of competition"— that is to say in filling in and administering the details embodied by that general standard—the commission acts in part quasi-legislatively and in part quasi-judicially. In making investigations and reports thereon for the information of Congress under § 6, in aid of the legislative power, it acts as a legislative agency. Under § 7, which authorizes the commission to act as a master in chancery under rules prescribed by the court, it acts as an agency of the judiciary. To the extent that it exercises any executive function—as distinguished from executive power in the constitutional sense—it does so in the discharge and effectuation of its quasi-legislative or quasi-judicial powers, or as an agency of the legislative or judicial departments of the government.

If Congress is without authority to prescribe causes for removal of members of the trade commission and limit executive power of removal accordingly, that power at once becomes practically all-inclusive in respect of civil officers with the exception of the judiciary provided for by the Constitution. The Solicitor General, at the bar, apparently recognizing this to be true, with commendable candor, agreed that his view in respect of the removability of members of the Federal Trade Commission necessitated a like view in respect of the Interstate Commerce Commission and the Court of Claims. We are thus confronted with the serious question whether not only the members of these quasi-legislative and quasi-judicial bodies, but the judges of the legislative Court of Claims, exercising judicial power continue in office only at the pleasure of the President.

We think it plain under the Constitution that illimitable power of removal is not possessed by the President in respect of officers of the character of those just named. The authority of Congress, in creating quasi-legislative or quasi-judicial agencies, to require them to act in discharge of their duties independently of executive control cannot well be doubted; and that authority includes, as an appropriate incident, power to fix the period during which they shall continue in office, and to forbid their removal except for cause in the meantime. For it is quite evident that one who holds his office only during the pleasure of another, cannot be depended upon to maintain an attitude of independence against the latter's will.

The fundamental necessity of maintaining each of the three general departments of government entirely free from the control or coercive influence, direct or indirect, of either of the others, has often been stressed and is hardly open to serious question. So much is implied in the very fact of the separation of the powers of these departments by the Constitution; and in the rule which recognizes their essential co-equality. The sound application of a principle that makes one master in his own house precludes him from imposing his control in the house of another who is master there. James Wilson, one of the framers of the Constitution and a former justice of this court, said that the independence of each department required that its proceedings "should be free from the remotest influence, direct or indirect, of either of the other two powers." And Mr. Justice Story in the first volume of his work on the Constitution, said that neither of the departments in reference to each other "ought to possess, directly or indirectly, an overruling influence in the administration of their respective powers."

The power of removal here claimed for the President falls within this principle, since its coercive influence threatens the independence of a commission, which is not only wholly disconnected from the executive department, but which, as already fully appears, was created by Congress as a means of carrying into operation legislative and judicial powers, and as an agency of the legislative and judicial departments.

In the light of the question now under consideration, we have reexamined the precedents referred to in the *Myers* case, and find nothing in them to justify a conclusion contrary to that which we have reached. The so-called "decision of 1789" had relation to a bill proposed by Mr. Madison to establish an executive Department of Foreign Affairs. The bill provided that the principal officer was "to be removable from office by the President of the United States." This clause was changed to read "whenever the principal officer shall be removed from office by the President of the United States" certain things should follow, thereby, in connection with the debates, recognizing and confirming, as the court thought in the *Myers* case, the sole power of the President in the matter. We shall not discuss the subject further, since it is so fully covered by the opinions in the *Myers* case, except to say that the office under consideration by Congress was not only purely executive, but the officer one who was responsible to the President, and to him alone, in a very definite sense. A reading of the debates shows that the President's illimitable power of removal was not considered in respect of other than executive officers. And it is pertinent to observe that when, at a later time, the tenure of office for the Comptroller of the Treasury was under consideration, Mr. Madison quite evidently thought that, since the duties of that office were not purely of an executive nature but partook of the judiciary quality as well, a different rule in respect of executive removal might well apply. 1 Annals of Congress, cols. 611–612.

In *Marbury v. Madison*, [5 U.S. 137 (1803),] it is made clear that Chief Justice Marshall was of opinion that a justice of the peace for the District of Columbia was not removable at the will of the President; and that there was a distinction between such an officer and officers appointed to aid the President in the performance of his constitutional duties. In the latter case, the distinction he saw was that "their acts are his acts" and his will, therefore, controls; and, by way of illustration, he adverted to the act establishing the Department of Foreign Affairs, which was the subject of the "decision of 1789."

The result of what we now have said is this: Whether the power of the President to remove an officer shall prevail over the authority of Congress to condition the power by fixing a definite term and precluding a removal except for cause, will depend upon the character of the office; the *Myers* decision, affirming the power of the President alone to make the removal, is confined to purely executive officers; and as to officers of the kind here under consideration, we hold that no removal can be made during the prescribed term for which the officer is appointed, except for one or more of the causes named in the applicable statute.

To the extent that, between the decision in the *Myers* case, which sustains the unrestrictable power of the President to remove purely executive officers, and our present decision that such power does not extend to an office such as that here involved, there shall remain a field of doubt, we leave such cases as may fall within it for future consideration and determination as they may arise.

Notes and Questions

1. **The FTC Act.** As discussed in Chapter 1, Congress enacted the Federal Trade Commission Act (FTC Act) in 1914 to expand the protections against anticompetitive conduct and unfair methods of competition provided in the 1890 Sherman Antitrust Act. The FTC Act established the Federal Trade Commission (FTC or Commission), a five-member body charged with enforcing many components of the Act. As the Court's opinion explains, FTC Commissioners can be removed only "for inefficiency, neglect of duty, or malfeasance in office." This standard is commonly known as "for-cause" removal protection.

What, according to the Court, were Congress's reasons for providing FTC Commissioners with for-cause removal protection? Protection from whom? From what? How would such protection help to accomplish the Act's objectives? Are there ways in which such protection might *undermine* the FTC Act's objectives? Does for-cause removal protection have any practical effect where Commissioners are appointed by the President, and Commissioners — at least those in the President's party — will not want to incur the President's disfavor?

2. **Posture of the Dispute?** What did Humphrey's executor want from the government? Why did that demand implicate the President's authority to remove a commissioner of the FTC without cause? What argument did Humphrey's executor make for why the President lacked such authority? What provisions of the Constitution would that argument have depended upon? What was the government's argument in response? What provisions of the Constitution would that argument have invoked? Note that the court below certified the questions to the Supreme Court, a procedure that today is rarely used.

3. **Distinguishing *Myers*?** The Court in *Humphrey's* emphasizes the differences between the Commissioner of the FTC and the first-class postmaster in Portland, Oregon, the agency head whose removal was at issue in *Myers v. United States*, 272 U.S. 52 (1926). The lengthy opinion was authored by Chief Justice Taft, himself a former President, and was a paean to broad executive power. The Court in *Myers* held that the President had authority to dismiss a first-class postmaster for any reason or no reason at all. The *Myers* Court thus held invalid the removal restrictions in the statute at issue. *See* Act of July 12, 1876, ch. 179, 19 Stat. 80, 81 ("Postmasters of the

first, second and third classes shall be appointed and may be removed by the President by and with the advice and consent of the Senate and shall hold their offices for four years unless sooner removed or suspended according to law.").

a. The *Humphrey's* Court purports to limit the holding in *Myers*, despite the breadth of its language: "[T]he narrow point actually decided was only that the President had power to remove a postmaster of the first class, without the advice and consent of the Senate as required by act of Congress." Even if the President arguably does have the power to ignore a for-cause limitation on removal of a postmaster, is it nevertheless constitutionally problematic for Congress to insert itself in a particular removal by requiring that its advice and consent be secured? See discussion of the Tenure of Office Acts, *infra* Note 7, and the legislative veto in the Notes following *INS v. Chadha*, in Section [B][2][a], below.

b. Is *Myers* also distinguishable, as the *Humphrey's* Court indicates, because of the difference in functions and place within the constitutional scheme of the two governmental agencies? The postmaster exercises executive authority over the operations of the post office he or she is charged with. But wouldn't the postmaster also have some quasi-adjudicative authority over discipline decisions involving the staff and some quasi-legislative authority over rulemaking decisions involving postal affairs? The FTC at the time of *Humphrey's* did not exercise legislative rulemaking authority but did have the quasi-executive authority to initiate enforcement proceedings either in the courts or through internal adjudication. Indeed, in these agency adjudications, the FTC would also be exercising a kind of quasi-adjudicative function, as the Court notes, in exercising its § 7 authority.

Are these "quasi" labels helpful? Dissenting in *FTC v. Ruberoid Co.*, 343 U.S. 470, 487-88 (1953), Justice Jackson stated: "Courts have differed in assigning a place to these seemingly necessary bodies in our constitutional system. Administrative agencies have been called *quasi*-legislative, *quasi*-executive, or *quasi*-judicial, as the occasion required, in order to validate their functions within the separation of powers scheme of the Constitution. The mere retreat to the qualifying '*quasi*' is implicit with confession that all recognized classifications have broken down, and '*quasi*' is a smooth cover which we draw over our confusion, as we might use a counterpane to conceal a disordered bed."

4. **The President's "Take Care" Responsibility?** How does the Court address the contention that the President's Article II, § 3 duty to "take care that the laws be faithfully executed" requires that he or she have unfettered discretion to dismiss inferior officers? What options would have been available to President Roosevelt if an FTC commissioner ruled consistently against the Administration's position in important cases? Note that, according to Kirti Datla & Richard L. Revesz, *Deconstructing Independent Agencies (And Executive Agencies)*, 98 CORNELL L. REV. 769, 788 (2013), "[n]o recent President has attempted to remove the head of an independent agency for cause, or at the very least, no such attempt has led to litigation that resulted in judicial interpretation of the terms in a removal protection clause."

Does the presence of this "headless fourth branch" infringe upon the vesting of executive authority in the President? Recall that an incoming President under most statutes can designate the chair of the agency and that the members of the multimember agency usually have staggering terms, so that within a year or so, the President will have the ability to nominate members of his or her choosing (subject to Senate confirmation). *See generally* Neal E. Devins & David Lewis, *Not-So-Independent Agencies*, 88 B.U. L. Rev. 459 (2008).

5. **The "Decision of 1789."** The Decision of 1789 mentioned in *Humphrey's Executor*, and relied on extensively in *Myers*, refers to an early debate in the House of Representative concerning Congress's power to remove the Secretary of Foreign Affairs:

> On June 16, 1789, the House resolved itself into a Committee of the Whole on a bill proposed by Mr. Madison for establishing an executive department to be denominated the Department of Foreign Affairs, in which the first clause, after stating the title of the officer and describing his duties, had these words: "to be removable from office by the President of the United States." 1 Annals of Congress, 455. After a very full discussion, the question was put: shall the words "to be removable by the President" be struck out? It was determined in the negative yeas 20, nays 34. 1 Annals of Congress, 576.

> On June 22, in the renewal of the discussion, Mr. Benson moved to amend the bill[.]***

> Mr. Benson's*** amendment to alter the second clause by the insertion of the italicized words, made that clause to read as follows:

> "That there shall be in the State Department an inferior officer to be appointed by the said principal officer, and to be employed therein as he shall deem proper, to be called the Chief Clerk in the Department of Foreign Affairs, *and who, whenever the principal officer shall be removed from office by the President of the United States,* or in any other case of vacancy, shall, during such vacancy, have charge and custody of all records, books and papers appertaining to said department."

> Th[is] amendment was then approved by a vote of thirty to eighteen. 1 Annals of Congress, 580. Mr. Benson then moved to strike out in the first clause the words "to be removable by the President," in pursuance of the purpose he had already declared, and this second motion of his was carried by a vote of thirty-one to nineteen. 1 Annals of Congress, 585.***

> After the bill as amended had passed the House, it was sent to the Senate, where it was discussed in secret session, without report. The critical vote there was upon the striking out of the clause recognizing and affirming the unrestricted power of the President to remove. The Senate divided by ten to ten, requiring the deciding vote of the Vice-President, John Adams, who voted against striking out, and in favor of the passage of the bill as it had left the House.*** The bill, having passed as it came from the House, was signed

by President Washington and became a law. Act of July 27, 1789, 1 Stat. 28, c. 4.

Myers, 272 U.S. at 112–15 (emphasis in original).

For the *Myers* Court, this history confirmed the executive's absolute power of removal, "except only as granted therein to Congress in the matter of inferior offices."

> It is very clear from this history that the exact question which the House voted upon was whether it should recognize and declare the power of the President under the Constitution to remove the Secretary of Foreign Affairs without the advice and consent of the Senate. That was what the vote was taken for. Some effort has been made to question whether the decision carries the result claimed for it, but there is not the slightest doubt, after an examination of the record, that the vote was, and was intended to be, a legislative declaration that the power to remove officers appointed by the President and the Senate vested in the President alone, and, until the Johnson Impeachment trial in 1868, its meaning was not doubted even by those who questioned its soundness.

272 U.S. at 114.

Is the *Myers* Court's reading of this historical evidence persuasive? Scholarly opinion on what Congress decided in the Decision of 1789 and its significance for modern governance is divided to this day. *Compare, e.g.*, Saikrishna Prakash, *New Light on the Decision of 1789*, 91 CORNELL L. REV. 1021, 1026 (2006), *with* DAVID CURRIE, THE CONSTITUTION IN CONGRESS: THE FEDERALIST PERIOD 1789–1801, at 39 (1999).

6. **"Unitary Executive" Theory.** *Myers'* reading of the Decision of 1789 is often associated with the so-called "unitary executive" theory. Proponents of this theory contend that, by reason of the President's position as Chief Executive and Commander in Chief, the President has nearly unlimited control over the actions of administrative agencies, including independent agencies. The argument is that such control is implied by the original meaning of the Constitution, particularly the provisions of Article II providing that "[t]he executive power shall be vested in a President of the United States of America," and that "he shall take care that the laws be faithfully executed." U.S. Const. Art. II, §§ 1, 3. At a functional level, advocates of the unitary executive theory contend that unfettered presidential control of administrative agencies is necessary to the proper functioning of a constitutional democracy. If the President cannot control the actions of administrative functionaries, voters will have difficulty holding the President accountable for agencies' actions. *See generally* STEPHEN G. CALABRESI & CHRISTOPHER S. YOO, THE UNITARY EXECUTIVE: PRESIDENTIAL POWER FROM WASHINGTON TO BUSH (2003); Symposium, *Executive Branch Interpretation of the Law*, 15 CARDOZO L. REV. 21 (1993); Morton Rosenberg, *Congress's Prerogative over Agencies and Agency Decisionmakers: The Rise and Demise of the Reagan Administration's Theory of the Unitary Executive*, 57 GEO. WASH. L. REV. 627 (1989).

How does this view of the President's executive authority square with Congress's legislative authority in Article I of the Constitution, which includes the authority to establish administrative agencies, confer on them particular responsibilities and resources, and regulate the terms of their compensation and tenure of office?

7. **The Tenure of Office Acts.** Congress's use of for-cause removal protection in the FTC Act was an example of a line of legislation seeking to insulate agency heads from presidential control. In 1820, Congress enacted the first Tenure of Office Act, 3 Stat. 582, ch. 102, which provided that "all district attorneys, collectors of the customs, naval officers and surveyors of the customs, navy agents, receivers of public moneys for lands, registers of the land offices, paymasters in the army, the apothecary general, the assistant apothecaries general, and the commissary general of purchases . . . shall be appointed for the term of four years, but shall be removable."

Following the Civil War, Congress enacted the Tenure of Office Act of 1867, 14 Stat. 430, ch. 154, in response to President Andrew Johnson's threats to remove Secretary of War Edwin Stanton from office. Johnson favored quick re-integration of the confederate states, a position that was directly contrary to Congress's goal of using readmission to "reconstruct" the South and require southern governments to respect the rights of newly freed slaves. To prevent Johnson from removing Stanton, a Lincoln appointee who supported the Republican Congress's reconstruction policies, Section 1 of the 1867 Act provided "[t]hat every person holding any civil office to which he has been appointed by and with the advice and consent of the Senate . . . shall be entitled to hold such office until a successor shall have been in like manner appointed and duly qualified," except as provided in the Act. Section 2 authorized the President to suspend an officer who was "guilty of misconduct in office, or crime, or for any reason shall become incapable or legally disqualified to perform his duties." But the officer could not be removed until the Senate returned and gave its consent.

In August 1867, Johnson suspended Stanton while the Senate was in recess. When the Senate returned, it rejected Johnson's request to remove Stanton by a vote of 35–16. Ignoring the vote, Johnson on February 21, 1868, appointed Lorenzo Thomas as Secretary of War — an apparent violation of both sections of the Tenure in Office Act. As alleged in articles of impeachment brought against Johnson, Thomas boasted that he would physically remove Stanton from the War Office. Stanton refused to relinquish his office or to vacate the War Office. The House responded by impeaching Johnson. After a three-month trial, the Senate acquitted Johnson by a single vote.

In 1887, Congress repealed the 1867 statute in its entirety. Act of Mar. 3, 1887, 24 Stat. 500, ch. 353. Despite the fact that its validity was moot, Chief Justice Taft's opinion in *Myers* opined that the Act "in so far as it attempted to prevent the President from removing executive officers who had been appointed by him by and with the advice and consent of the Senate, was invalid, and that subsequent legislation of the same effect was equally so." 272 U.S. at 176. For histories of the Act and Johnson's impeachment, see David O. Stewart, Impeached: The Trial of President Andrew Johnson and the Fight for Lincoln's Legacy (2009); William H. Rehnquist,

GRAND INQUESTS: THE HISTORIC IMPEACHMENTS OF JUSTICE SAMUEL CHASE AND PRESIDENT ANDREW JOHNSON (1993).

8. **"Independent" vs. Executive Department Agencies?** Following *Humphrey's Executor*, courts and commentators have tended to assume that an agency like the FTC is "independent" if the members of the agency sit for a fixed term and can be removed only for cause, and not because of political or ideological disagreement. In contrast, an agency is considered to be an "executive" agency if its heads can be removed by the President at will and it is assigned, by statute or a matter of custom, to a position within the Executive. "Independent" agencies tend to be multimember bodies, with the majority belonging to the President's party and the minority belonging to the opposition party. Executive agencies, the theory goes, are subject to plenary presidential control, because the President has the authority to dismiss a recalcitrant agency head if the agency does not follow the President's wishes. This distinction is also reflected in the Paperwork Reduction Act, which contains a list of "independent regulatory agenc[ies]." 44 U.S.C. § 3502(5).

But is the dividing line between independent and Executive agencies so clear? Kirti Datla and Richard L. Revesz, in *Deconstructing Independent Agencies (And Executive Agencies)*, 98 CORNELL L. REV. 769, 788 (2013), survey the organic statutes of eighty-one federal agencies, and find that there is no single set of characteristics that is shared by agencies commonly thought to be independent. The organic statutes of the most "independent" agencies exhibit removal protection, commissioners with specified tenure, a multimember structure, partisan balance requirements, litigation authority, budget and congressional communication authority, and adjudication authority. The least independent agencies on Datla and Revesz's scale — among them the Central Intelligence Agency, the National Aeronautics and Space Administration, and the Peace Corps — had none of the above-mentioned indicia of independence. Agencies commonly thought of as independent and falling within the Executive Branch include the Environmental Protection Agency. *See also* Rachel Barkow, *Insulating Agencies: Avoiding Capture Through Institutional Design*, 89 TEX. L. REV. 15 (2010); Daniel A. Crane, *Debunking* Humphrey's Executor, 83 GEO. WASH. L. REV. 1835 (2016).

Is the linchpin for an agency's "independence" its multimember structure rather than removal protection per se? Ordinarily, Congress couples a multimember structure and removal protection when it intends to establish an agency relatively independent of the President. In establishing the Consumer Financial Protection Bureau (CFPB) as part of the Dodd-Frank Act, Congress created an agency headed by a single Administrator with a fixed term and for-cause removal protection. In *PHH Corp. v. CFPB*, 839 F.2d 1 (D.C. Cir. 2016), *vac'd in rebey en banc granted*, 2017 U.S. App LEXIS 2733 (D.C. Cir. Feb. 16, 2017), the court of appeals (2–1) declared the independent single-member structure an unconstitutional derogation of the President's Article I power and struck the for-cause removal provision to remedy the violation. As this book went to press, the D.C. Circuit set the *PHH* case for rehearing *en banc*.

9. Removal Protections for "Core" Executive Officers? May *Humphrey's Executor*-style removal protections be extended to officers such as prosecutors who exercise traditional executive functions? In *Morrison v. Olson*, 487 U.S. 654 (1988), the Court rejected constitutional challenges to Title VI of the Ethics in Government Act, 28 U.S.C. §§ 49, 591-599 (Act). The Act was passed in the aftermath of the Watergate scandal and aimed "to preserve and promote the accountability and integrity of public officials and of the institutions of the Federal Government." S. Rep. No. 95-170, at 1 (1st Sess., 1977). Its first five titles create a disclosure regime for federal employees, establish the Office of Government Ethics, and provide rules that limit federal employees' outside employment. Title VI expired by its terms in 1999. While it was in effect, Title VI provided a mechanism for the Attorney General to investigate alleged offenses by the President, Vice-President, and certain high-level executive branch officials, and to seek the appointment of an independent counsel where the Attorney General concluded that allegations of wrongdoing warranted further investigation. The Supreme Court in *Morrison* summarized the way Title VI operated as follows (487 U.S. at 660–62):

> [Title VI] allows for the appointment of an "independent counsel" to investigate and, if appropriate, prosecute certain high-ranking Government officials for violations of federal criminal laws. The Act requires the Attorney General, upon receipt of information that he determines is "sufficient to constitute grounds to investigate whether any person [covered by the Act] may have violated any Federal criminal law," to conduct a preliminary investigation of the matter. When the Attorney General has completed this investigation, or 90 days has elapsed, he is required to report to a special court (the Special Division) created by the Act "for the purpose of appointing independent counsels." 28 U. S. C. § 49 (1982 ed., Supp. V). If the Attorney General determines that "there are no reasonable grounds to believe that further investigation is warranted," then he must notify the Special Division of this result. In such a case, "the division of the court shall have no power to appoint an independent counsel." § 592(b)(1). If, however, the Attorney General has determined that there are "reasonable grounds to believe that further investigation or prosecution is warranted," then he "shall apply to the division of the court for the appointment of an independent counsel."*** Upon receiving this application, the Special Division "shall appoint an appropriate independent counsel and shall define that independent counsel's prosecutorial jurisdiction." § 593(b).
>
> With respect to all matters within the independent counsel's jurisdiction, the Act grants the counsel "full power and independent authority to exercise all investigative and prosecutorial functions and powers of the Department of Justice, the Attorney General, and any other officer or employee of the Department of Justice." § 594(a).***

Two statutory provisions govern the length of an independent counsel's tenure in office. The first defines the procedure for removing an independent counsel. Section 596(a)(1) provides:

> "An independent counsel appointed under this chapter may be removed from office, other than by impeachment and conviction, only by the personal action of the Attorney General and only for good cause, physical disability, mental incapacity, or any other condition that substantially impairs the performance of such independent counsel's duties."

If an independent counsel is removed pursuant to this section, the Attorney General is required to submit a report to both the Special Division and the Judiciary Committees of the Senate and the House "specifying the facts found and the ultimate grounds for such removal." § 596(a)(2). Under the current version of the Act, an independent counsel can obtain judicial review of the Attorney General's action by filing a civil action in the United States District Court for the District of Columbia. Members of the Special Division "may not hear or determine any such civil action or any appeal of a decision in any such civil action." The reviewing court is authorized to grant reinstatement or "other appropriate relief." § 596(a)(3).

The other provision governing the tenure of the independent counsel defines the procedures for "terminating" the counsel's office. Under § 596(b) (1), the office of an independent counsel terminates when he or she notifies the Attorney General that he or she has completed or substantially completed any investigations or prosecutions undertaken pursuant to the Act. In addition, the Special Division, acting either on its own or on the suggestion of the Attorney General, may terminate the office of an independent counsel at any time if it finds that "the investigation of all matters within the prosecutorial jurisdiction of such independent counsel . . . have been completed or so substantially completed that it would be appropriate for the Department of Justice to complete such investigations and prosecutions." § 596(b)(2).

Acting pursuant to Title VI, the Attorney General appointed an independent counsel to investigate whether Theodore Olson (who would later argue *Bush v. Gore* on behalf of George W. Bush) gave false testimony to Congress in a congressional investigation of the Environmental Protection Agency's decision to invoke executive privilege in response to a congressional subpoena. Olson contended that Title VI violated the Appointments Clause, Article III, and "impermissibly interfere[d] with the President's authority under Article II in violation of the constitutional principle of separation of powers."

With respect to the Appointments Clause challenge, the Court concluded that the independent counsel "clearly falls on the 'inferior officer' side" of the principal/inferior officer line. The independent counsel was "subject to removal by a higher Executive Branch official." She was "empowered by the Act to perform only certain, limited duties." And while Title VI "delegate[d] to appellant 'full power and independent authority to exercise all investigative and prosecutorial functions and powers of the Department of Justice,' § 594(a),*** this grant of authority [did] not include any authority to formulate policy for the Government or the Executive Branch, nor [did] it give appellant any administrative duties outside of those necessary to operate her office."

The Court also rejected Olson's claim that the functions the independent counsel performed made it improper for the office to carry removal protection. The Court reasoned that, "[u]nlike *Bowsher* [*v. Synar*, 478 U.S. 71 (1986), *infra* Section [B][2]] and *Myers*, this case does not involve an attempt by Congress itself to gain a role in the removal of executive officials other than its established powers of impeachment and conviction." Title VI's removal restrictions were instead more analogous to those in *Humphrey's Executor* and *Wiener v. United States*, 357 U.S. 349 (1958), which upheld provisions of the War Claims Act of 1948, 62 Stat. 1240, providing that members of the War Claims Commission established to pay claimants injured by the Axis powers could not be removed from office. Those cases' approval of removal protection did not depend on officials performing "executive" functions. Although *Humphrey's Executor* and *Wiener* stressed the "quasi-legislative" and "quasi-judicial" nature of the officials who enjoyed removal protections, "the determination of whether the Constitution allows Congress to impose a 'good cause'-type restriction on the President's power to remove an official cannot be made to turn on whether or not that official is classified as 'purely executive.' The analysis contained in our removal cases is designed not to define rigid categories of those officials who may or may not be removed at will by the President, but to ensure that Congress does not interfere with the President's exercise of the 'executive power' and his constitutionally appointed duty to 'take care that the laws be faithfully executed' under Article II.*** [B]ecause the independent counsel may be terminated for 'good cause,' the Executive, through the Attorney General, retain[ed] ample authority to assure that the counsel is competently performing his or her statutory responsibilities in a manner that comports with the provisions of the Act."

The Court also rejected Olson's argument that "taken as a whole, the Act violates the separation of powers by reducing the President's ability to control the prosecutorial powers wielded by the independent counsel." Congress "retained for itself no powers of control or supervision of an independent counsel." And Title VI gave the Attorney General "several means of supervising or controlling the prosecutorial powers that may be wielded by an independent counsel"—most prominently, the power to remove an independent counsel for good cause.

Justice Scalia alone dissented. He maintained, citing *Heckler v. Chaney*, 470 U.S. 821 (1985), *infra* Chapter 5[C], *Buckley v. Valeo*, 424 U. S. 1 (1976), *supra* p. 286, and *United States v. Nixon*, 418 U. S. 683 (1974), that "the conduct of a criminal prosecution (and of an investigation to decide whether to prosecute)" was a "purely executive power," because "[g]overnmental investigation and prosecution of crimes" was a "quintessentially executive function." Title VI "deprive[d] the President of the United States of exclusive control over the exercise of that power," Justice Scalia objected. "Congress has effectively compelled a criminal investigation of a high-level appointee of the President in connection with his actions arising out of a bitter power dispute between the President and the Legislative Branch.*** If to describe this case is not to decide it, the concept of a government of separate and coordinate powers no longer has meaning."

In 1994, Kenneth Starr was appointed as an independent counsel under Title VI to investigate allegations that Bill and Hillary Clinton violated the law in connection with investments in the Whitewater Development Corporation, a failed real estate company, while Bill Clinton was governor of Arkansas in the 1970s. Starr's investigation expanded to cover allegations that Clinton committed perjury when testifying about his relationship with White House intern Monica Lewinsky and ultimately led to the President's impeachment by the House of Representatives.

10. **"Double For-Cause" Removal Protection?** As a practical matter, *Humphrey's Executor* settles the constitutionality of for-cause removal protections for most agency heads (with the possible exception of key advisers to the President such as the Attorney General and the Secretaries of Defense and State). Even jurists who adhere to the so-called "unitary executive" theory, see Note 6 following *Humphrey's Executor v. United States, supra* p. 309, appear to concede it may be too late in the day to revisit *Humphrey's Executor's* approval of that practice. *See Freytag v. Commissioner* (Scalia, J., concurring), Section [B][1][c], *supra* p. 288. However, the Supreme Court has objected to congressional efforts to insulate inferior officers from supervision by agency heads already protected by for-cause removal provisions. As described in Note 7 following *Edmond v. United States, supra* p. 295, the Sarbanes-Oxley Act effectively granted members of the Public Company Accounting Oversight Board "double for-cause" protection. A member could only be removed for cause by the SEC, whose Commissioners by convention also enjoy for-cause removal protection. The Supreme Court held in *Free Enterprise Fund v. PCAOB*, 130 S. Ct. 3138 (2010), that such "double for-cause" protection violated Article II:

> The added layer of tenure protection makes a difference. Without a layer of insulation between the Commission and the Board, the Commission could remove a Board member at any time, and therefore would be fully responsible for what the Board does. The President could then hold the Commission to account for its supervision of the Board, to the same extent that he may hold the Commission to account for everything else it does.
>
> A second level of tenure protection changes the nature of the President's review. Now the Commission cannot remove a Board member at will. The President therefore cannot hold the Commission fully accountable for the Board's conduct, to the same extent that he may hold the Commission accountable for everything else that it does. The Commissioners are not responsible for the Board's actions.

To remedy this defect, the Court invalidated the provision of the Sarbanes-Oxley Act that gave Board members for-cause removal protection, allowing them to be removed at the SEC's discretion. The *Free Enterprise Fund* opinion also contained dicta indicating disagreement with the underlying reasoning in *Humphrey's Executor*. For example, the Court noted that,

> The diffusion of power carries with it a diffusion of accountability. The people do not vote for the "Officers of the United States." Art. II, § 2, cl. 2. They instead look to the President to guide the "assistants or deputies . . . subject to his superintendence." The Federalist No. 72, p. 487 (J. Cooke ed. 1961) (A. Hamilton). Without a clear and effective chain of command, the public cannot "determine on whom the blame or the punishment of a pernicious measure, or series of pernicious measures ought really to fall." That is why the Framers sought to ensure that "those who are employed in the execution of the law will be in their proper situation, and the chain of dependence be preserved; the lowest officers, the middle grade, and the highest, will depend, as they ought, on the President, and the President on the community." 1 Annals of Cong., at 499 (J. Madison).

Even so, *Free Enterprise Fund* hesitated to follow this logic to its conclusion, noting that it was not questioning the validity of federal civil service laws, and that "[n]o one doubts Congress's power to create a vast and varied federal bureaucracy."

It should be noted that the Court in *Free Enterprise Fund* purported not to disturb multimember independent agencies' use of administrative law judges (ALJ) in adjudicative proceedings, even though ALJs operate under a double for-cause removal protection regime, insofar as they cannot be removed except for cause under federal civil service laws and the members of agencies themselves serve for fixed terms and cannot be removed except for cause. Dissenting in *Free Enterprise Fund*, Justice Breyer cited research which showed that "the Federal Government relies on 1,584 ALJs to adjudicate administrative matters in over 25 agencies. These ALJs adjudicate Social Security benefits, employment disputes, and other matters highly important to individuals." Breyer asked whether "every losing party before an ALJ now [has] grounds to appeal on the basis that the decision entered against him is unconstitutional?" 130 S. Ct. at 3181. The majority responded: "our holding also does not address that subset of independent agency employees who serve as administrative law judges. . . . [U]nlike members of the Board, many administrative law judges of course perform adjudicative rather than enforcement or policymaking functions, see §§ 554(d), 3105, or possess purely recommendatory powers." *Id.* at 3161 n.10.

As noted above, lower courts since *Free Enterprise Fund* have reached conflicting conclusions about whether the current system of appointments and job protections for SEC ALJs is constitutional. *See* Note 10 following *Edmond v. United States*, *supra* p. 297.

Note on the Federal Civil Service

The cases in the preceding two sections all concern the appointment and removal of high-level or "political" appointees — employees that are viewed as "officers of the United States" and fall within the scope of the Appointments Clause because they exercise "significant authority pursuant to the laws of the United States." *Free Enter. Fund v. Pub. Co. Accounting Oversight Bd.*, 561 U.S. 477, 477 (2010). Most federal employees, however, do not fall within this category.

Within a given department or agency, personnel are divided among "political" positions and other appointees who are not. Political positions are typically identified by the department or agency's organic statute—the statute that formally establishes the agency and defines its institutional structure. For example, following the Civil War, Congress passed the Act to Establish the Department of Justice, 16 Stat. 162, ch. 150 (1870). The Act established the Department of Justice (DOJ) as "an executive department of the government of the United States . . . of which the Attorney General shall be the head." *Id.*§ 1. (The post of Attorney General of the United States was established in the Judiciary Act of 1789, ch. 20, 1 Stat. 73). The 1870 Act further created the Office of the Solicitor General, which litigates cases on behalf of the United States in the Supreme Court, and transferred lawyers from other departments to the DOJ, classifying them as "assistants" to the Attorney General. *Id.*§§ 2, 3, 7. As to these positions, the Act provided that the persons holding them "shall be appointed by the President, by and with the advice and consent of the Senate." *Id.*§ 9. The appointment of a United States Attorney (also a creation of the 1789 Judiciary Act) requires Senatorial confirmation, *see* 28 U.S.C. § 546(b); that of assistant United States Attorneys do not.

With respect to lower-level employees, a government-wide statute, 5 U.S.C. § 3101, authorizes agency heads to hire any number of employees permitted by the agency's most recent budget appropriation. Non-political, civil-service employees are paid according to one of several "schedules." The most common of the schedules, the General Schedule (GS), is used for white-collar employees. As of 2015, pay under the schedule ranges from $17,803 to $129,517 per year before "locality" adjustments based on the region an employee works in take effect.[7]

Appointment of civil service employees is governed by the Civil Service Reform Act of 1978, Pub. L. No. 95-454, 92 Stat. 1111. The Act, one of several statutes passed in the aftermath of the Watergate scandal during the Nixon Administration, generally seeks to protect civil-service employees from politically motivated employment actions. It created the Office of Personnel Management (OPM), an agency within the Office of Management and Budget in the Executive Office of the President. OPM serves as the federal government's employment agency, interprets the civil service laws, and provides guidance to other agencies on the operation of the civil service system. The Act also created the Merit Systems Protection Board (MSPB), an agency charged with adjudicating violations of the civil service laws. These agencies supersede the former Civil Service Commission.

Non-political civil service employees enjoy significant job-security protections. In addition to the usual protections of the collective bargaining agreement, antidiscrimination law, and statutory protection against dismissal or other discipline without

---

7. Office of Personnel Management, 2012 General Schedule (GS) Locality Pay Tables, http://www .opm.gov/policy-data-oversight/pay-leave/salaries-wages/2012/general-schedule/ (last visited Feb. 11, 2014).

"cause," it is unlawful for a federal government employer to "coerce the political activity of any person . . . or take any action against any employee or applicant for employment as a reprisal for the refusal of any person to engage in such political activity"; to retaliate against the employee for exposing wrongdoing, testifying, or disclosing evidence of wrongdoing; or to "grant any preference or advantage not authorized by law . . . for the purpose of improving or injuring the prospects of any particular person for employment," among other things. 5 U.S.C. § 2302(b). Civil service employees may appeal a wide variety of adverse employment actions to the MSPB. *See* 5 U.S.C. § 7701; 5 C.F.R. § 1201, pt. 1201.A. *See generally Kloeckner v. Solis*, 133 S. Ct. 596 (2012). Even managerial-level employees in the "Senior Executive Service" enjoy protections under the 1978 Civil Service Act. On the role of unions within the federal sector, see Samuel Estreicher, *The Paradox of Federal-Sector Labor Relations: Voluntary Unionism without Colletive Bargaining over Wages and Employee Benefits*, 19 EMPLOY. RTS. OF EMP. POL. J. 283 (2015).

Notes and Questions

1. **The Policy Logic of Civil Service Laws.** What is Congress's rationale for giving most federal employees significant protections against discharge and other discipline? Is that decision premised on the assumption that, if it were not for employment protections, politicians would interfere with the hiring and work of civil servants? That employees in secure civil service positions will carry out the work of the government more effectively? Might it be driven by concerns about Congress's ability to pay employees at rates competitive with private sector employers? Traditionally public employees were paid less than their private-sector counterparts but received some degree of job security and better benefits.

2. **The Civil Service and the Presidency.** According to decisions such as *Free Enterprise Fund v. PCAOB*, 561 U.S. 477 (2010), the President must have a high degree of control over the bureaucracy in order to carry out his or her constitutional functions. Moreover, such control is necessary to the effective functioning of our democracy because the President is the only official directly elected by all of the people, and the hence the individual the public should be able to hold accountable for major policy developments and mishaps. According to *Free Enterprise Fund*, for-cause removal protections are in tension with the presidential control and accountability contemplated by Article II. Can the civil service laws be squared with this conception of presidential authority?

3. **Further Reading.** For further reading on the federal bureaucracy, see, e.g, JAMES Q. WILSON, BUREAUCRACY: WHAT GOVERNMENT AGENCIES DO AND WHY THEY DO IT (2000); PAUL C. LIGHT, THICKENING GOVERNMENT: FEDERAL HIERARCHY AND THE DIFFUSION OF ACCOUNTABILITY (1995); STEPHEN SKOWRONEK, BUILDING A NEW AMERICAN STATE: THE EXPANSION OF NATIONAL ADMINISTRATIVE CAPACITIES, 1877–1920 (1982); WILLIAM A. NISKANEN, BUREAUCRACY AND REPRESENTATIVE GOVERNMENT (1974).

2. Limits on Congressional Control of Agency Action

A distinct set of questions raised by the Constitution's silence on administrative agencies involves their working relationship with Congress, and particularly, the extent to which Congress can control the actions of agencies once they are created by law. *Humphrey's Executor* observed with the respect to the FTC that "the commission acts in part quasi-legislatively and in part quasi-judicially." Does it follow that, insofar as the Commission is performing a legislative function, Congress should have the power to negative its actions? Should Congress have the authority to remove an agency head it is dissatisfied with? The following cases take up these questions.

Immigration and Naturalization Service v. Chadha
462 U.S. 919 (1983)

CHIEF JUSTICE BURGER delivered the opinion of the Court.

***Each [case] presents a challenge to the constitutionality of the provision in §244(c)(2) of the Immigration and Nationality Act, 66 Stat. 216, as amended, 8 U.S.C. §1254(c)(2), authorizing one House of Congress, by resolution, to invalidate the decision of the Executive Branch, pursuant to authority delegated by Congress to the Attorney General of the United States, to allow a particular deportable alien to remain in the United States.

I

Chadha is an East Indian who was born in Kenya and holds a British passport. He was lawfully admitted to the United States in 1966 on a nonimmigrant student visa. His visa expired on June 30, 1972. On October 11, 1973, the District Director of the Immigration and Naturalization Service ordered Chadha to show cause why he should not be deported for having "remained in the United States for a longer time than permitted." Pursuant to §242(b) of the Immigration and Nationality Act (Act), 8 U.S.C. §1252(b), a deportation hearing was held before an Immigration Judge on January 11, 1974. Chadha conceded that he was deportable for overstaying his visa and the hearing was adjourned to enable him to file an application for suspension of deportation under §244(a)(1) of the Act, 8 U.S.C. §1254(a)(1). Section 244(a)(1), at the time in question, provided:

> "As hereinafter prescribed in this section, the Attorney General may, in his discretion, suspend deportation and adjust the status to that of an alien lawfully admitted for permanent residence, in the case of an alien who applies to the Attorney General for suspension of deportation and—
>
> "(1) is deportable under any law of the United States except the provisions specified in paragraph (2) of this subsection; has been physically present in the United States for a continuous period of not less than seven years immediately preceding the date of such application, and proves that during all of such period he was and is a person of good moral character; and is a person whose deportation would, in the opinion of the Attorney General, result in extreme

hardship to the alien or to his spouse, parent, or child, who is a citizen of the United States or an alien lawfully admitted for permanent residence."[1]

After Chadha submitted his application for suspension of deportation, the deportation hearing was resumed on February 7, 1974. On the basis of evidence adduced at the hearing, affidavits submitted with the application, and the results of a character investigation conducted by the INS, the Immigration Judge, on June 25, 1974, ordered that Chadha's deportation be suspended. The Immigration Judge found that Chadha met the requirements of §244(a)(1): he had resided continuously in the United States for over seven years, was of good moral character, and would suffer "extreme hardship" if deported.

Pursuant to §244(c)(1) of the Act, 8 U.S.C. §1254(c)(1), the Immigration Judge suspended Chadha's deportation and a report of the suspension was transmitted to Congress.*** Once the Attorney General's recommendation for suspension of Chadha's deportation was conveyed to Congress, Congress had the power under §244(c)(2) of the Act, 8 U.S.C. §1254(c)(2), to veto the Attorney General's determination that Chadha should not be deported. Section 244(c)(2) provides:

"(2) In the case of an alien specified in paragraph (1) of subsection (a) of this subsection—

"if during the session of the Congress at which a case is reported, or prior to the close of the session of the Congress next following the session at which a case is reported, either the Senate or the House of Representatives passes a resolution stating in substance that it does not favor the suspension of such deportation, the Attorney General shall thereupon deport such alien or authorize the alien's voluntary departure at his own expense under the order of deportation in the manner provided by law. If, within the time above specified, neither the Senate nor the House of Representatives shall pass such a resolution, the Attorney General shall cancel deportation proceedings."

The June 25, 1974, order of the Immigration Judge suspending Chadha's deportation remained outstanding as a valid order for a year and a half. For reasons not disclosed by the record, Congress did not exercise the veto authority reserved to it under §244(c)(2) until the first session of the 94th Congress. This was the final session in which Congress, pursuant to §244(c)(2), could act to veto the Attorney General's determination that Chadha should not be deported. The session ended on December 19, 1975. 121 Cong. Rec. 42014, 42277 (1975). Absent congressional action, Chadha's deportation proceedings would have been canceled after this date and his status adjusted to that of a permanent resident alien. *See* 8 U.S.C. §1254(d).

---

1. Congress delegated the major responsibilities for enforcement of the Immigration and Nationality Act to the Attorney General. 8 U.S.C. §1103(a). The Attorney General discharges his responsibilities through the Immigration and Naturalization Service, a division of the Department of Justice.

On December 12, 1975, Representative Eilberg, Chairman of the Judiciary Subcommittee on Immigration, Citizenship, and International Law, introduced a resolution opposing "the granting of permanent residence in the United States to [six] aliens," including Chadha. H. Res. 926, 94th Cong., 1st Sess.; 121 Cong Rec. 40247 (1975). The resolution was referred to the House Committee on the Judiciary. On December 16, 1975, the resolution was discharged from further consideration by the House Committee on the Judiciary and submitted to the House of Representatives for a vote. 121 Cong. Rec. 40800. The resolution had not been printed and was not made available to other Members of the House prior to or at the time it was voted on. So far as the record before us shows, the House consideration of the resolution was based on Representative Eilberg's statement from the floor that

"[i]t was the feeling of the committee, after reviewing 340 cases, that the aliens contained in the resolution [Chadha and five others] did not meet these statutory requirements, particularly as it relates to hardship; and it is the opinion of the committee that their deportation should not be suspended."

The resolution was passed without debate or recorded vote. Since the House action was pursuant to § 244(c)(2), the resolution was not treated as an Art. I legislative act; it was not submitted to the Senate or presented to the President for his action.

After the House veto of the Attorney General's decision to allow Chadha to remain in the United States, the Immigration Judge reopened the deportation proceedings to implement the House order deporting Chadha. Chadha moved to terminate the proceedings on the ground that § 244(c)(2) is unconstitutional. The Immigration Judge held that he had no authority to rule on the constitutional validity of § 244(c)(2). On November 8, 1976, Chadha was ordered deported pursuant to the House action.

Chadha appealed the deportation order to the Board of Immigration Appeals, again contending that § 244(c)(2) is unconstitutional. The Board held that it had "no power to declare unconstitutional an act of Congress" and Chadha's appeal was dismissed.

Pursuant to § 106(a) of the Act, 8 U.S.C. § 1105a(a), Chadha filed a petition for review of the deportation order in the United States Court of Appeals for the Ninth Circuit . . . . [T]he Court of Appeals held that the House was without constitutional authority to order Chadha's deportation; accordingly it directed the Attorney General "to cease and desist from taking any steps to deport this alien based upon the resolution enacted by the House of Representatives.***

III

A

We turn now to the question whether action of one House of Congress under § 244(c)(2) violates strictures of the Constitution.*** Explicit and unambiguous provisions of the Constitution prescribe and define the respective functions of the Congress and of the Executive in the legislative process. Since the precise terms of those familiar provisions are critical to the resolution of these cases, we set them out verbatim. Article I provides:

"All legislative Powers herein granted shall be vested in a Congress of the United States, which shall consist of a Senate *and* House of Representatives." Art. I, § 1. (Emphasis added.)

"Every Bill which shall have passed the House of Representatives *and* the Senate, *shall*, before it becomes a law, be presented to the President of the United States . . . ." Art. I, § 7, cl. 2. (Emphasis added.)

"*Every* Order, Resolution, or Vote to which the Concurrence of the Senate and House of Representatives may be necessary (except on a question of Adjournment) shall be presented to the President of the United States; and before the Same shall take Effect, *shall be* approved by him, or being disapproved by him, *shall be* repassed by two thirds of the Senate and House of Representatives, according to the Rules and Limitations prescribed in the Case of a Bill." Art. I, § 7, cl. 3. (Emphasis added.)

These provisions of Art. I are integral parts of the constitutional design for the separation of powers.***

B

The Presentment Clauses

The records of the Constitutional Convention reveal that the requirement that all legislation be presented to the President before becoming law was uniformly accepted by the Framers. Presentment to the President and the Presidential veto were considered so imperative that the draftsmen took special pains to assure that these requirements could not be circumvented. During the final debate on Art. I, § 7, cl. 2, James Madison expressed concern that it might easily be evaded by the simple expedient of calling a proposed law a "resolution" or "vote" rather than a "bill." As a consequence, Art. I, § 7, cl. 3, was added.

The decision to provide the President with a limited and qualified power to nullify proposed legislation by veto was based on the profound conviction of the Framers that the powers conferred on Congress were the powers to be most carefully circumscribed. It is beyond doubt that lawmaking was a power to be shared by both Houses and the President. In The Federalist No. 73 (H. Lodge ed. 1888), Hamilton focused on the President's role in making laws:

"If even no propensity had ever discovered itself in the legislative body to invade the rights of the Executive, the rules of just reasoning and theoretic propriety would of themselves teach us that the one ought not to be left to the mercy of the other, but ought to possess a constitutional and effectual power of self-defence."

The President's role in the lawmaking process also reflects the Framers' careful efforts to check whatever propensity a particular Congress might have to enact oppressive, improvident, or ill-considered measures. The President's veto role in the legislative process was described later during public debate on ratification:

"It establishes a salutary check upon the legislative body, calculated to guard the community against the effects of faction, precipitancy, or of any impulse unfriendly to the public good, which may happen to influence a majority of that body.

". . . The primary inducement to conferring the power in question upon the Executive is, to enable him to defend himself; the secondary one is to increase the chances in favor of the community against the passing of bad laws, through haste, inadvertence, or design." The Federalist No. 73, *supra*, at 458 (A. Hamilton).

See also The Pocket Veto Case, 279 U.S. 655, 678 (1929); *Myers v. United States*, 272 U.S. 52, 123 (1926).***

C

Bicameralism

The bicameral requirement of Art. I, §§ 1, 7, was of scarcely less concern to the Framers than was the Presidential veto and indeed the two concepts are interdependent. By providing that no law could take effect without the concurrence of the prescribed majority of the Members of both Houses, the Framers reemphasized their belief, already remarked upon in connection with the Presentment Clauses, that legislation should not be enacted unless it has been carefully and fully considered by the Nation's elected officials.***

However familiar, it is useful to recall that apart from their fear that special interests could be favored at the expense of public needs, the Framers were also concerned, although not of one mind, over the apprehensions of the smaller states. Those states feared a commonality of interest among the larger states would work to their disadvantage; representatives of the larger states, on the other hand, were skeptical of a legislature that could pass laws favoring a minority of the people. It need hardly be repeated here that the Great Compromise, under which one House was viewed as representing the people and the other the states, allayed the fears of both the large and small states.

We see therefore that the Framers were acutely conscious that the bicameral requirement and the Presentment Clauses would serve essential constitutional functions. The President's participation in the legislative process was to protect the Executive Branch from Congress and to protect the whole people from improvident laws. The division of the Congress into two distinctive bodies assures that the legislative power would be exercised only after opportunity for full study and debate in separate settings. The President's unilateral veto power, in turn, was limited by the power of two-thirds of both Houses of Congress to overrule a veto thereby precluding final arbitrary action of one person. It emerges clearly that the prescription for legislative action in Art. I, §§ 1, 7, represents the Framers' decision that the legislative power of the Federal Government be exercised in accord with a single, finely wrought and exhaustively considered, procedure.

IV***

[W]e must nevertheless establish that the challenged action under §244(c)(2) is of the kind to which the procedural requirements of Art. I, §7, apply.*** Examination of the action taken here by one House pursuant to §244(c)(2) reveals that it was essentially legislative in purpose and effect. In purporting to exercise power defined in Art. I, §8, cl. 4, to "establish an uniform Rule of Naturalization," the House took action that had the purpose and effect of altering the legal rights, duties, and relations of persons, including the Attorney General, Executive Branch officials and Chadha, all outside the Legislative Branch. Section 244(c)(2) purports to authorize one House of Congress to require the Attorney General to deport an individual alien whose deportation otherwise would be canceled under §244. The one-House veto operated in these cases to overrule the Attorney General and mandate Chadha's deportation; absent the House action, Chadha would remain in the United States. Congress has acted and its action has altered Chadha's status.

The legislative character of the one-House veto in these cases is confirmed by the character of the congressional action it supplants. Neither the House of Representatives nor the Senate contends that, absent the veto provision in §244(c)(2), either of them, or both of them acting together, could effectively require the Attorney General to deport an alien once the Attorney General, in the exercise of legislatively delegated authority, had determined the alien should remain in the United States. Without the challenged provision in §244(c)(2), this could have been achieved, if at all, only by legislation requiring deportation.***

The nature of the decision implemented by the one-House veto in these cases further manifests its legislative character. After long experience with the clumsy, time-consuming private bill procedure, Congress made a deliberate choice to delegate to the Executive Branch, and specifically to the Attorney General, the authority to allow deportable aliens to remain in this country in certain specified circumstances. It is not disputed that this choice to delegate authority is precisely the kind of decision that can be implemented only in accordance with the procedures set out in Art. I. Disagreement with the Attorney General's decision on Chadha's deportation — that is, Congress' decision to deport Chadha — no less than Congress' original choice to delegate to the Attorney General the authority to make that decision, involves determinations of policy that Congress can implement in only one way; bicameral passage followed by presentment to the President. Congress must abide by its delegation of authority until that delegation is legislatively altered or revoked.[19]

---

19. This does not mean that Congress is required to capitulate to "the accretion of policy control by forces outside its chambers." Javits & Klein, *Congressional Oversight and the Legislative Veto: A Constitutional Analysis*, 52 N.Y.U. L. Rev. 455, 462 (1977). The Constitution provides Congress with abundant means to oversee and control its administrative creatures. Beyond the obvious fact that Congress ultimately controls administrative agencies in the legislation that creates them, other means of control, such as durational limits on authorizations and formal reporting requirements, lie well within Congress' constitutional power.

Finally, we see that when the Framers intended to authorize either House of Congress to act alone and outside of its prescribed bicameral legislative role, they narrowly and precisely defined the procedure for such action. There are four provisions in the Constitution, explicit and unambiguous, by which one House may act alone with the unreviewable force of law, not subject to the President's veto:

(a) The House of Representatives alone was given the power to initiate impeachments. Art. I, § 2, cl. 5;

(b) The Senate alone was given the power to conduct trials following impeachment on charges initiated by the House and to convict following trial. Art. I, § 3, cl. 6;

(c) The Senate alone was given final unreviewable power to approve or to disapprove Presidential appointments. Art. II, § 2, cl. 2;

(d) The Senate alone was given unreviewable power to ratify treaties negotiated by the President. Art. II, § 2, cl. 2.

Clearly, when the Draftsmen sought to confer special powers on one House, independent of the other House, or of the President, they did so in explicit, unambiguous terms.***

Since it is clear that the action by the House under § 244(c)(2) was not within any of the express constitutional exceptions authorizing one House to act alone, and equally clear that it was an exercise of legislative power, that action was subject to the standards prescribed in Art. I.*** To accomplish what has been attempted by one House of Congress in this case requires action in conformity with the express procedures of the Constitution's prescription for legislative action: passage by a majority of both Houses and presentment to the President.

The veto authorized by § 244(c)(2) doubtless has been in many respects a convenient shortcut; the "sharing" with the Executive by Congress of its authority over aliens in this manner is, on its face, an appealing compromise. In purely practical terms, it is obviously easier for action to be taken by one House without submission to the President; but it is crystal clear from the records of the Convention, contemporaneous writings and debates, that the Framers ranked other values higher than efficiency.***

Justice Powell, concurring in the judgment.

The Court's decision, based on the Presentment Clauses, Art. I, § 7, cls. 2 and 3, apparently will invalidate every use of the legislative veto. The breadth of this holding gives one pause. Congress has included the veto in literally hundreds of statutes, dating back to the 1930's. Congress clearly views this procedure as essential to controlling the delegation of power to administrative agencies. One reasonably may disagree with Congress' assessment of the veto's utility, but the respect due its judgment as a coordinate branch of Government cautions that our holding should be no more extensive than necessary to decide these cases. In my view, the cases may be decided on a narrower ground. When Congress finds that a particular person does not satisfy the statutory criteria for permanent residence in this country it has assumed a judicial function in violation of the principle of separation of powers. Accordingly, I concur only in the judgment.***

The Constitution does not establish three branches with precisely defined boundaries. Rather, as Justice Jackson wrote: "While the Constitution diffuses power the better to secure liberty, it also contemplates that practice will integrate the dispersed powers into a workable government. It enjoins upon its branches separateness but interdependence, autonomy but reciprocity." *Youngstown Sheet & Tube Co. v. Sawyer*, 343 U.S. 579, 635 (1952) (concurring in judgment). The Court thus has been mindful that the boundaries between each branch should be fixed according to common sense and the inherent necessities of the governmental coordination. But where one branch has impaired or sought to assume a power central to another branch, the Court has not hesitated to enforce the doctrine.

Functionally, the doctrine may be violated in two ways. One branch may interfere impermissibly with the other's performance of its constitutionally assigned function. Alternatively, the doctrine may be violated when one branch assumes a function that more properly is entrusted to another. These cases present the latter situation.***

On its face, the House's action appears clearly adjudicatory. The House did not enact a general rule; rather it made its own determination that six specific persons did not comply with certain statutory criteria. It thus undertook the type of decision that traditionally has been left to other branches. Even if the House did not make a *de novo* determination, but simply reviewed the Immigration and Naturalization Service's findings, it still assumed a function ordinarily entrusted to the federal courts. Where, as here, Congress has exercised a power that cannot possibly be regarded as merely in aid of the legislative function of Congress, the decisions of this Court have held that Congress impermissibly assumed a function that the Constitution entrusted to another branch.***

Chief Justice Marshall observed: "It is the peculiar province of the legislature to prescribe general rules for the government of society; the application of those rules to individuals in society would seem to be the duty of other departments." *Fletcher v. Peck*, 6 Cranch 87, 136 (1810). In my view, when Congress undertook to apply its rules to Chadha, it exceeded the scope of its constitutionally prescribed authority. I would not reach the broader question whether legislative vetoes are invalid under the Presentment Clauses.

Notes and Questions

1. **Posture of the Dispute?** How did the legislative veto in § 244 of the Immigration and Nationality Act (INA) function? What actions were taken within the Justice Department before Congress was presented with the decision to suspend an alien's deportation? How did Chadha's case end up in Congress? What happened with respect to the case in Congress?

After Congress determined that Chadha's deportation should not have been suspended, the immigration judge reopened his case and ordered that Chadha be deported. Chadha was able to access the Article III courts by filing a petition for review of the immigration judge's order under 8 U.S.C. § 1105a (now 8 U.S.C. § 1252). What legal argument would Chadha have raised in his petition for review?

How did the dispute over Chadha's deportability end up before the Supreme Court? What did the Ninth Circuit conclude as to whether Chadha should be deported, and the validity of the House resolution that purported to cancel the immigration judge's decision granting Chadha suspension of deportation?

In the Ninth Circuit and the Supreme Court, the Immigration and Naturalization Service (INS) took the position that the legislative veto was unconstitutional. Accordingly, the INS *supported* Chadha's petition for review of the IJ's deportation order. To ensure an adversary presentation of the case, the House of Representatives and Senate appeared as *amici curiae*. The Ninth Circuit (per then-Judge Kennedy) found the legislative veto unconstitutional, 634 F.2d 408 (1980), and the House and Senate petitioned the Supreme Court to review its judgment.

2. **The Immigration and Nationality Act's Mode of Regulation.** The Immigration and Nationality Act, 8 U.S.C. § 1101 et seq., delegates vast regulatory authority to the Attorney General and the INS, at the time of *Chadha* a unit of Justice Department but now rechristened Immigration and Customs Enforcement (ICE) and placed within the U.S. Department of Homeland Security. Homeland Security Act of 2002, Pub. L. No. 107-296, 116 Stat. 2135.

As a general matter, an alien can be deported ("removed" in the language of the current act) if he or she is not lawfully authorized to be present in the United States. *See* 8 U.S.C. §§ 1182(a); 1227(a). The Act's "cancellation of removal" provision, currently found at 8 U.S.C. § 1229b, authorizes the Attorney General, acting through an immigration judge, to allow an otherwise deportable alien to remain in the country if among other things the alien has been physically present in the United States for ten years and has been "a person of good moral character" during that time. Cancellation of removal replaces a practice known as "suspension of deportation," which was at issue in *Chadha* and permitted some aliens to remain in the United States notwithstanding the fact that they technically lacked authority to remain in the country.

The Executive Office for Immigration Review (EOIR) was created on January 9, 1983, through an internal Department of Justice (DOJ) reorganization that combined the Board of Immigration Appeals with the Immigration Judge function previously performed by the former INS. The director of the EOIR reports to the Deputy Attorney General. As a result of the reorganization, immigration judges are independent of the enforcement authority of the INS (now ICE).

Under INA § 244, an immigration judge's decision to award suspension of deportation was forwarded to Congress for review. In the batch of cases at issue in *Chadha*, the House disagreed with the Department of Justice's decision to suspend deportation in

6 out of 340 cases, or 1.7% of the cases it reviewed. Given this seemingly low reversal rate, why did Congress include a process for a legislative veto in § 244? Would the possibility of legislative veto have affected immigration judges' decisions even if the absolute number of decisions reversed by Congress was low? If so, why?

3. **The "Private Bill" Analogy.** Suspension of deportation and cancellation of removal supplement "private bills" in which Congress addresses the immigration status of particular aliens or classes of aliens through legislation specific to them. Such "private bills" are legislative acts requiring approval of both houses and are subject to presentment. Because they affect a specific individual or entity or a few individuals or entities, they generally receive less scrutiny than public laws. Between 1995 and 2007, 451 private bills affecting non-citizens' legal status were introduced; Congress enacted 36 such bills. *See* Margaret Mikyung Lee, Congressional Research Service, Private Immigration Legislation, at 29 (August 9, 2007). Could Congress have used private bills to accomplish the same ends as § 244? Which is the preferable procedure?

Justice Powell's concurrence observed on this score (462 U.S. at 966):

> In deciding whether Chadha deserves to be deported, Congress is not subject to any internal constraints that prevent it from arbitrarily depriving him of the right to remain in this country.[9] Unlike the judiciary or an administrative agency, Congress is not bound by established substantive rules. Nor is it subject to the procedural safeguards, such as the right to counsel and a hearing before an impartial tribunal, that are present when a court or an agency adjudicates individual rights. The only effective constraint on Congress' power is political, but Congress is most accountable politically when it prescribes rules of general applicability. When it decides rights of specific persons, those rights are subject to "the tyranny of a shifting majority."

Footnote 9 of the concurrence stated: "Congress may authorize the admission of individual aliens by special Acts, but it does not follow that Congress unilaterally may make a judgment that a particular alien has no legal right to remain in this country." What in the Constitution limits Congress's power to unilaterally make a judgment that a particular alien has no legal right to remain in this country? *Compare Calder v. Bull*, 3 U.S. 386 (1798) (holding that Ex Post Facto Clause applies only to criminal punishments), *with Kennedy v. Mendoza-Martinez*, 372 U.S. 144, 195 (1963) (invalidating statute that stripped draft evaders of citizenship as a violation of due process).

4. **Why is the Legislative Veto Unconstitutional?** What was the specific constitutional defect with the legislative veto created by INA § 244? Consider three possibilities:

a. **Procedurally Defective Exercise of "Legislative" Power: Unicameral Action and Failure of Presentment to the President?** According to the majority, § 244 was unconstitutional because it permitted the House to exercise legislative power without complying with the bicameralism and presentment requirements of Article I, § 7. This conclusion is premised on the assumption that, when the House disapproved Chadha's suspension of deportation, it enacted legislation. What, according to the Court, was the legislation passed in violation of Article I, § 7? When the House expressed disapproval of Chadha's suspension of deportation, was it making law or, in *Yakus*'s terms, formulating "subsidiary administrative policy within the prescribed statutory framework?" 321 U.S. at 414.

Insofar as the House was formulating subsidiary administrative policy, is it possible to distinguish its actions from those of an administrative agency? In a portion of the opinion not excepted above, the Court claims that when the Attorney General decides to suspend an alien's deportation, "he does not exercise 'legislative' power. The bicameral process is not necessary as a check on the Executive's administration of the laws because his administrative activity cannot reach beyond the limits of the statute that create it—a statute duly enacted pursuant to Art. I, §§ 1, 7." 462 U.S. at 953 n.16. Isn't the same true of the House when it passes a resolution reversing the Attorney General's decision to suspend an alien's deportation? Yet, the Court says that "[a] one-House veto is clearly legislative in both character and effect and is not so checked; the need for the check provided by Art. I, §§ 1,7, is therefore clear."

b. **Impermissible Encroachment on Executive Power?** None of the Justices contended that § 244 impermissibly intruded on the President's Article II authority to take care that the laws—here, the INA—be faithfully executed. But doesn't the legislative veto effectively replace the Executive with Congress as the governmental body ultimately responsible for enforcement of the law? Professor Alan Morrison, who represented Chadha in the Ninth Circuit and the Supreme Court, argues that the legislative veto had this effect. Alan B. Morrison, *A Non-Power Looks at Separation of Powers*, 79 Geo. L.J. 281, 285 (1990). Is he correct? Is his position consistent with the general view that even "independent" administrative agencies can play a law enforcement role?

Is the President necessarily in a stronger position after *Chadha*? Consider Louis Fisher, *The Legislative Veto: Invalidated, It Survives*, 56 L. & Contemp. Prob. 273, 286 (1993):

> Following the Court's ruling in 1983, Congress amended a number of statutes by deleting legislative vetoes and replacing them with joint resolutions. Congress replaced the one-house veto in the executive reorganization statute with a joint resolution of approval. Although this satisfied the twin requirements of *Chadha* (bicameralism and presentment), the President's position was actually worsened. The President now had to obtain the approval of both houses within a specified number of days in order to reorganize executive agencies. Under the procedure that operated before *Chadha*, a reorganization plan automatically became effective within a fixed number of days unless one house acted to disapprove. The shift to a joint resolution of approval meant that Congress had, in effect, a negative one-house veto. The refusal of one House to support a joint resolution of approval would spell defeat for a reorganization proposal. The new procedure was so onerous that the Reagan Administration decided not to request a renewal of reorganization authority after it expired.

Is this joint-resolution requirement — in effect, a one-house veto — constitutional after *Chadha*? Is the reorganization context different?

c. **A Norm Against Self-Delegation?** The Court observes that "Congress' decision to deport Chadha . . . involves determinations of policy that Congress can implement in only one way; bicameral passage followed by presentment to the President." On this account, the problem with § 244 is that Congress engaged in impermissible self-dealing when it delegated *to itself* authority to carry out the INA. This would seem to be a formal separationist concern. Thus, even where the executive welcomes the change from private immigration bills to the cancellation of deportation procedure (though subject to a legislative veto) or, in another context, may welcome the ability to initiate an executive reorganization (even at the price of a legislative veto provision), *see* Fisher, *supra*, the Constitution's commitment to separation of powers precludes Congress's ongoing formal involvement in execution of the laws. Congress can affect funding decisions and engage in oversight, Section [C], below, but it cannot without bicameral action be a formal barrier to executive action. This also appears to be the gloss the *Humphrey's* Court attached to the *Myers* decision: Congress can place ex ante restrictions on the President's removal authority but its consent cannot be required ex post for any given removal decision. In other words, Congress cannot insert itself directly into the process of executing the laws. This is so even where the overall effect of the legislative veto does not directly diminish the President's authority.

5. **"Laying Before" Statutes.** The Rules Enabling Act, 28 U.S.C. § 2072, authorizes the Supreme Court "to prescribe general rules of practice and procedure and rules of evidence for cases in the United States district courts . . . and courts of appeals." When the Supreme Court adopts a new rule of procedure or evidence, it transmits the proposed rule to Congress by May 1 of the year on which the rule is to become effective. "Such rule shall take effect no earlier than December 1 of the year in which such rule is so transmitted unless otherwise provided by law" — that is, unless Congress enacts a law that modifies the proposed rule.

The Congressional Review Act of 1996 (CRA or Act), 5 U.S.C. § 801 et seq., enacted as part of the Small Business Regulatory Enforcement Fairness Act of 1996, Pub. L. No. 104-121, 110 Stat. 847, requires agencies to notify Congress of new major regulations, and extends the 30-day waiting period for new regulations under the Administrative Procedure Act, 5 U.S.C. § 553(d), to 60 days. Under the CRA, Congress can "veto" a new regulation if the House and Senate pass a joint disapproval resolution and the resolution is signed by the President or the President's veto is overridden by a two-thirds majority of the House and Senate. The Act provides for expedited consideration of disapproval resolutions that have been passed by one house of Congress, and allows for Senate floor votes (without filibuster) on resolutions that have not been reported out of committee within twenty days of a rule being submitted to Congress. Under the procedures established by the Act, a disapproval resolution may only target a single regulation, and may be debated for "not more than 10 hours." The 60-day waiting period allows a new Congress to disapprove so-called "midnight rules" that are issued in the final days of an outgoing presidential administration.

Does *Chadha* call into question the validity of these "laying before" statutes? What would you argue if you were retained to challenge them? Does the CRA allow Congress to step into the shoes of agency decisionmakers exercising delegated regulatory authority? As a functional matter, does it allow Congress to accomplish the same thing as the legislative veto?

Before 2017, the Congressional Review Act was invoked successfully a single time, to block a rule on workplace ergonomics promulgated by the Occupational Health and Safety Administration during the final days of President Bill Clinton's presidency, 66 Fed. Reg. 20,403 (Apr. 23, 2001). In the first months of the 115th Congress, however, congressional Republicans used the Act to block a number of Obama-era rules, among them an FCC rule that prohibited internet service providers from selling data about customers' internet usage, 81 Fed. Reg. 87,274 (Dec. 2, 2016), a Department of Labor rule that governed the reporting of injuries and illnesses, 81 Fed. Reg. 91,792 (Dec. 19, 2016), and regulations implementing Preisdent Obama's Fair Pay and Safe Workplaces Executive Order, which strengthened legal protections for employees of federal contractors, 81 Fed. Reg. 58,562 (Aug. 25, 2016). As this book went to press, thirteen Obama-era regulations had been blocked via the Congressional Review Act. George Washington University's Regulatory Studies Center maintains a current list of blocked regulations at http://regulatorystudies.columbian.gwu.edu. For further analysis, see Morton Rosenberg, The Congressional Review Act After 15 Years: Background and Considerations for Reform Draft Report Prepared for the Administrative Conference of the United States (Sept. 16, 2011); Note, *The Mysteries of the Congressional Review Act*, 122 Harv. L. Rev. 2162 (2009).

6. Ex Ante Presentment?: *Chadha* and Executive Reorganization Acts. The Supreme Court's decision in *Chadha* had major implications for Congress's use of Reorganization Acts to help streamline the federal bureaucracy:

> Between 1932 and 1981, Congress periodically delegated authority to the President that allowed him to develop plans for reorganization of portions of the federal government and to present those plans to Congress for consideration under special parliamentary procedures. Under these procedures, the President's plan would go into effect unless one or both houses of Congress passed a resolution rejecting the plan, a process referred to as a "legislative veto."

Henry B. Hogue, Congressional Research Service, Presidential Reorganization Authority: History, Recent Initiatives, and Options for Congress 1 (Dec. 11, 2012).

In 1977, Congress, at President Carter's request, enacted revised reorganization legislation that retained a legislative veto but allowed a reorganization to take effect if Congress did not exercise the veto within sixty days. Pub. L. No. 95-17, 91 Stat. 29. The legislation also required the introduction of a disapproval motion in both houses of Congress, and included procedural provisions designed to ensure the swift consideration of such motions. As the Congressional Research Service study notes:

President Carter submitted ten plans under the new statute, all of which went into effect. Among these were a plan to reorganize the federal personnel management system, including the creation of an Office of Personnel Management, a Merit Systems Protection Board, and a Federal Labor Relations Authority; the establishment of a Federal Emergency Management Agency, to which were transferred functions and entities from various parts of the government; and to reorganize international trade functions, centering policy coordination and negotiation in this area in a United States Trade Representative in the Executive Office of the President.

Hogue, *supra*, at 2.

Following the Supreme Court's decision in *Chadha*, Congress in 1984 enacted legislation that required an affirmative vote of Congress before a reorganization plan submitted by the President took effect. 98 Stat. 3192. The 1984 statute provided that Congress would consider a joint resolution for approval of the plan under an expedited procedure that limited the time for committee consideration and for floor debate, and limited amendments to the joint resolution. The statute set a deadline of December 31, 1984, for the submission of reorganization plans. President Reagan did not submit any plans before the statutory deadline, but the lapsed statute remains in the U.S. Code at 5 U.S.C. §§ 901–913.

The decision in *Chadha* raised the alarming possibility that agencies that had been created by prior reorganization plans and their actions were void. To confirm the lawfulness of prior reorganization plans and agency actions taken under them, Congress on October 19, 1984, passed "An Act to prevent disruption of the structure and functioning of the Government by ratifying all reorganization plans as a matter of law." Pub. L. No. 98-532, 98 Stat. 2705.

7. **Ex Ante Presentment?:** *Chadha* **and the Line Item Veto.** Thirteen years after the Court decided *Chadha*, Congress in April 1996 enacted the Line Item Veto Act, Pub. L. No. 104-130, 110 Stat. 1200. Long sought by "good government" advocates, the Act aimed "to ensur[e] greater fiscal accountability in Washington," H.R. Conf. Rep. 104-491, at 15 (2d Sess. 1996), by counteracting collective action problems thought to prevent Congress from keeping federal spending within appropriate limits. In particular, the Act sought to address the fact that individual members of Congress have strong incentives to secure "pork" that benefits their constituencies but weak incentives to police other members' pork-barrel spending or the overall federal budget. To counteract this tendency, the Act gave the President the power to "cancel in whole" three types of provisions contained within a law that had passed Congress and was presented to the President for signing: "(1) any dollar amount of discretionary budget authority; (2) any item of new direct spending; or (3) any limited tax benefit."

To cancel a spending provision, the President was required to certify that the cancellation would "(i) reduce the Federal budget deficit; (ii) not impair any essential Government functions; and (iii) not harm the national interest." A cancellation took effect when Congress received a message from the President identifying the cancelled item and certifying that he found the item satisfied the above requirements. Congress could override the cancellation of a budget item if both houses of Congress passed a "disapproval bill" under expedited procedures provided in the Act. If a disapproval bill did not pass, the cancelled provision would have no "legal force or effect."

The Supreme Court (per Justice Stevens) ruled that the Act violated the Presentment Clause because it effectively authorized the President to create a statute that was not voted on by both houses and presented to the President. Quoting *Chadha*, the Court stated: "[T]he power to enact statutes may only 'be exercised in accord with a single, finely wrought and exhaustively considered procedure.'" The laws that resulted from the exercise of the line-item veto were "not the product of the 'finely wrought' procedure that the Framers designed." *Clinton v. City of New York*, 524 U.S. 417, 440 (1998).

The Court distinguished *Field v. Clark*, 143 U.S. 649 (1892), which upheld § 3 of the Tariff Act of 1890, 26 Stat. 567, against a constitutional challenge. That section directed the President to suspend a statutory tariff exemption for sugar, molasses, coffee, tea, and hides "whenever, and so often" as the President found that a country producing and exporting those items imposed duties on U.S. agricultural products that were "reciprocally unequal and unreasonable." According to the Court in *Clinton*, the Tariff Act differed from the Line Item Veto Act in that the President was implementing a policy established by Congress as opposed to revisiting a decision made in law: "whenever the President suspended an exemption under the Tariff Act, he was executing the policy that Congress had embodied in the statute. In contrast, whenever the President cancels an item of new direct spending or a limited tax benefit he is rejecting the policy judgment made by Congress and relying on his own policy judgment. Thus, the conclusion in *Field v. Clark* that the suspensions mandated by the Tariff Act were not exercises of legislative power does not undermine our opinion that cancellations pursuant to the Line Item Veto Act are the functional equivalent of partial repeals of Acts of Congress that fail to satisfy Article I, § 7."

8. **Postscript.** Despite *Chadha*'s holding that the legislative veto violates Article I, § 7, "Congress continues to add legislative vetoes to bills and Presidents continue to sign them into law, although often in their signing statements they object to these legislative vetoes and regard them as unconstitutional under the Supreme Court's ruling." Louis Fisher, Congressional Research Service, Legislative Vetoes After *Chadha*, at 5 (May 2, 2005) (citing more than 400 post-*Chadha* laws that contain legislative-veto provisions). Moreover, conference committee reports on appropriations measures sometimes contain statements to the effect that an agency may not expend appropriated funds, or undertake particular initiatives, until it consults with the congressional committees that oversee it.

———

Of course, Congress has many mechanisms other than the legislative veto available to it for overseeing and influencing administrative action. Section [C] below surveys mechanisms that are not thought to raise constitutional problems. But first, it is necessary to consider another mechanism of congressional control that raises constitutional questions—the selection of agency heads.

Bowsher v. Synar

478 U.S. 714 (1986)

CHIEF JUSTICE BURGER delivered the opinion of the Court.***

I

A

On December 12, 1985, the President signed into law the Balanced Budget and Emergency Deficit Control Act of 1985, Pub. L. 99-177, 99 Stat. 1038, 2 U.S.C. § 901 et seq. (1982 ed., Supp. III), popularly known as the "Gramm-Rudman-Hollings Act." The purpose of the Act is to eliminate the federal budget deficit. To that end, the Act sets a "maximum deficit amount" for federal spending for each of fiscal years 1986 through 1991. The size of that maximum deficit amount progressively reduces to zero in fiscal year 1991. If in any fiscal year the federal budget deficit exceeds the maximum deficit amount by more than a specified sum, the Act requires across-the-board cuts in federal spending to reach the targeted deficit level, with half of the cuts made to defense programs and the other half made to nondefense programs. The Act exempts certain priority programs from these cuts. § 255.

These "automatic" reductions are accomplished through a rather complicated procedure, spelled out in § 251, the so-called "reporting provisions" of the Act. Each year, the Directors of the Office of Management and Budget (OMB) and the Congressional Budget Office (CBO) independently estimate the amount of the federal budget deficit for the upcoming fiscal year. If that deficit exceeds the maximum targeted deficit amount for that fiscal year by more than a specified amount, the Directors of OMB and CBO independently calculate, on a program-by-program basis, the budget reductions necessary to ensure that the deficit does not exceed the maximum deficit amount. The Act then requires the Directors to report jointly their deficit estimates and budget reduction calculations to the Comptroller General.

The Comptroller General, after reviewing the Directors' reports, then reports his conclusions to the President. § 251(b). The President in turn must issue a "sequestration" order mandating the spending reductions specified by the Comptroller General. § 252. There follows a period during which Congress may by legislation reduce spending to obviate, in whole or in part, the need for the sequestration order. If such reductions are not enacted, the sequestration order becomes effective and the spending reductions included in that order are made.

Anticipating constitutional challenge to these procedures, the Act also contains a "fallback" deficit reduction process to take effect "[i]n the event that any of the reporting procedures described in section 251 are invalidated." § 274(f). Under these provisions, the report prepared by the Directors of OMB and the CBO is submitted directly to a specially created Temporary Joint Committee on Deficit Reduction, which must report in five days to both Houses a joint resolution setting forth the content of the

Directors' report. Congress then must vote on the resolution under special rules, which render amendments out of order. If the resolution is passed and signed by the President, it then serves as the basis for a Presidential sequestration order.

B

Within hours of the President's signing of the Act,[1] Congressman Synar, who had voted against the Act, filed a complaint seeking declaratory relief that the Act was unconstitutional. Eleven other Members later joined Congressman Synar's suit. A virtually identical lawsuit was also filed by the National Treasury Employees Union. The Union alleged that its members had been injured as a result of the Act's automatic spending reduction provisions, which have suspended certain cost-of-living benefit increases to the Union's members.

A three-judge District Court, appointed pursuant to 2 U.S.C. § 922(a)(5) (1982 ed., Supp. III), invalidated the reporting provisions. *Synar v. United States*, 626 F. Supp. 1374 (DC 1986) (Scalia, Johnson, and Gasch, JJ.).*** Although the District Court concluded that the Act survived a delegation doctrine challenge, it held that the role of the Comptroller General in the deficit reduction process violated the constitutionally imposed separation of powers.***

III

The Constitution does not contemplate an active role for Congress in the supervision of officers charged with the execution of the laws it enacts. The President appoints "Officers of the United States" with the "Advice and Consent of the Senate . . . ." Art. II, § 2. Once the appointment has been made and confirmed, however, the Constitution explicitly provides for removal of Officers of the United States by Congress only upon impeachment by the House of Representatives and conviction by the Senate. An impeachment by the House and trial by the Senate can rest only on "Treason, Bribery or other high Crimes and Misdemeanors." Art. II, § 4. A direct congressional role in the removal of officers charged with the execution of the laws beyond this limited one is inconsistent with separation of powers.

To permit the execution of the laws to be vested in an officer answerable only to Congress would, in practical terms, reserve in Congress control over the execution of the laws. As the District Court observed: "Once an officer is appointed, it is only the authority that can remove him, and not the authority that appointed him, that he must fear and, in the performance of his functions, obey." The structure of the Constitution does not permit Congress to execute the laws; it follows that Congress cannot grant to an officer under its control what it does not possess.

Our decision in *INS v. Chadha*, 462 U.S. 919 (1983), supports this conclusion.*** To permit an officer controlled by Congress to execute the laws would be, in essence, to permit a congressional veto. Congress could simply remove, or threaten to remove,

---

1. In his signing statement, the President expressed his view that the Act was constitutionally defective because of the Comptroller General's ability to exercise supervisory authority over the President. Statement on Signing H. J. Res. 372 Into Law, 21 Weekly Comp. of Pres. Doc. 1491 (1985).

an officer for executing the laws in any fashion found to be unsatisfactory to Congress. This kind of congressional control over the execution of the laws, *Chadha* makes clear, is constitutionally impermissible.***

With these principles in mind, we turn to consideration of whether the Comptroller General is controlled by Congress.

IV

Appellants urge that the Comptroller General performs his duties independently and is not subservient to Congress. We agree with the District Court that this contention does not bear close scrutiny.

The critical factor lies in the provisions of the statute defining the Comptroller General's office relating to removability.[5] Although the Comptroller General is nominated by the President from a list of three individuals recommended by the Speaker of the House of Representatives and the President pro tempore of the Senate, *see* 31 U.S.C. § 703(a)(2),[6] and confirmed by the Senate, he is removable only at the initiative of Congress. He may be removed not only by impeachment but also by joint resolution of Congress "at any time" resting on any one of the following bases:

"(i) permanent disability;

"(ii) inefficiency;

"(iii) neglect of duty;

"(iv) malfeasance; or

"(v) a felony or conduct involving moral turpitude."

31 U.S.C. § 703(e)(1)(B).[7]

***The removal provision was an important part of the legislative scheme, as a number of Congressmen recognized. Representative Hawley commented: "[H]e is our officer, in a measure, getting information for us . . . . If he does not do his work properly, we, as practically his employers, ought to be able to discharge him from his office." 58 Cong. Rec. 7136 (1919). Representative Sisson observed that the removal provisions would give "[t]he Congress of the United States . . . absolute control of the man's destiny in office." The ultimate design was to "give the legislative branch of the Government

---

5. We reject appellants' argument that consideration of the effect of a removal provision is not "ripe" until that provision is actually used. As the District Court concluded, "it is the Comptroller General's presumed desire to avoid removal by pleasing Congress, which creates the here-and-now subservience to another branch that raises separation-of-powers problems." The Impeachment Clause of the Constitution can hardly be thought to be undermined because of nonuse.

6. Congress adopted this provision in 1980 because of "the special interest of both Houses in the choice of an individual whose primary function is to provide assistance to Congress." S. Rep. No. 96-570, p. 10.

7. Although the President could veto such a joint resolution, the veto could be overridden by a two-thirds vote of both Houses of Congress. Thus, the Comptroller General could be removed in the face of Presidential opposition. Like the District Court, we therefore read the removal provision as authorizing removal by Congress alone.

control of the audit, not through the power of appointment, but through the power of removal." 58 Cong. Rec. 7211 (1919) (Rep. Temple).

[The contention that the Comptroller General is not subservient to Congress because the grounds for removal are limited] fails to recognize the breadth of the grounds for removal. The statute permits removal for "inefficiency," "neglect of duty," or "malfeasance." These terms are very broad and, as interpreted by Congress, could sustain removal of a Comptroller General for any number of actual or perceived transgressions of the legislative will.***

[We add] that the political realities reveal that the Comptroller General is [not] free from influence by Congress. The Comptroller General heads the General Accounting Office (GAO), "an instrumentality of the United States Government independent of the executive departments," 31 U.S.C. § 702(a), which was created by Congress in 1921 as part of the Budget and Accounting Act of 1921, 42 Stat. 23. Congress created the office because it believed that it "needed an officer, responsible to it alone, to check upon the application of public funds in accordance with appropriations." H. Mansfield, The Comptroller General: A Study in the Law and Practice of Financial Administration 65 (1939).***

Against this background, we see no escape from the conclusion that, because Congress has retained removal authority over the Comptroller General, he may not be entrusted with executive powers. The remaining question is whether the Comptroller General has been assigned such powers in the Balanced Budget and Emergency Deficit Control Act of 1985.

V

The primary responsibility of the Comptroller General under the instant Act is the preparation of a "report." This report must contain detailed estimates of projected federal revenues and expenditures. The report must also specify the reductions, if any, necessary to reduce the deficit to the target for the appropriate fiscal year. The reductions must be set forth on a program-by-program basis.

In preparing the report, the Comptroller General is to have "due regard" for the estimates and reductions set forth in a joint report submitted to him by the Director of CBO and the Director of OMB, the President's fiscal and budgetary adviser. However, the Act plainly contemplates that the Comptroller General will exercise his independent judgment and evaluation with respect to those estimates. The Act also provides that the Comptroller General's report "shall explain fully any differences between the contents of such report and the report of the Directors." § 251(b)(2).

Appellants suggest that the duties assigned to the Comptroller General in the Act are essentially ministerial and mechanical so that their performance does not constitute "execution of the law" in a meaningful sense. On the contrary, we view these functions as plainly entailing execution of the law in constitutional terms. Interpreting a law enacted by Congress to implement the legislative mandate is the very essence of "execution" of the law. Under § 251, the Comptroller General must exercise judgment concerning facts that affect the application of the Act. He must also interpret the provisions of the Act to determine precisely what budgetary calculations are required. Decisions of that kind are typically made by officers charged with executing a statute.*** [A]s *Chadha* makes clear, once Congress makes its choice in enacting legislation, its participation ends. Congress can thereafter control the execution of its enactment only indirectly—by passing new legislation. *Chadha*, 462 U.S., at 958. By placing the responsibility for execution of the Balanced Budget and Emergency Deficit Control Act in the hands of an officer who is subject to removal only by itself, Congress in effect has retained control over the execution of the Act and has intruded into the executive function. The Constitution does not permit such intrusion.***

VI

We now turn to the final issue of remedy. Appellants urge that rather than striking down § 251 and invalidating the significant power Congress vested in the Comptroller General to meet a national fiscal emergency, we should take the lesser course of nullifying the statutory provisions of the 1921 Act that authorizes Congress to remove the Comptroller General. At oral argument, counsel for the Comptroller General suggested that this might make the Comptroller General removable by the President. All appellants urge that Congress would prefer invalidation of the removal provisions rather than invalidation of § 251 of the Balanced Budget and Emergency Deficit Control Act.***

Severance at this late date of the removal provisions enacted 65 years ago would significantly alter the Comptroller General's office, possibly by making him subservient to the Executive Branch. Recasting the Comptroller General as an officer of the Executive Branch would accordingly alter the balance that Congress had in mind in drafting the Budget and Accounting Act of 1921 and the Balanced Budget and Emergency Deficit Control Act, to say nothing of the wide array of other tasks and duties Congress has assigned the Comptroller General in other statutes. Thus appellants' argument would require this Court to undertake a weighing of the importance Congress attached to the removal provisions in the Budget and Accounting Act of 1921 as well as in other subsequent enactments against the importance it placed on the Balanced Budget and Emergency Deficit Control Act of 1985.

Fortunately this is a thicket we need not enter. The language of the Balanced Budget and Emergency Deficit Control Act itself settles the issue. In § 274(f), Congress has explicitly provided "fallback" provisions in the Act that take effect "[i]n the event . . . *any* of the reporting procedures described in section 251 are invalidated." § 274(f)(1) (emphasis added). The fallback provisions are fully operative as a law. Assuming that appellants are correct in urging that this matter must be resolved on the basis of congressional intent, the intent appears to have been for § 274(f) to be given effect in this situation.***

Accordingly, rather than perform the type of creative and imaginative statutory surgery urged by appellants, our holding simply permits the fallback provisions to come into play.[10]***

---

10. Because we conclude that the Comptroller General, as an officer removable by Congress, may not exercise the powers conferred upon him by the Act, we have no occasion for considering

JUSTICE STEVENS, with whom JUSTICE MARSHALL joins, concurring in the judgment.

When this Court is asked to invalidate a statutory provision that has been approved by both Houses of the Congress and signed by the President, particularly an Act of Congress that confronts a deeply vexing national problem, it should only do so for the most compelling constitutional reasons. I agree with the Court that the "Gramm-Rudman-Hollings" Act contains a constitutional infirmity so severe that the flawed provision may not stand. I disagree with the Court, however, on the reasons why the Constitution prohibits the Comptroller General from exercising the powers assigned to him by § 251(b) and § 251(c)(2) of the Act. It is not the dormant, carefully circum-scribed congressional removal power that represents the primary constitutional evil. Nor do I agree with the conclusion*** that the analysis depends on a labeling of the functions assigned to the Comptroller General as "executive powers." Rather, I am convinced that the Comptroller General must be characterized as an agent of Congress because of his longstanding statutory responsibilities; that the powers assigned to him under the Gramm-Rudman-Hollings Act require him to make policy that will bind the Nation; and that, when Congress, or a component or an agent of Congress, seeks to make policy that will bind the Nation, it must follow the procedures man-dated by Article I of the Constitution—through passage by both Houses and present-ment to the President. In short, Congress may not exercise its fundamental power to formulate national policy by delegating that power to one of its two Houses, to a legisla-tive committee, or to an individual agent of the Congress such as the Speaker of the House of Representatives, the Sergeant at Arms of the Senate, or the Director of the Congressional Budget Office. That principle, I believe, is applicable to the Comp-troller General.***

Article I of the Constitution specifies the procedures that Congress must follow when it makes policy that binds the Nation: its legislation must be approved by both of its Houses and presented to the President.*** If Congress were free to delegate its poli-cymaking authority to one of its components, or to one of its agents, it would be able to evade the carefully crafted restraints spelled out in the Constitution. That danger—congressional action that evades constitutional restraints—is not present when Congress delegates lawmaking power to the executive or to an independent agency.

The distinction between the kinds of action that Congress may delegate to its own components and agents and those that require either compliance with Article I pro-cedures or delegation to another branch pursuant to defined standards is reflected in the practices that have developed over the years regarding congressional resolutions. The joint resolution, which is used for "special purposes and . . . incidental matters," 7 Deschler's Precedents of the House of Representatives 334 (1977), makes binding policy and "requires an affirmative vote by both Houses and submission to the President for approval"—the full Article I requirements. A concurrent resolution, in contrast,

---

appellees' other challenges to the Act, including their argument that the assignment of powers to the Comptroller General in § 251 violates the delegation doctrine, *see, e.g., A.L.A. Schechter Poultry Corp. v. United States*, 295 U.S. 495 (1935); *Yakus v. United States*, 321 U.S. 414 (1944).

makes no binding policy; it is "a means of expressing fact, principles, opinions, and purposes of the two Houses," Jefferson's Manual and Rules of the House of Representatives 176 (1983), and thus does not need to be presented to the President. It is settled, however, that if a resolution is intended to make policy that will bind the Nation and thus is "legislative in its character and effect," S. Rep. No. 1335, 54th Cong., 2d Sess., 8 (1897) — then the full Article I requirements must be observed. For "the nature or substance of the resolution, and not its form, controls the question of its disposition."

In my opinion, Congress itself could not exercise the Gramm-Rudman-Hollings functions through a concurrent resolution. The fact that the fallback provision in § 274 requires a joint resolution rather than a concurrent resolution indicates that Congress endorsed this view. I think it equally clear that Congress may not simply delegate those functions to an agent such as the Congressional Budget Office. Since I am persuaded that the Comptroller General is also fairly deemed to be an agent of Congress, he too cannot exercise such functions.***

Notes and Questions

1. **The Comptroller General's Office.** The Comptroller General heads the Government Accountability Office (GAO), an important arm of Congress. Created in 1921, the GAO's principal function is to help Congress monitor the work of the government. *See* Budget and Accounting Act of 1921, Pub. L. No. 67-13, 42 Stat. 20. The Comptroller General is appointed by the President for a 15 year term with the advice and consent of the Senate, and selected from a list of three candidates chosen by the Speaker of the House and the President pro tempore of the Senate. He or she can be removed only for cause, through a joint resolution of the House and Senate that is presented for presidential veto in the same manner as an enrolled bill. *See* 31 U.S.C. § 703.

2. **The Gramm-Rudman-Hollings Act.** As the Court explains, the Gramm-Rudman-Hollings Act of 1985 (GRH), Pub. L. No. 99-177, 99 Stat. 1037, aimed to reduce the federal deficit, which at the time of GRH's enactment was the largest in history. To do so, GRH provided for automatic spending cuts if federal spending was projected to exceed a "maximum deficit amount" specified in the Act. GRH thus served as kind of mast-binding mechanism. If the total spending authorized by Congress exceeded the ceilings specified in GRH, government-wide spending cuts would take effect to bring spending down to previously established levels.

To determine the amount and distribution of these "automatic" reductions, GRH created what the Court describes as a "rather complicated procedure." First, the Office of Management and Budget (see Section [C], below) and Congressional Budget Office, an executive arm (see Section [C], below), would estimate the amount of the projected deficit and calculate spending reductions needed to reduce it to the level permitted by GRH. The Comptroller General would review those estimates, reconcile them according to "economic calculation standards," and make a report to the President regarding the spending cuts needed to bring the total federal budget in line with the ceiling specified in GRH. Upon receiving the Comptroller General's report, the President would issue a "sequestration order" that set budget levels for specific federal programs. Finally, the sequestration order would be forwarded to Congress. If Congress failed to enact a substitute measure, the President's sequestration order would take effect.

From the perspective of a lawmaker concerned with controlling federal spending, how is the process created by GRH an improvement over the ordinary appropriations process? (See Note 11 accompanying *TVA v. Hill*, in Chapter 2[B][2][a], *supra* p. 180, for a review of that process.) What pathologies of the legislative process does the GRH process correct? Does the GRH process force Congress to make difficult trade-offs among competing budget priorities? Or does it rather encourage members of Congress to spend without regard to deficits, confident that in the end their decisions would be shoehorned into a budget whose overall size is within reasonable limits? Some states have enacted balanced budget amendments to their constitutions that prohibit expenditures in excess of revenue for a given fiscal year. From a public policy standpoint, are such amendments preferable to the process created by GRH?

3. **Why Was the GRH Budget Process Held Unconstitutional: Non-delegation Concerns?** Plaintiffs argued that GRH was unconstitutional because it delegated legislative authority to the Comptroller General in violation of *Schechter* and *Yakus*. Is the kind of authority delegated by GRH — i.e., authority to set the budget of many federal regulatory agencies — one that raises non-delegation concerns? What is the "intelligible principle" that guided the Comptroller General's decisions when setting the funding levels for federal programs?

The three-judge district court held that GRH's delegation to the Comptroller General did not violate the non-delegation doctrine. As an initial matter, the court rejected the contention that the delegation of budget authority was per se impermissible because establishing the federal budget was a core congressional function. "*Synar v. United States*, 626 F. Supp. 1374, 1375 (D.D.C. 1986). With respect to the intelligible principle underlying Congress's delegation, the district court noted that "the economic calculation standards, which might seem vague and confusing to laymen, will have more precise meaning to officials accustomed to making such determinations." On the whole, "the totality of the Act's standards, definitions, context, and reference to past administrative practice provide[d] an adequate 'intelligible principle' to guide and confine administrative decisionmaking." *Id.* at 1389.

Are these conclusions persuasive? Is the setting of the budget a non-delegable legislative function as Justice Stevens argues? Could Congress delegate authority to a committee to decide conclusively whether to impeach a particular official?

4. **Why Was the GRH Budget Process Held Unconstitutional: Self-Delegation Concerns?** Despite rejecting plaintiffs' non-delegation argument, the district court and Supreme Court concluded that the GRH's budget process was unconstitutional because of the relationship between Congress and the Comptroller General. The Supreme Court's analysis proceeds in three steps.

a. The Court first reiterated the self-delegation prohibition of *Chadha*—that "once Congress makes its choice in enacting legislation, its participation ends." Note that the Court read *Chadha* to establish an anti-self-delegation norm rather than resting on the conclusion that the legislative veto permits Congress to exercise legislative power without satisfying the bicameralism and presentment requirements.

Does the Court in *Bowsher* overstate this point? Article I gives the House and Senate authority to impeach executive officers. To know whether an officer should be impeached, Congress must be able to monitor the activities of the executive branch and independent agencies. This requires a monitoring and reporting apparatus, and *Chadha* went out of its way to emphasize the constitutionality of statutory monitoring and reporting mechanisms. In any event, many agencies are in a symbiotic relationship with Congress because they depend on year-to-year appropriations to support their work. As discussed below, these relationships give Congress significant influence over agency decisionmaking.

What is the "active role" in law-execution that the Court is worried about? Are the Comptroller General's responsibilities under GRH an example of Congress impermissibly assigning law-executing responsibility to itself?

b. The Court next concludes that, because Congress cannot take an active role in enforcement of the law, it cannot have authority to remove an officer who is responsible for execution of the law. The Court reasons that "[t]o permit an officer controlled by Congress to execute the laws would be, in essence, to permit a congressional veto. Congress could simply remove, or threaten to remove, an officer for executing the laws in any fashion found to be unsatisfactory to Congress."

Is this conclusion sufficiently responsive to the dynamics of the legislative process? Suppose that Congress had legal authority to remove the Comptroller General for any reason or no reason at all by passing a joint resolution. What other conditions would have to be satisfied for Congress to "remove*** an officer for executing the laws in any fashion found to be unsatisfactory to Congress." Consider, in particular, the partisan makeup of Congress and the ability of a minority to block removal at a number of steps in the process, *see* Note on the Dynamics of Legislation, *supra* Section [2][A][2][a]. Moreover, since the removal resolution would be presented to the President, it would require a two-thirds vote of both houses to override a veto. Is it a sufficient basis for concern that whatever the formal removal mechanism, the GAO was established to serve and views itself as an arm of Congress?

c. Finally, the Court concludes that GRH's budget process is unconstitutional because the Comptroller General is responsible for execution of the law, and Congress had the authority to remove him. What is the basis for the Court's conclusion that the Comptroller General "executes" the law? The Court observes that "[i]nterpreting a law enacted by Congress to implement the legislative mandate is the very essence of 'execution' of the law." Which "law" does GRH require the Comptroller general to interpret? Is what the Comptroller General does in connection with that law comparable to what, say, a prosecutor does when enforcing the federal criminal code? What kind of judgments did the Comptroller General have to make under GRH to determine the funding level for federal programs? Is it clear why those judgments require the exercise of "executive" as opposed to judicial or legislative judgment?

To the extent that GRH requires the performance of "executive" functions, does it matter that OMB—an agent of the President—was involved from the beginning of the budget process, in drafting reports and estimates that formed the basis for the Comptroller General's report to the President? Does it matter that the sequestration order was issued by the President as a formal matter? Could the President decline to issue a sequestration order? Could the President insist on an order to the President's liking through control of the OMB?

In the Court's view, the Comptroller General's removal protections did not give him constitutionally adequate insulation from congressional control to be able to exercise an executive role: the terms "inefficiency," "neglect of duty," and "malfeasance" are "very broad and, as interpreted by Congress, could sustain removal of a Comptroller General for any number of actual or perceived transgressions of the legislative will." Is this a plausible interpretation of 31 U.S.C. § 703, which governs the Comptroller General's tenure in office? How does the Comptroller General differ from the head of a *Humphrey's Executor*-style independent agency? Isn't it clear that § 703 intends to give the Comptroller General the same degree of protection from removal as the head of an independent agency?

How does Justice Stevens' analysis of the GRH budget process differ from the Court's? Would Justice Stevens have struck the budget process established by GRH if Congress did not have the authority to remove the Comptroller General? If so, why?

5. **Implications of the Remedy.** Having concluded that the GRH budget process violates the separation of powers, the Court stayed its judgment for 60 days to give Congress the opportunity to implement the act's fallback provisions. Under those provisions, the OMB and CBO's budget estimates would be forwarded to a special joint committee of Congress rather than to the Comptroller General. The Committee would have five days to issue a report that specified across-the-board spending cuts to federal programs, which, when issued, would be entitled to expedited consideration in both houses of Congress. Is there a functional difference between the procedure struck down in *Bowsher* and the procedure created by the fallback provisions?

Note: Recent Developments in Congressional Control of Agency Action

Beginning in 2011, when Republicans took control of a majority of seats in the House of Representatives, a variety of measures have been proposed that would give Congress a more prominent role in the federal regulatory process. Consider the following:

1. The proposed REINS Act, H.R. 427, 114th Cong. 1st Sess., would prohibit a "major" agency rule, defined as one that had an annual effect on the economy of $100 million or more, from taking effect unless Congress specifically approved the rule via joint resolution. Under the Act, a joint resolution seeking approval of an agency rule would be entitled to expedited consideration in both the House and Senate. In general, the pertinent committee of the House or Senate would have fifteen days to report on whether it recommended approval of the rule. Once reported by a committee, an approval resolution would come to a vote within three days of its introduction, and would be protected from amendments.

Does the procedure contemplated by the REINS Act contravene the principles articulated in *Chadha* and *Bowsher* even though the vetoed regulation has yet to go into effect? *Compare, e.g.*, Ronald M. Levin, *The REINS Act: Unbridled Impediment to Regulation*, 83 Geo. Wash. L. Rev. 1446, 1468 (2015) (REINS Act is unconstitutional because it "accomplish[es] virtually the same result as the 'traditional' one-house veto"), *with* Jonathan H. Adler, *Placing "REINS" on Regulations: Assessing the Proposed REINS Act*, 16 N.Y.U. J. Legis. & Pub. Pol'y 1, 24 (2013) (constitutional concerns "unfounded," because Act observes "the formal requirements for legislation in Article I").

2. The proposed SCRUB Act, H.R. 1155, 114th Cong., 2d Sess. (passed by House, Jan. 7, 2016), would establish a Retrospective Regulatory Review Commission and charge it with reviewing the entire *Code of Federal Regulations* to identify agency rules that should be repealed to lower the cost of regulation. In identifying candidates for repeal, the new commission would be required to consider a rule's original purposes, whether the rule accomplishes those purposes effectively, whether the rule involves excessive compliance costs, and the extent to which the rule overlaps, duplicates, or conflicts with other federal, state, or local rules. Once the commission identified a rule for repeal, it could be repealed through a "cut-go" process which would require an agency to rescind an old regulation as a condition of promulgating a new one. Alternatively, regulations identified by the commission could be repealed via a joint resolution that would be entitled to expedited consideration in the House and Senate. Once Congress repealed a rule under the Act, agencies would be prohibited from reissuing "substantially similar" rules without Congress's approval and issuing a new rule that results in the same adverse effects of a repealed rule.

Does the SCRUB Act reflect a sensible approach to identifying regulations that should be repealed? In testimony on the Act, Professor Ronald Levin argued that the review commission, whose members would be appointed by House and Senate leaders, would not be a "credible authority." Commission members "would not need to be experts in anything, and they could not possibly be experts in all of the areas that they would have the power to affect. That power would be breathtaking."[1] Is this a persuasive criticism? Is there a significant difference between the powers exercised by

---

1. Washington University in St. Louis, Prof. Levin Testifies Before U.S. House Subcommittee on SCRUB Act, http://law.wustl.edu/news/pages.aspx?id=9996 (last visited Jan. 25, 2017).

a member of the review commission, on the one hand, and those exercised by a member of Congress, on the other? Is the prohibition of "substantially similar" rules issued without congressional permission valid under *Chadha*?

Executive Order 13,771 of January 30, 2017, 82 Fed. Reg. 9339, adopted a version of the "cut-go" process as a direction to agencies that are subject to Presidential oversight. Section 2(a) of the order provides that, "[u]nless prohibited by law, whenever an executive department or agency*** publicly proposes for notice and comment or otherwise promulgates a new regulation, it shall identify at least two existing regulations to be repealed." For OMB's guidance on EO 13,771, see https://www.white-house.gov/the-press-office/2017/04/05/memorandum-implementing-executive-order-13771-titled-reducing-regulation.

3. The proposed Regulatory Accountability Act, Title I of H.R. 5, 115th Cong., 1st Sess. (passed by House, Jan. 11, 2017), would require agencies to issue an "advance notice of proposed rulemaking" above and beyond the notice required by the Administrative Procedure Act, *see infra* Chapter 4[C], for any "major" or "high-impact" rule, a "negative-impact-on-jobs-and-wages rule," or a rule that involves a novel legal or policy issue. A "major rule" is defined as a rule that the White House Office of Information and Regulatory Affairs (OIRA), *see infra* Chapter 3[D][1], determines is likely to impose an annual cost on the economy of $100 million or more. A "high-impact rule" is one that OIRA determines is likely to have an annual cost on the economy of $1 billion or more. A "negative-impact-on-jobs-and-wages rule" is a one that is likely to reduce employment or wages in certain economic sectors or industry areas.

In the advance notice of rulemaking, an agency would be required to identify "the nature and significance of the problem the agency may address with a rule, including data and other evidence and information on which the agency expects to rely for the proposed rule"; "the legal authority under which a rule may be proposed, including whether a rule making is required by statute"; "in the case of a rule that involves a novel legal or policy issue arising out of statutory mandates, the nature of and potential reasons to adopt the novel legal or policy position upon which the agency may base a proposed rule"; and "an achievable objective for the rule and metrics by which the agency will measure progress toward that objective." Before issuing a high-impact rule, the agency would be required to hold a hearing at which agency decisionmakers could be cross-examined. The Accountability Act would require agencies to reassess the costs and benefits of rules subject to Act every five years.

4. The proposed ALERT Act, H.R.75, 115th Cong., 1st Sess. (introduced Jan. 3, 2017), would require agencies to publish monthly updates on the internet that identify the regulations the agency expects to issue in the coming year. The bill prohibits a regulation from taking effect until six months after such an update is published, subject to exceptions.

As Chapter 4 explains, the Administrative Procedure Act already requires agencies to give advance notice of rules, and provides that a rule may not go into effect until

30 days after it is published in the *Federal Register*. 5 U.S.C. § 553(d). What is the purpose of the ALERT Act's further requirement that agencies give updates about their rulemaking activity via the internet? Consider how the ALERT Act would interact with other bills mentioned in this note if they were enacted.

Given the difficulties Congress has in acting decisively and the exposure of legislators to lobbying from pressure groups, is the checking function contemplated by these proposed measures better performed by the President?

C. Congressional Control of Agency Action

The legislative veto and control over agency personnel are only two of the mechanisms available to Congress to influence the actions of agencies. In contrast to those two levers, most mechanisms of congressional control do not raise any serious constitutional concerns. The following sections introduce two such mechanisms — the appropriations and oversight processes.

1. Appropriations

Agencies, like other organizations, require money to function. Congress's control over appropriations thus gives it a powerful mechanism for influencing agency actions. The following report, prepared by an analyst of the Congressional Research Service, introduces the process that Congress, agencies, and the President follow to determine how agencies will be funded on a year-to-year basis.

The Congressional Appropriations Process: An Introduction

Sandy Streeter, Congressional Research Service (Feb. 22, 2007)

***When considering appropriations measures, Congress is exercising the power granted to it under the Constitution, which states, "No money shall be drawn from the Treasury, but in Consequence of Appropriations made by Law." The power to appropriate is a legislative power. Congress has enforced its prerogatives with laws setting limits on U.S. government officials. A U.S. government employee, for example, may not commit the government to spend more than the amount appropriated by law and may not make such government funding obligations before an appropriation funding those activities becomes law, unless such action is statutorily authorized. An appropriation may be used only for the programs and activities for which Congress made the appropriation, except as otherwise provided by law.

The President has an important role in the appropriations process by virtue of his constitutional power to approve or veto entire measures, unless Congress overrides a veto. He also has influence, in part, because of various duties imposed by statute, such as submitting an annual budget to Congress.

The House and Senate Committees on Appropriations have jurisdiction over the annual appropriations measures. At the beginning of the 110th Congress, both committees reorganized their subcommittees. Each committee now has 12 subcommittees and each subcommittee has jurisdiction over an annual appropriations measure that provides funding for departments and agencies under the subcommittee's jurisdiction.***

Annual Appropriations Cycle

President Submits Budget

The President initiates the appropriations process by submitting his annual budget for the upcoming fiscal year to Congress. He is required to submit his annual budget on or before the first Monday in February. Congress has, however, provided deadline extensions; both statutorily and, sometimes, informally.

The President recommends spending levels for various programs and agencies of the federal government in the form of budget authority (or BA) because Congress provides budget authority instead of cash to agencies. Budget authority is the authority provided by federal law to incur financial obligations that will result in immediate or future expenditures (or outlays) involving federal funds. Examples of financial obligations include entering into contracts to build a submarine or purchase supplies. The resulting outlays are payments from the Treasury, usually in the form of checks or electronic funds transfers.

An FY2006 appropriations act, for example, provided $1.6 billion in new budget authority for FY2006 to the Department of Defense (DOD) to build a nuclear attack submarine. That is, the act gave DOD legal authority to sign contracts to build the submarine. The department could not commit the government to pay more than $1.6 billion. The outlays occur when government payments are made to the contractor.

An appropriation is a type of budget authority that not only provides the authority to make obligations, but also gives the agency legal authority to make the subsequent payments from the Treasury. Appropriations must be obligated in the fiscal year(s) for which they are provided. Appropriations measures provide new budget authority (as opposed to previously enacted budget authority).

Not all new budget authority provided for a fiscal year is expended that year. For example, in the case of construction projects, the outlays may occur over several years as various stages of the project are completed.***

As Congress considers appropriations measures providing new budget authority for a particular fiscal year, discussions on the resulting outlays only involve estimates. Data on the actual outlays for a fiscal year are not available until the fiscal year has ended.

When the President submits his budget to Congress, each agency generally provides detailed *justification* materials to the House and Senate appropriations subcommittees with jurisdiction over its funding.

Congress Adopts Budget Resolution

The Congressional Budget and Impoundment Control Act of 1974, as amended, [Pub. L. No. 93-344, 88 Stat. 297, 2 U.S.C. §§ 601-688] (the Congressional Budget Act) requires Congress to adopt an annual budget resolution. The budget resolution is Congress's response to the President's budget. The budget resolution must cover at least five fiscal years: the upcoming fiscal year plus the four subsequent fiscal years.***

The budget resolution is never sent to the President, nor does it become law. It does not provide budget authority or raise or lower revenues; instead, it is a guide for the House and Senate as they consider various budget-related bills, including appropriations and tax measures. Both the House and Senate have established parliamentary rules to enforce some of these spending ceilings when appropriations measures are considered on the House or Senate floor, respectively.*** The Congressional Budget Act provides an April 15 deadline for final congressional adoption of the budget resolution. However, during the 31 fiscal years Congress has considered budget resolutions (FY1976–FY2006), Congress frequently did not meet this deadline. For three of those years (FY1999, FY2003, and FY2005), Congress never completed a budget resolution.***

The Congressional Budget Act prohibits House consideration of appropriations measures for the first fiscal year of the budget resolution until Congress completes the budget resolution. But, it provides an exception. Even if the budget resolution is not in place, the House may begin considering most appropriations measures after May 15. No similar exception exists in the Senate. If Congress delays completion of the annual budget resolution (or does not complete the resolution), each chamber may adopt a deeming resolution to address these procedural difficulties.

Timetable for Consideration of Appropriations Measures

Traditionally, the House of Representatives initiated consideration of appropriations measures and the Senate subsequently amended the House-passed bills. For the FY1998 through FY2005 regular appropriations bills, the Senate appropriations subcommittees and committee did not generally wait for the House bill; instead, they reported original Senate bills. Under this non-traditional approach, both House and Senate appropriations committees and their subcommittees were often considering the regular bills simultaneously. The Senate returned to the traditional practice, however, for the FY2006 and FY2007 regular appropriations bills.***

During the fall, the appropriations committees are usually heavily involved in conferences to resolve differences between the two chambers. Relatively little or no time is left before the fiscal year begins to resolve what may be wide disparities between the House and Senate, to say nothing of those between Congress and the President. Congress is usually faced with the need to enact one or more temporary continuing resolutions pending the final disposition of the regular appropriations bills.

Work of the Appropriations Committees

After the President submits his budget, the House and Senate appropriations sub-committees hold hearings on the segments of the budget under their jurisdiction. They focus on the details of the agencies' justifications, primarily obtaining testimony from agency officials.

After the hearings have been completed and the House and Senate appropriations committees have generally received their spending ceilings, the subcommittees begin to mark up the regular bills under their jurisdiction and report them to their respective full committees.***

House and Senate Floor Action

After the House or Senate appropriations committee reports an appropriations bill to the House or Senate, respectively, the bill is brought to the floor. At this point, Representatives or Senators are generally provided an opportunity to propose floor amendments to the bill.

House. Prior to floor consideration of a regular appropriations bill, the House generally considers a special rule reported by the House Committee on Rules setting parameters for floor consideration of the bill. If the House adopts the special rule, it usually considers the appropriations bill immediately.

The House considers the bill in the Committee of the Whole House on the State of the Union (or Committee of the Whole) of which all Representatives are members. A special rule on an appropriations bill usually provides for one hour of general debate on the bill. The debate includes opening statements by the chair and ranking minority member of the appropriations subcommittee with jurisdiction over the regular bill, as well as other interested Representatives.

After the Committee of the Whole debates the bill, it considers amendments. A regular appropriations bill is generally read for amendment, by paragraph.*** After the Committee of the Whole completes consideration of the measure, it rises (dissolves) and reports the bill with any adopted amendments to the full House. The House then votes on the adopted amendments and passage. After House passage, the bill is sent to the Senate.

Senate. The full Senate considers the bill as reported by its appropriations committee. The Senate does not utilize the device of a special rule to set parameters for consideration of bills. Before taking up the bill, however, or during its consideration, the Senate sometimes sets parameters by unanimous consent.***

Committee and floor amendments to the reported bills must meet requirements under the Senate standing rules and precedents, congressional budget process, authorization-appropriation process, as well as requirements agreed to by unanimous consent. The specifics of the Senate and House requirements differ, including the waiver procedures.

The Senate, in contrast to the House, does not consider floor amendments in the order of the bill. Senators may propose amendments to any portion of the bill at any time unless the Senate agrees to set limits.

House and Senate Conference Action

Generally, members of the House and Senate appropriations subcommittees having jurisdiction over a particular regular appropriations bill, and the chair and ranking minority members of the full committees meet to negotiate over differences between the House- and Senate-passed bills.

Under House and Senate rules, the negotiators (or conferees or managers) are generally required to remain within the scope of the differences between the positions of the two chambers. Their agreement must be within the range established by the House- and Senate-passed versions. For example, if the House-passed bill appropriates $3 million for a program and a separate Senate amendment provides $5 million, the conferees must reach an agreement that is within the $3–$5 million range. However, these rules are not always followed.

The Senate typically passes a single substitute amendment to each House bill. In such instances, the conferees must reach agreement on all points of difference between the House and Senate versions before reporting the conference report in agreement to both houses. When this occurs, the conferees propose a new conference substitute for the bill as a whole. The conferees attach a joint explanatory statement (or *managers' statement*) explaining the new substitute.

Usually, the House considers conference reports on appropriations measures first because it traditionally considers the measures first. The first house to consider a conference report has the option of voting to recommit the report to the conference for further consideration, rejecting the conference report, or adopting it. After the first house adopts the conference report, the conference is automatically disbanded; therefore, the second house has two options — adopt or reject the conference report. Conference reports cannot be amended in either the House or Senate.

If the conference report is rejected, or is recommitted by the first house, the conferees negotiate further over the matters in dispute between the two houses. The measure cannot be sent to the President until both houses have agreed to the entire text of the bill.

Presidential Action

After Congress sends the bill to the President, he has 10 days to sign or veto the measure. If he takes no action, the bill automatically becomes law at the end of the 10-day period. Conversely, if he takes no action when Congress has adjourned, he may pocket veto the bill.

If the President vetoes the bill, he sends it back to Congress. Congress may override the veto by a two-thirds vote in both houses. If Congress successfully overrides the veto, the bill becomes law. If Congress is unsuccessful, the bill dies.

Types of Appropriations Measures

There are three major types appropriations measures: regular appropriations bills, continuing resolutions, and supplementals. Of the three types, regular appropriations bills typically provide most of the funding.

Regular Appropriations Bills

The House and Senate annually consider several regular appropriations measures. Each House and Senate appropriations subcommittee has jurisdiction over one regular bill. Due to the House and Senate appropriations committees' recent reorganization, therefore, each chamber will consider 12 regular bills.

Regular appropriations bills contain a series of unnumbered paragraphs with headings; each is generally an account. The basic unit of appropriation is the account. Under these measures, funding for each department and large independent agency is distributed among several accounts. Each account, generally, includes similar programs, projects, or items, such as a "research and development" account or "salaries and expenses" account. For small agencies, a single account may fund all of the agency's activities. These acts typically provide a lump-sum amount for each of these accounts. A few accounts include a single program, project, or item, which the appropriations acts fund individually.

In report language, the House and Senate Committees on Appropriations provide more detailed directions to the department and agencies on the distribution of funding among various activities funded within an account. Funding for most local projects are included in report language, as opposed to the text of the appropriations bill.***

Congress has traditionally considered and approved each regular appropriations bill separately, but Congress has recently combined bills together. For 18 of the past 31 years (FY1977–FY2007), Congress packaged two or more regular appropriation bills together in one measure, or, in the case of FY2001, into two measures. These packages are referred to as omnibus measures or mini-bus measures. In these cases, Congress typically began consideration of each regular bill separately, but generally in conference combined some of the bills together. During conference on a single regular appropriations bill, the conferees typically included in the conference report final agreements on other outstanding regular appropriations bills, thereby creating an omnibus or minibus appropriations measure.***

Continuing Resolutions

Regular appropriations bills expire at the end of the fiscal year. If action on one or more regular appropriations measures has not been completed by the deadline, the agencies funded by these bills must cease nonessential activities due to lack of budget authority. Traditionally, continuing appropriations have been used to maintain temporary funding to agencies and programs until the regular bills are enacted. Such appropriations continuing funding are usually provided in a joint resolution, hence the term *continuing resolution* (or CR).

On or before the deadline, Congress and the President generally complete action on an initial continuing resolution that temporarily funds the outstanding regular appropriations bills. In contrast to funding practices in regular bills (i.e., providing appropriations for each account), temporary continuing resolutions generally provide funding by a rate and/or formula. Recently, the continuing resolutions have generally provided a rate at the levels provided in the previous fiscal year. The initial CR typically provides temporary funding until a specific date or until the enactment of the applicable regular appropriations acts, if earlier. Once the initial CR becomes law, additional interim continuing resolutions are frequently utilized to sequentially extend the expiration date. These subsequent continuing resolutions sometimes change the funding methods. Over the past 31 fiscal years, Congress has approved, on average, four continuing resolutions each year***.

Supplementals

Congress frequently considers one or more supplemental appropriations measures for a fiscal year that provide additional funds for specified activities. Supplementals may provide funding for unforeseen needs (such as funds to recover from a hurricane, earthquake or flood); or increase or provide funding for other activities. These measures, like regular appropriations bills, provide specific amounts of funding for individual accounts in the bill. Sometimes Congress includes supplemental appropriations in regular bills and continuing resolutions.***

Rescissions

Rescissions cancel previously enacted budget authority. To continue the earlier example, after Congress enacted the $1.6 billion to construct the submarine, it could enact legislation canceling the budget authority prior to its obligation. Rescissions are an expression of changed or differing priorities. They may also be used to offset increases in budget authority for other activities.

The President may recommend rescissions to Congress, but it is up to Congress to act on them. Under Title X of the Congressional Budget Act, Congress must enact a bill approving the President's rescissions within 45 days of *continuous session of Congress* or the budget authority must be spent.

In practice, this usually means that funds proposed for rescission not approved by Congress must be made available for obligation after about 60 calendar days, although the period can extend to 75 days or longer.

In response to the President's recommendation, Congress may decide not to approve the amount specified by the President, approve the total amount, or approve a different amount. In 2005, the President requested a rescission of $106 million from the Department of Defense (DOD), Operations and Maintenance, Defense-Wide account and $48.6 million from DOD, Research, Development, Test, and Evaluation, Army account. Congress provided a rescission of $80 million from the first account in the Department of Defense, Emergency Supplemental Appropriations to Address Hurricanes in the Gulf of Mexico, and Pandemic Influenza Act, 2006. The act did not provide a rescission from the second account.

Congress may also initiate rescissions. In the above act, Congress also initiated a rescission of $10 million from the Department of State, Diplomatic and Consular Programs account.

As budget authority providing the funding must be enacted into law, so, too, a rescission canceling the budget authority must be enacted into law. Rescissions can be included in either separate rescission measures or any of the three types of appropriations measures.

Notes and Questions

1. **The Importance of Appropriations to Agencies.** Appropriations are the lifeblood of agencies. As a legal matter, this results from Congress's control over federal spending under Article I, § 9 ("No money shall be drawn from the treasury, but in consequence of appropriations made by law . . . .") and a pair of federal statutes that limit agencies' authority to accept money from outside sources and make financial commitments that are not backed by an appropriation. The Miscellaneous Receipts Act, 31 U.S.C. § 3302, provides that unless otherwise directed by law, "an official or agent of the Government receiving money for the Government from any source shall deposit the money in the Treasury as soon as practicable without deduction for any charge or claim." The Anti-Deficiency Act, 31 U.S.C. § 1341, provides that an officer or employee of the government may not "(A) make or authorize an expenditure or obligation exceeding an amount available in an appropriation or fund for the expenditure or obligation" or "(B) involve [the] government in a contract or obligation for the payment of money before an appropriation is made unless authorized by law."

To what extent may an agency reallocate money that is appropriated for one purpose to another? 31 U.S.C. § 1301(a) provides: "Appropriations shall be applied only to the objects for which the appropriations were made except as otherwise provided by law." Section (d) provides: "A law may be construed to make an appropriation out of the Treasury or to authorize making a contract for the payment of money in excess of an appropriation only if the law *specifically states* that an appropriation is made or that such a contract may be made" (emphasis added). Under a separate statute, 31 U.S.C. § 1502, appropriations must generally be spent during the fiscal year for which they were appropriated. Appropriations bills ordinarily authorize the expenditure of funds as opposed to directing an agency to spend money, a feature that Presidents exploited to "impound" appropriated money. *See generally* L. Harold Levinson & Jon L. Mills, *Impoundment: A Search for Legal Principles*, 26 U. Fla. L. Rev. 191 (1974). The Congressional Budget and Impoundment Control Act of 1974, Pub. L. No. 93-344, 88 Stat. 297, sought to curtail the President's impoundment power by establishing guidelines governing the impoundment of funds appropriated by Congress. *See* 2 U.S.C. §§ 682–688.

Violations of the Miscellaneous Receipts Act are punishable by restitution and removal from office. 31 U.S.C. § 3302(d). Violations of the Anti-Deficiency Act are a criminal offense, punishable by two years' imprisonment and a $5,000 fine. 31 U.S.C. § 1350. Civil plaintiffs generally lack a "personal stake" in securing compliance with appropriations acts, and thus lack standing to challenge the misuse of appropriated money. *See Raines v. Byrd*, 521 U.S. 811, 830 (1997) (holding individual members of Congress lacked standing to challenge the Line Item Veto Act). *See generally* Chapter 5[A], *infra*. Nonetheless, the district court in *House of Representatives v. Burwell*, 130 F. Supp. 3d 53 (D.D.C. 2015), concluded that the House of Representatives had standing directly under the Appropriations Clause to challenge the Treasury Department's payment of cost-sharing subsidies to insurers that, the House alleged, were not authorized by the Affordable Care Act. The district court ruled for the House on the merits and enjoined Treasury from making further payments. *House of Representatives v. Burwell*, 185 F. Supp. 3d 165 (D.D.C. 2016), *stay granted* 2016 U.S. App. LEXIS 23584 (D.C. Cir. Dec. 5, 2016).

2. **"Mandatory" vs. "Discretionary" Funding.** Appropriations are divided into two categories: "mandatory" funding is provided by substantive legislation (called "authorizing" legislation within Congress) and does not have to be re-authorized from year to year. "Discretionary" funding is provided by annual appropriations acts and must be reauthorized year to year. In recent years, mandatory funding has accounted for at least 60% of the federal budget. It is used to fund the major entitlement programs, most notably Social Security and Medicare.

In addition to being funded through mandatory appropriations that are not subject to yearly re-authorization, an agency can be funded through fees that are exempt from the Miscellaneous Receipts Act. For example, the Federal Reserve is funded through assessments against member banks, as is the Public Company Accounting Oversight Board (PCAOB), the subject of *Free Enterprise Fund v. PCAOB*, discussed in the Notes following *Edmond*, Section [B][1][c], *supra*. More recently, the Dodd-Frank Act provided that the Consumer Financial Protection Bureau (CFPB), discussed in Note 8 following *Humphrey's Executor v. United States*, *supra* p. 311, was to receive funding from the Federal Reserve, according to a fixed formula set out in the Dodd-Frank Act. *See* 12 U.S.C. § 5497. To receive funding, the CFPB need only make a request to the New York branch of the Federal Reserve. For the Federal Reserve Board, the PCAOB, and the CFPB, there is no requirement of congressional appropriation. Even if an agency does not have an independent source of funding, it might be permitted to submit budget requests directly to Congress rather than through the Office of Management and Budget, which, as discussed below, coordinates the budget requests of many agencies.

From the perspective of an agency that is designed to operate independent of political interference, which is more desirable — *Humphrey's Executor*-style removal protection or independent funding authority? More likely to promote independence from Congress or the President? *See* Rachel Barkow, *Insulating Agencies: Avoiding Capture Through Institutional Design*, 89 Tex. L. Rev. 15, 42–44 (2010).

3. **Budget Justification.** Agencies that are funded through discretionary appropriations must submit a yearly "budget justification" to the pertinent appropriations subcommittee of the House and Senate. Budget justifications are elaborate works of

advocacy that seek to explain the agency's need for funding as persuasively as possible. For example, the Federal Trade Commission's 2015 budget justification contains 23 single-spaced pages cataloging "highlights" of the Commission's accomplishments in the prior fiscal year. *See* Federal Trade Commission, Fiscal Year 2015 Congressional Budget Justification 5-28.

4. **Dictating Agency Action through the Appropriations Process.** Can Congress direct specific agency actions through appropriations measures? In *United States v. Will*, 449 U.S. 200 (1980), a case involving "a statutorily defined formula for annual cost-of-living increases in the compensation of federal judges," the Supreme Court held that it would not distinguish between appropriations measures and non-appropriations measures for purposes of determining whether a statutory directive had the force of law. "[W]hen Congress desires to suspend or repeal a statute in force, [t]here can be no doubt that*** it could accomplish its purpose by an amendment to an appropriation bill, or otherwise." *Id.* at 222 (citations and internal punctuation omitted). The Court characterized *TVA v. Hill*, 437 U.S. 153 (1978), *supra* Chapter 2[B][2][a], as a case involving a "repeal by implication." Citing *TVA*, the Court said (449 U.S. at 221–22) that the rule against repeals by implication "applies with especial force when the provision advanced as the repealing measure was enacted in an appropriations bill."

In recent decades, it has become common for Congress to prohibit appropriated funds from being used for purposes or agency programs that Congress (or more realistically, the relevant appropriations subcommittee) disfavors. For example, § 538 of the Consolidated and Further Continuing Appropriations Act, 2015, Pub. L. No. 113-235, 128 Stat. 2130 (Dec. 26, 2014), provides:

> None of the funds made available in this Act to the Department of Justice may be used, with respect to the States of Alabama [thirty-one other states, and the District of Columbia], to prevent such States from implementing their own State laws that authorize the use, distribution, possession, or cultivation of medical marijuana.

Does this limitation prohibit federal criminal prosecutions for using or distributing marijuana under the Controlled Substances Act, 21 U.S.C. § 812, which classifies marijuana as a Schedule 1 substance, along with drugs such as LSD and heroin? The Justice Department under President Obama took the position that "§ 538 says nothing about prosecuting individual violators of the CSA, and it therefore does not expressly or implicitly bar the Department from prosecuting individuals who are in violation of federal law." United States' Opposition to Defendant Tote's Motion to Dismiss, *United States v. Tote*, No. 1:14-mj-00212-SAB (E.D. Cal. Apr. 29, 2015). The Ninth Circuit, however, concluded that § 538 prosecutions prevent states from giving "practical effect" to their medical marijuana laws. Therefore, the appropriations rider bars prosecutions for uses of medical marijuana that are permitted by state law. *United States v. McIntosh*, 833 F.3d 1163 (9th Cir. 2016).

Section 552 of the Department of Homeland Security Appropriations Act of 2010 similarly provides that "[n]one of the funds made available in this or any other Act may be used to release an individual who is detained, as of June 24, 2009, at Naval Station, Guantanamo Bay, Cuba, into the continental United States." Pub. L. No. 111-83, § 552, 123 Stat. 2142, 2177 (2010). Note that the prohibition on using funds to transfer Guantanamo bay detainees applied to "any*** Act" passed by Congress. Is it appropriate for Congress to shape policy in this way given that appropriations measures are often part of omnibus statutes providing funding for a wide variety of agencies and programs, and the President lacks line-item veto authority? *See Clinton v. City of New York*, 524 U.S. 417 (1998), Note 7 following *INS v. Chadha, supra* p. 333.

In addition to prohibiting particular activities, appropriations legislation may direct that appropriated funds be used for particular purposes. Such directives are often contained not in a statute that becomes law, but in a committee report that accompanies an appropriations act. Committee reports also contain reporting instructions that, for example, require an agency to file a report with the pertinent congressional committees after expending appropriated funds. At times, committee reports direct agencies to consult with a committee or subcommittee prior to spending funds on a particular project.

It is well-established that such directives lack the force of law. "[W]here Congress merely appropriates lump-sum amounts without statutorily restricting what can be done with those funds, a clear inference arises that it does not intend to impose legally binding restrictions, and indicia in committee reports and other legislative history as to how the funds should or are expected to be spent do not establish any legal requirements on the agency." *Lincoln v. Vigil*, 508 U.S. 182, 192 (1993) (internal punctuation omitted). Nevertheless, "agencies make special efforts to catalogue and track all such statutory language." John C. Roberts, *Are Congressional Committees Constitutional?: Radical Textualism, Separation of Powers, and the Enactment Process*, 52 CASE W. RES. L. REV. 489, 562–63 (2001).

The most dramatic form of control that Congress can exercise in an appropriations act is to defund an agency entirely. A favorite target for defunding is the National Labor Relations Board. In the past decade, dozens of bills have been introduced that would have eliminated all funding for the Board. While *NLRB v. Noel Canning* was before the Supreme Court (see note 11 following *Edmond vs. United States, supra*), the House passed a bill that would have shut down the NLRB pending the Supreme Court's decision. *See* Preventing Greater Uncertainty in Labor-Management Relations Act, H.R. 1120, 113th Cong. (2013). Do threats to defund an agency have an effect, if perhaps subliminal, on the actions the agency is willing to undertake? A Former Acting General Counsel of the NLRB denied they do. *See* Lafe Solomon, *Administering Labor Law in Political Turbulence*, 34 BERKELEY J. EMP. & LAB. L. 273, 282 (2013).

5. *TVA v. Hill* **Revisited.** Recall the Court's statements in *TVA v. Hill* that (a) "[t]he doctrine disfavoring repeals by implication 'applies with full vigor [when] the subsequent legislation is an appropriations measure,'" and (b) "[e]xpressions of committees dealing with requests for appropriations cannot be equated with statutes enacted

by Congress." (*Supra*, p. 169.) Having considered the appropriations process in more detail, do these statements reflect the way in which the appropriations process in fact functions? What explains the Court's willingness to enforce appropriations *riders*— language in appropriation acts that modifies obligations created by substantive legislation? Given the way in which such riders are enacted and the difficulty Presidents have vetoing omnibus appropriations measures that contain such riders, should they be narrowly construed? Presumed not to modify or repeal inconsistent legislation? On what grounds?

2. Oversight

The power of the purse may be Congress's most important lever for controlling agency action, but it is not the only one. In addition to funding agencies, Congress exercises constitutional and statutory authority to investigate agencies and publicize their actions. The following case, which arose out of the Teapot Dome scandal, sheds light on some aspects of this "oversight" function.

McGrain v. Daugherty

273 U.S. 135 (1927)

MR. JUSTICE VAN DEVANTER delivered the opinion of the court.

This is an appeal from the final order in a proceeding in habeas corpus discharging a recusant witness held in custody under process of attachment issued from the United States Senate in the course of an investigation which it was making of the administration of the Department of Justice.***

Harry M. Daugherty became the Attorney General March 5, 1921, and held that office until March 28, 1924, when he resigned. Late in that period various charges of misfeasance and nonfeasance in the Department of Justice after he became its supervising head were brought to the attention of the Senate by individual senators and made the basis of an insistent demand that the department be investigated to the end that the practices and deficiencies which, according to the charges, were operating to prevent or impair its right administration might be definitely ascertained and that appropriate and effective measures might be taken to remedy or eliminate the evil. The Senate regarded the charges as grave and requiring legislative attention and action. Accordingly it formulated, passed and invited the House of Representatives to pass (and that body did pass) two measures taking important litigation then in immediate contemplation out of the control of the Department of Justice and placing the same in charge of special counsel to be appointed by the President; and also adopted a resolution authorizing and directing a select committee of five senators—

> "to investigate circumstances and facts, and report the same to the Senate, concerning the alleged failure of Harry M. Daugherty, Attorney General of the United States, to prosecute properly violators of the Sherman Anti-trust Act and the Clayton Act against monopolies and unlawful restraint of trade;

the alleged neglect and failure of the said Harry M. Daugherty, Attorney General of the United States, to arrest and prosecute Albert B. Fall, Harry F. Sinclair, E.L. Doheny, C.R. Forbes, and their co-conspirators in defrauding the Government, as well as the alleged neglect and failure of the said Attorney General to arrest and prosecute many others for violations of Federal statutes, and his alleged failure to prosecute properly, efficiently, and promptly, and to defend, all manner of civil and criminal actions wherein the Government of the United States is interested as a party plaintiff or defendant. And said committee is further directed to inquire into, investigate and report to the Senate the activities of the said Harry M. Daugherty, Attorney General, and any of his assistants in the Department of Justice which would in any manner tend to impair their efficiency or influence as representatives of the Government of the United States."

The resolution also authorized the committee to send for books and papers, to subpoena witnesses, to administer oaths, and to sit at such times and places as it might deem advisable.

In the course of the investigation the committee issued and caused to be duly served on Mally S. Daugherty—who was a brother of Harry M. Daugherty and president of the Midland National Bank of Washington Court House, Ohio,—a subpoena commanding him to appear before the committee for the purpose of giving testimony bearing on the subject under investigation, and to bring with him the "deposit ledgers of the Midland National Bank since November 1, 1920; also note files and transcript of owners of every safety vault; also records of income drafts; also records of any individual account or accounts showing withdrawals of amounts of $25,000 or over during above period." The witness failed to appear.

A little later in the course of the investigation the committee issued and caused to be duly served on the same witness another subpoena commanding him to appear before it for the purpose of giving testimony relating to the subject under consideration—nothing being said in this subpoena about bringing records, books or papers. The witness again failed to appear; and no excuse was offered by him for either failure.

The committee then made a report to the Senate stating that the subpoenas had been issued, that according to the officer's returns—copies of which accompanied the report—the witness was personally served; and that he had failed and refused to appear. After a reading of the report, the Senate adopted a resolution reciting these facts and proceeding as follows:

"Whereas the appearance and testimony of the said M.S. Daugherty is material and necessary in order that the committee may properly execute the functions imposed upon it and may obtain information necessary as a basis for such legislative and other action as the Senate may deem necessary and proper: Therefore be it

"Resolved, That the President of the Senate pro tempore issue his warrant commanding the Sergeant at Arms or his deputy to take into custody the body of the said M.S. Daugherty wherever found, and to bring the said M.S. Daugherty before the bar of the Senate, then and there to answer such questions pertinent to the matter under inquiry as the Senate may order the President of the Senate pro tempore to propound; and to keep the said M.S. Daugherty in custody to await the further order of the Senate."***

The warrant was issued agreeably to the resolution and was addressed simply to the Sergeant at Arms. That officer on receiving the warrant endorsed thereon a direction that it be executed by John J. McGrain, already his deputy, and delivered it to him for execution.

The deputy, proceeding under the warrant, took the witness into custody at Cincinnati, Ohio, with the purpose of bringing him before the bar of the Senate as commanded; whereupon the witness petitioned the federal district court in Cincinnati for a writ of habeas corpus. The writ was granted and the deputy made due return setting forth the warrant and the cause of the detention. After a hearing the court held the attachment and detention unlawful and discharged the witness, the decision being put on the ground that the Senate in directing the investigation and in ordering the attachment exceeded its powers under the Constitution, 299 Fed. 620. The deputy prayed and was allowed a direct appeal to this Court under § 238 of the Judicial Code as then existing.***

The first of the principal questions—the one which the witness particularly presses on our attention—is, as before shown, whether the Senate—or the House of Representatives, both being on the same plane in this regard—has power, through its own process, to compel a private individual to appear before it or one of its committees and give testimony needed to enable it efficiently to exercise a legislative function belonging to it under the Constitution.

The Constitution provides for a Congress consisting of a Senate and House of Representatives and invests it with "all legislative powers" granted to the United States, and with power "to make all laws which shall be necessary and proper" for carrying into execution these powers and "all other powers" vested by the Constitution in the United States or in any department or officer thereof. Art. I, secs 1, 8. Other provisions show that, while bills can become laws only after being considered and passed by both houses of Congress, each house is to be distinct from the other, to have its own officers and rules, and to exercise its legislative function independently. Art. I, secs. 2, 3, 5, 7. But there is no provision expressly investing either house with power to make investigations and exact testimony to the end that it may exercise its legislative function advisedly and effectively. So the question arises whether this power is so far incidental to the legislative function as to be implied.

In actual legislative practice power to secure needed information by such means has long been treated as an attribute of the power to legislate. It was so regarded in the British Parliament and in the Colonial legislatures before the American Revolution;

and a like view has prevailed and been carried into effect in both houses of Congress and in most of the state legislatures.***

We are of opinion that the power of inquiry—with process to enforce it—is an essential and appropriate auxiliary to the legislative function. It was so regarded and employed in American legislatures before the Constitution was framed and ratified. Both houses of Congress took this view of it early in their history—the House of Representatives with the approving votes of Mr. Madison and other members whose service in the convention which framed the Constitution gives special significance to their action—and both houses have employed the power accordingly up to the present time.***

We are further of opinion that the provisions are not of doubtful meaning, but, as was held by this Court in the cases we have reviewed, are intended to be effectively exercised, and therefore to carry with them such auxiliary powers as are necessary and appropriate to that end. While the power to exact information in aid of the legislative function was not involved in [earlier] cases, the rule of interpretation applied there is applicable here. A legislative body cannot legislate wisely or effectively in the absence of information respecting the conditions which the legislation is intended to affect or change; and where the legislative body does not itself possess the requisite information—which not infrequently is true—recourse must be had to others who do possess it. Experience has taught that mere requests for such information often are unavailing, and also that information which is volunteered is not always accurate or complete; so some means of compulsion are essential to obtain what is needed. All this was true before and when the Constitution was framed and adopted. In that period the power of inquiry—with enforcing process—was regarded and employed as a necessary and appropriate attribute of the power to legislate—indeed, was treated as inhering in it. Thus there is ample warrant for thinking, as we do, that the constitutional provisions which commit the legislative function to the two houses are intended to include this attribute to the end that the function may be effectively exercised.

The contention is earnestly made on behalf of the witness that this power of inquiry, if sustained, may be abusively and oppressively exerted. If this be so, if affords no ground for denying the power. The same contention might be directed against the power to legislate, and of course would be unavailing. We must assume, for present purposes, that neither house will be disposed to exert the power beyond its proper bounds, or without due regard to the rights of witnesses.***

We come now to the question whether it sufficiently appears that the purpose for which the witness's testimony was sought was to obtain information in aid of the legislative function. The court below answered the question in the negative[.]*** We are of opinion that the court's ruling on this question was wrong, and that it sufficiently appears, when the proceedings are rightly interpreted, that the object of the investigation and of the effort to secure the witness's testimony was to obtain information for legislative purposes.

It is quite true that the resolution directing the investigation does not in terms avow that it is intended to be in aid of legislation; but it does show that the subject to be investigated was the administration of the Department of Justice—whether its functions were being properly discharged or were being neglected or misdirected, and particularly whether the Attorney General and his assistants were performing or neglecting their duties in respect of the institution and prosecution of proceedings to punish crimes and enforce appropriate remedies against the wrongdoers—specific instances of alleged neglect being recited. Plainly the subject was one on which legislation could be had and would be materially aided by the information which the investigation was calculated to elicit. This becomes manifest when it is reflected that the functions of the Department of Justice, the powers and duties of the Attorney General and the duties of his assistants, are all subject to regulation by congressional legislation, and that the department is maintained and its activities are carried on under such appropriations as in the judgment of Congress are needed from year to year.***

We think the resolution and proceedings give no warrant for thinking the Senate was attempting or intending to try the Attorney General at its bar or before its committee for any crime or wrongdoing. Nor do we think it a valid objection to the investigation that it might possibly disclose crime or wrongdoing on his part.***

We conclude that the investigation was ordered for a legitimate object; that the witness wrongfully refused to appear and testify before the committee and was lawfully attached; that the Senate is entitled to have him give testimony pertinent to the inquiry, either at its bar or before the committee; and that the district court erred in discharging him from custody under the attachment.

Notes and Questions

1. **Origins of the Dispute.** *McGrain* arose out of the Teapot Dome scandal—until Watergate, perhaps the greatest scandal in the history of American politics. Prompted by the Navy's switch from coal-powered ships to those powered by oil, President Warren Harding in 1921 issued an order transferring control of three oil fields, including the Teapot Dome field in Natrona, Wyoming, from the Department of the Navy to the Department of the Interior. The next year, Secretary of Interior Albert Fall leased production rights for Teapot Dome to Harry Sinclair, the founder of the Sinclair Oil Corporation, and the rights for two others fields to oilmen who were personal friends of Fall. In awarding the leases, Fall did not comply with the Mineral Leasing Act of 1920, 41 Stat. 437, ch. 85, § 1, which required that production rights be awarded through competitive bidding. Thereafter, Sinclair and other beneficiaries of no-bid leases made large personal loans and gifts to Secretary Fall. A Wall Street Journal article drew attention to the process through which the leases were awarded, and on April 15, 1922, Senator John B. Kendrick (D-WY), introduced the first of many resolutions calling for investigations of the Harding administration's actions. The resulting investigations caused enormous controversy, as Fall attempted to cover up evidence of the kickbacks he received. In 1929, he was finally convicted of receiving bribes and sentenced to one year of imprisonment.

The specific congressional investigation at issue in *McGrain* focused on Attorney General Harry Daughtery's actions in connection with the Teapot Dome scandal. Daughtery did not prosecute Fall, Sinclair, or the lessees of the two other fields involved in the scandal. The Senate's investigation sought to discover whether Daughtery was involved in the illegal transactions, and whether he declined to prosecute Fall for political reasons.

2. **Posture of the Dispute.** The event that precipitated the *McGrain* suit was the arrest of Attorney General Daugherty's brother Mally pursuant to a resolution of the Senate. Why did the Senate want Mally to testify? How did Mally obtain judicial review of the lawfulness of his arrest? What did the court below conclude?

3. **Why Can Congress Compel Testimony from Private Individuals?** The first issue the Court addresses in *McGrain* is whether a house of Congress has authority to compel the testimony of private individuals when investigating the actions of a government agency. What reasons did the Court give for answering affirmatively? What is the constitutional basis for Congress's authority in this area? In the Court's view, does the extent of Congress's authority vary depending on the public or private status of a person from whom it demands information?

The Court is unmoved by Daugherty's argument that Congress's "power of inquiry*** may be abusively and oppressively exerted." In a portion of the opinion not excerpted above, the Court refers to *Kilbourn v. Thompson*, 103 U.S. 168 (1881), and *Marshall v. Gordon*, 243 U.S. 521 (1917), as examples of Congress' use of its subpoena power. *Kilbourn* considered the scope of material that could be discovered by a House committee and concluded that the committee could investigate only matters relevant to a subject over which it exercised jurisdiction. Neither house of Congress possessed "a general power of making inquiry into the private affairs of the citizen." Moreover, Congress's investigative power did not extend to "a matter wherein relief or redress could be had only by a judicial proceeding." In *Kilbourn* itself, the Court evaluated the "resolution under which the committee acted" to determine that it had crossed the line and conducted an impermissible inquiry.

The question in *Marshall* was whether the House had authority to punish the author of an "ill-tempered" letter, "which was well calculated to arouse the indignation not only of the members of the subcommittee but of those of the House generally." The Court concluded that while the House generally has authority to punish persons who interfere with its business, the author of the letter did not fall within this category. The letter did not interfere with the House's business, but merely produced a "sense of indignation" in representatives and the mind of the public.

Do these cases meaningfully constrain Congress's investigative powers? Suppose you were advising a House or Senate committee whose members expressed a desire to reveal the inner workings of a politically unpopular company. What steps would the committee need to take to ensure that it did not violate *Marshall* and *Kilbourn*?

McGrain also invoked *In re Chapman*, 166 U.S. 661 (1897). There, the Court rejected a constitutional challenge to a statute that made the refusal to testify before Congress a criminal offense. Upholding Chapman's conviction under the statute, the Court concluded that a resolution directing a witness to testify need not identify the "legislative function" Congress was carrying out in express terms. If a "legitimate object" could be inferred from the questions put to the witness, Congress would be presumed to be acting within the scope of its authority.

4. **When Is an Investigation "In Aid of the Legislative Function"?** The second issue *McGrain* addresses is the standard for determining whether an investigation is "in aid of the legislative function," the basic standard of relevancy established in *Kilbourn*. Why did the court below determine that the subpoena directed at Mally Daugherty was not in aid of the legislative function? Why did the Supreme Court reject that conclusion? According to the Supreme Court, when is a congressional effort to secure testimony in aid of the legislative function? Why was that standard satisfied with respect to Mally?

5. **Privileges.** As a practical matter, the most important constraint on Congress's ability to obtain information is not the scope of its investigative power (which *McGrain* shows to be very broad) but testimonial privileges. The question of privilege did not arise in *McGrain*, because Mally had not yet been questioned by the House and the House had withdrawn its demand that he produce records, books and papers of the Midland National Bank. But in cases where a witness appears in a congressional investigation, the witness frequently resists testifying or handing over information on the ground that Congress has asked for something that is privileged.

Perhaps the most important privilege in congressional investigations is the Fifth Amendment privilege against self-incrimination. That privilege may be asserted "when there is reasonable apprehension on the part of the witness that his answer would furnish some evidence upon which he could be convicted of a criminal offense*** or which would reveal sources from which evidence could be obtained that would lead to such conviction or to prosecution therefor.*** Once it has become apparent that the answers to a question would expose a witness to the danger of conviction or prosecution, wider latitude is permitted the witness in refusing to answer other questions." *United States v. Jaffee*, 98 F. Supp. 191, 193–94 (D.D.C. 1951). Congress may overcome the privilege by conferring use immunity on a witness through a procedure outlined in 18 U.S.C. § 6002, et seq. If a witness refuses to testify on the ground of the privilege, an authorized representative of the House or Senate may apply to the federal district court for an order compelling the witness's testimony. After the court issues the order, the witness may no longer refuse to testify on the grounds of privilege. Any information that the witness reveals may not be used to prosecute her. *See* § 6002.

The statutory privilege confers a use immunity, not a transactional immunity. Thus, the statutory immunity does not prevent the Justice Department from prosecuting a witness based on evidence obtained through other means. To facilitate such prosecutions, the Attorney General is notified when Congress petitions the district court for an immunity order. The government's evidence against the witness at that point is filed under seal, establishing that it was not derived from the witness's congressional testimony. *Id.* § 6005(a). On the government's difficulty in making such proof, see, e.g., *United States v. North*, 910 F.2d 843 (D.C. Cir. 1990).

The attorney-client and work product privileges also figure prominently in many congressional investigations. The decision to honor these privileges rests in the discretion of the investigating committee, and is not controlled by court precedents. "In practice, committee resolutions of claims of these privileges have involved a pragmatic assessment of the needs of the individual committee to accomplish its legislative mission and the potential burdens and harms that may be imposed on a claimant of the privilege if it is denied." Morton Rosenberg, Investigative Oversight: An Introduction to the Law, Practice, and Procedure of Congressional Inquiry 32 (Cong. Res. Serv., Apr. 7, 1995).

In investigations of the President and executive branch agencies, the target of a congressional inquiry may also invoke "executive privilege"—a claimed right to confidentiality implied from the Constitution. In *United States v. Nixon*, 418 U.S. 683 (1974), the Supreme Court held that while the President's communications with close advisors are presumptively privileged, the privilege could be overcome by showing that information within the President's possession—in *Nixon*, the President's famous tape-recordings of oval office phone calls and conversations—is needed to prosecute a case or controversy. Though *Nixon* recognizes the existence of some form of executive privilege, the Supreme Court has never addressed a claim of executive privilege in a congressional investigation. Most such disputes are instead settled through informal negotiations between Congress and the President. Where courts have been asked to resolve claims of executive privilege arising out of a congressional investigation, they have been extremely reluctant to rule on the merits. *See, e.g., United States v. AT&T*, 551 F.2d 384 (D.C. Cir. 1976) (remanding with directions that the district court supervise negotiations between the executive branch and Congress over the scope of discoverable information); *United States v. AT&T*, 567 F.2d 121 (D.C. Cir. 1977) (remanding for further negotiations under a procedure devised by the Court of Appeals).

6. **The Scale of Congressional Oversight.** *McGrain* illustrates Congress's power of investigation. Through oversight hearings, Congress can investigate the operation of the government to determine, inter alia, whether the law is being implemented consistently with congressional intent and assess the need for new legislation. A large number of committees and sub-committees have oversight responsibilities. *See* Jack M. Beermann, *Congressional Administration*, 43 SAN DIEGO L. REV. 61, 124 (2006).

7. **Relief Against Legislative Abuse?** Because of the Speech and Debate Clause protection and doctrines of official immunity, it is difficult to obtain redress for abuse by a legislator. *See, e.g. McSurely v. McClellan*, 753 F.2d 88 (D.C. Cir. 1985).

D. Presidential Control of Agency Action

Congress, of course, is not the only institution with power to oversee agencies' actions. The majority of agencies are legally part of the Executive Branch and thus subject to formal control by the President. Even nominally "independent" agencies are susceptible to the President's influence, through a mix of legal and informal mechanisms. The following sections introduce these mechanisms.

1. Formal Oversight

Perhaps the most important mechanism of presidential control is the President's power, through the Office of Management and Budget (OMB) and OMB's Office of Information and Regulatory Affairs (OIRA), to vet agency regulations before they take effect. As discussed below, agencies can implement legislative policy through rule-making (i.e., by promulgating regulations having the force of law); through adjudication; and through more informal practices such as providing guidance to regulated industries. Before an executive department or agency promulgates a rule, it must clear the process established in the following Executive Order, giving the White House a powerful opportunity to affect the final form of the regulation.

Executive Order 12866 of September 30, 1993

Regulatory Planning and Review

***[B]y the authority vested in me as President by the Constitution and the laws of the United States of America, it is hereby ordered as follows:

Section 1. Statement of Regulatory Philosophy and Principles.

(a) *The Regulatory Philosophy*. Federal agencies should promulgate only such regulations as are required by law, are necessary to interpret the law, or are made necessary by compelling public need, such as material failures of private markets to protect or improve the health and safety of the public, the environment, or the well-being of the American people. In deciding whether and how to regulate, agencies should assess all costs and benefits of available regulatory alternatives, including the alternative of not regulating. Costs and benefits shall be understood to include both quantifiable measures (to the fullest extent that these can be usefully estimated) and qualitative measures of costs and benefits that are difficult to quantify, but nevertheless essential to consider. Further, in choosing among alternative regulatory approaches, agencies should select those approaches that maximize net benefits (including potential economic, environmental, public health and safety, and other advantages; distributive impacts; and equity), unless a statute requires another regulatory approach.

(b) *The Principles of Regulation*. To ensure that the agencies' regulatory programs are consistent with the philosophy set forth above, agencies should adhere to the following principles, to the extent permitted by law and where applicable:

(1) Each agency shall identify the problem that it intends to address (including, where applicable, the failures of private markets or public institutions that warrant new agency action) as well as assess the significance of that problem.

(2) Each agency shall examine whether existing regulations (or other law) have created, or contributed to, the problem that a new regulation is intended to correct and whether those regulations (or other law) should be modified to achieve the intended goal of regulation more effectively.

(3) Each agency shall identify and assess available alternatives to direct regulation, including providing economic incentives to encourage the desired behavior, such as user fees or marketable permits, or providing information upon which choices can be made by the public.

(4) In setting regulatory priorities, each agency shall consider, to the extent reasonable, the degree and nature of the risks posed by various substances or activities within its jurisdiction.

(5) When an agency determines that a regulation is the best available method of achieving the regulatory objective, it shall design its regulations in the most cost-effective manner to achieve the regulatory objective. In doing so, each agency shall consider incentives for innovation, consistency, predictability, the costs of enforcement and compliance (to the government, regulated entities, and the public), flexibility, distributive impacts, and equity.

(6) Each agency shall assess both the costs and the benefits of the intended regulation and, recognizing that some costs and benefits are difficult to quantify, propose or adopt a regulation only upon a reasoned determination that the benefits of the intended regulation justify its costs.

(7) Each agency shall base its decisions on the best reasonably obtainable scientific, technical, economic, and other information concerning the need for, and consequences of, the intended regulation.

(8) Each agency shall identify and assess alternative forms of regulation and shall, to the extent feasible, specify performance objectives, rather than specifying the behavior or manner of compliance that regulated entities must adopt.

(9) Wherever feasible, agencies shall seek views of appropriate State, local, and tribal officials before imposing regulatory requirements that might significantly or uniquely affect those governmental entities. Each agency shall assess the effects of Federal regulations on State, local, and tribal governments, including specifically the availability of resources to carry out those mandates, and seek to minimize those burdens that uniquely or significantly affect such governmental entities, consistent with achieving regulatory objectives. In addition, as appropriate, agencies shall seek to harmonize Federal regulatory actions with related State, local, and tribal regulatory and other governmental functions.

(10) Each agency shall avoid regulations that are inconsistent, incompatible, or duplicative with its other regulations or those of other Federal agencies.

(11) Each agency shall tailor its regulations to impose the least burden on society, including individuals, businesses of differing sizes, and other entities (including small

communities and governmental entities), consistent with obtaining the regulatory objectives, taking into account, among other things, and to the extent practicable, the costs of cumulative regulations.

(12) Each agency shall draft its regulations to be simple and easy to understand, with the goal of minimizing the potential for uncertainty and litigation arising from such uncertainty.

Section 2. *Organization.* An efficient regulatory planning and review process is vital to ensure that the Federal Government's regulatory system best serves the American people.

(a) *The Agencies.* Because Federal agencies are the repositories of significant substantive expertise and experience, they are responsible for developing regulations and assuring that the regulations are consistent with applicable law, the President's priorities, and the principles set forth in this Executive order.

(b) *The Office of Management and Budget.* Coordinated review of agency rulemaking is necessary to ensure that regulations are consistent with applicable law, the President's priorities, and the principles set forth in this Executive order, and that decisions made by one agency do not conflict with the policies or actions taken or planned by another agency. The Office of Management and Budget (OMB) shall carry out that review function. Within OMB, the Office of Information and Regulatory Affairs (OIRA) is the repository of expertise concerning regulatory issues, including methodologies and procedures that affect more than one agency, this Executive order, and the President's regulatory policies. To the extent permitted by law, OMB shall provide guidance to agencies and assist the President, the Vice President, and other regulatory policy advisors to the President in regulatory planning and shall be the entity that reviews individual regulations, as provided by this Executive order.***

Section 3. *Definitions.****

(b) "Agency," unless otherwise indicated, means any authority of the United States that is an "agency" under 44 U.S.C. 3502(1),[a] other than those considered to be independent regulatory agencies, as defined in 44 U.S.C. 3502(10).[b]***

---

a. 44 U.S.C. § 3502(1) provides:
   (1) the term "agency" means any executive department, military department, Government corporation, Government controlled corporation, or other establishment in the executive branch of the Government (including the Executive Office of the President), or any independent regulatory agency, but does not include—
      (A) the Government Accountability Office;
      (B) Federal Election Commission;
      (C) the governments of the District of Columbia and of the territories and possessions of the United States, and their various subdivisions; or
      (D) Government-owned contractor-operated facilities, including laboratories engaged in national defense research and production activities[.]
   —Eds.
b. 44 U.S.C. § 3502(5) (previously § 3502(10)) provides:
   (5) the term "independent regulatory agency" means the Board of Governors of the Federal Reserve System, the Commodity Futures Trading Commission, the Consumer Product Safety

(d) "Regulation" or "rule" means an agency statement of general applicability and future effect, which the agency intends to have the force and effect of law, that is designed to implement, interpret, or prescribe law or policy or to describe the procedure or practice requirements of an agency.

(e) "Regulatory action" means any substantive action by an agency (normally published in the Federal Register) that promulgates or is expected to lead to the promulgation of a final rule or regulation, including notices of inquiry, advance notices of proposed rulemaking, and notices of proposed rulemaking.

(f) "Significant regulatory action" means any regulatory action that is likely to result in a rule that may:

> (1) Have an annual effect on the economy of $100 million or more or adversely affect in a material way the economy, a sector of the economy, productivity, competition, jobs, the environment, public health or safety, or State, local, or tribal governments or communities;

> (2) Create a serious inconsistency or otherwise interfere with an action taken or planned by another agency;

> (3) Materially alter the budgetary impact of entitlements, grants, user fees, or loan programs or the rights and obligations of recipients thereof; or

> (4) Raise novel legal or policy issues arising out of legal mandates, the President's priorities, or the principles set forth in this Executive order.

Section 4. *Planning Mechanism.* In order to have an effective regulatory program, to provide for coordination of regulations, to maximize consultation and the resolution of potential conflicts at an early stage, to involve the public and its State, local, and tribal officials in regulatory planning, and to ensure that new or revised regulations promote the President's priorities and the principles set forth in this Executive order, these procedures shall be followed, to the extent permitted by law:

(a) *Agencies' Policy Meeting.* Early in each year's planning cycle, the Vice President shall convene a meeting of the Advisors and the heads of agencies to seek a common understanding of priorities and to coordinate regulatory efforts to be accomplished in the upcoming year.

(b) *Unified Regulatory Agenda.* For purposes of this subsection, the term "agency" or "agencies" shall also include those considered to be independent regulatory agencies,

---

Commission, the Federal Communications Commission, the Federal Deposit Insurance Corporation, the Federal Energy Regulatory Commission, the Federal Housing Finance Agency, the Federal Maritime Commission, the Federal Trade Commission, the Interstate Commerce Commission, the Mine Enforcement Safety and Health Review Commission, the National Labor Relations Board, the Nuclear Regulatory Commission, the Occupational Safety and Health Review Commission, the Postal Regulatory Commission, the Securities and Exchange Commission, the Bureau of Consumer Financial Protection, the Office of Financial Research, Office of the Comptroller of the Currency, and any other similar agency designated by statute as a Federal independent regulatory agency or commission[.]
— Eds.

as defined in 44 U.S.C. 3502(10). Each agency shall prepare an agenda of all regulations under development or review, at a time and in a manner specified by the Administrator of OIRA. The description of each regulatory action shall contain, at a minimum, a regulation identifier number, a brief summary of the action, the legal authority for the action, any legal deadline for the action, and the name and telephone number of a knowledgeable agency official.***

(c) *The Regulatory Plan.* For purposes of this subsection, the term "agency" or "agencies" shall also include those considered to be independent regulatory agencies, as defined in 44 U.S.C. 3502(10).

(1) As part of the Unified Regulatory Agenda, beginning in 1994, each agency shall prepare a Regulatory Plan (Plan) of the most important significant regulatory actions that the agency reasonably expects to issue in proposed or final form in that fiscal year or thereafter. The Plan shall be approved personally by the agency head and shall contain at a minimum:

(A) A statement of the agency's regulatory objectives and priorities and how they relate to the President's priorities;

(B) A summary of each planned significant regulatory action including, to the extent possible, alternatives to be considered and preliminary estimates of the anticipated costs and benefits;

(C) A summary of the legal basis for each such action, including whether any aspect of the action is required by statute or court order;

(D) A statement of the need for each such action and, if applicable, how the action will reduce risks to public health, safety, or the environment, as well as how the magnitude of the risk addressed by the action relates to other risks within the jurisdiction of the agency;

(E) The agency's schedule for action, including a statement of any applicable statutory or judicial deadlines; and

(F) The name, address, and telephone number of a person the public may contact for additional information about the planned regulatory action.

(2) Each agency shall forward its Plan to OIRA by June 1st of each year.

(3) Within 10 calendar days after OIRA has received an agency's Plan, OIRA shall circulate it to other affected agencies, the Advisors, and the Vice President.

(4) An agency head who believes that a planned regulatory action of another agency may conflict with its own policy or action taken or planned shall promptly notify, in writing, the Administrator of OIRA, who shall forward that communication to the issuing agency, the Advisors, and the Vice President.

(5) If the Administrator of OIRA believes that a planned regulatory action of an agency may be inconsistent with the President's priorities or the principles set forth in this Executive order or may be in conflict with any policy or

action taken or planned by another agency, the Administrator of OIRA shall promptly notify, in writing, the affected agencies, the Advisors, and the Vice President.

(6) The Vice President, with the Advisors' assistance, may consult with the heads of agencies with respect to their Plans and, in appropriate instances, request further consideration or inter-agency coordination.

(7) The Plans developed by the issuing agency shall be published annually in the October publication of the Unified Regulatory Agenda. This publication shall be made available to the Congress; State, local, and tribal governments; and the public. Any views on any aspect of any agency Plan, including whether any planned regulatory action might conflict with any other planned or existing regulation, impose any unintended consequences on the public, or confer any unclaimed benefits on the public, should be directed to the issuing agency, with a copy to OIRA.***

Section 6. *Centralized Review of Regulations.* The guidelines set forth below shall apply to all regulatory actions, for both new and existing regulations, by agencies other than those agencies specifically exempted by the Administrator of OIRA:

(a) *Agency Responsibilities.*

(1) Each agency shall (consistent with its own rules, regulations, or procedures) provide the public with meaningful participation in the regulatory process. In particular, before issuing a notice of proposed rulemaking, each agency should, where appropriate, seek the involvement of those who are intended to benefit from and those expected to be burdened by any regulation (including, specifically, State, local, and tribal officials). In addition, each agency should afford the public a meaningful opportunity to comment on any proposed regulation, which in most cases should include a comment period of not less than 60 days. Each agency also is directed to explore and, where appropriate, use consensual mechanisms for developing regulations, including negotiated rulemaking.***

(3) In addition to adhering to its own rules and procedures and to the requirements of the Administrative Procedure Act, the Regulatory Flexibility Act, the Paperwork Reduction Act, and other applicable law, each agency shall develop its regulatory actions in a timely fashion and adhere to the following procedures with respect to a regulatory action:***

(B) For each matter identified as, or determined by the Administrator of OIRA to be, a significant regulatory action, the issuing agency shall provide to OIRA:

(i) The text of the draft regulatory action, together with a reasonably detailed description of the need for the regulatory action and an explanation of how the regulatory action will meet that need; and

(ii) An assessment of the potential costs and benefits of the regulatory action, including an explanation of the manner in which the regulatory action is consistent with a statutory mandate and, to the extent permitted by law, promotes the President's priorities and avoids undue interference with State, local, and tribal governments in the exercise of their governmental functions.

(C) For those matters identified as, or determined by the Administrator of OIRA to be, a significant regulatory action within the scope of section 3(f)(1), the agency shall also provide to OIRA the following additional information developed as part of the agency's decision-making process (unless prohibited by law):

(i) An assessment, including the underlying analysis, of benefits anticipated from the regulatory action (such as, but not limited to, the promotion of the efficient functioning of the economy and private markets, the enhancement of health and safety, the protection of the natural environment, and the elimination or reduction of discrimination or bias) together with, to the extent feasible, a quantification of those benefits;

(ii) An assessment, including the underlying analysis, of costs anticipated from the regulatory action (such as, but not limited to, the direct cost both to the government in administering the regulation and to businesses and others in complying with the regulation, and any adverse effects on the efficient functioning of the economy, private markets (including productivity, employment, and competitiveness), health, safety, and the natural environment), together with, to the extent feasible, a quantification of those costs; and

(iii) An assessment, including the underlying analysis, of costs and benefits of potentially effective and reasonably feasible alternatives to the planned regulation, identified by the agencies or the public (including improving the current regulation and reasonably viable nonregulatory actions), and an explanation why the planned regulatory action is preferable to the identified potential alternatives.

(D) In emergency situations or when an agency is obligated by law to act more quickly than normal review procedures allow, the agency shall notify OIRA as soon as possible and, to the extent practicable, comply with subsections (a)(3)(B) and (C) of this section. For those regulatory actions that are governed by a statutory or court-imposed deadline, the agency shall, to the extent practicable, schedule rulemaking proceedings so as to permit sufficient time for OIRA to conduct its review, as set forth below in subsection (b)(2) through (4) of this section.***

(b) *OIRA Responsibilities.* The Administrator of OIRA shall provide meaningful guidance and oversight so that each agency's regulatory actions are consistent with applicable law, the President's priorities, and the principles set forth in this Executive order and do not conflict with the policies or actions of another agency. OIRA shall, to the extent permitted by law, adhere to the following guidelines:

(1) OIRA may review only actions identified by the agency or by OIRA as significant regulatory actions under subsection (a)(3)(A) of this section.

(2) OIRA shall waive review or notify the agency in writing of the results of its review within the following time periods:

(A) For any notices of inquiry, advance notices of proposed rulemaking, or other preliminary regulatory actions prior to a Notice of Proposed Rulemaking, within 10 working days after the date of submission of the draft action to OIRA;

(B) For all other regulatory actions, within 90 calendar days after the date of submission of the information set forth in subsections (a)(3)(B) and (C) of this section, unless OIRA has previously reviewed this information and, since that review, there has been no material change in the facts and circumstances upon which the regulatory action is based, in which case, OIRA shall complete its review within 45 days; and

(C) The review process may be extended (1) once by no more than 30 calendar days upon the written approval of the Director and (2) at the request of the agency head.

(3) For each regulatory action that the Administrator of OIRA returns to an agency for further consideration of some or all of its provisions, the Administrator of OIRA shall provide the issuing agency a written explanation for such return, setting forth the pertinent provision of this Executive order on which OIRA is relying. If the agency head disagrees with some or all of the bases for the return, the agency head shall so inform the Administrator of OIRA in writing.

(4) Except as otherwise provided by law or required by a Court, in order to ensure greater openness, accessibility, and accountability in the regulatory review process, OIRA shall be governed by the following disclosure requirements:

(A) Only the Administrator of OIRA (or a particular designee) shall receive oral communications initiated by persons not employed by the executive branch of the Federal Government regarding the substance of a regulatory action under OIRA review;

(B) All substantive communications between OIRA personnel and persons not employed by the executive branch of the Federal Government regarding a regulatory action under review shall be governed by the following guidelines: (i) A representative from the issuing agency shall be invited to any meeting between OIRA personnel and such person(s); (ii) OIRA shall forward to the issuing agency, within 10 working days of receipt of the communication(s), all written communications, regardless of format, between OIRA personnel and any person who is not employed by the executive branch of the Federal Government, and the dates and names of individuals involved in all substantive oral communications (including meetings to which an agency representative was invited, but did not attend, and telephone conversations between OIRA personnel and any such persons); and (iii) OIRA shall publicly disclose relevant information about such communication(s), as set forth below in subsection (b)(4)(C) of this section.

(C) OIRA shall maintain a publicly available log that shall contain, at a minimum, the following information pertinent to regulatory actions under review:

(i) The status of all regulatory actions, including if (and if so, when and by whom) Vice Presidential and Presidential consideration was requested;

(ii) A notation of all written communications forwarded to an issuing agency under subsection (b)(4)(B)(ii) of this section; and

(iii) The dates and names of individuals involved in all substantive oral communications, including meetings and telephone conversations, between OIRA personnel and any person not employed by the executive branch of the Federal Government, and the subject matter discussed during such communications

(D) After the regulatory action has been published in the Federal Register or otherwise issued to the public, or after the agency has announced its decision not to publish or issue the regulatory action, OIRA shall make available to the public all documents exchanged between OIRA and the agency during the review by OIRA under this section.

(5) All information provided to the public by OIRA shall be in plain, understandable language

Section 7. *Resolution of Conflicts.* To the extent permitted by law, disagreements or conflicts between or among agency heads or between OMB and any agency that cannot be resolved by the Administrator of OIRA shall be resolved by the President, or by the Vice President acting at the request of the President, with the relevant agency head (and, as appropriate, other interested government officials). Vice Presidential and Presidential consideration of such disagreements may be initiated only by the Director, by the head of the issuing agency, or by the head of an agency that has a significant interest in the regulatory action at issue. Such review will not be undertaken at the request of other persons, entities, or their agents.***

Section 8. *Publication.* Except to the extent required by law, an agency shall not publish in the Federal Register or otherwise issue to the public any regulatory action that is subject to review under section 6 of this Executive order until (1) the Administrator of OIRA notifies the agency that OIRA has waived its review of the action or has completed its review without any requests for further consideration, or (2) the applicable time period in section 6(b)(2) expires without OIRA having notified the agency that it is returning the regulatory action for further consideration under section 6(b)(3), whichever occurs first. If the terms of the preceding sentence have not been satisfied and an agency wants to publish or otherwise issue a regulatory action, the head of that agency may request Presidential consideration through the Vice President, as provided under section 7 of this order.***

Section 10. *Judicial Review.* Nothing in this Executive order shall affect any otherwise available judicial review of agency action. This Executive order is intended only to improve the internal management of the Federal Government and does not create any right or benefit, substantive or procedural, enforceable at law or equity by a party against the United States, its agencies or instrumentalities, its officers or employees, or any other person.

Notes and Questions

1. **The Legal Status of Executive Orders.** An "executive order" is a formal order issued by the President. Although a great deal of lawyering generally goes into executive orders, there is no set process an order must go through before it is released. An order takes effect when it is signed by the President. Of course, an executive order has no legal effect if the President lacked authority to issue it or the order conflicts with law. *See Youngstown Sheet & Tube Co. v. Sawyer*, 343 U.S. 579 (1952); Samuel Estreicher & Steven Menashi, *Taking* Steel Seizure *Seriously: The Iran Nuclear Agreement and the Separation of Powers*, 86 Ford L. Rev. (forthcoming 2017).

Consider *Chrysler Corp. v. Brown*, 441 U.S. 281 (1979). Respondents sought to obtain reports that Chrysler submitted to the Department of Labor (DOL) pursuant to DOL regulations that required companies doing business with the federal government to provide information about their compliance with federal civil rights laws, including companies' use of affirmative action plans. Chrysler objected to the disclosure of the reports on the ground that disclosure was barred by the Trade Secrets Act, 18 U.S.C. § 1905, which bars government employees from disclosing confidential information they receive from private parties "to any extent not authorized by law." Respondents and DOL contended that the release of Chrysler's reports was "authorized by law" because it was required by a provision of DOL's regulations that permitted disclosure of reports submitted to DOL, "if it is determined that the requested inspection or copying furthers the public interest and does not impede any of the functions of the [agencies monitoring civil rights compliance]." 40 C.F.R. § 60.40.2(a) (1978). As authority for this regulation, DOL invoked Executive Order 11,246, 30 Fed. Reg. 12,319 (Sept. 24, 1965), which directed federal agencies in general terms to end discrimination in employment by the federal government and by contractors who did business with the government.

The Supreme Court concluded that DOL's regulations were not "law" for purposes of the Trade Secrets Act, because they could not be traced to a delegation of authority from Congress. Insofar as DOL relied on Executive Order 11,246, the Court reasoned that even if the order implemented the civil rights statutes, those statutes did not authorize the President to formulate subsidiary policy regarding the release of confidential information: "[T]he thread between these regulations and any grant of authority by the Congress is so strained that it would do violence to established principles of separation of powers to denominate these particular regulations 'legislative' and credit them with the 'binding effect of law.'" 441 U.S. at 308.

2. **The Origins of Executive Order 12,866.** As developed in later Chapters, the basic procedural framework for agency rulemaking is defined by the Administrative Procedure Act, 5 U.S.C. § 551 et seq. Executive Order 12,866 establishes a structure within the executive branch that permits the President to review agency rules at various stages of their development.

The order originated in Executive Order 12,291, promulgated by President Ronald Reagan on February 17, 1981. That order established a "Presidential Task Force on Regulatory Relief" and required agencies to submit a "Regulatory Impact Analysis" to the Director of the Office of Management and Budget (OMB) for all "major" rules. Major rules were defined, in a formulation borrowed by Executive Order 12,866, as those that (1) had an annual effect on the economy of $100 million or more; (2) caused a "major increase" in costs or prices for consumers, individual industries, federal, state, or local government agencies, or geographic regions; or (3) caused "significant adverse effects" on competition, employment, investment, productivity, innovation, or on the ability of United States-based enterprises to compete with foreign-based enterprises in domestic or export markets. Agencies were required to submit a Regulatory Impact Analysis at two points in the rulemaking cycle: when the agency issued a "notice of proposed rulemaking" and before the rule became final. When OMB received a Regulatory Impact Analysis, it was authorized, in conjunction with President's Regulatory Relief Taskforce, to seek changes to the rule or remand it to the agency for further analysis. In general, an agency rule could not take effect without OMB approval.

Executive Order 12,498 was promulgated after President Reagan's 1984 reelection and further consolidated White House control over agency rulemaking. That order required agencies to submit a statement of regulatory policies, objectives, and goals to the Director of OMB on an annual basis. The order required that agencies' rulemaking plans be consistent with "the Administration's regulatory principles," which generally required that agencies undertake cost-benefit analyses and promulgate regulations only when "the potential benefits to society for the regulation outweigh the potential costs to society."

Critics charged that, as practiced by the Reagan and George H.W. Bush administrations, presidential review of rulemaking was little more than a pretense for a deregulatory program that had not been authorized by law and conflicted with the statutory mandates of many administrative agencies. They furthermore criticized the lack of transparency in the OMB review process. OMB's contacts with regulated entities were not made public, and the OMB process was perceived in this account to provide a "second bite at the apple" for industries opposed to new regulations.[8]

Given these criticisms, President Bill Clinton's decision to revoke both orders in the first year of office was unsurprising. More surprising was Clinton's decision to preserve the basic features of the Reagan orders in Executive Order 12,866: ex ante review of regulations by the OMB, a requirement that agencies submit a regulatory agenda for OMB approval, and an emphasis on cost-benefit analysis in the agenda-setting and rulemaking phases of the regulatory process.

Executive Order 12,866 made four main changes to the regime established by President Reagan's orders. First, the role of the Office of Information and Regulatory Affairs (OIRA) was formalized. Second, Executive Order 12,866 included measures designed to make OMB/OIRA review of regulations more transparent by, for example, mandating that an agency representative participate in communications between OIRA and private individuals, and requiring OIRA to keep a log of its communications with regulatory agencies and private parties. Third, the order imposed a 90-day limit on OMB/OIRA review, preventing OMB from holding up regulations by inaction. Fourth and perhaps most significantly, Executive Order 12,866 reduced the number of agency rules that were subject to searching cost-benefit review. For rules deemed significant because they were likely to have an annual economic effect of $100 million or more, the agency was required to provide "[a]n assessment, *including the underlying analysis*, of benefits anticipated from the regulatory action ... together with, to the extent feasible, a quantification of those benefits." § 6(C)(i) (emphasis added). For other significant rules, the agency was required to provide only "[a]n assessment of the *potential* costs and benefits of the regulatory action." *See generally* Steven Croley, *White House Review of Agency Rulemaking: An Empirical Investigation*, 70 U. Chi. L. Rev. 821 (2003).

Note that, by cross-reference to the Paperwork Reduction Act, 44 U.S.C. §§ 3502(1) and (5), the review process for specific rules applies only to executive agencies, departments, and government-controlled corporations. Independent agencies including the Federal Reserve, the FTC and the SEC, are exempt. Both executive and independent agencies are obligated, however, to submit an annual regulatory agenda for OMB review.

3. **Executive Order 13,771.** On February 3, 2017, President Trump signed Executive Order 13,771, entitled "Reducing Regulation and Controlling Regulatory Costs." OMB guidance on the order stated that "EO 12,866 remains the prmary governing EO regarding regulatory planning and review." *See* 82 Fed. Reg. 9339 (Feb. 3, 2017).

4. **What Problem Is Executive Order 12,866 Trying to Solve?** The preamble to Executive Order 12,866 speaks broadly about the need for effective and efficient federal

---

8. *See, e.g.*, E. Donald Elliot, *TQM-ing OMB: Or Why Regulatory Review under Executive Order 12,291 Works Poorly and What President Clinton Should Do About It*, 57 L. & Contemp. Probs. 167 (1994); Erik D. Olson, *The Quiet Shift of Power: Office of Management & Budget Supervision of Environmental Protection Agency Rulemaking under Executive Order 12,291*, 4 Va. J. Nat. Resources L. 1 (1984).

regulation, that respects the concerns of state, local, and tribal governments. Looking specifically at the order's operative provisions, what does the order seek to accomplish? To the extent that the order seeks to improve the effectiveness and efficiency of agency regulations, is ex ante review by a centralized bureaucracy a reasonable way of accomplishing those objectives?

a. One objective served by Executive Order 12,866 is to rationalize the regulations promulgated by different agencies operating in "shared regulatory space." In *TVA v. Hill*, for example, the Tennessee Valley Authority proposed to complete a project that would result in the elimination of the snail darter — an outcome the Department of Interior, exercising authority newly delegated by the Endangered Species Act, believed to be unlawful. Centralized regulatory review can be understood as an effort to head off such conflicts at a relatively early stage of the policymaking process.

Professor Sunstein observes that very soon after a proposed regulation is received by OIRA, "the relevant OIRA desk officer . . . will generally circulate the rule to a wide range of offices and departments, both within the Executive Office of the President and outside of it." This process is intended to give other agencies an opportunity to comment on the proposed regulation, and note conflicts among the reviewing agency's regulations and the proposed regulation. This process follows informal coordination that may occur prior to the formal OIRA review process. "In important but unusual cases, a White House policy office will initiate a process to consider or promote rule-making and to help coordinate discussions long before OIRA review begins." Cass R. Sunstein, *The Office of Information and Regulatory Affairs: Myths and Realities*, 126 Harv. L. Rev. 1838, 1849 (2013).

The problem of coordinating the regulatory initiatives of several administrative agencies dealing with the same industry has been with us since at least the New Deal. Consider, for example, the unsuccessful attempt of President Franklin D. Roosevelt's Secretary of the Interior Harold Ickes to corral all regulation of water power into his department. *See* Laura Kalman, Abe Fortas: A Biography 71 (1990). Ickes was keen on managing inter-agency conflict by amassing power within a single agency. *See* Bruce Allen Murphy, Fortas: The Rise and Ruin of a Supreme Court Justice 53–60 (1988). Are objections and proposals that originate in other agencies likely to be seen as an obstacle to the agency's objectives, as TVA concluded with respect to the Tellico Dam, or good faith efforts to improve the coherence of federal law? Might the answer depend on whether agencies operate under statutes that share similar regulatory objectives? The existence of informal professional networks among the agencies' personnel? How would a successful private corporation seek to ensure that a new product or service accounted for the views of the corporation's internal stakeholders?

For more on the problem of coordinating agency action, see Jody Freeman & Jim Rossi, *Agency Coordination in Shared Regulatory Space*, 125 Harv. L. Rev. 1131 (2012); Daphna Renan, *Pooling Powers*, 115 Colum. L. Rev. 211 (2015).

b. Consider also the possibility that Executive Order 12,866 had the primary purpose of increasing the President's management authority over the actions of regulatory agencies. In an influential article, then-Professor Elena Kagan argued that, particularly in its dispute resolution provisions, the order implied the President had authority over "discretionary decisions assigned by Congress to specified executive branch officials (other than the President)." As a result, "the President would not need to resort to his power of removal over executive branch heads to ensure a certain rule-making result: that result would—or at least should—follow by virtue of a presidential (displacing a secretarial) order. For the Clinton executive order to make this claim was to say something significant about the nature of the relationship between the agencies and the President—to say that they were *his* and so too were their decisions." Elena Kagan, *Presidential Administration*, 114 HARV. L. REV. 2245, 2290 (2001).

5. **The Regulatory Agenda.** The first affirmative requirement Executive Order 12,866 imposes on agencies is to develop an annual regulatory plan. Agency plans are to include "the most important significant regulatory actions that the agency reasonably expects to issue in proposed or final form in that fiscal year or thereafter." They are subject to OMB review, particularly for consistency with other agencies' regulatory plans, and incorporated into an OMB-created "Unified Regulatory Agenda," a kind of blueprint for the regulations that the government will implement in the coming year. The Unified Regulatory Agenda is now available online at www.reginfo.gov.

According to Executive Order 12,866, this process is designed to improve coordination among agencies, head off conflicts among agency regulations at an early stage, provide an opportunity for state, local, and tribal officials to participate in regulatory planning, and ensure that new or revised regulations promote the President's priorities. The order does not mention that the regulatory agenda process also provides advance warning to regulated industries of the government's rulemaking initiatives, and permits them to mobilize opposition to agency rulemaking at an early stage of a rule's development.

Given that agencies must submit early-stage rules for OMB review, is there any practical reason to require agencies to also submit a yearly regulatory plan? Spend a few minutes browsing the current Unified Regulatory Agenda at the website cited above. Does the site contain information that would be useful to state, local, and tribal governments? Other federal agencies? Regulated industries?

6. **Pre-Release Vetting of Agency Regulations.** The most important feature of Executive Order 12,866 is the vetting process it creates for agency regulations. Agencies are required to submit regulations for OIRA review at three main points in the rulemaking process: (a) when the agency announces it intends to engage in rulemaking; (b) when the agency issues a proposed rule (a public draft of a rule that interested parties may comment upon); and (c) before the agency issues a final rule. The vetting requirement applies only to executive agencies and departments. Independent agencies are exempted from the process by Executive Order 12,866's definition of "agencies."

Prior to the creation of the OMB review process, agency rules would become effective 30 days after they were published in the Federal Register under § 553(d) of the Administrative Procedure Act, 5 U.S.C. § 553(d). The OMB process creates an additional layer of review, beyond that mandated by statute. Review of proposed regulations is coordinated by a desk officer employed by OIRA, a branch of OMB intended to serve as a repository of information and expertise about regulation. OIRA review focuses on a rule's consistency with other regulations and, crucially, the agency's determination that the regulation is cost-justified. Where OIRA finds a rule deficient in some respect, it can negotiate changes with the agency, or remand the rule for further agency consideration. As a practical matter, a regulation OIRA objects to will not become final. *See* Sunstein, *supra*, 126 HARV. L. REV. at 1848.

A recent study by the Administrative Conference of the United States, an independent federal agency that conducts research on the federal bureaucracy, found that in calendar year 2013, OIRA review of an economically significant rule took on average 93 days. Review of other significant rules took an average of 162 days. These periods were notably longer than the historical average for significant rules (economic and non-economic), which hovered between 40 and 60 days. Some reviews took as long as two years to complete, notwithstanding the 90 day time-limit for reviews under Executive Order 12,866. Curtis W. Copeland, Admin. Conf. of the United States, Length of Rule Reviews by the Office of Information and Regulatory Affairs, at 26, 29 (Dec. 2, 2013). In 2013, OIRA reviewed a total of 418 rules: 40 rules were approved without change, 349 were approved with changes, and 24 were withdrawn from OIRA review by the agency.[9] These statistics likely understate the extent of OIRA's influence, because the office encourages agencies to submit draft rules for "informal" review before formally invoking the OIRA review process.

7. **Presidential vs. Congressional Oversight.** How does formal presidential oversight of agency rulemaking compare to congressional oversight conducted via the Congressional Review Act, oversight hearings, and the budget and appropriations process? Consider specifically (a) the timeframe for oversight (ex ante versus ex post); (b) the criteria used when reviewing agency action; (c) the institutional bureaucracy involved in the oversight process; and (d) the likelihood that oversight will result in changes to agency action. Does Congress or the President have a clear edge in influencing agency action?

Note on the Office of Management and Budget

Formal presidential oversight of administrative agencies occurs largely through the Office of Management Budget (OMB), an office within the Executive Office of the President created in a 1970 government reorganization from the former Bureau of the Budget. *See* 31 U.S.C. § 501 note. The Bureau of the Budget was originally created by the Budget and Accounting Act of 1921, Pub. L. No. 67-13, 42 Stat. 20. The director of OMB is appointed by the President, with the advice and consent of the Senate. The Office has two principal functions—preparing and implementing the President's annual budget, and supervising the President's regulatory policies.

---

9. Data derived from Office of Information and Regulatory Affairs, Review Counts, http://www .reginfo.gov/public/do/eoCountsSearchInit?action=init.

Preparation of the President's budget is performed by the "budget" side of OMB. This side of the office consists of five resource management offices (RMOs), which are organized by agency and program area. These offices work with agencies to develop budget requests for the coming fiscal year. Each spring, agencies submit formal budget requests to OMB. Through the RMOs, OMB reviews and revises the requests, and incorporates them into a master budget that the President submits to Congress. The President's master budget also includes appropriations requests from Congress and the Judiciary; by custom, these requests are transmitted to Congress with no changes by OMB. The President is required by law to submit a budget to Congress "[o]n or after the first Monday in January but not later than the first Monday in February of each year." 31 U.S.C. § 1105(a). That deadline, however, is often violated and sometimes extended formally or informally.

Prior to the 1921 Budget and Accounting Act, agencies submitted their budgets directly to Congress. When the Bureau of the Budget began to compile a consolidated budget, independent agencies resisted participating in the process on the ground that doing so would compromise their independence. The Reorganization Act of 1939, Pub. L. No. 76-19, 53 Stat. 561, 565, clarified that independent agencies were required to transmit budget requests to the Bureau of the Budget in the same manner as executive department agencies. The legislation thereby brought independent agencies within the unified budget process that applies to other agencies.

Nonetheless, some agencies' appropriations requests are not subject to OMB vetting or incorporated in the President's unified budget. In the 1970s, Congress began to enact statutes that permitted certain independent agencies to transmit budget requests directly to Congress. Most prominently, 12 U.S.C. § 250 exempts the SEC, the Board of Governors of the Federal Reserve System, the Federal Deposit Insurance Corporation, the Comptroller of the Currency, the Director of the Office of Thrift Supervision, the Director of the Federal Housing Finance Agency, and the National Credit Union Administration from OMB budget oversight and authorizes those agencies to submit budget requests directly to Congress. Other statutory provisions direct agencies to submit appropriations requests simultaneously to Congress and OMB, or direct that the President's budget note the agency's original appropriations request. *See, e.g.*, 42 U.S.C. § 7171(j). Some agencies, such as the Nuclear Regulatory Commission, submit appropriations requests directly to Congress without statutory authorization, based on their view that they are independent of the Executive.

Formal oversight of regulatory policy occurs through the "management" side of OMB. The management side is headed by the Deputy Director for Management, a political appointee, and consists of five offices: the Office of Federal Financial Management, the Office of Federal Procurement Policy, the Office of E-Government and Information Technology, the Office of Performance and Personnel Management, and the Office of Information and Regulatory Affairs (OIRA). As detailed above, the last of these offices, OIRA, is responsible for the President's oversight of agency rulemaking.

OIRA is a comparatively small bureaucracy. Its director is appointed by the President with the advice and consent of the Senate. In the Obama administration, OIRA also has an Associate Administrator and Chief of Staff who are political appointees. OIRA's remaining staff consists of "desk officers" who are civil servants. In Fiscal Year 2014, OIRA's budget had funding for 44 "full time equivalent" positions. In recent years, OIRA has reviewed between 500 and 700 "significant" rules per year. However, staff shortages at OIRA have contributed to delays in the office's review of agency rulemaking.

OMB coordinates the submission of proposed legislation to Congress, through its Legislative Reference Division. Under OMB Circular A-19, first promulgated in September 1979, all bills that an executive agency wishes to transmit to Congress must be sent to OMB for pre-clearance. When an agency sends a bill to OMB, OMB reviews it and circulates it to other interested agencies. OMB may propose substantive or technical amendments, or a complete substitute for the agency's bill. When the review process is complete, OMB clears the bill by advising the agency that it has "no objection" to the bill, or that the bill is "in accord with the President's program," if it implements a presidential proposal. If the agency bill conflicts with an important administrative objective, the agency may not transmit it to Congress. "In practically all instances, however, disagreements are resolved through discussions at the policy levels of OMB and the agencies." Memorandum from Jeffrey D. Zients to Heads of Departments and Agencies re: Legislative Coordination and Clearance, Apr. 15, 2013, available at http://www.whitehouse.gov/sites/default/files/omb/memoranda/2013/m-13-12.pdf.

OMB's stance on the bill is transmitted to Congress along with the agency's proposed bill. Independent agencies customarily submit proposed legislation to OMB for pre-clearance in the same manner as executive agencies. However, some independent agencies have statutory authority to transmit legislation to Congress directly.

Notes and Questions

1. **Significance of the OIRA Administrator.** Since the OIRA Administrator became responsible for White House review of new regulations, "Presidents have tended to nominate to this position relatively independent figures, rather than individuals with close ties to interest groups." Michael A. Livermore & Richard L. Revesz, *Can Executive Review Help Prevent Capture?*, *in* Preventing Regulatory Capture: Special Interest Influence and How to Limit It 420, 442 (Daniel Carpenter & David Moss eds., 2013). Does this diminish the President's control over the rulemaking process? *See* Adrian Vermuele, *Conventions of Agency Independence*, 113 Colum. L. Rev. 1163, 1206–07 (2013).

2. **Executive Review and "Ossification" of Administrative Law?** The formal presidential review processes supervised by OMB and OIRA are frequently criticized for contributing to the "ossification" of administrative law—i.e., the tendency of administrative regulations, once enacted, to continue in the same form, and the failure of agencies to enact new or amended regulations in response to changed circumstances. *See, e.g.*, Michael A. Livermore & Richard L. Revesz, *Regulatory Review, Capture, and*

Agency Inaction, 101 Geo. L.J. 1337, 1342 (2013); Thomas O. McGarity, *Some Thoughts on "Deossifying" the Rulemaking Process*, 41 Duke L.J. 1385, 1431 (1991). When reading the materials on agency rulemaking and judicial review in the following sections, bear this critique in mind and consider the extent to which ossification results from the procedural framework created by the Administrative Procedure Act, the requirements imposed by court-created doctrine governing judicial review, and the requirements imposed by formal presidential review.

3. **Cost-Benefit Analysis.** Executive Order 12,866 and its predecessor have promoted acceptance of cost-benefit analysis (CBA), within the limits of the agency's policymaking authority, as an important analytic approach to assessing the desirability of agency rulemaking. *See* Note on Cost-Benefit Analysis following *Motor Vehicle Manufacturers Association of the United States, Inc. v. State Farm Mutual Automobile Insurance Co.*, *infra* Chapter 5[D].

4. **Further Reading.** OMB—and to an even greater extent OIRA—are the subjects of substantial literatures. For entry points into those literatures, see, e.g., Cass R. Sunstein, *The Office of Information and Regulatory Affairs: Myths and Realities*, 126 Harv. L. Rev. 1838 (2013); Sally Katzen, *OIRA at Thirty: Reflections and Recommendations*, 63 Admin. L. Rev. 103 (2011); Nicholas Bagley & Richard L. Revesz, *Centralized Oversight of the Regulatory State*, 106 Colum. L. Rev. 1260 (2006); Lisa Schultz Bressman & Michael P. Vandenbergh, *Inside the Administrative State: A Critical Look at the Practice of Presidential Control*, 105 Mich. L. Rev. 47 (2006); James F. Blumstein, *Regulatory Review by the Executive Office of the President: An Overview and Policy Analysis of Current Issues*, 51 Duke L.J. 851, 867 (2001); Richard H. Pildes & Cass R. Sunstein, *Reinventing the Regulatory State*, 62 U. Chi. L. Rev. 1 (1995).

2. Informal Oversight

Of course, it would be naïve to think that the formal oversight mechanisms created by law and executive order are the President's only tools for influencing the actions of administrative agencies. As famously expressed by President Truman and historian Richard E. Neustadt, "presidential power is the power to persuade." The materials that follow give a sense of the President's informal influence over administrative agencies and introduce some of the legal questions raised by informal presidential oversight: Does the President have authority to direct agency actions? Is informal Presidential control consistent with the rule of law?

Tummino v. Torti

603 F. Supp. 2d 519 (E.D.N.Y. 2009)

Korman, District Judge:***

Plan B is an emergency contraceptive that can be used to reduce the risk of unwanted pregnancy after sexual intercourse. When used as directed, it can reduce the risk of pregnancy by up to 89 percent.*** Plaintiffs—individuals and organizations advocating wider distribution of and access to emergency contraceptives, as well as parents and their minor children seeking access to the same — brought this action challenging the denial of a Citizen Petition, which requested that the Food and Drug Administration ("FDA") make Plan B available without a prescription to women of all ages.***

Under the Federal Food, Drug, and Cosmetic Act ("FDCA"), 21 U.S.C. §§ 301 et seq., no new drug product may be sold in the United States unless the Secretary of Health and Human Services ("Secretary") first approves a new drug application ("NDA") submitted by the drug's sponsor. *Id.* § 355. The Secretary delegated primary responsibility over drug regulation to the Commissioner of the FDA ("Commissioner"). *Id.* § 393(d).***

Many new drugs are initially approved for prescription-only status and then later considered for non-prescription status, i.e., an over-the-counter or OTC switch. A drug is suitable for OTC use when found to be safe and effective for self-administration and when its labeling clearly provides directions for safe use and warnings regarding unsafe use, side effects, and adverse reactions.***

There are two means by which the FDA can switch a prescription-only drug to non-prescription status. First, it can promulgate a regulation changing the drug's status. *See* 21 U.S.C. § 353(b)(3). This rulemaking process may be initiated by the Commissioner, 21 C.F.R. § 310.200(b), or by any interested person who files a citizen petition. *Id.* § 10.25(a). Within 180 days of receipt of the petition, the Commissioner must either approve or deny the petition or provide "a tentative response [to the petitioner], indicating why the agency has been unable to reach a decision on the petition." *Id.* § 10.30(e)(2)(iii). Alternatively, a drug sponsor may request an over-the-counter switch. *Id.* § 310.200(b). Unlike the first mechanism, this process does not require rulemaking. *See* 21 U.S.C. §§ 355(c), (d); 21 C.F.R. § 314.71. Nevertheless, only the drug sponsor can supplement its initial new drug application. 21 C.F.R. § 314.71(a).***

In February 1997, the FDA announced that certain combined oral contraceptives are safe and effective for emergency use, and requested sponsors to submit new drug applications for that use. On July 28, 1999, the FDA approved an NDA for Plan B submitted by the Plan B sponsor. Plan B then became available to consumers in the United States on a prescription-only basis.

1. Filing of the Citizen Petition and First OTC Switch Application

On February 14, 2001, one of the named plaintiffs, the Association of Reproductive Health Professionals ("ARHP"), and sixty-five other organizations (together the "petitioners") filed a Citizen Petition, asking the FDA to switch Plan B, and all emergency contraceptives like it, from prescription-only to over-the-counter status without age or point-of-sale restrictions. The petition included affidavits from Dr. David Grimes, the chair of the World Health Organization task force that had conducted the largest and most definitive trials on Plan B to date, and Dr. Elizabeth Raymond, who conducted the label comprehension and actual use studies which the Plan B sponsor would ultimately submit in support of its [Supplemental New Drug Application ("SNDA")].***

On September 6, 2001, the FDA advised the petitioners that it had not yet resolved the issues raised in the Citizen Petition, but that it would respond "as soon as we have reached a decision on your request." The FDA did not respond for nearly five more years, when it announced, on June 9, 2006, that it had denied the petition. During this period, however, the FDA communicated regularly with the Plan B sponsor about its anticipated SNDA.***

2. Review of First OTC Switch Application: OTC Access Without Age Restriction

[W]hile the Plan B sponsor did not formally submit the SNDA until April 2003, the FDA was aware of and anticipated the application well in advance. Indeed, at an Office of the Commissioner's meeting in June 2002, FDA officials — including then Deputy Commissioner Dr. Lester Crawford — and review staff discussed the "political sensitivity" of a potential switch to OTC status for Plan B. These discussions regarding the political implications of the switch applications were not limited to intra-agency meetings: On the very same day that the Plan B sponsor first formally requested OTC status, then-FDA Commissioner Dr. Mark McClellan discussed the pending application with Jay Lefkowitz, the Deputy Assistant to the President for Domestic Policy at the White House. Commissioner McClellan testified that he had provided several updates on the Plan B application to relevant policy staff at the White House.***

During [a meeting in late December 2003 or early January 2004], Dr. Woodcock, Acting Deputy Commissioner, and Dr. Steven Galson, Acting Director for the Center for Drug Evaluation and Research (CDER), told their subordinates, Drs. Jenkins and Kweder, "that Plan B could not be approved on this round," and that the decision was to be made at the level of CDER Director or at the Commissioner's level. This was a departure from usual FDA procedures because under its "normal schema" a switch to OTC of a first in class drug, such as Plan B, would be handled at the Office Director level and would not require approval or sign off by the Commissioner's office. Moreover, they were told that the White House had been involved in the decision on Plan B. Dr. Kweder testified that Dr. Woodcock had told her at that meeting that:

> Dr. McClellan had [not] made [the decision] on his own but . . . the White House was involved . . . we were told, and that it was made very clear that there were a lot of constituents who would be very unhappy with . . . an over-the-counter Plan B, and . . . there] was part of the public that needed to have the message that we were taking adolescents and reproductive issues seriously.

Moreover, the pressure coming from the White House appears to have been transmitted down by the Commissioner's office in such a way as to significantly affect Dr. Galson's position on the over-the-counter switch application. While Dr. Galson would ultimately concur with Commissioner McClellan's decision and sign the Not-Approvable letter in May 2004,*** Dr. Jenkins testified*** that "there were occasions where . . . Dr. Galson . . . told me that he felt that he didn't have a choice, and . . . that he wasn't sure that he would be allowed to remain as Center Director if he didn't agree with the [Not-Approvable] Action."***

Nevertheless, FDA review staff continued their "first review cycle" for the OTC switch application submitted by the Plan B sponsor. On January 9, 2004, Dr. Curtis

Rosebraugh, Deputy Director of the Division of OTC Drugs, recommended approval of the application submitted by the Plan B sponsor, concluding that Plan B has a "low misuse and abuse potential" and is "safe and effective." Moreover, he suggested that Plan B could decrease unwanted teen pregnancy by up to 70 percent and reduce teen abortions.

On January 15, 2004, less than a week after Rosebraugh circulated his memorandum, and before other FDA offices had completed their respective reviews, Dr. Galson met with and informed members of the ODE III, ODE V and OND that the Commissioner's office had decided that the FDA would issue a Not-Approvable letter because of a lack of adequate data to support appropriate use of Plan B by adolescents under 16. There is evidence that Commissioner McClellan made this decision before FDA staff had completed their scientific reviews of that data.***

[O]n May 6, 2004, Dr. Galson, Acting Director of the Center for Drug Evaluation and Research, sent the Plan B sponsor a Not-Approvable letter on the initial SNDA. Dr. Galson told the sponsor that before the OTC switch could be approved it needed to provide more information on safe use by women under 16, or more information in support of a dual marketing plan that would sell Plan B as a prescription-only product to women under 16. Central to this decision was Dr. Galson's refusal to extrapolate the findings from the actual use study in the 17 and older age group (with 518 enrollees) to the 16 and younger age group (with 22 enrollees). Dr. Galson reasoned that it is "very difficult to extrapolate data on behavior from older ages to younger ages" because of the diminished capacity of adolescents to make rational decisions and the "large developmental differences" between early- and mid-adolescence. This conclusion was a departure from the FDA's "long history" of extrapolating data for other contraceptives, including prescription oral contraceptives.***

3. Review of Second OTC Switch Application: OTC Access for 16 and Older

After it received the May 6, 2004 Not-Approvable letter, the Plan B sponsor submitted an amended SNDA in July 2004, formally proposing a dual marketing plan for Plan B that would allow non-prescription sales to persons age 16 and over who presented a valid identification to a pharmacist, and prescription-only sales to women 15 years and younger. The amended SNDA proposed that Plan B be kept behind-the-counter ("BTC") at pharmacies so as to enforce the age restriction on non-prescription use. This marketing approach is referred to as the behind-the-counter or "BTC" regime."***

In January 2005, notwithstanding review staff's continued view that OTC access should be approved without age restriction, Dr. Galson, Acting Director of the Center for Drug Evaluation and Research, asked Dr. Jenkins to draft an approvable letter for the Plan B OTC switch application approving OTC status for women age 17 and over. Dr. Galson had concluded and informed Acting Commissioner Crawford that he was "comfortable with the science" and that OTC use of Plan B "should be approved over the counter for 17 and up." Acting Commissioner Crawford testified at his deposition that he concurred with Dr. Galson's recommendation. Nevertheless, in January or February 2005, before Dr. Galson could issue the letter he had instructed

Dr. Jenkins to draft, Acting Commissioner Crawford removed Dr. Galson's authority to make a decision on the OTC switch application. This was the only time Dr. Galson had had his authority to make such a decision removed and the only time he is aware of it happening to any Center of Drug Evaluation and Research Director.***

Notwithstanding assurances that the FDA would act by September 1, 2005, Commissioner Crawford announced in late August 2005 that he would put off the decision yet again. In a letter dated August 26, 2005, Commissioner Crawford stated that, although the "scientific data [is] sufficient to support the safe use of Plan B as an OTC product . . . for women who are 17 years of age and older," the FDA is unable to reach a decision on the approvability of the application—even as to women 17 and older—because of "unresolved issues" related to the FDA's authority to approve the BTC regime of Plan B and the logistics of enforcing the age based and point-of-sale restrictions. That same day, the FDA announced its intention to issue an advance notice of a 60-day public comment period on whether rulemaking procedures were necessary to resolve and clarify these unresolved issues. This decision presented a new obstacle to the Senate deadline of September 1, 2005 for a decision on Plan B, which had been a condition of the Senate's confirmation of Commissioner Crawford.***

The 60-day period for public comment on whether rulemaking procedures were necessary closed on November 1, 2005. The FDA received approximately 47,000 public comments and hired an outside company to review and summarize those comments. That review was completed six months later on May 19, 2006. After reviewing these materials, the FDA finally concluded—more than eleven months after halting its review of the OTC switch application to seek public comment—that it was not necessary after all to engage in agency rulemaking before deciding the Plan B sponsor's OTC switch application. Instead, on July 31, 2006, the FDA announced that "[n]on-prescription sales of [Plan B] could be approved for women 18 and older within weeks," although it requested more information regarding the Plan B sponsor's plan to enforce the age and point-of-sale restrictions, which required that Plan B be kept behind the pharmacy counter. By this point in time, Commissioner Crawford had resigned and Dr. von Eschenbach had been made Acting Commissioner and nominated to replace him. This change in policy was announced a day before Dr. von Eschenbach's confirmation hearing.***

4. Denial of Citizen Petition

In June 2006, less than two months before the FDA announced that it would approve non-prescription use of Plan B only for women over the age of 18, the FDA issued a final agency decision denying the Citizen Petition—which had requested non-prescription access to Plan B for women of all ages—finding that petitioners had failed to provide sufficient data or information to meet the statutory and regulatory requirements for an OTC switch for any age group, much less the under 16 age group.***

C. GAO Investigation

At the request of members of Congress, including 19 Senators and 29 Representatives, the Government Accountability Office ("GAO") initiated an investigation into the process which led to the issuance of the May 6, 2004, Not-Approvable letter, denying the initial supplemental new drug application filed by the Plan B sponsor.***

[T]he GAO concluded that "there are no age-related marketing restrictions for safety reasons for any of the prescription or OTC contraceptives that FDA has approved, and FDA has not required pediatric studies for them." In particular, it noted, "[a]ll FDA-approved OTC contraceptives are available to anyone, and all FDA-approved prescription contraceptives are available to anyone with a prescription." Finally, the GAO noted that the "FDA did not identify any issues that would require age-related restrictions in its review of the original application for prescription Plan B, and prescription Plan B is available to women of any age."***

[DISCUSSION]

[Plaintiffs brought this action in January 2005 against the Commissioner of the FDA, pursuant to the Administrative Procedure Act and the Constitution. Plaintiffs challenged the FDA's denial of the Citizen Petition seeking to make Plan B available on an over-the-counter basis without age or point-of-sale restriction.]***

1. Improper Political Influence***

[The district court found the FDA had been subjected to improper political influence (even though no APA or statutory violation was found). The court noted that "the Advisory Committee and FDA scientific review staff strongly recommended approving Plan B OTC without age restriction, finding that restricting access to young adolescents would present greater health risks that making Plan B freely available." And yet, "despite this recommendation, the FDA refused to approve the Citizen Petition and first SNDA submitted by the Plan B sponsor. Instead, before the scientific reviews were complete, the Commissioner decided that unrestricted OTC access could not be approved, because of his concern about the inadequacy of data available for young adolescents."]

2. Departures from Its Own Policies

The evidence of lack of good faith is also confirmed by the manner in which the FDA departed from its normal procedures for evaluating OTC switch applications when it considered the Plan B applications. The most glaring procedural departure was the decision to act against the Advisory Committee's recommendation to approve the Plan B OTC switch application without age restriction. While advisory committees do not have the final say on OTC switch applications, the fact remains that in every such application in the last decade, the FDA has followed committee recommendations.

The FDA's decision regarding Plan B departed from its general policies and practices in at least four other respects. The first is the placement of additional members on the Reproductive Health Drugs Advisory Committee for the purpose of achieving ideological balance. This goal of ideological diversity does not aid the FDA in its obligation to examine the safety and effectiveness of a drug's use in self-medication. 21 U.S.C. §§ 353(b)(1), 355(d).*

The second departure was the unusual involvement of the White House in the Plan B decision-making process. Whether or not it was permissible for the FDA to discuss such questions with the White House, these discussions were not the norm for the FDA with respect to this type of decision.

The third departure concerns the timing of the decision to deny OTC use without age restriction. Plaintiffs presented evidence and the GAO made findings which indicate that the decision regarding the OTC status of Plan B may have been made before the scientific reviews of the OTC switch application were complete, and without consultation with FDA scientists. If the decision was made prior to the completion of the scientific reviews, this would certainly be evidence of a departure from the typical FDA decision-making process. Moreover, such a premature decision would lend further support to plaintiffs' theory that FDA upper management were pressured by the White House to deny young adolescents OTC access to Plan B regardless of whether the scientific evidence supported a finding that they could use Plan B safely and effectively.

The fourth departure was the FDA's refusal to extrapolate actual use study data from the older age group to the 16 and younger age group. There is evidence in the record that the FDA routinely extrapolated such data when reviewing the safety and effectiveness of various other contraceptives.***

[The district court directed the FDA to make Plan B available to women over the age of 17 immediately, and remanded for further consideration of whether Plan B should be made available to younger women. By December 2011, the FDA was set to approve over the counter sales of Plan B with no age restriction. However, Secretary of HHS Kathleen Sebelius—who was appointed by President Obama—overruled the agency's decision on the ground that "the data submitted by [the Plan Sponsor] do not conclusively establish that Plan B One-Step should be made available over the counter for all girls of reproductive age." Gardiner Harris, *Plan to Widen Availability of Morning-After Pill Is Rejected*, N.Y. TIMES, Dec. 7, 2011, at A1. The district court ordered FDA to permit Plan B sales with no age restriction. After losing a motion for a stay in the U.S. Court of Appeals for the Second Circuit, the FDA ultimately approved Plan B for over-the-counter and off-the-shelf sales with no age restrictions. See News Release, FDA Approves Plan B One-Step Emergency Contraceptive for Use

---

* Section 353(b)(1) provides:

  (1) A drug intended for use by man which—

    (A) because of its toxicity or other potentiality for harmful effect, or the method of its use, or the collateral measures necessary to its use, is not safe for use except under the supervision of a practitioner licensed by law to administer such drug; or

    (B) is limited by an approved application under section 355 of this title to use under the professional supervision of a practitioner licensed by law to administer such drug;

  shall be dispensed only [by prescription].

Section 355(d) sets out the "[g]rounds for refusing" a new drug application, including that "the results of*** tests show that such drug is unsafe for use***."—Eds.

Without a Prescription for all Women of Child-Bearing Potential (June 20, 2013). The availability of Plan B does not appear to have had a substantial effect on adolescents' sexual practices.]

Notes and Questions

1. **FDA Regulation of Pharmaceuticals Revisited.** Recall from Chapter 1 that, although the FDA is formally part of an executive department agency (the Department of Health and Human Services, or "HHS"), it has a tradition of independent, science-based decisionmaking. Decisions on whether to switch a prescription drug to over-the-counter status are made by Offices of Drug Evaluation within the FDA's Center for Drug Evaluation and Research, often with the assistance of advisory panels of outside experts.

What is the line of authority between the President and the FDA's Offices of Drug Evaluation? Which offices and divisions of the FDA were involved in the decision not to approve Plan B for over the counter (OTC) sales?

2. **The Regulatory Issue.** Under regulations promulgated by HHS, "[a]ny drug limited to prescription use*** remains so limited" until its status is changed by regulation or in response to a petition by the drug's sponsor. 21 C.F.R. § 310.200(a). A petition to make a prescription drug available OTC may be approved if "the Commissioner finds [prescription] requirements are not necessary for the protection of the public health by reason of the drug's toxicity or other potentiality for harmful effect, or the method of its use, or the collateral measures necessary to its use, and he finds that the drug is safe and effective for use in self-medication as directed in proposed labeling." *Id.* § 310.200(b). At issue in *Tummino* is whether Plan B satisfies this standard.

Note the role that "proposed labeling" plays in the decision to approve an OTC switch application. The safety of a drug is evaluated in relation to its proposed labelling; thus, a drug that may be unsafe for some uses may be made available OTC if its labelling restricts uses to those that are safe. The initial choice of which labelling to propose lies with a drug's sponsor, not the FDA, though as *Tummino* suggests, the labelling the sponsor proposes can be affected by the FDA's views.

3. **Informal vs. Formal Executive Oversight of Agency Decisionmaking.** How does the form of executive oversight illustrated by *Tummino* compare to formal presidential oversight through the OMB and the OIRA? In particular, consider the following factors:

- The *timing* of the oversight. Does review occur before, during, or after the agency acts in the first instance?

- The transparency of the presidential oversight. Are regulated actors or beneficiaries of regulation aware of the executive's involvement? Are other branches of government?

- The *effectiveness* of the oversight as a means of implementing the administration's policies and heading off conflicts among the regulatory actions of different agencies. Is the White House better able to accomplish its regulatory objectives through formal or informal oversight?

With respect to transparency, note that the Bush administration's involvement in the regulation of Plan B is an exceptional case. More often, the President is able to influence administrative policy in ways that do not necessarily leave a public record. The influence is transmitted through the President's political appointees in each executive department or employees within the Executive Office of the President. *See* Jo Becker & Barton Gellman, *Leaving No Tracks*, WASH. POST, June 27, 2007, at A01.

4. Is Executive Involvement in FDA Decisionmaking a Problem? The district court in *Tummino* is clearly bothered by the White House's involvement in the decision whether to make Plan B available over the counter. What is the district court's specific objection to the White House's involvement in the decision? According to the district court, did the White House act in excess of its legal authority? Did the FDA violate the law by taking the White House's views into account? As we will see, the Administrative Procedure Act permits a reviewing court to upset an agency's regulatory decision if the decision is "arbitrary" or "capricious." Is it arbitrary and capricious to restrict access to emergency contraception based on a mix of safety concerns and moral-religious beliefs that are not necessarily based on scientific considerations. What guidance can we glean from the agency's organic statute on this concern?

Would the district court's objections apply to a decision that was not fundamentally one of a scientific nature? Recall the question presented by *Morrison v. National Australia Bank*, in Chapter 2[B][2][e], above: do the anti-fraud provisions of the Securities Exchange Act apply to a securities transaction between a foreign purchaser and foreign seller that took place on a foreign securities exchange, which impacted a U.S.-based investor? Suppose that, at a summit meeting in Brussels, European leaders complained to the President that securities litigation under the Act was interfering with their ability to regulate their countries' securities markets and that, prior to the Court's decision in *Morrison*, the President directed the SEC to issue a directive that restricted the Act's anti-fraud restrictions to transactions on U.S. exchanges. If the SEC followed the President's suggestion, would the district court's objections apply to its action? Does it matter that the SEC is a so-called independent agency? What if the President, through his or her Secretary of State, conveyed the President's "strongly held concerns" to the SEC? Would it matter if the Attorney General conveyed to the SEC that it would not support any SEC court actions that involved transactions on non-U.S. exchanges?

5. FCC "Net Neutrality" Regulation. For many years, the Federal Communications Commission (FCC), telecommunications companies, internet content providers, and technology enthusiasts have debated whether internet backbone operators (companies that maintain high-speed links that make up the internet's backbone) and internet service providers (ISPs) (companies that connect end users to the internet) must treat all internet traffic equally. In practical terms, an equal treatment or "net neutrality" rule would prohibit ISPs from providing a fast lane for certain preferred content. For example, an ISP operating under an equal-treatment rule could not favor content from YouTube over content from HBO or Disney. *See Verizon v. FCC*, 740 F.3d 623 (D.C. Cir. 2014).

In the *Open Internet Order*, 24 F.C.C.R. 13064 (2009), the FCC imposed transparency requirements on ISPs which required disclosure of "accurate information regarding the[ir] network management practices, performance, and commercial terms of [service]." The *Open Internet Order* also prohibited ISPs from blocking certain services and imposed an anti-discrimination requirement that barred ISPs from "unreasonably discriminat[ing] in transmitting lawful network traffic" to end users.

On a petition for review, the D.C. Circuit in *Verizon* vacated the rule. The D.C. Circuit acknowledged that the FCC had statutory authority to issue a net-neutrality rule and advanced permissible reasons for doing so. However, the court concluded that the FCC could not simultaneously impose an anti-discrimination requirement on ISPs and treat them as "information-service" providers for purposes of the Telecommunications Act of 1996, Pub. L. No. 104-104, 110 Stat. 56, as it had done for many years prior to the *Open Internet Order*. This was the because the 1996 Act does not treat information-service providers as common carriers who are barred from discriminating among customers. To subject ISPs to an anti-discrimination regime, the FCC would have to reclassify them as "telecommunications carriers," which the Act treats as common carriers. *Verizon*, 740 F.3d at 659. *See also National Cable & Telecommunications Ass'n v. Brand X Internet Servs.*, 545 U.S. 967 (2005) (describing FCC's classification of cable broadband providers as information service providers).

On remand from the D.C. Circuit, the FCC reopened its rulemaking. The newly installed Chair, Tom Wheeler, stated that his mind was open on the net neutrality issue, but it appeared unlikely that the Commission would take quick action. On June 1, 2014, the late night talk show host John Oliver dedicated a segment of his show to explaining net neutrality and urged viewers to submit comments supporting net neutrality to the FCC. *See* https://youtu.be/fpbOEoRrHyU. Oliver's video went viral and hundreds of thousands of comments supporting net neutrality were submitted to the Commission. On November 10, 2014, President Obama released a YouTube video "urging" the FCC to "implement the strongest possible rules to protect net neutrality." *See* https://youtube/uKcjQPVwfDk. In January 2015, Chairman Wheeler announced that he supported common carrier regulation of ISPs. On February 26, 2015, the FCC adopted an order to that effect. *Protecting and Promoting the Open Internet*, 30 FCC Rcd. 5601.

Can President Obama's actions with respect to net neutrality be distinguished from the Bush administration's actions in *Tummino*? Did not the President do the very thing in the net neutrality episode that Judge Korman criticized the White House for doing *Tummino*? Or did the transparency of President Obama's request, and his formal recognition of the FCC's independent decisionmaking authority, distinguish his "request" from the actions of the Bush White House? Is the problem the transparency of the White House's efforts to influence agency policy as opposed to the fact of those efforts? For discussion, see Kathryn A. Watts, *Controlling Presidential Control*, 114 MICH. L. REV. 683 (2016).

In *Chevron v. NRDC*, 467 U.S. 837, 865 (1984), in Chapter 5[C][3], below, the Supreme Court noted that "an agency to which Congress has delegated policymaking responsibilities may, within the limits of that delegation, properly rely upon the incumbent administration's views of wise policy to inform its judgments." Does the district court give sufficient attention to this consideration?

6. **Executive Oversight and Statutory Design.** How was the Bush administration able to influence FDA decisionmaking? Does the FDA Administrator have for-cause job protection? Would that have made a difference? What are the implications of Congress's decision to place the FDA within the HHS, an executive department, and to have the FDA run by a single officer answerable to the Secretary of HHS?

7. **Executive Oversight and the Administrative Procedure Act.** The district court is also bothered that the White House's involvement in the regulation of Plan B caused the FDA to depart from its usual procedures, and potentially violate the Administrative Procedure Act (APA). We turn to the APA in the next Chapter. As you read the materials, consider whether the procedural framework created by the APA is adequate to protect the integrity of the regulatory process from White House pressure.

Note on the President's Authority to Direct the Actions of Administrative Agencies

The White House's efforts to control the FDA's regulation of Plan B highlight a recurring question regarding the President's authority over administrative agencies: does the President have legal authority to *direct* the way an agency carries out its statutory mandate? The question is presented in sharpest form by presidential efforts to direct the actions of an independent agency. Does the President have authority to, say, require the Securities Exchange Commission or Nuclear Regulatory Commission to promulgate a regulation addressing a problem of interest to the White House?

Debate on this question occurs at both the constitutional and statutory level. At the constitutional level, unitary-executive theorists contend that presidential control is required by a proper understanding of Article II. *See* Note 6 following *Humphrey's Executor v. United States*, Section [B][1][d], *supra* p. 309. This understanding of the President's authority was famously endorsed in *Myers v. United States*, 272 U.S. 52 (1926). Chief Justice Taft there wrote: "The ordinary duties of officers prescribed by statute come under the general administrative control of the President by virtue of the general grant to him of the executive power, and he may properly supervise and guide their construction of the statutes under which they act in order to secure that unitary and uniform execution of the laws which Article II of the Constitution evidently contemplated in vesting general executive power in the President alone."

However, *Myers* recognized two exceptions to the President's authority to direct agency action. First, "there may be duties so peculiarly and specifically committed to the discretion of a particular officer as to raise a question whether the President may overrule or revise the officer's interpretation of his statutory duty in a particular instance." *Id.* at 135. Second, "there may be duties of a quasi-judicial character imposed on executive officers and members of executive tribunals whose decisions after hearing affect interests of individuals, the discharge of which the President cannot in a particular case properly influence and control." *Id.*

In the past decade, unitary-executive theory, see Note 6 following *Humphrey's Executor v. United States*, *supra* p. 309, has attracted a large amount of academic and popular attention, particularly after it was invoked to justify human rights abuses in the aftermath of the September 11, 2001, terrorist attacks. Nevertheless, the theory's actual impact on the law has been modest. Decisions such as *Freytag* and *Edmond*, in Section [B][1][c], and *Free Enterprise Fund v. PCAOB*, 130 S. Ct. 3138 (2010), while invoking the rhetoric of unitary-executive theory, have shown some reluctance to embrace it to its logical consequences. This reluctance is likely explained by the fact that, as its proponents concede, a complete embrace of unitary-executive theory would require reconsideration of *Humphrey's Executor* and its conclusions on the status of independent agencies.[10]

An important question regarding the President's authority to direct agency action is whether, as a matter of statutory interpretation, the President has authority to control the actions of an officer to whom a statute delegates regulatory authority. Often legislation is written in terms that state the decisionmaker is the agency or the agency head. For example, the Federal Trade Commission Act "empower[s]" and "direct[s]" the FTC "to prevent persons, partnerships, or corporations . . . from using unfair methods of competition" by promulgating "rules which define with specificity acts or practices which are unfair or deceptive." 15 U.S.C. §§ 45(a)(2), 57(a)(1)(B). Section 105(a) of the Truth in Lending Act, 5 U.S.C. § 1604(a), directs the Consumer Financial Protection Bureau to "prescribe regulations to carry out the purposes of this subchapter." The Immigration and Nationality Act directs the Director of Homeland Security to "establish such regulations; . . . issue such instructions; and perform such other acts as he deems necessary for carrying out his authority" under the statute. 8 U.S.C. § 1103(a)(3). The Clean Air Act directs "the Administrator" of the Environmental Protection Agency to promulgate national ambient air quality standards. 42 U.S.C. § 7409(a). Does the President have authority, as Chief Executive, to step into the shoes of the agency decisionmaker and exercise the authorities delegated in these and many other statutes?

One school of thought interprets these statutes essentially to mean what they say.[11] If, for example, the Director of Homeland Security is directed to promulgate regulations, the President may not step into the Director's shoes and exercise that authority. On this view, the President serves as an overseer and supervisor of administrative action, not "the decider." This view finds support in an early opinion by Attorney General William Wirt. Addressing the President's authority to revise accountings

---

10. *See* Stephen G. Calabresi & Kevin H. Rhodes, *The Structural Constitution: Unitary Executive, Plural Judiciary*, 105 Harv. L. Rev. 1153, 1165–66 (1992).

11. *See, e.g.*, Peter L. Strauss, *Overseer, or "The Decider"? The President in Administrative Law*, 75 Geo. Wash. L. Rev. 696 (2007); Kevin M. Stack, *The President's Statutory Power to Administer the Laws*, 106 Colum. L. Rev. 263 (2006); Robert V. Percival, *Presidential Management of the Administrative State: The Not-so-Unitary Executive*, 41 Duke L.J. 963 (2001).

performed by Treasury Department officials, Wirt concluded that "[i]f the laws ... require a particular officer by name to perform a duty, not only is that officer bound to perform it, but no other officer can perform it without a violation of the law; and were the President to perform it, he would not only be not taking care that the laws were faithfully executed, but he would be violating them himself."[12] Even if the President cannot step into the shoes of the congressionally designated decisionmaker, to what extent can the President or his or her aides strongly influence the decision, including by threatening to dismiss the official?

Another school of thought holds that delegations—at least to executive department agencies—should be read presumptively to permit the President to direct the officer's decision.[13] This view rests on the premise that when Congress assigns an agency to the executive branch, it contemplates coordination and direction by the President. Otherwise, it would assign authority to a multimember agency protected from removal without cause.

This view has also been adopted by the Executive Branch. In response to congressional efforts to influence decisions of the Secretary of Interior in the 1850s, President Franklin Pierce asked his Attorney General Caleb Cushing, "Are instructions issued by the Heads of Department to officers, civil or military, within their respective jurisdictions, valid and lawful, without containing express reference to the direction of the President; and is or not such authority implied in any order issued by the competent Department?" Cushing responded that such officers are always subject to presidential control:

> [N]o Head of Department can lawfully perform an official act against the will of the President; and that will is by the Constitution to govern the performance of all such acts. If it were not thus, Congress might by statute so divide and transfer the executive power as utterly to subvert the Government, and to change it into a parliamentary despotism, like that of Venice or Great Britain, with a nominal executive chief utterly powerless,—whether under the name of Doge, or King, or President, would then be of little account, so far as regards the question of the maintenance of the Constitution.[14]

The Supreme Court has yet to address squarely the President's statutory authority to direct agency action, but the question sometimes arises when White House officials are alleged to have engaged in improper ex parte contacts with congressionally designated decisionmakers. Consider *Portland Audubon Soc. v. Endangered Species Committee*, 984 F.2d 1534 (1993). The Ninth Circuit was asked to review a decision of the Endangered Species Committee to grant an exemption from the Endangered Species Act to the Bureau of Land Management for sales of thirteen forests in western Oregon. As discussed in connection with *TVA v. Hill*, in Chapter 2[B][2][a], the Committee (popularly known as the "God Squad") may authorize projects that would

---

12. The President and Accounting Officers, 1 Op. Att'y Gen. 624, 625 (1823).

13. Elena Kagan, *Presidential Administration*, 114 HARV. L. REV. 2245 (2001).

14. Relation of the President to the Executive Departments., 7 Op. Atty. Gen. 453, 469–70 (1855).

destroy an endangered species or its critical habitat if the Committee determines among other things that the "benefits of such action clearly outweigh the benefits of alternative courses of action." 16 U.S.C. § 1536(h)(1). The Committee is made up of high-ranking officials: the Secretaries of Agriculture, the Army, and Interior, the Chairman of the Council of Economic Advisors, the Administrators of the Environmental Protection Agency and National Oceanic and Atmospheric Administration, and an individual from "each affected State" who is selected by the President.

The Secretary of Interior initially considers applications for exemptions and is required to forward an application to the Committee if certain threshold requirements are satisfied. 16 U.S.C. §§ 1536(g)(1)–(3). An Administrative Law Judge (ALJ) then holds a hearing on the application and prepares a report for the Committee's consideration. §1536(g)(4). The Committee is directed to "make a final determination whether or not to grant an exemption within 30 days" after receiving the ALJ's report. The Endangered Species Act expressly describes the ALJ hearing as a formal adjudication. § 1536(g)(4). But the Act is silent regarding the form of administrative process the Committee is required to follow. It provides only that "[a]ll meetings and records resulting from activities pursuant to this subsection shall be open to the public." § 1536(g)(8).

The exemption at issue in *Portland Audubon* was the second that had ever been granted in the history of the Committee. After it was approved, an environmental group contended, based on two news reports and an affidavit written by its lawyer, that "at least three Committee members had been 'summoned' to the White House and pressured to vote for the exemption." The White House pressure "may have" changed the vote of at least one Committee member, the environmental group maintained.

The Ninth Circuit concluded, per Reinhardt, J., that the Committee was subject to the APA's prohibition of ex parte communications in formal adjudication, 5 U.S.C. § 557(d)(1), and that the alleged White House contacts, if proven, violated that prohibition. This issue is discussed further in Chapter 4[C], *infra*. The court remanded to the Committee with instructions that an ALJ conduct a new evidentiary hearing to determine the extent and impact of the White House's communications with Committee members. Before that hearing was held, the Bureau of Land Management withdrew the underlying application for an exemption, which mooted the case.

Chapter 4

The Work of Administrative Agencies

The preceding chapters discussed the constitutional position of administrative agencies and described some of the mechanisms available to Congress and the President for influencing agencies' actions. Here we narrow our focus, and turn to the day-to-day work of agencies.

Like all complex organizations, administrative agencies engage in a wide range of activities. Many of these activities are not visible to outside observers. Insofar as their actions affect the legal rights of regulated or beneficiary parties, however, agencies are required to follow procedures set out in the statutes they administer and the Administrative Procedure Act (APA), 5 U.S.C. §§ 551–559. A separate chapter of the APA, 5 U.S.C. §§ 701–706, governs judicial review of agency action.

A. The Administrative Procedure Act: Historical Background

The APA was enacted in 1946, following more than a decade of debate over what the legal and policy response should be to the growing phenomenon of federal administrative agencies.[1] In 1934, a committee of the American Bar Association (ABA) began work on a framework statute for administrative procedure. The ABA committee was highly critical of existing administrative practice. In 1938, the ABA committee, then chaired by Harvard Law School Dean Roscoe Pound, released a report identifying ten "tendencies" of administrative agencies, including "an obstinate tendency to decide without a hearing, or without hearing one of the parties, or after conference with one of the parties in the absence of the other whose interests are adversely affected."[2] The ABA proposed new legislation governing administrative procedure, which was introduced with minor alterations in 1939 by Senator Marvel Mills Logan (D-KY) and Representative Francis Walter (D-PA).[3]

---

1. *See generally* Walter Gellhorn, *The Administrative Procedure Act: The Beginnings,* 72 Va. L. Rev. 219 (1986); George B. Shepherd, *Fierce Compromise: The Administrative Procedure Act Emerges from New Deal Politics,* 90 Nw. U. L. Rev. 1557, 1598 (1996).

2. Kenneth Culp Davis, *Dean Pound and Administrative Law,* 42 Colum. L. Rev. 89, 90 (1942) (quoting the ABA report).

3. *See* 86 Cong. Rec. 5561 (1939) (introduction of H.R. 6324, 76th Cong., 1st Sess. (1939)).

The stated purpose of the Logan-Walter bill was "to stem and, if possible, to reverse the drift into parliamentarism which, if it should succeed in any substantial degree in this country, could but result in totalitarianism with [the] complete destruction of the division of governmental power between the Federal and the State Governments and with the entire subordination of both the legislative and judicial branches of the Federal Government to the executive branch wherein are included the administrative agencies and tribunals of that Government."[4] The bill's central features were a requirement that agencies issue implementing regulations within one year of a statute's passage; a new administrative appeal mechanism under which a person aggrieved by agency action could request reconsideration by a board created within the agency for that purpose; and a requirement that agencies follow uniform "trial" procedures, to be established by the Supreme Court in the same manner as the Federal Rules of Civil Procedure. The bill provided for expedited judicial review of agency action in the U.S. Court of Appeals for the D.C. Circuit. An agency decision could be set aside on seven enumerated grounds, including "that the [agency] decision is not supported by the findings of fact."[5]

The Logan-Walter bill moved through Congress swiftly. In an effort to derail it, President Franklin Roosevelt asked his Attorney General (and later Justice) Frank Murphy to create a committee to study the work of the administrative agencies.[6] The committee's study is a landmark of American public law. In the course of producing it, the committee held hearings on forty agencies and executive departments, and produced detailed monographs on twenty-seven of the agencies that it studied.

While the Attorney General's committee was performing its work, Congress passed the Logan-Walter bill. President Roosevelt vetoed the bill, citing the ongoing work of the Attorney General's committee.[7] The report of the Attorney General's committee was released on January 24, 1941.[8] Its descriptive sections drew on the monographs that the committee had published and described the evolution of administrative process, informal and formal adjudication, rulemaking, and the prevailing standards for judicial review. The committee's members did not reach agreement on the form new legislation should take. Thus, the report included two different proposed bills for Congress's consideration.

---

4. Report to Accompany S. 915, S. Rep. No. 76-442, at 5 (1st Sess. 1939).

5. *Id.* at 4.

6. The committee had twelve members: future Secretary of State Dean Acheson; Third Circuit Judge Francis Biddle; Washington University law professor Ralph F. Fuchs; Lloyd K. Garrison, the chair of the National Labor Relations Board; D. Lawrence Groner, a judge of the Court of Appeals for the District of Columbia Circuit; Harvard Law School professor Henry M. Hart, Jr.; Assistant Attorney General Carl McFarland; James W. Morris, a judge of the U.S. District Court for the District of Columbia; Yale Law School professor Harry Shulman; University of Michigan Law School Dean E. Blythe Stason; and Arthur T. Vanderbilt, Dean of New York University School of Law and future New Jersey Supreme Court Justice. The committee's director was Columbia University law professor Walter Gellhorn.

7. Veto Message, Walter-Logan Bill, *reprinted in* 86 Cong. Rec. 13,942-43 (1940).

8. *See* United States Attorney General's Committee on Administrative Procedure, Final Report, S. Doc. No. 8, 77th Cong., 1st Sess. app. A (1941).

The bill endorsed by a majority of the committee would have established a Federal Office of Administrative Procedure that was authorized to supervise the appointment of agency "hearing commissioners" and investigate complaints of agency misconduct. The bill did not require that agencies give notice of proposed regulations or provide an opportunity for public comment. Nor did it address judicial review, instead leaving courts to review agency action under the prevailing common law standards.

The "minority bill"—endorsed by Assistant Attorney General Carl McFarland, University of Michigan Law School Dean E. Blythe Stason, and Arthur T. Vanderbilt, the Dean of New York University School of Law and future Chief Justice of New Jersey—imposed greater controls on the administrative process. Most notably, it provided that regulations could be promulgated only following notice to the public and an opportunity to comment. The minority bill also required that agency rules be published in the Federal Register, and specified standards for judicial review of agency action. Courts were authorized to void agency decisions that were not supported "upon the whole record, by substantial evidence," and to invalidate rules found to be "unreasonable."[9]

After the report was released in 1941, progress on administrative procedure legislation stalled for the duration of World War II. As the war came to a close, Attorney General Francis Biddle and his successor (and later Justice) Tom Clark negotiated an agreement with congressional leaders on the content of a new administrative procedure bill. In early 1944, Senator Pat McCarran (D-NV) and Rep. Hatton Sumners (D-TX), the chairs of the Senate and House Judiciary Committees, introduced the bill as S. 2030 and H.R. 5081. On January 6, 1945, the bill was reintroduced by Senator McCarran as S. 7, which would become the APA. Three days of hearings on S. 7 were held before the House Committee on the Judiciary in June 1945.[10] By the spring of 1946, the new bill had widespread support. It passed the House in March 1946 and the Senate in May 1946. On June 11, 1946, President Harry Truman signed it into law. In 1947, the Attorney General published a "Manual" on the APA, which is often consulted as a guide to interpreting the Act.

In final form, the APA largely codified best practices that had been identified by the Attorney General's study committee. The Act applies of its own force to rulemaking and adjudication by "agencies," which are defined in 5 U.S.C. § 551(1) as "each authority of the Government of the United States" excepting Congress, the courts, certain territorial governments, and the certain entities within the military. Many substantive statutes cross-reference the APA, providing that an agency may regulate a problem via the procedures there specified.

The APA is largely a gap-filler. In the event of a conflict between the statute that authorized an agency (often called the "organic statute") and the APA, the organic statute always controls. Where the organic statute is silent, the APA's procedures apply.

---

9. *Id.* at 230.

10. Administrative Procedure: Hearings Before the House Comm. on the Judiciary on the Subject of Federal Administrative Procedure, 79th Cong., 1st Sess. (1945).

Section 559 of the APA states that the Act does not "limit or repeal additional requirements imposed by statute or otherwise recognized by law." Subsequent legislation is deemed not to "supersede or modify" the APA except to the extent it does so "expressly."

Under the APA, three principal forms of agency action are expressly recognized: rulemaking; adjudication; and the development of interpretative rules, general statements of policy, and agency procedural rules. The sections below introduce these categories of agency activity, as well as the relationship between rulemaking and adjudication, agency elaboration of statutory policy, and litigation by administrative agencies. The text of the APA is reproduced in the documentary supplement. To understand the cases and materials that follow, it is essential to first read the statute.

B. Adjudication

An agency charged with administering a statute must make countless determinations of fact and law. Is a particular activity within the scope of the statute? What did a regulated actor do? Did the actor's actions violate a standard established by the statute? In the argot of the Administrative Procedure Act, answering such questions requires the agency to engage in "adjudication." The cases below introduce the two forms of agency adjudication—"formal" adjudication and "informal" adjudication.

1. Formal Adjudication

Richardson v. Perales

402 U.S. 389 (1971)

Mr. Justice Blackmun delivered the opinion of the Court.

In 1966 Pedro Perales, a San Antonio truck driver, then aged 34, height 5'11", weight about 220 pounds, filed a claim for disability insurance benefits under the Social Security Act. Sections 216(i)(1), 68 Stat. 1080, and 223(d)(1), 81 Stat. 868, of that Act, 42 U.S.C. § 416(i)(1) and 42 U.S.C. § 423(d)(1) (1964 ed., Supp. V), both provide that the term "disability" means "inability to engage in any substantial gainful activity by reason of any medically determinable physical or mental impairment . . . ." Section 205(g), 42 U.S.C. § 405(g), relating to judicial review, states, "The findings of the Secretary as to any fact, if supported by substantial evidence, shall be conclusive . . . ."

The issue here is whether physicians' written reports of medical examinations they have made of a disability claimant may constitute "substantial evidence" supportive of a finding of nondisability, within the § 205(g) standard, when the claimant objects to the admissibility of those reports and when the only live testimony is presented by his side and is contrary to the reports.

I

In his claim Perales asserted that on September 29, 1965, he became disabled as a result of an injury to his back sustained in lifting an object at work. He was seen by a neurosurgeon, Dr. Ralph A. Munslow, who first recommended conservative treat-ment. When this provided no relief, myelography was performed and surgery for a possible protruded intervertebral disc at L-5 was advised. The patient at first hesitated about surgery and appeared to improve. On recurrence of pain, however, he con-sented to the recommended procedure. Dr. Munslow operated on November 23.*** No disc protrusion or other definitive pathology was identified at surgery. The post-operative diagnosis was: "Nerve root compression syndrome, left." The patient was discharged from Dr. Munslow's care on January 25, 1966, with a final diagnosis of "Neuritis, lumbar, mild."

Mr. Perales continued to complain, but Dr. Munslow and Dr. Morris H. Lam-pert, a neurologist called in consultation, were still unable to find any objective neurological explanation for his complaints. Dr. Munslow advised that he return to work.

In April 1966 Perales consulted Dr. Max Morales, Jr., a general practitioner of San Antonio. Dr. Morales hospitalized the patient from April 15 to May 2. His final dis-charge diagnosis was: "Back sprain, lumbo-sacral spine."

Perales then filed his claim. As required by § 221 of the Act, 42 U.S.C. § 421, the claim was referred to the state agency for determination. The agency obtained the hos-pital records and a report from Dr. Morales. The report set forth no physical findings or laboratory studies, but the doctor again gave as his diagnosis: "Back sprain — lumbo-sacral spine," this time "moderately severe," with "Ruptured disk not ruled out." The agency arranged for a medical examination, at no cost to the patient, by Dr. John H. Langston, an orthopedic surgeon. This was done May 25.

Dr. Langston's ensuing report to [New Mexico's] Division of Disability Determina-tion* was devastating from the claimant's standpoint. The doctor referred to Perales' being "on crutches or cane" since his injury. He noted a slightly edematous condition in the legs, attributed to "inactivity and sitting around"; slight tenderness in some of the muscles of the dorsal spine, thought to be due to poor posture; and "a very mild sprain [of those muscles] which would resolve were he actually to get a little exercise and move." Apart from this, and from the residuals of the pantopaque myelography and hemilaminectomy, Dr. Langston found no abnormalities of the lumbar spine. Otherwise, he described Perales as a "big physical healthy specimen . . . obviously holding back and limiting all of his motions, intentionally. . . . His upper extremities, though they are completely uninvolved by his injury, he holds very rigidly as though he were semi-paralyzed. His reach and grasp are very limited but intentionally so. . . . Neurological examination is entirely normal to detailed sensory examination with pin-wheel, vibra-tory sensations, and light touch. Reflexes are very active and there is no atrophy anywhere."***

---

* Under 42 U.S.C. § 421, the initial determination of whether an individual is disabled is made by a state agency applying standards and criteria promulgated by the Social Security Administration. States are entitled to compensation from the Social Security trust fund for the costs of adjudicating disability claims. — Eds.

The state agency denied the claim.*** The state agency then arranged for an examination by Dr. James M. Bailey, a board-certified psychiatrist with a subspecialty in neurology. Dr. Bailey's report to the agency on August 30, 1966, concluded with the following diagnosis:

> "Paranoid personality, manifested by hostility, feelings of persecution and long history of strained interpersonal relationships.
>
> "I do not feel that this patient has a separate psychiatric illness at this time. It appears that his personality is conducive to anger, frustrations, etc."

***The Bureau of Disability Insurance of the Social Security Administration [(SSA)] made its independent review. The report and opinion of Dr. Morales, as the claimant's attending physician, were considered, as were those of the other examining physicians. The claim was again denied.

Perales requested a hearing before a hearing examiner. The agency then referred the claimant to Dr. Langston and to Dr. Richard H. Mattson for electromyography studies.*** Dr. Langston advised the agency that Dr. Mattson's finding of "very poor effort" verified what Dr. Langston had found on the earlier physical examination.

The requested hearing was set for January 12, 1967, in San Antonio. Written notice thereof was given the claimant with a copy to his attorney. The notice contained a definition of disability, advised the claimant that he should bring all medical and other evidence not already presented, afforded him an opportunity to examine all documentary evidence on file prior to the hearing, and told him that he might bring his own physician or other witnesses and be represented at the hearing by a lawyer.

The hearing took place at the time designated. A supplemental hearing was held March 31. The claimant appeared at the first hearing with his attorney and with Dr. Morales. The attorney formally objected to the introduction of the several reports of Drs. Langston, Bailey, Mattson, and Lampert, and of the hospital records. Various grounds of objection were asserted, including hearsay, absence of an opportunity for cross-examination, absence of proof the physicians were licensed to practice in Texas, failure to demonstrate that the hospital records were [authenticated as business records,] and the conclusory nature of the reports. These objections were overruled and the reports and hospital records were introduced. The reports of Dr. Morales and of Dr. Munslow were then submitted by the claimant's counsel and admitted.

At the two hearings oral testimony was submitted by claimant Perales, by Dr. Morales, by a former fellow employee of the claimant, by a vocational expert, and by Dr. Lewis A. Leavitt, a physician board-certified in physical medicine and rehabilitation, and chief of, and professor in, the Department of Physical Medicine at Baylor University College of Medicine. Dr. Leavitt was called by the hearing examiner as an independent "medical adviser," that is, as an expert who does not examine the claimant but who hears and reviews the medical evidence and who may offer an opinion. The adviser is paid a fee by the Government. The claimant, through his counsel, objected to any testimony by Dr. Leavitt not based upon examination or upon a hypothetical.

Dr. Leavitt testified over this objection and was cross-examined by the claimant's attorney. He stated that the consensus of the various medical reports was that Perales had a mild low-back syndrome of musculo-ligamentous origin.

The hearing examiner, in reliance upon the several medical reports and the testimony of Dr. Leavitt, observed in his written decision, "There is objective medical evidence of impairment which the heavy preponderance of the evidence indicates to be of mild severity . . . . Taken altogether, the Hearing Examiner is of the conclusion that the claimant has not met the burden of proof."***

It is to be noted at this point that § 205(d) of the Act, 42 U.S.C. § 405(d), provides that the Secretary has power to issue subpoenas requiring the attendance and testimony of witnesses and the production of evidence and that the Secretary's regulations, authorized by § 205(a), 42 U.S.C. § 405(a), provide that a claimant may request the issuance of subpoenas, 20 CFR § 404.926. Perales, however, who was represented by counsel, did not request subpoenas for either of the two hearings.

The claimant then made a request for review by the [SSA] Appeals Council and submitted as supplemental evidence a judgment dated June 2, 1967, in Perales' favor against an insurance company for workmen's compensation benefits aggregating $11,665.84, plus medical and related expenses, and a medical report letter dated December 28, 1966, by Dr. Coyle W. Williams, apparently written in support of a welfare claim made by Perales. In his letter the doctor noted an essentially negative neurological and physical examination except for tenderness in the lumbar area and limited straight leg raising. He observed, "I cannot explain all his symptoms on a physical basis. I would recommend he would re-condition himself and return to work. My estimation, he has a 15% permanent partial disability the body as a whole." The Appeals Council ruled that the decision of the hearing examiner was correct.

Upon this adverse ruling the claimant instituted the present action for review pursuant to § 205(g). Each side moved for summary judgment on the administrative transcript. The District Court stated that it was reluctant to accept as substantial evidence the opinions of medical experts submitted in the form of unsworn written reports, the admission of which would have the effect of denying the opposition an opportunity for cross-examination; that the opinion of a doctor who had never examined the claimant is entitled to little or no probative value, especially when opposed by substantial evidence including the oral testimony of an examining physician; and that what was before the court amounted to hearsay upon hearsay. The case was remanded for a new hearing before a different examiner. On appeal the Fifth Circuit noted the absence of any request by the claimant for subpoenas and held that, having this right and not exercising it, he was not in a position to complain that he had been denied the rights of confrontation and of cross-examination. It held that the hearsay evidence in the case was admissible under the Act; that, specifically, the written reports of the physicians were admissible in the administrative hearing; that Dr. Leavitt's testimony also was admissible; but that all this evidence together did not constitute substantial evidence when it was objected to and when it was contradicted by evidence from the only live witnesses.***

III***

Congress has provided that the Secretary [of HHS]

> "shall have full power and authority to make rules and regulations and to establish procedures ... necessary or appropriate to carry out [the SSA's] provisions, and shall adopt reasonable and proper rules and regulations to regulate and provide for the nature and extent of the proofs and evidence and the method of taking and furnishing the same in order to establish the right to benefits hereunder." § 205(a), 42 U.S.C. § 405(a).

Section 205 (b) directs the Secretary to make findings and decisions; on request to give reasonable notice and opportunity for a hearing; and in the course of any hearing to receive evidence. It then provides:

> "Evidence may be received at any hearing before the Secretary even though inadmissible under rules of evidence applicable to court procedure."

In carrying out these statutory duties the Secretary has adopted regulations that state, among other things:

> "The hearing examiner shall inquire fully into the matters at issue and shall receive in evidence the testimony of witnesses and any documents which are relevant and material to such matters. ... The ... procedure at the hearing generally ... shall be in the discretion of the hearing examiner and of such nature as to afford the parties a reasonable opportunity for a fair hearing." 20 CFR § 404.927.

From this it is apparent that (a) the Congress granted the Secretary the power by regulation to establish hearing procedures; (b) strict rules of evidence, applicable in the courtroom, are not to operate at social security hearings so as to bar the admission of evidence otherwise pertinent; and (c) the conduct of the hearing rests generally in the examiner's discretion. There emerges an emphasis upon the informal rather than the formal. This, we think, is as it should be, for this administrative procedure, and these hearings, should be understandable to the layman claimant, should not necessarily be stiff and comfortable only for the trained attorney, and should be liberal and not strict in tone and operation. This is the obvious intent of Congress so long as the procedures are fundamentally fair.

IV

With this background and this atmosphere in mind, we turn to the statutory standard of "substantial evidence" prescribed by § 205(g). The Court has considered this very concept in other, yet similar, contexts. The National Labor Relations Act, § 10(e), in its original form, provided that the NLRB's findings of fact "if supported by evidence, shall be conclusive." 49 Stat. 454. The Court said this meant "supported by substantial evidence" and that this was

> "more than a mere scintilla. It means such relevant evidence as a reasonable mind might accept as adequate to support a conclusion." *Consolidated Edison Co. v. NLRB*, 305 U.S. 197, 229 (1938).

The Court has adhered to that definition in varying statutory situations. *See NLRB v. Columbian Enameling & Stamping Co.*, 306 U.S. 292, 300 (1939); *Universal Camera Corp. v. NLRB*, 340 U.S. 474, 477–487 (1951); *Consolo v. Federal Maritime Comm'n*, 383 U.S. 607, 619–620 (1966).

V***

We conclude that a written report by a licensed physician who has examined the claimant and who sets forth in his report his medical findings in his area of competence may be received as evidence in a disability hearing and, despite its hearsay character and an absence of cross-examination, and despite the presence of opposing direct medical testimony and testimony by the claimant himself, may constitute substantial evidence supportive of a finding by the hearing examiner adverse to the claimant, when the claimant has not exercised his right to subpoena the reporting physician and thereby provide himself with the opportunity for cross-examination of the physician.

We are prompted to this conclusion by a number of factors that, we feel, assure underlying reliability and probative value:

1. The identity of the five reporting physicians is significant. Each report presented here was prepared by a practicing physician who had examined the claimant.***

2. The vast workings of the social security administrative system make for reliability and impartiality in the consultant reports. We bear in mind that the agency operates essentially, and is intended so to do, as an adjudicator and not as an advocate or adversary. This is the congressional plan. We do not presume on this record to say that it works unfairly.[7]

3. One familiar with medical reports and the routine of the medical examination, general or specific, will recognize their elements of detail and of value. The particular reports of the physicians who examined claimant Perales were based on personal consultation and personal examination and rested on accepted medical procedures and tests.*** These are routine, standard, and unbiased medical reports by physician specialists concerning a subject whom they had seen. That the reports were adverse to Perales' claim is not in itself bias or an indication of nonprobative character.

4. The reports present the impressive range of examination to which Perales was subjected. A specialist in neurosurgery, one in neurology, one in psychiatry, one in orthopedics, and one in physical medicine and rehabilitation add up to definitive opinion in five medical specialties, all somewhat related, but different in their emphases. It is fair to say that the claimant received professional examination and opinion on a scale beyond the reach of most persons and that this case reveals a patient and careful endeavor by the state agency and the examiner to ascertain the truth.

---

7. We are advised by the Government's brief that in fiscal 1968, 515,938 disability claims were processed; that, of these, 343,628 (66.601%) were allowed prior to the hearing stage; that approximately one-third of the claims that went to hearing were allowed; and that 320,164 consultant examinations were obtained.

5. So far as we can detect, there is no inconsistency whatsoever in the reports of the five specialists. Yet each result was reached by independent examination in the writer's field of specialized training.

6. Although the claimant complains of the lack of opportunity to cross-examine the reporting physicians, he did not take advantage of the opportunity afforded him under 20 CFR § 404.926 to request subpoenas for the physicians.***

7. Courts have recognized the reliability and probative worth of written medical reports even in formal trials and, while acknowledging their hearsay character, have admitted them as an exception to the hearsay rule.***

9. There is an additional and pragmatic factor which, although not controlling, deserves mention. This is what Chief Judge Brown has described as "[t]he sheer magnitude of that administrative burden," and the resulting necessity for written reports without "elaboration through the traditional facility of oral testimony." With over 20,000 disability claim hearings annually, the cost of providing live medical testimony at those hearings, where need has not been demonstrated by a request for a subpoena, over and above the cost of the examinations requested by hearing examiners, would be a substantial drain on the trust fund and on the energy of physicians already in short supply.

VI

Perales relies heavily on the Court's holding and statements in *Goldberg v. Kelly*, [397 U.S. 254, 267–68 (1970),] particularly the comment that due process requires notice "and an effective opportunity to defend by confronting any adverse witnesses. . . ." *Kelly*, however, had to do with termination of [federal welfare] benefits without prior notice. It also concerned a situation, the Court said, "where credibility and veracity are at issue, as they must be in many termination proceedings." The Perales proceeding is not the same. We are not concerned with termination of disability benefits once granted. Neither are we concerned with a change of status without notice. Notice was given to claimant Perales. The physicians' reports were on file and available for inspection by the claimant and his counsel. And the authors of those reports were known, and were subject to subpoena and to the very cross-examination that the claimant asserts he has not enjoyed. Further, the specter of questionable credibility and veracity is not present; there is professional disagreement with the medical conclusions, to be sure, but there is no attack here upon the doctors' credibility or veracity. *Kelly* affords little comfort to the claimant.

[T]he claimant complains of the system of processing disability claims. He suggests, and is joined in this by the briefs of *amici*, that the Administrative Procedure Act [(APA)], rather than the Social Security Act, governs the processing of claims and specifically provides for cross-examination, 5 U.S.C. § 556(d) (1964 ed., Supp. V).***

We need not decide whether the APA has general application to social security disability claims, for the social security administrative procedure does not vary from that prescribed by the APA.*** [The APA's provisions for formal adjudication] conform, and are consistent with, rather than differ from or supersede, the authority given the Secretary by the Social Security Act's §§ 205(a) and (b) "to establish procedures," and "to regulate and provide for the nature and extent of the proofs and evidence and the method of taking and furnishing the same in order to establish the right to benefits," and to receive evidence "even though inadmissible under rules of evidence applicable to court procedure." Hearsay, under either Act, is thus admissible up to the point of relevancy.

The matter comes down to the question of the procedure's integrity and fundamental fairness. We see nothing that works in derogation of that integrity and of that fairness in the admission of consultants' reports, subject as they are to being material and to the use of the subpoena and consequent cross-examination. This precisely fits the statutorily prescribed "cross-examination as may be required for a full and true disclosure of the facts."

Notes and Questions

1. **The Social Security Act.** We have already encountered the Social Security Disability Insurance (SSDI) program in *Heckler v. Campbell*, in Chapter 1[C][3]. SSDI is a form of social disability insurance for workers who suffer an injury that prevents them from returning to work. To receive SSDI benefits, an employee must suffer from a "disability," defined as an "inability to engage in any substantial gainful activity by reason of any medically determinable physical or mental impairment which can be expected to result in death or which has lasted or can be expected to last for a continuous period of not less than 12 months." 42 U.S.C. § 423(d)(1). The SSDI program is "designed primarily to aid workers who, after having made a contribution to the nation's work force, are unable to continue" to work. *Coleman v. Gardner*, 264 F. Supp. 714, 718 (S.D. W. Va. 1967).

2. **The Disability Adjudication Process.** What were the main features of the process the SSA established to adjudicate claims for SSDI insurance? Who determined whether Perales was entitled to benefits in the first instance? Who reviewed that decision? In total, how many levels of review were provided? What kind of evidence did the hearing officer (now called an ALJ) rely on? What form did the examiner's decision take? Was it written or oral? Cursory or detailed? From beginning to end, how long did it take to adjudicate Perales' claim to SSDI benefits?

3. **The Task for the Agency?** Recalling the discussion in *Heckler*, why did Congress assign responsibility for adjudicating disability claims to states and ALJs employed by the SSA as opposed to the courts?

Summary statistics provide a sense of the scale of the task for the agency. Social Security ALJs adjudicate approximately 800,000 cases per year. In fiscal year 2012, the SSA issued a report ranking 165 hearing offices by the average number of ALJ dispositions issued per day. In the most productive office (Mayaguez, Puerto Rico), ALJs averaged 3.86 dispositions per day. In the least productive office (Queens, New York), ALJs averaged 1.55 dispositions per day. The median rate was 2.41 dispositions per day.[11]

---

11. Soc. Sec. Admin., Hearing Office Dispositions Per ALJ Per Day Ranking Report, FY 2012, available at http://www.ssa.gov/appeals/DataSets/archive/04_FY2012/04_September_Disposition _Per_Day_Per_ALJ_Ranking_Report.pdf.

In fiscal year 2014, ALJs awarded benefits in approximately 31% of cases. The grant rate has been gradually declining; in 2004, the grant rate was 37%, and in 2000, it was 47%.[12]

In Fiscal Year 2012, the Social Security Appeals Council, an appellate body comprised of some 125 judges, processed over 166,000 requests for review. Though the council has authority to review cases on its own motion, the overwhelming majority of cases it decides were appeals filed by individuals who had been denied benefits by an ALJ. In Fiscal Year 2014, the average time from filing to a benefits decision was 422 days. That year, the Council had a backlog of approximately 1 million cases. *See* Administrative Conference of the United States, Improving Consistency in Social Security Disability Adjudications, 78 Fed. Reg. 41,352 (July 10, 2013); David Fahrenthold, *The Biggest Backlog in the Federal Government*, Wash. Post, Oct. 26, 2014, at B13.

4. **Perales' Argument.** What defect did Perales identify in the process for adjudicating his disability claim? What did he want the hearing examiner to do in his case?

The district court judge who reviewed the SSA's denial of Perales' claim stated that the word-for-word reliance by the hearing examiner (now the ALJ) on the recommendations of the medical adviser gave him "nausea." 402 U.S. at 414 (Douglas, J., dissenting). Dissenting from the Supreme Court's decision, Justice Douglas wrote that "[c]ross-examination of doctors in*** physical injury cases is*** essential to a full and fair disclosure of the facts.*** The use of circuit-riding doctors who never see or examine claimants to defeat their claims should be beneath the dignity of a great nation." *Id.* at 413–14.

Is the dissent's objection compelling? When making important life decisions, do people ordinarily insist on an opportunity to cross-examine the individuals who make recommendations based on medical judgments? For example, if a doctor told her patient that she had six months to live on the basis of a standardized blood test, how would the patient go about verifying the accuracy of the doctor's conclusion? Would it be reasonable for the patient to demand an opportunity to cross-examine the laboratory analyst who performed the blood test? The researchers who devised the test?

In any event, didn't Perales have the opportunity to subpoena the doctors and examine them during the hearing before the ALJ? Is there a good reason to place the burden on Perales rather than requiring the government to present testimony by the doctors and make them available for cross-examination? Should the calculus for whether this degree of process is required take into account the number of hearings the agency has to conduct (see footnote 7 of the Court's opinion) and that there is generally no reason to believe that the ALJ is biased against SSDI claimants? *But cf.* Samuel Estreicher & Richard L. Revesz, *Nonacquiescence by Federal Administrative Agencies*, 98 Yale L.J. 679, 699 (1989) (describing SSA's efforts to reduce disability payments during 1980s, including its refusal to follow adverse circuit precedent).

---

12. Soc. Sec. Admin., Selected Data From Social Security's Disability Program, Disabled Worker Beneficiary Statistics by Calendar Year, Quarter & Month, www.ssa.gov/oact/STATS/dibStat.html.

What is the statutory basis for Perales' argument? Why, according to the Supreme Court, is Perales' argument misplaced? What provisions of the SSA and APA does the Court rely on? In the Court's view, was Perales foreclosed from cross-examining the doctors whose reports formed the basis for the denial of his disability claim? What can an attorney representing SSDI claimants do if she wishes to cross-examine doctors who write reports used to decide the claims?

5. **Weight to be Given to Claimant's Treating Physician's Views?** There has been considerable litigation over how much weight the SSA must give to the claimant's treating physician's views. The Second Circuit has insisted, and by threat of injunction has compelled the SSA to concede, that—

> [A] treating physician's opinion on the subject of medical disability, i.e., diagnosis and nature and degree of impairment, is: (i) binding on the fact-finder unless contradicted by substantial evidence; and (ii) entitled to some extra weight because the treating physician is usually more familiar with a claimant's medical condition than are other physicians, although resolution of genuine conflicts between the opinion of the treating physician, with its extra weight, and any substantial evidence to the contrary remains the responsibility of the fact-finder.

Schisler v. Heckler, 787 F.2d 76, 81 (2d Cir. 1986). Some decisions also maintain that "opinions of non-examining medical personnel cannot, in themselves, constitute substantial evidence to override the opinion of the treating source." *Stieberger v. Sullivan*, 738 F. Supp. 716 (S.D.N.Y. 1990). Is the courts' approach here consistent with the Supreme Court's decision in *Richardson*? Is this an area where the courts should be guided by the agency's intuitions based on experience with these kinds of claims? What are the reasons for courts to be skeptical of agency determinations in this context?

6. **Requirements for Formal "On the Record" Adjudication.** The Supreme Court resolves Perales' claim that the Social Security Administration should have followed the APA rather than the Social Security Act in adjudicating his claim by reasoning that "the social security administrative procedure does not vary from that prescribed by the APA."

The requirements for formal adjudication under the APA are set forth in §§ 554, 556, and 557 of the Act. The trigger for formal adjudication is statutory language to the effect that an agency must decide a matter "on the record after opportunity for an agency hearing." *See Steadman v. SEC*, 450 U.S. 91, 97 n.13 (1981); *United States v. Florida East Coast R. Co.*, 410 U.S. 224 (1973); *United States v. Allegheny-Ludlum Steel Corp.*, 406 U.S. 742 (1972), discussed in Note 6 following *Portland Cement Ass'n v. Ruckelshaus, infra* Section [C].

Where a statute uses such language, the APA requires the agency to follow a hearing procedure to adjudicate claims. In particular, the claimant is entitled to an oral hearing, at which she can present evidence and argument, § 554(c)(2). "Subject to published rules of the agency," the claimant is entitled to be confronted with and cross-examine witnesses, § 556(c). A transcript of the hearing is created by a court reporter or videographer. Under § 556(e), "[t]he transcript of testimony and exhibits, together with all papers and requests filed in the proceeding, constitutes the exclusive record for decision." When the agency decisionmaker relies on a material fact that is not part of the hearing record, the claimant is entitled to an opportunity to contest the fact.

Ex parte contacts among the agency decisionmaker, outside parties, and the agency's non-adjudicatory personnel are regulated strictly. Under § 554(d)(1), the individual presiding at the reception of the evidence, usually the ALJ, may not "consult a person or party on a fact in issue, unless on notice and opportunity for all parties to participate." *See also* § 557(d)(1) (except where a statute authorizes disposition of matters ex parte, neither the agency nor anyone involved in the decisional process may engage in ex parte communications regarding the merits of a proceeding with any "interested person outside the agency"). The ALJ may not "be responsible to or subject to the supervision or direction of an employee or agent engaged in the performance of investigative or prosecuting functions for an agency." § 554(d)(2). If the ALJ or other employee involved in the decisional process receives an ex parte communication or causes one to be made, that information must be placed on the record, § 557(d)(1)(C), and the ALJ may sanction the party who made the ex parte submission, § 557(d)(1)(D).

7. **Administrative Law Judges.** We have already encountered ALJs in connection with the controversy over the manner of their appointment by the SEC. *See* Note on the Controversy Over SEC ALJs, Note 10 following *Edmond v. United States* in Section 3[B][1][c], *supra* p.297. Typically, an ALJ is the employee presiding at a hearing governed by APA §§ 554, 556, and 557. The agency head or other decisionmaker is not present at the hearing but makes the decision on the basis of an interim or recommended decision issued by the ALJ after the record closes, § 557(b). ALJs are employees of the agency and are required to apply agency policy. They are responsible for maintaining the integrity of the record, ruling on evidentiary matters, and issuing preliminary findings of fact and conclusions of law in their initial or recommended decision. As a formal matter, the ALJ functions as a "transmission belt" for the agency. Unless a statute provides otherwise, the agency is the decisionmaker, not the ALJ, except for when no party appeals from the ALJ's decision. *See Universal Camera Corp. v. NLRB*, 340 U.S. 474 (1951).

By law, ALJs cannot be supervised by agency employees engaged in investigative or prosecutorial functions. In most agencies, they are supervised by a separate division of judges within the agency. In addition, a separate administrative agency, the Office of Personnel Management, formerly the Civil Rights Commission, handles ALJ hiring, classification, promotion, and compensation. *See* 5 U.S.C. §§ 3105; 5372. *See also* 5 U.S.C. § 3344 (providing for transfer of ALJs among agencies when an agency experiences a temporary staffing shortage). The Merit Systems Protection Board has exclusive jurisdiction to adjudicate disciplinary actions against ALJs, who may be dismissed only for "good cause." *See* 5 U.S.C. § 7521.

Is it problematic to separate the hearing of evidence from the decision of administrative claims? Must "he who hears" also "decide"? The Supreme Court flirted with this position before the APA's enactment, but would soon abandon it. *See Morgan v.*

United States, 304 U.S. 1 (1938); Daniel Ernst, Morgan *and the New Dealers*, 20 J. Pol'y Hist. 447 (2008).

8. **Social Security Administration ALJs.** Are SSA ALJs too inclined to grant benefits or unduly predisposed to deny benefits? According to a news report, a single administrative law judge "who sits in the impoverished intersection of West Virginia, Kentucky and Ohio, decided 1,284 cases [in fiscal year 2010] and awarded benefits in all but four. For the first six months of fiscal 2011, [the same judge] approved payments in every one of his 729 decisions, according to the Social Security Administration." Damian Paletta, *Judge Can Rarely Rule 'No'*, Wall St. J., May 19, 2011, at A1.

In *Stieberger v. Heckler*, 615 F. Supp. 1315, 1321 (S.D.N.Y. 1985), plaintiffs challenged the Social Security Administration's "Bellmon Review" policy, under which decisions of ALJs with a high percentage of pro-claimant determinations were subject to agency-initiated review by the agency's Appeals Council. Defending the policy, the agency introduced a study in which 3,600 randomly selected disability determinations that awarded benefits were reviewed by the Appeals Council, using the same standards applied by ALJs. "The major finding*** was that significant differences in decision results were produced when these different decisionmakers were presented with the same evidence on the same cases. The ALJs allowed 64 percent of the cases. The Appeals Council, applying ALJ standards, allowed 48 percent." The Appeals Council demonstrated the same allowance rate regardless of the ALJ who originally decided the case.

The district court in *Stieberger* determined that the Bellmon Review process had compromised ALJ impartiality in a manner that was inconsistent with the APA. This was due in part to the *in terrorem* effect on ALJs of knowing that too much generosity toward claimants would single out an ALJ for scrutiny. *See id.* at 1390 ("[O]nly approximately 50% of all ALJ denials are subject to claimant-initiated Appeals Council review. Under Bellmon Review, however, an ALJ with an unusually high allowance*** rate had up to 100% of his or her allowance decisions subject to the scrutiny of the agency for possible review, a procedure which was not necessarily confined in its alleged impact solely to ALJs actually under individual Bellmon Review but which may well have reverberated among other ALJs whose allowance rates were approaching unacceptable levels."). Following protracted court proceedings, the SSA elected to discontinue the program.

Professor Richard Pierce contends that ALJs' decisions on SSDI disability claims "are making a significant contribution to the economic problems the [United States] is now experiencing." Richard J. Pierce Jr., *What Should We Do About Social Security Disability Appeals?* 34 Regulation 34, 34 (Fall 2011). Pierce observes that annual payments from the SSDI trust fund are presently $124 billion dollars, or one per cent of the United States' gross domestic product. This phenomenon, Pierce contends, is linked to the rise of disability cases based on "nonexertional restrictions" such as anxiety, depression, or pain attributable to a musculoskeletal condition. Pierce suggests that many of these claims are bogus or at the very least questionable, and that ALJs are predisposed toward granting them because doing so improves their standing in the communities they work in and insulates their decisions from further review. (Aside from cases the Appeals Council reviews on its own motion, SSA does not appeal the grant of benefits.)

Moreover, Pierce argues, an ALJ's effective insulation from oversight violates the Appointments Clause. That conclusion "flows inevitably" from four characteristics of the present disability adjudication process:

> First, ALJs make final decisions to grant disability benefits. Second, SSA ALJs are employed by SSA, which, in turn, is an independent agency headed by a Commissioner who serves a six-year term and who can only be removed by the President for "neglect of duty or malfeasance in office." Third, ALJs can be removed only by the MSPB and only for "good cause." Fourth, the MSPB is an independent agency headed by three members who serve seven-year terms and who can be removed by the President only for "inefficiency, neglect of duty, or malfeasance in office."

According to Pierce, this structure violates the Appointments Clause as interpreted in *Free Enterprise Fund v. Public Company Accounting Oversight Board*, 130 S. Ct. 3138 (2010), discussed in Note 10 following *Humphrey's Executor*, Chapter 3[B][1][d], *supra* p. 315. "Because ALJs make final decisions to grant benefits, they are 'officers of the United States' rather than employees." ALJs, however, are not appointed using the procedures required by the Appointments Clause, and are subject to multiple layers of insulation from presidential control.

Is Professor Pierce's argument convincing? Consider (a) whether SSA ALJs are indeed officers of the United States for purposes of the Appointments Clause; (b) whether the reasoning in *Free Enterprise Fund* applies to individuals who are formally charged with applying agency policy fairly and impartially as opposed to formulating such policy; (c) whether, as the Court recognized in *Myers v. United States*, 272 U.S. 52, 135 (1926), *supra* p. 392, "there may be duties of a quasi-judicial character imposed on executive officers and members of executive tribunals whose decisions after hearing affect interests of individuals, the discharge of which the President cannot in a particular case properly influence and control"; and (d) whether Pierce's argument extends to use of ALJs to adjudicate other agencies' cases, such as the FTC, NLRB or SEC. Would appointment by the agency head cure the Appointments Clause problem or would ALJs' for-cause removal protection under the civil service system have to be eliminated? If the latter, would such a change make ALJs more responsible to agency heads? Is that desirable?

9. **Agency Self-Imposed Procedures.** Consider the Court's discussion of the SSA's internal regulations for disability claims. As a general matter, procedures adopted by the agency are binding on the agency until revoked even if those procedures are not otherwise required by law. *See Accardi v. Shaughnessy*, 349 U.S. 280 (1955), discussed in the Note on Rulemaking's Consequences for Adjudication in Section [D], below.

10. **The Due Process Check.** Whether engaged in formal adjudication, informal adjudication, or another form of action, an agency's procedures must satisfy due process in any proceeding that affects "life, liberty, or property." U.S. Const. amend. V. This raises several questions.

a. Is the interest affected by the agency's action protected by the Due Process Clause? An initial question is whether the interest affected by an agency's action falls within the scope of the Due Process Clause. The meaning of "life" and "liberty" is obvious. With respect to "property," current Supreme Court doctrine holds that the Due Process Clause protects any interest to which an individual has a "legitimate claim of entitlement":

> To have a property interest in a benefit, a person clearly must have more than an abstract need or desire for it. He must have more than a unilateral expectation of it.*** It is a purpose of the ancient institution of property to protect those *claims upon which people rely in their daily lives*, reliance that must not be arbitrarily undermined. It is a purpose of the constitutional right to a hearing to provide an opportunity for a person to vindicate those claims.

Board of Regents of State Colleges v. Roth, 408 U.S. 564, 577 (1972) (emphasis added).

b. Is the agency action a "public act" for which a legislative hearing provides all the process due? In *Londoner v. Denver*, 210 U.S. 373 (1908), and *Bi-Metallic Inv. Co. v. State Bd. of Equalization*, 239 U.S. 441 (1915), the Supreme Court recognized a distinction for due process purposes between administrative actions that affect a relatively small number of individuals and actions that affect many people on common grounds.

Londoner was a due process challenge to a tax assessment that the Denver city council imposed on the recommendation of its board of public works, which identified the taxpayers responsible for the costs of public works projects using a formula established by state law. Petitioners argued that "the assessment was made without notice and opportunity for hearing to those affected by it, thereby denying to them due process of law." While denying that petitioners were entitled to a full, trial-type hearing before the assessment was imposed, the Court ruled they were entitled "to support [their] allegations by argument however brief, and, if need be, by proof, however informal."

Bi-Metallic was "a suit to enjoin the State Board of Equalization and the Colorado Tax Commission from putting in force, and the defendant Pitcher as assessor of Denver from obeying, an order of the boards increasing the valuation of all taxable property in Denver forty per cent." In an opinion by Justice Holmes, the Court distinguished *Londoner* as a case that involved "[a] relatively small number of persons . . . who were exceptionally affected, in each case upon individual grounds." In contrast to such a case, due process did not require that the state provide a hearing before imposing an across-the-board tax increase:

> Where a rule of conduct applies to more than a few people it is impracticable that every one should have a direct voice in its adoption. The Constitution does not require all public acts to be done in town meeting or an assembly

of the whole. General statutes within the state power are passed that affect the person or property of individuals, sometimes to the point of ruin, without giving them a chance to be heard. Their rights are protected in the only way that they can be in a complex society, by their power, immediate or remote, over those who make the rule.

c. What procedures does due process require? If agency action affects an interest that is protected by due process and the action is not a generally applicable rule that is covered by *Bi-Metallic*, the final question is whether the agency procedures are adequate. To answer this question, courts essentially balance the costs of the additional procedures demanded by the challenger against the anticipated benefits of these procedures. *See Connecticut v. Doehr*, 501 U.S. 1, 11 (1991). As articulated in *Mathews v. Eldridge*, 424 U.S. 319, 335 (1976), three factors are relevant to the analysis:

> First, the private interest that will be affected by the official action; second, the risk of an erroneous deprivation of such interest through the procedures used, and the probable value, if any, of additional or substitute procedural safeguards; and finally, the Government's interest, including the function involved and the fiscal and administrative burdens that the additional or substitute procedural requirement would entail.

In *Richardson*, Perales challenged the SSA's reliance on reports by non-testifying physicians as a violation of due process as well as the Social Security Act and the APA. Are you persuaded by the Court's reasons for rejecting his due process claim? Note that in *Goldberg v. Kelly*, 397 U.S. at 267–68, which involved *termination* of welfare benefits, the Court ruled that due process required "an effective opportunity to defend by confronting any adverse witnesses. . . ." Why is the initial determination of eligibility context different from a constitutional standpoint? What was Perales' private interest in cross-examining the physicians who examined him and evaluated his disability claim? What was the SSA's interest in *not* producing those physicians at a hearing? Would producing the physicians have measurably improved the reliability of the disability determination? On due process in agency proceedings, *see generally* Henry J. Friendly, *"Some Kind of Hearing,"* 123 U. Pa. L. Rev. 1267 (1973); Jerry L. Mashaw, *The Supreme Court's Due Process Calculus for Administrative Adjudicating: Three Factors in Search of a Theory of Value*, 44 U. Chi. L. Rev. 28 (1976).

2. Informal Adjudication

APA § 551(7) defines the term "adjudication" to mean the "agency process for the formulation of an order." The term "order" is, in turn, defined as "the whole or a part of a final disposition*** of an agency in a matter other than rulemaking," § 551(6). Adjudication is thus all final agency action other than rulemaking. Although, as we have seen, the APA contains several provisions dealing with formal or on-the-record adjudication, it has almost nothing to say about informal adjudication, i.e., adjudication that is not the product of an on-the-record proceeding.

Citizens to Preserve Overton Park, Inc. v. Volpe

401 U.S. 402 (1971)

Opinion of the Court by MR. JUSTICE MARSHALL, announced by MR. JUSTICE STEWART.

The growing public concern about the quality of our natural environment has prompted Congress in recent years to enact legislation designed to curb the accelerating destruction of our country's natural beauty. We are concerned in this case with § 4(f) of the Department of Transportation Act of 1966, as amended, and § 18(a) of the Federal-Aid Highway Act of 1968, 82 Stat. 823, 23 U.S.C. § 138 (1964 ed., Supp. V) (hereafter § 138). These statutes prohibit the Secretary of Transportation from authorizing the use of federal funds to finance the construction of highways through public parks if a "feasible and prudent" alternative route exists. If no such route is available, the statutes allow him to approve construction through parks only if there has been "all possible planning to minimize harm" to the park.

Petitioners, private citizens as well as local and national conservation organizations, contend that the Secretary has violated these statutes by authorizing the expenditure of federal funds for the construction of a six-lane interstate highway through a public park in Memphis, Tennessee. Their claim was rejected by the District Court, which granted the Secretary's motion for summary judgment, and the Court of Appeals for the Sixth Circuit affirmed.*** We now reverse the judgment below and remand for further proceedings in the District Court.

Overton Park is a 342-acre city park located near the center of Memphis. The park contains a zoo, a nine-hole municipal golf course, an outdoor theater, nature trails, a bridle path, an art academy, picnic areas, and 170 acres of forest. The proposed highway, which is to be a six-lane, high-speed, expressway, will sever the zoo from the rest of the park. Although the roadway will be depressed below ground level except where it crosses a small creek, 26 acres of the park will be destroyed. The highway is to be a segment of Interstate Highway I-40, part of the National System of Interstate and Defense Highways. I-40 will provide Memphis with a major east-west expressway which will allow easier access to downtown Memphis from the residential areas on the eastern edge of the city.

Although the route through the park was approved by the Bureau of Public Roads in 1956 and by the Federal Highway Administrator in 1966, the enactment of § 4(f) of the Department of Transportation Act prevented distribution of federal funds for the section of the highway designated to go through Overton Park until the Secretary of Transportation determined whether the requirements of § 4(f) had been met. Federal funding for the rest of the project was, however, available; and the state acquired a right-of-way on both sides of the park. In April 1968, the Secretary announced that he concurred in the judgment of local officials that I-40 should be built through the park. And in September 1969 the State acquired the right-of-way inside Overton Park from the city. Final approval for the project—the route as well as the design—was not announced until November 1969, after Congress had reiterated in § 138 of the Federal-Aid Highway Act that highway construction through public parks was to be restricted. Neither announcement approving the route and design of I-40 was accompanied by a statement of the Secretary's factual findings. He did not indicate why he believed there were no feasible and prudent alternative routes or why design changes could not be made to reduce the harm to the park.

Petitioners contend that the Secretary's action is invalid without such formal findings and that the Secretary did not make an independent determination but merely relied on the judgment of the Memphis City Council. They also contend that it would be "feasible and prudent" to route I-40 around Overton Park either to the north or to the south. And they argue that if these alternative routes are not "feasible and prudent," the present plan does not include "all possible" methods for reducing harm to the park. Petitioners claim that I-40 could be built under the park by using either of two possible tunneling methods, and they claim that, at a minimum, by using advanced drainage techniques the expressway could be depressed below ground level along the entire route through the park including the section that crosses the small creek.

Respondents argue that it was unnecessary for the Secretary to make formal findings, and that he did, in fact, exercise his own independent judgment which was supported by the facts. In the District Court, respondents introduced affidavits, prepared specifically for this litigation, which indicated that the Secretary had made the decision and that the decision was supportable. These affidavits were contradicted by affidavits introduced by petitioners, who also sought to take the deposition of a former Federal Highway Administrator who had participated in the decision to route I-40 through Overton Park.

The District Court and the Court of Appeals found that formal findings by the Secretary were not necessary and refused to order the deposition of the former Federal Highway Administrator because those courts believed that probing of the mental processes of an administrative decisionmaker was prohibited. And, believing that the Secretary's authority was wide and reviewing courts' authority narrow in the approval of highway routes, the lower courts held that the affidavits contained no basis for a determination that the Secretary had exceeded his authority.

We agree that formal findings were not required. But we do not believe that in this case judicial review based solely on litigation affidavits was adequate.*** Even though there is no *de novo* review in this case and the Secretary's approval of the route of I-40 does not have ultimately to meet the substantial-evidence test, the generally applicable standards of § 706 [of the APA] require the reviewing court to engage in a substantial inquiry. Certainly, the Secretary's decision is entitled to a presumption of regularity. But that presumption is not to shield his action from a thorough, probing, in-depth review.

The court is first required to decide whether the Secretary acted within the scope of his authority. This determination naturally begins with a delineation of the scope of the Secretary's authority and discretion. As has been shown, Congress has specified only a small range of choices that the Secretary can make. Also involved in this initial inquiry is a determination of whether on the facts the Secretary's decision can reasonably be said to be within that range. The reviewing court must consider whether the Secretary properly construed his authority to approve the use of parkland as limited to situations where there are no feasible alternative routes or where feasible alternative routes involve uniquely difficult problems. And the reviewing court must be able to find that the Secretary could have reasonably believed that in this case there are no feasible alternatives or that alternatives do involve unique problems.

Scrutiny of the facts does not end, however, with the determination that the Secretary has acted within the scope of his statutory authority. Section 706(2)(A) requires a finding that the actual choice made was not "arbitrary, capricious, an abuse of discretion, or otherwise not in accordance with law." 5 U.S.C. § 706(2)(A) (1964 ed., Supp. V). To make this finding the court must consider whether the decision was based on a consideration of the relevant factors and whether there has been a clear error of judgment. Although this inquiry into the facts is to be searching and careful, the ultimate standard of review is a narrow one. The court is not empowered to substitute its judgment for that of the agency.

The final inquiry is whether the Secretary's action followed the necessary procedural requirements. Here the only procedural error alleged is the failure of the Secretary to make formal findings and state his reason for allowing the highway to be built through the park.

Undoubtedly, review of the Secretary's action is hampered by his failure to make such findings, but the absence of formal findings does not necessarily require that the case be remanded to the Secretary. Neither the Department of Transportation Act nor the Federal-Aid Highway Act requires such formal findings. Moreover, the Administrative Procedure Act requirements that there be formal findings in certain rulemaking and adjudicatory proceedings do not apply to the Secretary's action here. *See* 5 U.S.C. §§ 553(a)(2), 554(a) (1964 ed., Supp. V). And, although formal findings may be required in some cases in the absence of statutory directives when the nature of the agency action is ambiguous, those situations are rare. Plainly, there is no ambiguity here; the Secretary has approved the construction of I-40 through Overton Park and has approved a specific design for the project.

Petitioners contend that although there may not be a statutory requirement that the Secretary make formal findings and even though this may not be a case for the reviewing court to impose a requirement that findings be made, Department of Transportation regulations require them. This argument is based on DOT Order 5610.1, which requires the Secretary to make formal findings when he approves the use of parkland for highway construction but which was issued after the route for I-40 was approved.***

While we do not question that DOT Order 5610.1 constitutes the law in effect at the time of our decision,*** there is an administrative record that allows the full, prompt review of the Secretary's action that is sought without additional delay which would result from having a remand to the Secretary.

That administrative record is not, however, before us. The lower courts based their review on the litigation affidavits that were presented. These affidavits were merely "post hoc" rationalizations, *Burlington Truck Lines v. United States*, 371 U.S. 156, 168–169 (1962), which have traditionally been found to be an inadequate basis for review. *Burlington Truck Lines v. United States, supra; SEC v. Chenery Corp.*, 318 U.S. 80, 87 (1943). And they clearly do not constitute the "whole record" compiled by the agency: the basis for review required by § 706 of the Administrative Procedure Act.

Thus it is necessary to remand this case to the District Court for plenary review of the Secretary's decision. That review is to be based on the full administrative record that was before the Secretary at the time he made his decision. But since the bare record may not disclose the factors that were considered or the Secretary's construction of the evidence it may be necessary for the District Court to require some explanation in order to determine if the Secretary acted within the scope of his authority and if the Secretary's action was justifiable under the applicable standard.

The court may require the administrative officials who participated in the decision to give testimony explaining their action. Of course, such inquiry into the mental processes of administrative decisionmakers is usually to be avoided. *United States v. Morgan*, 313 U.S. 409, 422 (1941). And where there are administrative findings that were made at the same time as the decision, as was the case in *Morgan*, there must be a strong showing of bad faith or improper behavior before such inquiry may be made. But here there are no such formal findings and it may be that the only way there can be effective judicial review is by examining the decisionmakers themselves.

The District Court is not, however, required to make such an inquiry. It may be that the Secretary can prepare formal findings including the information required by DOT Order 5610.1 that will provide an adequate explanation for his action. Such an explanation will, to some extent, be a "post hoc rationalization" and thus must be viewed critically. If the District Court decides that additional explanation is necessary, that court should consider which method will prove the most expeditious so that full review may be had as soon as possible.

[Separate opinions of JUSTICE BLACK and JUSTICE BLACKMUN omitted.]

Notes and Questions

1. **The Procedural Context?** What is the specific action of the Secretary of Transportation that petitioners challenged in this case? What procedure had the Secretary followed? Petitioners sought judicial review of the Secretary's action in the U.S. District Court for the District Columbia, and the case was transferred to the district court for the Western District Tennessee, where Overton Park is located. Which statute did petitioners sue under? How did the courts below rule on petitioners' challenge to the Secretary's action? What was the basis for their rulings?

2. **The Statutory Context?** As the Court's opinion in *Overton Park* explains, § 4(f) of the Department of Transportation Act of 1966, 82 Stat. 824, and § 18(a) of the Federal-Aid Highway Act of 1968, 82 Stat. 823, prohibited the Secretary of Transportation from using federal funds to finance construction of highways in public parks if a "feasible and prudent" alternative existed. Recall from above, Chapter 3[C][1], that

conditions on the use of federal funding are a powerful — and commonly used — mechanism for Congress to advance its policies.

Why would Congress have made use of such a funding directive as opposed to, say, prohibiting the construction of highways in specified parks? Would Congress have authority under Article I, Section 8 to issue such a flat-out prohibition? If we assume Congress would have such authority, isn't it more respectful of state and local authority to place conditions on federal funding rather than directly supplanting local decisionmaking? Given the limited tax base of many localities and the leverage the federal government enjoys from the federal income tax, is there any practical difference to the local governments?

3. **Informal Adjudication Under the APA?** The decision in *Overton Park* assumes that the Secretary's decision to route I-40 through Overton Park was an "adjudication" for purposes of the APA. What issue did the Secretary "adjudicate" in deciding to route I-40 through the park? When did this adjudication occur? Is it possible to tell from the *Overton Park* decision? Note that the APA recognizes two different forms of adjudication. The procedures for formal, on-the-record adjudication are specified in §§ 554, 556 and 557. Informal adjudication is an "ancillary matter" governed, if at all, by § 555 (other than, of course, the authorizing statute and the agency's own regulations and policies).

4. **Procedural Requirements for Informal Adjudication?** In contrast to formal adjudication, the APA does not specify the procedures that an agency must follow when adjudicating a matter informally. Section 555 provides only that a person compelled to appear before an agency is entitled to assistance of counsel, that subpoenas and other demands for information must be consistent with law, and that the agency should promptly inform interested persons of "the denial in whole or in part of a written application, petition, or other request."

Despite the fact that the APA says relatively little about informal adjudication, the Court in *Overton Park* implies certain procedural requirements for agency decisionmaking from the fact that agency decisions are subject to judicial review under APA § 706. According to the Supreme Court, what questions must a reviewing court answer to determine whether an agency has acted lawfully? How as a practical matter are these judicial review requirements likely to affect the agency's decisionmaking process in the first instance? How would you advise the Secretary of Transportation to proceed in the first instance?

a. **Agency's Authority.** The *Overton Park* Court says that a reviewing court must first "decide whether the Secretary acted within the scope of his authority." From where did the Secretary's authority derive? How were reviewing courts to know whether the Secretary acted within the scope of his authority?

b. **Consideration of Relevant Factors.** Next, a reviewing court "must consider whether the decision was based on a consideration of the relevant factors and whether there has been a clear error of judgment." What statutory provision does this standard derive from? What source should the agency consult to identify the relevant factors and the appropriate weight they should be given? Suppose an agency wishes to avoid having its employees testify in court every time that a decision to fund highway construction is challenged in the courts. What should it do?

c. **Following Necessary Procedure.** Finally, a reviewing court must assure itself that the agency "followed the necessary procedural requirements." This would include any procedures required by statute, the agency regulations, and due process. Note the Court's analysis of DOT Order 5610.1 in *Overton Park*; could it provide a basis for the Court's ruling? *See United States ex rel. Accardi v. Shaugnessy*, 347 U.S. 260 (1954); Note on Rulemaking's Consequences for Adjudication—And Vice Versa, *infra* Section [D].

5. **Backfilling the Agency's Justification?** In *Overton Park*, the Supreme Court remanded to the district court to review the Secretary of Transportation's decision "based on the full administrative record that was before the Secretary at the time he made his decision." If the "bare record" did not reveal whether the Secretary's decision satisfied the standards articulated by the Supreme Court, the district court was to "require some explanation" for the Secretary's decision, such as through testimony of administrative officials who participated in the decision. Alternatively, the district court could remand to the agency to permit the Secretary to make formal findings explaining his decision to route I-40 through the park. Is *Overton Park* consistent with the Court's general position, often associated with *SEC v. Chenery*, 318 U.S. 80 (1943), *infra* Chapter 4[D], that courts review agency action on the ground provided by the agency at the time of decision? Is it clear why the Court is giving the agency a second chance via the remand rather than invalidating the agency action for failure to make a legally required explanation?

In *Florida Power & Light Co. v. Lorion*, 470 U.S. 729, 744 (1985), the Court clarified that in the ordinary course, the appropriate disposition in a case involving an inadequate administrative record or inadequate contemporaneous agency explanation is to remand the case back to the agency: "[I]f the reviewing court simply cannot evaluate the challenged agency action on the basis of the record before it, the proper course, except in rare circumstances, is to remand to the agency for additional investigation or explanation." Why is a remand preferable to having agency officials testify regarding the basis for a challenged decision? Is a remand likely to generate better evidence of the reasons for the agency's decision? Does it have desirable effects for the agency's relationship with regulated parties? Keep these questions in mind when reading *SEC v. Chenery*, *infra* Section [D].

6. **Exemptions from Judicial Review.** The APA exempts two forms of agency action from judicial review. First, judicial review is unavailable when a "statute[] preclude[s] judicial review." Second, judicial review is unavailable when "agency action is committed to agency discretion by law." 5 U.S.C. §701(a). As Chapter 5 explains, both exceptions are narrow. The presumption under the APA is that most "final" agency will be subject judicial review in some forum. *See* Chapter 5[B], *infra*. The *Overton Park* Court found the Secretary of Transportation's action reviewable under the APA because there was law to apply: "The language [of §4(f) of the Transportation Act

and § 138 of the Federal-Aid-to-Highways Act] is a plain and explicit bar to the use of federal funds for construction of highway financing through parks—and only the most unusual situations are exempted." Is this clear from the statutes? For criticism of the Court's reasoning on this point, see Peter L. Strauss, *Revisiting* Overton Park, 39 UCLA L. Rev. 1251 (1992).

————

U.S. Customs Service Ruling in *United States v. Mead Corp.*, 533 U.S. 218 (2001)

To provide a sense of what an informal agency adjudicative determination looks like, consider the following letter ruling issued by the Customs Service, now U.S. Customs and Border Protection (Customs), which at the time of the letter was part of the Department of the Treasury and is now located within the Department of Homeland Security (DHS).

First, some background. Duties on goods imported into the United States are determined according to the Harmonized Tariff Schedule of the United States (HTSUS), 19 U.S.C. § 1202. HTSUS is the U.S. implementation of the Harmonized System, a standardized system of names and numbers used to classify goods in international trade that was created by the International Convention on the Harmonized Commodity Description and Coding System, June 14, 1983, 1035 U.N.T.S. 3 (entered into force, Jan. 1, 1988).

Customs is responsible for assessing and collecting duties under the HTSUSA. The agency is authorized to "fix the final classification and rate of duty applicable to [imported] merchandise*** under rules and regulations prescribed by the Secretary [of the Treasury]." 19 U.S.C. § 1500(b). Customs rulings are issued by attorneys in the Office of Regulations and Rulings at Customs Headquarters, by National Import Specialists of the National Commodity Specialist Division at the Port of New York, and by Field National Import Specialists located at the 46 service ports located throughout the United States. *See* 19 C.F.R. § 177.2(a); 19 C.F.R. § 101.3(b)(2). Most rulings are issued before goods are imported into the United States. Alternatively, protests may be filed at the port of entry where the decision being protested was made, as occurred in the adjudication that follows. *See* 19 C.F.R. § 174.12(d).

U.S. Customs Service

RE: Decision on Application for Further Review of Protest No. 4501-93-100016*

October 21, 1994*

District Director, U.S. Customs Service,

4477 Woodson Road, Rm. 200

St Louis, MO 63134-3716

Dear Sir:

This is a decision on application for further review of a protest timely filed on March 26, 1993, by Sidney H. Kuflik of the law firm of Lamb & Lerch, on behalf of his client, the Mead Corporation, against your decision regarding the classification of day/week planners, also referred to as organizers or agendas. Four entries of the subject merchandise were made at the port at Kansas City, Missouri, between the dates of September 3 and October 14, 1992. These entries were liquidated [*i.e.*, the amount of duty was fixed—Eds.] between December 28, 1992, and January 29, 1993.***

Counsel*** raises substantive legal arguments pertaining to the validity of the classification of these articles under subheading 4820.10.2010, [Harmonized Tariff Schedule of the United States (HTSUSA)].****

The articles at issue are described as "day planners."*** Samples of style numbers 47062 and 47104 were submitted to this office along with generalized information about the day planners. Some of the day planners contain three-ring binders which are inserted into a pocket on the inside of the jacket cover. These articles contain calendar planners, daily planners, sections designated for address/telephone information, blank note pads, rulers, plastic business card holders and graph note pads. Four entries of the subject merchandise were liquidated by Customs under subheading 4820.10.2010, HTSUSA, as bound diaries, dutiable at a rate of 4 percent ad valorem.

[Mead] contends that the day planners are properly classifiable under subheading 4820.10.4000, HTSUSA, and entitled to duty free entry. In support of this contention, [Mead] states*** the day planners at issue are not diaries per se, but rather articles "similar to" diaries, and therefore classification is precluded from subheading 4820.10.20, HTSUSA[.]***

The determinative issue is whether the subject merchandise is classifiable as bound "diaries" under subheading 4820.10.2010, HTSUSA, or as "similar to" diaries under subheading 4820.10.4000, HTSUSA. This issue has been addressed in several rulings by this office.*** In these rulings this office has consistently determined that articles similar in design and/or function to the instant merchandise are classifiable as diaries. The rationale for this determination was based on lexicographic sources, as well as extrinsic evidence of how these types of articles are treated in the trade and commerce of the United States.

In all of [these] rulings***, Customs held that articles synonymously referred to as diaries, planners, agendas, organizers and engagement books, most of which

---

* At the time this ruling was issued, heading 4820 and subheadings 4820.10, 4820.10.20 and 4820.10.40 of the HTSUS provided as follows:

> 4820 Registers, account books, notebooks, order books, receipt books, letter pads, memorandum pads, diaries and similar articles, exercise books, blotting pads, binders (loose-leaf or other), folders, file covers, manifold business forms, interleaved carbon sets and other articles of stationery, of paper or paperboard; albums for samples or for collections and book covers (including cover boards and book jackets) of paper or paperboard:
>
> 4820.10 Registers, account books, notebooks, order books, receipt books, letter pads, memorandum pads, diaries and similar articles:
>
> 4820.10.20 Diaries, notebooks and address books, bound; memorandum pads, letter pads and similar articles 3.6%
>
> 4820.10.40 Other 0%

—Eds.

incorporated the same or similar components as the subject merchandise, (i.e., day/week planners, address/telephone sections, blank sections for notes), fit squarely within the definition of "diary" as set forth in the Compact Edition of the Oxford English Dictionary, 1987. That definition reads:

> 2. A book prepared for keeping a daily record, or having spaces with printed dates for daily memoranda and jottings; also applied to calendars containing daily memoranda on matters of importance to people generally or to members of a particular profession, occupation, or pursuit.

In counsel's supplementary submission to this office, dated September 22, 1994, it is argued that Customs should base its classification of the subject merchandise solely on the first definition of "diary" presented in the Oxford English Dictionary, which reads:

> 1. A daily record of events or transactions, a journal, specially, a daily record of matters affecting the writer personally, or which come under his personal observation.

In response to this claim, we wish to stress two points. First, Customs is not obligated to limit its reliance on lexicographic sources to the first definition presented for a given word. Reference to lexicographic sources is a means to ascertain the commonly accepted definition or definitions, for a word or term. It broadens our understanding of a word so as to arrive at a more accurate classification. Many words have several definitions and Customs may consider any or all of them when making a classification determination. Second, we note that the narrower definition of "diary," as set forth in the Oxford English Dictionary's first definition, connotes an article containing blank pages used to record extensive notations of one's daily activities. This is not the sole format for a diary. The word "diary" also connotes a more formal and comprehensive approach to record-keeping.

The broader concept of diary includes those articles classified in HRL's 955636 and 955637, both dated April 6, 1994. In those rulings Customs determined that the classification of day planners as diaries reflects the common and commercial identity of these items in the marketplace. In HRL 955636, Customs classified day planners that were similar in function to the articles currently at issue. The covers of the day planners classified in HRL 955636 were conspicuously and indelibly printed with the legend "1994 Desk Diary." As we noted in that ruling, it stands to reason that the publisher would not have gone to the added expense of printing "1994 Desk Diary" on these articles' covers, nor risked alienating potential customers, if the articles were not indeed recognized as diaries in the marketplace. The fact remains that these articles must be considered a recognized form of diary if a manufacturer in the industry labels the articles as such and purposely presents them in such a manner to the consumer. This fact is pertinent in the instant analysis because the articles marketed as diaries in HRL 955636 and the Mead planners at issue are similar in material respects; both articles contain day and week planners with spaces to record appointments and various notations, sections for address and telephone numbers and blank sections for notes. As the overall design and function of the HRL 955636 diaries and the Mead planners are the same, and the former are marketed to consumers as diaries and recognized in the trade as such, it is reasonable to conclude that the Mead planners are similarly deemed to be diaries in the trade and commerce of the United States.

Further evidence that day planners are treated as a form of diary in the trade and commerce of the United States is provided by current advertisements run in The New Yorker magazine. The New Yorker regularly displays full-page advertisements for its "1994 New Yorker Desk Diary." The diary depicted in the advertisement appears to have a similar function to the planners under review. The advertisement's copy reads: "Since you depend on a diary every day of the year, pick the one that's perfect for you ... Recognize what's important to you: a week at a glance, a ribbon marker, lie flat binding (spiral), lots of space to write."***

The Court of International Trade has spoken to the issue of what constitutes a diary for classification purposes. In *Fred Baumgarten v. United States*, [49 Cust. Ct. 275 (1962),] the court dealt with the classification of a plastic-covered book which was similar in overall function to the articles currently under review. In *Baumgarten*, the court determined the correct classification of an article which measured approximately 4-1/4 inches by 7-3/8 inches and contained pages for "Personal Memoranda," calendars for the years 1960–1962, statistical tables, and 20-odd pages set aside for telephone numbers and addresses. The majority of the book consisted of ruled pages allocated to the days of the year and the hours of the day. A blank lined page, inserted at the end of each month's section, was captioned "Notes." The court held that this article was properly classified by Customs under item 256.56, Tariff Schedules of the United States, which provided for "Blank books, bound: diaries," at a duty rate of 20 percent ad valorem. In that ruling, the court held:

> "the particular distinguishing feature of a diary is its suitability for the receipt of daily notations; and in this respect, the books here in issue are well described. By virtue of the allocation of spaces for hourly entries during the course of each day of the year, the books are designed for that very purpose. That the daily events to be chronicled may also include scheduled appointments would not detract from their general character as appropriate volumes for the recording of daily memoranda."

The *Baumgarten* Court's analysis and holding, if applied to the merchandise at issue, yields a similar finding: the articles at issue are properly classifiable as bound diaries of subheading 4820.10.2010, HTSUSA, inasmuch as their distinguishing feature is their suitability for the receipt of daily notations. As with the articles at issue in *Baumgarten*, the Mead day planners contain allocated spaces for daily and hourly entries.***

The primary design and function of an article controls its classification. Hence, the determinative criteria as to whether these types of articles are deemed "diaries" for classification purposes is whether they are primarily designed for use as, or primarily function as, articles for the receipt of daily notations, events and appointments.

Sincerely,

John Durant, Director, Commercial Rulings

Notes and Questions

1. **Regulatory Framework and Judicial Review.** Note the similarities between this regulatory structure and its predecessor discussed in *Nix v. Hedden*, *supra* Chapter 2[B][2][c]. What explains Congress's decision to delegate authority to fix customs duties to Customs? Is this a function that, as a practical matter, the courts could perform?

A party that objects to Customs' classification of imported goods may seek review in the U.S. Court of International Trade (CIT), an Article III court with nine judges that sits in New York City. *See* 28 U.S.C. § 1581 (defining CIT's jurisdiction); 28 U.S.C. § 1585 (granting CIT all the powers in law and equity of, or as conferred by statute upon, a district court of the United States). Appeals from decisions of the Court of International Trade are heard by the U.S. Court of Appeals for the Federal Circuit. *See* 28 U.S.C. § 1295(a)(5).

Why is judicial review of customs rulings centralized in the Court of International Trade instead of occurring in federal trial courts, as it was at the time of *Nix*? Why are appeals heard only in the Federal Circuit?

2. **The Issue for the Agency?** At issue in this letter ruling is whether Mead Corp.'s day planners are classifiable as "diaries" under HTSUS subheading 4820.10.4000. If so, the day planners were subject to a 3.6% import tax. If not, the planners could be imported without duty. Customs resolves similar issues in thousands of cases per year. Between 1998 and 1999, it issued a total of 11,898 classification rulings. 10,986, or approximately 92%, of the rulings were issued by the National Commodity Specialist Division at the Port of New York or by Field National Import Specialists at service ports. Brief of the Customs and International Trade Bar Ass'n at 6, *United States v. Mead Corp.*, 533 U.S. 218 (2001).

3. **The Agency's Reasoning?** Why does the Customs Service conclude that the day planners are diaries for purposes of HTSUS subheading 4820.10.4000?

a. **Lexicographic sources.** The agency first turns to the dictionary definition of the term "diary." Customs relies on a definition from the Compact Oxford English Dictionary, while Mead relies on the full OED. What is the rationale for relying on these dictionaries? Do they demonstrate the way in which the authors of the HTSUS used the term "diaries"? The way the term is used in common usage? The way it is used among a specialized community of diary users? Is the classification of diaries an example of the lay versus ordinary meaning problem illustrated by *Nix v. Hedden*? Why or why not?

b. **Treatment of day planners in trade and commerce.** Customs notes that it has previously classified day planners as diaries. As a formal matter, Customs is not bound by its prior rulings. It can change its mind and reverse prior decisions but can it ignore those rulings while they are in effect? *Cf. NLRB v. Wyman-Gordon Co.*, 394 US 759, 766 (1969), *infra* Section [D] ("Subject to the qualified role of *stare decisis* in the administrative process, [adjudicated cases] may serve as precedents. But this is far from saying . . . that commands, decisions, or policies announced in adjudication are 'rules' in the sense that they must, without more, be obeyed by the affected public."). Could Customs as a practical matter keep track of the thousands of letter rulings it issues every year?

Customs notes an advertisement in *The New Yorker* for a day planner that is advertised as a "desk diary." Customs reasons that, because the New Yorker day planner is a diary, Mead's day planners, which are similar to it, are also diaries. Why is the *New Yorker* diary relevant to the issue before the agency? Does it show how the drafters of the HTSUS understood the term "diary"? How the term is used in general usage?

c. **Judicial Precedent.** Customs also relies on the Court of Internal Trade's 1962 decision in *Baumgarten v. United States*. There, the court observed that "the particular distinguishing feature of a diary is its suitability for the receipt of daily notations." What was the court interpreting in *Baumgarten*? Is the court's statement regarding the "distinguishing feature" of diaries in *Baumgarten* good evidence of the meaning of HTSUS subheading 4820.10?

As a general matter, does the Customs Service's resolution of Mead's protest require the application of agency expertise? Does it reflect the value of assigning policy implementation to an institution that is relatively free from improper political influences? Is it an example of an agency providing "mass justice," as in the Social Security context?

4. **The Impact of Judicial Review?** Recall from *Overton Park* that an agency adjudicating a statutory requirement must demonstrate that it is acting within the scope of its delegated authority; considered the "relevant" factors; and followed the necessary procedures. Does the format of the Customs Service's letter ruling reflect the influence of the Court's holdings in *Overton Park*? If so, how?

5. **Judicial Deference to Informal Agency Adjudications?** The letter ruling reproduced here is the subject of a notable Supreme Court decision addressing the legal status of such agency determinations and the pertinent standards for judicial review. *See United States v. Mead Corp.*, 533 U.S. 218 (2001), in Chapter 5[C][3].

C. Rulemaking

In the terminology of the Administrative Procedure Act, all agency action subject to its provisions falls into one of two categories, "adjudication" or "rulemaking." Having considered informal and formal forms of adjudication, we turn now to rulemaking.

Portland Cement Association v. Ruckelshaus

486 F.2d 375 (D.C. Cir. 1973)

LEVENTHAL, CIRCUIT JUDGE:

Portland Cement Association seeks review of the action of the Administrator of the Environmental Protection Agency (EPA) in promulgating stationary source standards for new or modified portland cement plants, pursuant to the provisions of Section 111 of the Clean Air Act. Medusa Corporation and Northwestern States Portland Cement Company were granted leave to intervene by this court and they together with petitioner, will be referred to as the cement manufacturers. Long Island Lighting Company has filed a brief as an *Amicus Curiae.****

Section 111 of the Clean Air Act, [42 U.S.C. § 7411,] directs the Administrator to promulgate "standards of performance" governing emissions of air pollutants by new stationary sources constructed or modified after the effective date of pertinent regulations. The focus of dispute in this case concerns EPA compliance with the statutory language of Section 111(a) which defines "standard of performance" as follows:

(1) The term "standard of performance" means a standard for emissions of air pollutants which reflects the degree of emission limitation achievable through the application of the best system of emission reduction which (taking into account the cost of achieving such reduction) the Administrator determines has been adequately demonstrated.

After designating portland cement plants* as a stationary source of air pollution which may "contribute significantly to air pollution which causes or contributes to the endangerment of public health or welfare", under Section 111(b)(1)(A) of the Act, the Administrator published a proposed regulation establishing standards of performance for portland cement plants. The proposed regulation was accompanied by a document entitled "Background Information For Proposed New-Source Performance Standards," which set forth the justification. Interested parties were afforded an opportunity to participate in the rule making by submitting comments, and more than 200 interested parties did so. The "standards of performance" were adopted by a regulation, issued December 16, 1971, which requires, inter alia, that particulate matter emitted from portland cement plants shall not be:

(1) In excess of 0.30 lb. per ton of feed to the kiln (0.15 Kg. per metric ton), maximum 2-hour average. (2) Greater than 10% opacity, except that where the presence of uncombined water is the only reason for failure to meet the requirements for this subparagraph, such failure shall not be a violation of this section.

The standards were justified by the EPA as follows:

---

* "Portland" cement is the most common form of cement in common use around the world, and is named for its similarity to Portland stone, which is quarried on the Isle of Portland in Dorset, England. — Eds.

> The standards of performance are based on stationary source testing conducted by the Environmental Protection Agency and/or contractors and on data derived from various other sources, including the available technical literature. In the comments of the proposed standards, many questions were raised as to costs and demonstrated capability of control systems to meet the standards. These comments have been evaluated and investigated, and it is the Administrator's judgment that emission control systems capable of meeting the standards have been adequately demonstrated and that the standards promulgated herein are achievable at reasonable costs.

On March 21, 1972, EPA published a "Supplemental Statement in Connection With Final Promulgation", amplifying the justification for its standards and indicating that it had been prompted by the action of this court in *Kennecott Copper Corp. v. E.P.A.*, 462 F.2d 846 (1972), to offer "a more specific explanation of how [the Administrator] had arrived at the standard." This statement relied principally on EPA tests on existing portland cement plants to demonstrate that the promulgated standards were achievable.

The action of the Administrator has been challenged [on the ground that t]he achievability of the standards was not adequately demonstrated.***

Section 111 of the Act requires "the degree of emission limitation achievable [which] ... the Administrator determines has been adequately demonstrated." Petitioners contend that the promulgated standard for new stationary sources has not been "adequately demonstrated", raising issues as to the interpretation to be given to this requirement, the procedures followed by the agency in arriving at its standard, and the scientific evidence upon which it was formulated. An examination of these questions requires a brief description of the process used to manufacture portland cement and the devices presently employed to control emissions.

A. Present Types of Emission Control in the Manufacture of Portland Cement

In the manufacturing process for portland cement, the principal ingredients, limestone and clay, are combined, after having been reduced to a powdery fineness, to make a substance known as raw feed. The powdered limestone and clay are mixed by either the wet process or the dry process. In the wet process, water is added to the limestone and clay to make a slurry, which is then introduced into a kiln. In the dry process, the two substances are mixed mechanically and by use of air before the mix is introduced into a kiln.

Raw feed is introduced to the kiln at ambient air temperature and is then heated to a temperature of about 2700° Fahrenheit, produced within the kiln by the use of various fuels. The emission standards under challenge here relate solely to the control of particulate matter produced by the kiln operation.

The kiln operation involves the chemical process known as calcining limestone; carbon dioxide is driven from the limestone, converting calcium carbonate ($CaCO_3$) into calcium oxide (CaO), ($CaCO_3$ yields $CO_2 + CaO$). The calcium oxide later combines with the clay to form a substance known as "clinker", the basic component of cement. The calcination process produces gases and dust as by-products. The particulate matter is suspended in the hot exhaust gas and the various types of emission control devices remove this matter from the gas, before it is emitted into the atmosphere through a stack.

The two types of equipment principally used in removing particulate matter from the exhaust gas are electrostatic precipitators and glass fabric bags, impregnated with graphite, located in a "bag house." When the precipitator is used, dust particles are charged and pass through an electrical field of the opposite charge, thus causing the dust to be precipitated out of the exhaust gas and thereafter collected by the device. When glass fabric bags are used, the exhaust gas is cooled, sometimes by a water spray, so that the bags will operate without damage from excessive heat. The bag filters out the particulate dust, though sometimes the coolant combines with the dust to form a gummy substance as residue in the bags, which must be continuously cleaned out in order to avoid impairing the permeability of the bag.

It is the ability of control devices such as precipitators and bags to separate out a sufficient amount of particulate from the exhaust—in accord with the proposed standards—which is under challenge by the manufacturers. The standard requires that the particulate matter emitted from portland cement plants not be "in excess of 0.30 lb. per ton of feed to the kiln . . . maximum 2-hour average".

B. Technology Available For New Plants

We begin by rejecting the suggestion of the cement manufacturers that the Act's requirement that emission limitations be "adequately demonstrated" necessarily implies that any cement plant now in existence be able to meet the proposed standards. Section 111 looks toward what may fairly be projected for the regulated future, rather than the state of the art at present, since it is addressed to standards for new plants—old stationary source pollution being controlled through other regulatory authority. It is the "achievability" of the proposed standard that is in issue.

The language in section 111 was the result of a Conference Committee compromise, and did not incorporate the language of either the House or Senate bills.[58] The House bill would have provided that "the Secretary . . . [give] appropriate consideration to technological and economic feasibility", while the Senate would have required that standards reflect "the greatest degree of emission control which the Secretary determines to be achievable through application of the latest available control technology, processes, operating methods, or other alternatives."

The Senate Report made clear that it did not intend that the technology "must be in actual routine use somewhere." The essential question was rather whether the technology would be available for installation in new plants. The House Report also refers to "available" technology. Its caution that "[i]n order to be considered 'available' the technology may not be one which constitutes a purely theoretical or experimental means of preventing or controlling air pollution" merely reflects the final language

---

58. The Conference Committee considered S.4358, 91st Cong., 2d Sess., 113 (1970) and H.R. 17255, 91st Cong., 2d Sess. sec. 112 (1970). The Report of the Conference does not discuss the language finally adopted, H.Rep.No.91-1783, 91st Cong., 2d Sess. 9, 45 (1970).

adopted, that it must be "adequately demonstrated" that there will be "available technology".

The resultant standard is analogous to the one examined in *International Harvester* [*v. Ruckelshaus*, 478 F.2d 615 (D.C. Cir. 1973)]. The Administrator may make a projection based on existing technology, though that projection is subject to the restraints of reasonableness and cannot be based on "crystal ball" inquiry. As there, the question of availability is partially dependent on "lead time", the time in which the technology will have to be available. Since the standards here put into effect will control new plants immediately, as opposed to one or two years in the future, the latitude of projection is correspondingly narrowed. If actual tests are not relied on, but instead a prediction is made, "its validity as applied to this case rests on the reliability of [the] prediction and the nature of [the] assumptions."

C. Right to Comment on EPA Methodology

We find a critical defect in the decision-making process in arriving at the standard under review in the initial inability of petitioners to obtain—in timely fashion—the test results and procedures used on existing plants which formed a partial basis for the emission control level adopted, and in the subsequent seeming refusal of the agency to respond to what seem to be legitimate problems with the methodology of these tests.

1. Unavailability of Test Methodology

The regulations under review were first proposed on August 3, 1971 and then adopted on December 16, 1971. Both the proposed and adopted rule cited certain portland cement testing as forming a basis for the standards. In the statements accompanying the proposed rule, the Administrator stated:***

> The standards of performance are based on stationary source testing conducted by the Environmental Protection Agency and/or contractors . . . .

As indicated in the earlier statement of the case, the proposed standard was accompanied by a Background Document which disclosed some information about the tests, but did not identify the location or methodology used in the one successful test conducted on a dry-process kiln. Further indication was given to petitioners that the Administrator was relying on the tests referred to in the Background Document, when the statement of reasons accompanying the adopted standard were expanded in mid-March of 1972, in the supplemental statement filed while this case was pending on appeal to our court. The Administrator there stated:

> The proposed standard was based principally on particulate levels achieved at a kiln controlled by a fabric filter.

For the first time, however, another set of tests was referred to, as follows:

> After proposal [of the regulation], but prior to promulgation a second kiln controlled by a fabric filter was tested and found to have particulate emissions in excess of the proposed standard. However, based on the revised particulate test method, the second installation showed particulate emissions to be less than 0.3 pound per ton of kiln feed.

These two testing programs were referred to in the March 1972 supplemental statement, but the details, aside from a summary of test results, were not made available to petitioners until mid-April 1972. At that time, it was revealed that the first set of tests was conducted April 29–30, 1971, by a contractor for EPA, at the Dragon Cement Plant, a dry process plant in Northampton, Pennsylvania, and that the second set was performed at the Oregon Portland Cement plant, at Lake Oswego, Oregon, a wet process plant, on October 7 and 8, 1971. The full disclosure of the methodology followed in these tests raised certain problems, in the view of petitioners, on which they had not yet had the opportunity to comment. Their original comments in the period between the proposal and promulgation of the regulation could only respond to the brief summary of the results of the tests that had been disclosed at that time.

After intervenor Northwestern States Portland Cement Company received the detailed test information in mid-April 1972, it submitted the test data, for analysis of reliability and accuracy, to Ralph H. Striker, an engineer experienced in the design of emission control systems for portland cement plants.

He concluded that the first series of tests run at the Dragon Cement Company were "grossly erroneous" due to inaccurate sampling techniques to measure particulate matter. Northwestern States then moved this Court to remand the record to EPA so that the agency might consider the additional comments on the tests. This motion was granted on October 31, 1972.***

We are aware that EPA was required to issue its standards within 90 days of the issuance of the proposed regulation, and that this time might not have sufficed to make an adequate compilation of the data from the initial tests, or to fully describe the methodology employed. This was more likely as to the second tests, which were begun during the pendency of the proposed regulation. In contrast, more than three months intervened between the conduct of the first tests and the issuance of the proposed regulation. Even as to the second tests*** the fact that the agency chose to perform additional tests and release the results indicates that it did not believe possible agency consideration was frozen. It is not consonant with the purpose of a rule-making proceeding to promulgate rules on the basis of inadequate data, or on data that, [to a] critical degree, is known only to the agency.

2. The EPA Response to the Remand

In this case, EPA made no written submission as to the additional comments made by petitioners. Our remand was ordered, as to Northwestern, on October 31, 1972. All that EPA did was to comply with the mandate that the analysis of Mr. Striker be added to the certified record. It may be that EPA considers Mr. Striker's analysis invalid—but we have no way of knowing this. As the record stands, all we have is Mr. Striker's repudiation of the test data, without response. The purpose of our prior remand cannot be realized unless we hear EPA's response to his comments, and the record must be remanded again, for that purpose.

We are not establishing any broad principle that EPA must respond to every comment made by manufacturers on the validity of its standards or the methodology and scientific basis for their formulation. In the case of the Striker presentation, however, our prior remand reflects this court's view of the significance, or at least potential significance, of this presentation. If this were a private lawsuit, we might reverse the order under appeal for failure of its proponent to meet the burden of refutation or explanation. Since this is a matter involving the public interest, in which the court and agency are in a kind of partnership relationship for the purpose of effectuating the legislative mandate, we remand. This agency, particularly when its decisions can literally mean survival of persons or property, has a continuing duty to take a "hard look" at the problems involved in its regulatory task, and that includes an obligation to comment on matters identified as potentially significant by the court order remanding for further presentation. Manufacturers' comments must be significant enough to step over a threshold requirement of materiality before any lack of agency response or consideration becomes of concern. The comment cannot merely state that a particular mistake was made in a sampling operation; it must show why the mistake was of possible significance in the results of the test. This was certainly done by Mr. Striker, who on the basis of some extensive mathematical calculations stated:

> It is my personal opinion that the particulate matter emissions of .202 pounds in test 1 per ton of kiln feed reported in the summary sheet on Page vii and again on Page 6 of Exhibit 4-A is grossly erroneous, and that the correct emission of particulate matter is in the neighborhood of .404 pounds per ton of kiln feed.

In order that rule-making proceedings to determine standards be conducted in orderly fashion, information should generally be disclosed as to the basis of a proposed rule at the time of issuance. If this is not feasible, as in case of statutory time constraints, information that is material to the subject at hand should be disclosed as it becomes available, and comments received, even though subsequent to issuance of the rule—with court authorization, where necessary. This is not a requirement that the rule be suspended, though the court may consider an application for stay based on probability of success and furtherance of the public interest.

Conversely, challenges to standards must be limited to points made by petitioners in agency proceedings. To entertain comments made for the first time before this court would be destructive of a meaningful administrative process.

There are claims made in this court which were not presented to EPA. For example, petitioner Portland Cement Association states in its brief, in regard to the first set of tests at the Dragon Cement Plant:

> Mistakes and conditions occurred which prevented the test from using observed, measured values. Encrusted solids were thought to cause a high reading in Run 1 so lower readings from other tests were substituted. The area of a duct was calculated rather than measured due to the presence of deposits. And liquid from Run 3 was erroneously poured into a beaker from Run 2.

From the reference supplied in petitioner's brief, we discern that this criticism of testing procedure was based upon data released on the testing after the 45 day period of comment had passed, and so there was no opportunity at that time to bring this sampling error to the attention of the agency. However, our October 1972 remand gave EPA an opportunity, in its updating and ongoing reexamination, to make a specific comment on petitioner's objection to the Dragon plant test. Instead, only the comment of Mr. Striker was presented.

Ordinarily, we would not consider comments not presented to EPA. But here there was belated disclosure by EPA of back-up testing, and remand will be necessary concerning the Striker criticism. Accordingly, we will provide that EPA should, on remand, consider the contentions presented in briefs to this court, though not previously raised, unless EPA explains why they are not material. It will be for EPA, on the remand, to examine the relevancy and import of petitioners' criticisms of the Administrator's methodology.

Notes and Questions

1. **The Procedural Posture?** What decisionmaking procedure was the EPA using when it determined that a Portland cement plant could emit pollution at a rate of "0.30 lb. per ton of feed to the kiln (0.15 Kg. per metric ton), maximum 2-hour average"? Who were the petitioners challenging the agency action? What precisely were petitioners challenging? What did petitioners want from the EPA?

Prior to taking the action under review, how long had the issue been under consideration by the EPA? When did the comment period begin and end? What actions had the Court of Appeals taken? When? What was the appeals court's rationale? What was the statutory basis in the Clean Air Act (CAA) and the APA for those actions?

2. **The Statutory Context.** Section 111 of the CAA directs the EPA to develop performance standards for new "stationary sources" of emissions, such as power plants and factories. Why was it necessary for Congress to delegate authority to develop new source performance standards to the EPA? Could these standards have been established by Congress after appropriate hearings?

3. **The Regulatory Issue?** What is the basic defect the D.C. Circuit identifies in the EPA's determination that Portland cement plants may not emit pollution "[i]n excess of 0.30 lb. per ton of feed to the kiln (0.15 Kg. per metric ton), maximum 2-hour average"?

4. **"Adjudicative Fact" vs. "Legislative Fact."** Agency adjudication often involves the determination of "adjudicative facts." These are "facts concerning [the] immediate parties—what the parties did, what the circumstances were, what the background conditions were***." Kenneth Culp Davis, *An Approach to Problems of Evidence in the Administrative Process*, 55 HARV. L. REV. 364, 402 (1942). Such factual determinations—who did or said what, to whom, when, where, and why—are normally made by courts or in agency adjudications. For example, in *Richardson v. Perales*, *supra* Section [B][1], the central factual questions were Perales' physical and mental condition and whether it prevented him from being able to return to work. To determine these facts, the SSA heard from Perales, reviewed notes from doctors who treated

him, and consulted the Social Security grids, which aggregated information about the availability of work in the national economy, see *Heckler v. Campbell, supra* Chapter 1[C][3].

In contrast, agency rulemaking often depends upon data about general social conditions and may require the agency to make prospective determinations about what is likely to happen to a large number of people in many locations. These are often called "legislative" facts: "When an agency wrestles with a question of law or policy, it is acting legislatively*** and the facts which inform its legislative judgment may conveniently be denominated legislative facts." Davis, *supra*, at 402. For example, in *Portland Cement*, the Administrator's determination of "the degree of emission limitation achievable through the application of the best system of emission reduction" is necessarily forward-looking and is based on technological, logistic and cost considerations that would generally be applicable to all Portland cement plants. This is considered a legislative fact and resembles the kinds of determinations legislatures usually make when considering the necessity for legislation and the form that legislation takes. *But cf.* Note 3 to *INS v. Chadha, supra* Chapter 3[B][2][a], p. 328 (discussing private bills).

5. **Rulemaking Requirements vs. Adjudication Requirements.** Recall from *Overton Park* that when "adjudicating" a statutory issue, an agency must consider "relevant factors" and avoid making "a clear error of judgment." To withstand judicial review, an agency as a practical matter must maintain a contemporaneous record of the factors it considered, the legal authorities that support its action, and the reasons why it adjudicated an issue the way it did. How do the requirements for rulemaking recognized by the D.C. Circuit in *Portland Cement* compare to the *Overton Park* requirements? What is the legal basis for the *Portland Cement* requirements?

6. **Formal versus Informal Rulemaking under the APA.** The APA uses the term "rulemaking" to refer to the process of promulgating forward-looking, quasi-legislative rules. These are sometimes referred to as "substantive" or "legislative" rules. An agency may be directed to engage in rulemaking by law or do so of its own motion. In addition, APA § 553(e) requires "[e]ach agency [to] give an interested person the right to petition for the issuance, amendment, or repeal of a rule."

As with adjudication, the APA recognizes both formal and informal modes of rulemaking. *See* 5 U.S.C. §§ 553, 556–557. Formal rulemaking is relatively rare today, and is governed by §§ 556 and 557. Formal rulemaking proceedings involve hearings and resemble agency adjudications. The agency has authority to issue subpoenas, take testimony, and hear presentations of evidence and argument. After a record is compiled, a rule is promulgated.

When is an agency required to follow formal rulemaking procedures instead of following § 553? In *United States v. Florida East Coast Railway Co.*, 410 U.S. 224 (1973), the Supreme Court considered the process that the Interstate Commerce Commission (ICC) followed in promulgating a rule that required railroads to make an incentive payment when using another railroad's boxcars. The rule sought to address a nationwide boxcar shortage and was issued under § 1(14)(a) of the Interstate

Commerce Act, 24 Stat. 379, as amended, which provided: "The Commission may, after hearing, on a complaint or upon its own initiative without complaint, establish reasonable rules, regulations, and practices with respect to car service by common carriers by railroad subject to this chapter . . . ."

Before promulgating the rule, the ICC held informal meetings with railroads to discuss the boxcar shortage and elicited their views on how the Commission should respond to it. The Commission also published a report that contained the text of its proposed rule and invited railroads to submit "statements of facts, briefs, and statements of position" supporting or opposing the rule. The Commission did not hold an oral hearing on the rule, however.

On petitions for review of the rule, the Supreme Court held that the opportunity to submit written evidence and argument satisfied § 1(14)(a)'s "hearing" requirement, and that neither that section nor the APA required the agency to hold an oral hearing. Relying on *United States v. Allegheny-Ludlum Steel Corp.*, 406 U.S. 742 (1972), the Court reasoned that formal hearing procedures in rulemaking were only obligatory when a statute contained language to the effect that a decision had to be made "on the record after opportunity for an agency hearing." Absent such language, agency procedures that complied with § 553 satisfied the statutory requirement to hold a "hearing." Demanding an oral hearing in the absence of language calling for an on-the-record hearing would elevate form over substance, the Court reasoned. "The parties had fair notice of exactly what the Commission proposed to do, and were given an opportunity to comment, to object, or to make some other form of written submission. . . . Given the 'open-ended' nature of the proceedings, and the Commission's announced willingness to consider proposals for modification after operating experience had been acquired, we think the hearing requirement of § 1(14)(a) of the Act was met." The Court distinguished a situation where an "effort was made to single out any particular railroad for special consideration based on its own peculiar circumstances." In contrast to such a rule, the incentive-payment rule was "applicable across the board to all of the common carriers by railroad subject to the Interstate Commerce Act."

The decisions in *Florida East Coast Railway* and *Allegheny-Ludlum* had the effect of making notice-and-comment rulemaking available under pre-APA statutes. *See* Kent Burnett, *How the Supreme Court Derailed Formal Rulemaking*, 85 Geo. Wash. L. Rev. ARGUENDO (2017); Nathaniel L. Nathanson, *Probing the Mind of the Administrator: Hearing Variations and Standards of Judicial Review Under the Administrative Procedure Act and Other Federal Statutes*, 75 Colum. L. Rev. 721 (1975). On the advantages of formal, on-the-record rulemaking, see Aaron L. Nielson, *In Defense of Formal Rulemaking*, 75 Ohio St. L.J. 231 (2014).

7. **The Informal Rulemaking Process.** Informal or "notice and comment" rulemaking, under APA § 553, is the bread and butter of many agencies' regulatory efforts. As suggested by the "notice and comment" label, the process of informal rulemaking is structured around three events: notice that an agency intends to promulgate a rule, the receipt of comments on the proposed rule, and the agency's response to the comments, including, eventually, the release of a final rule.

a. **Notice of Proposed Rulemaking; "Paper Hearing" Requirement.** Under § 553(b), informal rulemaking begins when an agency publishes a "notice of proposed rule-making" or NOPR in the Federal Register. The notice must contain "either the terms or substance of the proposed rule or a description of the subjects and issues involved."

One important issue raised by the notice requirement concerns the scope of the agency's disclosure. *Portland Cement* holds that prior to finalizing a rule, an agency must give notice of the data and technical methodologies it relied on in formulating the rule. According to *Portland Cement*, disclosure of this information is inherent in the rulemaking process created by § 553: "It is not consonant with the purpose of a rule-making proceeding to promulgate rules on the basis of inadequate data, or on data that, [to a] critical degree, is known only to the agency." Is the court's assertion to this effect persuasive? If we analogize informal rulemaking to a legislative process, would we expect legislatures to reveal their data and methodology prior to passing a statute? Should we consider the notice and comment requirement as more of an informational device for *the agency*, with the agency giving as much notice of its proposed rule and supporting information as it finds useful for its purposes? Is this the appropriate analogy for considering APA § 553?

In Professor Stewart's view, *Portland Cement* and related decisions from the early 1970s require "a 'paper hearing' that combines many of the advantages of a trial-type adversary process (excepting oral testimony and cross-examination) while avoiding undue delay and cost." He maintains the paper-hearing requirement "has been an outstanding success in improving the quality of decisionmaking at EPA and providing a realistic basis for judicial review without unduly hobbling the agency's ability to get its job done." Richard B. Stewart, *The Development of Administrative and Quasi-Constitutional Law in Judicial Review of Environmental Decisionmaking: Lessons from the Clean Air Act*, 62 Iowa L. Rev. 713, 731–32 (1977). Do reviewing courts have statutory authority to impose such a requirement? What provisions of the APA does *Portland Cement* invoke in establishing the paper-hearing requirement?

Another issue raised by the notice requirement involves the relationship between a NOPR and the final agency rule: did the NOPR provide adequate notice of the rule that the agency ultimately adopted? The Attorney General's 1947 Manual stated with respect to this issue:

> Where able to do so, an agency may state the proposed rule itself or the substance of the rule in the notice required by section [553(a)]. On the other hand, the agency, if it desires, may issue a more general "description of the subjects and issues involved." It is suggested that each agency consider the desirability of using the latter method if publication of a proposed rule in full would unduly burden the Federal Register or would in fact be less informative to the public. In such a case, the agency may inform interested persons that copies of the proposed rule may be obtained from the agency upon request — this, of course, in addition to the "description of the subjects and issues involved" in the Federal Register. Where there is a "description of the subjects and issues involved," the notice should be sufficiently informative to

assure interested persons an opportunity to participate intelligently in the rule making process.

U.S. DEP'T OF JUSTICE, ATTORNEY GENERAL'S MANUAL ON THE ON THE ADMINISTRATIVE PROCEDURE ACT 29–30 (1947).

In a leading decision on the adequacy of a NOPR, the Seventh Circuit considered whether the Internal Revenue Service (IRS) had provided adequate notice of a rule governing the tax treatment of medical associations' membership dues. *American Med. Ass'n v. United States*, 887 F.2d 760 (7th Cir. 1989). The IRS's NOPR listed seven factors that the IRS would *consider* in allocating dues to a category of taxable income. The agency's final rule contained three mathematical tests that would be used to do so and set out bright-line rules for the circumstances in which those tests would be used.

Interpreting § 553, the court of appeals reasoned it was "clear that the notice need not identify every precise proposal which the agency may ultimately adopt; notice is adequate if it apprises interested parties of the issues to be addressed in the rule-making proceeding with sufficient clarity and specificity to allow them to participate in the rulemaking in a meaningful and informed manner. Stated another way, a final rule is not invalid for lack of adequate notice if the rule finally adopted is 'a logical outgrowth' of the original proposal." The IRS's final rule satisfied this standard, because the NOPR apprised the public of the options the agency was considering, even if it did not identify the precise manner in which the IRS would treat medical association dues:

> The approach finally adopted by the IRS, while substantially different from the N[O]PR, was a "logical outgrowth" of the original proposal. The final rule dealt with the identical issue of dues allocation, merely altering the allocation regime to assure greater consistency and fairness. The allocation rules finally adopted were not a wholly new approach to the issue of dues allocation. Instead the final rule was "contained" in the proposed version, and merely eliminated some of the alternative calculation methods specified in the N[O]PR.

Id. at 769.

Although *American Medical Association* tolerated foreseeable changes between a NOPR and a final rule, other decisions have adopted a much stricter attitude. *See, e.g.,* *CSX Transp., Inc. v. Surface Transp. Bd.*, 584 F.3d 1076 (D.C. Cir. 2009) (invalidating Surface Transportation Board rule that set benchmark rates for railroads based on the past four years of waybill data, where agency initially proposed to determine rates using a benchmark derived from the past year of waybill data); *United Mine Workers of Am. v. Mine Safety & Health Admin.*, 407 F.3d 1250, 1261 (D.C. Cir. 2005) (invalidating Mine Safety and Health Administration rule that established a *maximum* air velocity for belt air courser ventilators, where the agency's NOPR originally suggested a *minimum* air velocity for such ventilators).

The D.C. Circuit has also stated that a notice may be "too general to be adequate. Agency notice must describe the range of alternatives being considered with reasonable specificity. Otherwise, interested parties will not know what to comment on, and notice will not lead to better-informed agency decision-making." *Small Ref. Lead Phase-Down Task Force v. USEPA*, 705 F.2d 506, 549 (1983). Given the requirement of reasonable specificity, on the one hand, and courts' willingness to vacate regulations for failing to provide reasonable notice, on the other, what is the safest strategy for an agency seeking to promulgate a major new regulation, particularly a rule that could be challenged in multiple courts of appeals? What did EPA do in *Portland Cement*?

b. **Comments.** After the NOPR issues, "the agency shall give interested persons an opportunity to participate in the rule making through submission of written data, views, or arguments with or without opportunity for oral presentation," § 553(c). The comment period is to be "not less than 30 days," § 553(d). In practice, agencies frequently provide a much longer period for comment, and many extend the comment period at the request of commenters. (Extensions are noted in the Federal Register.)

Almost all agencies today accept comments through Regulations.gov, a website developed by the Environmental Protection Agency under authority of the E-Government Act of 2002, Public Law No. 107-347, 116 Stat. 2899. Rules with broad impact tend to generate a large number of comments. In a study of final rules published in the Federal Register in November and December 2003, such rules prompted an average of 2,408 comments. Stuart Shapiro, *Two Months in the Life of the Regulatory State*, 30 ADMIN. & REG. L. NEWS 12 tbl. 1 (Spring 2005).

c. **Responding to Comments.** After the comment period closes, an agency reviews the comments that have been received, organizes them, and decides how to respond. After consolidating duplicate comments, an agency will generally respond to a comment in three ways. It may (1) ignore the comment; (2) respond to the comment when it promulgates a final rule; or (3) modify the proposed rule in response to the comment and note the change when the final rule is released.

In *Portland Cement*, the court denied that it was "establishing any broad principle that EPA must respond to every comment made by manufacturers on the validity of its standards or the methodology and scientific basis for their formulation." Instead, the agency need only respond to comments that satisfy "a threshold requirement of materiality." Why did Mr. Striker's comments satisfy this standard in *Portland Cement*? How does an agency identify the comments to which it must respond?

Consider *Portland Cement*'s description of the duty to respond to comments from the perspective of a regulated firm or an organization representing beneficiaries of a statutory scheme seeking to preserve the regulatory status quo. What incentives does *Portland Cement* create for such a firm or organization? What incentives does *Portland Cement* create for an agency engaged in rulemaking? Does the answer depend on the agency's perception that a rule will be challenged via judicial review? Suppose an agency such as EPA has undertaken to promulgate a high-profile rule that is virtually certain to be challenged in the D.C. Circuit. What is the agency's safest strategy for responding to comments?

8. **What is the "Record" in Informal Rulemaking?** In formal rulemakings and adjudications, the APA specifies that the administrative "record" consists of "[t]he transcript of testimony and exhibits, together with all papers and requests filed in the proceeding." 5 U.S.C. § 556(e). The APA further specifies that "[w]hen an agency decision rests on official notice of a material fact not appearing in the evidence in the record, a party is entitled, on timely request, to an opportunity to show the contrary." *Id.*

The APA does not specifically speak to what the record consists of in informal rulemaking proceedings. Section 553(c) says only that "the agency shall give interested persons an opportunity to participate in the rule making through submission of written data, views, or arguments with or without opportunity for oral presentation." The totality of this material, along with material the information the agency identified through its own efforts, constitutes the "record" for purposes of informal rulemaking. *See Solite Corp. v. EPA*, 952 F.2d 473, 485 (D.C. Cir. 1991). Today, some agencies maintain web-based rulemaking dockets, which provide a real-time view of the information that has been submitted in connection with a rulemaking. *See, e.g.*, Federal Communications Commission, Docket No. 14–28, http://apps.fcc.gov/ecfs/comment_search/execute?proceeding=14-28.

As a result of *Portland Cement*'s disclosure regime, interested parties as well as the agency generally will have access to the information and commentary that the agency relies upon in formulating a rule. At the judicial-review stage, these materials arrive at the court in appendices to the parties' briefs. Under the local rules of the D.C. Circuit, for example, the agency has the initial burden of filing the record in a petition for review of agency action. *See* D.C. Cir. Local Rule 17(b)(1) ("The agency must file: (A) the original or a certified copy of the entire record or parts designated by the parties; or (B) a certified list adequately describing all documents, transcripts of testimony, exhibits, and other material constituting the record, or describing those parts designated by the parties.").

9. **Models of the Court-Agency Relationship.** Note *Portland Cement*'s contention that in the rulemaking context, "the court and agency are in a kind of partnership relationship for the purpose of effectuating the legislative mandate." As we encounter more cases in which a court is reviewing agency action, consider whether other courts share the same view. What is an alternative to the partnership model? On Judge Leventhal's "partnership" model of the court-agency relationship, see Harold Leventhal, *Environmental Decisionmaking and the Role of the Courts*, 122 U. Pa. L. Rev. 509 (1974); Samuel Estreicher, *Pragmatic Justice: The Contributions of Judge Harold Leventhal to Administrative Law*, 80 Colum. L. Rev. 894 (1980).

10. **Postscript.** Following the D.C. Circuit's remand in *Portland Cement*, the EPA tested five more plants. All seven plant tests—the two initial tests and five post-remand tests—showed that the .30 lb emissions standard was achievable. In a challenge to

EPA's final rule, the D.C. Circuit upheld the rule in its entirety. *See Portland Cement Ass'n v. Train*, 513 F.2d 506, 509 (D.C. Cir. 1975).

———

Portland Cement makes use of the same move that *Overton Park* invoked to impose procedural requirements on informal agency adjudication. According to Judge Leventhal's opinion, disclosure of the data and analytic methods the agency relied on in drafting a rule is required not only by § 553, but also to enable meaningful judicial review of an agency's actions. Virtually any procedural requirement can be justified on the ground that it would improve judicial review, however. This in turn raises questions about how far courts can intrude in agency processes in the name of improving judicial review. Stated differently, does the prospect of judicial review authorize reviewing courts to develop a general federal "administrative common law"? The decision below, issued following a decade in which the D.C. Circuit and other courts imposed additional requirements on informal rulemaking, not specified in an organic statute or the APA, takes up that question.

Vermont Yankee Nuclear Power Corp. v. Natural Resources Defense Council, Inc.

435 U.S. 519 (1978)

Mr. Justice Rehnquist delivered the opinion of the Court.

***

I

A

Under the Atomic Energy Act of 1954, 68 Stat. 919, as amended, 42 U.S.C. § 2011 et seq., the Atomic Energy Commission[2] was given broad regulatory authority over the development of nuclear energy. Under the terms of the Act, a utility seeking to construct and operate a nuclear power plant must obtain a separate permit or license at both the construction and the operation stage of the project. *See* 42 U.S.C. §§ 2133, 2232, 2235, 2239. In order to obtain the construction permit, the utility must file a preliminary safety analysis report, an environmental report, and certain information regarding the antitrust implications of the proposed project. *See* 10 CFR §§ 2.101, 50.30(f), 50.33a, 50.34(a) (1977). This application then undergoes exhaustive review by the Commission's staff and by the Advisory Committee on Reactor Safeguards (ACRS), a group of distinguished experts in the field of atomic energy. Both groups submit to the Commission their own evaluations, which then become part of the

———

2. The licensing and regulatory functions of the Atomic Energy Commission (AEC) were transferred to the Nuclear Regulatory Commission (NRC) by the Energy Reorganization Act of 1974, 42 U.S.C. § 5801 et seq. (1970 ed., Supp. V). Hereinafter both the AEC and NRC will be referred to as the Commission.

record of the utility's application.[3] *See* 42 U.S.C. §§ 2039, 2232(b). The Commission staff also undertakes the review required by the National Environmental Policy Act of 1969 (NEPA), 83 Stat. 852, 42 U.S.C. § 4321 et seq., and prepares a draft environmental impact statement, which, after being circulated for comment, 10 CFR §§ 51.22–51.25 (1977), is revised and becomes a final environmental impact statement. § 51.26. Thereupon a three-member Atomic Safety and Licensing Board conducts a public adjudicatory hearing, 42 U.S.C. § 2241, and reaches a decision[4] which can be appealed to the Atomic Safety and Licensing Appeal Board, and currently, in the Commission's discretion, to the Commission itself. 10 CFR §§ 2.714, 2.721, 2.786, 2.787 (1977). The final agency decision may be appealed to the courts of appeals. 42 U.S.C. § 2239; 28 U.S.C. § 2342. The same sort of process occurs when the utility applies for a license to operate the plant, 10 CFR § 50.34(b) (1977), except that a hearing need only be held in contested cases and may be limited to the matters in controversy. *See* 42 U.S.C. § 2239(a); 10 CFR § 2.105 (1977); 10 CFR pt. 2, App. A, V(f) (1977).

[The Court of Appeals for the District of Columbia Circuit] remanded a decision of the Commission to grant a license to petitioner Vermont Yankee Nuclear Power Corp. to operate a nuclear power plant.***

B

In December 1967, after the mandatory adjudicatory hearing and necessary review, the Commission granted petitioner Vermont Yankee a permit to build a nuclear power plant in Vernon, Vt. See 4 A.E.C. 36 (1967). Thereafter, Vermont Yankee applied for an operating license. Respondent Natural Resources Defense Council (NRDC) objected to the granting of a license, however, and therefore a hearing on the application commenced on August 10, 1971. Excluded from consideration at the hearings, over NRDC's objection, was the issue of the environmental effects of operations to reprocess fuel or dispose of wastes resulting from the reprocessing operations.[6] This ruling was affirmed by the Appeal Board in June 1972.

In November 1972, however, the Commission, making specific reference to the Appeal Board's decision with respect to the Vermont Yankee license, instituted rule-making proceedings "that would specifically deal with the question of consideration

---

3. ACRS is required to review each construction permit application for the purpose of informing the Commission of the "hazards of proposed or existing reactor facilities and the adequacy of proposed reactor safety standards." 42 U.S.C. § 2039.

4. The Licensing Board issues a permit if it concludes that there is reasonable assurance that the proposed plant can be constructed and operated without undue risk, 42 U.S.C. § 2241; 10 CFR § 50.35(a) (1977), and that the environmental cost-benefit balance favors the issuance of a permit.

6. The nuclear fission which takes place in light-water nuclear reactors apparently converts its principal fuel, uranium, into plutonium, which is itself highly radioactive but can be used as reactor fuel if separated from the remaining uranium and radioactive waste products. Fuel reprocessing refers to the process necessary to recapture usable plutonium. Waste disposal, at the present stage of technological development, refers to the storage of the very long lived and highly radioactive waste products until they detoxify sufficiently that they no longer present an environmental hazard. There are presently no physical or chemical steps which render this waste less toxic, other than simply the passage of time.

of environmental effects associated with the uranium fuel cycle in the individual cost-benefit analyses for light water cooled nuclear power reactors." The notice of proposed rulemaking offered two alternatives, both predicated on a report prepared by the Commission's staff entitled Environmental Survey of the Nuclear Fuel Cycle. The first would have required no quantitative evaluation of the environmental hazards of fuel reprocessing or disposal because the Environmental Survey had found them to be slight. The second would have specified numerical values for the environmental impact of this part of the fuel cycle, which values would then be incorporated into a table, along with the other relevant factors, to determine the overall cost-benefit balance for each operating license.

Much of the controversy in this case revolves around the procedures used in the rulemaking hearing which commenced in February 1973. In a supplemental notice of hearing the Commission indicated that while discovery or cross-examination would not be utilized, the Environmental Survey would be available to the public before the hearing along with the extensive background documents cited therein. All participants would be given a reasonable opportunity to present their position and could be represented by counsel if they so desired. Written and, time permitting, oral statements would be received and incorporated into the record. All persons giving oral statements would be subject to questioning by the Commission. At the conclusion of the hearing, a transcript would be made available to the public and the record would remain open for 30 days to allow the filing of supplemental written statements. More than 40 individuals and organizations representing a wide variety of interests submitted written comments. On January 17, 1973, the Licensing Board held a planning session to schedule the appearance of witnesses and to discuss methods for compiling a record. The hearing was held on February 1 and 2, with participation by a number of groups, including the Commission's staff, the United States Environmental Protection Agency, a manufacturer of reactor equipment, a trade association from the nuclear industry, a group of electric utility companies, and a group called Consolidated National Intervenors which represented 79 groups and individuals including respondent NRDC.

After the hearing, the Commission's staff filed a supplemental document for the purpose of clarifying and revising the Environmental Survey. Then the Licensing Board forwarded its report to the Commission without rendering any decision. The Licensing Board identified as the principal procedural question the propriety of declining to use full formal adjudicatory procedures. The major substantive issue was the technical adequacy of the Environmental Survey.

In April 1974, the Commission issued a rule which adopted the second of the two proposed alternatives described above. The Commission also approved the procedures used at the hearing, and indicated that the record, including the Environmental Survey, provided an "adequate data base for the regulation adopted." Finally, the Commission ruled that to the extent the rule differed from the Appeal Board decisions [regarding the] Vermont Yankee [license,] "those decisions have no further

presidential [sic] significance," but that since "the environmental effects of the uranium fuel cycle have been shown to be relatively insignificant, . . . it is unnecessary to
apply the amendment to applicant's environmental reports submitted prior to its
effective date or to Final Environmental Statements for which Draft Environmental
Statements have been circulated for comment prior to the effective date."

Respondents appealed from both the Commission's adoption of the rule and its
decision to grant Vermont Yankee's license to the Court of Appeals for the District of
Columbia Circuit.***

D

With respect to the challenge of Vermont Yankee's license, the court first ruled
that in the absence of effective rulemaking proceedings,[13] the Commission must
deal with the environmental impact of fuel reprocessing and disposal in individual
licensing proceedings. The court then examined the rulemaking proceedings and,
despite the fact that it appeared that the agency employed all the procedures
required by 5 U.S.C. §553 (1976 ed.) and more, the court determined the proceedings to be inadequate and overturned the rule. Accordingly, the Commission's
determination with respect to Vermont Yankee's license was also remanded for further proceedings.***

II

A

Petitioner Vermont Yankee first argues that the Commission may grant a license
to operate a nuclear reactor without any consideration of waste disposal and fuel
reprocessing. We find, however, that this issue is no longer presented by the record in
this case. The Commission does not contend that it is not required to consider the
environmental impact of the spent fuel processes when licensing nuclear power plants.
Indeed, the Commission has publicly stated subsequent to the Court of Appeals'
decision in the instant case that consideration of the environmental impact of the
back end of the fuel cycle in "the environmental impact statements for individual LWR's
[light-water power reactors] would represent a full and candid assessment of costs
and benefits consistent with the legal requirements and spirit of NEPA." 41 Fed. Reg.
45849 (1976).***

B

We next turn to the invalidation of the fuel cycle rule.*** [T]he majority of the Court
of Appeals struck down the rule because of the perceived inadequacies of the procedures employed in the rulemaking proceedings. The court first determined [the
primary argument here] to be "that the decision to preclude 'discovery or

---

13. In the Court of Appeals no one questioned the Commission's authority to deal with fuel cycle
issues by informal rulemaking as opposed to adjudication. Neither does anyone seriously question
before this Court the Commission's authority in this respect.

cross-examination' denied them a meaningful opportunity to participate in the proceedings as guaranteed by due process."***

The court conceded that absent extraordinary circumstances it is improper for a reviewing court to prescribe the procedural format an agency must follow, but it likewise clearly thought it entirely appropriate to "scrutinize the record as a whole to insure that genuine opportunities to participate in a meaningful way were provided . . . ." The court also refrained from actually ordering the agency to follow any specific procedures, but there is little doubt in our minds that the ineluctable mandate of the court's decision is that the procedures afforded during the hearings were inadequate. This conclusion is particularly buttressed by the fact that after the court examined the record, particularly the testimony of Dr. Pittman, and declared it insufficient, the court proceeded to discuss at some length the necessity for further procedural devices or a more "sensitive" application of those devices employed during the proceedings.***

In prior opinions we have intimated that even in a rulemaking proceeding when an agency is making a "'quasi-judicial'" determination by which a very small number of persons are "'exceptionally affected, in each case upon individual grounds,'" in some circumstances additional procedures may be required in order to afford the aggrieved individuals due process. *United States v. Florida East Coast R. Co.*, [410 U.S. 224, 242, 245 (1973)], quoting from *Bi-Metallic Investment Co. v. State Board of Equalization*, 239 U.S. 441, 446 (1915). It might also be true, although we do not think the issue is presented in this case and accordingly do not decide it, that a totally unjustified departure from well-settled agency procedures of long standing might require judicial correction.

But this much is absolutely clear. Absent constitutional constraints or extremely compelling circumstances the "administrative agencies 'should be free to fashion their own rules of procedure and to pursue methods of inquiry capable of permitting them to discharge their multitudinous duties.'"

Respondent NRDC argues that § 4 of the Administrative Procedure Act, 5 U.S.C. § 553 (1976 ed.), merely establishes lower procedural bounds and that a court may routinely require more than the minimum when an agency's proposed rule addresses complex or technical factual issues or "Issues of Great Public Import." We have, however, [rejected] this view. We also think the legislative history, even the part which [NRDC] cites, does not bear out its contention. The Senate Report explains what eventually became § 4 thus:

> "This subsection states . . . the minimum requirements of public rule making procedure short of statutory hearing. Under it agencies might in addition confer with industry advisory committees, consult organizations, hold informal 'hearings,' and the like. Considerations of practicality, necessity, and public interest . . . will naturally govern the agency's determination of the extent to which public proceedings should go. Matters of great import, or those where the public submission of facts will be either useful to the agency

or a protection to the public, should naturally be accorded more elaborate public procedures." S. Rep. No. 752, 79th Cong., 1st Sess., 14–15 (1945).

The House Report is in complete accord:***

"The bill is an outline of minimum essential rights and procedures. . . . It affords private parties a means of knowing what their rights are and how they may protect them . . . .

". . . [The bill contains] the essentials of the different forms of administrative proceedings . . . ." H.R. Rep. No. 1980, 79th Cong., 2d Sess., 9, 16–17 (1946).

And the Attorney General's Manual on the Administrative Procedure Act 31, 35 (1947), a contemporaneous interpretation previously given some deference by this Court because of the role played by the Department of Justice in drafting the legislation, further confirms that view. In short, all of this leaves little doubt that Congress intended that the discretion of the agencies and not that of the courts be exercised in determining when extra procedural devices should be employed.

There are compelling reasons for construing §4 in this manner. In the first place, if courts continually review agency proceedings to determine whether the agency employed procedures which were, in the court's opinion, perfectly tailored to reach what the court perceives to be the "best" or "correct" result, judicial review would be totally unpredictable. And the agencies, operating under this vague injunction to employ the "best" procedures and facing the threat of reversal if they did not, would undoubtedly adopt full adjudicatory procedures in every instance. Not only would this totally disrupt the statutory scheme, through which Congress enacted "a formula upon which opposing social and political forces have come to rest," *Wong Yang Sung v. McGrath*, 339 U.S., at 40, but all the inherent advantages of informal rulemaking would be totally lost.

Secondly, it is obvious that the court in these cases reviewed the agency's choice of procedures on the basis of the record actually produced at the hearing, and not on the basis of the information available to the agency when it made the decision to structure the proceedings in a certain way. This sort of Monday morning quarterbacking not only encourages but almost compels the agency to conduct all rulemaking proceedings with the full panoply of procedural devices normally associated only with adjudicatory hearings.

Finally, and perhaps most importantly, this sort of review fundamentally misconceives the nature of the standard for judicial review of an agency rule. The court below uncritically assumed that additional procedures will automatically result in a more adequate record because it will give interested parties more of an opportunity to participate in and contribute to the proceedings. But informal rulemaking need not be based solely on the transcript of a hearing held before an agency. Indeed, the agency need not even hold a formal hearing. *See* 5 U.S.C. §553(c) (1976 ed.). Thus, the adequacy of the "record" in this type of proceeding is not correlated directly to the type of procedural devices employed, but rather turns on whether the agency has followed the statutory mandate of the Administrative Procedure Act or other relevant statutes. If the agency is compelled to support the rule which it ultimately adopts with the type of record produced only after a full adjudicatory hearing, it simply will have no choice but to conduct a full adjudicatory hearing prior to promulgating every rule. In sum, this sort of unwarranted judicial examination of perceived procedural shortcomings of a rulemaking proceeding can do nothing but seriously interfere with that process prescribed by Congress.

Respondent NRDC also argues that the fact that the Commission's inquiry was undertaken in the context of NEPA somehow permits a court to require procedures beyond those specified in §4 of the APA when investigating factual issues through rulemaking. The Court of Appeals was apparently also of this view, indicating that agencies may be required to "develop new procedures to accomplish the innovative task of implementing NEPA through rulemaking." But we search in vain for something in NEPA which would mandate such a result. We have before observed that "NEPA does not repeal by implication any other statute." In fact, just two Terms ago, we emphasized that the only procedural requirements imposed by NEPA are those stated in the plain language of the Act. Thus, it is clear NEPA cannot serve as the basis for a substantial revision of the carefully constructed procedural specifications of the APA.***

There remains, of course, the question of whether the challenged rule finds sufficient justification in the administrative proceedings that it should be upheld by the reviewing court. Judge Tamm, concurring in the result reached by the majority of the Court of Appeals, thought that it did not. There are also intimations in the majority opinion which suggest that the judges who joined it likewise may have thought the administrative proceedings an insufficient basis upon which to predicate the rule in question. We accordingly remand so that the Court of Appeals may review the rule as the Administrative Procedure Act provides. We have made it abundantly clear before that when there is a contemporaneous explanation of the agency decision, the validity of that action must "stand or fall on the propriety of that finding, judged, of course, by the appropriate standard of review. If that finding is not sustainable on the administrative record made, then the Comptroller's decision must be vacated and the matter remanded to him for further consideration." *Camp v. Pitts*, 411 U.S. 138, 143 (1973). *See also SEC v. Chenery Corp.*, 318 U.S. 80 (1943). The court should engage in this kind of review and not stray beyond the judicial province to explore the procedural format or to impose upon the agency its own notion of which procedures are "best" or most likely to further some vague, undefined public good.[21]

---

21. Of course, the court must determine whether the agency complied with the procedures mandated by the relevant statutes. *Citizens to Preserve Overton Park v. Volpe*, 401 U.S. 402, 417 (1971). But, as we indicated above, there is little doubt that the agency was in full compliance with all the applicable requirements of the Administrative Procedure Act.

Notes and Questions

1. **Regulatory Context: The Dilemmas of Atomic Energy.** Nuclear energy presents unique regulatory problems. Nuclear power plants provide a cheap and virtually pollution-free source of electricity once the massive front-end investment required to construct a plant is made. However, as the 2011 meltdown of the Fukushima, Japan plant illustrates, nuclear plants present a small but real risk of devastating losses to the environment and human life. Given these concerns, some groups have opposed any use of nuclear power as a matter of principle.

Federal lawmakers have not adopted this stance. To promote the development of nuclear energy, the Price-Anderson Nuclear Industries Indemnity Act, Pub. L. No. 85-256, 71 Stat. 576 (1957), established a no-fault liability insurance program for injuries caused by nuclear accidents. At the administrative level, the Atomic Energy Act of 1946, Pub. L. No. 79-585, 60 Stat. 755, created the Atomic Energy Commission (AEC) and charged the AEC with regulating as well as promoting the use of nuclear energy in the United States. The AEC was widely criticized for being too cozy with industry and shortchanging its regulatory responsibilities. Recognizing that the combination of promotion and regulatory functions in a single agency created a conflict of interest, Congress separated responsibility for those tasks in the Energy Reorganization Act of 1974, 42 U.S.C. § 5801 et seq. Authority to promote nuclear energy was lodged in the Department of Energy. Regulatory authority was given to the newly-created Nuclear Regulatory Commission (NRC).

The NRC consists of five commissioners who are appointed by the President with advice and consent of the Senate for five-year terms. No more than three commissioners may be members of the same political party. The chair of the Commission is selected by the President and serves at the President's pleasure. *See* 42 U.S.C. § 5841.

2. **The Procedural Posture and Regulatory Context: The Agency Procedure.** The NRC uses a two-part process to regulate safety at nuclear plants. A permit is required both to construct a nuclear plant and to operate a plant. *See* 42 U.S.C. § 2131. Permitting or licensing is formal adjudication for purposes of the APA. *See* §§ 551(5), (6).

To obtain a construction permit, a plant builder is required to complete a preliminary safety and environmental analysis. That analysis is reviewed by the Advisory Committee on Reactor Safeguards (ACRS), a committee of technical experts. The Commission's staff separately prepare a report on the proposed plant's environmental impact, as required by the National Environmental Policy Act (NEPA), 42 U.S.C. § 4321 et seq. As discussed in connection with *TVA v. Hill*, in Chapter 2[B][2][a], NEPA generally requires agencies undertaking a major project to analyze and document the project's impact on the environment.

When these reports are complete, a three-member Atomic Safety and Licensing Board, a panel comprised of Administrative Law Judges that conducts hearings at the direction of the Commission, conducts a "public adjudicatory hearing" on whether to grant a permit and, if so, the conditions to include in it. The Licensing Board's decision can be appealed to an Atomic Safety and Licensing Appeal Board and then to the NRC itself. Judicial review of the NRC's final action on the permit application is in the courts of appeals.

The same process is followed when an operator applies to operate a plant or renew a license. But a hearing need not be held if no one opposes a plant's continued operation, and may be limited to the matters in controversy. Initial licenses may last for up to 40 years. A renewal may last for up to 20 years.

The permitting process thus incorporates both informal rulemaking (in establishing a framework for licensing decisions, such as with respect to the spent-fuel issue) and formal adjudication (in making the permitting/licensing decisions). What design choices are reflected in this process? What objectives are served by having so many "hands" involved in the approval of a permit application? Does the agency's review process seem well-structured to identify potential safety problems, particularly problems that an engineering team working in isolation might overlook? Does the process seem well-structured to allow for political debate about the wisdom of installing a nuclear plant at a specific location?

Since 1998, NRC has approved 42 renewal licenses. The last new nuclear plant to enter service in the United States is the Watts Bar plant in Rhea County, Tennessee. It was first licensed in the early 1970s and went online in 1996. *See* Nuclear Regulatory Commission, Fact Sheet on Reactor License Renewal, http://www.nrc.gov/reading-rm /doc-collections/fact-sheets/fs-reactor-license-renewal.html (last visited Aug. 26, 2015).

3. **The Vermont Yankee Proceeding.** The petitioners' objection in *Vermont Yankee* focused on how the NRC accounted for the environmental effects of spent-fuel waste. As footnote 6 of the Court's opinion explains, spent fuel can be reprocessed for further use, but ultimately must be stored for an indefinite period of time. It is highly toxic.

The focus in *Vermont Yankee* is the NRC's decision to grant the Vermont Yankee plant an operating permit, after construction of the plant had been approved. In an initial on-the-record hearing on Vermont Yankee's application for an operating permit, the Licensing Board excluded evidence about the environmental effects of reprocessing and disposing of spent reactor fuel. The Licensing Board granted Vermont Yankee's application for an operating permit and the decision was affirmed by the Appeal Board. Thereafter, the NRC initiated a new informal rulemaking "that would specifically deal with the question of consideration of environmental effects associated with the fuel cycle in the individual cost-benefit analyses for light water cooled nuclear power reactors." (Can you see why NRC initiated this rulemaking rather than stand by its earlier decision to exclude evidence of the environmental effects of spent and reprocessed fuel?)

The NRC considered two options for accounting for the effects of spent fuel in proceedings on individual plants' operating permits. Under the first approach, the environmental effects of fuel processing and disposal would essentially be disregarded, because an Environmental Survey of the Nuclear Fuel Cycle prepared by the NRC's staff found those effects to be de minimis when fuel was stored properly. Under the second approach, numerical values would be assigned to account for the environmental effects of fuel processing and disposal. Those values would be incorporated into a table with other factors to determine the overall cost-benefit balance for the operating permit. The NRC adopted the second approach in the "fuel cycle rule" that petitioners challenged in *Vermont Yankee*.

What specifically did petitioners object to in the fuel-cycle rule? Note that NRDC challenged the rule on both procedural and substantive grounds. NRC had conceded the substantive point by the time *Vermont Yankee* reached the Supreme Court. NRC acknowledged it was required to account for the environmental costs of fuel processing and disposal when considering the environmental impact of a new plant and evaluating operation applications.

4. **What Is Wrong with the D.C. Circuit's Procedural Creativity?** Although the D.C. Circuit's opinion was not perfectly clear, the Supreme Court understood it to have vacated the fuel-cycle rule on the ground that the NRC did not follow appropriate procedures prior to promulgating it. The D.C. Circuit specifically objected to the fact that NRDC was not given an opportunity to take discovery or cross-examine the NRC's staff regarding the assumptions and methodology they used when quantifying the costs of fuel processing and disposal for the Vermont Yankee plant.

The Supreme Court plainly rejected the D.C. Circuit's conclusion that the agency's procedure was inadequate and chastised the court of appeals for imposing discovery and cross-examination rights not based on the AEA, the APA, the agency's regulations, or due process. What, specifically, is wrong with what the D.C. Circuit had tried to do?

a. **Lack of Statutory Authority?** The Supreme Court notes that the D.C. Circuit's demands for discovery and cross-examination lack a basis in the APA or the Atomic Energy Act. Does it follow that the D.C. Circuit's procedural demands were illegitimate? Some commentators have drawn a parallel between *Vermont Yankee* and *Erie R. v. Tompkins*, 304 U.S. 64 (1938), insofar as both decisions disclaim the federal judiciary's authority to make common law that does not derive its authority from the Constitution or a statute. *See, e.g.*, Cass R. Sunstein, *Is the Clean Air Act Unconstitutional?*, 98 MICH. L. REV. 303, 342 (1999) ("[T]here is no common law of administrative law."). Is the contention that there is no common law of administrative law consistent with *Overton Park* and *Portland Cement*? *See generally* Kenneth Culp Davis, *Administrative Common Law and the* Vermont Yankee *Opinion*, 1980 UTAH L. REV. 3 (1980); Emily S. Bremer, *The Unwritten Administrative Constitution*, 66 FLA. L. REV. 1215 (2014).

b. **Unpredictable Judicial Review?** Is the Supreme Court correct that the D.C. Circuit's procedural innovations will make judicial review unpredictable? Can judicial review be entirely predictable when APA § 706 directs reviewing courts to set aside agency action that is "arbitrary, capricious, an abuse of discretion, or otherwise not in accordance with law"? If you were counsel to the NRC following the D.C. Circuit's decision in *Vermont Yankee*, what would you have advised the Commission to do in future proceedings for individual plant operating permits?

c. **Substitution of Proceduralist Review for Review of the Merits?** The Supreme Court notes that, although it disapproves the D.C. Circuit's practice of imposing novel procedural requirements on agencies, the D.C. Circuit is free on remand to consider whether the fuel-cycle rule "finds sufficient justification in the administrative proceedings." The Court's analysis here resonates with a long-running debate between Judges Bazelon and Leventhal, who both sat on the D.C. Circuit, over whether judicial review of agency action should focus on the merits of the agency's decision or the process used to reach that decision. Are the "substance" and "process" labels helpful here? Does *Vermont Yankee* show conclusively that judicial review should focus on the merits of the agency's action to the exclusion of process concerns? *See generally* Ronald J. Krotoszynski, Jr., *"History Belongs to the Winners": The Bazelon-Leventhal Debate and the Continuing Relevance of the Process/Substance Dichotomy in Judicial Review of Agency Action*, 58 Admin. L. Rev. 995 (2006).

d. **Impelling Agencies to Use Trial-Type Procedures?** Finally, the Supreme Court observes that the D.C. Circuit's procedural interventions may skew the administrative record in ways that are problematic. The Court predicts that agencies operating under a "vague injunction to employ the 'best' procedures and facing the threat of reversal if they [do] not [will] undoubtedly adopt full adjudicatory procedures in every instance." Such procedures may undermine the agency's ability to discharge its statutory mandate. In addition, they may result in the agency compiling a suboptimal record for the particular decision the agency has to make. The Court writes, "the adequacy of the 'record' in this type of proceeding is not correlated directly to the type of procedural devices employed, but rather turns on whether the agency has followed the statutory mandate of the Administrative Procedure Act or other relevant statutes."

Is the Supreme Court's concern justified? Consider the problem before the agency in *Vermont Yankee*—how to account for the costs of reprocessing and storing spent nuclear fuel in the decision to approve a new nuclear plant. What kind of information is a trial-type adjudicatory process likely to produce? Is this the same kind of information that, say, a responsible technical expert would seek out when considering how to manage spent nuclear fuel? Is it possible that trial-type procedures would *frustrate* the production of high-quality scientific and technical information? If so, how? Consider the fact that, in some jurisdictions, the only physicians who will testify in medical malpractice cases are "professional experts" who no longer practice in their field of expertise.

5. **"Paper Hearing" Requirements After Vermont Yankee.** Despite *Vermont Yankee*'s injunction that reviewing courts are not to impose procedure requirements on agencies, courts continue to apply the requirements of *Overton Park* and *Portland Cement*. Indeed, *Vermont Yankee* has not dissuaded the D.C. Circuit and other courts from interpreting other §553 requirements somewhat expansively. *See, e.g., Home Box Office, Inc. v. FCC*, 567 F.2d 9 (D.C. Cir. 1977) (elaborating non-statutory limits on ex parte contacts in informal rulemaking); *Association of Nat'l Advertisers v. FTC*, 627 F.2d 1151, 1170 (D.C. Cir. 1979) (same; pre-judgment of matters under consideration

in a quasi-legislative rule). *See generally* Jack M. Beermann & Gary Lawson, *Reprocessing* Vermont Yankee, 75 GEO. WASH. L. REV. 856 (2007) (describing and criticizing the Circuit's record of procedural innovation).

Recognizing the tension between *Overton Park*, *Portland Cement*, and other judicial-review-enhancing doctrines on the one hand, and *Vermont Yankee* on the other, the court in *Occidental Petroleum Corp. v. SEC*, 873 F.2d 325, 338–39 (D.C. Cir. 1989) (D. Ginsburg, J.), stated:

> Nothing in the general principles of *Vermont Yankee* is inconsistent . . . with the standards for judicial review set forth in *Overton Park*. Section 706, as interpreted in the latter case, establishes a performance standard for informal action by an agency: in order to allow for meaningful judicial review, the agency must produce an administrative record that delineates the path by which it reached its decision. If the record does not meet the *Overton Park* standard, the district court may insist that the agency produce, by whatever means the agency chooses, a record that does meet the required level of performance. The general principles of *Vermont Yankee*, on the other hand, would simply forbid the reviewing court from imposing upon the agency specific procedural steps that must be followed in order to create a reviewable record, i.e., a design standard.*** [W]e see nothing in the broad statements in the latter opinion to indicate any lowering of the performance standard mandated by *Overton Park*.

Does this analysis succeed in reconciling *Overton Park* and *Vermont Yankee*? Is it consistent with Justice Rehnquist's opinion in *Vermont Yankee*? Does the claim that reviewing courts may impose "performance standards" find support in text of APA §§ 553 and 706?

6. **Postscript.** Following the Supreme Court's decision, the NRC adopted an interim rule which specified that fuel processing and storage generated no pertinent costs for purposes of environmental impact statements, because spent fuel would be stored in a location where it was permanently isolated from the natural environment and inaccessible to human beings. The D.C. Circuit invalidated the rule on the ground that the assignment of zero costs to fuel storage was inconsistent with NEPA. *Natural Res. Def. Council, Inc. v. U.S. Nuclear Regulatory Comm'n*, 685 F.2d 459 (D.C. Cir. 1982). The Supreme Court again reversed. *Baltimore Gas & Elec. Co. v. Natural Res. Def. Council, Inc.*, 462 U.S. 87 (1983). The Supreme Court criticized the D.C. Circuit for arrogating to itself authority to decide "whether development of nuclear generation facilities should proceed in the face of uncertainties about their long-term effects on the environment." *Id.* at 97.

In the 1980s and 1990s, the Vermont Yankee Plant, located five miles south of Brattleboro, Vermont supplied about 75% of the electricity used in the state of Vermont. Its current owner, Entergy Corp., announced that the plant ceased operations on December 29, 2014, due in part to Vermont lawmakers' hostility to the plant's continued operation and the availability of cheap electricity from non-nuclear sources. *See* Mathew L. Wald, *Vermont Yankee Plant to Close Next Year as the Nuclear Industry Retrenches*, N.Y. Times, Aug. 28, 2013, at A14.

D. The Relationship Between Rulemaking and Adjudication

As we have seen, the APA imposes different procedural requirements for rulemaking and adjudication. The end products of rulemaking and adjudication, however, can be quite similar. Both rulemaking and adjudication provide an opportunity for an agency to elaborate statutory policy and, in so doing, to establish standards of conduct for regulated individuals and firms.

The three decisions that follow grapple with whether certain agency actions can be undertaken only through rulemaking. Before reading the decisions, review the definitions of "adjudication" and "rule making" in APA § 551.

Securities & Exchange Commission v. Chenery Corp.

332 U.S. 194 (1947)

Mr. Justice Murphy delivered the opinion of the Court.

***When the case was first here, we emphasized a simple but fundamental rule of administrative law. [*See SEC v. Chenery*, 318 U.S. 80 (1943).] That rule is to the effect that a reviewing court, in dealing with a determination or judgment which an administrative agency alone is authorized to make, must judge the propriety of such action solely by the grounds invoked by the agency. If those grounds are inadequate or improper, the court is powerless to affirm the administrative action by substituting what it considers to be a more adequate or proper basis. To do so would propel the court into the domain which Congress has set aside exclusively for the administrative agency.

We also emphasized in our prior decision an important corollary of the foregoing rule. If the administrative action is to be tested by the basis upon which it purports to rest, that basis must be set forth with such clarity as to be understandable. It will not do for a court to be compelled to guess at the theory underlying the agency's action; nor can a court be expected to chisel that which must be precise from what the agency has left vague and indecisive. In other words, "We must know what a decision means before the duty becomes ours to say whether it is right or wrong."

Applying this rule and its corollary, the Court was unable to sustain the [Securities & Exchange] Commission's [(SEC's)] original action. The Commission had been dealing with the reorganization of the Federal Water Service Corporation (Federal), a holding company registered under the Public Utility Holding Company Act of 1935, 49 Stat. 803. During the period when successive reorganization plans proposed by the management were before the Commission, the officers, directors and controlling stockholders of Federal purchased a substantial amount of Federal's preferred stock on the over-the-counter market. Under the fourth reorganization plan, this preferred stock was to be converted into common stock of a new corporation; on the basis of the purchases of preferred stock, the management would have received more than 10% of this new common stock. It was frankly admitted that the management's purpose in buying the preferred stock was to protect its interest in the new company. It was also plain that there was no fraud or lack of disclosure in making these purchases.

But the Commission would not approve the fourth plan so long as the preferred stock purchased by the management was to be treated on a parity with the other preferred stock. It felt that the officers and directors of a holding company in [a] process of reorganization under the Act were fiduciaries and were under a duty not to trade in the securities of that company during the reorganization period. And so the plan was amended to provide that the preferred stock acquired by the management, unlike that held by others, was not to be converted into the new common stock; instead, it was to be surrendered at cost plus dividends accumulated since the purchase dates. As amended, the plan was approved by the Commission over the management's objections.

Th[is] Court interpreted the Commission's order approving this amended plan as grounded solely upon judicial authority. The Commission appeared to have treated the preferred stock acquired by the management in accordance with what it thought were standards theretofore recognized by courts. If it intended to create new standards growing out of its experience in effectuating the legislative policy, it failed to express itself with sufficient clarity and precision to be so understood. Hence the order was judged by the only standards clearly invoked by the Commission. On that basis, the order could not stand. The opinion pointed out that courts do not impose upon officers and directors of a corporation any fiduciary duty to its stockholders which precludes them, merely because they are officers and directors, from buying and selling the corporation's stock. Nor was it felt that the cases upon which the Commission relied established any principles of law or equity which in themselves would be sufficient to justify this order.

The opinion further noted that neither Congress nor the Commission had promulgated any general rule proscribing such action as the purchase of preferred stock by Federal's management. And the only judge-made rule of equity which might have justified the Commission's order related to fraud or mismanagement of the reorganization by the officers and directors, matters which were admittedly absent in this situation.

After the case was remanded to the Commission, Federal Water and Gas Corp. (Federal Water), the surviving corporation under the reorganization plan, made an application for approval of an amendment to the plan to provide for the issuance of new common stock of the reorganized company. This stock was to be distributed to the members of Federal's management on the basis of the shares of the old preferred stock which they had acquired during the period of reorganization, thereby placing them in the same position as the public holders of the old preferred stock. The intervening members of Federal's management joined in this request. The Commission denied the application in an order issued on February 8, 1945. That order was reversed by the Court of Appeals, which felt that our prior decision precluded such action by the Commission.

The latest order of the Commission definitely avoids the fatal error of relying on judicial precedents which do not sustain it. This time, after a thorough reexamination of the problem in light of the purposes and standards of the Holding Company Act, the Commission has concluded that the proposed transaction is inconsistent with the standards of §§ 7 and 11 of the Act. It has drawn heavily upon its accumulated experience in dealing with utility reorganizations. And it has expressed its reasons with a clarity and thoroughness that admit of no doubt as to the underlying basis of its order.***

It is true that our prior decision explicitly recognized the possibility that the Commission might have promulgated a general rule dealing with this problem under its statutory rule-making powers, in which case the issue for our consideration would have been entirely different from that which did confront us. But we did not mean to imply thereby that the failure of the Commission to anticipate this problem and to promulgate a general rule withdrew all power from that agency to perform its statutory duty in this case. To hold that the Commission had no alternative in this proceeding but to approve the proposed transaction, while formulating any general rules it might desire for use in future cases of this nature, would be to stultify the administrative process. That we refuse to do.

Since the Commission, unlike a court, does have the ability to make new law prospectively through the exercise of its rule-making powers, it has less reason to rely upon ad hoc adjudication to formulate new standards of conduct within the framework of the Holding Company Act. The function of filling in the interstices of the Act should be performed, as much as possible, through this quasi-legislative promulgation of rules to be applied in the future. But any rigid requirement to that effect would make the administrative process inflexible and incapable of dealing with many of the specialized problems which arise. See Report of the Attorney General's Committee on Administrative Procedure in Government Agencies, S. Doc. No. 8, 77th Cong., 1st Sess., p. 29. Not every principle essential to the effective administration of a statute can or should be cast immediately into the mold of a general rule. Some principles must await their own development, while others must be adjusted to meet particular, unforeseeable situations. In performing its important functions in these respects, therefore, an administrative agency must be equipped to act either by general rule or by individual order. To insist upon one form of action to the exclusion of the other is to exalt form over necessity.***

Hence we refuse to say that the Commission, which had not previously been confronted with the problem of management trading during reorganization, was forbidden from utilizing this particular proceeding for announcing and applying a new standard of conduct. Cf. *Federal Trade Commission v. Keppel & Bro.*, 291 U.S. 304 [Chapter 1[C][2], above]. That such action might have a retroactive effect was not necessarily fatal to its validity. Every case of first impression has a retroactive effect, whether the new principle is announced by a court or by an administrative agency. But such retroactivity must be balanced against the mischief of producing a result which is contrary to a statutory design or to legal and equitable principles. If that mischief is greater than the ill effect of the retroactive application of a new standard, it is not the type of retroactivity which is condemned by law. *See Addison v. Holly Hill Co.*, 322 U.S. 607, 620.

And so in this case, the fact that the Commission's order might retroactively prevent Federal's management from securing the profits and control which were the objects of the preferred stock purchases may well be outweighed by the dangers inherent in such purchases from the statutory standpoint. If that is true, the argument of retroactivity becomes nothing more than a claim that the Commission lacks power to enforce the standards of the Act in this proceeding. Such a claim deserves rejection.***

Drawing upon its experience, the Commission indicated that [the] normal and special powers of the holding company management during the course of a § 11(e) reorganization placed in the management's command "a formidable battery of devices that would enable it, if it should choose to use them selfishly, to affect in material degree the ultimate allocation of new securities among the various existing classes, to influence the market for its own gain, and to manipulate or obstruct the reorganization required by the mandate of the statute."***

Turning to the facts in this case, the Commission noted the salient fact that the primary object of Federal's management in buying the preferred stock was admittedly to obtain the voting power that was accruing to that stock through the reorganization and to profit from the investment therein. That stock had been purchased in the market at prices that were depressed in relation to what the management anticipated would be, and what in fact was, the earning and asset value of its reorganization equivalent. The Commission admitted that the good faith and personal integrity of this management were not in question; but as to the management's justification of its motives, the Commission concluded that it was merely trying to "deny that they made selfish use of their powers during the period when their conflict of interest, vis-a-vis public investors, was in existence owing to their purchase program." Federal's management had thus placed itself in a position where it was "peculiarly susceptible to temptation to conduct the reorganization for personal gain rather than the public good" and where its desire to make advantageous purchases of stock could have an important influence, even though subconsciously, upon many of the decisions to be made in the course of the reorganization. Accordingly, the Commission felt that all of its general considerations of the problem were applicable to this case.

The scope of our review of an administrative order wherein a new principle is announced and applied is no different from that which pertains to ordinary administrative action. The wisdom of the principle adopted is none of our concern. Our duty is at an end when becomes evident that the Commission's action is based upon substantial evidence and is consistent with the authority granted by Congress.

We are unable to say in this case that the Commission erred in reaching the result it did.***

Mr. Justice Jackson, dissenting***

The essential facts are few and are not in dispute. This corporation filed with the Securities and Exchange Commission a voluntary plan of reorganization. While the reorganization proceedings were pending sixteen officers and directors bought on the open market about 7½% of the corporation's preferred stock. Both the Commission and the Court admit that these purchases were not forbidden by any law, judicial precedent, regulation or rule of the Commission. Nevertheless, the Commission has ordered these individuals to surrender their shares to the corporation at cost, plus 4% interest, and the Court now approves that order.***

The Court's reasoning adds up to this: The Commission must be sustained because of its accumulated experience in solving a problem with which it had never before been confronted!

Of course, thus to uphold the Commission by professing to find that it has enunciated a "new standard of conduct" brings the Court squarely against the invalidity of retroactive law-making. But the Court does not falter. "That such action might have a retroactive effect was not necessarily fatal to its validity."

If it is of no consequence that no rule of law be existent to support an administrative order, and the Court of Appeals is obliged to defer to administrative experience and to sustain a Commission's power merely because it has been asserted and exercised, of what use is it to print a record or briefs in the case, or to hear argument? Administrative experience always is present, at least to the degree that it is here, and would always dictate a like deference by this Court to an assertion of administrative power.***

Whether, as matter of policy, corporate managers during reorganization should be prohibited from buying or selling its stock, is not a question for us to decide. But it is for us to decide whether, so long as no law or regulation prohibits them from buying, their purchases may be forfeited, or not, in the discretion of the Commission. If such a power exists in words of the statute or in their implication, it would be possible to point it out and thus end the case. Instead, the Court admits that there was no law prohibiting these purchases when they were made, or at any time thereafter. And, except for this decision, there is none now.

Mr. Justice Frankfurter joins in this opinion.

Notes and Questions

1. **Justification for Regulation?** The SEC in *Chenery* was acting pursuant to the Public Utility Holding Company Act of 1935 (PUHCA or Act), 49 Stat. 803, ch. 687, repealed by the Energy Policy Act of 2005, Pub. L. 109-58, 119 Stat. 594, subtit. F, §§ 1261–1277 (July 29, 2005). The PUHCA limited the scope of public utilities' operations in response to concerns that utility holding companies had grown too large to regulate effectively and were operating as ungovernable trusts. *See* Joel Seligman, The Transformation of Wall Street 122 (3d ed. 2003). It is one of the many

securities regulation statutes passed in the aftermath of the Great Depression. Regulated utilities were required either to operate within a single state or as an integrated system that served a defined geographic area. Section 11 required utility holding companies to divest assets and businesses to accomplish these objectives, and charged the SEC with overseeing holding company reorganizations. The SEC was to approve a reorganization if, following notice and an opportunity for a hearing, it found the reorganization plan necessary to effectuate the Act's mandate "and fair and equitable to the persons affected by such plan."

2. **The Procedural Posture.** Note that the *Chenery* decision above was the Supreme Court's second encounter with the case. In *Chenery I*, the SEC concluded that Federal's managers were subject to a common law duty of fair dealing that arose out of their position as fiduciaries of the company. In the SEC's view, that duty precluded the managers from acquiring a stake in the reorganized company by converting preferred shares of the old firm into common stock of the new company at a time when successive reorganization plans were being submitted by the managers to the SEC. The Supreme Court read the SEC's decision to rest on general equitable principles and concluded that while the managers were indeed fiduciaries, their actions were not inconsistent with equitable principles that had been recognized by courts. *See SEC v. Chenery Corp.*, 318 U.S. 80, 86–87 (1943).

Justice Frankfurter's opinion for the Court in *Chenery I* reasoned that because "[t]he grounds upon which an administrative order must be judged are those upon which the record discloses that its action was based," the SEC's order had to be vacated. At the same time, Justice Frankfurter made clear that the SEC was not limited to enforcing general equitable principles, and that "Congress certainly did not mean to preclude the formulation by the Commission of standards expressing a more sensitive regard for what is right and what is wrong than those prevalent at the time the Public Utility Holding Company Act of 1935 became law." To give the Commission an opportunity to articulate a permissible basis for its order, the case was remanded to the SEC.

What purposes are served by requiring the agency to reconsider its decision in light of its previous erroneous ground when a new sufficient ground has been offered in the courts by government counsel (and presumably agreed to by the agency)? Did the SEC in *Chenery II* in fact advance a materially different ground for voiding the management stock purchase? When is the "*Chenery* remand" appropriate? Judge Friendly observed that *Chenery* permits courts to ask agencies, "Do you really mean it?", and to suggest lines of inquiry that the agency overlooked or did not deal with in a satisfactory manner. However, "*Chenery* does not mean that any assignment of a wrong reason calls for reversal and remand; this is necessary only when the reviewing court concludes there is a significant chance that but for the error the agency might have reached a different result." Henry J. Friendly, Chenery *Revisited: Reflections on Reversal and Remand of Administrative Orders*, 1969 DUKE L.J. 199, 211 (1969).

3. **Retrospective vs. Prospective Decisionmaking?** Given the Court's conclusion in *Chenery I* that general equitable principles did not bar the stock purchases, what basis did SEC advance for its prohibition? If this is an issue of first impression under the

PUHCA, should the prohibition be announced in an adjudication or in a prospective declaration of agency policy such as a rulemaking or agency guidance? Does it matter that the managers' stock purchases were not a *malum in se* punishable by the criminal law (see Note 10 to *Yates v. United States, supra* Chapter 2[B][1], p. 127?) Should the agency have provided that, in order to avoid unfair surprise, its order would operate on a prospective-only basis? Can the agency do so consistently with the APA? *See* Emily S. Bremer, *The Agency Declaratory Judgment*, 78 Ohio St. L. J. (forthcoming 2017).

NLRB v. Wyman-Gordon Co.
394 U.S. 759 (1969)

Mr. Justice Fortas announced the judgment of the Court and delivered an opinion in which The Chief Justice, Mr. Justice Stewart, and Mr. Justice White join.

On the petition of the International Brotherhood of Boilermakers and pursuant to its powers under §9 of the National Labor Relations Act, 49 Stat. 453, 29 U.S.C. §159, the National Labor Relations Board ordered an election among the production and maintenance employees of the respondent company. At the election, the employees were to select one of two labor unions as their exclusive bargaining representative, or to choose not to be represented by a union at all. In connection with the election, the Board ordered the respondent to furnish a list of the names and addresses of its employees who could vote in the election, so that the unions could use the list for election purposes. The respondent refused to comply with the order, and the election was held without the list. Both unions were defeated in the election.

The Board upheld the unions' objections to the election because the respondent had not furnished the list, and the Board ordered a new election. The respondent again refused to obey a Board order to supply a list of employees, and the Board issued a subpoena ordering the respondent to provide the list or else produce its personnel and payroll records showing the employees' names and addresses. The Board filed an action in the United States District Court for the District of Massachusetts seeking to have its subpoena enforced or to have a mandatory injunction issued to compel the respondent to comply with its order.

The District Court held the Board's order valid and directed the respondent to comply. The United States Court of Appeals for the First Circuit reversed. The Court of Appeals thought that the order in this case was invalid because it was based on a rule laid down in an earlier decision by the Board, *Excelsior Underwear Inc.*, 156 N.L.R.B. 1236 (1966), and the *Excelsior* rule had not been promulgated in accordance with the requirements that the Administrative Procedure Act prescribes for rule making, 5 U.S.C. §553.***

The *Excelsior* case involved union objections to the certification of the results of elections that the unions had lost at two companies. The companies had denied the unions a list of the names and addresses of employees eligible to vote. In the course of the proceedings, the Board "invited certain interested parties" to file briefs and to participate in oral argument of the issue whether the Board should require the employer to furnish lists of employees [who were eligible to vote in the representation election]. Various employer groups and trade unions did so, as amici curiae. After these proceedings, the Board issued its decision in *Excelsior*. It purported to establish the general rule that such a list must be provided, but it declined to apply its new rule to the companies involved in the *Excelsior* case. Instead, it held that the rule would apply "only in those elections that are directed, or consented to, subsequent to 30 days from the date of [the] Decision."

Specifically, the Board purported to establish "a requirement that will be applied in all election cases. That is, within 7 days after the Regional Director has approved a consent-election agreement entered into by the parties . . . , or after the Regional Director or the Board has directed an election . . . , the employer must file with the Regional Director an election eligibility list, containing the names and addresses of all the eligible voters. The Regional Director, in turn, shall make this information available to all parties in the case. Failure to comply with this requirement shall be grounds for setting aside the election whenever proper objections are filed."

Section 6 of the National Labor Relations Act empowers the Board "to make . . . , in the manner prescribed by the Administrative Procedure Act, such rules and regulations as may be necessary to carry out the provisions of this Act." 29 U.S.C. § 156. The Administrative Procedure Act contains specific provisions governing agency rule making, which it defines as "an agency statement of general or particular applicability and future effect," 5 U.S.C. § 551(4).[2] The Act requires, among other things, publication in the Federal Register of notice of proposed rule making and of hearing; opportunity to be heard; a statement in the rule of its basis and purposes; and publication in the Federal Register of the rule as adopted. *See* 5 U.S.C. § 553. The Board asks us to hold that it has discretion to promulgate new rules in adjudicatory proceedings, without complying with the requirements of the Administrative Procedure Act.

The rule-making provisions of that Act, which the Board would avoid, were designed to assure fairness and mature consideration of rules of general application. See H.R. Rep. No. 1980, 79th Cong., 2d Sess., 21–26 (1946); S. Rep. No. 752, 79th Cong., 1st Sess., 13–16 (1945). They may not be avoided by the process of making rules in the course of adjudicatory proceedings. There is no warrant in law for the Board to replace the statutory scheme with a rule-making procedure of its own invention. Apart from the fact that the device fashioned by the Board does not comply with statutory command, it obviously falls short of the substance of the requirements of the Administrative Procedure Act. The "rule" created in *Excelsior* was not published in the Federal Register, which is the statutory and accepted means of giving notice of a rule as adopted; only selected organizations were given notice of the "hearing," whereas notice in the Federal

---

2. We agree with the opinion of Chief Judge Aldrich below that the *Excelsior* rule involves matters of substance and that it therefore does not fall within any of the Act's exceptions. *See* 5 U.S.C. § 553(b)(A).

Register would have been general in character; under the Administrative Procedure Act, the terms or substance of the rule would have to be stated in the notice of hearing, and all interested parties would have an opportunity to participate in the rule making.

The Solicitor General does not deny that the Board ignored the rule-making provisions of the Administrative Procedure Act. But he appears to argue that *Excelsior*'s command is a valid substantive regulation, binding upon this respondent as such, because the Board promulgated it in the *Excelsior* proceeding, in which the requirements for valid adjudication had been met. This argument misses the point. There is no question that, in an adjudicatory hearing, the Board could validly decide the issue whether the employer must furnish a list of employees to the union. But that is not what the Board did in *Excelsior*. The Board did not even apply the rule it made to the parties in the adjudicatory proceeding, the only entities that could properly be subject to the order in that case. Instead, the Board purported to make a rule: i. e., to exercise its quasi-legislative power.

Adjudicated cases may and do, of course, serve as vehicles for the formulation of agency policies, which are applied and announced therein. See H. Friendly, The Federal Administrative Agencies 36–52 (1962).[4] They generally provide a guide to action that the agency may be expected to take in future cases. Subject to the qualified role of stare decisis in the administrative process, they may serve as precedents. But this is far from saying, as the Solicitor General suggests, that commands, decisions, or policies announced in adjudication are "rules" in the sense that they must, without more, be obeyed by the affected public.

In the present case, however, the respondent itself was specifically directed by the Board to submit a list of the names and addresses of its employees for use by the unions in connection with the election. This direction, which was part of the order directing that an election be held, is unquestionably valid. Even though the direction to furnish the list was followed by citation to "*Excelsior Underwear Inc.*, 156 NLRB No. 111," it is an order in the present case that the respondent was required to obey. Absent this direction by the Board, the respondent was under no compulsion to furnish the list because no statute and no validly adopted rule required it to do so.

Because the Board in an adjudicatory proceeding directed the respondent itself to furnish the list, the decision of the Court of Appeals for the First Circuit must be reversed.***

---

4. Mr. Justice Harlan's dissent argues that because the Board improperly relied upon the *Excelsior* "rule" in issuing its order, we are obliged to remand. He relies on *SEC v. Chenery Corp.*, 318 U.S. 80 (1943). To remand would be an idle and useless formality. *Chenery* does not require that we convert judicial review of agency action into a ping-pong game. In *Chenery*, the Commission had applied the wrong standards to the adjudication of a complex factual situation, and the Court held that it would not undertake to decide whether the Commission's result might have been justified on some other basis. Here, by contrast, the substance of the Board's command is not seriously contestable. There is not the slightest uncertainty as to the outcome of a proceeding before the Board, whether the Board acted through a rule or an order. It would be meaningless to remand.

Mr. Justice Black, with whom Mr. Justice Brennan and Mr. Justice Marshall join, concurring in the result.

***I am convinced that the *Excelsior* practice was adopted by the Board as a legitimate incident to the adjudication of a specific case before it, and for that reason I would hold that the Board properly followed the procedures applicable to "adjudication" rather than "rule making." Since my reasons for joining in reversal of the Court of Appeals differ so substantially from those set forth in the prevailing opinion, I will spell them out at some length.

Most administrative agencies, like the Labor Board here, are granted two functions by the legislation creating them: (1) the power under certain conditions to make rules having the effect of laws, that is, generally speaking, quasi-legislative power; and (2) the power to hear and adjudicate particular controversies, that is quasi-judicial power. The line between these two functions is not always a clear one and in fact the two functions merge at many points. For example, in exercising its quasi-judicial function an agency must frequently decide controversies on the basis of new doctrines, not theretofore applied to a specific problem, though drawn to be sure from broader principles reflecting the purposes of the statutes involved and from the rules invoked in dealing with related problems. If the agency decision reached under the adjudicatory power becomes a precedent, it guides future conduct in much the same way as though it were a new rule promulgated under the rule-making power, and both an adjudicatory order and a formal "rule" are alike subject to judicial review. Congress gave the Labor Board both of these separate but almost inseparably related powers. No language in the National Labor Relations Act requires that the grant or the exercise of one power was intended to exclude the Board's use of the other.

Nor does any language in the Administrative Procedure Act require such a conclusion.*** [A]lthough it is true that the adjudicatory approach frees an administrative agency from the procedural requirements specified for rule making, the Act permits this to be done whenever the action involved can satisfy the definition of "adjudication" and then imposes separate procedural requirements that must be met in adjudication. Under these circumstances, so long as the matter involved can be dealt with in a way satisfying the definition of either "rule making" or "adjudication" under the Administrative Procedure Act, that Act, along with the Labor Relations Act, should be read as conferring upon the Board the authority to decide, within its informed discretion, whether to proceed by rule making or adjudication. Our decision in *SEC v. Chenery Corp.*, 332 U.S. 194 (1947), though it did not involve the Labor Board or the Administrative Procedure Act, is nonetheless equally applicable here. As we explained in that case, "the choice made between proceeding by general rule or by individual, ad hoc litigation is one that lies primarily in the informed discretion of the administrative agency."

In the present case there is no dispute that all the procedural safeguards required for "adjudication" were fully satisfied in connection with the Board's *Excelsior* decision, and it seems plain to me that that decision did constitute "adjudication" within the meaning of the Administrative Procedure Act, even though the requirement was to be prospectively applied. The Board did not abstractly decide out of the blue to announce a brand new rule of law to govern labor activities in the future, but rather established the procedure as a direct consequence of the proper exercise of its adjudicatory powers. Sections 9(c)(1) and (2) of the Labor Relations Act empower the Board to conduct investigations, hold hearings, and supervise elections to determine the exclusive bargaining representative that the employees wish to represent them. This is a key provision of the plan Congress adopted to settle labor quarrels that might interrupt the free flow of commerce. A controversy arose between the Excelsior Company and its employees as to the bargaining agent the employees desired to act for them. The Board's power to provide the procedures for the election was invoked, an election was held, and the losing unions sought to have that election set aside. Undoubtedly the Board proceeding for determination of whether to confirm or set aside that election was "agency process for the formulation of an order" and thus was "adjudication" within the meaning of the Administrative Procedure Act.

The prevailing opinion seems to hold that the *Excelsior* requirement cannot be considered the result of adjudication because the Board did not apply it to the parties in the *Excelsior* case itself, but rather announced that it would be applied only to elections called 30 days after the date of the *Excelsior* decision. But the *Excelsior* order was nonetheless an inseparable part of the adjudicatory process.***

Apart from the fact that the decisions whether to accept a "new" requirement urged by one party and, if so, whether to apply it retroactively to the other party are inherent parts of the adjudicatory process, I think the opposing theory accepted by the Court of Appeals and by the prevailing opinion today is a highly impractical one. In effect, it would require an agency like the Labor Board to proceed by adjudication only when it could decide, prior to adjudicating a particular case, that any new practice to be adopted would be applied retroactively. Obviously, this decision cannot properly be made until all the issues relevant to adoption of the practice are fully considered in connection with the final decision of that case. If the Board were to decide, after careful evaluation of all the arguments presented to it in the adjudicatory proceeding, that it might be fairer to apply the practice only prospectively, it would be faced with the unpleasant choice of either starting all over again to evaluate the merits of the question, this time in a "rule-making" proceeding, or overriding the considerations of fairness and applying its order retroactively anyway, in order to preserve the validity of the new practice and avoid duplication of effort. I see no good reason to impose any such inflexible requirement on the administrative agencies.

Mr. Justice Douglas, dissenting.

***The "substantive" rules described by § 553(d) may possibly cover "adjudications," even though they represent performance of the "judicial" function. But it is no answer to say that the order under review was "adjudicatory." For as my Brother Harlan says, an agency is not adjudicating when it is making a rule to fit future cases. A rule like the one in *Excelsior* is designed to fit all cases at all times. It is not particularized to special facts. It is a statement of far-reaching policy covering all future representation elections.

It should therefore have been put down for the public hearing prescribed by the [APA].***

Mr. Justice Harlan, dissenting.

The language of the Administrative Procedure Act does not support the Government's claim that an agency is "adjudicating" when it announces a rule which it refuses to apply in the dispute before it. The Act makes it clear that an agency "adjudicates" only when its procedures result in the "formulation of an *order*." 5 U.S.C. § 551(7). (Emphasis supplied.) An "order" is defined to include "the whole or a *part* of a final disposition . . . of an agency *in a matter other than rule making* . . . ." 5 U.S.C. § 551(6). 551 (Emphasis supplied.) This definition makes it apparent that an agency is not adjudicating when it is making a rule, which the Act defines as "an agency statement of general or particular applicability and *future effect* . . . ." 5 U.S.C. § 551(4). (Emphasis supplied.) Since the Labor Board's *Excelsior* rule was to be effective only 30 days after its promulgation, it clearly falls within the rule-making requirements of the Act.

Nor can I agree that the natural interpretation of the statute should be rejected because it requires the agency to choose between giving its rules immediate effect or initiating a separate rule-making proceeding. An agency chooses to apply a rule prospectively only because it represents such a departure from pre-existing understandings that it would be unfair to impose the rule upon the parties in pending matters.***

Before the Board may be permitted to adopt a rule that so significantly alters pre-existing labor-management understandings, it must be required to conduct a satisfactory rule-making proceeding, so that it will have the benefit of wide-ranging argument before it enacts its proposed solution to an important problem.***

Chenery's teachings are applicable here. The Regional Office that issued the order under review refused to consider the merits of the arguments against the *Excelsior* rule which were raised by Wyman-Gordon on the ground that they had been rejected by the Board in the *Excelsior* case itself[.] The Board denied review of this decision on the ground that "it raises no substantial issues warranting review."***

Since the major reason the Board has given in support of its order is invalid, *Chenery* requires remand.*** Since the *Excelsior* rule was invalidly promulgated, it is clear that, at a minimum, the Board is obliged on remand to recanvass all of the competing considerations before it may properly announce its decision in this case. We cannot know what the outcome of such a reappraisal will be. Surely, it cannot be stated with any degree of certainty that the Board will adopt precisely the same solution as the one which was embraced in *Excelsior*. The plurality simply usurps the function of the National Labor Relations Board when it says otherwise.

Notes and Questions

1. **The Logic of Prospective-Only Overruling?** The validity of the Board's order in *Wyman-Gordon* depended upon the validity of its earlier order in *Excelsior*, holding on a prospective basis that the employer must provide a list of employees to a union in a representation election. What were the Board's reasons for making its *Excelsior* ruling prospective only? In general, what are the benefits of a prospective "adjudicative" ruling compared to a regulation promulgated through notice-and-comment rulemaking? The costs? Does an order that applies on a prospective-only basis fit within the definition of "adjudication" in 5 U.S.C. § 551(6) ("'adjudication' means agency process for the formulation of an order") and "order" in 5 U.S.C. § 551(7) ("'order' means the whole or a part of a final disposition, whether affirmative, negative, injunctive, or declaratory in form, of an agency in a matter other than rule making but including licensing")? Does the Justices' disquiet with the Board's prospective-only order reflect implicit reliance on an idealized, platonic concept of adjudication? *See generally* Lon Fuller, *The Forms and Limits of Adjudication*, 92 Harv. L. Rev. 353 (1978); Owen M. Fiss, *Foreword: The Forms of Justice*, 93 Harv. L. Rev. 1 (1979).

2. **Does *Wyman-Gordon* Prevent an Agency from Issuing a Prospective-Only Overruling of a Past Precedent via Adjudication?** The Court splinters off in four different positions, but a plurality of the Court sustains the agency's order refusing to certify Wyman-Gordon's victory in the representation election because the company refused to comply with the *Excelsior* list requirement. Does this result mean that an agency can be confident that a prospective-only overruling of agency precedent will be enforced by the courts? Is the agency under an obligation to not abuse its discretion when overruling past policy and, in such cases, to make its policy change prospective only? If the agency intends to change positions, does it make sense to require it to halt its adjudication in midstream and embark on a rulemaking?

NLRB v. Bell Aerospace Co.

416 U.S. 267 (1974)

Mr. Justice Powell delivered the opinion of the Court.

This case presents two questions: first, whether the National Labor Relations Board properly determined that all "managerial employees," except those whose participation in a labor organization would create a conflict of interest with their job responsibilities, are covered by the National Labor Relations Act; and second, whether the Board must proceed by rulemaking rather than by adjudication in determining whether certain buyers are "managerial employees." We answer both questions in the negative.***

Respondent Bell Aerospace Co., Division of Textron, Inc. (company), operates a plant in Wheatfield, New York, where it is engaged in research and development in the design and fabrication of aerospace products. On July 30, 1970, Amalgamated

Local No. 1286 of the United Automobile, Aerospace and Agricultural Implement Workers of America (union) petitioned the National Labor Relations Board (Board) for a representation election to determine whether the union would be certified as the bargaining representative of the 25 buyers in the purchasing and procurement department at the company's plant. The company opposed the petition on the ground that the buyers were "managerial employees" and thus were not covered by the Act.

The relevant facts adduced at the representation hearing are as follows. The purchasing and procurement department receives requisition orders from other departments at the plant and is responsible for purchasing all of the company's needs from outside suppliers. Some items are standardized and may be purchased "off the shelf" from various distributors and suppliers. Other items must be made to the company's specifications, and the requisition orders may be accompanied by detailed blueprints and other technical plans. Requisitions often designate a particular vendor, and in some instances the buyer must obtain approval before selecting a different one. Where no vendor is specified, the buyer is free to choose one.

Absent specific instructions to the contrary, buyers have full discretion, without any dollar limit, to select prospective vendors, draft invitations to bid, evaluate submitted bids, negotiate price and terms, and prepare purchase orders. Buyers execute all purchase orders up to $50,000. They may place or cancel orders of less than $5,000 on their own signature. On commitments in excess of $5,000, buyers must obtain the approval of a superior, with higher levels of approval required as the purchase cost increases. For the Minute Man missile project, which represents 70% of the company's sales, purchase decisions are made by a team of personnel from the engineering, quality assurance, finance, and manufacturing departments. The buyer serves as team chairman and signs the purchase order, but a representative from the pricing and negotiation department participates in working out the terms.

After the representation hearing, the Regional Director transferred the case to the Board. On May 20, 1971, the Board issued its decision holding that the company's buyers constituted an appropriate unit for purposes of collective bargaining and directing an election. Relying on its recent decision in *North Arkansas Electric Cooperative, Inc.*, 185 N.L.R.B. 550 (1970), the Board first stated that even though the company's buyers might be "managerial employees," they were nevertheless covered by the Act and entitled to its protections. The Board then rejected the company's alternative contention that representation should be denied because the buyers' authority to commit the company's credit, select vendors, and negotiate purchase prices would create a potential conflict of interest between the buyers as union members and the company.***

On June 16, 1971, a representation election was conducted in which 15 of the buyers voted for the union and nine against. On August 12, the Board certified the union as the exclusive bargaining representative for the company's buyers. That same day, however, the Court of Appeals for the Eighth Circuit denied enforcement of another Board order [in a different case] and held that "managerial employees" were not covered by the Act and were therefore not entitled to its protections.

Encouraged by the Eighth Circuit's decision, the company moved the Board for reconsideration of its earlier order. The Board denied the motion, stating that it disagreed with the Eighth Circuit***. In the Board's view, Congress intended to exclude from the Act only those "managerial employees" associated with the "formulation and implementation of labor relations policies." In each case, the "fundamental touchstone" was "whether the duties and responsibilities of any managerial employee or group of managerial employees do or do not include determinations which should be made free of any conflict of interest which could arise if the person involved was a participating member of a labor organization."***

The company stood by its contention that the buyers, as "managerial employees," were not covered by the Act and refused to bargain with the union. An unfair labor practice complaint resulted in a Board finding that the company had violated §§ 8(a)(5) and (1) of the Act, 29 U.S.C. §§ 158(a)(5) and (1), and an order compelling the company to bargain with the union. Subsequently, the company petitioned the United States Court of Appeals for the Second Circuit for review of the order and the Board cross-petitioned for enforcement.

The Court of Appeals denied enforcement.***

[The Supreme Court initially held that Congress had categorically, though implicitly, excluded managerial employees from the NLRA's coverage when it enacted the Taft-Hartley amendments to the NLRA in 1947. This part of the Court's opinion appears *infra* in Chapter 5[C][2], page 572.]

The Court of Appeals also held that, although the Board was not precluded from determining that buyers or some types of buyers were not "managerial employees," it could do so only by invoking its rulemaking procedures under § 6 of the Act, 29 U.S.C. § 156. We disagree.***

[T]he present question is whether on remand the Board must invoke its rulemaking procedures if it determines, in light of our opinion, that these buyers are not "managerial employees" under the Act. The Court of Appeals thought that rulemaking was required because any Board finding that the company's buyers are not "managerial" would be contrary to its prior decisions and would presumably be in the nature of a general rule designed "to fit all cases at all times."***

The views expressed in *Chenery II* and *Wyman-Gordon* make plain that the Board is not precluded from announcing new principles in an adjudicative proceeding and that the choice between rulemaking and adjudication lies in the first instance within the Board's discretion. Although there may be situations where the Board's reliance on adjudication would amount to an abuse of discretion or a violation of the Act, nothing in the present case would justify such a conclusion. Indeed, there is ample indication that adjudication is especially appropriate in the instant context. As the Court of Appeals noted, "there must be tens of thousands of manufacturing, wholesale and retail units which employ buyers, and hundreds of thousands of the latter." Moreover, duties of buyers vary widely depending on the company or industry. It is doubtful whether any generalized standard could be framed which would have more than marginal utility. The Board thus has reason to proceed with caution, developing its standards in a case-by-case manner with attention to the specific character of the buyers' authority and duties in each company. The Board's judgment that adjudication best serves this purpose is entitled to great weight.

The possible reliance of industry on the Board's past decisions with respect to buyers does not require a different result. It has not been shown that the adverse consequences ensuing from such reliance are so substantial that the Board should be precluded from reconsidering the issue in an adjudicative proceeding. Furthermore, this is not a case in which some new liability is sought to be imposed on individuals for past actions which were taken in good-faith reliance on Board pronouncements. Nor are fines or damages involved here. In any event, concern about such consequences is largely speculative, for the Board has not yet finally determined whether these buyers are "managerial."

It is true, of course, that rulemaking would provide the Board with a forum for soliciting the informed views of those affected in industry and labor before embarking on a new course. But surely the Board has discretion to decide that the adjudicative procedures in this case may also produce the relevant information necessary to mature and fair consideration of the issues. Those most immediately affected, the buyers and the company in the particular case, are accorded a full opportunity to be heard before the Board makes its determination.

The judgment of the Court of Appeals is therefore affirmed in part and reversed in part, and the cause remanded to that court with directions to remand to the Board for further proceedings in conformity with this opinion.***

Notes and Questions

1. **The Regulatory Context.** We have already encountered the National Labor Relations Act (NLRA), 49 Stat. 449, codified as amended at 29 U.S.C. § 151–169, in connection with *NLRB v. Catholic Bishop of Chicago*, Chapter 2[B][1][f]. The Act established the National Labor Relations Board (NLRB or Board) and authorized the Board to regulate "unfair" labor practices. From its creation, the Board has possessed statutory authority "from time to time to make, amend, and rescind, in the manner prescribed by [the Administrative Procedure Act], such rules and regulations as may be necessary to carry out [the NLRA]." 29 U.S.C. § 156. Despite this authorization, the Board has rarely engaged in substantive rulemaking. *But see American Hospital Assn. v. NLRB*, 499 U.S. 606 (1991) (unanimously upholding Board rule that defined bargaining units for acute care hospital facilities).

2. **When Must an Agency Engage in Rulemaking?** The Supreme Court in *Bell Aerospace* unanimously reaffirmed the *Chenery II* holding that the agency has broad discretion whether to use rulemaking or adjudication in elaborating policy under its organic statute. (Of course, the organic statue would control, but it rarely speaks to

the subject.) In a number of decisions authored by Judge Friendly, including the ruling overturned in *Bell Aerospace*, the Second Circuit had taken the contrary position that an agency abuses its discretion when it changes a longstanding policy affecting reliance interests via adjudication; in such cases, the court of appeals held, the agency must use rulemaking. Judge Friendly's view was based in part on concerns about notice to the regulated industry:

> There must be tens of thousands of manufacturing, wholesale and retail units which employ buyers, and hundreds of thousands of the latter. Yet the Board did not even attempt to inform industry and labor organizations, by means providing some notice though not in conformity with section 4, of its proposed new policy and to invite comment thereon***.

Bell Aerospace Co. v. NLRB, 475 F.2d 485, 496 (1973).

Moreover, the fact that the Board was *changing* policy articulated in prior adjudications weighed heavily, in the court of appeals' view, in favor of rulemaking:

> [W]hen the Board has so long been committed to a position, it should be particularly sure that it has all available information before adopting another, in a setting where nothing stands in the way of a rule-making proceeding except the Board's congenital disinclination to follow a procedure which*** enables the agency promulgating the rule to educate itself before establishing rules and procedures which have a substantial impact on those regulated.

Id. at 497.

The Supreme Court decidedly rejected Judge Friendly's position in *Bell Aerospace*. How does the Court address Judge Friendly's concerns? Are those concerns valid at a time when, thanks to electronic communications, it is relatively simple for regulated parties and their lawyers to keep track of agencies' activities? Is it fair to require employers throughout the country to assume the costs of monitoring developments at the Board? To require employees or unions to do so? Are there mechanisms that allow management and labor to spread monitoring costs among themselves?

3. **"Abuse of Discretion" in the Decision to Proceed Through Adjudication?** It is well-established that a decisionmaker "necessarily abuse[s] its discretion if it based its ruling on an erroneous view of the law." *Cooter & Gell v. Hartmarx Corp.*, 496 U.S. 384, 405 (1990). Thus, a decision to proceed by adjudication when a statute required rulemaking, or vice versa, would presumably be an abuse of discretion.

In addition, the Court in *Bell Aerospace* noted two other circumstances in which the use of adjudication could be an abuse of discretion. First, "adverse consequences" caused by industry reliance on an agency's prior position may be "so substantial" that the agency is precluded from reconsidering its position through adjudication. Second, adjudication may cause a "new liability*** to be imposed for past actions which were taken in good-faith reliance" on the agency's prior positions. Why did the SEC's decision in *Chenery* not fall within the latter exception? Was a "good-faith reliance" interest disturbed in that case? Are the reliance concerns weighty in the *Bell Aerospace* context where the issue is whether a particular group of employees may seek collective representation and employers do not incur economic penalties as a consequence of the agency's change in policy?

How significant must reliance interests be for the imposition of retroactive liability based on a new agency policy to be an abuse of agency discretion? In *FCC v. Fox Televisions Stations, Inc.*, 132 S. Ct. 2307 (2012), the Supreme Court approached the question from the perspective of due process. At issue in *Fox* were three orders of the FCC finding that television broadcasts of expletives and nudity violated the prohibition on broadcasts of obscenity in 18 U.S.C. § 1464. Prior to the *Fox* orders, the Commission had long held that only deliberate or repeated broadcasts of obscenity and nudity violated § 1464. Under the leadership of Commissioners appointed by President George W. Bush, the Commission changed position and held that the broadcast of a "fleeting" expletive or depiction of fleeting nudity violated the indecency ban. In two of the orders, the Commission found a violation of § 1464 but declined to assess monetary penalties; in the third, the Commission imposed a forfeiture of $27,500 on each of 45 stations that aired the indecent episode.

In the first round of litigation challenging the orders, the Supreme Court held that the FCC's change of position was not arbitrary and capricious because the agency acknowledged it was changing positions and offered reasonable justifications for the change. *FCC v. Fox Television Stations, Inc.* 129 S. Ct. 1800 (2009), *infra* Chapter 5[D], p. 641. In the second round of litigation, the Supreme Court ruled that the FCC's application of the policy as applied in the specific cases under review violated due process. This was because the FCC's prior decisions "fail[ed] to provide a person of ordinary intelligence fair notice of what is prohibited." *FCC v. Fox Television Stations, Inc.*, 132 S. Ct. 2307, 2317 (2012).

4. When Should an Agency Make Use of Rulemaking as a Matter of Good Practice? Although *Bell Aerospace* teaches that agencies have no legal obligation to use rulemaking in many circumstances, it might still be a good idea for agencies to do so. Following Judge Friendly's suggestion in *Bell Aerospace*, one of this volume's authors has argued that rulemaking is particularly appropriate when an agency seeks to change established policy. In this context, rulemaking promotes stability in the law, provides the agency an opportunity to elicit empirical information from a broad range of parties, and generally provides a superior procedural format for public participation in the agency's policymaking process. *See* Samuel Estreicher, *Policy Oscillation at the Labor Board: A Plea for Rulemaking*, 37 ADMIN. L. REV. 163 (1985); Samuel Estreicher, *"Depoliticizing" the National Labor Relations Board: Administrative Steps*, 64 EMORY L.J. 1611 (2015). Given these advantages, why might an agency be reluctant to engage in rulemaking when changing its position? Would resort to rulemaking expose the agency to political scrutiny that it might not otherwise encounter were it to proceed via adjudication? What other costs might an agency incur by engaging in rulemaking?

5. Further Reading. For more on the relationship between adjudication and rulemaking, *see, e.g.*, Elizabeth M. Magill, *Agency Choice of Policymaking Form*, 71 U. CHI.

L. Rev. 1384 (2004); Glen O. Robinson, *The Making of Administrative Policy: Another Look at Rulemaking and Adjudication and Administrative Procedure Reform*, 118 U. Pa. L. Rev. 513 (1970); Colin S. Diver, *Policymaking Paradigms in Administrative Law*, 95 Harv. L. Rev. 395 (1981); David L. Shapiro, *The Choice of Rulemaking or Adjudication in the Development of Administrative Policy*, 78 Harv. L. Rev. 921 (1965).

Note on Rulemaking's Consequences for Adjudication — and Vice Versa

Though agencies are generally free to make administrative policy through rulemaking or adjudication, an agency's choice of policymaking format may affect its freedom to act in the future. In particular, an agency's decision to engage in rulemaking may preclude it from taking actions inconsistent with its own regulations in future adjudications.

In *United States ex rel. Accardi v. Shaugnessy*, 347 U.S. 260 (1954), the Supreme Court considered the effect of a regulation promulgated by the Attorney General under the Immigration Act of 1917, Pub. L. 64-301, 39 Stat. 874, as amended. Under § 19(c) of the Act, the Attorney General was authorized to suspend deportation of an otherwise deportable alien if certain statutory conditions were satisfied and the Attorney General determined that the alien had a good moral character. The Attorney General's decisions, however, were reviewable by Congress, under a procedure similar to the one-house veto later invalidated in *INS v. Chadha*, Chapter 3[B][2][a], above.

By regulation, the Attorney General delegated authority to make the initial decision on applications for suspension of deportation to "hearing officers," who today are known as immigration judges. Immigration judges' decisions were reviewable by the Board of Immigration Appeals (BIA), a unit of the Justice Department. Under the regulation, the BIA was directed to "exercise such discretion and power conferred upon the Attorney General by law as is appropriate and necessary for the disposition of the case. The decision of the Board*** shall be final except in those cases reviewed by the Attorney General***." 8 C.F.R. § 90.3(c) (1949 ed.).

The petitioner conceded he was deportable and applied for suspension of deportation, which the hearing officer denied. Before his appeal was heard by the BIA, the Attorney General allegedly promulgated a list of 100 "unsavory characters" who were to be deported. As a result, the BIA did not consider the petitioner's petition for suspension of deportation on the merits because it had already been decided by the Attorney General. The Supreme Court concluded that the Attorney General's actions were unlawful as a violation of his own regulation and directed that a writ of habeas corpus issue for the benefit of the petitioner. The Court reasoned:

> [T]he Board was required*** to exercise its own judgment when considering appeals. The clear import of broad provisions for a final review by the Attorney General himself would be meaningless if the Board were not expected to render a decision in accord with its own collective belief. In

unequivocal terms the regulations delegate to the Board discretionary authority as broad as the statute confers on the Attorney General; the scope of the
Attorney General's discretion became the yardstick of the Board's. And if
the word "discretion" means anything in a statutory or administrative grant
of power, it means that the recipient must exercise his authority according to
his own understanding and conscience. This applies with equal force to the
Board and the Attorney General. In short, as long as the regulations remain
operative, the Attorney General denies himself the right to sidestep the Board
or dictate its decision in any manner.

Id. at 266–67.

Accardi establishes that, having promulgated a regulation, an agency must comply
with it until the regulation is repealed or modified. For example, courts reviewing the
denial of claims for Social Security Disability Insurance regularly consider whether
the Social Security Administration has followed the procedures it has established by
regulation for adjudicating such claims. An Administrative Law Judge's failure to correctly apply the grids devised by the agency (*see Heckler v. Campbell*, Chapter 1[C][3])
is an established ground for vacating or reversing the denial of benefits. *See Seavey v.
Barnhart*, 276 F.3d 1 (1st Cir. 2001).

Despite the seeming simplicity of *Accardi*'s command, the limits of the principle it
established remain uncertain. Professor Schwartz observes:

> Disputed points include whether agencies are bound by all regulations, or
> only by legislative regulations; by procedural or only by substantive regula-
> tions; and in all proceedings, only in civil cases, or only in proceedings for
> judicial review of administrative action[.] Uncertainty about the scope of this
> principle is also reflected in controversy as to its exceptions: Are agencies
> bound only by regulations designed for the protection of members of the
> public (rather than internal agency governance), or only by those on which
> a member of the public has relied?

Joshua I. Schwartz, *The Irresistible Force Meets the Immovable Object: Estoppel Remedies for an Agency's Violation of Its Own Regulations or Other Misconduct*, 44 Admin.
L. Rev. 653, 669–70 (1992). For further analysis, see Thomas W. Merrill, *The* Accardi
Principle, 74 Geo. Wash. L. Rev. 569 (2006); Peter Raven-Hansen, *Regulatory Estoppel: When Agencies Break Their Own "Laws,"* 64 Tex. L. Rev. 1 (1985).

What of the converse situation in which an agency takes a position on a question
of administrative policy in an adjudication or series of adjudications: does this constrain the agency's ability to revise its position through rulemaking? Given *Bell Aerospace*'s conclusion that the NLRB was free to change its position on the coverage of
managerial employees via adjudication, an agency would seem to be free to change a
position established by adjudication through a rulemaking. Indeed, rulemaking provides a degree of notice and public participation that commentators contend is particularly appropriate when an agency undertakes a major change in policy. As we will
see, however, changes to an agency's position on a question of administrative policy

must be supported to the same degree as the initial policy determination. *See Motor Vehicle Mfrs. Assn. v. State Farm Mut. Auto. Ins. Co.*, 463 U.S. 29 (1983), *infra* Chapter 5[D]. Moreover, while estoppel does not generally run against the government, it can potentially do so in narrow circumstances, and some statutes, *see, e.g.*, 29 U.S.C. § 259, establish safe harbors for action taken in good faith reliance on agency action. *See* Note 8 to *Perez v. Mortgage Bankers Ass'n*, *infra* Section [F], p. 505.

E. Policy Elaboration

In *Yakus v. United States*, 321 U.S. 414, 425 (1944), Chapter 3[B][1][a], the Supreme Court wrote that the Emergency Price Administrator was charged with "the formulation of subsidiary administrative policy within the prescribed statutory framework." This is generally what is entailed when Congress delegates policymaking authority to an agency. The agency is subject to the requirements and limitations of its organic statute, but not all of the details of the envisioned regulatory scheme are spelled out in the terms of the statute. Where the details are not spelled out, there is a question who fills them out — the agency or the court. The following two cases illustrate the way in which two different agencies formulate subsidiary policy within their statutory frameworks, and how their work is received in the courts.

General Electric Co. v. Gilbert
429 U.S. 125 (1976)

Mr. Justice Rehnquist delivered the opinion of the Court.

Petitioner, General Electric Co., provides for all of its employees a disability plan which pays weekly nonoccupational sickness and accident benefits. Excluded from the plan's coverage, however, are disabilities arising from pregnancy. Respondents, on behalf of a class of women employees, brought this action seeking, inter alia, a declaration that this exclusion constitutes sex discrimination in violation of Title VII of the Civil Rights Act of 1964, 78 Stat. 253, as amended, 42 U.S.C. § 2000e et seq.***

I

As part of its total compensation package, General Electric provides nonoccupational sickness and accident benefits to all employees under its Weekly Sickness and Accident Insurance Plan (Plan) in an amount equal to 60% of an employee's normal straight-time weekly earnings. These payments are paid to employees who become totally disabled as a result of a nonoccupational sickness or accident. Benefit payments normally start with the eighth day of an employee's total disability (although if an employee is earlier confined to a hospital as a bed patient, benefit payments will start immediately), and continue up to a maximum of 26 weeks for any one continuous period of disability or successive periods of disability due to the same or related causes.

The individual named respondents are present or former hourly paid production employees at General Electric's plant in Salem, Va. Each of these employees was pregnant during 1971 or 1972, while employed by General Electric, and each presented a claim to the company for disability benefits under the Plan to cover the period while absent from work as a result of the pregnancy. These claims were routinely denied on the ground that the Plan did not provide disability-benefit payments for any absence due to pregnancy. Each of the respondents thereafter filed charges with the Equal Employment Opportunity Commission (EEOC) alleging that the refusal of General Electric to pay disability benefits under the Plan for time lost due to pregnancy and childbirth discriminated against her because of sex. Upon waiting the requisite number of days, the instant action was commenced in the District Court. The complaint asserted a violation of Title VII. Damages were sought as well as an injunction directing General Electric to include pregnancy disabilities within the Plan on the same terms and conditions as other nonoccupational disabilities.

Following trial, the District Court made findings of fact and conclusions of law, and entered an order in which it determined that General Electric, by excluding pregnancy disabilities from the coverage of the Plan, had engaged in sex discrimination in violation of § 703(a)(1) of Title VII, 42 U.S.C. § 2000e-2(a)(1).*** The ultimate conclusion of the District Court was that petitioner had discriminated on the basis of sex in the operation of its disability program in violation of Title VII. An order was entered enjoining petitioner from continuing to exclude pregnancy-related disabilities from the coverage of the Plan, and providing for the future award of monetary relief to individual members of the class affected. Petitioner appealed to the Court of Appeals for the Fourth Circuit, and that court by a divided vote affirmed the judgment of the District Court.

Between the date on which the District Court's judgment was rendered and the time this case was decided by the Court of Appeals, we decided *Geduldig v. Aiello*, 417 U.S. 484 (1974), where we rejected a claim that a very similar disability program established under California law violated the Equal Protection Clause of the Fourteenth Amendment because that plan's exclusion of pregnancy disabilities represented sex discrimination. The majority of the Court of Appeals felt that *Geduldig* was not controlling because it arose under the Equal Protection Clause of the Fourteenth Amendment, and not under Title VII. The dissenting opinion disagreed with the majority as to the impact of *Geduldig*.***

II

Section 703(a)(1) provides in relevant part that it shall be an unlawful employment practice for an employer

> "to discriminate against any individual with respect to his compensation, terms, conditions, or privileges of employment, because of such individual's race, color, religion, sex, or national origin," 42 U.S.C. § 2000e-2(a)(1).

While there is no necessary inference that Congress, in choosing this language, intended to incorporate into Title VII the concepts of discrimination which have evolved from court decisions construing the Equal Protection Clause of the Fourteenth Amendment, the similarities between the congressional language and some of those decisions surely indicate that the latter are a useful starting point in interpreting the former. Particularly in the case of defining the term "discrimination," which Congress has nowhere in Title VII defined, those cases afford an existing body of law analyzing and discussing that term in a legal context not wholly dissimilar to the concerns which Congress manifested in enacting Title VII. We think, therefore, that our decision in *Geduldig v. Aiello, supra*, dealing with a strikingly similar disability plan, is quite relevant in determining whether or not the pregnancy exclusion did discriminate on the basis of sex. In *Geduldig*, the disability insurance system was funded entirely from contributions deducted from the wages of participating employees, at a rate of 1% of the employee's salary up to an annual maximum of $85. In other relevant respects, the operation of the program was similar to General Electric's disability benefits plan.

We rejected appellee's equal protection challenge to this statutory scheme. We first noted:

> "We cannot agree that the exclusion of this disability from coverage amounts to invidious discrimination under the Equal Protection Clause. California does not discriminate with respect to the persons or groups which are eligible for disability insurance protection under the program. The classification challenged in this case relates to the asserted underinclusiveness of the set of risks that the State has selected to insure."

This point was emphasized again, when later in the opinion we noted:

> "[T]his case is thus a far cry from cases like *Reed v. Reed*, 404 U.S. 71 (1971), and *Frontiero v. Richardson*, 411 U.S. 677 (1973), involving discrimination based upon gender as such. The California insurance program does not exclude anyone from benefit eligibility because of gender but merely removes one physical condition — pregnancy — from the list of compensable disabilities. While it is true that only women can become pregnant, it does not follow that every legislative classification concerning pregnancy is a sex-based classification like those considered in *Reed, supra*, and *Frontiero, supra*. Normal pregnancy is an objectively identifiable physical condition with unique characteristics. Absent a showing that distinctions involving pregnancy are mere pretexts designed to effect an invidious discrimination against the members of one sex or the other, lawmakers are constitutionally free to include or exclude pregnancy from the coverage of legislation such as this on any reasonable basis, just as with respect to any other physical condition.

> "The lack of identity between the excluded disability and gender as such under this insurance program becomes clear upon the most cursory analysis. The program divides potential recipients into two groups — pregnant women and nonpregnant persons. While the first group is exclusively female, the second includes members of both sexes."

The quoted language from *Geduldig* leaves no doubt that our reason for rejecting appellee's equal protection claim in that case was that the exclusion of pregnancy from coverage under California's disability-benefits plan was not in itself discrimination based on sex.***

The instant suit was grounded on Title VII rather than the Equal Protection Clause, and our cases recognize that a prima facie violation of Title VII can be established in some circumstances upon proof that the effect of an otherwise facially neutral plan or classification is to discriminate against members of one class or another. *See Washington v. Davis*, 426 U.S. 229, 246–248 (1976).*** As in *Geduldig*, respondents have not attempted to meet the burden of demonstrating a gender-based discriminatory effect resulting from the exclusion of pregnancy-related disabilities from coverage.***

The Plan, in effect (and for all that appears), is nothing more than an insurance package, which covers some risks, but excludes others. The "package" going to relevant identifiable groups we are presently concerned with—General Electric's male and female employees—covers exactly the same categories of risk, and is facially non-discriminatory in the sense that "[t]here is no risk from which men are protected and women are not. Likewise, there is no risk from which women are protected and men are not." As there is no proof that the package is in fact worth more to men than to women, it is impossible to find any gender-based discriminatory effect in this scheme simply because women disabled as a result of pregnancy do not receive benefits; that is to say, gender-based discrimination does not result simply because an employer's disability-benefits plan is less than all-inclusive. For all that appears, pregnancy-related disabilities constitute an additional risk, unique to women, and the failure to compensate them for this risk does not destroy the presumed parity of the benefits, accruing to men and women alike, which results from the facially evenhanded inclusion of risks.***

III

We are told, however, that this analysis of the congressional purpose underlying Title VII is inconsistent with the guidelines of the EEOC, which, it is asserted, are entitled to "great deference" in the construction of the Act, [*Griggs v. Duke Power Co.*, 401 U.S. 424, 431, 433–34 (1971)]; *Phillips v. Martin Marietta Corp.*, 400 U.S. 542, 545 (1971) (Marshall, J., concurring). The guideline upon which respondents rely most heavily was promulgated in 1972, and states in pertinent part:

> "Disabilities caused or contributed to by pregnancy, miscarriage, abortion, childbirth, and recovery therefrom are, for all job-related purposes, temporary disabilities and should be treated as such under any health or temporary disability insurance or sick leave plan available in connection with employment. . . . [Benefits] shall be applied to disability due to pregnancy or childbirth on the same terms and conditions as they are applied to other temporary disabilities." 29 CFR § 1604.10(b) (1975).

In evaluating this contention it should first be noted that Congress, in enacting Title VII, did not confer upon the EEOC authority to promulgate rules or regulations pursuant to that Title. *Albemarle Paper Co. v. Moody*, 422 U.S. 405, 431 (1975). This does not mean that EEOC guidelines are not entitled to consideration in determining legislative intent. But it does mean that courts properly may accord less weight to such guidelines than to administrative regulations which Congress has declared shall have the force of law, or to regulations which under the enabling statute may themselves supply the basis for imposition of liability, *see, e.g.,* § 23(a), Securities Exchange Act of 1934, 15 U.S.C. § 78w(a).***

The EEOC guideline in question*** is not a contemporaneous interpretation of Title VII, since it was first promulgated eight years after the enactment of that Title. More importantly, the 1972 guideline flatly contradicts the position which the agency had enunciated at an earlier date, closer to the enactment of the governing statute. An opinion letter by the General Counsel of the EEOC, dated October 17, 1966, states:

> "You have requested our opinion whether the above exclusion of pregnancy and childbirth as a disability under the long-term salary continuation plan would be in violation of Title VII of the Civil Rights Act of 1964.
>
> "In a recent opinion letter regarding pregnancy, we have stated, 'The Commission policy in this area does not seek to compare an employer's treatment of illness or injury with his treatment of maternity since maternity is a temporary disability unique to the female sex and more or less to be anticipated during the working life of most women employees.' Therefore, it is our opinion that according to the facts stated above, a company's group insurance program which covers hospital and medical expenses for the delivery of employees' children, but excludes from its long-term salary continuation program those disabilities which result from pregnancy and childbirth would not be in violation of Title VII."

A few weeks later, in an opinion letter expressly issued pursuant to 29 CFR § 1601.30 (1975), the EEOC's position was that "an insurance or other benefit plan may simply exclude maternity as a covered risk, and such an exclusion would not in our view be discriminatory."

We have declined to follow administrative guidelines in the past where they conflicted with earlier pronouncements of the agency.*** There are also persuasive indications that the more recent EEOC guideline sharply conflicts with other indicia of the proper interpretation of the sex-discrimination provisions of Title VII. The legislative history of Title VII's prohibition of sex discrimination is notable primarily for its brevity. Even so, however, Congress paid especial attention to the provisions of the Equal Pay Act, 29 U.S.C. § 206(d), when it amended § 703(h) of Title VII by adding the following sentence:

> "It shall not be an unlawful employment practice under this subchapter for any employer to differentiate upon the basis of sex in determining the amount of the wages or compensation paid or to be paid to employees of such employer if such differentiation is authorized by the provisions of section 206(d) of Title 29." 42 U.S.C. § 2000e-2(h).

This sentence was proposed as the Bennett Amendment to the Senate bill, 110 Cong. Rec. 13647 (1964), and Senator Humphrey, the floor manager of the bill, stated that the purpose of the amendment was to make it "unmistakably clear" that "differences of treatment in industrial benefit plans, including earlier retirement options for women, may continue in operation under this bill, if it becomes law." Because of this amendment, interpretations of § 6(d) of the Equal Pay Act are applicable to Title VII as well, and an interpretive regulation promulgated by the Wage and Hour Administrator under the Equal Pay Act explicitly states:

> "If employer contributions to a plan providing insurance or similar benefits to employees are equal for both men and women, no wage differential prohibited by the equal pay provisions will result from such payments, even though the benefits which accrue to the employees in question are greater for one sex than for the other. The mere fact that the employer may make unequal contributions for employees of opposite sexes in such a situation will not, however, be considered to indicate that the employer's payments are in violation of section 6(d), if the resulting benefits are equal for such employees." 29 CFR § 800.116(d) (1975).

Thus, even if we were to depend for our construction of the critical language of Title VII solely on the basis of "deference" to interpretative regulations by the appropriate administrative agencies, we would find ourselves pointed in diametrically opposite directions by the conflicting regulations of the EEOC, on the one hand, and the Wage and Hour Administrator, on the other. Petitioner's exclusion of benefits for pregnancy disability would be declared an unlawful employment practice under § 703(a)(1), but would be declared not to be an unlawful employment practice under § 703(h).

We are not reduced to such total abdication in construing the statute. The EEOC guideline of 1972, conflicting as it does with earlier pronouncements of that agency, and containing no suggestion that some new source of legislative history had been discovered in the intervening eight years, stands virtually alone. Contrary to it are the consistent interpretation of the Wage and Hour Administrator, and the quoted language of Senator Humphrey, the floor manager of Title VII in the Senate. They support what seems to us to be the "plain meaning" of the language used by Congress when it enacted § 703(a)(1).***

MR. JUSTICE BRENNAN, with whom MR. JUSTICE MARSHALL concurs, dissenting.

[T]he demonstration of purposeful discrimination is not the only ground for recovery under Title VII. [T]his Court, and every Court of Appeals now have firmly settled that a prima facie violation of Title VII, whether under § 703(a)(1) or § 703(a)(2), also is established by demonstrating that a facially neutral classification has the effect of discriminating against members of a defined class.

General Electric's disability program has three divisible sets of effects. First, the plan covers all disabilities that mutually afflict both sexes. Second, the plan insures against all disabilities that are male-specific or have a predominant impact on males. Finally, all female-specific and female-impacted disabilities are covered, except for the most prevalent, pregnancy. The Court focuses on the first factor—the equal inclusion of mutual risks—and therefore understandably can identify no discriminatory effect arising from the plan. In contrast, the EEOC and plaintiffs rely upon the unequal exclusion manifested in effects two and three to pinpoint an adverse impact on women. However one defines the profile of risks protected by General Electric, the determinative question must be whether the social policies and aims to be furthered by Title VII and filtered through the phrase "to discriminate" contained in § 703(a)(1) fairly forbid an ultimate pattern of coverage that insures all risks except a commonplace one that is applicable to women but not to men.

As a matter of law and policy, this is a paradigm example of the type of complex economic and social inquiry that Congress wisely left to resolution by the EEOC pursuant to its Title VII mandate. See H.R. Rep. No. 92-238, p. 8 (1972). And, accordingly, prior Title VII decisions have consistently acknowledged the unique persuasiveness of EEOC interpretations in this area. [The Court's rejection of the EEOC's 1972 guideline] is attributed to two interrelated events: an 8-year delay between Title VII's enactment and the promulgation of the Commission's guideline, and interim letters by the EEOC's General Counsel expressing the view that pregnancy is not necessarily includable as a compensable disability. Neither event supports the Court's refusal to accord "great deference" to the EEOC's interpretation.***

[W]hile some eight years had elapsed prior to the issuance of the 1972 guideline, and earlier opinion letters had refused to impose liability on employers during this period of deliberation, no one can or does deny that the final EEOC determination followed thorough and well-informed consideration. Indeed, realistically viewed, this extended evaluation of an admittedly complex problem and an unwillingness to impose additional, potentially premature costs on employers during the decisionmaking stages ought to be perceived as a practice to be commended. It is bitter irony that the care that preceded promulgation of the 1972 guideline is today condemned by the Court as tardy indecisiveness, its unwillingness irresponsibly to challenge employers' practices during the formative period is labeled as evidence of inconsistency, and this indecisiveness and inconsistency are bootstrapped into reasons for denying the Commission's interpretation its due deference.

Notes and Questions

1. **The Regulatory Context.** Under Title VII of the Civil Rights Act of 1964, 42 U.S.C. § 2000e et seq., it is an unlawful employment practice for an employer "to discriminate against any individual with respect to his compensation, terms, conditions, or privileges of employment, because of such individual's race, color, religion, sex, or national origin." *Id.* § 2000e-2. Recall from Chapter 1[C][3], *supra*, that enforcement authority is divided between private litigants and the Equal Employment Opportunity Commission (EEOC). Discrimination claims are initially investigated by the EEOC's regional offices or state agencies operating under agreement with the EEOC. After such investigation, the EEOC may decide to bring suit on behalf of the charging

party or issue a "right to sue" letter, *id.* § 2000e-5(f)(1), allowing the charging party to file an action in court. The EEOC also has authority to bring an action to remedy a pattern or practice of discrimination. *Id.* §§ 2000e-4 through 6.

The General Counsel is responsible for the conduct of litigation by the EEOC and "shall have such other duties as the Commission may prescribe or as may be provided by law." *Id.* § 2000e-4(b)(1). By regulation, "[a]ny interested person desiring a written interpretation or opinion from the Commission may make a request therefore." 29 C.F.R. § 1601.28 (1975). Good-faith reliance upon an opinion letter signed by the General Counsel on behalf of the Commission provides a defense to liability in an action for employment discrimination under 42 U.S.C. § 2000e-12(b)(1). That provision provides: "In any action or proceeding based on any alleged unlawful employment practice, no person shall be subject to any liability or punishment for or on account of*** the commission by such person of an unlawful employment practice if he pleads and proves that the act or omission complained of was in good faith, in conformity with, and in reliance on any written interpretation or opinion of the Commission***." *See generally* Samuel Estreicher, *Achieving Antidiscrimination Objectives Through "Safe Harbor" Rules in Cases of Chronic Hiring Aversion*, 2 J. LAW OF PUB. AFF. (forthcoming 2017).

Under Title VII, the EEOC lacks the authority to promulgate substantive rules as well as the authority to bring agency adjudications against law violators.* The agency has long issued guidance explaining how it will interpret Title VII in enforcement actions. Such guidance is published in the Federal Register or the EEOC's Compliance Manual. Because it constitutes a "general statement[] of policy," 5 U.S.C. § 553(b)(3)(A), it is not subject to the APA's notice-and-comment requirements.

2. **The Procedural Posture?** What relief were the plaintiffs in *Gilbert* seeking? What was the procedural posture of the case when it reached the Supreme Court? What had the lower courts concluded regarding the lawfulness of GE's disability plan? On what basis?

3. **The Task for the Agency?** To support their contention that General Electric's disability plan discriminated on the basis of sex, plaintiffs relied on a guideline promulgated by the EEOC in 1972. That guideline was published in the Code of Federal Regulations and indicated that it was issued under 42 U.S.C. § 2000e-12, which provides that "[t]he Commission shall have authority from time to time to issue, amend, or rescind suitable procedural regulations to carry out the provisions of this subchapter." The Court notes that the EEOC General Counsel took a position contrary to the position EEOC took in the 1972 guideline in a letter dated October 17, 1966. Does the Court describe the circumstances under which the letter was written? Was the letter an official pronouncement of the EEOC triggering the good-faith reliance provision of 42 U.S.C. § 2000e-12(b)(1)? The Court also relies on an opinion letter issued a few weeks after the October 17 letter "expressly issued pursuant

---

* With one exception—the EEOC may use adjudication for discrimination claims against federal-sector employers. *See* 42 U.S.C. § 2000e-16(b).

to 29 C.F.R. 1601.30" that took the same position. That procedural regulation provides that a letter from the General Counsel does not establish a defense to liability under Title VII unless it is signed by the EEOC General Counsel on behalf of the Commission.

4. **Dueling Agency Pronouncements.** The Court quotes an interpretative regulation promulgated by the Department of Labor's Wage and Hour Administrator, which opines that an employer does not violate the Equal Pay Act, 29 U.S.C. § 206, by making equal contributions to an insurance plan that provides different benefits to men and women. Why does the Court believe that the Wage and Hour Administrator's interpretation of the Equal Pay Act is pertinent to the meaning of Title VII? Under the Wage and Hour Administrator's regulation, could an employer contribute $100 per employee per month to an insurance plan that paid unemployment benefits only to men, on the theory that unemployed women will be "taken care of" by a man? Note that the Equal Pay Act is now enforced by the EEOC rather than the Labor Department.

5. **Why Does the Court Reject EEOC's Interpretation?** Although the Court cites precedents which hold that the EEOC's interpretation of Title VII is entitled to "great deference," it undertakes an independent analysis of whether Title VII requires disability plans to cover pregnancy-related disability and reaches a conclusion opposite to the EEOC. What tools of statutory interpretation does the Court rely on when considering whether the exclusion of pregnancy-related disabilities from GE's plan violates Title VII? Does the Court's interpretation place most weight on text, history, or purpose? Is it compelled by the "plain meaning" of Title VII, as the Court contends?

Why does the Court decide not to give "great deference" to the EEOC's conclusion in its 1972 guidance that the exclusion of pregnancy from a disability insurance plan constitutes discrimination on account of sex? Was EEOC acting within the scope of its delegated authority? Did it consider factors pertinent to whether non-coverage of pregnancy constituted discrimination on the basis of sex? Did it follow any procedures required by law?

6. **Judicial Deference and the Absence of Rulemaking or Adjudicatory Authority.** Should the EEOC's lack of rulemaking authority be an important factor in deciding how much deference a court owes to the EEOC's view of how the prohibition of sex discrimination applies in the benefits context? Does the lack of such authority evidence a lower level of congressional respect for or trust of the agency or, put differently, a congressional design to have the elaboration of subsidiary policy under the statute be made by courts rather than the agency? Does the statutory question — whether discrimination on account of sex includes discrimination on account of pregnancy — change depending on the functions or authority of the agency?

7. **Postscript.** Two year after the decision in *Gilbert*, Congress enacted the Pregnancy Discrimination Act, Pub. L. No. 95-555, 92 Stat. 2076 (1978). The Act amended Title VII's definitions section to include a new subsection, 42 U.S.C. § 2000e(k), that provides as follows:

The terms "because of sex" or "on the basis of sex" include, but are not limited to, because of or on the basis of pregnancy, childbirth, or related medical conditions; and women affected by pregnancy, childbirth, or related medical conditions shall be treated the same for all employment-related purposes*** as other persons not so affected but similar in their ability or inability to work***.

The Supreme Court acknowledged that the Act was intended to overrule "both the holding and the reasoning of the Court in the *Gilbert* decision." *Newport News Shipbuilding & Dry Dock Co. v. EEOC*, 462 U.S. 669, 678 (1983). *See also* Report of the Senate Committee on Human Resources on S. 995, S. Rep. No. 95-331, at 8 (1st Sess. 1977) (Act intended to "reestablis[h] the law as it was understood prior to" *Gilbert*). Courts divided, however, over how to interpret the Act's second clause. Who was in the comparator class of "other persons not so affected but similar in their ability or inability to work" to "women affected by pregnancy, childbirth, or related medical conditions"?

In *Young v. United Parcel Service*, 135 S. Ct. 1338 (2015), the Supreme Court again declined to follow an EEOC guideline which purported to answer that question. The guideline, contained in the July 2014 version of the EEOC's Compliance Manual, stated that "[a]n employer may not refuse to treat a pregnant worker the same as other employees who are similar in their ability or inability to work by relying on a policy that makes distinctions based on the source of an employee's limitations***." 2 EEOC Compliance Manual § 626-I(A)(5), p. 626:0009 (July 2014). The manual illustrated this interpretation with the following example, which EEOC concluded was a violation of Title VII:

> An employer has a policy or practice of providing light duty, subject to availability, for any employee who cannot perform one or more job duties for up to 90 days due to injury, illness, or a condition that would be a disability under the ADA. An employee requests a light duty assignment for a 20-pound lifting restriction related to her pregnancy. The employer denies the light duty request.

The Supreme Court declined to defer to the guideline because the EEOC issued the guideline after the Supreme Court had granted certiorari in the instant case, and because the guideline contradicted prior litigating positions taken by the Justice Department without offering reasons for "the" government's change of position. Interpreting the comparator clause *de novo*, the Supreme Court concluded that in disparate treatment cases, the clause required a showing of intentional discrimination because of pregnancy. A plaintiff could make out a prima facie case of disparate treatment "by providing sufficient evidence that the employer's policies impose a significant burden on pregnant workers, and that the employer's 'legitimate, nondiscriminatory' reasons are not sufficiently strong to justify the burden, but rather—when considered along with the burden imposed—give rise to an inference of intentional discrimination." A plaintiff could "create a genuine issue of material fact as to whether a significant burden exists," so as to withstand a motion for summary judgment, "by providing evidence that the employer accommodates a large percentage of nonpregnant workers while failing to accommodate a large percentage of pregnant workers." What is the practical difference between the standard promulgated by the EEOC and the standard the Court announces?

Chevron USA, Inc. v. NRDC: **The Regulatory Background**

The proposed EPA regulation that follows led to the Supreme Court's decision in *Chevron USA, Inc. v. NRDC*, widely considered "one of the most important decisions in the history of [American] administrative law." 1 RICHARD J. PIERCE, JR., ADMINISTRATIVE LAW TREATISE 140 (4th ed. 2002). The *Chevron* opinion and its framework for judicial review of agency action are presented in Chapter 5. Here, we focus on the regulatory background to the case.

A precursor to the Clean Air Act, the Air Pollution Control Act of 1955,[1] provided research support and financial assistance to states to address air pollution but had little effect on air quality. Congress enacted two air-pollution laws in 1963[2] and 1967,[3] but regulation of air pollution continued to be seen as ineffective. In the late 1960s, the popular press and scientific studies attributed hundreds of deaths to air pollution. Pollution caused by meteorological inversions — phenomena in which pollution is trapped in the part of the atmosphere closest to the earth — was a particular source of concern.[4] In the face of continuing public pressure to address the air pollution crisis, Congress in 1970 enacted amendments to the Air Pollution Control Act that created the modern Clean Air Act.[5]

The 1970 Clean Air Act established a comprehensive regulatory system governing air pollution that was jointly administered by the new Environmental Protection Agency[6] and the states. It created three major programs:

1. The *National Ambient Air Quality Standards* (NAAQS) program, established by section 109 of the Act, required EPA to promulgate national air quality standards for six pollutants: ozone, particulate matter, carbon monoxide, nitrogen oxide, sulfur dioxide, and lead. The 1970 Act did not authorize EPA to regulate these pollutants directly, but instead directed states to put in place State Implementation Plans (SIPs), subject to EPA review, to bring pollution down to the levels specified in the NAAQS.

----

1. Pub. L. No. 84-159, ch. 360, 69 Stat. 322.

2. Clean Air Act of 1963, Pub. L. No. 88-206, 77 Stat. 392.

3. Air Quality Act of 1967, Pub. L. No. 90-148, 81 Stat. 485.

4. *See* Senate Report No. 91-1196, at 1 (2d. Sess. 1970) (citing "air quality criteria documents for five major pollutants" that "indicate[d] that the air pollution problem is more severe, more pervasive, and growing at a more rapid rate than was generally believed"); Peter Hiss, *S.I. Deaths Linked to Air Pollution: Jersey Is Called Probable Source Affecting Lung Cancer in North Area*, N.Y. TIMES, Jan. 12, 1967, at A1 (citing studies linking air pollution in New Jersey to increased mortality in Staten Island).

5. Clean Air Amendments of 1970, Pub. L. No. 91-604, 84 Stat. 1676.

6. The Environmental Protection Agency was established in an executive reorganization plan on July 9, 1970. Reorganization Plan No. 3, 35 Fed. Reg. 15623, 84 Stat. 2086.

2. The *New Source Performance Standards* (NSPS) program, established in section 111 of the Act, required EPA to promulgate guidelines for emissions from new and modified stationary sources of pollution such as factories and power plants. The guidelines would be enforced through "state plans." (Confusingly, these states plans are different than the SIPs required by the NAAQS program.)

3. The *Hazardous Air Pollutants Program*, established in section 112 of the Act, authorized EPA to promulgate emissions standards for pollutants that were not governed by a NAAQS that "may cause, or contribute to, an increase in mortality or an increase in serious irreversible, or incapacitating reversible, illness."

EPA published the first set of NAAQS in April 1971.[7] The 1970 Act generally gave states until 1975 to comply with them. But by 1975, it was clear that many states would fail to do so.

In December 1976, EPA promulgated a regulation, known as the Emissions Offset Ruling, that addressed states' failure to achieve compliance with the NAAQS. The ruling imposed new conditions on the construction or modification of major stationary pollution sources in "nonattainment" states that were out of compliance with the NAAQS.[8] The ruling also requested that states in nonattainment areas submit revised SIPs to EPA.

In August 1977, Congress passed the Clean Air Amendments Act of 1977.[9] The 1977 amendments established new deadlines for states to comply with the NAAQS and adopted the Offset Ruling's distinction between "attainment" areas that were in compliance with the NAAQS and "nonattainment" areas that were not. The Act created two new programs regulating pollution from new and modified pollution sources, which applied depending on whether a state fell within an attainment or nonattainment area.

New Part C, entitled "Prevention of Significant Deterioration" (PSD), aimed to prevent air quality in attainment areas from deteriorating toward the NAAQS levels. New Part D, entitled "Plan Requirements for Nonattainment Areas" (the nonattainment program), governed nonattainment areas and was designed to force states to bring their air quality up to the level contemplated by the NAAQS. Both the PSD program and nonattainment program required states to implement technology-based standards for new and modified sources of pollution. Under Part D, nonattainment states were further required to submit revised SIPs to the EPA administrator by July 1, 1979. The revised plans had to comply with a lengthy list of requirements set out in § 172(b) of the 1977 amendments. One of these was that the state have in place a permitting program — known as "New Source Review" — that governed the construction of "new or modified stationary sources" of air pollution. Neither the 1977 act nor its legislative history defined "source." But the Act imposed a

---

7. 36 Fed. Reg. 8186 (Apr. 1971).

8. 41 Fed. Reg. 55,524 (1976).

9. Pub. L. No. 95-95, 91 Stat. 685.

moratorium on the construction of new or modified sources in nonattainment states that did not have a revised state implementation plan in place by July 1, 1979.

The definition of "source" turned out to be a major issue in implementing the 1977 amendments. The controversy had to do with how broadly the term swept. As the government later explained, two competing definitions emerged, one of which allowed a facility such as a power plant to be treated as a single "source":

> Under a plantwide definition, a so-called "bubble" concept is employed to treat the entire plant as a source; that is, the plant is viewed as if it were encased in a bubble that has a single emission point for the plant as a whole. Under this definition, when emissions from one unit within a plant are increased or a new unit is added, the change need not undergo formal new source review if the operator can reduce emissions of the same pollutant elsewhere within the plant so that total emissions do not increase by more than a *de minimis* amount. In contrast, under a dual definition, each process unit within a plant, as well as the plant as a whole, is viewed as a "source." Thus, any major new unit or any significant increase in emissions from an existing unit triggers formal new source review, even if aggregate emissions from the plant decrease or remain the same.[10]

Power plants and regulatory reformers favored using the bubble concept in the PSD and nonattainment programs. The concept encouraged plant operators to find the most efficient way of reducing pollution, and thus created an early market-based system for controlling air pollution. Environmentalists and their allies at EPA opposed the bubble concept, based on their belief that forcing plants to upgrade specific pieces of technology was the most effective way to control air pollution.[11]

The D.C. Circuit entered the controversy in 1978, in a case challenging a pre-1977 regulation that had been issued under the NSPS program. That regulation established performance standards for the nonferrous smelting industry and made limited use of the bubble concept in defining when a source underwent a "modification" so as to require a new permit.[12] Although the regulation treated each piece of equipment within a plant as a unique source, it provided that a "modification" would not occur where an "existing facility undergoes a physical or operational change" and the facility demonstrated that "the total emission rate of any pollutant has not increased from all facilities within the stationary source."[13]

---

10. Brief of the United States at 8, *Chevron USA, Inc. v. NRDC*, 467 U.S. 837 (1984).

11. *See generally* Jody Freeman, *The Story of* Chevron: *Environmental Law and Administrative Discretion, in* ADMINISTRATIVE LAW STORIES (Richard J. Lazarus & Oliver A. Houck, Eds. 2005).

12. 40 Fed. Reg. 58,416 (Dec. 16, 1975).

13. *Id.* at 58,418–58,419.

In *ASARCO Inc. v. EPA*, a divided panel of the D.C. Circuit vacated the rule.[14] Judge J. Skelly Wright wrote for the majority. He concluded that the bubble concept was inconsistent with both the language and the purpose of the NSPS program.

Following *ASARCO*, EPA had to decide whether the bubble concept could be used in the new PSD and nonattainment programs created by the 1977 Act. In June 1978, EPA issued a regulation implementing the PSD program, which took the same approach to the bubble concept as the regulation invalidated in *ASARCO*.[15] The agency reasoned that Congress had been aware of how EPA understood "modification" when it enacted the 1977 amendments, and adopted the EPA's usage in the amendments.

In informal guidance and a proposed rule, EPA indicated it would take a different approach to the bubble concept in the nonattainment program.[16] Here, the agency would allow the bubble concept to be used, but only if a state had a revised SIP in place. EPA reasoned that where a state had a revised SIP in place, the SIP would ensure that the state was making adequate progress toward coming into compliance with NAAQS. Furthermore, use of the bubble concept in these states would "provide greater flexibility to sources to effectively manage their air emissions at least cost."[17]

Power companies petitioned for review of the PSD regulation in the D.C. Circuit, and the petitions were consolidated in *Alabama Power Co. v. Costle*. The court issued an order summarizing its conclusions in June 1979[18] and issued its final opinion in April 1980.[19] The three judges on the panel which heard the petition divided the opinion into separate sections. Judge Malcolm Wilkey wrote the section addressing challenges to the EPA's use of the bubble concept.

Judge Wilkey concluded, contrary to EPA, that Congress had not intended to adopt the agency's definition of a "modification" in the PSD program but instead intended the term to have the same meaning as in section 111. Under *ASARCO*, the agency therefore could not ground its use of the bubble concept in the definition of "modification." But EPA was free, Judge Wilkey suggested, to rely on the bubble concept in determining whether there had been an "increase" in pollution from a "source." In Wilkey's view, "Congress wished to apply the permit process . . . only where industrial changes might *increase* pollution in an area, not where an existing plant changed its operations in ways that produced no pollution increase."[20] Wilkey's opinion in *Alabama Power* reflected a completely different attitude toward the bubble concept than Judge Wright's opinion in *ASARCO*. "Whereas Judge Wright had implied that the

---

14. 578 F.2d 319, 325 (D.C. Cir. 1978).
15. 43 Fed. Reg. 26,380 (June 19, 1978).
16. 44 Fed. Reg. 3274 (Jan. 16, 1979); 44 Fed. Reg. 20,372 (Apr. 4, 1979).
17. 44 Fed. Reg. at 3276.
18. 606 F.2d 1068 (D.C. Cir. 1979).
19. 636 F.2d 323 (D.C. Cir. 1980).
20. *Id.* at 401 (emphasis added).

bubble was *unlawful* in any form under Section 111, the Wilkey opinion seemed to say that the bubble concept was *required* under the PSD program."[21]

In response to *Alabama Power*, EPA issued a revised regulation on August 7, 1980, that adopted the bubble concept for purposes of the PSD program.[22] In the same regulation, EPA indicated that it would use the dual definition of "source" in implementing the nonattainment program. Following Judge Wilkey's logic, EPA reasoned that the nonattainment program was intended to *improve* existing air quality. Because the bubble concept allowed emissions to remain constant, it was necessary to define "source" more narrowly for purposes of the nonattainment program. That, in turn, would force technology improvements that reduced the amount of pollution that power plants in nonattainment states released.

In November of that year, Ronald Reagan was elected President on a platform of government deregulation. Upon taking office in January 1981, Reagan ordered "a Government-wide reexamination of regulatory burdens and complexities," which led to EPA promulgating the proposed rule that follows.

EPA Requirements for Preparation, Adoption, and Submittal of Implementation Plans; Approval and Promulgation of Implementation Plans
PROPOSED RULE

46 Fed. Reg. 16,278 (Mar. 12, 1981)

On August 7, 1980 EPA published amended rules affecting PSD new source review, nonattainment area new source review and the construction moratorium. The Prevention of Significant Air Quality Deterioration (PSD) program requires new or modified "major" air pollution sources locating in areas where national ambient air quality standards (NAAQS) are being attained (or where air quality data is insufficient to determine whether or not NAAQS are being attained) to obtain construction permits which meet the requirements of Part C of Title I of the Clean Air Act. The basic purpose of the PSD program is to protect air quality in clean air areas. In areas where NAAQS are not being attained, new or modified "major" sources which would emit the pollutant(s) for which the area is nonattainment must obtain construction permits under Section 173 of the Act.

EPA's amended rules define "source" differently for PSD and nonattainment purposes. The difference revolves around the treatment of a plant that contains a number of individual pieces of process equipment that themselves each emit more than 100 tons per year. For PSD, EPA generally defines "source" in terms of an entire plant.

---

21. Thomas W. Merrill, *The Story of* Chevron: *The Making of an Accidental Landmark*, 66 ADMIN. L. REV. 253, 264 (2014) (emphasis added).

22. 45 Fed. Reg. 52,676 (Aug. 7, 1980).

For the nonattainment program, however, EPA defines "source" as both the entire plant and each of those "major" pieces of process equipment within it.***

The Proposed Amendment

EPA today is proposing to change the definition of "source" contained in the rules governing nonattainment area new source review and the construction moratorium so as to make that definition conform to that contained in the PSD rules. The result will be to eliminate the differences in coverage between the PSD and nonattainment programs that were described above. The change is being carried out by amending the definition of the terms "building", "structure", "facility" and "installation", which are the components of the term "source." EPA is also proposing to delete the definition of "reconstruction."

Discussion

The decision to reconsider the scope of nonattainment area new source review has been made in the context of a Government-wide reexamination of regulatory burdens and complexities that is now in progress. EPA has also reevaluated all of the arguments on all sides of these definitional issues. The Agency has concluded that the amendments to the August 7 rules being proposed today will substantially reduce the burdens imposed on the regulated community without significantly interfering with timely achievement of the goals of the Clean Air Act.

The issue of the proper scope of the nonattainment area definition of "source" is not a clear-cut legal question. The statute does not provide an explicit answer, nor is the issue squarely addressed in the legislative history. The D.C. Circuit (in *Alabama Power Co. v. Costle*) has stated by implication that EPA has substantial discretion to define the constituent elements of this term.

The question thus involves a judgment as to how to best carry out the Act. Two issues have been reexamined here. The first is whether the definition of "source" in nonattainment areas should be modified to conform to the one in PSD areas. The second is whether new source review based on "reconstruction" should be required at all.

EPA believes for the following reasons that the proposed change in the definition of "source" is appropriate.

1. The August 7 definition forbids any construction or modification of major pieces of process equipment in areas where the construction moratorium is in effect, even where no increase in emissions at a plant would result. There are a substantial number of such nonattainment areas nationwide at present.

2. Even outside of these "construction moratorium" areas under the present regulatory scheme the August 7 definition can act as a disincentive to new investment and modernization by discouraging modifications to existing facilities.

3. For both these reasons, under the current overall regulatory system, the August 7 definition can actually retard progress in air pollution control by discouraging replacement of older, dirtier processes or pieces of equipment with new, cleaner ones.

4. The proposed definition would simplify EPA's rules by using the same definition of "source" for PSD, nonattainment new source review and the construction moratorium. This reduces confusion and inconsistency.

5. States will remain subject to the requirement that for all nonattainment areas they demonstrate attainment of NAAQS as expeditiously as practicable and show reasonable further progress toward such attainment. Thus, the proposed change in the mandatory scope of nonattainment new source review should not interfere with the fundamental purpose of Part D of the Act.

6. New Source Performance Standards (NSPS) will continue to apply to many new or modified facilities and will assure use of the most up-to-date pollution control techniques regardless of the applicability of nonattainment area new source review.

7. In order to avoid nonattainment area new source review, a major plant undergoing modification must show that it will not experience a significant net increase in emissions. Where overall emissions increase significantly, review will continue to be required.

For these reasons EPA has reconsidered the concerns it expressed in the August 7 preamble and has decided that the "dual definition" is excessively and unnecessarily burdensome.

In light of the change to the nonattainment area definition of source, there is good reason to abandon the "reconstruction" test for nonattainment area new source review. That test by itself only requires review in cases where there is reconstruction, but a "significant" increase in emissions is absent. With a plant-wide definition of source, the reconstruction provision would only trigger review in cases of plant-wide reconstruction. Few instances of plant-wide reconstruction are expected. Thus, there is little justification for the added complexity this provision entails. Moreover, this change will further reduce inconsistency with the PSD rules which do not have a reconstruction provision.

The Clean Air Act, in Section 111, recognizes an independent, long-term interest in making sure that new facilities install state-of-the-art pollution controls when they are built. This results in the most cost-effective long-term air quality improvement by controlling pollution at the design stage, rather than requiring costly retrofits. Of course, this approach, unlike the nonattainment area requirements of Part D, is not based on the location of particular sources.

For these reasons, EPA believes that a "reconstruction" definition is appropriate for the new source performance standards under Section 111. However, the arguments for it are considerably weaker where a program of review basically designed to meet air quality standards in particular places is at issue, and EPA proposes to drop it there.

EPA solicits comments on the proposed rule. All such comments will be carefully considered prior to any final action.***

Dated: March 6, 1981

Walter C. Barber, Jr.

Acting Administrator.

Notes and Questions

1. **The Design of the Regulatory Scheme?** Why did Congress adopt a bi-level, federal-state permitting scheme in the New Source Review provision of the 1977 Clean Air Act Amendments? Is controlling air pollution from power plants and other stationary sources of pollution the kind of regulatory problem that benefits from experimentation by states acting as "laboratories of democracy"? Are there plausible arguments why, for example, Texas can sustain higher levels of arsenic in its air than New York? Might Congress have enlisted states because, given the size of the country, federal permitting would be too unwieldy? Are any efficiencies of scale achieved by giving states authority to enforce plant licensing requirements? Might the state role in new source permitting reflect a political compromise designed to take the edge off a federal regulatory scheme perceived as a federal intrusion on state prerogatives? Note that Congress only enacted federal legislation addressing air pollution after two decades of ineffective state efforts.

On EPA's role in coordinating states' response to air pollution, see *EPA v. EME Homer City Generation, LP*, 134 S. Ct. 1584 (2014). The Court in *EME* rejected industry challenges to EPA rules that restricted emissions in "upwind" states such as Pennsylvania and Ohio, whose effects were felt by "downwind" states such as New York and New Jersey where pollution would travel after being released in upwind states. *See also* Richard L. Revesz, *Federalism and Interstate Environmental Externalities*, 144 U. Pa. L. Rev. 2341 (1996).

2. **The Agency's Choice of Policymaking Form?** Note that the EPA promulgated its new position on the use of the bubble concept in the nonattainment program via regulation rather than by adjudication or informal guidance. Why did EPA act via regulation? Would it have gone down well with environmental activists and the courts if EPA announced the new position in an adjudication? Would this have been allowed under *Bell Aerospace*? Recall that the regulation reflected a change in administrative policy, and that EPA did not issue permits directly, but defined standards for state regulators responsible for individual permitting decisions.

3. **Why Did EPA Adopt the "Bubble Concept" for Both Attainment and Non-Attainment Areas?** As explained above, EPA took two stances on the bubble concept between January 1979 and March 1981, when it issued the rule adopting the bubble concept nationwide. EPA's first stance applied different definitions of "stationary source" based on whether a state was covered by an existing State Implementation Plan (SIP) or had adopted a revised SIP. On this view, the bubble concept did not apply to

existing SIPs, but the concept could be used in new or modified SIPs if they otherwise complied with the 1977 Clean Air Amendments and regulations thereunder.

What is the rationale behind this interpretation of the stationary-source concept? Is the interpretation based primarily on technical considerations? Practical considerations? Legal considerations?

In August 1980, EPA shifted positions and promulgated a regulation in which the meaning of "stationary source" varied based on whether a plant was located in a part of the country that was in attainment with the air quality standards EPA had set out in NAAQS. What is the reasoning behind *this* interpretation of the stationary concept? Consider the reasoning of the D.C. Circuit:

> The nonattainment program's *raison être* is to ameliorate the air's quality in nonattainment areas sufficiently to achieve expeditious compliance with the NAAQSs. This purpose*** rules out application of the bubble concept to the nonattainment program.

NRDC v. Gorsuch, 685 F.2d 718, 726–27 (1982) (R. Ginsburg, J.).*

Finally, in its October 1981 regulation, EPA adopted the bubble concept on a nationwide basis, regardless of whether a facility was located in an attainment or nonattainment area, and regardless of whether a state was required to develop a new SIP under the 1977 amendments. Was EPA's position supported by a compelling rationale?

EPA explained that if "stationary source" were construed too narrowly, the permitting requirement could ""act as a disincentive to new investment and modernization by discouraging modifications to existing facilities." Doesn't this conclusion depend on a number of difficult assumptions? Consider the possibility that the bubble concept permits a plant to "bank" pollution credits for equipment that it is retiring for reasons unrelated to air pollution (so-called "anyway" equipment). Through such banking, the bubble concept permits plants to maintain present pollution levels indefinitely, regardless of changes in the efficiency of technology. In its final rule, promulgated in October 1981, EPA dismissed this "banking" argument as speculative and said that it "contradict[ed] a central principle of economic efficiency, under which [sic] the cheapest and most cost-effective emission reductions should be allowed to be used first, not saved until some hypothetical future need develops while more expensive controls are used first." 46 Fed. Reg. 50,768.

The agency also contended that nationwide use of the bubble concept would simplify administration of the Clean Air Act. Is this kind of simplicity consistent with Congress's goals in the 1977 Clean Air Act Amendments? Did EPA give any answer to the Court of Appeals' argument that use of the bubble concept was inappropriate in nonattainment areas, where Congress sought not simply to maintain existing air quality but improve it?

---

*The respondent, Anne Gorsuch, was the mother of Supreme Court Justice Neil Gorsuch.

4. **The "Bubble Concept" Rule in the Courts.** After EPA promulgated the final regulation, 46 Fed. Reg. 50766 (Oct. 14, 1981), the Natural Resources Defense Council (NRDC) challenged it in court. The D.C. Circuit vacated the rule insofar as it extended the bubble concept to nonattainment areas, on the ground that doing so was foreclosed by *ASARCO* and *Alabama Power. NRDC v. Gorsuch*, 685 F.2d 718 (1982). The Supreme Court reversed, reasoning that use of the bubble concept was a question of subsidiary administrative policy that the Congress had implicitly left to the agency in the 1977 Clean Air Act Amendments. *Chevron USA, Inc. v. NRDC*, 467 U.S. 837 (1984), *infra* Chapter 5[C][3]. Setting aside the degree of deference that courts owe to an agency's interpretation of a statute it administers, why might the Supreme Court have accepted the EPA's oscillation regarding the use of the bubble concept when the Court was so critical in *Gilbert* of the EEOC's oscillation on the exclusion of pregnancy-related disabilities from employer-provided disability insurance? What features, if any, distinguish the EPA's decision and regulatory challenge from the EEOC's?

F. Exceptions to APA § 553: Interpretive Rules and Policy Statements

One significant difference between the EEOC interpretation at issue in *Gilbert* and the EPA regulation at issue in *Chevron* is that the EPA sought to promulgate a regulation with the force of law whereas the EEOC was merely providing non-binding guidance and, moreover, lacked substantive rulemaking authority with respect to Title VII, the statute at issue in that case. Such nonbinding guidance, which presumably does not require an express authorization from Congress, falls within APA § 553's exception for "interpretative rules, general statements of policy, or rules of agency organization, procedure, or practice," 5 U.S.C. § 553(b)(3)(A), and, insofar as the APA is concerned, can be promulgated without notice and comment.

The idea that agencies issue interpretative rules or guidance predates the APA. The Attorney General's Report on Administrative Procedure noted:

> Some of these, such as many of the rulings of the Treasury Department under the tax laws, take the form of opinions upon specific statements of fact and should hardly be called regulations; but they often operate as effective precedents. Others, such as the rulings of the Board of Governors of the Federal Reserve System, refer to hypothetical facts and become in effect somewhat generalized opinions of what is lawful and what is unlawful. Some agencies which issue interpretations couched in general terms rather than rulings upon particular facts are careful to distinguish them from regulations that have the force of law; other agencies simply promulgate their interpretations as regulations which are indistinguishable in form from those that have statutory force.

FINAL REPORT OF THE ATTORNEY GENERAL'S COMMITTEE ON ADMINISTRATIVE PROCEDURE 99–100 (1941).

An agency's interpretation of its own regulations is likely to be influential, and may be entitled to judicial deference, *see Auer v. Robbins*, 519 U.S. 452 (1997), *infra* Chapter 5[C][3], raising the possibility that agencies will issue interpretations that will have a practical binding effect but without following notice-and-comment procedures. Is this practice lawful under the APA? Consider the approaches of the D.C. Circuit and the Supreme Court in the case below.

Perez v. Mortgage Bankers Association

135 S. Ct. 1199 (2015)

JUSTICE SOTOMAYOR delivered the opinion of the Court.

When a federal administrative agency first issues a rule interpreting one of its regulations, it is generally not required to follow the notice-and-comment rulemaking procedures of the Administrative Procedure Act (APA or Act). *See* 5 U.S.C. § 553(b)(A). The United States Court of Appeals for the District of Columbia Circuit has nevertheless held, in a line of cases beginning with *Paralyzed Veterans of Am. v. D.C. Arena L.P.*, 117 F.3d 579 (1997), that an agency must use the APA's notice-and-comment procedures when it wishes to issue a new interpretation of a regulation that deviates significantly from one the agency has previously adopted. The question in these cases is whether the rule announced in *Paralyzed Veterans* is consistent with the APA. We hold that it is not.

I

A

The APA establishes the procedures federal administrative agencies use for "rule making," defined as the process of "formulating, amending, or repealing a rule." § 551(5). "Rule," in turn, is defined broadly to include "statement[s] of general or particular applicability and future effect" that are designed to "implement, interpret, or prescribe law or policy." § 551(4).

Section 4 of the APA, 5 U.S.C. § 553, prescribes a three-step procedure for so-called "notice-and-comment rulemaking."* First, the agency must issue a "[g]eneral notice of proposed rule making," ordinarily by publication in the Federal Register. § 553(b). Second, if "notice [is] required," the agency must "give interested persons an opportunity to participate in the rule making through submission of written data, views, or arguments." § 553(c). An agency must consider and respond to significant comments received during the period for public comment. Third, when the agency promulgates the final rule, it must include in the rule's text "a concise general statement of [its] basis and purpose." § 553(c). Rules issued through the notice-and-comment process are often referred to as "legislative rules" because they have the "force and effect of law."

---

* Justice Sotomayor's opinion refers to sections of the version of the APA enacted in 1946. Because Title 5 of the U.S. Code which contains the APA has been enacted into positive law, Pub. L. No. 89-554, 80 Stat. 378, writers more commonly refer to the sections of the U.S. Code.

Not all "rules" must be issued through the notice-and-comment process. Section 4(b)(A) of the APA provides that, unless another statute states otherwise, the notice-and-comment requirement "does not apply" to "interpretative rules, general statements of policy, or rules of agency organization, procedure, or practice." 5 U.S.C. § 553(b) (A). The term "interpretative rule," or "interpretive rule,"[1] is not further defined by the APA, and its precise meaning is the source of much scholarly and judicial debate. We need not, and do not, wade into that debate here. For our purposes, it suffices to say that the critical feature of interpretive rules is that they are "issued by an agency to advise the public of the agency's construction of the statutes and rules which it administers." *Shalala v. Guernsey Memorial Hospital*, 514 U.S. 87, 99 (1995) (internal quotation marks omitted). The absence of a notice-and-comment obligation makes the process of issuing interpretive rules comparatively easier for agencies than issuing legislative rules. But that convenience comes at a price: Interpretive rules "do not have the force and effect of law and are not accorded that weight in the adjudicatory process." *Ibid.*

B

These cases began as a dispute over efforts by the Department of Labor to determine whether mortgage-loan officers are covered by the Fair Labor Standards Act of 1938 (FLSA), 52 Stat. 1060, as amended, 29 U.S.C. § 201 et seq. The FLSA "establishe[s] a minimum wage and overtime compensation for each hour worked in excess of 40 hours in each workweek" for many employees. Certain classes of employees, however, are exempt from these provisions. Among these exempt individuals are those "employed in a bona fide executive, administrative, or professional capacity . . . or in the capacity of outside salesman. . . ." § 213(a)(1). The exemption for such employees is known as the "administrative" exemption.

The FLSA grants the Secretary of Labor authority to "defin[e]" and "delimi[t]" the categories of exempt administrative employees. *Ibid.* The Secretary's current regulations regarding the administrative exemption were promulgated in 2004 through a notice-and-comment rulemaking. As relevant here, the 2004 regulations differed from the previous regulations in that they contained a new section providing several examples of exempt administrative employees. *See* 29 CFR § 541.203. One of the examples is "[e]mployees in the financial services industry," who, depending on the nature of their day-to-day work, "generally meet the duties requirements for the administrative exception." § 541.203(b). The financial services example ends with a caveat, noting that "an employee whose primary duty is selling financial products does not qualify for the administrative exemption."

In 1999 and again in 2001, the Department's Wage and Hour Division issued letters opining that mortgage-loan officers do not qualify for the administrative exemption. In other words, the Department concluded that the FLSA's minimum wage and maximum hour requirements applied to mortgage-loan officers. When the

---

1. The latter is the more common phrasing today, and the one we use throughout this opinion.

Department promulgated its current FLSA regulations in 2004, respondent Mortgage Bankers Association (MBA), a national trade association representing real estate finance companies, requested a new opinion interpreting the revised regulations. In 2006, the Department issued an opinion letter finding that mortgage-loan officers fell within the administrative exemption under the 2004 regulations. Four years later, however, the Wage and Hour Division again altered its interpretation of the FLSA's administrative exemption as it applied to mortgage-loan officers. Reviewing the provisions of the 2004 regulations and judicial decisions addressing the administrative exemption, the Department's 2010 Administrator's Interpretation concluded that mortgage-loan officers "have a primary duty of making sales for their employers, and, therefore, do not qualify" for the administrative exemption. The Department accordingly withdrew its 2006 opinion letter, which it now viewed as relying on "misleading assumption[s] and selective and narrow analysis" of the exemption example in § 541.203(b). Like the 1999, 2001, and 2006 opinion letters, the 2010 Administrator's Interpretation was issued without notice or an opportunity for comment.

C

MBA filed a complaint in Federal District Court challenging the Administrator's Interpretation. MBA contended that the document was inconsistent with the 2004 regulation it purported to interpret, and thus arbitrary and capricious in violation of § 10 of the APA, 5 U.S.C. § 706. More pertinent to this case, MBA also argued that the Administrator's Interpretation was procedurally invalid in light of the D.C. Circuit's decision in *Paralyzed Veterans*. Under the *Paralyzed Veterans* doctrine, if "an agency has given its regulation a definitive interpretation, and later significantly revises that interpretation, the agency has in effect amended its rule, something it may not accomplish" under the APA "without notice and comment." *Alaska Professional Hunters Assn., Inc. v. FAA*, 177 F.3d 1030, 1034 (CADC 1999). Three former mortgage-loan officers— Beverly Buck, Ryan Henry, and Jerome Nickols—subsequently intervened in the case to defend the Administrator's Interpretation.

The District Court granted summary judgment to the Department. *Mortgage Bankers Assn. v. Solis*, 864 F. Supp. 2d 193 (DC 2012).*** The D. C. Circuit reversed.*** In the court's view, "[t]he only question" properly before it was whether the District Court had erred in requiring MBA to prove that it relied on the Department's prior interpretation. Explaining that reliance was not a required element of the *Paralyzed Veterans* doctrine, and noting the Department's concession that a prior, conflicting interpretation of the 2004 regulations existed, the D.C. Circuit concluded that the 2010 Administrator's Interpretation had to be vacated.

II

The *Paralyzed Veterans* doctrine is contrary to the clear text of the APA's rule-making provisions, and it improperly imposes on agencies an obligation beyond the "maximum procedural requirements" specified in the APA, *Vermont Yankee Nuclear Power Corp. v. Natural Resources Defense Council, Inc.*, 435 U.S. 519, 524 (1978).

A

The text of the APA answers the question presented. Section 4[(b)(3)(A)] of the APA*** states that unless "notice or hearing is required by statute," the Act's notice-and-comment requirement "does not apply . . . to interpretative rules." § 553(b)(3)(A). This exemption of interpretive rules from the notice-and-comment process is categorical, and it is fatal to the rule announced in *Paralyzed Veterans*.

Rather than examining the exemption for interpretive rules contained in § 4(b)(A) of the APA, the D.C. Circuit in *Paralyzed Veterans* focused its attention on § 1 of the Act. That section defines "rule making" to include not only the initial issuance of new rules, but also "repeal[s]" or "amend[ments]" of existing rules. *See* § 551(5). Because notice-and-comment requirements may apply even to these later agency actions, the court reasoned, "allow[ing] an agency to make a fundamental change in its interpretation of a substantive regulation without notice and comment" would undermine the APA's procedural framework.

This reading of the APA conflates the differing purposes of §§ 1 and 4 of the Act. Section 1 defines what a rulemaking is. It does not, however, say what procedures an agency must use when it engages in rulemaking. That is the purpose of § 4. And § 4 specifically exempts interpretive rules from the notice-and-comment requirements that apply to legislative rules. So, the D.C. Circuit correctly read § 1 of the APA to mandate that agencies use the same procedures when they amend or repeal a rule as they used to issue the rule in the first instance. *See FCC v. Fox Television Stations, Inc.*, 556 U.S. 502, 515 (2009) [*infra*, Chapter 5[D]] (the APA "make[s] no distinction . . . between initial agency action and subsequent agency action undoing or revising that action"). Where the court went wrong was in failing to apply that accurate understanding of § 1 to the exemption for interpretive rules contained in § 4: Because an agency is not required to use notice-and-comment procedures to issue an initial interpretive rule, it is also not required to use those procedures when it amends or repeals that interpretive rule.

B

The straightforward reading of the APA we now adopt harmonizes with longstanding principles of our administrative law jurisprudence. Time and again, we have reiterated that the APA "sets forth the full extent of judicial authority to review executive agency action for procedural correctness."*** We explained in *Vermont Yankee* that § 4 of the Act "established the maximum procedural requirements which Congress was willing to have the courts impose upon agencies in conducting rulemaking procedures." "Agencies are free to grant additional procedural rights in the exercise of their discretion, but reviewing courts are generally not free to impose them if the agencies have not chosen to grant them."

The *Paralyzed Veterans* doctrine creates just such a judge-made procedural right: the right to notice and an opportunity to comment when an agency changes its interpretation of one of the regulations it enforces. That requirement may be wise policy. Or it may not. Regardless, imposing such an obligation is the responsibility of Congress or the administrative agencies, not the courts.***

III***

There may be times when an agency's decision to issue an interpretive rule, rather than a legislative rule, is driven primarily by a desire to skirt notice-and-comment provisions. But regulated entities are not without recourse in such situations. Quite the opposite. The APA contains a variety of constraints on agency decisionmaking—the arbitrary and capricious standard being among the most notable. As we held in *Fox Television Stations*, and underscore again today, the APA requires an agency to provide more substantial justification when "its new policy rests upon factual findings that contradict those which underlay its prior policy; or when its prior policy has engendered serious reliance interests that must be taken into account. It would be arbitrary and capricious to ignore such matters."[4]

In addition, Congress is aware that agencies sometimes alter their views in ways that upset settled reliance interests. For that reason, Congress sometimes includes in the statutes it drafts safe-harbor provisions that shelter regulated entities from liability when they act in conformance with previous agency interpretations. The FLSA includes one such provision: As amended by the Portal-to-Portal Act of 1947, 29 U.S.C. § 251 et seq., the FLSA provides that "no employer shall be subject to any liability" for failing "to pay minimum wages or overtime compensation" if it demonstrates that the "act or omission complained of was in good faith in conformity with and in reliance on any written administrative regulation, order, ruling, approval, or interpretation" of the Administrator of the Department's Wage and Hour Division, even when the guidance is later "modified or rescinded." §§ 259(a), (b)(1). These safe harbors will often protect parties from liability when an agency adopts an interpretation that conflicts with its previous position.[5]***

C

MBA changes direction in the second half of its brief, contending that if the Court overturns the *Paralyzed Veterans* rule, the D. C. Circuit's judgment should nonetheless

---

4. MBA*** suggests that interpretive rules have the force of law because an agency's interpretation of its own regulations may be entitled to deference under *Auer v. Robbins*, 519 U.S. 452 (1997), and *Bowles v. Seminole Rock & Sand Co.*, 325 U.S. 410 (1945). Even in cases where an agency's interpretation receives *Auer* deference, however, it is the court that ultimately decides whether a given regulation means what the agency says. Moreover, *Auer* deference is not an inexorable command in all cases. *See Christopher v. SmithKline Beecham Corp.*, 132 S. Ct. 2156, 2166 (2012) (*Auer* deference is inappropriate "when the agency's interpretation is plainly erroneous or inconsistent with the regulation" or "when there is reason to suspect that the agency's interpretation does not reflect the agency's fair and considered judgment" (internal quotation marks omitted)); *Thomas Jefferson Univ. v. Shalala*, 512 U.S. 504, 515 (1994) ("[A]n agency's interpretation of a . . . regulation that conflicts with a prior interpretation is entitled to considerably less deference than a consistently held agency view" (internal quotation marks omitted)). [Location of footnote changed from original.—Eds]

5. The United States acknowledged at argument that even in situations where a statute does not contain a safe-harbor provision similar to the one included in the FLSA, an agency's ability to pursue enforcement actions against regulated entities for conduct in conformance with prior agency interpretations may be limited by principles of retroactivity. *See* Tr. of Oral Arg. 44–45. We have no occasion to consider how such principles might apply here.

be affirmed. That is so, MBA says, because the agency interpretation at issue—the 2010 Administrator's Interpretation—should in fact be classified as a legislative rule.

We will not address this argument. From the beginning, the parties litigated this suit on the understanding that the Administrator's Interpretation was—as its name suggests—an interpretive rule.***

JUSTICE SCALIA, concurring in the judgment.

I agree with the Court's decision, and all of its reasoning demonstrating the incompatibility of the D. C. Circuit's *Paralyzed Veterans* holding with the Administrative Procedure Act. *Paralyzed Veterans of Am. v. D.C. Arena L.P.*, 117 F. 3d 579 (CADC 1997). I do not agree, however, with the Court's portrayal of the result it produces as a vindication of the balance Congress struck when it "weighed the costs and benefits of placing more rigorous . . . restrictions on the issuance of interpretive rules." That depiction is accurate enough if one looks at this case in isolation. Considered alongside our law of deference to administrative determinations, however, today's decision produces a balance between power and procedure quite different from the one Congress chose when it enacted the APA.***

[T]he Act provides that "the *reviewing court* shall . . . interpret constitutional and statutory provisions, and determine the meaning or applicability of the terms of an agency action." § 706 (emphasis added). The Act thus contemplates that courts, not agencies, will authoritatively resolve ambiguities in statutes and regulations.***

Heedless of the original design of the APA, we have developed an elaborate law of deference to agencies' interpretations of statutes and regulations. Never mentioning § 706's directive that the "reviewing court . . . interpret . . . statutory provisions," we have held that agencies may authoritatively resolve ambiguities in statutes. *Chevron U.S.A. Inc. v. Natural Resources Defense Council, Inc.*, 467 U.S. 837, 842–843 (1984) [*infra* Chapter 5[C][3]]. And never mentioning § 706's directive that the "reviewing court . . . determine the meaning or applicability of the terms of an agency action," we have—relying on a case decided before the APA, *Bowles v. Seminole Rock & Sand Co.*, 325 U.S. 410 (1945)—held that agencies may authoritatively resolve ambiguities in regulations. *Auer v. Robbins*, 519 U.S. 452, 461 (1997) [*infra* Chapter 5[C][3]].*

By supplementing the APA with judge-made doctrines of deference, we have revolutionized the import of interpretive rules' exemption from notice-and-comment rulemaking. Agencies may now use these rules not just to advise the public, but also to bind them. After all, if an interpretive rule gets deference, the people are bound to obey it on pain of sanction, no less surely than they are bound to obey substantive rules, which are accorded similar deference. Interpretive rules that command deference do have the force of law.

***Of course an interpretive rule must meet certain conditions before it gets deference—the interpretation must, for instance, be reasonable—but once it does

---

* The opinion in *Auer* was authored by Justice Scalia for a unanimous Court.—Eds.

so it is every bit as binding as a substantive rule. So the point stands: By deferring to interpretive rules, we have allowed agencies to make binding rules unhampered by notice-and-comment procedures.

The problem is bad enough, and perhaps insoluble if *Chevron* is not to be uprooted, with respect to interpretive rules setting forth agency interpretation of statutes. But an agency's interpretation of its own regulations is another matter. By giving that category of interpretive rules *Auer* deference, we do more than allow the agency to make binding regulations without notice and comment. Because the agency (not Congress) drafts the substantive rules that are the object of those interpretations, giving them deference allows the agency to control the extent of its notice-and-comment-free domain. To expand this domain, the agency need only write substantive rules more broadly and vaguely, leaving plenty of gaps to be filled in later, using interpretive rules unchecked by notice and comment. The APA does not remotely contemplate this regime.

Still and all, what are we to do about the problem? The *Paralyzed Veterans* doctrine is a courageous (indeed, brazen) attempt to limit the mischief by requiring an interpretive rule to go through notice and comment if it revises an earlier definitive interpretation of a regulation. That solution is unlawful for the reasons set forth in the Court's opinion: It contradicts the APA's unqualified exemption of interpretive rules from notice-and-comment rulemaking.

But I think there is another solution — one unavailable to the D. C. Circuit since it involves the overruling of one this Court's decisions***. [T]here are weighty reasons to deny a lawgiver the power to write ambiguous laws and then be the judge of what the ambiguity means. I would therefore restore the balance originally struck by the APA with respect to an agency's interpretation of its own regulations, not by rewriting the Act in order to make up for *Auer*, but by abandoning *Auer* and applying the Act as written. The agency is free to interpret its own regulations with or without notice and comment; but courts will decide — with no deference to the agency — whether that interpretation is correct.

[Justice Thomas issued a separate opinion concurring in the judgment, contending that judicial deference to an agency's interpretation of its own regulation was unwise and unconstitutional. Justice Alito joined the opinion of the Court except as to Part III-B. He invited litigants to bring a case in which the validity of *Auer* deference could be reconsidered.]

Notes and Questions

1. **The Statutory Framework.** As we have seen, the Fair Labor Standards Act (FLSA), 29 U.S.C. § 201 et seq., requires covered employers to pay time-and-a-half for work in excess of 40 hours per week. *See* Note 2 following *Brooklyn Savings Bank v. O'Neil*, *supra* Chapter 1[C][1], p. 33. Employees who work in a bona fide "administrative" capacity are exempt from the overtime-pay requirement. § 213(a)(1). The same statutory provision that exempts administrative employees from the overtime-pay requirement provides that FLSA exemptions are to be "defined and delimited from

time to time by regulations of the Secretary, subject to the provisions of [the Administrative Procedure Act]."

Why would Congress have delegated authority to identify jobs that fall within the administrative exception to the Labor Department as opposed to leaving the task to the courts? Does identification of administrative professionals require information or technical expertise that judges cannot readily access? How does the Department acquire this information or expertise? Note that, as discussed below, DOL rarely issued regulations that did anything other than repeat the pertinent statutory language until the Bush 43 administration.

2. **The Regulatory Posture?** The regulation at issue in *Mortgage Bankers*, 29 C.F.R. § 541.200, was promulgated April 23, 2004, to "update[] the regulations defining and delimiting the exemptions for 'white collar' executive, administrative and professional employees." 69 Fed. Reg. 22,122. When it issued the regulation, DOL noted that while "[t]he minimum wage and overtime pay requirements of the Fair Labor Standards Act (FLSA) are among the nation's most important worker protections," those protections had been "eroded" by DOL's failure to explain the exceptions for white collar employees. The intent of the regulation was to "restore the overtime protections intended by the FLSA." In practice, the 2004 regulations also provided cover to regulated industries. For example, one regulation promulgated together with § 541.200 created an exemption for any employee who earned more than $100,000 per year. *See* 29 C.F.R. § 541.601.

Prior to the 2004 rulemaking, the agency's regulations tended merely to repeat the statutory language; guidance was provided by "interpretations" that accompanied the regulations. *See, e.g., Freeman v. National Broadcasting Company, Inc.*, 80 F.3d 78, 84 (2d Cir. 1996) (rejecting reliance on "out-of-date" and "nonbinding" interpretations concerning "professional employee" exemption). The 2004 regulations eliminated the distinction between "regulations" and "interpretations" in place of a unitary set of regulations. Case-by-case guidance was provided by opinion letters that responded to queries about the FLSA's applicability to situations described the by the requester of the opinion. Both the 2004 regulation and the 2006 letter addressing whether mortgage loan officers fell within the FLSA's administrative exception were promulgated during the tenure of Secretary of Labor Elaine Chao, who served under President George W. Bush from 2001 to 2009, and now serves as Secretary of Transportation.

a. **The 2006 Opinion Letter.** The opinion issued by DOL in 2006 was arguably part of a broader effort on the part of the DOL under Secretary Chao to restrict the scope of employer liability under the FLSA. *See* Deborah Thompson Eisenberg, *Regulation by* Amicus: *The Department of Labor's Policy Making in the Courts*, 65 FLA. L. REV. 1223, 1259 (2013).

The 2006 letter contained a disclaimer that stated:

> This opinion is based exclusively on the facts and circumstances described in your request and is given based on your representation, express or implied, that you have provided a full and fair description of all the facts and circumstances

that would be pertinent to our consideration of the question presented. Existence of any other factual or historical background not contained in your letter might require a conclusion different from the one expressed herein.

The disclaimer anticipates the possibility that an employer will seek to take advantage of the "good faith defense" created by the Portal to Portal Act, ch. 52, § 1, 61 Stat. 84, codified at 29 U.S.C. § 258. The Act provides that "no employer shall be subject to any liability or punishment for or on account of the failure of the employer to pay minimum wages or overtime compensation*** if he pleads and proves that the act or omission complained of was in good faith in conformity with and in reliance on any administrative regulation, order, ruling, approval, or interpretation, of any agency of the United States, or any administrative practice or enforcement policy of any such agency with respect to the class of employers to which he belonged." *Id.*

The Act further provides: "Such a defense, if established, shall be a bar to the action or proceeding, notwithstanding that after such act or omission, such administrative regulation, order, ruling, approval, interpretation, practice, or enforcement policy is modified or rescinded or is determined by judicial authority to be invalid or of no legal effect." *Id.*

Given the 2006 letter's disclaimer, how could any employer rely on the letter to conclude that mortgage loan officers were generally exempt administrative employees? Won't there always be "factual or historical background" that is different between the employer that requested the interpretation and other, similarly situated employers? Or was the position taken by the letter sufficiently broad so as to negate the disclaimer?

Compare the Customs Service's analysis in the letter ruling reproduced *supra* Chapter 4[B][2]. Did Customs' ruling have a broader or narrower scope than DOL's 2006 opinion letter? Should it?

b. **The 2010 Administrator Interpretation.** Under the Obama Administration's Secretary of Labor Hilda L. Solis, the DOL stopped issuing opinion letters. In its March 2010 Administrator Interpretation, DOL explained that the 2006 opinion letter incorrectly assumed that 29 C.F.R. § 541.203(b) created an alternative standard for determining whether financial services employees were covered by the administrative exemption. That provision, the 2010 Interpretation said, "merely provides an example to help distinguish between those employees in the financial services industry whose primary duty is related to the management or general operations of the employer's customers and those whose primary duty is selling the employer's financial products."

Does this disagreement over the semantic meaning of the regulation justify a change in DOL's position? Had anything changed on the ground that necessitated revisiting the status of mortgage-loan officers? Would it have been preferable for DOL to have acknowledged that, as a result of the change in administration, it now took a narrower view of FLSA exemptions, and that this had prompted it to reexamine the 2006 opinion letter? *See* Note 5 following *Motor Vehicle Mfrs. Assn. of United States, Inc. v. State Farm Mut. Automobile Ins. Co., infra* Chapter 5[D], p. 634.

3. **The "*Paralyzed Veterans*" Doctrine.** In the decision below, the D.C. Circuit invalidated the 2010 Administrator Interpretation because it had been issued as a policy statement rather than promulgated through APA-compliant notice-and-comment rulemaking. In the court of appeals' view, the Administrator Interpretation "significantly revised" the 2006 opinion letter, which was a "definitive interpretation" of 29 C.F.R. § 541.200. If DOL wished to revisit the position it took in the 2006 opinion letter, the D.C. Circuit ruled, it could only do so by issuing a new regulation. *Mortgage Bankers Ass'n v. Harris*, 720 F.3d 966, 971 (D.C. Cir. 2013). The "issue a new regulation" requirement applied even if regulated parties did not rely on the prior "definitive interpretation." *Id.* at 968.

The principle that an agency could not significantly revise a prior authoritative interpretation except through notice-and-comment rulemaking was announced in *Paralyzed Veterans of America v. DC ARENA LP*, 117 F.3d 579, 586 (1997):

> Under the APA, agencies are obliged to engage in notice and comment before formulating regulations, which applies as well to "repeals" or "amendments." *See* 5 U.S.C. § 551(5). To allow an agency to make a fundamental change in its interpretation of a substantive regulation without notice and comment obviously would undermine those APA requirements.

4. **Why Does the *Perez* Court Reject the *Paralyzed Veterans* Doctrine?** The Supreme Court unanimously rejects the *Paralyzed Veterans* doctrine. The Court first says that the doctrine "is contrary to the clear text of the APA." This conclusion is based on the fact that the APA does not require notice-and-comment before an agency issues an interpretative rule: "Because an agency is not required to use notice-and-comment procedures to issue an initial interpretative rule, it is also not required to use those procedures when it amends or repeals that interpretative rule."

Is this a satisfactory response to the D.C. Circuit's concern? The appeals court maintained that, *in substance*, an "authoritative" interpretative statement fixed the meaning of the regulation it interpreted. Does this mean that the interpretation is, in fact, binding? Because a significant change from a prior interpretative statement would alter the meaning of the regulation, the change could only be effected through notice-and-comment procedures, the D.C. Circuit held. Does the Supreme Court address this concern? Is its response satisfactory?

The Supreme Court also reasons that the *Paralyzed Veterans* doctrine runs afoul of *Vermont Yankee*, because it imposes a procedural requirement on agencies that is not required by the APA. Does *this* point address the D.C. Circuit's concern that an authoritative interpretative statement in substance is equivalent to a new regulation? If an authoritative interpretative statement is actually equivalent to a new regulation, wasn't the D.C. Circuit correct to insist on notice and comment before the interpretative statement was amended? Can the D.C. Circuit's position be reconciled with *Vermont Yankee*'s bar on administrative common law? Consider also Justice Scalia's argument that the source of mischief is the courts' practice of deferring to agency interpretations that, by statute, are not supposed to bind the public.

5. When Do Interpretive Rules or Policy Statements Have the Force of Law and Require Compliance with § 553? Following the Supreme Court's decision in *Mortgage Bankers*, what is the legal status of the DOL's 2010 Administrator Interpretation? Does the Interpretation bind financial institutions as a matter of law? The 2006 opinion letter? The 2004 regulation? If a mortgage loan officer brings a private, civil action seeking overtime pay and contends that she is not covered by the administrative exception, how will the courts approach the question?

Note that in *Auer v. Robbins*, 519 U.S. 452, 462 (1997), *infra* Chapter 5[C][3], the Supreme Court, per Scalia, J., held that an agency's interpretation of its own regulation set out in an *amicus curiae* brief was "controlling" unless the interpretation was "plainly erroneous"; "inconsistent with the regulation"; "a *post hoc* rationalization advanced by an agency seeking to defend past agency action against attack"; or an interpretation that "[did] not reflect the agency's fair and considered judgment on the matter in question."

The Supreme Court in *Mortgage Bankers* does not address when interpretive rules or policy statements must be promulgated using § 553 notice and comment, because the question was not presented in the courts below. The question, however, has been a major source of confusion for courts and commentators. *See generally* David Franklin, *Legislative Rules, Nonlegislative Rules, and the Perils of the Short Cut*, 120 YALE L.J. 276 (2010). Consider the following approaches to the problem.

a. The "Effect on Agency" Test. Professor Anthony suggests that "a nonlegislative document" should be treated as a legislative rule and therefore subject to notice-and-comment procedures if "as a practical matter the agency treats it the same way it treats a legislative rule—that is, as dispositive of the issues that it addresses." Robert A. Anthony, *Interpretative Rules, Policy Statements, Guidances, Manuals, and the Like—Should Federal Agencies Use Them to Bind the Public*, 41 DUKE L.J. 1311, 1328–29 (1992). To determine whether an agency is treating a document this way, "certain indicia" should be consulted: "agency enforcement action based upon nonobservance of the nonlegislative document"; "regular application of the standards set forth in the document"; and the agency's representations to the public. *Id.* (emphasis in original omitted).

In *Texas v. United States*, 809 F.3d 134 (5th Cir. 2015), the Fifth Circuit applied a version of the effect on agency test in upholding a preliminary injunction that barred implementation of the Obama administration's Deferred Action for Parents of Americans and Lawful Permanent Residents (DAPA) program. Memorialized in memoranda issued by the Justice Department and the Department of Homeland Security (DHS), DAPA established a process through which qualifying aliens who lacked lawful immigration status could apply for a three-year deferral of enforcement proceedings, a concept that immigration law refers to as "deferred action." Under a longstanding Justice Department regulation, a deferred action recipient is entitled to a temporary work authorization. 8 C.F.R. § 274a. 12(C)(14). As a result of a provision in the Real ID Act, Pub. L. No. 109-13, 119 Stat. 302, securing a work authorization allows a deferred action recipient to apply for a driver's license in many states.

The Fifth Circuit panel majority concluded that the DAPA program could only be established through notice-and-comment rulemaking because the program did not "genuinely" leave agency decisionmakers free to evaluate applications for deferred action on a case-by-case basis. The majority emphasized that, under DAPA, aliens applied for deferred action using a "check the box" form, and that the leadership of U.S. Customs and Immigration Services (CIS) had promulgated a 150-page manual with detailed instructions specifying how CIS staff should process DAPA applications. Certain denials of deferred action required the approval of a supervisor. In the predecessor DACA (Deferred Action for Childhood Arrivals) program, only 5% of 723,000 applications for deferred action were denied. While the DHS memoranda establishing DAPA "purport[ed] to grant discretion" to frontline personnel, the program was in fact a legislative rule because it was "applied by the agency in a way that indicates it is binding." The dissenting judge disagreed with the district court's finding that DAPA left front-line decisionmakers without meaningful authority to deny applications on a case-by-case basis and concluded that the program's "channeling of agency enforcement discretion—through the use of non-exhaustive, flexible criteria—is entirely consistent with a non-substantive rule."

As a remedy for DHS's failure to follow notice-and-comment procedures, the Fifth Circuit approved the entry of a preliminary injunction that halted implementation of DAPA on a nationwide basis, even though the plaintiffs had not sought to have a class action certified. Are such injunctions an appropriate exercise of the courts' remedial authority? *See generally* Samuel L. Bray, *Multiple Chancellors: Reforming the National Injunction*, 130 Harv. L. Rev. (forthcoming 2017); Getzel Berger, Note, *Nationwide Injunctions Against the Federal Government: A Structural Approach*, 92 N.Y.U. L. Rev. (forthcoming 2017).

The Supreme Court granted certiorari to review the Fifth Circuit's decision upholding the district court's preliminary injunction on January 19, 2016. On June 23, 2016, the judgment was affirmed by an equally divided Court. 136 S. Ct. 2271, 2272 (2016). On June 15, 2017, DHS rescinded the memoranda establishing the DAPA program. *See* Rescission of Memorandum Providing for Deferred Action for Parents of Americans and Lawful Permanent Residents ("DAPA"), https://www.dhs. gov/news/2017/06/15/rescission-memorandum-providing-deferred-action-parents-americans-and-lawful.

For further discussion of DAPA, see Note 6 following *Heckler v. Chaney*, *infra* Chapter 5[B], p. 558.

b. **The "Legal Effect" Test.** In *American Mining Congress v. Mine Safety & Health Administration*, 995 F.2d 1106 (1993), the D.C. Circuit held that "Program Policy Letters" issued by the Department of Labor's Mine Safety and Health Administration (MSHA) were valid interpretative rules even though they were not themselves the product of notice-and-comment procedures under § 553 of the APA. The letters provided guidance on how MSHA would interpret its "Part 50" regulations promulgated under the Federal Mine Safety and Health Act, 30 U.S.C. § 801, that covered the "Notification, Investigation, Reports and Records of Accidents, Injuries, Illnesses,

Employment, and Coal Production in Mines." One of them provided that when certain illnesses were diagnosed, a mine operator was required to report the "diagnosis" to MHSA in the same manner as mine operators are required to report accidents, occupational injuries, and occupational illnesses. The Program Policy Letters at issue in *American Mining Congress* provided that certain x-ray readings indicative of mesothelioma constituted a "diagnosis" within the meaning of the regulation.

The appeals court reasoned that the distinction between notice-and-comment regulations and interpretative rules turned "almost exclusively on the basis of whether the purported interpretive rule has 'legal effect.'" That, in turn, was "best ascertained by asking (1) whether in the absence of the rule there would not be an adequate legislative basis for enforcement action or other agency action to confer benefits or ensure the performance of duties, (2) whether the agency has published the rule in the Code of Federal Regulations, (3) whether the agency has explicitly invoked its general legislative authority, or (4) whether the rule effectively amends a prior legislative rule. If the answer to any of these questions is affirmative, we have a legislative, not an interpretive rule." Because the Program Policy Letters merely clarified the Part 50 diagnosis regulation and did not satisfy any of the above tests, they were valid interpretative rules.

Under this test, would the 2006 opinion letter in *Perez* be classified as a legislative rule? The 2010 Administrator Interpretation?

c. The "Arbitrary Legislative Choice" Test. In *Hoctor v. United States Department of Agriculture*, 82 F.3d 165 (7th Cir. 1996) (Posner, J.), the Seventh Circuit considered an interpretative rule issued by the Department of Agriculture which stated that all "dangerous animals," including lions, tigers, and leopards, must be contained within a perimeter fence at least eight feet high. The rule interpreted a Department of Agriculture regulation promulgated following notice-and-comment procedures, which provided that a "facility [housing dangerous animals] must be constructed of such material and of such strength *as appropriate* for the animals involved. The indoor and outdoor housing facilities shall be structurally sound and shall be maintained in good repair to protect the animals from injury and to contain the animals." (Emphasis added.)

Petitioner Patrick Hoctor was a dealer of wild animals including "Big Cats" such as lions, tigers, and ligers (a cross between a male lion and a female tiger). He kept his animals in pens, which in turn were surrounded by a containment fence. Hoctor's entire compound was surrounded by a six-foot high perimeter fence. He was cited repeatedly by the Department of Agriculture for failing to maintain an eight-foot high fence. He challenged the citations on the ground that the eight-foot high requirement — as opposed to the more general requirement of structural strength appropriate to contain the animals — was not legally enforceable.

The Seventh Circuit agreed. The court distinguished between "normal" or "routine" interpretation and interpretations based on arbitrary "legislative" choices. The former elaborate the meaning of terms in a statute or regulation and would not necessarily benefit from public input, because an agency is constantly interpreting the language of the statute and regulations it administers. The latter were "consistent with the statute or regulation which the rules are promulgated under but not derived from it, because they represent an arbitrary choice among methods of implementation." This type of interpretation would benefit from the public participation provided by notice-and-comment rulemaking, because it is analogous to the kind of line-drawing performed by a legislature. The court concluded, "When agencies base rules on arbitrary choices they are legislating, and so these rules are legislative or substantive and require and comment rulemaking***."

The Department of Agriculture's eight-foot-fence requirement was such a rule. Although the requirement implemented the Department's structural-strength regulation, it represented "an arbitrary choice among methods of implementation." As such, the fact that Hoctor violated the eight-foot rule did not prove that he violated the "structural strength" requirement in the Department's regulation. If the Department wanted violation of the eight-foot requirement to ipso facto establish a violation of the law, it would have to promulgate the requirement through notice-and-comment rulemaking.

Under this test, would the 2006 Opinion Letter in *Perez* be classified as a legislative rule? The 2010 Interpretation?

Which of these three approaches has the strongest foundation in the APA? Which is preferable as a policy matter? Analysis of whether an interpretative rule or policy statement should have been promulgated through notice-and-comment procedures has parallels to the analysis required by *United States v. Mead, infra* Chapter 5[C][3]. When reading *Mead*, consider whether it, *American Mining Congress*, or *Hoctor* offer a better approach to identifying agency work product with the force of law.

6. **Agency Avoidance of Rulemaking Procedures?** The Court in *Perez* observes "[t]here may be times when an agency's decision to issue an interpretive rule, rather than a legislative rule, is driven primarily by a desire to skirt notice-and-comment provisions." How prevalent is this practice? For varying perspectives, compare Richard A. Epstein, *The Role of Guidances in Modern Administrative Procedure*, 8 J. LEG. ANAL. 47 (2015), with Connor Raso, *Agency Avoidance of Rulemaking Procedures*, 67 ADMIN. L. REV. 65 (2015).

7. **The Publication Requirement.** APA § 553 recognizes four situations in which an agency may promulgate a rule of general applicability without following notice-and-comment procedures. Section 553(a) provides that "[t]his section applies*** except to the extent there is involved*** [1] a military or foreign affairs function of the United States" or [2] "a matter relating to agency management or personnel or to public property, loans, grants, benefits, or contracts." Section 553(b)(3) exempts from the notice requirement [3] "interpretative rules, general statements of policy, or rules of agency organization, procedure, or practice." Finally, § 553(b)(3) provides that an agency may promulgate a rule without notice "when the agency for good cause finds (and incorporates the finding and a brief statement of reasons therefor in the rules issued) that notice and public procedure thereon are impracticable, unnecessary, or contrary to the public interest."

Even if a rule is promulgated without notice and comment, it must be published in the Federal Register. Section 552(a)(1), added to the APA by the Freedom of Information Act of 1966, Pub L. No. 89-487, 80 Stat. 250, requires agencies to "separately state and currently publish in the Federal Register for the guidance of the public*** substantive rules of general applicability adopted as authorized by law, and statements of general policy or interpretations of general applicability formulated and adopted by the agency" and "each amendment, revision, or repeal of the foregoing."

8. Estoppel Against the Government? The *Paralyzed Veterans* doctrine was based in part on a recognition that, because regulated parties rely on informal policy statements to organize their affairs, changes in agency policy may be unfair. For example, in the *Alaskan Hunters* case, 177 F.3d 1030 (D.C. Cir. 1999), hunting lodge operators in remote parts of Alaska opened new businesses in reliance on the regional Federal Aviation Administration office's representation that they did not have to comply with all of the FAA's aviation regulations. A new policy promulgated by the agency, which was at issue in *Alaskan Hunters*, would have required some of those lodges to shut down. To prevent such unfairness, *Paralyzed Veterans* said that an "authoritative" interpretation of a regulation can only be modified through a new notice-and-comment rulemaking. In *Perez*, the Supreme Court noted "[t]he United States['] acknowledge[ment] at argument that even in situations where a statute does not contain a safe-harbor provision similar to the one included in the FLSA, an agency's ability to pursue enforcement actions against regulated entities for conduct in conformance with prior agency interpretations may be limited by principles of retroactivity."

A similar concern with reliance underlies the common law doctrine of estoppel, which holds that in some circumstances a party may not assert a claim or right that is inconsistent with her prior actions. Estoppel, however, is generally thought not to lie against the government.

The reasons for this are discussed in *Office of Personnel Management v. Richmond*, 496 U.S. 414 (1990). Under the Civil Service Reform Act of 1978, Pub. L. No. 95-454, 92 Stat. 1111, the Office of Personnel Management (OPM) administers an insurance program for government employees who retire because of a disability. Under the program, a disabled employee is entitled to benefits provided that the employee has accumulated five years of federal government service. The program continues to pay benefits until the employee is "restored to an earning capacity fairly comparable to" his pay at the time of retirement. 5 U.S.C. §8337(d). By regulation, OPM delegates authority to other federal agencies to administer the program. *See* 5 C.F.R. ch. I, subch. B, pt. 250, subpt. A.

Prior to 1982, a retiree met the earning-capacity test if he made 80% of his earning capacity in each of the two succeeding calendar years. The 1982 Omnibus Budget Reconciliation Act, Pub. L. No. 97-253, 96 Stat. 792, changed the measuring period to one year. Pursuant to a delegation from OPM, the Navy established a Civilian Personnel Department within its Navy Public Works Center in San Diego, California.

Charles Richmond asked an "employee relations specialist" at the Center how much he could earn without exceeding the 80% eligibility limit. The specialist mistakenly told Richmond that his earning capacity would be calculated using the two-year period. Relying on the specialist's advice, Richmond took on additional work that put him above the eligibility limit. When OPM found out, it discontinued Richmond's disability benefits for the period in which he exceeded the limit.

The Supreme Court rejected Richmond's claim that OPM was estopped from doing so. "[L]eav[ing] for another day whether an estoppel claim could ever succeed against the Government," the Court reasoned that estoppel would not lie when it would cause the expenditure of government funds not authorized by statute. Payment of money in these circumstances, the Court reasoned, would violate the Appropriations Clause insofar as government money would be expended without an "Appropriation[] made by Law." U.S. Const. art. 1, § 9, cl. 7. Moreover, accepting Richmond's claim of estoppel would discourage government officers from communicating advice to the public. In the Court's view, "[t]he natural consequence of a rule that made the Government liable for the statements of its agents would be a decision to cut back and impose strict controls upon Government provision of information in order to limit liability."

Concurring in the judgment on the ground that it was required by the Court's precedent, Justice Stevens complained that the majority's Appropriations Clause argument was a makeweight, because the disability insurance program was authorized by law and Congress could not have expected that the program would operate 100% free of error. What of the Court's claim that estoppel will discourage agency officials from providing guidance? Does the availability of estoppel prevent private companies from providing guidance and support to their customers? OPM regulations that took effect after *Richmond* provide that, if OPM erroneously *pays* disability benefits to a retiree, recovery of the overpayment may be waived "when the annuitant (a) is without fault and (b) recovery would be against equity and good conscience." 5 C.F.R. § 845.301. "A recipient of an overpayment is without fault if he/she performed no act of commission or omission which resulted in the overpayment." 5 C.F.R. § 831.1402. The regulations do not provide a way for retirees in Richmond's position to obtain authoritative advice about retirement benefits. Does the existence of the waiver provision suggest there is no need for courts to recognize estoppel against the government?

Can the Court's strong position against estoppel in *Richmond* be reconciled with the holding of *United States ex rel. Accardi v. Shaugnessy*, 347 U.S. 260 (1954) (discussed in Note on Rulemaking's Consequences for Adjudication, in Section [D], *supra*, p. 470), that an agency must follow its own regulations until they are repealed or modified? What distinguishes the agency action at issue in *Accardi* from the agency action in *Richardson*?

Might *Accardi* and *Richmond* be read as an effort to circumscribe the kind of agency actions that regulated parties can reasonably rely upon in order to balance regulated parties' need for certainty, on the one hand, and the government's need to control the actions of "rogue" employees, on the other? Recall *Chenery II*'s observation that the retroactivity inherent in establishing administrative policy through adjudication "must be balanced against the mischief of producing a result which is contrary to a statutory design or to legal and equitable principles. If that mischief is greater than the ill effect of the retroactive application of a new standard, it is not the type of retroactivity which is condemned by law." *SEC v. Chenery*, 332 U.S. 194, 203 (1947), *supra* Section [D]. Also recall *Bell Aerospace*'s observation that, while an agency is generally free to choose between rulemaking and adjudication when elaborating statutory policy, the agency might be constrained to use rulemaking if "adverse consequences ensuing from such reliance are so substantial that the [agency] should be precluded from reconsidering the issue in an adjudicative proceeding." *NLRB v. Bell Aerospace Co.*, 416 U.S. 267, 295 (1974), *supra* Section [D].

G. Litigation

In addition to adjudicating cases and promulgating regulations, interpretive rules, guidance documents, and statements of policy, an agency may elaborate administrative policy through litigation. Agency litigation can take a number of forms.

1. **Independent Litigating Authority.** First, an agency may have authority to file civil or criminal actions to enforce a statute the agency administers. For example, § 707 of the Civil Right Act of 1964 authorizes the Equal Employment Opportunity Commission (EEOC) to bring an action on behalf of the charging party, 42 U.S.C. § 2000e-5(f)(1), or to remedy "a pattern or practice of resistance to the full enjoyment of any of the rights secured by [the Civil Right Act]." 42 U.S.C. § 2000e-6(a). EEOC pattern-and-practice actions are not subject to Federal Rule of Civil Procedure 23. Thus, the agency may pursue aggregate remedies more easily than a private plaintiff who must demonstrate that his or her claim is "typical" of the class the plaintiff seeks to represent. *See generally Teamsters v. United States*, 431 U.S. 324 (1977); *General Telephone Co. v. EEOC*, 446 U.S. 318 (1980). Thirty-odd agencies possess some degree of authority to conduct litigation on their own behalf. *See* Susan M. Olson, *Challenges to the Gatekeeper: The Debate over Federal Litigating Authority*, 68 JUDICATURE 70 (1984).

2. **Intervention.** As an alternative to bringing an action on its own behalf, an agency might intervene in an action filed by another party. Intervention is specifically authorized in a number of substantive regulatory statutes. *See, e.g.,* 42 U.S.C. 2000e-4(g) (EEOC may intervene in individual employment discrimination actions "against a respondent other than a government, governmental agency or political subdivision"); 28 U.S.C. § 2403 (Justice Department may intervene "wherein the constitutionality of any Act of Congress affecting the public interest is drawn in question"). In addition, an agency may intervene under the general authority provided by Federal Rule of Civil Procedure 24.

When an agency intervenes in a lawsuit, it will ordinarily have all the powers and responsibilities of a party to the suit. The agency may participate in discovery, present evidence and argument to the court, and will be bound by the court's judgment. A district court, however, has authority under the Federal Rules to impose limitations or conditions on an agency's intervention. *See Stringfellow v. Concerned Neighbors in Action*, 480 U.S. 370 (1987).

3. **Case Screening.** The False Claims Act (FCA) allows a plaintiff known as a "relator" to sue on behalf of the government to recover funds that were paid in response to "a false or fraudulent claim for payment or approval." 31 U.S.C. § 3729(a)(1)(A). The FCA requires litigants to file a complaint alleging violations of the Act with the Justice Department before the complaint is filed in court. The Department then has the opportunity to review the complaint and investigate the allegations, and to take over prosecution of the case or intervene in the action. If the Justice Department declines to take over prosecution of the case, the plaintiff is allowed to bring the action on behalf of the government. Regardless of whether the government takes over the case, the relator is entitled to a bounty of up to "25 percent of the proceeds of the action or settlement of the claim" if the case succeeds. A handful of other federal and state statutes allow a party to sue on the government's behalf subject to pre-screening by a government agency. *See generally* David Freeman-Engstrom, *Agencies as Litigation Gatekeepers*, 123 YALE L.J. 530 (2013).

4. **"Friend of the Court" Submissions.** Short of formally intervening in an action, an agency may file a brief *amicus curiae* to offer its views on the meaning of a statute the agency administers or a regulation that it promulgated. Courts often ask agencies to file *amicus* briefs presenting their views. But an agency may also monitor litigation and file a brief on its own initiative or in coordination with a party.

In *Auer v. Robbins*, 519 U.S. 452, 461 (1997), *infra* Chapter 5[C][3], the Supreme Court stated that an agency's interpretation of a regulation the agency promulgated is "controlling" unless the agency interpretation is "plainly erroneous or inconsistent with the regulation" even if the interpretation is set out in an *amicus* brief. Since *Auer*, it has become commonplace for agencies to appear as *amici* in cases where the meaning of an agency regulation is at issue, offer the agency's views, and argue that those views are entitled to considerable weight. *See, e.g., Christopher v. SmithKline Beecham Corp.*, 132 S. Ct. 2156 (2012); *Chase Bank v. McCoy*, 131 S. Ct. 871 (2011); *Christensen v. Harris County*, 529 U.S. 576 (2000).

In *Auer*, the Court rejected the argument that deference was inappropriate because the agency's positions were developed in response to litigation. The Court stated, however, that agency views lack persuasive authority if they represent a "'post hoc rationalizatio[n]' advanced by an agency seeking to defend past agency action against attack" or there was "reason to suspect that the interpretation does not reflect the agency's fair and considered judgment on the matter in question." *Auer* is discussed more fully in Chapter 5[C][3], *infra*.

4. **The Department of Justice's Role in Agency Litigation.** Although litigation can provide an important opportunity for an agency to elaborate subsidiary statutory policy, it must be remembered that most agency litigation is not conducted by agencies themselves, but by the Department of Justice. This is the case both for independent agencies and for those within the executive branch. *See* Kirti Datla & Richard L. Revesz, *Deconstructing Independent Agencies (And Executive Agencies)*, 98 Cornell L. Rev. 769, 800 tbl. 5 (2013). DOJ's responsibility for agency litigation results from two statutes. 5 U.S.C. §3106 restricts "the head of an Executive department or military department" from employing attorneys "for the conduct of litigation in which the United States, an agency, or employee thereof is a party." It also requires the agency head to refer lawsuits involving the agency to the Department of Justice. The presumption that agency litigation be conducted by the Justice Department is underscored by a provision of the Judicial Code, 28 U.S.C. §516, which provides: "Except as otherwise authorized by law, the conduct of litigation in which the United States, an agency, or officer thereof is a party, or is interested, and securing evidence therefor, is reserved to officers of the Department of Justice, under the direction of the Attorney General."

Through the Solicitor General, the Justice Department is responsible for representing agencies in the Supreme Court. To ensure that government agencies and departments do not take positions the Solicitor General is unwilling to defend, the Solicitor General's office reviews all cases decided adversely to the government in the lower courts. Generally, an appeal by an agency to a higher court may not be taken without the Solicitor General's permission, although a handful of agencies have authority to pursue appeals without Solicitor General authorization. *See, e.g.,* 2 U.S.C. §437c(f)(4) (Federal Election Commission); 2 U.S.C. §288c (Senate Office of Legal Counsel).

As we saw in *TVA v. Hill, supra* Chapter 2[B][2][a], the Solicitor General's office does not always agree with agencies on the position "the" government should take in the Supreme Court. Occasionally, conflicts among the Solicitor General's office, executive agencies, and independent agencies boil over into public view. In *Sheet Metal Workers' International Association v. EEOC*, 478 U.S. 421 (1986), EEOC attorneys successfully defended a district court order that required a union with a history of race discrimination to adopt an affirmative action plan in the U.S. Court of Appeals for the Second Circuit. In the Supreme Court, the EEOC was represented by the Solicitor General's office, and took the position that the district court order was invalid. Noting that "EEOC present[s] this challenge from a rather curious position," the Supreme Court adopted the position EEOC advanced in the lower courts and upheld the district court's order.

Such cases, however, are not the norm. Typically, differences among the Department of Justice and agencies are resolved informally, and the Solicitor General's office files a single brief representing the views of the entire government. Former Solicitor General Seth P. Waxman describes the process for approving appeals and formulating "the" government's position as follows:

In every instance, the process begins with a written analysis and recommendation, which is then circulated to every government component that might conceivably have an interest in the matter. [Agencies and departments] in turn prepare their own analyses and share them with each other. I recall cases from my tenure in which as many as a dozen different agencies and components have expressed views.

After all of these memos are in, an Assistant to the Solicitor General prepares an independent analysis and recommendation; a Deputy writes another; and the entire package lands on the Solicitor General's desk for decision. Ordinarily, between five and ten of these recommendation packages arrive every day. Most are reasonably straightforward, but sometimes the recommendations differ widely. Meetings are convened in which representatives of each component gather to consider each other's views, with the Solicitor General trying to reconcile differences and fashion a single coherent position.

***[I]n a surprisingly large percentage of cases, a position can be developed that leaves everyone satisfied—or at least equally dissatisfied. The beauty of the system is that each government component reflects a unique conception of what constitutes the interest of the United States. In that way, the government acts as a microcosm of the country as a whole, mirroring the complexity and diversity of American views.

Seth P. Waxman, *Defending Congress*, 79 N.C. L. Rev. 1073, 1076–77 (2001).

How does litigation authority compare to other protections of agency independence, such as removal protection and authority to submit budget requests directly to Congress? Is an agency's ability to litigate on its own behalf likely to improve the agency's ability to function without improper partisan influence? How might DOJ authority to litigate on an agency's behalf affect the agency's decisionmaking?

Chapter 5

Judicial Review

To this point, this volume has not directly engaged one of the central questions of federal administrative law: what is the appropriate relationship between reviewing courts and administrative agencies? On the one hand, some degree of judicial oversight of agency action seems essential to ensuring that administrative agencies do not go beyond the limits of their statutory authority or abuse their discretion. On the other hand, an overly aggressive system of judicial review could impede the kind of effective government that Congress seeks to encourage in delegating authority to an administrative agency.

This chapter considers the statutory and constitutional doctrines governing judicial review of agency action. We begin with threshold limitations on judicial review: the requirements of a "case" or "controversy" that supports federal court jurisdiction under Article III of the Constitution and "final" agency action under the Administrative Procedure Act (APA). We then turn to the standards governing judicial review of final agency action under the APA. The chapter closes by examining judicial review of discretionary agency action. Before proceeding, students should read Article III and the APA provisions on judicial review, 5 U.S.C. §§ 701–706.

A. Justiciability

The most basic questions regarding judicial review of agency action are "who" and "when": which *parties* may seek judicial review of agency action, and to what extent can parties seeking review of agency action challenge an agency rule or policy *before* it has been applied in a concrete dispute? As a constitutional matter, these present questions of "justiciability": they go to whether a challenge to agency action can be entertained under Article III of the Constitution. Section 1 introduces the doctrine of "standing," which controls who may challenge an agency's action and the type of actions that are reviewable. Section 2 turns to the doctrine of "ripeness," which governs the timing of judicial review.

1. Standing

Lujan v. Defenders of Wildlife
504 U.S. 555 (1992)

Justice Scalia delivered the opinion of the Court with respect to Parts I, II, III-A, and IV, and an opinion with respect to Part III-B, in which The Chief Justice, Justice White, and Justice Thomas join.

This case involves a challenge to a rule promulgated by the Secretary of the Interior interpreting §7 of the Endangered Species Act of 1973 (ESA), 87 Stat. 892, as amended, 16 U.S.C. §1536, in such fashion as to render it applicable only to actions within the United States or on the high seas. The preliminary issue, and the only one we reach, is whether respondents here, plaintiffs below, have standing to seek judicial review of the rule.

I

The ESA, 87 Stat. 884, as amended, 16 U.S.C. §1531 et seq., seeks to protect species of animals against threats to their continuing existence caused by man. *See generally TVA v. Hill*, 437 U.S. 153 (1978) [*supra* Chapter 2[B][2][a]]. The ESA instructs the Secretary of the Interior to promulgate by regulation a list of those species which are either endangered or threatened under enumerated criteria, and to define the critical habitat of these species. 16 U.S.C. §§1533, 1536. Section 7(a)(2) of the Act then provides, in pertinent part:

> "Each Federal agency shall, in consultation with and with the assistance of the Secretary [of the Interior], insure that any action authorized, funded, or carried out by such agency . . . is not likely to jeopardize the continued existence of any endangered species or threatened species or result in the destruction or adverse modification of habitat of such species which is determined by the Secretary, after consultation as appropriate with affected States, to be critical." 16 U.S.C. §1536(a)(2).

In 1978, the Fish and Wildlife Service (FWS) and the National Marine Fisheries Service (NMFS), on behalf of the Secretary of the Interior and the Secretary of Commerce respectively, promulgated a joint regulation stating that the obligations imposed by §7(a)(2) extend to actions taken in foreign nations. 43 Fed. Reg. 874 (1978). The next year, however, the Interior Department began to reexamine its position. A revised joint regulation, reinterpreting §7(a)(2) to require consultation only for actions taken in the United States or on the high seas, was proposed in 1983, 48 Fed. Reg. 29990, and promulgated in 1986, 51 Fed. Reg. 19926; 50 CFR 402.01 (1991).

Shortly thereafter, respondents, organizations dedicated to wildlife conservation and other environmental causes, filed this action against the Secretary of the Interior, seeking a declaratory judgment that the new regulation is in error as to the geographic scope of §7(a)(2) and an injunction requiring the Secretary to promulgate a new regulation restoring the initial interpretation. The District Court granted the Secretary's motion to dismiss for lack of standing. The Court of Appeals for the Eighth Circuit reversed by a divided vote. On remand, the Secretary moved for summary judgment on the standing issue, and respondents moved for summary judgment on the merits. The District Court*** granted respondents' merits motion, and ordered the Secretary to publish a revised regulation. The Eighth Circuit affirmed.***

II

While the Constitution of the United States divides all power conferred upon the Federal Government into "legislative Powers," Art. I, §1, "[t]he executive Power,"

Art. II, § 1, and "[t]he judicial Power," Art. III, § 1, it does not attempt to define those terms. To be sure, it limits the jurisdiction of federal courts to "Cases" and "Controversies," but an executive inquiry can bear the name "case" (the Hoffa case) and a legislative dispute can bear the name "controversy" (the Smoot-Hawley controversy). Obviously, then, the Constitution's central mechanism of separation of powers depends largely upon common understanding of what activities are appropriate to legislatures, to executives, and to courts.*** Though some [aspects of standing] express merely prudential considerations that are part of judicial self-government, the core component of standing is an essential and unchanging part of the case-or-controversy requirement of Article III.

Over the years, our cases have established that the irreducible constitutional minimum of standing contains three elements. First, the plaintiff must have suffered an "injury in fact"—an invasion of a legally protected interest which is (a) concrete and particularized,[1] and (b) "actual or imminent, not 'conjectural' or 'hypothetical.'" Second, there must be a causal connection between the injury and the conduct complained of—the injury has to be "fairly . . . trace[able] to the challenged action of the defendant, and not . . . th[e] result [of] the independent action of some third party not before the court." Third, it must be "likely," as opposed to merely "speculative," that the injury will be "redressed by a favorable decision."

The party invoking federal jurisdiction bears the burden of establishing these elements.***

III ***

A

Respondents' claim to injury is that the lack of consultation with respect to certain funded activities abroad "increas[es] the rate of extinction of endangered and threatened species." Complaint ¶ 5. Of course, the desire to use or observe an animal species, even for purely esthetic purposes, is undeniably a cognizable interest for purpose of standing. *See, e. g., Sierra Club* [*v. Morton*, 405 U.S. 727, 740–41 n.16 (1972)]. "But the 'injury in fact' test requires more than an injury to a cognizable interest. It requires that the party seeking review be himself among the injured." To survive the Secretary's summary judgment motion, respondents had to submit affidavits or other evidence showing, through specific facts, not only that listed species were in fact being threatened by funded activities abroad, but also that one or more of respondents' members would thereby be "directly" affected apart from their "'special interest' in th[e] subject."

With respect to this aspect of the case, the Court of Appeals focused on the affidavits of two Defenders' members—Joyce Kelly and Amy Skilbred. Ms. Kelly stated that she traveled to Egypt in 1986 and "observed the traditional habitat of the endangered nile crocodile there and intend[s] to do so again, and hope[s] to observe the crocodile directly," and that she "will suffer harm in fact as the result of [the] American . . .

---

1. By particularized, we mean that the injury must affect the plaintiff in a personal and individual way.

role . . . in overseeing the rehabilitation of the Aswan High Dam on the Nile . . . and [in] develop[ing] . . . Egypt's . . . Master Water Plan." Ms. Skilbred averred that she traveled to Sri Lanka in 1981 and "observed th[e] habitat" of "endangered species such as the Asian elephant and the leopard" at what is now the site of the Mahaweli project funded by the Agency for International Development (AID), although she "was unable to see any of the endangered species"; "this development project," she continued, "will seriously reduce endangered, threatened, and endemic species habitat including areas that I visited . . . [, which] may severely shorten the future of these species"; that threat, she concluded, harmed her because she "intend[s] to return to Sri Lanka in the future and hope[s] to be more fortunate in spotting at least the endangered elephant and leopard."*** We shall assume for the sake of argument that these affidavits contain facts showing that certain agency-funded projects threaten listed species—though that is questionable. They plainly contain no facts, however, showing how damage to the species will produce "imminent" injury to Mses. Kelly and Skilbred. That the women "had visited" the areas of the projects before the projects commenced proves nothing. As we have said in a related context, "'Past exposure to illegal conduct does not in itself show a present case or controversy regarding injunctive relief . . . if unaccompanied by any continuing, present adverse effects.'" And the affiants' profession of an "inten[t]" to return to the places they had visited before—where they will presumably, this time, be deprived of the opportunity to observe animals of the endangered species—is simply not enough. Such "some day" intentions—without any description of concrete plans, or indeed even any specification of when the some day will be—do not support a finding of the "actual or imminent" injury that our cases require.***

B

A[n] impediment to redressability is the fact that the agencies generally supply only a fraction of the funding for a foreign project. AID, for example, has provided less than 10% of the funding for the Mahaweli project. Respondents have produced nothing to indicate that the projects they have named will either be suspended, or do less harm to listed species, if that fraction is eliminated. As in *Simon* [*v. Eastern Kentucky Welfare Rights Organization*, 426 U.S. 26 (1976)], it is entirely conjectural whether the nonagency activity that affects respondents will be altered or affected by the agency activity they seek to achieve. There is no standing.

IV

The Court of Appeals found that respondents had standing for an additional reason: because they had suffered a "procedural injury." The so-called "citizen-suit" provision of the ESA provides, in pertinent part, that "any person may commence a civil suit on his own behalf (A) to enjoin any person, including the United States and any other governmental instrumentality or agency . . . who is alleged to be in violation of any provision of this chapter." 16 U.S.C. § 1540(g). The court held that, because § 7(a)(2) requires interagency consultation, the citizen-suit provision creates a "procedural righ[t]" to consultation in all "persons"—so that *anyone* can file suit in federal court to challenge the Secretary's (or presumably any other official's) failure to follow the assertedly correct consultative procedure, notwithstanding his or her inability to allege any discrete injury flowing from that failure. To understand the remarkable nature of this holding one must be clear about what it does not rest upon: This is not a case where plaintiffs are seeking to enforce a procedural requirement the disregard of which could impair a separate concrete interest of theirs (e. g., the procedural requirement for a hearing prior to denial of their license application, or the procedural requirement for an environmental impact statement before a federal facility is constructed next door to them).[7] Nor is it simply a case where concrete injury has been suffered by many persons, as in mass fraud or mass tort situations. Nor, finally, is it the unusual case in which Congress has created a concrete private interest in the outcome of a suit against a private party for the Government's benefit, by providing a cash bounty for the victorious plaintiff. Rather, the court held that the injury-in-fact requirement had been satisfied by congressional conferral upon *all* persons of an abstract, self-contained, non-instrumental "right" to have the Executive observe the procedures required by law. We reject this view.

We have consistently held that a plaintiff raising only a generally available grievance about government—claiming only harm to his and every citizen's interest in proper application of the Constitution and laws, and seeking relief that no more directly and tangibly benefits him than it does the public at large—does not state an Article III case or controversy.*** "The province of the court," as Chief Justice Marshall said in *Marbury v. Madison*, 1 Cranch 137, 170 (1803), "is, solely, to decide on the rights of individuals." Vindicating the *public* interest (including the public interest in Government observance of the Constitution and laws) is the function of Congress and the Chief Executive.***

Nothing in this contradicts the principle that "[t]he . . . injury required by Art. III may exist solely by virtue of 'statutes creating legal rights, the invasion of which creates standing.'" [Where we have so held, Congress elevated] to the status of legally cognizable injuries concrete, *de facto* injuries that were previously inadequate in law (namely, injury to an individual's personal interest in living in a racially integrated community, and injury to a company's interest in marketing its product free from competition. As we said in *Sierra Club* [*v. Morton*, 405 U.S. 727, 738 (1972)], "[Statutory] broadening [of] the categories of injury that may be alleged in support of

---

7. There is this much truth to the assertion that "procedural rights" are special: The person who has been accorded a procedural right to protect his concrete interests can assert that right without meeting all the normal standards for redressability and immediacy. Thus, under our case law, one living adjacent to the site for proposed construction of a federally licensed dam has standing to challenge the licensing agency's failure to prepare an environmental impact statement, even though he cannot establish with any certainty that the statement will cause the license to be withheld or altered, and even though the dam will not be completed for many years. (That is why we do not rely, in the present case, upon the Government's argument that, *even if* the other agencies were obliged to consult with the Secretary, they might not have followed his advice.) What respondents' "procedural rights" argument seeks, however, is quite different from this: standing for persons who have no concrete interests affected—persons who live (and propose to live) at the other end of the country from the dam.

standing is a different matter from abandoning the requirement that the party seeking review must himself have suffered an injury."***

We hold that respondents lack standing to bring this action and that the Court of Appeals erred in denying the summary judgment motion filed by the United States. The opinion of the Court of Appeals is hereby reversed, and the cause is remanded for proceedings consistent with this opinion.

JUSTICE KENNEDY, with whom JUSTICE SOUTER joins, concurring in part and concurring in the judgment.***

The Court's holding that there is an outer limit to the power of Congress to confer rights of action is a direct and necessary consequence of the case and controversy limitations found in Article III. I agree that it would exceed those limitations if, at the behest of Congress and in the absence of any showing of concrete injury, we were to entertain citizen suits to vindicate the public's nonconcrete interest in the proper administration of the laws. While it does not matter how many persons have been injured by the challenged action, the party bringing suit must show that the action injures him in a concrete and personal way. This requirement is not just an empty formality. It preserves the vitality of the adversarial process by assuring both that the parties before the court have an actual, as opposed to professed, stake in the outcome, and that "the legal questions presented . . . will be resolved, not in the rarified atmosphere of a debating society, but in a concrete factual context conducive to a realistic appreciation of the consequences of judicial action." In addition, the requirement of concrete injury confines the Judicial Branch to its proper, limited role in the constitutional framework of Government.***

JUSTICE STEVENS, concurring in the judgment.***

In this case,*** the likelihood that respondents will be injured by the destruction of the endangered species is not speculative. If respondents are genuinely interested in the preservation of the endangered species and intend to study or observe these animals in the future, their injury will occur as soon as the animals are destroyed. Thus the only potential source of "speculation" in this case is whether respondents' intent to study or observe the animals is genuine. In my view, Joyce Kelly and Amy Skilbred have introduced sufficient evidence to negate petitioner's contention that their claims of injury are "speculative" or "conjectural."*** [A] reasonable finder of fact could conclude, from their past visits, their professional backgrounds, and their affidavits and deposition testimony, that Ms. Kelly and Ms. Skilbred will return to the project sites and, consequently, will be injured by the destruction of the endangered species and critical habitat.

The plurality also concludes that respondents' injuries are not redressable[.]*** We must presume that if this Court holds that §7(a)(2) requires consultation, all affected agencies would abide by that interpretation and engage in the requisite consultations. Certainly the Executive Branch cannot be heard to argue that an authoritative construction of the governing statute by this Court may simply be ignored by any agency head.*** [In the remainder of his opinion, Justice Stevens concluded that, although respondents had standing, "the Government is correct in its submission that §7(a)(2) does not apply to activities in foreign countries."]

[Dissenting opinion of JUSTICE BLACKMUN, joined by JUSTICE O'CONNOR, omitted.]

Notes and Questions

1. **The Statutory Framework.** Section 7 of the Endangered Species Act (ESA), 16 U.S.C. § 1536, requires federal agencies to consult with the Secretary of Interior before taking actions that threaten endangered species or their critical habitat and prohibits agencies from taking such actions. Recall from *TVA v. Hill*, 437 U.S. 153 (1978), *supra* Chapter 2[B][2][a], that responsibility for implementing the ESA spans multiple agencies. The Secretary of the Interior, acting through the Fish and Wildlife Service, is responsible for identifying ("listing") endangered species and their critical habitat, a process performed using notice-and-comment rulemaking. 16 U.S.C. § 1533(a). (The Secretary of Commerce, through the National Marine Fisheries Service, is responsible for listing decisions concerning certain marine species. *See* § 1533(a)(2).) Once a species is listed, all federal agencies are subject to § 7's consultation requirement and prohibition on jeopardizing endangered species. 16 U.S.C. § 1536(a)(2). The ESA directs the Secretary of the Interior to "establish, and publish in the Federal Register, agency guidelines to insure that the purposes of this section are achieved efficiently and effectively." 16 U.S.C. § 1533(h). "The Secretary shall provide to the public notice of, and opportunity to submit written comments on, any guideline (including any amendment thereto) proposed to be established under" § 1533(h).

2. **The ESA's Citizen Suit Provision.** After giving notice to the Secretary of the Interior and following a sixty-day waiting period during which the agency may remedy the perceived violation, "any person may commence a civil suit on his own behalf—"

> (A) to enjoin any person, including the United States and any other governmental instrumentality or agency (to the extent permitted by the eleventh amendment to the Constitution), who is alleged to be in violation of any provision of this chapter or regulation issued under the authority thereof; or***

> (C) against the Secretary where there is alleged a failure of the Secretary to perform any act or duty under section 1533 of this title which is not discretionary with the Secretary.

16 U.S.C. § 1640(g).

Given that the Secretary of Interior is responsible for overseeing federal agencies' compliance with the ESA, why would Congress have concluded that the Secretary's actions should also be subject to judicial review at the behest of "any person"? Without the citizen-suit provision, would beneficiaries of environmental regulation otherwise be able sue? What interests are served by enabling private suits by beneficiaries of the regulatory scheme? Does the citizen suit provision reflect a high degree of confidence in the agencies that Congress directed to carry out the Act's mandates? (Recall the background to the ESA discussed in Note 2 following *TVA v. Hill*, *supra* p. 173.)

How would Congress have expected citizen suits to work with the provisions of the Act enforced by the interior secretary? Does the role played by the citizen-suit provision depend on whether the current Secretary generally supports the Act's objectives, is indifferent to those objectives, or affirmatively opposes them? Do you see any problems for the administration of the ESA if citizen suits are the primary movers in ESA litigation?

Assuming that Congress intended citizen suits to protect against maladministration of the Act, what conditions must hold for citizen suits to perform this function successfully? What assumptions is Congress making about the persons who choose to file citizen suits? About the judiciary? For an overview of the mechanisms Congress has used to encourage private citizens to check agencies, see Richard B. Stewart & Cass R. Sunstein, *Public Programs and Private Rights*, 95 Harv. L. Rev. 1193 (1981).

3. **Statutory "Zone of Interest" Standing?** As the Court explains, the plaintiff environmental organizations brought a facial, pre-enforcement challenge to the Commerce-Interior regulation limiting ESA § 7 to projects in the United States and on the high seas. Does the Court question whether plaintiffs had *statutory* standing to sue under the ESA's citizen-suit provision — that is, whether the ESA authorized the organizations to sue for violations of the Act? Is there a basis for arguing that plaintiffs *lacked* statutory standing?

When a substantive statute does not provide a right of action, plaintiffs in certain circumstances may be able to proceed under § 702 of the Administrative Procedure Act (APA), which provides, "[a] person suffering legal wrong because of agency action . . . is entitled to judicial review thereof." This is often termed "nonstatutory review" as contrasted with the review process specified in the agency's authorizing statute. Section 702 also provides that a person "adversely affected or aggrieved by agency action within the meaning of a relevant statute" is entitled to judicial review thereof. In applying this section, courts traditionally looked to whether the party seeking judicial review fell within the "zone of interests" a statute sought to protect. *See, e.g., Lujan v. Nat'l Wildlife Fed'n*, 497 U.S. 871, 883 (1990) (observing that "the failure of an agency to comply with a statutory provision requiring 'on the record' hearings would assuredly have an adverse effect upon the company that has the contract to record and transcribe the agency's proceedings; but since the provision was obviously enacted to protect the interests of the parties to the proceedings and not those of the reporters, that company would not be 'adversely affected within the meaning' of the statute").

Confusingly, the Supreme Court has also used the "zone of interests" test to determine whether the federal courts as a prudential matter should decline to exercise jurisdiction over a dispute that presented a case-or-controversy under Article III — a doctrine known as "prudential standing." In *Lexmark International, Inc. v. Static Control Components, Inc.*, 134 S. Ct. 1377 (2014), however, the Supreme Court appeared to repudiate this aspect of the Article III standing doctrine, stating: "Whether a plaintiff comes within the 'zone of interests' is an issue that requires us to determine, using traditional tools of statutory interpretation, whether a legislatively conferred cause of action encompasses a particular plaintiff's claim."

4. Elements of Constitutional Standing—"Injury-in-Fact." As the *Lujan* Court explains, the concept of Article III standing requires that the party seeking judicial relief show an "injury in fact" that is concrete and particularized. Where the plaintiff is an organization seeking to vindicate its members' interests, the injury must be suffered by the members. *See Summers v. Earth Island Institute*, 129 S. Ct. 1142, 1151–52 (2009).

The plaintiff organizations in *Lujan* averred that, as result of the Interior-Commerce regulation, their members would no longer be able to observe the endangered Nile crocodile, the Asian elephant, and the leopard in their native habitats. Plaintiffs' focus on *observing* endangered species reflects the influence of an earlier Article III standing case, *Sierra Club v. Morton*, 405 U.S. 727, 735 (1972). There, the Court concluded that the Sierra Club lacked standing to challenge the Interior Department's permitting of a ski resort that Disney planned to open in the Mineral King Valley of the Sierra Nevada mountains:

> The impact of the proposed changes in the environment of Mineral King will not fall indiscriminately upon every citizen. The alleged injury will be felt directly only by those who use Mineral King and Sequoia National Park, and for whom the aesthetic and recreational values of the area will be lessened by the highway and ski resort. The Sierra Club failed to allege that it or its members would be affected in any of their activities or pastimes by the Disney development. Nowhere in the pleadings or affidavits did the Club state that its members use Mineral King for any purpose, much less that they use it in any way that would be significantly affected by the proposed actions of the respondents.

Why does the Court in *Lujan* conclude that plaintiffs had not suffered an injury in fact? Is the Court's problem with the *type* of injury that plaintiffs claimed they would suffer or the *time frame* in which they claimed they would experience that injury? Isn't Justice Stevens correct that, if plaintiffs genuinely intended to observe endangered animals, they would inevitably be affected by the joint regulation? If the Court accepted this "inevitable impact" argument, would there be any limit on the listing decisions that plaintiff organizations could challenge in a given proceeding?

5. Elements of Constitutional Standing—"Causation." The second requirement of constitutional standing is that there be "a causal connection between the injury and the conduct complained of." Why is causation not at issue in *Lujan*? For a case where the causation requirement proved fatal to the plaintiff's standing, see *Simon v. Eastern Ky. Welfare Rights Organization*, 426 U.S. 26, 42–43 (1976) (denying standing to plaintiffs challenging an Internal Revenue Service ruling that hospitals could limit services to indigent patients without jeopardizing their tax-exempt status). "The complaint here alleged only that petitioners, by the adoption of Revenue Ruling 69–545, had 'encouraged' hospitals to deny services to indigents.*** But it does not follow*** that the denial of access to hospital services in fact results from petitioners' new Ruling, or that a court-ordered return by petitioners to their previous policy would result in these respondents' receiving the hospital services they desire. It is purely speculative whether the denials of service specified in the complaint fairly can be traced to petitioners' 'encouragement' or instead result from decisions made by the hospitals without regard to the tax implications.").

6. **Elements of Constitutional Standing—"Redressability."** Constitutional standing finally requires a likelihood "that the injury will be 'redressed by a favorable decision.'" The *Lujan* Court faults plaintiffs' showing on this point, positing that an injunction against the Interior Secretary would not necessarily bind other agencies of the government, and that foreign projects which harm endangered species could go forward even if a U.S. court ruled that § 7 applied worldwide. In contrast, Justice Steven posits that "all affected agencies" would abide by the courts' interpretation of the ESA, and that "foreign governments, when faced with the threatened withdrawal of United States assistance, will modify their projects to mitigate the harm to endangered species." What is the empirical basis for these predictions from the Court and Justice Stevens? On the government's general duty to obey decisions of the Supreme Court, see *Cooper v. Aaron*, 358 U.S. 1 (1958); Edwin Meese, *The Law of the Constitution*, 61 TULANE L. REV. 979 (1986).

7. **Organizational Standing.** An organization has standing and may bring suit in place of an individual plaintiff if at least one member of the organization has standing to sue, the organization's purposes are germane to the suit, and neither the claim asserted nor the relief requested requires the participation in the lawsuit of individual members. *See Hunt v. Wash. State Apple Adver. Comm'n*, 432 U.S. 333, 335 (1977) (Washington State Apple Advertising Commission had standing to challenge statute restricting sales of sub-food-grade apples). *Cf. Warth v. Seldin*, 422 U.S. 490, 494 (1975) (civil rights group and homebuilders association, none of whose members intended to purchase housing, lacked standing to challenge town zoning restrictions). What is the binding effect of a losing decision on the members of an organization who served as a representative of its members? *See McCrory v. Harris*, No. 15-1262 (U.S. 2016).

8. **Litigating the Standing Issue.** The *Lujan* Court states that standing is litigated in the same manner as any other showings a plaintiff is required to make to prevail on the merits. Thus, for example, well-pled allegations to the effect that a plaintiff has suffered an injury-in-fact are sufficient to withstand a motion to dismiss for failure to state a claim challenging the plaintiff's standing. In one respect, however, standing differs from other showings the plaintiff is required to make. Because standing goes to a federal court's subject matter jurisdiction, an alleged defect in standing may be raised at any point in the lifecycle of a civil case, including on appeal. *See, e.g., FW/PBS, Inc. v. Dallas*, 493 U.S. 215, 230 (1990) (*sua sponte* dismissing First Amendment challenge to civil disability provisions of city zoning ordinance because plaintiffs lacked standing). On the other hand, Article III standing concepts do not apply to proceedings before administrative agencies or in state courts. *See generally* Helen Hershkoff, *State Courts and the "Passive Virtues": Rethinking the Judicial Function*, 114 HARV. L. REV. 1833 (2001).

9. **Congress's Power to Establish Article III Injuries.** The Court accepts that Congress may "elevate to the status of legal cognizable injuries concrete, *de facto* injuries that were previously inadequate in law," but denies that the Interior Department's alleged failure to comply with the ESA's inter-agency consultation requirements before promulgating the regulation injured the plaintiffs in a manner that created an Article III injury in fact. What is the difference between "an individual's interest in living in a racially integrated community" and "injury to a company's interest in marketing its product free from competition," which the Court accepts as injuries in fact, and the "procedural" injury that plaintiffs sought to vindicate in *Lujan*, which the Court finds insufficient?

Twice in recent years, the Supreme Court has granted certiorari to consider the extent of Congress's power to create rights the violation of which creates an injury in fact. In *First American Financial Corp. v. Edwards*, No. 10-708, the Court granted certiorari to consider whether a private purchaser of real estate settlement services has standing under the Real Estate Settlement Procedures Act of 1974 (RESPA), 12 U.S.C. §§ 2601–2617, to maintain an action in federal court in the absence of any claim that the alleged violation affected the price, quality, or other characteristics of the settlement services provided. RESPA aims to eliminate kickbacks and referral fees in the settlement process for home mortgage loans. To that end, it creates a private right of action for any person who is charged an undisclosed "fee, kickback, or thing of value" and directs courts to award "an amount equal to three times the amount of any charge paid for such settlement service" to prevailing plaintiffs. 12 U.S.C. §§ 2607(a), (d). The plaintiff was charged an undisclosed fee for title insurance but did not allege that she paid more than prevailing market rate as a result. Following *Warth v. Seldin*, 422 U.S. 490, 500 (1975), a pre-*Lujan* case which concluded that civil rights organizations lacked standing to challenge a zoning ordinance that excluded low- and moderate-income individuals from Penfield, New York, the Ninth Circuit held that "[t]he injury required by Article III can exist solely by virtue of 'statutes creating legal rights, the invasion of which creates standing.'" *Edwards v. First Am. Corp.*, 610 F.3d 514, 517 (9th Cir. 2010). After granting certiorari to review the Ninth Circuit's judgment, the Supreme Court dismissed the writ as improvidently granted on June 28, 2012.

In *Spokeo v. Robbins*, 136 S. Ct. 1540 (2016), the Court granted certiorari to consider the standing of a plaintiff whose credit history was reported on a website in violation of the Fair Credit Reporting Act, 15 U.S.C. § 1681-1681x, in a manner that made the plaintiff appear *more* creditworthy than he in fact was. Following *Edwards*, the Ninth Circuit found standing because "the violation of a statutory right is usually a sufficient injury in fact to confer standing." *Robins v. Spokeo, Inc.*, 742 F.3d 409, 412 (9th Cir. 2014). The Supreme Court, operating with only eight Justices as a result of Justice Scalia's death, vacated and remanded for further analysis of whether the complaint satisfied both the "concreteness" and "particularity" aspects of the standing analysis. The Court did not specifically address the extent of Congress's authority to create rights the violation of which creates injury in fact.

Does the Court in *Lujan* suggest a judicially manageable standard for determining when a statutory violation also gives rise to a "concrete," "*de facto*," "particularized" injury-in-fact? Is the definition of which injuries allow a party to obtain judicial relief better understood as one of the "legislative powers" that Article I grants to Congress? For a skeptical account of judicial efforts to define the type of injuries that parties may vindicate through private litigation, see William A. Fletcher, *The Structure of Standing*, 98 YALE L.J. 221 (1988). On standing to enforce statutory violations, see generally Mark Seidenfeld & Allie Akre, *Standing in the Wake of Statutes*, 57 ARIZ. L. REV. 745 (2015); Cass R. Sunstein, *What's Standing after* Lujan? *Of Citizen Suits, "Injuries," and Article III*, 91 MICH. L. REV. 163 (1992); Samuel Estreicher, *Congressional Power and Constitutional Rights: Reflections on Proposed "Human Life" Legislation*, 68 VA. L. REV. 333 (1982).

10. **Other Limitations on Justiciability: Mootness, the Political Question Doctrine, and Ripeness.** The doctrine of standing is one of several doctrines that seek to ensure that courts do not intrude on matters that the Constitution assigns to other departments of government. The "mootness" doctrine captures the intuition that courts should not adjudicate disputes that no longer present a live case or controversy, even if the dispute satisfied the case-and-controversy requirement when it was filed. *See De Funis v. Odegaard*, 416 U.S. 312 (1974). To determine whether an action is moot, courts examine whether there has been a change in circumstances that removes the controversy that existed at the beginning of the litigation. This can occur, for example, because the dispute has been resolved through other means; an intervening event removes the plaintiff's interest in the controversy; or action by another court or administrative agency gives the plaintiff all the relief sought. The Supreme Court has recognized exceptions to mootness for claims, such as in challenges to restrictive abortion legislation, that are "capable of repetition, yet evading review," and situations where the defendant voluntarily ceases conduct that is allegedly illegal. *Id.* at 318–19.

The "political question" doctrine recognizes that some questions that arise under the Constitution and laws should not be adjudicated by courts because the Constitution contemplates that they will be finally resolved by other branches of government. In the leading modern case, the Supreme Court summarized the doctrine as follows:

> Prominent on the surface of any case held to involve a political question is found a textually demonstrable constitutional commitment of the issue to a coordinate political department; or a lack of judicially discoverable and manageable standards for resolving it; or the impossibility of deciding without an initial policy determination of a kind clearly for nonjudicial discretion; or the impossibility of a court's undertaking independent resolution without expressing lack of the respect due coordinate branches of government; or an unusual need for unquestioning adherence to a political decision already made; or the potentiality of embarrassment from multifarious pronouncements by various departments on one question.

Baker v. Carr, 369 U.S. 186, 217 (1962).

The "ripeness" doctrine involves the *timing* of litigation challenging agency action and informs the availability of "pre-enforcement" challenges—i.e., challenges to an agency regulation or policy that are filed before the regulation or policy is applied in a concrete case. Ripeness can be viewed as a constitutional issue but, as in the decision that follows, it often arises as a question of whether an action can be brought sooner than the specific review procedure set out in the agency's organic statue.

2. Ripeness

Abbott Laboratories v. Gardner

387 U.S. 136 (1967)

Mr. Justice Harlan delivered the opinion of the Court.

In 1962 Congress amended the Federal Food, Drug, and Cosmetic Act (52 Stat. 1040, as amended by the Drug Amendments of 1962, 76 Stat. 780, 21 U.S.C. § 301 et seq.), to require manufacturers of prescription drugs to print the "established name" of the drug "prominently and in type at least half as large as that used thereon for any proprietary name or designation for such drug," on labels and other printed material, § 502(e)(1)(B), 21 U.S.C. § 352(e)(1)(B). The "established name" is one designated by the Secretary of Health, Education, and Welfare pursuant to § 502(e)(2) of the Act, 21 U.S.C. § 352(e)(2); the "proprietary name" is usually a trade name under which a particular drug is marketed. The underlying purpose of the 1962 amendment was to bring to the attention of doctors and patients the fact that many of the drugs sold under familiar trade names are actually identical to drugs sold under their "established" or less familiar trade names at significantly lower prices. The Commissioner of Food and Drugs, exercising authority delegated to him by the Secretary published proposed regulations designed to implement the statute, 28 Fed. Reg. 1448. After inviting and considering comments submitted by interested parties the Commissioner promulgated the following regulation for the "efficient enforcement" of the Act, § 701(a), 21 U.S.C. § 371(a):

> "If the label or labeling of a prescription drug bears a proprietary name or designation for the drug or any ingredient thereof, the established name, if such there be, corresponding to such proprietary name or designation, shall accompany each appearance of such proprietary name or designation." 21 CFR § 1.104(g)(1).

A similar rule was made applicable to advertisements for prescription drugs, 21 CFR § 1.105(b)(1).

The present action was brought by a group of 37 individual drug manufacturers and by the Pharmaceutical Manufacturers Association, of which all the petitioner companies are members, and which includes manufacturers of more than 90% of the Nation's supply of prescription drugs. They challenged the regulations on the ground that the Commissioner exceeded his authority under the statute by promulgating an order requiring labels, advertisements, and other printed matter relating to prescription drugs to designate the established name of the particular drug involved every time its trade name is used anywhere in such material.

The District Court, on cross motions for summary judgment granted the declaratory and injunctive relief sought, finding that the statute did not sweep so broadly as to permit the Commissioner's "every time" interpretation. The Court of Appeals for the Third Circuit reversed without reaching the merits of the case. It held first that under the statutory scheme provided by the Federal Food, Drug, and Cosmetic Act pre-enforcement[1] review of these regulations was unauthorized and therefore beyond the jurisdiction of the District Court. Second, the Court of Appeals held that no "actual case or controversy" existed and, for that reason, that no relief under the Administrative Procedure Act. 5 U.S.C. §§ 701–704 (1964 ed., Supp. II), or under the Declaratory Judgment Act, 28 U.S.C. § 2201, was in any event available.***

I

The first question we consider is whether Congress by the Federal Food, Drug, and Cosmetic Act intended to forbid pre-enforcement review of this sort of regulation promulgated by the Commissioner. The question is phrased in terms of "prohibition" rather than "authorization" because a survey of our cases shows that judicial review of a final agency action by an aggrieved person will not be cut off unless there is persuasive reason to believe that such was the purpose of Congress. Early cases in which this type of judicial review was entertained have been reinforced by the enactment of the Administrative Procedure Act, which embodies the basic presumption of judicial review to one "suffering legal wrong because of agency action, or adversely affected or aggrieved by agency action within the meaning of a relevant statute," 5 U.S.C. § 702, so long as no statute precludes such relief or the action is not one committed by law to agency discretion, 5 U.S.C. § 701(a). The Administrative Procedure Act provides specifically not only for review of "[a]gency action made reviewable by statute" but also for review of "final agency action for which there is no other adequate remedy in a court," 5 U.S.C. § 704. The legislative material elucidating that seminal act manifests a congressional intention that it cover a broad spectrum of administrative actions,[2] and this Court has echoed that theme by noting that the Administrative Procedure Act's "generous review provisions" must be given a "hospitable" interpretation. *Shaughnessy v. Pedreiro*, 349 U.S. 48, 51. [O]nly upon a showing of "clear and convincing evidence" of a contrary legislative intent should the courts restrict access to judicial review. See also Jaffe, Judicial Control of Administrative Action 336–359 (1965).

Given this standard, we are wholly unpersuaded that the statutory scheme in the food and drug area excludes this type of action. The Government relies on no explicit statutory authority for its argument that pre-enforcement review is unavailable,

---

1. That is, a suit brought by one before any attempted enforcement of the statute or regulation against him.

2. *See* H.R. Rep. No. 1980, 79th Cong., 2d Sess., 41 (1946): "To preclude judicial review under this bill a statute, if not specific in withholding such review, must upon its face give clear and convincing evidence of an intent to withhold it. The mere failure to provide specially by statute for judicial review is certainly no evidence of intent to withhold review." *See also* S. Rep. No. 752, 79th Cong., 1st Sess., 26 (1945).

but insists instead that because the statute includes a specific procedure for such review of certain enumerated kinds of regulations, not encompassing those of the kind involved here, other types were necessarily meant to be excluded from any pre-enforcement review.* The issue, however, is not so readily resolved; we must go further and inquire whether in the context of the entire legislative scheme the existence of that circumscribed remedy evinces a congressional purpose to bar agency action not within its purview from judicial review.***

In this case the Government has not demonstrated such a purpose; indeed, a study of the legislative history shows rather conclusively that the specific review provisions were designed to give an additional remedy and not to cut down more traditional channels of review. At the time the Food, Drug, and Cosmetic Act was under consideration, in the late 1930's, the Administrative Procedure Act had not yet been enacted, the Declaratory Judgment Act was in its infancy, and the scope of judicial review of administrative decisions under the equity power was unclear. It was these factors that led to the form the statute ultimately took. There is no evidence at all that members of Congress meant to preclude traditional avenues of judicial relief. Indeed, throughout the consideration of the various bills submitted to deal with this issue, it was recognized that "There is always an appropriate remedy in equity in cases where an

---

* Section 701(b) of the Act, 21 U.S.C. § 371 (1964), provided: "The Secretary of the Treasury and the Secretary of Health, Education, and Welfare shall jointly prescribe regulations for the efficient enforcement of the provisions of section 381 of this title [relating to imports and exports of pharmaceuticals], except as otherwise provided therein." Section 701(e) created an administrative procedure for challenging regulations issued under § 701(b). Section 701(f) provided as follows:

(f) **Review of order.**

(1) In a case of actual controversy as to the validity of any order under subsection (e) of this section, any person who will be adversely affected by such order if placed in effect may at any time prior to the ninetieth day after such order is issued file a petition with the United States court of appeals for the circuit wherein such person resides or has his principal place of business, for a judicial review of such order.***

(2) If the petitioner applies to the court for leave to adduce additional evidence, and shows to the satisfaction of the court that such additional evidence is material and that there were reasonable grounds for the failure to adduce such evidence in the proceeding before the Secretary, the court may order such additional evidence (and evidence in rebuttal thereof) to be taken before the Secretary, and to be adduced upon the hearing, in such manner and upon such terms and conditions as to the court may seem proper. The Secretary may modify his findings as to the facts, or make new findings, by reason of the additional evidence so taken, and he shall file such modified or new findings, and his recommendation, if any, for the modification or setting aside of his original order, with the return of such additional evidence.

(3) Upon the filing of the petition referred to in paragraph (1) of this subsection, the court shall have jurisdiction to affirm the order, or to set it aside in whole or in part, temporarily or permanently.***

(4) The judgment of the court affirming or setting aside, in whole or in part, any such order of the Secretary shall be final, subject to review by the Supreme Court of the United States upon certiorari or certification***.

(5) Any action instituted under this subsection shall survive notwithstanding any change in the person occupying the office of Secretary or any vacancy in such office.

(6) The remedies provided for in this subsection shall be in addition to and not in substitution for any other remedies provided by law.—Eds.

administrative officer has exceeded his authority and there is no adequate remedy of law, . . . [and that] protection is given by the so-called Declaratory Judgments Act . . . ." H.R. Rep. No. 2755, 74th Cong., 2d Sess., 8. It was specifically brought to the attention of Congress that such methods had in fact been used in the food and drug area, and the Department of Justice, in opposing the enactment of the special-review proce- dures of § 701, submitted a memorandum which was read on the floor of the House stating: "As a matter of fact, the entire subsection is really unnecessary, because even without any express provision in the bill for court review, any citizen aggrieved by any order of the Secretary, who contends that the order is invalid, may test the legality of the order by bringing an injunction suit against the Secretary, or the head of the Bureau, under the general equity powers of the court." 83 Cong. Rec. 7892 (1938).

The main issue in contention was whether these methods of review were satisfac- tory.*** The supporters of the special-review section sought to include it in the Act primarily as a method of reviewing agency *factual* determinations. For example, it was argued that the level of tolerance for poisonous sprays on apple crops, which the Sec- retary of Agriculture had recently set, was a factual matter, not reviewable in equity in the absence of a special statutory review procedure. Some congressmen urged that challenge to this type of determination should be in the form of a de novo hearing in a district court, but the Act as it was finally passed compromised the matter by allow- ing an appeal on a record with a "substantial evidence" test, affording a considerably more generous judicial review than the "arbitrary and capricious" test available in the traditional injunctive suit.

A second reason for the special procedure was to provide broader venue to litigants challenging such technical agency determinations. At that time, a suit against the Sec- retary was proper only in the District of Columbia, an advantage that the Govern- ment sought to preserve. The House bill, however, originally authorized review in any district court, but in the face of a Senate bill allowing review only in the District of Columbia, the Conference Committee reached the compromise preserved in the pres- ent statute authorizing review of such agency actions by the courts of appeals.

Against this background we think it quite apparent that the special-review proce- dures provided in § 701(f), applying to regulations embodying technical factual deter- minations, were simply intended to assure adequate judicial review of such agency decisions, and that their enactment does not manifest a congressional purpose to elim- inate judicial review of other kinds of agency action.

This conclusion is strongly buttressed by the fact that the Act itself, in § 701(f)(6), states, "The remedies provided for in this subsection shall be in addition to and not in substitution for any other remedies provided by law."*** The Government deals with the clause by arguing that it should be read as applying only to review of regula- tions under the sections specifically enumerated in § 701(e). This is a conceivable read- ing, but it requires a considerable straining both of language and of common understanding. The saving clause itself contains no limitations, and it requires an artificial statutory construction to read a general grant of a right to judicial review begrudgingly, so as to cut out agency actions that a literal reading would cover.***

The only other argument of the Government requiring attention on the preclusive effect of the statute is that *Ewing v. Mytinger & Casselberry, Inc.*, 339 U.S. 594, counsels a restrictive view of judicial review in the food and drug area. In that case the Food and Drug Administrator found that there was probable cause that a drug was "adulterated" because it was misbranded in such a way as to be "fraudulent" or "misleading to the injury or damage of the purchaser or consumer." § 304(a), 21 U.S.C. § 334(a). Multiple seizures were ordered through libel actions. The manufacturer of the drug brought an action to challenge directly the Administrator's finding of probable cause. This Court held that the owner could raise his constitutional, statutory, and factual claims in the libel actions themselves, and that the mere finding of probable cause by the Administrator could not be challenged in a separate action. That decision was quite clearly correct, but nothing in its reasoning or holding has any bearing on this declaratory judgment action challenging a promulgated regulation.***

The drug manufacturer in *Ewing* was quite obviously seeking an unheard-of form of relief which, if allowed, would have permitted interference in the early stages of an administrative determination as to specific facts, and would have prevented the regular operation of the seizure procedures established by the Act. That the Court refused to permit such an action is hardly authority for cutting off the well-established jurisdiction of the federal courts to hear, in appropriate cases, suits under the Declaratory Judgment Act and the Administrative Procedure Act challenging final agency action of the kind present here.***

II

A further inquiry must, however, be made. The injunctive and declaratory judgment remedies are discretionary, and courts traditionally have been reluctant to apply them to administrative determinations unless these arise in the context of a controversy "ripe" for judicial resolution.*** The problem is best seen in a twofold aspect, requiring us to evaluate both the fitness of the issues for judicial decision and the hardship to the parties of withholding court consideration.

As to the former factor, we believe the issues presented are appropriate for judicial resolution at this time. First, all parties agree that the issue tendered is a purely legal one: whether the statute was properly construed by the Commissioner to require the established name of the drug to be used every time the proprietary name is employed. Both sides moved for summary judgment in the District Court, and no claim is made here that further administrative proceedings are contemplated.***

Second, the regulations in issue we find to be "final agency action" within the meaning of § 10 of the Administrative Procedure Act, 5 U.S.C. § 704, as construed in judicial decisions. An "agency action" includes any "rule," defined by the Act as "an agency statement of general or particular applicability and future effect designed to implement, interpret, or prescribe law or policy," §§ 2(c), 2(g), 5 U.S.C. §§ 551(4), 551(13).

The cases dealing with judicial review of administrative actions have interpreted the "finality" element in a pragmatic way.***

***The regulation challenged here, promulgated in a formal manner after announcement in the Federal Register and consideration of comments by interested parties is quite clearly definitive. There is no hint that this regulation is informal, or only the ruling of a subordinate official, or tentative. It was made effective upon publication, and the Assistant General Counsel for Food and Drugs stated in the District Court that compliance was expected.

The Government argues, however, that the present case can be distinguished from cases like *Frozen Food Express* [*v. United States*, 351 U.S. 40 (1956),] on the ground that in those instances the agency involved could implement its policy directly, while here the Attorney General must authorize criminal and seizure actions for violations of the statute. In the context of this case, we do not find this argument persuasive. These regulations are not meant to advise the Attorney General, but purport to be directly authorized by the statute. Thus, if within the Commissioner's authority, they have the status of law and violations of them carry heavy criminal and civil sanctions. Also, there is no representation that the Attorney General and the Commissioner disagree in this area; the Justice Department is defending this very suit. It would be adherence to a mere technicality to give any credence to this contention. Moreover the agency does have direct authority to enforce this regulation in the context of passing upon applications for clearance of new drugs, § 505, 21 U.S.C. § 355, or certification of certain antibiotics, § 507, 21 U.S.C. § 357.

This is also a case in which the impact of the regulations upon the petitioners is sufficiently direct and immediate as to render the issue appropriate for judicial review at this stage. These regulations purport to give an authoritative interpretation of a statutory provision that has a direct effect on the day-to-day business of all prescription drug companies; its promulgation puts petitioners in a dilemma that it was the very purpose of the Declaratory Judgment Act to ameliorate. As the District Court found on the basis of uncontested allegations[:] "Either they must comply with the every time requirement and incur the costs of changing over their promotional material and labeling or they must follow their present course and risk prosecution." The regulations are clear-cut, and were made effective immediately upon publication; as noted earlier the agency's counsel represented to the District Court that immediate compliance with their terms was expected. If petitioners wish to comply they must change all their labels, advertisements, and promotional materials; they must destroy stocks of printed matter; and they must invest heavily in new printing type and new supplies. The alternative to compliance—continued use of material which they believe in good faith meets the statutory requirements, but which clearly does not meet the regulation of the Commissioner—may be even more costly. That course would risk serious criminal and civil penalties for the unlawful distribution of "misbranded" drugs.

It is relevant at this juncture to recognize that petitioners deal in a sensitive industry, in which public confidence in their drug products is especially important. To require them to challenge these regulations only as a defense to an action brought by the Government might harm them severely and unnecessarily. Where the legal issue presented is fit for judicial resolution, and where a regulation requires an immediate and significant change in the plaintiffs' conduct of their affairs with serious penalties attached to noncompliance, access to the courts under the Administrative Procedure Act and the Declaratory Judgment Act must be permitted, absent a statutory bar or some other unusual circumstance, neither of which appears here.

The Government contends that if the Court allows this consolidated suit, then nothing will prevent a multiplicity of suits in various jurisdictions challenging other regulations. The short answer to this contention is that the courts are well equipped to deal with such eventualities. The venue transfer provision, 28 U.S.C. § 1404(a), may be invoked by the Government to consolidate separate actions. Or, actions in all but one jurisdiction might be stayed pending the conclusion of one proceeding. A court may even in its discretion dismiss a declaratory judgment or injunctive suit if the same issue is pending in litigation elsewhere.***

Further, the declaratory judgment and injunctive remedies are equitable in nature, and other equitable defenses may be interposed. If a multiplicity of suits are undertaken in order to harass the Government or to delay enforcement, relief can be denied on this ground alone. The defense of laches could be asserted if the Government is prejudiced by a delay. And courts may even refuse declaratory relief for the nonjoinder of interested parties who are not, technically speaking, indispensable.

In addition to all these safeguards against what the Government fears, it is important to note that the institution of this type of action does not by itself stay the effectiveness of the challenged regulation. There is nothing in the record to indicate that petitioners have sought to stay enforcement of the "every time" regulation pending judicial review. *See* 5 U.S.C. § 705. If the agency believes that a suit of this type will significantly impede enforcement or will harm the public interest, it need not postpone enforcement of the regulation and may oppose any motion for a judicial stay on the part of those challenging the regulation. It is scarcely to be doubted that a court would refuse to postpone the effective date of an agency action if the Government could show, as it made no effort to do here, that delay would be detrimental to the public health or safety.

Mr. Justice Fortas, with whom The Chief Justice and Mr. Justice Clark join, dissenting.*

The Court has opened Pandora's box. Federal injunctions will now threaten programs of vast importance to the public welfare.***

Since enactment of the Federal Food, Drug, and Cosmetic Act in 1938, the mechanism for judicial review of agency actions under its provisions has been well understood. Except for specific types of agency regulations and actions to which I shall refer, judicial review has been confined to enforcement actions instituted by the Attorney

---

* Justice Fortas's dissent was filed in a companion case to *Abbott Laboratories, Gardner v. Toilet Goods Association, Inc.*, 387 U.S. 167 (1967). — Eds.

General on recommendation of the agency. As the recurrent debate over this technique demonstrates, this restricted avenue for challenge has been deemed necessary because of the direct and urgent relationship of the field of regulation to the public health. It is this avenue that applies with respect to the regulations at issue in the present cases.

The scheme of the Act, in this respect, is as follows: "Prohibited acts" are listed in § 301, 52 Stat. 1042, as amended, 21 U.S.C. § 331. Subsequent sections authorize the Attorney General to institute three types of proceedings. First, under § 302, 52 Stat. 1043, as amended, 21 U.S.C. § 332, he may apply to the district courts of the United States for injunctive relief. If an injunction is violated, jury trial is assured on demand of the accused. Second, under § 304, 52 Stat. 1044, as amended, 21 U.S.C. § 334, the Attorney General may institute libel proceedings in the district courts and seek orders for seizure of any misbranded or adulterated food, drug, device, or cosmetic. Third, criminal prosecution is authorized for violations, but before the Secretary may report a violation to the Attorney General for criminal prosecution, he must afford the affected person an opportunity to present his views. §§ 303, 305, 52 Stat. 1043, 1045, as amended, 21 U.S.C. §§ 333, 335.

The present regulations concededly would be reviewable in the course of any of the above proceedings. Apart from these general provisions, the Act contains specific provisions for administrative hearing and review in the courts of appeals with respect to regulations issued under certain, enumerated provisions of the Act—not including those here involved. These appear in § 701(f) of the Act, 52 Stat. 1055, as amended, 21 U.S.C. § 371(f). Section 701, by subdivision (a), contains the Secretary's general authority, exercised in the present cases, to promulgate "regulations for the efficient enforcement of [the Act]." Subdivisions (e) and (f) provide for public hearings, administrative findings, and judicial review in a court of appeals with respect to those regulations specifically enumerated in subsection (e). The Court agrees that this procedure applies only to the enumerated types of regulations and that the present regulations are unaffected. Then, as to the enumerated regulations which are subject to judicial review—and only as to them—subparagraph (6) of subsection (f) specifies that "[t]he remedies provided for in this subsection shall be in addition to and not in substitution for any other remedies provided by law." This "saving clause" does not apply or refer to regulations other than those enumerated, and the Court's argument to the contrary is inconsistent with the clear wording and placement of the clause.

In evaluating the destructive force and effect of the Court's action in these cases, it is necessary to realize that it is arming each of the federal district judges in this Nation with power to enjoin enforcement of regulations and actions under the federal law designed to protect the people of this Nation against dangerous drugs and cosmetics. Restraining orders and temporary injunctions will suspend application of these public safety laws pending years of litigation—a time schedule which these cases illustrate.[10] They are disruptive enough, regardless of the ultimate outcome. The Court's validation

---

10. The "every time" regulation was published about four years ago, on June 20, 1963, 28 Fed. Reg. 6375. As a result of litigation begun in September of 1963, it has not yet been put into force.***

of this shotgun attack upon this vital law and its administration is not confined to these suits, these regulations, or these plaintiffs—or even this statute. It is a general hunting license; and I respectfully submit, a license for mischief because it authorizes aggression which is richly rewarded by delay in the subjection of private interests to programs which Congress believes to be required in the public interest.***

Where a remedy is provided by statute, I submit that it is and has been fundamental to our law, to judicial administration, to the principle of separation of powers in our Constitution, that the courts will withhold equitable or discretionary remedies unless they conclude that the statutory remedy is inadequate.***

The regulation*** relates to a 1962 amendment to the Act requiring manufacturers of prescription drugs to print on the labels or other printed material, the "established name" of the drug "prominently and in type at least half as large as that used thereon for any proprietary name or designation for such drug." § 502(e)(1), 76 Stat. 790, 21 U.S.C. § 352(e)(1). Obviously, this requires some elucidation, either case-by-case or by general regulation or pronouncement, because the statute does not say that this must be done "every time," or only once on each label or in each pamphlet, or once per panel, etc., or that it must be done differently on labels than on circulars, or doctors' literature than on directions to the patients, etc. This is exactly the traditional purpose and function of an administrative agency. The Commissioner, acting by delegation from the Secretary, took steps to provide for the specification. He invited and considered comments and then issued a regulation requiring that the "established name" appear every time the proprietary name is used. A manufacturer—or other person who violates this regulation—has mislabeled his product. The product may be seized; or injunction may be sought; or the mislabeler may be criminally prosecuted. In any of these actions he may challenge the regulation and obtain a judicial determination.

The Court, however, moved by petitioners' claims as to the expense and inconvenience of compliance and the risks of deferring challenge by noncompliance, decrees that the manufacturers may have their suit for injunction at this time and reverses the Third Circuit. The Court says that this confronts the manufacturer with a "real dilemma." But the fact of the matter is that the dilemma is no more than citizens face in connection with countless statutes and with the rules of the SEC, FTC, FCC, ICC, and other regulatory agencies. This has not heretofore been regarded as a basis for injunctive relief unless Congress has so provided. The overriding fact here is—or should be—that the public interest in avoiding the delay in implementing Congress' program far outweighs the private interest; and that the private interest which has so impressed the Court is no more than that which exists in respect of most regulatory statutes or agency rules.*** The courts cannot properly—and should not—attempt to judge in the abstract and generally whether this regulation is within the statutory scheme. Judgment as to the "every time" regulation should be made only in light of specific situations, and it may differ depending upon whether the FDA seeks to enforce it as to doctors' circulars, pamphlets for patients, labels, etc.***

Mr. Justice Clark, dissenting.

I join my Brother Fortas' dissent. As he points out the regulations here merely require common honesty and fair dealing in the sale of drugs. The pharmaceutical companies, contrary to the public interest, have through their high-sounding trademarks of long-established medicines deceitfully and exorbitantly extorted high prices therefor from the sick and the infirm. Indeed, I was so gouged myself just recently when I purchased some ordinary eyewash drops and later learned that I paid 10 times the price the drops should have cost.***

Notes and Questions

1. **Regulatory and Procedural Posture?** *Abbott Laboratories v. Gardner* and *Gardner v. Toilet Goods Association*, from which Justice Fortas's dissent is taken, were two of three cases on the availability of pre-enforcement judicial review that the Supreme Court decided on May 22, 1967. *See also Toilet Goods Ass'n v. Gardner*, 387 U.S. 158 (1967). *Abbott Labs* involved a Food & Drug Administration (FDA) regulation, known as the "every time" regulation, 28 Fed. Reg. 6375 (1963), that was issued under 1962 amendments to the Federal Food, Drug, and Cosmetic Act. The regulation required prescription drug labels to include the "established" name for name-brand pharmaceuticals. For example, it would have required that the label for Tylenol® identify the drug as acetaminophen. What was the status of the Secretary's regulation at the time the *Abbott Laboratories* case was filed? What process did the Secretary follow in promulgating the regulation? Did the agency engage in notice-and-comment rulemaking? Did pharmaceutical companies have an opportunity to present objections to the proposed regulation at the agency level? What other opportunities did the trade association representing these companies have to challenge the regulation other than the pre-enforcement action they brought?

Abbot challenged the regulation in an action filed under the APA and the Declaratory Judgment Act in the U.S. District Court for the District of New Jersey. What was the basis for the federal court's subject matter jurisdiction? As a strategic matter, why did Abbot file suit there instead of in Washington, D.C., where the Department of Health, Education, and Welfare (FDA's parent Department at the time) was located? What was at issue in the district court litigation? What did the district court conclude with respect to the regulation's validity? What did the Third Circuit conclude?

The *Toilet Goods* cases involved an FDA regulation regulating "diluents" used to color food and cosmetics. The regulation was issued under the Color Additive Amendments to the Food, Drug, and Cosmetics Act, Pub. L. No. 86-618, 74 Stat. 397 (1960). Among other things, the regulation subjected all cosmetics to a regime of pre-market review. The Second Circuit, per Judge Friendly, concluded that an industry association could challenge the lawfulness of the regulation before it was enforced. *Toilet Goods Ass'n v. Gardner*, 360 F.2d 677 (2d Cir. 1966).

2. **The Parties' Positions?** Why did Abbott Laboratories seek judicial review *before* the Secretary's regulation took effect? What harm did it claim it would suffer (if any) if it was required to challenge the validity of the Secretary's regulation in an

action where it was accused of violating the regulation? Why did the government oppose pre-enforcement review? Justice Harlan's opinion for the Court notes the potential that pre-enforcement review will lead to "a multiplicity of suits in various jurisdictions challenging other regulations." Pre-enforcement review might also "harass the Government or [be a means to] delay enforcement." Are Justice Harlan's responses to these concerns convincing?

Justice Fortas's dissent observes that if judicial review is deferred until a regulation is applied in the context of an individual enforcement proceeding, the need for judicial review may disappear entirely. Will this be because the regulation will exert an *in terrorem* effect and never go challenged, because no party is willing to risk being sanctioned for violating it? Is this consideration salient in the case of regulated industries who are repeat players before the agency and can collectivize the costs of opposing agency action, through trade association representation, and think they have a strong case on the merits and benefit, in any event, from delaying a regulation? In assessing the costs and benefits of allowing pre-enforcement review, does the Court draw a distinction between well-resourced regulated industries who are able to share the costs of representation and less well-resourced beneficiaries of regulation? Can such a line be drawn under the statute in question or the APA? For the case in favor of judicial attention to such concerns, see Marc Galanter, *Why the "Haves" Come out Ahead: Speculations on the Limits of Legal Change*, 9 Law & Soc. Rev. 95 (1974).

Justice Fortas was a former general counsel of the Public Works Administration and Under-Secretary of the Interior in the Roosevelt administration, a founding member of the Arnold & Porter firm in Washington, D.C., and one of President Johnson's principal advisors. *See generally* Laura Kalman, Fortas: A Biography (1990). He laments that the Court's decision "arm[s] each of the federal district judges in this Nation with power to enjoin enforcement of regulations and actions under the federal law designed to protect the people of this Nation against dangerous drugs and cosmetics." Is he correct that — without some screening mechanism to coordinate where pre-enforcement challenges may be entertained — regulated industries will engage in blatant forum- and judge-shopping in an attempt to frustrate the implementation of federal regulatory policy? Does the course of the *Abbot Laboratories* and *Toilet Goods* litigation support his position? See footnote 10 to Justice Fortas's dissent. What sort of screening mechanism would you propose?

More broadly, is Justice Fortas right that the Court's tolerance for pre-enforcement review elevates the interests of regulated industries opposing regulation over those whom regulation is intended to protect and the public at large? Should the availability of pre-enforcement review be decided in terms of whose ox is gored, or is it better to approach the issue in terms of articulating the best background rule for legislation: In the absence of express language in the particular statute, when is agency action sufficiently "final" that it makes sense to allow judicial review?

3. **Final vs. Non-Final Agency Action.** Judicial review under the APA is limited to "final" agency action. *See* 5 U.S.C. § 704 ("Agency action made reviewable by statute and *final* agency action for which there is no other adequate remedy in a court are

subject to judicial review."). In contrast, "[a] preliminary, procedural, or intermediate agency action or ruling not directly reviewable is subject to review on the review of the final agency action." *Id.*

The Attorney General's 1947 Manual stated the following with respect to the finality of agency rules:

> Since "agency action" is defined to include "rule", the question arises as to whether the phrase, "final agency action for which there is no other adequate remedy in any court", provides for direct judicial review of all rules. Many statutes which give rule making powers (particularly rules of general applicability) to agencies make no provision for judicial review of such rules. The validity of such rules has generally been open to challenge in proceedings for their enforcement. In addition, it has been suggested that in appropriate circumstances, review could be obtained in proceedings under the Declaratory Judgment Act. It is clear from the legislative history that section 10(c) [5 U.S.C. § 704(c)] was not intended to provide for judicial review in the abstract of all rules.*** [Moreover], the Declaratory Judgments Act does not altogether fit the subject and needs some limitation (not, it may be noted, extension) to care for the determination of fact issues, since under the Declaratory Judgments Act juries determine the facts under instructions from the presiding judge.

U.S. Dep't of Justice, Attorney General's Manual on the on the Administrative Procedure Act 102 (1947).

The Court in *Abbot Laboratories* identifies several situations in which an agency decision will *not* be considered final: when the regulation is "informal, or only the ruling of a subordinate official, or tentative." Why, by contrast, is the regulation at issue in *Abbott Laboratories* considered final? If we look at the regulation standing alone, is it "final" action? How is the regulation "final" if it has no practical effect until it is enforced?

4. **The "Presumption of Reviewability."** The Court's statutory analysis proceeds in two steps. The Court first posits that agency action is presumptively reviewable "because a survey of our cases shows that judicial review of a final agency action by an aggrieved person will not be cut off unless there is persuasive reason to believe that such was the purpose of Congress." Is there an "aggrieved person" in *Abbott Laboratories*? In what sense? Compare the concept of standing, discussed in Section [A] [1], *supra*.

The presumption of reviewability is "reinforced" by two provisions of the APA, the Court maintains. Section 702 creates a cause of action for any person "suffering legal wrong because of agency action, or adversely affected or aggrieved by agency action within the meaning of a relevant statute." Section 704 authorizes the review of "[a]gency action made reviewable by statute and final agency action for which there is no other adequate remedy in a court."

Is the Court correct that these provisions support a presumption that agency action is reviewable pre-enforcement? Recall 5 U.S.C. § 704's limitation of judicial review to "final agency action" and the pre-APA practice, averted to in the Attorney General's Manual, of reviewing the validity of agency action in enforcement proceedings. Even if the provisions reflects Congress's intent that agency action be reviewable *at some point* in time, do they address the availability of *pre-enforcement* review? Does the Court offer persuasive evidence that, in enacting the APA, Congress intended to make agency regulations reviewable *before* they were applied in a specific context? Do any of the materials discussed by the Court support the opposite inference — that Congress intended agency action to be reviewable, but only when a regulated party was threatened with a sanction in a concrete proceeding? For the history of judicial review of agency action in the pre-*Abbott Labs* era, see Thomas W. Merrill, *Article III, Agency Adjudication, and the Origins of the Appellate Review Model of Administrative Law*, 111 COLUM. L. REV. 939 (2011).

Regardless of the accuracy of the Court's claims regarding Congress's intent in the APA, the Court's discussion in *Abbott Laboratories* has become the *locus classicus* for the principle that final agency action is presumptively subject to judicial review; to preclude review, a statute must clearly express Congress's intention to do so. *See, e.g., Board of Governors of Fed. Reserve Sys. v. MCorp Fin., Inc.*, 502 U.S. 32, 44 (1991); *Japan Whaling Ass'n v. Am. Cetacean Soc.*, 478 U.S. 221, 230 (1986); *Block v. Community Nutrition Institute*, 467 U.S. 340, 345 (1984). For a comprehensive criticism of that principle, see Nicholas Bagley, *The Puzzling Presumption of Reviewability*, 127 HARV. L. REV. 1285 (2014).

5. **Statutory Bars to Pre-Enforcement Review.** The second step in the Court's analysis in *Abbott Labs* focuses on the Food, Drug, and Cosmetics Act (FDCA). The Court considers whether anything in the FDCA overcame the presumption of reviewability prior to agency enforcement and concludes that the Act did not preclude such review. Much of the Court's attention is focused on § 705 of the FDCA. Section 705(e) provided that Secretary was to hold public hearings when determining how to regulate specified drugs, and § 705(f) specified a procedure for obtaining pre-enforcement judicial review of the Secretary's actions under § 705(e). Justice Fortas reads these and other provisions allowing for pre-enforcement review as a sign that Congress did not intend to authorize pre-enforcement review of other actions: "the Act contains specific provisions for administrative hearing and review in the courts of appeals with respect to regulations issued under certain, enumerated provisions of the Act." How does the Court respond? Why does the Court not apply the *expressio unius* canon, which teaches that the availability of review for actions under § 705(e) is a signal that Congress, having focused on review of agency action in this statutory scheme, did not intend other actions of the Secretary to be subject to pre-enforcement review? Are the Court's reasons for rejecting the *expressio unius* inference persuasive?

6. Does Pre-Enforcement Review Necessarily Suspend Agency Action? The debate in *Abbott Laboratories* is premised on the assumption that, in some significant fraction of cases where a party seeks pre-enforcement judicial review, the agency or the reviewing court will stay the challenged regulation pending review. Courts traditionally have considered four factors in deciding whether to stay administrative action pending review: "(1) whether the stay applicant has made a strong showing that he is likely to succeed on the merits; (2) whether the applicant will be irreparably injured absent a stay; (3) whether issuance of the stay will substantially injure the other parties interested in the proceeding; and (4) where the public interest lies." *Nken v. Holder*, 556 U.S. 418, 425–26 (2009) (quoting *Hilton v. Braunskill*, 481 U.S. 770, 776 (1987)).

Is it likely that once a petition for review has been filed in the courts, an agency will postpone the effective date of the agency action on its own motion, *see* 5 U.S.C. § 705, or defer enforcement proceedings until the pre-enforcement challenge permitted by *Abbott Laboratories* is resolved? In addition to the scenario illustrated by *Abbott Laboratories*, the problem arises where agency action is self-enforcing, as where, say, the Nuclear Regulatory Commission (NRC) has approved a license for low-power testing of a nuclear power facility. In such circumstances, the testing can proceed without an NRC enforcement action, and the opponent of agency action will likely attempt to convince the reviewing court to stay the agency action. *See, e.g., Cuomo v. U.S. Nuclear Regulatory Comm'n*, 772 F.2d 972 (D.C. Cir. 1985) (per curiam). The problem also arises where the agency does not itself pursue enforcement actions, but sets standards applicable in private actions. *Cf. Perez v. Mortgage Banks Ass'n*, 135 S. Ct. 1199 (2015), *supra* Chapter 4[F].

7. Is the Dispute "Ripe" for Decision? Having established that pre-enforcement review is available as a matter of statutory construction, the *Abbott* Court turns to whether the lower courts should have exercised their discretion to entertain a pre-enforcement challenge to the Secretary's regulation. The Court frames this issue as whether the dispute is "ripe" for adjudication. Ripeness depends on two factors: (1) "the fitness of the issues for judicial decision" and (2) "the hardship to the parties of withholding court consideration." Although *Abbott Labs* does not discuss the legal basis for the ripeness requirement, the Court more recently approached it as a requirement of Article III jurisdiction as well as a self-imposed prudential limitation on the federal courts' power to decide cases and controversies. *National Park Hospitality Ass'n v. Dep't of Interior*, 538 U.S. 803, 808 (2003) ("The ripeness doctrine is drawn both from Article III limitations on judicial power and from prudential reasons for refusing to exercise jurisdiction, but, even in a case raising only prudential concerns, the question of ripeness may be considered on a court's own motion.").

In *National Parks*, the Court concluded that a facial challenge to a National Park Service regulation determining that the Contract Disputes Act of 1978, 92 Stat. 2383, 41 U.S.C. § 601 et seq., did not apply to concession contracts was not ripe, because the regulation was merely an interpretative rule that did not "affect a concessioner's primary conduct." As such, there was no hardship in denying review until the regulation was applied in the context of a concrete dispute. The Court further stated that, except for cases covered by *Abbott Laboratories*, "a regulation is not ordinarily considered the type of agency action 'ripe' for judicial review under the [APA] until the scope of the controversy has been reduced to more manageable proportions, and its factual components fleshed out, by some concrete action applying the regulation to the claimant's situation in a fashion that harms or threatens to harm him." (538 U.S. at 808 (quoting *Lujan v. National Wildlife Federation*, 497 U.S. 871, 891 (1990)).

Why does the Court in *Abbott Labs* conclude that the issues are fit for judicial decision? As the Court indicates, the case involved a purely legal issue. To what extent does the case for judicial review differ when the challenge to agency policy depends on the factual sufficiency of the agency's grounds for acting, *cf. National Ass'n of Mfrs. v. SEC*, 748 F.3d 359, 369 (D.C. Cir. 2014), or the validity of the agency's required cost-benefit analysis, *cf. Business Roundtable v. SEC*, 647 F.3d 1144 (D.C. Cir. 2011)?

Why does the *Abbott Labs* Court conclude that the balance of hardships favors entertaining a pre-enforcement challenge rather than entertaining a challenge to the validity of the regulation in the context of a concrete enforcement proceeding? What hardships would drug manufacturers endure if they were not permitted to bring a pre-enforcement challenge to the Secretary's regulation? The Court says that "[t]o require them to challenge these regulations only as a defense to an action brought by the Government might harm them severely and unnecessarily." How precisely? Is this kind of "harm" something that every actor subject to a new regulatory policy will experience?

In practice, the requirements that agency action be fit for judicial decision and that a party seeking judicial review suffer "hardship" if review is delayed have not been a major obstacle to judicial review of agency action. Indeed, in many pre-enforcement challenges, the government does not argue and the reviewing court does not consider whether the challenge should be heard in the exercise of the reviewing court's discretion. *See, e.g., National Ass'n of Mfrs. v. SEC*, 748 F.3d 359 (D.C. Cir. 2014) (pre-enforcement challenge to SEC "conflict mineral" rule, 77 Fed. Reg. 56,274 (Sept. 12, 2012)); *American Meat Inst. v. U.S. Dep't of Agric.*, 746 F.3d 1065, 1072 (D.C. Cir. 2014) (pre-enforcement challenge to USDA country-of-origin labeling rule, 78 Fed.Reg. 31,367 (May 24, 2013)). *Abbott Laboratories* has thus come to stand for the general proposition that significant regulations may generally be challenged before they are enforced, notwithstanding the limitations on pre-enforcement review that are expressly stated in the *Abbott Labs* decision.

8. **The *Ewing* Case.** The Court in *Abbott Labs* distinguishes *Ewing v. Mytinger & Casselberry, Inc.*, 339 U.S. 594 (1950). In that case, the FDA Administrator instituted multiple libel proceedings in the federal courts to seize shipments of "Nutrilite Food Supplement" that were travelling in interstate commerce. At the time, Section 334 of the Food, Drug, and Cosmetics Act permitted the FDA to bring libel proceedings "when the Administrator has probable cause to believe from facts found, without hearing, by him or any officer or employee of the Agency that the misbranded article is dangerous to health, or that the labeling of the misbranded article is fraudulent, or

would be in a material respect misleading to the injury or damage of the purchaser or consumer." The manufacturer of Nutrilite brought a freestanding lawsuit challenging the Food and Drug Administrator's administrative finding that there was probable cause to believe Nutrilite was misbranded. It sought an injunction prohibiting the FDA from initiating further libel proceedings. The Supreme Court held that the district court was without jurisdiction to entertain the manufacturer's action. The Court reasoned that "[j]udicial review of such a preliminary step in a judicial proceeding is so unique that we are not willing easily to infer that it exists.*** Multiple seizures are the means of protection afforded the public. Consolidation of all the libel suits so that one trial may be had is the relief afforded the distributors of the articles." 339 U.S. at 600, 602.

9. May Congress Require Regulated Parties to Seek Judicial Review Within a Specified Time Frame? As noted in Chapter 3, the Emergency Price Control Act of 1942, Pub. L. No. 77-420, 56 Stat. 23, directed the Office of Price Administration to set maximum prices for commodities trading in interstate commerce during World War II. To do so, the Price Administrator would promulgate regulations fixing prices that "in his judgment [were] generally fair and equitable and [would] effectuate the purposes of this Act." *Id.* § 2(a). Knowing violations of a price regulation were a criminal offense, punishable by a $5,000 fine and two years' imprisonment.

Section 203 of the Act provided that "any person subject to any provision of a regulation or order" was entitled to "file a protest specifically setting forth objections to any such provision and affidavits or other written evidence in support of such objections." A regulated party could file a protest after the sixty day period expired if the grounds for the protest were not apparent until then. If the protest was denied, judicial review was available in the Emergency Court of Appeals, an Article III court created by the Act. Review of the Emergency Court of Appeals' judgments was available in the Supreme Court.

In *Yakus v. United States*, 321 U.S. 414 (1944), *supra* Chapter 3[B][1][a], the Supreme Court concluded that the protest mechanism was meant to be the exclusive avenue for challenging the validity of price regulations promulgated by the Office of Price Administration. The Court further concluded that a criminal defendant who failed to take advantage of the protest mechanism could not defend against prosecution on the ground that the order he violated was invalid. Rejecting the defendants' argument that the exclusive review procedure violated due process, the Court said that the procedure "affords to those affected a reasonable opportunity to be heard and present evidence." Defendants could not complain about being precluded from challenging the regulation, because they "failed to seek the administrative remedy and the statutory review which were open to them." *Id.* at 434.

The Court stressed, however, the extraordinary circumstances in which the act was passed. It was "adopted January 30, 1942, shortly after our declaration of war against Germany and Japan, when it was common knowledge, as is emphasized by the legislative history of the Act, that there was grave danger of wartime inflation and the disorganization of our economy from excessive price rises. Congress was under pressing necessity of meeting this danger by a practicable and expeditious means which would operate with such promptness, regularity and consistency as would minimize the sudden development of commodity price disparities, accentuated by commodity shortages occasioned by the war." *Id.* at 432. Does this suggest a different result for cases in which Congress's use of an exclusive-review scheme is not motivated by a national emergency? Recall the interest balancing framework of *Mathews v. Eldridge*, 424 U.S. 319 (1976), see Note 10 to *Richardson v. Perales*, *supra* Chapter 4[B][1].

10. **Implied Rights of Action to Remedy Statutory Violations.** The Supreme Court's permissive attitude toward judicial review of agency action under the APA contrasts with its willingness to imply private rights of action to remedy violations of federal law. Of course, many statutes expressly create a private action for persons harmed by a violation of the statute. Where a statute establishes substantive standards of conduct but does not create a private right of action in express terms, the Supreme Court uses a four-part test to determine whether one should be implied:

> First, is the plaintiff one of the class for whose especial benefit the statute was enacted — that is, does the statute create a federal right in favor of the plaintiff? Second, is there any indication of legislative intent, explicit or implicit, either to create such a remedy or to deny one? Third, is it consistent with the underlying purposes of the legislative scheme to imply such a remedy for the plaintiff? And finally, is the cause of action one traditionally relegated to state law, in an area basically the concern of the States, so that it would be inappropriate to infer a cause of action based solely on federal law?

Cort v. Ash, 422 U.S. 66, 78 (1975) (citations and internal punctuation omitted). Since *Cort* was decided, the Court has rarely found the test satisfied. *See Cannon v. University of Chicago*, 441 U.S. 677 (1979) (applying *Cort* to find a private right of action to enforce § 901(a) of Title IX of the Education Amendments of 1972, 20 U.S.C. § 1681); *id.* at 731 (Powell, J. dissenting) (criticizing *Cort* as "an open invitation to federal courts to legislate causes of action not authorized by Congress").

On the viability of actions seeking only injunctive relief against state action violating federal law, see *Armstrong v. Exceptional Child Ctr., Inc.*, 135 S. Ct. 1378 (2015). The case involved a dispute over payment for services provided by a Medicaid provider. Under Idaho's Medicaid plan, the state's Department of Health and Welfare reimburses providers of "habilitation services" for covered expenses. Section 30(A) of the Medicaid Act, 42 U.S.C. § 1396a(a)(30)(A), requires Idaho's plan to "assure that payments are consistent with efficiency, economy, and quality of care" while "safeguard[ing] against unnecessary utilization of . . . care and services." Medicaid providers sued Idaho Health and Welfare Department officials, claiming that Idaho reimbursed them at rates lower than what § 30(A) permits, and seeking an injunction directing the officials to increase the reimbursement rates.

In an opinion joined in full by three other Justices, Justice Scalia rejected the argument that the Constitution's Supremacy Clause, Art. VI, cl. 2, created a cause of action that private litigants could invoke to ensure that state officials complied with federal law. He then turned to whether "this suit can proceed against Idaho in equity," and concluded that "the Medicaid Act implicitly precludes private enforcement of § 30(A)." This was because "the sole remedy Congress provided for a State's failure to comply with Medicaid's requirements . . . is the withholding of Medicaid funds by the Secretary of Health and Human Services," and because § 30(A)'s mandate that state plans provide for payments that are "consistent with efficiency, economy, and quality of care" while "safeguard[ing] against unnecessary utilization of . . . care and services" did not supply a judicially manageable rule of decision.

Justice Breyer provided the fifth vote rejecting a private cause of action. He suggested that the case did not turn on the general availability of a cause of action to enforce compliance with federal law under the Supremacy Clause or the federal question statute, 28 U.S.C. § 1331, but on the fact that private civil litigation over reimbursement rates was inconsistent with the statutory scheme in § 30(A). Justice Breyer noted that respondents could ask the federal Department of Health and Human Services (HHS) to promulgate a rule specifying appropriate compensation rates, and that HHS's resolution of that petition would be subject to judicial review under the APA.

For analysis of federal requirements enforced through funding conditions, see Eloise Pasachoff, *Agency Enforcement of Spending Clause Statutes: A Defense of the Funding Cut-Off*, 124 YALE L.J. 248 (2014).

B. Unreviewable Action "Committed to Agency Discretion"

Abbott Laboratories highlights the presumption that final agency action is subject to judicial review, even when a new agency policy has not been applied in the context of a concrete enforcement proceeding. What forms of agency action does this presumption extend to? Does the presumption of reviewability extend to an agency's failure to act, too?

Citizens to Preserve Overton Park, Inc. v. Volpe
401 U.S. 402 (1971)

[Recall from the prior excerpt from this decision in Chapter 4[B][2], that petitioners in *Overton Park* challenged the Secretary of Transportation's decision to route Interstate Highway I-40 through Overton Park in Memphis, Tennessee. Petitioners contended that the decision to route the highway through Overton Park violated § 4(f) of the Department of Transportation Act of 1966, as amended, and § 18(a) of the Federal-Aid Highway Act of 1968, 82 Stat. 823, 23 U.S.C. § 138 (1964 ed., Supp. V). Those statutes prohibited the Secretary of Transportation from authorizing the use of federal funds to finance the construction of highways through public parks if a "feasible and prudent" alternative route existed. If no such route was available, the Secretary was permitted to approve construction of highways in parks on condition that "all possible planning to minimize harm" to the park was performed.]

A threshold question—whether petitioners are entitled to any judicial review—is easily answered. Section 701 of the Administrative Procedure Act, 5 U.S.C. § 701 (1964 ed., Supp. V), provides that the action of "each authority of the Government of the United States," which includes the Department of Transportation, is subject to judicial review except where there is a statutory prohibition on review or where "agency action is committed to agency discretion by law." In this case, there is no indication that Congress sought to prohibit judicial review and there is most certainly no "showing of 'clear and convincing evidence' of a . . . legislative intent" to restrict access to judicial review. *Abbott Laboratories* v. *Gardner*, 387 U.S. 136, 141 (1967).

Similarly, the Secretary's decision here does not fall within the exception for action "committed to agency discretion." This is a very narrow exception. The legislative history of the Administrative Procedure Act indicates that it is applicable in those rare instances where "statutes are drawn in such broad terms that in a given case there is no law to apply." S. Rep. No. 752, 79th Cong., 1st Sess., 26 (1945).

Section 4(f) of the Department of Transportation Act and § 138 of the Federal-Aid Highway Act are clear and specific directives. Both the Department of Transportation Act and the Federal-Aid Highway Act provide that the Secretary "shall not approve any program or project" that requires the use of any public parkland "unless (1) there is no feasible and prudent alternative to the use of such land, and (2) such program includes all possible planning to minimize harm to such park . . . ." 23 U.S.C. § 138 (1964 ed., Supp. V); 49 U.S.C. § 1653(f) (1964 ed., Supp. V). This language is a plain and explicit bar to the use of federal funds for construction of highways through parks—only the most unusual situations are exempted.

Despite the clarity of the statutory language, respondents argue that the Secretary has wide discretion. They recognize that the requirement that there be no "feasible" alternative route admits of little administrative discretion. For this exemption to apply the Secretary must find that as a matter of sound engineering it would not be feasible to build the highway along any other route. Respondents argue, however, that the requirement that there be no other "prudent" route requires the Secretary to engage in a wide-ranging balancing of competing interests. They contend that the Secretary should weigh the detriment resulting from the destruction of parkland against the cost of other routes, safety considerations, and other factors, and determine on the basis of the importance that he attaches to these other factors whether, on balance, alternative feasible routes would be "prudent."

But no such wide-ranging endeavor was intended. It is obvious that in most cases considerations of cost, directness of route, and community disruption will indicate that parkland should be used for highway construction whenever possible. Although it may be necessary to transfer funds from one jurisdiction to another, there will always be a smaller outlay required from the public purse when parkland is used since the public already owns the land and there will be no need to pay for right-of-way. And since people do not live or work in parks, if a highway is built on parkland no one will have to leave his home or give up his business. Such factors are common to substantially all highway construction. Thus, if Congress intended these factors to be on an equal footing with preservation of parkland there would have been no need for the statutes.

Congress clearly did not intend that cost and disruption of the community were to be ignored by the Secretary. But the very existence of the statutes[29] indicates that protection of parkland was to be given paramount importance. The few green havens that are public parks were not to be lost unless there were truly unusual factors present in a particular case or the cost or community disruption resulting from alternative routes reached extraordinary magnitudes. If the statutes are to have any meaning, the Secretary cannot approve the destruction of parkland unless he finds that alternative routes present unique problems.

Plainly, there is "law to apply" and thus the exemption for action "committed to agency discretion" is inapplicable.***

Notes and Questions

1. **Statutory Basis for the Government's Argument?** The government's argument in *Overton Park* invokes 5 U.S.C. § 701(a), which sets out definitions applicable to the chapter of the APA that governs judicial review. It provides:

> (a) This chapter applies, according to the provisions thereof, except to the extent that—
>
> > (1) statutes preclude judicial review; or
> >
> > (2) *agency action is committed to agency discretion by law.*

5 U.S.C. § 701(a) (emphasis added).

2. **"Committed to Agency Discretion"?** Why is the Secretary of Transportation's decision to route I-40 through Overton Park not covered by § 701(a)(1)? After *Abbott Laboratories* and this decision, what must a statute say to trigger the § 701(a)(1) bar on judicial review?

Why is review of the Secretary's decision not barred by § 701(a)(2)? The Court concedes that cost, disruption of the community, and preservation of parkland are all

---

29. The legislative history of both § 4(f) of the Department of Transportation Act, 49 U.S.C. § 1653(f) (1964 ed., Supp. V), and § 138 of the Federal-Aid Highway Act, 23 U.S.C. § 138 (1964 ed., Supp. V), is ambiguous. The legislative committee reports tend to support respondents' view that the statutes are merely general directives to the Secretary requiring him to consider the importance of parkland as well as cost, community disruption, and other factors. See, e. g., S. Rep. No. 1340, 90th Cong., 2d Sess., 19; H.R. Rep. No. 1584, 90th Cong., 2d Sess., 12. Statements by proponents of the statutes as well as the Senate committee report on § 4(f) indicate, however, that the Secretary was to have limited authority. See, e. g., 114 Cong. Rec. 24033–24037; S. Rep. No. 1659, 89th Cong., 2d Sess., 22. See also H.R. Conf. Rep. No. 2236, 89th Cong., 2d Sess., 25. Because of this ambiguity it is clear that we must look primarily to the statutes themselves to find the legislative intent.

relevant to the decision where to route a highway. The Court also concedes that the statutory reference to "feasible and prudent" alternative routes requires the Secretary to exercise discretion in making routing decisions. Why then is the Secretary's decision not one that is "committed to agency discretion by law"? If as the Court concedes the Secretary is entitled to exercise discretion when determining where to route a highway, why is his decision not "agency action*** committed to agency discretion by law"? What function does the Court envision judicial review performing when the underlying agency decision requires the exercise of discretion? (Refer also to the excerpt from *Overton Park* reproduced in Chapter 4[B][2], *supra*.)

3. **"No Law to Apply"?** Quoting the report of Senate Committee on the Judiciary on the APA, the Court states that § 701(a)(2) bars judicial review of agency action only if a statute is "drawn in such broad terms that in a given case there is no law to apply." For cases in which this section has been found to bar review, see, e.g., *Webster v. Doe*, 486 U.S. 592 (1988) (section of National Security Act, 50 U.S.C. § 403(c), authorizing termination of the employment of Central Intelligence Agency employees "when necessary or advisable in interest of United States," held nonreviewable); *Merida Delgado v. Gonzales*, 428 F.3d 916 (10th Cir. 2005) (section of Aviation and Transportation Security Act of 2001, Pub. L. No. 107-71, § 113(a), 115 Stat. 597, that permitted Attorney General to prohibit aliens who presented "an aviation or national security risk" from taking flight training classes; same).

Compare *Dunlop v. Bachowski*, 421 U.S. 560 (1975), which sustained reviewability. A provision of the Labor-Management Reporting and Disclosure Act of 1959 (LMDRA), 29 U.S.C. § 482, requires the Secretary of Labor to investigate complaints of irregularities in union elections. "[I]f he finds probable cause to believe that a violation . . . has occurred and has not been remedied," the Secretary must "bring a civil action against the labor organization as an entity in the district court of the United States." Bachowski filed a complaint with the Secretary of Labor complaining that a February 1973 election to fill a district officer position at the United Steelworkers of America violated the Act. The Secretary conducted an investigation and advised Bachowski that "[b]ased on the investigative findings . . . [a] civil action to set aside the challenged election is not warranted."

On Bachowski's petition for judicial review, the Supreme Court rejected the government's contention that the Secretary's decision was unreviewable because there was no law to apply. The Court surveyed the LMDRA and found no "congressional purpose to prohibit judicial review." While acknowledging that "the statute relies upon the special knowledge and discretion of the Secretary for the determination of both the probable violation and the probable effect," it ruled that "to enable the reviewing court intelligently to review the Secretary's determination [not to bring suit], the Secretary must provide the court and the complaining witness with copies of a statement of reasons supporting his determination." *Id.* at 571. The Court nonetheless rejected the argument that the complaining witness must have the opportunity to challenge the factual findings underpinning the Secretary's determination in an action for judicial review.

In *Mach Mining, LLC v. EEOC*, 135 S. Ct. 1645 (2015), the Court reached a similar conclusion with respect to the Equal Employment Opportunity Commission (EEOC)'s duty to conciliate claims under Title VII of the Civil Rights Act of 1964. The Title VII complaint process generally begins when "a person claiming to be aggrieved" files a charge of an unlawful employment practice with the EEOC or a state agency exercising its powers. 42 U.S.C. § 2000e-5(b). The EEOC is then required to notify the employer of the charge and investigate. If the EEOC finds reasonable cause to believe the employer engaged in an unlawful practice, it must "endeavor to eliminate [the] alleged unlawful employment practice by informal methods of conference, conciliation, and persuasion." § 2000e-5(b).

The Court in *Mach Mining* concluded that EEOC's compliance with this requirement was subject to judicial review. Relying on statutory provisions that protected the confidentiality of conciliation efforts and granted the EEOC discretion over the kind of conciliation efforts to pursue, the Court concluded, however, that the scope of review was narrow:

> The statute demands*** that the EEOC communicate in some way (through "conference, conciliation, and persuasion") about an "alleged unlawful employment practice" in an "endeavor" to achieve an employer's voluntary compliance. § 2000e-5(b). That means the EEOC must inform the employer about the specific allegation, as the Commission typically does in a letter announcing its determination of "reasonable cause." Such notice properly describes both what the employer has done and which employees (or what class of employees) have suffered as a result. And the EEOC must try to engage the employer in some form of discussion (whether written or oral), so as to give the employer an opportunity to remedy the allegedly discriminatory practice.***

> A sworn affidavit from the EEOC stating that it has performed the obligations noted above but that its efforts have failed will usually suffice to show that it has met the conciliation requirement. If, however, the employer provides credible evidence of its own, in the form of an affidavit or otherwise, indicating that the EEOC did not provide the requisite information about the charge or attempt to engage in a discussion about conciliating the claim, a court must conduct the factfinding necessary to decide that limited dispute.

Id. at 1656.

4. Is Unreviewable Agency Action Constitutional? Does the Court's interpretation of § 701 in *Overton Park* reflect an unstated premise that agency action *must* be subject to judicial review to be compatible with the Constitution? This idea is sometimes invoked in support of the "presumption of reviewability" thought to have been established by *Abbott Laboratories. See* Thomas W. Merrill, *Delegation and Judicial Review*, 33 Harv. J.L. & Pub. Pol'y 73 (2010). If agency action *must* be subject to judicial review, what is the constitutional basis for the requirement? Does it follow from structural concerns? Due process? *Cf. Crowell v. Benson*, 285 U.S. 22, 87–88 (1932)

(Brandeis, J., dissenting) ("[U]nder certain circumstances, the constitutional require-ment of due process is a requirement of judicial process.").

In *Clapper v. Amnesty International*, 133 S. Ct. 1138 (2013), the Supreme Court con-sidered whether journalists and human rights activists had standing under Article III to bring a constitutional challenge to § 702 of the Foreign Intelligence Surveillance Act of 1978 (FISA), 50 U.S.C. § 1881a (2006 ed., Supp. V), as amended by the Foreign Intelligence Surveillance Amendment Act of 2008, Pub. L. No. 110-261, 122 Stat. 2436. Amended § 702 created "a new framework under which the Government may seek the [Foreign Intelligence Surveillance Court's] authorization of certain foreign intel-ligence surveillance targeting the communications of non-U.S. persons located abroad. Unlike traditional FISA surveillance, § 1881a does not require the Government to demonstrate probable cause that the target of the electronic surveillance is a foreign power or agent of a foreign power." Rather, the amended section permits the govern-ment to collect certain electronic communications upon making a showing that, inter alia, its systems are reasonably designed to avoid collecting communications from U.S. persons. The Second Circuit found standing based on the fact that the respondents would incur expenses to avoid having their communications monitored. *Amnesty Int'l USA v. Clapper*, 638 F.3d 118 (2d Cir. 2011).

The Supreme Court concluded, by a 5-4 vote, that respondents' fear of being tar-geted for surveillance was too speculative to establish constitutional standing. The Court emphasized, however, that "our holding today by no means insulates § [702] from judicial review." This was because decisions of the Foreign Intelligence Surveil-lance Court (FISC) and Foreign Intelligence Court of Review provided an avenue for judicial review; the constitutionality of § 702 would arise in criminal prosecutions in which the government used evidence collected under § 702; and telecommunica-tions companies could challenge certain "collection" orders under a separate FISA provision. Note that the FISC is an unusual tribunal. Established in 1978 by the Foreign Intelligence Surveillance Act, 50 U.S.C. § 1801 et seq., the court is comprised of eleven federal judges who are designated by the Chief Justice of the United States and sit for seven-year terms. Most of the Court's work is conducted ex parte in response to requests by the government for approval of electronic surveillance. *See generally* David S. Kris, *Modernizing the Foreign Intelligence Surveillance Act* (Brook-ing Inst. Working Paper, Nov. 15, 2007).

In *ACLU v. Clapper*, 785 F.3d 787 (2015), the Second Circuit considered a facial challenge to "the bulk telephone metadata collection program*** under which the National Security Agency ('NSA') collects in bulk 'on an ongoing daily basis' the metadata associated with telephone calls made by and to Americans, and aggregates those metadata into a repository or data bank that can later be queried." Like the plaintiffs in *Amnesty International*, the *ACLU* plaintiffs' basic complaint was that the NSA was engaged in unlawful surveillance of American's phone calls and electronic communications. In contrast to *Amnesty International*, plaintiffs in *ACLU* could demonstrate that their personal information—specifically, "details about telephone calls, including, for example, the length of a call, the phone number from which the call was made, and the phone number called"—had been collected by the NSA. Relying on a secret order of the FISC revealed by Edward Snowden, plaintiffs averred that each of the major U.S. phone companies was required "to produce call detail records, every day, on all telephone calls made through its systems or using its services where one or both ends of the call are located in the United States."

The Second Circuit distinguished *Amnesty International* on the ground that the plaintiffs had shown more than a speculative risk of harm: "[T]he government's own orders demonstrate that [plaintiffs'] call records are indeed among those collected as part of the telephone metadata program." The government argued "that any alleged injuries here depend on the government's reviewing the information collected, and that [plaintiffs] have not shown anything more than a 'speculative prospect that their telephone numbers would ever be used as a selector to query, or be included in the results of queries of, the telephony metadata.'" But the mere collection of the telephone data was an injury that conferred Article III standing. The data was "seized," as a Fourth Amendment matter, when it was stored in a government database.

On the merits, the Second Circuit ruled that bulk collection of telephone metadata was not authorized by § 215 of the PATRIOT Act, Pub. L. No. 107-56, 115 Stat. 272 (2001), as reauthorized. Three weeks after the Second Circuit issued its decision, on June 1, 2015, the current version of § 215 expired. On June 2, Congress enacted and President Obama signed the USA Freedom Act, Pub. L. No. 114-23. The Act temporarily reauthorized the metadata collection program for 180 days, following which it prohibited large-scale bulk collection of call metadata. On June 29, the Foreign Intelligence Surveillance Court issued an order authorizing the government to resume bulk collection of telephone metadata during the 180-day reauthorization period. *In re Application of the Federal Bureau of Investigation for an Order Requiring the Production of Tangible Things*, No. B.R. 15–75 (F.I.S.C. June 29, 2015).

APA § 551 defines "agency action" to include "failure to act." Section 706 directs reviewing courts to "compel agency action unlawfully withheld or unreasonably delayed." Does it follow that an agency's decision not to pursue a violation of a statute it is charged with administering is subject to judicial review?

Heckler v. Chaney

470 U.S. 821 (1985)

JUSTICE REHNQUIST delivered the opinion of the Court.***

I

Respondents have been sentenced to death by lethal injection of drugs under the laws of the States of Oklahoma and Texas. Those States, and several others, have recently adopted this method for carrying out the capital sentence. Respondents first petitioned the [Food and Drug Administration (FDA)], claiming that the drugs used by the States for this purpose, although approved by the FDA for the medical purposes stated on their labels, were not approved for use in human executions. They alleged that the drugs had not been tested for the purpose for which they were to be used, and that, given that the drugs would likely be administered by untrained personnel, it was also likely that the drugs would not induce the quick and painless death intended. They urged that use of these drugs for human execution was the "unapproved use of an approved drug" and constituted a violation of the Act's prohibitions against "misbranding."[1] They also suggested that the [Food, Drug, and Cosmetic Act, 52 Stat. 1040, as amended, 21 U.S.C. § 301 et seq. (FDCA)] requirements for approval of "new drugs" applied, since these drugs were now being used for a new purpose. Accordingly, respondents claimed that the FDA was required to approve the drugs as "safe and effective" for human execution before they could be distributed in interstate commerce. *See* 21 U.S.C. § 355. They therefore requested the FDA to take various investigatory and enforcement actions to prevent these perceived violations; they requested the FDA to affix warnings to the labels of all the drugs stating that they were unapproved and unsafe for human execution, to send statements to the drug manufacturers and prison administrators stating that the drugs should not be so used, and to adopt procedures for seizing the drugs from state prisons and to recommend the prosecution of all those in the chain of distribution who knowingly distribute or purchase the drugs with intent to use them for human execution.

The FDA Commissioner responded, refusing to take the requested actions. The Commissioner first detailed his disagreement with respondents' understanding of the scope of FDA jurisdiction over the unapproved use of approved drugs for human execution, concluding that FDA jurisdiction in the area was generally unclear but in any event should not be exercised to interfere with this particular aspect of state criminal justice systems. He went on to state:

> "Were FDA clearly to have jurisdiction in the area, moreover, we believe we would be authorized to decline to exercise it under our inherent discretion to decline to pursue certain enforcement matters. The unapproved use of approved drugs is an area in which the case law is far from uniform. Generally, enforcement proceedings in this area are initiated only when there is a serious danger to the public health or a blatant scheme to defraud. We cannot conclude that those dangers are present under State lethal injection laws, which are duly authorized statutory enactments in furtherance of proper State functions. . . ."

Respondents then filed the instant suit in the United States District Court for the District of Columbia, claiming the same violations of the FDCA and asking that the FDA be required to take the same enforcement actions requested in the prior petition. Jurisdiction was grounded in the general federal-question jurisdiction statute, 28 U.S.C. § 1331, and review of the agency action was sought under the judicial review provisions of the APA, 5 U.S.C. §§ 701–706. The District Court granted summary

---

1. *See* 21 U.S.C. § 352(f): "A drug or device shall be deemed to be misbranded . . . [u]nless its labeling bears (1) adequate directions for use . . . ."

judgment for petitioner.*** A divided panel of the Court of Appeals for the District of Columbia Circuit reversed.***

II

The Court of Appeals' decision addressed three questions: (1) Whether the FDA had jurisdiction to undertake the enforcement actions requested, (2) whether if it did have jurisdiction its refusal to take those actions was subject to judicial review, and (3) whether if reviewable its refusal was arbitrary, capricious, or an abuse of discretion. In reaching our conclusion that the Court of Appeals was wrong, however, we need not and do not address the thorny question of the FDA's jurisdiction. For us, this case turns on the important question of the extent to which determinations by the FDA not to exercise its enforcement authority over the use of drugs in interstate commerce may be judicially reviewed. That decision in turn involves the construction of two separate but necessarily interrelated statutes, the APA and the FDCA.

The APA's comprehensive provisions for judicial review of "agency actions" are contained in 5 U.S.C. §§ 701–706. Any person "adversely affected or aggrieved" by agency action, see § 702, including a "failure to act," is entitled to "judicial review thereof," as long as the action is a "final agency action for which there is no other adequate remedy in a court," see § 704. The standards to be applied on review are governed by the provisions of § 706. But before any review at all may be had, a party must first clear the hurdle of § 701(a). That section provides that the chapter on judicial review "applies, according to the provisions thereof, except to the extent that — (1) statutes preclude judicial review; or (2) agency action is committed to agency discretion by law." Petitioner urges that the decision of the FDA to refuse enforcement is an action "committed to agency discretion by law" under § 701(a)(2).

This Court has not had occasion to interpret this second exception in § 701(a) in any great detail. On its face, the section does not obviously lend itself to any particular construction; indeed, one might wonder what difference exists between §(a)(1) and §(a)(2). The former section seems easy in application; it requires construction of the substantive statute involved to determine whether Congress intended to preclude judicial review of certain decisions.*** But one could read the language "committed to agency discretion by law" in §(a)(2) to require a similar inquiry. In addition, commentators have pointed out that construction of §(a)(2) is further complicated by the tension between a literal reading of §(a)(2), which exempts from judicial review those decisions committed to agency "discretion," and the primary scope of review prescribed by § 706(2)(A) — whether the agency's action was "arbitrary, capricious, or an abuse of discretion." How is it, they ask, that an action committed to agency discretion can be unreviewable and yet courts still can review agency actions for abuse of that discretion? See 5 K. Davis, Administrative Law § 28:6 (1984) (hereafter Davis); Berger, Administrative Arbitrariness and Judicial Review, 65 Colum. L. Rev. 55, 58 (1965). The APA's legislative history provides little help on this score. Mindful, however, of the common-sense principle of statutory construction that sections of a statute generally should be read "to give effect, if possible, to every clause . . . ," we think there is a proper construction of § (a)(2) which satisfies each of these concerns.

This Court first discussed § (a)(2) in *Citizens to Preserve Overton Park v. Volpe*, 401 U.S. 402 (1971).*** [We initially] addressed the "threshold question" of whether the agency's action was at all reviewable. After setting out the language of § 701(a), the Court stated:

> "In this case, there is no indication that Congress sought to prohibit judicial review and there is most certainly no 'showing of 'clear and convincing evidence' of a . . . legislative intent' to restrict access to judicial review. *Abbott Laboratories v. Gardner*, 387 U.S. 136, 141 (1967). . . .
>
> "Similarly, the Secretary's decision here does not fall within the exception for action 'committed to agency discretion.' This is a very narrow exception. . . . The legislative history of the Administrative Procedure Act indicates that it is applicable in those rare instances where 'statutes are drawn in such broad terms that in a given case there is no law to apply.' S. Rep. No. 752, 79th Cong., 1st Sess., 26 (1945)."

The above quote answers several of the questions raised by the language of § 701(a), although it raises others. First, it clearly separates the exception provided by § (a)(1) from the § (a)(2) exception. The former applies when Congress has expressed an intent to preclude judicial review. The latter applies in different circumstances; even where Congress has not affirmatively precluded review, review is not to be had if the statute is drawn so that a court would have no meaningful standard against which to judge the agency's exercise of discretion. In such a case, the statute ("law") can be taken to have "committed" the decisionmaking to the agency's judgment absolutely. This construction avoids conflict with the "abuse of discretion" standard of review in § 706 — if no judicially manageable standards are available for judging how and when an agency should exercise its discretion, then it is impossible to evaluate agency action for "abuse of discretion." In addition, this construction satisfies the principle of statutory construction mentioned earlier, by identifying a separate class of cases to which § 701(a)(2) applies.

To this point our analysis does not differ significantly from that of the Court of Appeals. That court purported to apply the "no law to apply" standard of *Overton Park*. We disagree, however, with that court's insistence that the "narrow construction" of § (a)(2) required application of a presumption of reviewability even to an agency's decision not to undertake certain enforcement actions.***

Overton Park did not involve an agency's refusal to take requested enforcement action. It involved an affirmative act of approval under a statute that set clear guidelines for determining when such approval should be given. Refusals to take enforcement steps generally involve precisely the opposite situation, and in that situation we think the presumption is that judicial review is not available.***

The reasons for this general unsuitability are many. First, an agency decision not to enforce often involves a complicated balancing of a number of factors which are peculiarly within its expertise. Thus, the agency must not only assess whether a violation has occurred, but whether agency resources are best spent on this violation or another, whether the agency is likely to succeed if it acts, whether the particular enforcement action requested best fits the agency's overall policies, and, indeed, whether the agency has enough resources to undertake the action at all. An agency generally cannot act against each technical violation of the statute it is charged with enforcing. The agency is far better equipped than the courts to deal with the many variables involved in the proper ordering of its priorities. Similar concerns animate the principles of administrative law that courts generally will defer to an agency's construction of the statute it is charged with implementing, and to the procedures it adopts for implementing that statute. *See Vermont Yankee Nuclear Power Corp. v. Natural Resources Defense Council, Inc.*, 435 U.S. 519, 543 (1978).

In addition to these administrative concerns, we note that when an agency refuses to act it generally does not exercise its coercive power over an individual's liberty or property rights, and thus does not infringe upon areas that courts often are called upon to protect. Similarly, when an agency does act to enforce, that action itself provides a focus for judicial review, inasmuch as the agency must have exercised its power in some manner. The action at least can be reviewed to determine whether the agency exceeded its statutory powers. Finally, we recognize that an agency's refusal to institute proceedings shares to some extent the characteristics of the decision of a prosecutor in the Executive Branch not to indict—a decision which has long been regarded as the special province of the Executive Branch, inasmuch as it is the Executive who is charged by the Constitution to "take Care that the Laws be faithfully executed." U.S. Const., Art. II, § 3.

We of course only list the above concerns to facilitate understanding of our conclusion that an agency's decision not to take enforcement action should be presumed immune from judicial review under § 701(a)(2). For good reasons, such a decision has traditionally been "committed to agency discretion," and we believe that the Congress enacting the APA did not intend to alter that tradition. In so stating, we emphasize that the decision is only presumptively unreviewable; the presumption may be rebutted where the substantive statute has provided guidelines for the agency to follow in exercising its enforcement powers.[4] Thus, in establishing this presumption in the APA, Congress did not set agencies free to disregard legislative direction in the statutory scheme that the agency administers. Congress may limit an agency's exercise of enforcement power if it wishes, either by setting substantive priorities, or by

---

4. We do not have in this case a refusal by the agency to institute proceedings based solely on the belief that it lacks jurisdiction. Nor do we have a situation where it could justifiably be found that the agency has "consciously and expressly adopted a general policy" that is so extreme as to amount to an abdication of its statutory responsibilities. See, *e.g., Adams v. Richardson*, 480 F.2d 1159 (1973) (en banc). Although we express no opinion on whether such decisions would be unreviewable under § 701(a)(2), we note that in those situations the statute conferring authority on the agency might indicate that such decisions were not "committed to agency discretion."

otherwise circumscribing an agency's power to discriminate among issues or cases it will pursue.***

III

To enforce the various substantive prohibitions contained in the FDCA, the Act provides for injunctions, 21 U.S.C. § 332, criminal sanctions, §§ 333 and 335, and seizure of any offending food, drug, or cosmetic article, § 334. The Act's general provision for enforcement, § 372, provides only that "[t]he Secretary is *authorized* to conduct examinations and investigations . . ." (emphasis added). Unlike the statute at issue in *Dunlop* [*v. Bachowski*, 421 U.S. 560 (1975)], § 332 gives no indication of when an injunction should be sought, and § 334, providing for seizures, is framed in the permissive—the offending food, drug, or cosmetic "shall be liable to be proceeded against." The section on criminal sanctions states baldly that any person who violates the Act's substantive prohibitions "shall be imprisoned . . . or fined." Respondents argue that this statement mandates criminal prosecution of every violator of the Act but they adduce no indication in case law or legislative history that such was Congress' intention in using this language, which is commonly found in the criminal provisions of Title 18 of the United States Code. See, e. g., 18 U.S.C. § 471 (counterfeiting); 18 U.S.C. § 1001 (false statements to Government officials); 18 U.S.C. § 1341 (mail fraud). We are unwilling to attribute such a sweeping meaning to this language, particularly since the Act charges the Secretary only with recommending prosecution; any criminal prosecutions must be instituted by the Attorney General. The Act's enforcement provisions thus commit complete discretion to the Secretary to decide how and when they should be exercised.***

Respondents' [most substantial counter-argument is] based upon § 306 of the FDCA***. That section provides:

> "Nothing in this chapter shall be construed as requiring the Secretary to report for prosecution, or for the institution of libel or injunction proceedings, minor violations of this chapter whenever he believes that the public interest will be adequately served by a suitable written notice or ruling." 21 U.S.C. § 336.

Respondents seek to draw from this section the negative implication that the Secretary is required to report for prosecution all "major" violations of the Act, however those might be defined, and that it therefore supplies the needed indication of an intent to limit agency enforcement discretion. We think that this section simply does not give rise to the negative implication which respondents seek to draw from it. The section is not addressed to agency proceedings designed to discover the existence of violations, but applies only to a situation where a violation has already been established to the satisfaction of the agency. We do not believe the section speaks to the criteria which shall be used by the agency for investigating possible violations of the Act.

IV

We therefore conclude that the presumption that agency decisions not to institute proceedings are unreviewable under 5 U.S.C. § 701(a)(2) is not overcome by the enforcement provisions of the FDCA.*** No colorable claim is made in this case that the agency's refusal to institute proceedings violated any constitutional rights of respondents, and we do not address the issue that would be raised in such a case. The fact that the drugs involved in this case are ultimately to be used in imposing the death penalty must not lead this Court or other courts to import profound differences of opinion over the meaning of the Eighth Amendment to the United States Constitution into the domain of administrative law.***

JUSTICE BRENNAN, concurring.

[T]he Court properly does not decide today that nonenforcement decisions are unreviewable in cases where (1) an agency flatly claims that it has no statutory jurisdiction to reach certain conduct; (2) an agency engages in a pattern of nonenforcement of clear statutory language***; (3) an agency has refused to enforce a regulation lawfully promulgated and still in effect;[1] or (4) a nonenforcement decision violates constitutional rights. It is possible to imagine other nonenforcement decisions made for entirely illegitimate reasons, for example, nonenforcement in return for a bribe, judicial review of which would not be foreclosed by the nonreviewability presumption. It may be presumed that Congress does not intend administrative agencies, agents of Congress' own creation, to ignore clear jurisdictional, regulatory, statutory, or constitutional commands, and in some circumstances including those listed above the statutes or regulations at issue may well provide "law to apply" under 5 U.S.C. § 701(a)(2). Individual, isolated nonenforcement decisions, however, must be made by hundreds of agencies each day. It is entirely permissible to presume that Congress has not intended courts to review such mundane matters, absent either some indication of congressional intent to the contrary or proof of circumstances such as those set out above.***

JUSTICE MARSHALL, concurring in the judgment.

When a statute does not mandate full enforcement, I agree with the Court that an agency is generally "far better equipped than the courts to deal with the many variables involved in the proper ordering of its priorities." As long as the agency is choosing how to allocate finite enforcement resources, the agency's choice will be entitled to substantial deference, for the choice among valid alternative enforcement policies is precisely the sort of choice over which agencies generally have been left substantial discretion by their enabling statutes. On the merits, then, a decision not to enforce that is based on valid resource-allocation decisions will generally not be "arbitrary, capricious, an abuse of discretion, or otherwise not in accordance with law," 5 U.S.C. § 706(2)(A). The decision in this case is no exception to this principle.

The problem of agency refusal to act is one of the pressing problems of the modern administrative state, given the enormous powers, for both good and ill, that agency inaction, like agency action, holds over citizens. As *Dunlop v. Bachowski*, 421 U.S. 560 (1975), recognized, the problems and dangers of agency inaction are too important,

---

1. Cf. *Motor Vehicle Manufacturers Assn. v. State Farm Mutual Ins. Co.*, 463 U.S. 29, 40–44 (1983) (failure to revoke lawfully a previously promulgated rule is reviewable under the APA).

too prevalent, and too multifaceted to admit of a single facile solution under which "enforcement" decisions are "presumptively unreviewable." Over time, I believe the approach announced today will come to be understood, not as mandating that courts cover their eyes and their reasoning power when asked to review an agency's failure to act, but as recognizing that courts must approach the substantive task of reviewing such failures with appropriate deference to an agency's legitimate need to set policy through the allocation of scarce budgetary and enforcement resources. Because the Court's approach, if taken literally, would take the courts out of the role of reviewing agency inaction in far too many cases, I join only the judgment today.

Notes and Questions

1. **Regulatory and Procedural Posture?** As footnote 1 of the opinion for the Court notes, the Food, Drug, and Cosmetics Act (FDCA) provides that "[a] drug or device shall be deemed to be misbranded*** [u]nless its labeling bears (1) adequate directions for use***." 21 U.S.C. § 352(f). "An interested person may petition the Commissioner to issue, amend, or revoke a regulation or order, or to take or refrain from taking any other form of administrative action." 21 C.F.R. § 10.25. Where a petition points out new information or risks that are not addressed in a drug's existing labeling, the agency may require the manufacturer to take corrective action. *See, e.g., Reckis v. Johnson & Johnson*, 28 N.E.3d 445 (Mass. 2015) (describing successful petition to require makers of children's ibuprofen to amplify warnings about risks of a rare skin disorder triggered by use of ibuprofen). Petitioners contended drugs used in lethal injections were misbranded because they were distributed without adequate instructions for their use and petitioned the Food and Drug Administration (FDA) to initiate enforcement proceedings against states that used such drugs. Does the petitioners' complaint allege a serious violation of the FDCA? Are persons sentenced to death within the "zone of interests" protected by the FDCA? Before answering "no," consider that drugs used by veterinarians to euthanize animals are subject to FDA regulation. *See* Food & Drug Administration, Compliance Policy Guide § 650.100: Animal Drugs for Euthanasia (1995).

Which provisions of the APA did petitioners invoke in seeking judicial review of the FDA's decision not to initiate enforcement proceedings? Was the FDA's decision an exercise of formal or informal rulemaking? Formal or informal adjudication? If the decision been subject to review, which of the standards of review in APA § 706 would have been applicable?

2. **The Court's Analysis: Failure to Act vs. Decision Not to Enforce?** The Court begins its analysis of whether the FDA's decision not to initiate enforcement proceedings can be reviewed by offering a gloss on sections 701(a)(1) and 701(a)(2) of the APA. Section 701(a)(1) provides that "[t]his chapter [governing judicial review] applies*** except to the extent that*** statutes preclude judicial review." In the Court's view, when does this section apply? Section 701(a)(2) exempts from judicial review "agency action*** committed to agency discretion by law." When in the

Court's view does this section apply? What difference is there between the coverage of § 701(a)(1) and § 702(a)(2)?

The Court then distinguishes between "an affirmative act of approval under a statute that sets clear guidelines for determining when such approval should be given" and "an agency's refusal to take requested enforcement action." Where the former kind of action is presumed to be reviewable under *Overton Park*, the latter is not. The Court observes that decisions not to enforce "often involve[] a complicated balancing of a number of factors which are peculiarly within its expertise." Isn't this true of much action agency? Consider the EPA's decision to recognize the plant-wide "bubble" concept in *Chevron USA, Inc. v. NRDC*, Chapter 4[E], *supra*. Didn't that decision involve a "complicated balancing" of environmental, legal, administrative, and political concerns?

The Court next observes that the decision not to prosecute "implicates property and liberty interests, whereas a mere failure to act does not." Is the Court correct? Isn't there a significant liberty interest at stake in FDA's decision not to regulate lethal injection drugs?

In any event, why is an impact on property or liberty interests determinative of the availability of judicial review? Recall Justice Fortas's argument in *Abbott Laboratories* that courts should take into account the interests of those who benefit from regulation and the public, as well as the interests of regulated parties. Insofar as judicial review seeks to ensure that agency action is exercised consistently with law, is there any reason to single out affirmative agency regulation for scrutiny? The Court says that when an agency acts, "that action itself provides a focus for judicial review." Is a requisite "focus" missing when, as Justice Marshall notes, "requests for administrative enforcement typically seek to prevent concrete and future injuries that Congress has made cognizable — injuries that result, for example, from misbranded drugs, such as alleged in this case, or unsafe nuclear powerplants — or to obtain palpable benefits that Congress has intended to bestow — such as labor union elections free of corruption"?

Finally, the Court notes that "an agency's refusal to institute proceedings shares to some extent the characteristics of the decision of a prosecutor in the Executive Branch not to indict — a decision which has long been regarded as the special province of the Executive Branch, inasmuch as it is the Executive who is charged by the Constitution to 'take Care that the Laws be faithfully executed.'" Is the analogy sound?

APA § 551(13) provides that "'agency action' includes the whole or a part of an agency rule, order, license, sanction, relief, or the equivalent or denial thereof, or *failure to act*" (emphasis added). Section 706(1) in turn authorizes reviewing courts to "compel agency action unlawfully withheld or unreasonably delayed." How can this APA provision be squared with the Court's recognition in *Heckler* of a presumption of non-reviewability of agency refusals to act? Compare *Overton Park*'s analysis of the exception to reviewability for action "committed to agency discretion" where there is "no law to apply."

3. **Presumptive Non-Reviewability of FDA Enforcement Decisions?** The Court in *Heckler* emphasizes that agency non-enforcement decisions are only presumptively non-reviewable: "Congress may limit an agency's exercise of enforcement power if it wishes, either by setting substantive priorities, or by otherwise circumscribing an agency's power to discriminate among issues or cases it will pursue." Why does the Court conclude that Congress has not limited the FDA's enforcement discretion in this manner in the FDCA?

4. **What Overcomes the *Heckler* Presumption that Agency Non-Enforcement Decisions Are Not Reviewable?** Justice Brennan's concurrence highlights four situations in which the decision not to initiate an enforcement proceeding is (in his view) subject to judicial review notwithstanding *Heckler*: (1) when an agency disclaims jurisdiction to reach a particular category of action; (2) when the agency engages in a "pattern of nonenforcement"; (3) when the agency acts in violation of its own regulation; and (4) when the decision to not enforce violates a constitutional right.

What is the theory behind the first and second exceptions? As to the third, note the connection between the availability of judicial review and *United States ex rel. Accardi v. Shaughnessy*, 347 U.S. 260 (1954), discussed in the Note on Rulemaking's Consequences for Adjudication in Chapter 4[D], *supra* p. 470. *Accardi* holds that, having promulgated a regulation, an agency must comply with it until the regulation is validly repealed or modified.

5. **Statutory Guidelines or Controls on the Exercise of Enforcement Discretion?** The *Heckler* Court recognizes that legislation may establish limits on an agency's choice to prosecute, or decline to prosecute, particular categories of action. For example, a statute might provide that violations satisfying specified objective criteria must be prosecuted; that interested parties may petition the agency to begin enforcement proceedings and that the resulting decisions will be subject to judicial review; or that all violations of a particular provision that are brought to the agency's attention must be prosecuted. *See generally* Richard B. Stewart & Cass Sunstein, *Public Programs and Private Rights*, 95 HARV. L. REV. 1193 (1982).

In a section of the *Heckler* opinion not reproduced above, the Court wrote that *Dunlop v. Bachowski*, 421 U.S. 560 (1975), discussed in Note 3 following *Citizens to Preserve Overton Park*, *supra* p. 545, "present[ed] an example of statutory language which supplied sufficient standards to rebut the presumption of unreviewability.*** The statute being administered quite clearly withdrew discretion from the agency and provided guidelines for exercise of its enforcement power." 470 U.S. at 834–35.

In *Massachusetts v. EPA*, 549 U.S. 497 (2007), the Court considered whether the EPA's denial of a citizen petition asking the agency to promulgate regulations governing greenhouse gases released from motor vehicles was subject to judicial review. Section 202(a)(1) of the Clean Air Act provides:

The [EPA] Administrator shall by regulation prescribe (and from time to time revise) in accordance with the provisions of this section, standards

> applicable to the emission of any air pollutant from any class or classes of
> new motor vehicles or new motor vehicle engines, which in his judgment
> cause, or contribute to, air pollution which may reasonably be anticipated
> to endanger public health or welfare.

42 U.S.C. § 7521(a)(1). The Act's citizen-suit provision states that "any person may commence a civil action . . . against the Administrator where there is alleged a failure of the Administrator to perform any act or duty under this chapter which is not discretionary with the Administrator." 42 U.S.C. § 7604(a)(2).

In denying the petition for rulemaking, EPA determined that it lacked authority under § 202 to regulate greenhouse gases. EPA further maintained that, assuming it had authority to regulate greenhouse gas emissions from motor vehicles, it would decline to do so in the exercise of its discretion. The EPA explained this decision by citing a purported lack of scientific consensus on whether greenhouse gases contribute to global warming. It also stated that the regulation of greenhouse gases was such a serious problem that regulatory efforts should be led by the White House and Congress, not the agency.

The Supreme Court found statutory jurisdiction to review EPA's denial of the rulemaking petition and distinguished *Heckler*. It reasoned:

> In contrast to nonenforcement decisions, agency refusals to initiate rulemaking
> "are less frequent, more apt to involve legal as opposed to factual analysis,
> and subject to special formalities, including a public explanation." They
> moreover arise out of denials of petitions for rulemaking which (at least in
> the circumstances here) the affected party had an undoubted procedural right
> to file in the first instance. Refusals to promulgate rules are thus susceptible
> to judicial review, though such review is "extremely limited" and "highly
> deferential."

549 U.S. at 527–28 (citation omitted).

6. *Heckler* **and the Obama "Deferred Action" Initiatives.** In January 2010, Secretary of Homeland Security Janet Napolitano announced a program known as Deferred Action for Childhood Arrivals (DACA). *See generally* Dep't of Homeland Security, Deferred Action for Childhood Arrivals, http://web.archive.org/web/20170119172353 /https://www.dhs.gov/deferred-action-childhood-arrivals. Her memorandum announcing the program explained that, as an exercise of DHS's enforcement discretion under the immigration laws, "certain young people who were brought to this country as children and know only this country as home" were entitled to "deferred action" that temporarily exempted them from being removed from the United States. Individuals who were not in removal proceedings who submitted to a background check could formalize their status as beneficiaries of deferred action. *See* Memorandum from Janet Napolitano, Exercising Prosecutorial Discretion with Respect to Individuals who Came to the United States as Children, June 15, 2012, available at http://www .dhs.gov/xlibrary/assets/s1-exercising-prosecutorial-discretion-individuals-who -came-to-us-as-children.pdf.

President Obama in November 2014 announced an expansion of the DACA program to include parents of U.S. citizens and lawful permanent residents who lacked lawful immigration status. *See* Note 5 following *Perez v. Mortgage Bankers Ass'n, supra* Chapter 4[F], p. 502. Under this program—known as Deferred Action for Parents of Americans and Lawful Permanent Residents (DAPA)—qualifying individuals could apply for a three-year deferral of their removal and authorization to work in the United States. A contemporaneous memorandum issued by DHS Secretary Jeh Johnson explained that DACA beneficiaries would be eligible for three-year deferrals, and could also apply for work authorization. Like the Napolitano memo, the Johnson memo presented DAPA as an exercise of DHS's prosecutorial discretion. See Memorandum from Jeh Charles Johnson, Nov. 20, 2014.

Following the President's announcement, Texas and twenty-five other states brought suit under the APA challenging DAPA's legality. On February 16, 2015, a judge of the U.S. District Court for the Southern District of Texas issued a nationwide preliminary injunction enjoining DHS from implementing the program. *Texas v. United States*, 2015 U.S. Dist. LEXIS 45482 (S.D. Tex. Feb. 16, 2015).

On appeal from the district court's injunction, the Fifth Circuit held, by a 2-1 vote, that Texas had Article III standing because it would be required under federal law to issue driver's licenses to DAPA beneficiaries and would incur costs of $130.89 for each license it issued. *Texas v. United States*, 809 F.3d 134 (5th Cir. 2015). The appellate court ruled that DAPA was subject to judicial review despite *Heckler*. How is this case distinguishable from *Heckler*, if at all? The court of appeals stated that "If 500,000 unlawfully present aliens residing in Texas were reclassified as lawfully present pursuant to DAPA, they would become eligible for driver's licenses at a subsidized fee. Congress did not intend to make immune from judicial review an agency action that reclassifies millions of illegal aliens. . . ." *Id.* at 165. *See generally* Adam B. Cox & Cristina M. Rodríguez, *The President and Immigration Law Redux*, 125 YALE L.J. 104 (2015).

On the merits, the Fifth Circuit determined that Texas was likely to prevail on its claim that DAPA was a substantive regulation that could only be promulgated through notice-and-comment under 5 U.S.C. § 553, not a memorandum directing DHS personnel how to process requests for deferred action. *See* Note 5 following *Perez v. Mortgage Bankers Ass'n, supra* Chapter 4[F], p. 502. On June 23, 2016, the Supreme Court affirmed the court of appeals' decision by an equally-divided vote. *United States v. Texas*, 136 S. Ct. 2271 (2016).

C. Review of Final Agency Action

Assuming that there is final agency action that does not fall within a bar on judicial review, the question becomes *how* judicial review is performed, not whether it is available. In approaching that question, it is helpful to keep in mind the policymaking form an agency made use of in the action under review (rulemaking or adjudication, formal or informal) and the provision of APA § 706 that the reviewing court is applying. We begin with the standard § 706 proscribes for review of factual findings: "substantial evidence."

1. Findings of Fact

Universal Camera Corp. v. NLRB

340 U.S. 474 (1951)

Mr. Justice Frankfurter delivered the opinion of the Court.

The essential issue raised by this case*** is the effect of the Administrative Procedure Act and the legislation colloquially known as the Taft-Hartley Act [Pub. L. No. 80-101, 61 Stat. 136 (1947)] on the duty of Courts of Appeals when called upon to review orders of the National Labor Relations Board.

The Court of Appeals for the Second Circuit granted enforcement of an order directing, in the main, that petitioner reinstate with back pay an employee found to have been discharged because he gave testimony under the Wagner Act and cease and desist from discriminating against any employee who files charges or gives testimony under that Act.***

I

The Wagner Act provided: "The findings of the Board as to the facts, if supported by evidence, shall be conclusive." Act of July 5, 1935, § 10(e), 49 Stat. 449, 454, 29 U.S.C. § 160(e). This Court read "evidence" to mean "substantial evidence," *Washington, V. & M. Coach Co. v. Labor Board*, 301 U.S. 142, and we said that "[s]ubstantial evidence is more than a mere scintilla. It means such relevant evidence as a reasonable mind might accept as adequate to support conclusion." *Consolidated Edison Co. v. Labor Board*, 305 U.S. 197, 229. Accordingly, it "must do more than create a suspicion of the existence of the fact to be established. . . . [I]t must be enough to justify, if the trial were to a jury, a refusal to direct a verdict when the conclusion sought to be drawn from it is one of fact for the jury."

The very smoothness of the "substantial evidence" formula as the standard for reviewing the evidentiary validity of the Board's findings established its currency. But the inevitably variant applications of the standard to conflicting evidence soon brought contrariety of views and in due course bred criticism. Even though the whole record may have been canvassed in order to determine whether the evidentiary foundation of a determination by the Board was "substantial," the phrasing of this Court's process of review readily lent itself to the notion that it was enough that the evidence supporting the Board's result was "substantial" when considered by itself.***

Criticism of so contracted a reviewing power reinforced dissatisfaction felt in various quarters with the Board's administration of the Wagner Act in the years preceding the war. The scheme of the Act was attacked as an inherently unfair fusion of the functions of prosecutor and judge. Accusations of partisan bias were not wanting. The "irresponsible admission and weighing of hearsay, opinion, and emotional speculation in place of factual evidence" was said to be a "serious menace." No doubt some, perhaps even much, of the criticism was baseless and some surely was reckless. What is here relevant, however, is the climate of opinion thereby generated and its effect on Congress. Protests against "shocking injustices" and intimations of judicial "abdication" with which some courts granted enforcement of the Board's orders stimulated pressures for legislative relief from alleged administrative excesses.

The strength of these pressures was reflected in the passage in 1940 of the Walter-Logan Bill.* It was vetoed by President Roosevelt, partly because it imposed unduly rigid limitations on the administrative process, and partly because of the investigation into the actual operation of the administrative process then being conducted by an experienced committee appointed by the Attorney General. It is worth noting that despite its aim to tighten control over administrative determinations of fact, the Walter-Logan Bill contented itself with the conventional formula that an agency's decision could be set aside if "the findings of fact are not supported by substantial evidence."

The final report of the Attorney General's Committee was submitted in January, 1941. The majority concluded that "[d]issatisfaction with the existing standards as to the scope of judicial review derives largely from dissatisfaction with the fact-finding procedures now employed by the administrative bodies." Departure from the "substantial evidence" test, it thought, would either create unnecessary uncertainty or transfer to courts the responsibility for ascertaining and assaying matters the significance of which lies outside judicial competence. Accordingly, it recommended against legislation embodying a general scheme of judicial review.

Three members of the Committee registered a dissent. Their view was that the "present system or lack of system of judicial review" led to inconsistency and uncertainty. They reported that under a "prevalent" interpretation of the "substantial evidence" rule "if what is called 'substantial evidence' is found anywhere in the record to support conclusions of fact, the courts are said to be obliged to sustain the decision without reference to how heavily the countervailing evidence may preponderate — unless indeed the stage of arbitrary decision is reached. Under this interpretation, the courts need to read only one side of the case and, if they find any evidence there, the administrative action is to be sustained and the record to the contrary is to be ignored."***

One is tempted to say "uncritical" because the legislative history of that Act hardly speaks with that clarity of purpose which Congress supposedly furnishes courts in order to enable them to enforce its true will. On the one hand, the sponsors of the legislation indicated that they were reaffirming the prevailing "substantial evidence" test. But with equal clarity they expressed disapproval of the manner in which the courts were applying their own standard. The committee reports of both houses refer to the

---

* As noted in Chapter 4[A], *supra*, the Walter-Logan bill was introduced prior to the bill that became the Administrative Procedure Act, and incorporated recommendations from the American Bar Association's committee on administrative practice. — Eds.

practice of agencies to rely upon "suspicion, surmise, implications, or plainly incredible evidence," and indicate that courts are to exact higher standards "in the exercise of their independent judgment" and on consideration of "the whole record."

Similar dissatisfaction with too restricted application of the "substantial evidence" test is reflected in the legislative history of the Taft-Hartley Act. The bill as reported to the House provided that the "findings of the Board as to the facts shall be conclusive unless it is made to appear to the satisfaction of the court either (1) that the findings of fact are against the manifest weight of the evidence, or (2) that the findings of fact are not supported by substantial evidence." The bill left the House with this provision. Early committee prints in the Senate provided for review by "weight of the evidence" or "clearly erroneous" standards. But, as the Senate Committee Report relates, "it was finally decided to conform the statute to the corresponding section of the Administrative Procedure Act where the substantial evidence test prevails. In order to clarify any ambiguity in that statute, however, the committee inserted the words 'questions of fact, if supported by substantial evidence on the record considered as a whole . . . .'"

This phraseology was adopted by the Senate. The House conferees agreed.*** The Senate version became the law.

It is fair to say that in all this Congress expressed a mood.*** From the legislative story we have summarized, two concrete conclusions do emerge. One is the identity of aim of the Administrative Procedure Act and the Taft-Hartley Act regarding the proof with which the Labor Board must support a decision. The other is that now Congress has left no room for doubt as to the kind of scrutiny which a Court of Appeals must give the record before the Board to satisfy itself that the Board's order rests on adequate proof.

It would be mischievous word-playing to find that the scope of review under the Taft-Hartley Act is any different from that under the Administrative Procedure Act. The Senate Committee which reported the review clause of the Taft-Hartley Act expressly indicated that the two standards were to conform in this regard, and the wording of the two Acts is for purposes of judicial administration identical. And so we hold that the standard of proof specifically required of the Labor Board by the Taft-Hartley Act is the same as that to be exacted by courts reviewing every administrative action subject to the Administrative Procedure Act.*** The substantiality of evidence must take into account whatever in the record fairly detracts from its weight. This is clearly the significance of the requirement in both statutes that courts consider the whole record.***

To be sure, the requirement for canvassing "the whole record" in order to ascertain substantiality does not furnish a calculus of value by which a reviewing court can assess the evidence. Nor was it intended to negative the function of the Labor Board as one of those agencies presumably equipped or informed by experience to deal with a specialized field of knowledge, whose findings within that field carry the authority of an expertness which courts do not possess and therefore must respect. Nor does it mean that even as to matters not requiring expertise a court may displace the Board's choice between two fairly conflicting views, even though the court would justifiably have made a different choice had the matter been before it *de novo*. Congress has merely made it clear that a reviewing court is not barred from setting aside a Board decision when it cannot conscientiously find that the evidence supporting that decision is substantial, when viewed in the light that the record in its entirety furnishes, including the body of evidence opposed to the Board's view.

[T]he Administrative Procedure Act and the Taft-Hartley Act direct that courts must now assume more responsibility for the reasonableness and fairness of Labor Board decisions than some courts have shown in the past. Reviewing courts must be influenced by a feeling that they are not to abdicate the conventional judicial function. Congress has imposed on them responsibility for assuring that the Board keeps within reasonable grounds. That responsibility is not less real because it is limited to enforcing the requirement that evidence appear substantial when viewed, on the record as a whole, by courts invested with the authority and enjoying the prestige of the Courts of Appeals. The Board's findings are entitled to respect; but they must nonetheless be set aside when the record before a Court of Appeals clearly precludes the Board's decision from being justified by a fair estimate of the worth of the testimony of witnesses or its informed judgment on matters within its special competence or both.

II***

The decision of the Court of Appeals is assailed on two grounds. It is said (1) that the court erred in holding that it was barred from taking into account the report of the examiner on questions of fact insofar as that report was rejected by the Board, and (2) that the Board's order was not supported by substantial evidence on the record considered as a whole, even apart from the validity of the court's refusal to consider the rejected portions of the examiner's report.

The latter contention is easily met.*** [I]t is clear from the court's opinion in this case that it in fact did consider the "record as a whole," and did not deem itself merely the judicial echo of the Board's conclusion. The testimony of the company's witnesses was inconsistent, and there was clear evidence that the complaining employee had been discharged by an officer who was at one time influenced against him because of his appearance at the Board hearing. On such a record we could not say that it would be error to grant enforcement.

The first contention, however, raises serious questions to which we now turn.

III

***Section 10 (c) of the Labor Management Relations Act provides that "if upon the preponderance of the testimony taken the Board shall be of the opinion that any person named in the complaint has engaged in or is engaging in any such unfair labor practice, then the Board shall state its findings of fact . . . ." 61 Stat. 147, 29 U.S.C. (Supp. III) § 160(c). The responsibility for decision thus placed on the Board is wholly inconsistent with the notion that it has power to reverse an examiner's findings only when they are "clearly erroneous." Such a limitation would make so drastic a departure from prior administrative practice that explicitness would be required.

The Court of Appeals concluded from this premise "that, although the Board would be wrong in totally disregarding his findings, it is practically impossible for a court, upon review of those findings which the Board itself substitutes, to consider the Board's reversal as a factor in the court's own decision. This we say, because we cannot find any middle ground between doing that and treating such a reversal as error, whenever it would be such, if done by a judge to a master in equity." Much as we respect the logical acumen of the Chief Judge of the Court of Appeals,* we do not find ourselves pinioned between the horns of his dilemma.

We are aware that to give the examiner's findings less finality than a master's and yet entitle them to consideration in striking the account, is to introduce another and an unruly factor into the judgmatical process of review. But we ought not to fashion an exclusionary rule merely to reduce the number of imponderables to be considered by reviewing courts.

The Taft-Hartley Act provides that "The findings of the Board with respect to questions of fact if supported by substantial evidence on the record considered as a whole shall be conclusive." 61 Stat. 148, 29 U.S.C. (Supp. III) § 160(e). Surely an examiner's report is as much a part of the record as the complaint or the testimony. According to the Administrative Procedure Act, "All decisions (including initial, recommended, or tentative decisions) shall become a part of the record . . . ." § 8(b), 60 Stat. 242, 5 U.S.C. § 1007(b). We found that this Act's provision for judicial review has the same meaning as that in the Taft-Hartley Act. The similarity of the two statutes in language and purpose also requires that the definition of "record" found in the Administrative Procedure Act be construed to be applicable as well to the term "record" as used in the Taft-Hartley Act.

It is therefore difficult to escape the conclusion that the plain language of the statutes directs a reviewing court to determine the substantiality of evidence on the record including the examiner's report.***

We do not require that the examiner's findings be given more weight than in reason and in the light of judicial experience they deserve. The "substantial evidence" standard is not modified in any way when the Board and its examiner disagree. We intend only to recognize that evidence supporting a conclusion may be less substantial when an impartial, experienced examiner who has observed the witnesses and lived with the case has drawn conclusions different from the Board's than when he has reached the same conclusion. The findings of the examiner are to be considered along with the consistency and inherent probability of testimony. The significance of his report, of course, depends largely on the importance of credibility in the particular case. To give it this significance does not seem to us materially more difficult than to heed the other factors which in sum determine whether evidence is "substantial."

---

* Learned Hand—Eds.

We therefore remand the cause to the Court of Appeals. On reconsideration of the record it should accord the findings of the trial examiner the relevance that they reasonably command in answering the comprehensive question whether the evidence supporting the Board's order is substantial. But the court need not limit its reexamination of the case to the effect of that report on its decision. We leave it free to grant or deny enforcement as it thinks the principles expressed in this opinion dictate.***

MR. JUSTICE BLACK and MR. JUSTICE DOUGLAS concur with parts I and II of this opinion but as to part III agree with the opinion of the court below, 179 F.2d 749, 753.

Notes and Questions

1. **Regulatory and Procedural Posture?** As we have seen, the Wagner Act, ch. 372, 49 Stat. 449 (1935), and Taft-Hartley Act, Pub. L. No. 80-101, 61 Stat. 136 (1947) (collectively known as the National Labor Relations Act or NLRA), are the major framework statutes governing labor-management relations in the United States. The NLRA created the National Labor Relations Board (NLRB) and charged it with prosecuting and adjudicating claims of unfair labor practices. 29 U.S.C. § 160(a). Among those practices is an employer's act of retaliation against an employee for exercising rights protected by the NLRA, including the giving of testimony to the NLRB. *See* NLRA § 8(a)(4), 29 U.S.C. § 158(a)(4).

At issue in *Universal Camera* was the Board's finding that Universal Camera retaliated against an employee, Imre Chairman, for giving testimony to the agency in violation of § 8(a). 179 F.2d 749, 750 (2d Cir. 1950). The specific question for the Supreme Court was whether the agency's findings were supported by "substantial evidence on the record considered as a whole," as required by NLRA § 10(e), 29 U.S.C. § 160(e).

2. **Substantial Basis in Evidence vs. Substantial Evidence on the Record as a Whole?** Justice Frankfurter's opinion observes that the substantial evidence standard originated in Supreme Court decisions applying the Wagner Act's instruction that courts were to review decisions of the Board to ensure that they were supported by "evidence." The Court in these prior decisions read "evidence" to mean "substantial evidence." In *Universal Camera*, the Court considered the effect of the 1947 Taft-Hartley amendment which required (in § 10(e)) that the Board's "findings with respect to question of fact" be supported by "substantial evidence on the record considered as a whole . . . ." What was the problem Congress was attempting to address by this amendment? When would looking at the entire record as opposed to the evidence that supported the Board's decision make a difference?

3. **"Historical" or "Adjudicative" vs. "Legislative" Facts?** Does the scope of judicial review change when a court is reviewing an agency finding involving a general social or historical condition (a so-called "legislative" fact) as opposed to the specific controversy before the agency (an "adjudicative" fact)? *See* Note 4 to *Portland Cement Ass'n v. Ruckelshaus, supra* Chapter 4[C], p. 433. In *NLRB v. United Insurance Co.*, 390 U.S. 254 (1968), which appears below, the Supreme Court vacillates on the standard of review applicable to an agency's application of law to fact. While suggesting that the legal import of facts found by the agency is a pure question of law, subject to review

de novo, the Court also says that the agency's view should prevail if it represents a "choice between two fairly conflicting views." *Id.* at 260.

Should courts take the same deferential approach when reviewing agency decisions that rest on the agency's view of legislative facts? To what extent does the APA speak to the issue? What are the costs and benefits of *de novo* court review? Of deferring to the agency when the issue could be resolved in more than one way? In *Zamora v. Immigration & Naturalization Serv.*, 534 F.2d 1055 (2d Cir. 1976), the Second Circuit considered what weight to give to letters the State Department submitted to Immigration Judges (IJs) that (1) described general conditions in the home countries of petitioners seeking asylum and (2) made non-binding recommendations about the disposition of petitioners' applications for asylum. The court stated, per Friendly, J., that "[t]he attitude of the country of prospective deportation toward various types of former residents is a question of legislative fact, on which the safeguards of confrontation and cross-examination are not required and on which the IJ needs all the help he can get." In contrast, the State Department's views on individual petitioners' eligibility for asylum were not entitled to deference—from either the IJ or the courts—because the adjudication of specific cases was the responsibility of the IJ and the Board of Immigration Appeals. *See also American Airlines, Inc. v. Civilian Aeronautics Boards*, 359 F.2d 624, 626 (D.C. Cir. 1966) (Leventhal, J.) (rejecting argument that Civilian Aeronautics Board was required to use trial-type procedures to determine industry-wide conditions in air cargo industry; agency proceedings, including the opportunity to submit data and argument, "gave the parties [the] opportunity to persuade and enlighten the Board").

4. **The Role of ALJs?** Unfair labor practice charges are initially adjudicated by an Administrative Law Judge (ALJ), who, at the time of the Court's decision in *Universal Camera*, was referred to as a "trial examiner." 61 Stat. 140. The ALJ prepares "a proposed report, together with a recommended order," 29 U.S.C. § 160(c), that sets forth findings of fact and conclusions of law. After it receives the ALJ's report, the Board is free to accept, modify, or reject it. The Board's decision is the final action of the agency. *Id. See also* 5 U.S.C. § 557(b) (providing generally that "[w]hen the [ALJ] makes an initial decision, that decision then becomes the decision of the agency without further proceedings unless there is an appeal to, or review on motion of, the agency within time provided by rule").

The Second Circuit in the decision on review in *Universal Camera* concluded that the fact that the full Board rejected the ALJ's proposed findings of fact had no effect on the scope of judicial review of the Board's decision. "We hold that, although the Board would be wrong in totally disregarding his findings, it is practically impossible for a court, upon review of those findings which the Board itself substitutes, to consider the Board's reversal as a factor in the court's own decision. This we say, because we cannot find any middle ground between doing that and treating such a reversal as error, whenever it would be such, if done by a judge to a master in equity." 179 F.2d at 753.

Why does the Supreme Court reject the Second Circuit's position? What, in the Supreme Court's view, is the relevance of the Board's rejection of the examiner's findings? What if the findings are based on credibility assessments? Even if the Board is the statutory decisionmaker, not the ALJ, how can the Board make reasonable credibility assessments if it is not present at the hearing where evidence is taken? If, for example, the ALJ credits testimony by supervisors that the employee engaged in a heated dispute on the day he was discharged, is the Board to accept that finding in determining whether the employee was fired because of his conduct or because he had previously given testimony to the agency? Is the Board also required to accept that the ALJ's determination that the employee was fired because of that conduct?

On remand, the Second Circuit accepted the trial examiner's finding that the employee's dismissal was not in retaliation for his having given testimony to the NLRB. Accordingly, the Court did not enforce the Board's order. 190 F.2d 429 (1951). Concurring, Judge Jerome Frank (a former SEC chairman under President Roosevelt and proponent of legal realism) offered the following gloss (*id.* at 432) on what the Supreme Court decided in *Universal Camera*:

> An examiner's finding binds the Board only to the extent that it is a "testimonial inference," or "primary inference," *i.e.*, an inference that a fact to which a witness orally testified is an actual fact because that witness so testified and because observation of the witness induces a belief in that testimony. The Board, however, is not bound by the examiner's "secondary inferences," or "derivative inferences," *i.e.*, facts to which no witness orally testified but which the examiner inferred from facts orally testified by witnesses whom the examiner believed. The Board may reach its own "secondary inferences," and we must abide by them unless they are irrational; in that way, the Board differs from a trial judge (in a juryless case) who hears and sees the witnesses, for, although we are usually bound by his "testimonial inferences," we need not accept his "secondary inferences" even if rational, but, where other rational "secondary inferences" are possible, we may substitute our own. Since that is true, it is also true that we must not interfere when the Board adopts either (1) its examiner's "testimonial inferences" and they are not absurd, or (2) his rational "secondary inferences."

2. Application of Law to Fact

Questions of law, including the substantive reach of a statute, are for the *de novo* consideration of the court (subject to whatever deference is owed the agency's views under *Chevron U.S.A., Inc. v. NRDC*, Section [C][3], *infra*, and subsequent cases). Questions of historical adjudicative fact—who did or said what to whom, when, where, why and how—are for the plenary consideration of the agency (although they must be grounded in substantial evidence in the record considered as a whole). When the question is whether the agency has properly applied the law to the facts, the inquiry is twofold: (1) whether the agency has applied the proper legal principles, and

(2) whether its application of those principles to the facts is grounded in substantial evidence. Consider the Supreme Court's attempts to deal with agency application of law in the following two cases.

NLRB v. United Insurance Co. of America

390 U.S. 254 (1968)

MR. JUSTICE BLACK delivered the opinion of the Court.

In its insurance operations respondent United Insurance Company uses "debit agents" whose primary functions are collecting premiums from policyholders, preventing the lapsing of policies, and selling such new insurance as time allows. The Insurance Workers International Union, having won a certification election, seeks to represent the debit agents, and the question before us is whether these agents are "employees" who are protected by the National Labor Relations Act or "independent contractors" who are expressly exempted from the Act.[1] Respondent company refused to recognize the Union, claiming that its debit agents were independent contractors rather than employees. In the ensuing unfair labor practice proceeding the National Labor Relations Board held that these agents were employees and ordered the company to bargain collectively with the Union. On appeal the Court of Appeals found that the debit agents were independent contractors and refused to enforce the Board's order.***

At the outset the critical issue is what standard or standards should be applied in differentiating "employee" from "independent contractor" as those terms are used in the Act. Initially this Court held in *NLRB v. Hearst Publications*, 322 U.S. 111, that "Whether . . . the term 'employee' includes [particular] workers . . . must be answered primarily from the history, terms and purposes of the legislation." Thus the standard was one of economic and policy considerations within the labor field. Congressional reaction to this construction of the Act was adverse and Congress passed an amendment specifically excluding "any individual having the status of an independent contractor" from the definition of "employee" contained in § 2(3) of the Act. The obvious purpose of this amendment was to have the Board and the courts apply general agency principles in distinguishing between employees and independent contractors under the Act. And both petitioners and respondents agree that the proper standard here is the law of agency. Thus there is no doubt that we should apply the common-law agency test here in distinguishing an employee from an independent contractor.

Since agency principles are to be applied, some factual background showing the relationship between the debit agents and respondent company is necessary. These basic facts are stated in the Board's opinion and will be very briefly summarized here. Respondent has district offices in most States which are run by a manager who usually has several assistant managers under him. Each assistant manager has a staff of four or five debit agents, and the total number of such agents connected with

---

1. The National Labor Relations Act, as amended (61 Stat. 136, 73 Stat. 519, 29 U.S.C. § 151 et seq.), protects an "employee" only and specifically excludes "any individual having the status of an independent contractor." (§ 2(3).)

respondent company is approximately 3,300. New agents are hired by district managers, after interviews; they need have no prior experience and are assigned to a district office under the supervision of an assistant district manager. Once he is hired, a debit agent is issued a debit book which contains the names and addresses of the company's existing policyholders in a relatively concentrated geographic area. This book is company property and must be returned to the company upon termination of the agent's service. The main job of the debit agents is to collect premiums from the policyholders listed in this book. They also try to prevent the lapsing of policies and sell new insurance when time allows. The company compensates the agents as agreed to in the "Agent's Commission Plan" under which the agent retains 20% of his weekly premium collections on industrial insurance and 10% from holders of ordinary life, and 50% of the first year's premiums on new ordinary life insurance sold by him. The company plan also provides for bonuses and other fringe benefits for the debit agents, including a vacation-with-pay plan and participation in a group insurance and profit-sharing plan. At the beginning of an agent's service an assistant district manager accompanies the new agent on his rounds to acquaint him with his customers and show him the approved collection and selling techniques. The agent is also supplied with a company "Rate Book," which the agent is expected to follow, containing detailed instructions on how to perform many of his duties. An agent must turn in his collected premiums to the district office once a week and also file a weekly report. At this time the agent usually attends staff meetings for the discussion of the latest company sales techniques, company directives, etc. Complaints against an agent are investigated by the manager or assistant manager, and, if well founded, the manager talks with the agent to "set him straight." Agents who have poor production records, or who fail to maintain their accounts properly or to follow company rules, are "cautioned." The district manager submits a weekly report to the home office, specifying, among other things, the agents whose records are below average; the amounts of their debits; their collection percentages, arrears, and production; and what action the district manager has taken to remedy the production "letdown." If improvement does not follow, the company asks such agents to "resign," or exercises its rights under the "Agent's Commission Plan" to fire them "at any time."

There are innumerable situations which arise in the common law where it is difficult to say whether a particular individual is an employee or an independent contractor, and these cases present such a situation. On the one hand these debit agents perform their work primarily away from the company's offices and fix their own hours of work and work days; and clearly they are not as obviously employees as are production workers in a factory. On the other hand, however, they do not have the independence, nor are they allowed the initiative and decision-making authority, normally associated with an independent contractor. In such a situation as this there is no shorthand formula or magic phrase that can be applied to find the answer, but all of the incidents of the relationship must be assessed and weighed with no one factor being decisive. What is important is that the total factual context is assessed in light of the pertinent common-law agency principles. When this is done, the decisive factors in these cases become the following: the agents do not operate their own independent businesses, but perform functions that are an essential part of the company's normal operations; they need not have any prior training or experience, but are trained by company supervisory personnel; they do business in the company's name with considerable assistance and guidance from the company and its managerial personnel and ordinarily sell only the company's policies; the "Agent's Commission Plan" that contains the terms and conditions under which they operate is promulgated and changed unilaterally by the company; the agents account to the company for the funds they collect under an elaborate and regular reporting procedure; the agents receive the benefits of the company's vacation plan and group insurance and pension fund; and the agents have a permanent working arrangement with the company under which they may continue as long as their performance is satisfactory. Probably the best summation of what these factors mean in the reality of the actual working relationship was given by the chairman of the board of respondent company in a letter to debit agents about the time this unfair labor practice proceeding arose:

> "if any agent believes he has the power to make his own rules and plan of handling the company's business, then that agent should hand in his resignation at once, and if we learn that said agent is not going to operate in accordance with the company's plan, then the company will be forced to make the agents final [sic].
>
> "The company is going to have its business managed in your district the same as all other company districts in the many states where said offices are located. The other company officials and I have managed the United Insurance Company of America's operations for over 45 years very successfully, and we are going to continue the same successful plan of operation, and we will not allow anyone to interfere with us and our successful plan."

The Board examined all of these facts and found that they showed the debit agents to be employees. This was not a purely factual finding by the Board, but involved the application of law to facts—what do the facts establish under the common law of agency: employee or independent contractor? It should also be pointed out that such a determination of pure agency law involved no special administrative expertise that a court does not possess. On the other hand, the Board's determination was a judgment made after a hearing with witnesses and oral argument had been held and on the basis of written briefs. Such a determination should not be set aside just because a court would, as an original matter, decide the case the other way. As we said in *Universal Camera Corp. v. NLRB*, 340 U.S. 474, "Nor does it [the requirement for canvassing the whole record] mean that even as to matters not requiring expertise a court may displace the Board's choice between two fairly conflicting views, even though the court would justifiably have made a different choice had the matter been before it de novo." 340 U.S., at 488. Here the least that can be said for the Board's decision is that it made a choice between two fairly conflicting views, and under these circumstances the Court of Appeals should have enforced the Board's order. It was error to refuse to do so.

Notes and Questions

1. **The Statutory Issue?** At issue in *United Insurance* was whether the company's "debit agents" were covered by the NLRA as amended by the 1947 Taft-Hartley Act, Pub. L. No. 80-101, § 2(3), 61 Stat. 136, 137–38 (1947). That question, in turn, depended on whether the agents were "employees" or "independent contractors" for purposes of the Act. The Act provided: "The term 'employee' shall include any employee*** and shall include any individual whose work has ceased as a consequence of, or in connection with, any current labor dispute or because of any labor practice, and who has not obtained any other regular and substantially equivalent employment, but shall not include*** any individual having the status of an independent contractor***." 29 U.S.C. § 152(3).

In the 1947 Taft-Hartley Act, Congress overrode the Supreme Court's earlier interpretation in the *Hearst* case through an amendment that excluded independent contractors from the NLRA's coverage. Justice Black says the "obvious" purpose of this amendment was to make "general agency principles" applicable in proceedings before the NLRB and the courts where an individual's status as an employee or an independent contractor was at issue. Although the Taft-Hartley amendments to the NLRA do not define the term "independent contractor," the relevant House committee states: "In the law, there always had been a difference, and a big difference, between 'employees' and 'independent contractors.' 'Employees' work for wages or salaries under direct supervision. 'Independent contractors' undertake to do a contract for a price, decide how the work will be done, usually hire others to do the work, and depend for their income not upon wages, but upon the difference between what they pay for goods, materials, and what they receive for the end result, that is, upon profits." It would seem that Congress intended to restore agency principles to the employee-status determination. How those principles apply in factual settings where employees are paid commissions rather than for time served and where they are not directly supervised because they work off-site is a question of the application of law to fact, subject to, the *United Insurance* Court tells us, substantial evidence review.

2. **Regulatory and Procedural Posture?** How was the question of the debit agents' status raised before the NLRB? What did the Board conclude? Who sought review of the Board's order? What did the Court below conclude?

3. **General Principles of the Common Law of Agency?** The Court states that the status of debit agents turns on "common-law" agency principles. Does the Court explain what the NLRB's authority is where "the common law of agency" does not clearly provide a clear answer? Is the Board required simply to canvas court decisions on agency law or does it have authority in these open areas to develop subsidiary principles that give effect to statutory objectives? Reconsider this question when reading *Chevron*, Section [C][3], *infra*, and cases elaborating the deference regime it established. For the pertinent agency principles in this area as applied to the employment context, see Restatement of Employment Law § 1.01 (2015).

From where do such principles derive? In *Erie R. Co. v. Tompkins*, 304 U.S. 64, 78 (1938), the Supreme Court famously held "[t]here is no federal general common law." Given *Erie*'s rejection of general federal common law, does *United Insurance* hold that state-law agency principles control the determination of whether an individual is an employee? If so, which state? Is the Taft-Hartley amendment best read as directing the Board and the courts to apply state law? *See generally* Michael C. Harper, *Fashioning a General Common Law for Employment in an Age of Statutes*, 100 CORNELL L. REV. 1281, 1284 (2015) ("[T]he determination of the common law to be incorporated into [federal] statutes [that reference common law concepts] affords the [Supreme] Court the opportunity to influence the development of the general common law."); Caleb Nelson, *The Persistence of General Law*, 106 COLUM. L. REV. 503, 503–04 (2006) ("[W]ithin the interstices of written federal law, courts often articulate federal rules of decision that*** draw their substance from state law. Rather than tracking the local law of any single state, though, these federal rules reflect state law *in general*; what matters is how *most* states do things, not whatever the policymakers in one particular state have said.").

4. **A Choice Between "Two Fairly Conflicting Views"?** Having articulated the legal framework, the Court elaborates the facts relevant to the classification of United Insurance's debit agents. The agents did not maintain independent businesses; performed an "essential" function for United Insurance; did not have prior training or experience; and did business in the company's name. Moreover, United had total control over debit agents' compensation, and provided a benefits package similar to those that full-time employees traditionally receive.

The Court says that "the least that can be said for the Board's decision is that it made a choice between two fairly conflicting views." For that reason, the Supreme Court opines, the Board's decision should have been enforced by the Court of Appeals. Which provision of APA § 706 does the Supreme Court believe governs review of the Board's decision regarding debit agents?

NLRB v. Bell Aerospace Co.

416 U.S. 267 (1974)

MR. JUSTICE POWELL delivered the opinion of the Court.

[Recall from the prior excerpt in Chapter 4[D], *supra* p. 464, that the Court granted certiorari to consider two questions: "first, whether the National Labor Relations Board properly determined that all 'managerial employees,' except those whose participation in a labor organization would create a conflict of interest with their job responsibilities, are covered by the National Labor Relations Act (NLRA); and second, whether the Board must proceed by rulemaking rather than by adjudication in determining whether certain buyers at Bell Aerospace were 'managerial employees.'"]

II

We begin with the question whether all "managerial employees," rather than just those in positions susceptible to conflicts of interest in labor relations, are excluded from the protections of the Act.[4]*** [W]e draw on several established principles of statutory construction. In addition to the importance of legislative history, a court may accord great weight to the longstanding interpretation placed on a statute by an agency charged with its administration. This is especially so where Congress has re-enacted the statute without pertinent change. In these circumstances, congressional failure to revise or repeal the agency's interpretation is persuasive evidence that the interpretation is the one intended by Congress. We have also recognized that subsequent legislation declaring the intent of an earlier statute is entitled to significant weight.***

A

The Wagner Act [Pub. L. No. 74-196, 49 Stat. 449 (1935)] did not expressly mention the term "managerial employee." After the Act's passage, however, the Board developed the concept of "managerial employee" in a series of cases involving the appropriateness of bargaining units. The first cases established that "managerial employees" were not to be included in a unit with rank-and-file employees. In *Freiz & Sons*, 47 N.L.R.B. 43, 47 (1943), for example, the Board excluded expediters from a proposed unit of production and maintenance workers because they were "closely related to the management." Similarly, in *Spicer Mfg. Corp.*, 55 N.L.R.B. 1491, 1498 (1944), expediters were again excluded from a unit containing office, technical, clerical, and professional employees because "the authority possessed by [the expediters] to exercise their discretion in making commitments on behalf of the Company stamps them as managerial." This rationale was soon applied to buyers. See, *e.g.*, *Hudson Motor Car Co.*, 55 N.L.R.B. 509, 512 (1944); *Vulcan Corp.*, 58 N.L.R.B. 733, 736 (1944); *Barrett Division, Allied Chem. & Dye Corp.*, 65 N. L. R. B. 903, 905 (1946); *Electric Controller & Mfg. Co.*, 69 N.L.R.B. 1242, 1245–1246 (1946). The Board summarized its policy on "managerial employees" in *Ford Motor Co.*, 66 N.L.R.B. 1317, 1322 (1946):

---

4. Section 2(3) of the Act defines the term "employee" as follows:

"The term 'employee' shall include any employee, and shall not be limited to the employees of a particular employer, unless this subchapter explicitly states otherwise, and shall include any individual whose work has ceased as a consequence of, or in connection with, any current labor dispute or because of any unfair labor practice, and who has not obtained any other regular and substantially equivalent employment, but shall not include any individual employed as an agricultural laborer, or in the domestic service of any family or person at his home, or any individual employed by his parent or spouse, or any individual having the status of an independent contractor, or any individual employed as a supervisor, or any individual employed by an employer subject to the Railway Labor Act, as amended from time to time, or by any other person who is not an employer as herein defined." 29 U.S.C. § 152(3).

Supervisory employees are expressly excluded from the protections of the Act. That term is defined in § 2(11):

"The term 'supervisor' means any individual having authority, in the interest of the employer, to hire, transfer, suspend, lay off, recall, promote, discharge, assign, reward, or discipline other employees, or responsibility to direct them, or to adjust their grievances, or effectively to recommend such action, if in connection with the foregoing the exercise of such authority is not of a merely routine or clerical nature but requires the use of independent judgment." 29 U.S.C. § 152(11).

"We have customarily excluded from bargaining units of rank and file workers executive employees who are in a position to formulate, determine and
effectuate management policies. These employees we have considered and still
deem to be 'managerial,' in that they express and make operative the decisions of management."

Whether the Board regarded all "managerial employees" as entirely outside the protection of the Act, as well as inappropriate for inclusion in a rank-and-file bargaining
unit, is less certain. To be sure, at no time did the Board certify even a separate unit of
"managerial employees" or state that such was possible.***

During this period the Board's policy with respect to the related but narrower category of "supervisory employees" manifested a progressive uncertainty. The Board first
excluded supervisors from units of rank-and-file employees, but in *Union Collieries
Coal Co.*, 41 N.L.R.B. 961, supplemental decision, 44 N.L.R.B. 165 (1942), it certified a
separate unit composed of supervisors who were to be represented by an independent
union. Shortly thereafter, the Board approved a unit of supervisors whose union was
affiliated with a union of rank-and-file employees. This trend was soon halted, however,
by *Maryland Drydock Co.*, 49 N.L.R.B. 733 (1943), where the Board held that supervisors, although literally "employees" under the Act, could not be organized in any unit.***

Maryland Drydock was subsequently overruled in *Packard Motor Car Co.*, 61
N.L.R.B. 4, 64 N.L.R.B. 1212 (1945), where the Board held that foremen could constitute an appropriate unit for collective bargaining. The Board's position was upheld
5-4 by this Court in *Packard Co. v. NLRB*, 330 U.S. 485 (1947). In view of the subsequent legislative reversal of the *Packard* decision, the dissenting opinion of Mr. Justice Douglas is especially pertinent. He stated:

"The present decision . . . tends to obliterate the line between management and labor. It lends the sanctions of federal law to unionization at all
levels of the industrial hierarchy. It tends to emphasize that the basic opposing forces in industry are not management and labor but the operating
group on the one hand and the stockholder and bondholder group on the other.
The industrial problem as so defined comes down to a contest over a fair division of the gross receipts of industry between these two groups. The struggle
for control or power between management and labor becomes secondary to
a growing unity in their common demands on ownership.

"I do not believe this is an exaggerated statement of the basic policy
questions which underlie the present decision. For if foremen are 'employees' within the meaning of the National Labor Relations Act, so are vice-
presidents, managers, assistant managers, superintendents, assistant
superintendents — indeed, all who are on the payroll of the company,
including the president; all who are commonly referred to as the management, with the exception of the directors. If a union of vice-presidents
applied for recognition as a collective bargaining agency, I do not see how we

could deny it and yet allow the present application. But once vice-presidents, managers, superintendents, foremen all are unionized, management and labor will become more of a solid phalanx than separate factions in warring camps."***

Mr. Justice Douglas also noted that the Wagner Act was intended to protect "laborers" and "workers" whose right to organize and bargain collectively had not been recognized by industry, resulting in strikes, strife, and unrest. By contrast, there was no similar history with respect to foremen, managers, superintendents, or vice presidents. Furthermore, other legislation indicated that where Congress desired to include managerial or supervisory personnel in the category of employees, it did so expressly. See, e.g., Railway Labor Act of 1926, 44 Stat. 577, 45 U.S.C. § 151; Merchant Marine Act, 1936, as amended, 52 Stat. 953, 46 U.S.C. § 1101 et seq.; Social Security Act, § 1101, 49 Stat. 647.

B

The *Packard* decision was a major factor in bringing about the Taft-Hartley Act of 1947, 61 Stat. 136. The House bill, H.R. 3020, 80th Cong., 1st Sess. (1947), provided for the exclusion of "supervisors," a category broadly defined to include any individual who had authority to hire, transfer, promote, discharge, reward, or discipline other employees or effectively to recommend such action. It also excluded (i) those who had authority to determine or effectively recommend the amount of wages earned by other employees; (ii) those employed in labor relations, personnel, and employment departments, as well as police and timestudy personnel; and (iii) confidential employees. The Senate version of the bill, S. 1126, 80th Cong., 1st Sess. (1947), also excluded supervisors, but defined that category more narrowly than the House version, distinguishing between "straw bosses, leadmen, set-up men, and other minor supervisory employees, on the one hand, and the supervisor vested with such genuine management prerogatives as the right to hire or fire, discipline, or make effective recommendations with respect to such action." S. Rep. No. 105, 80th Cong., 1st Sess., 4 (1947). It was the Senate's view that employees such as "straw bosses," who had only minor supervisory duties, should be included within the Act's protections.

Significantly, both the House Report and the Senate Report voiced concern over the Board's broad reading of the term "employee" to include those clearly within the managerial hierarchy. Focusing on Mr. Justice Douglas' dissent in *Packard*, the Senate Report specifically mentioned that even vice presidents might be unionized under the Board's decision. It also noted that unionization of supervisors had hurt productivity, increased the accident rate, upset the balance of power in collective bargaining, and tended to blur the line between management and labor. The House Report echoed the concern for reduction of industrial output and noted that unionization of supervisors had deprived employers of the loyal representations to which they were entitled.[11] And in criticizing the Board's expansive reading of the Act's definition of the term "employees," the House Report noted that "[w]hen Congress passed the Labor Act, we were concerned, as we said in its preamble, with the welfare of 'workers' and 'wage earners,' not of the boss." H.R. Rep. No. 245, 80th Cong., 1st Sess., 13 (1947).

The Conference Committee adopted the Senate version of the bill. H.R. Conf. Rep. No. 510, 80th Cong., 1st Sess., 35 (1947). The House Managers' statement in explanation of the Conference Committee Report stated:

> "The conference agreement, in the definition of 'supervisor,' limits such term to those individuals treated as supervisors under the Senate amendment. In the case of persons working in labor relations, personnel and employment departments, it was not thought necessary to make specific provision, as was done in the House bill, since the Board has treated, and presumably will continue to treat, such persons as outside the scope of the act.***"

The legislative history of the Taft-Hartley Act of 1947 may be summarized as follows. The House wanted to include certain persons within the definition of "supervisors," such as straw bosses, whom the Senate believed should be protected by the Act. As to these persons, the Senate's view prevailed. There were other persons, however, who both the House and the Senate believed were plainly outside the Act. The House wanted to make the exclusion of certain of these persons explicit. In the conference agreement, representatives from both the House and the Senate agreed that a specific provision was unnecessary since the Board had long regarded such persons as outside the Act. Among those mentioned as impliedly excluded were persons working in "labor relations, personnel and employment departments," and "confidential employees." But assuredly this did not exhaust the universe of such excluded persons. The legislative history strongly suggests that there also were other employees, much higher in the managerial structure, who were likewise regarded as so clearly outside the Act that no specific exclusionary provision was thought necessary. For example, in its discussion of confidential employees, the House Report noted that "[m]ost of the people who would qualify as 'confidential' employees are *executives and are excluded from the act in any*

---

11. The Report also makes evident that Congress was concerned with more than just the possibility of a conflict of interest in labor relations if supervisors were unionized:

> "Supervisors are management people. They have distinguished themselves in their work. They have demonstrated their ability to take care of themselves without depending upon the pressure of collective action. No one forced them to become supervisors. They abandoned the 'collective security' of the rank and file voluntarily, because they believed the opportunities thus opened to them to be more valuable to them than such 'security.' It seems wrong, and it is wrong, to subject people of this kind, who have demonstrated their initiative, their ambition and their ability to get ahead, to the leveling processes of seniority, uniformity and standardization that the Supreme Court recognizes as being fundamental principles of unionism. It is wrong for the foremen, for it discourages the things in them that made them foremen in the first place. For the same reason, that it discourages those best qualified to get ahead, it is wrong for industry, and particularly for the future strength and productivity of our country." H.R. Rep. No. 245, 80th Cong., 1st Sess., 16–17 (1947).

event." H.R. Rep. No. 245, p. 23 (emphasis added). We think the inference is plain that "managerial employees" were paramount among this impliedly excluded group.***

C

Following the passage of the Taft-Hartley Act, the Board itself adhered to the view that "managerial employees" were outside the Act.*** Until its decision in *North Arkansas* in 1970, the Board consistently followed this reading of the Act. It never certified any unit of "managerial employees," separate or otherwise, and repeatedly stated that it was Congress' intent that such employees not be accorded bargaining rights under the Act. And it was this reading which was permitted to stand when Congress again amended the Act in 1959. 73 Stat. 519.

The Board's exclusion of "managerial employees[,]" defined as those who "formulate and effectuate management polices by expressing and making operative the decisions of their employer," has also been approved by courts without exception.

D

In sum, the Board's early decisions, the purpose and legislative history of the Taft-Hartley Act of 1947, the Board's subsequent and consistent construction of the Act for more than two decades, and the decisions of the courts of appeals all point unmistakably to the conclusion that "managerial employees" are not covered by the Act. We agree with the Court of Appeals below that the Board "is not now free" to read a new and more restrictive meaning into the Act.

In view of our conclusion, the case must be remanded to permit the Board to apply the proper legal standard in determining the status of these buyers. *SEC v. Chenery Corp.*, 318 U.S. 80, 85 (1943); *FTC v. Sperry & Hutchinson Co.*, 405 U.S. 233, 249 (1972). We express no opinion as to whether these buyers fall within the category of "managerial employees."

[Justice White, joined by Justices Brennan, Stewart, and Marshall, dissented from this part of the Court's opinion]

Notes and Questions

1. **The Statutory Issue?** At issue in *Bell Aerospace* is whether "managerial" employees are statutory "employees" protected by the NLRA. Why is that question not answered by the text of § 2(3), quoted in footnote 4? Given the Act's distinction between ordinary employees and supervisory employees, why is the status of managerial employees even relevant? Could the case have been decided on the ground that Bell Aerospace's buyers were supervisory employees? Do all managerial employees supervise other people? Are Bell's buyers an example of managerial employees who do meet the statutory definition of supervisors? Does the express exclusion of supervisors from the NLRA's coverage make it harder to find an implied exclusion for non-supervisory managers?

2. **Regulatory and Procedural Posture?** Recall from Chapter 4 that the buyers at Bell Aerospace sought to form a union to engage in collective bargaining. The company declined to recognize a union on the ground that the buyers were managerial

employees excluded from statutory protection, leading the buyers to file an unfair labor practice charge before the NLRB. The NLRB ordered Bell to recognize the union, and the company sought judicial review.

3. **The NLRB's Non-Acquiescence in the Eighth Circuit's Views.** Note the Board's refusal to conform its view of whether managerial employees were covered by the Act to the contrary view of the Eighth Circuit. If the Board had refused to apply the Eighth Circuit's view in a subsequent case and the employer sought review in that court of appeals, the Board would be engaged in "non-acquiescence," a practice it engaged in from time to time to preserve its view of national labor policy despite contrary circuit rulings. When if ever is such "non-acquiescence" legitimate? Does the answer depend on whether the agency adheres to a circuit court's views for cases arising within the circuit? Does it matter whether review of the agency's decisions can be sought in multiple venues, as is the case with the NLRB, *see* 29 U.S.C. § 160(e), or only in a single district court, as with the Social Security Administration, *see* 42 U.S.C. § 405(g)? Does it depend on whether the agency is actively engaged in seeking Supreme Court review? For extended analyses, *see* Samuel Estreicher & Richard L. Revesz, *Nonacquiescence by Federal Administrative Agencies*, 98 YALE L.J. 679 (1989); Matthew Diller & Nancy Morawetz, *Intracircuit Nonacquiescence and the Breakdown of the Rule of Law: A Response to Estreicher and Revesz*, 99 YALE L.J. 801 (1990); and Samuel Estreicher & Richard L. Revesz, *The Uneasy Case Against Intracircuit Nonacquiescence: A Reply*, 99 YALE L.J. 831 (1990).

4. **Appropriate Legal Standard vs. Application of Appropriate Legal Standard in a Given Case?** Why does the Supreme Court not take the same "two fairly conflicting views" approach to the NLRB's interpretation of employee status in *Bell Aerospace* as it did in *United Insurance*? What is the difference between asking whether an individual is an employee or independent contractor, on the one hand, and whether Congress implicitly excluded managerial employees from the NLRA, on the other? Was the Board applying the appropriate legal standard in *United Insurance*? Was it in *Bell Aerospace*? How can we tell when the issue is whether the agency is applying the appropriate legal standard and when it is not? Which provision of APA § 706 does the Court apply in *United Insurance*? In *Bell Aerospace*?

5. **The Court's Statutory Analysis?** In finding an implied exception for nonsupervisory managerial employees, the Court places virtually no weight on the text and purpose of the Act. Instead, the Court's analysis takes the form of articulating or discerning implied premises of the congressional drafters of the legislation. The aspect of the NLRA's history that the Court considers in greatest depth is the enactment of the Taft-Hartley amendments of 1947, Pub. L. No. 80-101, 61 Stat. 136. Among other things, the Taft-Hartley Act responded to the Board's decision in *Packard Motor Car Co.*, 61 N.L.R.B. 4, 64 N.L.R.B. 1212 (1945). The Supreme Court sustained the *Packard* ruling in *Packard Motor Car Co. v. NLRB*, 330 U.S. 485 (1947), holding that factory foremen constituted an appropriate unit for collective bargaining purposes. The decision occasioned a powerful dissent by Justice William O. Douglas, former chair of the SEC during the Roosevelt administration, warning of unionized coalitions of

executive and rank-and-file employees joining forces against corporate owners. How in the Court's telling did members of Congress react to that decision? Is the evidence of congressional "intent" cited by the Court persuasive evidence of how a majority of the House and Senate saw the *Packard Motor* decision? Recall the "hierarchy" of legislative history discussed in Note 5 following *Hanrahan v. Hampton*, *supra* Chapter 2[B][1][c], p. 154.

6. **Impact of the Agency's Longstanding Interpretation?** Why is the NLRB's "longstanding" interpretation of whether the NLRA applies to managerial employees relevant to the meaning of the statute? What is the rationale for interpreting a statute consistently with a longstanding agency interpretation? Does it depend on Congress having amended or revisited the statute after the agency interpretation became well-established? Does Congress have to in fact focus on the issue when revisiting the statute? What weight should be given to the fact that a change in the agency's interpretation may disrupt significant reliance interests? Were such interests implicated in the *Bell Aerospace* case? *Compare Perez v. Mortgage Bankers' Association*, 135 S. Ct. 1199 (2015), Chapter 4[F], *supra*; *Motor Vehicle Mfrs. Assn. v. State Farm Mut. Auto. Ins. Co.*, 463 U.S. 29 (1983) *infra* Section [D]; *FCC v. Fox Television Stations*, 556 U.S. 502 (2008), *infra* Section [D].

In light of the Court's position that post-enactment legislative "history" generally is not probative of statutory meaning (see Note 10 following *TVA v. Hill*, Chapter 2[B][1][a], *supra* p. 179, why does the Court conclude that the Taft-Hartley amendments clarified the meaning of the Wagner Act even though those amendments did not expressly create an exclusion from coverage for nonsupervisory managers? Are the amendments legitimate evidence of the Wagner Act's meaning because they were part of an actual change in the statute in a related context?

3. Policy Elaboration: "*Chevron* Deference" and "*Skidmore* Respect"

As the preceding sections suggest, agencies at times make administrative policy through factfinding and the application of law to concrete disputes. Other times the establishment of administrative policy is more deliberate and obvious. The status of such policy, and the deference to which it is entitled from courts, are the subjects of an important line of Supreme Court decisions that, more than any other area of doctrine, attempt to delineate the proper relationship between the courts and the administrative state.

Skidmore v. Swift & Co.

323 U.S. 134 (1944)

[Reread the Court's decision, which appears in Chapter 1[C][3], *supra* p. 41, then proceed to the Notes and Questions that follow.]

Notes and Questions

1. **The Statutory Issue?** The question presented by *Skidmore* was whether the time "plaintiffs spent in the fire hall subject to call to answer fire alarms constituted hours worked, for which overtime compensation [was] due under the FLSA." The relevant provision of the Act required time-and-a-half compensation for "a workweek longer than forty hours." Pub. L. No. 75-718, § 7(a), ch. 676, 52 Stat. 1060 (1938), *codified at* 29 U.S.C. § 207(a).

What textual arguments would petitioners have made to support their claim that they were entitled to compensation for time spent in the fire hall? What textual arguments would Swift have made in response? Recall from Chapter 1 that the FLSA seeks to guaranty minimum terms and conditions of employment for employees within its scope, and to overcome collective-action and economic-power problems that prevent individual workers from demanding such terms and conditions on an individual basis. Do these statutory objectives have any bearing on the petitioners' entitlement to compensation? If there were no administrative agency, how would the courts address this question? If there is an agency involved, what weight, if any, should be given to its views?

2. **The Procedural Posture?** Did the *Skidmore* petitioners turn to a court or an agency to enforce their right to statutory overtime? How were they able to bypass the Department of Labor (DOL)? At what point in the proceedings did the DOL's Wage and Hour Administrator offer his views of how the FLSA's time-and-a-half provision applied to on-call time? In what form were the Administrator's views articulated?

3. **The DOL's Interpretative Bulletins.** Recall from Note 2 following *Perez v. Mortgage Bankers Association*, Chapter 4[F], *supra* p. 499, that DOL issues guidance about the applicability of the FLSA and other statutes it administers in addition to issuing substantive regulations under § 553 of the APA. At present, DOL guidance is promulgated via "Administrator Interpretations" that "set forth a general interpretation of the law and regulations, applicable across-the-board to all those affected by the provision in issue." U.S. Dep't of Labor, Wage & Hour Division, Rulings and Interpretations, http://www.dol.gov/whd/opinion/opinion.htm (last visited Feb. 5, 2015).

At the time of *Skidmore*, DOL guidance appeared in an "Interpretative Bulletin" published by DOL's Wage and Hour Division. Interpretative Bulletin No. 13, cited by the Court in *Skidmore*, was first issued in July 1939 and revised in October 1939, October 1940, and November 1940. It was—

> intended to indicate the course which the Administrator will follow with respect to the determination of employees' hours of work in the performance of his administrative duties under the act, unless he is directed otherwise by the authoritative rulings of the courts or unless he shall subsequently decide that his interpretation is incorrect.

The bulletin addressed such matters as the use of time clocks; "waiting time and employees subject to call"; travel time; meetings, lectures, and training programs; and employees who had more than one job. U.S. Department of Labor, Wage and Hour Division, Office of the Administrator, Interpretative Bulletin No. 13 ¶ 1, app. A to Brief of the U.S. Dep't of Labor, *Skidmore v. Swift & Co.*, 323 U.S. 134 (1944).

4. **What Is *Skidmore* "Respect" or "Weight"?** The Supreme Court in *Skidmore* does not decide the bottom-line question of whether the petitioners are entitled to overtime for time spent in the fire hall or within hailing distance. However, the Court reverses the decision below and remands for further proceedings in which the Secretary of Labor's views will be afforded the "respect" to which they are "entitled."

What does the Supreme Court mean in instructing the lower courts to afford the Secretary's views the "respect" to which they are entitled? Are the Secretary's views legally binding on the lower courts? Must the courts follow the Secretary's lead? Should the courts regard the Secretary's views any differently than a treatise or law review article written by a prominent academic? Recall Justice Scalia's dissent in *Perez v. Mortgage Banker's Ass'n, supra* Chapter 4[F].

In general, the Court invokes *Skidmore* when it decides that the question is one of "pure" statutory interpretation in which the courts have plenary interpretive authority and no deference is owed as a legal matter to the agency's views. *Bell Aerospace* is such a case, as are many others discussed in this book. In such cases, are the agency's views relevant? Why if so? When are the agency's views especially persuasive? Professor Strauss calls the consideration to which the Administrator's views are entitled *Skidmore* "weight." By this, he means that "an agency's view on a given statutory question may in itself warrant respect by judges who themselves have ultimate interpretive authority." Peter L. Strauss, *"Deference" Is Too Confusing—Let's Call Them "Chevron Space" and "Skidmore Weight"*, 112 COLUM. L. REV. 1143, 1145 (2012).

Consider the Supreme Court's observation that "[g]ood administration of the [FLSA] and good judicial administration alike require that the standards of public enforcement and those for determining private rights shall be at variance only where justified by very good reasons." Why does good administration of the Act require that it be interpreted consistently by courts and the Department of Labor (at least presumptively)? Why is such consistency beneficial to "good judicial administration"? Consider the fact that FSLA cases are heard in twelve, geographically disperse circuits.

5. **Factors Affecting Respect—Consistency Over Time.** The *Skidmore* Court writes that the "weight" to be given the Secretary's views will vary based on a number of factors. One such factor is an interpretation's consistency over time. Why is this relevant?

In *Norwegian Nitrogen Products Co. v. United States*, 288 U.S. 294 (1933), the Supreme Court considered a challenge to a rate setting under the flexible tariff provisions of the Tariff Act of 1922, ch. 356, 42 Stat. 858. The Act directed the President, upon the recommendation of the U.S. Tariff Commission, to increase or decrease the duty on imported goods upon finding that doing so was necessary to equalize differences in the cost of production in the United States and its chief foreign competitor. Petitioners, foreign manufacturers of sodium nitrate, contended that the Commission had violated the law by denying them an opportunity to examine U.S. producers' confidential price data before recommending a new tariff of 4.5 cents per pound, which the President adopted. The Commission maintained that it was required only to give petitioners an opportunity to be heard and present evidence, not to examine U.S. producers' price data. The relevant provisions of the Tariff Act provided that the Commission was to give interested parties "reasonable public notice of its hearings [and] reasonable opportunities*** to be present, to produce evidence, and to be heard."

Rejecting petitioners' challenge, the Court approvingly noted that the practice of denying interested parties access to confidential price information "developed before the Act of 1922 [and has been] continued and confirmed with the tacit approval of the President and the acquiescence of the Congress." 288 U.S. at 315. "From the beginning there has been an administrative policy to treat the costs or investments of identified producers as akin to a trade secret, with the result that disclosure, even if not strictly within the prohibition of the statute, was forbidden in the view of the Commission by persuasive considerations of fair dealing and expediency.*** Consistently through all its hearings the Commission has acted upon the principle that the cost of production will not be made known to competitors if the producers are so few that there can be no disclosure of the cost without disclosing the identity of those producing at that cost." *Id.* at 311.

Does a change in agency position always weigh against *Skidmore* respect? Consider the following:

> [I]f an agency's views vacillate over time, that detracts from, if it does not entirely eliminate, any *Skidmore* weight to which they might otherwise be entitled. . . . In considering how persistent a particular agency interpretation or finding has been, *Skidmore* treats variances occurring with the changing of the political guard as a negative, not a positive, factor. Under *Skidmore*, courts credit findings that are likely to be politically neutral, that may have lasted through a number of political changes. This is not just a matter of efficiency; it also respects the complex relationship amongst the legislature, executive, and judiciary.

Strauss, *supra*, at 1146–47. What "complex relationship" does Professor Strauss have in mind here?

6. **Factors Affecting Respect — The Agency's Expertise.** Another factor that affects the weight to which an agency's views are entitled under *Skidmore* is the extent to which those views are informed by the agency's expertise in a subject area. An interpretation that is informed by expertise in the administration of the statute is, all other things being equal, entitled to more respect.

In *Skidmore*, the Supreme Court repeatedly emphasizes the context-sensitive, fact-dependent nature of the inquiry into whether time spent on-call is working time. Might an agency's views carry special weight in such circumstances? On what theory? Is respect less appropriate when a legal question is straightforward and does not require extensive knowledge or experience? Why?

7. Factors Affecting Respect—Validity of Agency Reasoning. The final factor *Skidmore* instructs courts to consider is the "validity" of an agency's reasoning. Consider *University of Texas Southwest Medical Center v. Nassar*, 133 S. Ct. 2517 (2013). At issue was which standard of causation a plaintiff had to meet to establish a claim under Title VII's anti-retaliation provision. The EEOC's Title VII compliance manual stated that a plaintiff needed to show only that retaliation was a motivating factor in an adverse employment action, not that retaliation was the but for cause of the action. This was so, the EEOC reasoned, because "an interpretation*** that permits proven retaliation to go unpunished undermines the purpose of the anti-retaliation provisions of maintaining unfettered access to the statutory remedial mechanism." 2 EEOC Compliance Manual § 8-II(E)(1), at 614:0008, n. 45 (Mar. 2003).

The Court rejected the government's contention that the EEOC's view was entitled to *Skidmore* respect because the manual's reasoning was circular. The manual "assert[ed] the lessened causation standard is necessary in order to prevent 'proven retaliation' from 'go[ing] unpunished.' Yet this assumes the answer to the central question at issue here, which is what causal relationship must be shown in order to prove retaliation." 133 S. Ct. at 2533–54.

———

Justice Jackson's opinion in *Skidmore* is careful to note that the Wage and Hour Administrator's views of the FLSA "do not constitute an interpretation of the Act or a standard for judging factual situations which binds a district court's processes, as an authoritative pronouncement of a higher court might do." The Administrator's views were "not controlling upon the courts by reason of their authority."

How should courts approach an agency's view of appropriate policy when Congress has delegated to the agency a measure of discretion to set policy within statutory limits? How should courts determine whether Congress has in fact delegated policymaking authority to the agency? If the agency has authority to speak with the force of law, what is the role of the reviewing court? Before reading the decision that follows, review the regulatory history of the "bubble rule" that was at issue in *Chevron*, in Chapter 4[E], *supra* p. 482.

Chevron U.S.A. Inc. v. Natural Resources Defense Council
467 U.S. 837 (1984)

JUSTICE STEVENS delivered the opinion of the Court.

[Section 172(b)(6) of the Clean Air Amendments of 1977, Pub. L. 95-95, 91 Stat. 685, required "nonattainment states" that were out of compliance with National Ambient Air Quality Standards (NAAQS) promulgated by the EPA to establish a permit program, known as "New Source Review," governing "the construction and operation of new or modified major stationary sources in accordance with section 173 (relating to permit requirements)." Among other things, § 173 required the proposed source to achieve the lowest achievable emission rate (LAER). Section 173 defined LAER as "(A) the most stringent emission limitation which is contained in the implementation plan of any State for such class or category of source, unless the owner or operator of the proposed source demonstrates that such limitations are not achievable, or (B) the most stringent emission limitation which is achieved in practice by such class or category of source, whichever is more stringent."]

***The question presented by these cases is whether EPA's decision to allow States to treat all of the pollution-emitting devices within the same industrial grouping as though they were encased within a single "bubble" is based on a reasonable construction of the statutory term "stationary source."

I

The EPA regulations containing the plantwide definition of the term stationary source were promulgated on October 14, 1981. 46 Fed. Reg. 50766. Respondents[3] filed a timely petition for review in the United States Court of Appeals for the District of Columbia Circuit pursuant to 42 U.S.C. § 7607(b)(1). The Court of Appeals set aside the regulations.

The court observed that the relevant part of the amended Clean Air Act "does not explicitly define what Congress envisioned as a 'stationary source,' to which the permit program . . . should apply," and further stated that the precise issue was not "squarely addressed in the legislative history."*** Since the purpose of the permit program—its "raison d'etre," in the court's view—was to improve air quality, the court held that the bubble concept was inapplicable in these cases under its prior precedents. It therefore set aside the regulations embodying the bubble concept as contrary to law. We granted certiorari to review that judgment, and we now reverse.***

II***

When a court reviews an agency's construction of the statute which it administers, it is confronted with two questions. First, always, is the question whether Congress has directly spoken to the precise question at issue. If the intent of Congress is clear, that is the end of the matter; for the court, as well as the agency, must give effect to the unambiguously expressed intent of Congress.[9] If, however, the court determines Congress has not directly addressed the precise question at issue, the court does not simply impose its own construction on the statute,[10] as would be necessary in the absence of an administrative interpretation. Rather, if the statute is silent or

---

3. National [*sic*] Resources Defense Council, Inc., Citizens for a Better Environment, Inc., and North Western Ohio Lung Association, Inc.

9. The judiciary is the final authority on issues of statutory construction and must reject administrative constructions which are contrary to clear congressional intent. See, *e.g.*, *FEC v. Democratic Senatorial Campaign Committee*, 454 U.S. 27, 32 (1981); *SEC v. Sloan*, 436 U. S. 103, 117–118 (1978); *FMC v. Seatrain Lines, Inc.*, 411 U.S. 726, 745–746 (1973); *Volkswagenwerk v. FMC*, 390 U.S. 261, 272 (1968); *NLRB v. Brown*, 380 U.S. 278, 291 (1965); *FTC v. Colgate-Palmolive Co.*, 380 U.S. 374, 385 (1965); *Social Security Board v. Nierotko*, 327 U.S. 358, 369 (1946); *Burnet v. Chicago Portrait Co.*, 285 U.S. 1, 16 (1932); *Webster v. Luther*, 163 U.S. 331, 342 (1896). If a court, employing traditional tools of statutory construction, ascertains that Congress had an intention on the precise question at issue, that intention is the law and must be given effect.

10. See generally, R. Pound, The Spirit of the Common Law 174–175 (1921).

ambiguous with respect to the specific issue, the question for the court is whether the agency's answer is based on a permissible construction of the statute.[11]

"The power of an administrative agency to administer a congressionally created ... program necessarily requires the formulation of policy and the making of rules to fill any gap left, implicitly or explicitly, by Congress." *Morton v. Ruiz*, 415 U.S. 199, 231 (1974). If Congress has explicitly left a gap for the agency to fill, there is an express delegation of authority to the agency to elucidate a specific provision of the statute by regulation. Such legislative regulations are given controlling weight unless they are arbitrary, capricious, or manifestly contrary to the statute. Sometimes the legislative delegation to an agency on a particular question is implicit rather than explicit. In such a case, a court may not substitute its own construction of a statutory provision for a reasonable interpretation made by the administrator of an agency.

We have long recognized that considerable weight should be accorded to an executive department's construction of a statutory scheme it is entrusted to administer, and the principle of deference to administrative interpretations

> "has been consistently followed by this Court whenever decision as to the meaning or reach of a statute has involved reconciling conflicting policies, and a full understanding of the force of the statutory policy in the given situation has depended upon more than ordinary knowledge respecting the matters subjected to agency regulations. See, *e.g., National Broadcasting Co. v. United States*, 319 U.S. 190; *Labor Board v. Hearst Publications, Inc.*, 322 U.S. 111; *Republic Aviation Corp. v. Labor Board*, 324 U.S. 793; *Securities & Exchange Comm'n v. Chenery Corp.*, 332 U.S. 194; *Labor Board v. Seven-Up Bottling Co.*, 344 U.S. 344.

> "... If this choice represents a reasonable accommodation of conflicting policies that were committed to the agency's care by the statute, we should not disturb it unless it appears from the statute or its legislative history that the accommodation is not one that Congress would have sanctioned." *United States v. Shimer*, 367 U.S. 374, 382, 383 (1961).

In light of these well-settled principles it is clear that the Court of Appeals misconceived the nature of its role in reviewing the regulations at issue. Once it determined, after its own examination of the legislation, that Congress did not actually have an intent regarding the applicability of the bubble concept to the permit program, the question before it was not whether in its view the concept is "inappropriate" in the general context of a program designed to improve air quality, but whether the

---

11. The court need not conclude that the agency construction was the only one it permissibly could have adopted to uphold the construction, or even the reading the court would have reached if the question initially had arisen in a judicial proceeding. *FEC v. Democratic Senatorial Campaign Committee*, 454 U.S., at 39; *Zenith Radio Corp. v. United States*, 437 U.S. 443, 450 (1978); *Train v. Natural Resources Defense Council*, Inc., 421 U.S. 60, 75 (1975); *Udall v. Tallman*, 380 U.S. 1, 16 (1965); *Unemployment Compensation Comm'n v. Aragon*, 329 U.S. 143, 153 (1946); *McLaren v. Fleischer*, 256 U.S. 477, 480–481 (1921).

Administrator's view that it is appropriate in the context of this particular program is a reasonable one. Based on the examination of the legislation and its history which follows, we agree with the Court of Appeals that Congress did not have a specific intention on the applicability of the bubble concept in these cases, and conclude that the EPA's use of that concept here is a reasonable policy choice for the agency to make.***

VII

In this Court respondents expressly reject the basic rationale of the Court of Appeals' decision. That court viewed the statutory definition of the term "source" as sufficiently flexible to cover either a plantwide definition, a narrower definition covering each unit within a plant, or a dual definition that could apply to both the entire "bubble" and its components. It interpreted the policies of the statute, however, to mandate the plantwide definition in programs designed to maintain clean air and to forbid it in programs designed to improve air quality. Respondents place a fundamentally different construction on the statute. They contend that the text of the Act requires the EPA to use a dual definition—if either a component of a plant, or the plant as a whole, emits over 100 tons of pollutant, it is a major stationary source. They thus contend that the EPA rules adopted in 1980, insofar as they apply to the maintenance of the quality of clean air, as well as the 1981 rules which apply to nonattainment areas, violate the statute.

Statutory Language

The definition of the term "stationary source" in § 111(a)(3) refers to "any building, structure, facility, or installation" which emits air pollution. This definition is applicable only to the NSPS program by the express terms of the statute; the text of the statute does not make this definition applicable to the permit program.*** Although the definition in that section is not literally applicable to the permit program, it sheds as much light on the meaning of the word "source" as anything in the statute. As respondents point out, use of the words "building, structure, facility, or installation," as the definition of source, could be read to impose the permit conditions on an individual building that is a part of a plant. A "word may have a character of its own not to be submerged by its association." *Russell Motor Car Co. v. United States,* 261 U.S. 514, 519 (1923). On the other hand, the meaning of a word must be ascertained in the context of achieving particular objectives, and the words associated with it may indicate that the true meaning of the series is to convey a common idea. The language may reasonably be interpreted to impose the requirement on any discrete, but integrated, operation which pollutes. This gives meaning to all of the terms—a single building, not part of a larger operation, would be covered if it emits more than 100 tons of pollution, as would any facility, structure, or installation. Indeed, the language itself implies a "bubble concept" of sorts: each enumerated item would seem to be treated as if it were encased in a bubble. While respondents insist that each of these terms must be given a discrete meaning, they also argue that § 111(a)(3) defines "source" as that term is used in § 302(j).* The latter section, however, equates a source with a facility, whereas the former defines "source" as a facility, among other items.

We are not persuaded that parsing of general terms in the text of the statute will reveal an actual intent of Congress. We know full well that this language is not dispositive; the terms are overlapping and the language is not precisely directed to the question of the applicability of a given term in the context of a larger operation. To the extent any congressional "intent" can be discerned from this language, it would appear that the listing of overlapping, illustrative terms was intended to enlarge, rather than to confine, the scope of the agency's power to regulate particular sources in order to effectuate the policies of the Act.

Legislative History

In addition, respondents argue that the legislative history and policies of the Act foreclose the plantwide definition, and that the EPA's interpretation is not entitled to deference because it represents a sharp break with prior interpretations of the Act.

Based on our examination of the legislative history, we agree with the Court of Appeals that it is unilluminating. The general remarks pointed to by respondents "were obviously not made with this narrow issue in mind and they cannot be said to demonstrate a Congressional desire. . . ." *Jewell Ridge Coal Corp. v. Mine Workers*, 325 U.S. 161, 168–169 (1945). Respondents' argument based on the legislative history relies heavily on Senator Muskie's observation that a new source is subject to the LAER requirement. But the full statement is ambiguous and like the text of § 173 itself, this comment does not tell us what a new source is, much less that it is to have an inflexible definition. We find that the legislative history as a whole is silent on the precise issue before us. It is, however, consistent with the view that the EPA should have broad discretion in implementing the policies of the 1977 Amendments.

More importantly, that history plainly identifies the policy concerns that motivated the enactment; the plantwide definition is fully consistent with one of those concerns — the allowance of reasonable economic growth — and, whether or not we believe it most effectively implements the other, we must recognize that the EPA has advanced a reasonable explanation for its conclusion that the regulations serve the

---

* Section 302 appears in Title III of the Clean Air Act and contains definitions that are applicable to the entire Act. Section 302(j) defined a "major stationary source" as follows:

> Except as otherwise expressly provided, the terms "major stationary source" and "major emitting facility" mean any stationary facility or source of air pollutants which directly emits, or has the potential to emit, one hundred tons per year or more of any air pollutant (including any major emitting facility or source of fugitive emissions of any such pollutant, as determined by rule by the Administrator).

91 Stat. 770.

environmental objectives as well. Indeed, its reasoning is supported by the public record developed in the rulemaking process,[36] as well as by certain private studies.[37]

Our review of the EPA's varying interpretations of the word "source"—both before and after the 1977 Amendments—convinces us that the agency primarily responsible for administering this important legislation has consistently interpreted it flexibly— not in a sterile textual vacuum, but in the context of implementing policy decisions in a technical and complex arena. The fact that the agency has from time to time changed its interpretation of the term "source" does not, as respondents argue, lead us to conclude that no deference should be accorded the agency's interpretation of the statute. An initial agency interpretation is not instantly carved in stone. On the contrary, the agency, to engage in informed rulemaking, must consider varying interpretations and the wisdom of its policy on a continuing basis. Moreover, the fact that the agency has adopted different definitions in different contexts adds force to the argument that the definition itself is flexible, particularly since Congress has never indicated any disapproval of a flexible reading of the statute.

Significantly, it was not the agency in 1980, but rather the Court of Appeals that read the statute inflexibly to command a plantwide definition for programs designed to maintain clean air and to forbid such a definition for programs designed to improve air quality. The distinction the court drew may well be a sensible one, but our labored review of the problem has surely disclosed that it is not a distinction that Congress ever articulated itself, or one that the EPA found in the statute before the courts began to review the legislative work product. We conclude that it was the Court of Appeals, rather than Congress or any of the decisionmakers who are authorized by Congress to administer this legislation, that was primarily responsible for the 1980 position taken by the agency.

Policy

The arguments over policy that are advanced in the parties' briefs create the impression that respondents are now waging in a judicial forum a specific policy battle which they ultimately lost in the agency and in the 32 jurisdictions opting for the "bubble concept," but one which was never waged in the Congress. Such policy arguments are more properly addressed to legislators or administrators, not to judges.[38]

---

36. See, for example, the statement of the New York State Department of Environmental Conservation, pointing out that denying a source owner flexibility in selecting options made it "simpler and cheaper to operate old, more polluting sources than to trade up...."

37. "Economists have proposed that economic incentives be substituted for the cumbersome administrative-legal framework. The objective is to make the profit and cost incentives that work so well in the marketplace work for pollution control.... [The 'bubble' or 'netting' concept] is a first attempt in this direction. By giving a plant manager flexibility to find the places and processes within a plant that control emissions most cheaply, pollution control can be achieved more quickly and cheaply." L. Lave & G. Omenn, Cleaning the Air: Reforming the Clean Air Act 28 (1981) (footnote omitted).

38. Respondents point out if a brand new factory that will emit over 100 tons of pollutants is constructed in a nonattainment area, that plant must obtain a permit pursuant to § 172(b)(6) and in order to do so, it must satisfy the § 173 conditions, including the LAER requirement. Respondents argue if an old plant containing several large emitting units is to be modernized by the replacement

In these cases the Administrator's interpretation represents a reasonable accommodation of manifestly competing interests and is entitled to deference: the regulatory scheme is technical and complex, the agency considered the matter in a detailed and reasoned fashion, and the decision involves reconciling conflicting policies. Congress intended to accommodate both interests, but did not do so itself on the level of specificity presented by these cases. Perhaps that body consciously desired the Administrator to strike the balance at this level, thinking that those with great expertise and charged with responsibility for administering the provision would be in a better position to do so; perhaps it simply did not consider the question at this level; and perhaps Congress was unable to forge a coalition on either side of the question, and those on each side decided to take their chances with the scheme devised by the agency. For judicial purposes, it matters not which of these things occurred.

Judges are not experts in the field, and are not part of either political branch of the Government. Courts must, in some cases, reconcile competing political interests, but not on the basis of the judges' personal policy preferences. In contrast, an agency to which Congress has delegated policymaking responsibilities may, within the limits of that delegation, properly rely upon the incumbent administration's views of wise policy to inform its judgments. While agencies are not directly accountable to the people, the Chief Executive is, and it is entirely appropriate for this political branch of the Government to make such policy choices—resolving the competing interests which Congress itself either inadvertently did not resolve, or intentionally left to be resolved by the agency charged with the administration of the statute in light of everyday realities.

When a challenge to an agency construction of a statutory provision, fairly conceptualized, really centers on the wisdom of the agency's policy, rather than whether it is a reasonable choice within a gap left open by Congress, the challenge must fail. In such a case, federal judges—who have no constituency—have a duty to respect legitimate policy choices made by those who do. The responsibilities for assessing the wisdom of such policy choices and resolving the struggle between competing views of the public interest are not judicial ones: "Our Constitution vests such responsibilities in the political branches." *TVA v. Hill,* 437 U.S. 153, 195 (1978).

We hold that the EPA's definition of the term "source" is a permissible construction of the statute which seeks to accommodate progress in reducing air pollution with economic growth. "The Regulations which the Administrator has adopted provide what the agency could allowably view as . . . [an] effective reconciliation of these two-fold ends. . . ." *United States v. Shimer,* 367 U.S., at 383.***

---

of one or more units emitting over 100 tons of pollutant with a new unit emitting less—but still more than 100 tons—the result should be no different simply because "it happens to be built not at a new site, but within a pre-existing plant."

Notes and Questions

1. **Regulatory and Procedural Posture?** Recall from Chapter 4 that *Chevron* involved a challenge to the EPA's adoption of the "bubble concept" for purposes of the New Source Review program established by the Clean Air Act Amendments of 1977, Pub. L. 95-95, 91 Stat. 685. What was the status of the bubble rule when the Supreme Court granted certiorari in *Chevron*? The basis for the lower court's action?

2. **The Agency's Authority When Acting Under an Express Delegation?** *Chevron* sets out a seemingly comprehensive framework for judicial review of agency statutory interpretations that takes account of the statute the agency is acting under, the APA, the form of administrative action that the court is reviewing, and the perceived quality of the agency's action, among other factors.

Justice Stevens' analysis begins in Part II by describing the relationship between the courts and the agency when the agency has acted under a statutory provision that expressly delegates authority to the agency to promulgate policy with the force of law. In this scenario, "legislative regulations are given controlling weight unless they are arbitrary, capricious, or manifestly contrary to the statute." From where does this standard of review derive? See the standards of review listed in 5 U.S.C. § 706.

Why didn't the Court in *Chevron* review EPA's adoption of the bubble concept under the standard for express delegations of regulatory authority? Note that, in its 1981 regulation adopting the bubble concept, EPA did not cite a statutory provision that expressly directed it to define a "source." *See* Requirements for Preparation, Adoption and Submittal of Implementation Plans and Approval and Promulgation of Implementation Plans, 46 Fed. Reg. 50,766 (Oct. 14, 1981).

3. **The Agency's Authority When Acting Within the Permissible Range of Discretion or "*Chevron* Space"?** Justice Stevens next observes that "[s]ometimes the legislative delegation to an agency on a particular question is implicit rather than explicit." This occurs when the pertinent statute does not express a "specific intention" on the question addressed by the agency — i.e., when the statute is ambiguous or leaves a "gap" to be filled. When Congress impliedly delegates interpretative authority to an agency, "a court may not substitute its own construction of a statutory provision for a *reasonable* interpretation made by the administrator of an agency" (emphasis added). Professor Strauss calls this area of agency authority "*Chevron* space." It is "the area within which an administrative agency has been statutorily empowered to act in a manner that creates legal obligations or constraints — that is, its delegated or allocated authority." Peter L. Strauss, *"Deference" Is Too Confusing — Let's Call Them "Chevron Space" and "Skidmore Weight"*, 112 Colum. L. Rev. 1143, 1145 (2012).

Why does indeterminate statutory language create "space" for an agency to promulgate interpretations that carry the force of law (if reasonable)? The Court's opinion can be read in at least two ways. First, Justice Stevens might be saying that when Congress uses indeterminate language, it *intends or should be presumed to intend* to delegate to the agency authority to implement the meaning of the statutory text it enacts. On this account, *Chevron* establishes a canon or presumption that indeterminate language delegates interpretative authority; when the agency exercises that authority, its interpretation, if reasonable, is controlling because this is what the statute contemplated.

Why in the Court's view should ambiguous or incompletely specified language presumptively be read as a delegation to the EPA rather than to the courts? For example, the relevant statutory text in *Skidmore* ("a workweek longer than forty hours") was also indeterminate as applied to the issue of "on call" time, yet the issue was considered one for the courts. Does the *Chevron* Court's presumption reflect the frequency with which agencies and the courts are called upon to interpret the statute? The relative expertise of the courts and the agency vis-à-vis the subjects of the statute? Can the Court's presumption be reconciled with 5 U.S.C. § 706 ("To the extent necessary to decision and when presented, the reviewing court shall decide all relevant questions of law, interpret constitutional and statutory provisions, and determine the meaning or applicability of the terms of an agency action.")? With § 706(2)(A), which directs courts to set aside agency action that is "arbitrary, capricious, an abuse of discretion, *or otherwise not in accordance with law*"? Can the presumption be reconciled with § 706(2)(C), directing courts to set aside agency action found to be "in excess of statutory jurisdiction, authority, or limitations, or short of statutory right"?

Second, Justice Stevens might be saying that the agency has authority to make subsidiary or supplemental policy decisions within the space allowed by the statute. On this account, the agency's authority to make subsidiary policy derives from its organic act and from statutory provisions that grant the agency general authority to promulgate rules and interpretations. *See, e.g.*, 42 U.S.C. § 7601(a)(1) ("The [EPA] Administrator is authorized to prescribe such regulations as are necessary to carry out his functions under [the Clean Air Act, as amended].").The agency's reasonable interpretation of an ambiguous statutory provision is controlling because it is an exercise of its background authority. The requirement that the agency interpretation be reasonable ensures that the interpretation is not inconsistent with the meaning of the statutory provision the agency interpretation implements.

Which of these views of *Chevron* best accounts for the opinion? Which is more attractive as a normative matter? Are they necessarily exclusive of one another?

4. **Agencies as Politically Accountable Interpreters?** In what is perhaps *Chevron*'s most famous passage, Justice Stevens sets out a political theory argument for reading indeterminate statutory language to delegate interpretative authority to the agency. Compared to the courts, he says, the agency has greater democratic accountability:

> Judges are not experts in the field, and are not part of either political branch of the Government. Courts must, in some cases, reconcile competing political interests, but not on the basis of the judges' personal policy preferences. In contrast, an agency to which Congress has delegated policymaking responsibilities may, within the limits of that delegation, properly rely upon the incumbent administration's views of wise policy to inform its judgments.

> While agencies are not directly accountable to the people, the Chief Execu-
> tive is, and it is entirely appropriate for this political branch of the Government
> to make such policy choices — resolving the competing interests which
> Congress itself either inadvertently did not resolve, or intentionally left to be
> resolved by the agency charged with the administration of the statute in light
> of everyday realities.

Assume the Supreme Court is correct that agencies are more accountable to the political branches than courts. What does the accountability of an interpreter have to do with whether a piece of legislation delegated interpretive authority to that interpreter? In general, do we want the political branches to decide what the law is, or do we count on relatively neutral, principled courts for this task? Why should Congress be presumed to "punt" to an agency rather than the Article III courts when it cannot settle for itself how a specific problem should be addressed? Is it likely Congress when enacting legislation expects administrative agencies to have final interpretive say over ambiguous points in that legislation even when the heads of those agencies are appointed by a President from a different party?

5. **Consistency of Agency Interpretation with Congressional Intent ("***Chevron*** Step 1").** *Chevron* famously establishes a two-step framework to determine the effect of an agency's statutory interpretation. *Chevron* Step 1 goes to whether the agency interpretation is consistent with enacted law. The question here is whether "Congress has directly spoken to the precise question at issue. If the intent of Congress is clear, that is the end of the matter; for the court, as well as the agency, must give effect to the unambiguously expressed intent of Congress."

a. **How to Determine Congressional Intent?** In answering whether Congress has directly spoken to the precise question at issue, *Chevron* instructs reviewing courts to employ "traditional tools of statutory construction." *Chevron*, at n. 9, *supra* p. 584. Which of these "traditional tools" does the Court employ in *Chevron*? Does the Court take a position on the kinds of evidence that can legitimately be consulted to determine statutory meaning, or does it rather use *all* of the traditional tools of statutory interpretation?

Isn't the lower court in *Chevron* correct that use of the bubble concept in nonattainment areas conflicts with Congress's objectives in the Clean Air Act Amendments insofar as the concept permits regulated sources in non-attainment areas to continue rather than reduce their current levels of pollution? Does the Supreme Court dispute the court of appeals' conclusion that use of the bubble concept in nonattainment areas is inconsistent with the objectives of the Clean Air Act Amendments? Is the Supreme Court's difficulty rather with the weight that the court of appeals gave to the amendments' general purpose? Stated differently, does Congress's general goal of reducing pollution in non-attainment zones show definitively that the statutory definition of "source" is incompatible with the bubble concept?

b. **Role of Prior Lower-Court Precedent?** If a lower court previously decided a statutory question in a manner contrary to the agency's current interpretation, is the agency's action unlawful? In *National Cable & Telecommunications Ass'n v.*

Brand X Internet Servs., 545 U.S. 967, 982 (2005), the Supreme Court ruled that "[a] court's prior judicial construction of a statute trumps an agency construction otherwise entitled to *Chevron* deference only if the prior court decision holds that its construction follows from the unambiguous terms of the statute and thus leaves no room for agency discretion."

Brand X involved a dispute over the Federal Communications Commission's (FCC) regulation of internet service providers. The Communications Act of 1934, Pub. L. No. 73-416, 48 Stat. 1064, as amended by the Telecommunications Act of 1996, Pub. L. No. 104-104, 110 Stat. 56, regulates two categories of communications and media businesses. "Information service" providers—those "offering*** a capability for [processing] information via telecommunications," 47 U.S.C. § 153(20)—are subject to mandatory FCC regulation and treated as common carriers. Telecommunications carriers—those "offering*** telecommunications for a fee directly to the public*** regardless of the facilities used," § 153(46)—are not subject to common-carrier FCC regulation. Prior to the FCC order at issue in *Brand X*, the Ninth Circuit had ruled, in a case in which the FCC was not a party, that internet service delivered via a cable modem was a telecommunications service. *AT&T Corp. v. City of Portland*, 216 F.3d 871 (9th Cir. 2000). In the order at issue in *Brand X*, the FCC classified broadband cable modem service as an information service. On review, the Ninth Circuit held that the FCC order was contrary to law because of the *City of Portland* precedent.

The Supreme Court found the Ninth Circuit's approach inconsistent with *Chevron*:

> *Chevron* established a "presumption that Congress, when it left ambiguity in a statute meant for implementation by an agency, understood that the ambiguity would be resolved, first and foremost, by the agency, and desired the agency (rather than the courts) to possess whatever degree of discretion the ambiguity allows." Yet allowing a judicial precedent to foreclose an agency from interpreting an ambiguous statute, as the Court of Appeals assumed it could, would allow a court's interpretation to override an agency's. *Chevron*'s premise is that it is for agencies, not courts, to fill statutory gaps. The better rule is to hold judicial interpretations contained in precedents to the same demanding *Chevron* step one standard that applies if the court is reviewing the agency's construction on a blank slate: Only a judicial precedent holding that the statute unambiguously forecloses the agency's interpretation, and therefore contains no gap for the agency to fill, displaces a conflicting agency construction.

545 U.S. at 982–83. Since the Ninth Circuit had not made clear in *City of Portland* that the FCC lacked statutory authority to classify broadband cable modem service as an "information service," the case was remanded for the appeals court to engage in the requisite *Chevron*-Step 1 inquiry. Would the case have come out the same if the FCC had been a party in the prior *City of Portland* case and was unable to obtain Supreme Court review?

c. **Role of Canons?** Another issue that arises at Step 1 involves the relationship between the agency's interpretation and the canons of construction. *See Yates v. United States,* 135 S. Ct. 1074 (2015), *supra* Chapter 2[B][1][a]. If the pertinent canon (or canons) point to an interpretation other than the one put forward by the agency, is the agency interpretation contrary to "the unambiguously expressed intent of Congress"? Is there a basis for concluding that an interpretation suggested by a canon clearly establishes the intent of Congress? Are they ever fully dispositive of statutory authority issues at Step 1? What if the canon embodies a deeply-held constitutional or other substantive norm requiring clear language from Congress before that norm can be displaced? *See generally* Kenneth A. Bamberger, *Normative Canons in the Review of Administrative Policymaking,* 118 Yale L.J. 64 (2008).

6. **Reasonableness of Agency Interpretation ("*Chevron* Step 2").** If the agency is acting within the scope of its delegated authority and its interpretation is not inconsistent with the clear intent of Congress, the final question "is whether the agency's answer is based on a permissible construction of the statute." Importantly, there is no requirement that the agency advance the "best" interpretation of the statute: "The court need not conclude that the agency construction was the only one it permissibly could have adopted to uphold the construction, or even the reading the court would have reached if the question initially had arisen in a judicial proceeding." *Chevron,* at n.11, *supra* p. 585.

Why in the Supreme Court's view is the EPA regulation adopting the bubble concept a "permissible construction" of the Clean Air Act Amendments? The Court emphasizes that the regulation balances allowance of reasonable economic growth, on the one hand, with environmental objectives, on the other. Does it follow that *any* regulation that balanced these competing concerns would pass muster at Step 2? What would be the result under *Chevron* if EPA had determined that the value of the natural environment is incalculable and disallowed use of the bubble concept because it led to marginally greater destruction of the environment?

How does the Supreme Court's review of the reasonableness of the EPA's regulation compare to the analysis required by *Skidmore*? Does the *Chevron* Court consider "the thoroughness evident in [EPA's] consideration, the validity of its reasoning, its consistency with earlier and later pronouncements, and all those factors which give it power to persuade"? Does the EPA's oscillation on the bubble concept preclude *Skidmore* respect?

Is the inquiry under *Chevron* Step 2 here any different from what the Court required in *Overton Park, supra* Section [B], or what is entailed in review under APA § 706(2)(a)? For an argument that all three standards are essentially the same, *see* Ronald M. Levin, *The Anatomy of* Chevron: *Step Two Reconsidered,* 72 Chi.-Kent L. Rev. 1253 (1997).

The Court says that "an agency to which Congress has delegated policymaking responsibilities may, within the limits of that delegation, properly rely upon the incumbent administration's views of wise policy to inform its judgments." Does it follow that EPA would be free to revise its reliance on the bubble concept if, say, an ardent environmentalist was elected President and appointed the head of Greenpeace as EPA Administrator? Why not? Does the answer to this question suggest that what is going on in *Chevron* Step 2 is not so much an "interpretation" of the statutory text as a policy determination within the agency's authority? Does that policy determination within those limits nevertheless have the force of law?

7. **Does the Agency Have Interpretive or Subsidiary Policymaking Authority ("*Chevron* Step Zero")?** Note that not all indeterminate statutory provisions trigger *Chevron*'s presumption that such provisions indicate a delegation of interpretative authority to the agency, or, alternatively, *Chevron*'s recognition that the agency has a range of policymaking discretion within which its decisions have the force of law. The agency which claims such authority must be "charged with the administration of the statute." In addition, the agency must be authorized to promulgate rules, engage in adjudication, or otherwise issue interpretations of the statute it administers. Agencies typically receive such authorization in their organic statutes or in newly enacted regulatory statutes. *See, e.g.,* 12 U.S.C. § 5521(b)(1) (granting the Consumer Financial Protection Bureau Director authority to "prescribe rules and issue orders and guidance, as may be necessary or appropriate to enable the Bureau to administer and carry out the purposes and objectives of the Federal consumer financial laws, and to prevent evasions thereof"); 42 U.S.C. § 7607 (granting EPA similar rulemaking authority for programs established by the Clean Air Act). On this point, compare the treatment of the EEOC in *General Electric v. Gilbert, supra* Chapter 4[E].

––––––––

Despite setting out a seemingly comprehensive framework for judicial review of agency statutory interpretations, *Chevron* did not address a number of threshold questions about when its framework applied. *See generally* Thomas W. Merrill & Kristin E. Hickman, Chevron's *Domain*, 89 Geo. L.J. 833 (2001). At the front end, *Chevron* did not establish a hard-and-fast test for determining when Congress implicitly delegated interpretative authority to the implementing agency. To the contrary, *Chevron*'s endorsement of all "traditional" tools of statutory interpretation invited debate about when the intent of Congress was sufficiently clear to preclude an agency from further elaborating the meaning of a statute. At the back end, *Chevron* did not address the form in which an agency must act if it intends its statutory interpretation to have the force of law. Suppose, for example, that EPA set forth its views concerning the bubble concept in a letter to the regulatory community or a Facebook post rather than a regulation promulgated following notice-and-comment procedures. Would its views still be binding on the courts? And what of *Skidmore*? If an agency interpretation was not entitled to *Chevron* "deference," might it still warrant *Skidmore* "respect" or "weight"? How, for example, would a court applying *Chevron* evaluate the Customs Service's tariff ruling reproduced in Chapter 4[B][2]?

Following a decade and a half in which the Supreme Court and lower courts applied *Chevron* ever more expansively, the Supreme Court turned to these questions in 2001.

Before reading the decision that follows, review the customs letter ruling reproduced in Chapter 4[B][2], *supra* p. 421.

United States v. Mead Corp.

533 U.S. 218 (2001)

JUSTICE SOUTER delivered the opinion of the Court.

The question is whether a tariff classification ruling by the United States Customs Service deserves judicial deference. The Federal Circuit rejected Customs's invocation of *Chevron U.S.A. Inc. v. Natural Resources Defense Council, Inc.*, 467 U.S. 837 (1984), in support of such a ruling, to which it gave no deference. We agree that a tariff classification has no claim to judicial deference under *Chevron*, there being no indication that Congress intended such a ruling to carry the force of law, but we hold that under *Skidmore v. Swift & Co.*, 323 U.S. 134 (1944), the ruling is eligible to claim respect according to its persuasiveness.

I

A

Imports are taxed under the Harmonized Tariff Schedule of the United States (HTSUS), 19 U.S.C. § 1202. Title 19 U.S.C. § 1500(b) provides that Customs "shall, under rules and regulations prescribed by the Secretary [of the Treasury,] . . . fix the final classification and rate of duty applicable to . . . merchandise" under the HTSUS. Section 1502(a) provides that

> "[t]he Secretary of the Treasury shall establish and promulgate such rules and regulations not inconsistent with the law (including regulations establishing procedures for the issuance of binding rulings prior to the entry of the merchandise concerned), and may disseminate such information as may be necessary to secure a just, impartial, and uniform appraisement of imported merchandise and the classification and assessment of duties thereon at the various ports of entry."[1]

See also § 1624 (general delegation to Secretary to issue rules and regulations for the admission of goods).

The Secretary provides for tariff rulings before the entry of goods by regulations authorizing "ruling letters" setting tariff classifications for particular imports. 19 CFR § 177.8 (2000). A ruling letter

> "represents the official position of the Customs Service with respect to the particular transaction or issue described therein and is binding on all Customs Service personnel in accordance with the provisions of this section until

---

1. The statutory term "ruling" is defined by regulation as "a written statement . . . that interprets and applies the provisions of the Customs and related laws to a specific set of facts." 19 CFR § 177.1(d) (1) (2000).

modified or revoked. In the absence of a change of practice or other modification or revocation which affects the principle of the ruling set forth in the ruling letter, that principle may be cited as authority in the disposition of transactions involving the same circumstances." § 177.9(a).

After the transaction that gives it birth, a ruling letter is to "be applied only with respect to transactions involving articles identical to the sample submitted with the ruling request or to articles whose description is identical to the description set forth in the ruling letter." § 177.9(b)(2). As a general matter, such a letter is "subject to modification or revocation without notice to any person, except the person to whom the letter was addressed," § 177.9(c), and the regulations consequently provide that "no other person should rely on the ruling letter or assume that the principles of that ruling will be applied in connection with any transaction other than the one described in the letter," *ibid.* Since ruling letters respond to transactions of the moment, they are not subject to notice and comment before being issued, may be published but need only be made "available for public inspection," 19 U.S.C. § 1625(a), and, at the time this action arose, could be modified without notice and comment under most circumstances, 19 CFR § 177.10(c) (2000).***

Any of the 46 port-of-entry Customs offices may issue ruling letters, and so may the Customs Headquarters Office, in providing "[a]dvice or guidance as to the interpretation or proper application of the Customs and related laws with respect to a specific Customs transaction [which] may be requested by Customs Service field offices . . . at any time, whether the transaction is prospective, current, or completed," 19 CFR § 177.11(a) (2000). Most ruling letters contain little or no reasoning, but simply describe goods and state the appropriate category and tariff. A few letters, like the Headquarters ruling at issue here, set out a rationale in some detail.

B

Respondent, the Mead Corporation, imports "day planners," three-ring binders with pages having room for notes of daily schedules and phone numbers and addresses, together with a calendar and suchlike. The tariff schedule on point falls under the HTSUS heading for "[r]egisters, account books, notebooks, order books, receipt books, letter pads, memorandum pads, diaries and similar articles," HTSUS subheading 4820.10, which comprises two subcategories. Items in the first, "[d]iaries, notebooks and address books, bound; memorandum pads, letter pads and similar articles," were subject to a tariff of 4.0% at the time in controversy. Objects in the second, covering "[o]ther" items, were free of duty. HTSUS subheading 4820.10.40.

Between 1989 and 1993, Customs repeatedly treated day planners under the "other" HTSUS subheading. In January 1993, however, Customs changed its position, and issued a Headquarters ruling letter classifying Mead's day planners as "Diaries . . . , bound" subject to tariff under subheading 4820.10.20. That letter was short on explanation, but after Mead's protest, Customs Headquarters issued a new letter, carefully reasoned but never published, reaching the same conclusion. This letter considered two definitions of "diary" from the Oxford English Dictionary, the first covering a daily journal of the past day's events, the second a book including "'printed dates for daily memoranda and jottings; also . . . calendars . . . .'" *Id.*, at 33a–34a (quoting Oxford English Dictionary 321 (Compact ed. 1982)). Customs concluded that "diary" was not confined to the first, in part because the broader definition reflects commercial usage and hence the "commercial identity of these items in the marketplace." As for the definition of "bound," Customs concluded that HTSUS was not referring to "bookbinding," but to a less exact sort of fastening described in the Harmonized Commodity Description and Coding System Explanatory Notes to Heading 4820, which spoke of binding by "'reinforcements or fittings of metal, plastics, etc.'"

Customs rejected Mead's further protest of the second Headquarters ruling letter, and Mead filed suit in the Court of International Trade (CIT). The CIT granted the Government's motion for summary judgment, adopting Customs's reasoning without saying anything about deference.

Mead then went to the United States Court of Appeals for the Federal Circuit. While the case was pending there this Court decided *United States v. Haggar Apparel Co.*, 526 U.S. 380 (1999), holding that Customs regulations receive the deference described in *Chevron U.S.A. Inc.* v. *Natural Resources Defense Council, Inc.*, 467 U.S. 837 (1984). The appeals court requested briefing on the impact of *Haggar*, and the Government argued that classification rulings, like Customs regulations, deserve *Chevron* deference.

The Federal Circuit, however, reversed the CIT and held that Customs classification rulings should not get *Chevron* deference, owing to differences from the regulations at issue in *Haggar*. Rulings are not preceded by notice and comment as under the Administrative Procedure Act (APA), 5 U.S.C. § 553, they "do not carry the force of law and are not, like regulations, intended to clarify the rights and obligations of importers beyond the specific case under review."***

The Court of Appeals accordingly gave no deference at all to the ruling classifying the Mead day planners and rejected the agency's reasoning as to both "diary" and "bound." It thought that planners were not diaries because they had no space for "relatively extensive notations about events, observations, feelings, or thoughts" in the past. And it concluded that diaries "bound" in subheading 4810.10.20 presupposed "unbound" diaries, such that treating ring-fastened diaries as "bound" would leave the "unbound diary" an empty category.

We granted certiorari in order to consider the limits of *Chevron* deference owed to administrative practice in applying a statute. We hold that administrative implementation of a particular statutory provision qualifies for *Chevron* deference when it appears that Congress delegated authority to the agency generally to make [pronouncements] carrying the force of law, and that the agency interpretation claiming deference was promulgated in the exercise of that authority. Delegation of such authority may be shown in a variety of ways, as by an agency's power to engage in adjudication or notice-and-comment rulemaking, or by some other indication of a comparable congressional intent. The Customs ruling at issue here fails to qualify, although the possibility that it deserves some deference under *Skidmore* leads us to vacate and remand.

II

A

When Congress has "explicitly left a gap for an agency to fill, there is an express delegation of authority to the agency to elucidate a specific provision of the statute by regulation," *Chevron*, 467 U.S., at 843–844, and any ensuing regulation is binding in the courts unless procedurally defective, arbitrary or capricious in substance, or manifestly contrary to the statute. *See id.*, at 844; *United States v. Morton*, 467 U.S. 822, 834 (1984); APA, 5 U.S.C. §§ 706(2)(A), (D). But whether or not they enjoy any express delegation of authority on a particular question, agencies charged with applying a statute necessarily make all sorts of interpretive choices, and while not all of those choices bind judges to follow them, they certainly may influence courts facing questions the agencies have already answered. "[T]he well-reasoned views of the agencies implementing a statute 'constitute a body of experience and informed judgment to which courts and litigants may properly resort for guidance,'" *Bragdon v. Abbott*, 524 U.S. 624, 642 (1998) (quoting *Skidmore*, 323 U.S., at 139–140), and "[w]e have long recognized that considerable weight should be accorded to an executive department's construction of a statutory scheme it is entrusted to administer . . . ." *Chevron, supra*, at 844. The fair measure of deference to an agency administering its own statute has been understood to vary with circumstances, and courts have looked to the degree of the agency's care, its consistency, formality, and relative expertness, and to the persuasiveness of the agency's position. The approach has produced a spectrum of judicial responses, from great respect at one end, see, *e.g.*, *Aluminum Co. of America v. Central Lincoln Peoples' Util. Dist.*, 467 U.S. 380, 389–390 (1984) ("'substantial deference'" to administrative construction), to near indifference at the other, see, *e.g.*, *Bowen v. Georgetown Univ. Hospital*, 488 U.S. 204, 212–213 (1988) (interpretation advanced for the first time in a litigation brief). Justice Jackson summed things up in *Skidmore v. Swift & Co.*:

> "The weight [accorded to an administrative] judgment in a particular case will depend upon the thoroughness evident in its consideration, the validity of its reasoning, its consistency with earlier and later pronouncements, and all those factors which give it power to persuade, if lacking power to control."

Since 1984, we have identified a category of interpretive choices distinguished by an additional reason for judicial deference. This Court in *Chevron* recognized that Congress not only engages in express delegation of specific interpretive authority, but that "[s]ometimes the legislative delegation to an agency on a particular question is implicit." Congress, that is, may not have expressly delegated authority or responsibility to implement a particular provision or fill a particular gap. Yet it can still be apparent from the agency's generally conferred authority and other statutory circumstances that Congress would expect the agency to be able to speak with the force of law when it addresses ambiguity in the statute or fills a space in the enacted law, even one about which "Congress did not actually have an intent" as to a particular result. When circumstances implying such an expectation exist, a reviewing court has no business rejecting an agency's exercise of its generally conferred authority to resolve a particular statutory ambiguity simply because the agency's chosen resolution seems unwise, but is obliged to accept the agency's position if Congress has not previously spoken to the point at issue and the agency's interpretation is reasonable, cf. 5 U.S.C. § 706(2) (a reviewing court shall set aside agency action, findings, and conclusions found to be "arbitrary, capricious, an abuse of discretion, or otherwise not in accordance with law").

We have recognized a very good indicator of delegation meriting *Chevron* treatment in express congressional authorizations to engage in the process of rulemaking or adjudication that produces regulations or rulings for which deference is claimed. See, *e.g.*, *EEOC v. Arabian American Oil Co.*, 499 U.S. 244, 257 (1991) (no *Chevron* deference to agency guideline where congressional delegation did not include the power to "promulgate rules or regulations"). It is fair to assume generally that Congress contemplates administrative action with the effect of law when it provides for a relatively formal administrative procedure tending to foster the fairness and deliberation that should underlie a pronouncement of such force. Thus, the overwhelming number of our cases applying *Chevron* deference have reviewed the fruits of notice-and-comment rulemaking or formal adjudication. That said, and as significant as notice-and-comment is in pointing to *Chevron* authority, the want of that procedure here does not decide the case, for we have sometimes found reasons for *Chevron* deference even when no such administrative formality was required and none was afforded, see, *e.g.*, *NationsBank of N.C., N.A. v. Variable Annuity Life Ins. Co.*, 513 U.S. 251, 256–257, 263 (1995). The fact that the tariff classification here was not a product of such formal process does not alone, therefore, bar the application of *Chevron*.

There are, nonetheless, ample reasons to deny *Chevron* deference here. The authorization for classification rulings, and Customs's practice in making them, present a case far removed not only from notice-and-comment process, but from any other circumstances reasonably suggesting that Congress ever thought of classification rulings as deserving the deference claimed for them here.

B

No matter which angle we choose for viewing the Customs ruling letter in this case, it fails to qualify under *Chevron*. On the face of the statute, to begin with, the terms of the congressional delegation give no indication that Congress meant to delegate authority to Customs to issue classification rulings with the force of law. We are not, of course, here making any global statement about Customs's authority, for it is true that the general rulemaking power conferred on Customs, *see* 19 U.S.C. § 1624, authorizes some regulation with the force of law, or "legal norms"***. It is true as well that Congress had classification rulings in mind when it explicitly authorized, in a parenthetical, the issuance of "regulations establishing procedures for the issuance of binding rulings prior to the entry of the merchandise concerned," 19 U.S.C. § 1502(a). The reference to binding classifications does not, however, bespeak the legislative type of activity that would naturally bind more than the parties to the ruling, once the goods classified are admitted into this country. And though the statute's direction to disseminate "information" necessary to "secure" uniformity seems to assume that a ruling may be precedent in later transactions, precedential value alone does not add up to *Chevron* entitlement; interpretive rules may sometimes function as precedents, *see* Strauss, *The Rulemaking Continuum*, 41 Duke L.J. 1463, 1472–1473 (1992), and they enjoy no *Chevron* status as a class. In any event, any precedential claim of a classification ruling is counterbalanced by the provision for independent review of Customs classifications by the CIT, *see* 28 U.S.C. §§ 2638–2640; the scheme for CIT review includes a provision that treats classification rulings on par with the Secretary's rulings on "valuation, rate of duty, marking, restricted merchandise, entry requirements, drawbacks, vessel repairs, or similar matters," § 1581(h); *see* § 2639(b). It is hard to imagine a congressional understanding more at odds with the *Chevron* regime.

It is difficult, in fact, to see in the agency practice itself any indication that Customs ever set out with a lawmaking pretense in mind when it undertook to make classifications like these. Customs does not generally engage in notice-and-comment practice when issuing them, and their treatment by the agency makes it clear that a letter's binding character as a ruling stops short of third parties; Customs has regarded a classification as conclusive only as between itself and the importer to whom it was issued, 19 CFR § 177.9(c) (2000), and even then only until Customs has given advance notice of intended change, §§ 177.9(a), (c). Other importers are in fact warned against assuming any right of detrimental reliance. § 177.9(c).

Indeed, to claim that classifications have legal force is to ignore the reality that 46 different Customs offices issue 10,000 to 15,000 of them each year. Any suggestion that rulings intended to have the force of law are being churned out at a rate of 10,000 a year at an agency's 46 scattered offices is simply self-refuting. Although the circumstances are less startling here, with a Headquarters letter in issue, none of the relevant statutes recognizes this category of rulings as separate or different from others; there is thus no indication that a more potent delegation might have been understood as going to Headquarters even when Headquarters provides developed reasoning, as it did in this instance.***

In sum, classification rulings are best treated like interpretations contained in policy statements, agency manuals, and enforcement guidelines. They are beyond the *Chevron* pale.

C

To agree with the Court of Appeals that Customs ruling letters do not fall within *Chevron* is not, however, to place them outside the pale of any deference whatever. *Chevron* did nothing to eliminate *Skidmore*'s holding that an agency's interpretation may merit some deference whatever its form, given the "specialized experience and broader investigations and information" available to the agency, and given the value of uniformity in its administrative and judicial understandings of what a national law requires.

There is room at least to raise a *Skidmore* claim here, where the regulatory scheme is highly detailed, and Customs can bring the benefit of specialized experience to bear on the subtle questions in this case: whether the daily planner with room for brief daily entries falls under "diaries," when diaries are grouped with "notebooks and address books, bound; memorandum pads, letter pads and similar articles," HTSUS subheading 4820.10.20; and whether a planner with a ring binding should qualify as "bound," when a binding may be typified by a book, but also may have "reinforcements or fittings of metal, plastics, etc.," Harmonized Commodity Description and Coding System Explanatory Notes to Heading 4820. A classification ruling in this situation may therefore at least seek a respect proportional to its "power to persuade." Such a ruling may surely claim the merit of its writer's thoroughness, logic, and expertness, its fit with prior interpretations, and any other sources of weight.

D***

Although we all accept the position that the Judiciary should defer to at least some *** administrative action, we have to decide how to take account of the great range of its variety. If the primary objective is to simplify the judicial process of giving or withholding deference, then the diversity of statutes authorizing discretionary administrative action must be declared irrelevant or minimized. If, on the other hand, it is simply implausible that Congress intended such a broad range of statutory authority to produce only two varieties of administrative action, demanding either *Chevron* deference or none at all, then the breadth of the spectrum of possible agency action must be taken into account.*** The Court's choice has been to tailor deference to variety. This acceptance of the range of statutory variation has led the Court to recognize more than one variety of judicial deference, just as the Court has recognized a variety of indicators that Congress would expect *Chevron* deference.[18]***

JUSTICE SCALIA, dissenting.

* * * The doctrine of *Chevron*—that all authoritative agency interpretations of statutes they are charged with administering deserve deference—was rooted in a legal presumption of congressional intent, important to the division of powers between the Second and Third Branches. When, *Chevron* said, Congress leaves an ambiguity in a statute that is to be administered by an executive agency, it is presumed that Congress meant to give the agency discretion, within the limits of reasonable interpretation, as to how the ambiguity is to be resolved. By committing enforcement of the statute to an agency rather than the courts, Congress committed its initial and primary interpretation to that branch as well.***

---

18. It is, of course, true that the limit of *Chevron* deference is not marked by a hard-edged rule. But *Chevron* itself is a good example showing when *Chevron* deference is warranted, while this is a good case showing when it is not. Judges in other, perhaps harder, cases will make reasoned choices between the two examples, the way courts have always done.

The basis in principle for today's new doctrine can be described as follows: The background rule is that ambiguity in legislative instructions to agencies is to be resolved not by the agencies but by the judges. Specific congressional intent to depart from this rule must be found — and while there is no single touchstone for such intent it can generally be found when Congress has authorized the agency to act through (what the Court says is) relatively formal procedures such as informal rulemaking and formal (and informal?) adjudication, and when the agency in fact employs such procedures.*** [T]he Court's principal criterion of congressional intent to supplant its background rule seems to me quite implausible. There is no necessary connection between the formality of procedure and the power of the entity administering the procedure to resolve authoritatively questions of law. The most formal of the procedures the Court refers to — formal adjudication — is modeled after the process used in trial courts, which of course are not generally accorded deference on questions of law. The purpose of such a procedure is to produce a closed record for determination and review of the facts — which implies nothing about the power of the agency subjected to the procedure to resolve authoritatively questions of law.***

Notes and Questions

1. **The Regulatory Posture?** We have now encountered the tariff dispute that gave rise to *Mead* two times. *See supra* Chapter 4[B][2]. What occurred at the agency level before Mead sought judicial review of the tariff classification of its day planners? What did the agency conclude? Which of the APA policymaking formats — rulemaking or adjudication, formal or informal — did the Customs Service follow in determining that Mead's day planners were properly classified as "diaries"?

2. **The Procedural Posture?** Mead challenged the Customs Service's classification in the U.S. Court of International Trade, which has exclusive jurisdiction to hear civil actions challenging tariff determinations of the Customs Service (now U.S. Customs and Border Protection, a unit of the Department of Homeland Security). *See* 28 U.S.C. § 1581. What did the Court of International Trade conclude regarding the classification of day planners? What did the U.S. Court of Appeals for the Federal Circuit conclude? Did the Court of International Trade give any weight to the views expressed by the Customs Service in the letter ruling reproduced in chapter 4? Did it find that Customs' ruling was entitled to *Chevron* "deference"? *Skidmore* "respect"? What about the Court of Appeals?

3. **When Does the *Chevron* Framework Apply? — Front-End Considerations.** *Chevron* holds that when a statute is indeterminate with respect to the question addressed in an agency interpretation, Congress delegated authority to the agency charged with administering the statute to promulgate a reasonable interpretation that has the force of law. In *Mead*, the Supreme Court clarifies that not all statements by the agency about the meaning of the statute it administers are covered by *Chevron*. Rather, a reviewing court must assure itself that Congress delegated interpretative authority, and that the agency interpretation that claims deference is, in fact, an exercise of the agency's delegated interpretative authority.

The Supreme Court notes that the Customs Service through the Secretary of the Treasury has "general rulemaking power" that "authorizes some regulation with the force of law." *See* 19 U.S.C. § 1624 ("In addition to the specific powers conferred by this chapter the Secretary of the Treasury is authorized to make such rules and regulations as may be necessary to carry out the provisions of this chapter."). In addition, 19 U.S.C. § 1502(a) provides:

> The Secretary of the Treasury shall establish and promulgate such rules and regulations not inconsistent with the law (including regulations establishing procedures for the issuance of binding rulings prior to the entry of the merchandise concerned), and may disseminate such information as may be necessary to secure a just, impartial, and uniform appraisement of imported merchandise and the classification and assessment of duties thereon at the various ports of entry.

Why, in the Supreme Court's view, are these provisions insufficient to show that Congress intended Customs' letter rulings to have the force of law? Is the difficulty that the statutes do not speak to the legal effect of letter rulings? That while Customs has authority to issue "rules and regulations" with the force of law, it did not exercise that authority when it issued the letter ruling in *Mead*, or with respect to tariff classifications as a general matter?

What must a statute say, post-*Mead*, to trigger the *Chevron* presumption that an agency interpretation carries the force of law? Consider note 18 to the Court's opinion. Consider also the views of Justice Breyer, concurring in part and concurring in the judgment in *City of Arlington, Tex. v. FCC*, 133 S. Ct. 1863 (2013). (The majority opinion in *City of Arlington* appears in Section [C][3], *infra*.) Justice Breyer stated (133 S. Ct. at 1875–76):

> [T]he existence of statutory ambiguity is sometimes not enough to warrant the conclusion that Congress has left a deference-warranting gap for the agency to fill because our cases make clear that other, sometimes context-specific, factors will on occasion prove relevant. (And, given the vast number of government statutes, regulatory programs, and underlying circumstances, that variety is hardly surprising.) In *Mead*, for example, we looked to several factors other than simple ambiguity to help determine whether Congress left a statutory gap, thus delegating to the agency the authority to fill that gap with an interpretation that would carry "the force of law." Elsewhere, we have assessed
>
>> "the interstitial nature of the legal question, the related expertise of the Agency, the importance of the question to administration of the statute, the complexity of that administration, and the careful consideration the Agency has given the question over a long period of time." *Barnhart v. Walton*, 535 U.S. 212, 222 (2002).

The subject matter of the relevant provision — for instance, its distance from the agency's ordinary statutory duties or its falling within the scope of another agency's authority — has also proved relevant. *See Gonzales* [*v. Oregon*, 546 U.S. 243, 265–266 (2006)]. *See also* Gellhorn & Verkuil, *Controlling* Chevron-*Based Delegations*, 20 Cardozo L. Rev. 989, 1007–1010 (1999).

Moreover, the statute's text, its context, the structure of the statutory scheme, and canons of textual construction are relevant in determining whether the statute is ambiguous and can be equally helpful in determining whether such ambiguity comes accompanied with agency authority to fill a gap with an interpretation that carries the force of law. Statutory purposes, including those revealed in part by legislative and regulatory history, can be similarly relevant.

4. When Does the *Chevron* Framework Apply? — Back-End Considerations. Perhaps the more significant holding of *Mead* is that, even if an agency possesses delegated interpretative authority, not all statements by the agency about the meaning of the statute it administers have the force of law. Instead, an agency statutory interpretation must reflect an exercise of the agency's delegated authority to bind courts and regulated parties.

The Court stated that when an agency proceeds through "a relatively formal administrative procedure tending to foster the fairness and deliberation that should underlie a pronouncement of such force," the agency is presumed to be exercising its delegated interpretative authority. Which of the APA's policymaking formats does the Court here have in mind? Although formal procedure is a signal that the agency is exercising delegated interpretative authority, it is neither necessary nor sufficient to establish that fact, "for we have sometimes found reasons for *Chevron* deference when no such administrative formality was required and none was afforded." The Court here cites *NationsBank of N. Carolina, N.A. v. Variable Annuity Life Ins. Co.*, 513 U.S. 251 (1995). In *NationsBank*, the Court extended *Chevron* deference to a decision by the Comptroller of the Currency granting a bank's application to serve as a sales agent for annuity contracts issued by a third-party insurer. The Comptroller's decision was set out in a lengthy and closely reasoned letter issued under the signature of a Senior Deputy Comptroller. *See* Petition for Certiorari, app. D, *NationsBank of N. Carolina, N.A. v. Variable Annuity Life Ins. Co.*, 513 U.S. 251 (1995).

Does *NationsBank* suggest why the Court is unwilling to hold, as least as a per se matter, that to qualify for the *Chevron* presumption, an agency's statutory interpretation *must* be promulgated through rulemaking or formal adjudication? Also recall the regulatory framework at issue in *Yakus v. United States*, 321 U.S. 414 (1944), *supra* Chapter 3[B][1][a].

Why does the Court conclude that the tariff ruling in *Mead* does not reflect an exercise of Customs' delegated interpretative authority?

5. **The Status of Customs' Letter Rulings?** The Court says that Customs' classification rulings "are beyond the *Chevron* pale.*** [They] are best treated like interpretations contained in policy statements, agency manuals, and enforcement guidelines." What then is the legal status of Customs' letter ruling? Is it binding on Customs? Mead? Other parties who import diaries? Note Customs' express refusal to give letter rulings stare decisis effect that extends beyond the parties to the ruling and "the reality that 46 different Customs offices issue 10,000 to 15,000 of them each year."

Recall also the debate over when agency "guidance" is effectively a substantive regulation and must be promulgated using notice-and-comment procedures. *See* Note 2 following *Perez v. Mortgage Bankers' Ass'n*, Chapter 4[F], *supra* p. 502. That debate is premised on the idea that because some instances of agency guidance "effectively" or "in substance" function as substantive regulations that carry the force of law, they must be promulgated using 5 U.S.C. § 553's notice-and-comment procedures. Is that premise consistent with the Court's analysis in *Mead*? Does the Court in *Mead* endorse the idea that because a document issued by an agency functions in a particular way, it is subject to notice and comment? Or does *Mead* take the perspective that the process through which an agency document is issued determines its legal status?

6. **The *Skidmore* "Respect" Fallback.** Having concluded that Customs' letter ruling is not entitled to *Chevron* deference, the Court nevertheless finds that it is a candidate for *Skidmore* respect. The letter is reproduced in Chapter 4[B][2], *supra* p. 421. How does it fare when one evaluates "the thoroughness evident in its consideration, the validity of its reasoning, its consistency with earlier and later pronouncements, and all those factors which give it power to persuade, if lacking power to control"?

On remand, the Federal Circuit refused to afford *Skidmore* respect to Customs' ruling because it relied on judicial and agency precedents the Circuit thought inapt and disregarded dictionary definitions the court found pertinent. Interpreting the Harmonized Tariff Schedules *de novo*, the court accepted Mead's claim that its day planners fell under the duty-free "other" heading and not the "diary" heading. 283 F.3d 1342, 1344 (Fed. Cir. 2002). The government did not petition for certiorari.

7. **The Post-*Mead* Landscape of Deference to Agency Statutory Interpretation.** Evaluate whether after *Mead*, agency statutory interpretations are subject to at least three standards of review:

a. If the agency statutory interpretation is promulgated under an express statutory delegation of interpretative authority, it is "binding in the courts unless procedurally defective, arbitrary or capricious in substance, or manifestly contrary to the statute."

b. If the agency interpretation falls within the permissible range of discretion or "*Chevron* space," it is binding if it is reasonable. A reviewing court, however, must assure itself that Congress delegated interpretative authority to the agency and that the agency interpretation reflects an exercise of that authority.

c. If the agency interpretation does not fall within the above two categories, it is afforded *Skidmore* respect or weight commensurate with its
power to persuade.

Does this scheme follow from the APA or has the Court "abandoned all pretense
of ascertaining congressional intent . . . , building instead, case by case, an edifice of
its own creation," as Justice O'Connor wrote in a different context? *Allied-Bruce Ter-
minix Cos., Inc. v. Dobson*, 513 U.S. 265, 283 (1995) (O'Connor, J. concurring). As a
matter of policy, does the three-tiered structure reflect a sensible allocation of interpretative authority between courts and agencies?

While *Mead* clarified that not all agency statutory interpretations are candidates
for *Chevron* deference, it left other questions about the scope of the *Chevron* framework unanswered. A persistent question involved agency statutory interpretations that
affected the agency's jurisdiction or authority to act. Could an agency expand the scope
of its authority through an interpretation of a statute it administered, or did such
interpretations present too great of a fox-guarding-the-henhouse problem to qualify
for *Chevron* deference?

City of Arlington v. FCC

133 S. Ct. 1863 (2013)

JUSTICE SCALIA delivered the opinion of the Court.

We consider whether an agency's interpretation of a statutory ambiguity that
concerns the scope of its regulatory authority (that is, its jurisdiction) is entitled to
deference under *Chevron U.S.A. Inc. v. Natural Resources Defense Council, Inc.*, 467
U.S. 837 (1984).

I

Wireless telecommunications networks require towers and antennas; proposed sites
for those towers and antennas must be approved by local zoning authorities. In the
Telecommunications Act of 1996, Congress "impose[d] specific limitations on the traditional authority of state and local governments to regulate the location, construction, and modification of such facilities," and incorporated those limitations into the
Communications Act of 1934, see 110 Stat. 56, 151. Section 201(b) of that Act empowers the Federal Communications Commission to "prescribe such rules and regulations
as may be necessary in the public interest to carry out [its] provisions." Ch. 296, 52
Stat. 588, codified at 47 U.S.C. § 201(b). Of course, that rulemaking authority
extends to the subsequently added portions of the Act. See *AT&T Corp. v. Iowa Utilities
Bd.*, 525 U.S. 366, 377–378 (1999).

The Act imposes five substantive limitations, which are codified in 47 U.S.C. § 332(c)(7)(B); only one of them, § 332(c)(7)(B)(ii), is at issue here.* That provision requires state or local governments to act on wireless siting applications "within a reasonable period of time after the request is duly filed." Two other features of § 332(c)(7) are relevant. First, subparagraph (A), known as the "saving clause," provides that nothing in the Act, except those limitations provided in § 332(c)(7)(B), "shall limit or affect the authority of a State or local government" over siting decisions. Second, § 332(c)(7)(B)(v) authorizes a person who believes a state or local government's wireless-siting decision to be inconsistent with any of the limitations in § 332(c)(7)(B) to "commence an action in any court of competent jurisdiction."

In theory, § 332(c)(7)(B)(ii) requires state and local zoning authorities to take prompt action on siting applications for wireless facilities. But in practice, wireless providers often faced long delays. In July 2008, CTIA—The Wireless Association,[1] which represents wireless service providers, petitioned the FCC to clarify the

---

* Section 332(c)(7) provides:

(7) Preservation of local zoning authority

   (A) General authority

Except as provided in this paragraph, nothing in this chapter shall limit or affect the authority of a State or local government or instrumentality thereof over decisions regarding the placement, construction, and modification of personal wireless service facilities.

   (B) Limitations

      (i) The regulation of the placement, construction, and modification of personal wireless service facilities by any State or local government or instrumentality thereof—

         (I) shall not unreasonably discriminate among providers of functionally equivalent services; and

         (II) shall not prohibit or have the effect of prohibiting the provision of personal wireless services.

      (ii) A State or local government or instrumentality thereof shall act on any request for authorization to place, construct, or modify personal wireless service facilities within a reasonable period of time after the request is duly filed with such government or instrumentality, taking into account the nature and scope of such request.

      (iii) Any decision by a State or local government or instrumentality thereof to deny a request to place, construct, or modify personal wireless service facilities shall be in writing and supported by substantial evidence contained in a written record.

      (iv) No State or local government or instrumentality thereof may regulate the placement, construction, and modification of personal wireless service facilities on the basis of the environmental effects of radio frequency emissions to the extent that such facilities comply with the Commission's regulations concerning such emissions.

      (v) Any person adversely affected by any final action or failure to act by a State or local government or any instrumentality thereof that is inconsistent with this subparagraph may, within 30 days after such action or failure to act, commence an action in any court of competent jurisdiction. The court shall hear and decide such action on an expedited basis. Any person adversely affected by an act or failure to act by a State or local government or any instrumentality thereof that is inconsistent with clause (iv) may petition the Commission for relief.***—Eds.

1. This is not a typographical error. CTIA—The Wireless Association was the name of the petitioner. CTIA is presumably an (unpronounceable) acronym, but even the organization's website does

meaning of § 332(c)(7)(B)(ii)'s requirement that zoning authorities act on siting requests "within a reasonable period of time." In November 2009, the Commission, relying on its broad statutory authority to implement the provisions of the Communications Act, issued a declaratory ruling responding to CTIA's petition. The Commission found that the "record evidence demonstrates that unreasonable delays in the personal wireless service facility siting process have obstructed the provision of wireless services" and that such delays "impede the promotion of advanced services and competition that Congress deemed critical in the Telecommunications Act of 1996." A "reasonable period of time" under § 332(c)(7)(B)(ii), the Commission determined, is presumptively (but rebuttably) 90 days to process a collocation application (that is, an application to place a new antenna on an existing tower) and 150 days to process all other applications.

Some state and local governments opposed adoption of the Declaratory Ruling on the ground that the Commission lacked "authority to interpret ambiguous provisions of Section 332(c)(7)." Specifically, they argued that the saving clause, § 332(c)(7)(A), and the judicial review provision, § 337(c)(7)(B)(v), together display a congressional intent to withhold from the Commission authority to interpret the limitations in § 332(c)(7)(B). Asserting that ground of objection, the cities of Arlington and San Antonio, Texas, petitioned for review of the Declaratory Ruling in the Court of Appeals for the Fifth Circuit.

Relying on Circuit precedent, the Court of Appeals held that the *Chevron* framework applied to the threshold question whether the FCC possessed statutory authority to adopt the 90- and 150-day timeframes. Applying *Chevron*, the Court of Appeals found "§ 332(c)(7)(A)'s effect on the FCC's authority to administer § 332(c)(7)(B)'s limitations ambiguous," and held that "the FCC's interpretation of its statutory authority" was a permissible construction of the statute. On the merits, the court upheld the presumptive 90- and 150-day deadlines as a "permissible construction of § 332(c) (7)(B)(ii) and (v) . . . entitled to *Chevron* deference."***

II

A

As this case turns on the scope of the doctrine enshrined in *Chevron*, we begin with a description of that case's now-canonical formulation. "When a court reviews an agency's construction of the statute which it administers, it is confronted with two questions." First, applying the ordinary tools of statutory construction, the court must determine "whether Congress has directly spoken to the precise question at issue. If the intent of Congress is clear, that is the end of the matter; for the court, as well as the agency, must give effect to the unambiguously expressed intent of Congress." But "if the statute is silent or ambiguous with respect to the specific issue, the question for

---

not say what it stands for. That secret, known only to wireless-service-provider insiders, we will not disclose here. [Cellular Telephone Industries Association—Eds.]

the court is whether the agency's answer is based on a permissible construction of the statute."

Chevron is rooted in a background presumption of congressional intent: namely, "that Congress, when it left ambiguity in a statute" administered by an agency, "understood that the ambiguity would be resolved, first and foremost, by the agency, and desired the agency (rather than the courts) to possess whatever degree of discretion the ambiguity allows." *Smiley v. Citibank (South Dakota), N.A.*, 517 U.S. 735, 740–741 (1996). *Chevron* thus provides a stable background rule against which Congress can legislate: Statutory ambiguities will be resolved, within the bounds of reasonable interpretation, not by the courts but by the administering agency. Congress knows to speak in plain terms when it wishes to circumscribe, and in capacious terms when it wishes to enlarge, agency discretion.

B

The question here is whether a court must defer under *Chevron* to an agency's interpretation of a statutory ambiguity that concerns the scope of the agency's statutory authority (that is, its jurisdiction). The argument against deference rests on the premise that there exist two distinct classes of agency interpretations: Some interpretations—the big, important ones, presumably—define the agency's "jurisdiction." Others—humdrum, run-of-the-mill stuff—are simply applications of jurisdiction the agency plainly has. That premise is false, because the distinction between "jurisdictional" and "nonjurisdictional" interpretations is a mirage. No matter how it is framed, the question a court faces when confronted with an agency's interpretation of a statute it administers is always, simply, whether the agency has stayed within the bounds of its statutory authority.

The misconception that there are, for *Chevron* purposes, separate "jurisdictional" questions on which no deference is due derives, perhaps, from a reflexive extension to agencies of the very real division between the jurisdictional and nonjurisdictional that is applicable to courts. In the judicial context, there is a meaningful line: Whether the court decided correctly is a question that has different consequences from the question whether it had the power to decide at all. Congress has the power (within limits) to tell the courts what classes of cases they may decide but not to prescribe or superintend how they decide those cases. A court's power to decide a case is independent of whether its decision is correct, which is why even an erroneous judgment is entitled to res judicata effect. Put differently, a jurisdictionally proper but substantively incorrect judicial decision is not ultra vires.

That is not so for agencies charged with administering congressional statutes. Both their power to act and how they are to act is authoritatively prescribed by Congress, so that when they act improperly, no less than when they act beyond their jurisdiction, what they do is ultra vires. Because the question—whether framed as an incorrect application of agency authority or an assertion of authority not conferred — is always whether the agency has gone beyond what Congress has permitted it to do, there is no principled basis for carving out some arbitrary subset of such claims as "jurisdictional."***

One of the briefs in support of petitioners explains, helpfully, that "[j]urisdictional questions concern the who, what, where, and when of regulatory power: which subject matters may an agency regulate and under what conditions." But an agency's application of its authority pursuant to statutory text answers the same questions. Who is an "outside salesman"? What is a "pole attachment"? Where do the "waters of the United States" end? When must a Medicare provider challenge a reimbursement determination in order to be entitled to an administrative appeal? These can all be reframed as questions about the scope of agencies' regulatory jurisdiction — and they are all questions to which the *Chevron* framework applies. *See Christopher v. SmithKline Beecham Corp.*, 132 S. Ct. 2156, 2162, 2165 (2012); *National Cable & Telecommunications Assn., Inc. v. Gulf Power Co.*, 534 U.S. 327 (2002); *United States v. Riverside Bayview Homes, Inc.*, 474 U.S. 121, 123, 131 (1985); *Sebelius v. Auburn Regional Medical Center*, 133 S. Ct. 817, 821, 826–827 (2013).

In sum, judges should not waste their time in the mental acrobatics needed to decide whether an agency's interpretation of a statutory provision is "jurisdictional" or "non-jurisdictional." Once those labels are sheared away, it becomes clear that the question in every case is, simply, whether the statutory text forecloses the agency's assertion of authority, or not.***

C

Those who assert that applying *Chevron* to "jurisdictional" interpretations "leaves the fox in charge of the henhouse" overlook the reality that a separate category of "jurisdictional" interpretations does not exist. The fox-in-the-henhouse syndrome is to be avoided not by establishing an arbitrary and undefinable category of agency decisionmaking that is accorded no deference, but by taking seriously, and applying rigorously, in all cases, statutory limits on agencies' authority. Where Congress has established a clear line, the agency cannot go beyond it; and where Congress has established an ambiguous line, the agency can go no further than the ambiguity will fairly allow. But in rigorously applying the latter rule, a court need not pause to puzzle over whether the interpretive question presented is "jurisdictional."

CHIEF JUSTICE ROBERTS, with whom JUSTICE KENNEDY and JUSTICE ALITO join, dissenting.

If a congressional delegation of interpretive authority is to support *Chevron* deference, that delegation must extend to the specific statutory ambiguity at issue. The appropriate question is whether the delegation covers the "specific provision" and "particular question" before the court. *Chevron*, 467 U.S., at 844. A congressional grant of authority over some portion of a statute does not necessarily mean that Congress granted the agency interpretive authority over all its provisions.

An example that might highlight the point concerns statutes that parcel out authority to multiple agencies, which "may be the norm, rather than an exception." See, e.g., *Gonzales* [*v. Oregon*, 546 U.S. 243 (2006)] (describing shared authority over the [Controlled Substances Act] between the Attorney General and the Secretary of Health and Human Services); *Sutton v. United Air Lines, Inc.*, 527 U.S. 471, 478 (1999) (authority to issue regulations implementing the Americans with Disabilities Act "is split primarily among three Government agencies"). The Dodd-Frank Wall Street Reform and Consumer Protection Act [Pub. L. No. 111–203, 124 Stat. 1376 (2010)], for example, authorizes rulemaking by at least eight different agencies. When presented with an agency's interpretation of such a statute, a court cannot simply ask whether the statute is one that the agency administers; the question is whether authority over the particular ambiguity at issue has been delegated to the particular agency.

By the same logic, even when Congress provides interpretive authority to a single agency, a court must decide if the ambiguity the agency has purported to interpret with the force of law is one to which the congressional delegation extends. A general delegation to the agency to administer the statute will often suffice to satisfy the court that Congress has delegated interpretive authority over the ambiguity at issue. But if Congress has exempted particular provisions from that authority, that exemption must be respected, and the determination whether Congress has done so is for the courts alone.***

In these cases, the FCC issued a declaratory ruling interpreting the term "reasonable period of time" in 47 U.S.C. § 332(c)(7)(B)(ii). The Fifth Circuit correctly recognized that it could not apply *Chevron* deference to the FCC's interpretation unless the agency "possessed statutory authority to administer § 332(c)(7)(B)(ii)," but it erred by granting *Chevron* deference to the FCC's view on that antecedent question. Because the court should have determined on its own whether Congress delegated interpretive authority over § 332(c)(7)(B)(ii) to the FCC before affording *Chevron* deference, I would vacate the decision below and remand the cases to the Fifth Circuit to perform the proper inquiry in the first instance.

[Opinion of JUSTICE BREYER, concurring in part and concurring in the judgment, omitted.]

Notes and Questions

1. **The Regulatory and Procedural Posture?** At issue in *City of Arlington* is the FCC's conclusion that it had authority to state a presumptive period of time for what would constitute "a reasonable period of time" during which a state or local government was required to act on a wireless siting application under 47 U.S.C. § 332(c)(7)(B)(ii). The City claimed that the FCC lacked authority to promulgate such an interpretation because of § 332(c)(7)'s savings clause. The savings clause stated that § 332(c)(7) provided the exclusive authority to "limit or affect the authority of a State or local government" over a siting decision. The FCC responded that it had authority to state

a period of time that was presumptively reasonable and that its statement was entitled to *Chevron* treatment.

How did the city obtain judicial review over the FCC's decision in question? What standard of review did the court below apply in reviewing the FCC's decision?

2. **Antecedents for the Court's Decision.** The dispute in *City of Arlington* was not the first time the Supreme Court confronted an argument that it should distinguish between "nonjurisdictional" agency determinations that were entitled to comparatively greater deference and "jurisdictional" determinations that were entitled to less deference. In *Crowell v. Benson*, 285 U.S. 22 (1932), *supra* Chapter 3[B][1][b], the Court held that determinations of "jurisdictional" fact—by which it meant facts that underpinned an agency's power to regulate consistently with Article I—were subject to *de novo* review. The rationale was that, given their effect on the federal government's regulatory authority, such facts were too important to leave to agency decisionmaking.

3. **Administrability of the Line Between Jurisdictional and Non-Jurisdictional Determinations?** The Supreme Court's conclusion that the FCC's conclusion is governed by *Chevron* is driven in large part by its belief that there is no administrable line between statutory provisions that give an agency jurisdiction over a particular subject area and those that direct an agency how to exercise its delegated authority. Does Chief Justice Roberts' dissent put forward a workable test for drawing that line? Is the Chief Justice's suggestion that courts determine whether the statutory delegation to the agency "extend[s] to the specific statutory ambiguity at issue" consistent with the *Chevron* presumption that indeterminate statutory language delegates interpretative authority to the agency charged with administering the statute? Was there a statutory provision in *Chevron* that specifically delegated authority over the definition of a pollution "source" to the EPA?

4. **"Foxes Guarding the Henhouse"?** A classic criticism of federal administrative agencies posits that agencies are "power maximizers" that seek to maximize their budget and regulatory power. *See* WILLIAM A. NISKANEN, BUREAUCRACY AND REPRESENTATIVE GOVERNMENT (1971). Is the Court sufficiently attentive to the possibility that an agency might seek to expand its regulatory authority—here, at the expense of state and local government authority—through expansive interpretations of vague statutory provisions? On the other hand, when Congress requires state and local authorities to act "within a reasonable period of time," it is imposing a federal limitation on their discretion the specific parameters of which have to be interpreted either case-by-case in the courts or through a FCC regulation. Is it clear that state and local authorities are necessarily worse off with the clarity of the latter? Can it be assumed that the FCC's dominant or likely motivation is to grab power for itself?

5. *Chevron* **Deference in Shared Regulatory Space?** As Chief Justice Roberts observes in his *Arlington* dissent, an increasing number of statutes are administered by multiple agencies. *See also* Note 4 following Executive Order 12,866, Chapter 3[D], *supra* p. 376 (describing the phenomenon of "shared regulatory space"). The way in which

Chevron applies to such statutes—if at all—is not obvious. *Chevron*, of course, was a case in which a single agency was charged with administering the pertinent statute. Moreover, the precedents *Chevron* built upon in establishing its two-step framework were likewise single-agency, single-statute cases. *See, e.g., INS v. Jong Ha Wang*, 450 U.S. 139, 144 (1981) (Attorney General's regulation promulgated under the Immigration and Nationality Act); *Train v. Natural Resources Defense Council, Inc.*, 421 U.S. 60 (1975) (EPA guidelines promulgated under 1970 Clean Air Act).

Does it make sense to apply the *Chevron* presumption that Congress intends the implementing agency to fill statutory gaps when a statute is administered by more than one agency? Is the Chief Justice's "specific question" approach more attractive in this setting? For efforts to apply *Chevron* to statutes administered by multiple agencies, *see, e.g.*, William Weaver, Note, *Multiple-Agency Delegations & One-Agency* Chevron, 67 VAND. L. REV. 275 (2014); Catherine M. Sharkey, *Agency Coordination in Consumer Protection*, 2013 U. CHI. L. FORUM 329; Jody Freeman & Jim Rossi, *Agency Coordination in Shared Regulatory Space*, 125 HARV. L. REV. 1131 (2012); Jacob E. Gersen, *Overlapping and Underlapping Jurisdiction in Administrative Law*, 2006 SUP. CT. REV. 201 (2006).

Chevron, *Mead*, and *City of Arlington* consider the weight that should be given to an agency's interpretation of a statute it administers, set out in a format that suggests the agency intends to speak with the force of law. Do the deference principles elaborated in those decisions also apply to an agency's interpretation of a *regulation* that the agency issues via notice-and-comment rulemaking? In other words, does ambiguity in a regulation create a kind of "*Chevron* space" where the agency's views—expressed in a legal brief, interpretive rule, or guidance document—authoritatively determine the meaning of the regulation?

Auer v. Robbins

519 U.S. 452 (1997)

JUSTICE SCALIA, delivered the opinion of the Court.

　　* * *

I

Petitioners are sergeants and a lieutenant employed by the St. Louis Police Department. They brought suit in 1988 against respondents, members of the St. Louis Board of Police Commissioners, seeking payment of overtime pay that they claimed was owed under § 7(a)(1) of the [Fair Labor Standards Act (FLSA)], 29 U.S.C. § 207(a)(1). Respondents argued that petitioners were not entitled to such pay because they came within the exemption provided by § 213(a)(1) for "bona fide executive, administrative, or professional" employees.

Under regulations promulgated by the Secretary, one requirement for exempt status under § 213(a)(1) is that the employee earn a specified minimum amount on a "salary basis." 29 CFR §§ 541.1(f), 541.2(e), 541.3(e) (1996). According to the regulations, "[a]n employee will be considered to be paid 'on a salary basis' . . . if under his employment agreement he regularly receives each pay period on a weekly, or less frequent basis, a predetermined amount constituting all or part of his compensation, which amount is not subject to reduction because of variations in the quality or quantity of the work performed." § 541.118(a). Petitioners contended that the salary-basis test was not met in their case because, under the terms of the St. Louis Metropolitan Police Department Manual, their compensation could be reduced for a variety of disciplinary infractions related to the "quality or quantity" of work performed. Petitioners also claimed that they did not meet the other requirement for exempt status under § 213(a)(1): that their duties be of an executive, administrative, or professional nature. See §§ 541.1(a)-(e), 541.2(a)-(d), 541.3(a)-(d).

The District Court found that petitioners were paid on a salary basis and that most, though not all, also satisfied the duties criterion. The Court of Appeals affirmed in part and reversed in part, holding that both the salary-basis test and the duties test were satisfied as to all petitioners.***

II

The FLSA grants the Secretary broad authority to "defin[e] and delimi[t]" the scope of the exemption for executive, administrative, and professional employees. § 213(a)(1). Under the Secretary's chosen approach, exempt status requires that the employee be paid on a salary basis, which in turn requires that his compensation not be subject to reduction because of variations in the "quality or quantity of the work performed," 29 CFR § 541.118(a) (1996). Because the regulation goes on to carve out an exception from this rule for "[p]enalties imposed . . . for infractions of safety rules of major significance," § 541.118(a)(5), it is clear that the rule embraces reductions in pay for disciplinary violations. The Secretary is of the view that employees whose pay is adjusted for disciplinary reasons do not deserve exempt status because as a general matter true "executive, administrative, or professional" employees are not "disciplined" by piecemeal deductions from their pay, but are terminated, demoted, or given restricted assignments.***

III

A primary issue in the litigation unleashed by application of the salary-basis test to public-sector employees has been whether, under that test, an employee's pay is "subject to" disciplinary or other deductions whenever there exists a theoretical possibility of such deductions, or rather only when there is something more to suggest that the employee is actually vulnerable to having his pay reduced. Petitioners in effect argue for something close to the former view; they contend that because the police manual nominally subjects all department employees to a range of disciplinary sanctions that includes disciplinary deductions in pay, and because a single sergeant was actually subjected to a disciplinary deduction, they are "subject to" such deductions and hence nonexempt under the FLSA.

The Court of Appeals rejected petitioners' approach, saying that "[t]he mere possibility of an improper deduction in pay does not defeat an employee's salaried status" if no practice of making deductions exists.***

The Secretary of Labor, in an *amicus* brief filed at the request of the Court, interprets the salary-basis test to deny exempt status when employees are covered by a policy that permits disciplinary or other deductions in pay "as a practical matter." That standard is met, the Secretary says, if there is either an actual practice of making such deductions or an employment policy that creates a "significant likelihood" of such deductions. The Secretary's approach rejects a wooden requirement of actual deductions, but in their absence it requires a clear and particularized policy — one which "effectively communicates" that deductions will be made in specified circumstances.***

Because the salary-basis test is a creature of the Secretary's own regulations, his interpretation of it is, under our jurisprudence, controlling unless "'plainly erroneous or inconsistent with the regulation.'" *Robertson v. Methow Valley Citizens Council*, 490 U.S. 332, 359 (1989) (quoting *Bowles v. Seminole Rock & Sand Co.*, 325 U.S. 410, 414 (1945)). That deferential standard is easily met here. The critical phrase "subject to" comfortably bears the meaning the Secretary assigns. See American Heritage Dictionary 1788 (3d ed. 1992) (def. 2: defining "subject to" to mean "prone; disposed"; giving as an example "a child who is subject to colds"); Webster's New International Dictionary 2509 (2d ed. 1950) (def. 3: defining "subject to" to mean "[e]xposed; liable; prone; disposed"; giving as an example "a country subject to extreme heat").

The Secretary's approach is usefully illustrated by reference to this case. The policy on which petitioners rely is contained in a section of the police manual that lists a total of 58 possible rule violations and specifies the range of penalties associated with each. All department employees are nominally covered by the manual, and some of the specified penalties involve disciplinary deductions in pay. Under the Secretary's view, that is not enough to render petitioners' pay "subject to" disciplinary deductions within the meaning of the salary-basis test. This is so because the manual does not "effectively communicate" that pay deductions are an anticipated form of punishment for employees *in petitioners' category*, since it is perfectly possible to give full effect to every aspect of the manual without drawing any inference of that sort. If the statement of available penalties applied solely to petitioners, matters would be different; but since it applies both to petitioners and to employees who are unquestionably not paid on a salary basis, the expressed availability of disciplinary deductions may have reference only to the latter. No clear inference can be drawn as to the likelihood of a sanction's being applied to employees such as petitioners. Nor, under the Secretary's approach, is such a likelihood established by the one-time deduction in a sergeant's pay, under unusual circumstances.

Petitioners complain that the Secretary's interpretation comes to us in the form of a legal brief; but that does not, in the circumstances of this case, make it unworthy of deference. The Secretary's position is in no sense a "*post hoc* rationalizatio[n]" advanced by an agency seeking to defend past agency action against attack, *Bowen v. Georgetown Univ. Hospital*, 488 U.S. 204, 212 (1988). There is simply no reason to suspect that the interpretation does not reflect the agency's fair and considered judgment on the matter in question. Petitioners also suggest that the Secretary's approach contravenes the rule that FLSA exemptions are to be "narrowly construed against . . . employers" and are to be withheld except as to persons "plainly and unmistakably within their terms and spirit." But that is a rule governing judicial interpretation of statutes and regulations, not a limitation on the Secretary's power to resolve ambiguities in his own regulations. A rule requiring the Secretary to construe his own regulations narrowly would make little sense, since he is free to write the regulations as broadly as he wishes, subject only to the limits imposed by the statute.***

Notes and Questions

1. **The Interpretive Question?** *Auer* involves the FLSA exemption for "employee[s] employed in a bona fide executive, administrative, or professional capacity," 29 U.S.C. § 213(a)(1), and the DOL's requirement—the validity of which is not challenged in *Auer*— that exempt employees be paid on a "salary basis." Section 213 of the FLSA gives the Secretary of Labor authority to "defin[e] and delimit[t]" the scope of FLSA exemptions. The salary basis test is set out in a regulation, 29 C.F.R. § 541, that was first promulgated by the Secretary of Labor in 1940. See 29 C.F.R. §§ 541.2(a); 541.3(b) (1940 Supp.); 5 Fed. Reg. 4077 (1940). What is the specific issue regarding the salary basis that the Court in *Auer* undertakes to resolve?

2. **Deference to DOL's Interpretation of its own Regulation?** Section 706 of the APA provides that "[t]o the extent necessary to decision and when presented, the reviewing court shall decide all relevant questions of law, interpret constitutional and statutory provisions, and determine the meaning or applicability of the terms of an agency action." In light of this command, why does the Supreme Court defer to the DOL's interpretation of its regulation setting out the salary-basis test? Would a court interpreting the text of the FLSA and DOL's regulation arrive at the same middle-ground approach that DOL advocated? Could it, following traditional principles of statutory interpretation?

Should DOL be presumed to have delegated interpretive authority to itself when it drafted the salary basis regulation in the same manner that, per *Chevron*, Congress delegates interpretive authority to the agency charged with administering a statute? Does DOL have authority to issue binding interpretations of regulations that it issues in the manner that *Mead* thought necessary for an agency to speak with the force of law when interpreting a statute? If neither the regulation nor the legal authorities under which the Department operates reflect the expectation that the agency's views will carry the force of law, why does the Court state that the Department's views are "controlling"? Consider the views of Professors Sunstein and Vermeule:

> [I]nterpretation of ambiguous regulations is really an exercise in policymaking, at least much of the time. A regulatory term like "subject to" calls for further specification in a diverse array of cases, an exercise that in turn requires judgments of policy. Agencies have technical expertise as well as political accountability, and so long as a regulation is ambiguous, it should be "interpreted" by them (policy should be made by them), not by courts, which lack those advantages.

Cass R. Sunstein & Adrian Vermeule, *The Unbearable Rightness of* Auer, 84 U. Chi. L. Rev. (forthcoming 2017) (manuscript at 11).

Do these functional considerations support the conclusion that the agency's view is authoritative as opposed to merely persuasive? If the agency regulation is ambiguous, agencies presumably have the comparative advantage vis-à-vis courts in determining what it means, and what is the best policy under the statute the agency administers. On this reasoning, courts should respect agency judgments informed by their experience applying the regulation. But in what sense is deference to the agency's view called for in the *Chevron* sense — that the scope of a regulation is a matter of policymaking discretion that was committed to the agency for final resolution rather than an interpretive matter for the court's plenary decision? Stated differently, is there a view of the agency's *authority* as opposed to its policymaking expertise that justifies full-fledged deference?

Does it matter how the agency's interpretation was delivered? Is *Auer* correct to reject the suggestion that interpretations of administrative policy set out in litigation briefs are different in kind from statements of administrative policy delivered via regulation, adjudication, or interpretive letter?

3. **The Origins of *Auer* Deference.** The Supreme Court stated as early as 1898 that "[t]he interpretation given to the regulations by the department charged with their execution, and by the official who has the power, with the sanction of the President, to amend them is entitled to the greatest weight . . . ." *United States v. Eaton*, 169 U.S. 331, 343 (1898). In the post-World War II era, the principle that courts should defer to an agency's interpretation of its own regulation is usually traced to *Bowles v. Seminole Rock & Sand Co.*, 325 U.S. 410 (1945) (*Seminole Rock*), which upheld the Office of Price Administration's interpretation of a maximum price regulation issued under the Emergency Price Control Act of 1942, Pub. L. No. 77-421, 56 Stat. 23. *See* Notes 1–2 following *Yakus v. United States*, *supra* Chapter 3[B][1][a].

Seminole Rock's understanding of the deference due to an agency's interpretation of its own regulation is somewhat more nuanced than *Auer*'s quotation of the case might suggest:

> Since [determining the highest price charged by the respondent for crushed stone] involves an interpretation of an administrative regulation a court must necessarily look to the administrative construction of the regulation if the meaning of the words used is in doubt. The intention of Congress or the principles of the Constitution in some situations may be relevant in the first instance in choosing between various constructions. But the ultimate

criterion is the administrative interpretation, which becomes of controlling weight unless it is plainly erroneous or inconsistent with the regulation. The legality of the result reached by this process, of course, is quite a different matter.

325 U.S. at 413–14.

Seminole Rock thus suggests that a regulation should be read in light of "the intention of Congress" and "the principles of the Constitution." Although an agency is entitled to insist on its own interpretation, this is a "criterion" of the regulation's meaning— and the court remains free to say that interpretation is unlawful or simply wrong. Does this statement of the standard of review more closely resemble *Chevron* deference or the "respect" due to the agency's views under *Skidmore v. Swift & Co., supra* Chapter 1[C][3]?

4. **Exceptions to *Auer* Deference.** As the opinions in *Auer* and *Seminole Rock* explain, an agency's interpretation of a regulation is not "controlling" if it is "plainly erroneous," "inconsistent with the regulation," or there is "reason to suspect that the interpretation does not reflect the agency's fair and considered judgment on the matter in question." In addition, the Supreme Court has said that *Auer* deference is inappropriate for regulations that merely "parrot" the controlling statute. *Gonzales v. Oregon*, 546 U.S. 243, 257 (2006). It has declined to give controlling weight to an interpretation that it viewed as creating "unfair surprise" for regulated parties. *Christopher v. SmithKline Beecham Corp.*, 567 U.S. 142 (2012). And in *Perez v. Mortgage Banker's Association*, the Court stated that an agency's interpretation of its own regulation is subject to arbitrary-and-capricious review. *See Perez v. Mortg. Bankers Ass'n*, 135 S. Ct. 1199, 1208 n.4 (2015), *supra* p. 496.

The issue in *Christopher* was whether pharmaceutical sales representatives fell within the FLSA exemption for "outside salesman." 29 U.S.C. § 213(a)(1). DOL regulations promulgated in 1938, 1940, and 1949 and reissued with minor amendments in 2004, defined an "outside employee" as an any employee whose primary duty was making any sale, exchange, contract to sell, consignment for sale, shipment for sale, or other disposition. Petitioners were pharmaceutical sales representatives, known as "detailers," who worked more than forty hours a week and did not receive statutory overtime. *See* 29 U.S.C. § 207(a). They sued to recover overtime in the U.S. District Court for the District of Arizona. While their case was pending, DOL filed an amicus brief in a Second Circuit appeal that also raised the question whether pharmaceutical detailers fell within the outside salesman exception. DOL's brief took the position that detailers were not covered by the outside salesman exception and thus had to be paid overtime.

The Supreme Court concluded that DOL's interpretation of its regulation was not entitled to any weight whatsoever. The Court found it significant that "despite the industry's decades-long practice of classifying pharmaceutical detailers as exempt employees, the DOL never initiated any enforcement actions with respect to detailers or otherwise suggested that it thought the industry was acting unlawfully." Acknowledging that enforcement decisions are informed by many factors other than an agency's legal interpretation of the statute and regulations it administers, the Court concluded "no explanation for the DOL's inaction is plausible . . . [o]ther than acquiescence" in classifying detailers as exempt.

5. **The Continuing Viability of** *Auer*? Despite authoring the *Auer* opinion, Justice Scalia decided late in his career that the principle the case announced was mistaken. Consider his opinion concurring in part and dissenting in part in *Decker v. Northwest Environmental Defense Center*, 133 S. Ct. 1326 (2013):

> [W]hen an agency interprets its own rules*** the power to prescribe is augmented by the power to interpret; and the incentive is to speak vaguely and broadly, so as to retain a "flexibility" that will enable "clarification" with retroactive effect. "It is perfectly understandable" for an agency to "issue vague regulations" if doing so will "maximiz[e] agency power."*** *Auer* deference encourages agencies to be "vague in framing regulations, with the plan of issuing 'interpretations' to create the intended new law without observance of notice and comment procedures." *Auer* is not a logical corollary to *Chevron* but a dangerous permission slip for the arrogation of power.

Justice Thomas has endorsed the later Scalia's view. *See United Student Aid Funds, Inc. v. Bible*, 136 S. Ct. 1607, 1608 (2016) (Thomas, J., dissenting from the denial of a petition for certiorari asking the Court to overrule *Auer* and *Seminole Rock*).

Are Justice Scalia's criticisms persuasive in light of the many exceptions to the rule that an agency's interpretation of its own regulation is controlling? Does not the availability of arbitrary-and-capricious review provide a way for courts to control the very type of gamesmanship that concerns Justice Scalia? If *Auer* were overruled, would courts interpret agency regulations *de novo* or would they extend something like *Skidmore* respect to the agency's interpretation of its own regulation? On the second-order effects of overruling *Auer*, see Aaron Nielson, *Beyond* Seminole Rock, 105 Geo. L.J. (forthcoming 2017).

D. Review of Discretionary Agency Action

To this point, we have considered judicial review of final agency action that results from an agency's adjudication of a particular matter or the imposition of a regulatory requirement. *Chevron*, however, teaches that one of the principal benefits of agency regulation is the agency's ability to update the regulatory scheme over time, within statutory limits. Within the limits of the statutory delegation, an agency may even "rely upon the incumbent administration's views of wise policy to inform its judgments." *Chevron*, 467 U.S. at 865.

What is the burden of justification on an agency when it makes such a policy determination? Is the burden different when the agency changes its policy determination as opposed to establishing it in the first instance? The final set of materials in this chapter grapples with those questions.

Motor Vehicle Manufacturers Association v. State Farm Mutual Automobile Insurance Co.

463 U.S. 29 (1983)

JUSTICE WHITE delivered the opinion of the Court.

The development of the automobile gave Americans unprecedented freedom to travel, but exacted a high price for enhanced mobility. Since 1929, motor vehicles have been the leading cause of accidental deaths and injuries in the United States. In 1982, 46,300 Americans died in motor vehicle accidents and hundreds of thousands more were maimed and injured. While a consensus exists that the current loss of life on our highways is unacceptably high, improving safety does not admit to easy solution. In 1966, Congress decided that at least part of the answer lies in improving the design and safety features of the vehicle itself. But much of the technology for building safer cars was undeveloped or untested. Before changes in automobile design could be mandated, the effectiveness of these changes had to be studied, their costs examined, and public acceptance considered. This task called for considerable expertise and Congress responded by enacting the National Traffic and Motor Vehicle Safety Act of 1966 (Act), 80 Stat. 718, as amended, 15 U.S.C. § 1381 et seq. (1976 ed. and Supp. V). The Act, created for the purpose of "reduc[ing] traffic accidents and deaths and injuries to persons resulting from traffic accidents," 15 U.S.C. § 1381, directs the Secretary of Transportation or his delegate to issue motor vehicle safety standards that "shall be practicable, shall meet the need for motor vehicle safety, and shall be stated in objective terms." 15 U.S.C. § 1392(a) (1976 ed., Supp. V). In issuing these standards, the Secretary is directed to consider "relevant available motor vehicle safety data," whether the proposed standard "is reasonable, practicable and appropriate" for the particular type of motor vehicle, and the "extent to which such standards will contribute to carrying out the purposes" of the Act. 15 U.S.C. §§ 1392(f)(1), (3), (4).[3]

The Act also authorizes judicial review under the provisions of the Administrative Procedure Act (APA), 5 U.S.C. § 706, of all "orders establishing, amending, or revoking a Federal motor vehicle safety standard," 15 U.S.C. § 1392(b). Under this authority, we review today whether NHTSA acted arbitrarily and capriciously in revoking the requirement in Motor Vehicle Safety Standard 208 that new motor vehicles produced after September 1982 be equipped with passive restraints to protect the safety of the occupants of the vehicle in the event of a collision.***

---

3. The Secretary's general authority to promulgate safety standards under the Act has been delegated to the Administrator of the National Highway Traffic Safety Administration (NHTSA). 49 CFR § 1.50(a) (1982). This opinion will use the terms NHTSA and agency interchangeably when referring to the National Highway Traffic Safety Administration, the Department of Transportation, and the Secretary of Transportation.

I

The regulation whose rescission is at issue bears a complex and convoluted history. Over the course of approximately 60 rulemaking notices, the requirement has been imposed, amended, rescinded, reimposed, and now rescinded again.

As originally issued by the Department of Transportation in 1967, Standard 208 simply required the installation of seatbelts in all automobiles. It soon became apparent that the level of seatbelt use was too low to reduce traffic injuries to an acceptable level. The Department therefore began consideration of "passive occupant restraint systems"—devices that do not depend for their effectiveness upon any action taken by the occupant except that necessary to operate the vehicle. Two types of automatic crash protection emerged: automatic seatbelts and airbags. The automatic seatbelt is a traditional safety belt, which when fastened to the interior of the door remains attached without impeding entry or exit from the vehicle, and deploys automatically without any action on the part of the passenger. The airbag is an inflatable device concealed in the dashboard and steering column. It automatically inflates when a sensor indicates that deceleration forces from an accident have exceeded a preset minimum, then rapidly deflates to dissipate those forces. The lifesaving potential of these devices was immediately recognized, and in 1977, after substantial on-the-road experience with both devices, it was estimated by NHTSA that passive restraints could prevent approximately 12,000 deaths and over 100,000 serious injuries annually.

In 1969, the Department formally proposed a standard requiring the installation of passive restraints, thereby commencing a lengthy series of proceedings. In 1970, the agency revised Standard 208 to include passive protection requirements, and in 1972, the agency amended the Standard to require full passive protection for all front seat occupants of vehicles manufactured after August 15, 1975. In the interim, vehicles built between August 1973 and August 1975 were to carry either passive restraints or lap and shoulder belts coupled with an "ignition interlock" that would prevent starting the vehicle if the belts were not connected.***

In preparing for the upcoming model year, most car makers chose the "ignition interlock" option, a decision which was highly unpopular, and led Congress to amend the Act to prohibit a motor vehicle safety standard from requiring or permitting compliance by means of an ignition interlock or a continuous buzzer designed to indicate that safety belts were not in use. Motor Vehicle and Schoolbus Safety Amendments of 1974, Pub. L. 93-492, § 109, 88 Stat. 1482, 15 U.S.C. § 1410b(b). The 1974 Amendments also provided that any safety standard that could be satisfied by a system other than seatbelts would have to be submitted to Congress where it could be vetoed by concurrent resolution of both Houses. 15 U.S.C. § 1410b(b)(2).

The effective date for mandatory passive restraint systems was extended for a year until August 31, 1976. But in June 1976, Secretary of Transportation William T. Coleman, Jr., initiated a new rulemaking on the issue. After hearing testimony and reviewing written comments, Coleman extended the optional alternatives indefinitely and suspended the passive restraint requirement. Although he found passive restraints technologically and economically feasible, the Secretary based his decision on the expectation that there would be widespread public resistance to the new systems. He instead proposed a demonstration project involving up to 500,000 cars installed with passive restraints, in order to smooth the way for public acceptance of mandatory passive restraints at a later date.

Coleman's successor as Secretary of Transportation disagreed. Within months of assuming office, Secretary Brock Adams decided that the demonstration project was unnecessary. He issued a new mandatory passive restraint regulation, known as Modified Standard 208. The Modified Standard mandated the phasing in of passive restraints beginning with large cars in model year 1982 and extending to all cars by model year 1984. The two principal systems that would satisfy the Standard were airbags and passive belts; the choice of which system to install was left to the manufacturers. In *Pacific Legal Foundation v. Department of Transportation*, 593 F.2d 1338, *cert. denied*, 444 U.S. 830 (1979), the Court of Appeals upheld Modified Standard 208 as a rational, nonarbitrary regulation consistent with the agency's mandate under the Act. The Standard also survived scrutiny by Congress, which did not exercise its authority under the legislative veto provision of the 1974 Amendments.

Over the next several years, the automobile industry geared up to comply with Modified Standard 208. As late as July 1980, NHTSA reported:

> "On the road experience in thousands of vehicles equipped with air bags and automatic safety belts has confirmed agency estimates of the life-saving and injury-preventing benefits of such systems. When all cars are equipped with automatic crash protection systems, each year an estimated 9,000 more lives will be saved, and tens of thousands of serious injuries will be prevented."
> NHTSA, Automobile Occupant Crash Protection, Progress Report No. 3, p. 4.

In February 1981, however, Secretary of Transportation Andrew Lewis reopened the rulemaking due to changed economic circumstances and, in particular, the difficulties of the automobile industry. Two months later, the agency ordered a one-year delay in the application of the Standard to large cars, extending the deadline to September 1982, and at the same time, proposed the possible rescission of the entire Standard. After receiving written comments and holding public hearings, NHTSA issued a final rule (Notice 25) that rescinded the passive restraint requirement contained in Modified Standard 208.

II

In a statement explaining the rescission, NHTSA maintained that it was no longer able to find, as it had in 1977, that the automatic restraint requirement would produce significant safety benefits. Notice 25. This judgment reflected not a change of opinion on the effectiveness of the technology, but a change in plans by the automobile industry. In 1977, the agency had assumed that airbags would be installed in 60% of all new cars and automatic seatbelts in 40%. By 1981 it became apparent that automobile manufacturers planned to install the automatic seatbelts in approximately 99% of the new cars. For this reason, the lifesaving potential of airbags would not be realized. Moreover, it now appeared that the overwhelming majority of passive belts planned to be installed by manufacturers could be detached easily and left that way permanently. Passive belts, once detached, then required "the same type of affirmative action that is the stumbling block to obtaining high usage levels of manual belts." For this reason, the agency concluded that there was no longer a basis for reliably predicting that the Standard would lead to any significant increased usage of restraints at all.

In view of the possibly minimal safety benefits, the automatic restraint requirement no longer was reasonable or practicable in the agency's view. The requirement would require approximately $1 billion to implement and the agency did not believe it would be reasonable to impose such substantial costs on manufacturers and consumers without more adequate assurance that sufficient safety benefits would accrue. In addition, NHTSA concluded that automatic restraints might have an adverse effect on the public's attitude toward safety. Given the high expense and limited benefits of detachable belts, NHTSA feared that many consumers would regard the Standard as an instance of ineffective regulation, adversely affecting the public's view of safety regulation and, in particular, "poisoning . . . popular sentiment toward efforts to improve occupant restraint systems in the future."

State Farm Mutual Automobile Insurance Co. and the National Association of Independent Insurers filed petitions for review of NHTSA's rescission of the passive restraint Standard. The United States Court of Appeals for the District of Columbia Circuit held that the agency's rescission of the passive restraint requirement was arbitrary and capricious. While observing that rescission is not unrelated to an agency's refusal to take action in the first instance, the court concluded that, in this case, NHTSA's discretion to rescind the passive restraint requirement had been restricted by various forms of congressional "reaction" to the passive restraint issue. It then proceeded to find that the rescission of Standard 208 was arbitrary and capricious for three reasons. First, the court found insufficient as a basis for rescission NHTSA's conclusion that it could not reliably predict an increase in belt usage under the Standard. The court held that there was insufficient evidence in the record to sustain NHTSA's position on this issue, and that, "only a well justified refusal to seek more evidence could render rescission non-arbitrary." Second, a majority of the panel concluded that NHTSA inadequately considered the possibility of requiring manufacturers to install nondetachable rather than detachable passive belts. Third, the majority found that the agency acted arbitrarily and capriciously by failing to give any consideration whatever to requiring compliance with Modified Standard 208 by the installation of airbags.

The court allowed NHTSA 30 days in which to submit a schedule for "resolving the questions raised in th[e] opinion." Subsequently, the agency filed a Notice of Proposed Supplemental Rulemaking setting forth a schedule for complying with the court's mandate. On August 4, 1982, the Court of Appeals issued an order staying the compliance date for the passive restraint requirement until September 1, 1983, and requested NHTSA to inform the court whether that compliance date was achievable. NHTSA informed the court on October 1, 1982, that based on representations by manufacturers, it did not appear that practicable compliance could be achieved before September 1985. On November 8, 1982, we granted certiorari, and on November 18, the Court of Appeals entered an order recalling its mandate.

III

Unlike the Court of Appeals, we do not find the appropriate scope of judicial review to be the "most troublesome question" in these cases. Both the Act and the 1974 Amendments concerning occupant crash protection standards indicate that motor vehicle safety standards are to be promulgated under the informal rulemaking procedures of the Administrative Procedure Act. 5 U.S.C. § 553. The agency's action in promulgating such standards therefore may be set aside if found to be "arbitrary, capricious, an abuse of discretion, or otherwise not in accordance with law." 5 U.S.C. § 706(2)(A); *Citizens to Preserve Overton Park v. Volpe*, 401 U.S. 402, 414 (1971); *Bowman Transportation, Inc. v. Arkansas-Best Freight System, Inc.*, 419 U.S. 281 (1974). We believe that the rescission or modification of an occupant-protection standard is subject to the same test. Section 103(b) of the Act, 15 U.S.C. § 1392(b), states that the procedural and judicial review provisions of the Administrative Procedure Act "shall apply to all orders establishing, amending, or revoking a Federal motor vehicle safety standard," and suggests no difference in the scope of judicial review depending upon the nature of the agency's action.

Petitioner Motor Vehicle Manufacturers Association (MVMA) disagrees, contending that the rescission of an agency rule should be judged by the same standard a court would use to judge an agency's refusal to promulgate a rule in the first place — a standard petitioner believes considerably narrower than the traditional arbitrary-and-capricious test. We reject this view. The Act expressly equates orders "revoking" and "establishing" safety standards; neither that Act nor the APA suggests that revocations are to be treated as refusals to promulgate standards. Petitioner's view would render meaningless Congress' authorization for judicial review of orders revoking safety rules. Moreover, the revocation of an extant regulation is substantially different than a failure to act. Revocation constitutes a reversal of the agency's former views as to the proper course. A "settled course of behavior embodies the agency's informed judgment that, by pursuing that course, it will carry out the policies committed to it by Congress. There is, then, at least a presumption that those policies will be carried out best if the settled rule is adhered to." *Atchison, T.&S.F.R. Co. v. Wichita Bd. of Trade*, 412 U.S. 800, 807–808 (1973). Accordingly, an agency changing its course by rescinding a rule is obligated to supply a reasoned analysis for the change beyond that which may be required when an agency does not act in the first instance.

In so holding, we fully recognize that "[r]egulatory agencies do not establish rules of conduct to last forever," and that an agency must be given ample latitude to "adapt their rules and policies to the demands of changing circumstances." But the forces of change do not always or necessarily point in the direction of deregulation. In the abstract, there is no more reason to presume that changing circumstances require the rescission of prior action, instead of a revision in or even the extension of current regulation. If Congress established a presumption from which judicial review should start, that presumption — contrary to petitioners' views — is not against safety regulation, but against changes in current policy that are not justified by the rulemaking record. While the removal of a regulation may not entail the monetary expenditures and other costs of enacting a new standard, and, accordingly, it may be easier for an agency to justify a deregulatory action, the direction in which an agency chooses to move does not alter the standard of judicial review established by law.

The Department of Transportation accepts the applicability of the "arbitrary and capricious" standard. It argues that under this standard, a reviewing court may not set aside an agency rule that is rational, based on consideration of the relevant factors, and within the scope of the authority delegated to the agency by the statute. We do not disagree with this formulation. The scope of review under the "arbitrary and capricious" standard is narrow and a court is not to substitute its judgment for that of the agency. Nevertheless, the agency must examine the relevant data and articulate a satisfactory explanation for its action including a "rational connection between the facts found and the choice made." *Burlington Truck Lines, Inc. v. United States*, 371 U.S. 156, 168 (1962). In reviewing that explanation, we must "consider whether the decision was based on a consideration of the relevant factors and whether there has been a clear error of judgment." *Citizens to Preserve Overton Park v. Volpe, supra*, at 416. Normally, an agency rule would be arbitrary and capricious if the agency has relied on factors which Congress has not intended it to consider, entirely failed to consider an important aspect of the problem, offered an explanation for its decision that runs counter to the evidence before the agency, or is so implausible that it could not be ascribed to a difference in view or the product of agency expertise. The reviewing court should not attempt itself to make up for such deficiencies; we may not supply a reasoned basis for the agency's action that the agency itself has not given. *SEC v. Chenery Corp.*, 332 U.S. 194, 196 (1947). We will, however, "uphold a decision of less than ideal clarity if the agency's path may reasonably be discerned." *Bowman Transportation, Inc. v. Arkansas-Best Freight System, Inc., supra*, at 286. For purposes of these cases, it is also relevant that Congress required a record of the rulemaking proceedings to be compiled and submitted to a reviewing court, 15 U.S.C. § 1394, and intended that agency findings under the Act would be supported by "substantial evidence on the record considered as a whole."

IV

The Court of Appeals correctly found that the arbitrary-and-capricious test applied to rescissions of prior agency regulations, but then erred in intensifying the scope of its review based upon its reading of legislative events. It held that congressional reaction to various versions of Standard 208 "raise[d] doubts" that NHTSA's rescission "necessarily demonstrates an effort to fulfill its statutory mandate," and therefore the agency was obligated to provide "increasingly clear and convincing reasons" for its action.***

[T]his Court has never suggested that the standard of review is enlarged or diminished by subsequent congressional action. While an agency's interpretation of a statute may be confirmed or ratified by subsequent congressional failure to change that interpretation, in the cases before us, even an unequivocal ratification — short of statutory incorporation — of the passive restraint standard would not connote approval or disapproval of an agency's later decision to rescind the regulation. That decision remains subject to the arbitrary-and-capricious standard.***

V

The ultimate question before us is whether NHTSA's rescission of the passive restraint requirement of Standard 208 was arbitrary and capricious. We conclude, as did the Court of Appeals, that it was. We also conclude, but for somewhat different reasons, that further consideration of the issue by the agency is therefore required. We deal separately with the rescission as it applies to airbags and as it applies to seatbelts.

A

The first and most obvious reason for finding the rescission arbitrary and capricious is that NHTSA apparently gave no consideration whatever to modifying the Standard to require that airbag technology be utilized. Standard 208 sought to achieve automatic crash protection by requiring automobile manufacturers to install either of two passive restraint devices: airbags or automatic seatbelts. There was no suggestion in the long rulemaking process that led to Standard 208 that if only one of these options were feasible, no passive restraint standard should be promulgated. Indeed, the agency's original proposed Standard contemplated the installation of inflatable restraints in all cars. Automatic belts were added as a means of complying with the Standard because they were believed to be as effective as airbags in achieving the goal of occupant crash protection. At that time, the passive belt approved by the agency could not be detached. Only later, at a manufacturer's behest, did the agency approve of the detachability feature — and only after assurances that the feature would not compromise the safety benefits of the restraint. Although it was then foreseen that 60% of the new cars would contain airbags and 40% would have automatic seatbelts, the ratio between the two was not significant as long as the passive belt would also assure greater passenger safety.

The agency has now determined that the detachable automatic belts will not attain anticipated safety benefits because so many individuals will detach the mechanism. Even if this conclusion were acceptable in its entirety, standing alone it would not justify any more than an amendment of Standard 208 to disallow compliance by means of the one technology which will not provide effective passenger protection. It does not cast doubt on the need for a passive restraint standard or upon the efficacy of airbag technology. In its most recent rulemaking, the agency again acknowledged the lifesaving potential of the airbag:

"The agency has no basis at this time for changing its earlier conclusions in 1976 and 1977 that basic air bag technology is sound and has been sufficiently demonstrated to be effective in those vehicles in current use . . . . " NHTSA Final Regulatory Impact Analysis (RIA) XI-4 (Oct. 1981).

Given the effectiveness ascribed to airbag technology by the agency, the mandate of the Act to achieve traffic safety would suggest that the logical response to the faults of detachable seatbelts would be to require the installation of airbags. At the very least this alternative way of achieving the objectives of the Act should have been addressed and adequate reasons given for its abandonment. But the agency not only did not require compliance through airbags, it also did not even consider the possibility in its 1981 rulemaking. Not one sentence of its rulemaking statement discusses the airbags-only option. Because, as the Court of Appeals stated, "NHTSA's . . . analysis of airbags was nonexistent," what we said in *Burlington Truck Lines, Inc. v. United States*, 371 U.S., at 167, is apropos here:

> "There are no findings and no analysis here to justify the choice made, no indication of the basis on which the [agency] exercised its expert discretion.***

The automobile industry has opted for the passive belt over the airbag, but surely it is not enough that the regulated industry has eschewed a given safety device. For nearly a decade, the automobile industry waged the regulatory equivalent of war against the airbag and lost—the inflatable restraint was proved sufficiently effective. Now the automobile industry has decided to employ a seatbelt system which will not meet the safety objectives of Standard 208. This hardly constitutes cause to revoke the Standard itself. Indeed, the Act was necessary because the industry was not sufficiently responsive to safety concerns. The Act intended that safety standards not depend on current technology and could be "technology-forcing" in the sense of inducing the development of superior safety design. If, under the statute, the agency should not defer to the industry's failure to develop safer cars, which it surely should not do, *a fortiori* it may not revoke a safety standard which can be satisfied by current technology simply because the industry has opted for an ineffective seatbelt design.

Although the agency did not address the mandatory airbag option and the Court of Appeals noted that "airbags seem to have none of the problems that NHTSA identified in passive seatbelts," petitioners recite a number of difficulties that they believe would be posed by a mandatory airbag standard. These range from questions concerning the installation of airbags in small cars to that of adverse public reaction. But these are not the agency's reasons for rejecting a mandatory airbag standard. Not having discussed the possibility, the agency submitted no reasons at all. The short—and sufficient—answer to petitioners' submission is that the courts may not accept appellate counsel's post hoc rationalizations for agency action. It is well established that an agency's action must be upheld, if at all, on the basis articulated by the agency itself. *SEC v. Chenery Corp.*, 332 U.S., at 196.[15]

---

15. The Department of Transportation expresses concern that adoption of an airbags-only requirement would have required a new notice of proposed rulemaking. Even if this were so, and we need not decide the question, it would not constitute sufficient cause to rescind the passive restraint requirement.***

B

Although the issue is closer, we also find that the agency was too quick to dismiss the safety benefits of automatic seatbelts. NHTSA's critical finding was that, in light of the industry's plans to install readily detachable passive belts, it could not reliably predict "even a 5 percentage point increase as the minimum level of expected usage increase." 46 Fed. Reg. 53423 (1981). The Court of Appeals rejected this finding because there is "not one iota" of evidence that Modified Standard 208 will fail to increase nationwide seatbelt use by at least 13 percentage points, the level of increased usage necessary for the Standard to justify its cost. Given the lack of probative evidence, the court held that "only a well justified refusal to seek more evidence could render rescission non-arbitrary."

Petitioners object to this conclusion. In their view, "substantial uncertainty" that a regulation will accomplish its intended purpose is sufficient reason, without more, to rescind a regulation. We agree with petitioners that just as an agency reasonably may decline to issue a safety standard if it is uncertain about its efficacy, an agency may also revoke a standard on the basis of serious uncertainties if supported by the record and reasonably explained. Rescission of the passive restraint requirement would not be arbitrary and capricious simply because there was no evidence in direct support of the agency's conclusion. It is not infrequent that the available data do not settle a regulatory issue, and the agency must then exercise its judgment in moving from the facts and probabilities on the record to a policy conclusion. Recognizing that policymaking in a complex society must account for uncertainty, however, does not imply that it is sufficient for an agency to merely recite the terms "substantial uncertainty" as a justification for its actions. As previously noted, the agency must explain the evidence which is available, and must offer a "rational connection between the facts found and the choice made." *Burlington Truck Lines, Inc. v. United States, supra*, at 168. Generally, one aspect of that explanation would be a justification for rescinding the regulation before engaging in a search for further evidence.

In these cases, the agency's explanation for rescission of the passive restraint requirement is *not* sufficient to enable us to conclude that the rescission was the product of reasoned decisionmaking.*** We start with the accepted ground that if used, seatbelts unquestionably would save many thousands of lives and would prevent tens of thousands of crippling injuries.*** [T]he safety benefits of wearing seatbelts are not in doubt, and it is not challenged that were those benefits to accrue, the monetary costs of implementing the Standard would be easily justified. We move next to the fact that there is no direct evidence in support of the agency's finding that detachable automatic belts cannot be predicted to yield a substantial increase in usage. The empirical evidence on the record, consisting of surveys of drivers of automobiles equipped with passive belts, reveals more than a doubling of the usage rate experienced with manual belts. Much of the agency's rulemaking statement—and much of the controversy in these cases—centers on the conclusions that should be drawn from these studies. The agency maintained that the doubling of seatbelt usage in these studies could not be extrapolated to an across-the-board mandatory standard because the passive seatbelts were guarded by ignition interlocks and purchasers of the tested cars are somewhat atypical. Respondents insist these studies demonstrate that Modified Standard 208 will substantially increase seatbelt usage. We believe that it is within the agency's discretion to pass upon the generalizability of these field studies. This is precisely the type of issue which rests within the expertise of NHTSA, and upon which a reviewing court must be most hesitant to intrude.

But accepting the agency's view of the field tests on passive restraints indicates only that there is no reliable real-world experience that usage rates will substantially increase. To be sure, NHTSA opines that "it cannot reliably predict even a 5 percentage point increase as the minimum level of expected increased usage." Notice 25, 46 Fed. Reg. 53423 (1981). But this and other statements that passive belts will not yield substantial increases in seatbelt usage apparently take no account of the critical difference between detachable automatic belts and current manual belts. A detached passive belt does require an affirmative act to reconnect it, but—unlike a manual seatbelt—the passive belt, once reattached, will continue to function automatically unless again disconnected. Thus, inertia—a factor which the agency's own studies have found significant in explaining the current low usage rates for seatbelts—works in *favor* of, not *against*, use of the protective device. Since 20% to 50% of motorists currently wear seatbelts on some occasions, there would seem to be grounds to believe that seatbelt use by occasional users will be substantially increased by the detachable passive belts. Whether this is in fact the case is a matter for the agency to decide, but it must bring its expertise to bear on the question.

The agency is correct to look at the costs as well as the benefits of Standard 208. The agency's conclusion that the incremental costs of the requirements were no longer reasonable was predicated on its prediction that the safety benefits of the regulation might be minimal.*** When the agency reexamines its findings as to the likely increase in seatbelt usage, it must also reconsider its judgment of the reasonableness of the monetary and other costs associated with the Standard. In reaching its judgment, NHTSA should bear in mind that Congress intended safety to be the pre-eminent factor under the Act:

> "The Committee intends that safety shall be the overriding consideration in the issuance of standards under this bill. The Committee recognizes . . . that the Secretary will necessarily consider reasonableness of cost, feasibility and adequate lead-time." S. Rep. No. 1301, 89th Cong., 2d Sess., 6 (1966).*

> "In establishing standards the Secretary must conform to the requirement that the standard be practicable. This would require consideration of all relevant factors, including technological ability to achieve the goal of a particular standard as well as consideration of economic factors.

---

* As indicated above, this report was issued by the Senate Commerce Committee.—Eds.

"Motor vehicle safety is the paramount purpose of this bill and each standard must be related thereto." H.R. Rep. No. 1776, 89th Cong., 2d Sess., 16 (1966).[†]

The agency also failed to articulate a basis for not requiring nondetachable belts under Standard 208. It is argued that the concern of the agency with the easy detachability of the currently favored design would be readily solved by a continuous passive belt, which allows the occupant to "spool out" the belt and create the necessary slack for easy extrication from the vehicle. The agency did not separately consider the continuous belt option, but treated it together with the ignition interlock device in a category it titled "Option of Adopting Use-Compelling Features." The agency was concerned that use-compelling devices would "complicate the extrication of [an] occupant from his or her car." "[T]o require that passive belts contain use-compelling features," the agency observed, "could be counterproductive[, given] . . . widespread, latent and irrational fear in many members of the public that they could be trapped by the seat belt after a crash." In addition, based on the experience with the ignition interlock, the agency feared that use-compelling features might trigger adverse public reaction.

By failing to analyze the continuous seatbelts option in its own right, the agency has failed to offer the rational connection between facts and judgment required to pass muster under the arbitrary-and-capricious standard. We agree with the Court of Appeals that NHTSA did not suggest that the emergency release mechanisms used in nondetachable belts are any less effective for emergency egress than the buckle release system used in detachable belts. In 1978, when General Motors obtained the agency's approval to install a continuous passive belt, it assured the agency that nondetachable belts with spool releases were as safe as detachable belts with buckle releases. NHTSA was satisfied that this belt design assured easy extricability: "[t]he agency does not believe that the use of [such] release mechanisms will cause serious occupant egress problems . . . ." While the agency is entitled to change its view on the acceptability of continuous passive belts, it is obligated to explain its reasons for doing so.

The agency also failed to offer any explanation why a continuous passive belt would engender the same adverse public reaction as the ignition interlock, and, as the Court of Appeals concluded, "every indication in the record points the other way." We see no basis for equating the two devices: the continuous belt, unlike the ignition interlock, does not interfere with the operation of the vehicle. More importantly, it is the agency's responsibility, not this Court's, to explain its decision.

VI

"An agency's view of what is in the public interest may change, either with or without a change in circumstances. But an agency changing its course must supply a reasoned analysis . . . ." *Greater Boston Television Corp. v. FCC*, 444 F. 2d 841, 852 (1970)

---

† This report was issued by the House Committee on Interstate and Foreign Commerce. — Eds.

(footnote omitted), *cert. denied*, 403 U.S. 923 (1971). We do not accept all of the reasoning of the Court of Appeals but we do conclude that the agency has failed to supply the requisite "reasoned analysis" in this case. Accordingly, we vacate the judgment of the Court of Appeals and remand the cases to that court with directions to remand the matter to the NHTSA for further consideration consistent with this opinion.

Justice Rehnquist, with whom The Chief Justice, Justice Powell, and Justice O'Connor join, concurring in part and dissenting in part.

I agree that, since the airbag and continuous spool automatic seatbelt were explicitly approved in the Standard the agency was rescinding, the agency should explain why it declined to leave those requirements intact. I do not believe, however, that NHTSA's view of detachable automatic seatbelts was arbitrary and capricious.***

The agency chose not to rely on a study showing a substantial increase in seatbelt usage in cars equipped with automatic seatbelts and an ignition interlock to prevent the car from being operated when the belts were not in place and which were voluntarily purchased with this equipment by consumers. It is reasonable for the agency to decide that this study does not support any conclusion concerning the effect of automatic seatbelts that are installed in all cars whether the consumer wants them or not and are not linked to an ignition interlock system.

It seems to me that the agency's explanation, while by no means a model, is adequate. The agency acknowledged that there would probably be some increase in belt usage, but concluded that the increase would be small and not worth the cost of mandatory detachable automatic belts. The agency's obligation is to articulate a "'rational connection between the facts found and the choice made.'" I believe it has met this standard.***

The agency's changed view of the standard seems to be related to the election of a new President of a different political party. It is readily apparent that the responsible members of one administration may consider public resistance and uncertainties to be more important than do their counterparts in a previous administration. A change in administration brought about by the people casting their votes is a perfectly reasonable basis for an executive agency's reappraisal of the costs and benefits of its programs and regulations. As long as the agency remains within the bounds established by Congress, it is entitled to assess administrative records and evaluate priorities in light of the philosophy of the administration.

Notes and Questions

1. **The Statutory and Regulatory Design Question?** The Department of Transportation (DOT) is an executive branch agency. Established in 1966, the Department's mandate is "to assure the coordinated, effective administration of the transportation programs of the Federal Government" and to develop "national transportation policies and programs conducive to the provision of fast, safe, efficient, and convenient

transportation at the lowest cost consistent therewith." 49 U.S.C. § 102 note. The Secretary of Transportation is appointed by the President with the advice and consent of the Senate.

As the Court notes, the national Traffic and Motor Vehicle Safety Act of 1966, Pub. L. No. 89-563, 80 Stat. 718, directed the Secretary to promulgate safety standards that "shall be practicable, shall meet the need for motor vehicle safety, and shall be stated in objective terms." *Id.* § 103(a). The Act further provided that "[t]he Administrative Procedure Act shall apply to all orders establishing, amending, or revoking a Federal motor vehicle safety standard under this title." *Id.* § 103(b). Why did Congress find it necessary to delegate authority to regulate motor vehicle safety to an administrative agency? Is vehicle safety regulation an area that benefits from decisionmaking by an expert decisionmaker? Where delegation to an agency permits an updating of regulatory requirements over time? Why did Congress delegate authority to an executive department rather than a multimember "independent" agency?

2. **Regulatory and Procedural Posture?** "Modified Standard 208" was promulgated by Secretary of Transportation Brock Adams in 1977 and required vehicle manufacturers to use passive restraint systems — automatic seatbelts or airbags — by model year 1984. The question presented by *State Farm* was whether Secretary of Transportation Andrew Lewis's rescission of Modified Standard 208 in February 1981 was consistent with the Traffic and Motor Vehicle Safety Act and APA.

Modified Standard 208 is notable among other reasons because it reflects an early example of a *performance* standard. "Although the [standard] presumed the existence of a particular type of equipment [it] did not mandate its use. Instead it permitted the use of any 'passive' technology*** that would meet the standard's performance criteria.*** [T]he proposal was framed in terms of the effects produced on an anthropomorphic dummy in the frontal barrier crashes at 30 miles per hour." JERRY L. MASHAW & DAVID L. HARFST, THE STRUGGLE FOR AUTO SAFETY 86 (1990).

What happened at the Department of Transportation between the 1977 promulgation of Modified Standard 208 and the Standard's rescission in 1981? What happened in Congress? The courts? What did the court below conclude regarding the rescission of Modified Standard 208? What standard of review did it apply? What was the basis for its decision? Mashaw and Harfst point out (at 208) that "[t]he agency was particularly concerned that the current phase-in schedule*** might exacerbate the economic troubles of the domestic automobile industry," which was facing intense competition from Japanese and European manufacturers. Why did the agency not rely more heavily on this argument in *State Farm*? Is a desire to protect domestic manufacturers from foreign competition a permissible basis for action under the Traffic and Motor Vehicle Safety Act?

3. **DOT's Burden of Justification?** In the Supreme Court's view, what burden of justification did the DOT have to carry in rescinding Modified Standard 208? Was the agency required to make use of a specific process prior to rescinding the standard?

For example, was it required to conduct new hearings, or give interested parties a new opportunity to submit evidence and argument? Was Secretary Lewis free simply to reevaluate the conclusions of Secretary Adams in light of the Reagan administration's deregulatory philosophy? If Jimmy Carter had prevailed in the 1980 presidential election and run on a platform of reducing threats to health and safety, would his new Secretary of Transportation have been entitled to replace Modified Standard 208 with a more stringent standard—say, one that required airbags in all new vehicles by model year 1985? According to *State Farm*, would DOT have been required to follow a specific procedure?

4. **The Standard of Review?** Petitioners contended that "the rescission of an agency rule should be judged by the same standard a court would use to judge an agency's refusal to promulgate a rule in the first instance, and that this standard was "considerably narrower than the traditional arbitrary-and-capricious test." What standard of review did petitioners have in mind? See Note 5 following *Heckler v. Chaney*, Section [B], *supra* p. 557 (discussing judicial review of petition for rulemaking in *Massachusetts v. EPA*, 127 S. Ct. 1438 (2007)).

Why does the Supreme Court reject petitioners' argument? For purposes of the APA, what distinguishes an agency's rescission of a rule from its failure to promulgate a rule in the first instance? The Supreme Court implies that an agency declining to promulgate a rule in the first instance may not have an obligation "to supply a reasoned analysis" for its decision. Is that correct? *See* APA § 551(13) ("'agency action' includes the whole or a part of an agency rule, order, license, sanction, relief, or the equivalent or denial thereof, or failure to act"); APA § 706(1) ("reviewing court shall*** compel agency action unlawfully withheld or unreasonably delayed").

At the other end of the spectrum, the D.C. Circuit concluded that DOT could rescind Modified Standard 208 only if it adduced "clear and convincing reasons" for doing so. Why did the court of appeals conclude this was the relevant standard? Does it make sense to apply the clear and convincing standard—an evidentiary standard that requires more proof than the preponderance-of-the-evidence standard but less than that required by the beyond-a-reasonable-doubt standard—to any agency's rescission of a legislative rule? Why does the Supreme Court reject the D.C. Circuit's clear-and-convincing standard?

Which standard of review does the Supreme Court apply to review the rescission of Modified Standard 208? Which provision of APA § 706 does this standard derive from? Does the fact that the Department proceeded by rulemaking as opposed to adjudication affect the standard of review? *Compare Citizens to Preserve Overton Park v. Volpe*, 401 U.S. 402 (1971), Chapter 4[B], *supra*.

5. **Why Was the DOT's Airbag Analysis Arbitrary and Capricious?** The Court analyzes the rescission of Modified Standard 208 as it applied to airbags separately from the rescission as it applied to automatic seatbelts. Why does the Court conclude that the rescission vis-à-vis airbags was arbitrary and capricious?

The Court faults the Department's failure to consider an airbags-only standard after having concluded that Modified Standard 208 readily would not achieve its intended safety objectives because automatic seatbelts could be detached. Why does the Court believe that the airbags-only option is an alternative that the agency was required to consider? Was the agency required to consider *other* alternatives to Modified Standard 208 that would have overcome the problem created by detachable seatbelts?

Is the Court, in effect, faulting DOT for allowing itself to be "captured" by the motor vehicle industry? The Court observes that, in the form originally adopted by the Department, automatic seatbelts could not be detached. "Only later, at a manufacturer's behest, did the agency approve of the detachability feature." The possibility that drivers would detach seatbelts and leave them detached then became the basis for the Department's conclusion that the Modified Standard 208 would not achieve its intended safety benefits. On the general phenomenon of capture, see Preventing Regulatory Capture: Special Interest Influence and How to Limit It (Daniel Carpenter & David A. Moss, eds. 2013).

The D.C. Circuit was troubled by the fact that the rescission of the standard was motivated in part by Secretary of Transportation Lewis's desire to implement President Reagan's regulatory philosophy. Does this fact trouble the Supreme Court? What is its relevance, if any, to whether the rescission of the standard was arbitrary and capricious? To what extent can the President influence the regulatory decisions of its executive department heads? Did the Traffic and Motor Vehicle Act bar such influence? Can it do so constitutionally? *See* Note on the President's Authority to Direct the Actions of Administrative Agencies, Chapter 3[D][2], *supra*; Kathryn A. Watts, *Proposing a Place for Politics in Arbitrary and Capricious Review*, 119 Yale L.J. 85 (2009).

6. Why Was DOT's Decision Not To Require Automatic Seatbelts Arbitrary and Capricious? Why does the Supreme Court conclude that the rescission of Modified Standard 208 was arbitrary and capricious insofar the automatic seatbelt requirement was concerned? The D.C. Circuit thought it significant that Department lacked an empirical basis for its conclusion that adoption of the standard would not, in fact, increase seat belt use. Does the Supreme Court adopt the D.C. Circuit's view on this point? The Supreme Court reasons that because of inertia, automatic seatbelts would increase seatbelt use even if the seatbelts were detachable. Is this an objection that the Department should have anticipated in the process of rescinding the rule? What could it have done to rebut the argument?

The Court also faults the Department for failing to provide a reasoned explanation for not requiring non-detachable automatic seatbelts. What did the agency say on this point? Again, was its error its uncritical adoption of the motor vehicle manufacturers' position on the feasibility of non-detachable automatic seatbelts? Is the Department's failure a failure "to explain its decision," or a failure to make a good policy decision?

7. The Role of Cost-Benefit Analysis in Arbitrary and Capricious Review? Can *State Farm* be understood to rest on the Court's conclusion that DOT did not properly account for the costs and benefits of rescinding Modified Standard 208? To the extent that arbitrary and capricious review requires courts to consider an agency's evaluation of costs and benefits, how does judicial review of the agency's action differ from the review performed by the Office of Information and Regulatory Affairs (OIRA) under Executive Order 12,866? *See* Chapter 3[D][1], *supra*.

Consider *Michigan v. EPA*, 135 S. Ct. 2699 (2015). A provision of the Clean Air Act Amendments of 1990, 42 U.S.C. § 7412, directed EPA to "perform a study of the hazards to public health reasonably anticipated to occur as a result of emissions by [power plants] of [hazardous air pollutants]," and to regulate power plants' release of hazardous pollutants if EPA found "that regulation is appropriate and necessary after considering the results of the study." Congress required the agency to make this finding because other provisions of the Clean Air Act Amendments imposed new restrictions on power plants, and legislators were uncertain whether regulation of power plants was also warranted under the Hazardous Air Pollutants Program, which was at issue in *Michigan*.

After performing the § 7412 study, the EPA concluded that regulation of power plants was indeed appropriate and necessary. The finding announcing this conclusion, 65 Fed. Reg. 79,825, did not weigh the anticipated costs and benefits of regulating power plants' release of hazardous pollutants but stated (at 79,830) that "the effectiveness and costs of [potential] controls will be examined" at later stages in the regulatory process. The agency's final regulation established new controls on power plants' release of hazardous substances, based on detailed analysis of the costs of different pollution-control technologies. With the final regulation, 77 Fed. Reg. 9363, the EPA issued a Regulatory Impact Analysis as required by Executive Order 12,866, which estimated the direct financial costs of the new regulation at $9.6 billion per year, and the direct financial benefits at $4 to $6 million per year. The Regulatory Impact Analysis noted that many benefits of regulating power plants—such as preventing neurological illness from mercury exposure—could not be reduced to dollars and cents figures.

The Supreme Court vacated the EPA's final regulation for failure to consider costs at the initial stage of its regulatory process by a 5-4 vote. Justice Scalia's opinion for the Court reasoned (135 S. Ct. at 2707) that it was not "rational, never mind 'appropriate,' to impose billions of dollars in economic costs in return for a few dollars in health or environmental benefits." Although the EPA explicitly weighed the costs and benefits of its regulation at later stages of the administrative process, the Court believed this did not cure the agency's initial failure to consider costs. "It is unreasonable to infer that, by expressly making cost relevant to other decisions, the Act implicitly makes cost irrelevant to the appropriateness of regulating power plants." The Court distinguished *Whitman v. American Trucking Assns., Inc.*, 531 U.S. 457 (2001), *supra* Chapter 3[B][1][a], on the ground that the statutory language at issue there only "encompasse[d] health and safety." The disallowance of cost consider-ations in that case "has no application here. 'Appropriate and necessary' is a far more comprehensive criterion than 'requisite to protect the public health'; read fairly and in context*** the term plainly subsumes consideration of cost."

Can *Michigan* be squared with *Vermont Yankee*'s prohibition of administrative common law, or is the Court in effect requiring the agency to conduct multiple rounds of cost-benefit analysis on pain of having its regulation vacated on judicial review? Was the Court right to focus on monetizable costs of the agency regulation? *See generally* Jonathan S. Masur & Eric A. Posner, *Unquantified Benefits and Bayesian Cost-Benefit Analysis*, Coase-Sandor Institute for Law & Econ. Working Paper No. 730 (Aug. 17, 2015). EPA re-promulgated the rule at issue in *Michigan* in April 2016. Following Trump's inauguraton, the agency in February 2017 announced that it would consider revoking the rule.

In *Business Roundtable v. SEC*, 647 F.3d 1144 (D.C. Cir. 2011), the D.C. Circuit relied on a form of cost-benefit analysis with strong parallels to OIRA review to invalidate Exchange Act Rule 14a–11, 75 Fed. Reg. 56,668 (2010). To select directors, most pub-lic companies send proxy materials to shareholders that list candidates for board posi-tions and solicit votes. Traditionally, the only candidates listed in a company's proxy materials were those selected by the incumbent board. To challenge the company slate, a shareholder had to distribute an alternative set of proxy materials at significant per-sonal expense.

Exchange Act Rule 14a–11 required companies subject to the Securities Act's proxy provisions, 15 U.S.C. §78n, to include certain shareholder nominees for board posi-tions in the firm's proxy materials. In the SEC's view, the rule would increase the com-petitiveness of board elections and thereby improve shareholder value by reducing the costs of challenging the company's incumbent board. A shareholder seeking to distribute proxy materials under the rule nonetheless was required to satisfy a num-ber of conditions:

> To use Rule 14a–11, a shareholder or group of shareholders must have con-tinuously held "at least 3% of the voting power of the company's securities entitled to be voted" for at least three years prior to the date the nominating shareholder or group submits notice of its intent to use the rule, and must continue to own those securities through the date of the annual meeting. The nominating shareholder or group must submit the notice, which may include a statement of up to 500 words in support of each of its nominees, to the Commission and to the company.

In promulgating the rule, the SEC considered its general costs and benefits, and quantified some of them. The SEC did not, however, develop an econometric model for comparing the rules costs and benefits. As explained by the court of appeals (*id.* at 1149):

[T]he Commission predicted Rule 14a–11 would lead to "[d]irect cost savings" for shareholders in part due to "reduced printing and postage costs" and reduced expenditures for advertising compared to those of a "traditional" proxy contest. The Commission also identified some intangible, or at least less readily quantifiable, benefits, principally that the rule "will mitigate collective action and free-rider concerns," which can discourage a shareholder from exercising his right to nominate a director in a traditional proxy contest, and "has the potential of creating the benefit of improved board performance and enhanced shareholder value." The Commission anticipated the rule would also impose costs upon companies and shareholders related to "the preparation of required disclosure, printing and mailing . . . , and [to] additional solicitations," and could have "adverse effects on company and board performance," for example, by distracting management. The Commission nonetheless concluded the rule would promote the "efficiency of the economy on the whole," and the benefits of the rule would "justify the costs" of the rule.

The Commission relied on two studies that found positive effects on shareholder value from "hybrid boards" that included dissident directors, and from proxy contests in general, Chris Cernich et al., IRRC Inst. for Corporate Responsibility, Effectiveness of Hybrid Boards (May 2009); and J. Harold Mulherin & Annette B. Poulsen, *Proxy Contests & Corporate Change: Implications for Shareholder Wealth*, 47 J. Fin. Econ. 279 (1998). The Commission discounted another study that found negative effects on shareholder value from the election of dissident board members, Elaine Buckberg, NERA Econ. Consulting, & Jonathan Macey, Yale Law School, Report on Effects of Proposed SEC Rule 14a–11 on Efficiency, Competitiveness and Capital Formation 9 (2009).

On review, the D.C. Circuit invalided the rule under Administrative Procedure Act, 5 U.S.C. § 706, and provisions of the Exchange Act and Investment Company Act that require the Commission to consider the effect of a new rule upon "efficiency, competition, and capital formation," 15 U.S.C. §§ 78c(f), 78w(a)(2), 80a–2(c). The court concluded that the SEC's reliance on the Cernich and Mulherin studies was inappropriate, because the studies' long-term implications for shareholder value were unclear. The Commission's reliance on those studies, the court opined, revealed that the Commission lacked an adequate empirical basis for the conclusion "that increasing the potential for election of directors nominated by shareholders will result in improved board and company performance and shareholder value." 647 F.3d at 1151.

The court criticized the SEC for not quantifying all of the costs and benefits of Rule 14a–11, failing to develop a sufficient empirical basis for the rule, and performing an economic analysis that, in the court's view, reflected an improper approach to cost-benefit analysis. For example, the court noted that—

the Commission discounted the costs of Rule 14a–11—but not the benefits—as a mere artifact of the state law right of shareholders to elect directors.*** [W]ith reference to the potential costs of Rule 14a–11, such as management distraction and reduction in the time a board spends "on strategic and long-term thinking," the Commission thought it "important to note that these costs are associated with the traditional State law right to nominate and elect directors, and are not costs incurred for including shareholder nominees for director in the company's proxy materials." As we have said before, this type of reasoning, which fails to view a cost at the margin, is illogical and, in an economic analysis, unacceptable.

Is it appropriate for a reviewing court to engage in the same style of cost-benefit review that the OIRA performs under Executive Order 12,866? Cass R. Sunstein, *The Real World of Cost-Benefit Analysis: Thirty-Six Questions (And Almost as Many Answers)*, 114 COLUM. L. REV. 167 (2014), observes that as practiced in the executive branch, cost-benefit analysis relies heavily on "authoritative documents that are both meant and understood to bind executive agencies even though they lack the force of law." These documents reflect inter-agency conventions or presumptions and are sometimes approved by the President or the President's advisors. Does the Executive Branch's reliance on such conventions call into question the wisdom of the decision in *Business Roundtable? See generally* John C. Coates IV, *Cost-Benefit Analysis of Financial Regulation: Case Studies and Implications*, 124 YALE L.J. 882 (2015); Bruce Kraus & Connor Raso, *Rational Boundaries for SEC Cost-Benefit Analysis*, 30 YALE J. REG. 289 (2013); Grant M. Hayden & Matthew T. Bodie, *The Bizarre Law and Economics of* Business Roundtable v. SEC, 38 J. CORP. L. 101 (2012); James D. Cox & Benjamin J. C. Baucom, *The Emperor Has No Clothes: Confronting the D.C. Circuit's Usurpation of SEC Rulemaking Authority*, 90 TEX. L. REV. 1811 (2012).

8. *State Farm* **and "Hard Look Review."** Prior to the Supreme Court's decision in *State Farm*, the U.S. Court of Appeals for the District of Columbia Circuit had long understood 5 U.S.C. §706 to require reviewing courts to ensure that agencies took a "hard look" at regulatory alternatives before making a decision. In the leading decision, Judge Harold Leventhal explained the standard as follows:

> Assuming consistency with law and the legislative mandate, the agency has latitude not merely to find facts and make judgments, but also to select the policies deemed in the public interest. The function of the court is to assure that the agency has given reasoned consideration to all the material facts and issues. This calls for insistence that the agency articulate with reasonable clarity its reasons for decision, and identify the significance of the crucial facts, a course that tends to assure that the agency's policies effectuate general standards, applied without unreasonable discrimination.***

> Its supervisory function calls on the court to intervene not merely in case of procedural inadequacies, or bypassing of the mandate in the legislative charter, but more broadly if the court becomes aware, especially from a combination of danger signals, that the agency has not really taken a "hard look" at the salient problems, and has not genuinely engaged in reasoned decision-making. If the agency has not shirked this fundamental task, however, the court exercises restraint and affirms the agency's action even though the court would on its own account have made different findings or adopted different standards.

Greater Boston Television Corp. v. FCC, 444 F.2d 841, 851 (D.C. Cir. 1970). *See generally* Samuel Estreicher, *Pragmatic Justice: The Contributions of Judge Harold Leventhal to Administrative Law*, 80 COLUM. L. REV. 894 (1980).

Several court of appeals decisions have understood *State Farm* to endorse this form of review. *See, e.g., Neighborhood TV Co. v. FCC*, 742 F.2d 629, 639 (D.C. Cir. 1984); *Frisby v. U.S. Dep't of Hous. & Urban Dev.*, 755 F.2d 1052, 1055 (3d Cir. 1985); *Long Island Head Start Child Dev. Servs. v. NLRB*, 460 F.3d 254, 257 (2d Cir. 2006). In particular, courts of appeals understood *State Farm* to require additional scrutiny of the agency's reasons for acting when it rescinded a prior regulation or changed its approach to regulating an issue. As expressed in a 2002 restatement of administrative law principles, reviewing courts were to set aside agency action that "without legitimate reason and adequate explanation" was "inconsistent with prior agency policies or precedents." Section of Admin. Law & Regulatory Practice, Am. Bar Ass'n, *A Blackletter Statement of Federal Administrative Law*, 54 ADMIN. L. REV. 1, 43 (2002).

Not everyone shared this understanding of *State Farm*, however. In 1982, then-Professor Scalia argued, commenting on the D.C. Circuit's decision in *State Farm*, that "[m]ore needs to be done" to make agencies responsive to political considerations and, likewise, make the influence of such considerations visible to outside observers.

> When NHTSA comes to reconsider the passive-restraint rule recently remanded by the D.C. Circuit, and if it chooses to adhere to its prior course, it would be refreshing and instructive if, instead of (or at least in addition to) blowing smoke in our eyes with exhaustive technical and economic data, it said flat-out: "It is our judgment that people should not be strapped in cars if they don't want to be; nor should they have to spend substantial sums for airbags if they choose otherwise." A political judgment, the retribution or reward for which will be meted out by Congress, or at the polls, but not in the courts.

Antonin Scalia, *Rulemaking as Politics*, 34 ADMIN. L. REV. v, xi (1982).

Seven years later, Justice Scalia argued in a lecture on *Chevron* that policy oscillation at the agency level was not necessarily a bad thing:

> If Congress is to delegate broadly, as modern times are thought to demand, it seems to me desirable that the delegee be able to suit its actions to the times, and that continuing political accountability be assured, through direct political pressures upon the Executive and through the indirect political pressure of congressional oversight. All this is lost if "new" or "changing" agency interpretations are somehow suspect. There are of course well established restrictions upon sudden and irrational changes of interpretation through adjudication, and statutorily prescribed procedures (including a requirement of reasoned justification) for changes of interpretation through rulemaking. And at some point, I suppose, repeated changes back and forth may rise (or descend) to the level of "arbitrary and capricious," and thus unlawful, agency action. But so long as these limitations are complied with, there seems to me no reason to value a new interpretation less than an old one.

Antonin Scalia, *Judicial Deference to Administrative Interpretations of Law*, 1989 DUKE L.J. 511, 518 (1989).

The debate between these two understandings of *State Farm*—one calling for searching reviewing of changes in agency policy, the other broadly supportive of such changes, within statutory limits—reached the Supreme Court in 2009.

FCC v. Fox Television Stations, Inc.
129 S. Ct. 1800 (2009)

JUSTICE SCALIA delivered the opinion of the Court, except as to Part III-E.

Federal law prohibits the broadcasting of "any . . . indecent . . . language," 18 U.S.C. § 1464, which includes expletives referring to sexual or excretory activity or organs, *see FCC v. Pacifica Foundation*, 438 U.S. 726 (1978). This case concerns the adequacy of the Federal Communications Commission's explanation of its decision that this sometimes forbids the broadcasting of indecent expletives even when the offensive words are not repeated.

I. Statutory and Regulatory Background

The Communications Act of 1934, 48 Stat. 1064, 47 U.S.C. § 151 et seq. (2000 ed. and Supp. V), established a system of limited-term broadcast licenses subject to various "conditions" designed "to maintain the control of the United States over all the channels of radio transmission," § 301 (2000 ed.). Twenty-seven years ago we said that "[a] licensed broadcaster is granted the free and exclusive use of a limited and valuable part of the public domain; when he accepts that franchise it is burdened by enforceable public obligations." *CBS, Inc. v. FCC*, 453 U.S. 367, 395 (1981) (internal quotation marks omitted).

One of the burdens that licensees shoulder is the indecency ban—the statutory proscription against "utter[ing] any obscene, indecent, or profane language by means of radio communication," 18 U.S.C. § 1464—which Congress has instructed the Commission to enforce between the hours of 6 a.m. and 10 p.m. Public Telecommunications Act of 1992, § 16(a), 106 Stat. 954, note following 47 U.S.C. § 303. Congress has given the Commission various means of enforcing the indecency ban, including civil fines, *see* § 503(b)(1), and license revocations or the denial of license renewals, *see* §§ 309(k), 312(a)(6).

The Commission first invoked the statutory ban on indecent broadcasts in 1975, declaring a daytime broadcast of George Carlin's "Filthy Words" monologue actionably indecent. *Pacifica Foundation*, 56 F.C.C.2d 94. At that time, the Commission announced the definition of indecent speech that it uses to this day, prohibiting "language that describes, in terms patently offensive as measured by contemporary community standards for the broadcast medium, sexual or excretory activities or organs, at times of the day when there is a reasonable risk that children may be in the audience."

In *FCC v. Pacifica Foundation, supra,* we upheld the Commission's order against statutory and constitutional challenge. We rejected the broadcasters' argument that the statutory proscription applied only to speech appealing to the prurient interest, noting that "the normal definition of 'indecent' merely refers to nonconformance with accepted standards of morality." And we held that the First Amendment allowed Carlin's monologue to be banned in light of the "uniquely pervasive presence" of the medium and the fact that broadcast programming is "uniquely accessible to children."

In the ensuing years, the Commission took a cautious, but gradually expanding, approach to enforcing the statutory prohibition against indecent broadcasts. Shortly after *Pacifica,* Commission expressed its "inten[tion] strictly to observe the narrowness of the *Pacifica* holding," which "relied in part on the repetitive occurrence of the 'indecent' words" contained in Carlin's monologue. When the full Commission next considered its indecency standard, however, it repudiated the view that its enforcement power was limited to "deliberate, repetitive use of the seven words actually contained in the George Carlin monologue." The Commission determined that such a "highly restricted enforcement standard ... was unduly narrow as a matter of law and inconsistent with [the Commission's] enforcement responsibilities under Section 1464."***

Although the Commission had expanded its enforcement beyond the "repetitive use of specific words or phrases," it preserved a distinction between literal and non-literal (or "expletive") uses of evocative language. The Commission explained that each literal "description or depiction of sexual or excretory functions must be examined in context to determine whether it is patently offensive," but that "deliberate and repetitive use ... is a requisite to a finding of indecency" when a complaint focuses solely on the use of nonliteral expletives.

Over a decade later, the Commission emphasized that the "full context" in which particular materials appear is "critically important," but that a few "principal" factors guide the inquiry, such as the "explicitness or graphic nature" of the material, the extent to which the material "dwells on or repeats" the offensive material, and the extent to which the material was presented to "pander," to "titillate," or to "shock." "No single factor," the Commission said, "generally provides the basis for an indecency finding," but "where sexual or excretory references have been made once or have been passing or fleeting in nature, this characteristic has tended to weigh against a finding of indecency."

In 2004, the Commission took one step further by declaring for the first time that a nonliteral (expletive) use of the F- and S-Words could be actionably indecent, even when the word is used only once. The first order to this effect dealt with an NBC broadcast of the Golden Globe Awards, in which the performer Bono commented, " 'This is really, really, f***ing brilliant.' " *In re Complaints Against Various Broadcast Licensees Regarding Their Airing of the "Golden Globe Awards" Program,* 19 FCC Red. 4975, 4976, n. 4 (*Golden Globes Order*). Although the Commission had received numerous complaints directed at the broadcast, its enforcement bureau had concluded that the material was not indecent because "Bono did not describe, in context, sexual or excretory organs or activities and . . . the utterance was fleeting and isolated." The full Commission reviewed and reversed the staff ruling.

The Commission first declared that Bono's use of the F-Word fell within its indecency definition, even though the word was used as an intensifier rather than a literal descriptor. "[G]iven the core meaning of the 'F-Word,'" it said, "any use of that word . . . inherently has a sexual connotation." The Commission determined, moreover, that the broadcast was "patently offensive" because the F-Word "is one of the most vulgar, graphic and explicit descriptions of sexual activity in the English language," because "[i]ts use invariably invokes a coarse sexual image," and because Bono's use of the word was entirely "shocking and gratuitous."

The Commission observed that categorically exempting such language from enforcement actions would "likely lead to more widespread use." Commission action was necessary to "safeguard the well-being of the nation's children from the most objectionable, most offensive language." The order noted that technological advances have made it far easier to delete ("bleep out") a "single and gratuitous use of a vulgar expletive," without adulterating the content of a broadcast.

The order acknowledged that "prior Commission and staff action have indicated that isolated or fleeting broadcasts of the 'F-Word' . . . are not indecent or would not be acted upon." It explicitly ruled that "any such interpretation is no longer good law." It "clarif[ied] . . . that the mere fact that specific words or phrases are not sustained or repeated does not mandate a finding that material that is otherwise patently offensive to the broadcast medium is not indecent." Because, however, "existing precedent would have permitted this broadcast," the Commission determined that "NBC and its affiliates necessarily did not have the requisite notice to justify a penalty."

II. The Present Case

This case concerns utterances in two live broadcasts aired by Fox Television Stations, Inc., and its affiliates prior to the Commission's Golden Globes Order. The first occurred during the 2002 Billboard Music Awards, when the singer Cher exclaimed, "I've also had critics for the last 40 years saying that I was on my way out every year. Right. So f*** 'em." The second involved a segment of the 2003 Billboard Music Awards, during the presentation of an award by Nicole Richie and Paris Hilton, principals in a Fox television series called "The Simple Life." Ms. Hilton began their interchange by reminding Ms. Richie to "watch the bad language," but Ms. Richie proceeded to ask the audience, "Why do they even call it 'The Simple Life?' Have you ever tried to get cow s*** out of a Prada purse? It's not so f***ing simple." Following each of these broadcasts, the Commission received numerous complaints from parents whose children were exposed to the language.

On March 15, 2006, the Commission released Notices of Apparent Liability for a number of broadcasts that the Commission deemed actionably indecent, including the two described above. Multiple parties petitioned the Court of Appeals for the Second Circuit for judicial review of the order, asserting a variety of constitutional and statutory challenges. Since the order had declined to impose sanctions, the

Commission had not previously given the broadcasters an opportunity to respond to the indecency charges. It therefore requested and obtained from the Court of Appeals a voluntary remand so that the parties could air their objections. The Commission's order on remand upheld the indecency findings for the broadcasts described above. See *In re Complaints Regarding Various Television Broadcasts Between February 2, 2002, and March 8, 2005*, 21 FCC Rcd. 13299 (2006) (*Remand Order*).

The order first explained that both broadcasts fell comfortably within the subject-matter scope of the Commission's indecency test because the 2003 broadcast involved a literal description of excrement and both broadcasts invoked the "F-Word," which inherently has a sexual connotation. The order next determined that the broadcasts were patently offensive under community standards for the medium. Both broadcasts, it noted, involved entirely gratuitous uses of "one of the most vulgar, graphic, and explicit words for sexual activity in the English language." It found Ms. Richie's use of the "F-Word" and her "explicit description of the handling of excrement" to be "vulgar and shocking," as well as to constitute "pandering," after Ms. Hilton had playfully warned her to "'watch the bad language.'" And it found Cher's statement patently offensive in part because she metaphorically suggested a sexual act as a means of expressing hostility to her critics. The order relied upon the "critically important" context of the utterances, noting that they were aired during prime-time awards shows "designed to draw a large nationwide audience that could be expected to include many children interested in seeing their favorite music stars." Indeed, approximately 2.5 million minors witnessed each of the broadcasts.

The order asserted that both broadcasts under review would have been actionably indecent under the staff rulings and Commission dicta in effect prior to the *Golden Globes Order*— the 2003 broadcast because it involved a literal description of excrement, rather than a mere expletive, because it used more than one offensive word, and because it was planned; and the 2002 broadcast because Cher used the F-Word not as a mere intensifier, but as a description of the sexual act to express hostility to her critics. The order stated, however, that the pre-*Golden Globes* regime of immunity for isolated indecent expletives rested only upon staff rulings and Commission dicta, and that the Commission itself had never held "that the isolated use of an expletive ... was not indecent or could not be indecent." In any event, the order made clear, the *Golden Globes Order* eliminated any doubt that fleeting expletives could be actionably indecent, and the Commission disavowed the bureau-level decisions and its own dicta that had said otherwise. Under the new policy, a lack of repetition "weigh[s] against a finding of indecency," but is not a safe harbor.

The order explained that the Commission's prior "strict dichotomy between 'expletives' and 'descriptions or depictions of sexual or excretory functions' is artificial and does not make sense in light of the fact that an 'expletive's' power to offend derives from its sexual or excretory meaning." In the Commission's view, "granting an automatic exemption for 'isolated or fleeting' expletives unfairly forces viewers (including children)" to take "'the first blow'" and would allow broadcasters "to air expletives at all hours of a day so long as they did so one at a time." Although the Commission determined that Fox encouraged the offensive language by using suggestive scripting in the 2003 broadcast, and unreasonably failed to take adequate precautions in both broadcasts, the order again declined to impose any forfeiture or other sanction for either of the broadcasts.

Fox returned to the Second Circuit for review of the *Remand Order*, and various intervenors including CBS, NBC, and ABC joined the action. The Court of Appeals reversed the agency's orders, finding the Commission's reasoning inadequate under the Administrative Procedure Act. The majority was "skeptical that the Commission [could] provide a reasoned explanation for its 'fleeting expletive' regime that would pass constitutional muster," but it declined to reach the constitutional question. Judge Leval dissented.***

III. Analysis

A. Governing Principles

*** In overturning the Commission's judgment, the Court of Appeals here relied in part on Circuit precedent requiring a more substantial explanation for agency action that changes prior policy. The Second Circuit has interpreted the Administrative Procedure Act and our opinion in *State Farm* as requiring agencies to make clear "'why the original reasons for adopting the [displaced] rule or policy are no longer dispositive'" as well as "'why the new rule effectuates the statute as well as or better than the old rule.'" The Court of Appeals for the District of Columbia Circuit has similarly indicated that a court's standard of review is "heightened somewhat" when an agency reverses course.

We find no basis in the Administrative Procedure Act or in our opinions for a requirement that all agency change be subjected to more searching review. The Act mentions no such heightened standard. And our opinion in *State Farm* neither held nor implied that every agency action representing a policy change must be justified by reasons more substantial than those required to adopt a policy in the first instance. That case, which involved the rescission of a prior regulation, said only that such action requires "a reasoned analysis for the change beyond that which may be required when an agency does not act in the first instance." Treating failures to act and rescissions of prior action differently for purposes of the standard of review makes good sense, and has basis in the text of the statute, which likewise treats the two separately. It instructs a reviewing court to "compel agency action unlawfully withheld or unreasonably delayed," 5 U.S.C. § 706(1), and to "hold unlawful and set aside agency action, findings, and conclusions found to be [among other things] ... arbitrary [or] capricious," § 706(2)(A). The statute makes no distinction, however, between initial agency action and subsequent agency action undoing or revising that action.

To be sure, the requirement that an agency provide reasoned explanation for its action would ordinarily demand that it display awareness that it *is* changing position. An agency may not, for example, depart from a prior policy *sub silentio* or simply disregard rules that are still on the books. And of course the agency must show that there are good reasons for the new policy. But it need not demonstrate to a court's satisfaction that the reasons for the new policy are *better* than the reasons for the old one; it suffices that the new policy is permissible under the statute, that there are good reasons for it, and that the agency *believes* it to be better, which the conscious change of course adequately indicates. This means that the agency need not always provide a more detailed justification than what would suffice for a new policy created on a blank slate. Sometimes it must—when, for example, its new policy rests upon factual findings that contradict those which underlay its prior policy; or when its prior policy has engendered serious reliance interests that must be taken into account. It would be arbitrary or capricious to ignore such matters. In such cases it is not that further justification is demanded by the mere fact of policy change; but that a reasoned explanation is needed for disregarding facts and circumstances that underlay or were engendered by the prior policy.

In this appeal from the Second Circuit's setting aside of Commission action for failure to comply with a procedural requirement of the Administrative Procedure Act, the broadcasters' arguments have repeatedly referred to the First Amendment. If they mean to invite us to apply a more stringent arbitrary-and-capricious review to agency actions that implicate constitutional liberties, we reject the invitation.*** If the Commission's action here was not arbitrary or capricious in the ordinary sense, it satisfies the Administrative Procedure Act's "arbitrary [or] capricious" standard; its lawfulness under the Constitution is a separate question to be addressed in a constitutional challenge.

B. Application to This Case

Judged under the above described standards, the Commission's new enforcement policy and its order finding the broadcasts actionably indecent were neither arbitrary nor capricious. First, the Commission forthrightly acknowledged that its recent actions have broken new ground, taking account of inconsistent "prior Commission and staff action" and explicitly disavowing them as "no longer good law." *Golden Globes Order*, 19 FCC Rcd., at 4980, ¶ 12. To be sure, the (superfluous) explanation in its *Remand Order* of why the Cher broadcast would even have violated its earlier policy may not be entirely convincing. But that unnecessary detour is irrelevant. There is no doubt that the Commission knew it was making a change. That is why it declined to assess penalties; and it relied on the *Golden Globes Order* as removing any lingering doubt.

Moreover, the agency's reasons for expanding the scope of its enforcement activity were entirely rational. It was certainly reasonable to determine that it made no sense to distinguish between literal and nonliteral uses of offensive words, requiring repetitive use to render only the latter indecent. As the Commission said with regard to expletive use of the F-Word, "the word's power to insult and offend derives from its sexual meaning." And the Commission's decision to look at the patent offensiveness of even isolated uses of sexual and excretory words fits with the context-based approach we sanctioned in *Pacifica*. Even isolated utterances can be made in "pander[ing,] . . . vulgar and shocking" manners, and can constitute harmful "'first blow[s]'" to children. It is surely rational (if not inescapable) to believe that a safe harbor for single words would "likely lead to more widespread use of the offensive language."

When confronting other requests for per se rules governing its enforcement of the indecency prohibition, the Commission has declined to create safe harbors for particular types of broadcasts. The Commission could rationally decide it needed to step away from its old regime where nonrepetitive use of an expletive was per se nonactionable because that was "at odds with the Commission's overall enforcement policy."

The fact that technological advances have made it easier for broadcasters to bleep out offending words further supports the Commission's stepped-up enforcement policy. And the agency's decision not to impose any forfeiture or other sanction precludes any argument that it is arbitrarily punishing parties without notice of the potential consequences of their action.

C. The Court of Appeals' Reasoning

The Court of Appeals*** criticized the Commission for failing to explain why it had not previously banned fleeting expletives as "harmful 'first blow[s].'" In the majority's view, without "evidence that suggests a fleeting expletive is harmful [and] ... serious enough to warrant government regulation," the agency could not regulate more broadly.***

There are some propositions for which scant empirical evidence can be marshaled, and the harmful effect of broadcast profanity on children is one of them. One cannot demand a multiyear controlled study, in which some children are intentionally exposed to indecent broadcasts (and insulated from all other indecency), and others are shielded from all indecency. It is one thing to set aside agency action under the Administrative Procedure Act because of failure to adduce empirical data that can readily be obtained. *See, e.g., State Farm*, 463 U.S., at 46–56 (addressing the costs and benefits of mandatory passive restraints for automobiles). It is something else to insist upon obtaining the unobtainable. Here it suffices to know that children mimic the behavior they observe—or at least the behavior that is presented to them as normal and appropriate. Programming replete with one-word indecent expletives will tend to produce children who use (at least) one-word indecent expletives. Congress has made the determination that indecent material is harmful to children, and has left enforcement of the ban to the Commission. If enforcement had to be supported by empirical data, the ban would effectively be a nullity.***

[T]he Court of Appeals found unconvincing the agency's prediction (without any evidence) that a per se exemption for fleeting expletives would lead to increased use of expletives one at a time. But even in the absence of evidence, the agency's predictive judgment (which merits deference) makes entire sense. To predict that complete immunity for fleeting expletives, ardently desired by broadcasters, will lead to a substantial increase in fleeting expletives seems to us an exercise in logic rather than clairvoyance. The Court of Appeals was perhaps correct that the Commission's prior policy had not yet caused broadcasters to "barrag[e] the airwaves with expletives." That may have been because its prior permissive policy had been confirmed (save in dicta) only at the staff level. In any event, as the *Golden Globes* order demonstrated, it did produce more expletives than the Commission (which has the first call in this matter) deemed in conformity with the statute.***

IV. Constitutionality

The Second Circuit did not definitively rule on the constitutionality of the Commission's orders, but respondents nonetheless ask us to decide their validity under the First Amendment. This Court, however, is one of final review, "not of first view."*** We see no reason to abandon our usual procedures in a rush to judgment without a lower court opinion. We decline to address the constitutional questions at this time.***

[Opinions of JUSTICE THOMAS, concurring; JUSTICE STEVENS, dissenting; JUSTICE GINSBURG, dissenting; and JUSTICE BREYER (joined by JUSTICE STEVENS, Souter, Ginsburg), dissenting, omitted.]

Notes and Questions

1. **Regulatory and Procedural Posture?** The Federal Communications Commission (FCC) was created by the Communications Act of 1934 to regulate "communication by wire and radio." 47 U.S.C. § 151. The FCC consists of five members, who are appointed by the President with the advice and consent of the Senate to serve five-year terms. One of the commissioners is designated by the President as the chair. The Communications Act is silent regarding the reasons a commissioner may be removed from office; however, commissioners are understood to enjoy *Humphrey's Executor*-style protections. *See* 556 U.S. at 547 (Breyer, J., dissenting) ("Commissioners*** enjoy*** an independence expressly designed to insulate them, to a degree, from the exercise of political oversight" (internal quotation marks omitted)).

As the Supreme Court's opinion explains, the FCC has authority to enforce the statutory ban on "utter[ing] any obscene, indecent, or profane language by means of a radio communication." 18 U.S.C. § 1464. The FCC receives indecency complaints via mail and its website. (Interested readers may file a complaint and review past complaints at https://consumercomplaints.fcc.gov/.) Indecency complaints are reviewed initially by the FCC's Enforcement Bureau (referred to in the court's opinion as the FCC's "staff"), which is authorized to close complaints that clearly fall outside the FCC's authority, such as those complaining of indecency broadcast after 10:00 p.m. In other matters, the Enforcement Bureau investigates the complaint and forwards a recommendation to the Commission for decision.

Complaints forwarded by the Enforcement Bureau are reviewed by the Commission at regular meetings. If the Commission determines that a broadcast was obscene, indecent or profane, it issues a Notice of Apparent Liability, a preliminary finding that a broadcast violated the law. This preliminary finding may be confirmed or rescinded when the FCC issues a Forfeiture Order. The Commission is authorized by law to "conduct its proceedings in such manner as will best conduce to the proper dispatch of business and to the ends of justice." 47 U.S.C. § 154(j). Thus, enforcement proceedings are considered informal adjudications under the APA. *See Action for Children's Television v. FCC*, 852 F.2d 1332, 1337 (D.C. Cir. 1988).

As the Supreme Court's opinion also explains, *Fox* arose out of an enforcement proceeding against the Fox television network following the network's broadcast of the words "fuck" and "shit" during the 2002 Billboard Music Awards and 2003 Billboard Music Awards. Both broadcasts involved a "fleeting" expletive—one that was unplanned and unscripted, which the network failed to bleep out successfully at the time of the original live broadcast. What was the FCC's position on such expletives at the time of its order in *Fox*? How long had that been the FCC's position? What sanction did the FCC impose against Fox?

2. **The Standard of Review—Does "Hard Look" Review Survive *Fox*?** When it reviewed the FCC's order, the Second Circuit relied on circuit precedent that required the FCC to show "why the original reasons for adopting the [displaced] rule or policy are no longer dispositive," *Brae Corp. v. United States*, 740 F.2d 1023, 1038 (D.C. Cir. 1984), as well as "why the new rule effectuates the statute as well as or better than the old rule," *New York Council, Ass'n of Civ. Tech. v. FLRA*, 757 F.2d 502, 508 (2d Cir. 1985).

Do these requirements follow from *State Farm*? Did the Supreme Court in *State Farm* require the Department of Transportation to show that the original reasons for adopting Modified Standard 208 no longer required adoption of the standard? Did the Court in *State Farm* require the Department of Transportation to show that a standard that required no passive restraints better effectuated the Traffic and Motor Vehicle Safety Act of 1966? What does the Supreme Court in *Fox* conclude?

3. **The Standard of Review—Changes in Agency Position?** Despite criticizing certain aspects of hard look review, the Supreme Court concedes that judicial review of a change in agency policy differs from judicial review of agency action undertaken on a blank slate. The Court observes that an agency must acknowledge it is changing position; "[a]n agency may not*** depart from a prior policy *sub silentio* or simply disregard rules that are on the books." What is the rationale underlying this requirement? Consider Judge Friendly's views:

> What gives concern is the manner, alas not atypical of the agencies, in which
> [a] change was made—slipped into an opinion in such a way that only careful readers would know what had happened, without articulation of reasons, and with prior authorities not overruled, so that the opinion writers remain free to pull them out of the drawer whenever the agency wishes to reach a result supportable by the old rule but not the new.

HENRY J. FRIENDLY, THE FEDERAL ADMINISTRATIVE AGENCIES 63 (1962).

An example of Judge Friendly's critique is the NLRB action under review in *Allentown Mack Sales & Service, Inc. v. NLRB*, 522 U.S. 359 (1998). On the surface, *Allentown Mack* presented a straightforward question of whether the Board's factual findings regarding whether the employer had a sufficient basis for doubting the union's majority support were supported by substantial evidence. "Under longstanding Board precedent, an employer who believes that an incumbent union no longer enjoys the support of a majority of its employees has three options: to request a formal, Board-supervised election, to withdraw recognition from the union and refuse to bargain, or to conduct an internal poll of employee support for the union. The Board has held that the latter two are unfair labor practices unless the employer can show that it had a 'good-faith reasonable doubt' about the union's majority support." *Id.* at 361.

In the proceedings at issue in *Allentown Mack*, the ALJ and Board applied evidentiary presumptions derived from prior Board decisions involving the good-faith reasonable doubt standard. One such presumption held that anti-union statements made in the context of an interview for a job with a new employer who prefers a non-unionized workforce are not entitled to credit. Another of the Board's presumptions held that statements by one employee about the preferences of other employees were not entitled to credit.

In a scathing opinion authored by Justice Scalia, a five-Justice majority rejected the Board's reliance on the presumptions because they had been applied inconsistently and were inconsistent with the ultimate question of whether the employer had a good-faith reasonable doubt about whether the union enjoyed majority support. The majority also endorsed in strong terms the petitioner's complaint that "although 'the Board continues to cite the words of the good faith doubt branch of its withdrawal of recognition standard,' a systematic review of the Board's decisions reveal[s] that 'it has in practice eliminated the good faith doubt branch in favor of a strict head count.'" *Id.* at 372. The Court concluded that the Board's adoption of evidentiary presumptions through case-by-case adjudication amounted to a form of "policymaking by factfinding" that violated rule-of-law values. "An agency should not be able to impede judicial review, and indeed even political oversight, by disguising its policymaking as factfinding." *Id.* at 326. Are there benefits to a one-case-at-a-time approach that *Allentown Mack*'s strong endorsement of policymaking transparency fails to take into account? *See generally* Joan Flynn, *The Costs and Benefits of "Hiding the Ball": NLRB Policymaking and the Failure of Judicial Review*, 75 B. U. L. REV. 387 (1995).

The Supreme Court in *Fox* concedes that an agency must provide "a more detailed justification" when "its new policy rests upon factual findings that contradict those which underlay its prior policy." Why? Do the agency's original findings in this scenario effectively function as an especially persuasive comment that the agency must take into account prior to taking new action? Was the Court's concession necessary to maintain consistency with *State Farm*?

The Fox Court also concedes that more detailed justification is required "when [the agency's] prior policy has engendered serious reliance interests." Does the Court explain why? Aren't reliance interests more appropriately addressed through the agency's choice of remedy? *Cf. Perez v. Mortgage Bankers Ass'n*, 135 S. Ct. 1199, 1209 n.5 (2015) (noting government's acknowledgment that "even in situations where a statute does not contain a safe-harbor provision*** an agency's ability to pursue enforcement actions against regulated entities for conduct in conformance with prior agency interpretations may be limited by principles of retroactivity").

4. **Why Was the FCC's Order Upheld?** The Supreme Court concludes that the FCC's order withstands scrutiny because the Commission acknowledged it was changing its regulatory stance in the *Golden Globes Order*, the reasons adduced for the change were rational, and sanctioning broadcasts of fleeting expletives was consistent with the Commission's broader enforcement program. Does the Court accept all of the reasons the FCC advanced for its change in policy? For example, does the Court accept that any use of the word "'fuck'" "inherently has a sexual connotation"? That Bono's use of the word in the 2004 Golden Globes broadcast was "shocking and gratuitous"? *Cf.* Jocelyn Noveck, *In Public, Expletive is Rarely Deleted Anymore*, Columbus Dispatch, Mar. 29, 2006 (reporting that, in a March 2006 Associated Press poll, sixty-four percent of respondents reported using the term).

The Second Circuit faulted the FCC for not adducing empirical evidence that exposure to a fleeting expletive harms children. Recalling the distinction between legislative and adjudicative facts (*see* Note 4 to *Portland Cement Ass'n v. Ruckelshaus, supra* Chapter 4[C] p. 433), is fleeting expletives' effect on children a legislative fact or an adjudicative one? Why does the Supreme Court conclude that the court of appeals' objection is not well taken? Is the Supreme Court correct that empirical evidence cannot be marshaled regarding the effects, if any, of exposing children to expletives? *Cf., e.g.,* Cynthia Hoffner & Joanne Cantor, *Developmental Differences in Responses to a Television Character's Appearance and Behavior*, 21 Developmental Psychol. 1065, 1065 (1985) (describing results of studies which found "that young children seem to recall more of the *visual* than the *auditory* (mainly verbal) components of television programs"). Even if the Supreme Court is wrong that the effects of exposing children to expletives cannot be measured empirically, was the Second Circuit correct to demand such evidence? Consider Justice Scalia's claim that "*Congress* has made the determination that indecent material is harmful to children" (emphasis added).

The Second Circuit also faulted the FCC's prediction that use of expletives would increase if the broadcast of fleeting expletives did not result in a sanction. Was the appellate court's objection well taken? If the broadcast of an expletive is unplanned, what is the deterrent value of punishing it? What in the Supreme Court's view is wrong with the lower court's analysis?

5. **Postscript.** On remand, the Second Circuit took up the broadcaster's constitutional challenges to the FCC's indecency policy. The court concluded, this time with Judge Leval joining the majority, that the entire policy, not simply the agency's position on fleeting expletives, violated due process because the regime did not provide fair notice of when the broadcast of an expletive would lead to the broadcaster being sanctioned. *Fox Television Stations, Inc. v. FCC*, 613 F.3d 317 (2d Cir. 2010). The Supreme Court agreed that the policy failed to provide constitutionally adequate notice as to the specific broadcasts at issue in *Fox*, but did not address its facial constitutionality. The Supreme Court nonetheless suggested that the FCC consider "modify[ing] its current indecency policy in light of its determination of the public interest and applicable legal requirements." *FCC v. Fox Television Stations, Inc.*, 132 S. Ct. 2307, 2320 (2012).

On April 1, 2013, the FCC issued a public notice seeking comment on "whether the full Commission should make changes to its current broadcast indecency policies or maintain them as they are." The notice announced that, while FCC staff built a record for the Commission's consideration, the Commission would focus enforcement on "egregious" indecency cases. Federal Communications Commission, FCC Cuts Indecency Complaints By 1 Million; Seeks Comment on Policy (Apr. 1, 2013). More than 10,000 comments have been submitted in response to the FCC's notice to date. *See* http://apps.fcc.gov/ecfs/comment_search/execute?proceeding=13-86. Many are form complaints submitted via organizations that are morally opposed to profanity and obscenity. Many others appear to have been submitted by individuals who are mentally unstable. As this volume went to press, the Commission had not yet adopted a new policy.

Index

653